W9-AGU-131

THE PHILOSOPHY OF

CHARLES HARTSHORNE

THE LIBRARY OF LIVING PHILOSOPHERS

PAUL ARTHUR SCHILPP, FOUNDER AND EDITOR 1938–1981
LEWIS EDWIN HAHN, EDITOR 1981–

Paul Arthur Schilpp, Editor

THE PHILOSOPHY OF JOHN DEWEY (1939, 1971, 1989)
THE PHILOSOPHY OF GEORGE SANTAYANA (1940, 1951)
THE PHILOSOPHY OF ALFRED NORTH WHITEHEAD (1941, 1951)
THE PHILOSOPHY OF G. E. MOORE (1942, 1971)
THE PHILOSOPHY OF BERTRAND RUSSELL (1944, 1971)
THE PHILOSOPHY OF ERNST CASSIRER (1949)
ALBERT EINSTEIN: PHILOSOPHER-SCIENTIST (1949, 1970)
THE PHILOSOPHY OF SARVEPALLI RADHAKRISHNAN (1952)
THE PHILOSOPHY OF KARL JASPERS (1957; aug. ed., 1981)
THE PHILOSOPHY OF C. D. BROAD (1959)
THE PHILOSOPHY OF RUDOLF CARNAP (1963)
THE PHILOSOPHY OF C. I. LEWIS (1968)
THE PHILOSOPHY OF KARL POPPER (1974)
THE PHILOSOPHY OF BRAND BLANSHARD (1980)
THE PHILOSOPHY OF JEAN-PAUL SARTRE (1981)

Paul Arthur Schilpp and Maurice Friedman, Editors

THE PHILOSOPHY OF MARTIN BUBER (1967)

Paul Arthur Schilpp and Lewis Edwin Hahn, Editors

THE PHILOSOPHY OF GABRIEL MARCEL (1984)
THE PHILOSOPHY OF W. V. QUINE (1986)
THE PHILOSOPHY OF GEORG HENRIK VON WRIGHT (1989)

Lewis Edwin Hahn, Editor

THE PHILOSOPHY OF CHARLES HARTSHORNE (1991)

In Preparation:

Lewis Edwin Hahn, Editor

THE PHILOSOPHY OF A. J. AYER
THE PHILOSOPHY OF PAUL RICOEUR

THE LIBRARY OF LIVING PHILOSOPHERS
VOLUME XX

THE PHILOSOPHY OF

CHARLES HARTSHORNE

EDITED BY

LEWIS EDWIN HAHN

SOUTHERN ILLINOIS UNIVERSITY AT CARBONDALE

LA SALLE, ILLINOIS • OPEN COURT • ESTABLISHED 1887

THE PHILOSOPHY OF CHARLES HARTSHORNE

OPEN COURT and the above logo are registered in the U.S. Patent and Trademark Office.

© 1991 by The Library of Living Philosophers
First printing 1991

Printed and bound in the United States of America.

Library of Congress Cataloging-in-Publication Data

The Philosophy of Charles Hartshorne / edited by Lewis Edwin Hahn.
    p.   cm. — (The Library of living philosophers ; v. 20)
    Includes bibliographical references and index.
    ISBN 0-8126-9147-4.—ISBN 0-8126-9148-2 (pbk.)
    1. Hartshorne, Charles, 1897–   . I. Hartshorne, Charles 1897–
II. Hahn, Lewis Edwin, 1908–   III. Series.
B945.H354P48   1991
191—dc20   91-10824
                                                               CIP

The Library of Living Philosophers is published under the sponsorship of Southern Illinois University at Carbondale.

GENERAL INTRODUCTION
TO
THE LIBRARY OF LIVING PHILOSOPHERS

Founded in 1938 by Professor Paul Arthur Schilpp and edited by him until July 1981, when the present writer became editor, the Library of Living Philosophers is devoted to critical analysis and discussion of some of the world's greatest living philosophers. The format for the series provides for setting up in each volume a dialogue between the critics and the great philosopher. The aim is not refutation or confrontation but rather fruitful joining of issues and improved understanding of the positions and issues involved. That is, the goal is not overcoming those who differ from us philosophically but interacting creatively with them.

The basic idea for the series, according to Professor Schilpp's general introduction to each of the earlier volumes, came from the late F. C. S. Schiller, who declared in his essay on "Must Philosophers Disagree?" (In *Must Philosophers Disagree?* London: Macmillan, 1934) that the greatest obstacle to fruitful discussion in philosophy is "the curious etiquette which apparently taboos the asking of questions about a philosopher's meaning while he is alive." The "interminable controversies which fill the histories of philosophy," in Schiller's opinion, "could have been ended at once by asking the living philosophers a few searching questions." And while he may have been overly optimistic about ending "interminable controversies" in this way, it seems clear that directing searching questions to great philosophers about what they really mean or how they think certain difficulties in their philosophy can be resolved while they are still alive can produce more comprehensible understanding and more fruitful philosophizing than might otherwise be had.

And to Paul Arthur Schilpp's undying credit, he acted on this basic thought in launching in 1938 the Library of Living Philosophers. It is planned that each volume in the Library of Living Philosophers shall include preferably an intellectual autobiography by the principal philosopher or an authorized biography as well as a bibliography of that thinker's publications, a series of expository and critical essays written by a wide range of leading exponents and opponents of the philosopher's thought, and the philosopher's replies to the interpretations and queries in these articles. The intellectual autobiographies usually shed light on both how the philosophies of the great thinkers developed and the major philosophical movements and issues of their time; and many of our great philosophers seek to orient their outlook not merely to their contemporaries but also to what they find most important in earlier philosophers. The bibliography will help provide ready access to the featured scholar's writings and thought.

With this format in mind, the Library expects to publish at more or less regular intervals a volume on one of the world's greater living philosophers.

In accordance with past practice, the editor has deemed it desirable to secure the services of an Advisory Board of philosophers to aid him in the selection of subjects of future volumes. The names of eight prominent American philosophers who have agreed to serve appear on the page following the Introduction. To each of them the editor is most grateful.

Future volumes in this series will appear in as rapid succession as is feasible in view of the scholarly nature of this Library. The next volume in the series will be devoted to the philosophy of Sir Alfred J. Ayer, and it will be followed by one on Paul Ricoeur.

Throughout its career, since its founding in 1938, the Library of Living Philosophers, because of its scholarly nature, has never been self-supporting. We acknowledge gratefully that the generosity of the Edward C. Hegeler Foundation has made possible the publication of many volumes, but for support of future volumes additional funds are needed. On 20 February 1979 the Board of Trustees of Southern Illinois University contractually assumed sponsorship of the Library, which is therefore no longer separately incorporated. Gifts specifically designated for the Library, however, may be made through the Southern Illinois University Foundation, and inasmuch as the latter is a tax-exempt institution, such gifts are tax-deductible.

LEWIS E. HAHN
EDITOR

DEPARTMENT OF PHILOSOPHY
SOUTHERN ILLINOIS UNIVERSITY AT CARBONDALE

ADVISORY BOARD

ACKNOWLEDGMENTS

The editor hereby gratefully acknowledges his obligation and sincere gratitude to all the publishers of Charles Hartshorne's books and publications for their kind and uniform courtesy in permitting us to quote—sometimes at some length—from Professor Hartshorne.

LEWIS E. HAHN

TABLE OF CONTENTS

PREFACE

It is fitting that Volume XX of the Library of Living Philosophers should be devoted to the philosophy of Charles Hartshorne. He has participated as critic in eight of our earlier volumes, more than any other philosopher; and this volume affords opportunity for searching criticism and clarification of his major tenets. He is internationally known for his contributions to philosophy of creativity and for his distinctive brand of process philosophy and theology; and for more than six decades he has presented his theses ever more persuasively, comparing and contrasting them in illuminating fashion with those of major historical figures and movements from Plato, Aristotle, Democritus, and Ancient Buddhism through Epicurus, Anselm, Socinus, Leibniz, Hume, and Kant to Emerson, Bergson, James, Peirce, Dewey, Royce, W. E. Hocking, Whitehead, Husserl, Merleau-Ponty, Heidegger, Ayer, and Popper. And he has learned from each of them, both from their positive contributions and their limitations or mistakes, which may be one of his reasons for holding that great philosophers should state their theses definitely and clearly enough that their soundness can be defended, if they are sound, or their error shown, if they are in error. His increasingly rich and precise statements of his views over the years, moreover, support Plato's idea of the importance of longevity for philosophical inquiry; and what other nonagenarians have maintained his level of philosophical production?

In his psychicalistic process philosophy he distinguishes sharply between a priori metaphysics and empirical cosmology. The former seeks necessary positive general truths about existence which are not falsifiable by any conceivable observations. The latter helps develop a world view which combines the abstract and the concrete, the logical and the actual. The present volume helps spell out his view. But central for his outlook are fresh interpretations of such notions as God, feeling and feeling of feeling, freedom, chance, and creativity, the primacy of aesthetic meaning, or affective tone, the social character of experience, sympathy as self-creative, the unity of life and an ecological approach to the world, inclusive polar contrasts, doctrinal matrices, relatedness and asymmetry, and generalized causal possibility with a place for probabilities and open possibilities.

Charles Hartshorne also enjoys an international reputation as an ornithologist. He is a foremost expert on bird song, and his birding has taken him all over the world. His Intellectual Autobiography affords an interesting account of how this interest developed and how it is related to his philosophical concerns; and a special feature of this volume is dialogue between Professor Hartshorne and various of his critics on his ornithological contributions.

I am grateful, of course, to Charles Hartshorne and the other contributors for their co-operation in producing an unusually illuminating and fruitful set of exchanges which highlight the major foci of his thought. Special thanks are due also to Dorothy C. Hartshorne for her work on his bibliography. Unhappily, one contributor, H. G. Hubbeling, died suddenly on 7 October 1986. His essay for our volume, I am told, was his last piece of philosophical writing.

I am also thankful for the hearty support, encouragement, and co-operation of our publisher, Open Court Publishing Company, particularly M. Blouke Carus, David R. Steele, and Kerri Mommer.

For welcome and much needed support and encouragement provided by the administration of Southern Illinois University I am also most grateful.

As always, moreover, my grateful appreciation goes to the staff of the Morris Library for their help with references.

To Sharon Grissom, Vernis Shownes, and the Philosophy Department secretariat I extend my warm thanks for help in many ways and on numerous projects, and I give special thanks to Sharon R. Langrand for help with manuscripts and proofs. For unfailing support and counsel I am deeply grateful to my colleagues, especially Elizabeth R. Eames, John Howie, and Matthew J. Kelly.

LEWIS EDWIN HAHN
EDITOR

DEPARTMENT OF PHILOSOPHY
SOUTHERN ILLINOIS UNIVERSITY AT CARBONDALE
JUNE 1990

PART ONE

INTELLECTUAL AUTOBIOGRAPHY OF CHARLES HARTSHORNE

Charles Wheeler, my grandfather after whom I was named, designed part of a transcontinental railroad and held terms as president of one RR, and vice-president of another. (The town, Oklahoma, was named after him.) So my father grew up in comfortable circumstances. In his youth the family lived in a large, well-landscaped estate in Merion, a suburb of Philadelphia.

SOME CAUSES OF
MY INTELLECTUAL GROWTH

I. Some not wholly Serious Preliminaries on Modesty and Its Opposite

Before I begin this more or less chronological account of my intellectual coming to be, I wish to confess an apprehension that the reader will find the account self-serving and self-flattering. He might, however, remember that an illustrious board of elder statesmen of the honorable profession of teaching philosophy has declared me an illustrious person. Who am I, a single individual, to disagree with them? Moreover, there has long been a question of whether it is humanly possible to write about one's own past without a certain prettifying of the events and behaviors described. Perhaps the reader has read the remark of Kenneth Galbraith, after he had given a glowing account of an achievement of his as Ambassador to India: "Modesty is an overrated virtue." It is also, I add, a virtue it is contradictory to boast of, and I have therefore always been careful not to boast of it (said, I suppose, somewhat boastingly). Certainly, a philosopher should, and I do, try to face reality, and it is my intention to admit some of the less creditable facts and behaviors in my past. "It is not wisdom to be only wise," wrote Santayana. Whatever this cryptic saying meant, one exegesis might be, "To represent oneself as never having been foolish is to suggest that one is either more or less than a human being, that is, a thinking animal but still an animal, and of a kind that has largely lost the wisdom of instinct tested by countless centuries of natural selection."

There is another limitation in the effort toward modest self-characterization. "It is more important that a proposition be interesting than that it be true"; for, if it is not interesting, who cares if it is true? Here is a related thought, "It is more important that Einstein's theory of relativity is beautiful than that it is true," said by Dirac to an audience of whom I was one. I shall in what follows hope to be interesting, and to achieve some touches of beauty as well as a reasonable amount of truth.

In a lighter vein, I recall three definitely modest autobiographies. Two were by persons who made a living by writing humorously; the titles were, *My World and Welcome to It* and *My Life and Hard Times*. The third work was also humorous, but by a well-liked and respected professor of geography, Robert Platt, a teacher, as it happened, of my brother Richard, who rose rapidly to fame as a geographer himself. Platt was also my colleague at the University of Chicago. Retired from that institution, he accepted an invitation to another university. There he was asked to introduce himself to his new academic community by writing an account of his career for the campus newspaper. He was not accustomed to thinking about his life and accomplishments as particularly notable. He knew he was capable and well-thought-of but also that others were more distinguished. So how to present his rather humdrum life history? He decided to have some fun. His entire life he presented as a series of failures. He had tried this—with no great success. He had tried that—with mediocre results. He wrote a book—it was only so-so. He got married—no great success there. The campus paper published it all. Soon thereafter he received a letter from a sympathetic reader of his sad account of his disappointments in life. The letter ended with the suggestion that he try to look more on the bright side of things. "Very well," he seems to have said to himself, "I see how I can have fun a second time." So he rewrote his life story, this time presenting his career as a sequence of glorious triumphs, including his marriage. This account, too, was published.

If the professor who could see his role in life in two opposite ways, each equally unreal and absurd, was not modest, who is? He is no longer living, but he was a good friend to many, including Richard and me. In many talks with him I recall only one boastful remark. "I," he said, "am the only person who understands both Hartshornes," meaning the geographer and the philosopher. It was true that he read Richard's writings as they came out and, for a number of years, my books as they came out, and appreciated both. I know of no other person of whom this has been true.

Concerning the length of these recollections, perhaps it will be borne in mind that I did not seek the opportunity to write them. I was required by the editor to furnish an autobiography, "short or long"—but how can one be short on so interesting and complex a subject? Were I a person like Whitehead it would be different. He did not boast of his modesty; but his wife did it for him, and with reason. He was one of the greatest persons I have encountered, and one of the most modest. He carefully destroyed all evidence that might tempt anyone to write about his life; he really thought that whatever was important for posterity in himself was in his writings as already published and he was happy that he had been able to put his intellectual self into permanent form. Peirce was less modest, though also great; yet he did say that since his "brain was small" he was unable "to consider more than one idea at a time", and that people only become logicians (as he had) because they have trouble thinking well. In retrospect he once described his youthful manner as he entered the London Athenaeum Club, "I am Charles Peirce (etc., etc.), and above all I yield to no one in my ineffable modesty."

II. Causal Explanation

As I have elsewhere suggested (in an essay called, "How I Got That Way"), to explain a philosopher's development causally is one thing, to assert or imply that the development was fully determined by its causal conditions is quite another. A cause of an event is, by the least question-begging definition, a necessary condition, a *sine qua non*, without which the event could not have happened as it did. Even the totality of such conditions, some of us hold, only makes what concretely happens possible, it does not make it necessary. As for what turns the possibility into fully concrete actuality, that is precisely what is meant by freedom or spontaneity in the libertarian sense. Strictly speaking, of concrete actualities there are no temporally antecedent yet "sufficient" conditions. Emergence is involved in *all* causation. Many quantum physicists admit this, although some do not. Even some classical physicists saw it: Peirce for one; and Maxwell at least strongly hinted at it. That the idea of sufficient conditions has been taken so literally comes from the fact, first sharply pointed to by Whitehead, that the "fallacy of misplaced concreteness" is extremely difficult to avoid. The role of language makes this more or less inevitable.

From William James, first, then, years later, Peirce and Whitehead I derived the conviction that it is not the past that determines the present (at least the present of a human consciousness); rather the present determines itself, using past process as necessary condition. *Either* present process is its own sufficient condition, given the past, or there is no such thing as sufficient condition for the present process taken in its fully concrete actuality. For various abstract aspects of it, the past may indeed be sufficient condition. And much of the time it is these aspects that we talk about causally. James saw the point in connection with the freedom of human beings. Peirce, and later Whitehead, saw it as a general truth about causation as such and actuality as such, with the human example as a special, intensive case. Atomic freedom is insignificant in comparison with human freedom; but it is not zero freedom. People are far too casual in affirming zero where "very little" is all that the evidence supports. Maxwell, Peirce, and Whitehead have all made this point in this connection. I got it first from Peirce.

A vigorously and complexly thinking animal, thinking not only about things but about thinking itself, lives largely—in its imagination—in a world of more or less abstract universals, the specific or individual instances of which are never deducible from the universals. 'I must have protein' does not entail 'I must have meat', still less, 'I must have *this* meat'. The more abstract our goals, the less can they determine concrete actions or decisions. If 'motive' in 'the strongest motive' is a universal (and if it can be put into words it is universal), then no concrete act uniquely follows logically. So careless of elementary logical truth is a certain deterministic argument.

I hope to make plausible that what happened before and around my childhood, youth, and early manhood causally conditioned, made possible, my philosophical career, but left it concretely free in specifics and details. Of course, my account of causal conditions will be far from complete; but that is a different point, entirely compatible with the presence of chance or causal indeterminacy as a negative but necessary aspect of significant freedom. The doctrine of compatibilism (freedom *with* strict causal determinism) is a doctrine of the total insignificance of our freedom, giving human beings no greater scope (because zero in both cases) of creative options than the lowest creatures. Not they nor we make effective decisions, settle what was previously unsettled, thus enriching the definiteness of reality; rather, the omnipotent past, or an omnipotent Something or Someone, makes its and our decisions — unless (Spinoza) there has never been anything to decide, since the necessary, the possible, and the actual are indistinguishable.

For me this issue was settled by James's "Dilemma of Determinism." In its cosmic, fully general form, the libertarian view was confirmed and nailed down by Peirce's "Doctrine of Necessity Examined." After reading the latter, I had other things to do than to worry about the details of "compatibilist" arguments. Whitehead saw the general point, without help from Peirce but with some from James, and wove it into a much more complete and comprehensive scheme. Obviously, he was working on my problems. I had to become (more or less) Whiteheadian, as well as Peircean. I told Whitehead this, whereupon he gave me a gracious bow.

III. The Ancestral Families

Charles Hartshorne, the grandfather after whom I was named, designed part of a transcontinental railroad and served terms as president of one railroad and vice-president of another. (The town Hartshorne, Oklahoma, was named after him.) So my father grew up in comfortable circumstances. In his youth the family lived in a large, well-landscaped estate in Merion, a suburb of Philadelphia. There was nothing vulgar, so far as I could or can see, about the paternal aunts (three) or the one uncle, or seven first cousins, of mine. The two grandparents died too early in my life to be recalled later.

The Hartshorne family had been Quakers until Phillips Brooks converted Mrs. Charles Hartshorne to the Episcopal Church. My father had his B.A. and M.A. from Haverford (then definitely Quaker) and a law degree; however—partly because he did not want to be obliged to represent his father's railroad in law cases, partly because he did want to marry a very pious daughter of a scholarly Episcopal clergyman, and perhaps mostly because he was interested in theology—he decided to become an Episcopal clergyman himself. His youngest sister, my Aunt Amy, became an Episcopalian, and so did his older brother, my Uncle Ned. In contrast the other sisters, Aunts Mary and Nanna, between them married three Ethical Culture Society leaders, Nanna being widowed by the first of her two husbands. One of Uncle Ned's daughters, cousin Tina (Mrs. Richard Jenney), an admirable little person, good all through, lived as a loyal member of the Society of Friends. I grew up knowing about three forms of Protestantism (or at least of nonfundamentalist forms of the Judaeo-Christian tradition) encountering a fourth, Unitarianism, first from reading Emerson, and then when I went to Harvard as a Junior. No relative was anything like a fundamentalist. One family retainer was an intelligent Roman Catholic, Lillie Zietz, Aunt Amy's companion.

Mother's family was less wealthy than Father's but equally refined and even more religious. They were wholly Episcopalian. Mother's father, the Rev. James Haughton, author of a book on The Holy Spirit (consisting mostly of quotations), I recall as a gentle, kindly person. His parish was at Bryn Mawr, not far from Merion. Some of the Haughtons of previous generations had been wealthy, although a fortune had been lost through an untrustworthy partner.

Through my relatives alone I could learn nothing about the illiterate or semi-literate portions of the population, nothing about the vulgar rich, about alcoholics, dissolute people, nothing about notably stupid, bad-mannered, or violent people. I am not boasting, just trying to state facts about my sheltered upbringing. The sole hint of scandal about relatives that came my way while I was growing up, or indeed until recently, was that one distant cousin (second or once removed) was of a man who came in shabby clothes to a family reunion because, it was said, he thought he had committed the unforgivable sin—whatever that may be. On the other hand, another distant cousin, Anna C. Hartshorne, was the author of a carefully researched two-volume work, *Japan and its People* (1902), a founder of Tsuda College for Women (first in, now near, Tokyo), for which she raised money and in which she taught English for several decades. My wife and I visited this college, and learned that one of its principal buildings was named after Anna. We recall her as a delightful and obviously brilliant elderly person.

The two families whose merging brought me into being included, within recent generations, several clergymen, several doctors, one of whom, an amateur poet, was among the first to advocate medical education for women and served as a faculty member at the Woman's Medical College of Pennsylvania. There was a distinguished paleontologist, E. D. Cope, and a shipowner who was also an amateur poet all his life.

Recently, I have been surprised by evidence (perhaps inconclusive) of two not easily defensible actions in my childhood or youth by relatives. One of these actions brought misfortune to the individual himself. In sum, my relatives were not faultless; but, as the world goes, they were remarkably close to that. If not in the best sense sheer aristocrats, they were well in the "upper upper" middle class. On the other hand, my parents were not isolated from the poor, the lower middle class, or the proletariat. My mother treated everyone as a fellow human being. As a clergyman and thoughtful reader of newspapers, my father knew and was concerned about what went on in the world. Across the street from us in Phoenixville, Pennsylvania, began a large section of the town where lived, in company houses, poor, presumably ignorant laborers in the steel mill, who had been imported from Central Europe. Father was indignant that they had to be at work twelve hours a day. He knew the rationalizations given by the owners of the mill, one of them prominent in his church. Father's criticism of Billy Sunday, the evangelist, was, "He preaches against the sins of the poor, not of the rich."

IV. CHILDHOOD AND EARLY YOUTH

a) My Family and Its Residences

My first twenty years were spent almost entirely in Pennsylvania; that is, in the only one of the thirteen original colonies that was founded essentially by Quakers. Two towns (without Quakers, I think) were the primary environments of my family while I grew up. The smaller town, Kittanning (population 4000) in western Pennsylvania, on the Allegheny River, saw me through infancy (that prepersonal stage of life) and childhood (the time of becoming a person) to the end of my eleventh year in June, 1907. The two-and-one-half times larger Phoenixville, in eastern Pennsylvania on the Skuylkill River, was the scene of my last two years of grade school, after which, aged fourteen, I began spending large parts of each year elsewhere, though still being in the town for some days or weeks each year.

In summers (from 1911 until 1916, when the war began changing things), we all went to a mountain resort called Eaglesmere in the northeastern part of the state. It was ideal for observing Canadian-zone nature, supplementing the different climatic conditions in Phoenixville, and in Lancaster County, where, for the high school years, I went to a private boarding-school called Yeates. This diversity of habitats was one of many pieces of luck (the right word in my philosophy) favoring my eventually becoming a fairly sophisticated field naturalist and almost a zoögeographer.

To keep this account within reasonable limits I shall say little about Kittanning, making only incidental retrospective references to it. This is the more appropriate in that I am trying to explain how my becoming the sort of philosopher that I am was causally possible. For this, my youth is more obviously relevant and more readily cited than my childhood. I remember no childhood anticipations of the philosophical problems that will be the concerns of my readers. My mother thought I philosophized as a child; but I have no recollections that confirm this. I loved nature in a rather uninformed way, listened to Father's sermons (according to Mother), but tended to forget them later when I was beginning to deal intellectually with religion. I read Kipling's *Jungle Books* with fascination, also Long's nature stories, and Hawthorne's account of Greek mythology, learned about electricity from reading *Popular Electricity* and playing with electric toys, but recall nothing of any childish philosophical puzzling over these or other experiences.

b) Public and Private Schools: Holidays; Books and Birds; Becoming a Writer

As the oldest of five boys, with Frances, the one sister, eighteen months older, I enjoyed certain advantages. Three of the other boys were so close to my age (two of them identical twins) that when, in Phoenixville, we formed a baseball team, we needed only five additional boys. The playing field "belonged" to us since it was part of the church property, Father being an Episcopal minister. As oldest Hartshorne boy I naturally became the secretary-treasurer, however we called it. In general, in my late childhood and early teens, I was, without any special effort to be so, the leader of three brothers. (Alfred, the youngest boy of the five of us, tended to be left out and made his own friends.) Father got an admirable man to establish in our area the first (or second?) Boy Scout troop in the country (about 1909). Somehow also, I got hold of a book, a wonderful book, by Horace Kephart, *Camping and Woodcraft*. So I began to plan camping trips for myself and the twins, James and Henry, (next to me in age). Eventually Richard, the fourth boy, wanted to be included when it came to the longest trip, lasting a week. We fished and carried our tents and food other than fish on our backs. I planned it all. When I decided I wanted a microscope (a rather low power, cheap one) I got the others to contribute to the cost, though I do not recall that they greatly shared my interest in the tiny creatures we were thereby able to observe. So with some other things. The twins and I never quarreled.

Of course, being the oldest of the boys in question is the barest beginning of an explanation of the fact that I (and not the twins) became something of an intellectual leader as an adult. But some of the missing factors, so far as they were environmental (not genes), can be supplied. Father decided to send two of us boys, sister having been already so treated, to a private school for our four precollege years. He passed over the twins since they had done less well in public school than Richard and I. (Alas, they knew why this was done.) So I first, and Richard a year later, went to a remarkably good, small private boarding school in Pennsylvania, called Yeates, where we had small classes, excellent teachers, intelligent individual attention, stimulating rewards for achievement. The more I have read about American high schools and about the "public schools" in England as they used to be, the more I marvel at the luck Richard and I had in being sent to *that* school. Richard is now a world-famous geographer.

In my first year at Yeates I was, as had not happened before, away from relatives or family attendants (all of them understanding and helpful), or previously known peer friends. I recall no shock from this change; and I did find passable friends quickly among both students and teachers. Still, it put me in a position in which I had to learn to develop even more self-reliance. No longer could I enjoy effortless leadership.

By chance, the first Christmas at home from Yeates with the family for the holiday, I saw, in a store in Philadelphia (an hour by train from Phoenixville) to which I had gone to look for presents for the family, a book that changed my life from then on. It was a pocket bird guide, the first good one—and it was very good—in this country, possibly in the world. This was Chester A. Reed's *Song and Insectivorous Birds East of the Rockies*. It looked interesting, and I bought it as a present to myself. It pictured a three-power field glass as available for five dollars postpaid. I sent for that. I was now, as I returned to Yeates, in an ideal position to *begin* to learn a science, ornithology.

Yeates was an almost tiny but well-equipped establishment, surrounded by farms and wood lots, in a principal migratory bird flyway, on a stream in rich Lancaster County, with a variety of habitats within a short walk in any direction. Also, the school had a rule that nicely fitted the purpose I had acquired from Reed's book, that of learning the birds of my part of the world. Not *all* the birds! The book concentrated on birds endowed with good organs for controlling sounds, the group of species called true songbirds or oscines. So I began my birding as a specialist. This too was lucky, for, had I not done so, I could never have achieved very much, since my main vocation lay elsewhere. I could not have been responsible for learning all the species ill-equipped to sing (hawks, owls, ducks, shorebirds, sea-birds, etc., etc.) and have become, as I eventually did, an authority on bird song.

The school rule referred to was that students achieving fairly high grades were excused from the otherwise required study hour-and-a-quarter following breakfast. This gave me a splendid time for birding. Nor was this all. The season was midwinter, the ideal time for learning to know the year-round birds and the winter visitors, since the number of species is then small. Learning these was quickly done. Then, as spring migrants began to arrive, I could add them to the list of those already learned. In spring, in startling contrast to autumn, birds are in full mature plumage and are beginning to sing. Identification is therefore at its easiest, and on a good day exciting, since the birds come in waves as the weather favors their flight, and chances of securing food when they descend from the skies of a morning. (They migrate mostly at night.) Altogether, without having ever intended to do so before finding that book, I was almost forced by circumstances to become a field naturalist, a form of empirical scientist. No teacher suggested it. But Reed did it. From this, and also from Kephart's book on wood-craft, I learned a lesson some seem never to learn: If you want to find out how to do something or understand something, there is probably a book that will give you a good chance of accomplishing this.

Dr. Gardiner, the founder and headmaster of Yeates, strongly favored my new interest and urged me never to lose it. He was an Episcopal clergyman and a Yale athlete; he taught science, including the theory of evolution, and so far as Richard or I can recall he never suggested that it contradicted belief in God. My father had thought this issue through in the 1880s and reached the same conclusion. So had Charles Kingsley, an Anglican clergyman, still earlier. Fundamentalist arguments on this matter—but why bother my readers with this antique controversy?

The school offered a prize for an essay in observation of nature, which I won. There was a school periodical to which I contributed my first bird article, perhaps my first publication; also a short story, and a poem I wrote as class poet in my last year at the school. These three writings are lost, but they were the beginnings of a writing-publishing career that has lasted now for more than seventy years. My first full-time teaching came thirteen years later in Chicago. In my case "publish or perish" has never been relevant. For me it was, as I came to see later, teach or perish. In those years also I wrote an account of a camping trip by four Hartshorne boys for a sporting magazine, which published it. From then on the only years in which I did not publish something were probably the two spent in the army medical corps in WWI and (four years later) two in England and Europe doing postdoctoral study on a fellowship from Harvard. In these four years I was absorbing and digesting new impressions, not giving out results for others. I was reading some, and writing long letters to relatives and a friend or two.

Yeates School gave me: a fine introduction to literature (the English teacher was something of a poet and an interesting man); a basically sound though very elementary introduction to natural science; good training in elementary geometry and algebra, a fine course on the geography of South America, on which I wrote an essay for a prize contest. I won the prize, but for another essay which, to my present astonishment, bore the title, "The Psychology of Advertising"! These writings, too, are lost. Obviously I had a fine momentum going as a writer before even reaching college. I fear the public high school in Phoenixville would not have done this for me. However, the teaching in the grades in Phoenixville for the two years I attended was, so far as I recall, quite acceptable, and I have no complaint whatever about it.

Although at Phoenixville and Eaglesmere I was sometimes the leader of several younger brothers, Yeates brought out the fact that I was not naturally a leader, as the term is usually intended. At Yeates I shone or excelled, but did not lead. Thus, an annual prize for junior football fell to me, not because I was quarterback or captain or made goals but because, as right end I prevented the other side from making one by chasing after their runner (who had broken through our lines) and bringing him down—although he was normally faster than I was, as I knew from playing tag with him.

No dream of becoming president—of anything—came my youthful way. I did hope for some years that I would be a great poet. In the long run five learned societies have elected me president, the largest of these being the Western (now Central) Division of the American Philosophical Association and the Southern Society for Philosophy and Psychology. However, the secretaries of all these societies did the real work (bless them), except in the Metaphysical Society, whose founder, Paul Weiss, is a more managerial person and one to whom I am ever grateful, since his work opened doors for my favorite subject. I merely made the presidential addresses.

At Yeates I told brother Richard, who was my roommate one year, "You will become a college president; I never will." This prediction has in essence been fulfilled. For example, during WWII Richard was put in charge of the geographical section of the OSS, with seventy salaries under his control. I could scarcely imagine doing such a thing. The urge to tell others what theoretical positions to take in various matters comes naturally to me, but not what practical steps to take. I have even found it difficult to tell a class what books to read, having trouble enough deciding which of many relevant books to read myself.

What I was at Yeates was a "loner," though without ceasing to be sociable and a team player. Even at Kittanning, I recall bicycle trips, at least one for miles in the country alone, and one long trip with a single companion. Kit Carson and Daniel Boone, solitary in a wilderness, were childish heroes of mine. Being alone has for me not usually meant being lonely. Partly this was because of a Wordsworthian feeling for nature. When I came to read that poet, I felt I knew what he was talking about. At Yeates this became vividly apparent.

I have elsewhere explained why I think both science and philosophy make Wordsworth easier to take seriously now than when he wrote. Not that he was describing physical nature as it is in itself; rather he was describing nature so far as given to our direct intuitions, apart from pragmatic and presumably scientific abstractions. The "ocean of feelings" that Whitehead ascribes to physical reality is not only thought; so far as our bodies are made of this reality, it is intuited. What is not intuited but only thought is nature as consisting of absolutely insentient stuff or process. No such nature is directly given to us. The individual subjects of the feelings in subanimal and subplant nature are not *distinctly* intuited, being too minute and rapidly changing. Hence the idea of the simply insentient.

Wordsworth was doing a phenomenology of direct experience far better than Husserl ever did. The famous phenomenologist was too addicted to certain abstractions for that. Wordsworth seems to have influenced Whitehead much as he did me. He saved both of us from materialism and even dualism. Both result from an inadequate phenomenology and a now antiquated physics. At least so I have thought for decades and so Whitehead, in effect, told me, and in his writings implies, that he thought.

At Yeates School three developments were under way in my case. There was the first stage of a long process of becoming a practitioner of an empirical science, ornithology, involving taxonomy in a limited branch, the study of one group of animal forms, plus a specialized aspect of what came later to be called ethology, or the study of animal behavior. The specialization was what Szöke has termed biomusicology, the science of animal music. Then there was making a start in the incomparable career, as it has always been to me, of writer. Finally, there was a first step in the long journey toward maturity in the philosophy of life, or of religion. That all this implied an academic career as teacher of philosophy was a concession to practical requirements and was the last aspect to be fully decided in my mind.

Two events, not yet mentioned, both connected with books that effected life-changes, occurred during the Yeates years. The first was finding, in my father's library, a copy of *Emerson's Essays*. I read it through; it must have had great effect because, some time later, engaged in writing poetry, I happened upon the book again and was surprised to find that the ideas I had thought my own creations were those of Emerson. I had so far internalized the great prose poet! For all that I can ever know, Emerson had as much to do with my present philosophy as any single professional philosopher whom some may regard as my teacher or master. I am not an Emersonian, but I could not have been what I am without him. This is what a cause is, a *sine qua non*, not an element in an all-determining power making our decisions for us in advance. Until we have something like a consensus on this point, we philosophers are, I think, going to remain as confused as we have lately been. Determinism is as old as philosophy (Democritus). It has never permanently convinced any society in which discussion was at all free and is farther from doing so now than ever. There seems no hope of consensus there.

The third book that changed much for me was Matthew Arnold's *Literature and Dogma*, a vigorous attack on traditional Christianity. How I got hold of it I do not know; but it broke my dogmatic slumber. Any religious belief I could henceforth accept would have to be a philosophical one, with reasons that I could grasp as convincing. This took several years to find, even in vague outlines. I reached those outlines only after two years at Haverford College and the first of my two years in France in the U.S. Army Medical Corps in WWI.

The summer following graduation from Yeates was the time of my first but not quite last experience in hiring myself out as laborer. Two maternal uncles owned a farm with a hired farmer in charge of the actual farming. I worked under him, and then, as all the hay was taken care of, went to another farm and then another. My idea was to see what things were like outside the schools and the towns I had previously known. I learned about a number of personality types quite outside my previous experience.

V. HAVERFORD COLLEGE: THE SEARCH FOR A PHILOSOPHY OF RELIGION

The choice of college was Father's. I do not recall being consulted in the matter, nor that I had any wish to the contrary.

At Haverford I listened to many addresses and lectures by Rufus Jones, the most outstanding professional philosopher and theologian that the American Society of Friends has produced. Reputed a mystic and a scholarly student of mysticism, Jones was also a robustly commonsensical, humorous, and knowledgeable disciple of Royce and, through reading, of the Cornell school of idealism. I took a course of his on the history of Christian doctrines in which the assigned reading was Royce's extraordinary book, *The Problem of Christianity*. This was the first book by a professional philosopher that I read. The great essay on "Community" definitely settled once and for all in my mind the falsity of the doctrine of enlightened self-interest as *the* motivation. Without a sense of and sympathy for others there is no personal self. Nothing is more directly natural and rational than interest in others. Eventually, this carried me beyond Royce and anything I recall of Jones to something more and more like the Whiteheadian-Buddhist (and to some extent Peircean) notion of the conscious self as a "personally-ordered society" of momentary actualities, all related to their predecessors in the series by the same principle, though not in the same degree, as relates them to members of some other series. The simplest description of this principle is feeling of feeling, or sympathy. This issue was in the main already settled during my second year at Haverford, after a brief time during which I argued vigorously with my father for the self-interest doctrine. During my first year in the army, when I was twenty or twenty-one years old, the matter grew quite clear. I related my view to a fellow occupant of a tent in which slept those of us who, at the time, were on night-duty. He was a law student, and his comment was, "That's a perfectly good little doctrine." I don't know about the 'little', but otherwise I still accept his evaluation.

Another occurrence of importance while at Haverford was coming to read Coleridge's *Aids to Reflection*, in which he paraphrases, or as DeQuincey put it, "plagiarizes," Schelling's philosophy. Otherwise I then knew nothing of German idealism. Eventually, years later, at Harvard (and while studying in Germany) I read much of the literature in English (and some in German) and took a course with C. I. Lewis on the subject. But Coleridge was my introduction to it and presumably had some effect, though my recollections of the book are faint and slight.

Haverford did some other things for me. I heard the great scholar and superb human being F. B. Gummere (whom Harvard tried vainly to attract) in his eloquent lecture course on English literature. My debt to that literature is immense.

I also took a course on composition in which I wrote an essay, "On Taking Things for Granted." This, too, is lost; but it set forth the risks of lightly assuming as known what is in truth not known. Perhaps I was at that time as close to Sextus Empiricus as I have ever come in my questionings.

At Haverford I encountered a group of sophisticated agnostics or atheists, readers of Nietzsche, and took a look at the latter's writings. They did not appeal to me, partly, I think, because of the writer's somewhat repellent personality, as I felt it in reading him. He still does not appeal to me. His crass male chauvinism is unforgivable. I can, however, see now much better than I could then why religion as he found it around him repelled him. And I find sympathetic his scorn of philosophers who fail to see that being is a mere abstraction from becoming. The "eternal recurrence" that so enraptured him seems, on the contrary, a regression into the traditional Greek overestimation of mere being.

I roomed for seven months with William Henry Chamberlin, a senior, two classes ahead of me, a highly intellectual person, without religious beliefs but also without any wish to destroy beliefs of mine. This was my first chance to show that I can associate closely with others without requiring or being required to share their religious ideas. With Phoenixville associates and at Yeates this had scarcely been an issue, except that my parents had become aware of the effects on me of reading Arnold's book and had shown that they would avoid harassing me about the change in my conviction that it had occasioned.

My summer vacation between the first and second years at Haverford was mostly spent at the Plattsburg volunteer military training school for civilians. It was clear that there would be conscription, since we had entered the war; and after a spell with absolute pacifism I had come to view that extreme doctrine (I had read Tolstoi's defense of it) as not for me the solution of the war-peace problem. The simulated military life interested me, and I wrote long letters about it. But I did not fancy myself as a warrior in the business of killing. So the question of my role in or during the war was moot. The matter was settled and my time at Haverford was somewhat shortened by the following events. Recruiting officers for the U.S. Army Medical Corps came to the institution, with its pacifist tendencies, to ask for volunteers for the status of orderlies, with the rank of privates, to join a group of doctors and nurses to take over from the British a base hospital in France (at Le Tréport, a seaside summer resort). I have in my book of recollections explained why I responded to this appeal. It ended my second year at Haverford in March. Since I had already decided to change to Harvard for my further education, only a few weeks of Haverford were sacrificed by the decision. I have never regretted the time I did spend at Haverford, but I wanted something else from then on.

VI. Army Life as Educative (1917–1919)

a) I Think about God, Mind, and Matter

The reader may have noticed, in this account, how meeting books has for me rivaled, perhaps surpassed, meeting people as stimulus. The last intellectually important event before my spell in the military was reading (of all things!) H. G. Wells's novel *Mr. Britling Sees it Through*. Wells had read William James's *Varieties of Religious Experience* and found in James's idea of a "finite God" what he took, for a few years, as the solution to the theological problem of evil, which, for so many at the time, was dramatically illustrated by WWI. In the novel he expresses this new faith with astonishing and for me then—and indeed even now if I reread it—convincing eloquence. Rarely indeed has any novelist so explicitly and powerfully argued for a definite theological view. Later, as we learn from Wells's *Experiment in Autobiography*, he changed his mind and became an agnostic, if not outright atheist. As, during my menial labors in an army hospital, I thought over the notion of a simply finite God, I began to see that, no more than simply asserting, was simply renouncing, God's infinity the solution to any theological problem.

I will, howevever, say that, as I found out later, my father had, probably before I was born, himself renounced what had usually been meant by the divine infinity, absoluteness, utter independence, and omnipotence, without substituting for it an equally unqualified divine finitude, relativity, dependence, or "limited" power. Since, in my late childhood and early youth, I heard many sermons by my father, though I recall little of these experiences, it is reasonable to suppose that in my attitude toward the classical problem of evil, which has never been, for me, a major reason for regarding God's existence as problematic—given a reasonable connotation for 'God'—I have almost certainly been profoundly influenced by the fact that my father was no uncritical defender of, rather he vigorously rejected, what I call classical theism. There is ample evidence, some of which I intend to publish, of my father's thought about this idea of God. It shows the vigor of an informed and highly trained mind (he had a master's degree, and both a divinity and a law degree). He was also that not very common phenomenon at the time of a pious religious person (with Episcopal and also Quaker background) who in the 1880s accepted Darwinian evolution. For all I know, my philosophy derives as much from him as from Peirce, or Whitehead, by both of whose philosophies I have obviously been strongly influenced.

That James's finitism does not furnish a credible theology became my conclusion soon after reading Wells, and then James's *Varieties*. (I had that book with me in the army, along with a small library of books of philosophical-theological relevance that I managed to smuggle in a second case besides the single one that was our standard equipment. Or so my memory seems to tell me: I do not recall anyone else having two cases in the hut in which I slept during most of those two years.)

What moved me beyond Wells was that he thought of God only as the supermind of humanity, not as the spirit of the cosmos as a whole; and his main reason appeared to be the idea of inanimate nature as mindless—in short a mind-matter dualism. Briefly I accepted this, until the following happening.

One day, looking at a beautiful French landscape, I had a vivid experience. A phrase of Santayana (coming to me second hand, I think) defining beauty as "objectified pleasure" popped into my mind. "No," I said to myself, and then something like the following: "the pleasure is not first in me as subject of this experience and then projected onto the object as in the experience. It is *given as in the object*, or at any rate some sort of feeling is so given. Nature comes to us as constituted by feelings, not as constituted by mere lifeless, insentient matter. *That* is a product of thought, not of perception. Matter as dualists describe it is never a datum, it is a construct. And how can we form a valid concept of something we could never experience and without analogy to what we can experience? So, if God is, as Wells says, the spirit or supermind of humanity, God may be the supermind of inanimate nature (so-called) as well.''

From this time on I never took very seriously the notion of God as radically finite in the sense that Wells derived from James. Learning later that Wells gave up the idea seemed confirmation, so far as it went. Always since then, I have thought of James's empiricism as a classical example of the utterly inconclusive or inadequate philosophical results to be expected from unqualified empiricism. If there is no a priori metaphysical knowledge, then I think agnosticism is the right conclusion.

No further definite step toward a philosophical theology came to me while in the army. I thought a lot about the problem of Christology (I had Augustine's *Confessions* with me) and found that for me the idea that we know God only, or even chiefly by knowing how to think about Jesus failed to speak to my condition. I felt that I had some clues about life and our basic relation to nature and to something superhuman and cosmic. I had had a course on the New Testament by a distinguished scholar, H. J. Cadbury; from none of this however, could I derive an affirmative answer to the question of a radically supernatural status distinguishing Jesus from all the rest of humanity. I responded positively to the two Great Commandments, to the manifestations of love depicted in the accounts of Jesus, and Paul's great prose poem on the subject; but the essential problem seemed to me the relation of God to nature, and man as included in nature, not the special relation of God to Jesus. I fear that is where I am still. I felt somewhat sad about it. I had been brought up otherwise.

b) *My Military Relations with the At Least Equal Sex*

The two years in an army hospital were spent with five groups of people: male doctors, all mature persons; male orderlies like myself, mostly in their twenties or not much older; male patients, in age like the orderlies; female nurses doing their jobs, some middle-aged; a few occasional female patients in a separate room, two at a time, either sick nurses or British ambulance drivers. The nurses had the rank of second lieutenant, we orderlies were mostly privates. For two years, then, my female associates were all mature people, trained, disciplined, career women. There were *no* very young women, no teen-agers! (The one French family I came to know a little included a refined young lady with a child or two, a grandmother, and a husband in the army whom I met on my second and last visit at their house.) Some of the nurses became good friends; and one of these friendships was a more perfect non-erotic relation than I would have believed possible. I feel grateful for this prolonged unique relationship to the opposite sex. In addition to encounters with the galaxy of gifted, intelligent, educated, female relatives in my father's and mother's families, my two years of steady experience with professional women—not all with the refinement of my relatives—is a major causal condition making it possible for me, through my entire adult life, to look upon both sexes as human in the full sense.

If there is a difference, I hold that it is women who most completely sum up human potentialities. I agree with Ashley Montagu on this and am prepared to argue the matter. The science of genetics has disproved what Aristotle and Aquinas took as the sign of women's inferiority: that the "seed" comes only from the father. We now know that genes, the formative factors, come from both parents. Only from women, however, come the supports to the embryo and infant furnished by womb and mammary glands. Nor are these all the uniquely feminine contributions. It is women who have the net addition, the physiological plus. A woman is not an incomplete man—on the contrary.

In the long past, with no science of genetics, poor sanitation, and poor medical knowledge, the burden of bearing multitudes of infants—and in many cases dying during or soon after the end of the childbearing and nursing period—it was almost beyond the capacity of human nature to grasp the truth that women can, in favorable circumstances, do about as well as men in the arts and sciences. No one of us can know exactly how well they might do in a society that had overcome the traditional ignorance and prejudice in these matters. The remaining need for moderate birth rates—to match, in a crowded world, the moderate death rates—would still limit the number of women who enjoyed the favorable circumstances referred to. Plato was wiser than Aristotle here: some women, many women, can and should attain high levels of cultural activity. To deny this is prescientific error, selfish meanness, or the kind of religion that makes obtuseness to new knowledge a divine demand.

VII. HARVARD UNIVERSITY: I BECOME A PHILOSOPHER

a) Interlude in California: My First Harvard Professor

After leaving the army, in the spring of 1919, came a summer in California, partly with Frank Morley, a brilliant and delightful Haverford classmate and his likewise wonderful English parents, via the Canadian Rockies. Included was a bicycle and camping trip by myself in the Sierras. The small number of automobiles made this possible; it would scarcely be so now. I had seen France and England; I thought I should see my own country. I attended a few lectures at the University of California at Berkeley and heard C. I. Lewis on Fichte and Schelling. He charmed me, as he did to the end of my career at Harvard, which began that autumn. (Lewis was not yet a professor at Harvard but was trained there and began his teaching there in my second or senior year. He again gave his course, which I took, on post-Kantian idealism.) A course on typing at Berkeley has been useful ever since. On my bicycle trip I saw a sign about a job in a small lumber mill; feeling that my money might give out otherwise, I took the job for about ten days. This was enough for a task that one had fully learned after a day or two. It was definitely unskilled labor. I also picked prunes for a day. That, too, was unskilled.

b) Harvard Teachers; Doctoral Dissertation

William James, Royce, and Santayana were only memories (or photographs) at Harvard, but R. B. Perry, favorite pupil of James and aggressive critic of idealism, was there and so was W. E. Hocking, a charismatic proponent of idealism. He was a disciple of Royce but was influenced also by James. Flashes of insight, striking epigrams ("pluralism is an unfinished thought," meaning *extreme* pluralism—or was it dualism he was thus dismissing?) were his forte, rather than careful, rigorous chains of reasoning. Lewis, student of James and Royce, Kant scholar, exponent of symbolic logic and its first historian, as well as a wise thinker about *The Analysis of Knowledge and Valuation*, to use the title of his best book (besides his history of symbolic logic) taught me the most. I had five courses with him. H. M. Sheffer, an emotionally troubled person but a brilliant logician, gave courses on his own way of doing logic, one of which I took. I listened to another. I also took his fine course on British Empiricism.

At Harvard I had a minor in English literature with two distinguished teachers, a standard course on zoölogy, and W. E. Hocking's famous metaphysics course. (I heard a few lectures of his in other courses.) I also had two courses that were (at last!) my introduction to the history of philosophy. I took the course on ancient philosophy and the course on modern philosophy in the same semester. This juxtaposition worked well, so far as I could see. I kept being thrilled to find ideas I had come to by myself in vaguer form being set forth and defended by writers of centuries or more ago; thrilled also by many ideas new to me. James Haughton Woods, named after my maternal grandfather, became a friend and guide in my philosophical studies. Woods was a Sanskrit scholar, a generally learned man (I had a course with him on Greek philosophy), and a wonderful person, as well as the best departmental chairman I have known.

Neither of us had previously known about the other. Woods was the academic statesman who later conceived and executed the brilliant idea of asking Whitehead to teach philosophy, thereby changing the intellectual history of this country and, in time, the world. (But this was in 1924, when I was in Europe.) Woods told me to read F. H. Bradley rather than Bernard Bosanquet—I did, but gave Bosanquet a try, too—and above all to study logic, "The coming thing." How right he was in all this!

Hocking encouraged me to develop my interest in metaphysical problems; and Lewis warmly praised an essay I wrote on Fichte. Lewis and Perry kept me critical of Hocking's too easy ways of establishing his beliefs. Lewis had a proof that I still accept for the impossibility that reality could be an absolute, mutually implicative system. Perry went to the opposite extreme of universally external relations. Hocking had learned from James to give up Royce's unqualified doctrine of internal relations; also to admit a future open even for God and allow for freedom in the libertarian sense. I worked out a doctrine of relations as, in many cases, strictly external for some, though not for all (or both) their terms but genuinely internal for one term. It was not, I think, wholly satisfactory; but it did avoid the two extremes, as found in Russell and Hume on one side and Bradley and Royce, later Blanshard, on the other. Much of this prepared me for Peirce and Whitehead, especially the former, who very obviously and definitely avoided these extremes.

My rejection of a mind-matter dualism, already settled while I was in the army, was encouraged not only by Hocking's idealism but even more directly by the psychologist, L. T. Troland, with whom I took a course and who was later of central importance for my first book, on sensation. Troland was a convinced psychicalist, influenced by Fechner. On my oral examination he expressed his agreement with me on the point.

Two undergraduate and two graduate years as student at Harvard produced a somewhat definite epistemological and metaphysical scheme in my dissertation on "the unity of all things" (in God). I attempted to prove by argument the positions I affirmed. There is no mention of Whitehead, who was still in London and of whose writings I had read only some parts of *The Concept of Nature*. This did convince me (if I needed convincing), that reality is essentially becoming or process, not mere being. Also I did write for one class an essay called "The Self Its Own Maker" (before I knew anything of Lequier's "Thou hast created me creator of myself," or Whitehead's "the self-created creature"). My dissertation contained little that is contradictory of Whitehead's or Peirce's views; but this came about otherwise than through their influence. The same world, and many of the same influences, worked on me as had worked on Whitehead and Peirce. None of us would have been possible a century earlier. But I am getting ahead of my story.

c) In Europe as Postdoctoral Student; Husserl, Heidegger, et al. (1923–1925)

A Sheldon Fellowship for study abroad came after my Ph.D. degree. I remained abroad for two years and more, mostly in Germany, but with some intensive experience in England, Austria (Moritz Schlick, Heinrich Gomperz), France (Lucien Lévy-Bruhl—whom I had heard lecture at Harvard—Edouard Le Roy, Lucien Laberthonnière). I met or at least heard a number of other famous people: S. Alexander, R. G. Collingwood, J. S. Haldane (father of J. B. S. Haldane the great biologist) G. E. Moore, G. F. Stout, Harold H. Joachim, with whom I had a good talk (his book *Truth* I thought wrong-headed, but I felt that, like Bernard Bosanquet, he was a man of good will), Richard Kroner, Oskar Becker, Julius Ebbinghaus, Max Scheler. In Berlin I heard one lecture each by Max Planck and Adolf Harnack. In Freiburg, I learned about the history of philosophy from Kroner, Ebbinghaus, and Jonas Cohn ("*Cohn weiss Alles*" was the saying; I remember him as especially good on Plato). Edmund Husserl I saw and heard many times, read several of his early books, especially *Ideen*. Heidegger I barely met, but heard him lecture many times and read some of his early writings. Neither of the two satisfied me. Husserl seemed naive in his basic program, partly as he did to Heidegger, because of his idea that we can achieve absolute evidence, utter clarity and distinctness, by suspending belief and attending to the given. Heidegger was not naive, but—as it seemed to me—much of the time he was either saying pretentiously what I already knew or was retreating back and back into the philosophic past, as though Aristotle was closer to the truth than the Scholastics, the pre-Socratics than Aristotle, and someone or something, I'm still not sure what, truer than the pre-Socratics—perhaps the poet J. C. F. Hölderlin.

It was only five or more years later, when I read and reviewed *Sein und Zeit*, that I began to see with some clarity what Heidegger was driving at. Against Husserl he seemed right; *being in the world* is indeed the basic datum, present even in dreams, as Bergson has shown. Ortega y Gasset had this same agreement with Heidegger. But beyond that, how much did the latter give us that James, Bergson, or various others had not already said in other words? Also I did not especially admire Heidegger's character, nor can I greatly like a philosopher who offers so nearly nothing in ethics!

In Marburg, whither Heidegger had gone, taking with him most of his students, including me, I heard, besides Heidegger, the neo-Kantian Paul Natorp and Nicolai Hartmann. Natorp was a learned man and I found his *Psychologie* stimulating. Hartmann, too, was learned and an effective critic of the idealisms that then existed in Germany, but his positive proposals left me somewhat cold. Later, when I had known Whitehead and read his American writings, Hartmann seemed at best a much weakened analogy, in cosmology, to Whitehead, closer to Alexander, and worth attending to only in ethics. His character or personality, too, I disliked. Kroner, Ebbinghaus, Scheler, Cohn, Oskar Becker, Alexander Pfänder, and Rickert were my favorite German philosophers. In Austria I respected Schlick, and Heinrich Gomperz (who later taught at the University of Southern California).

One of my objections to Husserl was also that expressed by Gilbert Ryle—his lack of humor. To see no wisdom in the history of philosophy is to be benighted, to see no comic foolishness in it, ditto. In this respect Ebbinghaus was exemplary. He was deeply serious, but also humorous and witty. He had in succession two wonderful wives (the first died of tuberculosis) and he knew it both times. I knew both wives, especially the second, who at this writing may be still alive.

I returned from my student wanderings with some ideas about the direction that phenomenological inquiry should take, in contrast to Husserl, but in partial agreement with Heidegger. My chief quarrel with Husserl (which I expressed to him on one occasion, whereupon he said, "Perhaps you have something," [*Vielleicht haben Sie Etwas*]) was over his dualism of sensation and feeling. I do not see Heidegger as endorsing this dualism. For me sensation has always been, since my experience in France in the war years, a special form of feeling or intuitive valuation. The sweetness of fruit and other sugars is an organism's sense of "good to eat." Even horses have it. The bitterness or sourness of some substances found in nature is a feeling of "bad to eat," the saltiness of sea water, a feeling of "bad to drink." This is a biologically intelligible view of sensation, which is more than can be said of the way many, but far from all, philosophers and psychologists have viewed the matter. I hold that color and sound qualities are, less obviously but still truly, to be similarly interpreted. My first book was on this subject. I still think its basic argument and broad conclusions are sound and unrefuted. Sensory qualities are intrinsically adaptive. Evolution has brought this about.

Most intellectuals are too far from nature and the primitive modes of human and primate existence (in which sense organs and related parts of brains were much as they are now) to easily see the point. Wordsworth poetically expressed the affective content of sense impressions; and Whitehead and I, before we knew each other, got help from Wordsworth, and also Shelley. Berkeley and Goethe both hinted at the basically emotive content of perception. The famous psychologist C. Spearman was well aware of it, as was the American experimentalist F. R. Bichowsky.

I recall no further definite progress in my own philosophical doctrines while a traveling Harvard fellow. I was concentrating somewhat on the sensation problem, of which Husserl's dualistic account (which he seemed to take for granted while declaring his presuppositionlessness) had reminded me.

*d) Harvard Instructor and Research Fellow: Peirce, Whitehead
   (1925–1928)*

I returned to Harvard with the triple assignment: instructing a course; assisting
Whitehead (whom for the first time I would hear lecture) in his metaphysics
course by helping him grade papers; and beginning to edit the unpublished as
well as the already published philosophical writings of Charles S. Peirce. By
sheer luck—for I had not asked for these assignments—I was to be intensively
exposed, virtually simultaneously, to the thought of perhaps the two greatest
philosophical geniuses who ever worked primarily in this country. There was a
price for this. It took me a long time to digest, and then only partially, the
technical knowledge and insight of these two thinkers.

   The department, as was usual, I think, asked me to give a talk on my
European experiences and impressions. This was my first occasion of talking to
so large a professional group. I told about Husserl and I little remember what
else, except that I did quote Heidegger in a phrase not common with him, I
believe, (but then congenial, it seems, to me): the problem of Christianity is to
determine "the significance of the Cross." I was shocked to learn from Perry
that my talk had lasted an hour and fifteen minutes. (He tactfully said that he
thought about the time only because Professor DeWulf had to catch a plane.)
This was the beginning of my acquiring what every professor should have,
although I know of at least one who never acquired it, a sense of how long one
is taking with a speech. (Two presidents of the Eastern Division gave talks of far
more than two hours, one because, knowing what he was doing and being an
egotist, he made the most of a captive audience, the other for what reason I cannot imagine. He was supposed to be an experienced and well-intentioned man.)

   After my talk, Whitehead, addressing me for perhaps the first time, spoke
cordially about what I had said. He expressed surprise concerning Husserl's
stress on essences, the pseudo-Cartesian rationalism I have referred to above.
Clearly, he felt as I did that Husserl never understood the fully concrete
phenomena. He also complimented me publicly on my remark about German as
a language in which it is all too easy to express philosophical ideas (*Umwelt* and
Mitwelt, for example), tending perhaps to give one a specious sense of
intellectual command of the truth.

   Both Whitehead's lectures that year in the class in which I was his assistant
and Peirce's papers began to impress me more than any of my teachers so far had
done. Besides Whitehead's class lectures that year, there were those in Boston on
Religion in the Making, of which I recall hearing at least one. During my three
years as a junior member of the Harvard faculty, those were the only lectures by
Whitehead that I recall hearing, except one on mathematical logic and one in the
elementary history of philosophy in which, one year, I instructed a section. How-

ever, I read *Religion in the Making*, also *Symbolism, Its Meaning and Effect* (which I reviewed in a student magazine), and *Science and the Modern World*. Deeply as I was impressed by Whitehead's personality—the most all-round perfect one that I have met in a person of genius, or as Victor Lowe has said, "the most civilized man"—I am not convinced that my preference on the whole for his thought to that of Peirce is primarily explained by my visual and auditory encounters with him. As already remarked, my intellectual stimuli have been primarily books.

I had no need to meet Peirce. As with all great writers, what counted most in him was there in his writings. But Peirce came to his ideas thirty or forty years before Whitehead, and in that time great intellectual changes occurred. In addition, Peirce, by a mixture of bad luck, personal mistakes, and mistakes by others, had a difficult time of it, and did not quite "get his act together." He lacked the steady communication with students and competent colleagues that a scholar needs. Supposing the two comparable in genius, Whitehead had several advantages. That is my explanation for agreeing more with him. Paul Weiss came to the opposite conclusion. But he, too, had never seen Peirce! It remains true that one will have to have Peirce in mind to understand thoroughly my thought or Paul's.

My career at Harvard was lucky in another respect than that of exposure to Peirce and Whitehead. Paul Weiss did me, also himself to be sure, a great favor by offering to help in the editing of Peirce. He was just the kind of helper that was needed. Neither of us was putting all his eggs in that basket; we both wanted to get through with the job and go on to doing independent work. Both deeply admired Peirce from the first moment, Weiss (I imagine) even before that as student of Morris Cohen in New York. Both viewed our task as an obligation to the profession.

Weiss had more facility at the time in formal logic than I did, but was, as he has said himself, less mature as a philosopher (he was also four years younger). In religious interest and in some other ways I was closer to Peirce than was Weiss. Peirce had an episcopal background, was an experimental psychologist and this country's first phenomenologist, well before Husserl. But Weiss had traits the job needed. I was hesitating between two procedures, though I preferred one; Weiss who later in his career made numerous bold decisions, urged me to stop debating with myself and do what I wanted to do, which was to adopt the systematic, instead of chronological, procedure. I knew there could be objections either way. But we had to decide and I give Weiss credit for easing the process. Above all he did a great amount of detailed work, not only for the two years or so that we worked together in Cambridge but for some years afterward. The way of numbering smaller portions than chapters was his, adapted from Wittgenstein. It was he who discovered the Sheffer stroke function in three pages of Peirce, written long before Sheffer. It was also Weiss who saw to it that he and I received full credit for our work on the title page of the volumes, even though some graduate students had a hand in it after I left the scene. In every way I can think of, Weiss's part was beneficial.

My teaching at Harvard was found disappointing, in comparison with the high expectations arising from my work in courses and the dissertation, as well as the written and oral examinations leading up to the Ph.D. degree. There are several reasons for my lack of any great success as a teacher in those years. One was that my first course was badly, uninvitingly entitled (not by me but by someone while I was in Europe). Few, and no excellent, students took it; I did not do teaching as naturally and easily as writing, and I never, in my own eyes, reached the same level of almost steady excellence in it that I (and some others) attribute to myself in the other function. But I did reach a higher level after leaving Harvard.

I never received an offer from Harvard after leaving it in 1928 to go to Chicago. The possibility was discussed in the department; but, as Whitehead, I think, told me, there were "two groups." On one issue Weiss and I have long agreed: by failing to take either of us the department did not necessarily show its wisdom! In all such matters there is an element of luck. Such things can never be purely rational. Even when one is in a department as decisions are made, it is not always clear why they go as they do. Nor am I entirely sure that in this case luck was bad, so far as I was concerned. And if it was, this is nothing in comparison with the good luck that had already occurred.

Perhaps here is as good a place as any to say something about the fact that, so far, my causal explanations have been environmental rather than genetic. In other words, next to nothing has been said about the unique gene combination (since I have no twin) that must be in me. It is silly to say that this factor amounts to little and environment does everything (apart from the element of freedom I referred to at the outset). It is silly because there is no conceivable way of proving it, and it contradicts in principle, I incline to think, what we do know about the genes and their consequences. The reason for not trying to go further to specify what the innate factor may be in my case is that there is so little secure knowledge by which to relate genes and philosophical differences. If anything transcends easy scientific knowledge, surely this does.

VIII. The University of Chicago (1928–1955)

a) The Chicago Pragmatists; A Friend for Life

In this, my first full-time teaching, I found myself in a different climate of opinion. At Harvard only Lewis took John Dewey seriously, not to mention Mead, whose views resembled Dewey's. But in Chicago it was precisely these two whose views dominated. There was, however, great respect for Peirce and James. I had already heard, and had been impressed by, Dewey when he gave a lecture to a meeting of the Eastern Division of the American Philosophical Association. I may have read something of his writings. I had also seen and heard Mead give brief comments on a talk by Whitehead at the World Congress of philosophers in 1928 at Harvard. The Chicago experience led me to go deeply into the forms that pragmatism took after Peirce and James, especially in Dewey, Mead, Tufts, and their admirers and students, chiefly those in Chicago. If I differ from this "Chicago School," I know rather well just how and why. Had I remained at Harvard, this might have been much less true, and, I suspect, to my loss.

It is quite possible that nothing occurring in the twenty-seven years I spent at the University of Chicago had more effect on my intellectual development than my engagement and (in my first December in the city) marriage to Dorothy Eleanore Cooper. She did not come to me with an already defined philosophy, except in the sense of having an unorthodox religious perspective (Universalism), of being a theist in a not sharply formulated sense, and of having had some training in Biblical scholarship and in the history of philosophy. She was also a trained botanist and a trained musician (pianist and singer) who was sincerely devoted to the ideals of art *and* science (especially in the biological form). What more could a philosopher who was also an embryo-ornithologist wish for in an intellectual companion? As for an unintellectual one, I have managed rather well without that!

It was an advantage that my wife, who, for partly accidental reasons, had given up any scientific ambitions she may have had, though not her respect for science, was ambitious not in philosophy but in music, especially opera. This implied no rivalry to my philosophical aims. Rather the contrary! My first book, the gist of which was in my dissertation written ten years before the book, was on sensation interpreted as a form of feeling. And the art to which I chiefly related the idea was music. Bird song, a special case of what I call animal music, fitted into the same picture. My book was in principle credible to Dorothy before it was to anyone else.

Besides all this, I had long ago renounced male chauvinism in principle and expected to do part of the household chores, no matter whom I married. So a wife with ambitions was in order. This is not all. Dorothy had lived through a classic case of a wife (her mother), a career woman in the early days of career women, being married but happy only in her career rather than as wife or even mother. The marriage was stable, but as a relationship endured rather than enjoyed by the two spouses. Dorothy understood this sufficiently to wish either for no marriage or for one very different for both parties than the one she had ob-

served and suffered from since she was old enough to realize what was going on.
I had grown up in a far more normally happy marriage than Dorothy had and my
experiences in the military corps had prepared me for the male role in such a
marriage. I had never expected *not* to wash dishes as husband, for example. I had
done it for months under one or another woman, my military superior, in the
army!

One of the advantages of marriage is that one may, with luck, acquire much
knowledge of the intimacies of life from in-laws, as well as from other intimates
of one's spouse. I can think of a number of families, Hartshornes, Haughtons,
Coopers, their subfamilies, and at least one other, that I believe I know more
intimately than I could under a less strongly stable family system.

Our honeymoon was our first experience of sexual union and was, as Dorothy
explicitly predicted to me beforehand, about as happy as we can imagine. True
we both had read an excellent book on the subject. To make no use of books
in such a matter I view as not very intelligent in a society in which writing
and printing has such importance in every other aspect of life. Societies without writing work out oral ways of preparing the young. Many in our society
lack both methods of being prepared. Margaret Mead had things to say about
this. Edith Wharton's mother flatly refused Edith's request for such help. Poor
genius-endowed Edith; stupid, wicked, or dismally unfortunate mother! Or, read
H. G. Wells's account of his first wife: "she submitted."

I should say that I had known Dorothy for some months while I was at
Harvard and she at Wellesley College and had exchanged a letter or two after
illness ended her stay at Wellesley. So our short engagement in Chicago did
not mean love "at first sight." I was not, at that stage in my life, so perceptive
as all that. I did know that she was talented and appealing and that we were
natural, and at ease with each other. I thought about her as possible life partner, but did not reach a positive decision. We might never have married had
Dorothy not seen my name as new instructor at the University of Chicago (from
which her father had his Ph.D.). I had not known that she was then living
in Chicago with her family. Her mother, told about my presence in the city,
said, "Invite him to dine with us." So chancy are some of the important things
in life!

I have not exhausted the reasons why my marriage was favorable to the
development of my philosophy and my writing. Dorothy had been a teacher, as
both her parents were or had been (her mother, with an M.A. in Classics, only
for a short time). Thus she had grown up much closer to academic life than I had.
Also she was, at the time, like her mother, a professional editor and proofreader,
with a brilliant record as such. Since I was even more naturally a writer than a
teacher, an editor and proofreader was something I could use and she volunteered
to meet the need. Above all, Dorothy is one of the rare people with so wide a

range of knowledge, so nimble an intelligence, and so tactful and generous in friendship as to make her an always interesting partner for an academic person. Not least of all, her chosen friends, men or women, are always good to have as also one's own.

Robert Frost said, "The woman always loses." I fear Dorothy lost something by marrying an ambitious professor-writer. She did however enjoy some professional opportunities in music, including opera, and some splendid opportunities in high-class amateur musical comedy, the Faculty Revels in the University of Chicago. She became much more universally known to the academic body than I ever did, and altogether favorably known. So if she lost, it was not everything.

Since neither Dorothy nor I were or are faultless, our marriage has definitely not been trouble-free. But since it was always perfectly obvious that the marriage was fantastically to my advantage in every essential way, I never wavered in my conviction that it could and should be preserved. It has, for more than 60 years. Unless at least one partner has this conviction, the endurance of a union "till death us do part" is at best problematic. The rewards for sharing happy memories for so many years have to be experienced to be appreciated.

With a different or no marriage who knows what might have happened to my mental growth? I can imagine many ways in which it might have been slowed down—energy lost in emotional stress, various distractions from intellectual and literary ambitions and primary interests—but no probable way in which it could have gone so well as it has. My writing has been criticized by experts for its content, but I think I am correct in saying that no one has objected to its style, to *how* those contents were expressed. Had I not had a gifted editor reading nearly everything, I might still have escaped severe censure on stylistic matters, but certainly not have won the praise frequently bestowed on the readability of my publications. One distinguished biologist told his secretary to read my *Born to Sing* "if only for its style." (He was also supportive about the content.)

This reminds me, had I married a person little interested in nature, or in empirical science, it is very possible that my interest in birds would have led to no such entry into a scientific community as the ornithologists constitute around the world, scores of them well known to me. It was my wife who warmly encouraged me to take advantage of a circular sent to me by the University of Michigan Biological Station about courses in ornithology and other branches of biology given in summer in Northern Michigan. Result, I spent two summers (in my fifty-fifth and fifty-sixth years) surrounded by empirical scientists and *no* philosophers, participating in a class taught by a noted teacher of ornithology, O. Sewall Pettingill, Jr., author of a number of significant books in the subject and an ideal person from whom to learn the essentials of scientific study of birds.

Thus I moved beyond a mere bird watcher and casual reader of bird books and became a person trying to form and test hypotheses by observed facts. So, when I philosophize, I know vividly what is meant by the behavioristic method, and a number of other aspects of study that transcend mere armchair speculating. At the end of the first summer I finally hit upon my major discovery, a tentative generalization to be tested the following summer. It was called "the monotony threshold," and was a contingent and empirically testable specialization of my metaphysical belief that the aim of all nature is beauty, aesthetic value. Whitehead said so; I would show how the facts of a branch of psychology or biology, animal behavior and animal mind, illustrated this principle and were illuminated by it. With minor reasonable qualifications it still stands unrefuted, and some experts accept it.

I must add one more contribution made by Dorothy Eleanore Cooper to the mental growth I am trying to explain. J. S. Mill's protest against "the subjection of women" had something, or much, to do with his experience of a remarkable woman who became his wife. Without help then from Mill I was on his side of this issue long before I knew any woman I wanted to marry. However, the remarkable woman I eventually married certainly reënforced my pro-women's-rights attitude. In addition, our only offspring—apart from several sad cases of still-birth—was a powerful further reënforcement. Both Dorothy and Emily (now Mrs. Nicolas D. Goodman) have taken careers and motherhood with dedicated seriousness, without allowing either to interfere with the career or happiness of the husband. Emily and Nicolas have Stanford Ph.D.'s, he in mathematics, she in history. As I have tried to be, so my son-in-law, professor in the University of New York at Buffalo, has been cooperative and fair in sharing family chores. He even attended the births, and was as fatherly a father as I can easily imagine, of the two children, a boy and then a girl, now aged twelve and eight. Emily teaches (part-time) courses on medicine in general or psychiatry in particular and has taught the history of feminism. Her Stanford dissertation was in French history, a subject for which the demand has fallen off since WWII. I believe she has found the right specialization. She has her mother's capacity for research, without Dorothy's musical gifts but with greater capacity for mathematics. She met her husband in Quine's logic class at Harvard. Even more easily than her mother she could have been a scientist—or a philosopher, for that matter. (So could her husband.) She easily grasps the gist of my philosophy.

b) Hutchins, Adler, McKeon; A Club of Scientists

In the next academic year after I arrived in Chicago, Robert Maynard Hutchins became president of the University. Through two friends and admirers of his,

Mortimer J. Adler and Richard P. McKeon, this soon brought about considerable changes in the way philosophy was taught there. Among the results were the departures of Mead, who had been chairman, Edwin Arthur Burtt, and, a year or two afterwards, Everett W. Hall. Hall, then a Cornellian type of idealist, a friend and a helpful critic of a draft of my first book, was a considerable loss. He later gave up his idealism.

Mead, soon after my arrival, lost his wife by death, and a year or so later was terminally ill himself. I heard but one lecture by him. The few personal encounters were unimportant in my case. What was important was the argument between Hutchins, Adler, and McKeon, on the one hand, and the pragmatists and most of the faculty on the other. The dispute seemed at first, far more than it really was, between partisans of neoscholasticism or Thomism and the then dominant form of American philosophy. It led me to think more than I otherwise might have about the issue between medieval theology, represented by Jacques Maritain, friend of Hutchins, who visited in Chicago and was introduced by another friend of Hutchins (not a professional philosopher) as the "greatest living philosopher." (One wondered how the introducer had ascertained this preëminence.) If I have harped a good deal in my writings on my differences from Aquinas, this controversy surrounding me had something to do with it. I had, however, encountered Etienne Gilson, both in France and at Harvard, had had a course with M. DeWulf on neoscholasticism, and had listened to lectures on the subject while 'postdoctoring' in Germany and Austria. So the topic was not new to me but was made to seem relevant by the actual situation.

Burtt's leaving the department was in one way lucky for me. He was the sole philosopher who had been taken into a scientific group called the X-Club (with wives designated XS). I replaced him. This group became for my intellectual growth a second set of primary colleagues. Through it I met several of the finest (and one of the truly great) scientific minds, Sewall Wright. He is now as I type the still living dean of geneticists with countless honorary degrees and medals to show the extent of his fame. He and his wife became our best friends in the university community. In the club he was the one whose grasp seemed to span all the branches of natural science, and who was also impressive as a scientist well aware of the distinction between scientific results and philosophical beliefs and with definite things to say about both.

In his philosophy, although agnostic about God (because of what seemed to him a conflict between it and relativity physics), Wright shared with me a firm belief in what I call psychicalism. He thought a mind-matter dualism unintelligible, as I have done for nearly seventy years; and if he was not even interested in a monistic materialism, I recall no word from him about it. Only some form of psychicalism was left. He was pleased by my hearty agreement with him in this. He also had ideas about freedom as subtly more than mere voluntariness, mere doing what one wishes. Rather, he thought it had causal significance in the creative sense. He had worked all this out for himself. He learned about panpsychism by reading Karl Pearson's criticism of it and decided the doctrine was better than the criticism. Years later he thought he remembered Pearson as an exponent of the psychical view, but rereading the passage found that Pearson opposed it. Still, the view was for him the right one and the opposition mistaken.

I cannot hope ever to know well a better scientific mind than Sewall's. Our agreement about mind and matter of course pleased me. Another member of the club, the fine physiologist Ralph Gerard, also inclined toward psychicalism. (He, however, was a strict determinist.) Alfred Emerson, the world expert on termites, was an emergent dualist. I think few would see in him a genius comparable to Wright's. He was, however, stimulating. If I have much general sense of what natural science has been in recent times, I thank chiefly three groups of people for this sense, so far as it goes; first, the pair Peirce and Whitehead, (the former much the stronger of the two as experimentalist); second, the X-Club; and third, the ornithologists I have known. I have also had some friendly acquaintance with physicists, particularly the great Robert Mullikan. But my mathematical illiteracy limits what I can gain from talking to them.

In his autobiography Mortimer Adler discusses the turmoil that began with his coming to the department of philosophy (at Hutchins's initiative), then led to his being transferred to the Law School (since he had written on *evidence* at Columbia) and ended finally by his leaving the university. I was on a trip in Europe part of this time. I have no quarrel with Adler's account of these matters. His philosophical difference from McKeon is somewhat similar to my difference. Adler and I are less willing than McKeon to allow the effort to understand the writings of past philosophers to largely crowd out philosophical understanding of nature and supernature (perhaps even of the great philosophers in their insights *and oversights*). This does not mean that I learned nothing from McKeon. It is partly because of exposure to his influence that my thinking has acquired so strong an historical slant. I have also learned from his way of contrasting and classifying philosophical approaches, especially about the contrast between Plato and Aristotle, also between Plato and the Neoplatonists, and between Aristotle and medieval disciples of Aristotle.

A friend of mine in Greek studies at Chicago, Brooks Otis, edited a student magazine for which I wrote a two-part essay on my position as neither Thomistic nor close to the Chicago version of Pragmatism. Hutchins wrote me an appreciative response. I had not particularly attacked him. I find it difficult to feel negative about very witty people. It soon became apparent that neither Adler nor McKeon was a Thomist. McKeon was not nearly so far from Dewey in his beliefs as some have supposed.

c) I Become Departmental Secretary; Visit to Stanford University

Having been made Dean within a few years of his arrival, McKeon found no one in the department who suited him as chairman, and proposed me as "acting secretary." I told him I did not like the role but he said, "the best administrators are the unwilling ones," or something like that, with Plato in mind. This was my only administrative experience. It lasted four quarters and was most fortunately ended by my being invited for two quarters to Stanford. Everyone knew I was more than willing to let someone else take the job. McKeon also was more than willing. So everyone was satisfied. The position was given to Charner Perry, to whom no one objected.

One important thing was accomplished while I was secretary. We invited Rudolf Carnap, after much struggle with the administration, to join the department. The idea was Charles Morris's, between whom and me there have always been friendly feelings. He wanted to invite Reichenbach also, and I, perhaps foolishly, supported this. It would have made the department lopsidedly logical positivist (or logical empiricist). It had one advantage though, it made it possible for the administration to split the difference and resolutely reject Reichenbach but, grudgingly, accept Carnap. I thought Carnap would strengthen the department and that I might learn from him. In both respects I believe I was right. But my supporting Reichenbach also must have made a negative impression on the administration. I agreed with the choice of Carnap over Reichenbach.

It became clear before my two quarters at Stanford were over that I was being considered for a position there and that the decision was negative. Again, my teaching was found less impressive than my writing. I was not upset by this. I had some fine students in a fair-sized aesthetics class. Two of the Stanford students I had became more or less successful teachers of philosophy, both emphasizing aesthetics and one, also Whitehead. A third became a now famous abstract painter. Anyway, I did not then feel a need to change jobs.

d) The Federated Theological Faculty; Carnap

One of the important influences that going to U. of C. brought to bear upon me was that of the Divinity School and the three theological seminaries associated with it. Four forms of Protestantism, liberal, highly literate representatives of each form, and all different from the two forms I had been largely brought up on, were involved. These groups became well aware of me and I of them within a few years of my arrival as I began to publish my reflections on the philosophy of religion, after finishing my book on sensation. Dean McKeon disapproved of this turn, saying that philosophy of religion was "less exact" than other aspects of philosophy. However, it was precisely this lack of precision that I saw a chance to correct.

It may well be that had I kept away longer or farther from religious topics than I did my writings might have seemed more relevant to the numerous philosophers who thought as McKeon did about religion, or were still more negative on the subject. On the other hand, I would have seemed less relevant to the likewise numerous scholars who looked upon philosophy primarily for the light it casts upon the validity of religious beliefs. There is some truth in Fritz Marti's remark that the mass base of a philosophy, if it has one, is in religious people. Anyhow, as theological students began more and more to take courses with me, the Dean of the Divinity School (first Ernest Cadman Colwell and then, as Colwell was promoted to the second highest office in the university, Bernard Loomer, ex-student of mine) felt the need to take me into account in the institutional arrangements. So it came about that, although I taught, with one exception, the same courses as I would have taught anyway, I had a joint appointment, at least financially; half my salary would come from the divinity side. Charner Perry, as chairman, thought this advantageous to the department; for, as he said, "We all know that all your courses are philosophical." I wish here to say that Perry, in my judgment, agnostic as he was himself, did not underrate my abilities. He once called me a great philosopher, gave my first book high praise, and I recall his saying that I was "more important to the department than Carnap."

The exception, the one course that was more religious, and perhaps less philosophical, than I would have taught without the theological half of my salary, was a course once taught jointly by me and Daniel Day Williams. His philosophy of religion was largely a deeply felt and well documented version of mine. His *The Spirit and Forms of Love* is a noble work. He died prematurely.

Considering how different my interests were from those of its other members, I do not charge the department—which I eventually decided to leave—with unfairness or lack of appreciation. T. V. Smith, another agnostic or nontheist whose testimony could be trusted, told me, "We all respect your intellectual abilities." The member (for some years after Mead left he was chairman) whose interest in religion had most in common with mine was Edward Scribner Ames, author of *The Psychology of Religion* and pastor of the Disciples Church near the university. He felt it wise to leave his theism vaguer, less rationalized; but he called my attempts in this direction "fascinating," and he admired me for my editing of and writing about Peirce and called it "Foundation Work." He did find my claims for Peirce, and by implication for myself, "almost awe-inspiring," and once told someone how, when he had asked me a question about physics, I had said he should ask Carnap, who knew much more about physics, Ames's reported comment, somewhat disconcerting to me, was, "For once he was modest." I've had many years now to reflect on that remark.

T. V. Smith and I had remarkably different backgrounds. He grew up in a Texas village of six hundred people where almost no one was educated. (His father did know the Bible but not much more.) After work in the Young Men's Christian Association, he left all religious affiliations and followed Mead in accepting a wholly nontheistic world view. With fantastic brilliance, considering his start in life, he became a professor at thirty and was elected twice to political office, the second time to a United States Senator's seat. His writings deal with religion, politics, and ethics. One striking book is on the harm that good men do and is called *Beyond Conscience*. Perhaps that is the source of my second book's title, *Beyond Humanism*. I found his political writings admirable and the rest worth reading. His comment on my work was, "When I can distract my attention from what you are saying enough to notice how you say it, I find your style rather intimately satisfying." In my speech at the farewell banquet before he left for the University of Syracuse I quoted this remark and said that my experience with T. V.'s writing was, "When I can distract attention sufficiently from the odd way in which he expresses himself, I find what he is saying generally makes good sense." As an example of the odd style, he entitled an article on the Deweyan ideal ("use your freedom to increase your freedom") "Always on the Grow." This was for an article in the *Ladies Home Journal*. He called his autobiography *The Nonexistent Man*, on the ground that no one tells the truth about his own past. Actually, it seemed to me, where I also had experienced the facts, that he told the truth pretty well.

With Carnap I had reasonably good relations. He was a rather solemn man of essential good will, but deadly serious about his own importance—rather like Husserl in this—an attitude which, some feel, caused him to give inadequate heed to the concerns of his second wife, who nursed him for years because of a back injury. But he was a considerate colleague. He and I could exchange ideas, provided we both, especially I, made a special effort to adapt to the other's language. In two ways my thinking did interest him somewhat. I had a disproof of the Thomistic idea of God as having complete knowledge of a contingently existing world, although in God there is nothing contingent. Whatever God could be, God is. Yet had there been a different world, God would have had knowledge (which in fact God does not have) that this other possible world existed. Carnap was interested in this as test case of the question, "Can such a view as Thomism be refuted by mere logic?" He helped me to formalize my argument so that it seemed to both of us cogent. I still think so.

The other idea of mine that was interesting to Carnap was a generalized parallel to his more limited doctrine: whatever can be expressed by using logical constants alone must be noncontingent, either contradictory and necessarily false or else consistent and necessarily true. My generalization broadened the doctrine to include metaphysical categories, ideas in a certain sense as universal as logical constants but not usually included in a list of the latter. This expresses my view of metaphysics as the search for necessary, because strictly universal, concepts. The extralogical terms include modal ones taken as more than merely syntactical, also ideas of experience or knowledge in its most general sense. Carnap knew, and either I then already did, or he made me, know, that the following paradox arises from the doctrine, whether in his or in my form. Consider such propositions as, "Only one individual exists," or "Only ten individuals exist." No extralogical ideas are involved, yet these propositions are not, and could not be, necessarily true. His solution: always and necessarily there is an infinity of individuals, at least the points in empty space-time. Mine is: the entire reality must always include an infinity of already elapsed events or Whiteheadian actual entities. In either case the propositions stated above are always and necessarily false. Moreover, if one says, "Suppose the proposition is, 'The total reality *now* (a problem in relativity physics to be sure) is such and such a finite number of individuals,' " then I reply; there is no definite meaning for "now," from a merely eternal point of view, and all definite fixing of a "now" requires empirical, nonlogical, and nonmetaphysical terms and is contingent.

It seems clear to me that Carnap was closer to my metaphysical position than Quine has been. The two once argued in Chicago about the distinction between a priori and empirical, and the department was unable to see that Quine made his case for rejecting the distinction. Nor am I convinced that he has made his case against modal logic.

Among my students in Chicago, none have been more important to me personally than John Cobb and Schubert Ogden, both internationally known theologians with Methodist backgrounds. Both have excellent understanding of my thought; both are effective teachers and have had significant disciples. Cobb began his teaching and writing career as a philosopher and wrote a fine book on Whitehead. He founded the Center for Process Studies and, with Lewis Ford (for one year my student at Emory University), the journal *Process Studies*. Cobb has exhibited remarkable ingenuity and organizing ability in bringing together groups of people to consider Whitehead's or my kind (or kinds) of philosophy in its (or their) bearings on Buddhism, Chinese philosophy, biology, psychiatry, ecology—on the last topic of which he has written a small, characteristically lucid and readable book. I add a third Chicago student, also enrolled in the divinity school, the late Eugene Peters, careful student of my writings and author of two very readable books on process thought. Finally, Eugene Freeman, known to countless philosophers as editor of *The Monist* and of Open Court (publisher of many philosophical books, including some of mine), was the first doctoral student for whom I was primarily responsible.

Two other students who have since been influential are W. L. Reese and Bernard Loomer, the former with Disciples of Christ religious origins and the latter brought up as a Baptist. There is no denying that response to my teaching has come easier to those with positive religious concerns than to those without them. However, Milton Singer became an important anthropologist who would scarcely fit this pattern. Nor would Lucio Chiaraviglio, who studied with me in both Chicago and Atlanta. He is a philosopher of science and an expert on artificial intelligence.

IX. EMORY UNIVERSITY (1955–1962) MY THIRD, AND THE UNIVERSITY OF TEXAS (1962–   ) MY FINAL, UNIVERSITY HOME

Twice in my career I have left one university for another entirely voluntarily. I left Harvard nonvoluntarily, since they told me they had "no job" for me after my three years as teacher, research worker on Peirce, and, for one year, paper-grader for Whitehead. But in 1955 I left U. of C. voluntarily. No one even hinted that I ought to go elsewhere, and there were some gasps and unmistakable groans when I said that I was leaving for Emory. I did not ask for a raise; I said I was accepting Emory's offer. Why? It was not for the money, though financial gain there was. It was not rank: I had at last been made a professor, although only with an unexplained delay of a year after Perry assured me my final promotion would go through. The reason for my leaving was none of this. It was my status in relation to the graduate students. I had become aware that, apart from a substantial and much valued portion of my graduate students that came to me from the three theological seminaries joined together with the U. of C. Divinity School under the Federated Theological Faculty (put together by my ex-student Bernard Loomer), most of the graduate students interested in philosophy looked elsewhere than to me for their main intake of wisdom. Either I must resign myself to a hard struggle to overcome this disadvantaged position or admit defeat (for it was a defeat) and make a fresh start, a clear opportunity for which had become available. I thought that the struggle, whatever the probabilities for success, would be a waste of my time and energy.

Who was to blame for the situation? Many people, or no one. One thing was clear, of any blame I must take a share, and I said so at the farewell dinner. In general too much energy goes into blaming someone, some scapegoat, for social troubles. It is usually, if not always, the actions, decisions, inactions, failures to decide, of several, often many persons, in conjunction—and this conjunction is seldom very close to what anyone intended—that has produced or constituted the situation. From any one person's perspective it is always partly bad or good luck.

I learned from Peirce, once and for all, that chance is the negative side of what Peirce called "spontaneity," others call freedom, and Bergson, Berdyaev, Whitehead, called creativity; and that both chance and some spontaneity are universal in nature. I did not need Whitehead to teach me this. My first suspicion of it came from William James, though only in relation to the human form of awareness or behavior

I came to Peirce five years later than to James and found that he had, for partly different and more comprehensive reasons, generalized causal freedom infinitely beyond the merely human part of reality. I found Whitehead doing the same, and eventually learned of others who had done this. All of these, with one exception, were writers whose work was done during the last ten or twelve decades. The exception, curiously enough, was Epicurus. He was more than twenty centuries ahead of the world in this respect. Believing that he himself had causal freedom, not the mere voluntariness that some think is all that is needed for responsibility and importance in our behavior, but in a sense involving some degree of randomness, chance, absence of complete determination by the past, he thought that the atoms, fundamental to everything, must also have some degree of this freedom.

Peirce knew about Epicurus, but, unlike a myriad others, he saw that modern science (laws of gases particularly) gives new reasons for such a view, and that it can be cogently argued for on various metaphysical and phenomenological, as well as pragmatic, grounds. Consistently with this, Peirce rated the Stoics, whose logic he knew, lowest of the ancient Greek schools. They fell in love with necessity, absolutized it superstitiously, as though (principle of contrast) necessity would make sense if nonnecessity, contingency, did not. Contingency, Peirce saw, is no mere negation. It is creation, additional definiteness to enrich reality. The created new becomes past and the past is immune to destruction. The past is "the sum of accomplished facts." These cannot be de-accomplished but are permanent parts of the cosmic poem.

My second voluntary leaving of a good university was for very different reasons. The teaching situation at Emory suited me well the entire time. As at Chicago, there were financial advantages in the move, but they were not *the* reasons. It happened that the Emory retirement rules (I was then 65) compared very unfavorably to those in Texas, thanks to the philosopher-dean, Albert Brogan, good in both roles, who had put through the most attractive retirement scheme I know of in the country. This was almost reason enough, but not quite. I would have felt more obligated to Emory had not a colleague had a car without seat belts. The statistical facts had been made clear enough by that time (I had even published my view on it), and any adult should have learned that "probability is the guide of life" (again the reality of chance). I am not impressed when someone says, "I do not believe in seat belts." That only says to me, "He or she does not believe in an elementary bit of the minimal wisdom without which we human beings, by our lack of instinctive guidance, are doubly handicapped." Anyhow, my wife suffered grievous and not wholly reparable injury partly caused by someone's or two people's lack of elementary good sense or thoughtfulness, and by bad luck in a combination of poor drivers in two cars. I put the decision up to Dorothy, asking her to go to Austin (which I had twice visited alone) to see how she liked the people she met and the housing available."If you like what you find, we'll go, if not not." She did like it, bought a house, and we went.

John Silber, departmental chairman who had persuaded me to take the idea of going to Texas seriously, promised that I would be permitted to return to Emory in the late spring for two weeks to help students doing dissertations. The promise, which (like all Silber's promises to me) was kept, a little diminished the shock of my departure, from what was and is an admirable institution, in some ways better now than it was then.

We now intend to remain in Austin because of many good friends in and out of the university, in which I have status as Ashbel Smith Professor Emeritus (since 1978), also because of a home and neighborhood that suit our lifestyle (neither of us wants to drive a car, for one thing), and because we are too busy to face the monstrous task of relocating. As Big Bill Tilden, of tennis fame, whom I once saw play, said: "Never change a winning game" (but— "Always change a losing game").

X. MY FOREIGN JOURNEYS AND SOJOURNS

In 1948 in Chicago, Ernest Cadman Colwell, president and second to Hutchins, the Chancellor, insisted that I go to Germany for the fall and winter semesters to teach in German at the University at Frankfurt. He said someone in philosophy was needed and that I was the one who could do it. Reluctantly I agreed. It meant leaving wife and daughter for months. I did teach in German, no English at all. I also lectured in half a dozen other universities there, giving the German lecture I had written, with some help from the wife of Wilhelm Pauck of the U. of C. Divinity School. She, like her husband, was bilingual. This new task meant that I was forced to do my thinking in another language than previously. In the years 1923 to 1925, as postdoctoral student in Germany, I had thought philosophically in German; but then I was chiefly taking in what was going on in Europe, not working much at developing the philosophy I had put into English in my dissertation at Harvard.

One of my criteria for creativity in philosophers is whether or not they can express their thought in more than one way and are not dependent entirely upon any single word. I have often taught Whitehead without using his terminology at all closely—though in his case I have also found how difficult it is to find other terms as good as those he mostly used. Somewhat similarly with Peirce, who was much more given to inventing wholly new words (*sinsign, qualisign,* as examples, out of scores). In Frankfurt I could no longer depend upon my previous terminology. I think this must have helped me to become clearer about the difference between verbal and more than verbal disagreements. I have known at least one philosopher who without a certain word had little left to say. Take any technical word from me, and I shall still have much the same things to say, even in English.

To have common ground with my advanced German students (I also taught an elementary course) I chose as seminar topic Leibniz and Whitehead. So I had to figure out how one goes from a seventeenth- and for fourteen years eighteenth-century thinker to a twentieth-century one, or vice versa. It made me vividly aware of the problem of progress in philosophy, since I was comparing two thinkers with similar concerns (mathematics, logic, physics, biology, metaphysics, theology) and with similar aims at clarity and logical cogency, but separated by two and a quarter centuries of intense intellectual effort. I also became aware of the difference between two philosophers who can be imagined to come fairly quickly to an understanding of the relations between their philosophies and to have a good chance of learning from one another, and other pairs of philosophers who could not be expected to do this. Leibniz could have learned from Whitehead much more easily, I think, than from Hegel; Whitehead could hardly be himself and give time and energy to understanding Hegel. The ideals of clarity—crediting Hegel with such an ideal—are not sufficiently close in the two philosophers for this to be conceivable. (Analogously, I have been plentifully exposed to Heidegger and his writings, and to many writings about him, but learned little.) It is arguable that one can learn more from Leibniz than from Kant, considering how much more energy must be put into penetrating the latter's less clear analyses. Peirce took a hard youthful look at Hegel and gave up. It was not his idea of intellectual method. He did admire Kant. If political philosophy were my specialty, I might feel differently about Hegel than I do.

In vacation I visited Sweden, where Alf Nyman was a reader of my first book and a very astute and learned scholar, interested in one of my problems, indeed several of them. I also visited Basel, Switzerland, and talked to Barth (Karl and his philosophical brother Heinrich) and briefly with Jaspers. I got little from the last, but something rather exciting from Karl: that he very definitely did agree with my contention that there is "change in God." Later I found it in his *Churchly Dogmatics* (Edinburgh, 1953–1964, II, 1, pp. 604–640), Barth writes also: [There is] "supreme necessity" as well as "supreme contingency" in God (p. 548). Even Barth thinks partly in twentieth-century terms! I see this as a classical example of what I call "cultural change." Centuries earlier Socinian theologians said similar things, but who paid any attention to them then on this point? Kant was utterly convinced that God, and any reality beyond mere appearances, must be wholly nontemporal and immutable, and he denied that we could know the contingency even of changing appearances. Aristotle thought (and I think) that he did know this. Here and there, in Germany, France, Italy, the U.S.A., cloudily in Hegel, more clearly in Schelling, still more clearly in Fechner and some other Germans in the last century, in Peirce (somewhat hesitantly and ambiguously), the idea of a temporal aspect of deity began to be taken seriously; but Whitehead was, after Plato, the first major metaphysician to commit himself to the doctrine that God, the eternal reality, is also "in a sense temporal." At nearly the same time, perhaps wholly independently, Berdyaev expressed a similar view. It was left to me to try to make a better worked out, fully-explicated version of the doctrine in my Dual Transcendence (stimulated by Morris Cohen's Principle of Polarity and Whitehead's Dipolarity). It is also a doctrine of dual immanence, and it transforms all sorts of not obviously theological problems in metaphysics. What had been a cry in the wilderness became a worldwide movement, not confined to any religion or denomination. It can be found in one branch of Hinduism, or Islam (via Bergson), or Judaism (the late A. J. Heschel).

In 1951–52 we went to Australia on a Fulbright Professorship. The aim was partly ornithological; I already knew a lot about Eurasian birds, which differ from ours vastly less than the Australian birds do. In Australia, I learned about the influence of Wittgenstein and G. E. Moore, but also much about the avifauna of Australia and (on the way to or from Australia) something of that of the Fiji Islands, New Zealand, and Hawaii. I also made friends with Charles Birch, the biologist who knew of my thought from his professor of biology. I met J. J. C. Smart and J. L. Mackie, who later became much more famous than they were then. Besides teaching in Melbourne, I gave lectures in Sydney, Adelaide, and Tasmania. With Alexander Boyce Gibson, who was responsible for my invitation to Melbourne, I had interesting discussions. He was especially good on Plato's philosophy of religion.

I met some professional ornithologists in Australia. Eighteen months after the end of my stay in the country, *The Emu*, the leading Australian journal in the subject, published a long essay of mine on "Musical Values in Australian Bird Songs." It was my most serious attempt at ornithological writing up to that time. In New Zealand, also, I enjoyed admirable and generous ornithological help, besides giving a philosophical lecture and meeting interesting philosophers in two universities.

The next big trip was in 1958, to Japan, via Hawaii, the Philippines, and Taiwan. The dual interests were to find birds and bird people, and learn Japanese thought, especially Buddhist. I lectured in English, but in Japan almost always with a translator. Again the ornithological aim was achieved nicely, and the philosophical one fairly well. In any case we earned the Fulbright money because my wife was extremely useful, teaching English in the Doshisha University and to Fulbright grantees to the U.S.A., and teaching American school subjects to a group of seventeen children of English-speaking parents, in four different grades, whose teacher had been withdrawn with the occupation forces. I managed to put in some birding in Hawaii, the Philippines and Taiwan on the way to Japan, and to give two lectures in Taipei on my philosophy.

In 1966 occurred our third and last Fulbright journey, first to India, where I gave lectures in several cities and spent two months in Banaras Hindu University as a visiting professor. The stimulus at the latter place was discussing with T. R. V. Murti (who likes to argue) and a number of other scholars, including some disciples of Sri Aurobindo. J. L. Mehta, scholarly writer on Heidegger, and one of the most likable persons we have met, made the unforgettable remark: "Your philosophy and Heidegger's are so different that they cannot even be compared." This is a little like the quaint phrase 'not to mention', thereby mentioning whatever follows. After India, several places were visited for the birds, on the way to Japan, where I had a Fulbright commission to teach a "summer seminar," coming between university sessions and meeting for three hours five days a week for several weeks. Ever since I have thought this was and is the right way to teach. Alas, colleges do not do it (with the sole exception of Colorado College, Colorado Springs, where I have taught twice for that very reason). Intellectual creation depends much on concentration. Our standard courses, each meeting for fifty minutes once, twice, or three times a week, do not promote this.

On the way to Japan in 1958, with wonderful luck for us, Arthur Murphy had me teach at the University of Washington for a quarter. Dorothy intensely enjoyed taking courses on Japan. One student in a class I taught there is now the publisher of my books. He never forgot me and my ideas.

A more recent far journey was to Australia in 1974 to attend a World Congress in Ornithology, and at nearly the same time, a meeting of the Australasian Philosophical Society. I gave one philosophical talk at the University of Sydney and a talk to the ornithologists. I came to know D. M. Armstrong, a professed and intelligent materialist, and Keith Campbell, whose interesting *Body and Mind* defends a "new epiphenomenalism," according to which "spirit" or "awareness by phenomenal properties" is a nonmaterial effect of certain material causes; but there are no material effects of these nonmaterial effects acting as causes. All causes are material, but some effects are irreducible to anything material. There is no mention of Peirce or Whitehead—or of myself—in the argument given against universal psychicalism, nor is any understanding exhibited of the way these writers argue for a psychical monism. I wonder, too, if the new epiphenomenalism is essentially different from Santayana's doctrine of spirit.

In 1984 occurred our most recent and I hope last journey to the other side of the world. The reasons for it were two invitations to give keynote addresses: one to a meeting in Hawaii of the Society for Asian and Comparative Philosophy, the other to a meeting in Nagoya of the Japan Society for Process Studies. Both were given to clearly cordial audiences surpassing my hopes. In the first, my subject was "Sankara, Nagarjuna, and Fa Tsang, with Some Western Analogues." In the second it was, "The Convergence of Eastern and Western Thought." At both meetings we met many old friends and made some new ones. In Japan we once again admired the extraordinary abilities of the Japanese people and the beauty, the pervasive aesthetic appeal, of the country. On Japanese television we saw a musical comedy that seemed clearly an original Japanese creation, but delightfully melodious, a little as though Gilbert and Sullivan had been reborn as Japanese. Without being able to get many of the words we felt that it showed a high level of public entertainment.

The Japanese papers on Whitehead, one on Husserl, seemed competent, some more so than others. None was specifically about my views, but an ex-student of mine, Seisaku Yamamoto, gave a paper on Whitehead. Yutaka Tanaka favorably compared Whitehead's idea of God and his own Japanese Christian idea which he had acquired from our late Japanese friend Professor Ariga, who invented the word 'hyathology' (derived from a Hebrew word) as substitute for 'ontology', to indicate that the concrete reality is becoming, not mere being. Ariga and I had agreed that there is in the Bible no ontology, only hyathology. The Hawaiian group, with some scholars representing Buddhism and others Vedantism (one of the latter an old friend from India but half Spanish), was perhaps the most exciting one. The question of intercultural communication was discussed from widely varying perspectives into which my own seemed to fit constructively.

I think the conference gave some support to my view that, profound as the barriers to understanding between languages or cultures may be, the individual or group perspectives within each culture are not much less profound. Everywhere there are the more monistically and the more pluralistically inclined, as well as those who hold a position between the extremes in these respects; also, those who can reasonably be viewed as theists and those either too monistic or too naturalistic, humanistic, or undecided to acknowledge a deity. Everywhere there are those who believe they can accept death as the nullification of our earthly careers (apart from our influences on posterity) and those who hope for the continuation of our individualities in posthumous careers either on earth or in some supernatural heaven.

It is not yet clear how widespread is the Whiteheadian middle ground of "objective immortality in the Consequent Nature of God," which does not mean any posthumous enjoyments (or sufferings) by us, but rather the everlasting divine appreciation of whatever beauty, aesthetic value, there was in our lives and the lives of those we influence. God becomes the ultimate posterity. I expect this view to gain ground in other cultures; for it is a logical medium between prolongation of personal careers beyond death and mere ceasing to be with death. If all we have ever been, we have been for divine love, we can never cease to be that, since in the divine life, while there is acquisition of novelty, there is no loss. Cumulative divine experience, enjoying all nondivine experience everlastingly (not eternally), is the doctrine that is clearly "this worldly" in one sense and yet answers the question, "How can it matter that or how we have lived if the living just ceases to be, not only for us, but in the end for all others? Indeed, what then remains to make it even true that we have lived as we have?" Objective immortality is a positive answer, and it takes absolutely seriously the proposition, we are to love God, who cherishes all creatures, with *all* our being. If for God we are to be there forevermore, then death has nullified *nothing* that we have ever actually achieved or been. And we are to live for no rewards for our actions other than those we can enjoy in this life and with no punishments save those that occur to us before death. We are to love our fellows not for our own or their posthumous advantage, but for their actual or potentional experiences in this life as contributions to the divine life, and to love ourselves for the same reason. Thus we are in ideal to love others literally "as (we love) ourselves." I see in this a subtle and profound though partial analogy with Buddhism.

I have said nothing about my nine months (1941–42) of teaching at the New School for Social Research in New York City. This was a time of learning from some brilliant German refugee scholars, also of enjoying the wit and wisdom of Horace Kallen, one of the most delightful disciples of William James one could meet. The school was strong in sociology. I wrote for its journal an essay on the Group Mind.

I will mention here my lecturing in England, Scotland, France, Belgium (University of Leuven), Hong Kong, Canada. The Belgian experience was the most recent and intensive of these, a semester's work in two courses, one taught together with Jan Van der Veken, an extremely intelligent and charming priest, expert on the philosophy of Merleau-Ponty and on that of Whitehead. To some extent the philosophical world is beginning to be one world, with the almost complete exception of Soviet Russia, Communist China, and some parts of the Arab world.

In metaphysical questions, given political and religious freedom, individual differences seem ineradicable. But, and here I agree with the late Richard

McKeon, this should not make peace impossible between groups. Metaphysical insight—I believe there is such a thing—is a privilege, and brute force is not the way to promote it. Of all the great international traditions, the Buddhist has shown the most consistent understanding of this truth. Theist though I am, I never long forget that the misuse of force has rather persistently occurred in groups very free with the name of God. There are tyrant ideas of deity and tyrant ways of professedly doing the will of God. In the nuclear age we must take a fresh look at these matters. The price of mistakes has reached a new high.

PART TWO

DESCRIPTIVE AND CRITICAL ESSAYS ON THE PHILOSOPHY OF CHARLES HARTSHORNE

A. EMPIRICAL INQUIRIES

1

Charles Birch

CHANCE, PURPOSE, AND DARWINISM

"Neither pure chance nor the pure absence of chance can explain the world."

CHARLES HARTSHORNE (1984, P. 69)

Charles Darwin went on his epic voyage of the Beagle a convinced determinist and moreover a deist at that. He had read Paley's "Natural Theology" when a student at Cambridge University and was impressed by its argument for the existence of God from the design of nature (Darwin, F., 1888, vol. 1, p. 309). How better explain the wonderful order of nature than as the product of a designer outside nature? This designer, God, had a relationship to nature as that of a carpenter to a table he designs and then constructs. The world in all its infinite detail was constructed by an all powerful God. This was the simple doctrine of divine carpentry. Bishops promulgated it from their pulpits. Students at the great universities were expected to believe it. Scientists were expected to provide more and more evidence for it. In that respect Darwin appeared a traitor, for the voyage of the Beagle around the world changed completely his view of the source of the order in nature. The author of *On the Origin of Species* had failed to perform what the public expected of its biologists. It was as if the Archbishop of Canterbury had announced his conversion to Buddhism. Darwin had discovered that nature was not made complete and perfect once and for all time. Nature was still in process of being made. Moreover, the process involved a "struggle for existence". And, perhaps even

I acknowledge gratefully the assistance of Dorothy Hartshorne in providing me with references to all of Charles Hartshorne's writings on Darwinism. I also acknowledge the helpful criticism and comments of John Cobb of an early draft of the manuscript.

more devastating for the design thesis, the process involved chance. The element of chance in Darwin's theory was the genetic variations on which natural selection acted. Instead of the tiger being designed with its stripes for camouflage, once and for all, Darwin invoked the notion that originally tigers had all sorts of patterns on their coats. This was a consequence of chance variation. But only that pattern persisted that gave the animal an advantage in its struggle for existence.

Neo-Darwinism, the dominant view of biologists today, is an interpretation of Darwinism in terms of a modern understanding of genetics. The basic source of genetic variation in the living world is chance variation of the DNA molecule. It can come in an infinite variety of forms. Which form is a matter of chance. Darwinism thus introduces an indeterminacy into the history of nature which, coupled with natural selection, necessarily leads to evolution of types. The most thoroughgoing analysis of evolution in terms of molecular genetics is Jacques Monod's *Chance and Necessity*. "Chance alone," says Monod (1974, p. 69), "is at the source of every innovation, of all creation in the biosphere." For Monod this is the one and only principle in nature. He contrasts his position with those who seek to find in every detail of nature evidence of deterministic design.

Charles Hartshorne is a thoroughgoing evolutionist. He accepts the role of chance events as the most fundamental contribution Darwin made to the theory of evolution. Indeed, as I indicate below, he is more emphatic in his emphasis on the role of chance than even Darwin was. But unlike Jacques Monod, Hartshorne argues that chance alone cannot explain the world. Chance and purpose can. Whereas Darwin (somewhat uncomfortably) and Monod (with complete conviction) embrace a world of chance in place of a world of design, Hartshorne interprets the natural order in terms of both chance and purpose. These two words have precise meanings in his argument which are explored below.

THE ROLE OF CHANCE IN EVOLUTIONARY TRANSFORMATION

The Neo-Darwinist speaks of chance mutations as being the source of all genetic variation in the living world. The meaning of chance in this context is quite specific, yet often misunderstood. It does not imply that mutation has no cause. We know many of the causes of mutation such as radiation and certain chemicals. Most mutations are deleterious to the organism that possesses them. Some few only confer on their possessors an increased chance to survive and reproduce. Whether or not a particular mutation increases the chance of its possessor to survive and reproduce is dependent upon a second chain of events which is quite independent of the event of mutation itself. The second chain of events has to do with the environment in which the organism finds itself. Each DNA molecule in the reproductive organs replicates to produce DNA in the sex cells. But once in several thousand times the DNA doesn't produce an exact copy of itself. It mutates. Most, but not necessarily all of these mutations, are deleterious to the organisms that possess them. Some may happen to confer resistance to poisons such as cyanide or DDT and even to poisons not yet synthesised by man!

Consider just one such mutation that happens to confer resistance to the insecticide DDT. The chain of events that leads to the production of the insect that has a mutant gene that confers resistance to DDT is quite unrelated to whether or not the environment contains DDT. If the environment is free of DDT, the mutation confers no advantage upon the organism. The DDT does not itself cause the mutation. All it does is to kill off those insects that don't have the gene for resistance, allowing those that have it to survive and reproduce. DDT is, in Darwinian terms, simply the selecting agent. The particular mutation that occurs at any time and the presence or absence of DDT in the environment are quite unrelated. So the geneticist says the sort of mutation that occurs is chance or random in relation to the needs of the organism at the time it occurs. How do we know this? Experiments have demonstrated quite conclusively that DNA mutates to confer resistance to DDT in the complete absence of DDT. Indeed, it is now evident that this mutation was occurring long before DDT was invented by man. And so it is for other mutations. A determinist might want to say that there is an omnipotent observer who sees that the appropriate mutation occurs at the appropriate time so that the two chains of events interact with benefit to the organism. That this is not the case is a scientific fact known from careful experimentation. There are no two ways about it. All sorts of mutations occur all the time, most are deleterious, but by chance some are not. In this context the word chance means, as Hartshorne (1984a, p. 16) says, "not decided by any agent and not determined by the past." No agent and no history determine that the intersection of the two causal chains will be advantageous to the organism concerned. The result of the interaction is not predictable from either chain of events taken separately.

Hartshorne's view is that the two such chains of causes involve creativity, choice, and decision. The presence or absence of DDT in the environment involves human choice. The changes in DDT from one form to another is not completely determined by the past history of DNA. There is an indeterminancy here in the sense that a choice is made to become this sort of DNA rather than that sort. This will be explained in more detail later. The point to make here is that purpose in some sense is posited to be present in each chain.

But the result of the intersection of the two chains of purposive events is not foreseen or purposed by either. This schematisation tends to exaggerate the separation of purpose and chance. In a process universe, every event involves intersections that introduce the element of chance, and every event has elements of purpose, expressing itself in choice, or decision, or self-creativity.

The recognition of chance and accident in the natural order is critically important in Hartshorne's philosophy of nature. For without chance there could be no freedom. If the universe and all happenings were fully determined by some omnipotent power, attributed by some to God, then there could be no freedom. As Hartshorne (1984a, p. 16) says, "Agent X decides to perform act A, agent Y independently decides to perform act B. So far as both succeed, what happens is the combination AB. Did X decide that AB should happen? No. Did Y decide the combination? No. Did any agent decide it? No. Did God, as supreme agent, decide it? No, unless 'decide' stands for sheer illusion in at least one of its applications to God and the creatures . . . the word chance is the implication of the genuine idea of free or creative decision making— 'creative' meaning, adding to the definiteness of the world, settling something previously unsettled, partly undefined or indeterminate." The recognition of chance and accident as part of the natural order, including human life, is the basis of Hartshorne's arguments against the notion of divine omnipotence that has plagued theology and so prevented it from coming to terms with science. And it is at the basis of his argument for the existence of a degree of freedom at all levels of the natural order from electrons and the like to humans.

I did not appreciate the centrality of chance and accident in Hartshorne's philosophy of nature until one occasion when we were together at the University of California at Berkeley. Hartshorne was doing work in the department of philosophy and I was teaching in the department of genetics. I had access to one of the first copies of Monod's (1970) book *Le Hasard et la Nécessité*, later published as *Chance and Necessity*. I loaned Hartshorne the copy I had. I might have thought he would have been perturbed by the dominance of chance in Monod's argument. On the contrary, he was mightily elated. Here, he said to me, was a biologist who was really taking chance seriously. The fact that Monod conceived chance alone as the one principle in nature was beside the point, at least at that stage of Hartshorne's assimilation of the book.

To take chance seriously is the first important step in moving away from the concept of deterministic design, whether by an omnipotent designer or as some inbuilt principle of nature. And, for Hartshorne, that is also the first step in moving toward a realistic concept of purpose, a step which Monod neither took nor even so much as contemplated.

To my knowledge Hartshorne is the only person to point out clearly that Charles Darwin could not admit the reality of chance, despite the role he attributed to it. In this respect Darwin was like Einstein when he said "God does not throw dice." And he probably greatly admired the deterministic universe of Newton and the sort of thinking that led Newton to that concept. At least we know that he had studied and admired the life of Newton (Darwin, F., 1902, p. 229). Perhaps he saw himself as the Newton of biology. The key to Darwin's thinking on chance and determinism is not to be found in *On the Origin of Species* but in Darwin's correspondence, especially that with the Harvard botanist Asa Gray in 1860 and 1861. Hartshorne's discussion of this is in Hartshorne (1962, Chapter 7 and 1984a, Chapter 3). The critical passage in Darwin's letter to Asa Gray is the following: "I cannot think that the world . . . is the result of chance; and yet I cannot look at each separate thing as the result of Design. . . . I am, and shall ever remain, in a hopeless muddle" (Darwin, F., 1888, vol. 2, pp. 353–54). And (p. 378), "But I know that I am in the same sort of muddle . . . as all the world seems to be in with respect to freewill, yet with everything supposed to have been foreseen or pre-ordained." Darwin repeatedly declared in his letters to Asa Gray, as well as to others, that chance cannot explain the world as an ordered whole. To a Mr. Graham, for example, he wrote "you have expressed my inward conviction far more vividly and clearly than I could have done, that the Universe is not the result of chance" (Darwin, F., 1888, vol. 1, p. 316). Again and again his letters reiterate this refrain; is it all ordained, or is it all a result of chance? Because of this dilemma Darwin gave up theism. At the same time he could see that there must be pervasive limitations upon chance, since unlimited chance is chaos. And as Hartshorne (1962, p. 207) points out, Darwin actually suggests that perhaps the solution is "designed laws" of nature, with all details, good and bad, depending upon "what we call chance." "I cannot persuade myself," wrote Darwin (Darwin, F., 1888, vol. 2, p. 312), "that a beneficient and omnipotent God would have designedly created the Ichneumonidae with the express intention of their feeding within the living bodies of Caterpillars, or that a cat should play with mice. Not believing this, I see no necessity in the belief that the eye was expressly designed. On the other hand, I cannot anyhow be contented to view this wonderful universe, and especially the nature of man, and to conclude that everything is the result of brute force. I am inclined to look at everything as resulting from designed laws, with the details, whether good or bad, left to the working out of what we may call chance. Not that this notion at all satisfies me. . . . But the more I think the more bewildered I become." Why? Hartshorne (1962, p. 207) has two suggestions. Darwin tended, like many others, to think of science as committed to determinism. What we call chance may not be chance at all. Secondly, it was not apparent to Dar-

win why cosmic purpose should leave anything to chance. God was identified
with absolute law and non-chance. The dominant theology of Darwin's day was
of no help to him in this respect. It had no clearly conceived creationist
philosophy. God must do everything or nothing. And if God is responsible for
everything, then why all the evil in the world? To Asa Gray Darwin writes
(Darwin, F., 1888, vol. 2, p. 382) about his dilemma thus. "You say that you
are in a haze; I am in thick mud; the orthodox would say in fetid, abominable
mud; yet I cannot keep out of the question." The "mud" in which Darwin said
he was immersed was, as Hartshorne (1962, p. 208) says, "the opacity which
always characterises a deterministic world-view."

Darwin argued correctly that the facts of evil are in conflict with a belief
in deterministic design (Darwin, F., 1888, vol. 1, p. 315; vol. 2, p. 312). But
only one of his correspondents suggested to him that God was other than an
omnipotent determiner of all the details of nature. That was the English vicar and
novelist Charles Kingsley. He wrote to Darwin, "I have gradually learnt to see
that it is just as noble a conception of Deity, to believe that He created primal
forms capable of self development into all forms needful . . . as to believe that
He required a fresh act of intervention to supply the lacunas which He Himself
made"(Darwin, F., 1888, vol. 2, p. 288). And elsewhere Kingsley wrote about
Darwin's contribution thus: "now they have got rid of an interfering God—a
master magician as I call it—they have to choose between the absolute empire
of accident and a living, immanent, ever-working God" (Quoted by Raven
1953, p. 177). In the evolutionary epic for children *The Water Babies* which
Kingsley wrote just four years after the publication of *On the Origin of Species*
he tells of how God "makes things make themselves" (Kingsley 1930 edition,
p. 248). At the time Kingsley's lonely voice must have been drowned out by the
voices of the majority of his fellow clerics who could see no saving grace in
Darwinism at all. There is no evidence that Darwin appreciated Kingsley's
alternative to the omnipotent deterministic God of deism.

Darwin needed a Monod to convince him that chance and accident were
essential to the order of nature. He needed also a Hartshorne to persuade him that
there was a credible alternative to the deism of Paley and other nineteenth-
century divines. But in fact he never did resolve his dilemma of chance and
determinism.

Darwin is commonly supposed to have shown that there is no room for
purpose in nature. He never showed anything of the sort. What he did show was
that existing concepts of design by an external agent were invalid. And as
Passmore (1959, p. 14) says so clearly, "Darwin's theory did nothing to *prove*
that God did not exist; but it did destroy the only argument, many men thought,
by which God's existence could possibly be established. That is why it
encouraged the development of agnosticism. . . ."

The Role of Purpose in Evolution

To suppose that Darwinism reduces the origin of biological order to pure chance is a mistake. For "there must be something positive limiting chance and something more than mere matter in matter, or Darwinism fails to explain life" (Hartshorne 1962, p. 210). What is "the positive something" that limits chance and what is "the something more than mere matter in matter "? Darwinism rules out the notion of an all determining orderer. It opens the door to another concept of ordering. Hartshorne (1984a, p. 71) insists that order implies the rule of one—"the only positive explanation of order is the existence of an orderer." But his is a very different concept of ordering from that of the deists which Darwin rightly rejected.

Darwinism led directly to Kingsley's notion that things tend to make themselves. Creativity exists within the entities of the creation. That is the first step in the argument for order. Many people find this a difficult concept to grasp. For as Hartshorne (1962, p. 209) says, "Since teleology had been thought of as unilateral creativity on the part of the deity, unshared in any appreciable degree with the creatures, indications that the world had far reaching potentialities for self-creation were naturally startling. But only because creativity had not been grasped in its proper universality, as the principle of existence itself." Today that should be a less startling concept, for science is leading more and more in that direction as witness, for example, the recognition of "self-organisation" in the natural order (Prigogine and Stengers 1984). The "something more than mere matter in matter" is the creativity of entities themselves, be they electrons, atoms, cells or bacteria or humans. Nuts and bolts can't evolve. For they have no intrinsic creativity. Only entities that have a degree of creativity can evolve. To have creativity is to have, in some sense, a goal or purpose. Future possibilities are causes of the present, both in sustaining the entity and in enabling it to evolve. In this philosophy, entities from electrons and the like to the most highly organised entities are sensate in some degree. This is their freedom to respond or not to respond to possibilities relevant to the entity. That is to say, they have in some sense experience or feelings. Creativity is not simply the rearrangement of bits and pieces of stuff. It is the anticipation and the move toward future possibilities. Possibilities or purposes are causes of the present as are also influences (akin to memories) of the past.

The creative evolution of entities is inconceivable if they are defined as permanent entities that maintain their identity throughout all evolution. As one moves up a level of organisation—electrons, atoms, molecules, cells, etc.—the properties of each larger whole are given not merely by the units of which it is composed but by the new relations between these units. It is not that the whole is more than the sum of its parts, but that its parts themselves are redefined and recreated in the process of evolution from one level to another. An electron in a lump of lead is not the same as an electron in a cell in a human brain. This means that the properties of matter relevant at, say, the atomic level do not begin to predict the properties of matter at the cellular level, let alone the level of complex organisms. That is why the Danish physicist Niels Bohr already fifty years ago advised his pupils that the new laws of physics were most likely to be discovered in biology. This view of the entities of nature calls not only for a new physics but for a biology too which—to use Lewontin's (1983, p. 36) felicitous terms—is "relational" rather than "constitutional". Up to now biology had been more constitutional than relational, though there are important exceptions which I refer to later.

In what sense does a multiplicity of creative agents imply the need for a rule of one? Precisely because too many cooks spoil the broth. There must be something that sets limits to the confusion and anarchy possible with a multiplicity of creative agents. Individual purposing agents need to be coordinated. In Hartshorne's view the order of that sort of world of entities requires a divine orderer. But how different that orderer is from the omnipotent orderer of deism! The key concept is no longer omnipotence but persuasiveness. The divine orderer is no manipulator of the world and its entities, be they electrons or people. The divine orderer works with entities that each have their degree of freedom to respond or not to respond to that influence. This may be tiny at the level of the electron. It is highly significant at the level of the human person. God, instead of being the all powerful manipulator of the creation, is its great persuader, providing its entities with specific goals or purposes and coordinating the activity of all. "What happens," says Hartshorne (1967, p. 59), is in no case the products of his creative acts alone. Countless choices, including the universally influential choices, intersect to make a world, and how, concretely, they intersect is not chosen by anyone, nor could it be. . . . Purpose, in multiple form, and chance are not mutually exclusive but complementary; neither makes sense alone."

Why then the partial disorder in the world and the evils of nature that Darwin was so sensitive to? There is but one answer in Hartshorne's philosophy. Order is not a consequence of dictatorial rule. Order is a consequence of "democratic" persuasion. There are no other sorts of ordering principle than these two. Darwinism makes belief in a dictator of the universe no longer credible. It opens the way to understanding order as a consequence of democratic persuasion and response. The analogy with a democracy is complete. Individual people in a democracy have their own degree of freedom (but not complete freedom) to respond or not to respond to the influence of the governing body. And the governing body is itself to be responsive to individuals in a democracy. So it must also be in a cosmic democracy. Applied to God there is what Hartshorne (1948, p. 50) appropriately calls "the metaphysics of democracy" — "a wholly absolute God is power divorced from responsiveness or sensitivity; a power which is not responsive is irresponsible." God's power is love that is responsive.

Besides the metaphysics of democracy another analogy of God's relation to the entities of creation is that of the human mind to the activities of the body (Hartshorne 1984a, p. 80). The human mind influences the organs and cells of the body and the cells in their turn influence the mind. Hurt my cells and you hurt me. Give my cells a healthy life and they give me a sense of vitality. I feel what my cells feel. This is good psychosomatic medicine. I am to a large extent, in sickness and in health, what I feel and think. There is circumstantial evidence, for example, that the onset of some sorts of cancer is initiated by sudden changes in the quality of one's experiences, either of great euphoria or of great disappointment or grief. There is nothing particularly mysterious about this. Thoughts influence the function of the brain both in changing impulses in the nerves and the hormones it secretes and which are sent all over the body. In putting such a strong emphasis on the mental, Hartshorne is in line with much of modern medical understanding of health and disease, but out of step with what is still the dominant mechanistic thinking in biology. This he fully realizes. "If there is a weakness in current evolutionary theory, it may derive, not from the admission of chance as pervasive, but from the tendency in science generally to limit itself to the supposedly merely physical, rather than psychical, aspects of reality" (Hartshorne 1984a, p. 81). However, the tide may be turning in science, ever so slowly, in Hartshorne's direction. Some biologists (e.g., Lewontin, Rose and Kamin 1984, Birch and Cobb 1981, and Hardy 1965) emphasise the role of choice in evolution in the following way. Animals are not simply at the mercy of their environment. They change their environment and in so doing determine to some extent the direction of their own evolution. One way they change their environment is by choosing a different one. Change in the populations' genes may then occur in consequence. For when an organism chooses a new environment it subjects itself to a new selective regime and hence a changed natural selection. In this way an individual's choice becomes a component of evolutionary change. This is not a Lamarckian change but strictly Darwinian. This mode of evolutionary change has long been recognized at the human level in what is called cultural evolution and the feed-back between cultural evolution and genetical evolution. An important principle, which biologists tend to ignore, is that individuals want to survive. They have an urge to live and to live well, to escape from predators and to seek out moments of quiet and repose. This perspective of the role of purpose applies in process thought to all individual entities. It is elaborated further in the section that follows this one.

The "something that limits pure chance" in Hartshorne's view is the persuasive influence of a divine orderer on the whole creation. "The something more in mere matter than matter" is the sentience of all entities allowed by their degree of freedom to both feel their world and to respond appropriately to it and in so responding to change.

Darwinism should have banished once and for all the notion of the universe as dictatorially governed. That it did not is largely due to the failure of people to recognize a second form of governance of the universe in which freedom and persuasion reign. Hartshorne more than anyone else in our time has led the way to this new dialogue with nature and with God.

THE UNITY OF ALL LIFE AND ALL CREATION

The evolution of the cosmos and especially the evolution of life provided for Hartshorne a major insight into the unity of the creation. In this Hartshorne was reflecting Darwin's own conviction as he well recognized when he wrote: "One of Darwin's deepest convictions, overlooked by many, was that all life is somehow one and that human attributes, such as sentience, are not to be supposed (as Descartes taught) abrupt supernatural additions to a merely mechanical nature. Darwin was troubled by his inability to see how there could be feeling in plants, thinking that this weakened his evolutionary argument. Somehow he did not realize the importance of the idea of cells, invisibly small individuals making up a vegetable organism and far better integrated than the entire organism. Darwin would have liked Whitehead . . . so far as this problem is concerned" (Hartshorne 1984b, p.129). Darwin wrote *The Expression of the Emotions in Man and Animals* (Darwin 1872) to elaborate his conviction that the sentient qualities of humans have their origins in those of our forebears. The world of nature was for Darwin a world of intense feeling. Hartshorne wrote his first book *The Philosophy and Psychology of Sensation* (Hartshorne 1934 and see especially p. 264) from this selfsame conviction. It was a guiding motivation for much of his global study of bird song. Birds, as a result of their singing, win and keep mates and, in some cases also territories. "But," says Hartshorne (1973, p. 10), "the energetic persistence of singing may be sustained partly by the feeling, however primitive, for the beauty (i.e., the "unity of contrast") of the sounds they are making." His global study of bird song showed to him that the evolution of singing had been toward an increasing sensitivity to the value of contrast and unexpectedness as balancing the value of sameness and repetition. In his theory of aesthetics of bird song he discovered evidence that birds tend to sing to avoid monotony. A bird that sings a few notes puts long intervals between them whereas a bird that sings many notes makes shorter intervals between them.

The bird sings for a purpose (its survival) no doubt unknown to the bird, but also for the enjoyment of singing. And why shouldn't animals besides humans enjoy life? As Walt Whitman wrote of animals in "Song of Myself":

> They bring me tokens of myself, they evince them plainly in their
> possession.
> I wonder where they get these tokens,
> Did I pass that way huge times ago and negligently drop them?

If we acknowledge that humans are sentient and are not just unfeeling robots, it is logical to extend this judgment to our closest relatives, such as the apes, and certainly our pets if not the rest of the mammals. But where to draw the line in sentience? Hartshorne's answer is that there is no line to be drawn. The alternative is to suppose that at some stage of evolution a mindless and feelingless world gave rise to mind and feeling. And that is to ask for a miracle. Logic forces him to insist on sentience in some form all down the line. For Darwin, that probably meant the first cell. For Hartshorne the line extends right down to the so-called ultimate particles, which in any case no longer look like particles at all. Biologists are today pretty well united in their conviction that it is impossible to draw a sharp boundary between the animate and the inanimate. Yet few seem to see the logic of extending mind and sentience in some form all down the line. It was a source of deep satisfaction for Hartshorne that one of the architects of the modern theory of Neo-Darwinism and one of the greatest evolutionists of our time and one of his closest friends agreed with him on this. I think Sewall Wright came to this conviction independently of Hartshorne (Wright 1953, 1964). But over many years, including some decades together as members of the faculty of the University of Chicago, Wright developed his ideas in close association with his revered friend and colleague. Another distinguished evolutionist who brought the Neo-Darwinian synthesis to his fellow biologists in Europe and who was at the same time a convinced pan-psychist is Rensch (1971). These and other biologists met together to share their ideas with Hartshorne and other process thinkers in Bellagio in Italy in 1974. The results of their deliberations were published in *Mind in Nature* (Cobb and Griffin 1977).

In Hartshorne's thinking the unity of life is no metaphor. It is the recognition of that which all entities share in common. Not everything is an entity, for some things like rocks and trees are aggregates of entities. An entity is precisely defined as that which acts and "feels" as one. It is the unit of feeling that makes an entity. And it is necessary to reiterate again and again that "feel" has a very different meaning at the level of the electron compared to our own elaborate feelings. Yet the connection and continuity remain.

Because of the unity of life Hartshorne sees human love as something that can be extended to the whole creation (Hartshorne 1934, p. 19). The humanist loves his fellow humans and appreciates nature. But for Hartshorne human love is to be extended to the rest of nature in the sense of sympathetic identification with the life of other sentient beings. Quite independently this view is now strongly promoted by "deep ecology" as a critical missing element in the conservation movement (Fox 1984, 1990).

The greatest scientists were not simply curious about nature. They too loved nature. Darwin loved animals as fellow creatures. The physicist J. J. Thomson said we couldn't know what an atom was unless we could be one. He regretted his inability to identify to that extent. Presumably God's knowledge of atoms is complete. To know is to possess and to be at one with that which is loved.

The consequences of extended love are enormous and deeply needed in our world in which so often humanity seems pitted against nature. We destroy nature to feed our appetites. Hartshorne (1937, p. 30) pointed out the consequences of our separation from nature well before conservation and deep ecology were thought of seriously. In addition to the disappearance of resources there is increased cruelty to animals when we fail to take animal feeling into account in our instrumental domination of nature. Today we have animal liberation movements and many sorts of conservation movements whose objective is to save nature from annihilation. But they all need a philosophy to deepen the extent of their concerns. I have for a long time found just such a philosophy in the thought of Charles Hartshorne.

CHARLES BIRCH

SCHOOL OF BIOLOGICAL SCIENCES
UNIVERSITY OF SYDNEY
SEPTEMBER 1985

REFERENCES

Birch, Charles and John B. Cobb, Jr. 1981. *The Liberation of Life: From Cell to Community*. Cambridge University Press.

Cobb, John B., Jr. and David R. Griffin, eds. 1977. *Mind in Nature, Essays on the Interface of Science and Philosophy*. Washington, D.C.: University Press of America.

Darwin, Francis, ed. 1888. *The Life and Letters of Charles Darwin*. Vols. I, II, and III. London: John Murray.

———, ed. 1902. *The Life of Charles Darwin*. London: John Murray.

Fox, Warwick. 1984. "Deep Ecology: A New Philosophy of Our Time?" *The Ecologist* 14:194–205.

———. 1990. *Toward a Transpersonal Ecology: Developing New Foundations for Environmentalism*. Boston: New Science Library.

Hardy, Alister C. 1965. *The Living Stream: A Restatement of Evolution Theory in Its Relation to the Spirit of Man.* Part I, Gifford Lectures (1963–65). London: William Collins.

Hartshorne, Charles. 1934. *The Philosophy and Psychology of Sensation.* The University of Chicago Press.

———. 1948. *The Divine Relativity.* New Haven: Yale University Press.

———. 1962. *The Logic of Perfection.* La Salle, Ill.: Open Court.

———. 1967. *A Natural Theology for Our Time.* La Salle, Ill.: Open Court.

———. 1973. *Born to Sing: An Interpretation and World Survey of Bird Song.* Bloomington, Ind.: Indiana University Press.

———. 1984a. *Omnipotence and Other Theological Mistakes.* Albany, N.Y.: State University of New York Press.

———. 1984b. *Creativity in American Philosophy.* Albany, N.Y.: State University of New York Press.

Kingsley, Charles. 1930. *The Water Babies.* London: Hodder and Stoughton.

Lewontin, Richard C. 1983. "The Corpse in the Elevator." *New York Review of Books* 30:14–37.

Lewontin, Richard C., Steven Rose, and Leon Kamin. 1984. *Not in Our Genes: Biology, Ideology and Human Nature.* New York, N.Y.: Pantheon Books.

Monod, Jacques. 1974. *Chance and Necessity: An Essay on the Natural Philosophy of Modern Biology.* London: Fontana/Collins.

Passmore, John. 1959. "Darwin and the Climate of Opinion." *Australian Journal of Science* 22:8–15.

Prigogine, Ilya and Isabelle Stengers. 1984. *Order Out of Chaos: Man's New Dialogue with Nature.* New York, N.Y.: Bantam Books.

Raven, Charles. 1953. *Natural Religion and Christian Theology.* The Gifford Lectures 1951. First series. Science and Religion. Cambridge University Press.

Rensch, Bernard. 1971. *Biophilosophy.* New York, N.Y.: Columbia University Press.

Wright, Sewall. 1953. "Gene and Organism." *American Naturalist* 87:5–18.

———. 1964. "Biology and the Philosophy of Science." In W. L. Reese and E. Freeman, eds. *Process and Divinity*, pp. 101–25. La Salle, Ill.: Open Court.

2

Alexander F. Skutch

BIRD SONG AND PHILOSOPHY

I first met Charles Hartshorne on July 10, 1961, when he and his wife, Dorothy, arrived at our farm in the Valley of El General in southern Costa Rica. They still looked fresh after a nine-mile ride from the nearest village over a rough road in a four-wheel-drive car, packed to capacity with people and their luggage, that served as a bus. They had arranged by correspondence to spend a few days with us after accompanying a birding tour in neighboring Panama.

Next morning, in the rain forest, I was introduced to Hartshorne's method of studying bird song. On a small tape recorder, he captured the voice of a bird, often one unseen amid dense vegetation. When he played back the recording, the singer, mistaking the reproduction of his own song for that of a rival invading his territory, advanced to meet the intruder, singing more loudly and profusely, often exposing himself to view for positive identification, while Charles made more adequate recordings of the songs for future study. On rainy afternoons, we sat on the porch while he, using a notation that he had developed, studied the voices of a pair of Rufous-breasted Wrens *(Thryothorus rutilus)* singing antiphonally in surrounding trees.

After five days on the farm, we stayed for two nights at an inn situated at an altitude of nearly 10,000 feet on the Cerro de la Muerte in the Cordillera de Talamanca. Here we heard, and Charles recorded, the songs of such high-altitude birds as the Timberline Wren *(Thryorchilus browni)* and the Black-billed Nightingale-Thrush *(Catharus gracilirostris)*. Then we continued along the Inter-American Highway to San José to attend the II Congreso Extraordinario Interamericano de Filosofía, where Hartshorne read papers on "Whitehead's Conception of God," and "Whitehead's Theory of Prehension." (The president of this congress was Abelardo Bonilla, vice-president of Costa Rica, and for the week of the congress its acting president, the elected president of the country, Mario Echandi, having temporarily resigned to honor philosophy, and realize briefly the Platonic ideal that philosophers should become heads of states.)

After the closure of the congress, we went down to the Inter-American Institute of Agricultural Sciences on the Caribbean slope to hear certain wrens. By recording their song and playing it back, Charles drew Black-throated Wrens *(Thryothorus atrogularis)* to the edges of the dense, lush thickets where they lurked unseen. Once he had two pairs of these wrens dueting simultaneously in plain view. Another Black-throated Wren, who apparently lacked a mate, repeated his lovely songs over and over. As we walked away from these superb musicians, Charles made a characteristic remark about the happy nature of the bird, who sang enchantingly instead of complaining about his solitary state.

Hartshorne's fortnight in Costa Rica was one of the briefer of his many visits to foreign countries, and an example of how he has combined his profession, philosophy, with his life-long avocation, bird study. Before writing *Born to Sing* he had spent more than fifty years reading about singing birds and listening to them in the field in about forty of the United States (including Hawaii), and in Australia, Japan, and India (in each of which he resided as a Fulbright professor). He had made less intensive but usually rather extensive observations in Nepal, England and several other European countries, Middle and South America, Jamaica, Uganda and Kenya, New Zealand, Fiji, the Philippines, Malaya, Hong Kong, and Taiwan—a breadth of field experience that few professional ornithologists can match. Moreover, he had listened to recordings of bird songs from many parts of the world and searched through regional bird books for descriptions of songs. Such was his ample preparation for writing his book.

Born to Sing: An Interpretation and World Survey of Bird Song, a book of 304 pages published in 1973 by Indiana University Press, contains the substance of earlier papers in ornithological and other journals and much more, so that we may regard it as the definitive exposition of his views. To appreciate the wide scope of this book, it should be considered from three aspects: (1) as a contribution to ornithology as a science based upon observation and experimentation, (2) as an essay in aesthetics or musicology as applied to bird song, and (3) as a contribution to the philosophy of nature. Let us take them in this order.

Basic to the scientific study of bird songs is their description in objective terms. The best way to convey to others what a bird sounds like is to play a record or tape-recording; but these are not available for every bird, nor can they be supplied with every book or article about bird songs. At the other extreme from the sensuous experience of hearing a bird song is the sonogram or audiospectrogram, made in a laboratory from a field recording, and indicating by rising and falling lines the frequencies and temporal distribution of all the notes in a complex song. Helpful to the trained investigator, they mean little to

BIRD SONG AND PHILOSOPHY 67

the uninitiated. Before portable tape recorders and sonograms were invented, students of bird songs tried to represent them by diverse systems of horizontal, vertical, and oblique lines, in a two-dimensional notation that could be made in the field. The musically educated found that they could record many birds' songs by staff notation, like any other music, but the verbal description is most often used by people able neither to interpret sonograms nor to read music. Many bird songs, like those of the Rufous-browed Peppershrike *(Cyclarhis gujanensis)* readily suggest brief phrases in one's native language; or they can be paraphrased by sequences of syllables, like the *choy che chee cheer cherít* of the Garden Thrush *(Turdus grayi)* that has been singing in our shade trees. Although no two people appear to hear a bird say exactly the same thing, when accompanied by adjectives such as "liquid" or "harsh," "cheerful" or "melancholy," this may be, despite its limitations, the best way to convey to most people some notion of the character of a bird's song. After explaining and illustrating each of these methods of describing songs, Hartshorne concludes that none satisfies everybody's needs and each has some value.

To carry out his project of selecting the world's best singers, Hartshorne developed a system of assessing their songs by relatively objective physical features. Those that he considered most relevant are (1) loudness or volume, (2) scope or complexity, (3) continuity or length of pauses in a song sequence, (4) tone or musical quality of the sounds composing a song, (5) organization or its coherence and structure, and (6) imitativeness, or the tendency to reproduce sounds that the singer has heard, to learn songs by listening to them. Each of these six qualities of a bird's song is rated on a scale of one to nine, giving a possible maximum of 54. Although no bird attains this high degree of perfection, some of the best singers make scores of 47 or 48.

Born to Sing deals principally with the Oscines or Songbirds, that great division of the Passeriform order with the most highly developed vocal organs and, therefore, the finest songs. After specifying the basis of his choice, Hartshorne prepared a world list of superior singers, with scores of 42 or more. It contains 192 species of Oscines, or nearly 5 percent of the approximately 4000 species in this suborder, plus the two suboscine lyrebirds or Australia. Each of the world's major zoogeographical regions contributes its share; but the "sometimes maligned" tropics, with only one third of Earth's land surface, contains about half of its highly musical species. The large families richest in superior singers, with more than 20 percent of their species in the list, are the mockingbirds and thrashers (Mimidae), confined to the New World; the wrens (Troglodytidae), with a single exception also confined to the Western Hemisphere; and the cosmopolitan thrushes (Turdidae), of which 65 of its 307 species (21 percent) are among the elite. The Old World warblers (Sylviidae) contribute 28 species to the distinguished group, but this is only 7 percent of their 398 species.

Families of Songbirds contrast greatly in the development of song. Wrens and tanagers are widespread in the Americas, where in many regions, especially in the tropics, several species of each occur in the same locality. Fourteen of the 59 species of wrens rank among the superior singers, but none of the 223 tanagers (although perhaps, if better known, some would merit inclusion). Why this great difference? Among tanagers are many of the most beautiful of tropical birds. As fruit-eaters who fly to trees and shrubs that, now here, now there, yield abundant crops of berries that are shared with many other birds, tanagers tend to be at most weakly territorial; they have little need of song to proclaim possession of territory. Brightly colored, mostly avoiding dense concealing vegetation, they maintain contact with their companions largely by sight, with a minimum of vocalizations. Many tanagers have no utterance worthy to be called song.

Lacking the bright colors so prominent among tanagers, wrens are often beautiful but never brilliant. The many nonmigratory species of warm lands live throughout the year in pairs or family groups that search for insects and spiders by hopping and flitting through dense foliage and vine tangles where visibility is narrowly restricted. Frequently unable to see each other when only a few yards apart, mates maintain contact by their voices. Often they sing antiphonally, the male often beginning a song that is continued by his partner, the two articulating their phrases so well that unless the listener is between them he seems to hear a single gifted singer. Moreover, wrens tend to be much more strongly territorial than tanagers. The development of song in these two families corresponds to their need of it.

In a wide survey of the relation of habits and habitats to the development of song, Hartshorne found that the most highly endowed singers live in situations and with habits that render visual means inadequate to attract and hold mates and secure territorial privacy. Birds who live in poorly lighted places, amid dense vegetation or near the ground, tend to have better songs than birds who spend more time in sunshine. Birds who glean insects amid concealing foliage, in the manner of Old World warblers, are more songful than aerial flycatchers like swallows. Although visibility is good amid the sparse vegetation of very arid country, meagerness of resources causes birds to be widely spaced, with voices well developed to proclaim their presence to distant neighbors. Solitary birds tend to sing better than the more social or gregarious species. Birds with inconspicuous plumage are more likely to sing well than those brilliantly attired. "The isolated and, at least when feeding, invisible individual is the typical singer, in touch with even one other of his kind only by voice." Although this is generally true, the rule is not without exceptions. Soberly attired Black-headed Brush-Finches *(Atlapetes atricapillus)* and other members of this neotropical genus sing poorly amid dense thickets and dim undergrowth;

Spotted-breasted Orioles *(Icterus pectoralis)* and Black-thighed Grosbeaks *(Pheucticus tibialis)*, both handsome in yellow and black, sing superbly in open crowns of trees.

Believing that birds who sing better should sing more, Hartshorne attempted to correlate the time a species spends singing with the quality of its songs. He developed a rather elaborate formula to calculate the numbers of hours a bird might devote to effective singing in the course of a year. As he expected, the correlation between song development and effective song season was high; but his data were hardly adequate for the undertaking.

A comparison of two birds who sing around me illustrates the difficulty of learning how much a bird sings. By far the best singer of the two is the Garden Thrush, who generously pours forth his sweetly varied songs during his breeding season from March to June, then falls silent for many months. The Orange-billed Nightingale-Thrush *(Catharus aurantiirostris)* repeats his quaint, short, less musical verses less freely, but he sings through much of the year. I would hesitate to say which of the two sings for more hours during the twelve months. It would require infinite patience to quantify the actual amount of singing of any individual or species throughout a year; and the undertaking would be more difficult for migratory birds, a few of which sing an appreciable amount in their winter homes, or while migrating. I agree with E. A. Armstrong that the thesis that birds who sing better sing more, probable as it appears, needs to be set upon a firmer foundation.[1]

Although *Born to Sing* deals chiefly with the Oscines, a chapter is devoted to the songs of the "less well-equipped singers," including birds of the "primitive" orders from tinamous to barbets and woodpeckers, and the suboscine Passeriform birds, from broadbills and woodcreepers to the American or "tyrant" flycatchers. To have painstakingly gathered, directly in the field and from recordings and published writings, such a vast amount of information on the songs of so many avian families, evaluated these songs by objective criteria wherever possible, and made much of this information readily available in carefully constructed tables, was a labor of love for which naturalists should be grateful. These tables should help those who delight in bird song, and have the means to travel, to hear the best singers in their native woods and fields. The analysis of the factors, behavioral and ecological, which favor the development of superior song is enlightening. These features, among others, make *Born to Sing* a substantial contribution to ornithology, the value of which is independent of its more controversial, but not for that reason less important, aspects, to which we now turn our attention.

One must be aesthetically insensitive not to recognize the beauty of bird songs, nor to be emotionally stirred by many of them, especially when heard in their natural settings, where they are most effective. Since many of these songs can be written in conventional musical notation, we think of them as music. Whether they are correctly so-called is a technical question to which Hartshorne addresses himself in the opening chapters of his book; as a student of aesthetics who wrote that "music is central to my life," he is well equipped for this undertaking. The main theme of his book is "the possible scientific uses of the aesthetic analogy between other animals, especially birds, and man with respect to music." Although the book's factual content is largely in the later chapters, it is underpinning for this main theme.

Order, our author holds, is the vast realm lying between the deadly extremes of chaos and mechanization. Beauty is created by the harmonious integration of diverse items. To be aesthetically satisfying and rank as music, a sequence of sounds must be neither wholly random nor dully repetitious but contain pleasing contrasts. The songs of many birds satisfy this requirement. Avian songs resemble human music in that every simple musical device, including transposition and simultaneous harmony, occurs in them. Perhaps the greatest difference between avian and human music is the brief span of the bird's repeatable patterns, commonly three seconds or less, rarely as much as fifteen seconds, whereas a human composer can develop a motif that lasts an hour.

I believe, with E. A. Armstrong, that Hartshorne, and others, underestimate the mentality of birds.[2] Their short-term memory, or conscious present, may encompass only a few seconds; but experiments reported by Edwin Boring suggest that man's conscious present is of the same order.[3] Birds certainly do not dismiss experiences from their minds as swiftly as is often supposed. Years ago I had a striking demonstration of their retentiveness. In a clearing amid a Panamanian forest, a snake that preys insatiably upon eggs and nestlings, lurking in the grass for a long while, kept a pair of Crimson-backed Tanagers *(Ramphocelus dimidiatus)* from attending their young in a nearby nest. For an hour after I removed the snake, unseen by the parents who flew away as I approached, they continued to peer down into the herbage from which it had vanished, neglecting the cries of their hungry nestlings. They did not promptly forget a distressing experience. And as to the memory that enables many migratory birds to alternate twice yearly between pin-points on the map thousands of miles apart—perhaps a certain nesting tree in Canada and a feeder in Costa Rica—it commands our admiration but baffles our understanding. When we recall that the bird's vital rhythm is more rapid than ours, with much swifter heartbeat, respiration, and metabolism, so that a second must seem longer to it than to us, we may conclude that the songs of the more highly endowed singers are respectably long. A longer, more involved song might defeat the song's purpose of facilitating rapid specific and individual recognition.

In conformity with his basic principle that aesthetic value lies between the extremes of chaotic multiplicity and mechanical regularity, Hartshorne emphasizes the monotony threshold, or limit of tolerance for repetition. Changes, or contrasts, stimulate attention; persistent repetition depresses response. However, if the interval between repetitions is longer than the song, or than an animal's span of immediate attention or conscious present, the repeated stimulus may fall upon its senses with a freshness that holds attention.

Singing birds have two methods of avoiding hypnotic monotony. Those that repeat the same simple song over and over tend to introduce pauses longer than the song between its repetitions. Those who sing more continuously vary their notes, or have a repertoire of different songs. Repetitious singers tend to perform discontinuously; those who sing more continuously tend to be versatile. Since normally a bird sings freely, without external constraint, it is not likely to perform so monotonously that the song's interest to the singer or his avian listener, mate or rival, is dulled to the point where its biological function is impaired. By avoiding monotony, a bird reveals its aesthetic sensitivity. Birds who, deficient in this sensitivity, repeat the same song hundreds of times in rapid succession are chiefly members of the more "primitive" orders. An example is the Whip-poor-will *(Caprimulgus vociferus)*, a nightjar who for many minutes together proclaims his name over and over with scarcely a pause. Perhaps his main interest is something other than the sounds he emits. The anti-monotony principle, which I believe Hartshorne was the first to recognize, certainly the first to develop, bears importantly upon the question of whether birds are aesthetically sensitive.

In the bird's ability to vary unpredictably the order of the songs in his repertoire, the number of times each is repeated, and the intervals between them, Hartshorne sees an example of the freedom, or indeterminacy, that he believes pervades all nature. These variations in the singer's performance are due to no external compulsion. Within the limits of the bird's repertoire, he is evidently free to sing as he pleases, just as we are free to choose between alternatives open to us. But if our choice were not determined by our character and needs, in relation to our opportunities, would we not more frequently make choices that we later regret? Perhaps the bird's song would be less satisfying to himself if it were not determined by factors within himself. With these brief remarks, we must dismiss a problem beyond the scope of this chapter.

Imitativeness, or the capacity to copy sounds, enters largely into Hartshorne's appraisal of bird song. It is one of the six features by which, on a scale of one to nine, he assesses the quality of songs. At one point in *Born to Sing* (p. 226), he declares that his principles would make him hesitate to designate as song the utterance of a bird with no capacity to learn sound production by hearing others sing. Elsewhere he wrote: "Perhaps we may go so far as to say that if birds ever act intelligently, they do so when imitating sounds and when improving their little musical patterns by practice."[4] However, birds, at least those that build the more elaborate nests, improve their productions by practice, as Nicholas and Elsie Collias demonstrated in the Village Weaver *(Ploceus cucullatus)*, so that, by the same criterion, this, too, must be viewed as intelligent behavior.[5]

Degrees of imitation may be recognized among birds. Their simple calls, including alarm and location notes, appear to be wholly innate, as are the less complex, but often enchantingly melodious, songs of some of the more "primitive" orders. The more elaborate songs of Oscines often contain an innate component that is polished and perfected in youth by hearing and copying older individuals of the same species, often their fathers, or even their contemporaries. We do not, as a rule, call these birds mimics, a term reserved for the minority of birds, including mockingbirds and mynahs, with a lifelong capacity for imitating sounds from a wide variety of living and lifeless sources and incorporating them in their vocal performances. This capacity undoubtedly reveals alert interest in sounds as such, regardless of their significance, and in perfecting their reproductions.

Although we admire the virtuosity of the accomplished mimic, his medley of liquid and harsh notes, trills, and chatters, often appearing to be thrown together at random, is hardly music of the highest order. He amuses us, and challenges us to identify the originals of his reproductions, but he often fails to move us deeply. If the true function of art is to stir exalting emotions, and the highest art is that which does this with the simplest means, then the simple purity of the notes of certain birds placed low in our systems of classification, such as the tinamous, is higher art than the flashy display of vocal flexibility in which mimics sometimes indulge.

Parrots are famed for their ability to imitate the human voice and other sounds, and we wonder why what we chiefly hear from them in the wild is harsh chatter and raucous calls. Many, perhaps most, species remain in pairs throughout the year. Mates appear to be bound together by sharing the same notes, different from those of other pairs in the flocks in which they usually travel, and which they learn from their partners. In captivity they learn from human companions words or brief phrases that sometimes they use in appropriate contexts, as when they say "Polly wants a cracker," or "Good morning"; but on the whole they are reputed to speak without understanding. Probably this is because we do not know how to teach them. When, instead of simply offering them words or short sentences to copy, their tutors demonstrate the meaning of a phrase by acting it with them, their learning is vastly improved. By such "social modeling," Irene Pepperberg taught an African Gray Parrot *(Psittacus erithacus)* to employ English words to request, refuse, identify, categorize, or quantify more than sixty items, to signify its wishes by phrases such as "come here," "I want x," and "wanna go y," and to refuse by saying "no."[6] We have hardly begun to probe the depths of the avian mind.

This brings us to the third and, I believe, most important aspect of Hartshorne's study of bird songs, its contribution to a philosophy of nature. His answers to the questions "Do birds have an aesthetic sense?" "Do birds enjoy their singing?" appear at first glimpse to have quite limited relevance, but, more profoundly viewed, they introduce us to a major problem of cosmology.

To demonstrate, as our author does, that birds' songs are not only beautiful but may properly be called music, does not prove that birds have aesthetic feeling. Flowers are beautiful, but we do not suppose that the plants which bear them have aesthetic sensibility and consciously design them. Bird song, for all its similarity to human music, might, conceivably, be an expression of the widespread tendency in the natural world to arrange its components into harmonious patterns, which I have called "harmonization."[7] Examples of such patterns are crystals (e.g., snowflakes), planetary systems, the filigree elegance of a tree-fern's leaf, the melodious song of a bird. Can we be certain that, unlike the other patterns, the last reveals aesthetic sensibility?

Before tackling the question of whether birds have aesthetic feeling and enjoy their songs, we must clarify the relation of art and its enjoyment to utility. It has commonly been assumed by the uncritical that birds sing when they are happy or contented. More than half a century before Eliot Howard published his classic *Territory in Bird Life*, Bernard Altum recognized the function of song in proclaiming possession of territory and attracting a mate. Falling into the far-too-common error of single-factor explanations, he denied that feeling entered into the exercise of this biologically necessary activity.[8] Would anyone maintain that because gardening, or cooking, or raising children are indispensable for the support and continuance of human life, one can find no pleasure in these occupations? Art and utility are not antithetic but complementary. The more useful an article that lends itself to decoration, the more likely it is to be embellished. Societies that lacked museums where works of art of no practical value might be exhibited, or houses with walls suitable for frescos or hanging pictures, lavished their artistic impulses, and expressed their aesthetic taste, by adorning their ceramics, so indispensable in their simple economy. Undoubtedly they found great satisfaction in molding and painting their artifacts of clay. To suppose that utility and aesthetic pleasure are incompatible is shallow thinking.

Hartshorne does not fall into this error. He sees no conflict between "birds sing for pleasure" and "they sing to maintain territory and attract mates." The more essential an activity is in the whole life of a bird, the more pleasure it is likely to find in it. This is in accord with evolutionary theory for, granted that animals feel, and that pleasant feeling reinforces the activity that engenders it, the more vitally necessary the activity, the more natural selection should make it a source of pleasure. Accordingly, we find that birds who most need song, especially those who can depend least upon visual communication because they live amid obstructing vegetation, and those that defend extensive territories, have developed the most elaborate and pleasing songs. Just as people like to hear themselves talk, birds seem to enjoy, most of all, hearing themselves sing. We would expect birds with the most pleasing songs, and the most exacting aesthetic sensibility that apparently accompanies its production, to sing most in a year, as Hartshorne tried to demonstrate. Unfortunately, because of the incompleteness of his data, the demonstration was not quite convincing.

It has been asserted that if birds have an aesthetic sense they should cluster around the finest singers to enjoy their performances. This overlooks the perils to which birds are exposed and the functions of their songs. While absorbed in listening to a superior performance, a gathering of birds might be too easily surprised by a raptor. A bird singing to assert his determination to defend his territory certainly would not permit another male of his kind to enter it, the better to hear his melodious notes. However, songbirds who have settled their territorial boundaries and dwell in peace with their neighbors may well enjoy singing back and forth with them, often copying all the intonations of their songs in a sort of vocal duel. "It is a stupendous fact about nature," Hartshorne wrote, "that the territorial disputes of thousands of species are something like artistic contests—song duels. The struggle is mainly musical (countersinging), not pugilistic. If only human beings could do so well!"

For the Neo-Darwinian evolutionists now predominant in biological circles, the measure of an organism's fitness is the number of viable offspring that it produces. Nothing else ultimately counts. Individuals of a species are engaged in an unremitting contest to produce the greatest number of descendants, for the most prolific lineage will eventually supplant its competitors. The thoughtful person who contemplates the long, harsh course of evolution will always ask, To what end all this strife and carnage, all this destruction of individuals, all this extinction and creation of species? What is gained by it? To answer this question, one must look to the psychic realm, for unless creatures find some satisfaction, some joys or values in their existence, it can make no slightest difference to them whether they live or cease to be. All their frantic efforts to multiply insentient creatures intrinsically incapable of finding the least satisfaction in their lives are wasted endeavor. As an objective science, biology would exceed its self-imposed limits if it tried to answer the question. It can minutely describe the structure of organisms, tell how they grow and reproduce and interact with each other, give a plausible account of their evolution, but it cannot find the slightest value, to themselves, in the lives of the creatures it studies.

When science reaches the end of its tether, philosophy must carry on. If there be significance and meaning in human life, or in the wider living world, it is the task of philosophy, not of science, to discover it. From its flowering in ancient Hellas, a major endeavor of philosophy has been to identify the true values available to humans, and to guide them in the realization of these values. Increasingly in recent times, philosophers, and philosophical biologists, have broadened the scope of this inquiry to explore the psychic lives of nonhuman animals, especially those highest in the evolutionary scale, birds and mammals, and to ask what experiences might enrich them. This is a hazardous undertaking, for we cannot demonstrate to the skeptic's satisfaction that these animals are conscious in the least degree. All we can say about them—or our fellow humans—is that they behave as though they feel and think; and we intuitively attribute consciousness to them.

Instead of vaguely asserting that animals as highly organized as birds, or dolphins, or elephants, or chimpanzees must certainly feel rather keenly, we do well to examine particular facets of their lives, such as their parental behavior, their social relations, their play, or their singing for indications of emotion or feeling in these contexts. Hartshorne has given us sound reasons for believing that birds aesthetically enjoy their singing. These reasons do not amount to unassailable proofs; but when we reflect that we cannot rigorously prove that our brothers are conscious, we will not lightly reject his arguments. I would go so far as to say that if gifted singers experience no gleam of pleasure in their singing they are not likely to find satisfaction in other aspects of their lives, in which case their evolution would have been a barren reorganization of matter, accomplishing nothing of importance. For it would be absurd to suppose that creatures who inhabited Earth so many millions of years before man appeared were created solely for his delectation.

Studies such as Hartshorne's *Born to Sing* and Donald Griffin's *The Question of Animal Awareness* help to exorcise the Cartesian specter of animal automatism, which lurks so stubbornly in certain minds, and has had such baneful consequences for nonhuman creatures. I marvel that any philosopher could have promulgated such a dogma, for we can as little disprove that animals feel as we can prove that they do, and there are more reasons, from analogy, from the continuity of evolution, from behavior, for preferring the second alternative.

A major concern of Hartshorne's philosophy has been values and their preservation. In *Born to Sing* he has felicitously wedded his philosophical and ornithological interests. By giving cogent reasons for believing that not only we who hear the songs of birds but they who sing them find aesthetic value in them, he makes feathered creatures seem close to us. For value is experienced only by beings that are conscious or feel. A universe devoid of feeling, therefore of value, no matter how many galaxies, stars, and planets were scattered through the vastitude of its space, would lack importance; its annihilation could cause no decrease of value, already at the zero point. The more reasons we have for believing that feeling and value are widely diffused through the cosmos, not only in living beings but perhaps, in a minor degree, in nonliving matter, the less alien it appears to us, the more it appears a congenial abode for us who enjoy, suffer, and aspire. And certainly the most promising place to begin the exploration of values beyond mankind is among creatures that have most in common with ourselves, especially the birds that, after man, are the most accomplished musicians in the animal kingdom—as Charles Hartshorne has done so well in his study of bird song.

ALEXANDER F. SKUTCH

COSTA RICA
JULY 1986

NOTES

1. Edward A. Armstrong, *A Study of Bird Song* (London: Oxford University Press, 1963), p. 243.

2. Edward A. Armstrong, Review of *Born to Sing. The Ibis* 116 (1974): 239–240.

3. Edwin G. Boring, *The Physical Dimensions of Consciousness* (New York: Dover Publications, 1963), pp. 135-136.

4. Charles Hartshorne, "The Relation of Bird Song to Music." *The Ibis* 100 (1958): 421–445, p. 435.

5. Nicholas E. Collias and Elsie C. Collias, *Nest Building and Bird Behavior* (Princeton, New Jersey: Princeton University Press, 1984), p. 216.

6. Irene M. Pepperberg, "Social Modeling Theory: A Possible Framework for Understanding Avian Vocal Learning," *The Auk* 102 (1985): 854–864, p. 856.

7. Alexander F. Skutch, *Life Ascending* (Austin: University of Texas Press, 1985).

8. Ernst Mayr, "Bernard Altum and the Territory Theory," *Proc. Linnaean Soc. N. Y.*, nos. 45–46, 1933–1934.

3

Lucio Chiaraviglio

HARTSHORNE'S AESTHETIC THEORY OF INTELLIGENCE

INTRODUCTION

Charles Hartshorne is the only philosopher who designed and carried out an empirical investigation that quantified certain aspects of the characteristic expressions of a group of species and correlated these quantities to aesthetic judgments of these expressions made by another species. The expressions in question were bird song and the judgments were human.[1]

This remarkable enterprise begins with the basic intuition that bird song is literally song and therefore is enjoyed by the singers. As in the human case, such enjoyment leads to observable and quantifiable dimensions of the singing behavior as well as qualitative rankings of song.

The basic quantity used to characterize species' song behavior is effective singing season. This quantity is obtained by correcting and normalizing the number of days of singing in the nesting region by such factors as the ratio of song length to the length of the song-pause cycle, the amount of daylight in the region, the amount of nocturnal song, and the amount of singing by migrants in winter quarters.

Two main ranking scales are used. The scaled score of song development is obtained as the sum of scores of six parameters: loudness, variety-complexity-scope, continuity, tonal purity, organization, and imitativeness. The scaled score of biological need of song is obtained by combining degree of territoriality, bird inconspicuousness, and gregariousness. Evidence is presented warranting the biological significance of the parameters that compose song development and need. Evidence is also given warranting the importance of the parameters of song development to the judgments of song quality.

The principal results of the investigation may be summarized as follows:

- annual amount of singing correlates with the degree of need for song;
- degree of need for song correlates with the score of song development;
- effective song season correlates with song development and the separate factors that constitute this scale;
- the factors that constitute song development correlate with human judgments of song goodness.

All the correlations listed are significant and in the right direction. Thus, aesthetically better singers have better developed songs, sing longer, and have greater biological need for song.[2]

Hartshorne explores numerous other issues including the correlation of song-supporting physiology to the quantities and scales mentioned. His remarks on the correlation of brain size and song development anticipate relevant discoveries by a decade.

This brief outline may suffice to indicate that part of the motivation of the investigation may be stated in the following hypotheses:

- if human aesthetic judgment reflects some aspects of feeling integration that are shared with birds and other singing animals, then the dimensions of songs that please humans should correlate with certain observable song quantities and scales;
- conversely, finding such a correlation is evidence that singing animals share with humans certain aspects of feelings as well as an aesthetic (musical) sense.

The enterprise is striking and highlights some of the recurring themes of Hartshorne's thought.[3] Taking "intelligence" in a broad sense, to be explained later, these themes may be stated as follows:

- intelligence is an active discretely granular process constituted by feelings that integrate other feelings;
- this active process is manifest in various degrees across the full evolutionary range;[4]
- the universe which is an aesthetic continuum of unity and contrast, bounded on one side by monotony and on the other by chaos, is a product of these processes.

These three themes are found in most of Hartshorne's work. Their presence in the investigation of bird song is evident. They also contribute substantially to his view of perfection. The necessary realization of perfection in the form of a harmonizer of contrasts—a perfect intelligence—has been one of his most enduring preoccupations. Thus, from birds to deity this trinity of themes plays a major role and constitutes the kernel of what is here termed "Hartshorne's theory of intelligence".

Following Hartshorne, "intelligence" is here taken as relational and applies primarily to processes. Generically, an intelligent process is one that steers a course between monotony and chaos. Processes integrate other processes within them and in so doing may generate stifling order, monotony, or disorder, chaos. Monotony and chaos are also relational. That is to say that a process may be monotonous relative to one integrating process and chaotic relative to another.

The relational view of monotony and chaos depends on notions of "work of intelligence" to be explained later. However, a concrete example taken from Hartshorne's treatment of monotony thresholds may clarify the basic idea.[5] He points out that some bird songs that are considered monotonous are sung with short pauses during which the birds attend to other matters. Singing with short pauses for intervening activities may produce a total process which, relative to the "intelligence" of that organism, maintains a proper balance of unity and contrasts. While the total production may still be monotonous to the human audience, the occurrence of pauses is evidence that the singer itself has monotony thresholds which were avoided by the total production. Thus, monotony thresholds may be quite different for organisms with different processing capabilities. Following Hartshorne, one may speculate that the height of the threshold is inversely related to the processing capabilities of the organisms. Hence, what is monotonous for humans may be acceptable to some birds.[6]

"Intelligence" is not here limited to conscious processes nor limited to those that include explicit reasoning. These processes may be included but are not necessary to intelligence. While much that has been said about mind and psyche is relevant to the present sense of "intelligence", there is the important caveat that these concepts often signify objects that are loci or receptacles of processes. The converse view is appropriate here: intelligences are processes that include such objects. Finally, "intelligence" is preferable to "mind", "psyche", and others because in the context of the computing sciences the term connotes processes that are open to investigation.[7]

The next section contains a brief sketch of some of the basic ideas of this new science.

THE WORK OF INTELLIGENCE

The externalization of physical work that occurred with the eighteenth- and nineteenth-century inventions of engines promoted the development of the science of thermodynamics. Work became a subject of scientific investigation and the science rapidly became a complex subject of interest much beyond the original bounds. Similarly, the contemporary externalization of intelligence promoted by the computing technologies is creating an as yet not well named subject with increasing interests well beyond the original settings. The new area brings together perceptions from many fields and is rapidly developing themes that repay with interest some of the borrowed intellectual capital.

Complexity theory is one such theme. One of its principal variations has the goal of measuring the relative hardness of problems. All kinds of problems are addressed provided there exist effective procedures, algorithms, to solve them.

This effort to quantify some of the work of intelligence has its historical antecedents in the foundational work of investigators such as Post, Gödel, Turing, Church, and others. These thinkers were concerned with the problems of mathematical proof, truth, computation, formal systems, and their inter-reducibilities.

The deservedly celebrated results of these concerns were that there exist no effective procedures for solving the general problem of mathematical proof or truth for many important senses of "mathematical", that there exist infinite hierarchies of non-computable functions, and that many apparently distinct formal senses of "proof" and "computation" are reducible to each other. This last result is encapsulated in what is known as "Church's Thesis" which proposes that these inter-reducible senses of "computation" are adequate formal counterparts of the corresponding intuitive ideas.

No generally accepted counterexample to Church's Thesis has been found. Thus, the described investigations led naturally to the identification of problems, their instances, and their solutions with their expression in suitable formal systems. The inter-reducibility of these systems gave confidence that the identification did not introduce artifacts that would nullify the enterprise.

Algorithms played an important role in the early investigations. However, the realization that their execution might consume resources at rates that were characteristic of the algorithms came much later. Discrete space and time were eventually identified as the abstract resources consumed in the execution of algorithms and thus also the resources consumed in the solutions of problems solved by the algorithms. Discrete time is the succession of steps taken and discrete space the memory occupied during algorithm execution. Since space, time, the formal expressions of problems, and their instances are all discrete entities, quantification of the work of intelligence involves counting and the rates at which such counts grow.

Time and space consumed in the execution of problem solving algorithms grow with the size of the problem instances being solved. For example, if the problem is one of recognizing or generating expressions in a language L based on an alphabet A, then recognizing whether a particular string S of elements of A is an expression of L is an instance of this problem. The size of this instance may be taken as the total number of occurrences of elements of A in S, the length of S. The recognition or generation of longer strings will generally consume more time and space. Thus, the rates of resource consumption for algorithms that solve such problems are monotonic non-decreasing time count and space count valued functions of the size of the instances.[8]

The rates at which algorithms consume resources may be said to characterize their efficiency. If among the algorithms that solve a problem there exist one that is most efficient, then the rate of resource consumption of this algorithm may be taken as characterizing the intrinsic complexity or hardness of the problem. Confidence in these concepts is gained by showing that problems that are appropriately reducible to each other have the same complexity.

The described quantification gives rise to the idea of feasible work that is similar to that of thermodynamics. In both cases there is no infinite refinment of efficiency nor unbounded supply of resources. Thus, for each process of resource deployment there exist a work of intelligence, a problem, whose intrinsic complexity exceeds the rates at which the resources are made available. Such work is unfeasible.

A problem is unfeasible if its most efficient solution has a high rate of resource consumption. Even so, unfeasibility is in practice relative to resources deployment. However, it is customary to say that problems whose complexity is given by functions that grow exponentially or faster are unfeasible. Fundamental physical facts such as the bounded speed of causal propagation and the essentially linear nature of addressable memory entail the unfeasibility of some such ranges of problems.

Complexity theory introduces a new boundary for intelligence and for what is intelligible. Unfeasibility joins the more traditional boundaries of inconsistency and undecidability. Using Hartshorne's terminology, one may be tempted to say that unfeasibility is a contingent boundary while the others are necessary. How much time and memory is available for works of intelligence depends on the particular state of some universe and is thus contingent.

Resolution of the metaphysical status of unfeasibility is just as difficult as the resolution of the status of the more traditional bounds of intelligibility. Philosophers who deny the possibility of instantaneous action at a distance or assert the necessity of a bounded speed of causal propagation, should find that certain classes of works of intelligence are necessarily unfeasible. Philosophers who find arithmetic more compelling should find that if some of the very basic laws of arithmetic are necessary, so is the non-existence of an upper bound for complexity. Hence, for every deployment of resources there must exist some unfeasible work of intelligence.

In the next sections the ideas sketched will be related to the triplet of themes selected from Hartshorne's work. The ideas will be illustrated and applied to problems that arise from the extremes of the spectrum of Hartshone's ontological interests.

INTEGRATIVE FEELINGS AND ALGORITHM EXECUTION

Hartshorne's aesthetic process view of reality and the concern with the work of intelligence share some basic ideas. Discrete processes are fundamental to both. For both the relations among process granules are asymmetrical and provide the relevant senses of "time" and "space" for processes.

Each but the first and last steps in algorithm-execution acquires data from previous steps and passes data to the next steps. The acquiring and passing relations are asymmetrical and furnish the primary sense of "time" relevant to execution. Space is the memory required for step synchronization. Data are held in memory until they can be utilized. Thus, memory space is the specious present of execution steps.

Similarly, in Hartshorne's theory, the feelings integrated are data acquired by the integrating feelings. This passing or acquiring of data is asymmetrical and provides the sense of "time" relevant to these processes. Space is the specious present of feelings.

Both processes of feeling integration and algorithm execution have anticipatory and terminal dimensions. In the case of algorithms the data acquired by each step must satisfy pre-conditions and the data passed on by each step must satisfy post-conditions. These conditions furnish an appropriate meaning of "correctness" for execution since correct execution must produce a step by step flow of data satisfying these conditions. Also, pre- and post-conditions specify what algorithms accomplish when executed correctly.

Anticipatory and consequent valuations are common in the flow of experience of complex organisms. Hartshorne's aesthetic view of processes generalizes this phenomenon to all levels of reality thus making the pre- and post-valued conditions characteristic of the ubiquitous aesthetic nature of reality. This is quite evident in the study of bird song where aesthetic sensibilities are found to regulate song but also in other works where aims and satisfactions structure the universe.

Those concerned with the work of intelligence are interested in externalizing intelligence in artifacts. Hartshorne's aesthetic process view of reality fosters an interest in those features of mind that are universal. Thus, the coincidence of views noted is not entirely accidental. However, there is also divergence of views. The notion of algorithm is central to all consideration of the work of intelligence but philosophers have been unaware of its importance. The prevalent view has been that declarative abstractions and associated valuations are sufficient for the analyses of processes.

This lacuna may be a residue of the static analysis of concreteness in terms of subjects and objects. Declarative language such as propositions and their true and false valuations are relevant to the analysis of processes but are also clearly insufficient. This should be readily apparent to anyone who has read a cookbook. Cookbooks contain recipes and while recipes do contain declarative expressions they are not declarative. Declarative expressions are not executable. In appropiate environments recipes may be executed yielding processes that produce gastronomic outputs. Such outputs may be desired and therefore anticipated. They may be appreciated and produce satisfactions. Accordingly, recipes are successful or otherwise but neither true nor false.

Recipes, plans, procedures, and algorithms are all more or less abstract specifications of processes. They are successful or unsuccessful according to whether the processes specified produce outputs which are anticipated and, if anticipated, according to whether they are satisfactory or otherwise. The successful-unsuccessful valuation of algorithms are to be contrasted to the true-false valuations of propositions. True-false valuations are completely independent of anticipations and satisfactions. They are independent of the relations between inputs and outputs of processes. Thus, propositions cannot bear the marks of a dynamic world. Algorithms bear these marks in their axiology. Furthermore, algorithms may be executed while propositions may not.

ALGORITHMS, ADAPTATION, LEARNING, AND PANPSYCHISM

As required by the aesthetic view, Hartshorne takes memory as a root paradigm for the organization of reality. Mounting ethological evidence shows that memory is preponderantly algorithmic rather than propositional. It is memories of procedures rather than facts. All organisms capable of learning acquire many algorithms that they execute in their daily rounds. This learned repertoire is a store of algorithmic memories that complement and build upon genetically programmed algorithms. The total store is largely unconscious and, without it, consciousness and propositional memories are probably impossible.

The acquired algorithms are most often learned via re-enaction or imitation of the processes of execution. In re-enaction, the organism is in an environment that constrains activity largely to the behavior required. The organism is put through the paces much as an industrial robot is programmed. The cost of such learning is probably at a minimum since the constraints limit trial and error.

Imitation is probably more costly since it uses rehearsal with trial and error and corrective feedback. Learning propositionally is probably the most costly of all.

The complexity of the task of recognizing or generating molecular behaviors composed of atoms from an already secure repertoire is linear in the number of repertoire elements occurring in the molecular behaviors. Song is often an example of a molecular behavior acquired by imitation. Bicycle riding is another example of such a behavior largely acquired by re-enaction. The complexity of the task of recognizing the satisfiability of a proposition is exponential in the number of its literals. Thus, learning behaviors via propositional descriptions has a cost which is at least exponential in the number of literals. Furthermore, if the propositions are to say much about the behaviors, then they must have as many or more literals than there are atoms in the behavior. Thus, learning via propositions has costs that grow exponentially with the numbers of elements to be dealt with. This is learning by the method of trying all alternatives which is almost always very costly.

The complexities of works of intelligence have associated physical costs. Generally, the more complex the algorithm the greater the cost of its physical execution. This is largely due to the fact that physical memories and processes consume energy. For example, the algorithms that embody the informational transactions that produce the genotypes of succeeding generations are physically realized in populations of organisms that consume energy to survive and reproduce. The energy budgets of these populations are the physical costs of the biological realizations of these algorithms.

Evolution is an obvious case where the most important interprocess relations are information transactions and thus, in a broad sense, are works of intelligence. Indeed, the complexity of evolution may be viewed in the same manner as that of any works of intelligence. The genetic macromolecules of reproducing populations are the memory spaces of the processes that lead from one generation to the next. These processes are the executions of mutation, recombination, replication, and selection algorithms that insure rapid fixation of favorable mutants. Mutation introduces new information, recombination disseminates it, and replication produces the large numbers on which selection acts. The total process is of exponential complexity.

The physical cost of exponential algorithms increases rapidly where selective pressures favor larger and more complex structures for supporting their memory spaces. For example, organisms which are composed of multiply differentiated cells require complex regulation of gene expression during development. Hence, longer genomes are needed for storing both regulatory and constitutive information. More complex structures are neccessary to support these genomes and the transcription and translation steps that express their information content. Furthermore, the generation time of such organisms must be longer to allow for the production of multiple generations of component cells.

Such considerations suggest that at some point along the scale of organismic complexity there is a crossover in the cost of genetic adaptation and the cost of adaptation by learning. However, for this to be so the costs of learning must be relatively low. Notice that learning is realized with cellular mechanisms of approximately the same order of physical costs as those that realize genetic adaptation. Hence, selection of learning would occur only if it is based on algorithms of lower complexity than those of genetic adaptation. Thus, only if learning most often occurs via algorithms of less than exponential complexity. Learning must be rarely propositional.

In organisms that learn, part of the work of intelligence necessary for survival is carried out at the level of gene expression and thus does not require genetic modification. So viewed, learning may appear to be an evolutionary strategy for keeping genetic information fixed. Those genes that are found on genomes that bear genes enabling learning could be locked into greater fixity than those not so blessed. If this were so, it would be reasonable to expect that molecular evolution would slow down with the increase in learning capabilities.

The facts do not warrant this expectation. The rate of molecular change seems roughly constant over many species and vast periods of time. Furthermore, learning that is cumulative across generations, learning that issues into culture, may accelerate biological evolution by rapidly altering selective pressures. The feedback path that leads from learning via culture to more rapid alteration of selective pressures may be itself a selective pressure that favors both learning and culture as modes of adaptation.

Genetic adaptation to rapidly changing selective pressures may be unfeasible for organisms that have developed the complexity required to support learning and culture. In the environments of these species there may not be enough physical resources to support very costly individuals in the large and exponentially growing populations required for genetic adaptation. So viewed, learning and culture appear to be specializations which, like all others, are genetic dead ends.

The existence of causal mechanisms that lead from learning and culture to potential evolutionary speed up and mechanisms that take the converse route from speed up to increased learning and dependence on culture suggests that intelligence may not be selected by any single set of pressures. The presence of intelligence in the evolutionary range may simply reflect a basic cost equilibrium between genotypic and phenotypic adaptation. This equilibrium may issue from the relative physical costs of the alternatives realized in a largely fixed and common range of basic physical devices. If this is so, the differences in costs are attributable to the complexity of the algorithms implemented. Since genotypic adaptation is obtained via exponential algorithms, then a fairly wide use of lower complexity learning algorithms may be expected throughout the evolutionary range. In other words, if learning is most often the cheaper alternative, then intelligence sufficient for learning may be the general case and some form of panpsychism, such as Hartshorne's, would be a reasonable doctrine.

It may be appropriate to end this section by commenting on some recent neurological discoveries that furnish concrete evidence of the costs of intelligence. The comment may be doubly appropriate since the discoveries were made in song birds and relate directly to the work of intelligence required to learn and process song repertoires. The main discoveries may be described as follows.

Song bird brains have special areas involved in song production. These areas are anatomically easily distinguished from the rest of the brain and appear to be specialized to song processing. Two forebrain nuclei, the hyperstriatum ventralis, pars caudalis (HVc) and the robust nucleus of the archistriatum (RA), are song control centers.[9] The HVc connects to the RA which in turn connect to the hypoglossal motor neurons that control voice production.[10] The HVc and RA areas are much larger and better developed in the singing males than in the nonsinging females.[11]

Canaries sing throughout the spring breeding season, stop singing in summer, and in autumn begin learning a new repertoire for the next spring. At onset of song development, at about the age of one month, immature canaries have HVc regions that are one-eighth as large as those of adults singing their full spring repertoires. In the fall as the adult begins to prepare a new repertoire just after the summer song rest the HVc is about half its spring size. Adult females can be induced to sing through the administration of male sex hormones and when this happens the HVc region and the nucleus RA increase by about fifty percent.

Male canaries with larger repertoires also have larger HVc and RA regions. Zebra finches and marsh wrens exhibit the same phenomenon. West coast marsh wrens that have three times the repertoire of the Eastern ones have forty percent larger HVc regions and thirty percent larger RA regions than their relatives.[12]

While the increases of the HVc and RA regions could be due to increases in the number of connections, the song birds studied grow new neurons both for replacement and for the mentioned brain increments. Twenty thousand new neurons appear each day in the canaries' forebrains which contain about seven million neurons. Thus, in just about one year there is a complete turn over of neurons in this area. Massive turn over of forebrain neurons has been observed in budgerigars and ringdoves. The forebrain is thought to be involved in complex learning.

Some of the discoveries mentioned have straightforward interpretations. The growth of selected areas of the brain so as to accommodate song is direct evidence of the physical costs of the algorithms involved in song production. The cost appears to be significant since it is avoided during the non-singing season by shrinking the involved areas of the brain.

Too little is known about neuron function, brain architecture, and the algorithms executed to say much about the relations between sizes of repertoires and the brain increments they appear to generate. Since the HVc region of canaries have fifteen thousand neurons in the shrunken state and double this quantity with the full repertoire, then it may be speculated that fifteen thousand neurons are directly required by this repertoire.[13] Fifteen thousand simple devices would be sufficient to form circuits to implement recognition and/or generation algorithms for the full repertoire. Similarly, the increments of brain size associated with larger repertoire of the Western marsh wren is consistent with known technology.

From the point of view of algorithm execution it is not a surprise that larger repertoires require greater processing capabilities. What is neurologically surprising is the high neuron turnover in birds and the apparent lack of it in other species. Some other species are known to respond to increased processing needs by expanding neuron connections but apparently they neither grow additional neurons nor replace them.[14]

The fact that increased processing needs are met by expansion of physical facilities, entails that facilities become saturated. Saturation may come about through a peak load as may happen during bird song season. Saturation may also come about through an accumulation of continuing processing requirements as may occur if there is a permanent need to learn novel things. Temporary expansion of facilities is a cost effective strategy for the first case and renovation of facilities may be a cost effective strategy for the second case.

In order to acquire new song repertoires for each spring, canaries may have evolved an expanding and contracting brain which provides new processing facilities at the time needed and reduced deadload during the intense foraging summer season. Rapid forebrain neuron turnover may have evolved to meet continuing learning challenges while maintaining low brain weight. Brain renovation may be a mandatory strategy for any organisms that require low weight and high learning capabilities thoughout life.

COMPLEXITY, CHAOS, AND ORDER

In Hartshorne's aesthetic view of reality, as well as in any other view that considers processes fundamental, order and chaos issue from interprocess relations. The purpose of this section is to give an example of such a relation in order to indicate how the work of intelligence generated by interprocess relations sets the bounds of chaos and order.

Re-enaction, reproduction, mimicry, and simulation are common and important interprocess relations. According to Whitehead, massive re-enaction is the foundation of all order. Hartshorne finds that mimicry is generally a sign of superior aesthetic sensibility and thus may be presumed to be instrumental to achieving the aesthetically satisfying middle ground between monotony and chaos, where song lies. Reproduction is certainly fundamental to all biological order. And the existence of universal simulators, algorithms capable of simulating any others, is central to the conception of algorithms.

Re-enaction, reproduction, mimicry, and simulation are closely related, share common structures and, for the purposes at hand, may all be considered as cases of replication. If process B is to replicate process A, then some information must flow from A to B which B must receive and process. Since B replicates A, the information that flows from A to B must include both the algorithm and data executed by A. The process B in turn must execute an algorithm which interprets this received information as consisting of an algorithm and its data and which then executes this algorithm against its data. Thus, the interpreting algorithm that B executes in order to replicate A increases the cost of B over that of A.

The complexity of B exceeds that of A. If A and B are realized in a similar physical fashion, then the physical costs of B will also surpass those of A. In a chain of replication costs accumulate and at some point exceed available resources. At such a point there is loss of information. Not all the information transmitted is received, processed, or re-transmitted. Forgetting is truly the general case. An unending accumulation of costs is unfeasible.

More generally, memory losses will occur whenever any processes inherit from others and the information transmitted by the parentals exceeds the processing capacity of the filials. The filials are more monotonous than the parentals if the information processed is simplified uniformly by all filials. The filials are more chaotic if the information is simplified differently by a sufficiently large number of filials. The first alternative decreases the diversity of the world and makes it available to processes with equal or greater resources than the filials. The second alternative increases the diversity of the world and makes it available only to processes with resources that exceed the combined resources of all the diverging filials. In a universe where there is no action at a distance the alternative worlds drift towards monotony and chaos. But they do so in relative isolation since shifting of resources and transmission of information takes time. Thus, the universe as a whole is buffered against large and pervasive changes.

A fuller statement of a theory of chaos and order is well beyond the scope of this essay. However, what has been barely sketched may suffice to illuminate one of Hartshorne's persistent ontological interests and the capstone of his process view of reality: the theory of perfection and deity.[15]

The existence of terminal elements in the field of the relation is-more-perfect-than depends on the properties of this relation. For example, if this relation is a non-terminating progression, then it has no terminal elements and to think Anselm's thoughts with respect to it is indeed to think contradictions. As Hartshorne has noted, those who wish to succeed with Anselm's arguments must provide construals of "is more perfect than" that have terminal elements.

From what has been said thus far it may be evident that the relations is-more-intelligent-than among processes or algorithms and requires-more-intelligence-than among problems have no terminal elements. A brief review of the associations of costs and intelligence may highlight these points.

Adequate memory and processing time are necessary but not sufficient conditions for intelligence. It is possible to consume great resources solving trivial problems. But it is not possible to spend trivial resources solving hard problems nor is it possible to spend small amounts of resources solving very large instances of easy problems. Furthermore, there are no upper bounds to the hardness of problems nor the size of the instances of most problems. Hence the relation requires-more-intelligence-than among problems and the relation is-more-intelligent-than among algorithms or processes have no terminal elements.

If there are most intelligent processes, hardest problems or largest instances that can be solved, their existence is a matter concerning resources available in some world. Such matters are not illuminated by Anselm's arguments.

Of course, one might try one's luck with Anselm's argument in connection with other interprocess relations. However, the idea of a perfect process as a universal binding agent, along whatever attributes, is poorly motivated in any process ontology. In ontologies of this kind, processes are what hold the universe together just by being processes. Perfection or even a modicum of adeptness is unneccessary to this end. For example, the processes of cooking assemble the ingredients of meals and while the results may be often unpalatable nothing else besides these processes is required for assembly. Notice that among the significant ingredients of cooking processes there are not only the food stuffs and other physical resources but also the cooks together with their aesthetic sensibilities and values. As this example illustrates, stuff, objects, persons and values are bound in processes independently of their perfection.

In summary, one may say that if processes are taken as fundamental, the idea that some receptacle is needed to hold them together is unneccessary. In such a view chaos and order as well as preservation and loss are relative to processes. Intelligence, in its broadest generalization, is the power of processes to accomplish many different tasks including preserving and ordering. However, intelligence is not free. The times of processing steps and the spaces of memories are consumed. Forgetting becomes a necessity and this limits the complexity of both chaos and order. In Hartshorne's territory, such are the lessons we learn from the birds.

LUCIO CHIARAVIGLIO
SCHOOL OF INFORMATION AND COMPUTER SCIENCE
GEORGIA INSTITUTE OF TECHNOLOGY
MARCH 1986

NOTES

1. C. Hartshorne, *Born to Sing: An Interpretation and World Survey of Bird Song* (Bloomington: Indiana University Press, 1973).
2. C. Hartshorne, *Bulletin of the Texas Ornithological Society* 8 (1975):2–5.
3. C. Hartshorne, "Metaphysics Contributes to Ornithology," *Theoria to Theory* 13 (1979):127–40.
4. In "Thinking About Thinking Machines," *Texas Quarterly* 7, 1 (Spring 1964):131–40, Hartshorne gives a very clear and concise statement of the rationale for the first two themes.
5. Hartshorne, *Born to Sing*, chap. 7, 119–56; C. Hartshorne, "The Monotony Threshold in Singing Birds," *Auk* 83 (1956):176–92; C. Hartshorne, Review of *North American Bird Songs, A World of Music* by Paul Bondeson, *The Wilson Bulletin* 90, 1 (1978):153–55.
6. R. A. Canady, D. E. Kroodsma, & F. Nottebohm, *Proc. Natl. Acad. Sci. U.S.A.* 81 (1984):6232–34.
7. P. J. Denning, *American Scientist* 74 (1984):18–20.
8. All singers and speakers have this kind of problem. It is a problem of linear complexity since the amount of memory or number of processing steps necessary to recognize or generate strings of morphemes increases linearly with the length of the strings.
9. P. J. Denning, *American Scientist* 74 (1984):18–20.
10. D. B. Kelley & F. Nottebohm, *J. Comp. Neurol.* 183 (1979):455–70; H. Williams & F. Nottebohm, *Soc. Neurosci. Abs.* 9 (1983):537; F. Nottebohm, *Condor* 86 (1984):227–36.
11. F. Nottebohm, S. Kasparrian, & C. Pandazis, *Brain Res.* 213 (1981):99–109.
12. R. A. Canady, D. E. Kroodsma, & F. Nottebohm, *Proc. Natl. Acad. Sci. U.S.A.* 81 (1984):6232–34.
13. F. Nottebohm, T. Stokes, & C. M. Leonard, *J. Comp. Neurol* 165 (1976): 457–86.
14. Enriched experimental environments change the structure of the cerebral cortex in young, adult, and old rats. Thus, these animals increase processing capabilities in response to increased load. See: M. Diamond, R. Johnson, A. N. Protti, C. Ott, & L. Kajisa, *Age* 6, 4 (1983):134–45.
15. C. Hartshorne, *The Logic of Perfection and Other Essays in Neoclassical Metaphysics* (La Salle, Ill.: Open Court Publishing Company, 1962).

4

Wayne Viney

CHARLES HARTSHORNE'S PHILOSOPHY AND PSYCHOLOGY OF SENSATION

In the early 1920s Charles Hartshorne completed his first course in psychology at Harvard University under Leonard Thompson Troland, one of the most versatile and productive scientists of his day.[1] Troland's course as well as his three-volume *Principles of Psychophysiology* reinforced Hartshorne's interests in sensory psychology and afforded an early and largely friendly climate that nurtured ideas that later culminated in *The Philosophy and Psychology of Sensation*.[2] Many of the other early general influences, especially on the philosophical side (e.g., Charles S. Peirce, Alfred North Whitehead, Josiah Royce, and William E. Hocking), are easily recognized. But while general influences can be traced, *The Philosophy and Psychology of Sensation*, Hartshorne's first book, is a highly original and comprehensive work setting forth ideas that occurred to its author on an independent basis. The purposes of this chapter are: (1) to summarize and evaluate the position set forth in Hartshorne's book and related short papers, and (2) to examine possible reasons for the neglect of a heuristic theory that anticipated many contemporary developments.

HARTSHORNE'S POSITION

Hartshorne's succinct statement of his thesis is that "the application of scientific and rational principles to the sensory qualities results in a new theory of these 'immediate data of consciousness,' considered both in themselves and in relation

The author expresses appreciation to Donald Wayne Viney for suggestions on bibliographical materials for this paper and for providing a helpful orientation to Hartshorne's philosophy. In more ways than one, the child is father of the man.

to their physical stimuli, organic conditions, biological significance, and evolutionary origin'' (6). Hartshorne characterizes his theory of the contents of sensation as "forming an 'affective continuum' of aesthetically meaningful, socially expressive, organically adaptive and evolving experience functions" (9). Chapters 1 and 2 set forth the theory and contrast it with classical sensory theory. Hartshorne's alternative to classical sensory theory is further elaborated in a chapter on philosophy (Ch. 3) devoted to the deadlock between realism and idealism, and a chapter on psychology that discusses theoretical conflicts in the discipline and the impact of materialistic and atomistic notions borrowed from nineteenth-century physics (Ch. 4). Evidence for the affective continuum is further elaborated in separate chapters entitled "Dualism in Aesthetics" (Ch. 5); "The Dimensions of Experience" (Ch. 6); "The Dimensions of Sensation" (Ch. 7); and "Sensation and the Environment" (Ch. 8). Appendices include discussions of the affective continuum in theology (A), the origin of Hartshorne's doctrine of pitch and loudness (B), brightness as a universal attribute (C), Goethe's Farbenlehre (D), and a helpful bibliographical note on major writings of the day on sensation (E).

The elaboration of Hartshorne's thesis is set forth under five assertions regarding sensory processes. These assertions, shortly to be described in more detail, are as follows: (1) there is mathematical continuity within and between sensory modalities; (2) affective tone is a part of the very essence of sensory quality; (3) experience is social, i.e., "feeling of feeling" accounts for communication between and within experiencing systems; (4) sensation is intricately related to adaptive behavior; and (5) sensory qualities have a developmental or evolutionary history from a common origin. These five assertions are clarified by first examining some of the contentions of classical sensory theory which serve as a foil for Hartshorne's work.

A major contention in the classical theory of Hermann von Helmholtz is that the sensory modalities operate in complete independence from each other. On the topic of the independence of modality, Helmholtz asserted "It is so profound that it excludes any transition from one to the other, any relation of greater or lesser similarity. For example, we cannot ask at all whether sweet is more similar to blue than to red."[3] Helmholtz acknowledged that comparisons are possible within a sensory modality or within a "quality circle," an expression he borrowed from Johann Gottlieb Fichte.[4] Thus we may say that green has more of a likeness to blue than it has to red, but by Helmholtz's reasoning we may not say that the taste of sweetness is inherently more like the smell of lilacs than the smell of rotten eggs. Though Helmholtz acknowledged the possibility of comparisons within quality circles, it is not clear how such intrasensory comparisons are possible if it is assumed that separate receptor systems are responsible for separate qualities such as red, green, and blue-violet. Another contention commonly encountered in classical sensory theories is that sensation and affect are separate conscious functions. Thus, if sensation is accompanied by affect, it is because the affect is somehow "added on" to the purely cognitive material of the sensation. This contention is defended in Oswald Külpe's *Outlines of Psychology*.[5] We turn now to a more detailed consideration of Hartshorne's alternative to classical theory.

Intersensory Continuity

If sensory qualities are radically isolated from each other, it follows that nothing except direct experience can ever reveal their inner nature. If the separation of sensory qualities is as complete as suggested in classical theory, then there is no analogy by which one could gain access to one quality from another. The assumption of discontinuity also poses difficult questions for those who are interested in the evolutionary history of sensory processes. If touch is the oldest sense, and if vision, audition, gustation, and olfaction evolved from this common parent, how can these newer elaborations of touch display qualities which forbid all meaningful transitions to their parent? Further, on what grounds would we expect the evolution of four offspring which are so heterogeneous that no transition from one to another is possible?

Hartshorne finds that the metaphors of common speech are sufficient to call attention to intersensory analogies and the possibility of an underlying continuity of experience. For example, sounds may be sweet, colorful, bright, or flat; colors may be loud, soft, warm, or cold; pain may be sharp or dull; a taste sensation may be bright or a smell may be sweet. We speak of the "blues" as an identifiable affective quality of a certain kind of music or we hear of a wine described as dry, bright, light, or flat. Hartshorne believes that these and the almost infinite variety of other combinations that we experience bespeak of objective affinities that point to an underlying continuity of experience. He does not deny that association or cultural conditioning may account for some combinations and these will not always be put together in the same way, that is, they will show variation as a function of culture or accidents of individual associations. Accordingly, it is not particularly surprising that studies on intersensory analogies may not always yield consistent results. Consistency of results is not possible until such time as we can control variability associated with conditioning.

One line of evidence pertinent to intersensory continuity comes from studies of individuals with congenital sensory defects. In an article entitled "The Intelligibility of Sensations" Hartshorne reviewed explanations of Helen Keller regarding her inferences concerning intersensory continuity. Keller, as quoted by Hartshorne, pointed out that:

The blind man carries with him into his dark environment all the faculties essential to the apprehension of the visible world whose door is closed behind him. He finds his surroundings everywhere homogeneous with those of the sunlit world; for there is an inexhaustible ocean of likenesses between the world within and the world without, and these likenesses, these correspondences, he finds equal to every exigency his life offers. . . .[6]

In her book, *The World I Live In*, Helen Keller provided many examples of how she anticipated the qualities of sights and sounds by analogy from her available senses. Hartshorne points out that Keller did enjoy vision and audition before these senses were destroyed by a brain fever before her second birthday. Accordingly, it could be argued that she was actually recalling very early experiences. But Keller's generalizations were undoubtedly influenced also by her extensive work with other handicapped people, many of whom were blind or deaf from birth.

It is tempting to believe that the test of Keller's claims for intersensory analogies is provided by research on individuals who were born blind, but who later have had sight bestowed by surgical intervention. It will be recalled that William Molyneux's question to John Locke in a letter dated 2 March 1693 anticipated such research on restoration of vision.[7] Both Locke and Molyneux came to the conclusion that a newly sighted individual would not be able to discriminate visually a sphere from a cube without first touching the objects. Unfortunately, as we will see, what appears to be a simple test is deceptive and the research on resighted and newly sighted individuals does not yield unequivocal data. We will find other reasons, however, to dispute the conclusions of Molyneux and Locke.

Just two years prior to the publication of Hartshorne's *Philosophy and Psychology of Sensation*, Marius von Senden published a monograph describing the history of research on those who have had vision restored or bestowed by surgical means.[8] Two of the classic cases have also been reprinted in Nicholas Pastore's *Selective History of Theories of Visual Perception: 1650–1950*[9] and additional studies are reviewed in a monograph by Gregory and Wallace.[10] Comment on Senden's case histories (e.g., see Wertheimer[11]) as well as comment on more recent cases (e.g., see Bennett,[12] Morgan[13]) provides insight into the difficulties of interpreting the results of these studies. Bennett points out that "many of the reports were fragmentary, and most of the reports were based on data that were collected in a haphazard informal manner."[14] Wertheimer calls attention to the aphikia or dazzle effects which follow the removal of the bandages and produce eye-muscle cramping, "cortical blindness," loss of voluntary eye movements due to muscle cramping, severe nystagmus, and problems with the normal functions of convergence and accommodation. He points out that the experience is so painful and the emotional reaction so strong that some patients give up trying to see. Wertheimer goes on to note that clinical and scientific interests in such cases are at odds with each other. Clinically, the problem of dazzle effects can be somewhat alleviated by introducing light on a gradual basis, but a graduated introduction of light works against scientific interests which are best served by assessing "the very first post-operative perception."[15]

In view of the difficulties of research on newly sighted individuals it is little wonder that results have not been reliable. In his book *Molyneux's Question*, Michael Morgan relates a case history in which transfer from previous tactile experience presumably made it possible for an individual to tell time from a clock on the wall, but another newly sighted individual showed no evidence of sensory substitution.[16] Morgan goes on to comment on additional problems associated with research on visual restoration. He notes that many individuals have had previous "visual" experiences of vague shapes, lightness, darkness and redness. Such individuals have typically had some form of corneal pathology along with a relatively intact retina which responds to diffuse light. Blindness in such individuals is different from blindness associated with severe pathology of the neural substrate of vision. In newly sighted individuals who have had corneal pathology it is difficult to assess whether there has been a transfer of information across sensory modalities or simple generalization within the visual modality based on previous limited visual experiences. Obviously, research on newly sighted individuals should be based on those who have lived in complete darkness, but there is strong evidence based on animal studies (e.g., Riesen,[17] Gottlieb[18]) that complete early visual deprivation results in atrophy of vital neural mechanisms in the visual system. Thus, normal sight following severe light deprivation may not be possible. From the time of Locke and Molyneux there has been an inclination to believe that studies on newly sighted individuals could provide evidence for or against intersensory continuity. At present, prudence counsels caution in interpreting such studies. There is, however, another kind of research on the blind which supports the concept of transition from the haptic to the visual systems.

In his book *Brain Mechanisms in Sensory Substitution*, Paul Bach-Y-Rita describes a "Tactile Visual Substitution System" (TVSS) that can deliver four hundred small vibrotactile points to a ten-inch square of skin on the abdomen or the back. The TVSS can deliver a pattern of stimulation that roughly corresponds to pictures, objects, or words that are picked up by a television camera and transduced by a commutator to the tactile stimulator. The blind subject, according to Bach-Y-Rita, is thus "able to read graphic material (such as bar graphs) and to identify geometric projections."[19] With a variation of the TVSS called the Linvell-Bliss Opticon it has also been demonstrated that blind subjects can read from the printed page.[20]

Morgan, commenting on these technological advances, asks, "Do the blind really see with a TVSS?" His reply is, "Either they do, or psychology as a science is impossible."[21] He contends that the differences between information provided by the skin and by the eye are not qualitative, but quantitative. Morgan concludes that "the 'sensationist' strand of empiricism has obstinately maintained that the way in which we perceive is entirely dependent on the way in which the message enters our brain: so much so, in fact, that there is no way in which to recognize that two messages coming over different pathways signify the same object, short of associating them by trial and error. This particular aspect of empiricism was wrong, and Locke's answer to Molyneux's question was mistaken."[22]

Hartshorne's first assertion, that there is continuity between sensory modalities, is much more likely to gain sympathetic audience among contemporary behavioral scientists than it was over fifty years ago when it was first argued in his *Philosophy and Psychology of Sensation*. Hartshorne contended at the time that intersensory analogies may have been ignored "partly because they have frequently been classified under an ambiguous or question-begging caption, namely, as cases of 'synesthesia,' which is regarded as a phenomenon peculiar to certain persons" (77). It is of interest that many recent general psychology texts do not discuss synesthesia. At the same time, one of the most respected contemporary texts in the field devotes a brief section to a discussion of "links between eye and ear."[23] The author conveys the results of recent studies that demonstrate intersensory connections in very young infants. For example, Spelke, in an article that discusses the development of intermodal perception, has demonstrated that four-month-old babies will spend far more time looking at a picture which is synchronized with a sound, than at another picture presented simultaneously which is out of synchrony with the sound.[24] Many other studies in recent years (e.g., Dodd;[25] Meltzoff and Borton;[26] and Wertheimer[27]) have demonstrated "cross talk" between sensory modalities. The old idea that sensory modalities operate in complete independence is no longer feasible. As Hartshorne pointed out, the classical theory never squared with evolutionary thought and it lacked the virtue of simplicity. Now there is increasing experimental evidence that demands that we take a more sympathetic look at alternatives such as the one proposed by Hartshorne.

The Affective Nature of Sensation

In his *Creative Synthesis and Philosophic Method*, Hartshorne reminds his readers that, "The mind is not a camera, merely recording facts. . . . The mere camera idea is a relic of the old faculty psychology, as Whitehead charges. There was 'cognition, volition, and affection.' But the best interpreters of this triad knew that mere cognition would be nothing at all.''[28] In opposition to association theories or to theories that emphasize cognition as mere non-connotative information, Hartshorne argues that affective tone is the primitive stuff of all human experience. He acknowledges that we can make a logical distinction between ''sense qualities'' and ''feeling tones'' but such logical distinctions should not be confused with the way the world of sensory experience actually works.[29] Hartshorne's theory represents a strong challenge to dualistic theory which separates sensation as mere action-indifferent information from feeling conceived as mood, ''emotional tone'' or that which we incline to do.

In contrast to the dualistic position, Hartshorne argues that there is not a qualitative chasm between sensation and feeling. Instead, they are so intimately connected that we cannot understand one without the other. One immediately implies the other, but affective tone has primacy. Hartshorne contends that ''of the two factors the affective is the more primitive and fundamental, and the sensory a specialization of this primordial function. Thus, between the two equations 'feeling is a form of sensation' and 'sensation is a form of feeling' there is reason . . . to emphasize the latter'' (128). Hartshorne argues that the old view of sensation as a mere faculty involving bare awareness stripped of all valuation, is the psychological counterpart of a long discredited atomism. Further, he contends that sensation as neutral awareness ''is a self-contradictory abstraction; that apart from factors of motive and valuation, apart from aesthetic and emotional aspects, nothing recognizable remains of consciousness or experience'' (108). Thus, conscious experience, according to Hartshorne, is valuational or affective in its very nature.

The case for Hartshorne's affective theory of sensation is argued most convincingly by drawing illustrative material from research on the somatosensory system, but Hartshorne believes that ''contact receptors'' do not operate by a fundamentally different set of rules than ''distance receptors.'' He believes that affective tone is inherent in all sensory activity though he concedes that ''the visual, [mode] is of all others the one which seems *prima facie* the most objective, the farthest removed from affection. . . .''[30] Accordingly, he is particularly interested in the search for evidence of affectivity in visual experiences and he devotes considerable space in his book to affective qualities particularly in colors. We begin here, nevertheless, with a consideration of affectivity in the haptic and gustatory systems and then we will turn our attention to vision.

Of all sensory experiences, pain appears as a centerpiece illustration of Hartshorne's contention that affective tone has primacy, that the principal defining characteristic of a sensation is affectional. Common qualifying adjectives (e.g., excruciating, racking, rending, tearing, stabbing, etc.) betray our understanding of pain as compelling emotional comment. The concept of "disinterested pain" is surely a contradiction in terms to most human beings; at the very least, such a concept is a paradox. Hartshorne's theory, however, allows space for the interesting vicissitudes of pain. He discusses some of the circumstances under which pain can be enjoyed (51–54) and circumstances under which we might develop the notion of "neutral" pain (54), but he argues that "pain as a major, dominant factor in awareness is revealed as in itself a relatively inexplicit or unintellectualized dislike" (55). As an aside, it may be that the function of any analgesic, whether chemically or stereotaxically induced, is to remove pain as "a major dominant factor" in awareness. Under such circumstances, and in hypnotic trances, we may develop the notion (illusion?) of "neutral" pain or we may displace pain.[31] Such analgesic effects do not count against Hartshorne's affective theory if they remove pain as "a major dominant factor" in awareness. The capacity of the body to produce opiate-like neurotransmitters, the so-called "endorphins," may also contribute to special or altered states of consciousness with respect to pain, but altered states of consciousness, whether naturally or artificially induced, do not undercut the validity of judgments about pain in itself. Hartshorne would also argue that, at a lower inaccessible level of consciousness, the body *is in fact in pain* as a consequence of a biological insult, even if such pain is temporarily blocked from the ordinary higher levels of conscious organization.

The other skin senses, like pain, are understood in experience primarily in terms of feeling tone. Ashley Montagu, in his book *Touching*, illustrates common understandings of the affective dimensions of the skin senses by calling attention to some wide-spread conventions of language. Thus, "We speak of 'rubbing' people the wrong way, and 'stroking' them the right way; of abrasive and 'prickly' personalities. . . . Some are 'thick-skinned,' others are 'thin-skinned,' some get 'under one's skin,'. . . . Some people are 'touchy,'. . . . A deeply felt experience is 'touching.'"[32] Georg V. Bekesy points out that Islamic scribes and medieval monks failed to transcribe "the too precise descriptions of skin sensations by the Greek and Roman authors."[33] Such descriptions were graphic reminders of the joys of sensual pleasure—joys which were often subject to censure or repression. It is of interest that most of our knowledge of the somatosensory system has been developed in the relatively liberal climate of the last one hundred years.

There is now a well-known large research literature indicating that an accumulation of quality tactile stimulation is necessary to long-term emotional well-being and that deprivation of quality stimulation results in arrested emotional development or even death. Studies by Renee Spitz[34] and Harry Harlow[35] have been particularly instructive regarding the critical role of tactile stimulation in emotional development. The results of such studies are clearly consistent with Hartshorne's theory, but such studies point to an additional fact, namely that tactile sensory stimulation is vital to well-being. Adults know through their own experience, the range of affectional or hedonic tones of touch. It is a source of comfort that results in a sense of well-being and on another extreme, a source of ecstasy. The research data indicate that infants from their birthdate have a sense of generally salutary and pleasureful effects of physical contact. The results of studies on the role of contact in emotional well-being are interpreted most parsimoniously by an affective theory of sensation such as proposed by Hartshorne. It is not clear how sensation as mere cognitive information could have long-term beneficial consequences on emotional development.

If we turn now to the gustatory system, we once again encounter examples of sensations that are intimately associated with rejection, aversion, consumption and enjoyment. Hartshorne points out that we acquire appreciation for certain complicated taste combinations such as sweet and sour or the subtle hint of bitterness as in beer. At the same time, many of the affective properties of taste are built into our very nature. Support for Hartshorne's position is provided by research that shows that affective or emotional dimensions of taste sensations are evident even in new born infants. Jacob Steiner,[36] for example, demonstrated the early hedonics of taste by supplying new born infants, prior to their first extrauterine feeding with solutions that were sweet, sour, or bitter. The sweet solution resulted in smiling, licking, and sucking activities while the bitter solution was followed by spitting and what could most reasonably be interpreted as a rejecting or negative facial expression. Sour solutions were followed by wrinkling the nose, puckering, and eye blinking. These responses could not have been "added on" through conditioning since they occurred in connection with the first extrauterine taste experiences. While there may be intrauterine conditioning to the taste of amniotic fluid, it is not clear how such conditioning could result in the specific approach and avoidance behaviors reported by Steiner. We will later turn attention to Hartshorne's explanation as to why the newborn should prefer the sweet solution and avoid bitter or sour solutions. For the present, however, it is sufficient to say that taste sensations, even in the newborn, are hedonically toned and lead to identifiable approach or avoidance behaviors.

A large volume of additional experimental evidence could be marshalled in support of the essentially affective nature of sensation in the haptic, gustatory, and olfactory systems. But we move now to the visual system where the evidence for affectivity in sensation is less easily established. The evidence for sensation, especially visual sensation, without affect is likely to have face validity for most observers. It is clear there are identifiable affective reactions to sounds, shapes, and colors, but in common experience, we may encounter claims that sensation is often devoid of affect. Researchers such as Michel Cabanac[37] and Paul Thomas Young[38] agree with Hartshorne that affective processes have objective claims, but these theorists have argued for a hedonic continuum with positive and negative poles and a middle range of stimuli to which we are indifferent. Such theories may have more appeal to common sense than Hartshorne's theory, though the latter may be more intelligible. Hartshorne points out "that bareness with respect to value [affect] turns out to be bareness with respect to intelligibility" (94).

Hartshorne admits there are dull sensations that appear to be devoid of affect, but he contends that the apparently missing affect can be discovered if the appropriate means of observation are established.[39] Thus, a "neutral" or dull patch of color in the background may appear altogether worthless and of no interest whatever. But if one closes one's eyes and imagines that the particular worthless color will never be seen again, one would become aware of a missing value, not just a missing stimulus. There would be a definite negative feeling of loss. It is of interest that profound sensory deprivation may evoke memories of rich sensory experiences of the past.[40] Those who have had vision restored following a period of blindness may also express deep appreciation for things that earlier seemed trivial or irrelevant.[41] Hartshorne also calls attention to the bias of classic theory which emphasized the separation of sensation and affect. Such an emphasis may influence the way we observe ourselves and thus contribute to the appearance that some sensations are of no interest. But we turn now to the positive side of Hartshorne's theory to consider the evidence for affect in visual sensations, particularly color sensations.

Hartshorne finds a natural gaiety, joy, and lighthearted quality in yellow. Furthermore, "the 'gaiety' of yellow (the peculiar highly specific gaiety) is the yellowness of the yellow" (7). He believes there are two strong colors, yellow and red (219). Red is naturally "warm, aggressive, insistent . . . the color of blood, the only important pervasively present red object in nature and an object of the highest and most immediate concern in many ways" (172). Red implies activity and "there is no other color which it is so necessary to take seriously" (256). In green, Hartshorne finds a quiet cheerfulness and in blue, a gentle affectionate quality (256). The particular affective properties inherent in the various colors are intimately connected with adaptation, but we will return to this topic later.

Hartshorne does not deny the importance of the role of conditioning in color preferences or meanings. Hence, it is predictable that there will be variability in color preferences. At the same time, he calls attention to the natural affective properties of color—properties that may sometimes be masked by conditioned preferences, but are nevertheless available to the careful observer.

The vicissitudes of color preference are well illustrated in early articles on the psychology of red[42] and the psychology of yellow[43] by Havelock Ellis. On the topic of yellow, Ellis contended that among many primitive peoples there was a particular delight with yellow and that red and yellow were the favorite colors of early Europeans. Yellow was also the most sacred and honored color in many early oriental cultures. In Greece and Rome, yellow was associated with a festive spirit and was a source of joy and delight. Hartshorne's views on the gaiety of yellow accurately reflect the way in which this color was regarded by primitive peoples. Yet, in recent times yellow is often the least preferred color. In 1941, Eysenck reassessed the results of some of the more than fifty experimental studies on color preference that had started with the work of J. Cohn[44] in 1894. Based on the reassessment of previous studies and his own data, Eysenck concluded that there was some agreement about color preference with yellow being overall (for many studies) the least preferred color. The order of preference was blue (most preferred), red, green, violet, orange, and yellow.[45] A more recent study by I. C. McManus, Amanda Jones, and Jill Cottrell on the aesthetics of color also found that yellow was the least preferred color and blue the most preferred.[46] Why has yellow moved to a less preferred position in modern times and are there natural positive feelings toward the color as Hartshorne contends—feelings that may be overshadowed by conditioned preferences?

Ellis concluded that yellow underwent a reversal because of the rejection of the early Christians of the ways of the world. Yellow or saffron, a color often worn by prostitutes in Rome, had stood for festive worldly celebration. The Christians justifiably rejected the symbols and values of a world largely hostile to their faith. Ellis points out that as late as 1833, yellow was prohibited in the garments of priests and he noted that at the turn of the century it was still avoided in Catholic and Protestant ecclesiastical proceedings. It still is. The use of a badge, typically yellow in color, to symbolize minority religious affiliation probably had its origin in Islamic countries, but was also practiced in many Christian countries.[47] In the Nazi period, Jews were required to wear large yellow triangles on their backs.[48] Yellow gradually became the symbol of treachery, inconstancy, jealousy, cowardice, and wantonness. Ellis notes that "Judas was painted in yellow garments . . . and in France in the sixteenth century, the doors of traitors and felons were daubed in yellow."[49] Paul Gauguin's "Yellow Christ" did nothing to endear him to the church. For whatever reasons, a color that was once a favorite and a special source of delight, fell into disfavor and was replaced by the color blue, the color of heaven.

The foregoing digression on the color yellow helps us frame Hartshorne's affective theory in a more cogent fashion. Color preferences, as well as other preferences, are subject to cultural influences but Hartshorne's theory calls us to a consideration of deeper feelings that should be distinguished from mere preferences. Hartshorne argues that "there is no evidence that culture determines color feeling, but only that it affects color preference or evaluation, a very different thing" (171). According to Hartshorne's theory, each color has special biological and psychological significance that transcends surface preferences. Experimental verification of such a contention is obviously fraught with difficulties. How does one construct a test that identifies a feeling that is not contaminated by a preference? If specific feeling tones can be identified with the redness of the red or the blueness of the blue, then these feelings should be more consistent, more universal, than mere preferences. But in a recent article on universal versus learned emotional responses to colors, Isolde D. Martin contends that to date, we have been unable to identify a learning or a universal factor as the overall variable in emotional responses to colors.[50] At the same time, there is now a large literature on emotional responses to color. Thus, one may find evidence that red illumination results in greater autonomic and cortical arousal than blue illumination.[51] Claims have been made that color may be used effectively as a therapeutic adjunct,[52] and fundamental judgments such as time estimation may be affected by color.[53] The findings of many of the studies are consistent with Hartshorne's affective theory, but alternative interpretations are often equally plausible. For example, greater physiological arousal to the color red as opposed to blue, may simply reflect a generalization effect from conditioning to stop lights or the flashing red lights of emergency vehicles. There is a need for cross cultural studies and for additional studies of color hedonics in very young infants and animals with color vision.

Additional evidence, especially from areas such as olfactory mediation of maternal or sexual behavior, aggressivity in response to sign stimuli, or the distress calls of infants could be employed to argue the essentially affective nature of specific sensations. The world of sound provides particularly rich examples of stimuli that appear to have an inherent capacity to startle, relax, activate, instill fear, or arrest attention. Hartshorne's section on hearing in chapter 8 on sensation and the environment is particularly relevant to his thesis. He calls attention to the vulnerability of an animal who has lost its hearing. Not only would such an animal be more subject to attack, it would also have more difficulty mating and caring for its young. He notes that distress calls of "dog or cat, of bird or human being, all show a family likeness. When the nest is being robbed, the parent-birds do not sing or merely utter usual call notes. Their voices take on strained, distressful, plaintive tones, appropriate to any human ears, to the situation. The songs, on the other hand, are usually joyous" (259). Affect in birdsong is, of course, a topic to which Hartshorne, as a capable ornithologist, has had long-standing interest. He has made numerous contributions to that literature (see, for example, representative articles such as "Do Birds Enjoy

Singing?"[54] "Some Biological Principles Applicable to Song-Behavior"[55] and "The Phenomenon of Bird Song"[56] or Hartshorne's book *Born to Sing*[57]).

Before considering Hartshorne's third assertion regarding sensory processes, it seems appropriate to inject a brief evaluative note regarding his position on the affective nature of sensation. It is clear there is a great deal of evidence from the laboratory, from conceptual analysis, and from common experience that supports affective theory. At the same time, there may still be some agreement with an early reviewer of *The Philosophy and Psychology of Sensation* who found a deficiency in the theory for "a want of consideration for those intermediate principles and 'middle-sized facts' which are required for balance and solidity."[58] In his preface, Hartshorne recognized that further analysis would suggest the need for elaborations and extensions of his theory. I believe that a strong emphasis on a concept of attenuation (defined here as the tendency of a specific affect to fatigue, fade, or weaken over time) would answer the aforementioned criticism and strengthen the theory without modifying any of its essential features. Granted, we are particularly resistant to attenuation in certain arenas such as pain. In other (most) arenas, however, we quickly attenuate so that an initial high level of affective tone is "adapted out" and followed by apparent disinterest.

Contemporary research has also suggested that attenuation of affect may play a role in various addictions and it contributes to the conditions under which we experience a reversal in the quality of affect, i.e., from pain to pleasure. In many passages, Hartshorne demonstrates his keen interest in reversals of affect as in cases of enjoyment accompanying or following pain (51–59, 204). In some important respects he anticipated contemporary opponent process theory (e.g., see Solomon[59]) which provides new leads about the machinery involved in reversals of affect. For example, painful, effortful, or unpleasant circumstances may stimulate the production of opiate-like neurotransmitters (endorphins) which result in quiescent, pleasant, or even euphoric moods. The motto "no pain, no gain" is often associated with activities such as running or weight lifting. Addiction to such activities may result partly from "pleasant affect" which inevitably follows the "pain" of the workout. However, through the benefits of conditioning, the effortful or painful quality of the workout is attenuated. Thus, the well conditioned individual may have to work harder to achieve a euphoric mood following a workout.

The Social Character of Experience

Hartshorne's philosophy and psychology of sensation assumes a fundamental continuity (where continuity is conceived as an abstract logical principle) between molar (whole) and cellular processes. Molar experience is thus informed by kindred or companion processes that share in the give and take of what is essentially community or social activity. In his article "Psychology and the Unity of Knowledge" Hartshorne argues that "Cells appear to be living individual organisms. They are thus remotely analogous to ourselves. So there is no warrant for supposing that their qualitative or inner aspect must be wholly different from ours."[60] Thus the molecular or cellular underpinnings of experience are not exempt from feeling-like qualities. Quite the contrary, they possess the primitive counterparts of the qualities we find in larger experience. There is then an essential continuity in the progression from simple to higher levels of organization.

The alternative materialistic hypothesis implies a radical discontinuity between molar experience and the molecular underpinnings of such experience. Blind structure, devoid of any feeling-like quality, is merely correlated with the rich varieties of personal experience. The concept of correlation at least avoids the conceptual hiatus created by any claim that there is intelligible communication between the molar world and the essentially alien molecular world.

Hartshorne's emphasis on continuity is well illustrated in his article entitled "The Social Theory of Feelings," where he calls attention to the experience of pain. The experience of pain "shares in the weal and woe of its cellular or subcellular individuals."[61] There are pain-like qualities in the cells which are subjected to physical or biological insult. The pain we feel is thus a feeling of feeling. The pain is "not just my subjective form but somehow an objective form, down there, 'over against' me."[62] There is then more than one suffering; suffering is participatory; it is a social sharing. The intimacy of such a view is apparent—molecular and cellular processes are sensitive to the molar realm and vice versa. Our knowledge is not of something radically alien, but of something kindred. In Hartshorne's view, feeling becomes the central psychological reality. We are "not primarily a knowing machine but an enjoying-suffering-striving member of a species that tends to perpetuate itself."[63]

There has never been good agreement about the scientific utility of psychical monism. It has had appeal to many eminent scientists and philosophers, but it is regarded with suspicion by others. It has the distinct advantage of suggesting an intelligible mode of causation in the psychical realm and of providing conceptual unity for a great range of phenomena, but it can be criticized for promising too much and delivering too little to testable scientific theories. Perhaps it is a task for the sociology or psychology of science to explore the relative benefits of materialistic and idealistic orientations.

Sensation and Adaptive Behavior

Hartshorne contends that "philosophy and psychology have been too little influenced by evolutionary considerations."[64] His contention may be especially appropriate to the field of sensation, the first topic in psychology that was explored in an intense experimental fashion. The senses were often viewed as the windows of the mind and as the foundation area for the establishment of a scientific psychology. It is true that much of the pioneering work on sensation (e.g., the work of Ernst Weber, Johannes Müller, and Thomas Young) was conducted prior to the publication of Darwin's *Origin of Species*. Such work was also largely pretheoretical with respect to any consideration of the crucial ties between sensory processes and adaptation.

Hartshorne, by contrast, calls attention to the functional or adaptive nature of sensory qualities. In his view, sensory qualities "express organic attitudes, or tend, of themselves, to incite modes of behavior; and these modes may be appropriate or useful, in relation to the physical circumstances generally accompanying the occurrence of stimuli productive of the respective sensations" (8). The expression "of themselves" is key because it tells us that sensory processes or qualities in themselves have adaptive significance. They need not be attached through association to a quality from another "compartment" or "faculty" of the mind. Thus, shapes, colors, odors, or sounds and the intrinsic feeling tones they evoke, are incitements to action that have adaptive significance. While Hartshorne titled his book *The Philosophy and Psychology of Sensation*, the theory it presents with its emphasis on adaptation is more clearly biological than many of its predecessors.

The emphasis on action and adaptation is closely connected to the assertion that there is intrinsic affect in sensation. Affect can incite action (a tendency to approach or avoid), but it is unclear how awareness alone or a mere registering of a thing without evaluation, could result in adaptive behavior. Hartshorne agreed with many of the contentions of Julius Pikler who held that "The supreme law of sensory response is the self-preservative tendency of the organic being" (147).

The biological slant of Hartshorne's theory is illustrated in his claim that "The usual view of the emotional aspects of sensations as accretions added to them after they were otherwise fully constituted is a profoundly unbiological doctrine. For the basis of these emotionalities is fully as old in the world as the sense organs themselves. The experience of the beneficient effects of moderate light, for example, is incomparably older than vision itself" (253). Hartshorne finds no accident in the very early tendency to approach and consume sweet things and to avoid bitter things. The former are usually nutritious and the latter often include poisonous objects. If the rule on sweet things doesn't hold for a given organism such as a cat, then we may expect to find a somewhat different organization and distribution of taste receptors, which we do.[65]

Evolution from a Common Origin

Hartshorne's final assertion regarding sensory processes is understood in the light of his distinction between emergence and pure emergence. Pure emergence implies a fundamental discontinuity resulting in a change in identity. Hartshorne insists that such a notion is pre-Darwinian and that "It is merely a less imaginative version of the special creation doctrine, involving the same objectionable denial of any possibility of a genetic explanation" (34). A less radical doctrine of emergence implies that a new quality is not entirely explained by antecedent events, but such events are nevertheless informative. The concept of emergence emphasizes differentiation, elaboration, or evolution while the concept of pure emergence emphasizes discontinuity and abrupt qualitative change.

Hartshorne's fifth assertion places emphasis on the importance of comparative and developmental psychologies of the senses. The comparative and developmental focus was in contrast to the early structural psychology of Titchener where the emphasis was on the study of sensory processes in normal adults. Hartshorne's genetic perspective was more consistent with American Functionalism, but by the time Functionalism was established, primary emphasis had shifted away from the senses to other topics such as learning, memory, motivation, and emotion. Accordingly, and unfortunately, the benefits of a well-coordinated and systematic genetic approach to sensory processes were not realized.

At a theoretical level, the issue of emergence versus pure emergence is very topical and is manifested in current discussions on topics such as disorderly growth processes (e.g., see Witten and Cates[66]) and punctuated equilibrium (e.g., see Hoffman[67]). Clearly, the debate continues on the rate and nature of biospheric change and may be more intense than it was when Hartshorne published his theory of sensation.

POSSIBLE REASONS FOR NEGLECT

We noted at the outset that Hartshorne has given us a heuristic theory that anticipated many subsequent developments in sensory psychology. Nevertheless, the theory has been overlooked or seriously neglected. This is unfortunate because Hartshorne's theory could have served, or for that matter could still serve, as the basis for a major programmatic research effort on sensory processes. One cannot read the book without being challenged with many ideas that could be tested in the laboratory. Had the book been written in a different setting and had the author had access to a laboratory and several experimentally oriented graduate students, it is very likely that articles on the affective continuum would have found their way into the appropriate journals. Even so, for reasons stated below, the success of the book would not have been assured.

William James

For all his catholicity and tolerance, sensation was one area of psychology for which William James could generate little enthusiasm. Indeed, Edwin G. Boring pointed out that James disliked the topic, found it unimportant, and neglected it as much as possible.[68] Boring, quoting from R. B. Perry's biography of James, points out that "James did not mention color mixture in the *Principles*, and put the topic into the *Briefer Course* only under protest."[69] James's attacks both on the questions investigated and the methods employed by German sensory psychologists are well known. He found that the German "microscopic psychology . . . taxes patience to the utmost, and could hardly have arisen in a country whose natives could be bored."[70] His even more scathing remarks on Fechner leave no doubt about his permanent disdain for the minutiae of such topics as thresholds, just noticeable differences, and after-images. Of Fechner, he said "it would be terrible if even such a dear old man as this could saddle our science forever with his patient whimsies, and, in a world so full of more nutritious objects of attention, compel all future students to plough through the difficulties, not only of his own works, but of the still drier ones written in his refutation."[71]

Hartshorne's approach to sensation would have likely been welcomed by James, but the sensory psychology of an earlier era did not satisfy his concerns with larger moral questions. The inspired chapters in the *Principles*, the book that influenced generations of American psychologists, were not the chapters on sensory processes, but chapters on subjects such as habit, the self, emotions, and the stream of thought. The direction of psychology, under James's leadership, thus shifted away from sensation and toward such topics as learning, psychopathology, educational improvement, and emotion.

Behaviorism

The major reason for the neglect of Hartshorne's book is that it was published at a time when Behaviorism was the dominant force in American psychology. There was no place within the rigid methodological and substantive prescriptions of behaviorism for a theory such as the one proposed by Hartshorne. In the first place, the topic was out of vogue, but even if there had been more interest in sensation, the panpsychism would have been sufficient to prejudice the case. Other topical areas (e.g., cognition, the psychology of religion, and species-specific behavior) suffered the same fate at the hands of a system that had an unusually truncating effect on the discipline.

Too Promissory?

A major virtue of Hartshorne's book, namely its multidisciplinary emphasis bringing biological, psychological, and philosophical perspectives together in one comprehensive treatment, turns out also to be a source of difficulty. Hartshorne's perspective may have been too sweeping, too promissory for the typical scientist, if not the typical philosopher. The point is illustrated in an early passage as follows: "The acceptance, as a hypothesis, of these five theses in the organically interrelated form in which they constitute, as will be shown, one coherent theory makes possible a binding-together of the results of many distinct lines of inquiry, embracing pure geometry, aesthetics, everyday social experience, biology, metaphysics, and religious experience, into a sweeping generalization capable of manifold empirical verifications as well as applicable to the clarification of numerous philosophical paradoxes. The merits claimed for the theory, however, may all be summed up in one—that it opens the way to the observation and explanation of facts hitherto unobserved or supposed 'inexplicable'" (8-9). Such a large claim may of course be true, but it very likely aroused suspicion and skepticism at a time marked by increasing specialization in psychological science.

CONCLUSION

Hartshorne's theory of sensation conveys the remarkable grasp of its author of several scientific fields and technical developments[72] within those fields which were integrated into his developing philosophy. The book, though largely unrecognized, is no less an intellectual achievement. Though unorthodox in its day, many of its claims have been explored and verified during the intervening years. Few people today would quarrel with its genetic emphasis (assertion 5) or its focus on the adaptive nature of sensations (assertion 4). The first two assertions pertaining to continuity and to the affective nature of sensation are highly relevant, as we tried to show, to a large body of research and much of the research is supportive of these assertions.

The third assertion, pertaining as it does to psychical monism, undoubtedly was, and remains, the most controversial. At the same time, this pivotal assertion lends coherence to the whole theory and provides an important larger perspective on the unity of knowledge. It is my belief that there is much to appreciate in the theory, even for those who cannot accept panpsychism.

WAYNE VINEY

DEPARTMENT OF PSYCHOLOGY
COLORADO STATE UNIVERSITY
AUGUST 1986

NOTES

1. Troland's achievements are remarkable, especially in view of his short life (1889–1932). He took his bachelor's degree from M.I.T. in 1912, his A.M. from Harvard in 1914, and his Ph.D. from Harvard in 1915. He was employed at Harvard until his death in 1932. He is remembered as the coinventer of technicolor movies and the author of numerous books including: *The Nature of Matter and Electricity*, 1917, coauthored with Daniel F. Comstock; *The Present Status of Visual Science*, 1922; *The Mystery of Mind*, 1926; *The Fundamentals of Human Motivation*, 1928; and his magnum opus, the three-volume *Principles of Psychophysiology*, 1929–1932. He was also author of many papers ranging over such diverse topics as psychical research, world peace, panpsychism, and optics. Troland served as president of the Optical Society of America and was a member or fellow of many other organizations. The *troland*, a unit of retinal illumination, was named after him.

2. *The Philosophy and Psychology of Sensation* was first published in 1934 by the University of Chicago Press. All quotes in this chapter will be from the 1968 reissue (Port Washington, N.Y.: Kennikat Press). Page references from this work will be indicated in parentheses.

3. Richard M. Warren and Roslyn P. Warren, *Helmholtz on Perception: Its Physiology and Development* (New York: John Wiley & Sons, 1968), p. 210.

4. Ibid., p. 210.

5. Oswald Külpe, *Outlines of Psychology: Based Upon the Results of Experimental Investigation*, trans. Edward Bradford Titchener (New York: Macmillan & Co., 1895). Reprint (New York: Arno Press, 1973), pp. 225–230.

6. Charles Hartshorne, "The Intelligibility of Sensations," *Monist* 44 (1934): 161–185.

7. For an excellent discussion of Molyneux's question and the background of that question in eighteenth-century philosophy see Michael J. Morgan, *Molyneux's Question* (New York: Cambridge University Press, 1977).

8. Marius von Senden, *Raum- und Gestaltauffassung bei operierten Blindgeborenen vor und nach der Operation* (Leipzig: Barth, 1932).

9. Nicholas Pastore, *Selective History of Theories of Visual Perception 1650–1950* (New York: Oxford University Press, 1971).

10. Richard L. Gregory and Jean G. Wallace, *Recovery from Early Blindness*, Experimental Psychology Society Monograph, no. 2 (Cambridge: Heffer, 1963).

11. Michael Wertheimer, "Hebb and Senden on the Role of Learning in Perception," *American Journal of Psychology* 64 (1951):133–137.

12. Thomas L. Bennett, *The Sensory World* (Monterey, CA: Brooks/Cole Publishing Co., 1978), pp. 174–175.

13. Morgan, pp. 180–191.

14. Bennett, p. 174.

15. Wertheimer, p. 135.

16. Morgan, p. 182.

17. Austin H. Riesen, "Arrested Vision," *Scientific American* 183 (1950): 16–19.

18. Gilbert Gottlieb, "The Role of Experience in the Development of Behavior and the Nervous System," in Gilbert Gottlieb, ed., *Neural and Behavioral Specificity* (New York: Academic Press, 1976), pp. 25–56.

19. Paul Bach-Y-Rita, *Brain Mechanisms in Sensory Substitution* (New York: Academic Press, 1972), p. 152.

20. Morgan, p. 204.

21. Ibid., p. 204.

22. Ibid., p. 207.

23. Henry Gletiman, *Psychology*, 2nd ed. (New York: W. W. Norton, 1986), pp. 477–479.

24. Elizabeth Spelke, "Infants' Intermodal Perception of Events," *Cognitive Psychology* 8 (1976):553–560.

25. Barbara Dodd, "Lip Reading in Infants: Attention to Speech Presented in-and-out-of-synchrony," *Cognitive Psychology* 11 (1979):478–484.

26. Andrew N. Meltzoff and Richard W. Borton, "Intermodal Matching by Human Neonates," *Nature* 282 (1979):403–404.

27. Michael Wertheimer, "Psychomotor Coordination of Auditory and Visual Space at Birth," *Science* 134 (1961):1692.

28. Charles Hartshorne, *Creative Synthesis and Philosophic Method* (La Salle, Ill.: Open Court, 1970), p. 300.

29. Charles Hartshorne, "Intelligibility of Sensations," p. 175.

30. Ibid., p. 184.

31. In a case known to the author, a woman during childbirth requested the induction of a hypnotic trance, a procedure that had been rehearsed many times prior to the actual delivery. After the trance was induced, the woman reported that she was no longer in pain, but that the delivery table was in terrible pain.

32. Ashley Montagu, *Touching: The Human Significance of the Skin* (New York: Harper and Row Publishers, 1978), pp. 5–6.

33. Georg V. Bekesy, "Similarities Between Hearing and Skin Sensations," *Psychological Review* 66 (1959):1–22.

34. Renee A. Spitz, "Hospitalism: An Inquiry into the Genesis of Psychiatric Conditions in Early Childhood," *Psychoanalytic Study of the Child* 1 (1945): 53–74.

35. Harry F. Harlow, "The Nature of Love," *American Psychologist* 13 (1958): 673–685.

36. Jacob E. Steiner, "Facial Expressions of the Neonate Infant Indicating the Hedonics of Food-Related Chemical Stimuli," in James M. Weiffenbach, ed., *Taste and Development: The Genesis of Sweet Preference* (DHEW Publication No. NIH 77–1068, 1977), Washington, D.C.: U. S. Government Printing Office, 173–188.

37. Michel Cabanac, "Sensory Pleasure," *Quarterly Review of Biology* 54 (1979):1–25.

38. Paul Thomas Young, "The Role of Affective Processes in Learning and Motivation," *Psychological Review* 66 (1959):104–125.

39. Hartshorne, "Intelligibility of Sensations," p. 176.

40. Jay T. Shurley, "Profound Experimental Sensory Isolation," *The American Journal of Psychiatry* 117 (1960):539–545.

41. Thomas J. Carroll, *Blindness* (Boston: Little, Brown and Company, 1961), p. 55.

42. Havelock Ellis, "The Psychology of Red," *Popular Science Monthly* 57 (1900):365–375.

43. _____, "The Psychology of Yellow," *Popular Science Monthly* 68 (1906):456–463.

44. Jonas Cohn, "Experimentelle Untersuchungen uber die Gefuhlsbetonung der Farben, Helligkeiten und ihren Combinationen," *Philosophische Studien* 10 (1894): 562–603.

45. Hans J. Eysenck, "A Critical and Experimental Study of Colour Preferences," *American Journal of Psychology* 54 (1941):385–394.

46. I. C. McManus, Amanda L. Jones, and Jill Cottrell, "The Aesthetics of Colour," *Perception* 10 (1981):651–666.

47. *Encyclopaedia Judaica*, vol. 4 (New York: Macmillan Co., 1971), pp. 62–70.

48. Ibid., p. 71.

49. Ellis, "The Psychology of Yellow," p. 461.

50. Isolde G. Martin, "Universal v. Learned Emotional Responses to Colors: Afterthoughts of Thesis Research," *Arts in Psychotherapy* 9 (1982):245–247.

51. Robert M. Gerard, "Color and Emotional Arousal," *American Psychologist* 13 (1958):340.

52. Faber Birren, *Color Psychology and Color Therapy* (New Hyde Park, N.Y.: University Books, Inc., 1961).

53. Ibid., p. 146.

54. Charles Hartshorne, "Do Birds Enjoy Singing? (An Ornitho-Philosophical Discourse)," *Bulletin of the Texas Ornithological Society* 8 (1975):2–5.

55. _____, "Some Biological Principles Applicable to Song Behavior," *The Wilson Bulletin* 70 (1958):41–56.

56. _____, "The Phenomenon of Birdsong," *Emory University Quarterly* 12 (1956):139–147.

57. _____, *Born to Sing: An Interpretation and World Survey of Bird Song* (Bloomington: Indiana University Press, 1973).

58. *Journal of Philosophy* 31 (1934):387–388.

59. Richard L. Solomon, "The Opponent-Process Theory of Acquired Motivation," *American Psychologist* 35 (1980):691–712.

60. Charles Hartshorne, "Psychology and the Unity of Knowlege," *Southern Journal of Philosophy* 5 (1967):81–90.

61. _____, "The Social Theory of Feelings," *Southern Journal of Philosophy* 3 (1965):87–93.

62. Ibid., p. 89.

63. Charles Hartshorne, personal communication, 18 June 1986.

64. Ibid.

65. Carl Pfaffmann, "Gustatory Afferent Impulses," *Journal of Cellular and Comparative Physiology* 17 (1941):243–258.

66. T. A. Witten and M. E. Cates, "Tenuous Structures and Disorderly Growth Processes," *Science* 232 (1986):1607–1612.

67. Antoni Hoffman, "Punctuated versus Gradual Mode of Evolution: A Reconsideration," in Max K. Hecht, Bruce Wallace, and Ghillean T. Prance, eds., *Evolutionary Biology*, vol. 15 (New York: Plenum Press, 1982), pp. 411–436.

68. Edwin G. Boring, "Human Nature vs. Sensation: William James and The Psychology of the Present," *The American Journal of Psychology* 55 (1942):310–327.

69. Ibid., p. 313.

70. William James, *The Principles of Psychology*, vol. 1 (New York: Henry Holt & Co., 1890), p. 192.

71. Ibid., p. 549.

72. It is to be regretted that Hartshorne's color theory involving four primaries (scarlet, buttercup yellow, blue-green, and violet) as well as his observations on the other senses could not be discussed in this chapter. His chapter, "The Dimensions of Sensation" (chapter 7), is recommended reading.

5

John Hospers

HARTSHORNE'S AESTHETICS

Hartshorne's philosophy casts a very wide net, and aesthetics is only a small part of it. But it would be equally correct to say that aesthetic principles also dominate the whole of his philosophy. At any rate, I shall attempt in this essay to limit my remarks to his aesthetics.

1. SENSATION AND FEELING

Hartshorne's first book, *The Philosophy and Psychology of Sensation*, begins with an analysis of the relation between sensation and feeling, and only later in the book do the implications of his view for aesthetics become manifest.[1] But these implications are powerful and all-pervasive.

According to a dominant philosophical tradition, human faculties are divided into knowing (cognition), feeling (emotion), and willing (volition). Where in this schema does sensation belong? Sensation has usually been included under cognition. " 'Cognition' means whatever mental characters function most helpfully to furnish man with information concerning the physical world. . . . Plainly, sensation and not feeling (as ordinarily conceived) is thus helpful."

Since "knowing" in the philosophical literature usually means knowing-*that* (this being what philosophers are primarily interested in), it is easy to see why sensation is placed where it is: through our senses we acquire information about the world outside us. If, however, we want to understand these distinctions phenomenologically—what they are "experienced as"—then sensation belongs with feeling and not with cognition. The *experience* of sensing is not a form of knowing at all, in spite of the fact that in the absence of sensation there are many things we could not know. Sensing is simply a kind of experience, as is feeling; both are immediate experiences, "given" in the sense that they are not the product of inference—"whereas willing, or better 'striving,' is conspicuously dual (an 'effort' is always sensed as correlative to 'resistance'), and whereas knowing or 'meaning' is irreducibly triadic (sign, thing signified, larger mental context or 'idea' for which it has this signification)."[2]

It is, in fact, often difficult to distinguish a sensation from a feeling. Is a pleasure a sensation or a feeling? We speak both of "a sensation of pleasure" and of "a feeling of pleasure." Is pain a sensation, or is it a feeling? "If one holds his hand in warm water, into which hot water is running, one experiences a transition from the sensation of warmth to that of heat. At the same time one also begins to experience a transition from a pleasant to a painful sensation. Now these two transitions are not given as sharply distinct, but, on the contrary, the intensification of the heat sensation and the more and more emphatic development of the painfulness appear as scarcely distinguishable changes. It is not merely that they occur simultaneously, but that as one compares the more vivid stages of the 'hotness' with those of the 'painfulness,' one intuits a close affinity or near identity somewhat like that which obtains between red and orange. Heat passes into practically pure pain as orange into red—the relationship between them is perceptibly one of continuity. Similar remarks apply to 'cold'."[3] Indeed, "if pain is a sensation and yet, as I believe every psychologist in the world would, under the relevant experimental conditions—that is to say, upon the rack!—admit, also a feeling, and if there is no sharp distinction between pain and the temperature sense, and if in general the alleged gulf between sense and feeling derives from the same type of evidence as that falsely employed to separate pain and feeling, then the whole system of discontinuous classes, together with its corollary of the 'ineffability' of sensations, begins to crumble before our eyes."[4]

It is difficult to make out whether Hartshorne is asserting an across-the-board identity between sensations and feelings. I agree with Hartshorne, against Price and other epistemologists, that sensing is not a form of knowing, and that sensing is *like* feeling in its utter immediacy and its non-inferential character. But to say that sensing is more like feeling than it is like knowing is not yet to say that sensing *is* feeling. It is true, as so often happens, that there are borderline cases in which we cannot make the distinction, or in which we could say indifferently that it is the one or the other—pleasure and pain being prime examples. But in other cases the distinction seems clear enough: color-experiences and sound-experiences are surely sensations, and exhilaration and depression are feelings. Does one really want to say that the experience of yellow *is* a feeling?

Indeed, the main task of *The Philosophy and Psychology of Sensation* is to trace the relation between sensations and feelings—an enterprise which would be redundant if there were not two kinds of entity between which a relation was to be traced. Hartshorne's most original achievement in this book is to give an account, sharply at odds with the traditional psychological account, of how sensations and feelings are related. I turn now to his account.

2. The Relation between Sensations and Feelings

In human experience, sensations and feelings are inextricably linked: not only in the arts (to be discussed later) but throughout all of our daily experience, sensations are constantly *suffused with affect*. High-pitched sounds are perceived as bright, just as much as colors are perceived as bright; and low tones are perceived as heavy. "Low notes are massive, dull, ponderous, and as it were earthy in tonality; high notes are thin, light, ethereal. . . . Colors also have apparent weight, and here certainly there is no bodily localization to explain this fact."[5]

Sensations in different sense-modalities are experienced as qualitatively similar: there is an *inter-sensory* similarity between one kind of sensation and another, as well as a similarity of sensations in these modalities with affective states. "A piercing shriek is qualitatively more intense than a groan could possibly be, even though the greater massiveness of the latter may render it quite as 'loud'."[6] "A sharp object is not merely a thin one, e.g., a thread, but one with an extremity both thin and firm, i.e., strong, intense. Hence only high notes can be 'sharp'."[7] The song of a wood thrush is "golden" and that of the (higher pitched) hermit thrush is "burnished silver."[8] In fact, "a sound may be far more like a certain color than it is like certain other sounds, or than the color is like certain other colors."[9] Psychologists habitually separate colors from sounds, and both from feelings, as "incommensurable data"—and yet may not "the plain man, any man not psychologizing, betray a deeper insight when by employing the 'metaphors' of speech he implies an underlying homogeneity of experience, such that sounds can really be 'sweet' or that sounds, colors, feelings, and temperature sensations can all be 'warm' or 'bright'? Science rests upon the discovery of unity; it is therefore a paradox that the speech of untrained men should postulate far more radical unities of the mental life than scientific psychology as yet recognizes."[10]

"Will anyone maintain that sweetness as a taste quality has no closer affinity of essence with sweetness of smell than it has with a putrid odor? Are there not sour-like smells and bitter-like? What blind dogmatism to deny that in the eating of ice cream the senses of taste, of cold, of smoothness, of smell, are all so interblended, and far indeed from absolutely heterogeneous, that it is not decided kinship but significant difference of quality that is hard to detect. It would be interesting to know what the tests of similarity are supposed to be by the defenders of the non-similarity of modes."[11] Moreover, "those who insist that the character—e.g., the gaiety—is not really in the color or the sound are stating theory and not observation. Subjects insist and are clear that they see the character and the color in the same place, and as somehow one thing, a thing readily and radically distinguishable from their own reactive feelings or attitudes toward the external sense-datum. They note frequently that the objective feeling may be in conflict with the observed reactive (intra-organic) feelings."[12] The testimony of mankind is that of the "pervasiveness of feeling, its immanence in the sensations."[13]

3. THE ATTACK ON ASSOCIATIONISM

The usual but mistaken view, says Hartshorne, is that sensations get connected with certain affects via association (after the manner of Hume and other empiricists). A woman wears only purple dresses because she associates purple with certain pleasant experiences she had years before; or, she experiences a banal tune as exhilarating because it was played during her honeymoon. Hartshorne certainly does not deny that this occurs: "A certain color might seem joyous because of some flowers of that color which recently had been received under happy circumstances. Should one's feelings toward the sender subsequently fade or undergo unfortunate reversal, the meaning of the color might then also change radically."[14] But these associations are purely personal—accidents of biography. Quite apart from such personal (and highly variable) associations, sensations are experienced as having certain affective qualities—not only by the human race, but, according to Hartshorne, by some of the higher animals as well.

> A conventional view would be that once the "highness" was established (by association) then brightness would follow, inasmuch as the sky is brighter than the earth, etc., etc. But one who attends to the phenomenon of sound brightness will perceive that this impression is quite as direct as that of elevation or lightness. It is curious too that this very word "light" should ambiguously suggest both comparisons. And in fact, light colors have less "weight" than dark. Is there any intrinsic qualitative reason for this, or must we accept the verdict: mere association? Now there is a perfectly definite test of the truth of the qualitative view. Namely, if brightness is really a common feature of visual and auditory data, then the most decisive consequence should be that "high" sounds should be more intense, since bright colors (as painters say, colors in a "high key") are intense in proportion to their brightness. . . . [15]

Thus far Hartshorne has explained the affect that is felt with certain percepts as the result of *qualitative similarities* that exist among the various modes of sensation and feeling. But then he goes on to account for the feeling-tones of various colors in terms of their connection with *pervasive features of our natural environment*. Hartshorne gives the following very plausible account of our affective response to green, blue, red, and yellow: "The vegetable covering of the normal foreground is not for the most part, to man or to animals akin to man, of direct significance as food or danger or other vital condition. . . . It is in no way an exciting fact, but a harmless and agreeable one. . . . The green vegetable covering of the earth is just the normal fact of existence. Psychologically, then, we should expect green to appear as a feeling of quiet cheerfulness. Who does not feel this to be in fact the character of green?"[16] As for blue (the bright blue of the sky, not the very different blue-violet of distant hills), "blue is bound up inseparably with that of an abundance of light, and is itself a luminous, 'ethereal' blue. Nevertheless, neither the sky nor the distant land is an object of important and frequent direct reaction. The one thing to do about them, normally speaking, is to pay them no attention. A strong preoccupation with them as objects of vision might easily and frequently have fatal results with no likelihood of as frequent compensating advantages . . ."[17] As for red,

> no other color can compare with it in the systematic way in which it stands for the dramatic crises of life, among all the higher animals. It is not merely that arterial blood, the central life-fluid, is of that color. We have to remember also that from the standpoint of vision it is chiefly by its color that blood is identified. Otherwise it cannot by sight be distinguished from water or other common fluids. Outside of vegetation nothing in nature probably is so readily and safely to be identified by its mere color as is the blood of the higher animals. But the identification of blood is the knowledge that edible flesh is at hand, or that foes or friends or members of the pack or the animal itself were in danger of pain. Blood is interwoven with success in the hunt, with consuming of the prey, with combat. . . . What is life for a higher animal but a shedding of blood and a struggle to conserve his own? . . . What, psychologically, do we find? That red is precisely the most dramatic and stirring of colors; that it lacks the light-hearted gaiety of yellow, the sunshine color; the cold intensity of white, the snow- and cloud-color; the quiet cheerfulness of green; the gentle affectionate quality of blue; and possesses, as no other color, the quality of excitement or activity.[18]

But, one might ask at this point, is not this an explanation of the affective qualities of certain colors in terms of association? Not the idiosyncratic associations mentioned before, of course, like the felt joyousness of the honeymoon tune, but association nonetheless—universal associations, common to the entire human race (and perhaps to higher animals as well), associations established through the common perception of pervasive features of our natural environment? It would still be true that green is felt as being "quietly cheerful" and so on, but the explanation of this affect would still be in terms of the association of these colors with recurring features of the environment. What is so objectionable about such "universal associationism"?

Not only is the relation (between color and affect) associational; it may be that the association occurs only if one has been raised in a certain kind of environment. Green is experienced as the normal background in temperate and tropical zones; but in deserts, wouldn't the color of sand be experienced as the normal background, rather than green? And in the Arctic, wouldn't the usual color of the environment be white, the color of snow? Would the affective character of various colors be the same for persons accustomed to such environments? One is tempted to say, not that color-affect is culturally variable (as in ethical relativism), but environment-variable, and thus that the connection between sensation and affect is not really universal.

Hartshorne himself notes that such

> uniformity of results, so far as it exists, would be due to the uniformity of environmental factors. Everyone sees much of the sky, most men see a good deal at least of foliage and of blood. And besides, these things enter into the tradition, so that the influence of literature and language and artistic usage would tend to extend their effects even, for example, upon a child of the city streets. And yet this account is not wholly satisfactory. It would imply, after all, rather drastic differences between city dwellers and country folk, between those living in regions where snow is common and those who have never seen snow. . . . Many will allege that precisely such variations occur. I am content here to urge that while the evidence is somewhat uncertain, it is clear that it would be an advantage to the artist if such variations were not to be feared, and that it is also doubtful whether any artist works with the possibility of them in mind.[19]

In the above passage, at any rate, Hartshorne leaves open the possibility that variation of affect is due to variation in one's pervasive environment. I suggest that one reason for Hartshorne's uncertainty about color-affect in different environments is that there is a factual uncertainty about the source of those affects. (1) If the color-affect is the result of the environment of the *individual*, then it would indeed seem to be subject to such variation. To someone growing up in an Arctic environment, where the prevailing color is white, green might not have the quality of "quiet cheerfulness" that it does in a grassy or forested environment. If there was only one green living thing every hundred square miles or so, one may well wonder what its typical affect would be: it might even be as dramatic as red is to residents of the tropics. On the other hand, (2) it is possible that the affect Hartshorne describes is already imprinted on the brains even of Arctic dwellers. Human beings lived in the tropics for many thousands of years before they migrated to colder climes, and the result of these centuries of tropical environment may well be a kind of "racial affect" in which even dwellers in the Arctic carried with them the residual affect of thousands of years of the accumulated affect of the race. In that case green would carry the same affect regardless of the particular environment of a particular person, and Hartshorne's assertion of universality of affect would be valid after all. I do not think the evidence is clear in this case. (I have seen an exhibition of Eskimo art, but since there was no green in it at all there was no opportunity even to speculate on what its affect to the artists in question might be.)

Elsewhere, however, Hartshorne expresses the view that artists cannot work with such possible variability in mind, and that they can count on a universality of affect: That in a painting cool colors will tend to recede and warm colors to come forward, that painting a small room a light color will tend to make it seem larger while painting it a dark color will tend to make it seem smaller, and so on. "Red is felt in artistic appreciation as warm, insistent, advancing; its bluish-green complementary is cool, gentle, receding. Yellow is lively, cheerful, light-hearted; blue-violet is quiet, wistful, earnest. . . ."[20] A painter, he says, must be able to rely on such effects in his audience, else his work could not be appreciated by others, at least outside his own region of the earth, whereas in fact it is.

It is easy to come down in favor of color-relativity if one fails to distinguish between color-*affect* and color-*evaluation*. The fact is, says Hartshorne, not that the same colors express different feelings to different peoples, but that different peoples have different feelings to express, and thus have expressed this difference of feeling in a difference of color. White is the color appropriate to funerals in the Orient (to take a stock example); does this show that the Chinese feeling for white is different from ours? Not at all; rather it shows that "the Chinese do not share our conviction that the symbols connected with a funeral should be such as to express solely the sheer negativity, destructiveness, and despair of death, which black does for us" (and also for the Chinese). And if a savage prefers cruder colors than we do, so are the feelings they express for him (and for us) more crude than those we enjoy. "There is no evidence that culture determines color-feeling, but only that it affects color preference or evaluation—a very different thing ."[21]

That color-preference and color-evaluation need to be distinguished from experienced color-affect, is a point well taken. But it still does not show that color-affects are universal within the human race. For example, I, with Hartshorne, experience yellow as bright and cheerful, and find it difficult to understand those who claim that they do not experience it thus. But to my surprise, yellow seems to be among the most disliked of colors; "I hate yellow" is a statement quite commonly heard. It is true, as Hartshorne says, that to like or dislike a color is one thing, and to agree on its affective quality is another. But it is difficult to believe that most people dislike brightness or cheerfulness. I have always found the epithet applied to cowards, "You're yellow," singularly inappropriate, yet it has been found sufficiently appropriate by many persons to keep the expression alive. Is only white "pure"? Is it that yellow is somehow too aggressive, that it "comes out at you" too much, at least for some people? But they don't mind bright blue, which also does this. It is at least a possibility that they don't find yellow in their experience to possess the same affect that Hartshorne and I find in it. Or perhaps they have in mind some "impure" shade of yellow.

Nor do I find the feeling-tone of black to be always that of negativity, deprivation, somberness, or death. The prevailing jet black of a Bacon painting may not exactly be cheerful, but it is nonetheless positive and exhilarating. A jet black metal desk is not felt by me to be as somber, lifeless, or "negative" (and certainly not reminiscent of death) as a dull brown one, and neither seems to me as utterly desolating as practically anything that is colored beige or olive green.

(Is this too a confusion of color-affect with color-preference? Perhaps, but I am inclined to doubt it. I am more inclined to think that the difference in color-preference is a consequence of a difference in color-affect.)

In summary, then, I agree with Hartshorne that percepts are constantly suffused with affect—that colors and sounds and smells are experienced as imbued with feeling-tones. And the connection between them is in some cases quite universal: clearly red is warm and not cold, and the sound of the piccolo is bright and sharp, not dull and flat. Red is more like the sound of a trumpet than like that of a flute, and the sound of the English horn is melancholy (witness its extensive use as a solo instrument in the Prelude to Act 3 of *Tristan und Isolde*, with its intimations of impending doom). In other cases I am less sure: "My own experience," says Hartshorne, "is that the most pronounced effect of warmth is in certain relatively low tones of stringed instruments, and in certain higher notes of the trumpet. The latter tones suggest scarlet, as long ago remarked; the former suggest a warm red-violet."[22] But in this case he is careful to qualify his assertion by saying "in my own experience." The chord of the major third (C-E) is felt by me, as apparently by most people, as cheerful, positive, uplifting. The chord of the minor third (C-E), by contrast, is felt as sad or melancholy. (It is not compositions in the minor key that are sad—they are often less so than those in the major key—but only the minor chord itself. What is built upon the chord may be as bright or tinkling as you please, as in many of Mozart's and Scarlatti's piano sonatas.) Yet it was not always so: many centuries ago, musicologists tell us, the minor third was experienced as a dissonance, and on that account was avoided.

I agree, then, that percepts are *experienced* as having affect. But to say this is not to say that the connection between a certain percept and a certain affect is *universal*—nor, which is still different, that it *should* be universal. A sensation may carry a certain feeling-tone for one person, or one culture, and not for another and it is not clear to me that there is anything particularly catastrophic about this. I am not even sure that creative artists have to assume that it is the same for everyone, or that to deny the universality is to "make nonsense of art."[23]

4. SENSATIONS AND AFFECT IN COMBINATION

Works of art are far different from single tones, shapes, colors, or words; they are extremely complex and intricate combinations of these elements. And the affective quality of a single component may be very different from that of the element occurring alone. Hartshorne himself gives an illustration of this: yellow, he says, is a bright, gay, happy color, but suppose "that in a prevailingly somber picture a large mass of strong yellow is introduced, without due regard to balance, transition, mediation, and the like. The yellow may then affront us as out of place; it may be felt as violent rather than as cheering or joyous."[24] No amount of such use of yellow, he says, can alter its character "so as to transform its good cheer into the feeling of sheer negativity, of deathlike evil, which is characteristic of black. . . . Yellow may appear hateful, but its hatefulness, so far as it is objective feeling at all, is emotionally far different, in any circumstances, from that of black, under any circumstances. . . . [Yellow's] light-heartedness may often jar too sharply with the prevailing melancholy of the picture."

People's judgments about the affective quality of works of art are notoriously at greater variance with one another than their judgments about the affective quality of single colors or tones. If Hartshorne's views about the universality of affect are to be at all sustained, it is important to come to some conclusion about the reasons for this difference. For example, (1) When Richard Strauss ends a tone-poem in two different keys, some experience this effect as mellow and satisfying, others as "bitter-sweet," others as merely dissonant, and still others as a frustrating and unsatisfying failure to effect a resolution—like someone playing seven white keys on the piano starting with middle C and never completing the octave. I suggest that those who experience the two last-mentioned effects are those who come to Strauss without having first listened to orchestral works by Mozart, Beethoven, and Brahms. He "goes them one better" by going in for great harmonic daring; but this daring is experienced as such only against the backdrop of the temporally prior compositions. Without that background of musical experience, the composition would be experienced as in some degree unsatisfying or repellent. (2) Edmund Gurney wrote in 1880, "Music which wears a definable expression to one person, does not wear it or wears a different one to another, though the music may be equally enjoyed by both. For instance, the great 'subject' of the first movement of Schubert's B-flat trio represents to me and many the *ne plus ultra* of energy and passion; yet this very movement was described by Schumann as 'tender, girlish, confiding.' "[25] (3) And Eduard Hanslick wrote in the following year,

> How many compositions by Mozart were thought by his contemporaries to be the most perfect expression of passion, warmth, and vigor of which music was capable. The placidity and moral sunshine of Haydn's symphonies were placed in contrast with the violent bursts of passion, the internal strife, the bitter and acute grief embodied in Mozart's music. Twenty or thirty years later, precisely the same comparison was made between Beethoven and Mozart. Mozart, the emblem of supreme and transcendent passion, was replaced by Beethoven, while he himself was promoted to the Olympic classicalness of Haydn. The musical merit of the many compositions which at one time made so deep an impression, and the aesthetic enjoyment which their originality and beauty still yield, are not altered in the least by this dissimilar effect on the feelings of different periods.[26]

If trained musical listeners, people who are not in the habit of projecting into the music whatever moods they may be experiencing at the moment, arrive at such diverse verdicts on the affective qualities of the music, what is one to say about the universality thesis—that not only is sensation A *felt* as being imbued with (or expressing, or objectifying, etc.) affect B, but that A *does* in fact embody affect B and that anyone who denies it is in error (as a person would be in error who said that red was a cool rather than a warm color)?

At this point it is customary to say things like "Well, responses to music are inescapably subjective"—"subjective" presumably meaning here that the response varies from person to person. But the question before us is not simply about responses to art, which of course do vary; the question is about the affective quality attributed to the work, which may remain constant even when responses such as liking or disliking, and feeling this or feeling that, may vary. It is not even what the music makes the listener *feel* that is in question (one can grant enormous variation in this also; the most joyous tune in the world may depress a person who is in the throes of personal grief), but what affective quality the listener would honestly attribute to the music: this may be happy music even though on the present occasion it doesn't make me *feel* happy.

Yet once all these issues, so easily confused with one another, have been carefully separated out, doesn't it remain the case that the affective qualities one attributes to works of art do vary enormously from one viewer or listener to another—far more than the simple cases of the sharpness of the piccolo or the warmth of the sound of a cello as compared with that of the flute, on which all might well agree?

Rather than reconciling ourselves to the "subjectivity of affect" which is so easy to do and so quickly puts an end to further discussion, I would suggest that our attribution of affective qualities to sounds and colors in works of art is *contextual*. To say that it is contextual is not at all the same as to say that it is subjective. Much of the affective quality we attribute to works of art depends on the "apperceptive background" in which our response is embedded. The Strauss passage *is* dissonant if we lack the acquaintance with other works of music which Strauss (probably quite consciously) presupposed in creating a musical ending without harmonic resolution. If we are acquainted only with Haydn, Mozart's music will indeed be "full of supreme and transcendent passion." Indeed, it may still be so after we have come to know Beethoven and Brahms, though the passion will be, if not more subdued, "more subtly expressed" when we perceive it through historical lenses which of course were not available in Mozart's time. The time may come when even Mahler's most violently agonized passages will come to seem less so when compared with still other music (which has yet to be written).

One wise motto, then, might well be, "For 'subjective' substitute 'contextual'." I have no doubt that this will carry us a long way in accounting for apparently disparate verdicts on the affective qualities of the same works of art. So much is the affect dependent upon the context that the very same dissonant chord in the Mahler Symphony No. 6 which is felt in one occurrence to be angry and aggressive, is felt in another movement of the same symphony to be a heart-rending agonized cry (not only by me, but by everyone I have asked about this). The difference in affect is accounted for not by the same chord in isolation having two different affects, but rather by the fact that the musical *context* (especially the musical progressions leading up to the chord) is quite different in the two cases. Nor is this difference limited to music: in certain paintings by Matisse in which the entire color-range is limited to shades of yellow, orange, and red, two warm colors within it may seem contrasting, even complementary, though if the painting contained even one hint of blue the apparent contrast among the warm colors would instantly vanish.[27]

There are other considerations as well which should be taken into account before we fall into the all-too-tempting pit of subjectivity:

1. If you ask a person "What is the prevailing mood of this symphony?" or even "What is the prevailing mood of this movement?" you are likely to get different answers because the affective qualities in a work of music are constantly shifting from one passage to the next; one might as well ask what is the true color of an iridescent gown. One listener will have in mind the quality of a passage which particularly strikes him, and another listener will give his verdict based upon another. For this reason it is important, in soliciting such verdicts, to consider only short passages. The shorter the passage, the more likely one is to elicit the same judgment on its affective quality.

2. Gurney wrote, "Music which wears a definable expression to one person, does not wear it or wears a different one to another."[28] The key word here may well be "definable." We may find a passage full of powerful affect but are unable to think of any words to describe this affect. And the words we do use to describe affective states (in life as well as in art) are not very precise, and often overlap. One person may say that a certain passage is triumphant and another that it is majestic, and they may differ only in the words they use to describe it. Not only is our use of affective words very sloppy, but there *is* no exact vocabulary for describing affective states as there is for describing the properties of physical objects. It is no wonder, then, that the people's verdicts on the affective quality of various passages at least *seem* to disagree, even more than that of the blind men trying to describe the elephant.

In view of the very great differences of context with which viewers and listeners come to a work of art, plus the difficulties in identifying the exact passage which is the subject of dispute, plus the difficulties of language in discovering whether we mean the same thing by the words we use, it is virtually impossible to say with certainty whether (and when) there are genuine differences in attribution of affective qualities. (Compare: are there really

differences in our considered moral judgments, or are the apparent differences the result of other factors, such as partial ignorance of the facts, differing
estimates of those facts, and different contexts of empirical or religious beliefs?) My guess is that there does remain a residue of genuine difference, just as
there remains a residue of difference in attribution of affect to simple sensory
qualities such as yellow. But it may be that I am less disturbed by this than
Hartshorne is.

It seems to me that our overall verdict on this issue must be somewhat
divided. It seems to me, for example, that there may be genuine differences in
affect to observers who are accustomed to radically differing environments.
Those qualities that depend on the environment can be expected to vary with the
environment. On the other hand, there are areas in which we can be more
positive. (1) Sometimes the basis for the affect is not environmental but
physiological, and thus will be the same for all creatures with human physiology.
Thus, horizontal lines will tend to be restful and peaceful (the normal position for
rest and sleep being horizontal), whereas jagged lines will not. We call some
tones ''high'' because their source is high in the throat. Or consider Hartshorne's
example: "Could a cat in a state of peaceful pleasure, as when being stroked,
growl fiercely, as it does when disturbed while gnawing a bone? How could a
general placidity be made physiologically consistent with the tense state of lung
muscles and vocal cords necessarily involved in growling?"[29] (2) A rejection of
subjectivity can also be sustained in those numerous cases in which there is an
objective resemblance between the elements being compared. A restless passage
of music will typically contain staccato passages, wide jumps in pitch, and rapid
accelerandos and crescendos, which greatly resemble in their general structure
the qualities of restless people (inability to keep still, rapid breathing and
heartbeat, etc.); is it any wonder that no one calls such music calm or restful?
And passages which we (rather vaguely) call ''sad'' do have many of the
qualities of people's behavior when they are sad: they move slowly, their sounds
are subdued and low, as is their walk (sad music is correspondingly slow, with
no sudden leaps in intervals, not strident or screaming, etc.); and is it any wonder
that no one calls such passages happy or excited?[30] There may yet remain cases
in which ''calm, careful, and collected'' students of the arts give conflicting
affective judgments. But such judgments are of course given in words, and in
view of the skimpiness of our emotion-vocabulary we are still far from being
justified in passing the judgment that in meaning, if not in words, our affective
judgments disagree—or, for that matter, that they do not.

It was easy for Santayana to say that beauty is pleasure seen as the quality of
the object; since different persons take pleasure in different objects, the
subjectivity of aesthetic judgments follows naturally. It is more difficult, but I
believe more in accord with the facts, to take Hartshorne's more heroic course:

to give a variety of reasons for insisting that in our judgments of affect it is not true that "anything goes." Many aestheticians, each in his or her own way (Langer, Sircello, Tormey, and others) have followed Hartshorne in pursuing and defending this more difficult course; but it was Hartshorne who blazed the trail and pioneered the attempt.

5. ART AND THE AESTHETIC

"Aesthetic value in the most general sense," writes Hartshorne in his paper "Aesthetics as Key to Ethics and Religion,"[31] "is intrinsic, immediately felt value. Economic value is at the opposite extreme, extrinsic and eventual." Most activities are combinations of the two: mathematics is usually pursued as a means to an end, yet one may also revel in the beauty of it. Moral virtue is a means toward an end (right action), yet it is also "intrinsically satisfying and beautiful to contemplate in others."

Aesthetic objects (scenes in nature, works of art) do not possess this intrinsic value; it is the *experience* of them that does. What is it, however, that makes these objects suitable for the enjoyment of intrinsic (immediately felt) value? Primarily, says Hartshorne, it is the feature of *unity-in-diversity*. "An aesthetically enjoyable object is given as coherent, as bound together into a more closely unified perceptual whole than are non-aesthetic objects. The only qualification is that this unity must not be so rigid as to exclude variety or create monotony. To take this condition into account we may employ the phrase 'coherent diversity'."[32] Coherent diversity, according to Hartshorne, comprises two main features: there are "more extensive likenesses between the parts than occur in non-aesthetic objects. . . . These repetitions of theme, of motif, with more or less variation are completely universal characters of art": and secondly, there is "interpenetration of the parts of the aesthetic whole in the sense that the perception of each includes the perception of all."[33] "The law of aesthetic order is then the twofold but inseparably unitary one of coherence as uniformity and coherence as mutual internality. The uniformity is, however, blended with the exceptional, the law-abiding with the irregular, necessity with freedom. . . ."[34] This characterization of the aesthetic is, of course, not original with Hartshorne; it has been a prominent feature of aesthetic theory from Aristotle to the present day, and has been most extensively set forth by many writers, in most detail by Stephen Pepper and by Harold Osborne.[35]

Though the general principle is familiar enough, it remained for Hartshorne to apply it to an unexpected and hitherto unexplored area: the songs of birds, in which he has become something of a specialist. Some birds, says Hartshorne, sing for hours on end, varying their songs considerably yet returning repeatedly to certain basic themes. Thus the aesthetic principle of unity-in-variety is preserved. On the other hand, there are birds who simply repeat a single brief song-pattern many times a day; they have no repertoire. Such warblings would seem to cross the "monotony threshold"—they have unity, but not enough variety to avoid monotony. But in fact, says Hartshorne, they do not, because these birds do not sing continuously. Even these birds "act as aesthetic principles require, although not by varying the singing; rather by interposing between successive utterances of their one song enough for other activities or experiences to occur and for the fading of immediate memory. Monotony in the aesthetic sense, especially in a creature with as short an attention span as a bird, need not arise from singing the same song over and over, provided there be sufficient pauses between utterances. In fact there is a strong correlation of length of pauses between utterances and repetitiousness of the singing."[36]

Indeed, Hartshorne ventures further and speculates that the laws governing the entire universe are aesthetic. Causal necessity would be monotonous; sheer chance would lack unity; but the universe in which we live is a kind of compromise between these two. "Probabilities are no mere makeshifts to cover our ignorance. They are in principle prudential rules for the everlasting game of chance which is existence itself. . . . Life, existence itself, is an art. Order sets rules for creative action; and the rules themselves must have been created and must be creatively altered in due course lest the universe peter out in deadly routine."[37]

Hartshorne cites an astronomer whose reason for being a determinist was aesthetic: the universe is more tidy and neat when thus conceived. But, Hartshorne very plausibly observes, "determinism is a theory of cosmic monotony, not of cosmic beauty. The very sense of intensity in scientific activity is essentially bound up with the unpredictability of future discoveries and the frequent surprises in experimental results."[38] If someone were to reply, "But science enables us to predict more phenomena all the time," I would reply, following Hartshorne, that as human knowledge increases, like a horizon ever opening up before us, new problems occur that had not arisen before, and in these we can often predict less and less. In order to predict Einstein's Theory of Relativity before Einstein conceived it, one would not only have to be able to predict *that* Einstein would devise it at such-and-such a date, but he would have to predict every detail of the theory itself (else his prediction would be incomplete), that is, to discover the theory before Einstein himself did. Creative acts are—in their vast detail—inherently incapable of prediction; to predict them would be to turn the creator into a copyist. Determinism—at least in its "everything is in principle predictable" version—is thus an impossible theory, and Hartshorne is right to say that "science makes many important things less predictable, not more."[39]

To attempt any remarks on the preceding quotations would take me too far from aesthetics. On Hartshorne's aesthetic theory, however, I shall venture a few comments.

1. Those scenes in nature, which people find worthy of repeated viewing (and photographing), and great works of art in all media, do seem to be characterized by the unity-in-variety principle; unity alone leads to monotony and sheer diversity to chaos. This has been the testimony of aestheticians and critics for more than two thousand years. In a musical composition, certain thematic material is introduced, then varied and combined with other themes (thus achieving diversity while retaining unity), all propelling one forward toward a climax in which the diverse elements are integrated. There is no doubt that people react positively to such patterns, as opposed to compositions which simply meander and "go nowhere," or in which the same thematic material is simply repeated without variation, or in which one can begin anywhere and end anywhere without any sense of progression or impending inevitability. *Why* human beings respond thus is a difficult question. I can think of no answer other than the rather inane one that the human psyche is so organized as to respond positively to this kind of pattern. Perhaps such patterns reflect various rhythms of organic life, or of the universe in general—but this fails to explain why certain works of art which have as much unity-in-diversity as other ones are nevertheless experienced as flat, inexpressive, and uninspiring. There should be much more to say on this subject, but I have never heard it said.

2. Hartshorne, quite correctly I believe, sees a connection between at least some aesthetic experiences and religious experiences. The feeling of religious exaltation experienced by a person listening to a performance of Bach's B Minor Mass has a considerable similarity to the exaltation felt by the devout worshiper in a cathedral. Still, there are differences: (1) the *object* of the experience in one case is a work of art, and in the other case God: and (2) the religious experience need not be characterized by formal features such as unity-in-variety which typically characterize the objects of aesthetic experience. Still, there is a kind of continuum among various kinds of experiences; consider a scientist in the process of creating a new scientific theory, and call this a "scientific experience"; surely there are similarities between such experiences and aesthetic experiences. They are not the same, and the product of such experiences is quite different, yet the experiences themselves, phenomenologically speaking, may well overlap and in some cases be difficult to distinguish from one another.

3. Works of art themselves have no intrinsic value—they are the objects which produce in us experiences of intrinsic value (experiences being the only things having such value). Yet it is important to recognize that works of art are usually *more* than sources of intrinsic value. Many works of literature, for example, have a good deal to tell us about human nature and the human

condition. Some works that do this to a high degree, such as Dostoyevsky's novels, may indeed have less *aesthetic* value than many lesser works of art. Many works of art have other fish to fry than simply being producers of aesthetic experiences. Those who desire works of art only as sources of aesthetic value should turn to Swinburne rather than to Dostoyevsky, to Gauguin rather than to Goya, to Haydn rather than to Gesualdo.

4. In some aesthetic objects the element of diversity appears to be almost absent, yet we may attribute to the object a high degree of aesthetic value. May not a diamond or a ruby be beautiful—but where is its complexity? Certain arias by Handel and Mozart consist of just a few tones; they are as simple as if any child could have written them, yet they are enduringly moving and memorable. If one considers the melodies alone, not the longer works of which they are a part, one is hard put to find any degree of complexity. I would describe such melodies as hauntingly beautiful, in spite of (or perhaps because of?) their extreme simplicity. Yet *most* simple melodies are inane and easily forgettable; and sometimes only a single note stands between the one and the other. No one, I think, has satisfactorily explained why one simple melody may be of enduring beauty whereas another melody, almost identical to it, is trivial, banal, and after a short time impossible to endure hearing. No general aesthetic criteria such as the unity-in-variety principle are sufficiently finely-honed to explain the difference.

5. In the house of art there are many mansions. Some works of art hardly touch ''the life of feeling'' at all, but simply tease the eye or the ear: their impact is perceptual rather than emotional; consider some of Gauguin's and Matisse's color-harmonies or Mondrian's arrangements of straight lines intersecting at right angles. On the other hand, there are many works of art, especially literature, that appeal to the intellect and not to the senses, such as the long stretches of informational material in Tolstoy's *War and Peace*. Thirdly, however, there are works of art whose primary appeal is not to the intellect nor to the senses but to the feelings. ''The entire warp and woof of aesthetic intuition, its sole content,'' says Hartshorne, ''is feeling.''[40] Hartshorne insists, as did Susanne Langer after him, throughout her book *Feeling and Form*, that the principal appeal of works of art is to ''the life of feeling.''

My own sympathies lie entirely with Hartshorne on this point. I want art to provide me a pipeline to the life of feeling; I want art to move me, not merely to titillate my senses or inform my intellect; I want art not only to be amusing or instructive but to impinge on me ''at the gut level''—to derive from it a memorable emotional experience—or at the very least, to provide me with some new insight into the life of feeling, as a novel may do even if it may not particularly move me emotionally. But I would resist the tendency to say that there is just one function of art, to be expressive or revelatory of some aspect of the life of feeling. I will take Mondrian for what he gives, and Tolstoy for what he gives, and not demand the same of every artist. Phrases such as "*the* function of . . ." are, I fear, usually preludes to a mistake.

For the same reason I find most charts, which attempt to provide us a neat and tidy arrangement of aesthetic categories, to be defective—they all try to make square pegs fit round holes. And this includes the provocative chart which Hartshorne has provided on more than one occasion:[41]

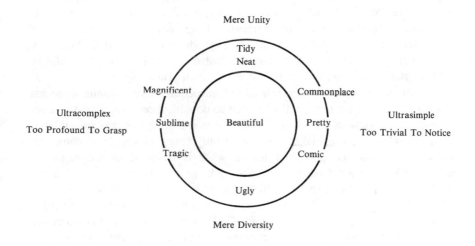

It seems to me that there are too many false symmetries in this diagram. It is true that something may be "tidy and neat" but not contain enough diversity to make it continuously interesting. But how is the ugly supposed to be connected with "mere diversity"? Can't a child's drawing be simple but ugly? Many persons would call a deep gash in the face of the earth ugly, but not because of "mere diversity"—many non-ugly things contain far more diversity than that. If a monotonously uniform pile of rubble is ugly (as some at least would say), it might be less ugly if it had more diversity. There are other theories of the ugly which don't fit in with Hartshorne's schema: for example, if Samuel Alexander is right, ugliness results from the unsuccessful *attempt* to create something beautiful, and consists in the lack of success of the attempt.[42] If this view is accepted, then only works of art can be ugly and nothing in nature can be (since there was no attempt that could fail). There may well be reasons for rejecting this theory of the ugly, but the fact that it exists is enough to give us pause before classifying something as ugly, and certainly before presenting "mere diversity" as an account of it.

If it is not clear what our basis is for calling something ugly, the same point can be made with regard to "pretty." It is possible that, at least in some cases, an object's lack of diversity may lead us to call it pretty whereas if it had more diversity we might be tempted to call it beautiful. But I am far from being convinced of this: in "She's pretty but not beautiful," is the difference owing to a lack of diversity, a diversity that is present when we don't withhold the judgment of beauty? I am not sure that it has anything to do with simplicity or diversity. Suppose I say that pale pink is pretty, but that Mediterranean blue (the color called "cerulean blue" that comes out of the painter's tube) is a beautiful color. Here there is no difference in diversity whatever, since both colors are simple percepts. Why can't something be (not merely pretty, but) beautiful in spite of great simplicity, like a shining jewel or an aria by Mozart?

Nor do I see how sublimity is related to "ultracomplexity." Sublimity seems to operate in a different arena entirely: it has to do with sheer size, vastness, awesomeness. The view of the Grand Canyon from the north rim may be sublime, but is it complexity that makes it so? Isn't our feeling of smallness compared with the vastness and power of nature what is essential in judgments of sublimity? When Kant described the sublime he mentioned "hurricanes leaving desolation in their track, the boundless ocean rising with rebellious force, the high waterfall of some mighty river . . . make our power of resistance of trifling moment in comparison with their might."[43] How is this related to complexity?

Comedy and tragedy are often mentioned as if they were as naturally opposite as left and right. There are of course many theories of the tragic, and a work that is tragic on one theory fails to be so on another. At any rate, tragedies on the whole fulfill very well the Aristotelian canons of unity-in-variety; indeed, the Greek tragedies are paradigm cases of it, and it is from these works that Aristotle generalized when he wrote his *Poetics*. The comic, however, is much more of a puzzle. It is said that in comedy, you can look down on people whom you consider less intelligent than yourself, and by laughing at their foibles you can engage in aggression without feelings of guilt. Or, the essence of comedy is some incongruity, some sudden unexpected twist or insight (though not all unexpected twists are comic). And so on. What constitutes the comic is an issue on which there is more disagreement than there is on tragedy.[44] My problem with the comic is that it seems difficult to fit it into accounts of the aesthetic at all: theories of the aesthetic seem to have been devised without any attention to the comic.

A Russian underground joke goes as follows: "What would happen if the Soviets took over the Sahara Desert? Answer: for two years, nothing; then there would be a shortage of sand.'' This joke probably seems funniest to those who are accustomed to constant shortages of consumer goods; but wherein lies the humor? In this case it is plausible to say that it lies in the absurd *exaggeration* in the description of a present condition, and the joke provides a welcome release for one's pent-up dissatisfaction. Yet other jokes do not share this pattern at all. Here is an underground Czech joke: ''The president of Czechoslovakia, a nation of fourteen million people, visits Mao, and asks him, 'How many people in China would you say are dissatisfied with your rule?' 'About fourteen million, I would say,' answers Mao; 'And how many would you say there are in Czechoslovakia?' 'Not more than that, I think,' is the reply.'' Is the source of the humor here the same? Is there any plausible account that will cover all cases? If so, I have never encountered it.

Most jokes are much too short to contain much diversity; they make one brief telling point and they are over. Where do they belong in the aesthetic hierarchy? Perhaps the unity-in-diversity criterion doesn't apply to them at all, as suggested in the example of the Mozart aria? Or perhaps a joke isn't enjoyed ''merely for its own sake,'' a feature which is supposed to characterize the entire realm of the aesthetic; perhaps it's an economical means of making some cognitive point (though not all quick-but-telling ways of making a point are funny—witness Aesop's fables). Perhaps then the comic doesn't belong under the heading of the aesthetic in the way the other arts do. But in that case, couldn't tragedy be plausibly excluded as well? Doesn't tragedy remind us of features of the human condition? ''What a waste, that the good should be destroyed with the bad'' is A. C. Bradley's theory of what all tragedy is [45]—or perhaps merely ''That could have been me'' or ''There, but for the grace of God and a favorable early environment, go I.'' In all these cases the tragedy is not merely ''enjoyed for its own sake'' but the experience points essentially to something beyond itself, which gives it its thrust and power. Yet whatever we may feel about the comic, few people would willingly exclude tragedy from the realm of the aesthetic.

Yet in so doing, a price must be paid: the usual conception of the aesthetic as that which is enjoyed for its own sake may require modification—first, as to enjoyment, and second, as to the phrase ''for its own sake.''

''Enjoyment'' is a rather vanilla-flavored word for characterizing our experience of many works of art, including the greatest ones. If we asked someone to report in a short sentence his response to Picasso's *Guernica*, or Penderecki's *Auschwitz Oratorio* or Dante's *Inferno* or Lumet's film *The Pawnbroker*, and he responded, ''I enjoyed it,'' we would feel that he has not responded appropriately, that he has failed to come to grips with the work. There is much art that deals with extremely painful emotions, and also evokes such emotions. Indeed, this can be said of most that one would label as ''profound.'' Of much art it would be true to say that he who has not suffered greatly cannot appreciate it. Tragedy is the principal genre of which such things can be said. How can we "enjoy" that which is so tragic, so painful, so distressing? Most of the traditional accounts will not suffice. (1) "The pain is weaker because we know it's only art and not real life." But weaker pain is still pain; and anyway, is it really weaker? The experience of great tragedy is often as strong and intense as that of any real-life experience. (2) The experience of tragedy is vivid, not diluted; but vividness itself is enjoyable. Some persons (but not all) enjoy vivid colors more than pastels. But is vividness itself enjoyed regardless of *what* it is that is vividly experienced? Is a vividly experienced gnawing toothache preferred to a mild discomfort? How about vividness of distress, revulsion, or disgust? (3) Eighteenth-century critics liked to say that the pain of the subject-matter is neutralized by the artist's skill in depiction, which causes pleasure. It is doubtless true that recognition of skill is pleasure-producing, but this view presents the experience of tragedy as if it were a kind of sugar-coated pill; the pill is swallowed because the pleasure in the depiction counterbalances the pain of the subject matter. Does this really describe one's experience of tragedy? (4) Aristotle's theory of catharsis provides at least a more plausible solution; a tragedy evokes painful emotions (not necessarily Aristotle's favorites, pity and fear), and a release of painful tensions, such as are developed in a tragedy, comes as a pleasurable relief. Tragedy is thus, Stephen Pepper says, an *art of relief*, as opposed to purely "pleasant" art, which he calls the *art of delight*.[46] Relief from pain, however, presupposes a prior experience of pain, and the fact remains that pain is not enjoyed for its own sake. (Not even in the case of the masochist, who enjoys not pain *per se* but the *pleasure* received from the *infliction* of pain—and then only the infliction of the pain of punishment: a masochist does not enjoy a headache or a toothache anymore than the rest of us do.)

We do appreciate the fine arts "for their own sake" in the sense that we do not use them for any practical purpose beyond themselves, such as acquiring knowledge or moral instruction (these are byproducts, when they occur at all): we do not use a painting to hide a crack in the wall, or prehistoric drawings on cave walls merely to gain anthropological knowledge, or even novels to give us historical facts. We go to the theater for the experience of seeing (enjoying?) the play, not for a lesson in morality, though such lessons may be there. But may not music release tensions and at the same time also be enjoyed as music? If Aristotle is right, there *is* a "practical purpose" involved in witnessing a tragedy, and the experience of tragedy is an *instrument toward a further end*: it is *medicinal*. Catharsis cleanses us emotionally—and is this not a practical effect, something sought beyond the experience itself, even if the spectator may not attend the play *in order* to obtain this effect?

If we are to include our experience of tragedy as aesthetic, then, I am inclined to think that even such a widely repeated formula as "being enjoyed for its own sake'' requires modification.[47] The trouble with aesthetics is that it is always being dominated by some general *theory*, and our acquaintance with the theory modifies the nature of our response to the arts. We then make our judgments within the framework of the theory, rather than frame the theory to fit the judgments. On this rock, it seems to me, all general aesthetic theories are in danger of breaking. This includes the unity-in-variety requirement, the ''for its own sake alone'' requirement, and even Hartshorne's requirement that all works of art must in some way explore ''the life of feeling.'' Yes, some art; perhaps most art; but not all. The ultimate fallacy in aesthetics is the fallacy of illicit generalization. But to indulge in such generalizations is a never-ending temptation.

JOHN HOSPERS

SCHOOL OF PHILOSOPHY
UNIVERSITY OF SOUTHERN CALIFORNIA
JANUARY 1987

NOTES

1. Charles Hartshorne, *The Philosophy and Psychology of Sensation* (University of Chicago Press, 1933), p. 39; hereafter referred to as *PPS*.

2. *PPS*, p. 37.

3. *PPS*, pp. 49–50. The point is similar to one made by Bishop Berkeley in *Three Dialogues between Hylas and Philonous* (first dialogue), which Hartshorne quotes on p. 92.

4. *PPS*, p. 57. One interesting feature of Hartshorne's discussion is his denial that sensory qualities can be mixtures of other sensory qualities. Orange is not a ''mixture'' of yellow and red; the only correct reference to ''mixture'' here is that you can mix red paint with yellow paint and get orange paint. It would be better to say that orange resembles red in one way and yellow in another way, without having either of them as a component. This is quite clear in the case of green: green doesn't resemble blue and yellow as orange resembles red and yellow, yet it is equally true that you can get green paint by mixing blue paint with yellow paint. But green doesn't look much like either of them: it is a perfectly distinct color, and only our knowledge of paint-mixtures and color-charts would lead us to say (what would otherwise come as a surprise) that green ''combines'' blue and yellow.

5. *PPS*, p. 60.

6. *PPS*, p. 66.

7. *PPS*, p. 74.

8. *PPS*, p. 84.

9. Ibid.

10. *PPS*, p. 73.

11. *PPS*, p. 80.

12. *PPS*, pp. 117–18.
13. *PPS*, p. 129.
14. *PPS*, p. 169.
15. *PPS*, pp. 60–61.
16. *PPS*, p. 254.
17. *PPS*, p. 255.
18. *PPS*, pp. 255–56.
19. *PPS*, p. 173.
20. *PPS*, p. 165.
21. *PPS*, p. 171.
22. *PPS*, p. 233.
23. *PPS*, p. 170.
24. *PPS*, p. 184.
25. Edmund Gurney, *The Power of Sound* (London: Smith, Elder & Co., 1880), p. 342.
26. Eduard Hanslick, *The Beautiful in Music* (New York: Novello, Ewer & Co., 1881), p. 25.
27. On context-dependence, see John Hospers, *Understanding the Arts* (Prentice-Hall, 1982), pp. 326–29.
28. Edmund Gurney, op. cit., p. 341.
29. *PPS*, p. 258.
30. See Carroll C. Pratt, *The Meaning of Music* (McGraw-Hill, 1931), p. 198.
31. Hartshorne, ''Aesthetics as the Key to Ethics and Religion,'' unpublished paper.
32. *PPS*, p. 159.
33. *PPS*, p. 160.
34. *PPS*, p. 161.
35. See Stephen Pepper, *Aesthetic Quality* (1936) and *Principles of Art Appreciation* (1949), and Harold Osborne, *The Theory of Beauty* (1952) and *Aesthetics and Art Theory* (1970).
36. Charles Hartshorne, ''Metaphysics Contributes to Ornithology.'' *Theoria to Theory*, 1979, vol. 13, p. 133.
37. Ibid., p. 139.
38. Charles Hartshorne, *Creative Synthesis and Philosophical Method* (Open Court), p. 306.
39. Ibid., p. 306.
40. *PPS*, p. 139.
41. For example in *Creative Synthesis and Philosophical Method*, p. 306.
42. Samuel Alexander, *Beauty and Other Forms of Value* (London: Macmillan, 1933).
43. Immanuel Kant, *Critique of Judgment*, Meredith translation (Oxford: Clarendon Press, 1911), p. 10.
44. Perhaps the best discussions of this remain those of Max Eastman in *The Sense of Humor* and *The Enjoyment of Laughter*.
45. A. C. Bradley, *Shakespearean Tragedy* (New York: Macmillan, 1914).
46. Stephen Pepper, *The Principles of Art Appreciation* (Harcourt, Brace, 1949), p. 141.
47. See John Hospers, *Understanding the Arts*, Chapter 8.

6

Robert H. Kane

FREE WILL, DETERMINISM, AND CREATIVITY IN HARTSHORNE'S THOUGHT

1. INTRODUCTION

Charles Hartshorne has said that his entire philosophy could be called a "metaphysics of freedom" or a "metaphysics of creativity." The essential connection between freedom and creativity in his writings is in no place more evident than in his treatment of the time honored problem of free will and determinism, which is the subject of this essay.

Hartshorne's treatment of free will and determinism is central to both his theological views and to his wider metaphysical commitments. In theology, the failure to reconcile divine attributes with human free will is for him a pivotal failing of classical theism (though not the only failing). Hartshorne's attempts to remedy the situation lead directly to his novel interpretations of divine power, omniscience and perfection, and to dual transcendence and other aspects of his neoclassical theology. He also argues that classical theism fails to adequately account for divine free will, which is a kind of self creation according to Hartshorne, and as such cannot be made coherent without admitting change in God.

In metaphysics generally, Hartshorne's views about free will and determinism are related to his views about creativity, time, perception, causality, individuality, and the world order. In his rejection of determinist views of all varieties, he aligns himself with (among many others) his major philosophical mentors, Peirce, Bergson, and Whitehead, along with James and Berdyaev, also with four obscure figures he would like to rehabilitate, Socinus, Cournot, Fechner, and Lequier, and one of the twentieth-century philosophers he most admires after Whitehead, namely Karl Popper. These are indeterminists all, though I think the positive account of free will offered by each of them leaves something to be desired. This is true to some extent of Hartshorne's view of free will also, as we will see, though I think he has had as many valuable and indispensable insights about free will as any philosopher of his generation.

My aim in this essay is threefold, first, to critically evaluate Hartshorne's views about free will and determinism in relation to theology, modern physics, psychology, ethics, and other fields, second, to discuss Hartshorne's views in relation to recent discussions of free will, and third, to make some constructive proposals about the free will issue itself that go beyond, but are in part inspired by, Hartshorne's views. The best compliment one can pay an important philosopher is to use his work as a stimulus to one's own thinking.

Hartshorne's discussions of free will and determinism are scattered throughout his writings, a fact that creates exegetical problems. I refer to his works throughout according to the letter code at the beginning of the footnotes.[1] But several essays and works stand out for this topic. They include chapters 6 and 8 of *The Logic of Perfection and Other Essays* (LP), chapter 5 of *Reality as Social Process* (RS), and chapter 1 of *Creative Synthesis and Philosophic Method* (CS). Two early essays are important, though superseded by others, namely chapters 9 and 10 of *Beyond Humanism* (BH). I also make considerable use of two recent books by Hartshorne, *Insights and Oversights of Great Thinkers* (IO) and *Creativity in American Philosophy* (CA).

2. FREE WILL AND DETERMINISM

The following theses are basic to (though they do not exhaust) Hartshorne's claims about free will.

    (I)   *Incompatibilism.* Free will is not compatible with determinism.
    (II)   *Indeterminism.* Determinism in all its varieties, logical, theological, and scientific, is false.
    (III) *Self-Creation.* Human free choices, though undetermined by antecedent circumstances, are not uncaused. They are brought about or created by rational beings. Freedom is a form of creativity; it is self-creation. (CS, 9)

On **I**, Hartshorne agrees with William James that compatibilist views of human freedom are an "evasion." (BH, 154–55) We touch on this issue in sections 4 and 7. On **II**, he has argued in different places against theological determinism as well as against physical, logical, and psychological forms of determinism. The theological issues are discussed in section 7, non-theological issues in sections 3 to 6. Finally, issues relating to thesis **III**, which bring in the notion of creativity, are discussed in sections 5 and 7.

These three theses define Hartshorne's view of free will (in terms now current) as a "libertarian" view, a designation we will use in deference to convention, despite its potentially misleading political connotations.

What does "determinism" mean in these theses? Hartshorne does not give as much attention to defining determinism as one might wish. But it is not difficult to reconstruct his meaning. The determined state or event is such that there are logically sufficient conditions for its occurrence at a given time among the circumstances occurring in its past and the laws of nature. (LP, 162–63; RS, 97–98; IO, 301) To put this schematically, the occurrence of a state or event E at a time t is determined in the relevant sense if and only if there are past circumstances (states and/or events occurring prior to t), or past circumstances and laws of nature, such that it is logically necessary that if the relevant circumstances and laws obtain, then E occurs at t. What Hartshorne often calls "absolute" or "strict" determinism (IO, 21–22; CS, 52; LP, 165) is, I believe, the view that all occurrences are determined in this sense. For reasons to be discussed, he agrees with James and other libertarians that free choices must be "ambiguous possibilities" in the sense that they might occur or not occur given all the same past circumstances and laws of nature.

3. PHYSICS, CAUSALITY, AND INDETERMINISM

In support of thesis **II** (that all forms of determinism are false), Hartshorne has attempted to refute traditional arguments for determinism and has also argued on theological and metaphysical grounds that determinism must be false. In general, I think that many of his arguments against traditional defenses of determinism are successful and important, though they leave some deeper problems in their wake. I have more serious reservations about some of his attempts to show that determinism must be false. In this section we discuss issues relating to physics and causality, in section 4, issues about psychology, motivation and rationality, in section 5, creativity and unconscious motivation, in section 6, metaphysical issues about time, actuality, and becoming, and in section 7, theological issues.

(i) *Causality and Sufficient Reason.* Some philosophers have defended determinism on a priori grounds, either in the manner of Leibniz, as a consequence of the principle of sufficient reason—everything must have a sufficient reason or explanation for its being—or, in the manner of Kant, as a consequence of the principle of causality—every event has a cause—

understood as a necessary presupposition or empirical or scientific inquiry. Hartshorne argues that in the light of modern physics these principles can no longer be accepted as a priori truths *in deterministic forms*. (LP, 162–68; BH, 142–47; RS, 89–90) He thinks that Kant in particular was misled by an uncritical faith in the implications of Newtonian physics and the alleged deterministic implications of that physics. (IO, 76–77) By contrast, Hartshorne insists that modern quantum physics discredits the assumption that "science *requires* us to think deterministically." (LP, 167) The uncertainty relations of quantum physics do not merely define the limits of our ability to know the physical world, they signify genuine indeterminacy in the physical world itself. (CA, 139) He notes that great physicists, like Einstein and Planck, resisted this conclusion to the end, but their view has not prevailed. (LP, 167)

Many would agree with these claims today. Though debates about the interpretation of quantum theory continue, the case for its irreducibly statistical character has, if anything, become stronger in recent decades. The early debates between Einstein and Bohr spawned a series of thought experiments and some actual experiments which have repeatedly supported the view that quantum uncertainties cannot be bypassed within the theory. (Among the most recent of such experiments are those conducted by Alain Aspect in Paris in 1981–82.[2]) Of course, quantum theory may be superseded by other theories, but the very conception of such a theory and its wide acceptance among physicists throws doubt on a priori arguments for determinism of either a Leibnizian or Kantian kind and gives the best kind of current scientific support for the claim that physical determinism is false. This does not mean the principle of causality must be given up entirely. Indeed, we will see in the next section that Hartshorne accepts it, but in an indeterministic form.

As for the principle of sufficient reason, I have argued that scientists continue to presuppose it as a heuristic principle, but again, not necessarily in a deterministic form.[3] One interesting thing about quantum theory is that while it denies the existence of deterministic explanations for all particular events, it does provide a sufficient (deductive nomological) explanation for *why there is no explanation* for these particular events (by way of the uncertainty principle). This gives the theory much of its power. For while physicists no longer require sufficient explanations for every particular event, they continue to require sufficient (i.e., deductive nomological) explanations *at some level* of explanation. If some things do not have a sufficient reason for being, there must be a sufficient reason for why there is no sufficient reason in these cases. The level at which they will settle for such an explanation depends on what the best available theory demands. This accords with Whitehead's dictum, often quoted by Hartshorne, "Seek simplicity, but distrust it." It also shows how figures like Einstein and Planck may have been correct in assuming that science requires sufficient explanations, but wrong in assuming that this requires the truth of determinism.

(ii) *Quantum Physics and Free Will*. But what relevance, if any, has quantum theory to free will? Hartshorne has also addressed this question, but not, I think, to date in a fully satisfactory way. Many who are willing to concede that quantum physics is indeterministic, nevertheless deny that it has any relevance to free will. They reason that, except in special cases, quantum indeterminacies are non-negligible only in the domain of microevents (quantum jumps, particle collisions, radioactive emissions, etc.). In larger systems like the human organism, where many atoms and molecules are involved, statistical uncertainties become negligibly small. And even if in rare cases undetermined events in the brain were to have large scale effects (say, a quantum jump in the brain causing a choice to be made or an arm to be raised), it would undermine freedom rather than enhancing it by diminishing the agent's control over the choice or action.

Hartshorne is aware of this dilemma and has attempted to respond to it in several ways. At one point he cites Niels Bohr: "As . . . Bohr suggests, one may reason by analogy: if individual events on the particle level are not determined by causal laws, then we should expect that on higher levels, where there is a greater depth of individuality and conscious alternatives to action, individual events will be less fully determined by their causal antecedents." (LP, 224) Unfortunately, what we know of brain function at present does not support such an analogy. If anything, there seems to be less non-negligible quantum uncertainty in the functioning of the brain than at the micro-level. The firing of an individual neuron, which is the basic unit of information processing, involves the movement of thousands of molecules across a synaptic cleft and of atoms near and through membranes. With such large numbers involved, uncertainties are reduced, not enlarged. In fact, there are good evolutionary reasons why the organism would want to reduce indeterminacies in the brain and behavior (rather than to increase them) in order to enhance its control over itself and the environment. This is part of the problem.

The other horn of the dilemma is no less daunting. If undetermined microevents in the brain *were* to have non-negligible large scale effects on choice or action, the agent's control over the choices or actions would be diminished, not enhanced. Such undetermined choices or actions would not be free choices or actions unless some higher level control by the agent were involved. Yet Hartshorne has only speculated about what such higher level control might involve. His clearest statements on the topic are the following. "A man is not identical with super billions of particles. He is one human individual. . . . The statistical laws of particles can hardly tell the whole story of human behavior, for there is at least one more entity present in the behavior besides particles, namely the human personality, or the stream of human experiences.'' (LP, 168; cf. RS, 96–97; BH, 146–47) In another place, he says, ''A human experience is a unitary individual event, not a mere mosaic of events on an electronic level. . . . Thus, the physics of . . . particles and their statistical regularities cannot be the whole truth about human behavior.'' (LP, 224)

The implication of these quotes is that Hartshorne, like other libertarians, supposes a kind of ''supervenience'' of the activity or experience of human agents on the microevents occurring in their bodies, the whole being somehow greater than the sum of its parts. But he has not explained how this supervenience is supposed to work in detail and has not answered certain objections to it that we will discuss in later sections. As a consequence his writings do not entirely allay fears of modern compatibilists that libertarian views of agency or causation like Hartshorne's are essentially mysterious. The whole question, therefore, of how, *if at all*, quantum theory is related to free will remains a piece of unfinished business in Hartshorne's philosophy.

4. PSYCHOLOGY, MOTIVATION, AND RATIONALITY

Hartshorne has also attacked determinist arguments in areas other than physics. He has been especially concerned to answer charges that indeterminist theories of human freedom do not make sense in psychological, motivational, or ethical terms. We will consider several such arguments in this section and the next.

(i) *Causality vs. Determinism*. Some determinists and compatibilists have argued that the only alternative to determination of choice or action is randomness or arbitrariness. In response to this, Hartshorne has argued that libertarians can grant a considerable influence of heredity and environment, past conditioning, character, and motivation, on human behavior without conceding that these influences determine the behavior to one outcome. (BH, 150–51; CS, 3; OT, 21) This response returns us to a point made in the previous section, namely that Hartshorne's rejection of determinism does not mean that he rejects the principle of causality in any form. All events have causes, or causal conditions, according to him, but these causes are necessary conditions for the occurrence of their effects, not sufficient, determining conditions. (LP, 162; IO, 301–2)

Does it make sense to talk in this way, as Hartshorne does, about undetermined events being caused or having ''causes''? Elizabeth Anscombe is another philosopher who thinks that it does make sense and her arguments have convinced many.[4] If, for example, it is undetermined that a board will break under the force of the karate master's blow, nevertheless if the board does break, it will make sense to say that its breaking was caused or produced by the force of the blow. This notion of being produced by certain conditions, as Anscombe points out, is basic to our ordinary notion of causation and is compatible with indeterminism. In general, we can say that X caused or produced Y in this sense even if Y might not have occurred given X. If this way of reconciling causality with indeterminism is what Hartshorne has in mind, and I think it is, then it does make sense. Of course, one could by stipulation restrict the meaning of "cause" to "determining cause," but this would not necessarily be in accord with ordinary usage, and it would not undermine the claim that an indeterminist can make sense of causation in an understandable sense.

Nevertheless, if we grant that (in principle) undetermined events can be caused, we are still left with special problems about how undetermined free choices are caused. To see what these problems are, let us look at Hartshorne's response to another traditional argument for determinism.

(ii) *The Strongest Motive Argument.* Many philosophers, including Hobbes, Jonathan Edwards, Hume, and Schopenhauer, have argued that rational choices must always be determined by a strongest motive. If among a set of options, A, B, C, one's strongest set of motives or reasons favors A, it would be irrational to choose B or C, and more irrational still if B or C were chosen by chance. Thus, rationality requires a strongest determining motive or sufficient reason for choice.

This argument has fascinated philosophers for centuries. But there are several telling objections to it which Hartshorne rightly endorses. (CA, 20; BH, 152; LP, 169–70) Thomas Reid pointed out that if the strongest motive is defined as the one that actually prevails, then the claim that every rational choice or action requires a strongest motive would be trivially true. But then the claim would imply nothing about whether or not the strongest or prevailing motive *determined* choice or action. Another way to put this is to say, as some libertarians have said, that the motives or reasons favoring one result over another, for example, the choice of A over B or C, may "incline without necessitating." One can consistently say that motives or reasons inclined one to choice of A without determining it. So the rationality of choice does not require a strongest *determining* motive.

To this argument, Hartshorne adds another. The above argument says that when there is a strongest motive, that motive may merely incline without determining. One may now add that there may not always *be* a strongest motive. Speaking against Leibniz, Hartshorne says, "it is not a sensible objection to a decision that it is not the best possible one [i.e., the one with the strongest motive]. It is quite enough justification that the decision be as *good* as any possible one. . . . 'As good as any possible choice' perfectly justifies a choice." (IO, 129; cf. RS, 93–94) That is to say, rational choice does not require a *unique* strongest motive. A justifiable reason for a choice may be as good as some other possible ones, so long as no others are better than it. This is an extremely important point which Hartshorne also uses in a theological context to refute

Leibniz's notorious claim that God must have created the best possible world. If there is no uniquely best world, then God would not be necessitated in choosing a world to create.

(iii) *Dual Rational Self Control.* These points are sufficient to refute traditional versions of the strongest motive argument. But they leave some deeper problems in their wake that Hartshorne and other libertarians have not yet solved. One of the most important of these problems is what I call the problem of dual rational self control.

To see it, assume that I have a choice to make between A (vacationing in Colorado) and B (staying home). I have been deliberating about this for several days, weighing pros and cons on either side and wavering between the options, until I come to believe that A (vacationing in Colorado) is the best option all things considered, and I choose it. If this was a free choice, then I could have chosen otherwise. Compatibilists will say that I "could have chosen otherwise" in this context means that if some circumstances involved in the deliberation had been different, if I had considered other options, or other consequences, if I had had different wants or attitudes, etc., I would have found B to be more favorable and chosen it. But libertarians like Hartshorne cannot accept this account of my freedom, because it is compatible with determinism: it may have been true that if some of my circumstances prior to choice had been different I would have chosen otherwise, and yet my choice was determined by the circumstances actually prevailing. What libertarians (and all incompatibilists) must hold is that I may have chosen otherwise, *all prior circumstances remaining the same.* (Cf. RS, 93) This requirement is inescapable for them because it is implied by the indeterminism of choice.

But the requirement creates problems about rationality. If the deliberation leading to choice is among the circumstances prior to choice (which seems undeniable), then it follows that I may have chosen B *given exactly the same deliberation* that actually led me to the choice of A—the same options considered, the same consequences inferred and assessed, the same wants and other motives, the same knowledge brought to bear, etc. That is to say, the same process of reasoning down to the minutest detail that led to the conclusion that A was the best option all things considered, might have issued in the choice of B. This undermines our conception of rational choice. For the choice of B in such circumstances would appear to be a fluke or accident. If such a strange happening did sometimes occur, it would not represent what we ordinarily understand by a free choice. We usually think that we may have chosen B in the same circumstances thinking it (i.e., B) to be the better option.

One can see the point of calling this the problem of "dual rational self control." For what is at issue is our deeply ingrained sense, not only that free choices can "go either way" but that they will be *rational whichever way they go*. If we choose A, we will have good reasons all things considered for choosing A *rather than* B and if we choose B we will have good reasons all things considered for choosing B *rather than* A. The problem is that the indeterminist requirement that all past circumstances remain the same seems to undermine this requirement of dual, or two-ways, rationality. For it requires that either choice could issue from *exactly* the same reasons and deliberation.

We can now see why the objections to traditional versions of the strongest motive argument will not handle this more subtle problem of dual rational self control. Motives or reasons may incline without necessitating, to be sure, as the first objection to the strongest motive argument suggested. But there is still a problem. If reasons incline to the choice of A over B, then the choice of A will be rational, though undetermined. But in these same circumstances, the choice of B, the choosing *otherwise*, would be irrational. And the same is true if reasons inclined to the choice of B. So *two-ways* rationality is lacking. Now consider the second objection to the strongest motive argument. There need not always *be* a unique strongest motive. Reasons may not incline clearly to the choice of A over B, or B over A. There may, for example, be good reasons favoring each option (A or B) over all others (C, D, etc.), but not clearly favoring one (A or B) over the other. This is a possible situation. But what it amounts to is the old idea of a "liberty of indifference" (*liberum arbitrium indifferentiae*), a free choice between options for which there is no clear preference. And aside from the problem that our ordinary free choices do not usually seem to be of this sort, there is the problem that the choice between options in such circumstances would be arbitrary, *whichever way it goes*. One cannot drag in an additional past motive to decide the issue, for the assumption is that all past circumstances remain the same. And if one brings in an additional deciding motive at the moment of choice, this will be as arbitrary, given the same past deliberation, as making one choice rather than another. One can see why the liberty of indifference has so often been criticized, and why libertarians have attempted to avoid the criticisms by postulating obscure or mysterious forms of agency, like noumenal selves, agent causes, transempirical power centers, (or Hartshorne's "unitary experiences") as supervenient causes to intervene and tilt the balance one way or the other. But if the operation of these unusual forms of agency or causation is not more clearly explained, it will not be clear how *they* solve the problem of dual rationality.

In summary, Hartshorne's responses to the traditional strongest motive argument are effective, but not to the deeper problem of dual rational self control. My own view is that the problem of dual rational self control is solvable, and I have tried to deal with it myself in a recent work on free will.[5] But its solution requires more powerful strategies than Hartshorne has yet brought to bear in his writings on free will.

5. Creativity and the Unconscious

Hartshorne has also addressed another well-known motivational argument for determinism, in this case an argument inspired by Freud. Some determinists have argued that even when we are not aware of conscious motives determining choice, our choices may nevertheless be determined by unconscious motives. Hartshorne responds to this familiar argument as follows: "Psychoanalysis may show that unconscious motivation molds our every act. This only proves what every indeterminist grants, that all parts of nature are subject to habits, laws, causes. It does not prove in the least that such habits or laws are absolute, determining to the last decimal point what will occur." (BH, 150) This correct point harks back to Hartshorne's distinction between causation and determination. One can admit that unconscious motives provide necessary causal conditions for many of our conscious choices without admitting that the unconscious motives are determining causes.

This is an important point, but it is only half the story about theories of the unconscious in relation to free will. It is important, I think, to add that unconscious motivation may play a positive role (and not merely a negative constraining role) in libertarian theories of free will; and this role can be fruitfully related to Hartshorne's views about creativity. It is worth noting that in theories of creativity in the arts and sciences the unconscious is often given the positive role of *multiplying* the possibilities available to the agent by suggesting novel associations and connections to the creative thinker, whereas in theories of free will the unconscious is often given the role of *limiting* the possibilities available to the agent, determining them to one outcome. The source of this strange duality may lie in the original concern of psychoanalytic theory with compulsive and neurotic behavior in which conscious processes are constrained by unconscious influences. But in normal persons who are making free choices, and in creative thinkers, the unconscious may well play a different, more creative or "inspirational," role.

This suggestion fits nicely with Hartshorne's views about free will as a form of creativity or self-creation (Thesis III of section 2). On Hartshorne's process view, all free creative experiences require "data" or something "given" to the experience from outside. (CS, 3–10) The data, or given, of any experience constitute its (necessary but not sufficient) causal conditions. Free creative activity is not only compatible with such causal conditions. It requires them, because it requires data to work with. (LP, 164, 180) (There is no creation *ex nihilo*. [IO, 76–77]) Yet the experience adds to the given something of its own, which is its creative contribution.

On this view, the unconscious mind would be an important source of the given in human free choices, a source of images, feelings, and associations which suggest new possibilities and consequences to the conscious deliberating agent. When we talk about creativity in the arts and sciences, this role is often called "inspiration"; and so it would be for the exercise of free will. For we need inspiration as much in *self* creation (i.e., free will) as in any other kind of creation. I have argued elsewhere that this is one important and indispensable way of making room for chance in accounts of free will,[6] and it underscores the important connection Hartshorne makes in Thesis **III** between free will and creativity.

6. TIME, ACTUALITY, AND BECOMING

The arguments considered thus far are attempts to refute traditional arguments for determinism. They are successful up to a point, I have argued, though some of them leave deeper problems in their wake that Hartshorne has not yet solved. But Hartshorne has also put forward stronger arguments of a metaphysical kind to show that determinism *must* be false, and these I think are more problematic. The main argument of this type concerns time and becoming.

(i) *Time*. On several occasions, Hartshorne cites Bergson's claim that time, if it is not creative (in an indeterminist sense), is nothing. (RS, 201; LP, 165) Behind this citation is an argument often made by Hartshorne that strict determinism is untenable because, if true, it would undermine the distinction between past and future and the very notion of temporal becoming. Several lines of thought seem to converge on this conclusion for Hartshorne.

The main line of argument appeals to deep themes in his metaphysics. He holds with Whitehead that actuality is definiteness. (CA, 193; IO, 265) To be actual is to be a definite this or that. For any predicate P that can meaningfully be ascribed to it, the actual thing either has P or does not have P. (RS, 88) The past is definite in this sense for Hartshorne, and the future indefinite, so that movement "forward in time consists in this, that reality grows richer in definiteness." (IO, 153) With these assumptions the argument proceeds as follows. "If becoming does not create new quality and quantity, new determinateness, then, we argue, it creates nothing and nothing ever becomes." (LP, 165) If nothing ever *becomes* then there is no temporal passage from past to future. Everything simply *is* all at once. As in Parmenides, being takes precedence over becoming and temporal passage is mere illusion, the "way of seeming." (CS, 17) But this is what determinism implies, according to Hartshorne, because, if determinism is true, all future occurrences are as definite as past occurrences. Everything simply is definite at all times and therefore actual; nothing ever becomes. (CN, 422–23)

It seems to me that this argument depends upon assumptions that determinists, *qua* determinists, need not accept (though if they were accepted the conclusion would indeed follow). Let us consider how determinists might respond to it. The reality of temporal becoming, they might say, depends upon the fact that moments of time related in the manner of McTaggart's B-series (according to the relations of before and after) successively take on the property of being *now*, thereby generating the A-series distinction between past, present, and future. The fact that a moment of time, or an event occurring at that moment, "is now" or "is now occurring" is an additional fact not countenanced by the B-series description of times or events and therefore adds some concreteness to the abstract B-series description. (Not all determinists hold this, but they could. The argument depends only upon its being consistent with their view.) This additional concreteness just is temporal becoming, they might add. Determinists can accept temporal becoming, because even though their view is that the entire series of events is determined, given the past and the laws of nature, so that the whole could be represented *sub specie aeternitatis* in a B-series, this does not imply that "everything simply *is* all at once," in Parmenidean fashion. For it is false to say that everything *is now* all at once, even if determinism is true, and the succession of nows added to the B-series description, represents temporal succession even if it follows a determinate pattern.

Hartshorne is aware of this general line of argument and seems to be responding to it when he says that, on the determinist view, if events are determined, then before they "happen, they lack nothing [in definiteness] except a totally transparent, featureless something called 'actual occurrence.'" (LP, 165) "To some of us," he adds, "this is truly an absurdity." But this dismissal of the determinist view is too easy. For one thing it has to be reconciled with something else Hartshorne has repeatedly claimed, namely that "concreteness is definiteness." (CA, 193) (Concreteness, definiteness, and actuality are all conceptually related for him.) The determinist might reply that no predicates are more concrete, or express concreteness (and hence definiteness and actuality), more evidently than "is now," "is now occurring," "is actually occurring," and the like. Being now or now occurring may therefore be "transparent" or "feature-less" properties in some sense, but they add concreteness, and therefore actuality.

Hartshorne would undoubtedly respond that by "definiteness" he means descriptive definiteness, so that only descriptive properties can add to the definiteness of something. (This is how he seems to understand the criterion for definiteness cited earlier.) Properties like being now are modal, not descriptive, and so do not add definiteness. This is the point of calling them "transparent" or "featureless." And if they do not add definiteness they do not add actuality. But there is a problem here for Hartshorne. If definiteness is restricted to descriptive properties, like "is red," and "is round," and if it excludes what we might call "modal" properties, like "is now" and "is actually occurring," then the connection between definiteness and *actuality* becomes problematic. For "is actual" is itself a modal ("transparent") property, and not a descriptive one. Properties like "is now" and "is actually occurring," express concreteness *and* actuality; so either they add definiteness, or definiteness cannot be identified with concreteness and actuality.

The upshot of these arguments if they are correct is that determinists *qua* determinists need not deny the reality of temporal becoming. They *need* not claim that everything simply *is* all at once, and nothing ever becomes. This is not to say that determinism is true, only that it cannot be shown to be necessarily false in this way.

(ii) *The Pragmatic Argument.* A different kind of argument sometimes used by Hartshorne to show that determinism must be false appeals to a "pragmatic" criterion of truth. The argument is stated most clearly in the following passage: "Determinism . . . has no consistent practical meaning [and therefore must be false]. *Before* I decide I may claim to know that my decision will be fully determined, whether by heredity and environment, or by God, but in what way can my decision take this alleged knowledge into account? *After* the decision I can say, See what I was preprogrammed to decide! But this in no way or degree helped me to make the decision. It was an idle retrospective application of a useless doctrine." (OT, 19; cf. CA, 51–52; IO, 373)

One might question the use of a "pragmatic" criterion of truth in this way. But even granting such a criterion for the sake of argument, there are problems with this argument. Determinism would have a very definite practical meaning for anyone *who had sufficient knowledge* of the past circumstances and laws of nature affecting the behavior of others. It would mean that he or she could predict the behavior of those others with certainty. That the doctrine has no such practical consequences for persons like us with limited knowledge is irrelevant, since we can define conditions under which it would have definite (and some would say unfortunate) practical consequences. Another point worth making is that determinism has indirect practical implications for persons like us with limited knowledge. A believer in determinism might be led more readily to a pessimistic view of life, or might become an atheist because he could not reconcile his belief in determinism with beliefs about his worth as a human being or about a loving and good God. These are the sorts of pragmatic consequences of belief in determinism that interested James, for example, and he did not believe they were necessarily irrational or illogical consequences for someone who believed in determinism. It would appear then that determinism is not a doctrine lacking practical significance,

either at the scientific level of prediction of human behavior or at the Jamesian
level of philosophical or religious commitment.

I may be misinterpreting this pragmatic argument against determinism which
Hartshorne has often used. But if so, I suspect many others will misinterpret it
in similar ways. At the very least Hartshorne should do more to clarify what he
means by it.

7. THEOLOGICAL ISSUES AND COMPATIBILISM

(i) *Theological Determinism.* We now turn to theological issues about free will
and determinism which obviously loom large in Hartshorne's writings. No claim
has seemed more pivotal or self evident to him than the claim that God could not
have created a strictly determined world. The reasoning behind this claim seems
to be the following.

> **(T)** *If God had created a strictly determined world, then no creature in that world
> would have free will. No creature would be ultimately responsible for the good or
> evil created; the ultimate responsibility would lie with God.* (DR, 138–39; OT,
> 10–11; IO, 351, 367; CA, 315)

From these assertions a host of theological problems are said to follow. Given a
strictly determined world, God would be ultimately responsible for the world's
evils, raising questions about divine power and goodness. (DR, 138) There
would be further questions about the justice and mercy of a being who would
punish us for our sins. (OT, 10–11) And there would be more subtle questions
about such a God being the God of love. Hartshorne tells us that he learned early
in life from his clergyman father to believe that "a God of love would respond
to the freedom of the creatures, would expect them to make their own decisions,
as a good parent with his or her children." (FU, 1)

Let us define theological determinism as the view that

> **(TD)** *God has created a strictly determined world (in the sense of "strictly
> determined" defined in section 2).*

In the light of the above arguments, Hartshorne believes that theological
determinism is necessarily false. For, given the claims of **T**, a being which
created a strictly determined world would not be a being of unsurpassable power
and goodness, of justice and mercy, and of love. Such a being could not
therefore be *God* in the sense of Anselm's "being than which none greater can
be conceived."

The claims of **T** are pivotal to this argument and I want to focus on them.
While Hartshorne has given a great deal of attention in his writings to drawing
out the diverse implications of **T** for theology, he has not given nearly as much

attention to the claims of **T** themselves. He proceeds almost as if the claims of **T** are self evident, and many persons would indeed be inclined to say that they are self evident. But the complexity of recent debates between "incompatibilists" and "compatibilists" about free will should make us wary. If the claims of **T** are true, we must ask why they are so.

Why, if at all, is it true that "if God had created a strictly determined world, then no creature in that world would have free will"? (Call this first claim of **T**, "**T1**".) Hartshorne has answered in a number of ways. He has said, for example, that to suppose God strictly determines "life's setting for each of us is to suppose that only one person really acts, God himself." (NT, 122) Elsewhere he says "the infinity of God's power would imply the sheer irrelevance of all creaturely choices" (NT, 74), and in another place, "if the past . . . determines what happens our notion of deciding is illusory." (OT, 15)

I think such claims are pointing to something important. But they will not suffice as they stand to establish **T1**. Those who believe that free will is compatible with determinism will argue that these claims are too strong and cannot be taken literally. Modern compatibilists would argue, for example, that deciding could still take place in a determined world. To decide is to form an intention as the result of practical reasoning; and this would still go on. Distinctions between deciding and remaining undecided, or deliberating and acting hastily, would still matter; they would not be "illusory." Nor would creaturely choices be "irrelevant" in a determined world. If God determined that many events in the world would come about *through* these choices and not otherwise, then they would be relevant. Nor would it be correct to say that creatures do not "act" in a determined world. To act is to bring something about in accordance with one's desires, beliefs and intentions, and beings would still be doing this in a determined world.

But, of course, what Hartshorne means is that creatures would not "really" be acting, deciding, and choosing in a strictly determined world, where the "really" has some honorific sense, and does not simply mean that creatures would not literally "do" these things in some ordinary sense. But what is this honorific sense of "really" acting or deciding? I think it can only be spelled out by focussing on the second two claims of **T**, namely, that in a determined world "no creature would be ultimately responsible for the good or evil created" (**T2**) and "the ultimate responsibility would lie with God" (**T3**). "Really" acting and deciding for Hartshorne and other libertarians is acting and deciding in a way that we have ultimate responsibility for what we do and decide.

But what does "ultimate responsibility" mean in these claims? This pivotal question needs to be addressed with more care than Hartshorne has given it to date in his writings. Without a clearer account of this notion, his arguments and those of other libertarians for the incompatibility of free will and determinism remain incomplete. In the remainder of this section, I want to suggest an answer to this question about ultimate responsibility and discuss its implications for Hartshorne's view.

(ii) *Ultimate Responsibility and Control.* I think the idea Hartshorne is reaching for, but has not adequately explicated in his writings, is the idea of a free action's being under the *ultimate control* of the agent's will. To get a grip on this notion we may quote another philosopher who has pointed toward it without also adequately explicating it. In his well known essay "Moral Luck,"[7] Thomas Nagel says, "If one cannot be responsible for consequences of one's acts due to factors beyond one's control, . . . or for properties of temperament not subject to one's will, or for the circumstances that pose one's moral choices, then how can one be responsible even for the stripped-down acts of the will itself, if *they* are the product of . . . circumstances outside of the will's control?" The idea is this. For ultimate responsibility, not only must the action be under the control of the agent's will, but also the control of the will itself cannot be "the product of . . . circumstances outside the will's control." Circumstances that influence the will to go one way rather than another must also be under the control of the will. This would be *ultimate* control. It is an odd idea. One may legitimately suspect that explicating it might lead to a regress or some other confusion. Yet I think it is the idea that Hartshorne's **T2** and **T3** require and that all incompatibilists need. John Hospers uses the same language as Nagel to state what the denial of it would come to. "When we plumb deeply . . . into the ultimate causes (what Hume called the 'secret springs') of human conduct, we shall become aware that people are what they are and do what they do because of circumstances outside the control of their wills."[8] For *ultimate* responsibility, libertarians must respond, this must not be so.

This gives us a rough idea of what is needed. "Ultimate responsibility," in the sense required by Hartshorne, Nagel, and other thinkers with incompatibilist intuitions, requires some sort of "ultimate control of the will" over choice or action. But many pitfalls attend a more careful analysis of such a notion—if one is possible at all. It is fair to say that, despite all that has been written about free will by contemporary philosophers, the analysis of this notion of ultimate control still remains in a formative state.[9] The following analysis is not complete. It depends, for example, upon more primitive notions of "intentional action," "explanation," and others which require more discussion than I can give them here. But I think it points in the right direction. And we can use it to make a final assessment of the claims of Hartshorne's **T** and of his incompatibilism.

We first define a notion of "control" of the agent's will over action (as opposed to the more complicated notion of "ultimate" control).

(C_A) *An action is* under the control of the agent's will *at a time t if and only if the action occurs at t only if the agent performs it intentionally at t and the action fails to occur at t only if the agent refrains from (or omits) performing it intentionally at t.*

In short, the action is "sensitive," as to its occurring or not occurring, to the voluntary or intentional influence of the agent. Clearly, this definition requires an account of intentional action (and omission), of which there are many in the literature, and this task is beyond us here. Suffice it to say that any number of current accounts of intentional action (e.g., those of Brand, L. Davis, Searle, Sellars, and others) which in themselves do not beg the question disputed by compatibilists and incompatibilists, would suit these definitions. Indeed, "control" as defined by C_A is compatible with determinism; it is "ultimate control" that will not be compatible with determinism.

We now expand upon C_A to give an account of an agent's control over states or events in general in terms of the agent's control over actions.

(C_E) *Its being the case that p is under the control of the agent's will at t if and only if there is an action (or set of actions) which (or each member of which) is under the control of the agent's will at t in the sense of* C_A *and which brings it about or causes it to be the case that p.*

This definition requires an account of event causation and of the manner in which actions can bring about or cause other events. In terms of it and C_A we can give a preliminary definition of ultimate control as follows.

(UC*) *An action A is under the* ultimate control *of the agent's will at t if and only if (a) the action A is under the control of the agent's will at t in the sense of* C_A *and (b) any set of conditions (states, events, laws of nature . . .) that would conjointly explain or prevent the occurrence of any exercise of the control of the agent's will at t over A is also relevantly under the control of the agent's will at t (in the sense of* C_E*).*

What does clause (b) add? Roughly, it means that the agent not only has intentional control over A at t, but also intentional control at t over *any circumstances that would explain or prevent the exercise of the agent's control over A at t.* In short, the agent has control not only over the action, but over the ultimate causes, or "springs of action."

One's immediate reaction is likely to be that this is a perfectly outrageous and unattainable requirement. But let us not jump to conclusions. We are still in the process of understanding it. The above definition requires an account of several further notions. By an "exercise of the control of the agent's will over A at t" is meant "either the agent's intentionally performing A at t or intentionally refraining from performing A at t." A set of conditions "prevents the occurrence of an event" means that the members of the set "conjointly provide a logically sufficient condition for the non-occurrence of the event.'' A set of conditions "explains" the occurrence of an event if its members conjointly provide an answer to the question "Why did the event occur rather than not?" This is meant to cover both explanations in terms of causes and explanations in terms of reasons. But the notion of explanation involved here is another that clearly needs further attention. Finally, by saying in clause (b) that the set of conditions is "relevantly" under the control of the agent's will I mean that the agent's control over these conditions is relevant to whether they do or do not explain or prevent the exercise of the agent's will. In other words, the agent can alter them in a way that would produce a relevantly different outcome (intentionally doing A *or* doing otherwise).

UC* is defective, as it stands, however. There is a potential regress. Note that the control of clause (a) over the action (call it "control$_1$") is not the same as the control of clause (b) over conditions that might influence the exercise of control$_1$. (Call clause (b) control "control $_2$".) **UC*** might be satisfied so that the exercise of control$_1$ is under the control of the agent's will, but the exercise of control$_2$ is not. Yet, to state that control$_2$ is under the control of the agent's will in terms of **UC*** would be to introduce another control$_3$, which must also be under the control of the agent's will, and so on *ad infinitum*. To account for this, let us say of any such sequence of controls, control$_1$ . . . control$_k$, that any control$_i$ in the sequence *depends* upon itself and each of the controls higher numbered than it, control$_{i+1}$ . . . control$_k$. We can then say that **(G)** the control of the agent's will over A at t is *grounded* upon any set of conditions which would explain or prevent the occurrence of any exercise of the control of the agent's will on which the control of the agent's will over A at t *depends*. We then have a final definition of ultimate control.

> **(UC)** *An action A is under the* ultimate control *of the agent's will at t if and only if (a) the action A is under the control of the agent's will at t in the sense of* C_A *and (b) any set of conditions upon which the control of the agent's will over A at t is grounded is also relevantly under the control of the agent's will at t in the sense of* C_E.

This would be ultimate control over action *and* the "springs of action." Note that if control over the action were determined by antecedent circumstances and laws of nature, condition (b) would fail, since these circumstances and laws would explain the occurrence of the action and prevent its non-occurrence and they would not be under the control of the agent's will at the time of action. But indeterminism is not something libertarians want for its own sake. It is a by-product of their desire for ultimate control.

(iii) *Self-creation.* Let us now return to Hartshorne's incompatibilism and the claims of **T**. I want to suggest that the "ultimate responsibility" of **T** presupposes "ultimate control" in the sense of **UC**. Thus, it is the incompatibility of ultimate control and determinism that underlies the claim of **T** that "free will could not exist in a determined world."

This suggests two final questions that Hartshorne has only partially answered. Why are ultimate responsibility and control so important? Can the condition of ultimate control really be satisfied by any coherent incompatibilist account of free will? For Hartshorne's answer to the first of these questions we must return to his notion of free will as self creation (thesis **III** of section 2). Our dignity as self creators is enhanced if we have ultimate control over at least some of our choices and actions. For then what we create can be explained by our wills *and by nothing else* that is not in turn explained by our wills. The genuinely free will is therefore *causa sola et finalis*; its action is indispensable, decisive, and *underived*. As Hartshorne says, quoting Bergson, it is this fact about it which is the source of our dignity. (LP, 232)

I believe this answer is essentially correct, though it needs more defense. But can one make sense of this ultimate or "underived" control of the will that ultimate responsibility requires? The condition **UC** is exceptionally strong, and I do not think anything less strong will do (for a variety of reasons, not all canvassed here). One may thus suspect with some justification that any theory of free will presupposing ultimate control in the sense of **UC** would be confused or mysterious. Compatibilists certainly think so. Many of them hold that libertarian or incompatibilist accounts of free will and free action are essentially mysterious. My own view is that an intelligible libertarian account of free will consistent with theses **I**, **II**, and **III** of section 2 and hence with Hartshorne's view can be formulated which satisfies the condition **UC** and hence the requirement of ultimate responsibility, without appealing to obscure or mysterious forms of agency or causation. I try to defend such a theory in a recent book which is mentioned in a previous note (see note 5). This theory goes well beyond anything Hartshorne has said on the subject, but I believe it preserves the spirit of his view of free will as self creation, if not the letter.

8. Conclusion

In summary, I have said the following for and against Hartshorne's treatment of the problem of free will. He is right to point out (a) that a priori arguments for determinism do not work, (b) that modern physics no longer requires us to think deterministically, (c) that indeterminists need not deny that all events have causes in an important sense, (d) that mere randomness or arbitrariness is not the only alternative to determinism, (e) that rational choice or action does not require a strongest motive, (f) that responsibility for choices or actions does not require that they be determined by character and motives, (g) that theories of unconscious motivation can be reconciled with indeterminist theories of free will, (h) that if creatures have free will, God could not have created a causally determined world, and (i) that the right model for free will is a form of self creativity or self creation. If these points are correct, they amply justify the statement made in section 2 that Hartshorne has had as many valuable and indispensable insights about free will as any philosopher of his generation.

I have criticized Hartshorne for not being clear about (a) how, if at all, quantum theory, or indeterminism in physics, is related to free will, (b) how the supervenience of human experience and activity upon statistical physical laws can be explained without mystery or obscurity, (c) how certain problems about the rationality of undetermined free choices—especially the problem of dual rational self control—can be solved. I also criticized two of his most important arguments against determinism, (d) the argument that determinism would undermine the distinction between past and future, and the idea of temporal succession, and (e) the argument from a pragmatic criterion of truth. Finally, (f) I criticized some of Hartshorne's arguments for the claim that free will is incompatible with determinism. He often claims that in a strictly determined world, creaturely choices would be "irrelevant," "illusory," or that agents would not "really" be choosing or acting. These claims, I think, are too strong and would rightly be rejected by compatibilists. To answer modern compatibilists one must go beyond what Hartshorne has said in his writings by spelling out the notions of ultimate responsibility and ultimate control over actions by the will. It is such ultimate responsibility and control that would be missing in a world in which all choices or actions were determined by nature or by God.

ROBERT H. KANE

DEPARTMENT OF PHILOSOPHY
THE UNIVERSITY OF TEXAS AT AUSTIN
JUNE 1986

NOTES

1. DR: *The Divine Relativity* (Yale, 1948); NT: *A Natural Theology for Our Time* (Open Court, 1967); MV: *Man's Vision of God* (Anchor, 1964); LP: *The Logic of Perfection and Other Essays* (Open Court, 1962); RS: *Reality as Social Process* (Free Press, 1953); OT: *Omnipotence and Other Theological Mistakes* (SUNY, 1984); CA: *Creativity in American Philosophy* (SUNY, 1984); IO: *Insights and Oversights of Great Thinkers* (SUNY, 1983); BH: *Beyond Humanism* (Willett, Clark, 1937); CS: *Creative Synthesis and Philosophic Method* (SCM Press, 1970); CN: "Contingency in the New Era

of Metaphysics" (*Journal of Philosophy*, 29, 1932); FU: "Freedom as Universal Principle" (Unpublished).

2. For discussion of the issues, see J. A. Wheeler and W. H. Zurek (eds.) *Quantum Theory and Measurement* (Princeton: Princeton University Press, 1983). The reference to Aspect is from Paul Davies, *Superforce* (Simon & Schuster, 1984).

3. See my "Nature, Plenitude and Sufficient Reason," *American Philosophical Quarterly* 13 (1976):23–33. And "Principles of Reason," *Erkenntnis* 24 (1986): 115–136.

4. Anscombe, *Causality and Determination* (Cambridge University Press, 1971). Cf. also Peter van Inwagen, *An Essay on Free Will* (Oxford: Clarendon Press, 1983, pp. 4–5).

5. R. Kane, *Free Will and Values* (SUNY Press, 1985). See especially chapter 4.

6. Ibid., chapter 6.

7. Reprinted in G. Watson, *Free Will* (Oxford, 1982), p. 183. Also in Nagel, *Mortal Questions* (Cambridge: Cambridge University Press, 1978).

8. Hospers, *Human Conduct* (New York: Harcourt, Brace & World, 1961), p. 521.

9. There are some efforts. See for example, Paul Gomberg, "Free Will as Ultimate Responsibility," *American Philosophical Quarterly* 15 (1975):205–12.

B. PHILOSOPHY OF RELIGION

7

H. Tristram Engelhardt, Jr.

NATURAL THEOLOGY AND BIOETHICS

I. INTRODUCTION: THE ROLE OF THE DIVINE PERSPECTIVE

The perspective or standpoint of God is important for other than religious reasons. It is the point of view of the best advantaged knower and the best informed valuer. To know from the viewpoint of God is to know without the limitations of particular finite knowers. God's knowledge is uniquely advantaged because He knows all perspectives there are to know, and because He creates all there is to know. Evaluations or moral judgments from God's point of view weigh all possible considerations. God is the actual ideal knower, observer, and moral judge. It is for this reason that the divine standpoint has played such a large role both indirectly and directly in accounts of explanation and evaluation. Though the standpoint of God has generally offered a privileged epistemic and evaluative perspective throughout the history of philosophy, this role became pronounced in the rationalist philosophies of René Descartes, Benedict Spinoza, and Gottfried Wilhelm Leibniz through their attempts to secure certainty in knowledge and to understand the presumptions involved in claims to true knowledge. As Spinoza argued in "De Mente" of his *Ethics*, reason is such that to know things is to know them under a form of eternity because they are included in the divine nature.[1] Or as Leibniz stated in "The Monadology," God is "*Knowledge*, which contains the detail of ideas. . . ."[2] For them as well as others the standpoint of God is important because it is the viewpoint from which idiosyncrasy has been maximally set aside. It is the lynchpin and cardinal standpoint for understanding objectivity or intersubjectivity in evaluations and explanations. "The object of religion as well as of philosophy is eternal truth in its objectivity, God and nothing but God . . ."[3] as Hegel put it. "The esoteric study of God and identity, as of cognitions, and notions, is philosophy itself."[4] Philosophy and, in an extended sense, natural theology are the higher truth of religion. The standpoint of God, as rationally conceived, affords the ultimate relation between the knower and the known, between the moral judge and the canons of morality.

As Charles Hartshorne shows, the divine standpoint is of importance, even if God is not omniscient or omnipotent and is instead constrained by the limitations of His free choices and the choices of His creatures.[5] With regard to knowledge, "God is the all-inclusive reality; his knowing, accordingly, must likewise be all-inclusive; ours, by contrast, is fragmentary, as our whole being is fragmentary; much remains outside us as knowers."[6] The same is the case with regard to evaluations. "We are intermediate and secondary makers of value, intermediate benefactors; are we not likewise intermediate and secondary recipients of value, intermediate beneficiaries? The supreme source, and as well the supreme result, of the entire process of value-making is, I suggest, the divine life, in its originative and its consummatory phases. . . ."[7] God knows most truly and judges best, even if He is not all-powerful and all-knowing.

Because the standpoint of God is so important to philosophical reflections on objectivity and intersubjectivity in evaluation and explanation, it has continued to play a role even after the Enlightenment and the partial abandonment of metaphysical reflections on God, freedom, and immortality occasioned by the arguments of David Hume, Immanuel Kant, and others. It is not just that the existence of God was maintained as a postulate of pure practical reason by philosophers such as Kant, but that a standpoint equivalent to that of the Deity has continued to be invoked both explicitly and implicitly in attempts to characterize true knowledge and correct moral judgment. Ideally advantaged knowers, ideal observers, observers who are fully informed concerning the consequences for others of possible choices, hypothetical moral decision-makers and hypothetical contractors are to a greater or lesser extent put in the standpoint previously explicitly accorded to the Deity. To take a rational point of view, to appeal to a point of view that sets aside particular historical, cultural, and individual biases, is to assume, as an element of intellectual reflection and analysis, the standpoint of God, whether or not one holds that the Deity exists. In this sense the rationalists were right: the concept of the Deity is central to the very notion of knowing truly and judging rightly.

In addition to providing the example of, or metaphor for, undistorted explanation and evaluation, natural theology offers a foil against which one can test the fabric of actual religious traditions. Prior to the development of Christian orthodoxy, natural theological reflections existed independently of a generally established theological orthodoxy. However, after Proclus, natural theology was domesticated in the sense that it was generally developed within the limits of Christian and, in a more extended sense, Judeo-Christian orthodoxy. Even philosophers such as Spinoza, who came into conflict with their religious traditions, remained committed to traditional elements of the Judeo-Christian account of

God such as omnipotence and omniscience. As a result of these circumstances, the West lost a source from which it could draw radically new perspectives regarding the Deity, and, derivatively, regarding Being, as was available even from Proclus through his influence on the Pseudo-Dionysus. There was no longer an independent scholarly tradition from which one could judge or criticize the anthropomorphisms of particular concrete religious traditions.

The domestication of natural theology during the Middle Ages and the weakening interest in natural theology after the Enlightenment have implications not only for the development of theologies within particular religious communities, but for philosophical reflection as well. In the absence of the ideal of a non-human perspective, ideal observers and hypothetical contractors are often overly bound to the particular interests of humans and the finite purposes of human culture. Invoking the divine perspective provides a protection against making man the measure of all things when one attempts to understand the character of ideal knowledge and value claims. Natural theology, by providing a God-centered portrayal of being, fashioned outside of particular religious traditions, can offer a view of values and of being with reference to a non-human perspective, that of God, in terms of which the importance of human values and even of the human race can be judged. Though human values and the human species must remain prominent in any account of morality and/or the universe, still there is a need to realize that the human species is, as all species, transient. Moreover, the particular characteristics of humans and their aspirations are at least in part a function of the results of evolution, a process that will set aside those particular characteristics in the same way it established them. "All individuals are dispensable; in the long run so are species. If nature has ends, the ends transcend 'self-interest' and even species interest. It is selfishness, conceit, and lack either of observation or of imagination that accounts for our failure to see this, for the facts are there."[8] God endures and individual humans, even the human species, come into existence and pass away.

These considerations lead to an evaluational perspective that values human life but does not make it central to final moral judgments. If humans are the only persons in the universe in the sense of moral agents, then we are of unique worth, but our singularity as a species would only be a contingent fact. There is no logical basis for excluding the existence of multitudes of species of persons spread through the vastness of the universe. In any event, the value of humans would not be derived from the idiosyncratic biological characteristics we have as a particular species, but rather because of our capacity as moral agents to act on values and to contribute experience and meaning to God.

[W]ithout us God would not be the same as he is. He would exist, and existence would be generically what it is now, namely, the self-identity of his all-participating life. But it is obvious that the details of the participation would be different if the things to be participated in were different, and that thus the divine dependence and independence are inseparable aspects of one mutual relationship.[9]

In summary, though humans are not of essential importance to God or the universe, humans as well as all life are of enduring significance. Still, all else being equal, the contribution of moral agents who can experience the world in a rich and deep sense will be greater than that of less developed and less complex experiencers of the world. We do not all equally contribute to God.

The God's-eye view is heuristic. It can suggest new ways in which we can understand ourselves as persons and as humans, and suggest ways in which we critically reassess our accepted religious and cultural presuppositions. Through his work in natural theology, Charles Hartshorne has shown how reality can be convincingly portrayed in terms novel to and corrective of inadequacies in traditional Judeo-Christian theological reflection. In particular, he has laid the foundations for a better appreciation of the significance of human life in the scope of things. Here I will restrict myself to one set of the implications of Hartshorne's work, from an area he has begun to explore during the last decade and a half: bioethics.

II. BIOETHICS: A GOD'S-EYE VIEW

Though Hartshorne has addressed a number of bioethical issues within his natural theological framework, one of the most interesting is that of abortion because it illustrates the special contribution made from a theological perspective. As Hartshorne has correctly observed, there is not an unambiguous sense to being alive, protecting life, or respecting the sacredness of life.[10] At the very least it is necessary to distinguish mere animal life from the life of persons. When one compares the life of sponges, fish, reptiles, cattle, dolphins, and great apes, one sees an increasing capacity to have pleasure, to experience pain, and to fashion plans. The life of great apes has greater worth, all else being equal, than the life of reptiles, fish, or sponges. The moral life of persons, as already noted, is even more complex and richer than that of other entities, leading to a variant of the great chain of being. This set of distinctions is important in understanding the significance for God of life in the universe. It is also of importance in understanding the stages through which human life develops, for the distinctions used in order to characterize different levels of non-human life can be imposed on human ontogeny. There are stages in the development of humans when human life is present prior to the development of human personal life. As Hartshorne has pointed out in comparing human embryos to human persons, "they [embryos] cannot [have] recognizably human feelings, much less human thoughts, and cannot compare with the feelings of a porpoise or chimpanzee in level of consciousness.''[11] As a consequence, they will contribute less to God than normal adults of other primate species. The differences lie not just in capacities for experiences but in capacities for the moral life. Our relations with moral agents have greater moral significance for us and for God than our relations with other entities. These distinctions can be elaborated without an appeal to a theological framework, but rather through considering what is involved in being a moral subject or object.[12]

Here one finds some of the most interesting developments of Hartshorne's views bearing on ethical issues: the character of relations between persons and fetuses. He argues that our relations with human fetuses must be judged, all else being equal, to be on a par with our relations to instances of life with a similar level of organization. "In sober truth, how can one love a fetus, by all evidence with less actual intelligence than a cat, *as one loves oneself*?"[13] The answer is, all else being equal, one cannot, though of course one can regard a fetus very highly because of the person it is likely to become. Moreover, one can conclude that actions against fetuses, all else being equal, are not equivalent to actions against normal adult mammals. As a result, Hartshorne holds that fetuses do not have robust rights not to be killed.

> The reader will not perhaps see why I am negatively impressed by the idea that the proper conclusion concerning the 'rights' of the 'innocent' in the womb is to be arrived at by looking with horror at moving pictures of a living, dying, or newly dead embryo. There are probably many people rather than few who would have trouble eating meat if they had spent an hour or two in some giant slaughter-house. The cattle also are 'innocent', and they may well suffer on their way to our tables, as much as, or more than, aborted fetuses. Cattle, too, are intricate, wonderfully organized creatures.[14]

It should be noted that Hartshorne does not conclude from those considerations that one is morally obliged to be a vegetarian. Moreover, it should be noted that all of these arguments are set within a consideration of God's experience of being, a point to which we will return below.

Hartshorne does conclude that the social role played by human infants may be sufficient to give them special moral standing, though they in many respects are more similar to fetuses than to adult humans. "I think it is clearly false that an infant has all the value of an adult or even of a normal year-old child. The 'beginning of a human life' is not, by any evidence, the actuality of a being on the human level of value."[15] It appears to be their role in a social nexus that conveys to infants their special importance.

> [T]here is no absolute rational proof that infanticide ought to be legally prohibited or viewed with the same horror as murder in the universally accepted sense. But our society has somehow made the decision to extend the connotations of "murder" or

utterly wrong homicide to infants that have by natural forces been freed from the womb. To tamper with this decision is to weaken the support of tradition for our moral and legal structures.[16]

As a result, Hartshorne, on the basis of social considerations, imputes to infants many of the rights possessed by adults, though the infants do not have a claim to those rights, in and of themselves. The result is that human life can be characterized under at least three major rubrics: (1) mere human biological life, (2) mere human biological life to which some of the rights of persons have been imputed (e.g., infants), and (3) human personal life in the strict sense.

This hierarchy reflects not just the intrinsic differences between a moral subject and a moral object, but also the significance that such entities have for God. Adult dolphins contribute more to the life of the Deity than human embryos, since the experience of the world by adult dolphins, great apes, and similar higher mammals is richer and more complex and nuanced than that of embryos, whether human or not. Because God knows the world, and therefore knows the experience of the entities in the world, the character of their experience contributes to God. The loss of the experience of an embryo will thus be, all else being equal, much less than the loss due to the death of a mature adult mammal.[17] Other considerations must also be taken into account, such as the variety and composition of the experiences and experiencers in the world. The variety in the world will be open to experience by the entities in the world, and thus contribute to and shape their experiences. The more complex and intricate the constellation of experiences in the world, the richer will be the contribution to God from the world. Since Hartshorne's arguments regarding divine relativity and sympathy lead us to conclude that the Deity depends on us and suffers and experiences with us, choices made in terms of what is morally right or wrong in the sense of violating rights or fulfilling obligations to other finite entities can be supplemented when they would otherwise be inconclusive. The character of one's life singly and with others can also be judged in terms of its contribution to the life of God. We can then ask what composition of experiences in the world is likely to compass the greatest range of diversity within the greatest amount of unity constitutable by the affinity of the elements of the experience. If no one's rights are violated in preventing the development of a fetus into an adult, and if the result of such interventions is a richer, more pleasing set of experiences for God, then one has a natural theological argument to sustain a wide range of choices to employ contraception and abortion.[18] From this perspective, their use may become not simply permissible, but laudatory. The proper religious choice will have been understood in terms of aesthetic values, in the sense of what is beautiful for God, not just in terms of moral obligations to finite beings. This special sense of aesthetic values can serve to underscore interest in the composition of value in the world as a whole.

One can illustrate this point by means of two examples, one on the micro-, the other on the macro-level. Consider a graduate student in theology who becomes pregnant while she is completing her dissertation. Her adviser will soon retire and leave the university and she must choose between the pregnancy and completing her dissertation, which is likely to make a major contribution to the field. In considering whether or not to have an abortion, she should in part weigh the difference between a world in which she (1) brings the fetus to term and never completes the dissertation, or (2) has an abortion, completes the dissertation, and plans to get pregnant again two years in the future. By appealing to God-centered considerations, her decision could be justified in terms of which of the two likely futures would realize the greatest richness of goods not only for her but for God.

Similarly, one could compare two different ways of approaching the needs of a developing country. One approach would attempt to increase the population to the point of maximum economic advantage for the country as a whole, the other would promote contraception and abortion, not just in order to maximize the quality of life of individual citizens, but also to maintain sufficient land and resources so as to preserve endangered species of plants and animals, which will then be open for enjoyment not only by residents of that country, but others throughout the world. In fact, a variety of floral and faunal species may itself be a contribution to the life of God. The choice to pursue a population and development policy aimed at supporting the quality of survival not just of humans but of non-human populations could thus have a God-centered basis.

In both pairs of options, not merely ethical but also aesthetic issues would be central to decision-making. The status of fetuses is important to judging the graduate student's decision, just as the protection of humans from starvation through the avoidance of over-population would also be an important factor in the choice of a population policy. But these considerations may not be sufficient in and of themselves to determine a final answer. Abstract moral considerations tend to provide, as Hegel has emphasized, only general restraints, not the basis for a concrete moral life. However, attempts to compare the consequences of different moral choices for God allow aesthetic criteria to suggest decisions in areas where moral constraints give latitude without guidance. Also, in seeking a world that will be most pleasing, most beautiful for God, one is brought to consider the cosmos as a whole. The appeal to the standpoint of the Deity thus broadens and deepens the process of evaluating consequences.

Utilitarians will recognize a similarity between this approach and that of a wide range of consequentialist accounts of moral decision-making. The similarity must be acknowledged; it is in fact with a consideration of the basis of that similarity that this essay began. To invoke the ultimate vantage point from which one can compare consequences and assess the significance of different possible worlds is to invoke, at least as an intellectual possibility, the standpoint of God. God's viewpoint is the position from which one could ultimately judge the comparability of different pleasures and pains, happinesses and sufferings, and weigh the consequences of their experience in different possible worlds. Of course, if God exists, the significance of such suffering and happiness takes on cosmic, enduring meaning. But even absent a decision on that point, the standpoint of the Deity is an intellectual device that can be forwarded in the attempt to choose among competing possible avenues of action.[19]

Invoking the Deity's standpoint has the advantage of enriching the perspective of the ideal observer invoked in much of moral theory, in that one must impute to the Deity not only concerns with rights and with moral goods in a narrow sense, but also a concern for the beauty and composition of the universe as a whole. Though concerns with aesthetic non-moral goods can be made a part of most consequentialist calculi, invoking the divine perspective is a prophylaxis against at least those forms of monistic consequentialism that attempt to reduce moral concerns to a mere calculus of human pleasures and pains. The Deity's perspective is plausibly not only broad but deep. It must include not only considerations of all involved, but of all the ways in which one can compare and appreciate all involved. The final judgment on the mosaic of experiences and experiencers who constitute the cosmos must in this sense be aesthetic, it must involve a choice among the contrasting possible beauties of alternative universes.

III. BIOETHICS RECONSIDERED

The great preponderance of theological reflections on bioethical issues has been elaborated within the embrace of particular religious traditions, which presuppose particular divine revelations. That is as would be expected, given the need of institutionalized religion to give guidance to particular communities of believers regarding the challenges engendered by modern biomedical advances. Hartshorne has offered a natural theological perspective through which such approaches can be critically reappraised and seen not only within a larger philosophical, but a broader theological, context. As has been noted, this leads to a God-centered understanding of bioethical dilemmas that gives great importance, but not singular standing, to human life. It introduces robustly aesthetic considerations, which may provide ways through which we can better understand the importance of bioethical decisions regarding ecological issues. If that were to occur, one would be able to realize the breadth implied in the term bioethics, the ethics of bios. There are, as this suggests, important implications in Hartshorne's work for bioethics, which are yet to be realized. Even when a revealed theological perspective sets final parameters and full content to theological understandings of bioethical issues, Hartshorne's approach will have provided an independent intellectual foil that has been absent since Christianity became the established religion of the Roman Empire.

Hartshorne has argued that "God acquires novelty by acquiring us as novel individuals. Our function is then to be novel. . . ."[20] Hartshorne through his work has fulfilled this function. He has helped us to appraise old issues anew and to see how we can approach new issues in terms of the enduring concerns of natural theology. Bioethics has a great deal to draw from his work.

H. TRISTRAM ENGELHARDT, JR.

CENTER OF ETHICS, MEDICINE AND PUBLIC ISSUES
BAYLOR COLLEGE OF MEDICINE
MARCH 1988

NOTES

1. "De natura Rationis est, res sub quadam aeternitatis specie percipere. De natura enim Rationis est, res ut necessarias, et non ut contingentes contemplari. Hanc autem rerum necessitatem vere, hoc est ut in se esto, percipit. Sed haec rerum necessitas est ipsa Dei aeternaae naturae necessitas. . . ." "De Mente," Propositio XLIV, Corollarium II. Benedict Spinoza, *Opera Quotquot Reperta Sunt*, 3rd ed., vol. 1 (Hague: Martinus Nijhoff, 1914), p. 110.

2. Philip P. Wiener (ed.), "The Monadology," *Leibniz Selections* (New York: Charles Scribner's Sons, 1951), #48, p. 542.

3. Georg Wilhelm Friedrich Hegel, *Lectures on the Philosophy of Religion*, vol. 1, trans. E. B. Speirs and J. B. Sanderson (New York: Humanities Press, 1974), p. 19.

4. Hegel, *Hegel's Philosophy of Mind*, trans. William Wallace (Oxford: Clarendon Press, 1971), sec. 573, p. 313.

5. Charles Hartshorne, *Omnipotence and Other Theological Mistakes* (Albany: State University of New York, 1984).

6. _____, *A Natural Theology for Our Time* (La Salle, Ill.: Open Court, 1967), p. 12.

7. _____, *The Divine Relativity* (New Haven: Yale University Press, 1964), p. 59.

8. _____, "Foundations for a Humane Ethics," in *On the Fifth Day: Animal Rights and Human Ethics*, ed. R. K. Morris and M. W. Fox (Washington, D.C.: Acropolis Books, 1978), p. 157.

9. _____, *Man's Vision of God* (Chicago: Willett, Clark & Co., 1941), p. 282.

10. _____, "Concerning Abortion: An Attempt at a Rational View," *The Christian Century* (Jan. 21, 1981):43.

11. _____, "Scientific and Religious Aspects of Bioethics," in *Theology and Bioethics*, ed. E. E. Shelp (Dordrecht: D. Reidel, 1985), p. 31.

12. H. Tristram Engelhardt, Jr., *The Foundations of Bioethics* (New York: Oxford, 1986), pp. 216–20.

13. Hartshorne, "Scientific and Religious Aspects of Bioethics," p. 35.

14. Ibid., p. 37.

15. Ibid., p. 32.

16. Ibid., p. 43.

17. One would also have to take into consideration whether there is a need for additional persons in the world, and if so, whether that need will be met by allowing some other embryo to develop into a human person, so as to contribute the experiences of a new person.

18. Hartshorne examined the issue of population control in an essay originally published in 1955 and reprinted in a collection of essays in 1962. There he argued that "[s]cience does make it possible to provide for an increasing population, but only with certain qualifications. The population growth must not be too fast and in crowded areas it may be that no growth, or even a decrease, would be the only, or the best, way to avoid misery." *The Logic of Perfection and Other Essays in Neoclassical Metaphysics* (La Salle, Ill.: Open Court, 1962), p. 301.

19. Appeal to the standpoint of God is a device through which one can attempt to resolve moral and aesthetic controversies when the participants in the controversy share sufficiently common understandings of how to characterize hierarchies of goods and harms and of the canons of beauty. Insofar as such common hierarchies are not available, controversies in ethics and aesthetics will in fact not be soluble by conclusive rational argument. See Engelhardt, *The Foundations of Bioethics*, pp. 23–49. However, the appeal to the viewpoint of God will still have heuristic force in pointing to the desideratum of a resolution in terms of a perspective that could weigh all consequences from a univocal perspective.

If it is the case, as I have argued elsewhere (*The Foundations of Bioethics*, pp. 32–49), that one cannot in fact establish from what moral perspective disinterested observers must regard reality, the same will hold with respect to specifying by reason alone the moral and aesthetic perspective of God. Hence, a number of what may appear as bizarre impossibilities must be entertained until a moral and aesthetic content can be specified for the mind of God. As a result, all of the questions addressed in this article that require a content-full answer will remain open, absent an appeal to revelation. In these matters, this author, as a Catholic, submits to the teachings of the Holy Fathers.

20. Hartshorne, *The Logic of Perfection*, p. 262.

8

John B. Cobb, Jr.

HARTSHORNE'S IMPORTANCE FOR THEOLOGY

In the years immediately after World War II, I returned to school along with many other veterans. During the war I had decided to enter some form of Christian ministry. That decision, while not discontinuous with my youthful piety, was quite new. I also determined that before entering seminary I should test my faith against the numerous objections the modern world raised against it. As the arena for this testing I chose the Committtee on the Analysis of Ideas and the Study of Methods at the University of Chicago. My announced project was a study of the modern critique of Christianity, and I envisioned a three-year program of such study.

It took only a couple of quarters, however, to undercut the mode of thought and faith that I had brought with me to the university. It was not so much that particular arguments against Christianity were especially convincing as that the whole way of thought, the sensibility, and the world view into which I was drawn by immersion into modernity made my beliefs incongruous and im-plausible. I could neither continue that program nor envision Christian ministry as an option for myself unless I could discover a formulation of Christian belief that successfully took the modern mind into account.

The crucial question for me was belief in God. There were other problems with Christian faith, but unless I could meaningfully and plausibly speak of God there seemed little point in wrestling with these other issues. The reality and nature of God were for me *the* intellectual and existential questions.

At that time the dominant form of theology was Neo-orthodoxy. I had found great stimulus and insight in the writings of Reinhold Niebuhr. But I could not find in him a convincing way of understanding God. When I turned to Karl Barth and Emil Brunner and others of that tradition, I was told that my desire to find whether there were reasons to believe in God was inappropriate, that it was an expression of lack of faith. This baffled me. They seemed content to affirm God on the basis of revelation. I did not find it plausible to speak of revelation unless I had some confidence that there was One to be revealed.

During the time I had been exposing myself to the problems that overwhelmed me, I had also encountered two thinkers who spoke seriously of God. They were Mortimer Adler and Charles Hartshorne. Of the two it was Hartshorne who really spoke to me, whose way of thinking seemed a real alternative to atheism. Over a period of years I felt and lived my way into a vision similar to his, and eventually I was able once again to affirm the reality of God with a confidence approaching his.

In writing of the importance of Hartshorne for theology, I have begun with his importance for me personally because my story is far from unique. Some dozens of contemporary philosophers and theologians owe to his conceptuality and reasoning their belief and their vocation. We do not constitute the mainstream of theology or philosophy of religion, but we do constitute a widely recognized school. Hartshorne's primary importance for theology has been the impression of his thought upon this group.

Both directly and through his theological followers, Hartshorne has influenced the general course of theology since World War II. Much of this influence has been in terms of ideas and concepts that were very much his own. But Hartshorne has played another role that has been equally important. That is, he has been the major mediator of Alfred North Whitehead's later thought. So closely did Hartshorne associate his own ideas with those of Whitehead that his students had difficulty in sorting them out sufficiently to give to Hartshorne full credit for his own originality.

Whitehead had focused on mathematical logic and philosophy of nature during his years in England. But when he came to the United States to teach at Harvard, he broadened his range. He introduced the knower into the nature the knower studied, and in fact allowed the activity of human experiencing to provide the model for understanding, by speculative generalization, the other units of nature. The cosmology that unfolded is a rich and complex one. In its expansion it came to include a fresh way of thinking of God.

During the period when Whitehead was working out his vision, both theology and philosophy were repudiating that kind of activity. Theology turned away from philosophy to found itself on independent grounds. Philosophy reinterpreted its role as analysis and thus rejected philosophy of nature and cosmology. Hence Whitehead's greatest work appeared at a time when no department or discipline considered that kind of intellectual activity worthy of attention.

Hartshorne was one of a small group of his generation who swam against the stream. He was convinced of the intrinsic importance of Whitehead's ideas about God and the world and he integrated them with his own. Chiefly through

Hartshorne's influence the intensive study of Whitehead was introduced into theology, and it has been in theology that, to date, it has had its largest role. Fortunately, it has gradually begun to get the attention it deserves in other fields.

The theological tradition in whose shaping Hartshorne played so key a role is usually called process (or process-relational) theology. Whitehead is the single most important philosopher for this movement, and some of its members have come to Whitehead independently of Hartshorne. There are others associated with the movement who look to Henry Nelson Wieman or Bernard Meland rather than to Whitehead or Hartshorne for their major inspiration. But the cohesion and vigor of the movement, its ability to survive during periods when it was rejected by both theology and philosophy, indeed, its very existence as a self-conscious movement, is due primarily to the work of Hartshorne.

In the remainder of this essay I will try to explain how Hartshorne's thinking enabled his theological disciples to remain or become believers. This might seem to indicate that his arguments for the existence of God would be of primary interest. But Hartshorne knew that arguments for God's existence could be convincing only if the idea of God for which they argued was itself intelligible. His primary contribution, therefore, has been in the introduction of a way of thinking of God that fits well with clear thinking about the world. But because the concepts and images of the world that have dominated the recent period provided no basis for speaking of God, especially Hartshorne's God, his project required a new way of thinking of the world. It is in the context of this new way of thinking about both the world and God that his reformulated arguments for the existence of God gain credibility. Accordingly, this exposition of Hartshorne's importance for theology will begin with his contribution to re-thinking the world, proceed to his specific contributions to thinking about God, and conclude with brief comments on his arguments for God's existence.

I. Hartshorne's View of the World

In the rise of modern science there was a struggle between two ways of viewing the world. One group saw things as having within themselves their own principle of motion. They believed that each entity was related to all the others, and that the world as a whole could be conceived as a living organism. The other group thought of the world as composed of matter in motion. In their view matter did not possess any principle of motion in itself; its motion had to be imposed upon it. They believed material entities could act upon one another only by contact. Pushes and pulls are the only means of altering or moving material objects. Hence, nature as a whole took on the shape of a machine.

We all know that it was the mechanistic view that won the day. It has been widely supposed that this victory was due to its close connection with the necessary implications of the science of the day; and certainly the mechanistic model did prove immensely fruitful in scientific advance. But the organic model was not incompatible with scientific advance or unproductive of fruitful hypotheses. The victory of the mechanistic model was not on purely scientific grounds.

Recent historical study has shown that in the victory of mechanism theology played its role as well. Christians in the voluntaristic tradition, who dominated the scene in the late Medieval and Reformation periods, thought of God as omnipotent will. This image did not fit well with a world in which every natural entity had its own principle of motion within itself. It fitted much better with a world of passive matter which moved only as it was moved from without. Such a world requires an external principle of motion which determines all motion whatsoever, none other than the omnipotent will of the voluntarists. Both Descartes and Newton propounded such arguments.

There were also political elements in the debate. A world in which every entity moves itself is one in which all might be thought rightfully to participate in the decisions determinative of their fate. A world in which real power is exercised only from without and from above fits better with the divine right of kings. Those who favored absolute monarchical power against the threat of anarchy often preferred the mechanistic model.

Whatever the reasons for the victory of mechanism, its consequences have been truly fateful. For one thing it made of the human mind something odd. Most people continued to believe that the human mind contained some principle of motion, some element of self-determination, and that thinking could not be fully explained by the laws governing material objects. Hence the human mind seemed to stand outside of the world machine. As a result the dominant thought of the modern world has been dualistic. Much of the most sophisticated thinking of the philosophers has been devoted to overcoming this dualism, but as long as the basic view of nature as machine remains, their effort cannot be successful.

Other problems have become equally acute. Empiricist philosophy in its culmination in Hume, showed that sense-experience provides no basis for positing a material substance underlying the sense-data. The mechanical principles hence are said not to apply to material objects but to the sense-data themselves! Empiricism also implies that causal relations must be discovered in sense-experience if anywhere, and yet nothing more can be found there than regular succession. Since it is unimaginable that we observe a regular succession of activities of God followed by worldly events, the whole notion of divine causality in the world vanishes from the discussion. Thus, although the modern, mechanistic world view was instituted in part to safeguard the sovereignty of divine Will, its empiricist form ended up by rendering any statement of divine agency nonsensical.

The natural sciences have on the whole continued to function as if there were causal relations in the world, and ordinary life takes this belief entirely for granted. The law courts could not function without such assumptions. But we are left in a situation in which the most rigorous thinking seems to undercut the beliefs apart from which society cannot function.

The dualistic separation of the human mind from the natural world suffered acutely from the emergence of evolutionary thinking. All the evidence suggests that the human mind evolved with the human body from animal minds in animal bodies. There is no indication that at some point a metaphysically unique entity, the human mind, suddenly appeared. Such a theory can be superimposed upon the data, but it finds no support from them. Everything indicates that human beings are fully part of the natural world. But if they are, then a purely mechanistic view of nature is clearly inadequate.

In more recent times the mechanistic view of nature has suffered severe setbacks also in physics. It does not apply to the subatomic level. This is not a minor difficulty, since it was part of the mechanistic view to understand the larger organizations of matter to be derivative from the laws governing the smaller units. The mechanistic vision can be sustained only with so many qualifications that one wonders what remains other than entrenched habits of thought.

Hartshorne's response to this situation has seemed to some of us both bold and convincing. It is the clear and unapologetic rejection of the mechanistic model. Against the view that the entities making up the world are little lumps of passive matter, analogous to billiard balls, he argues that they are little occasions of experience, analogous to moments of human experience. In the language used above, they all have some capacity for self-motion. They are all agents as well as patients receiving the action of other things. They are all subjects as well as objects.

Furthermore, causal relations are real. We experience them directly. Our experience grows out of bodily events and out of our own past experiences, which means that bodily events and past experiences are experienced as causally effective in the present. Conscious attention rarely focuses on these causal relations, but we are all pervasively aware of them. No one doubts them in practice.

The evidence for causal relations among the other entities that make up the natural world is readily explicable by this model. Against the mechanistic model of external relations, Hartshorne posits a model in which internal relations are primary. These internal relations are causal, but this is not the sort of causality that leads to determinism. Each entity must take account of its world, but each entity makes its own decision about just how to take account of that world and how to pass its influence on to others. This is organic causality, not the mechanistic causality that collapsed under empiricist analysis. It is only in relation to contemporaries and the future that relations are external.

Hartshorne has called his view a panpsychism or, more recently, "psychicalism". He does so for the very good reason that he takes the human psyche as a starting point for generalization about the nature of things. He is surely correct that if we truly wish to overcome dualism, we *must* see the human psyche as an example of the real things that make up the world!

Nevertheless, the term "panpsychism" (or "psychicalism") is problematic. Unquestionably it has been misleading to many and has invited irrelevant criticisms. Many characteristics of the psyche cannot be generalized, and we must be careful as to the entities to which generalization is made. Hence two caveats are in order.

First, the fact that the structure of human experience at a sufficient level of abstraction is also the structure of all unitary events does not mean that all the rich complexity of human experience can be found in molecules! Human experience is conscious; most experience is not. Human experience is richly informed with sense-data; most experience is not. Human experience includes thought; most experience does not.

Second, the generalization from human experience is to other unitary events. Many readers have supposed that it applies to a stone, but Hartshorne never suggests that a stone is a subject of experience. In the stone, it is only at the molecular, atomic, and subatomic levels that we find entities that appear to have organic unity and individuality. These are acted on and act in a unitary way. An object such as a stone, which is composed of vast numbers of such units, and which has no over-arching experience, behaves according to statistical principles derived from the behavior of its members. It is not like a primitive psyche.

Hartshorne's move at one stroke solves many of the most puzzling problems of modern thought. It fits with our knowledge of ourselves and of our bodies. It fits also with the results of modern scientific investigations. It supports intuitions that have been suppressed for several hundred years. Much of Hartshorne's importance for theology lies here.

Western theology, especially in its Protestant form, succumbed to dualism and even tried to read it back into the Bible. Hartshorne enables us to free ourselves from that heresy and to allow the Biblical understanding of the unity of creation to be seen again. He himself was early led by his vision to a deep concern for ecological issues at a time when the great majority of theologians ignored them. Gradually his vision of the interconnectedness of all creatures has helped theologians to reorient themselves away from purely anthropological concerns. Hartshorne's vision also helps to check the overwhelmingly individualistic ways of thinking that have dominated Western theology.

Hartshorne emphasizes the primacy of feeling over thought. This is, of course, not intended to encourage sentimentalism or to minimize the importance of careful intellectual activity. But it is a useful counter to the tendency to define human beings in terms of rationality and mind. It helps us to see how much of what we consider rational is influenced by emotion and purpose and thus to assimilate much that sociologists and psychologists have taught us.

Hartshorne shows that the human psyche is nothing but the flow of successive human experiences. This, too, has profound effects on theological anthropology. It helps to counter the apparent inevitability of egoism by showing that even our concern for our own future is for another. It also helps to open us to the profound wisdom of Buddhist thought which has understood the importance of rejecting substantialist thinking about the self. Thus Hartshorne has encouraged a dialogue between Christian process theology and Buddhist thought that has already proven fruitful for both.

II. The Whole

A mechanistic model for viewing the parts of the world suggests a view of the whole as a giant machine. With respect to this world, explanations must be in terms of necessity or chance. If one is to speak of God at all, it must be as an external maker of the machine. If such an external maker acts within the world, it must be as an exception to the laws that are otherwise universally effective. Such is the legacy of eighteenth-century thought for theology!

An organic and experiential model for viewing the units of which the world is composed suggests an organic and experiential view of the whole. Just as the parts are internally related to one another, so they are also internally related to the whole and the whole to them. The whole cannot be just what it is except as it has just the parts it has, and the parts cannot be just what they are except as parts of that whole. Thus the whole has characteristics unique to itself, and yet at the same time it shares many of the characteristics of the parts.

The uniqueness of the whole is illustrated by its necessity in contrast to the contingency of its parts. My existence and that of the sun or any other particular entity has a beginning and an ending. The sun and I might not have existed at all. But whatever the contingent parts may be, there will always be a whole. This is its metaphysical uniqueness. On the other hand, like the parts, just what the whole is in any moment depends on what the parts are. In this respect it is contingent.

In other respects the uniqueness of the whole consists in its perfection. Every entity within the world includes other entities within it. But this inclusion is fragmentary and limited. The whole, on the other hand, includes every entity perfectly. Similarly, every entity within the world can in principle be improved upon, can be superseded by something superior to it. But in the case of the whole, it can be surpassed only by later states of itself. No part could ever surpass the whole that completely includes it.

Clearly, this organic whole can also be written as Whole. It has the qualities of divinity. It is necessary and unsurpassable. Its inclusion of the world is a matter of knowledge and love. Thus it can be said to know and love the world perfectly. In short the Whole is God.

This identification of the whole with God must not be interpreted as pantheism. Pantheism ordinarily identifies the world with God in one of two ways. First, God may be conceived as simply the totality of worldly things having no characteristics or reality except those derived from its parts. Second, the whole that is God may be conceived as the one actuality, the one agent, in such a way that the parts have no real individuality or freedom. In short, pantheism either subsumes God into the world or the world into God. When the world is conceived mechanistically there is no alternative.

In the organic vision nothing like this occurs. The integrity of every creaturely organism is fully preserved, while God as the organism that includes all the other organisms is not the mere addition of these organisms. God is the unitary inclusive experience of the universe. God's knowledge is not the sum of the knowledge of the creatures, but infinitely superior to that. God's love is not the sum of creaturely loves, but the perfect love of all things. This is not pantheism but panentheism. All is in God, but God is much more than the additive totality of other things. Indeed, God is qualitatively different from all things.

III. God's Becoming, Receptivity, and Suffering

Philosophical theology has been deeply influenced by Greek thought, and Greek thought reflected Greek values. These values included the appraisal of eternity as superior to time, and of being as superior to becoming. In the Greek context this being could be interpreted as static, since the completely immutable was strongly favored over anything that was subject to change. Hartshorne polemicized against the tendency of classical Christian philosophical theology to adopt this Greek prejudice.

Many supporters of traditional Christian theology have criticized Hartshorne's criticisms as misrepresenting the tradition. They have argued that the theological understanding of being is far from static. Indeed, as pure act, it is completely dynamic. The immutability of God is the changelessness of dynamic activity not the changelessness of abstractions.

Especially in recent years Thomists have re-emphasized that the *esse* of Thomas is to be understood not as being-in-general but as the act of being, that act by virtue of which beings receive their being. Barthians have recently stressed that their emphasis on the sovereign freedom of the divine will is a radical denial that God is static. Indeed there have been arguments that the Thomistic and Barthian views of God avoid the image of a static God *more* successfully than does Hartshorne.

These arguments for the divine dynamism, however, do not fully respond to Hartshorne's point. In his critique of the tradition he has not been concerned solely with how God acts, but also with how God is acted upon. However dynamic God's activity in the world may be, if it is not responsive to the changing situation in the world, it cannot be the perfect form of action Hartshorne attributes to God. God's activity can be appropriately responsive to the world only as it results from perfect knowledge and love of the world. To have perfect knowledge and love of the world is to be affected by the world. To be perfectly affected by the world is to be perfectly receptive of what happens there and to be continuously changed by the continuously changing world. As long as Thomists and Barthians hedge on this point, Hartshorne's critique of the tradition is applicable.

Unlike Greek philosophers, all Christian theologians have affirmed God's love and knowledge of the world. They also recognize that from the human point of view the world changes. But they have refused to conclude that the changes in the world loved and known by God introduce changes into the loving and knowing. They have argued that what is loved and known by God does not change in the divine experience even though it seems to us to change.

This paradoxical position has been defended by distinguishing radically the divine from the creaturely perspective. For the divine perspective change does not occur, since the whole temporal process is always co-present. For God there is no distinction of past, present, and future, and time is unreal. These distinctions hold only from the creaturely point of view.

Hartshorne has devoted considerable energy to displaying the problems with such a doctrine. It implies that human experience is fundamentally illusory. It implies also that what is for us future is for God, and therefore in reality, already just what it is, fully determinate. That means that our sense of creativity, of rendering determinate what was, prior to that act, not determinate, is an illusion. Our sense of responsibility is undercut.

There is another, less common, mode of argument defending the divine immutability. It is asserted that although love and knowledge render the creatures affected by what is loved and known, this is not true for God. God loves and knows us in such a way that God remains unaffected by the objects loved and known.

Against this move Hartshorne can reply that a "love" that leaves the lover unaffected by the joys and sufferings of the one who is loved is not worthy of being called love at all. Similarly a "knowledge" that does not genuinely relate the knower to the known is not knowledge. Hartshorne deplores the widespread tendency in the tradition to apply certain words to God because of their prominence in the Biblical characterization of God but then to denude them of all meaning.

From a theological point of view Hartshorne enables us to see and name what has gone wrong in the tradition. In Biblical conceptuality God is *everlasting*, but not *eternal* in the Greek sense. God's character does not change. God is faithful to do what God promises. In these limited respects God is "immutable." But the Bible knows nothing of a timeless eternity.

The Biblical writers do not share the Greek prejudice against change and temporality. Even if they declare that God knows much about the future that we do not know, they do not suppose that the future is already present for God. The future is truly future.

When they write of God's knowledge and God's love, they mean what they say quite straightforwardly. For them there is the contrast between our very limited creaturely love and knowledge and God's perfect love and knowledge. But perfection does not deny temporality or mean that God is unaffected. It is only when God's everlastingness is reinterpreted as eternity that theologians are forced to make these moves.

Hartshorne shows us that these moves are necessitated not by reason as such but by Greek values which differ markedly from those of Israel. To return to Israel's values need not make us less rational, less rigorous in our conceptuality. It only leads to a different conceptuality, one that more appropriately expresses Biblical ways of thought and fits better as well with recent developments in many fields. It can liberate theology from a long captivity to features of the Greek mind that have weakened its ability to communicate its own message.

The discussion of God's receptivity, of the world's influence on God, makes contact with an ancient debate within the church. The question is whether God suffers. The early church knew that Jesus had suffered death on the cross, and there were those who drew the conclusion that God suffered in Jesus's suffering. But the church drew back from this conclusion. At least, its leading thinkers supposed, "God the Father" could not suffer.

This denial of divine suffering was not merely based on the doctrines of immutability and eternality. It reflected also a related but different Greek value. The Greeks generally felt that whereas to act is good, to be acted upon, that is, to be vulnerable to the actions of others over which one cannot exercise control, is a mark of weakness and inferiority. The Greek ideal, in both its Stoic and Epicurean forms, emphasized the independence of the happy person from others, the basic invulnerability necessary to excellence. The God of Aristotle is completely unaffected by what takes place in the world.

More consistently and vigorously than any other philosopher, Hartshorne has attacked this prejudice. True human excellence does not involve insensitivity or indifference to others but rather empathy with them. Alongside acting for the benefit of others, it includes feeling their feelings with them. This is especially important when others are suffering. In the human case this excellence is attained only very partially at best. But the divine perfection means that God perfectly receives all that happens in the world and perfectly responds to it. Far from being unaffected by our suffering and our joy, God suffers fully with us and rejoices fully with us.

It would be a mistake to suppose that only through Hartshorne's influence have theologians come to reject some of the Greek prejudices that have informed so much of the tradition. Over the centuries there have been protests against the dominant philosophical theology in the name of the authority of the Bible. The Protestant Reformation was one such protest. Pascal is famous for his contrast of the God of Abraham, Isaac, and Jacob with the God of the philosophers. Twentieth-century Neo-orthodoxy renewed the insistence on freeing theology from philosophical prejudices so as to allow the Bible to speak more directly to us. Dietrich Bonhoeffer wrote movingly that only a suffering God can help us now.

The special importance of Hartshorne's contribution to theology has been to show that one need not choose between a philosophical theology rife with Greek prejudices and a Biblical theology that avoids systematic employment of philosophically clarified concepts. By developing a dipolar view of God as eminently absolute but also eminently relational, Hartshorne has shown that a philosophical theology can be developed that is congenial in basic values and vision to Biblical modes of thought. He has shown that such a theology can be chosen on philosophical as well as theological grounds.

IV. Divine Power and the Problem of Evil

Hartshorne's critique of major features of traditional philosophical theology has found many points of contact in the popular piety of the churches and among students of scripture. Indeed, the doctrines he has criticized, while still widely taught, are on the defensive today. But many of those who appreciate some aspects of his thought reject it because of his denial to God of the type of power they are accustomed to attributing to God.

This debate, and Hartshorne's contribution, can best be understood by returning to the two world views described above. In the modern mechanistic world view, power is exercised externally by pushes and pulls. The most powerful being is the one that can move other bodies from place to place most successfully. God as the one who is infinitely powerful can relocate anything anywhere immediately.

In addition to the movement of objects there is also their generation and annihilation. God is conceived as the creator of the machine, the One who brought it into being and gave it its form and potentialities. God has also the power to destroy it, either by breaking it into parts or by simply abolishing the whole.

Of course, few theologians have thought of the whole of reality as simply a machine. The human mind is different, and often in talking of God's relation to the human person theologians have spoken of divine power in a very different way. But the analogy of the mode of power exercised on the machine and its parts is also influential. God's power brings the mind into being and can destroy it. God is also able directly to determine thoughts and feelings.

Hartshorne's psychicalist vision of reality leads to a very different notion of divine power. Every entity has some power of its own. This is both the power to be affected by others and the power to affect others. It is affected by others as they are appropriated into its own act of creative synthesis, the act by which it comes into being. It affects others by presenting itself for their appropriation through their acts of creative synthesis. The degree of its power is measured by how richly it appropriates its past and how much it contributes to the future. God perfectly appropriates the world and is immediately present for appropriation by all things.

Those whose view of power has been shaped in relation to the mechanistic vision complain that Hartshorne does not credit God with sufficient power. God does not move objects around by fiat. God does not bring things into being or destroy them except in collaboration with other powers. Indeed, God does not strictly determine what any entity will be.

A two-fold reply can be found in Hartshorne's work. First, there is a challenge to the idealization of the kind of control over others which is often attributed to God. That is a form of power that is not very admirable in the world. Why should we consider the extreme or absolute form of that power to be divine? The form of power that is most admirable is that which empathizes with others and empowers them. That power makes others free while contributing to the context of order within which they operate. Divine power does not interfere with the exercise of creaturely freedom but rather establishes the optimum freedom compatible with sufficient order for its effective exercise.

Second, there is a counter-attack upon the plausibility and intelligibility of the externalistic exercise of power. We have already seen that in the course of the development of empiricist philosophy external causation was seen to lack empirical warrant. No attribution of external causation to God makes sense in Humean terms. But even if all that is ignored, the very notion of omnipotence as it is developed in this context is self-destructive. It seems to mean that there is no power except God's power. But if creatures have no power at all then the power exercised by God in absolute control over them seems at best infinitesimal. We are impressed by God's power only because it seems effective in relation to great powers! Hence the insistence that all creatures have real power, even though it denies that God is in total control of events, attributes more power to God than does the doctrine of omnipotence when this is taken strictly.

Although some theologians have written as if they intended this extreme doctrine of divine omnipotence, most, when confronted with this critique, deny that anything of the sort was intended. God's omnipotence does not mean that everything else is wholly powerless. It means instead that God can achieve whatever God desires, that no resistance to God's will can be successful, that God can overrule all other powers. Omnipotence means that God has power over all other powers sufficient to prevent them from acting contrary to the divine will. This doctrine is not as immediately self-destructive.

However this doctrine still makes God completely responsible for every detail of history. Nothing can happen contrary to God's will. The Holocaust, too, must express God's purpose. Sin must be as much God's purpose as righteousness.

To avoid this consequence many theologians have adopted an additional doctrine. According to them, although God has the power to overrule all other powers, God does not use it. God limits the exercise of divine power so as to give real freedom to the creatures, or at least to the human ones. What happens in history, then, does not express God's purposes except in the very general sense that it is God's purpose that human beings exercise freedom and experience the consequences of their free acts.

This doctrine of divine self-limitation is designed to hold together divine omnipotence and human freedom and to avoid picturing God as the cause of sin and its consequences. But it, too, has its problems. It implies that God could, at any time, act to stop a particular course of events. God could have blocked Hitler's exercise of his freedom and thereby have saved the lives of six million Jews. Obviously God did not exercise power in that way. Why not? The usual answer is that God cares so much for human freedom and responsibility that God chooses not to intervene at all. But can we regard that as a loving and reasonable decision? Would an earthly parent stand by and watch while one child killed another out of respect for the former child's need to mature through exercising freedom? Surely an occasional intervention, perhaps a very subtle one not recognized by anyone, would be a small price to pay to save millions of Jews!

Hartshorne's different way of thinking of God's power does not do away with the question of theodicy, but it puts it in quite a different and much more manageable form. God is not responsible for the details of what happens. Not only human beings but all creatures act freely to some degree and shape the course of earthly and cosmic events. It is meaningless to ask why God does not intervene to prevent the worst abuses of freedom, since "intervention" presupposes a type of power that belongs only to creatures.

The question of theodicy for Hartshorne is only the question of whether the general cosmic principles are justified, including especially the balance of freedom and determination of risk and opportunity which characterize the world. One could challenge God's goodness by arguing that creatures have been granted too much freedom, that a better world would be a more tightly determined one. Or one could argue that God should have given creatures more freedom. But it is not evident that either argument would succeed. Few of us would want to be less free than we are, and yet we can all too easily see that the amount of freedom we possess is already extremely dangerous. We would hesitate to ask for more!

V. Eschatology

Dissatisfaction with Hartshorne's doctrine of divine power is often related to the need of many Christians to believe in a future fulfillment. Biblical imagery points primarily to a fulfillment coming at the end of history and bringing into being a New Age or Kingdom of Heaven on earth. In the nineteenth century many Christians came to hope for such a New Age as an outgrowth of progress in human history. Marxists translated this end into the classless society which would be the inevitable outcome of the dialectic of history. In the twentieth century, Teilhard de Chardin saw the New Age, Omega, as the end of the entire evolutionary process.

Hartshorne has never associated himself with such optimistic expectations about the course of history. He is impressed by Reinhold Niebuhr's critique. Although progress toward a better world is not inconsistent with his view of divine power, he sees the limits of human attainment. Many in their disillusionment with the earlier options have grown cynical with respect to the prospects of human history. It seems more likely to lead to decay or destruction than to fulfillment. If we are to hope for fulfillment in spite of this, it would have to be on the basis of a mode of divine action not employed in ordinary events. It would require an intervention. To accept Hartshorne's view of divine power is to forego any hope for such an intervention.

There is another form that hope for fulfillment often takes in Christian circles. This is hope for personal life after death, in some place or sphere quite different from earth. In this way of thinking the final fulfillment that is anticipated does not require any particular course of events on this planet.

It is not entirely clear that Hartshorne's metaphysics necessarily excludes personal survival of death, but it is very clear that Hartshorne himself does not believe in this kind of survival and has no interest in it. His philosophy works against this hope that is important to so many. Thus he rejects both an End of history and the hope of heaven. This does not mean that Hartshorne lacks interest in the deeper concerns which underlie these two forms of Christian eschatology. He senses the emptiness and loss of meaning that follow when hope is lost. But he believes that hope has been misplaced and that, by taking such questionable forms, it has aroused a skepticism which endangers hope itself. What is needed is a radical re-thinking of the human situation and the appropriate content of hope.

Hartshorne knows that our creaturely enjoyment of our experiences is fleeting indeed. Even in memory we can recall only tiny portions from the richness of the past. For us the past fades and most of its values are lost forever. If that were the whole story, the transitory attainments of life would lose their importance. The course of events would add up to nothing more than its fragmentary presence now in our histories, and with the eventual passing of human beings from the scene, most of that would be gone. The grounds for purposeful effort would be profoundly undercut.

But in Hartshorne's view this is only one side of the story. The Whole (God) jointly experiences with the part (the creature) all that happens in the creaturely life. In the fullest sense we are known by God and included in God. Whereas our experience as creatures involves a constant perishing, a perpetual loss of the immediacy of one experience as the next arises, the divine experience includes forever all that it has contained. The divine experience is enriched by its participation in new creaturely experiences, but not at the expense of the past. What is past in the world retains its immediacy in God.

To understand reality in this way is, for Hartshorne, to satisfy the real human need for hope. The need is to believe that what is attained in life is not lost, that it is important. To know that all we do and think and feel is forever felt in its immediacy by God is to know that it matters ultimately. Our lives are forever important because they matter forever to God.

Critics complain that the growing richness of the divine life does not satisfy the human hope. Human beings want to continue to be renewed as conscious subjects enjoying their own creaturely lives, only free from the evil and suffering that beset them here. This is the Heaven or the New Age to which they look forward. It is this they expect from a God of power and love.

Hartshorne's reply is that this desire for continuing personal existence expresses an immature stage of spiritual development. We are called to love God first and foremost. God is the one wholly adequate object of love. To whatever extent we love God our concern becomes God's blessedness above our own. We find our own fulfillment in loving God.

Similar doctrines have appeared before in the Christian tradition. But Hartshorne provides an enrichment that has not been clearly present before. Often we have been called to live for the glory of a God to whom it seems that our glorification makes no difference. Sometimes it has seemed that serving God in some measure turned attention away from serving creatures.

But for Hartshorne these limitations are abolished. We have the supreme privilege of contributing to the divine life. God does not depend on us for existence, as we depend on God, but God does depend on us for the specific form that the divine experience will take. We can add to its suffering or to its joy. But none of our contribution to the divine life can be in tension with love of our fellow creatures and service of them. What we do to the least of the creatures we do also to God. Love of God cannot be expressed except through service of creatures.

VI. ARGUMENTS FOR THE EXISTENCE OF GOD

Hartshorne has devoted a great deal of attention to arguments for the existence of God. Since such arguments cannot prove something that is internally incoherent or incompatible with the world we know, the first and prior question is whether there is a way of thinking about God that makes sense. Since that question depends on how we understand the world, I began by identifying some distinctive features of Hartshorne's view of the world and then showing how his view of God fits with that. When Hartshorne undertakes to prove the existence of God he is not trying to show that there exists a being alongside the world who acts upon it from without. Nor is he trying to prove the existence of a being inside the world who is one being among others only better and more powerful than the others. The arguments are rather for the unity and perfection of the whole.

Hartshorne's belief is that in fact our ordinary habits of thought presuppose the reality of this unified whole that is God. Hence, he is not intending to begin in his arguments with something familiar and then to show that it requires for its explanation a reality of a quite different order. All of the arguments intend to help us see that we always already implicitly believe in God, to make what is implicit explicit.

The question is not, therefore, whether arguments can be formulated that compel assent. Obviously this is impossible, since one can always deny the premises. Hartshorne does believe, however, that the arguments show the price that must be paid in order to avoid belief. The multiplicity of arguments has cumulative force in clarifying the scope of this price. Hartshorne thinks many people, if they fully understand what is being said, will not want to pay that price and will realize instead that the acknowledgment of belief in God is congruent with their deepest convictions.

The issue is not so much whether a particular argument can be so formulated as to coerce the mind. The issue is more whether one can fully understand what Hartshorne is saying and not find it basically convincing. At least among those who recognize that their experience seems to include the experience of God and/or experiences that point to God, the problem is chiefly to overcome obstacles to believing what, in itself, seems true. It is at this point that many have found Hartshorne's work so helpful. Those who had thought that "God", by definition referred to a being "up there" or "out there," and who had therefore, thought they could no longer believe, find that their positive experiences make sense when those strange hypotheses and images are replaced by this new view of God. Those who have found the sense of God's all-controlling power incongruent with their own awareness of freedom and responsibility discover that there is a far better way to think of God. Those who have found the reality of evil incompatible with what they have been taught about God's power find that another way of thinking of God enables them to respond realistically and hopefully to evil. The arguments work because they make contact with our sense of intelligibility, of meaning, of purpose, and of gratitude for life and freedom without asking us to believe what is incongruous with the remainder of our experience.

VII. An Appreciation

Looking back we often see that the most important thinkers of a generation are those who refused to take their cues from the dominant community. They have stubbornly pursued their own agenda, confident of the importance of the questions they asked even when they were of little interest to others. We can be grateful that during the heyday of renewed traditionalism in philosophical theology, of the rejection of philosophy by much of the rest of the theological community, and of the narrowing of the scope of its task to linguistic analysis, or to the phenomenological description of human existence within most of the philosophical community, there have been some who continued to ask the questions these traditions discouraged. Among them none have proved more creative, original, and important for Christian theology than Charles Hartshorne. The time of his greatest influence may still lie ahead.

John B. Cobb, Jr.

School of Theology at Claremont
July 1986

9

William L. Reese

THE "TROUBLE" WITH PANENTHEISM— AND THE DIVINE EVENT

That Charles Hartshorne should have invited me to share in the writing of *Philosophers Speak of God*, while I was still a graduate student at the University of Chicago, stands somewhere on the far side of wonder. The project had begun with a translation from Fechner's *Zend-Avesta*, initially suggested by Hartshorne to improve my German, looking to the language exams. Hartshorne would go over my drafts, making corrections. As the translation gained body we spoke, to be sure, of publishing a translation and commentary of the long chapter on God and the world ("Von Gott und Welt"). Then came a day when the editor of the University of Chicago Press, lunching with Professor Hartshorne, invited him to do an anthology of philosophical theism. He told the editor that the project had already begun, citing the translation, and arranged then and there for me to be co-author on an equal basis.

Despite the formal equality on which Hartshorne graciously insisted, I felt myself very much the underworker, especially at the start. We began with Charles marking passages in books from his own library, which we expected to include in the work. I would type out the passages, sometimes using more than the material marked, sometimes less, for the sake of a coherent entry. Eventually, we divided up the commentaries. The division of labor is detailed in the Preface of the book, omitting only the obvious point that the Index was by the underworker.

The master worker–underworker relationship can be read from the prose. I have not come upon a single ringing sentence in the material I contributed. All of the ringing sentences of the book belong to Professor Hartshorne. We had agreed that we were working out the implications of a theory about the nature of God, that the ability of the theory to generate plausible implications and to reveal difficulties in other theories about God would serve to confirm our hypothesis. That made me cautious and, I fear, tendentious; and the greater vigor of Hartshorne's prose flowed from his general élan, and probably also from his greater confidence in panentheism.

It seemed to me at the time, and still seems to me, that we were successful in establishing the greater coherence of the process view of God, as well as demonstrating inconsistencies in the classical conception. But our success seemed to me to derive more from the dipolarity of the hypothesis we espoused, harmonizing polar contraries by placing them on different levels of abstraction, than from the conception of panentheism even though the latter is one way of expressing the former.

And since the bankruptcy we noted in classical theism derived in large part from its inconsistencies, I felt a special commitment to avoid anything like inconsistency in the replacement doctrine. And yet I had noted what seemed to me a possible inconsistency in panentheism which troubled me then and to which I address myself now. I am not certain when I first mentioned the possible problem to Professor Hartshorne. I do recall that it came up during the oral on my doctoral dissertation. I also recall, although there is a chance that this bit of "memory" is projective, Professor Hartshorne's response. "Possibly," he said (or possibly he said), "space is Whiteheadian for us but Newtonian for God."

Fechner's view of a dipolar God, in one sense exclusive of reality, in another sense inclusive of it, certainly lends itself to the Newtonian present. In the metaphor, if that is what it is, the body of God now includes us; the mind or spirit in some sense excludes us. In that sense the metaphor appears already a bit non-Whiteheadian. Years before, a farmer in the Ozarks looking out across his fields had said to me: "Somehow pantheism doesn't feel quite right. One wants God to be available, but one doesn't want to be swallowed up by him." I shared the farmer's feeling and, although panentheistic inclusiveness was of a different kind, my animus against pantheism, however slight, may have spread to its more sophisticated relative.

In the first chapter of the book we had argued that dipolar panentheism explicated the Christian religion more faithfully than could classical theism, and that is the case, although once again it seemed to me that the superior explication came from dipolarity and not from panentheism. At times, although not in *Philosophers Speak of God*, Professor Hartshorne has quoted Acts 17.28: ". . . in Him we live and move and have our being," apparently to suggest that Christianity is panentheistic. But that quotation, the only one of its kind in the Bible, is presented by "Paul" as a Greek idea. What we have in the Areopagus speech is Stoic Pantheism, as Schweitzer among others has pointed out.[1] Jesus, to be sure, insisted upon a greater intimacy between the human and the divine than did Paul, but there is no statement in his teachings expressing the kind of inclusiveness required by the quotation from Acts. That conception is also absent from the Old Testament. And yet the doctrine of dipolarity is very much implicit in the view of God's relation to the world running through the entire Bible. The two doctrines, then, can stand apart.

Liking part of the conception but not the whole, and possibly shaken by the logical positivist attack on metaphysics itself, I turned from philosophy of religion for a time extending, as it turned out, through several decades. When I did return, it was through the seeing-as material of the later Wittgenstein. Following his injunction to put words back into the language-games they came from, I began to consider religious questions in very concrete contexts. And finding ordinary epistemology maladapted to religious questions, my criticism rested on ethical rather than epistemological grounds.

Finally, I came back to the problem of dipolarity and panentheism, arguing[2] that Whiteheadian relativity is not consistent with panentheism, and quoting with approval the suggestion of Teilhard de Chardin that God "invades" the world "as a ray of light does a crystal," that his presence is "very near and very distant at one and the same time."[3] I urged that the metaphor unpacks in a manner consistent with Whitehead's universal relativity "since my awareness of the light which bathes the crystal is a relation of an immediately past state of the crystal to an immediately past state of my body. I do not literally engulf the crystal nor the crystal me." And I mentioned "ridding ourselves of the sense of the uncanny which for many pervades the panentheistic analysis." Even so do old ideas hang on. The "many" may have included no more than an Ozark farmer and myself.

Given the Whiteheadian analysis that all contemporaries relate to each other through the immediate past, the criticism is valid with respect to any single state of the divine awareness, or any single state of awareness of the divine. It does not apply, however, to the world as the body of God, or my existence as a cell within that body. My criticism, then, was valid with respect to actual occasions. Consider any cell within my body. That cell is contemporary with the center of awareness which is the mind of that body. But mind and cell do not include each other. My mind can know of nothing more contemporary than the immediately past state of the cell. I might know of that through its signal of pain, or a less specific signal of satisfaction. Only pastnesses can be included in my awareness. Going the other way our cells are influenced in some sense by the signals our awareness sends them; but the cell can be aware at best of the immediately past state of my awareness. This interrelating of contemporaries through the immediate past provides the "elbow room" of Whitehead's universe.

For Whitehead the example is an instance of the irreducible plurality of the present moment. And since God is not "an exception to the metaphysical principles, invoked to save their collapse" but "their chief exemplification"

(405),[4] the principle applies to God as well. Some references in Whitehead appear to imply the contrary. The very definition of contemporaries as those events which do not contribute to each other, seems at first to yield a Newtonian present. Since those events which do contribute, or are contributed to, lie in the past or future of a given event M, the contemporaries of M all exist "now."[5] The sense that this defines a "now" for the entire universe is strengthened when Whitehead speaks of a "duration" as "a complete locus of actual occasions in 'unison of becoming' or in 'concrescent unison'. It is the old-fashioned 'present state of the world' " (375). Furthermore, it sounds like panentheism when he relates God to this state, saying that God is "in unison of becoming with every other creative act" (406).

On the other hand, he grants that "the peculiarity of the locus of contemporaries of M is that any two of its members, such as R and S, *need* not be contemporaries of each other. They *may* be mutually contemporaries, but not necessarily" (375). And somewhat later, and more generally: "According to modern relativistic views we must admit that there are many durations including M—in fact, an infinite number, so that no one of these contains all M's contemporaries" (375–76).

The conclusion I draw is that "unison of becoming" does not provide an old-fashioned Newtonian state of the universe, and that is what we should expect, in fact. When Whitehead related God to "unison of becoming" his reference was to God as "the beginning," that is, to the antecedent nature. This is treated below as the contribution of antecedent possibility to each event. And since the antecedent nature is "deficient in actuality," that identification does not yield panentheism; the consequent nature, on the other hand, is said specifically to be "in the past of all members."

Whitehead also has a doctrine of objectification in the extensive continuum which, if I understand it, requires spatial extensiveness of God. The space-time world of our experience is a contingent determination of the extensive continuum in which all actual occasions of this temporal epoch participate. In this "objectification" the extensive continuum is atomized spatially so that in this epoch, at least, "every actual entity in the temporal world is to be credited with a spatial volume for its perspective standpoint" (84). It should follow that the consequent nature of God, as temporal, possesses the most extensive spatial volume of any being, since that nature is involved with the perspective of each actual occasion. That would still not require a Newtonian present, since part of God's spatial volume might not be contemporary with another part. In that sense God's extensiveness would differ from ours. There are probably further complications in the doctrine of the "perspective standpoint." The "double fact" mentioned at the bottom of page 83 may be a double objectification, for example. In any case, the conclusion that one cannot support a divine Newtonian present within the set of Whitehead's affirmation stands firm. Up to this point my criticism is valid.

There is a suggestion in contemporary physics which goes beyond relativism. The 1964 Bell Interconnectedness Theorem requires the assumption of superluminal or instantaneous nonlocal interconnections.[6] Should the connections be instantaneous (in the model of Jung's synchronicity), an ultimate spatial perspective of Newtonian form would be conceivable once again; supposing that to be the divine perspective, each actual occasion of God's awareness would be contemporary with every contemporary actual occasion, and not merely antecedent or consequent. That is something like the suggestion I understood Hartshorne to have made during my oral, decades earlier.

And although my point is correct with respect to Whitehead, who could not have used the Bell theorem, I now believe it to be trivially so. It is trivial because our concern is not just with actual occasions but with personal order societies. My cell and my awareness are both personal order societies, and part of the more inclusive personal order society which is my body. Their character as enduring objects with overlapping actual occasions allows both inclusiveness and relativity. The problem changes into the old problem of analogy. It turns out that all we need to know is whether what is true of the cell in my body is also true of my life in relation to the Whiteheadian God. In the analogy God is the all-inclusive personal order society (even if completely subject to the relativity principle). We are dealing with the interrelation of two personal order societies, one more inclusive than the other, and both exemplifying the same categories.

The analogy is not incredible. Surely it is reasonable to believe that just as the life of my cell cannot be utterly unlike my own, so the process that is my life cannot be wholly unlike the process that is the universe. One might argue in Humian fashion that the upward gradient from cell to person might not be continued in the movement from person to universe. When Whitehead holds God to be the chief exemplification of the categories and when Hartshorne speaks of God's dual transcendence, they testify that the gradient does continue toward categorical perfection.

If God as exemplar of the categories requires continuation of the upward gradient, then it is appropriate to call the universe the body of God. Whether the phrase is appropriate as a productive analogy, a productive metaphor, or the literal truth, the processes of our lives are obviously not self-sufficient but require grounding in a fuller process. If it is reasonable to hold this ground of process to be both itself a process and the chief exemplification of the categories, we move from metaphor toward analogy and literal truth.

Certain foundational decisions require others. Once it has been decided that the issue of temporal passage is objective immortality rather than perpetual perishing, and that the pulses of that passage are defined by the subjective immediacies of feeling, then something must be done about the fading away of subjective immediacy as the present lapses into the past. What is done, and the only thing one could imagine happening in the Whiteheadian context, is that God saves the subjective immediacy of the past event. We are aware of our present moments sliding into the past, their subjective immediacies being replaced by new and different subjective immediacies. For Whitehead the consequent nature of God saves the subjective immediacy of those events in his own more adequate subjective immediacy, and so saves it for all time (or for eternality).

And if God is the agent keeping that subjective immediacy in the universe, it is reasonable to say that he knows the events he prehends in a manner infinitely more detailed than those events know themselves. For the events of my immediate past, or yours, are felt with the vagueness of that negative prehending that explains me through the absence of detailed characters in my constitution. The divine event senses not only the vagueness of my subjective immediacy. It senses as well the detailed positive prehensions which I feel only negatively. It senses these not in me, but in the past immediacy of those events which did feel the positive relatedness which is for me only vagueness. Or it senses those details in its own prior states where other immediacies, related to our own, are registered. There is no reason why the God event should not know the total immediate past of all events in one of these ways. As transcendent over our becoming, God (unlike us) will have no negative prehensions and no unconcious part. Just as our immediate present is constituted by our relations to whatever parts of the antecedent world we positively include, so God's immediate present will be constituted by positive relations to the entire antecedent world (perhaps even beyond the light cone, if we use the Bell theorem). His present will be our immediate past, and if we prehend him we would prehend in our present his immediate past. The present of each of us will be relative to that present's constitution in immediate pastness.

Without this saving grace of retained subjective immediacy, there would be incoherence in the system. Doubtless, we could understand what it is to be real under some other category. Then, of course, we would have a different system. We could understand "being real" under the category of extension, for example. That is one of the few alternative possibilities, in fact. Whether such a system can be worked out coherently seems doubtful. If Whitehead found incoherence in Cartesian dualism, he would have found still more in this option. In any case, he did not find this to be a live option, and it was not simply his interest in modern physics that closed it out.

When the reality of an entity is understood in terms of extension alone, nominalism sets in. When nominalism sets in, there is no place for real possibilities. One substitutes for them mental possibilities. But since extended things are real actualities, before they were actual they must have been really possible. How else could they have become actual? Extensionalism cannot provide the category of real possibility. It can think only mental possibilities and real actualities, and there is no indication of how a mental possibility could become a real actuality. That is a sign of the incoherence of nominalism.

Whitehead can, of course, provide real possibilities; and although all are real they grade spectrum-wise from the immediately to the remotely relevant. Just as the retention of subjective immediacy requires the consequent nature, so the provision for real possibilities requires the antecedent nature of God.

We shall suggest a problem with primordial valuation, but there is surely no problem with the idea of an antecedent valuation, meaning that by the time I come to the point of making a decision there is, over against the actual conditions of my life, a fan of alternative possibilities now relevant for actualization. We, and the antecedent world, provided the actual conditions; it was a function of the universe (and of the consequent nature) to have provided those relevant possibilities. Our task is simply to come upon them and understand what they are. In this sense we are always interacting with the universe. And if we know anything at all we know the universe will not run out of possibilities, that whatever we achieve there will be a correspondingly appropriate fan of unactualized possibilities relevant to those achievements, and leading out from them. This richness of possibility is the antecedent nature of God; or else the antecedent nature is the provider of these possibilities.

In these two ways the processes of our lives need to be completed by a cosmic process. We had already said that we relate to God through the immediate past. We also relate to him through the immediate future. But how is God the chief exemplification of the categories of process? There is no problem here with respect to the past. As chief exemplar God prehends the immediate past absolutely, that is, categorically, while we do so only more or less. Does the grounding of process by the antecedent nature likewise chiefly exemplify the categories?

Whitehead's doctrine is that there was a primordial valuation of possibility, and that God's antecedent nature is "unchanged by reason of its final completeness" (417). The unchanging nature and the primordial valuation require each other. But the primordial valuation does not provide, in my view, the subtlety of fit between achieved novelty and novel possibility which occurs in creative endeavor. No matter what has been achieved, appropriate novel possibilities now confront that achievement. Although not as transparently as in the case of the divine envisionment of all actualities, the primordial completion of possibilities also makes a shadow play of time. We could say of course that the creative person created not only the actual achievement but also the novel possibilities. But that isn't the sense one has. One's sense is that, having actually achieved x, one now finds y_1, y_2, y_3 confronting that achievement. The sense of the creative person is often, indeed, that he or she is no more than the instrument of that creativity. One does not create the possibilities, this is one's sense, one envisions real possibilities now in place as a result, or partly as a result, of one's past achievement. As in the case of the past, the fact seems to be an instance of divine-human cooperation.

So we would understand divine transcendence with respect to the possible in the following way: As God transcends our prehension of the immediate past, so he transcends our grasp of the possible, first of all in assuring the presence of relevant possibilities confronting achieved actuality, and second in creating possibilities. Given the category of real possibility, we have a role in making them relevant, that is, in making them potentialities, part of the *me on*. But the divine transcendence with respect to the possible goes beyond this. The divine role is not only that of cooperating with us in relevantizing possibilities in the *me on*, but in advance of this relevantizing, with an eye to the remote future, creating possibilities out of the *ouk on*, the nothing at all; that is, arranging the *me on* from the *ouk on*; and in this sense the divine activity is a *creatio ex nihilo*.

This slight change makes clearer the categorical power of creation in the divine activity. God creates from the *ouk on*! We as befits our lesser status only from the *me on*. He does what we do and does it better, that is, categorically, and that helps us in what we can do. Is this not a more faithful rendering of God's role as categorical exemplar of the category of the possible?

The divine event confronts us, one might say, at the two edges of the process of our lives. At its leading edge we sense how the possibilities of our lives lead out into something more. At its trailing edge we sense how our lives, so far achieved, fit into the total past.

An argument for the universe as the body of God now emerges. It arises in answer to the following puzzle: If we experience God through the immediate past, as we experience each other, why is it that we experience each other so obtrusively and God so unobtrusively? Why would not a being who transcends us categorically not be more obtrusive than our neighbor? The answer is that God is more obtrusive than our neighbor, for the universe is the body of God, and we sense the body of the universe more obtrusively than the body of our neighbor. On inspecting this claim it occurs to one that, given the difference of scale between my body and that of one of my cells, the same spread apartness I experience in the universe, with its vastness of space, would—could one of my cells experience as I experience—be experienced by the cell. And the differences would be almost wholly explicable by the difference of function and requirement on the part of various features of the environment, as Plato in fact argued in the *Timaeus*. In neither my neighbor nor the universe is the "awareness" possessed by that body obtrusively sensed. One point, indeed, on which philosophers agree, is the lack of direct awareness of other minds.

To my astonishment the sense of uncanniness I had long felt has been entirely dissipated by these considerations. The reason, I think, is both the "elbow room" provided by relativity and the fact that even though the divine event has as its instrument the entire body of the world, my chief concern is knowing the mind of God, not his body. The identification of the universe with the body of God has, however, an ethical advantage. Consider our obligation in caring for the universe, when the universe is so conceived, in preserving, that is to say, the eco system. Panentheism lends itself to the ecological ethic.

I conclude that the Whitehead-Hartshorne system works well metaphysically, and that the image of the universe as the body of God is not alien to the basic features of the system. When I put the total system in the world of practical concerns, however, ethical problems arise. Consider the assertion that God is motivated by ethical concerns. This surely implies that there are ethical absolutes in the divine nature. Whitehead does not affirm of God anything approaching ethical absolutes. Hartshorne's dual transcendence opens the way for them (functioning in relation to ethical relativities); but Hartshorne has concentrated more on the divine sensitivity to the world, that is, on God's ethical relativity.

The Whitehead-Hartshorne system is certainly adequate axiologically. It tells us how to develop our lives in terms of maximum value-enhancement. We are to work our lives into a finished whole. One begins with whatever random set of themes initially ingressed into one. These must be worked toward definitude. One sublimates, of course, but only in order to gain a higher transvaluation. One accepts other themes, introduces new themes, and works the whole toward some kind of logical, aesthetic, and valuational perfection. In doing this one is selecting relevant possibilities which make further possibilities relevant. This is helpful, and conforms elegantly to the dual transcendence of the divine.

One's transcendent sense in developing one's life is that one owes this much to the universe (or to God). It is really not enough to say that one's obligations are to society, although Kant put it so. Society doesn't care that much, nor know what if anything is owed it. But the Whiteheadian antecedent and consequent natures relate one both to a transcendent lure to go beyond one's past in the direction of value-enhancement, and to a transcendent appreciation for one's efforts and achievements. So beyond our relatedness to others is a sense of relatedness to the universe which adds to human life some of the amplitude of a "cosmic" purpose. In each actual occasion one relates to a divine event. Something like a constant dialogue with the divine is going on.

But while the Whiteheadian alternative tells us how we are to develop our lives, it is silent concerning the ethical dimensions of value-enhancement. And even though there is an ethical implication in panentheism, ethical absolutes have been hitherto scanted in the system. The divine functioning is universal. God saves the subjective immediacies of all events, of evil events as well as good. He adjusts possibilities into relevance for both saints and sinners. But better no God than one who is ethically neutral! Nor can Whitehead claim with Leibniz that this is the best of all possible worlds. One might be able to say that with the help of everyone it could become so. But if that is so then quite a few are not helping.

Plato said that God was perfect; and a saying of Jesus makes it clear that ethical perfection must be included in the kind of perfection appropriate to the divine nature. It is in the spirit of Hartshornian dual transcendence to insist on ethical perfection in God. But God saves the subjective immediacies of six million suffering Jews and along with this the ghoulish immediacies of their executioners and the satisfactions of a Hitler in the success of his plan. Is there point in saving the former? Is it ethical to save the latter?

How is this to be worked out? The first response is that if temporal passage is from possibility through discrete instantiation to objective immortality, everything must be saved. The Whiteheadian view is that conflicts must be turned into contrasts in the end. That is the axiological judgment; but what of the unfairness of these conflicts?

If follows from the metaphysics of the system that God feels the immediacy of the suffering of the six million Jews and always shall. It also follows that he feels the satisfactions of their tormenters and always will. When we add the requirement that God is necessarily ethical it follows that he cannot feel satisfaction in the satisfactions of the tormenters. He feels their satisfactions and is tormented by them. Part of God's transcendence is transcendence toward perfection, and ethical perfection implies ethical sensitivity. That is the relativistic point stressed by Hartshorne. God, then, is in torment, and will so remain until the sufferings of the six million shall have been expiated. How does one expiate the sufferings of six million men, women, and children? Not easily. And only by such a change in the world that the premises from which the final solution came are no longer in place, and are no longer even imaginable. But that supposes such a change in us and in our world that ethics is able to enter the marketplace, the world of politics, and even the world of religion. And since God is ethical, that is what he wishes. More, that is what he demands.

It also follows that those are doing the work of God who move us ever so slightly toward that changed situation. Elie Wiesel and others are doing the work of God by keeping the subjective immediacy of that suffering before us. Israel is doing the work of God by making it less imaginable than before that such an event can recur. Those Christians attempting to make their constituencies sense their constituent complicity in the final solution, those too are doing the work of God. And those indifferent to that suffering oppose the work of God.

But, meanwhile, what in the world is God doing? Surely, it is not in his nature to suffer passively. He would act against the evil. But when ever did he do that? And what would we have him do? Should he in the case of Hitler have simply arranged that one of the latter's epileptic seizures be terminal? Should he have taken advantage of Churchill's natural brio, luring him to order bombing raids against the rail lines leading to concentration camps? This is, of course, the type of the Humian Philo's suggestions: Why did God not arrange for a wave sufficiently higher than the rest, to send Catullus and his minions to the bottom? Indeed, why not? If his power does not extend to such matters, what can he do?

Jesus had already turned from such a thought, saying that the sun shone and the rain fell on good and bad alike. But he likewise held the belief, lacking in the Whiteheadian alternative, that in the end God would unmistakably intervene. Until then it is up to us. If Jesus is correct we should expect no special help now in bringing ethics into life, whatever might be the case at the end of the times.

One argument we might make is that it is appropriate for humans to accept total responsibility for what humans do. That would seem to be Whiteheadian. Someone might answer: But that is the way it has been in the past and consider what a mess we've made of it. We need special help.

To say that, the answer might continue, is to say we wish to be treated, or need to be treated, as children. We exempt children from full responsibility for what they do. If things begin going badly, we intervene to bring the matter out as it ought to be. One can't expect children to bear full responsibility for what they do, we say. Are we such children that this is the treatment we require?

Whatever we wish, or think we need, God has decided—one might put it so —to treat us as adults, leaving us totally responsible for what we and others do.

That solves at least part of the problem of theodicy while returning us to the appearance of God's ethical neutrality, since a world in which God treats us as adults will look exactly like a world with no God at all. In contrast, a world where God treats us as children will have a different look. In the nursery-type world of one's imagination we could be sure of God, so one might argue. In such a world God would be perhaps thirty-six feet tall so that we couldn't possibly miss him.

Our complaint, then, may amount to saying that God has chosen to treat us as though we were adults. And our complaint would be that we are so far from being adults that we cannot be counted upon to face up to adult responsibilities. But perhaps the truth is that we haven't faced up to adult responsibilities because, speaking of those who believe in God, it never occurred to us that God really would treat us as the adults we are (or ought to be) leaving us to perform on the high wire of life with no safety net whatever. If only we had known, we might have accepted adult responsibilities and saved God much of the torment he now experiences.

There does, then, exist an appropriate response to God's apparent inaction. He has assigned us total responsibility for our actions. This brings the metaphysics and the ethics into consistency; but if the universe in which God assigns us total responsibility is in every specifiable way exactly like a universe in which there is no God, the use of the term 'God' looks like a *façon de parler*, a claim made of Spinoza's use of *Deus sive natura*.

Still, it is consistent with the Whitehead-Hartshorne alternative to say that God's power is not of the kind that could send one wave a little higher than the rest or arrange for Hitler not to have come out of an epileptic seizure, any more than we have power to arrange specifically for an individual cell of our body to undertake a specific mission. Perhaps we can sometimes influence our cells in general, but surely not one by one. Where the mental pole of an individual is sufficiently high however, we might say, God is able to offer a lure toward goodness. One would have to suppose, then, that God did try to lure Churchill into bombing the railheads leading in to the concentration camps, and that Churchill did not respond. That is, perhaps, understandable. We are so deficient in rationality, and so swayed by prejudices on so many levels that we must often fail to respond to the divine lure.

Consider, for example, the fact that until the post–World War II period not a single Christian cried out a warning to the rest that putting the Jews in ghettoes, and practicing on them most of the inhuman anti-semitisms later used by Hitler, was irreligious. Not a single warning in over nineteen hundred years! Socrates pointed out that it is not what others do to you that harms your character. It is what you do to others.

On the hypothesis, these actions on our part keep God in ethical torment. That may mean little to a neutral observer but it would mean a great deal, I should think, to anyone with religious commitment. Such a person believes in the divine and is concerned about relating to the divine in an appropriate manner. The religious person is concerned about causing suffering anywhere. To cause suffering to the divine should leave this person likewise in torment.

But why then is there such apparent placidity in religious people? In the classical tradition it was only inconsistently believed that God could suffer. Many religious persons in that tradition do not believe that God can suffer. But the Whiteheadian God cannot avoid suffering. Perhaps many religious persons do not feel personally responsible for God's suffering. But if we are totally responsible as human beings for what humans do, we cannot avoid responsibility. Even if, *per impossibile*, we were in no way involved in any of the events which cause suffering in God, we would still be responsible because we are involved in humanity. And given the duplicity of human motives on so many levels, both conscious and unconscious, it is certain that we are actively involved in perpetuating many of the evils of the world. The only way we can reduce the extent of our responsibility, then, is to work actively on the problems, changing ourselves and our world, so that the evil is overcome. Otherwise we are not part of the solution but part of the problem.

The best explanation for the placidity of religious people derives, I now suggest, from their false view of divine providence. The religious person believes in providence, and often this amounts to the belief that whatever happens must have happened because God willed it.

Cromwell sat up with his friends seeking divine guidance concerning whether Charles I should after all be executed. While the praying went on, some functionary proceeded independently with the beheading. By the next morning Cromwell was saying that since the execution had occurred without its having been ordered, it must have been God's will. This supposes a notion of providence where everything that happens happens because God is in control. But such a view clearly needs to be modified on the Whitehead-Hartshorne view. The ordinary view opens itself to the duplicity which arises so easily in all of us, and in such hidden ways. Relate that to the fate of the six million! And it supports Hegel's comment about the truth that lies in power.

I think we need to suppose with Plato that God is the cause of a few things only, and not of the many things that happen in the world. But if that is so, Cromwell cannot properly take the circumstance that something has happened as a sign of divine approval. Religious people persist in doing this and thereby adulterate the purity of their faith.

Now, on the hypothesis, God is luring all of us in the direction of the good, and our resistance adds to the divine suffering. The fact that God's subjective immediacy retains the suffering of the past forever, introduces a perspective not available to some metaphysical alternatives. It is not the case, then, that time heals. Time heals, in common wisdom, because our retention of the past is inadequate. We forget and are healed. Given the eternality of the divine subjective immediacy, the only manner in which time can heal is by our overcoming the evil in the world. Given God's nature, there is no forgetting the past. Its evil must be expiated. And that expiation requires a radically new present in contrast to the past. The point is that from this standpoint we have not only our own karma to overcome but the karma, so to speak, of the world. And we cannot speak of our freedom from responsibility until we have overcome this world karma. Logically speaking, the Whitehead-Hartshorne alternative requires more ethical behavior, more social action, than its surrogates.

I have been using the Final Solution as the paradigm case of our responsibility for suffering. There are other cases I might have used. There is the manner in which we humans have thought of blacks as less than human in order to practice our dehumanizations against them in "good" conscience.

There is the manner in which New England puritans thought of the Indian villages as "the abode of Satan," partly at least for the sake of acquiring land. There is the manner in which Eve was thought of as being made from Adam's rib, partly at least for the sake of male domination. There is the manner in which future generations are simply not thought of, partly at least in order that our current exploitation of the environment may continue. But if the world around us is the body of God. . . . And if God is both ethical and in torment . . .

The divine lure entices us but we resist. Does this mean that God's program is not working? How has it gone thus far? He has achieved Socrates, Jesus, Albert Schweitzer, Gandhi, Raoul Wallenberg, and Martin Luther King. There have been others, of course; for example, Aristides de Sousa Mendes, second only to Wallenberg in the saving of Jewish lives. In addition, there are the underworkers who are as unobtrusive as the divine event itself. But suppose there have been just six. That averages out to one enlightened person each four hundred years. Given the immensity of time, that may be a good average. It may even be encouraging that two-thirds of those who qualify as God's human beings belong to the present century. Maybe God is making progress. The appearance of the six is enough in any case to provide patterns for what we must do, letting us know how our lives must testify.

These reasonable responses follow, I suggest, in the Whitehead-Hartshorne alternative when ethics is added to axiology. But there is a problem still. The credibility of the language of panentheism about the universe as the body of God rested partly on the ground that the working core of panentheism is the relation between the individual and the divine event. Let us follow this out a bit. There is in this alternative a relativistic equivalent to Newton's view of space as the divine sensorium. For process thought it would not be space, but space-time, which is the divine sensorium; indeed, we have held that divine and human interrelate in each space-time event. These events so much involve both sides that one's relation to the universe as inclusive of the divine event might be better called a "divine dialogicum" (or a divine-human dialogicum). Just as it does not seem improbable that the universe is the body of God, neither is it improbable that space-time should be the medium through which we experience God for this is the medium, to repeat an earlier point, through which we experience each other.

Everyone, then, is on this view engaged in a dialogue with the universe, not to say at times, a disputation. We talk to ourselves. We talk to each other, and sometimes just to the "other." In the same way that our sense of obligation relates, or seems to relate, beyond society so we sometimes have feelings of gratitude which are not appropriately directed to our parents, family, and friends, and so we direct them to the universe at large, hoping that the universe can somehow feel satisfaction in our satisfactions. We sometimes have complaints, too, not appropriately directed against family, friends, and society. It is the universe that is to blame. This is the kind of gratitude and complaint that is ordinarily directed to God.

Prayer is part of that dialogue; and prayers are addressed to God in every language. Are we then to say that among whatever else God is also the supreme linguist, the total Berlitz student, understanding every language and dialect? It would seem that we need to say something of the sort. How would the subjective immediacy of linguistic events be retained except in language, all of the languages of the world? We might reduce the strangeness of the saying by reflecting that speech and thought finally lead to action, and the dialogues we have in mind are at last dialogues of events. We think and speak and act, and then await a response from the world. We speak sometimes of a logic of events, as though what could happen now depends on what has happened already. And when we talk that way we mean that the events themselves support (and are supported by) some events, and are incompatible with others.

If we turn to Wittgenstein for a moment, although it was his view that the games of the world are language games, in his comments about religion the nonverbal is featured. He suggested that one should take note of the gestures of prayer behind the words. And he at least once asserted that Mozart and Beethoven are the actual sons of God. And musical inspiration, this is surely obvious, both begins and ends nonverbally. Perhaps there is a way of discounting words in relation to the divine event. But if through the logic of events the role of language is diminished, we must not allow that diminution to return us to the easy view of providence which we have rejected. Our view must be that only those events can reflect the divine will which are in harmony with the lure to the good. And certainly, however it may be with God, *we* must use language to parse out the subtle complexities of a logic of events which is counter-balanced against, while including, the ideally possible.

The problem arises from situating intentionality in the heart of the universe, and calls for clarity with respect to the manner in which divine and human intentions interrelate. This is, I suspect, a problem for all of theism; it certainly seems a problem for the Whitehead-Hartshorne framework. It perplexes me that, having worked my way through the problems troubling me in panentheism, I should now have come upon intractability where I had least expected it, in the relation between humans and the divine event.

At a certain point one's tendency is simply to bail out, one standard move being the leap of faith. One wants one's knight of faith to be warm-hearted. One also wants him to be clear-headed. One does not want him to be simple-minded.

WILLIAM L. REESE

DEPARTMENT OF PHILOSOPHY
STATE UNIVERSITY OF NEW YORK AT ALBANY
JULY 1986

NOTES

1. A. Schweitzer, *The Mysticism of Paul the Apostle*, trans. W. Montgomery (New York: Henry Holt & Co., 1931), pp.6–9.

2. In "Dipolarity and Monopolarity in the Idea of God," *Dialogos* (41 [1983], pp. 51–58).

3. *The Divine Milieu* (New York: Harper and Row, 1960), pp. 46–47.

4. A. N. Whitehead, *Process and Reality* (New York: Free Press, 1969), p. 405. Hereafter, the page number in parentheses, appearing in the text, shall refer to this book and edition.

5. Nothing is lost, I think, if at this point I use "event" rather than "occasion" language.

6. N. Herbert, *Quantum Reality* (New York: Anchor Books, Doubleday, 1985), pp. 211–31.

10

Jan Van der Veken

ULTIMATE REALITY AND GOD: THE SAME?

6 6 Ts 'cosmic wholeness' a religious conception?"[1] Charles Hartshorne thinks
I it is. The referent of worship—"Thou shalt love the Lord thy God with
all thy heart and with all thy mind and with all thy soul and with all thy
strength"—cannot be less than all-inclusive reality. Hence Hartshorne states
rather bluntly: "God is the all-inclusive reality."[2]

Admittedly, to say that God is more than all-inclusive reality is nonsensical. But does it follow from this that "God" and "all-inclusive reality," if
having the same referent, have exactly the same meaning? It seems to me that
the transition from all-inclusive reality to God is rather easy for Hartshorne
(and as I will try to show, for Anselm as well), and that it is more difficult for
many of us.

This article endeavors to show that a clearer distinction between the
philosophical absolute (all-inclusive reality) and the religious absolute (God)
contributes greatly to our clarification of the logic of all-inclusive reality and the
logic of God. As a conclusion I will show that this distinction highly illumines
and clarifies many of Hartshorne's own positions. In this sense, it is at the same
time a tribute offered to Hartshorne, an honorary doctor of the University of
Leuven, because the clarification of the relationship between the philosophical
absolute and the religious absolute has been the main focus of our discussions
and research with relation to process thought;[3] moreover, this reflection would
not have been possible without Hartshorne's basic inspiration.

I will state my position in an almost Hartshornian way, using a logic and
symbolism which is, I hope, congenial to his own.

Def. 1. Ultimate Reality (UR) is the philosophical Absolute, however it is
conceived. In the tradition of the West UR has been called the Absolute, Being,
Reality, Substance, Eternal Matter, Absolute Spirit, or something of the like.

Def. 2. The different ways of naming and conceiving UR are called *qualifications* of UR; hence UR-Q. From the historical point of view there have been many ways to conceive Ultimate Reality, and it seems that this is possible. What would be unthinkable is a conception where ultimate reality would not be qualified at all; this would move us closer to some Eastern conceptions of the Absolute, downgrading the reality of the many to sheer appearance or illusion.

Def. 3. The word *God* is used by the religious person in order to refer to the ultimate source of meaning and value. Ultimate Reality, religiously qualified (UR-Q$_r$) is often equated with God; God$_r$ stands for the God of religion. The question of the ultimate meaning of existence is closely related to the possibility of attributing certain religious qualifications to the Absolute.

Thesis 1. Ultimate Reality is in principle all-inclusive; this is expressed by the notion of "the Absolute." It is nonsensical to say that something "is" and does not belong to Reality. All-encompassivity is the first feature of Reality as a whole. That all-encompassive Reality is absolute means that it is not related to anything outside of itself. Absoluteness in this sense, of course, does not exclude but rather includes relations with each and every *r*eality; in principle they are included in all-encompassive *R*eality. All-encompassive Reality has been conceived by Parmenides as "complete on every side, like the mass of a well-rounded sphere,"[4] but more frequently it (Being) has been understood as infinite, because no boundaries (*finis*) to Reality as a whole can be conceived (Spinoza's argument for the uniqueness of Substance). For this reason, Reality as a whole can be seen without a beginning or an end and can be called infinite ("in-finite"; "*Un-endlich*").

Thesis 2. The affirmation of all-encompassive Reality is necessary, and as such belongs to modal logic.

> p stands for "Reality exists"; hence $\Box$p.
> It is impossible to deny the existence of p; $\Box p \rightarrow \neg \Diamond \neg p$.

I am not talking here about *a* reality *x*, which may or may not exist [∃ x(ax)], but about the necessary existence of all-encompassive Reality. The objection that "existence is not a predicate" applies only to particular, contingent realities, which may or may not exist, but *necessary* existence is rightly attributed to that which *cannot* fail to exist, hence to Reality as a whole. That Reality as a whole cannot conceivably not exist is what I propose to call "Parmenides' intuition": Being *is*, necessarily, or not at all.[5]

Thesis 3. Reality as a whole is "id quo majus cogitari nequit" (Anselm's phrase; hereafter "IQM"), provided that "majus" does not immediately convey the idea of perfection. It follows from Theses 1 and 2 that IQM is all-encompassive Reality and exists necessarily.

Given the *limited* understanding of IQM in Thesis 3, IQM cannot be contradictory, but it also follows that IQM does not necessarily have the religious qualifications that the believer would want to attach to God$_r$. Anselm's—and Hartshorne's —position is less convincing than it could be, because it does not make a sufficient distinction between the philosophical Absolute (Reality which exists necessarily) and the religious Absolute (God, conceived as [a] perfect, knowing, caring, loving Individual). It does not follow from the above three theses that IQM is also the source of ultimate meaning. IQM can be and has been understood in very different ways. To give just a few examples from the Western tradition, IQM has been conceived

- as Substance, God, or Nature, by Spinoza;
- as Spirit-expressing-Itself-in-the-world, by Hegel;
- as the God of classical theism, by Anselm and Aquinas;
- as the God of neo-classical theism (God surpassable only by Himself), by Fechner and Hartshorne.

I. The Logic of Paradoxical Theism

Anselm could equate IQM and God because he accepted the traditional Christian theistic framework. God himself is absolute Being, and the finite world does not add anything to him. Only within this particular context can IQM also be equated with God$_r$. This context is the result of the conflation between the philosophical Absolute (UR or all-that-is) and the [Creator-] God of both philosophy and theology, creating creatures which belong to Reality but are not included in IQM.

Hartshorne has convincingly pointed out that this position leads to paradoxical theism, because it has to face both philosophical and theological difficulties.

Let us first examine the philosophical difficulties. Anselm is looking for a modal proof (a proof that everyone who thinks would have to accept) for God$_r$. This is possible for Anselm because for him God$_r$ and IQM coincide, and IQM is that which cannot be thought as not existing: "And you, Lord our God, are this being."[7] On the contrary, Aquinas saw that a modal proof for the existence of God is not possible, because some philosophers have interpreted IQM differently, for example, along materialistic lines.[8] This is one reason why Thomas does not accept an a priori or modal proof for the existence of God.

The presupposition underlying the equation of God and IQM is that finite beings do not add anything at all to IQM. According to Anselm's presuppositions, IQM can exist without the created universe, so that, strictly speaking, created beings do not add anything at all to Being: "in that case, there are more beings, but there is not more Being" ("*dantur plura entia, non datur plus entis*"), according to a traditional saying of scholastic philosophy. If they did add something, indeed, then *God + creatures* would be greater than God, in which case this would be IQM. But how can something *be* without adding something to Being? How can there be something outside of IQM? The only logical conclusion is that IQM also includes finite beings.

In order to understand that God, even without creatures, could be conceived as IQM, we have to turn towards the origin of classical theism. The conceptualization of classical theism derives mainly from Aristotelian theism, combined with the Judeo-Christian doctrine of creation. Aristotle's Unmoved Mover is clearly *not* IQM, but rather the highest substance, a being amongst other beings. God, in this vision, is clearly not "all-there-is," but the highest (and most eminent) substance. For Aristotle, it makes no sense to say that God and Being coincide. The heavenly bodies are as eternal as the Unmoved Mover. Only when the Judeo-Christian doctrine of *creation ex nihilo* is accepted can the conception of God as the One Absolute Being arise.

The so-called onto-theological structure of Western metaphysics, pointed out by Heidegger, is a direct consequence of the cultural identification of the highest substance and God$_r$, conceived as the Creator or as the necessary ground of beings. The philosophical Absolute is here conceived as the available ground of all beings, and is equated at the same time with the first substance of Aristotle as well as with God$_r$ (who is admittedly also conceived as *a* Being or as *an* Individual). God is from now on conceived as *a* Being amongst beings, albeit the highest, and as the unshakeable ground of all becoming, though he himself is excluded from change.

Let us now turn to the religious difficulties. These are easily pointed out, because Hartshorne himself has convincingly done so many times. True enough, the equation between God and IQM has occurred primarily for religious reasons: the *Proslogion* is written in the context of a prayer. But unavoidably, to attribute unchangeability to God and to deny real relationships between him and his creatures leads towards difficulties; these have been adumbrated by the great theistic tradition, but they have never been solved. It does not suffice to say, as Anselm did, that God "is merciful according to [our] way of looking at things, and not according to [his]."[9]

It is Hartshorne's great merit to have shown that these logical difficulties can be solved to the benefit of religion. The claim that there are real relationships between God and his creatures (and not just between creatures and God) is probably the best way to characterize the difference between classical and neo-classical theism. All the rest follows from this recognition.

Although Hartshorne's theism is very different from Anselm's, he has been continuously attracted by Anselm's proof; God and IQM coincide for Hartshorne as well, albeit on the basis of quite different presuppositions. Hartshorne can equate IQM and God, since for him "God is the all-inclusive reality":[10] "I hold that God is unsurpassably inclusive and also unsurpassably integrated or unified. He is the all as an individual being."[11] In fact, IQM and God can be equated because God is conceived by Hartshorne in the way of absolute idealism, much in line with the position of Josiah Royce,[12] where God is the Absolute, conceived as an all-inclusive, perfect Knower. Hartshorne's version of the ontological argument clearly proves more than the existence of all-encompassive Reality: he gives IQM the richer meaning of *perfect inclusion through knowledge*. But it follows from this that Hartshorne's version of the ontological argument convinces only those who are willing to accept all-inclusiveness in the idealistic sense, i.e. as the perfect inclusion of the known by the Knower. However, when we give IQM the simpler meaning of all-inclusive Reality as such (Thesis 3), then it is obvious that Reality cannot fail to exist, and that, in principle, it must include realities. For this reason the ontological argument is much more solid if the meaning given to $\square$IQM is more modest than "perfection exists." "That which is such that greater cannot be conceived" cannot fail to exist, but *the way* in which all-inclusive Reality includes all realities cannot be decided on the basis of modal logic alone. Is there another way to say more about IQM?

II. Distinguishing Between the Philosophical Absolute and its Qualifications

A possible way out is a clearer distinction between Ultimate Reality (UR) and the Ultimate Qualifications (Q)—religious and non-religious (Q_r and Q_{nr})—which can/should be attributed to UR. According to this symbolism, God is represented not simply as UR but as UR-Q_r, i.e. Ultimate Reality, religiously qualified.

The problem of the necessity of an ontological foundation of all-there-is points towards the philosophical Absolute, which, as such, is neutral with regard to meaning and values. "Reality," "Substance," "All-there-is"—or, to use more dynamic notions, "Ongoingness," "Substantial Activity," "Creativity"—account for the fact "that there is something rather than nothing" (Leibniz's question), but they provide no clues about the way all-inclusive Reality should be conceived.

Ultimate Reality or the philosophical Absolute—Substantial Activity, Creativity (or, in other philosophies, Reality, Being, *Phusis*)—has all the modal features that most philosophers of the past have attributed to Reality as a whole. UR can be said to be

- absolute, i.e. not related to something outside itself: UR_1;
- all-encompassive in principle (otherwise it would not be ultimate): UR_2;
- one (or unifying the many): UR_3;
- necessarily existing: UR_4;
- eternal and/or including all temporal events: UR_5;
- omnipresent or including all space: UR_6;
- infinite (without boundaries): UR_7;
- etc.: UR_{7+n}.

Different conceptual frameworks are possible, but in any framework we must somehow account for the difference between Being and beings, between the One and the Many, the Absolute and the relative. Theistic philosophers cherish the idea that there is only one way to account for the being-there of finite beings, namely to appeal to God as the Creator of everything finite. But this need not be the only way to account for the fact "that there is something rather than nothing." Spinoza sees Substance for example as the ground of the finite modes. A materialistic philosopher would claim that eternal matter is the ground of all finite, material (and also of so-called spiritual) realities.

The equation of Substantial Activity, Creativity, or Self-developing Spirit with God is the basic idea behind pantheism. All that happens follows by necessity from the divine nature, "*ex necessitate divinae naturae*" (Spinoza's phrase): it happens necessarily, is as it ought to be, and hence is good. Classical theism also maintains that UR = the Absolute = God = the Creator of all finite beings. Here UR is subsistent Being, *Ipsum Esse Subsistens*, which does not require anything outside of itself in order to exist and can therefore be called *the* Absolute. As Hartshorne has shown, classical theism is therefore faced with the problem of an Absolute which is less than all-there-is, and of finite realities which do not add anything at all to Being.

Hartshorne also equates UR and God, but in a different framework. God now *includes* the temporal world; all-encompassivity appears to be the key difference between classical and neo-classical theism. Hartshorne thinks that the T-factor (Temporality) saves him from pantheism.[14] Indeed, he is not really a pantheist in the traditional sense, because he allows for creaturely freedom: God as eminent creativity includes freely acting agents and is qualified by their decisions. But in another sense God and all-there-is *do* coincide: God is at the same time eminently creative and in his concrete state he includes all other forms of creativity. This inclusion is effected by knowledge. Perfect knowledge for Hartshorne is not different than ontological inclusion; God includes everything because he is the perfect Knower, taking everything he knows into his own being.

Having difficulties with this idealistic type of inclusion, I suggest that Creativity itself should be conceived in terms of all-encompassivity. All that is is either Creativity, an instance of Creativity, or a qualification of Creativity; for this reason, Creativity = UR. But Creativity and God should not be identified. Creativity as such is neutral with regard to values: it is neither good nor bad. It is sheer ongoingness, accounting for the fact *that* beings are there, but saying nothing about how we are to evaluate them (except, probably, that it is better to be than not to be, as is expressed by the classical motto *ens et bonum convertuntur*). The world is, as far as I can see, not good enough to coincide with what the believer understands by "God"; God$_r$ is *not yet* "all in all" (1 Cor. 15:28). God is thus seen in my view not as all-there-is, but as a religious qualification of all-there-is, i.e. UR seen *as the believer sees it*. Seeing is always a "seeing as," as Wittgenstein has pointed out;[15] to see is to interpret or to add qualifications.

III. UR and God-talk

Let us now turn to a survey of some qualifications of UR which have been proposed, and try to determine in which cases "God$_r$-talk" would be appropriate.

It is clear that mankind has differed profoundly about the possibilities of attributing definite characteristics to Reality as a whole. Different interpretations of the philosophical Absolute have been given, some more theistic, some atheistic, some neutral. It may be doubted whether "reality as such," or "unqualified reality," can be at all if it is completely without any determination. Reality, in order to be definite (this, rather than that), needs some qualifications $(Q_{1, 2, \ldots n})$.

UR seems to be qualified by some order or mutual adjustment (Q_1). Without some order imposed upon the many, it is doubtful whether the many would be possible at all. This point has been made by Hartshorne many times, and implies that UR cannot exist without Q_1. Hence UR-Q_1 seems to apply whenever the problem of the One and the Many arises.

Logos seems to be a feature without which order, to whatever extent, is unthinkable. Some account of the observed regularities of our universe must be given, e.g. through the notion of an all-encompassive *Nous* (Anaxagoras). UR qualified by *Nous* or cosmic intellect is symbolized by UR-Q_2.

It is clear that from this point on the added qualifications and above all their interpretation are far more debatable than is that which can be said about UR on the basis of modal logic alone. Some have conceived Reality as permeated by reason: they believed in a World Soul (Plato), a cosmic intellect (Stoic philosophy), or a mathematical mind (Leibniz), etc. Some have conceived that intellect as personal, others as impersonal (anonymous thought). Most of what can be said about UR cannot be said on the basis of modal logic. Another universe is possible in the sense of being conceivable. This is to say that such characteristics do not belong necessarily to Ultimate Reality, and that our universe can be interpreted meaningfully in quite different ways. It follows that the more definite characteristics of UR can be attributed to it only on the basis of the *particular experiences* of mankind, religious or otherwise. These experiences are culturally determined, and deliver their message only when they are seen in their appropriate historical contexts.[16]

To say that UR is qualified by order and intellect does not yet seem to justify God-talk (provided that we give to "God" the *religious* meaning of that term). Some additional qualifications are necessary. These high-grade qualifications will bring us closer to Hartshorne's panentheistic world-view.

Can we recognize a "counter-agency" at work in the universe, a drive of Reason towards more complex structures (UR-Q_3)? Whitehead thinks that this is the case,[17] and Hartshorne agrees. But "Reason" in this context still has a very open-ended meaning; such a "counter-agency" has also been accepted by scientists, such as Ilya Prigogine.[18] They see a mystery at work in the universe which is ever open for new possibilities. For them, this upward trend is as "natural" as the movement towards the greatest possible disorder (entropy). Such a counter-agency can be conceived along theistic or non-theistic lines (as, e.g. in dialectical materialism, in which an upward trend is also recognized and said to be a qualification of "dialectical matter" itself). Nevertheless, the recognition of that counter-agency already moves us in a direction of the *more* than sheer matter, or more than the "eternal return of the same" (*Ewige Wiederkehr des Gleichen*; Nietzsche).

To say that the unity-in-diversity that is UR can best be conceived as an all-encompassing Experience, subjectively enjoying harmony, is a claim bringing us very close to Hartshorne's own position. But in the scheme given here, this is already UR-Q_4! The universe need not be conceived this way. Other *further* qualifications are the principle of the Good (UR-Q_5), unbounded love (UR-Q_6), and the overcoming of evil (UR-Q_7).

It seems to me that the minimal requirement for characterizing the philosophical Absolute (UP) as "divine" or for recognizing the God of religion at work in it, is that Reality be conceived as qualified or characterized not just by order and intelligence ($Q_{1 \text{ and } 2}$), but also by ethical demand, love and concern ($Q_{5, 6 \text{ and possibly } 7}$). The problem of philosophical theology is not to solve the question "whether there is a certain being called God" ("*un certain nommé, Dieu*"),[19] but whether there are enough reasons to conceive Reality, which exists anyway, as qualified by "divine" attributes, such as (minimally) rationality and concern, but probably ethical demand and the overcoming of evil as well.

Only extreme pantheism identifies UR and God without qualification. In all other systems there is a certain tension between all-there-is and God.

Traditional theism is one way to come to grips with this tension. On the one hand, God is not "all-there-is." He is conceived as subsistent being itself (on the basis of a literal interpretation of *Sum qui sum* in Exodus 3), and, as such, coincides with UR or with the Absolute. Yet through an act of free creation he brings about the whole created universe, which nevertheless adds nothing at all to subsistent being besides contributing to his external glory (*externa gloria Dei*).

My own position, which is a qualified Whiteheadianism or a Hartshorne-inspired "eschatological theo-en-pantism," could be summarized as follows:

1. Nothing can exist outside of UR; UR is *in principle* all-inclusive. UR is IQM (*id quo majus cogitari nequit*). "Majus" here has the limited meaning of "greater than" or "more encompassive than."
2. UR (Being, Substance, or in a more dynamic philosophy, Substantial Activity or Creativity) expresses itself, manifests itself, or appears in a manifold of beings, modes, or instances. All beings, realities, or instantiations of Creativity are not necessary, but because they are necessarily included in UR, they add concreteness to it (Hartshorne's "unsurpassable" insight).
3. On the basis of the spectacle of the universe (of which we are a part), we recognize that UR is qualified by order, intellect, directedness towards values. Because these concrete features or qualifications of UR are close to what a religious person understands by "God" or by the "divine," God-language is inchoatively appropriate at this level of qualification.
4. Here God is not a being amongst beings, nor Being itself, nor Reality. Reality as a whole seems too neutral, too ambiguous, to be addressed meaningfully by the word "God." The object of worship is not Reality itself, but rather that Instance at the ground of our being which seems directed towards beauty, goodness, and harmony and which lures us in that same direction. Because he cannot be outside of or "above" reality (as is the One for Plotinus), God, in this scheme, is to be seen as the objective ground in Reality itself of what the religious person intends to say: he/she believes that, taking everything into account, innermost Reality is lured towards truth, values, goodness, beauty, harmony, and that this directedness cannot be reduced to what we finite human beings can account for.
5. The religious person sees that the world and the Kingdom of God (the world as it *should be* from a religious point of view) do *not yet* coincide, but he/she hopes that God *will be* all in all (hence "eschatological theo-en-pantism").

Whereas traditional theism can be understood as the result of the conflation of the philosophical Absolute and the religious Absolute—which seemed necessary in the medieval philosophico-religious context—today it is advisable to make a clearer distinction between the problem of Being and the problem of God. Hartshorne asks himself the question, "What is metaphysics?" His answer: "I use it to refer to the study which seeks to clarify our conception of the absolute, necessary, strictly universal, infinite or perfect."[20] We need drop only one more metaphysical compliment, addressed to Absolute or all-encompassive Reality, namely that it has to be conceived as perfect in the religious sense of the word. Reality does not seem perfect, even as all-inclusive Reality—now. The believer, however, trusts that Reality is permeated by an Instance, Force, or loving, compassionate Concern which makes it worthwhile to hope *in spite of* the evident non-perfection of the world.

Wouldn't it be wise, in these less rationalistic times, to invert Hartshorne's contention, "I am saying that revelation defines the question, while philosophy or secular reason, gives the answer"?[21] Isn't it rather the other way around? Philosophy or secular reason asks the question and looks for possible conceptual frameworks. Religion—inspired by hope—gives a possible answer, upon which philosophical theology has to reflect as rationally as possible.

JAN VAN DER VEKEN

INSTITUTE OF PHILOSOPHY
CATHOLIC UNIVERSITY OF LEUVEN
OCTOBER 1986

NOTES

1. Charles Hartshorne, *A Natural Theology for Our Time* (La Salle, Ill.: Open Court, 1967), p. 7. Hereafter NTOT.
2. NTOT, p. 12.
3. *Whitehead's Legacy. Proceedings of the European Weekend on Process Philosophy, Leuven, November 10–12, 1978*, P. Jonkers and J. Van der Veken, eds., (Leuven: Center for Metaphysics and Philosophy of God, 1981). See also my "Whitehead's God is not Whiteheadian Enough" in *Whitehead and the Idea of Process. Proceedings of the First International Whitehead Symposium, 1981*, Harold Holz and Ernest Wolf-Gazo, eds., (Freiburg-München: Karl Alber, 1984). André Cloots, who wrote an M.A. thesis *Ch. Hartshorne's bipolair theisme. Een studie van de grondintuities van zijn denken* (1972), summarizes the main findings of his doctoral dissertation, *Van creativiteit naar allesomvattendheid: de vraag naar het ultieme in de proces-filosofie van Whitehead en Hartshorne* (1978), in a lecture, delivered at the European Weekend on Process Philosophy in the presence of Charles and Dorothy Hartshorne, under the title "Creativity and God in Whitehead and Hartshorne" (pp. 43–59).

4. Kathleen Freeman, *Ancilla to the Pre-Socratic Philosophers. A Complete Translation of the Fragments in Diels, Fragmente der Vorsokratiker* (Oxford: Blackwell, 1962), p. 44.

5. Id., p. 43: "Thus it must Be absolutely, or not at all."

6. M. P. Slattery, "The Negative Ontological Argument," *New Scholasticism* 43 (Autumn 1969), p. 615: "Parmenides' doctrine of Being has all the hall-marks of what was later to be known as the ontological argument for the existence of God. In fact, later forms of the argument merely repeat the substance of Parmenides' proof and differ from it only in details. They all amount to saying that when you think of absolute being, and do so correctly, then you see it cannot lack anything at all, above all it cannot lack existence."

7. M. J. Charlesworth, *St. Anselm's Proslogion with a Reply on Behalf of the Fool by Gaunilo and The Author's Reply to Gaunilo*, translated with an introduction and philosophical commentary by M. J. Charlesworth (Notre Dame-London: University of Notre Dame Press, 1979), p. 119.

8. Thomas Aquinas, *Summa Theologiae*, I^a, Q. 2, art. 1: Utrum Deum esse, sit per se notum. "Ad secundum dicendum quod forte ille qui audit hoc nomen Deus, non intelligit significari aliquid quo majus cogitari non possit, cum quidam crediderint Deus esse corpus."

9. *St. Anselm's Proslogion*, ed. cit., Proslogion VIII, p. 125.

10. NTOT, p. 12.

11. Charles Hartshorne, *Creative Synthesis and Philosophic Method* (London: SCM, 1970), p. 236.

12. A. Cloots, "De vraag naar het ultieme in de proces-filosofie" in *Tijdschrift voor Filosofie* 42:1 (1980), p. 69, quotes in this context the title of Hartshorne's Ph.D. dissertation, *An Outline and Defense of the Argument for the Unity of Being in the Absolute or Divine Good* (1923). Not only the title but the whole dissertation makes it clear that the original influences upon and the early insights of Hartshorne are not Whiteheadian, but idealistic-monistic. With respect to this see also W. L. Sessions, "Hartshorne's Early Philosophy" in *Two Process Philosophers. Hartshorne's Encounter with Whitehead*, L. S. Ford, ed., *AAS Studies in Religion* 5 (1973), pp. 10–34. It is interesting to see that Hartshorne at first labels his vision "teleological monism" (in his dissertation), then "pantheism" (in his book *Beyond Humanism* of 1937), and eventually "panentheism."

13. Charles Hartshorne, "A Conversation between Charles Hartshorne and Jan Van der Veken," *Louvain Studies* 8:2 (1980), p. 134 : "It depends upon how you conceive inclusion. Now I conceive inclusion in idealistic terms. To include something in the ultimate sense is to know it, to be aware of it, to have it as a context of awareness. If I knew, fully knew the happiness of someone else, I would have that happiness, it would be mine."

14. Charles Hartshorne, "Introduction: The Standpoint of Panentheism" in *Philosophers Speak of God*, Charles Hartshorne and W. L. Reese, eds., (Chicago-London: University of Chicago Press, 1969), 4th ed., p. 22: "Against all these difficulties the T factor [Temporality] is our safeguard. It makes the W factor [World], the pantheistic motive, innocuous and thus opens the door of escape from the paradoxes of a supreme reality which yet cannot intelligibly contain the totality of the actual."

15. L. Wittgenstein, *Philosophical Investigations* (Oxford: Blackwell, 1953), part II, XI, pp. 193–195. I. T. Ramsey also points to the importance of this passage, in his introduction to *Words about God. The Philosophy of Religion*, I. T. Ramsey, ed. (New

York: Harper & Row, 1971), pp. 9–10. The problem of the "justification of our ways of seeing" is a much debated issue here in Leuven. I would like to thank Herman De Dijn, Arnold Burms, and Brad Gregory for their stimulating discussions. I tend to agree with P. M. van Buren in his *Theological Explanations* (New York: Macmillan, 1968), when he says, "Surely we do not want to say that just every 'seeing as' 'goes', that since everyone has some perspective, anyone may have whatever he wants. . . . Hitler's way of seeing and the presumed perspective of Lee Harvey Oswald are cases of 'seeing as' which most of us condemn" (p. 172).

16. For R. J. Collingwood metaphysical propositions are purely historical, reflecting a cultural epoch's absolute presuppositions. Much of contemporary Parisian thought (M. Foucault, J. Derrida, et al.) implicitly accepts the same position, not only completely separating the issues of meaning and truth, but giving up the truth claim altogether.

17. A. N. Whitehead, *The Function of Reason* (Boston: Beacon Press, 1971), 7th ed., pp. 25–26. "The material universe has contained in itself, and perhaps still contains, some mysterious impulse for its energy to run upwards" (p. 24). "This counter-agency in its operation throughout the physical universe is too vast and diffusive for our direct observation" (p. 25).

18. I. Prigogine and Isabelle Stengers, *La Nouvelle Alliance. Métamorphose de la science* (Paris: Gallimard, 1979), p. 193. Teilhard de Chardin's basic intuition goes in the same direction; he also accepts a drive towards more complex structures.

19. R. J. Collingwood, in *An Essay on Metaphysics* (Chicago: Gateway edition, 1972), reacts forcefully against such a way of understanding "The proposition 'God Exists'," pp. 185–190.

20. Charles Hartshorne, "Metaphysics and the Modality of Existential Judgments," in *The Relevance of Whitehead. Philosophical Essays in Commemoration of the Centenary of the Birth of Alfred North Whitehead*, Ivor Leclerc, ed., p. 107.

21. Charles Hartshorne, "Can there be proofs for the existence of God?" in *Religious Language and Knowledge*, R. H. Ayers and W. Blackstone, eds. (Athens, Georgia: University of Georgia Press, 1972), pp. 62–75. Quoted passage on p. 62.

11

Jacquelyn Ann Kegley

THE DIVINE RELATIVITY AND
THE BELOVED COMMUNITY

To engage in a comparison of the thought of Josiah Royce and Charles Hartshorne is eminently appropriate, and it is so for several reasons. First, Royce was the first professional philosopher to be read by Charles Hartshorne as a college sophomore.[1] Secondly, Hartshorne acknowledges specific contributions of Royce to his own thought.[2] Thirdly, Royce and Hartshorne share a number of commonalities in background, spirit, and ideas. Some of these will be discussed in detail shortly, such as their idealism, their social view of reality, their ardent opposition to false individualism and self-interest, and their belief that the religious concern could not be ignored by philosophers and indeed was central to the metaphysical enterprise. Other commonalities need only be mentioned, namely, their study in Germany, their interest in phenomenology and logic, and their deep indebtedness to the thought of Charles Sanders Peirce. A fourth reason to produce a creative encounter between these two philosophical systems is that central to each system is the conviction that creative interchange, communication, ongoing expansion of meaning, truth, and experience are at the heart of reality. Royce's doctrine of interpretation is well known and his words fittingly establish why a Royce-Hartshorne dialogue is so apropos. He writes:

> . . . the philosopher's work is not lost when, in one sense, his system seems to have been refuted by death and when time seems to have scattered to scorn the words of his dust-filled mouth. His immediate end may have been unattained, but thousands of years may not be long enough to develop for humanity the full significance of his reflective thought.[3]

There is enough profundity in the thoughts of these two philosophers to engage the world in creative dialogue for years to come, if philosophy is still about at that time.

In what follows I shall do three things. First, I shall discuss common elements in Royce and Hartshorne's philosophical systems. Then, I shall illuminate some crucial and provocative differences. This then will enable me to raise critical questions about both philosophers' ideas and finally, as a result of the above, suggest several avenues of further exploration for Hartshorne and process thought.

SOME IMPORTANT COMMONALITIES

Turning to shared elements in the philosophies of Royce and Hartshorne, we find that one central aspect of their philosophies they have in common is that they are both idealists. However, it is also evident that this is only part of the story, for idealism has many forms and labels. Thus, Royce speaks of his philosophy as "Absolute Pragmatism" while others call it "Idealistic Pragmatism." Hartshorne labels his system in various ways, e.g., "Neoclassical Metaphysics," "Realistic Idealism," and "Panentheism."

What is needed, of course, is a definition of "idealism." Hartshorne provides one for us in one of his important essays on Royce, namely, "the doctrine that it is mind which explains matter. . . ."[4] On the other hand, in a recent essay on this article and Royce's influence on Hartshorne, Brent Stearns argues that the idealistic axiom which pervades Hartshorne's work and gives it its unique flavor, an axiom drawn from Royce, is "To be (or to be true or false) is to be known."[5] This axiom, Stern correctly notes, is stated by Hartshorne in a number of places as central to idealism.[6]

Although Royce nowhere, to my knowledge, announces this as the "idealistic axiom," and although I agree with Gene Reeves that it is not peculiar to Royce's version of idealism,[7] it is, however, an excellent place to begin to explore the common elements of the idealism of Royce and Hartshorne. Involved in the axiom, "To be is to be known," are the concept of "ideal knowledge" and Royce's famous argument from error which appeared first in his *The Religious Aspect of Philosophy*.[8] The argument starts from the fact that we do err, we can formulate false propositions about states of affairs. This possibility of error, not merely a contingent, but a logical one, can only be adequately explained through the actual existence of an absolute truth against which judgments can be measured as to their relative truth or falsity. Royce writes, "*the conditions that determine the logical possibility of error must themselves be absolute truth.*"[9] The only way that truth can exist is an actual correspondence between the idea and the experience that confirms it. The ideally adequate cognition must exist. The truth of a proposition is grounded in the fact that the ideally adequate knower knows it. Error exists in the lack of correspondence between our theoretical expectations and God's ideal experiential data. This is, in essence, Royce's argument from error.

Hartshorne presents an argument very similar to Royce's argument from error in the beginning of his "Ideal Knowledge Defines Reality: What Was True in Idealism," where he states, "Rather 'things as they are' is merely a verbal alternative for 'contents of the ideal knowledge.'"[10] Hartshorne will make some important qualifications to this statement in that article which will differentiate him from Royce and which we will discuss later, but it is important to stress that this argument from error and its notion of an "ideally adequate cognition" is something commonly shared by both philosophers.

That this is so can be seen in a number of ways. As Brent Stearns has shown, Hartshorne uses a form of Royce's argument from error and the model of God as the infallible knower in his ontological proof for God's existence.

Hartshorne contends that God's knowledge is modally coincident with the world. That is, God knows all actuals as actual and all possibles as possible. Now, says Hartshorne, try to hypothesize the possible non-existence of God. But on that case there would be one possible state of affairs that God, as the modally coincident being could not know as actual if it were actual. Hence, God the modally coincident being, if possible at all, logically must be actual. In other words, if God's non-existence were a possibility, then God would have to be able to know God's own non-existence. God could not do that, so God's non-existence cannot be possible. Therefore, God's existence is necessary. Thus God exists. This is basically the ontological proof of God's existence.[11] Further, Hartshorne uses a form of the argument from error to show that the existence of something is necessary, that there must be some world. If the existence of something is not necessary, argues Hartshorne, then the proposition "There is nothing" would be true. But that proposition can only be true under the condition that there is a correspondence between theory and experience in the mind of the ideal knower. However, this condition cannot be fulfilled; its fulfillment is incompatible with the truth of the proposition in question. Thus, the existence of something is necessary. Both Royce and Hartshorne use this kind of dialectical argument in which the will to deny a thesis wills its affirmation.[12] Hartshorne himself affirms the validity of Royce's insight in the argument from error, and sees it as central to Royce's adoption of idealism. He comments on this argument as follows:

> I believe this is a far better attempt than Augustine's to prove God from the idea of truth. Our efforts to know are efforts to share, as far as we can, in the divine life.[13]

And again, Hartshorne comments:

> Royce has two deep insights which, in my opinion, all idealists should have. First, nondivine modes of awareness cannot adequately understand their own essential

categories, such as "reality," apart from some insight, however dim and deficient into the idea of divine awareness. Second, the only concrete subject-object relations which make sense are in a broad sense social relations.[14]

This brings us to a second shared element between our two philosophers, namely, their social view of reality. Hartshorne again acknowledges Royce's contribution in this regard to his own thought in the Preface to his *Creative Synthesis and Philosophic Method*: "as a college sophomore I learned from Royce's great essay on 'Community' (in *The Problem of Christianity*) the most essential lesson of all this was to detect the element of illusion (or if you prefer, confusion) in the idea of a plurality of selves mutually external to each other. . . . in the centrality of the social structure of experience, I find the key to cosmology and epistemology, as well as ethics and religion."[15]

There is ample evidence of Hartshorne's commitment to the social structure of experience. It is necessary here to cite only a few elements of this idea as developed in his philosophy. "Experience," argues Hartshorne, "is social throughout, to its utmost fragments or 'elements.' Its every mode is a mode of sociability."[16] Involved with this assertion is his contention that no experience has itself as a datum. This leads to the conclusion that an other, an object or datum must somehow be present in every experience. Further related to his affirmation of "social organicism," is his theory of the "affective continuum." This argues that the contents of sensation form an "affective continuum" of "aesthetically meaningful, socially expressive, organically adaptive and evolving experience functions."[17] There are no completely isolated individuals, and one is literally talking about "feelings of feelings." "Creatures," says Hartshorne, "are social if they feel, and feel in relation to each others' feelings."[18] Experience, for Hartshorne, is "shared experience." Finally, in *The Logic of Perfection*, Hartshorne writes:

> The social point of view is the final point of view. All creatures are fellow creatures. Nothing is wholly alien to us or devoid of inner satisfactions with which, if we could grasp them, we might more or less sympathize. It is merely a question of how accessible to our perception and understanding the inner values may be.[19]

Hartshorne in a very recent reply to two articles on his idealism provides the consummate summary of the situation for us when he not only connects his social view of reality with idealism but also links it to Royce's view. Hartshorne writes: "Certainly nothing is more central to my view than that to be is to be for others. This is one way of expressing, the centrality for me as for Whitehead, of the concept of prehension."[20] He then cites a quotation from Whitehead: "The truth is only the way all things are together in the Consequent Nature of God"; and writes: "I do not see that this is farther from Royce's position than mine is."[21]

Although this will place us a little ahead in our discussion it does seem in order to discuss some aspects of Hartshorne's understanding of God, particularly as it relates to his social view of reality. (Other aspects of Hartshorne's panentheistic concept of God will be discussed as we enumerate crucial differences between Hartshorne and Whitehead.) Essentially, for Hartshorne, God is the supreme-eternal-temporal consciousness knowing and including the world. An important concept is inclusion. For Hartshorne, whatever is experienced is included, in its particularity, within the experience of it. The relation to x includes x though x does not thereby include the relation. This latter notion will be discussed later, but the important idea is that of inclusion. If John loves Mary, he shares her feeling, her life, her particularity, although admittedly the sharing is deficient. The essence, then, of experience, is to include data. This means that divine experience includes all data in a non-deficient way. Unqualified inclusion of all data can only be attributed to God. Hartshorne also contends that God preserves the entire past in all its detail and thus God is the ground of truth.

The notion of God's experience as inclusive further relates to Hartshorne's claim that God is the soul of the world.[22] Hartshorne writes: "we shall never conceive of a God of love unless we conceive of him as the all-sensitive mind of the world-body."[23] One cannot discuss in detail, at this point, Hartshorne's understanding of the mind-body relation except to point out that his is an organic monism. For him both reality as a whole and its parts are organic[24] and everything is both spatial and temporal. Moreover, from the lowest electronic event to the higher levels of being, including the highest, God, there are elements of what we call mind and matter, not abstracted from each other. To call God the soul of the universe, then, is to say that God is the soul-event in which is summed up all past and present reality. He is the whole universe as it happens, on the basis of its past as remembered by God at any given moment in the universal process. (He is more than that, as we shall see.)

Again, the relationship of God to the world is, therefore, an inclusive one. Everything is directly and omnisciently perceived because everything is both internal to him and consciously observed.[25] The world, therefore, can, for Hartshorne, be properly conceived as what happens within God: God is the soul of the world which is the body. There is more to be said about Hartshorne's concept of God, but it is now time to turn to Royce.

Hartshorne acknowledges Royce's contribution to his own thought about the social nature of reality in Royce's essay on "community" in *The Problem of Christianity*. This essay, however, represents the culmination of Royce's lifelong concern with "community" and the social aspects of reality. It was a lifelong Roycean conviction that knowledge involves both social and temporal extension of self. Knowledge of self as well as knowledge of nature is born out of a social context and is utterly dependent upon it. Throughout his philosophical career, Royce argued that self could never be considered a datum,[26] but rather self-consciousness arises out of a social contrast, via the contrast between what is mine and what is not mine, between the self and not self. I cannot even define my own experiences without contrasting them with other experiences that I take to be real. *"Our fellows,"* writes Royce, *"furnish us the constantly needed supplement to our own fragmentary meanings."*[27]

Not only does Royce see self-consciousness as fundamentally grounded in being-with-others, but he sees all knowledge of external reality as so grounded. It is community experience which distinguishes inner from outer, the outer world being the world whose presence can only be indicated to you by your definable, communicable experience. Further, social communication accounts for the importance of spatial definiteness to externality. The definably localizable in space can be independently verified and agreed upon by a number of socially communicating beings and thus externality stands the social test of common agreement.[28]

Further, for Royce, being-with-others is fundamentally bound up and inseparable from being-with-Nature. "Our belief in the reality of Nature," writes Royce, "when Nature is taken to mean the realm of physical phenomena known to common sense and to science, *is inseparably bound up with belief in the existence of our fellow men.* The one belief cannot be understood apart from the other."[29] With these views, it is not surprising that Royce throughout his philosophical writing recognized and pointed to the social, historical nature of science itself as well as to its role as a model of community.[30] Further he affirmed the creative nature of science. Science, he argued, works with certain leading ideas or guiding principles which are molded by but not predetermined in their details by experience. He states, "We report facts, we let the facts speak, but we, as we investigate, in the popular phrase, 'talk back to the facts.' We interpret as well as report."[31] And, "Science does indeed reveal to us not what the universe is apart from man, but *how man interprets his own experience.*"[32] I am reminded here of Hartshorne's excellent essay "Perception and the Concrete Abstractness of Science," where he writes, "Leibniz, not Hume or Kant, gave the clue to the double character of science just considered—that it enriches as well as impoverishes our world picture and is at once more and less abstract than common sense."[33]

This brings us directly to *The Problem of Christianity* with its doctrines of interpretation and community. In this book Royce outlines the conditions for existence of a community and, as he does so, indicates features of reality conceived of as social through and through. I shall discuss only three of these conditions at this time, as they are most relevant to our purpose here. The first condition of community is "the power of an individual to extend his life, in ideal fashion, so as to regard it as including past and future events which lie far away in time, and which he does not now personally remember."[34] This includes the ability to incorporate a past creatively into his own life plan as well as to recognize the possibility of new meaning of self in the future.

The second condition of community is that there be communication among selves. Community, for Royce, is the product of interpretation. Interpretation is a distinctive form of mental activity, a third form of knowledge, in addition to perception and cognition. The latter are dyadic relations whereas interpretation is triadic, involving a mediator between two minds. Thus, I am mediating the mind and thought of Royce, accessible through a set of signs contained in his works, to the mind of my hearer or reader. Three items are brought into a determinate relationship by this interpretation. (1) I, the interpreter, who must both understand Royce and know something of my audience; (2) the object, Royce's thought; and (3) a mind to whom the interpretation is addressed. The relationship is non-symmetrical, that is, unevenly arranged with respect to all three of the terms. If the order of the relationship were reversed, it would change the process.

Interpretation is a temporal process; each of the terms of the relation corresponds to the three dimensions of time: past, present, and future. Thus, what Royce wrote in the past I am at present interpreting to you for your future interpretation. The process is irreversible, partial, and ideally infinite. Once I have spoken, what I have said cannot be revoked. But what I have said is not the final words for there will be future interpretations of Royce, unless, for arbitrary purposes, the process of interpretation is interrupted or permanently stopped.

Royce's third condition of community is that unity actually is achieved, a shared interpretation of events is the result. What is gained from a process of interpretation is self-knowledge and community. Self-knowledge is achieved because we re-discover who we are and what our ideas and goals should be by contrasting them with the ideas and ideals of another. Community is achieved because our isolation has been transcended; a new vision and an experiential conspectus has come about. Further, community for Royce is both communal and individual, both one (guided by one ideal) and many (the individuals). Royce declares that "a community does not become one . . . by virtue of any reduction or melting of these various selves into a single merely present self or a mass of passing experience."[35]

Further, the building of community is a creative, active process which involves acts of self-will and commitment on the part of each self involved. Secondly, the selves are equal partners in the process—in the sense that each contribution is seen as having intrinsic worth. No one is seen as having higher status; it is a case of shared wisdom. Thirdly, all individuals retain their individuality. Even if conflicting interests or ideas are harmonized through the mediation of a third, all those interests (or ideas) remain irreducibly distinct. Indeed, the building of community through interpretation involves creative artistry and the unity to be achieved thereby is aesthetic unity, a "unity within

222 JACQUELYN ANN KEGLEY

variety.'' Royce speaks of the interpreter as a tragic artist looking down upon the many varying lives of his characters, and seeing their motives not interpenetrating, but cooperating in the dramatic action which constitutes his creation.[36] Further, all communities of intepretation have the structures of selves, and extended ones have an organic life of their own. A community is a living reality which is more than its members.[37] Royce writes: "We can compare a highly developed community, such as a state, either to the soul of a man or a living animal. A community is not a mere collection of individuals. It is a sort of live unit that has organs, as the body of an individual has organs.''[38]

Not only this, but Royce goes on in *The Problem of Christianity* to declare, "The World is the Community. The world contains its own interpreter. Its processes are infinite in their temporal varieties. But their interpreter, the spirit of the universal community—never absorbing varieties or permitting them to blend—compares and through a real life, interprets them all.''[39]

Before leaving Royce's social view of reality and its relation to Hartshorne's, some comment on objective immortality is in order. Hartshorne, in his notion of objective immortality, essentially holds that all shall be preserved in the experience (prehension) of God. Thus he declares, "to be is to be prehended." Hartshorne also writes: "To be is to have value (including disvalue), for valueless being could not be the object of any interest, any attention, any meaning.''[40] In this regard, I cite the following statement by Royce:

> . . . when viewed, as if I were alone, I, the individual, am not only doomed to failure, but I am lost in folly. The 'workings' of my ideas are events whose significance I cannot even remotely estimate in terms of their momentary existence, or in terms of my individual success. My life—means nothing, either theoretically or practically, unless I am a member of a community. I win no success worth having, unless it is also the success of the community to which I essentially and by virtue of my real relation to the whole universe belong. My deeds are not done at all, unless they are indeed done for all time and are irrevocable.[41]

Certainly, Royce here seems to argue that to be requires prehension or communal recognition (taking account by another). However, he does not seem to assert, as does Hartshorne, that everything has value merely by virtue of its creative act of becoming an actual entity. More on this later.

The commonalities which Royce and Hartshorne share in their social view of reality are indeed significant: reality is through and through social, to be is to be prehended or interpreted, and God or Ultimate Reality is both communal and personal, prehending and interpreting all. They also share a notion of experience as asymmetrical and the past as forever given, although there are important differences. We shall turn to crucial differences shortly, but first one more similarity, their shared belief that religious concerns are central to the philosophical enterprise. Such religious concern was, in fact, a lifelong one for both philosophers. Hartshorne's second book, *Beyond Humanism*, announced a new theology which he designated as "theistic naturalism or naturalistic theism," while *Man's Vision of God* formulated the logic of the new theism and demonstrated its superiority to Aquinas's classical theism. In *The Divine Relativity*, Hartshorne systematically formulated his now well known panentheistic conception of deity. Finally, in *Philosophers Speak of God*, jointly authored with William Reese, Hartshorne presents and discusses all the important possible conceptions of deity while at the same time arguing for the validity of panentheism. In *The Logic of Perfection* Hartshorne addresses the question of the validity of proofs for God's existence as well as concepts of freedom and organicism. Josiah Royce wrote three major works dealing with religion, *The Religious Aspect of Philosophy*, *The Sources of Religious Insight*, and *The Problem of Christianity*.[42] In the first two works Royce essentially argued two theses: (1) Religion is a way of unifying the emotional, practical, and theoretical sides of human experience, a way which must be understood and assessed by the philosopher; (2) The essential postulate of religion, of whatever religion, is that *man needs to be saved*. In *The Problem of Christianity* Royce addressed the question: "In what sense, if any, can modern man consistently be, in creed a Christian?"

Although the religious concern is central for both philosophers, one can already see differences in approach between Royce and Hartshorne. Hartshorne's concern is to develop an adequate theistic metaphysic while Royce's concern is to deal with what religion can and should mean for human experience. This leads us directly, then, to a discussion of enlightening differences between the two philosophers.

SUGGESTIVE DIFFERENCES

We turn first to the idealistic axiom, "To be is to be known," and the argument from error proving the ideally adequate cognition or knower. Hartshorne himself points to the crucial difference between his view and Royce's, noting it as an inadequacy in Royce's system. The difference is, says Hartshorne, that he denies truly objective, i.e., independent facts by allowing or arguing for some sort of dependence of the known upon the knower. This leads to a block universe in which no freedom or process is possible. Rather, says Hartshorne, the idealist should hold that "reality depends upon being known by some knower or knowers, but not upon just what particular knowers fulfill this requirement."[43] Hartshorne uses several analogies to illustrate this point. Thus, for example "humanity" is real because there are human beings. But in order for humanity to exist, you and I do not need to exist. In other words, there is no logical impossibility in something's depending upon there being instances of a property, without its depending in the least upon just what particular instances there are. Thus, though there may be a necessity that reality be known the case may be similar to a property and its instances. Shakespeare need not now be known by you or me in order to have been what he was. But to say that his having lived is a constituent of reality is to say that whatever suitable knowers, suitably situated, there are, will have the privilege of knowing about his life. And God, of course, in Hartshorne's view, is the one knower who is universally suitable and properly situated. So, God will in any case know Shakespeare's life, or anything else that has been or is real. But does this, then, make reality after all dependent upon a particular knower, God? No, says Hartshorne, this is Royce's view, but not his own. Rather, argues Hartshorne, I can be myself tomorrow whether it be cloudy or clear. My experiences would be different in those two cases. Though I would be the same individual, I would be the same individual in different states. Now the range of God's possible states is as wide as the possible states of the world. That is, no matter what other individuals may do, God will respond to them with some suitable state of his own awareness. The important point is that God's responses are free or partially independent of particulars. Thus, however God responds to Shakespeare, it will not be the only response he could make. What is necessary is only that he make some divinely adequate response. Hartshorne contends therefore that idealism should hold that individual identity, in all cases, including God's, has at least a partial independence from particulars."[44] Finally, Hartshorne says that he can accept Royce's assertion that "In God all questions are answered" only if it be understood that "some questions about the future are not proper questions and have no true answers, known or unknown."[45]

Hartshorne's concern here is to maintain elements of creativity, freedom, and realism. Thus, Hartshorne makes even clearer his objections to and differences from Royce in his essay, "The Synthesis of Idealism and Realism." There he argues that idealism is entirely compatible with a realistic view of the independence of the particular object and the dependence of the particular subject.[46] This argument, in my judgment, is cogent, and fits well with an observation made by Mary Mahowald concerning Royce. Royce, she argues, and I agree, approaches the formulation of his synthetic idealistic view in *The World and the Individual* after an inadequate and inconclusive critique of realism. She writes: ". . . Royce seems to read the realist as an idealist: he equates the existence of a thing with the knowing of an object, claiming that since the realist asserts the absolute independence of the thing known he therefore renders himself incapable of knowing it."[47]

The sum of all of this, for critics of Royce, is that he never, in spite of his emphasis on freedom, the responsibility of the individual, and love as a principle of individuation, succeeds in establishing the self as having worth other than in the entire explanation and fulfillment of his being as determined by the Absolute. Freedom, creativity, process, and chance, of course, have all been key ideas urging Hartshorne to adopt a social view of reality. "To be is to create," he declares, and the ultimate meaning of creation is "in the freedom or self-determination of any experience as a new 'one,' arising out of a previous many in terms of which it cannot, by any causal relationship, be fully described."[48] "Creative means," says Hartshorne, "additions to the definiteness of reality."[49]

Although they share deep convictions about the fundamentally social structure of reality, Hartshorne and Royce ultimately differ substantially on questions of freedom and creativity. Mahowald makes an interesting comment regarding Royce in this regard, namely, that he neglects establishing true individuality in his system because he focuses his philosophical consideration on false individualism, and, on diminishing and supplementing individual limitation.[50] It is true that Royce was concerned about rampant individualism, but he was equally concerned about stifling collectivism. In *The Problem of Christianity* he gives a careful analysis of these dual dangers and affirms again and again that the individual needs the community and the community needs unique individuals. The individual without the community is blind; community without individuals is empty.[51]

Royce also continually discusses interpretation, which builds community, as a creative artistic process producing a unity in variety, a new addition to reality. Indeed, it is fruitful to contrast Royce's doctrine of interpretation with Hartshorne's notion of "prehension." Particularly relevant in understanding this contrast is a criticism of Hartshorne raised by William Lad Sessions concerning the neglect of Peirce's thirdness.[52] Sessions is concerned about the way in which God's actuality includes all and yet is also perfect and unsurpassable. He asks: "Is the superiority and inclusion involved quantitative or qualitative?" Quantitative inclusion, argues Sessions, is dyadic while qualitative is triadic. Sessions summarizes his points as follows: "(1) Intentionality and transcendence (both triadic notions) are irreducible to inclusion (a dyadic notion); (2) Any metaphysical doctrine of God—especially that of DP—requires some irreducibly triadic notion in order to express the qualitative nature of God's categorical superiority. . . ."[53]

Sessions argues that Hartshorne has no adequate doctrine of irreducibly triadic relations[54] nor does he show how such a doctrine would relate to his doctrine of inclusion. Hartshorne, says Sessions, thus has an inadequate theory of knowledge and thus an inadequate metaphysic. Sessions's criticism of Hartshorne, on this score, relates to Hartshorne's interpretation of objective immortality. Hartshorne holds, he believes in concert with Whitehead, that all actual occasions are prehended and preserved everlastingly by God in their full immediacy.[55] Indeed, he writes: ". . . our adequate immortality can only be God's omniscience of us. . . . Now the meaning of omniscience is knowledge which is coextensive with reality, which can be taken as the measure of reality. Hence, if we can never be less than we have been to God, we can in reality never be less than we have been. Omniscience and the indestructibility of every reality are correlative aspects of one truth."[56] In other words, God completely preserves the *entire past*, all that has occurred exactly as it has occurred.[57] God totally includes the world.

This doctrine, of course, raises questions about pantheism, evil, and moral judgment. The question of pantheism probably will be adequately dealt with elsewhere in this volume, so it will not be discussed here. One will only note that Hartshorne's concept of deity is dipolar and thus God's abstract nature remains independent of reality, while the concrete nature includes it.[58] Turning to the problem of evil, it is quite clear that, for Hartshorne, God has knowledge of the tragedy, suffering, and pain of this world. All the good and evil that are actualized become part of God's prehensions. God suffers with us in our pain and rejoices with us in joy. All, both good and evil, are prehended adequately and impartially by God. The most wicked act is literally in God, and while wicked as regards the act's own self-decision, as divinely prehended, it is not subject to ethical description, positive or negative. In Hartshorne's words, "God is the concrete unity of the world, not the selected catalogue of its good aspects."[59]

Several problems arise. First, does this mean God is responsible for evil? Secondly, is there no sense of moral judgment involved in God's experience of the world? In answer to the question of God's responsibility for evil, it is Hartshorne's contention, as it is Whitehead's, that evil is the result of freedom, which in its multiplicity of self-determining acts means a degree of real chance. It also means a possible clash of goals, ends, etc., of "goods," says Hartshorne. Evil is discord over harmony, triviality over meaning. He writes: "The risks of evil which remain are not there because evil is in some mysterious way, good, but because without freedom, with its perils, there could be no world at all and neither good nor evil."[60] This is not seen as tragic for Hartshorne, for God remains as an actual entity within a community of actual entities and God is the process toward integration, the persuasive love, the tender companion. "He will," says Hartshorne, "elicit the utmost values even out of our failures. . . ."[61]

But will he? Readers of Hartshorne are not sure. First, there is his emphasis on adequate and impartial inclusion. Is this quantitative only or also qualitative? Is there judgment and selection involved in God's experience of the world? One is confused about this when Hartshorne, for example, seems to neglect God's inclusion of disvalues because of a belief that "every concrete experience as a whole is a value rather than a disvalue."[62] Surely this rings untrue if the term "value" is not more clearly specified, and it certainly gives credence to a lack of judgment in assessing the world and experiences in it. We are further disturbed by another of Hartshorne's statements: "That the tragedy [of life] would be less if we human beings went on developing new states of self-experience immortally is not at all clear to me."[63]

This statement is even more ironic in light of a recent discussion of evil in process thought which brings in the meliorism of William James. The author Randolph Crump Miller, speaks of human beings as authors of genuine novelty and thereby capable of moving toward increased harmony. They become seekers after values. Miller writes: "God does not undo the past. But because evil can be transformed by good in God's nature, it can become the basis for good in the present and can point to the future. God as persuasive love works for the increase of good and therefore of joy and peace. Our responsibility is to fulfill our roles, for our salvation is in a real sense up to us."[64]

My questions to Hartshorne are: Where is the persuasive lure and moral responsibility? How persuasive is an aesthetic vision to humans? Where is the hope, if no triumph of good over evil is ever guaranteed? Here the contrast between Royce and Hartshorne becomes enlightening. For Hartshorne God's work appears to me that of an artist, building unity in variety, balancing harmony and intensity, while Royce's God functions as interpreter of a world, also building unity in variety but with the ethical command on individuals in communities to be loyal to loyalty, i.e., to build ever-widening community and understanding, and the moral imperative on communities to build ever better environments for fostering individuality within a social context. Commitment to community, for Royce, is moral commitment. The moral self and the moral community, he claims, are committed to making the world even better.

> The best world for a moral agent is one that needs him to make it better. The purely metaphysical consciousness, in vain, therefore, says of the good. It is. The moral consciousness insists upon setting higher than every such assertion, the resolve. Let it be. The moral consciousness declines to accept, therefore, any metaphysical finality. It rejects every static world.[65]

Like James, Royce takes the emphasis on an open future as indicative of action that can be taken and should be taken. James writes: "Meliorism treats salvation as neither necessary nor impossible. It treats it as a possibility which becomes more of a probability the more numerous the actual conditions of salvation become."[66] Wherein lies salvation, surely a pre-eminent concern of religion, as Royce indicates, in the vision of aesthetic unity provided by Hartshorne? One suspects that Hartshorne's concern to overcome the limitations of the classical conception of God as well as its abuses, for example, in over-emphasizing judgment and punishment of sinners, has led him to neglect accounting for such notions as "grace," "salvation," "enlightenment," which are also part of a religious vision, whether theistic or not.

In this regard, it is interesting to recall that Whitehead, in speaking of God's persuasive love often refers to the Galilean vision of early Christianity. Here again another contrast between Hartshorne and Royce is instructive, and that concerns their discussion of religious matters. Hartshorne has been intent on explicating a conception of God so that it expresses and enhances "reverence or worship on a high ethical and cultural level."[67] In so doing he has criticized the classical notion of duty which emphasized abstractness, transcendence, aloofness, judgment. Royce, on the other hand, has been concerned with religious experience, with sin, guilt, and salvation. He also has given attention to Christology, at least to the role of Jesus and "the Galilean vision." Hartshorne clearly states, "I have no Christology to offer."[68] However, he does give attention to the cross as a symbol of the total involvement of God in the world[69] and has also given some consideration to the role of the church. Royce, on the other hand, has given considerable attention to the role and nature of the church in *The Problem of Christianity*.[70] Indeed, ecclesiology, for Royce, is at least as important as Christology if not even more important. Hartshorne has been interested in the church in terms of ecumenicity and thus Royce's statement is quite interesting in this regard: "*Look forward to the human and visible triumph of no form of the Christian Church.*"[71]

SUGGESTIONS FOR FURTHER EXPLORATION

This leads me to some closing suggestions for further exploration by Hartshorne and Process Thought of aspects of Royce's thought which may stimulate new developments in process thought itself. First of all, given some of the difficulties discussed above with Hartshorne's doctrine of inclusion, his lack of a developed sense of thirdness and difficulties with the problem of evil and hope and tragedy, a re-exploration of Royce's doctrine of interpretation could prove very fruitful. Hartshorne was much influenced by Bergson and thus Royce's critique of Bergson is certainly of some interest. Bergson, Royce claims, neglects interpretation as a third kind of cognition and yet, Royce points out, Bergson's own notion of reality as duration accessible only to intuition is itself an interpretation of reality.[72] Even the artists whom Bergson is so fond of using as examples, whom he recommends for their intuitive approach, are interpreters of reality.[73] Further, interpretation might be a more appropriate vehicle for expressing the work of God in his experience of the world in his endless enrichment of the world, while receiving things only for what they are worth and have been.[74] Thus, Royce tells us, "But interpretation, while always stimulated to fresh efforts by the inexhaustible wealth of the novel facts of the social world, demands, by virtue of its own nature, and even in the simplest conceivable case, an endless wealth of new interpretations."[75]

Finally, process thought could well benefit from Royce's careful study of the role of Christ and the church in *The Problem of Christianity* as well as his discussions of sin and guilt in other writings. His analysis of sin and guilt deserves attention for three reasons. He recognizes the universality and totality of sin and talks about it in both its individual and communal expressions; the latter emphasis is significantly missing in Hartshorne and process thought. Secondly, his analysis of sin and moral development is fully consonant with psychological analyses of guilt. Thirdly, Royce stresses the depth of sin and does justice to human freedom and human responsibility for sin.

As for Royce's analysis of the church as the Beloved Community, he provides a valuable insight into the need for community and the work of the Holy Spirit to fill out the ethic of Christian love. Further, Royce's analysis of interpretation has tremendous concrete possibilities for building communities and expressing Christian love. Hartshorne is one of the few process philosophers who has attempted to develop an ethics based on his thought.[76] Indeed an interesting comparison of his ethics with that of John Stuart Mill's utilitarianism demonstrates Hartshorne's disdain for action grounded in the motivation of self-interest.[77] Given the fundamentally social structure of reality, Hartshorne maintains that striving only to achieve one's future satisfaction is an irrational limitation of the scope of one's efforts.[78] A comparison of Royce's analyses of the failures of individualism and aspects of sin with Hartshorne's views would be in my judgment instructive and fruitful of new insights. Further, a new reading of Royce's ethical maxim "loyalty to loyalty" might result by placing it in juxtaposition with Hartshorne's concerns to expand our concerns for life in all its forms. Hartshorne writes:

> Not just tomorrow concerns me but my life as a whole if not just one human being which I am, or my little circle, but human beings generally, so far as I have dealings with them or can influence them. Indeed, not human life only but life as such is the final reference of thought.[79]

In addition, in his analysis of Hartshorne's ethic, in comparison with that of Mill, Moskop contends that both Hartshorne and Mill share the problem of subordination of justice to utility.[80] Although, Royce doesn't entirely escape this problem, I would suggest that his analysis of the subtle interactions of individualism—collectivism and his attempt to carefully balance rights of individual and community might provide help in this regard. Finally, Royce clearly posits a third alternative to individualism—collectivism, egoism, and altruism. In doing so, he gives us a base for developing a social philosophy based on creative interaction of self and community. Again, process thought has not given much attention to this area of philosophy, although apparently Hartshorne has begun such an investigation.[81]

A final area of attention for future developments out of the interaction of the thought of Hartshorne and Royce is that of science—its nature and its relation to religion and other endeavors. For example, Royce reasserts that morality is part of the core of religion and that science and religion are engaged in a common enterprise. He writes:

> The very existence of natural science, then, is an illustration of our thesis that the universe is endlessly engaged in the spiritual task of interpreting its own life.[82]

Hartshorne also has been much concerned with science and its relation to religion. Surely, however, more exploration of this is in order.

Thus, we have put into dialogue the philosophies of Royce and Hartshorne. Who knows what fecundity of new possibilities might result from the unity in variety produced by contemplation of the Beloved Community and the Divine Relativity?

JACQUELYN A. KEGLEY

DEPARTMENT OF PHILOSOPHY AND RELIGIOUS STUDIES
CALIFORNIA STATE UNIVERSITY, BAKERSFIELD
JULY 1986

NOTES

1. Cited as a fact in several sources. See: Eugene H. Peters, *Hartshorne & Neoclassical Metaphysics* (Lincoln: University of Nebraska Press, 1970), p. 41.

2. I cite two such acknowledgements. In "Replies" to "Interrogation of Charles Hartshorne, conducted by William Alston," contained in the volume, *Philosophical Interrogations, Interrogations of Martin Buber, John Wild, Jean Wahl, Brand Blanshard, Paul Weiss, Charles Hartshorne, Paul Tillich*, edited, with an introduction, by Sydney and Beatrice Rome (New York: Holt, Rinehart and Winston, 1964), Hartshorne says that he first encountered in Josiah Royce the idea that "while one of us has a single experience, some other enduring individual (event-sequence) on a non-human level may have a thousand or million. . . . (. . . though in him [Royce] the notion of unit-event seems lacking in focus)," p. 328. In his *Creative Synthesis and Philosophic Method* (London: SCM, 1970, University Press of America, 1983), Hartshorne praises Royce for his social view of reality. See pp. xvii–xviii.

3. Josiah Royce, *The Spirit of Modern Philosophy* (Boston and New York: Houghton Mifflin, 1892), p. 10.

4. Charles Hartshorne, "Royce and the Collapse of Idealism," *Revue internationale de Philosophie* 23 (1967):46.

5. Brent Stearns, "Hartshorne and Idealistic Philosophy," *American Journal of Theology & Philosophy* 7, no. 1 (January 1986):28.

6. See: Charles Hartshorne, "Ideal Knowledge Defines Reality: What Was True in Idealism," *Journal of Philosophy* 43 (1946):580.

7. Gene Reeves, "To Be Is To Be For Others," *American Journal of Theology and Philosophy* 7, no. 1 (January 1986):41.

8. Josiah Royce, *The Religious Aspect of Philosophy* (Boston: Houghton Mifflin and Co., 1885).

9. Royce, ibid., p. 385.

10. Hartshorne, "Ideal Knowledge Defines Reality," 574.

11. Stearns, "Hartshorne and Idealistic Philosophy," 31–32.

12. Ibid., 32.

13. Hartshorne, "Ideal Knowledge Defines Reality," 52.

14. Ibid., 57.

15. Charles Hartshorne, *Creative Synthesis and Philosophic Method*, pp. xvii–xviii.

16. Charles Hartshorne, *Reality as Social Process: Studies in Metaphysics and Religion* (Glencoe and Boston: Free Press and Beacon Press, 1953), p. 8.

17. Ibid., p. 9.

18. Ibid., p. 34.

19. *The Logic of Perfection* and *Other Essays in Neoclassical Metaphysics* (La Salle, Ill.: Open Court Publishing Co., 1962), pp. 309–310.

20. Charles Hartshorne, "Reeves and Stearns on My Idealism," *American Journal of Theology and Philosophy* 7, no. 1 (January 1986):46.

21. Ibid.

22. Charles Hartshorne, *Man's Vision of God and the Logic of Theism* (Chicago: Willet Clark & Co. 1941. Reprinted 1964 by Archon Books, Hamden, Conn.), chapter V.

23. Charles Hartshorne, *Beyond Humanism: Essays in the Philosophy of Nature* (Chicago: Willet & Clark Co., 1937. Nebraska: Bison Books Edition, 1968), p. 208.

24. Charles Hartshorne, *The Logic of Perfection*, pp. 191–215.

25. Charles Hartshorne, *Man's Vision of God*, pp. 177–92.

26. See: Josiah Royce, *The World and the Individual*, vol. II. (New York: Macmillan, 1900. New York: Dover Publications, 1959), p. 287 and Josiah Royce, *The Problem of Christianity*, vol. II (New York: Macmillan, 1918. Chicago: University of Chicago Press, 1968), p. 43.

27. Josiah Royce, *The World and the Individual*, vol. II, p. 172. Italics are Royce's.

28. Josiah Royce, "The External World and Social Consciousness," *Philosophical Review* III, no. 5 (September 1984):520.

29. Josiah Royce, *The World and the Individual*, vol. II, pp. 165–66. Italics are Royce's.

30. See: Josiah Royce, "The Social Factors of the Human Intellect." Unpublished papers, Folio 68, no. 3 (1897), pp. 18–19.

31. Josiah Royce, "Introduction to H. Poincare," *The Foundations of Science*, tr. G. B. Halsted (New York: Science Press, 1913), reprinted in *Royce's Logical Essays*, ed. D. S. Robinson (Dubuque, Iowa: Wm. C. Brown Co., 1951), pp. 279–80.

32. Josiah Royce, "Richmond Lectures," Unpublished papers, Folio 88, I (1904), pp. 20–21. Italics are Royce's.

33. Charles Hartshorne, "Perception and the 'Concrete Abstractness' of Science," *Philosophy and Phenomenological Research* 34.4 (June, 1974):465–476.

34. Josiah Royce, *The Problem of Christianity*, vol. II, pp. 60–61.
35. Ibid., p. 67.
36. Ibid., p. 188.
37. Regarding personality of community unpublished papers see vol. 91. "Spirit of the Community," 1900, p. 23. Concerning community as organic life see vol. 65, Lecture VII, p. 54.
38. Josiah Royce, *The Problem of Christianity*, vol. I, pp. 61–62.
39. Ibid., II, p. 324.
40. Charles Hartshorne, "Ideal Knowledge Defines Reality," 580.
41. Josiah Royce, *The Problem of Christianity*, vol. II, p. 313.
42. Josiah Royce, *The Religious Aspect of Philosophy* (Boston and New York: Houghton Mifflin & Company, 1885) *The Sources of Religious Insight* (The Brass Lectures, Lake Forest College, 1911. New York: Charles Scribner's Sons, 1912). *The Problem of Christianity* has already been cited.
43. Charles Hartshorne, "Royce and the Collapse of Idealism," 52.
44. Ibid., 53.
45. Ibid., 55.
46. Charles Hartshorne, "The Synthesis of Idealism and Realism," *Theoria*, vol. 15, Part I–III (12 March 1949):94.
47. Mary Briody Mahowald, *An Idealistic Pragmatism* (The Hague: Martinus Nijhoff, 1972), p. 171.
48. Charles Hartshorne, *Creative Synthesis and Philosophical Method*, p. 1 and p. 3.
49. Ibid., p. 3.
50. Mary Mahowald, *An Idealistic Pragmatism*, p. 170.
51. For a discussion of these issues see: Jacquelyn Ann K. Kegley, "Individual and Community: An American View," *Journal of Chinese Philosophy* II (1984):206–9.
52. William Lad Sessions, "Charles Hartshorne and Thirdness," *Southern Journal of Philosophy* 12 (Summer, 1974):239–52.
53. Ibid., 247.
54. This point is also supported by Derek Kelly in Peirce, Hartshorne and Weiss, *International Philosophical Quarterly* 4:48.
55. Charles Hartshorne, Review of John Blyth, *Whitehead: Theory of Knowledge*, in *Philosophy and Phenomenological Research* 3/3 (March 1948):373. For an extensive discussion of interpretations of Whitehead on objective immortality see: David R. Griffith, "Hartshorne's Differences From Whitehead," Chapter III in *Two Process Philosophers: Hartshorne's Encounter With Whitehead*, edited by Lewis S. Ford (Tallahasee, Florida: American Academy of Religion, 1973), pp. 52–55.
56. Charles Hartshorne, "Time, Death and Eternal Life," *Journal of Religion*, no. 2 (April 1952):101–2. See also, *The Logic of Perfection*, pp. 252–53.
57. Charles Hartshorne, "The Immortality of the Past: Critique of a Prevalent Misinterpretation," *Review of Metaphysics* VII, no. 1 (September 1953):98. Interestingly enough, Hartshorne tells us that the original influence for this view came from Royce.
58. Hartshorne replies in this regard: "The avoidance of pantheism is in the noninclusion of the world by God in his necessary individuality as well as in the mutual freedom of God and creature in relation to the other. God happens to include just this world; he did not have to in order to be himself" in "Interrogation of Charles Hartshorne" by William Alston, p. 344.
59. Charles Hartshorne, "The Immortality of the Past: Critique of a Prevalent Misinterpretation," 101–2.

60. Charles Hartshorne, *The Logic of Perfection*, p. 315.

61. Charles Hartshorne, *Man's Vision of God*, p. 331.

62. Charles Hartshorne, "The Immortality of the Past: Critique of a Prevalent Misinterpretation," 102.

63. Charles Hartshorne, "Interrogation of Charles Hartshorne" by William Alston, p. 344.

64. Randolph Crump Miller, "Process, Evil and God," *American Journal of Theology & Philosophy*, No. 3:69–70.

65. Josiah Royce, *The World and the Individual*, vol. II, p. 340.

66. William James, *Pragmatism* (New York: Longmans, 1907), p. 286.

67. Charles Hartshorne, *The Divine Relativity: A Social Conception of God*, The Terry Lectures, 1947 (New Haven: Yale University Press, 1948), p. 1.

68. Charles Hartshorne, "A Philosopher's Assessment of Christianity," *Religion and Culture: Essays in Honor of Paul Tillich*, ed. Walter Leibrecht (New York: Harper, 1959), p. 179.

69. For a discussion of these aspects of Hartshorne's thought, see: Ralph E. James, *The Concrete God* (New York, Indianapolis: Bobbs-Merrill Company, 1967), pp. 127–148 and pp. 149–169.

70. See *The Problem of Christianity*, vol. I and Jacquelyn Ann Kegley, "Josiah Royce, A New Source of Insight For Religion Today," *Religious Studies* 18:211–224.

71. Josiah Royce, *The Problem of Christianity*, II, p. 430.

72. Ibid., p. 334.

73. Ibid., p. 295.

74. Charles Hartshorne, "Whitehead and Berdyaev: Is There Tragedy in God?" *Journal of Religion* 37, no. 2 (April 1957):82.

75. Josiah Royce, *The Problem of Christianity*, II, p. 394.

76. See: Charles Hartshorne, "The Aesthetic Matrix," in *Creative Synthesis and Philosophic Method*, pp. 303–321 and Charles Hartshorne, "Beyond Enlightened Self-Interest: A Metaphysics of Ethics," *Ethics* 84/3 (April 1974):210–16.

77. John C. Moskop, "Mill and Hartshorne," *Process Studies* 10 (Spring-Summer, 1980):18–33.

78. Charles Hartshorne, "Beyond Enlightened Self Interest," 209 and 212–14.

79. Ibid., p. 205.

80. John C. Moskop, pp. 31ff.

81. See: Charles Hartshorne, "Indeterminism, Freedom as Universal Principle," *Journal of Social Philosophy* 15 (Fall, 1984):5–11.

82. Josiah Royce, *The Problem of Christianity*, II, p. 418.

12

Sallie B. King

BUDDHISM AND HARTSHORNE

There are deep and extensive areas of agreement shared by Hartshorne and Buddhism. Let us first try to convey the overall scope of the agreement and the enthusiasm behind it, along with something of its limitations. Hartshorne makes the following comment with respect to Whitehead, but he could have said it of himself: "Whitehead has profound points of agreement with Buddhism. It is almost harder to state the important differences than the aspects of agreement."[1] While he asserts that "I was already almost a Buddhist without knowing it long before I had read much about Buddhism or had any habit of relating my thinking to that tradition,"[2] it is clear that he sees certain philosophical deficiencies in that tradition which may be remedied by the encounter with process philosophy and especially process theology:

> It does seem to me that Western metaphysics, now at last, is in a position to find important ground with Buddhism . . . and from a global perspective, we can do better than either East or West was able to do in previous centuries. More than any other belief, it seems, the belief in Supreme creativity, inspiring, guiding and everlastingly cherishing lesser forms of creativity, can do more to explain reality and give us ideals.[3]

Elsewhere, in reflecting on his disagreement with Fa Tsang's Hua Yen school of Buddhism, Hartshorne remarks, "this makes me, if anything, more Buddhist than some Buddhists."[4] This willingness to identify himself as a qualified Buddhist while simultaneously desiring to improve Buddhism by moving it in the direction of certain key ideas of Christian process theology perhaps best captures Hartshorne's position. He expresses sincere and deep admiration for Buddhism with respect to those areas where the former and process philosophy coincide, but where they differ—notably with respect to God—he embraces Christianity in its process theology formulation. Given this set of enthusiasms and qualifications, Hartshorne may well identify himself as moving toward a "Buddhisto-Christian" religion.

Let us turn now to some specific topics for an overview of the Buddhist and Hartshorne positions with respect to each other. We will pass over those topics to be considered in more detail below, namely, self, motivation theory, and ethics.

1. Process.   Both Hartshorne's philosophy and Buddhism are thoroughgoing process systems, entirely lacking in substantialist elements. Buddhism mentions such concepts as substance, essence, or "self" only to deny their validity. In this respect, Buddhism and Hartshorne are very close indeed. Of course, this is a very general sort of affinity, but given the dominance of the world by substance philosophies, it is nonetheless significant.

2. God.   Hartshorne seems to feel that Buddhism's atheism is its most important difference from his own philosophy. There is much debate in the dialogue between process philosophy and Buddhism as to whether Buddhism is as atheistic as it claims and appears to be. Some question whether there are theistic elements in the Mahayana understanding of *nirvana* or Thusness, for example. Hartshorne himself often notes that D. T. Suzuki, the famous popularizer of Zen Buddhism in the West, once said that he was not sure that Buddhism is nontheistic. Certainly if there are subtle, theistic elements in Buddhism, they do not closely approach the kind of God we find so clearly articulated in Hartshorne.

3. Creativity.   Given their process orientations, Buddhism and Hartshorne are in general agreement that life is self-creating. In Buddhism this is more clearly articulated with respect to human than other forms of life. Nonetheless, there are some differences between the two with respect to freedom and determinism. These differences are, in fact, largely due to Buddhism's ambiguity on the subject. Hartshorne is always clear that life itself is creativity and that therefore an element of chance or freedom is present in every moment and aspect of the self-production of life. Potentiality becomes actuality in dependence on presently existing conditions but it is not completely determined by those conditions. Each actual event adds something new and unpredictable to what was previously given and this newness is possible because of the open, under-determined nature of creativity itself.

Buddhism, to its detriment, is not as clear on this subject as Hartshorne. In Buddhism this issue is shaped by the concept of *karma*, the law of cause and effect, according to which every event which occurs is conditioned by preceding events and every present event conditions future events. So far this idea concords with process philosophy ideas of prehension. But Buddhism, especially early Buddhism, is not clear as to the extent of this conditioning and the place of free, unconditioned creativity. How fully determined are consequent events? On this score, Buddhism equivocates. In some cases, Buddhism indicates that *karma* simply determines the conditions and events to which a person must respond in the course of living. The response itself, it is implied, is the undetermined act of the individual. Thus in practice Buddhist teachers stress to their disciples the necessity of enlightened responses to the challenges of life and the importance of practicing Buddhism to enable such enlightened responses. Buddhism is fairly clear as far as its practice goes, but it must be said that philosophically the status of such free responses to events in life is quite unclear. Moreover, there are many instances in the Buddhist literature where we read, for example, that a certain individual was enabled to achieve enlightenment because of the ''good'' karmic seeds sown by that individual over countless aeons of past lives. Furthermore, early Buddhism understands ordinary life, or *samsara*, to be a form of bondage; the goal is to attain *nirvana*, one aspect of which is freedom. But while *samsara* is bondage, it is we who create our own fetters and we who must undo them; the individual's responsibility for his or her state of being is complete. Thus the very existence of Buddhism is based upon the faith that it is possible to move from a state of bondage to a state of freedom, but the philosophical status of the acts which bring about such freedom is itself left unclarified.

Later Mahayana Buddhism takes up this issue in a very different form with its use of such concepts as *Tathagatagarbha*, Buddha nature, true self and original enlightenment. These terms refer to an enlightened, free and creative human nature possessed by all which is explicitly used to account for the possibility of enlightenment. This ''true self'' is not a substantial entity, but an ever-new, self-creating, absolutely free series of enlightened and compassionate acts.[5] Buddhism, however, retains the problem of relating the free acts of the true self to the universe of karmically conditioned (determined?) events.

Hartshorne's analysis of creativity in the midst of partial determination would seem to fit this aspect of Buddhist philosophy rather well, though it is unclear whether Hartshorne would affirm the possibility of a person actually living a life which consists of a series of nothing but enlightened and compassionate acts, as Zen affirms. In short, Buddhist philosophy stands in need of at least clarification and more probably reform with respect to the problem of freedom and determinism. Given their very large mutual affinities in other respects, Hartshorne's philosophy of creativity is a strikingly appropriate candidate to supply ideas for this reform.

4. Type of philosophy. Hartshorne is a metaphysician and theologian, a system constructor with a great deal of faith in the ability of reason to ponder the great questions and formulate accounts appropriate to the nature of things. The Buddhist attitude towards reason and metaphysics varies greatly across its breadth but generally speaking there is a deep suspicion of reason apparent in much of Buddhism. While there are metaphysical system builders in Buddhism, Buddhism is better characterized, for better or for worse, by its tendency to value and trust religious experience as the primary source of creative insight, while relegating reason to the role of destructive criticism (as in Nagarjuna) or analysis of experience.

As for Hartshorne, while it is true that one of his primary goals has been to create rationally adequate metaphysical notions, such as of God, Hartshorne makes clear that there is more to his system than the product of reasoning alone. For example, he states that his move into greater philosophical independence was one which entailed greater reliance on both his own intellect and his spiritual convictions,[6] plainly indicating the two as different sources of philosophical creativity. Elsewhere, he speaks a great deal of intuition, stating that "all proof rests on intuition somewhere."[7] He also speaks frequently of the influence which poetry and experiences with nature have had on him. It is obvious that Hartshorne is not chained to any narrowly conceived rationalism but rather simply requires his philosophical product, however multiple its ultimate sources, to take a rationally defensible form.

Buddhism, of course, has no use for plain nonsense. There are Buddhist logicians of great stature and in general Buddhism (especially Indian Buddhism) excels in sharply critical attacks on its opponents. This, however, is far from being the strong point of Buddhism, as Hartshorne rightly says.[8] Moreover, Buddhism does tend away from metaphysical system building, especially at some of its most creative points: in the teachings of the historical Buddha, in the revolutionary perspective of early Mahayana, and in the extreme emphasis on immediate experience in Zen. The Buddha's position, which came to characterize Buddhism, was that one had to experience reality directly in order to know it and that the ultimate nature of things could be known experientially through a form of experience which is non-verbal and non-rational, to be attained through meditation. This tendency is epitomized in the characteristic Mahayana assertion that Buddhist teachings do not contain the truth, that they are expedient means or devices designed to help the seeker to find the truth in direct experience.

It is easy to see that Hartshorne does want to express the truth in his writing and that he certainly has no patience with paradox. In this and the other disparities noted above we see something of the fundamental difference between Hartshorne and Buddhism with respect to the nature of the project in which each is engaged. One of the many remarkable things about the relationship between Hartshorne and Buddhism is the vast span of their agreement despite this fundamental difference in philosophical approach. While the two philosophies are built on drastically different foundations, it is still true that they have more in common than at odds, in terms of philosophical content as such. Nonetheless, a comparison of the two which refers only to the similarities and differences in content of the two philosophies without referring to this fundamental difference in the type of philosophy which each exemplifies overlooks the fact that the two function in different mental worlds. Certainly reading Hartshorne is a very different kind of experience from reading a Buddhist text.

With the above as background, let us now turn to the main subject of the present essay: a comparison of Hartshorne and Buddhism on the philosophy of self, motivation theory, and ethics. The concordance of the two philosophies on these related subjects and especially on the philosophy of self, which is the basis of the other two, is remarkable. Hartshorne refers to a single "Buddhist-Whiteheadian view of the self"; in his essay "Toward a Buddhisto-Christian Religion," he turns directly to these issues to illustrate the common ground between Buddhism and himself.

What, in brief, is the Buddhist-Hartshornian doctrine of self? Theirs is the "no soul, no substance" doctrine, according to which the human individual is a series of momentary acts, with no self, soul, essence, or substance of any kind performing the acts or inhering in the acts over time. As the great Buddhist thinker, Buddhaghosa, put it, there are deeds but no doer, suffering but no sufferer. What exist are complex series of linked acts, typically involving for the sentient individual conscious experiencing. Buddhism and Hartshorne see these series of acts as self-creating through a process of causation. Thus this moment of conscious experiencing shapes or conditions the next moment of conscious experiencing, which exists precisely as a response to the previous moment. Causality is the force which links together the inherently separate moments of experiencing and provides for the continuity in the process of becoming, or life.

While Hartshorne refers almost exclusively to the similarities between himself and Buddhism on the subject of the self, there are nonetheless differences between the two even on this issue which, while subtle, are still quite significant. For the Buddhist, strictly speaking the word "I," understood as a core of identity which endures over time, does not refer to anything in reality at all. There is no self, there is no experiencer, just moments of emotion, sensation, intellection, etc. Some contemporary Zen Buddhist teachers therefore avoid the use of the word "I" altogether in their speech (in English!).

Hartshorne escapes this radical position by pointing out that while the word "I" is highly ambiguous and thus its use can and does result in philosophical confusion there is nonetheless a valid sense in which it can be used in reference to "genetic identity."

> Genetic identity, which has only a relatively definite meaning, involves (1) some 'defining characteristic' reappearing in each member of a sequence or family of occasions; (2) direct inheritance by appreciably positive prehensions of this character from previous members.[9]

Thus there is a valid but limited sense in which Charles Hartshorne is Charles Hartshorne throughout his life and indeed thereafter, insofar as these words refer to a single series of experiences, linked by memory and causation. Hartshorne emphasizes that this genetic identity is an abstraction utterly lacking in the concrete reality of moment by moment experience but nonetheless its identification is a philosophical necessity.

Buddhism lacks a concept parallel to this. While it does not directly deny in philosophical terms the validity of what Hartshorne calls genetic identity, and indeed the doctrine of *karma* requires something like it, Buddhism nevertheless neglects clear and direct statements affirming such a thing. As a result, the status of the individual "series" is rather ambiguous in Buddhism. This may be illustrated in the following assertion of the Buddhist monk Nagasena:

> . . . in respect of me, Nagasena is but a way of counting, term, appellation, convenient designation, mere name for the hair of my head, hair of my body . . . brain of the head, form, sensation, perception, the predispositions, and consciousness. But in the Absolute sense there is no Ego [self] here to be found.[10]

Nagasena limits himself to denying the existence of a substantial self and concludes on this basis that he can find nothing to which the name "Nagasena" refers. This approach, while dramatic and forceful, is not as clear as Hartshorne's.

In parallel fashion, both Hartshorne and the Buddha observe that the human body endures longer than the human mind but build on this observation in rather different ways. The Buddha points out that while many people develop an aversion to their bodies because of the transience of those bodies and identify their minds as themselves, they would do better if they identified their bodies as themselves, insofar as the body lasts longer than the merely momentary existence of all mental states.[11] Hartshorne refers to this remark often and with approval. But the Buddha's remark is ironic; in the context of Buddhist teachings it is more than clear that the body also is no source of identity for the individual, indeed there is no such source. In Hartshorne, however, the body is an appropriate basis for individual identity in the sense of genetic identity:

> A social being needs suitable companions. Also, to preserve its (relative) identity through time it must have one ever-present group of such companions, in whose members and organization there is a high degree of constancy, but with sufficient influx of novelty to be interesting. This is precisely what a human body, especially in its neural portion, furnishes for human beings.[12]

Is Hartshorne simply clearer than the Buddhists in this? Or are the Buddhists more thoroughgoing than Hartshorne in their negation of the self?

It is important to consider the intention of Buddhism in this regard. While it is difficult to isolate a single first principle in Hartshorne's philosophy, in Buddhism such a principle is quite evident: the doctrine of no-self is the bedrock of Buddhist philosophy and practice. For the Buddhist, belief in self is the essence of ignorance and ignorance is the root cause of humanity's suffering. Eliminate belief in self and suffering disappears; the goal of Buddhism is attained. Thus Buddhist practice is designed to eliminate all forms of "clinging" to belief in self, whether conscious or unconscious, intellectual or emotional. Buddhist teachings are formulated accordingly: nothing is allowed which would permit the slightest grounds for grasping at a self. This is an absolute. Consequently, there is no room in Buddhist language for the slightest affirmation of self in any sense. To understand this is to understand the difference between Buddhism and Hartshorne on the self: the doctrine is very much the same, but the context of the doctrine in the two philosophies and their intended uses are different enough to result, ultimately, in significant discrepancies.

The difference becomes more explicit when we turn to Mahayana Buddhism. Here the doctrine of *sunyata* or emptiness is taken to "empty" the distinctions between pairs of opposites, including self and other. In Mahayana philosophy, the distinction between self and other is utterly nullified; from the absolute point of view there is no distinction whatsoever between the two: self is other and other is self. (From the relative point of view, a distinction is made for convenience, but this lacks in complete truth.) While philosophically this notion is the logical consequence of earlier Buddhist teachings on no-self and causation, it is even more important to recognize that it is the extension in practice of the intent of the earlier doctrine. If one is serious about eliminating all vestiges of "clinging" to self, this is the way to go.

Contrast this with Hartshorne's willingness to speak of the "series" of experiences or "career" of creative acts which constitutes an individual's life.

> Your or my career, meaning the event-sequence (a very complex combination of event-sequences in fact) making up your or my bodily-mental history, is clearly distinguishable from the career of any other human person.[13]

Buddhism and Hartshorne do not actually differ on this matter; the Buddhist doctrine amounts to the same thing. But Hartshorne is willing to speak in this way (for the sake of accuracy, clarity, and precision), while Buddhism is not (for the sake of religious practice or spiritual self-transformation).

The deep similarities together with subtly different nuances of application that we see between Buddhism and Hartshorne on the concept of self are found also in their respective theories of motivation and their ethical programs. Both are very strongly committed to the position that a self-interest theory of motivation is radically inadequate and false. In both cases the philosophical root of this position is their conviction that the mass of humanity is deluded in its belief that there is a concrete, substantial self, enduring over time, in whose interest one can act. To attempt to serve the "self" is to attempt the impossible. So far Buddhism and Hartshorne agree completely.

Theravada Buddhism adds the notion that a life lived on the basis of self-interest, ironically, results only in a life of suffering. Given human finitude, imperfection, and mortality, the ego-self's drive for individual happiness and satisfaction is doomed in all cases to utter failure. An echo of this idea is found in Hartshorne. He expresses in a number of places his delight in having given up attachment to self-interest as a theory of motivation and way of life.

> Long ago I made my decision: No one will ever compel me to shut myself up in a prison of self-interest; compel me to admit that others are for me mere means and myself the final and absolute end.[14]

He also speaks of the misery and hopelessness of the lives of those who attempt to live according to such a formula.

> In that case how ghastly an affair my death should appear! And how seriously I should have to take every misfortune to myself, and unseriously every misfortune to others. 'Writhing in delusion' — what else is it?[15]

These remarks are very much in the Theravada Buddhist spirit.

Buddhism, however, does not rest here and neither does Hartshorne. Mahayana Buddhists claimed to see vestiges of selfishness in the Theravada approach: I want to escape my suffering, therefore I practice Buddhism. They attack this position by means of their radical negation of the self-other distinction, reached by way of emptiness dialectics, as seen above. The new Buddhist ideal of the *bodhisattva* is epitomized in the form of the *bodhisattva*'s vow, ''I will not enter Nirvana (cessation of suffering, enlightenment) until all sentient beings can enter with me.'' Individual salvation is no longer contemplated as either desirable or possible. *Bodhisattvas* wed the wisdom of their insight into the non-existence of the self to a compassionate and absolutely altruistic way of life. Thus the basic form of motivation now is the desire to eliminate all suffering in all sentient beings universally and eternally and to replace that suffering with universal enlightenment.

Hartshorne, for his part, does not stop with a criticism of self-interest as the basis of a theory of motivation, but goes on to specify a more adequate theory on an entirely different basis. Again, there will be little here with which a Buddhist would disagree, but the language used and some of the implications are quite different. For Hartshorne, since there is no substantial self, the self-other distinction does break down on the immediate, concrete level of actual experience and this is the key to his theory of motivation.

> Motivation depends on much more concrete matters than substantial identity. The universal principle is not interest by and in oneself as always the same entity, nor is it interest in others as always others; it is interest by the self of the given moment . . . in other experiences or selves. . . . Some of these other selves will be continuations of the career to which the present self belongs, others will not. (That

distinction is not always very relevant.) Life is interested in life, experience in experience. Self-interest is a special case of this universal principle, altruism is another case. Not enlightened self-interest, but simply enlightened interest is the ultimate principle of right motivation, where enlightened means sufficiently future-regarding and sufficiently comprehensive of others' as well as one's own future.[16]

This moment of experience ("I") must always be experience of something else, other experiences. Whether these other experiences are part of one's own "career" or not is not an especially significant issue. The content of this moment's experience may be a memory (of "my" past experience); again, it may be a perception (of "your" face smiling in greeting). The salient point is that life reaches out to life; being inherently sentient and creative, our experiences of other experiences, moment by moment, are what we are. Thus life is a creative process of sympathetic feeling with other experiences. "Without sympathy there would be no human self and no social others."[17] The question of whether this moment's experience is a response to a past moment in my own "career" or another's pales in significance beside the fact that this moment's experience is always a sympathetic feeling-with and response to experience or life as such. This is the foundation of life, hence also of motivation and of ethics.

Clearly Hartshorne and Buddhism are very close in this matter. An important question does arise, however, regarding the place of altruism in the two philosophies. Certainly both philosophies strongly tend towards altruism; again, both ground altruism on a foundation which is far more solid than the notion of enlightened self-interest, i.e., acting on others' behalf in order to further one's own happiness or welfare. Nonetheless, a close reading reveals that Mahayana Buddhism's altruism is absolute, whereas Hartshorne's is qualified. This difference is based on the slight difference in their positions on the self.

Throughout Buddhism one finds a prominent thread of utter disregard for self. For example, in the *Jataka* tales of former lives of the Buddha, there is a story in which the Buddha-to-be, then living in the form of a rabbit, willingly—even eagerly—jumps into a stew pot to feed a hungry man. Again, the *Dhammapada* teaches that when one is struck or harmed by another, the proper response is not anger or self-pity, but compassion for the aggressor who has incurred bad *karma* through the act of aggression. This kind of thing, of which there are endless examples, is held as an ideal model which the Buddhist disciple should seek to emulate. And such acts are in fact emulated in the tradition, for example in the deaths of the Vietnamese monks who immolated themselves in an attempt to hasten the end of the war in their homeland. In short, there is in Buddhism a thread of absolute self-negation and self-sacrifice which very much colors the social ethics of that tradition. This is nothing but the expression in ethical form of the doctrine of no-self in its utterly uncompromising Buddhist form. Absolutely selfless acts are both an expression of and a means of realizing the utter non-existence of self.

Hartshorne's position differs from the Buddhist, again tending away from the extremeness of the Buddhist position to a more common-sensical or realistic position. We have seen that while for Hartshorne the ultimate basis of ethics is life's interest in and sympathy for life, both self-interest and altruism are special cases of this universal principle. Thus whereas self-interest has no place whatsoever in Buddhism (and this is especially clear in the Mahayana form) it does have a legitimate, albeit strictly limited, place in Hartshorne's philosophy. One is rationally and morally entitled to a degree of interest in the future of one's own ''career'' so long as that interest is placed in the perspective of one's similarly reasonable interest in the future of others and of life itself. An exclusive interest in one's own ''career'' is a distortion and irrational; likewise an interest in one's own future to a degree that relegates interest in others to a far secondary place is also a distortion. Clearly, the future of life or the cosmos is more important from a rational point of view than the future of any individual; my own future is of interest to me, but of relatively limited interest, in such a context. The soundest basis of my interest in myself is my interest in what I can contribute to the future of life.

> Of course, some relative differences are insuperable between self-sympathy and sympathy for others, but to absolutize the differences . . . is indeed lamentable. To be entirely rational is to love the whole ongoing universe, and oneself and one's future only as items in that universe—for that is to see things as they are. We are but pebbles on the cosmic beach.[18]

The contrast with Buddhism helps to bring out the point that in Hartshorne we have an ethic in which altruism is pre-eminent, while self-interest retains a minor but legitimate place. Hartshorne writes, ''I think . . . that there is a direct duty to promote one's own happiness, as well as that of others.''[19] The reason for this is partly that in making oneself happy one contributes to the happiness of others, partly that all of the experiences which constitute one are retained in the memory of God and enjoyed or suffered by God but also partly that in so far as life is sympathy I obviously do have sympathy for my own experiences as well as those of others. My happiness is one of several legitimate goals for me. My happiness has intrinsic value.

> . . . [T]here are only two ways we can fulfill the ultimate obligation: by achieving our own happiness and furthering future happiness in other persons or animals.[20]

As Hartshorne sees it, realistically speaking ''some relative differences are insuperable between self-sympathy and sympathy for others.''[21] Hartshorne expresses a sense of regret and even tragedy that this is the case, speaking of a "terribly real *relative* validity, as secondary derivative concepts, of the notions of self and self-advantage."[22] Nonetheless, it is hard to imagine Hartshorne embracing as realistic the image of the rabbit Buddha-to-be jumping in the stew pot as an ideal model to which humanity should aspire. Buddhism, however, simply does not accept Hartshorne's negative assessment of the possibility of a complete eradication of self-interest. In this respect, Buddhism is wildly optimistic about the intrinsic goodness of human nature and the ultimate perfectability of humanity.

Where Buddhism advocates the *bodhisattva* ideal, Hartshorne regards as ideal the Christian motto, "love thy neighbor as thyself." This contrast captures well the difference between the two. The *bodhisattva* is ideally utterly selfless, self-forgetting, self-negating, concerned exclusively with the welfare of others. To love others "as" oneself, however, assumes the validity of self-love but requires its universalization. Psychologically, this is a very different approach. Perhaps in the end the attitudes and behavior implicit in the two ideals amount to the same thing. I believe, however, that Buddhists would find the vestiges of self-interest remaining in Hartshorne to be impediments to the goal of utter selflessness which they, as Buddhists, strive to achieve. To the Mahayana Buddhist, my non-distinction from you is an unqualified truth; there can be no reality whatsoever attached to the concept of self-interest.

Let us now consider how these theoretical positions manifest themselves in the field of practical ethics. It should be mentioned here that while Buddhism is uncompromising in its altruism on a philosophical basis, it has not lived up to its promise in the practical realm. Generally, while various individuals have contributed in concrete ways to the welfare of others, Buddhism as a whole has tended (1) not to institutionalize acts of charity in the Buddhist church as such; and (2) to regard explicitly spiritual help (teaching, moral example, counseling, etc.) as more important than material help. There is evidence, though, that the Buddhist church is changing with respect to both of these points, and it is to be expected that as Buddhism modernizes and extends its familiarity with the Western world change of this kind will continue.

Turning to specific moral issues, we find the same general agreement between Hartshorne and Buddhism that we have seen with respect to the philosophy of self and the theory of motivation, but now some of the subtle differences between the two come to bear fruit. Generally speaking, both philosophies advocate an ethic in which concern for the individual person is replaced by concern for others, for the environing world, and for life itself. Most characteristically, both feel that a primary aim of life is to contribute in whatever way one can to the unfolding of the vast potential of life as such. Let us see to what degree this general agreement is maintained in two specific areas: environmental-ecological concern and animal ethics.

Hartshorne and Buddhism share a strong environmental ethic. Hartshorne has written a great deal on this subject, for example:

> We can try to view man and the rest of nature as one ecosystem in which our species is, so far as possible, complementary, rather than competitive, with the other creatures in the system. To this end we can take zero population growth, or even, eventually and for a time, population decrease, as desirable goals. We can put a burden of proof upon each proposed destruction of wild nature. We can weigh seriously the need for luxuries which use large amounts of energy. . . .[23]

Buddhism, likewise, is clear on this subject. The Sarvodaya Shramadana movement lists Ten Basic Needs for community development, prominent among which is "a, clean, safe, beautiful environment." Moreover, this is interpreted in terms of traditional Buddhist spiritual concerns as follows.

> If the Buddha taught that craving is at the root of human suffering, then so too are patterns of production and consumption that inflame this craving . . . . From the perspective of the Dharma, modest consumption is not only conservative of resources, but essential to spiritual health and self-reliance.[24]

A contemporary American Zen Roshi, Robert Aitken, has written an unusually clear book on Zen ethics. The ethical stance of the following passage and even much of the language of response to others is remarkably close to Hartshorne.

> Our task . . . is to respond generously to others. We can take as our models not only Shakyamuni . . . but also such humble beings as bushes and grasses. With every fiber, beings of the plant world are guiding others, perpetuating their species, beginning new species as circumstances permit, conveying their vitality to soil, waters, air, insects, animals, and people. . . . How do we actualize the oneness of all beings? Through responsibility, the ability to respond—like that of the clover.[25]

Let us take it, then, that Hartshorne and Buddhism are firm allies in the environmental cause. Not only do they share very similar values, they also base those values on their shared conviction that the non-substantial self constructs itself moment by moment as a living response to its environing world.

Turning to the issue of animal ethics, we will see that Buddhism and Hartshorne diverge substantially here and that this difference can be traced to philosophical grounds. To put the difference briefly, Hartshorne views life in hierarchical terms, with animals on the bottom, human beings in the middle, and God at the top of the hierarchy. This, of course, is the traditional Western view, a view which constitutes one of the great lines of demarcation between East and West. Buddhism is typical of Eastern views (with the prominent exception of Confucianism) in which human beings and animals are seen as one single category, "sentient beings." Without a God, this means there is no ontological hierarchy in Buddhism at all. As a result of this difference on ontology, we have different norms of behavior for human beings with regard to animals in the two philosophies.

For Hartshorne, the superiority of human beings as compared to other animals rests on the relatively greater intelligence, freedom, and creativity of humanity.

> The many important aspects of the difference between men and the other higher animals center in one: the symbolic capacity, shown obviously in language. . . . An effect of symbolic power is the enhancement of freedom in the partially indeterministic sense. . . . The ethical importance of the idea of freedom . . . is that it brings out the real nature of life. . . . If each moment of life is genuinely creative, at least in some slight degree, *then each creature is also a creator*. . . . Human beings do this to a far higher degree than the other animals. . . . I conclude . . . that in the sense in which any animal has intrinsic value, all animals have some of it, and the differences are matters of degree. Since man has the typical animal capacities . . . plus an enormous addition of reflective consciousness and technical power, it seems reasonable to assign him a far higher value than the other terrestrial creatures . . . at the same time it is also reasonable to proclaim the ideal that man should, where possible, regard himself and his value as additional or complementary to the others, rather than as competitive with them.[26]

Thus animals do have intrinsic value, but measured by the criteria of intelligence, freedom, and creativity, the intrinsic value of a human being is greater.

The obvious question here is why the criteria of intelligence, freedom, and creativity should be taken as the measures of the intrinsic value of a form of life. Certainly this question arises for a Buddhist, who, in fact, does not use these criteria. From a Buddhist point of view it would likely be argued that the reason for Hartshorne's use of these criteria is his Western, Christian bias. It is, in fact, hard to justify Hartshorne's position once the ontological hierarchy animals-humanity-God ceases to be assumed. For Hartshorne, just as animals possess a measure of intelligence, freedom, and creativity but humans possess more, so God, in turn, possesses more of these qualities than humanity. God embodies the highest values to the maximum possible degree. Thus again just as animals possess intrinsic value but less intrinsic value than human beings, so human beings possess less intrinsic value than God.

But here we must question Hartshorne. Just as the ultimate measure of a human life is what that life has contributed to God, so the ultimate measure of a nonhuman life is its contribution to God. Hartshorne himself says that God values both human and nonhuman experience, but goes on, "while rational animals make a special contribution to the Summum Bonum, every creature makes some contribution, however humble it may be."[27] While chastising Kant for his "museum piece" theology in which God is only interested in rational creatures, Hartshorne himself expounds a theology in which rational creatures make a "special" contribution and others a more "humble" one. What is this but a modified version of Kant's values, i.e., the projection onto God of the all-too-human act of measuring nonhuman life by human criteria, in particular, rationality and its consequences? Why should God not be like the Tao, to which a growing blade of grass, a dog chewing on a bone, and a human contemplating life are of equal, unmeasured value? Is Hartshorne justified in assuming that the intrinsic value of human experience is greater than that of the nonhuman? Can we assume that our relatively greater intelligence, freedom, and creativity give us greater inherent value?

The Buddhist approach to this issue is to determine the ethics of human behavior with respect to animals in terms of the capacity of the latter to suffer. They do not perceive any clear, intrinsic difference between the suffering of a human being in a given degree of pain and the suffering of an animal in a similar degree of pain. In accordance with the principle of *ahimsa*, they therefore refuse to sanction any acts which cause pain or suffering to other life forms, human or nonhuman. Being free of an ontological hierarchy which measures value in terms of other criteria, their position is as simple as that.

Thus we find, as one clear example, that many Buddhists advocate and practice vegetarianism. An American Zen Roshi, Philip Kapleau, argues cogently and authoritatively that any other position is inconsistent on Buddhist ethical grounds.[28] Hartshorne, on the contrary, argues that there may be a strong economic case to be made for partial vegetarianism (insofar as the production on a large scale of meat for human consumption is highly wasteful of the earth's resources), but does not make a case for complete vegetarianism on moral grounds.[29] Given the reality that human nutritional needs can be more than adequately met on a vegetarian diet, Hartshorne's disinclination to embrace the moral argument for vegetarianism becomes all the more problematic: human habit and aesthetic preference seem to count more heavily than animal suffering. Surely this can only be if the intrinsic value of animals is indeed far less than the intrinsic value of humans.

Hartshorne's position is made clear in his repeated use of the term "subhuman" rather than "nonhuman" to refer to nonhuman animals. It is well known that it is not possible on biological grounds to consider other animals inferior or "lower" than human animals. It is also not possible on Buddhist, Taoist, or Hindu grounds. It is, however, possible within the Christian world view in which God is conceived as like humanity but greater and animals as like humanity but lesser. Outside of this world view, it is difficult to justify the view that rationality, rather than capacity to suffer, should be the measure by which we judge our behavior towards other forms of life.

In conclusion, let us attempt a modest appraisal of what we have considered above. There is a great deal held in common by Hartshorne and Buddhism; with respect to the areas of shared ideas and values, how good is this position? Many will find the metaphysical analysis of self held in common by the two to be very convincing. At the least, it constitutes a radically different and stimulating alternative to the now largely discredited Cartesian view of the self and the philosophically problematic traditional Christian and Hindu views of the soul. Given the present search in Western philosophy for a viable alternative to traditional conceptions of human selfhood, the Buddhist-Hartshornian position deserves, and ultimately cannot help but receive, the most careful of consideration. The theory of motivation shared by the two philosophies, again, is a powerful and unique alternative to more popular theories of egotism and enlightened self-interest. If one is interested in a foundation for an ethics which is capable of asserting the reality and importance of altruistic behavior, some radically other-centered (as opposed to self-centered) philosophy such as this one will ultimately prove to be necessary.

As for the positions on actual ethical issues which result from these foundations, we have seen that Hartshorne and Buddhism are somewhat less in accord, though with their shared altruistic orientation there is again far more held in common here than in dispute. Probably no one but a hard-core egotist could doubt the ultimately salutary effects for humanity and for life itself of the ethical positions held in common in these philosophies. Such differences as do exist between them seem to me a fertile area for future Buddhist-process philosophy dialogue.

If we agree that this position is an attractive one, the question remains: can it be accepted? Buddhism has been deeply misunderstood on the issue of self and all its ramifications by Buddhists and non-Buddhists for twenty-five hundred years. Would the greater precision of the Hartshornian version of this idea be of help? Hartshorne himself seems to have faith in the power of rational argument. Buddhists, however, have written extensively on the great power of a threatened ego on the defensive and view this as the ultimate source of resistance to the Buddhist position. Buddhism claims that rational argument is rarely capable of penetrating deeply enough into the structure of the human psyche to dislodge fiercely held beliefs on personal identity and insist that it takes years of devoted meditation practice for most people to penetrate and appropriate this idea.

As for the future, both the Buddhist and the process philosophy camp look forward to the continuation of this dialogue. On the Buddhist side, it must be said that Buddhism has twenty-five hundred years of experience of working through its ideas on self, constructing a philosophical language to conceive its implications, and developing techniques for its realization. Its discussion of human identity and experience uses a language largely lacking in parallels in English and other Western languages. Moreover, Buddhist writings are extremely vast. All of this constitutes a gold mine for Western philosophers interested in working out a viable anthropological philosophy.

From the process philosophy side we can anticipate a positive contribution to the clarification of Buddhist ideas. Buddhist thought is rich and profound, but not always clear, consistent, or adequately worked out. It is rarely systematic. Process philosophy, and Hartshorne's work in particular, has much to contribute here.

Moreover, a process philosophy–Buddhism dialogue inevitably helps uncover cultural bias on both sides. We have seen above one way in which Buddhism may do this for Hartshorne. Obviously, a process philosopher studying Buddhism could perform the same service. Most exciting, those engaged in a process philosophy–Buddhism dialogue can explore together those issues outstanding between them, such as those discussed above, for their mutual benefit, and the benefit of all of us. What a pleasure to see the two sides debate the degree of absoluteness with which the no-self position, the position negating the distinction between self and other, should be taken! What a boon to have the two sides consider together issues such as animal ethics!

Last but far from least, the ongoing dialogue between Buddhism and process philosophy is one more contribution to the mutual recognition, understanding, and sympathetic acceptance of world cultures. Perhaps this is the greatest legacy of this dialogue for the future. Hartshorne's own words on the subject make a fitting closing:

> The provincialism of metaphysicians is nearing its end. . . . [P]racticing metaphysicians should from now on pay attention to the two great international, highly developed traditions in their subject, the Western . . . and the Buddhist. . . . As Whitehead well said, these two traditions should no longer be protected from each other.[30]

SALLIE B. KING

DEPARTMENT OF PHILOSOPHY
SOUTHERN ILLINOIS UNIVERSITY AT CARBONDALE
APRIL 1986

NOTES

1. Charles Hartshorne, "Whitehead's Differences from Buddhism," *Philosophy East and West* 25, 4 (October, 1975):407.

2. Charles Hartshorne, "Toward a Buddhisto-Christian Religion," in *Buddhism and American Thinkers*, ed. Kenneth K. Inada and Nolan P. Jacobson (Albany, NY: State University of New York Press, 1984), p. 2.

3. Ibid., p. 11.

4. Charles Hartshorne, "'Emptiness' and Fullness in Asiatic and Western Thought," *Journal of Chinese Philosophy* 6, 4 (December, 1979):419.

5. Sallie King, "The Buddha Nature: True Self as Action," *Religious Studies* 20 (June, 1984):255–67.

6. Charles Hartshorne, "The Development of My Philosophy," in *Contemporary American Philosophy: Second Series*, ed. John E. Smith (London: Allen and Unwin, 1970), p. 219.

7. Charles Hartshorne, "Could There Have Been Nothing? A Reply," *Process Studies* 1.1 (Spring, 1971):27.

8. Charles Hartshorne, "Process Themes in Chinese Thought," *Journal of Chinese Philosophy* 6,3 (September, 1979):330–31.

9. Charles Hartshorne, "Personal Identity from A to Z," *Process Studies* 2, 3 (Fall, 1972):211.

10. Translated from the *Milindapanha* in *Buddhism in Translations*, ed. Henry Clarke Warren (New York: Atheneum, 1979), p. 133. Second ellipsis in the original.

11. Samyutta Nikaya 12:62. Cited in ibid., p. 151.

12. Charles Hartshorne, "Panpsychism: Mind as Sole Reality," *Ultimate Reality and Meaning* 1, 2 (1978):122. The text has "neutral portion," but I have taken this as a typographical error for "neural portion."

13. "Buddhisto-Christian Religion," p. 4.

14. Charles Hartshorne, "Beyond Enlightened Self-Interest: A Metaphysics of Ethics," *Ethics* 84, 3 (April, 1974):207.

15. Ibid.

16. "Buddhisto-Christian Religion," p. 5.

17. Ibid.

18. Ibid.

19. Charles Hartshorne, "Ethics and the Process of Living," in *Man and His Conduct: Philosophical Essays in Honor of Risieri Frondizi*, ed. Jorge J. E. Gracia (Rio Piedras, Puerto Rico: Editorial Universitaria, 1980), p. 198.

20. Charles Hartshorne, "The Ethics of Contributionism," in *Responsibilities to Future Generations: Environmental Ethics*, ed. Ernest Partridge (Buffalo, NY: Prometheus Books, 1980), p. 104.

21. "Buddhisto-Christian Religion," p. 5.

22. Charles Hartshorne, "A Metaphysics of Individualism," in *Innocence and Power*, ed. Gordon Mills (Austin: University of Texas Press, 1965), p. 145.

23. Charles Hartshorne, "The Rights of the Subhuman World," *Environmental Ethics* 1.1 (Spring, 1979):57.

24. Joanne Macy, *Dharma and Development: Religion as Resource in the Sarvodaya Self-Help Movement*, Revised Edition (West Hartford, CT: Kumarian Press, 1985), p. 27 and pp. 45–46.

25. Robert Aitken, *The Mind of Clover: Essays in Zen Buddhist Ethics* (San Francisco: North Point Press, 1984), p. 136.

26. Charles Hartshorne, "Foundations for a Humane Ethics," in *On the Fifth Day: Animal Rights and Human Ethics*, ed. Richard Knowles Morris and Michael W. Fox (Washington, D.C.: Acropolis Books, 1978), pp. 160–63, 170.

27. ''Subhuman World,'' p. 50.

28. Philip Kapleau, *To Cherish All Life: A Buddhist Case for Becoming Vegetarian* (San Francisco: Harper and Row, 1931).

29. ''Subhuman World,'' p. 52.

30. ''Whitehead's Differences,'' p. 413.

13

John G. Arapura

HARTSHORNE'S RESPONSE TO VEDĀNTA

An Introductory Note

Our topic, "Hartshorne's Response to Vedānta", must be put in perspective, for ordinarily in the discussion of a leading Western philosopher or system such a topic would be considered quite outlandish. When we talk about Hartshorne's philosophy this is not the case. He is one of the very few great philosophers in Western history who have discussed and debated with Eastern systems and ideas as philosophy, with respect due to them as such, and in a well-informed manner. He has especially taken serious account of Buddhism and Hinduism among the Eastern traditions, looked deeply into them while laying stone upon stone, constructing his own system. He himself refers to his discussions with "philosophers of India and Japan".[1]

Of all Eastern traditions, Hartshorne finds the deepest affinity with Buddhism. In fact he finds himself closer to Buddhism than to most Western systems even, so much so that in some respects, for instance, on the question of genetic versus substantial identity of the individual, he says he is recommending a neo-Buddhist view.[2] It is also noteworthy that, on some metaphysical matters, to the degree to which he agrees with Buddhism, almost to the same degree does he disagree with Vedānta, i.e., its central system set forth by the great monist Śankara—and these two Indian traditions had engaged in an on-going debate for generations. As is to be expected, Hartshorne's positive appraisal, and use, of the one and critical appraisal of the other are conducted from an avowedly philosophical platform.

As Buddhism is venerated for being the greatest and truest precursor in antiquity of modern Process philosophy, so Vedānta is viewed in ways befitting an utter opponent and repository of antithetical ideas. The latter's radical monism (or non-dualism), its "static" view of reality, its extreme doctrine of permanent and unchanging substance and its theory of an eternally self-identical, substantial soul, which is also identical with ultimate reality (Brahman) itself and wholly beyond time, are all rated as the exact opposite of the ideas of Buddhism—and of Process philosophy: this is justly so because in these and such other matters the Vedānta of Śankara is surely the epitome and absolute paradigm, before which even those Western systems that in diverse respects are similar to it, pale. One has to gather Professor Hartshorne's comments on it from their sundry occurrences. But under what principle? There are several possibilities. Of these I have chosen as the most appropriate one the comprehension of a certain logical flow of Hartshorne's system, focussed on a few central strands, which have decisive bearing on how he responds to Vedāntic ideas, which he also sees as having bearing on the given points of his metaphysics. My effort will be directed towards achieving this comprehension, and I will insert my comments all along the way as occasions warrant.

The Strands of Hartshorne's Metaphysics Considered from the Point of View of His Response to Vedānta

Professor Hartshorne's response to Vedānta (as to all other systems) comes in the context of his working out his "neo-classical theism", or (as more commonly called now) "Process theology". For him, metaphysics ideally is theology. "The idea of God", he declares, "contains implicitly the entire contents of metaphysics".[3] In any case, Hartshorne's interest in Vedānta—and Buddhism—comes decidedly from his theistic concern, as he in one place remarks:

> In Buddhism a transcendent reality is recognized, but it is not, at least explicitly or obviously, taken to be God. In much Hindu thought a deity—Isvara—transcending the world is admitted, but it is distinguished from the still higher, or more strictly 'real' impersonal absolute or Brahman. I favor a more theistic view.[4]

All this shows that my discussion must be within the dimension of what may be broadly called Hartshorne's God question, picking up its appropriate strands, which are:

1. The Idea of God and the Problem of Proof

Professor Hartshorne, who may be rightly called the greatest living theistic philosopher, has set forth an appropriate global metaphysics—global primarily in the humanly significant sense of embracing, at least in principle, different civilizations and spiritual traditions of mankind. But his system is "neo-classical" in the historic, Western sense, because, as he declares: "While it is not an example of what most people mean by 'the great tradition', it has been thought out in intimate relation to the great metaphysical systems."[5]

Professor Hartshorne forges strong links between Process thought, of which he himself is one of the original makers, and the medieval roots of Western theology and metaphysics, yet squeezing novel possibilities out of the latter. That is how he can say that "the perspective upon Anselm alone should suffice to open a new era in metaphysics."[6] In tangible terms, it amounts to "the reconsideration given to the most famous of all metaphysical arguments, Anselm's proofs for God's existence."[7]

The paramount form in which the medieval thinkers of the West pursued the idea of God was through proofs for his existence—the assumption thereunder having been eventually challenged by Hume and Kant by refuting the proofs, although Kant (unlike Hume) believed that the idea had to be pursued by other means. Hartshorne's counter-refutation of Kant and Hume,[8] is rooted in his conviction that the proofs can be liberated for a much greater metaphysical mission, a conviction he translates into a meticulously worked out scheme, to be completed by his concept of the self-surpassing deity and all that goes with it. Theistic proofs were essentially deductive in character. As Hartshorne remarks: "Anselm was right in contending that existence was deducible from the definition of God, assuming that the definition is conceivable."[9] And "as for deduction" he clarifies, "what it does is to establish a price for rejecting its conclusions. Suppose P entails Q. Then those who initially accept P must either accept Q also, or reconsider their acceptance of P."[10] (Deduction of existence found its way into speculation too, even at its highest level, and not necessarily tied to divine existence. And interesting questions as to whether existence is a predicate or not a predicate came into vogue.)

2. Hartshorne's Less Restrictive Vision of Proof, as Having to Do with Divine Actuality

Hartshorne seems to argue that proofs for deity are not to be narrowly conceived in terms of the classical proofs for God's existence; rather they should be pointing to something more basic to the "religious" idea of God, i.e., divine actuality. He admits that the classical proofs have failed, and adds "but not all proofs, so that the impossibility of proofs has not been established".[11] The crux of the matter, it seems to me, lies in the fact that the nature of "proof" has been reconceived as a means of dealing with divine actuality. Attention is called to the "immeasurable gulf between existence and actuality".[12] Hartshorne lays down the proposition: "Actuality is always *more* than existence. Existence is *that* the defined abstract nature is *somehow* concretely actualized; but *how* it is actualized, in what particular state, with what *content* not deducible from abstract definition, constitutes the actuality."[13] "Actuality can never be deduced, not even in the divine case."[14] Actuality is, in other words, not a conclusion from an abstract definition, nor is it ever abstract[15] (like a definition). This position strongly reminds one of Śankara's (Vedāntic) dictum that philosophical showing (or proof) is nothing but clarification of what is already known,[16] rather than deduction through argument of what is unknown.

Hartshorne puts forward his own revolutionized definition of proof as something geared to divine actuality, in fact as the complete, rational working out of it. He calls it "global proof", which is squarely based on religion, both Western and Eastern. He describes it as "an argument from the rational necessity of religious experience and of God as its adequate referent."[17] Elsewhere, Hartshorne writes: "All arguments are phases of one 'global' argument, that the properly formulated theistically religious view of life and reality is the most intelligible, self-consistent and satisfactory one that can be conceived."[18]

Religion is viewed as a matter of achieving "individual integrity" or "wholeness".[19] In this respect "East Indian" religions (along with the religions of the West) offer positive testimony, despite Buddhism's refusal to rationalize (or theorize) what is given in "satori" or salvation, and Hinduism's tendency to view God "as an inferior manifestation of the mysterious ultimate",[20] which means also that they have, nonetheless, failed to work out a rational theory of God as the adequate referent of religious experience, which they have.

3. Criticism of Eastern Reliance on Intuition and of the Related (?) Problems of the Indefinite and the Absolute

Proof, whether in the sense applied to the restricted problem of existence, or in the wider—and more fundamental—sense of rationally working out the implications of divine actuality, intuitive knowledge of it being based on religious experience, is the pre-eminent act of theorizing. Failure in this respect on the part of Hinduism and Buddhism is attributed to their reliance on "sheer intuition".[21] Hartshorne cites the Māyā notion as an example of this failure:

> The contrast between Maya, correlative to ignorance, and Reality, correlative to true knowledge, resists conceptual analysis. Is Maya a form of being (and what form?), a form of non-being, a mixture of being and non-being, neither being nor non-being. . . . Press any statements by the followers of Sankara, and you will find, I am convinced, that the semblance of conceptual definiteness and logical structure is itself Maya.[22]

Now, in this statement there is something that needs to be clarified. The last sentence could mean—and is probably intended to mean—that Māyā got in the way of achieving conceptual definiteness and logical structure. Or it could mean that these things having been achieved, or in course of being achieved, Māyā pronounces them to be not really valid, measured by the criteria of a higher truth which is perhaps accessible to some intuition (or perhaps not). In fact, the latter is the better meaning, being true to what really happened in the Indian tradition. Furthermore, there was no failure to conceptualize or theorize even in respect of the very thing which may have pronounced all conceptualizing as inadequate for the highest truth, because that knowledge too is conceptually developed—and Māyā itself was theorized with the utmost definiteness that conceptual power could muster, as *the absolute indefinite*. This has a logic too, which is that there is a point of perfect development that definiteness of concept must reach, where alone can one clearly realize its inadequacy to the higher truth that still lies beyond. In that transaction there is a positive use of the indefinite: this is an achievement and not the aftermath of some failure. Furthermore, indefiniteness must be understood cosmologically and not merely epistemologically.[23] The classical and original enunciation of this whole principle is made by Śankara who writes (*Commentary on Brahma Sūtra*, 2.1.14): "The cosmos or Nature is the Māyā-power of divinity, a projection of Ignorance, and indefinable as either Being or other than Being . . .". Exceedingly subtle and elaborate developments followed from this in the Vedāntic tradition, the purpose of which was to show that there is a realm of the indefinite in which we are submerged and there can be no proper theory of Reality without taking it fully into account and dealing with it.

A modern Vedāntist, and the most original Indian philosopher of the present century, the late K. C. Bhattacharyya, in an article, "The Place of the Indefinite in Logic", describes[24] three ways in which the indefinite is usually understood: as explicitly epistemological; as provisionally definite; and as the function of truth itself, i.e., "as the function of negation which is neither a mere epistemological element nor a static truth by itself but still a constructive factor of definite truth only." But he goes further to argue for "a place for the absolute indefinite", which is historically found in the 'negative' matter of Plato, Māyā of Vedānta, and the Void (*Śūnyam*) of Buddhism. T. R. V. Murti tries to put the indefinite via Formal Logic as the exclusion of the Excluded Middle.[25] He cites as examples two propositions: "An integer between 3 and 4 is prime", An integer between 3 and 4 is composite and not prime", but adds that neither of these propositions is true though they are contradictories in the formal sense. He feels that the Excluded Middle is useless here.

Professor Hartshorne who had identified Māyā with the inability to conceptualize or theorize, in some other places, however, without pressing that point, speaks of the harm that the notion of the indefinite does to metaphysics, no doubt tacitly recognizing that it does have a theoretic base, inasmuch as the Greeks too, who could hardly be called non-theoretical, had it. And he feels that the harm is worsened in conjunction with its associate, the Absolute (in Greek and Indian form). To his mind it is evidence of a serious fault, namely, putting the abstract before the concrete in the attempt to grasp reality. Thus he remarks: "There is reason to charge both Greek and ancient Hindu and Buddhist philosophy with the tendency to invert the proper relation of abstract and concrete, to proceed as if the way to grasp reality is to equate it with indefiniteness."[26] Professor Hartshorne's logic is this: Although there can be determinate (concrete) forms of negation—and so Spinoza's motto that "all determination is negation" is partially correct—, indeterminateness is more complete negation because its form is abstract, and "the abstract is the more completely negative."[27]

A few spaces before we spoke of the positive use of the indefinite. Here we must think of the positive ways in which negation was employed in Vedānta (and allied systems). Professor Hartshorne too recognizes, "as Hegelians and Marxists and also Plato" have, that "an element of negation is inescapable" and says that "the problem is to locate it correctly."[28] The Vedāntists would go further with negation as they have with indefiniteness. As they, along with the Buddhists, believe that as indefinitness must be exploited thoroughly for philosophy, the various possibilities of negation must be used towards that end. Again, K. C. Bhattacharyya in another article, "Some Aspects of Negation",[29] discusses various possibilities. He believes that the primary equation of "the region of negation" with "the region of the indefinite" is itself subject to variations and he suggests that they must all be viewed as alternatives, which really means that they must all be taken together (for I find no other acceptable meaning for alternatives). The primary form, in which negation is equated with indefiniteness, according to the later definitions of Māyā at least, is the absence of identity and difference in a relation (to abstract being), which therefore is no relation at all. But then a second form of it is that which makes possible "the relation of two beings as set against some other relation", but these "not as the abstract beings but as related". (This form immediately calls Hartshorne too to mind.) A third form is one in which "each negation is at once the distinction." But then here "there is no *universal* negation, so there can be no universal fact-character also." "A whirl of negation then alone remains but it is still regarded as the positive." In the fourth form, "we definitely leave behind abstract being, which was our first starting point and start with contradiction itself or transcendent negation as our first principle." "Being" itself is here taken as something posited by this negation. "From this vortex of negation *any* particular may spring and so particulars have only to be accepted as they come and are related into a world, positive for all particular purposes but as an absolute inexplicability as the ground of it all."[30]

Now, even according to Bhattacharyya's account of the manifoldness of negation, it is, in the primary form at least, part and parcel of abstract Being, and hence the original equation of the region of negation with the region of the indefinite. To the extent that in most versions of Vedāntic metaphysics this primary equation is put forward rigidly with all its logical implications, Hartshorne is right in expressing his apprehension that the dominant intellectual doctrine (in Vedānta) "is the familiar Western doctrine (as in Plotinus) of 'the absolute', the formless 'infinite', viewed as superior to, but manifest in all definite, finite actuality, even divine actuality", which he holds "is an intellectual and religious mistake".[31] Why is it such a mistake? Because "God as actual is more than the absolute (which indeed is a mere abstraction) not less."

In fact, on the religious side at least, if not always on the intellectual side this mistake is corrected in Vedānta. And this not by virtue of the role assigned to Īśvara, or the personal form of the divine, rated as the lower form, but by reason of the ideas of power and concrete actuality through which Brahman is viewed. And insofar as the Absolute is still the indefinite, for the divine actuality to be more than it, it has also to be less than it. And I think Hartshorne's central point about the religious idea of God, namely, that it is based on wholeness and on conscious worship, for which he summons the testimony of Buddhism and Hinduism as well as the religions of the West, is apt here.

4. A Relativist Framework for the Religious Idea of God

Inasmuch as this article is focussed on what Hartshorne calls the religious idea of God, we shall confine ourselves to that and merely touch upon other aspects of his vast metaphysics and logic with direct relevance to it, and that too within the context of his response to Vedānta only. Hartshorne's criticism of the concept of the Absolute—as is well-known—is the general light in which his response to Vedānta is to be viewed. There are, however, special features to this response on account of Vedānta's "absolute" absolutism, of complete monism, of its extreme doctrines of eternally self-identical oneness of the individual with Brahman, of the non-reality of the world, and so on.

In this respect, it seems to me, Professor Hartshorne has discovered something of great significance within the Indian tradition itself—which is revealed largely by the way he discusses Buddhism's possibilities in his building the new metaphysical framework for the idea of God he has worked out on the basis of a religious principle. Neither the absolute nor in fact the abstract as such is shunned. There can be an absolute of Being and an absolute of Becoming: the choice of metaphysics is between them. In the departure of Buddhism from the Vedic-Vedāntic tradition this choice was first made clearly in the history of thought. Reflecting the Buddhist view, Hartshorne remarks: "If there is an eternal Being, it is some ultimate form of becoming."[32] Likewise, "relativity is the absolute principle" and "in a way it is *more* absolute".[33] As for abstractness, " 'Becoming' (like 'being') is also exceedingly abstract" (and so is 'relativity').[34]

Hartshorne too makes the Buddhist choice, in modern terms "the Buddhist-Whiteheadian type of philosophies", in answer to his own question: "In what kind of philosophy is the religious idea of God most at home?", because according to it, "the most concrete mode of reality is not existing substance, thing or person, but naturally occurring event, state, or experience".[35] This is the beginning of a metaphysical programme calculated to off-set "a bias" "philosophy early acquired" — found "both in ancient Greece and the Orient" — "from which it has been painfully struggling to free itself, a bias favoring one pole of certain ultimate contraries at the expense of the other pole, thus *being* at the expense of becoming, identity at the expense of diversity, the absolute or non-relative at the expense of the relative. . . ."[36]

At the risk of over-simplifying the programme that Professor Hartshorne works out in fine detail, I say it is basically a systematic obversion of the poles so that the ones so long under shadow, like becoming and relativity, may gain the upper hand. It is important to note that Hartshorne himself calls this scheme by the name "neo-classical metaphysics" or "neo-classical theology", which tells us much more about it than does the rather contrived flag name process philosophy.[37] However, there is no given order in which its terms of obversion like becoming, diversity, relativity, and so on are placed as might normally be expected in such a thoroughly speculative system. In any case that does not seem so essential, as Hartshorne notes, "it is not hard to translate talk about being and becoming into talk about absoluteness and relativity" — and one might add other associated pairs of contrasting concepts.

However, in replacing the concepts like being which had reigned in traditional metaphysics — and theology — help is drawn from Buddhism (well-experienced as the original champion who had fought against classical Hindu metaphysics);[38] in any case until modern Process came along there were no comparable combatants in the West. To quote Hartshorne:

> The earliest great tradition which espoused a philosophy of becoming was Buddhism. Heracleitos, who said things are new each moment, was isolated, and in addition obscure, for we have but fragmentary sayings. Only the followers of Buddha produced a great literature expressive of the doctrine that becoming is the universal form of reality. They carried this through, in some respects with admirable thoroughness, long before anything like it occurred in the West.[39]

So then, elsewhere Hartshorne shows that in Buddhism "and not in Heraclitus was the emergence of a radical philosophy of process"; for, "for one thing from the Greek we have some epigrams, from the Buddha and his followers, a library". And Hartshorne chides the West for neglecting "this great tradition".[40]

Both in the West and in India the concepts of being and its associates established their suzerainty first, and that very early in history. But while in the West their reign became a *sine qua non* in metaphysics, in India "Buddhism came to challenge it with a subtlety and persistence which had no counterpart in classical or medieval Europe."[41]

5. The Attack Upon Substance Doctrines with Emphasis Upon Events and States

As the system is neo-classical, given to obversion of leading classical concepts, in addition to the revolutionary new use of some classical doctrines themselves (such as Anselm's ontology), there is, in studying it, the freedom to choose from a number of contraries as focus. But on the whole, substance versus events (states) controversy has some reason to be preferred, for, after all, classical metaphysics has shown that when one talks long enough about being one starts talking about something like substance—for classical metaphysics the final term. Modern interpreters of Vedānta also see its doctrines in the light of substance, and so Buddhism is seen as opposing that in the name of events (states), or change.

The focus on the criticism of substance metaphysics as the primary mode of expressing the neo-classical approach is backed by some of Hartshorne's discussions. Together with substance goes the identity of the individual subject. From the event side arguments have been put forward to show that the alternative event view of individual identity and subject is more viable. Hartshorne argues that "the concept of substance, taken seriously and literally is an intellectual prison",[42] that "the universal category is event, not substance",[43] that "the most analytically complete way of speaking is event-speaking, not thing—or substance speaking".[44]

Professor Hartshorne believes that for our substance versus event controversy ancient India has provided an excellent example. And the ultimate philosophical adversaries may be substantial monists on the one side and event-pluralists on the other. Ancient India offers us the epitomes of both. Hartshorne observes: "It is, indeed, a significant fact that ancient India produced both the most radical of monisms and the most radical of pluralisms", and the fact that they both "first achieved wide acceptance in the same part of the world and at nearly the same time" is not "accidental".[45] The reference, of course, is to "the main stream of Hinduism [Vedānta]" and to Buddhism.

Reflecting Buddhism's position, and his own, he contends that "a unit of concrete or determinate reality" being "an event or experience",—and "person" to be understood as only "the same personal sequence"—"successive events are not mutually co-existent parts",[46] meaning that there can be no

substantial identity of the self (or personality). The key clause here is
"successive events are not mutually co-existent parts". This also expresses
the celebrated Buddhist view of momentariness and non-contiguity of events:
"the instant something appears that very instant [not even the next] it disappears". There is no overlap. Śankara, the opponent, rendering the issue into
the traditional cause-effect relation, argues (*Commentary on Brahma Sūtra*,
2.2.20) that if the Buddhists take this theory of theirs seriously they would
repudiate their own central doctrine of Becoming, because then there would be
nothing to become. Cause (or what exists at an earlier moment) must somehow come into contact with the effect (or what comes into existence the next
moment) if some process can be said to go on. (In fact, even concepts such as
earlier and later, as also real numbers, would be entirely impossible without
some continuity. And time too, likewise, can not be. Nāgārjuna, the great
Buddhist dialectician, actually drew the same logical conclusion from this, i.e.,
therefore, time does not exist—*tasmāt kalo na vidyate*—[*Mūlamadhyama-
kārikā, 19.3*]—including it in his famous doctrine of the Void, or *Śūnyatā*.)
Śankara continues on to the effect that an event as such is meaningless unless
understood in the sense of some entity coming into existence and passing out of
existence (theoretically, with or without enduring). Happening has to have
something that happens, and cannot itself be the something. (And to my
knowledge this has never been properly answered by the Buddhists.) Śankara
presses on to argue that if the happening (or the event of passing) has no relation
to the *something* (as a horse to a buffalo) then it would be entirely unaffected by
the happening, but would just remain eternal (contradicting the Buddhist theory
of Becoming!).

Hartshorne takes note of the standard objection that "without an enduring
subject of change there can be no change".[47] And he answers it by pointing out:
"The Buddhist or radical pluralist can simply say that 'change' in a single 'thing'
is shorthand for the *succession* of a number of contrasting events, where the
sequence of events has some connectedness and continuity of character which
leads us to verbalize it as the history of a single enduring individual."[48] As for
the concept of succession the preceding comment is relevant to it too. But we
have also the big problem of how the succeeding events are held together in some
kind of a logical unity so as to be the "history of a single enduring individual",
without being the scene of utterly transitory and unconnected episodes. This is an
important point for the Vedāntists, who see the inevitability of logos in this
relation of connected episodes. This must also put a new light upon Hartshorne's
position "that the most analytically complete way of speaking is event-
speaking". Take the famous saying of both Buddha and Heraclitus that one
cannot step into the same flowing stream twice. If this is completely broken into
event-speaking, then one cannot say this truth twice either. In the face of this

predicament, Hartshorne's statement: "Events have the relation which they have, whatever our language",[49] seems unsatisfactory.

Then, the words 'contrasting events' must also be looked at. Contrast is nothing but similarity in reverse, and must obey the same law. The Buddhists tried to argue that apprehension of 'similar (or contrasting) events' is independent of the events in question. (Professor Hartshorne does not lend himself to that.) Actually, it is a judgement based on simultaneous apprehension (or memory) of the events in question—and not otherwise: this Śankara relentlessly drives home (*Commentary on Brahma Sūtra*, 2.2.25), with the observation that philosophers have the fundamental obligation to use the common man's apprehension as a basis, lest sophistry be the result and they say things they do not themselves believe.

The issue of the enduring subject of change is tied in with the self-identity of the individual subject or person, involving the one who apprehends, along with the events (or entities) apprehended. This particular aspect is referred to by Hartshorne when he observes: "An old Hindu argument against event-pluralism ran: how could 'I' remember 'myself' doing such and such in the past if the self remembering and the self remembered were not the same? One remembers 'oneself', not another self, as doing, feeling, thinking, perceiving, such and such."[50] (The source of this, surely, is Śankara's *Commentary*, the reference just mentioned above.) Śankara's words are (in loose paraphrase): "It is never known to be the case that when a person has a perception of something, that perception is remembered by another person. Unless the person who perceives first and the person who perceives later (through memory) are one and the same, how can the cognition as to who perceived what be possible?" Supporting the Buddhist answer, Hartshorne continues: ". . . why should not 'myself', as in the past, refer to the special continuity of character connecting the experience in question to the remembering one?" The Vedāntist would counter that concepts like "special continuity of character" have a metaphorical flavour, and would, merely as such, have no capacity to connect experiences unless there is a person behind, around whom it is gathered predicatively. (This has bearing on Hartshorne's critique of Strawson too.)

Professor Hartshorne refers to, and criticizes,[51] the usual arguments of Vedāntists against event-pluralists (or any kind of pluralists) such as the one from dream (on waking, dream objects are found to be unreal), the one based on illusorily seeing the rope as snake, and the positive one in favour of permanent or indestructible entities. The most striking point in Hartshorne's arguments in favour of event-pluralism is the 'directional order'[52] of events, of "time's arrow". This is where the central Whiteheadian idea of "inheritance from past actions, our own and those of countless others",[53] attains its significance. The concept of asymmetry of events is crucial for this. One can appreciate

Hartshorne's objection to those parts of substantialist doctrines which may lend
themselves to "the prejudice in favour of symmetry". The distinction "between
directed or one-way relations and directionless or symmetrical ones"[54] is too
important to be neglected. In this respect, Hartshorne admits, the Buddhists,
despite all other successes failed.[55] They thought, like other Indians, that cause
and effect are reversible, symmetrical.[56] Nāgārjuna (Bradley, Śankara, and many
others) assumed the same. "The Buddhists tried to defend the doctrine of the
present reality of the past . . . they spoke in the same breath of the reality of the
past and also of future events", he observes, and adds that because they
symmetrically denied the past and future they could not become philosophers of
becoming, although they "meant to".[57] (Ultimately Hartshorne will restore
symmetry, in balance with non-symmetry.) In a way of speaking, despite
Buddhism's early promise, it stayed back as a retarded philosophy of becoming
and the "Whiteheadian" component of the original, hyphenated "Buddhist-
Whiteheadian" framework, of whose adequacy for the religious idea of God
Hartshorne had felt assured, must take over and complete the whole. The
Buddhists' failure "to do full justice to the relatedness of events" is attributed to
their still lingering "anti-relativist bias".[58] So then, "a metaphysics of becoming
and relativity is a modern philosophical task", "not accomplished in former
ages."[59]

Professor Hartshorne is right about Buddhism's anti-relativist bias, which,
however, is the consequence of its seeing the *relativity* of relativity—quite
divergent from his own principle of absoluteness of relativity, and perhaps more
thoroughly radical. The "absolute" for the Buddhists is the basis of their doubly
relativist perception and judgement, though still indistinguishable from Reality
as Becoming (and no way to be thought of as Being). However in some fashion,
the identity of language between Buddhism and Vedānta in respect of Ultimate
Reality (*paramārtha satya*) and all that mystical dialectics which comes from it
had turned out to be inevitable too. (Double relative is like double negative.)
This kind of Buddhism is no more congenial house for the pure Process deity
than is Vedānta.

We may still ask, if Buddhism still adheres to Reality as Becoming
and has also the principle of the absolute, the two being indistinguishable,
is it not the same as Hartshorne's Absolute of Becoming? The answer should
be 'no' because for Buddhism the Absolute is only the basis of the perception (or judgement) as to Becoming, and that is governed by the relativity of
relativity itself—and there is no direct, positive perception or speaking
of this Absolute except in the transcendent intuition (*prajñā*), which is not
speakable. Fundamentally, this is in agreement with the Vedānta of Śankara,
which has the same position with respect to its own Absolute (of Being), i.e.,
Brahman.

6. The Climactic Ideas of the Hartshorne Theology with Relevance to the Response of Vedānta

As students of Professor Hartshorne's system well know, all the stepping stones we have marked lead to his climactic theological ideas of transcendence (dual transcendence) and the self-surpassing of the deity, the latter based on a radical revision of Anselm—and related ones. They complete the meanings of the obverting concepts, beginning with relativity and becoming and going on to 'concrete', 'contingent', 'finite', etc., in themselves being made applicable to God, and also place them in new, creative combinations with their contraries so that God is spoken of (here, to make the order uniform) as Absolute and Relative;[60] infinite and finite;[61] unconditioned and conditioned;[62] immutable and mutable;[63] necessary and contingent;[64] most abstract and most concrete.[65] But on the whole, there remains the aversion to the exclusive prevalence of the traditional categories on the one side, 'absolute', 'infinite', 'immutable', etc., "with which we have been saddled for so long,"[66] as Hartshorne observes.

Now in combining them, the principle for it is dual transcendence, which is not the same as Cusanus's 'coincidence of opposites', for the abstract and concrete do not indistinguishably coincide but simply "are both in God."[67] Nonetheless, there is a "union of opposites"[68] but one in which the inner contrast between the contraries is incomparably greater than otherwise.[69] This tension (argument against Tillich's abolition of it) must be the secret of divine self-surpassing.

To conceive God through such contraries is also a practice in Vedānta. Thus Śankara writes: "Brahman is comprehended in two modalities, as qualified by the limiting adjuncts of name, form, change and modifications, and in the opposite manner; devoid of all adjuncts."[70] For Vedānta, however, this is just God *for us*, not God as he is in himself (itself). But Professor Hartshorne applies the contrary "modalities" (absolute-relative etc.), to describe God as he is *in himself*. In this connection one is tempted to turn Hartshorne's own question at him that he raised against Hegel: "Is his 'absolute idea' more than human thought in its most perfect form, or is it genuinely God . . . ?"[71]

Here is ushered in the question of negative theology, which Hartshorne criticizes, as did Hegel.[72] "Negation", he feels, "is parasitic on affirmation."[73] And negation is useful only if it joins up with affirmation (through some refraction, as it were). As for the transcendent, it is a mistake to describe it merely through negation, as "there must also be some positive aspects" of it.[74] The issue between Hartshorne and Vedānta in this matter is essentially whether what can be, must be, said positively about God must absorb the negative, or what cannot be said (hence negatively said) about God be the final absorbent. According to the Vedāntic logic, the negative gives contents to the concept of fullness or perfection, in comparison with which merely positive descriptions of perfection even when they come from Scripture, appear as depleted.[75]

Professor Hartshorne too deals with the perfection within the scope of transcendence (dual, for him) and rightly criticizes the concept of *ens realissimus*. Vedānta has this same concept as "the most real of the real" (*satyasya satyam*) but gives it no merely positive character, as it is permeated by "not this, not this" (*neti, neti*). As to perfection, Hartshorne's doctrine (put in my own words) is that it is *complete self-sufficiency that wants more, and creates what it wants, unceasingly*. No doubt, it is a doctrine that has a great appeal. But it can be countered by equally appealing alternatives. What obtains in non-dualist Vedānta is one such. Śankara (in *Commentary on Brahma Sūtra*, 2.1.32, 33) balances the proposition of Brahman's self-sufficiency with the proposition of his wanting (or desiring), and argues that the resultant (creation) is an activity without purpose (a sport) such that any positive contribution thereby must be put under the light of a higher negation.

But Hartshorne's theology says, "God is potentially inclusive of this coming creation", so that "remaining 'Himself', He (i.e., God) yet will endlessly require new content."[76] It indicates to him "absolute and utter togetherness" of the two and suggests that "if this were (but probably it is not) the meaning of the Vedantic doctrine of non-duality, we should have to accept it."[77] Professor Hartshorne's suspicion is right: it is not the Vedāntic non-duality. (However, he also takes note of the divergent Rāmānuja school of Vedānta in which such togetherness between God and the world as body and soul—*śarīra-śarīrī bhāva* in Sanskrit—obtains. But inasmuch as the world here is not strictly creation in Hartshorne's sense, but more akin to Plato's notion, he expresses his dissatisfaction with that doctrine.[78])

In retrospect, I have restricted myself to those issues which have been sharpened in the light of Professor Hartshorne's actual response. There are, no doubt, countless other issues which offer a fascinating prospect for debate between two systems that are so powerful and articulate and are in many ways polar opposites.

One fundamental problem (expressed in a scholastic mould, Indian and Western, within which Hartshorne surely thinks) is: God being himself plus all he creates—and create he must—and if what God creates is outside or other than himself, then the whole would be more than God; and yet that can not be. The Vedānta of Śankara which faces this, has the Māyā solution; Hartshorne has the solution of creative synthesis, of on-going Divine Process. As for the truth between them, at this point I simply say, let the process be the debate itself.

Strangely enough, some things said by Process theology are not entirely new to Vedānta. Hartshorne's view that God must be effect as well as cause is very familiar to Vedānta as the causal (*kāraṇa*) Brahman and effect (*kārya*) Brahman, but with a very different meaning. (Likewise, there is a derivation of the very word *Brahman*, meaning growth, process.) But the inner thrusts are different. Hartshorne's call to combine "sublime symmetry and sublime asymmetry in this (cause-effect) relationship"[79] is quite new.

In a sense the combination of symmetry and asymmetry could indicate breakthroughs even in the area of response to Vedānta, and it is something to be welcomed. There, then, is an alternative to the mere symmetrical collapse of effect into cause, on the one hand, and to the other extreme of denial of interaction and "dialogue" between creator and creature (usual in theology),[80] on the other.

But there is still a problem, for the essence of Vedāntic theology is not even the symmetry between cause and effect but the *identity* between Brahman and the individual being—"That thou art." Professor Hartshorne recognizes "That thou art", in Rāmānuja's fashion, as "deity *in* each of us", although "He (God) is more."[81] But, if one were to use Śankara's interpretation of it as the truth that stands behind every truth, inasmuch as "That" and "thou" (or "I") are one single existence, new creative possibilities come open. For, in that sense it refers to EXISTENCE pure and simple (God's and every one else's), and nothing that is concerned with divine actuality—the theme central to this paper—need conflict with it. That way of thinking has possibilities in conjunction with Professor Hartshorne's metaphysics, though not within its framework— something to be explored elsewhere.

JOHN G. ARAPURA

DEPARTMENT OF RELIGIOUS STUDIES
MCMASTER UNIVERSITY
SEPTEMBER 1986

NOTES

1. *Creative Synthesis and Philosophic Method* (Lanham, Md. and London: University Press of America, 1983), p. xviii.
2. Ibid., p. 183.
3. Ibid., p. 55.
4. Ibid., p. 227.
5. Ibid., p. xvi.
6. Ibid., p. 55.
7. Ibid., p. 54.
8. See for instance, *A Natural Theology for Our Time* (La Salle, Ill.: Open Court, 1981), p. 27f.

9. "What Did Anselm Discover?", *Insights and Oversights*, (Albany, N.Y.: State University of New York Press, 1983), p. 99.

10. *A Natural Theology*, p. 30.

11. Ibid., p. 29.

12. *Insights and Oversights*, p. 99.

13. Ibid., pp. 98–99.

14. Ibid., p. 99.

15. Loc. cit.

16. Cf. Śankara, *Commentary on Brahma Sūtra*, (1.1.1). See J. G. Arapura, *Gnosis and the Question of Thought in Vedānta*, (Dordrecht-Holland: Nijhoff, 1986), p. 148.

17. *A Natural Theology*, p. 45.

18. *Creative Synthesis*, p. 276.

19. *A Natural Theology*, p. 45.

20. Ibid., p. 22.

21. Ibid., p. 23.

22. Ibid., p. 23.

23. Note. For this see J. G. Arapura, *Gnosis and the Question of Thought in Vedānta*, pp. 187–191.

24. K. C. Bhattacharyya, *Studies in Philosophy* (originally published, Amalner: Indian Institute of Philosophy, 1929; as vol. II of the same; republished, Calcutta: Progressive Publishers, 1956), p. 227.

25. T. R. V. Murti, *The Central Philosophy of Buddhism* (London: Allen & Unwin, 1960, reprint), p. 147.

26. *Creative Synthesis*, p. 22.

27. Loc. cit.

28. Loc. cit.

29. Op. cit., pp. 205–217.

30. Ibid., pp. 209–210.

31. *A Natural Theology*, p. 24.

32. *Creative Synthesis*, p. 47.

33. Loc. cit.

34. Ibid., p. 46.

35. *A Natural Theology*, p. 25.

36. *Creative Synthesis*, p. 44.

37. See "Development of Process Philosophy", from *Philosophers of Process*, ed. Douglas Browning; reference here to the same, reproduced in E. H. Cousins, *Process Theology* (New York, Toronto: Newman Press, 1971), p. 47.

38. See *Creative Synthesis*, p. 177.

39. Ibid., "Development of Modern Process Philosophy", op. cit., p. 49.

40. *Creative Synthesis*, p. 177.

41. "Development of Process Philosophy", op. cit, p. 49.

42. *Creative Synthesis*, p. 189.

43. Ibid., p. 187.

44. Ibid., p. 175.

45. Ibid., p. 177.

46. Ibid., p. 181.

47. Loc. cit.

48. Ibid., pp. 181–182.

49. Ibid., p. 183.

50. Ibid., p. 182.
51. See "Śankara, Nāgārjuna and Fa Tsang—With Some Western Parallels", manuscript copy of lecture given at the Research Conference on Comparative Philosophy, Honolulu, Hawaii, Aug., 1984.
52. *Creative Synthesis*, p. 179; "Śankara, Nāgārjuna and Fa Tsang", pp. 10–11.
53. *Creative Synthesis*, p. 190.
54. *Creative Synthesis*, p. 205.
55. Ibid., p. 46.
56. "Śankara, Nāgārjuna and Fa Tsang", p. 10.
57. See, *The Logic of Perfection* (La Salle, Ill.: Open Court, 1973), p. 17.
58. *Creative Synthesis*, p. 46.
59. Loc. cit.
60. Cf. *Whitehead's Philosophy* (Lincoln and London: University of Nebraska Press, 1978), p. 88.; *A Natural Theology*, p. 36.
61. *A Natural Theology*, p. 36.
62. Loc. cit.
63. Loc. cit.
64. Loc. cit.; also ibid., p. 52.
65. *Creative Synthesis*, p. 237.
66. Cf. *A Natural Theology*, p. 28.
67. Cf. *Creative Synthesis*, p. 237.
68. Cf. *Whitehead's Philosophy*, p. 5.
69. Cf. *Creative Synthesis*, p. 237.
70. Śankara, *Commentary on Brahma Sūtra*, 1.1.11.
71. *Insights and Oversights*, p. 207.
72. *A Natural Theology*, p. 70; *Creative Synthesis*, p. 228.
73. *A Natural Theology*, p. 69.
74. *Creative Synthesis*, p. 228.
75. Note: I have discussed this issue in my *Gnosis and the Question of Thought in Vedānta*, p. 181.
76. *Logic of Perfection*, p. 79.
77. *Creative Synthesis*, p. 17.
78. *A Natural Theology*, p. 97.
79. *Creative Synthesis*, p. 221.
80. Cf. Loc. cit.
81. *A Natural Theology*, pp. 103–4.

C. LOGIC, PHENOMENOLOGY, AND METAPHYSICS

14

James P. Devlin

HARTSHORNE'S METAPHYSICAL ASYMMETRY

Hartshorne has always related his own thinking to his predecessors and contemporaries, with special emphasis on the latter. This style opposes, quite intentionally, that of metaphysical thinkers who display a carefully worked-out rhetoric of grandeur, such as Heidegger does. Today, Hartshorne wears the diadem of process theology in part because the modern age treats any philosopher who suffers deity gladly as a theologian; few distinguish even between revealed and natural theology. Almost all of Hartshorne's theological insights are accessible to the *lumen naturale*. A future age may well inherit, chiefly from him, a conception of deity that does not make a fool of every believer. Yet so original and well worked-out are his metaphysical doctrines, that his theology can well be regarded as secondary to these wider reflections. Better still is to recognize their seamless unity.

Hartshorne's metaphysics owes much to Whitehead and Peirce, but this debt has long been paid. For example, Peirce's error in considering time and actuality continuous, thanks to synechism, and Whitehead's reverse and somewhat less debauching error of regarding the domain of potentiality as discrete, via his eternal objects, cancel each other in Hartshorne's clearer thinking. Moreover, the mistakes are not trifling: they demonstrate that the underlying modal ideas must never have been fully grasped by either philosopher. Conceivably Hartshorne alone has adequately inferred metaphysical truth from modal logic; in other, earlier thinkers these truths remain inchoate. Moreover, Hartshorne draws more deeply from the wells of the Eastern and Western philosophical traditions than either Whitehead or Peirce.

In his primary metaphysical works Hartshorne develops theses I have arranged in eight clusters. All interrelate, all have modal-logical underpinnings, all display his drive towards asymmetry:

(A) The logic of ultimate contrasts;
(B) Metaphysics' logical cues;
(C) Asymmetric time as objective modality;
(D) The actual and the potential (quanta versus continua);
(E) The mind-body problem;
(F) The question of the 'individual';
(G) The ontological argument and God's consequent nature;
(H) The priority of the relative and the actual in ethics and aesthetics.

The key that unlocks all of these at once is Hartshorne's theory of relations, whether modal or material. This article focusses on one of his largest contributions to theory of relations, his logic of ultimate contrasts. Here he expounds the necessary place of the symmetric conception of relations and then reorients this conception through his doctrine of asymmetry. On the basis of this asymmetry, discoverable in formal logic, we shall turn to the theory of time—the basic ontological asymmetry. For this purpose we shall look at Hartshorne's ruminations upon an early opponent, Aristotle, whose contribution to modal theory Hartshorne has brought into sharp focus in recent years.

I. The Logic of Ultimate Contrasts

Hartshorne develops his theory of relations most persuasively under the heading, "A Logic of Ultimate Contrasts," in *Creative Synthesis*.[1] He argues that all binary relations that constitute ultimate contrasts are: (a) as sheer *abstraction*, mutually implicative, each internal to the other's definition; and (b) as *exemplified*, both internal and external, asymmetrically internal to the constitution of one term and external to the other. This definition is possible only because the denial of internal relations does not give a carte blanche to external relations. Refutation of Leibniz does not open the city's gates to Hume. If we recall the fallacy of the excluded middle and try to avoid its evils, we must note that relations may be either intrinsic to both terms, intrinsic to the first term and not the second, to the second and not the first, or intrinsic to neither. Apart from the two extreme cases stands the far too casually excluded middle: that the relation internally constitutes *only one term*. This is the asymmetrical option.

Examples of all three are familiar coin. Relationships of analytic identity, such as obtains for the relation of 'rational animal' to 'grammar learner,' are mutually internal, even if the consequences of the smaller notion are not evidently congruent with those of the larger, because each is a *sine qua non* for the other. At the other extreme, spatial relationships between objects exemplify relations simply external to the relata. They can be rightly considered internal or constitutive only of an *ensemble* that includes them both in a definitive and necessary way as parts of a whole. As for the third or middle option, this is shown by temporal relationships between non-simultaneous events. The events must be non-simultaneous else their relation would not be temporal at all, but spatial.[2] Temporal relations between events x and y invariably contribute to the constitution of the later event: x or y—one, but not both.

Binary relations between ultimate contrasts include a host of candidate pairs: relative-absolute, subject-object, particular-universal, dependent-independent, effect-cause, mind-matter, later-earlier, among others. The commonest dialectic insight reveals in the contrast of such terms a mutual dependency of sense between them, each taken as general concepts. Nothing could be emptier of ostensive reference than either side of these dichotomies, since even 'particular' refers to everything whatever, including all the various 'particular' examples of universals. 'Concrete' denotes everything and almost nothing. In the history of philosophical language in the West, from the classical through especially the medieval period, and on to the present day, the primary value of these *logoi* has derived from their context, but not only the context of their usage. There arises in addition to actual usage a context of anticipated contrast and contrariety: each term at least partly names the negation of the other term. The traditions of philosophical discourse have rarely made these special linguistic turns explicit, until the present era. Now their explicitation diminishes their power and reduces their importance.[3] However, the region of these terms remains the workplace of philosophical thought.

Granting the dialectical symmetry or abstract interdependence of these key pairs, Hartshorne lays them out schematically in a two-column list. Terms in the left column, like 'dependent,' 'relative,' and 'actual,' share the earmark of being traditionally the weaker term of the pair, the more deficient, the 'imperfect.' These are the relative or r-terms. The right-side column lists the traditionally honorific terms, 'independent,' 'absolute,' 'possible,' etc. These are the absolute or a-terms. Each pair is made up of one r-term and one a-term. Hartshorne shows that this schema displays the *proportionality* of these ultimate contrasts. 'Proportionality' means that the r-term in any pair relates to the a-term in that same pair in a way that is analogous to the relation of any other r-term to its a-term. If we take proportionality seriously, then if r_1 is to a_1 as r_2 is to a_2 we have $r_1 : a_1 :: r_2 : a_2$, from which it follows that $r_1 : r_2 :: a_1 : a_2$. Thus any r-term relates to another r-term in a way analogous to the relation between the two a-terms. Thus if the particular stands to the universal as the relative stands to the absolute, then the particular is to the relative as the universal is to the absolute. Moreover—and by increasing the variety of these dichotomies we enhance the interest of the exercise—the relative is to the absolute as mind is to matter, and as subject is to object, and as the consequent nature of God (all-knowing) is to the necessary or primordial nature.

This trellis of symmetries reveals too many interesting ontological relationships to be ignored by philosophers, but it is less than half the story. For this two-way symmetry between the terms of these 'ultimate' binary relations is set off against a one-way *a*symmetry. If the concepts on the trellis of symmetries are *exemplified*, then what results is a trellis of asymmetries. A *given* relative item necessitates a definite example of its absolute correlate, but not vice-versa! Rather, a specific a-term necessitates only the class of corresponding relative items. This is logical homomorphism, rather than isomorphism. Kant saw in the first *Critique* the strict internal interdependence of 'cause' and 'effect,' but missed the asymmetric imbalance for instances of cause and effect.[4] Any effect will require exactly a set of definite causes, but no cause can require an exactly definite effect, but rather a more or less narrow class of effects of 'such a kind.' Again, an experience requires exactly its objective contents, but the objects of the given experience merely require that there be some possible experiencer or other, animal, human, divine, or some rudimentary life.[5] A particular man necessitates the inclusion of the universal 'man' in his essential constitution, but each man is more or less irrelevant to the universal 'man.' It suffices that there be some possible examples of 'man.' An actuality necessitates a definite potentiality of which it is the actualization, but the potentiality is indifferent to the exact content of the actuality that corresponds to it: any such actualization will suffice.[6] The medievals may have toiled stintlessly at the fine points of the problem of universals versus particulars, but they did not see the inherent connection between this distinction and the distinction of potential and actual.[7] A universal is roughly speaking, a potentiality, whereas a particular is an actuality. The trellis of symmetries discloses such relations in advance.

A sense of the logic of these contrasts straightens out any number of confusions. The Platonic doctrine of participation or *methexis*, for example, confuses inclusion with class membership. Is Fred in the Idea 'man' or is the class-character 'man-ness' in Fred? The Platonic Idea must be *in* its instances; the instances can only be *in* the class named by the idea. The inclusion will be expressed by the contingent, dependent term. Plato here seemed to wish that Idea be more inclusive than things. Any instanced r-term (a particular *this*), however, is richer than its a-term (some universal). Any man possesses all the man-ness there is, and every man possesses it. The commonness of the independent Idea is the signature of its inexpensiveness. Any particular has all the value of the corresponding universals, but no knowledge of 'man,' however profound, can begin to specify a given man's actuality, much less exhaust it. The individual human being has an abundance of worth in excess of any *eidos*. The addition of a realm of Ideas adds not one jot of value to the universe. The world of particulars already possesses all such ideal value. The value of such a 'realm' lies in its aesthetic originality and complexity. The universals themselves are routinely exceeded by the humblest events. A relative term always has both its own relative and the corresponding absolute as constituents. For Hartshorne, the superior richness of the relative grounds divine personality, aesthetic beauty, love, and, more generally, the superiority of experience to its mere contents.

So whereas the relations between general categories are symmetrical and internal,[8] the order of instantiation is asymmetric and partially external, with specific necessity in the implication of absolute by relative, but only generic necessity (''some such'') in the implication of a relative term by an absolute one. The order of abstract relations like the order of quality and magnitude, and like space, is symmetric; the order of exemplification on the other hand, is, like time, asymmetric.[9] The relation of any abstraction to a concretum is asymmetrical in this typical sense. Meaningful general terms require the possibility of specific instances, but the character, timing, and context of these specific instances is in no way necessitated by the general terms. Contrary to Findlay, possibility is in no way more actual than actuality.[10] As general concepts each is perfectly general. But an actual instance, a concrete *this* is entirely actual and not merely more so than possibility. A possibility is not actual at all.

The type of contrast in which one term is inclusive of the other is shown in propositional logic by the relation of implication. $X \Rightarrow Y$ means that given X, Y is necessary, so that Y is the *sine qua non* of X, necessary to it (i.e., $-Y \Rightarrow -X$). Implication is exactly isomorphic to set inclusion, so $X \Rightarrow Y$ means $X \subseteq Y$. Both affirm that X is a sufficient condition for Y; Y is a necessary condition for X. X is here an r-term, inclus*ive* and imply*ing*; Y has the logical form of an a-term, the necessary condition in the relation. The only necessary and sufficient conditions, which Hartshorne rightly denies could exist in the realm of exemplification, would be set identity, $X = Y$, mutual inclusion, mutual dependence—but this is exactly the relation of symmetry between generic r- and a- terms. If the '=' relation held between a particular and its universal, then that particular would of necessity be 'in' every other particular—since they would both be the necessary and sufficient condition of the universal, and two things that are the necessary and sufficient condition of a third thing are the necessary and sufficient condition of each other, by the transitivity of the equivalence relation, '⇔.' Each white object would be in every other white object, which is nonsense.

But set inclusion is not an interesting enough case to *display* the concept of inclusion. It is more illuminating to consider the relation of implication between two terms, one of which is a compound of both, say RA, meaning R *and* A. Here the situation approximates the relation between r- and a- terms. RA $\Rightarrow$ A, but it is not true that A $\Rightarrow$ RA. RA is a sufficient condition for A, but A is not a sufficient condition for RA. The strangest and most convincing of Hartshorne's logical 'applications' may be this turn of thought, his playing with relations between one member of a pair, usually the a-term, and the pair itself. A could imply RA only if R were a trivially true term, or A were always false. But this would obtain only if R were necessarily true and necessary—but the r-terms are the contingent terms *par excellence*! Contingency implies necessity, not the other way around. A compound of necessary and contingent is not necessary but contingent.

A very special and extreme example is God. God, as both contingent and necessary, is contingent. Divine necessity becomes just an attribute, like 'white' or any other Peircean First. The divinity of God does not consist in God's being absolutely necessary (that is merely a condition, and an insufficient one); rather it consists in God's being absolutely relative, relative without qualification of scope, relative to everything. God (as consequent nature) stands as the supreme example of relativeness, dependency, and contingency, and in this is a sufficient condition for divinity. It represents the notion of God as all-knowing, which the medievals confused with God's essence as impassible, independent, suffering no contingency or dependency whatever. Moreover, this is not guesswork; the ontological argument, revealing God as inconceivable or else necessary, reveals the supremely relative God as absolutely necessary. If God were not absolutely relative (as well as absolutely absolute), this would be a genuinely deficient deity than which another could be conceived without this deficiency, because relativeness contributes all value. The 'all' of 'all-knowing' requires either contingency in God or else an utterly necessary universe with no novel value, but that too would be a deficiency. Aristotle's God is not all-knowing, but knows itself only *qua* necessary, as thought thinking itself. In this way, Aristotle defined an utterly necessary God with no trace of contingency, at the expense of all power, personality, and freedom. The Aristotelian God can exert no influence whatever. It is the doctrine of a caged deity.

A further feature of the trellis of symmetries is that the left- and right-hand terms may be given various names. By 'proportionality,' all the r-terms since they constitute an equivalence class,[11] could be designated by the name of any one of them, and the same goes for the a-terms. The relative terms could be called the 'mind' terms, the 'dependent' terms, or the 'temporal' terms; the a-terms could correspondingly be called, as a group, the 'matter' terms, the 'independent' terms, or the 'spatial' terms. The sense of play here is essential. As Hartshorne says, "The aim is less to demonstrate than to explicate. . . ."[12]

It may be objected that the *regulae* of Hartshorne's logic of relations remain at the level of schematics and do not descend to the subtler differences, for example, among proportional terms on the trellis of symmetries/asymmetries. The doctrine may be abstract, but is a 'logic' of this kind supposed to be otherwise? The clues available in this logic and its applications are formal, but the formality rectifies numerous mistakes casually made by assuming a symmetry that does not obtain or forgetting the difference between a general term and an instance of it (which may itself be a general term: 'man' is an instance of 'universal'). More importantly, it revives metaphysical speculation along more vigorous lines, beginning at the summit with Hartshorne's conception of God.

II. TIME

Time stands as the most decisive of relational concepts. As Hartshorne insists, the radical asymmetry of time bases all other asymmetries. He develops his analysis of time on several fronts, but most of its features retain the mark of his struggle against and agreement with Aristotle.

Aristotle offered at least two quite different conceptions of time, both capable of great power. Most of us are heirs to the view presented in the treatise on time in the *Physics*,[13] one of his consummate achievements. On this view, time is composed of two parts, past and future, divided by the *now*. The *now* is to time as a point to a line, and functions as a mere limit.[14] Aristotle sees in this presentation of the question no fundamental difference between the past and future that lie on either side of the *now*. The apparent adequacy of the line-image to the needs of time-measurement was such a positive discovery that it obscured the traps of viewing time as a continuum. This simple time-line anticipates the modern mathematical diagram of time as an x-axis in a Cartesian coordinate system, possessing the properties of the real numbers.[15] This model has prospered in mathematical analysis down the centuries, as a way of reducing time and chronology, or event-ordering, to chronometry, or time-measurement, making chronology exact and allowing various consequences as remote as time-trend analysis, and the graphical plotting of continuous measurements as functions of time. It also provides the theoretical underpinning for clock technology. Aristotle asserted the metric postulate that makes chronometry. possible: that there exists a unit-measure of time not itself subject to temporal decay, unchanging through space and time, a constant of comparison, a ruler with an 'end' in the past and another in the present. He defined time as a unit-measure, *metron*, countable in motion; and as 'what is counted in the count' of motion, its number, which turns out to be a count of the periods of some standard motion 'taken up' by a given notion.

The process of Aristotle's discovery was not smooth, however. By considering time a uniform magnitude, he skirted the difference between past and future, and the result was the knotty problem about time's ontological status that he left unanswered. He balks at this problem because he cannot answer the 'common' arguments that infer the non-existence of time from the non-existence of its parts.[16] If time has two parts, past, and future, and if the past does not exist because it 'is no more' and the future does not exist because it 'is not yet,' and the 'now' has no magnitude whatever, then what of time does exist? Aristotle might have argued here, but he does not, that 'past' and 'future' as classes of events (*kinesis*), have being; but he would still have foundered on the question of the being of the past events themselves, which he avoids discussing in his works—as though not wishing to commit either for or against the actuality of the past.

Augustine went further into the doubt about time via his analysis of the present, which was for him the psychological moment *par excellence*, providing the key to time's existence. Time becomes a kind of dilapidation on either side of a present, and presence becomes the sole access to what is real. Time has whatever being the present has. By the trellis of contrasts this is itself a profound move, in that Augustine took much further than Aristotle the dimension of soul or mind in time. Mind is to matter as time is to space, and as later events in time are to earlier ones. Aristotle also developed this theme, beginning a tradition that passed through Augustine down to Kant and Husserl. He did this with his discussion of the myth of the Sardinian Sleepers, who sleep for years, but so deeply that they cannot recognize any passage of time whatever, so for them there was no time.[17] Despite the careful introspection of the *Confessions*, though, Augustine also failed to capture the being of time. This may have been the result of the inadequacy of his modal apparatus. For to lay any claim to understanding time's being requires the introduction of modal considerations. Ironically but not surprisingly, the richer, modal view of time was suggested by none other than Aristotle, wearing his logical rather than physical hat, who adumbrated his modal time-theory chiefly in the *Categories* and *De Interpretatione*, as well as throughout the *Metaphysics*. Hartshorne rediscovers this conception of time in Aristotle, and has thus brought to closure his own conception of time as the order of asymmetry, and, with it, space as the order of symmetry.

Hartshorne's treatment of time has at least five facets: (i) it is non-spatial;[18] (ii) it is atomic or discrete, quantal; (iii) it is asymmetric; (iv) it is objectively modal; and (v) it is the root of freedom.

Non-spatial time. For process philosophy the present is spatially ordered. As presentational immediacy it is the zone of mental activity free from the causal efficacy of the body, the mind sojourning in possibility; as 'now,' in a time-sequence, it is a boundary but not a limit—it is the most recent past, the rim of actuality. The present has the thickness of a unit event, and a span numbered by the count of simultaneous actual occasions, and has the depth and density of the actual past. Actual occasions just out of prehensive reach of other actual occasions cannot influence one another at all, and that is sufficient for defining their relation as spatial, which is virtually the same as 'merely present.' The concept of 'simultaneity' expresses a kind of 'failure' of the time relation and is vital for relativity physics and for process philosophy. Two events, x and y, are simultaneous (and spatially related) just in case neither x can cause a change in y and nor can y in x. In Newtonian time, we would say that if event x occurred "a thousand years ago" so far away from a present-event that it would be detectable only in ten thousand years, they are *not* simultaneous events: epistemic considerations do not weigh in the scales of nature, and time-order and measure are treated as absolutes. On the other hand, for relativity as for process philosophy such events are simultaneous because actual effects from one to the other are impossible. The issue only has the appearance of being an epistemological one, for here epistemic limit equals ontological limit. But there is a difference of perspective between the two parties to the 'modern' definition of simultaneity: relativity physics is concerned with influence as limited by maximum signal speed, that of light; for process philosophy the principle is more proximate—all knowledge whatever is of the slightly past world, and the present act of knowing is simultaneous with and blind to new, unknown, events right in front of the knower. Knowledge and prehension are temporally ordered, and knowledge of actual presences is restricted to the mind's own musings, occurring as what Whitehead calls 'presentational immediacy.' Events mutually insusceptible of influence are spatially ordered, and will enter time-order only when included in a later actual occasion. An important historical note here, not heeded to my knowledge by Hartshorne, but of a piece with his other reflections on Aristotle, is that long before relativity physics Aristotle, in the *Categories*, defined simultaneous events as those incapable of influencing each other. So the most modern of notions, the seed of relativity, was announced in one of Aristotle's earliest works—a notion that could hardly be inferred from common sense. Hartshorne did not have to rediscover this in Aristotle, of course, but it has historical interest to recognize its Aristotelian origins—yet another Aristotelian insight duplicated by Whitehead.

Atomic time. The atomic characteristic is rudimentary to process philosophy, and its critique of perduring substance (in effect, a critique of Aristotle). Not only are the ultimate *concreta* of experience spatially very small, as all atomists believe, but for process philosophy temporally small as well. They are absolute minima, actual occasions. This denies change, by denying the subject of change, thought to 'endure' change; the individual is not the crude behemoth perceived through the senses as a large unity. Hartshorne locates process philosophy (and even Aristotle) between Hume for whom the individual is a mere 'association' of externals, and Leibniz, for whom the individual is absolutely self-same, with sheer internal relations stretching even into the future. These views of the individual and change can be refined a bit more, into four categories, depending on the acceptance or rejection of two predicates of the individual: that it have internal relations with its past or not; and that it be the same through time or not (that which is the same suffers no qualification on that part that remains the same; the same is thus a continuum). Leibniz postulates a self-same individual with internal relations to the past (and future); Aristotle postulates a self-same individual without internal relations to its past states—the past is not constitutive for an Aristotelian individual; Whitehead and Hartshorne postulate a non-self-same individual with internal relations to its past (the past is constitutive); and Hume postulates a non-self-same individual with only external relations. The pluralists are certainly those who orbit Hume, but is Aristotle or Whitehead more pluralist? Internal relations are powerfully non-pluralist, but in Whitehead, these are only one-way, and there are far more individuals in his universe than in Aristotle's. Aristotle more or less was ensnared by continuity throughout his work, in part because he was braced by the brutal Zenonian attack against continuity. His soldierly defense of continuity won victories such as the theory of infinitely divisible magnitudes (continua), another of Aristotle's firsts. But it also led to the canon of continuous change and the notion of the substrate.

Asymmetric time. Time's asymmetry follows in part from the logic of ultimate contrasts, and more deeply from modal reflections. Future and present-past both exist as genera, and have a two-way symmetrical relation to each other. The present is merely the most inclusive in a series of wholly actual occasions: the events of the past are not spread out externally to each other, much less nonexistent, but ordered, the more remote included within the more recent past. Inclusion here is, once again, that binary relation internal to one and external to the other term. Moreover, for Hartshorne time is divided modally. The past is the definite actual, the future the indefinite potential, which is to say, conditioned possibility. Among all distinctions modal distinctions express the greatest possible difference. They seem almost distinctions without similarity, as far as possible from distinctions without a difference. Most elements of contrast contain a common seed, but no seed can be on both sides of a modal fence. Thus nothing could be more distinct than these two time-domains. So while Aristotle can see only an 'obscure' being for time, Hartshorne sees two sorts of being for time, being as actuality and as potentiality.[19] Therefore he resolves Aristotle's *aporia*, and shows that 'matter' as substratum can be eliminated; by a principle of 'least paradox,' chance can then be explained as inclusion:

> The lack of a clear theory of constitutive relations is the origin of the opaque notion of matter; for if the past cannot enter the present, then there must be something, not the past itself, that does form part of the present as well as of the past to connect the two. The past is in the future, but the future is not in the past. In this sense, the relations between the past and the future are asymmetrical. It is an *internal relation*,

for the present or the later events, to include the earlier. Such events are inconceivable without their precedents. The contrary is not true.[20]

Objective-modality. On the other hand, Aristotle, despite his flawed conception of unreal time, was also the earliest philosopher to explore the possibility of time as objective modality—first in his equation between 'necessity' and 'eternity' and then in his isolation of the future as the realm of the indefinite, a realm to be cognitively approximated through probabilities. It is easy to see that if the eternal were what could not have failed to exist and what could not ever cease to exist, then the eternal means the necessary, modally definable as the 'not possibly not.' If some asserted the existence of an x such that it has always existed, it still *might* have not existed and could be contingent for all its longevity. But to assert that x will never cease to exist cannot be epistemologically sound unless there are compelling reasons[21] to adduce such a negation of possible non-being.

Hartshorne partly through Peirce rediscovers the great discoveries Aristotle made in modal logic: that *contingent, necessary*, and *impossible* form a triad such that any two of the three are negated by the third; that modal distinctions relate to temporal ones. Aristotle also argued that modal distinctions do not exist only because of the introduction of them into the universe through language. Hartshorne rightly criticizes modern linguistic philosophers and logicians for assuming that modal distinctions are linguistic distinctions rather than the linguistic expression of them being subsequent to their discovery through experience. Another way of putting this is that modal distinctions must exist in any language in all possible worlds. Aristotle has other ways of saying the same thing. For instance, since he makes the distinctions temporal, tense logic is the key to their explanation. One can hardly imagine Aristotle believing that tensed descriptions involve distinctions that are merely verbal. The sea battle tomorrow that has not happened yet can hardly be said not to have happened because it is described in the future tense. The temporal aspect of modality seems to be the most realistic aspect. Objective modality is the best argument against the often-held modern view that modal distinctions are verbal.

Hartshorne names five Aristotelian laws of modality. First, the equivalence of necessity and eternity. The second of these is that an occurrence strictly presupposes antecedents but not vice-versa: given the present state of affairs, the exact past is necessary, but not the future. Only general aspects of the future are free. There can no longer be a time in which Ronald Reagan had never been president. His presidency will have conditioned all subsequent presidencies. Years ago, however, the future by no means included his presidency. In this sense, the two directions of time are modally distinct. The third law Hartshorne discovers is that the future is a mixture of contingency and conditional necessity relative to the present. That the man will die is necessary, but just when or how is a matter of contingent factors. The fourth law is that truths about the future must be modally expressed, and if they concern anything contingent cannot be definitely true or false. The fifth and final modal law is remarkable: that something is perishable or imperishable is the same as its being contingent or necessary. Hartshorne says: "If I am not deluded, these five laws, taken as objective, are all correct and are among the most important truths that any philosopher has ever discovered. Not one is generally accepted today!"[22]

With regard to objective modality, Hartshorne makes several criticisms of Aristotle. On the modal side, the equivalence of necessary and eternal was not clearly understood epistemologically by Aristotle, who seems to think there could be a contingent knowing of something eternal, such as the heavens. But there is no way the heavens could be known to be necessary or eternal except by establishing their necessity in some way other than observation. The eternal, in other words, *appears* to be observationally available to us, but no observation, however long, could establish eternity as eternity. Aristotle seemed to miss this. Thus, Aristotle should never have affirmed the eternity of anything except the essential nature of God and the structure of the universe.

Time and freedom. The first condition of freedom is the asymmetry of time; the second is the modal character of time; the third is the priority of the relative over the absolute; the fourth is the predicability of the subject. Asymmetry means the future is indefinite and needs to be shaped and specified through action; modal argument shows even God cannot know the future, but merely makes far better predictions than creatures (and that this is no deficiency in God); the priority of the relative and the predicability of the (relative) subject taken together mean that actual value can be added to the world, through free action; and that the experiencing of this world itself becomes a datum for eternity, through the memory of deity, for example, or the eternity of the world itself. Freedom without the capacity to co-create the world and add to its value would be a paltry thing. For all these an understanding of the modal asymmetry of time is essential. Lack of a clear conception of the modal character of time, particularly the modal character of the future, will almost inevitably lead a given philosopher into determinism. The present and past taken together are actual as opposed to possible, and in this sense God or any other being can know them. But in what sense can God know the future? Very good predictive powers might give an extraordinarily accurate picture of a future, that is, a future that is highly probable. The future is never wholly unconditioned, since it must include the definite past; with its limitations, and because it is the product not of an autochthonous will, but of myriad conflicts among co-creators (including deity). God and brute fact propose; free agents merely dispose. But no future will be guaranteed and definite; 'some such future' may be necessary, but not its features or details.

Hartshorne remarks that Aristotle's idea that knowing is affected by the things known had to be completely reversed by Aquinas and other scholastics in order that they could characterize the unmoved mover as both knowing and unmoved. From this comes Kant's "calamitous doctrine" that from the paradigmatic knowledge of God, things are created by God's act of knowing them.[23] What Kant here did for knowledge, making an absolute also the 'knower,' which should be a relative term, he did just as badly for freedom. Creatures are unfree, except for a noumenal *deus ex machina*, because the phenomenal world is, for Kant, unfree and materially determined. The asymmetry of cause-effect is unmentioned in the Kantian corpus; but if freedom is noumenal, then it is also inherently noumenal in its effects; indeed, what phenomenal effects can noumenal freedom have? It would seem that for Kant time was the order of asymmetry, but actually his view of time, like Aristotle's in the *Physics*, is symmetrical; unlike Aristotle's, it is also deterministic.

III. Historical Note

Hartshorne's main criticisms of the Greeks are of their postulate of an enduring substrate and their depreciation of the temporal and contingent in the name of the eternal and necessary. The two are coeval as the result of the Greek preference for the Parmenidean 'One,' and a repugnance to all relativeness and dependency. Abhorrence in the face of the finitude of life may play a role in the origins of this Greek prejudice. But the prejudice can be refuted, particularly if one heeds logical cues, as Hartshorne does. It may seem, of course, that logic is one place that the primacy of the eternal is most demonstrable. Demonstration of necessity does not prevent recognition that the combination of the contingent and the necessary is contingent, and therefore that 'contingency' is the inclusive term. Similarly, Aristotle's theology shows the eternity and impassible necessity of God. But although it is demonstrably the most consistent theology in the history of thought this becomes a vice: in order to guarantee that every aspect of God is necessary rather than contingent, this theology must interpret deity as knowing nothing but itself. Aristotle's insight is sly and profound, because he sees that any richer conception of God would be world-dependent. If God were to know the contingent world, the knowledge of that contingent world would itself be contingent, and God, to the extent of that knowledge, would himself be contingent. Thus according to Aristotle God cannot know anything except the one eternal and necessary thing, to wit, his own essence, even though the version of God that must result is anathema to any religious worship. Nothing could be less true for either Aristotle or Plato than William Blake's dictum that "eternity is in love with the productions of time."[24] Deity cannot warrant the value of creature creativity. As Merleau-Ponty says, "Metaphysical and moral conscious-ness dies upon contact with the absolute. . . ."[25] — if by 'absolute' we mean the elimination of the relative.

Process philosophy is not developmental, as Hegelian thought is supposed to be. For the Hegeliens, an idealistic part-truth dominates the conception of philosophical knowledge: that the philosophical object becomes what it is thanks to the elucidation of it. If non-developmental philosophical theory suffers description as "typological" rather than "historical," then process philosophy and above all Hartshorne's view of philosophical history is decidedly typologi-cal. His underlying assumption is that the history of philosophy plays out in a neither random nor coherent fashion many of the possible options of philosoph-ical thought. Managing many such exhaustive disjunctions together is quite a feat, and Hartshorne has spent his whole life attempting this feat in larger and larger dimensions.

There is no question but that Hartshorne does not regard the great errors of philosophers as, in some subtle way, wheat: They are all chaff. Apparent errors might not be real errors, but a careful winnowing of accurate and profound thinking from inaccurate and lazy thinking would yield the authentic form of any thinker's thought. Hartshorne is therefore quite interested in careful reading, but only as it serves the thought and not as it serves the 'organic whole' of a thinker's philosophy.[26] Hartshorne in fact disbelieves in "organic wholes" when it comes to theory of any kind. Theory, rightly and deeply understood, is entirely inorganic. It would be safe to say that philosophy in its slipshod moments is not even literarily interesting. Therefore, Hartshorne knows what he is looking for in the history of philosophy, though he is not as uninterested in what he does not find as he is in what he discards.

Hartshorne's own metaphysics can in most of its dimensions be suggested by lines from Stevens: "There was no fury in transcendent forms./ But his actual candle blazed with artifice."[27] Actuality and its relational logic are hard to defend against legions of determinists, necessitarians, essentialists, materialists, idealists, synechists, skeptics, atheists, and worse. But still Hartshorne's blade is bright.

JAMES P. DEVLIN

DEPARTMENT OF PHILOSOPHY
BOSTON UNIVERSITY
DECEMBER 1986

NOTES

1. *Creative Synthesis and Philosophic Method*, ch. vi, especially pp. 100ff. According to Hartshorne, the historical origin of his theory lies somewhere in a discussion

of inclusion by Emerson. Crucial essays by Hartshorne include "The Neglect of Relative Predicates in Modern Philosophy," *The American Philosphical Quarterly* 14, no. 4 (1977), and "The Case for Idealism," *Philosophical Forum*, (Fall, 1968).

2. Events may overlap, if they are maxi-events (atomic events do not overlap), but if they overlap exactly they are the same event; two events separated spatially have no temporal relation—it may be impossible ever to verify their *order*, but that they have spatial relation is obvious.

3. However, we live for good and ill in an era when Wittgenstein is being remaindered and his skepticism has been shown inadequate. See Findlay's recantation, for example, or Rorty's defection. J. N. Findlay, *Wittgenstein: A Critique* (London: Routledge and Kegan Paul, 1984); Richard Rorty, *Philosophy and the Mirror of Nature* (Princeton: Princeton University Press, 1979).

4. *Critique of Pure Reason*, B, 5. Kant also missed the modal asymmetry of time even while he was attempting to ground metaphysics in modal distinctions in order to escape the wrath of Hume. Hartshorne's logical cues suggest a metaphysical prolegomenon. If Kant had read it, he would have rewritten half the *Critique*.

5. This is the final meaning of 'intentionality' whereby it was possible for Husserl to think that the contents of consciousness were assembled just in *this* act of consciousness, so that ". . . all real unities are unities of meaning." See *Ideen* I, §55. The *meaning* would always be unique and definite; the object would be available for various meanings. Intentionality is best understood as a type of inclusion.

6. For Peirce, any Second requires specifically the Firsts that enter into its composition, but not the other way around. Firsts are undefined by any given example.

7. Cf. Hartshorne, *Insights and Oversights of Great Thinkers: An Evaluation of Western Philosophy* (Albany: State University of New York Press, 1983), pp. 82ff.

8. Much confusion is introduced here by the Greeks for whom the trait's generality is often expressed in the neuter singular, and sounds like an *instance*. For example, the beautiful, *to kalon*, is both the beautiful thing and beauty itself.

9. For Whitehead, this distinction is expressed within prehension as the order of presentational immediacy (abstract, symmetric, continuous) versus the order of causal efficacy (concrete, asymmetric, discontinuous).

10. John Findlay asserts, apropos of a rescue of Leibniz, that "possibilities . . . are in a sense more actual than actualities," because of their exhaustiveness and permanence, and power to *instance themselves*, but how can the less rich produce something richer than itself? And why is the unexpressed permanent greater than an instance that actually and temporally expresses it? See J. N. Findlay, *Kant and the Transcendental Object* (Oxford: Clarendon Press, 1981), p. 31.

11. The equivalence class properly disjoins a larger group, and is of such an order that any member of such a class can 'stand for' the group. A row of students, Beth, John, Justine, etc., can be correctly called Beth's row or John's row.

12. *Creative Synthesis*, p. 99.

13. *Physics* Δ, 10–14.

14. *horos*. The limit has no magnitude whatever. It is a mere 'horizon.'

15. The first presentation of the real number 'continuum' in Western history is probably Aristotle's in the *Physics*' time-treatise and throughout his discussions of magnitude in *Physics* Zeta. That Aristotle should lay out the mathematical-conception of time and the real number series (as an infinitely divisible continuum) together in a small section of one book is doubtless astounding, but also unfortunate for the theory of time, which henceforward was invariably treated as a continuous magnitude.

16. Aristotle's reasoning is 'dialectical,' meaning for him the elaboration of 'common views,' but his resolution is aporetic; he cannot answer the argument that time cannot exist since its parts do not.

17. Here we also see a profound truth about the absence of mind during sleep—absence because the body (and especially brain) has not sustained mind, and reorganizes a unifying 'mind' only during dreams. The Sardinian Sleepers did not dream.

18. Space-time is an oblique conjunction; it too owes everything to the Aristotelian reduction of time to a neutral string of 'nows.'

19. He would be loath to say "being," but it is easy to convey the entire sense of Hartshorne's theory of objective modality in Aristotelian language.

20. *Insights and Oversights*, p. 107.

21. Jose Benardete in his dissertation explores an ontological argument in Aristotle, an argument from time to the being of the prime mover. Cf. *An Essay on Time: Wherein a Neglected Argument for the Prime Mover Is Shown to be Demonstrative* (University of Virginia, 1953).

22. *Insights and Oversights*, p. 47.

23. *Insights and Oversights,* p. 75.

24. Blake, *The Marriage of Heaven and Hell*, "Proverbs of Hell," ninth proverb.

25. Merleau-Ponty, "The Metaphysical in Man," *Sense and Non-Sense* (Evanston: Northwestern University Press, 1964; original 1964).

26. Merleau-Ponty expresses the contrary view: "The history of thought does not summarily pronounce: this is true; that is false. Like all history, it has its veiled decisions. It dismantles or embalms certain doctrines, changing them into 'message' or museum pieces. There are others, on the contrary, which it keeps active. These do not endure because there is some miraculous adequation or correspondence between them and an invariable 'reality'—such an exact and fleshless truth is neither sufficient nor necessary for the greatness of a doctrine—but because, as obligatory steps for those who want to go further, they retain an expressive power which exceeds their statements and propositions. These doctrines are the *classics*." *Signs* (Evanston: Northwestern University Press, 1964; original 1960), pp. 10–11.

27. Wallace Stevens, "A Quiet Normal Life," *The Collected Poems of Wallace Stevens* (New York: Alfred A. Knopf, 1982), p. 523.

15

Nancy Frankenberry

HARTSHORNE'S METHOD IN METAPHYSICS

Metaphysics has had a hard go of it in this century, for it has been distorted by both ends of an empiricist spectrum ranging from sharp assault to easy indifference. Logical positivism assumed that metaphysics moves and breathes in the polluted air of pure speculation, unclear meanings, and non-falsifiable theories. Analytic philosophy has operated on the equally erroneous assumption that having identified the presence of these pollutants, we have provided a sufficient explanation of metaphysics, discredited its pretensions, and replaced it with a more profitable form of argumentation. But to claim that metaphysics involves extravagant scope, limitations of language, and non-falsifiable claims does not discredit metaphysics; it merely states the obvious. The important questions are how metaphysicians find ways of protecting themselves against these liabilities and how, in some cases, they transform them into assets.

No other living philosopher has done more to eliminate the old liabilities and to elucidate the new assets of metaphysics in our time than Charles Hartshorne. The purpose of this essay is to examine critical features of Hartshorne's general method in metaphysics. I begin briefly by situating the inquiry in the context of a philosophy of process. In the next section I consider the formal characteristics of metaphysics according to Hartshorne's defense of its very possibility. The third section displays the chief methodological procedures that Hartshorne adopts, and the fourth section interprets the three most fundamental principles that govern the logic of his system, in particular, the key function of his doctrine of the primacy of asymmetrical relations. The concluding section raises some concerns about the harmony between the logical and phenomenological aspects of Hartshorne's method.

The Primacy of Becoming Over Being

One of the best routes to the center of Hartshorne's philosophy is to view it as an elaboration of answers to the following set of questions: What features are inherent in experience *as such*? What features are inherent in human experience but not essential to experience as such? How do we discover, or support a distinction between, what is contingent in human experience and what is essential to it? Or what is essential to human experience and what is essential to experience as such? Such questions lead to metaphysical analysis and the framing of general principles and categories which aim to be applicable to *all* experience. When the question is put this way, the phrase "human experience" is not a redundancy. The difference between "inherent in human experience" and "inherent in experience as such" is crucial to the question metaphysics asks, and is at the same time the source of the greatest difficulty in the kind of generalization it demands. Those who are unable to see this difference may be, as Hartshorne says, "not fitted for metaphysical inquiry."[1] But then, we may assume, those who *are* so fitted must possess something more publicly reliable than an extraordinary introspective power for surveying the inventory of experience in both its essential and contingent aspects. Systematic construction, dialectical defense, and logical candor, all of which Hartshorne has supplied in abundant measure, are indispensable to the method of metaphysics.

But if Hartshorne's method is in the service of exploring the universal and inescapable features of experience as such, it is experience conceived as *becoming* that is his focus. The hinge on which each of his major arguments turns is the important priority of becoming over being in experience, a radical inversion of the metaphysical ultimacy traditionally accorded to "being." In a philosophy of process, the crucially important difference between being and becoming cannot be overemphasized. Processive-relational becoming is construed, by Hartshorne as much as by Whitehead, as the ultimate principle of experience. It is ultimate in two senses: creativity cannot be explained in terms of anything more basic or more general than itself; and it is universally exemplified by every concrete actuality. Creativity, or the processive-relational becoming of experience, means, in Whitehead's succinct formula, "the many become one and are increased by one." As literally creative of new actualities, becoming is a process of emergent synthesis whereby the present, taking account of the past, adds novel incremental units, event by event. The spatial metaphor of the arrow of time captures the image of a "closed" past and an "open" future. Between the vanishing tail of the arrow and its expected head is the concreteness of the act of becoming of a new occasion of experience, a "now" which has its light of day.

Process philosophy's preference for the category of "becoming" over "being" is in no way arbitrary. Only becoming, Hartshorne argues, can be taken as inclusive of the contrast between being and becoming, without losing the contrast between them. Philosophies of being, on the other hand, are simply not capable of deriving the idea of becoming from the idea of being, not even through dialectical negation. From pure being, dialectics can arrive, at best, only at the idea of limited, determinate being—a far cry from becoming, or creativity. Hartshorne's preferential option for process, like liberation theology's "preferential option for the poor," is the result of a dialectical struggle between two opposing parties. The question is not, which can muscle out the other? Instead, the question is, which term is capable of including the legitimate interests of both sides, short of suppression? The primacy of becoming over being in a philosophy of process is the result of the insight, couched in the purely logical terms Hartshorne favors, that "given a variable V and a constant C, the togetherness of the two, VC, must be a variable."[2] The revolutionary implications of this insight for metaphysical method have yet to be fully registered.

THE FORMAL CHARACTERISTICS OF METAPHYSICAL INQUIRY

Questions about the logical status of metaphysical propositions, and their relation to the notions of truth and falsity, are so poorly understood today that one wonders how many contemporary philosophers in either the analytic or the continental tradition have bothered to investigate fairly Hartshorne's patient and thorough theory of metaphysics. When his statements on the subject are compared with current arguments within mainstream philosophy, there is good reason to believe that the "metaphysical veto" and the urge to "overcome metaphysics" are gestures directed against positions other than process metaphysics.

Hartshorne has proposed as many as twelve overlapping definitions of metaphysics, including the formula "the theory of experience as such."[3] In what is perhaps his most useful definition, he writes that metaphysics is properly understood as "the unrestrictive or completely general theory of concreteness" or of process *qua* process.[4] That is, metaphysical categories are an attempt to answer questions about the *generic* meaning of concreteness as such, or what can be said *universally* about the most concrete levels of reality.[5] Experience as such, process *qua* process, and concreteness may be taken as coextensive. "Concreteness" is obviously an abstraction, and the categories pertinent to its elucidation will be, like all categories, abstract. But they will be applicable to wholly *concrete* actualities, any one of which, as particular and unrepeatable, is "incomparably richer" qualitatively than the concept of it.[6] In this respect, the abstractions employed by process metaphysics are more fundamental, and thus more widely applicable, than the abstractions that are useful in other specialized disciplines. The physical sciences, mathematics, and formal logic all generalize spatio-temporal structures, quantities, and geometrical orders. But they omit quality. For this reason, Hartshorne views the *instances* of their abstractions as themselves abstract. When we repair to the metaphysical level, however, we have to do with the most fundamental level of abstraction, concreteness as such. Instances of *this* abstraction are wholly concrete. These are the actualities from which all else is abstractable as constituents or aspects. Abstractions, of course, are no substitute for concreteness, but without them we can hardly acquire knowledge of anything.

On the question of what constitutes knowledge, Hartshorne is firm. As recently as 1985, he reiterated his position that "Knowledge is of two kinds, empirical and *a priori*."[7] This is an old distinction, sustained with some difficulty in light of recent efforts to dissolve it, but Hartshorne uses it cautiously to clarify the logical status of metaphysical principles. Undaunted by those who assume with Quine that there is no way to tell the difference between a platitude grounded in "experience" and a "linguistic convention," and thus no point to the empirical/a priori distinction, Hartshorne has offered a strict account of the nature of empirical truths, of a priori truths, and of their difference. With Popper, he defines "empirical" as knowledge of the truth of propositions that actual experience corroborates to some extent and that some conceivable experience would falsify. Empirical propositions are always contingent, vulnerable to conceivable observational tests, and, in Hartshorne's terminology, "partially restrictive of existential possibilities."[8] They conflict with some possible state of affairs. "I am in Hanover," for example, conflicts with the conceivable state of affairs, "I am in Chicago." Contingent, empirical truths thus exclude actualization among alternative possibilities. From Hartshorne's use of the Leibnizian insight that the scope of disjunctive possibilities cannot all be actualized simultaneously or conjunctively, it follows that every positive empirical fact has negative implications, insofar as it excludes alternatives. Likewise, negative facts involve both exclusion and positive implications. The statement "I am not in Chicago" is not an assertion of an absence or a privation. It is an exclusion achieved by a positive state of affairs, i.e., my being elsewhere.

Are there nonempirical, noncontingent truths? Hartshorne finds three such classes: the truths of mathematics, those of formal logic, and those that metaphysics seeks to enunciate in its analysis of concreteness. Statements within all three classes of this severely limited type may be considered necessary or a priori. They are also alike in their immunity to falsification. Metaphysical assertions, if true, belong to the class of necessary truths, but this is not to say that all necessary truths are metaphysical ones. The best way to clarify the precise difference between metaphysical assertions and other necessary truths is to consider several important distinctions Hartshorne employs, most notably in *The Logic of Perfection* and in *Creative Synthesis and Philosophical Method*. In the first place, he distinguishes "conditional" and "unconditional" propositions in the mode of necessity.[9] Some necessary truths, such as "2 apples plus 2 apples are 4 apples," obtain upon certain conditions (in this case, the existence of apples). Unconditionally necessary truths, such as "2 plus 2 are 4," are those which depend upon no conditions whatsoever. In the second place, Hartshorne also distinguishes between those necessary propositions which are "non-existential" and those which are "existential." Mathematical statements, on these terms, are non-existential statements, even as they seek to be non-restrictive. But metaphysical assertions are distinguished from these by being existential, as well as non-restrictive, affirmations. Unlike mathematics, which affirms "relations between conceivable states of affairs, without affirming any such state to be actualized," metaphysics tries to express "what *all* possibilities of existence have in common."[10] Another way of expressing Hartshorne's distinction is to say that completely non-restrictive existential statements are necessarily true in at least this actual world, perhaps also in all possible worlds, and that completely non-restrictive, non-existential statements are necessarily true in possible worlds other than this actual one.

Combining the two sets of distinctions Hartshorne employs in *The Logic of Perfection* and in *Creative Synthesis and Philosophical Method*, we can admit as many as four kinds of necessary truths, only the last of which qualifies as properly metaphysical. Thus, the formally possible combinations of propositional types in the mode of necessity may be classified as: (1) conditional and non-existential, (2) conditional and existential, (3) unconditional and non-existential, and (4) unconditional and existential.[11] Examples of (1) are certain schemes of non-Euclidean geometry that are necessary, on the assumption of certain conditional postulates, and that are non-existential, stating what would be the case in some possible world, but not this one. Examples of (2) could be such propositions as "all triangles have three sides," "no dog is a cat," and "widows are unmarried women." They are conditionally necessary, given the existence of triangular objects, dogs, cats, and widows, which do in fact exist. Other examples of conditional and existential necessary truths may be difficult to decide, some falling within the purview of physics and scientific cosmology. But Hartshorne's view of classification (3) is exceptionally clear. No examples can be given of a necessary truth that is both unconditional and non-existential. Any candidate for such a status would have to be a truth which depends upon no conditions whatsoever. It will be true in all possible worlds, and therefore in the actual world as well. But if true in the actual world, it will be existential, and cannot be non-existential at all. We arrive, then, at (4) as the properly *metaphysical* class of necessary truths—those that are characterized as unconditional (completely non-restrictive) and so existential.

As existential, metaphysical truths are illustrated in the actual world. As unconditional, they are true in all possible worlds. And as necessary, they cannot be falsified in any possible world. Alternatively, Hartshorne can say that metaphysical truths are those that are bound to be verified by every actual or possible state of affairs. From this it follows that "Metaphysical truths may be described as such that no experience can contradict them, but also such that any experience must illustrate them."[12] The verifiability criterion holds specifically for metaphysical truth, while immunity to falsifiability holds generically as a criterion for necessary truth as such. All conceivable conditions are relevant to the verification of metaphysical truths, and no contingent conditions are relevant to their falsification. From this point of view, the only difficulty with the "verificationism" program espoused by Ayer, Hempel, Carnap, and Reichenbach was its much too narrow notion of observation, and *not* its requirement that meaningful statements be somehow related to observations of *some* sort. According to Hartshorne's theory, "verifiability (liberally enough construed) is valid as criterion of meaning in general; and falsifiability is valid as criterion of empirical meaning."[13]

A priori truths are simply those that contradict no conceivable observation, and hence may be taken as necessary principles.[14] "*All* truths will agree with experience," Hartshorne says, "hence the difference between contingent and necessary truths can show itself only in this, that the former could while the latter could not *conflict* with *conceivable* experiences."[15] The usual objection to this view is that a statement that claims to fit *any* conceivable experience must be vacuous because what is true of all things says nothing about any particular thing. Hartshorne agrees that a statement that no observation could count against says nothing *contingent* about reality. But this does not prevent it from being true of any and every such state, hence also of the actual state, even if perhaps only trivially true of it. He notes that "It is a strange logical lapse to infer 'describes no possible experience' from 'conflicts with no possible experience.' What could not be false under any circumstances is either nonsense or it is true under any and every circumstance."[16]

Given this understanding of metaphysics, it should be obvious that the a priori character of its assertions has nothing to do with Kant's definition of the a priori as independent of all experience. Nor does it have anything to do with truths that are known with absolute certainty. Hartshorne is explicit about maintaining a distinction between our formulations of metaphysical truth and the truth itself.[17] Errors frequently occur in metaphysics, just as they do in logic and mathematics. Is there, then, some *test* for weeding out mistakes in metaphysics? What would be a criterion for showing falsity in nonempirical matters? I suggest that Hartshorne's method permits falsification of putative metaphysical generalizations in the following two ways. First, empirical truths can discredit purportedly metaphysical assertions that are false of "actual nature," i.e., if they cannot comprehend cosmological or scientific laws of nature.[18] Thus, the empirical sciences have an important bearing on metaphysical issues, as Hartshorne's own interest in relativity physics shows. The bearing, however, is in terms of falsifiability. Second, the method of a priori falsification can be used in connection with nonempirical statements. This consists in demonstrating "confusion, inconsistency, or lack of definite meaning."[19] In actual practice, this is the method Hartshorne relies on most heavily. And that is why his defense of his own neo-classical metaphysics so frequently takes the form of exhibiting the "falsity" (i.e., incoherence) of all proposed alternatives, often through a series of brilliant *reductio* arguments.

Hartshorne's Popperian notion of the a priori as contradicting no conceivable experience thus involves him in a method that is broadly inductive. The inductive aspect of his method, like Whitehead's, consists in utilizing specific notions, chiefly taken from cases of memory and perception, and imaginatively generalizing these properties to infer generic notions applicable to all concrete facts. In so far as process philosophy, like science, employs the method of the "working hypothesis," it renounces the pretension that the metaphysician can begin with self-evident axioms and deduce from them the content of reality. The true role of deduction in metaphysics, Hartshorne says, "is not to bring out the content of the initially certain, but to bring out the meaning of tentative descriptions of the metaphysically ultimate in experience so that we shall be better able to judge if they do genuinely describe this ultimate."[20]

With these formal characteristics of metaphysics in mind, it is appropriate to ask for an *instance* of at least one such truth. What propositions are acceptable as candidates for the status of unconditionally necessary existential statements? Hartshorne's answer to this question takes several interchangeable forms, having to do with the propositions "something exists," "experience occurs," and "creative synthesis occurs."[21] With any one of these assertions Hartshorne is able to show the incoherence that lies behind the contemporary dogma that all existential claims are contingent. "Something exists," for instance, is not even conceivably falsifiable, and so it is on Hartshorne's terms a necessary truth. Furthermore, "something exists" denies that nothing exists, and Hartshorne argues that "nothing exists" is a literally inconceivable proposition, mere verbiage, which can therefore be ruled out on strictly logical grounds. He considers the notion that "there might have been nothing" a fine example of what Wittgenstein called "language idling."[22] To refer to absolutely nothing is not to refer at all. What could ever verify or exemplify the statement "nothing exists"? In order to verify or exemplify "nothing exists," at least something would have to exist, namely, the verifying experience itself.[23] And if that one experience exists, something exists.

Second, the statement "something exists" is verified or exemplified by absolutely everything which does exist, has existed, or could possibly exist. Not only does the statement have the general character of an a priori truth in that it is not conceivably falsifiable, but it also has the specific character of an a priori metaphysical truth in that it is always verified by whatever is so much as even possible. "Something exists" therefore meets the requirement of being unconditionally necessary. Third, from the fact that it is unconditionally necessary, it follows also that the proposition has application to the actual world. "Something exists" thus meets the requirement of being an existential affirmation as well.

With this demonstration that "something exists" (and its variants) is an unconditionally necessary, existential truth, Hartshorne has contributed a powerful new defense of the possibility of metaphysics. That he has also fashioned some definite methodological principles in support of his arguments is perhaps less well appreciated.

HARTSHORNE'S METHOD IN METAPHYSICS

Over a period of time, especially in his most mature reflections, Hartshorne has exhibited and employed a clear, consistent, and discernible method. However, the very employment has often proceeded at the expense of his clearly identifying and defending the methodological principles by which he operates. Hartshorne's methodological considerations are almost always so intertwined with his discussion of substantive issues that one rarely finds in his system a straightforward exposition or overall listing of his rules of philosophical procedure. In *Creative Synthesis and Philosophical Method*, a book he has cited as "the only close to definitive source"[24] for his philosophy, a chapter is devoted to the topic of "Some Principles of Method." Yet even here only four of the eight sections concern formal *principles*, while the other four sections contain statements of Hartshorne's metaphysical *conclusions*.[25] It is with some understatement, then, that Hartshorne warns readers that this chapter may appear "more like an outline of my metaphysical beliefs than like a listing of rules which everyone ought to follow whatever his beliefs."[26]

Nevertheless, what Hartshorne outlines in this chapter is crucial to understanding the exact meaning of his more recent claim elsewhere that "a metaphysician or ontologist should be a logician, phenomenologist, linguistic analyst, and pragmatist, and I can put my categorial commitments in all of these ways."[27] Hartshorne claims to accept each of these four aspects of philosophical method. In fact, the first three aspects—logical, phenomenological, and linguistic—correspond to the first three topics he considers at some length in "Some Principles of Method." (The fourth, "pragmatic," aspect is like the dodo in ornithology; one searches in vain for this bird anywhere in Hartshorne's *method*, although there are fleeting sightings of it in the company of remarks about the species known as "existentialism."[28]) Although the topics are treated in the order of "Language," "Experience," and "Formal Logic," their relative importance to Hartshorne's overall method is clearly in exactly reverse order.

The linguistic aspect of Hartshorne's method may be distilled, for the sake of convenience, in the form of these maxims: (1) Attend more to technical philosophical terminology than to ordinary language in dealing with the most general metaphysical questions, and take into account extreme cases of concreteness and of abstractness not normally recognized in ordinary language. (2) Employ the language of unit-events, rather than the language of enduring substances or individual things and persons, as the most indivisible units of concrete reality. (3) Distinguish clearly between the abstract *existence* of an individual (*that* it exists) and its concrete *actuality* of states or events (*how* it exists), a distinction recognized in ordinary language and one which is fundamental for clarity in metaphysics.[29] It is worth noting that the limitations he finds in ordinary language and its misleading metaphysical assumptions do not prevent Hartshorne from being splendidly able to argue various metaphysical points through "a careful study of ordinary cases," as, for example, in his discussion of the way the words "dependent" and "independent" each admit of positive and negative connotations that can be made mutually compatible in the dual view of transcendence.[30]

The phenomenological aspect of Hartshorne's philosophy is complex and intriguing. When he says that "The roots of all abstract ideas are to be sought in concrete experiencing of various kinds," he might almost be declaring a kind of radical empiricism in the spirit of William James.[31] But when he summons up, within a few short pages, the "principle of generality," we learn that human experience is to be divested of its "contingent specificities" so as to eliminate those "limitations that do not seem inherent in its meaning."[32] In the end, Hartshorne's discussion of the role of experience in philosophical method focuses only on the experiences of memory, perception, and imagination. These, he finds, "are three obvious aspects of concrete experiencing. A philosopher needs to make a careful examination of all three, in their essential or generic aspects."[33] The examination takes the form of looking for a generic trait that different kinds of experience have in common, comparing and assimilating cases, and then generalizing their properties to infer notions applicable to all concrete actualities. Comparing the two cases of memory and perception, he finds that "in some ways memory is a better key to the nature of experience than perception," mainly because "the temporal structure of memory is more obvious."[34] Attention to the mnemonic structure of experience yields a generalization of the abstract feature of socially structured, temporal inheritance seen *in* experience. Both memory and perception are offered as important cases of "prehension," the direct grasp of antecedent events upon which the perceiving or remembering events asymmetrically depend. Therefore, Hartshorne concludes:

> Common to the two is what Whitehead calls 'prehension,' intuition of the antecedently real. This is a specimen of what I mean by metaphysical discovery. It is no mere matter of human pyschology. There are good reasons for holding that only what is already real could be given to any experience in any world. Intuition of the past seems a paradox to some, but if they had really tried to conceive how something strictly simultaneous with the experience could be given they might see where the real paradox would be.[35]

However, no generalization from features found in human experience is alone sufficient to establish metaphysical claims about what is inherent in experience *as such*. Metaphysical method, in Hartshorne's view, must also employ strict logical devices. In the final analysis, Hartshorne generates clues to the structure of reality less from phenomenological evidence than from what he regards as basic truisms of formal and modal logic.

The logical aspect of Hartshorne's method is nowhere more evident than in his statement that "A basic procedure in all thinking is to *exhaust possible solutions* to a problem and arrive at the best or truest by elimination of those that are unsatisfactory."[36] The method of decision by elimination from exhaustive divisions of the doctrinal possibilities is for the sake of insuring the adequacy of the categories. Here the resources of formal logic become indispensable in formalizing the concepts exhaustively. In another variation on Popper, Hartshorne points out:

> The idea that one can somehow hit on the manifest truth and simply forget about alternatives as mere curiosities receives little support in experience. As Popper has so well shown, in empirical inquiry at least, falsification is the most crucial operation. I hold that this is true in non-empirical inquiry also. But unless possible solutions can be exhausted, there is no reason why elimination should bring us to our goal.[37]

In actual practice, the logical aspect of Hartshorne's method involves the procedure of using strict formal (mathematical) quantification, exhaustively listing the conceptual options, and severely testing each option by rational rules of conceptual coherence. The mode of argumentation thus becomes partly historical and partly systematic. The relevant sources in the history of philosophy supply the spectrum of conceptual hypotheses which have been or could be held. These can be put systematically into what Hartshorne calls a "position matrix," or a finite set of doctrines or combination of concepts traditionally applied to some problem.[38] To prove exhaustiveness, the position matrix can be formalized according to the three-cornered logic of quantification: all, some, and none. Otherwise, Hartshorne warns, formal possibilities that pertain to "some," lurking between the disjunction "all" or "none," may be improperly neglected. "Anyone who says 'all' must show why 'some'or 'none' would not be better. And he who says 'all or none' must justify the omission of 'some.' "[39]

The philosophical problem on which Hartshorne has most conspicuously honed the logical aspect of the method that I have just summarized is, of course, the ontological argument. Using the concepts "necessary" and "contingent," and the set $NC.nc$, he has shown nine mathematically possible theoretical options in conceiving the modal status of God and the world, where N or C stand for the transcendent forms of a category and n or c stand for the ordinary forms.[40] His own pantheistic or neo-classical view is one of the nine, and the only one to survive the test of conforming to all five of the rational rules he proposes.[41] Other options are eliminated as incoherent on the grounds that they are either contradictory or without clear meaning.

Under this same procedure, the use of similar universal contrasts, such as absolute (or independent) and relative (or dependent), infinite and finite, simple and complex, will again, we are assured, yield nine options and one highscorer: neo-classicism. The identical method is at work also in the argument for what Hartshorne calls "dual transcendence," where transcendence implies surpassing all possible others by being infinite, absolute, necessary, and also surpassing all others by being, in another respect, finite, relative, and contingent in uniquely excellent, unsurpassable ways. (Formal contradiction is avoided by maintaining a distinction of "aspects" or the different respects in which each is predicated.) Here too Hartshorne invokes the procedure of using mathematical structures, exhausting the conceptual options, and judging each option by rules of conceptual coherence. In this case the combinations of four concepts gives sixteen options, nine of which might be held to be broadly theistic.[42]

A rather different and, so far as I can see, unique *form* of Hartshorne's method appears in "Six Theistic Proofs" in *Creative Synthesis and Philosophical Method*. Whereas previously (and even within the same book) he had demonstrated with coercive techniques the logical necessity of his conclusion, thereby confounding nominalists, atheists, and empirical theists alike, here he states the arguments in the form of possible alternatives to this conclusion. As many as six theistic arguments are cast in a broadly similar form, stating either three or, in one case, four mutually exclusive possibilities of affirming *or denying* the neo-classical theistic conclusion. The standard Hartshornian positions all come into play in these brief twenty-three pages (to which I cannot do justice here), but the basic scheme itself is novel, allowing for the following set of options: "(*a*) reject premise p, (*b*) reject premise q, (*c*) reject premise r, (*d*) reject two or all of the premises, (*e*) accept the premises and the conclusion."[43] The ontological, cosmological, design, epistemic, moral, and aesthetic arguments are then each stated in the form of possible rejections (premises A1, A2, A3, A4) enabling one to avoid the (neoclassical theistic) conclusion (T) which Hartshorne proceeds to defend. With the use of this method, Hartshorne appears to have distanced himself from the fiction that fundamental questions can ever be settled by deductive logic, and to have offered, instead, a challenging form in which to consider the dilemmas, trilemmas, or quatrilemmas that are confronted in human beliefs or disbeliefs.

A Logic of Categorial Contrasts

The clarity of Hartshorne's philosophical method can best be captured by considering his use of the three principles I will interpret next: the principle of contrast, the principle of concrete inclusion, and the principle of asymmetry. These are the methodological principles basic to a revisionary mode of metaphysics in our time. Taken together, they serve to dismantle the dualistic assumptions inherited from Greek philosophy.

The acknowledged failure of classical metaphysics can be traced to its unsatisfactory handling of such categories as: relative-absolute, subject-objects, whole-constituents, effect-cause, becoming-being, temporal-eternal, particular-universal, actual-potential, complex-simple, finite-infinite, contingent-necessary. Over these conceptual pairs (or binary oppositions in contemporary terminology) philosophers in the West have long waged their inveterate disputes. Judging from the fate of historical cases, it is fair to say that classical metaphysics has proven persistently incapable of thinking the *togetherness* of these ultimate contrasts except by falling into invidious dichotomies. The chief reason for this failure consists in the monotonous "monopolar prejudice" that riddled the classical metaphysical imagination, according a special valorization to one member of each category (absolute, cause, being, eternal, universal, necessary, infinite, etc.) and disparaging the opposite pole (relative, effect, becoming, temporal, contingent, finite, etc.).

Hartshorne has advanced a theory of the relations of categorial contrasts that challenges us to rethink the traditional valorizations of but one pole of each pair, as well as the metaphysical dualism that has been the legacy of the monopolar prejudice. Every bit as radical as the method of deconstructionism, his "dipolar" method subverts the entire history of metaphysical dualism—and enjoys the added advantage of being intelligible.

The Principle of Contrast. According to Hartshorne, categorially universal contrasts, applicable to all reality, are to be seen as "correlatives, mutually interdependent, so that nothing real can be described by the wholly one-sided assertion of simplicity, being, actuality, and the like, each in a 'pure form,' devoid or independent of complexity, becoming, potentiality, and related contraries."[44] In general, strictly as concepts, polar contrasts such as abstract-concrete, universal-particular, cause-effect, are semantically interdependent terms. Their *conceptual* relations are symmetrical and irreducible. It makes no more sense to talk about the abstract apart from its contrasting term, the concrete, than to talk about the concrete independently of the category of the abstract. Hartshorne holds that "the two poles of each contrast stand or fall together; neither is simply to be denied or explained away or called 'unreal.' For if either pole is real the contrast itself, including both poles, is so."[45] The principle of contrast, which Hartshorne has sometimes called the principle of polarity,[46] asserts that far from being mere opposites or outright contradictions of each other, polar contrasts are logically irreducible. Each requires the other for its very meaning.

But dualism is not invalidated merely by considering categorial contrasts intensionally, or conceptually. When we ask the further question about the *togetherness* of being-and-becoming, concrete-and-abstract, necessary-and-contingent, we face the need for some principle of order or direction. What is the *relation* between the two poles? Which depends upon which? Of the two terms, which is capable of including the other without suppressing the contrast between them? What is the nature of the whole that is both-and? Dualism simply takes the relation between the two poles as a sheer conjunct or a mysterious "third." But mere conjunction in the form of "x *and* y" fails to explain the overall character of the whole that is both-and. It also fails to exhibit the metaphysical status of the concrete and the abstract as non-equivalent. This dilemma leads directly to Hartshorne's next principle.

The Principle of Concrete Inclusion. According to this principle, the relation between ultimate contrasts is not one of conjunction, but one of inclusion. This allows Hartshorne to make the claim that "the concept expressing the total reality is the entire truth, not because the correlative contrary concept can be dismissed or negated, but because the referents of the latter are included in those of the former, while the converse does not obtain."[47] Precisely which concepts are the ones that are capable of including their contrasts without dismissal or negation? Hartshorne's method points to the *concrete*, dependent pole as the inclusive one. Thus, the extraordinary 21-item table of ultimate contrasts, surely unique in intellectual history, that appears in chapter 6 of *Creative Synthesis and*

Philosophical Method, should be read according to the principle of concrete inclusion in order to see that the left-hand column lists the concrete terms, which find their correlative, abstract members in the right-hand column.[48] The concrete is related to the abstract as the inclusive to the included. The concrete or inclusive terms depend on the abstract or included as, for example, later effects depend on previous causes, or as subjects on given objects. With this insight, Hartshorne has effected a stunning shift of emphasis in modern metaphysics. It means, and here I must oversimplify, that we are to find the absolute only in the relative, objects only in subjects, causes only in effects, earlier events only in later ones, being only in becoming, the eternal only in the temporal, the potential only in the actual, the necessary only in the contingent, the infinite only in the finite, the simple only in the complex, the generic only in the specific, the universal only in the particular. It could be said that the principle of concrete inclusion is Hartshorne's version of Whitehead's "ontological principle." But Whitehead did not explicitly or systematically enunciate the next principle, of asymmetrical relativity, which is so central to Hartshorne's methodology that it deserves to be considered independently.[49]

The Principle of Asymmetrical Relations. Building on Whitehead's revolutionary concept of "prehension" and Peirce's category of "Secondness," Hartshorne has developed the notion of asymmetrical relations into a powerful tool for disposing of determinism, nominalism, stale debates between "realism" and "idealism" in epistemology, and equally unforced options between "monism" and "pluralism" in ontology. If it was Peirce's "logic of relatives," superceding the old subject-predicate logic, that started ontology on a new track, it is Hartshorne who has supplied the most detailed argumentation. And if it was Whitehead who had the first insight into a one-way causal relation of experience to things experienced, it is Hartshorne who has applied this insight most effectively across a broad range of traditional philosophical problems.

Indeed, the pattern of comprehensive asymmetry or directional order of relations, embracing a subordinate aspect of symmetry, is the very fulcrum of Hartshorne's philosophical method, so much so that he is able to claim it as "a paradigm for metaphysics" itself.[50] On this view, the basic relations that hold between momentary actualities are internal for one term and external for the other. Because relatedness is a function of causal connection, and causal connection means relation by inheritance, which is always temporal, the structure of relations is asymmetrical, allowing for a real dependence and a real independence.

Relations have always presented special problems for metaphysicians in the classical tradition. Neither a metaphysics of universal interdependent relations nor one of universal independent relations can be made rationally intelligible. Extreme monists (Spinoza, Bradley, Royce, Blanshard) make every dependent relation symmetrical, or a case of interdependence, so that if A is related to B, the relation is internal or constitutive of both A and B. Extreme pluralists (Ockham, Hume, Russell, Moore, Carnap) make every independent relation symmetrical, so that if A is related to B, the relation is external to both A and B, and a third entity, R, has to be imported to account for their relation, generating a vicious regress.

In a metaphysics of temporal process, however, there is no need to treat relations as either exclusively internal or as exclusively external. If "time's arrow" is fully real, relations may be internal in some cases and external in others, just as they may be internal to some terms but also external to some. Hartshorne's solution is to see that A (as temporally earlier) is independent of B (as temporally later), but *not vice versa*. This principle is a striking illustration of the value of Hartshorne's method of "three-cornered thinking," whereby neglected alternatives ("some") can be discovered to lie between the extremes of "all" and "none."

The principle of asymmetrical relations comprises the key to understanding not only Hartshorne's resolution of problems in cosmology, epistemology, religion, and ethics, but also his overcoming of classical metaphysics. The principle of contrast, which asserts the symmetrical *meaning* of the metaphysical polarities, gives way, under the conditions of concrete spatiotemporal events, to the principle of asymmetry. In general, simply as concepts, polar contrasts such as abstract-concrete, cause-effect, universal-particular, are symmetrical correlates. But Hartshorne maintains that when we move from the level of abstract concepts to the level of concrete instances or examples, employing these concepts to refer or to describe, they become radically asymmetrical in structure. At the level of temporal process, asymmetrical relations are ultimate, and symmetrical ones are derivative. Taken together, the principles of concrete inclusion and of ultimate asymmetry yield the further methodological insight that modal distinctions are ultimately coincident with temporal ones.[51] Thus, Hartshorne is able to claim that the actual-possible contrast, for example, coincides with the past-future distinction, so that to talk of an "actual future" which is causally necessary is a contradiction in terms.

To carry through the implications of taking asymmetry as primary in the causal, temporal process, granting to symmetrical conceptions only a partial truth, is to see the untenability of strict determinism, the doctrine that every event has both necessary and sufficient conditions in preceding events. That there are necessary conditions is undeniable. But if "sufficient" means "sufficient to make the event happen," there can be no such condition in preceding events. The event itself makes itself happen and is its own sufficient cause. This is the meaning of creative freedom, and it is unintelligible without the understanding of asymmetrical relations. Radioactive decay, the collisions of molecules in a gas, the flow of human speech—all have necessary causal constraints, and so there can be a fruitful causal analysis of them, but none is sufficient to fully determine the phenomena.

The methodological import of the primacy of asymmetrical relations for Hartshorne's philosophy as a whole is evident in the support it furnishes for a wide variety of substantive theses. Without entering into a discussion of the substantive issues themselves, I can note the following summary of theses Hartshorne defends with great passion and resourcefulness, all with the aid of this doctrine: (1) the reality of creative freedom, not fully determined by causal conditions; (2) the partial indeterminacy of the open future (even for the divine life); (3) memory, as givenness of the past; (4) a moderate pluralism of both internal and external, or dependent and independent, relations; (5) social relations, or Whitehead's "feeling of feeling," as pervasive in experience and reality; (6) perception and memory as two cases of "prehension," the direct grasp of antecedent events upon which the perceiving or remembering events asymmetrically depend, entailing the denial that perceiving and its data are simultaneous; (7) the Whiteheadian identification of prehension with causality; (8) the proportionality of the correlates considered as ultimate categorial contrasts; and (9) the process view of genetic identity as partial and relative. In particular, adherence to the principle of asymmetry influences the content and defense of Hartshorne's (10) idealism and psychicalism[52] and his (11) revision of Peirce's categories of Firstness, Secondness, and Thirdness.

There is no clearer place to see the overall importance of asymmetrical relationality in Hartshorne's philosophy than to consider the revisions he has proposed to Peirce's categories. Like Hartshorne, Peirce wanted to limit his own presuppositions to some elementary formal mathematical insights or categories which have instances in actual experiences. In his investigation of the general structures of process, Peirce modelled his category of Firstness after absolute independence, Secondness after dependence on one other, and Thirdness after dependence on two others, considering all higher numbers reducible to these. For Hartshorne, however, what is categorially relevant are the *kinds* of relations of dependence or independence, not, as Peirce seemed to think, the *number* of items on which an actual phenomenon depends or of which it is independent. Taking his clue from temporality, rather than a numerical model, Hartshorne locates Thirdness in futurity, or real possibility, probability, or law. This third relation in which a phenomenon can stand to others is an intermediate one of "nondependence with respect to definite particulars, dependence with respect to more or less general outlines."[53] Without the category of real possibility ("causality in the forward direction"), intermediate between sheer necessity and pure possibility, there could be no understanding of "time's arrow."[54] On this basis, Hartshorne is able to interpret Peirce's independence or Firstness not as unqualified zero-dependence but as sheer independence of *future details*. An event does not have to have any *particular successors*, but it does have to *have successors*, and Hartshorne holds that some general features of these are settled in advance. Likewise, Peirce's strict dependence or Secondness, when interpreted as primarily asymmetrical, means one-way dependence *on at least some* independent and previous events, no matter how many or how few.[55]

These revisions of Peirce's categories afford a special glimpse into Hartshorne's generalizing power and permit a convenient summary of his own categorial presuppositions. According to Hartshorne's method, the irreducible formal relations among experiences can be stated in three forms:

> (1) the positive form, strict dependence; (2) the negative form, strict independence (both holding asymmetrically among definite particulars); and (3) dependence that leaves the final particularity open and can be stated only in more or less general terms.[56]

Alternatively expressed, the categorial presuppositions of Hartshorne's entire philosophy are these: the non-inclusiveness of actuality with respect to successors (Firstness); the dependence of actuality on independent, previous events (Secondness); and the requirement that there be *some* suitable successors to any given actuality (Thirdness).

CONCLUDING REMARKS

In conclusion I would like to raise several very general questions about the kind of relation Hartshorne's methodology presupposes between the logical and the phenomenological aspects of process. In view of his strong claims on behalf of the use of formal logic, to which he assigns the fundamental responsibility for establishing the strict standards by which claims are to be judged as either possible or necessary, it may seem that logical considerations overshadow phenomenological ones in Hartshorne's method. Indeed, this tendency is probably to be expected in a philosophy that attempts to discover the abiding features of process itself. Reason's reach exceeds our observational grasp, or what's a metaphysics for?

At the same time, however, Hartshorne explicitly intends to hew to "a phenomenological aspect of philosophizing"[57] and has held since 1937 that "metaphysics is the generalization of phenomenology."[58] It would be interesting to know, therefore, just how Hartshorne currently understands the contribution that lived experience, phenomenologically considered, can make to philosophical method and how much weight is to be given to it. This question becomes especially interesting in light of Hartshorne's idealistic axiom that "to be is to be known," relativized in his system to mean, "to be is to be known by some conceivable observer," and in light of his theory of the modal coincidence of logical and real possibility. Radical empiricists, phenomenologists, and contextualists will want to know whether experiential phenomena are really given sufficient attention in Hartshorne's actual practice, despite his methodological stipulations, or whether they appear to serve primarily simply as suggestive stimuli for performing the *logical* moves relevant to inspecting the categories.

Those who recognize a subtle and important methodological difference between "experience seeking understanding" and "understanding seeking exemplification in experience" may wonder whether Hartshorne's masterful case for an a priori metaphysics has been advanced at the expense of elucidating concrete empirical and phenomenal contextuality. To the extent to which the whole methodological drift of his philosophy moves away from concreteness and toward abstractness, in the direction of logical invariance and away from contextual variables, it invites certain questions. Does methodological omission of what is concrete about "concreteness" have the effect of obscuring what is most vital to the principle of process? Is it the case that the "concrete" then becomes a distinction that makes no ultimate difference? How might such a method guard against giving the unwanted impression that concrete actuality serves mainly as a vehicle for displaying the a priori truths of which it is a mere instantiation? Hartshorne surely does not mean to endorse a kind of metaphysics of phenomenological redundancy, whereby human experience is important simply because it comes in handy for supplying concrete illustrations or instances of the most general *logical* truths that can be known a priori. The methodological issue, however, is whether his procedure so inflates the prerogatives of abstract logic as to risk attenuation of the principle of process.

This leads to the related question as to whether Hartshorne's method is primarily controlled by logical considerations whose phenomenological applicability is limited or inconclusive at just the points of most controversy. For example, on the difficult question of whether process is continuous or discrete, Hartshorne sides with Whitehead against Peirce and holds the metaphysical position that processes or concrete actualities are discrete units of experience. The phenomenological basis for this account, however, is hard to see. Hartshorne admits that perception of the non-human world reveals only "gross outlines" that are "vague in every spatial and temporal way as to exact details," and beyond a certain point perception is "neutral, or indefinite . . . in large part non-committal" on the question of whether experience is quantized or continuous.[59] He even acknowledges that experience is "not given as discrete," and that there is an "apparent continuity of process" and an "apparent lack of distinct units."[60] The problem then is that if no process directly exhibited in human experience seems to come in clearly discrete units, this phenomenological feature is in puzzling discrepancy with the metaphysical position that actualities are discrete units of experience. Hartshorne tells us: "Here is a splendid example of a seemingly strong (empirical) case for a philosophical view, a case which is nevertheless inconclusive, and indeed can be opposed by perhaps a still stronger though non-empirical case. No better example of the difficulty of philosophical issues is needed."[61] But he does not tell us, in the subsequent non-empirical defense he supplies on behalf of event pluralism, how exactly the metaphysical account of reality as composed of discrete, individual experiences or unit-events can find any clear basis in experience at all. If phenomenological analysis determines that the data of experience are vague or neutrally non-committal as to the question of continuity or discreteness, then why may not metaphysical generalization also leave open the question of whether the nature of experience as such is discrete or continuous?

Those of us who have learned as much, if not more, from Charles Hartshorne's writings as from Whitehead's can fully appreciate the way in which Hartshorne has brilliantly carried out the method Whitehead recommended when he advised "the use of . . . a matrix . . . to argue from it boldly and with rigid logic. The scheme should therefore be stated with utmost precision and definiteness, to allow of such argumentation."[62] There is another side, however, to Whitehead's own methodology, one in which both logical and phenomeno-logical aspects have the status of context-dependent factors in process. In some contrast to this, Hartshorne treats the a priori as indifferent to all temporal contexts. How far, then, we may wonder, does Hartshorne's method require the assumption that we context-conditioned creatures are indeed able to frame a scheme of philosophical categories with a logical rigor that evades the contingencies of our temporal context? In actual practice, of course, no philosopher will presume to ignore what Whitehead knew were the "unformu-lated qualifications, exceptions, limitations and new interpretations in terms of more general notions" which throw suspicion on any logical scheme of categories.[63] It would therefore be interesting to know what Charles Hartshorne himself would regard as the chief methodological qualifications, exceptions, limitations, or new interpretations in terms of more general notions that could conceivably confront his categories with the need for revision.

NANCY FRANKENBERRY

DEPARTMENT OF RELIGION
DARTMOUTH COLLEGE
MARCH 1987

NOTES

1. Charles Hartshorne, *Creative Synthesis and Philosophical Method* (La Salle, IL: Open Court, 1970), p. 25 (hereafter cited as *CSPM*).

2. *CSPM*, 14. Cf. Charles Hartshorne, *Whitehead's Philosophy: Selected Essays, 1935–1970* (Lincoln: University of Nebraska Press, 1972), p. 115 (hereafter cited as *WP*).

3. *CSPM*, 24, 33.

4. *CSPM*, 24, 22.

5. *CSPM*, 73f.

6. Cf. *CSPM*, 100, 64.

7. Charles Hartshorne, "Our Knowledge of God," in *Knowing Religiously*, ed. Leroy S. Rouner (Notre Dame: University of Notre Dame Press, 1985), p. 52.

8. *CSPM*, 159.

9. Charles Hartshorne, *The Logic of Perfection and Other Essays in Neoclassical Metaphysics* (La Salle, IL: Open Court, 1962), p. 53 (hereafter cited as *LP*). Hartshorne follows G. H. von Wright in this distinction. Cf. G. H. von Wright, *An Essay on Modal Logic* (Amsterdam: North-Holland Publishing Co., 1951), pp. 66–77.

10. *CSPM*, 162; cf. *LP*, 284 where Hartshorne suggests that "2 plus 2 are 4" may be metaphysical as well.

11. This schema is a working application of Hartshorne's own method of formal classification. The discussion here is indebted to George L. Goodwin, *The Ontological Argument of Charles Hartshorne* (Missoula: Scholar's Press, 1978), pp. 14–20, an interpretation endorsed by Hartshorne.

12. *LP*, 285.

13. *CSPM*, 21–22.

14. *CSPM*, 18, 31.

15. *CSPM*, 19–20.

16. Charles Hartshorne, "The Development of My Philosophy," in *Contemporary American Philosophy: Second Series*, ed. John E. Smith (London: Allen and Unwin, 1970), p. 220.

17. *CSPM*, 32, 282.

18. Charles Hartshorne, *Beyond Humanism: Essays in the Philosophy of Nature* (Chicago: Willet, Clark and Co., 1937; Lincoln: University of Nebraska Press, 1968), p. 292 (hereafter cited as *BH*).

19. *CSPM*, 69.

20. Charles Hartshorne, *Reality as Social Process* (Glencoe, IL: Free Press, 1953; New York: Hafner Publishing Co., 1971), p. 175 (hereafter cited as *RSP*).

21. *CSPM*, 72. Hartshorne offers two other examples in the form of the statements, "Necessarily, there are concrete actualities all of which are both externally and internally related, both absolute and relative," and "Necessarily, divine or infallible experience, having fallible experiences among its objects, occurs." He suggests that the last formulation sums up the others. I suggest that the statement that must qualify as a necessary existential truth, if one is to draw the theistic conclusion that Hartshorne himself draws, is the following: Necessarily, divine creative synthesis of all creative syntheses occurs. It is puzzling that no such formulation appears in Hartshorne's discussion at *CSPM*, 172.

22. Cf. Charles Hartshorne, "Response to Peters," in *Existence and Actuality, Conversations with Charles Hartshorne*, ed. John B. Cobb, Jr., and Franklin I. Gamwell (Chicago: University of Chicago Press, 1984), p. 15. Some would want to argue here that the alternative to necessity is not "nothing," but something else existing contingently. It

is not clear to me whether Hartshorne can rule out this move except by invoking his "principle of contrast."

23. *CSPM*, 159–162.

24. Charles Hartshorne, "The Neglect of Relative Predicates in Modern Philosophy," *American Philosophical Quarterly*, 14 (1977), p. 309, note 3 (hereafter cited as "NRP").

25. Two of the four principles referred to in this discussion are treated above. The other two, the "principle of balanced definiteness" and the "principle of least paradox" appear to be rather *ad hoc*. The former is an expression of an ideal aim and the latter is a sliding ruler for evaluating competing systems. With respect to the principle of balanced definiteness, Hartshorne advises that "the ideal of reasonableness is to combine balance with definiteness" in philosophical matters (*CSPM*, 93). I take this to mean: in the presence of extremists, try to split the difference! For a fine example of this principle in action, see "NRP": 309–318. With respect to the principle of least paradox, Hartshorne recognizes that "no position can be argued for merely on the ground that other positions present paradoxes," so he proposes that "one must decide which paradoxes are the really fatal ones, in comparison with those of contending postions" (*CSPM*, 88). The problem with this principle is the extreme difficulty of applying it. It tells us precious little, especially about *how* a philosopher might overcome the natural tendency to take his or her own position as the least paradoxical, shrugging off apparent problems as "not fatal" and levelling a *tu quoque* at contending positions. The prime systematic importance of this principle in Hartshorne's own philosophy, I believe, is that it helps him reject Kant's first antinomy rather than give up or modify his own psychicalism. Cf. "NRP": 317–318 and *CSPM*, 125, 235.

26. *CSPM*, 71.

27. Charles Hartshorne, "Categories, Transcendentals, and Creative Experiencing," *Monist*, 66, No. 3 (July 1983), p. 324.

28. For example, Hartshorne says that "From Peirce and James I accept a basic pragmatism (it is also a kind of existentialism): ideas must be expressible in living and behavior or they are merely verbal" (*CSPM*, xvi). Or see *CSPM*, 80: "Ideas are significant only if they can or could be believed, and there is no adequate test of the genuineness of belief other than this; can (and in suitable circumstances would) the belief be acted upon or in some sense lived by?" Cf. also *RSP*, p. 20–21.

29. Cf. *CSPM*, 71–75.

30. Cf. *CSPM*, 230ff.

31. *CSPM*, 75.

32. *CSPM*, 90, 91.

33. *CSPM*, 75.

34. *CSPM*, 75.

35. *CSPM*, 91f.

36. *CSPM*, 84.

37. *CSPM*, 85. Cf. his statement: "Mathematics, pure logical form, is almost as important in knowledge as observation. One reason for this is particularly significant for philosophy. The function of observation is not merely to decide for or against some hypothesis but ultimately to decide among possible hypotheses. We do not merely test explanations one at a time against facts; we bring to the facts a system of possible explanations to be evaluated against each other. The cogency of the procedure obviously depends, in part, upon whether or not the possibilities for explanation have been exhausted. To be sure of having surveyed all the possibilities, one must arrange them in a formal way, by means of a mathematical diagram, algebraic or geometrical" (*RSP*, 20).

38. *CSPM*, 85. The importance of intellectual history and of consulting both major

and minor figures in the history of philosophy (both East and West) is a major methodological motif of all Hartshorne's writings. See, most recently, his *Insights and Oversights of Great Thinkers* (Albany: State University of New York Press, 1983) and *Creativity in American Philosophy* (Albany: State University of New York, 1984).

39. *CSPM*, 85–86.

40. *CSPM*, 266.

41. The rules Hartshorne formulates for this purpose are the "principle of contrast," the principle of "contingent concreteness," the principle of "divine freedom," the principle of "divine inclusiveness," and the "classical principle." The last three deserve much closer critical scrutiny than I can give here. See *CSPM*, 264–65.

42. *CSPM*, 266, 271.

43. *CSPM*, 280.

44. Charles Hartshorne (with William L. Reese), *Philosophers Speak of God* (Chicago: University of Chicago Press, 1953), p. 2 (hereafter cited as *PSG*).

45. *CSPM*, 99.

46. This derives from the "law of polarity" found in the work of the American philosopher and logician Morris R. Cohen. Cf. Morris R. Cohen, *A Preface to Logic* (New York: Meridian, 1956), pp. 87–89, and *PSG*, 2. Hartshorne speaks also of the "principle of non-invidiousness," explaining at *CSPM*, 269: "The principle of contrast and that of non-invidiousness are closely connected and scarcely more than two ways of formulating one intuition."

47. *CSPM*, 100.

48. *CSPM*, 100–101. Hartshorne's logic of ultimate contrasts has only a very dim analogy to the Hegelian dialectic, as this table makes clear.

49. In several places, Whitehead does make explicit the idea that the relation between present and future is not symmetric, as when he states in *Adventures of Ideas* at p. 254: "Evidently this mutual immanence and constraint of a pair of occasions is not in general a symmetric relation. For, apart from contemporaries, one occasion will be in the future of the other. Thus the earlier will be immanent in the later according to the mode of efficient causality, and the later in the earlier according to the mode of anticipation. . . ."

50. *CSPM*, 210.

51. *CSPM*, 61.

52. The important qualification here is that Hartshorne's idealist assumption ("to be is to be known") is combined with an epistemological realism that recognizes objects of perception independent of the perceiver. Furthermore, it is the principle of asymmetrical relationality that allows Hartshorne explicitly to reject any notion of "organic wholes" that leads to absolute idealism (cf. *CSPM*, 212, 83, 104, 128, 197).

53. Charles Hartshorne, "A Revision of Peirce's Categories," *Monist*, 63, No. 3 (July, 1980), p. 280 (hereafter cited as "RPC").

54. "RPC", 280, 285–286.

55. "RPC," 282.

56. "RPC," 282.

57. *CSPM*, 75.

58. *BH*, 269.

59. *CSPM*, 194.

60. *CSPM*, 194, 192.

61. *CSPM*, 192.

62. Alfred North Whitehead, *Process and Reality*, David Ray Griffin and Donald Sherburne, eds. (New York: Free Press, 1978), p. 9 (hereafter cited as *PR*).

63. *PR*, 8.

16

Lewis S. Ford

HARTSHORNE'S INTERPRETATION OF WHITEHEAD

For many years Hartshorne has been among the foremost proponents and interpreters of Whitehead's philosophy. As early as July 1935 he responded to "Some Criticisms of Whitehead's Philosophy,"[1] and has written many other essays on Whitehead's philosophy over the years. Those from 1935 to 1970 have been conveniently collected in *Whitehead's Philosophy* (WPE).* On the strength of these publications Hartshorne has been primarily regarded as a disciple of Whitehead's who has assiduously sought to propagate the truths of the master.

This common perception of their relationship scarcely does justice to the independence and originality of Hartshorne's thought. He seems to have arrived at the basic philosophical convictions that have governed his career before he made any serious acquaintance with Whitehead. This can be documented by means of his dissertation, which was written at Harvard in 1922, before he had any personal contact with Whitehead or had read very much of Whitehead's besides *The Concept of Nature*. This dissertation has been analyzed for us by William Lad Sessions (TPP 10–34). What Whitehead seems to have taught Hartshorne was the asymmetrical character of prehension, enabling Hartshorne to organize his internal and external relations in terms of relations internal to one pole and external to the other, thereby enabling him to affirm both monism and pluralism in a more precise manner. Also, Whitehead's example of two natures for God enabled Hartshorne to conceive of God's absolute characteristics as abstract, while the relative characteristics were concrete (TPP 6–8).

Hartshorne once described his early philosophy as a synthesis of James and Royce, with an assist from William Ernest Hocking.[2] Nevertheless, it has remarkable affinities with Whitehead's philosophy, especially as modified

---

*See *A Note on References* for abbreviations of frequently cited works.

through contact with his thought. It is small wonder that Hartshorne should champion the other's philosophy, though not in the way that William A. Christian, Victor Lowe, Ivor Leclerc, and others have done. They are close students of the text of Whitehead, intent upon giving us a responsible and accurate interpretation of the texts. Hartshorne recognizes that his "primary aim has always been to arrive at truth through Whitehead, or to make truth accessible to others through him, more than to ascertain or communicate the truth about Whitehead" (WP 3).

While some divergence between Hartshorne and Whitehead has long been recognized, its extent was seldom appreciated until the differences were catalogued by David Ray Griffin (TPP 35–57). After a thorough study of those passages in which Hartshorne explicitly points out where he differs from Whitehead, Griffin proposes seven basic differences: (1) God is a single actual entity for Whitehead, but an unending temporal series of divine occasions for Hartshorne, each fully including its predecessors; (2) Hartshorne denies any need for eternal objects, seeing specific possibilities as temporally emergent; (3) Hartshorne takes secondary qualities (such as colors) to be first emergent in the experience of high-grade sentient organisms, while Whitehead argues that the same sensa are ingredient in the low-grade occasions (e.g. in human experience), though functioning in diverse ways; (4) Hartshorne's philosophic method and concept of metaphysical principles is more uncompromisingly rationalistic than Whitehead's (though Griffin—unlike myself—finds this contrast has been largely overdrawn, more apparent than real); (5) Hartshorne once held that contemporary occasions could prehend one another, but now agrees with Whitehead that they cannot; (6) Hartshorne denies that the subjective immediacy of an occasion is lost in being taken up into God's consequent nature, while it is a disputed point whether Whitehead thought otherwise; and (7) Hartshorne denies any real genetic succession within a single actual occasion, finding Whitehead's talk of 'earlier' and 'later' phases to be misleading.

In a companion essay, exploring these differences from a Whiteheadian stance which sought to affirm the existence of eternal objects, I noted four more differences: (8) the laws of nature are divinely imposed for Hartshorne, while they are immanent for Whitehead, expressing the regularities of causal inheritance; (9) lacking a doctrine of eternal objects, Hartshorne cannot explain divine persuasion in terms of providing initial subjective aims; (10) nor can subjectivity be understood in terms of subjective aim; finally, (11) their concepts of 'panpsychism' differ (TPP 58–83).

While taking into account both the profound similarity and the many differences between these two process thinkers, the present essay seeks to show how our interpretation of Whitehead could be affected by Hartshorne's approach. It does not attempt to revise or update that list of divergencies, except incidentally, since only some are important for the way we interpret Whitehead (primarily 1, 2, 6, 7, 9–11). As many, particularly process theologians, come to the reading of Whitehead after considerable study of Hartshorne, and thus read Whitehead through Hartshorne's spectacles, a close study of these spectacles is clearly in order.

We shall consider four topics: (a) God, (b) eternal objects, (c) prehension, and (d) 'perishing'.

(a) *God*. Whitehead speaks of God as a single actual entity, whose consequent experience of the world forms a single everlasting concrescence. At the same time, however, it is not at all clear how God, as a never ending concrescence, could influence the world. Actual occasions must first perish in order to be prehended by subsequent occasions. In 1936, years after the publication of *Process and Reality*, A. H. Johnson put the question to Whitehead: "If God never 'perishes', how can he provide data for other actual entities? Data are only available after the 'internal existence' of the actual entity 'has evaporated' " (PR 220/336). Whitehead responded, "This is a genuine problem. I have not attempted to solve it" (EWP 9f). Hartshorne does have a solution, although it requires that we modify the conception of God as an everlasting concrescence: let us reconceive God as a personally ordered society of divine occasions, each of which in turn is a cosmic unification of that present moment. Then each divine occasion, once past, can be prehended by the superseding occasions. This emendation may have its own problems, particularly in that this cosmic unification of the present moment defines a privileged meaning to simultaneity contrary to relativity physics.[3] Yet it overcomes a genuine difficulty in Whitehead's conception, and few alternative solutions have been proposed.[4]

Hartshorne's modification is facilitated by his understanding of the primordial nature as objective, which is not Whitehead's original understanding. Here we need to recognize that our two thinkers approach the theory of two divine natures in different ways. God, as first conceived by Whitehead, enjoyed the entire wealth of conceptual possibility, although this deity was only very thinly cerebral, absent-mindedly aloof from worldly affairs, akin to Aristotle's unmoved mover. The problem was to render him more personal, more involved in the world, and this was effected by adding physical feelings to his conceptual feelings and integrating the two. Hartshorne's God was already personal and all-inclusive. Dipolarity permitted a clear distinction between the universal and the concrete, such that the divine essence could be conceived as included within (by being prehended by) God's concrete states.

If this difference is overlooked, it becomes all too easy to conceive Whitehead's primordial nature along Hartshornean lines as a permanent atemporal abstract essence always included within the everlasting consequent nature. If the primordial nature embraces the complete multiplicity of eternal objects, these would be *always, everlastingly* present, because repeatedly prehended by an endless sequence of divine occasions. (Such everlasting subsistence is not required by Whitehead's original conception, because while all are nontemporally available, only those relevant to the given situation need be temporally present now.) In Hartshorne's own case, this permanent essence is streamlined down to those necessary properties God must at all times exemplify. If God is reconceived as an unending series of divine occasions bound together by a common characteristic, as in Hartshorne's modification, then the primordial nature becomes that 'defining characteristic', an objective element which every divine occasion embodies. Then the only subjective unifying element becomes the consequent nature, pure and simple, now quantized in terms of the physical feelings of the successive divine occasions. Since God can then unify his experience only by means of the consequent nature, it would appear that this could only be possible in terms of an unending series of divine temporal unifications.

But the primordial nature for Whitehead is not an inert, objective essence; it is a conceptual activity, a concrescence of conceptual feeling—a thinking on thinking, if you will. It is an abstraction from the total reality of God, to be sure, deficient in actuality and devoid of consciousness (PR 343/521), but this does not render it merely abstract in the sense of being an eternal object or a multiplicity of eternal objects. The consequent nature does not include the primordial nature in the sense in which a prehending occasion includes some datum it is prehending, for God's primordial feelings are aboriginal and hardly derived, particularly not from the world. The aboriginal conceptual and derived physical feelings are then woven together to constitute God's unified experience. This is a different kind of integration than that proposed by Hartshorne.[5]

(b) *Eternal Objects*. Hartshorne finds this doctrine a needless complication in a process metaphysics, one that may even compromise the ultimacy of creative process (WPE 163f; CSPM xv; RSP 20). As Griffin writes, "It makes the process seem to be not genuinely creative, but to involve only a shuffling of eternal realities, making the temporal world a mere duplicate reality" (TPP 40; cf. WPE 32). In my earlier essay (TPP 58–65) I defended Whitehead on this point, but it must be admitted that Hartshorne can make a very good case for the temporal emergence of quality (see TPP 37–45, 67–72). Yet to some extent here our two thinkers are arguing at cross-purposes. Despite his examples, Whitehead seems to have primarily in mind the mathematical 'patterns' for his paradigmatic eternal objects, while Hartshorne focusses upon qualities, which are Whitehead's 'sensa'.

Hartshorne has an unpublished but very telling argument against discrete eternal objects, telling because it is not an argument from some other perspective, but obtains its leverage from Whitehead's own theory of extension. In *The Philosophy and the Psychology of Sensation* (PPS), Hartshorne postulated an infinite affective continuum in which every quality could be coordinated with every other multidimensionally, supposing there to be a continuum of qualities between those which we have definite experience of. To consider just one dimension of this continuum, the color spectrum, we note that it is not constituted out of discrete elements, out of least parts. Hartshorne reports this conversation with Whitehead: "I asked him if possible qualities were not continuous, and he replied, 'Have I not said so?' I think he has said that possible forms of *extension* are continuous, but he forgets this when dealing with colors. Blue, he said, is an eternal object. But there is the color continuum; how small a part of this is the blue that is a single yet definite quality? I put this to him and he said: 'A very subtle argument. Perhaps you have something.'[6]

It is possible to conceive of continua such as this qualitative continuum as constituted from a dense infinity of eternal objects (TPP 65), but it is also possible to conceive of discrete eternal objects as emerging out of a continuous background. Which is derived from which? Now it is evident that Whitehead takes the continuum to be prior to discrete entities in the case of the extensive continuum. Were this not so, the extensive continuum would have been constituted by a dense infinity of points. Yet the elaborate procedures of extensive abstraction, refined in terms of extensive connection (PR, part IV, chapters 2–3), indicate that a point is to be defined by a progressive narrowing from a larger region. In the same way we can conceive of a definite shade of blue. It becomes progressively more defined as needed. The specific shade is derived from an antecedent continuous background; the background is not constituted from any dense infinity of sensa.

Hartshorne follows Peirce in generalizing this finding: all possibilities are continuous, there being no discrete eternal objects. This argument is very strong with respect to qualities, but does it apply equally well to that other species of eternal objects, the patterns? Can we be certain that all the patterns, without exception, can be derived from a background continuum?

It does seem, however, that the eternal objects are largely dispensable. The five functions Everett Hall enumerates (identity, permanence, universality, abstractness, and potentiality) can be accounted for without recourse to anything eternal or uncreated.[7] The category of conceptual derivation enables the abstraction of features from the concrete actualities physically prehended. We need only suppose that these concrete actualities are not antecedently constituted of eternal objects. To be sure, any incomplete abstraction from the concrete past will leave traces of its temporal origin behind, but that need not be true in instances of total abstraction. Because these 'objects' are abstracted from all temporal origination, they appear to be 'eternal', and they can function in all the ways in which eternal objects can, providing for the identity of various things, for permanence over time, for universality, for abstractness (certainly), and they can serve as the possibilities for further actualization. Insofar as their character is concerned, they are indistinguishable from ordinary eternal objects, as they bear no tales as to their temporal origin by means of derivation from past actuality.

While mostly dispensable in Whitehead's mature philosophy, the (eternal) objects were quite necessary in his early philosophy of nature. In seeking to overcome the bifurcation into the 'causal nature' of modern science and the 'apparent nature' of ordinary experience, he adopted what is to all intents and purposes a phenomenological approach. In place of the traditional space, time, and matter, he adopted two primitives for his description, events and objects. Events are limited segments of the temporal passage. They have various topological relationships among themselves, but have no characteristics apart from the objects. Objects were first variously classified as sense-objects, perceptual objects, percipient objects, etc. Sense-objects (sensa) were gradually discovered to have a different relationship to time than events (and the other objects) have, one which is properly outside time, timeless. Hence the reclassification into eternal and enduring objects, which had already taken place in the earliest compositional layer of *Science and the Modern World* (EWM 67f). Up to this point there is no attempt to account for either objects or events by causation or derivation. It is only a question of what is required for the description of that which is. While these objects were eternal, they were not yet transcendent, being simply the purely immanent characteristics of events.

That was changed, I have argued, by the introduction of the epochal theory of time, transforming the eternal objects into being primarily transcendent properties: possibilities for future actualization (EWM 69f). Later, a theory of causation was introduced in terms of concrescence. These two features go a long way toward providing a way in which characteristics such as were described by eternal objects could have been derived. Whitehead might have come finally to realize that the category of eternal objects had outlived its usefulness and perhaps should be abolished, as was the category of reversion (PR 249f/381f).

Yet there is one function not mentioned by Hall that suggests the eternal objects cannot easily be replaced by other means: novelty. God provides each nascent occasion with a novel subjective aim, and thus is the instrument of novelty for the world (PR 349/529). If all functions and characteristics Whitehead assigned to eternal objects were derived from past actualities, there could be no new forms for the world. From the past only old forms can be derived. If God is the source of these novel forms, it would seem that the forms would either have to be created or subsist eternally. If not created, then only an infinite reservoir of unactualized possibilities would appear to be adequate to the task.

As has been widely recognized, subjective aim plays an essential role in Whitehead's metaphysics. It is the basis for a new and distinctive argument for God's existence: concrescence requires subjective aim, which can only be derived from God (WM 170–74, 189–92). Hartshorne does not deny this form of divine persuasion (DR 142), but it plays only a greatly diminished role in his thought. I once thought that he could not account for subjective aim because it required the eternal objects he rejected (TPP 80), but there is no reason why God cannot temporally fashion whatever special purposes the occasions require. Hartshorne distinguishes between God's "(1) eternal and unchanging aspect, his purpose as laid down before all the worlds, or rather before each and every world, and (2) the more and more particular purposes which mark the approach to, and (3) the achievements of purpose which mark the arrival at, any given point of time": (MVG 237). Temporally created aims would seem to function as well as eternally uncreated ones.

It is often difficult to distinguish between nontemporal creation and eternal subsistence. Moreover, the dynamics of the primordial envisagement of the eternal objects might suggest their nontemporal creation.[8] Whitehead is insistent, however, that the eternal objects are uncreated. God "does not create eternal objects; for his nature requires them in the same degree that they require him" (PR 257/392). Whitehead appears to have rejected the traditional role of God as creator, perhaps in response to David Hume's *Dialogues Concerning Natural Religion*. It may well have been the primary reason for his earlier atheism (1898–1925), for as soon as he discovered in the principle of limitation a way in which God could be the source of cosmic order without being the world's creator, Whitehead declared himself to be a theist once again (EWM 113f, 127f). It seems that Whitehead's fierce objection to God as creator (which would introduce a divine determinism within an event ontology) may have caused him to overlook an increase in explanatory power for his basic principles. According to the ontological principle, "every condition to which the process of becoming conforms in any particular instance has its reason" either in past actualities or in the present concrescence (PR 24/36). Here the principle is restricted to processes of becoming, but Whitehead also extends it to explain the derivative existence of eternal objects as dependent upon the primary existence of actual entities, but why cannot it also explain the nature of these 'eternal objects' as emergent from divine decision? If "There is no justification for checking generalization at any particular stage" (PR 16/25), this particular generalization seems quite warranted.

The contrasting importance of subjective aim to our two thinkers stems in large part from their differing theories of actualization. Hartshorne's account, derived in part from C. S. Peirce's view of the possible as continuous, opposes future possibility as indefinite to the past actuality which is fully definite. The present is then actualization, for Hartshorne holds "with Bergson that actuality is pastness, since presentness is a becoming actual rather than a being actual" (CSPM 118). Actualization then is the process of rendering the indefinite perfectly definite. Since the near future is more definite than the distant future, the transition to the near future might be regarded as part of the process of actualization. Normally, however, actualization is understood as a process in the present, where the present is understood to be quantized. Otherwise, Hartshorne argues, the paradoxes of Zeno (and of G. H. von Wright) would apply against the process of becoming.

For Whitehead, however, actualization cannot be analyzed in terms of purely formal terms. Rather the past causal influences are appropriated in terms of a novel organizing principle, the subjective aim derived from God. Physical prehension is realistically understood as the appropriation of the past actualities themselves, as objectified for that novel concrescent. Within concrescence these physical prehensions initially constitute a multiplicity, which must be brought into unity in the final satisfaction.

It is helpful to conceive of these prehended past actualities as the proximate matter Aristotle talks about, that "out of which" the new occasion is constituted. Thus the occasion has matter derived from its situation in the world and a form ultimately derived from God. The final form unifies the disparate matter into one determinate actuality, while its fusion with matter realizes or actualizes the form. Thus an actualized form need not differ from itself as possible, since its actualization is not a question of any further definiteness, or of any other formal feature. Whitehead notes this difference by distinguishing between 'definiteness', "the illustration of select eternal objects," and 'determinateness' which is "analysable into 'definiteness' and 'position', where . . . 'position' is relative status in a nexus of actual entities" (PR 25/38, cat. expl. xx). 'Position' so concretely understood entails the unification of physical prehensions.

By giving a dynamic meaning to 'definition' as 'rendering something definite', we may distinguish between these two kinds of actualization in terms of 'definition' and 'determination'. Hartshorne likes to quote Whitehead's dictum that "definition is the soul of actuality" (PR 223/340), doubtless understanding definition to be the *essence* of actuality. Soul, however, can also be understood as an activity requiring a material substratum. Definition may be the soul of actuality, but this soul needs to be embodied by means of determination.

Definition can begin with a totally vague or indefinite (continuous) background and achieve in actuality complete definiteness. Possibility is then the indefinite, actuality is definite. The modal distinction is lost if there are definite eternal objects. "If all the 'forms of definiteness,' each perfectly definite in itself, are eternally given by God," Hartshorne writes, "it is not altogether clear to me what actualization accomplishes'' (WPE 95). ''Possibilities are not to be viewed as qualitatively identical with actualities, apart from some quality-free factor of actualization. Actualization must somehow be qualitative enhancement, or the concept is vacuous'' (NTT 73). Clearly definition, or any other purely formal theory of actualization is impossible if there are any prior eternal objects. It would therefore be impossible for Whitehead but then he does not need to make use of any formal theory of actualization. If we neglect any modification of subjective aim, so necessary for creaturely freedom, there is no *formal* difference between the initial and the final subjective aim. In this sense Hartshorne is correct: there is no qualitative enhancement, just as there is no formal difference between Kant's possible and actual hundred thalers.

While there is no formal difference, each being as perfectly definite as the other, an unrealized eternal object lacks any relationship with actualities, while the realized one forms the way in which the particular multiplicity of actualities constituting the world of the concrescent occasion are unified. Hartshorne's objections assume a purely formal view, but Whitehead opts for a hylomorphic perspective.[9]

For Whitehead, actualization as definition blurs the tasks of past causation and present decision too much. He notes that ''One task of a sound metaphysics is to exhibit final and efficient causes in their proper relation to each other'' (PR 84/129). ''Explanation by 'tradition,''' i.e. by past data, refers to efficient cause (PR 104/159), which can be distinguished from the final cause, which is the ''subjective aim'' (PR 210/320). The data provide the content, the aim, the unification. There is here a clear difference in the way these causes shape the final outcome, but in actualization as definition all the causes, whether objective or subjective, render the present occasion more and more definite. As Hartshorne remarks, ''All causation is persuasion, is final as well as efficient.''[10] All causation is persuasive in the sense that it renders something more definite without determining it; it does not coerce a given outcome. For Whitehead, however, only final causation is persuasive, that associated with final causation.

Divine persuasion in terms of the provision of subjective aim is essential to his theory of (self-) determination. While it is not clear how it can be essential for definition, Hartshorne forcefully argues for the divine provision of aim: ''I think without God ordinary actualities could not possibly arrive at a definite decision about their relation to the vast past from which the matter, the content, of their experience comes. How, without a hint, an 'initial subjective aim', from God would they sense the relevance of the innumerable items composing the initial data they must unify in the 'satisfaction', the felt aesthetic value, which constitutes their actuality, and do this in such fashion that they and all the other actualities solving this problem can together form a viable world and avoid the two deadly catastrophes of unbearable monotony and unbearable mutual discord?''[11]

This hint, for Hartshorne, would be an indefinite possibility which the occasion turns into a definite actuality. Whitehead's theory of unification, however, seems to need very definite eternal objects, for otherwise how could they specify just how a particular multiplicity might be unified? Every occasion faces a unique world, and only a definite form can unify its particular multiplicity of past actualities. A dense grouping of alternative ways of unifying might be given, such that the occasion in deciding modifies the aim to be just the one decided on, but each must be capable of forming the unity, and this requires a high degree of definiteness. Yet just this definiteness will be resisted by Hartshorne, because on the theory of definition there would be insufficient contrast between the possible and the actual. Such definite aims are practically actual, if definiteness is our criterion of actuality. Yet aims should be purely possible, providing highly specialized lures inviting free response.

So the characteristic way in which God influences the world is quite different: God sets the widest possible limits within which freedom can operate. ''Process would come to an end if limits were not imposed upon the development of incompatible lines of process. The comprehensive order of the world is enjoyed, but not determined or created, by ordinary actual entities. Since the particular order is logically arbitrary, it must be either a blind fact wholly opaque to explanation, or the result of a synthesis which deliberately selected it. The only alternative to such selection is the chance agreement of the multitude of acts of synthesis. The theistic explanation meets the difficulty head on. A divine prehension can use its freedom to create, and for a suitable period maintain, a particular world order. This selection then becomes a 'lure,' an irresistible datum, for all ordinary acts of synthesis'' (WPE 164).

This is a strange 'lure' if irresistible, for then all occasions must conform to the world order divinely imposed for that cosmic epoch. A lure for Whitehead must be capable of being resisted. In consequence the laws of nature are not divinely imposed but are an expression of the average general behavior of the occasions of a given epoch, their joint response to divine persuasion (see TPP 75–77). Though Hartshorne's theory of the laws of nature is far from Whitehead's final theory, it is markedly similar to his first concept of God as the 'principle of limitation' (SMW). In both cases God does not determine actuality, but sets the limits upon what can be actualized in the present. In his later theory, however, God is not seen as limiting what can be (the data of the past do that) but as suggesting an ideal, itself modifiable, in terms of which that actualization can be brought about.

(c) *Prehension*. Monistic philosophies have typically argued that all actualities are (symmetrically) internally relationed, these relations being constitutive of both entites so related. Extreme pluralistic philosophies have actualities that are externally related, the relations making no difference to the relata. Hartshorne has sought to mediate between these philosophies by means of an asymmetrical relation, internal to one relatum, but external to the other. Thus the causal relation is non-constitutive of the cause, but constitutive of the effect; the temporal relation makes no difference to the earlier event, but the later event cannot be what it is without the earlier; the knowledge relation is external to the known, but internal to the knower. The last-named relation has been used with devastating effect against Thomas Aquinas's contention that the knowledge relation has only a logical, not real, connection to God (cf. DR). Hartshorne holds the asymmetrical relations to be primary, from which symmetrical relations can be constructed.[12]

Hartshorne learned this asymmetry of relation from Whitehead, who taught that "the relationship between A [an eternal object] and a [an actual occasion] is external as regards A, and is internal as regards a" (SMW 160). Hartshorne extends this asymmetry to Whitehead's basic notion of 'prehension', but Whitehead never makes that identification explicit, despite the fact that in a great many particular instances, the prehension is internally constitutive of the subject, while remaining externally related to its datum. This is true of, e.g. physical, conceptual, propositional, and intellectual feelings.

Many following Hartshorne's identification of prehension with the asymmetrical relation find Whitehead to be seriously inconsistent when talking of mutual prehensions. They assume him to be speaking of mutual physical (i.e. causal) prehensions among contemporaries, which is impossible if contemporaries are causally independent, as relativity physics assures us. Yet we should notice that "the mutual prehensions of all the members of a nexus" (PR 253/387; cf. also 76/118, 194/295, 230/351) does not specify any particular type of 'prehensions'. Furthermore the only contexts to mention 'mutual prehensions' seem to be those examining the nature of a nexus. A nexus is a very general grouping of actualities, broader than a society although less general than a mere multiplicity. What rescues a nexus from being a mere multiplicity is the relatedness of its members to one another by means of 'mutual prehensions'. These relations are extremely general, not yet particularized as the causal relations that bind societies together. They are simply the spatiotemporally symmetrical internal relations (cf. EWM 23–31) that Whitehead first termed 'prehensions' (in SMW). While this understanding of 'prehension' was overlaid with all the more specialized types of prehension in *Process and Reality*, the earlier type is not repudiated, as long as 'prehensions' are broadly construed as "concrete facts of relatedness" (PR 22/32).

These relations are symmetrically constitutive of events in that its spatiotemporal position depends upon its relations to all other events. 'Substance' theory of actuality may disregard such relations as merely external because non-essential, but this is not the early theory of an event, which carries over into the later theory as well. Such spatiotemporal prehensions form the widest context for all more specialized events and prehensions as the extensive continuum: "The 'extensive' scheme is nothing else than the generic morphology of the internal relations which bind the actual occasions into a nexus, and which bind the prehensions of any one actual occasion into a unity, coordinately divisible" (PR 288/441).

Thus, for the sake of this one kind of prehension, itself something of a carry-over from the earliest theory of prehension, Whitehead does not make the identificaton of prehension with the asymmetrical internal/external relation that Hartshorne does.

(d) *Perishing and the Phases of Concrescence*. Hartshorne has never cared for Whitehead's "analysis of the becoming of an actual entity (a concrete unit-happening) into 'early' and 'late' phases. I never could see in the 'perishing' of actual entities anything more than a misleading metaphor which, taken literally, contradicts the dictum, entities 'become but do not change.' An entity becomes during (from an external point of view) a finite time and is succeeded by other actualities which objectify it along with their other predecessors, the objectifications being more or less abstract or deficient (qualified by 'negative prehensions') except for the divine objectifications, in which, as I construe Whitehead, 'there is no loss, no obstruction' or deficiency" (WPE 2).

These objections are interrelated, and reflect the differing theories of actualization we have just examined. Both treat the act of actualization as atomic and indivisible, which for Hartshorne means it cannot have parts in any sense. If so, there is an abruptness to the actualization in the present, which renders the actuality completely definite, in contrast to the gradual process of becoming increasingly more definite by degrees which characterizes the transition from the future to the present.

Despite his insistence upon the *physical* indivisibility of the act of becoming, Whitehead does divide it theoretically into earlier and later phases of concrescence. This need not cause difficulties, as long as Whitehead's qualification is taken into account: "the act [of becoming] is not extensive *in the sense that* it is divisible into earlier and later acts of becoming" (PR 69/107). Were this possible, there would be an infinite regress. Moreover, if the occasion were divisible into smaller acts of becoming, then as these smaller acts become determinate, the overall concrescence would become determinate at intermediate places. Yet concrescence is one process of determination, such that all the phases before final satisfaction are all indeterminate to differing degrees.[13]

Because Whitehead's analysis of concrescence is complex, involving the integration of the many physical feelings by meaning of the form supplied by the final subjective aim, and also requiring successive modification of this aim to account for freedom, the analysis in terms of earlier and later phases is helpful.

That terminology can be understood in a straightforward sense in terms of genetic division: the many become one, only gradually, by stages.[14] Earlier phases have greater multiplicity of physical feeling, less determinacy, in line with the initial phase, while later phases are more integrated, having more determinacy, approaching the complete determinateness of the final satisfaction. This ordering is obscured, however, if such a phase as conceptual valuation is regarded as 'later', since it is quite problematic to conceive of the relation between the concrete and the abstract as essentially temporal. Yet, as Whitehead tells us, the mental pole of conceptual feeling is "out of time" (PR 248/380). Only physical feelings are in time, and they alone should be reckoned in determining the degree of determinateness (and hence the 'lateness') of any phase.

The process of unification (concrescence) contrasts markedly from the unity of its product. The product is completely determinate, while the process is a complex affair of determination, integrating both physical and conceptual feeling. All determination ceases in the completion of determinateness. Whitehead describes this cessation of becoming as the 'perishing' of subjective immediacy. The notion of 'objective immortality' appears as early as the 1926 essay on "Time" (EWM 195), but Whitehead seems to have hit upon the idea of subjective 'perishing' while meditating on Locke's doctrine of time as a perpetual perishing (EWM 194f, 209 n16): "Locke's notion of time hits the mark better: time is 'perpetually perishing'. In the organic philosophy, [the becoming of] an actual entity has 'perished' when it is complete. The pragmatic use of the actual entity, constituting its static life, lies in the future. The creature perishes *and* is immortal" (PR 81f/126). This oxymoron degenerates into self-contradiction if the different senses in which the contrasting elements are intended is not taken into account. It is as being that the actuality is immortal, for it is a potential for every supervening becoming. In contrast the becoming perishes in order to achieve being.

Here Whitehead is groping towards what we regard as a momentous discovery in the history of metaphysics: the recognition that the subject/object distinction is best understood as a difference in temporal modality. If the subject perishes in order to be the object, and this perishing is the perishing of time, it is but a short step to recognize that subject means present immediacy, and object pastness. This is the root of Whitehead's insistence that the objectivity we experience is our immediate past, not part of our present, and the basis of his final pansubjectivity, for *every* occasion once was present, enjoying its own subjective immediacy.

Unfortunately, 'perishing' as exclusively applied to becoming is obscured by one reference to time as a 'perpetual perishing'. Here Whitehead is considering the dissipation of the influence of superjective being in ordinary finite occasions: "The ultimate evil in the temporal world . . . lies in the fact that the past fades, that time is a 'perpetual perishing'. Objectification involves elimination. The present fact has not the past fact with it in any full immediacy. The process of time veils the past below distinctive feeling'' (PR 340/517). This text apparently suggests that there is a perishing of being, but that would be contrary to the fourth category of explanation. If a being is ''a potential for *every* 'becoming''' (PR 22/33), it must exist in some sense for each generation of becoming, even if only in a very attenuated sense. It cannot have entirely perished. Rather it is the becoming which perishes, while the being gradually *fades* in the background. These are the two senses in which time, as described by Locke, is a 'perpetual perishing'.

These two issues, the perishing of subjective immediacy and the facing of the objective past, stem from different stages in the composition of *Process and Reality*. The reflections on Locke with respect to perishing and objective immortality are to be found in the Giffords draft (EWM 194–97C), although Whitehead was first able to realize the strict identification of present immediacy with subjectivity only after the adoption of the revised subjectivist principle that ''apart from the experience of the subjects there is nothing, nothing, nothing, bare nothingness'' (PR 167/254D). On the other hand, Whitehead's reflections on the fading of the past do not appear until after he has adopted the notion of a consequent, temporal divine nature (introduced in stage I in order to account for divine consciousness: see EWM 227–29). If God temporally experiences each phase of the creative advance as it occurs, and perfectly retains this experience forever in the everlasting divine concrescence, then there can be a remedy to the fading of the past, ubiquitously experienced on the finite level. If destruction is evil, then the relentless destruction of the past is the ultimate evil. Yet God can overcome such evil by exercising a tender care ''which loses nothing that can be saved'' (PR 346/525). Since all being is preserved by God forever perfectly, what cannot be saved? This would seem to be the becoming of subjective immediacy, which must perish in order to attain objective immortality. Even God, in order to prehend any occasion, can only prehend its objective determinateness, not its subjective process of determination.

Now it would be quite natural to describe what God experiences or remembers in terms of 'objective immortality', but since Whitehead had already used that term in analyzing the temporal shift from subjectivity to objectivity (and his methods of revision precluded altering his initial usage), he here uses the term 'everlasting',[17] a term not picked up in the process literature. In the light of this development, his continued use of 'objective immortality' solely for ordinary objectivity has been doubly misleading, since it totally neglects the sense in which objective being fades and has no necessary reference to divinity which 'immortality' connotes. (We must recognize that there would still be 'objective immortality' quite apart from God's consequent experience, since that doctrine of Whitehead's was conceived before there was any anticipation that God would have a temporal nature.)

Hartshorne's concern with 'objective immortality', as he uses the term, has been limited to the retention of objective being within the divine memory. This is the sense in which 'objective immortality' has been taken up into the process discussion, not in terms of Whitehead's original usage. This is quite understandably so, for we expect 'objective immortality' to have the perfect unfadingness only divine experience can bestow.

Hartshorne has been a staunch defender of Whitehead's contention that in God no objective being is lost. This means, in Hartshorne's terms, that nothing ultimately perishes. Paul Weiss once wrote: "To avoid affirming that God keeps past evils in existence, they [Whitehead and Hartshorne] are forced to suppose that God gives being only to that portion of the past that can be made part of a cosmic harmony. . . . But then something occurred, to wit past evils, which God does not preserve."[18]

Hartshorne's response amply shows that this interpretation is foreign to Whitehead's intent. I agree, particularly because evil is not an actuality, but arises from conflict between actualities.[19] If in the divine experience these conflicts can be resolved by being absorbed into a greater harmony, then all (objective) actualities can be incorporated into God without any loss. As Hartshorne notes, "Whitehead has explained how what is aesthetically incompatible on a simple level of prehension, can be made compatible by suitable supplementation of imaginative or conceptual material."[20]

Is not this precisely what is required by such passages as the following? God's "subjective aim prehends every actuality for what it can be in such a perfected system [the consequent nature]—its sufferings, its sorrows, its failures, its triumphs, its immediacies of joy—woven by rightness of feeling into the harmony of universal feeling, which is always immediate, . . . moving onward and never perishing. The revolts of destructive evil, purely self-regarding, are dismissed [but are not thereby eradicated] into their triviality of merely individual facts; and yet the good they did achieve in individual joy, in individual sorrow, in the introduction of needed contrast [i.e. the imaginative supplement] is yet saved by its relation to the completed whole [the total harmony]" (PR 346/525).[21] Thus we are explicitly told that the individual facts bearing the revolts of destructive evil are saved in the divine experience; they are not what cannot be saved.

Whitehead's speculative doctrine here profoundly confirms a very central doctrine of Christian experience, one most fully enunciated and reasserted by Martin Luther. As Paul Tillich expresses it, we are accepted by God despite our unacceptability. If God were to exclude all evil and other shortcomings from the divine experience, we would be only very fragmentarily prehended. If we are "to have a portion of the life to come," we have no secure place if this were to depend wholly on our merits, and not upon divine grace. Salvation, at least in any Christian sense, depends upon God fully and without reservation including within his experience all the being which we are, as Hartshorne so forcefully argues in this essay.

Yet what is that which is lost because it cannot be saved? Hartshorne notes: "This appears to imply that something is left out or lost. I think this is a misinterpretation, though a natural one."[22] He then backs up that claim by showing in considerable detail that no (objective) *being* is excluded from God's experience, but we are never told what cannot be saved. I have argued above that it is the perishing of subjective immediacy, but Hartshorne rejects this: "'Perishing,' as a sort of drying up of subjective immediacy, would be a change, or nothing that I can imagine" (WPE 166), and we are expressly told that actual entities become, but do not change (PR 80/124).

Perhaps his most explicit rejection occurs in a recent essay taking issue with Robert C. Neville concerning 'perishing': "I hold that the satisfaction contains its process of becoming ('the being cannot be abstracted from the becoming'), so that to prehend a past satisfaction is to prehend the becoming, the subjective immediacy itself, of the past actuality. The past presentness, the past becoming (which did not prehend itself, it simply was itself) is now prehended. And I see Neville's and others' arguments against this as verbal confusions. Prehending is retrospective, and past process is what is given. Nothing is lost, with the qualification that all nondivine prehending is more or less indistinct (Whitehead's 'negative prehensions') so that, except for God, much of the past is dismissed as irrelevant and in this sense is indeed lost. But not for God, by whose adequate prehending actualities 'live forevermore'" (PS 10:93f).

Several factors may account for Hartshorne's rejection of subjective perishing, among them four: (1) the relative status of the past, (2) the identification of being and becoming, (3) the particular way William A. Christian understands 'perishing', and (4) the differing ways our two thinkers conceive of actualization.

(1) As Hartshorne points out, succession does not depend "essentially upon perishing, upon the fading of immediacy as events cease to be present events," but occurs because later events include earlier events components. "It is the reality of the new *as added to that of the old*, rather that the unreality of the old, that constitutes process" (WPE 84). The present becomes past simply by being included in a new present event. Pastness is a shift in temporal status, not a change in the qualitative character of the actuality in question.

The fading of the immediate event as it recedes into the more distant past is a fading for us, but not ultimately. "The perishing [i.e. fading], taken anything like literally, is an illusion occasioned by the hiddenness of deity from us. But, as Whitehead at least sometimes explicates the terms, it has nothing to do with an internal change from vital actuality to a corpse or skeleton, but is merely the fact that the definite actual subject is now *also* object for further subjects. No longer is it the latest verge of actuality, since there is now a richer reality, including the once latest one. This has nothing to do, at least in my theory, with an inner shrinkage or impoverishment'' (CSPM 118). Thus while Hartshorne recognizes the temporal passage from subject to object, he questions whether the ontological transformation is as great as Whitehead is wont to suppose.

Although Whitehead is careful to place the occasion's satisfaction outside of its (present) concrescence (PR 84/129), it is very easy to interpret the satisfaction thus achieved as the present being of the actuality. If so, then the transition from the present to the past would be simply a shift in relative status, since it would be the same entity which is both the present outcome and the past datum prehended by successor actualities. Since present immediacy is paired with subjectivity, and pastness with objectivity by Whitehead, it would then make sense to see the shift from subjectivity to objectivity as involving merely a shift in relative status. But while the transition from present to past *could* be explained as simply a shift in relative status (this would make sense of *Science and the Modern World*), the shift as developed in *Process and Reality* requires a good bit more; in particular, the contrast between becoming as a process of determination and being as determinateness.

As to this distinction, Hartshorne remarks: ''When we are told that the indeterminacy of the actuality's self-creative process has 'evaporated' with the achieving of a determinate satisfaction,[23] this only means, I take it, that the particular resolution is henceforth definitive; i.e. the 'decision' cannot be made over again or otherwise. The process of deciding is not done away with, since it *is* the actual entity, and this, we are expressly told, can never change'' (WPE 166).

(2) The process of deciding *is* the actual entity, only if becoming is identical with being. This is precisely Hartshorne's position: ''the principle of process means that the entity *is* its activity, and to say that it lacks this activity is to say that the entity is not what it is'' (WPE 165).

Two ambiguities are involved here:

(i)   The principle of process says that an actuality's 'being' is *constituted* by its 'becoming', which could mean these are identical (so Hartshorne, Leclerc, Sherburne) or that the being is produced by the becoming (so Nobo, Kline, Ford).[24]

(ii)   Should 'being' be understood dynamically or not? Whitehead tries to use a simple dichotomy between becoming and being, where only a trichotomy will really do. (Unfortunately the terms necessary to describe such a trichotomy are not naturally available.) We need a triple contrast, between the static event (a), the dynamic event (b), and the coming into being or self creation of the event (c). Insofar as there is (a) unchanging endurance, there is similarity between successive events. (This similarity can be embraced within a single, larger event.) Insofar as there is (b) change, there is difference between successive events. Originally, this was Whitehead's sense of the flux of reality: ''the reality is the process'' (SMW 106). Process and becoming signified the dynamic flux of change characterizing the world. In this sense the being of the world *is* 'becoming'.

In the composition of *Process and Reality*, however, 'process' and 'becoming' came gradually to mean not the being achieved, but the way that being comes into being.[25] So much so, that the key terms are not now redundantly identified in the title, but contrasted: [Concrescent] *Process and* [Concrete] *Reality*, or *Concrescence and Concretum*.

Thus 'becoming' and 'being' can be contrasted either as the dynamic and static aspects of reality, or as the coming into being or self-creation of actualities, and the being so created. Unfortunately, the use of dynamic language to describe self-creation inevitably suggests that created being is somehow static. Thus Hartshorne speaks of God's remembering an occasion ''without any loss of its immediacy or vividness.''[26] If 'immediacy' is taken in the usual sense as meaning that no detail of (b) the dynamic being, including its sense of freshness and newness, is lost, this claim is surely true, but 'immediacy' in Whitehead invariably means (c) the occasion's own subjective immediacy of becoming. By making this distinction, we can say that (c) the subjective immediacy perishes in providing (b) an objective immediacy for God.

Hartshorne seeks to avoid any possible loss of [objective] immediacy in God by insisting that ''the entity *is* its activity'' (WPE 165). In this sense of 'activity', as the dynamic being we objectively experience, nothing has perished in God, although it quickly fades in the finite world. The being of the occasion is this activity (b), but this does not preclude there being another sense (c) in which the activity has come into being. While these distinctions can be observed, it must be recognized that Whitehead's decision to accommodate himself to ordinary language by expressing this complicated issue in terms of the simple contrast between 'becoming' and 'being' has contributed to the confusion on this point.

(3) In *An Interpretation of Whitehead's Metaphysics*, William A. Christian clearly recognizes the contrast between concrescent becoming (i.e. creation) and concrete being we have been urging. But one idiosyncrasy in his interpretation unfortunately requires the perishing of subjective immediacy (c) to entail the

perishing of [the being (b) of] the actual occasion itself as well. This is the teaching that the satisfaction is itself a subjective feeling which contains "the whole of the *temporal* duration of the occasion" (IWM 80).

This is affirmed despite those passages which assert the satisfaction lies beyond the process of concrescence (PR 84/129, 219f/335f), which Christian examines (IWM 43). To these we might add Whitehead's marginal note in his Cambridge copy: "i.e. the 'Satisfaction' is always objective. It never feels itself."[27] By assuming that the occasion subjectively enjoys its satisfaction for a duration after it has fully come into being, Christian makes it impossible to identify becoming with subjectivity or to interpret the perishing of subjective immediacy with the termination of the concrescence in the satisfaction. Rather the perishing of immediacy must now mean the termination of this being as felt in the final satisfaction (see EWP 318–21).

It is against Christian's interpretation that much of Hartshorne's critique is directed. Christian has, he argues, "mistaken the meaning of 'past' or 'perished'. 'Past' is a relative term, and cannot describe a quality of the actual entity, taken in itself. 'Perished' seems to describe such a quality, implying that the entity is dead, lacking in subjective activity. For this reason I think that the metaphor was an unfortunate one" (WPE 163). Perishing is not a qualitative change pertaining to particular characteristics of the being, but it is an ontological transformation from becoming to being. Hartshorne's criticisms are cogent insofar as they are directed against the perishing of an actuality itself and not just its subjectivity. Then perishing would clearly mean the loss of being.

(4) Perhaps the primary reason our two thinkers diverge with respect to 'perishing' can be found in their contrasting theories of actualization.* Hartshorne, with Peirce and Weiss, sees actualization primarily in terms of 'definition', the process whereby possibility, which insofar as it is indefinite includes many alternatives, is rendered more and more definite. The indefinite becomes fully definite and actual when it has excluded all alternatives. The final act transforming possibility into definite actuality occurs all at once, for Hartshorne subscribes to Whitehead's doctrine of the atomicity of becoming. Yet Hartshorne accepts this doctrine largely in order to meet Zeno's paradoxes, not because it is essential to actualization.

Hartshorne is committed to a purely formal approach to actuality. Consider the alternative, as expressed by his disciple Gene Peters: "To deny that a thing qua actual is its full definiteness or particularity is to commit oneself to the position that [sheer] actuality is a totally featureless something, a sheer surd—even for an omniscient knower."[28] If only the purely formal character of actuality were sufficient, concrete particularity could be replaced by eternal

---

*This point added in June 1988. LEH

objects. For Whitehead there must be something more, something by which eternal objects can pass from being unactualized to actualized. This something cannot simply be another eternal object.

Whitehead uses the quantum of time in order to explore the interiority and subjectivity of an occasion, an analysis which becomes focussed upon how determinate actuality comes into being. The process of definition is an important factor in actualization, but it is not the only factor. Definition is described in terms of the successive modifications of the subjective aim (PR 224ff/342ff) until its final form is reached. This is not enough in Whitehead's eyes, however, to constitute actuality. For the past actualities of the world as physically prehended at the outset must be synthesized together in a final contrast. The final subjective aim provides the formal means whereby the multiplicity of past actualities can be unified, while the actualities enable the form to stand out from among its near alternatives as the form actualized in that particular instance.

These past causal conditions play a role on Hartshorne's account, but only to serve as the means for achieving increasing definiteness. For Whitehead the past causes serve primarily as the content, or as we might even say, the matter of the final actuality. They are its matter, for it is out of these past actualities that the new occasion is made. In the end they provide no formal features, for these are already contained in the final form, but they provide the matter which transforms the final form from being a timeless possibility into a particular actuality.

While Whitehead does not use the term, we may properly characterize his as a theory of dynamic hylomorphism. It requires something more than form, and this "something" can be seen to be the matter out of which the actuality is formed. It is the difference between unactualized and actualized form.

In Whitehead's terms, if definiteness were sufficient, then actuality could be exhaustively analyzed in terms of conceptual prehensions. There would be no need for physical prehensions as well. The distinction seems necessary for there to be any divine temporal experience, because it is quite possible for a purely nontemporal actuality to know all the eternal objects. A timeless physical prehension is impossible, for it depends upon both the temporal emergence of the actual occasion prehended, and on the temporal subjective activity consequent to that emergence. Would Whitehead have come to affirm God's consequent nature had he not been already committed to a hylomorphic analysis requiring both timeless conceptual and temporal physical prehensions?[29]

Moreover, if actualization were only the progressive definition of the indefinite, then one stage would be as knowable as another. It would be subjective for its own process of actualization, while being objective for all others. But if concrescence is as complex as the hylomorphic account requires, then there would need be intermediate stages of concrescence.[30] We have no evidence that such intermediate stages can be experienced as objects by others, and this would violate the rule of relativity physics that only what is past can be prehended. Intermediate stages also lack the full unity required for objectification, having only the unity of propositions. Finally concrescence has the ontological status of becoming and hence is imprehensible, since only beings can be prehended.

None of these Whiteheadian reasons apply to Hartshorne's theory of actuality. Thus Hartshorne originally argued that God could even know contemporaries. Since the 1950s, however, he gave up this view, not because contemporaries as subjective were unknowable, but because relativity physics seemed to require it.[31]

As long as God was conceived as knowing contemporaries, divine prehension could be understood as strict inclusion. Whatever exists or existed, in the past or in the present, was included within the divine experience by means of prehension. This was strict panentheism, which Christian long ago argued was quite foreign to Whitehead's approach.[32] Contemporaries cannot be prehended, not only because of relativity physics, but because there is nothing to prehend. What God can and does prehend is the entirety of the past.

In treating present and past as relative terms, themselves correlated with the subjective and the objective, we have seen how Hartshorne's interpretation tends to diminish Whitehead's strong contrast. This may also follow from their differing understandings of what may loosely be called 'panpsychism'. Hartshorne's 'psychicalism' is really a form of pluralistic idealism, arguing that mentality is a feature of all actuality. It can be understood in terms of degrees of awareness, which extend to all actuality.[33] These degrees of awareness pertain to the being of each actuality, and need not be lost in the transition from present to past. Mind forms the primary category as the more inclusive, while matter is the derivative element so included.

Although Whitehead does not seem to have made the distinction explicit, the focus of his analysis is upon subjectivity rather that mentality. Thus the reformed subjectivist principle insists "that apart from the experiences of subjects there is nothing, nothing, nothing, bare nothingness" (PR 167/254). Thus subjects are primary, objects derivative. While the perishing of subjectivity involves no change in the character of an actuality, it does denote a shift from primary to derivative existence, for its past objective existence depends now upon the supervening actualities, including God. This is precisely the sense in which the occasions "perish and yet live forever more" (PR 351/533). By perishing in their subjective immediacy as primary existents in order to be objective, God can sustain them in the primacy of the divine experience forevermore.

For Whitehead, all present concrescences are equally subjective, but not all have the same mentality. The mental and the physical are properly characteristics pertaining to societies of occasions. Insofar as the occasions of a society actualize creative novelty, it is mental. Insofar as the occasions simply sustain the same enduring characteristic, the society is primarily physical. "This lowest form of slavish conformity pervades all nature. It is rather a capacity for mentality, than mentality itself. But it *is* mentality" (FR 33). I would rather say that it is not mentality, but subjectivity. For subjectivity is this capacity to be influenced by (novel) conceptual possibilities, including the capacity to decide between incompatible alternatives. Mentality first emerges, I think, in the actualization of novel possibilities.

Subjectivity rather than mentality is the necessary basis for becoming in Whitehead's theory. While mentality persists, subjectivity as present immediacy is precisely that which perishes in order to bring about being. Hartshorne has said of actualities (which would naturally include mentality): "They 'perish, yet live forevermore' is the final word of *Process and Reality*, and to this I adhere, whether or not Whitehead did" (CSPM 118). While it may be problematic in what sense they perish for Hartshorne, I hope I have demonstrated that both clearly affirm that they live forevermore in the divine life.

Most readers have noticed the differences with respect to (a) God and (b) eternal objects, but the distinctions with respect to (c) prehensions and (d) 'perishing' are quite subtle. Yet these differences may in the end be more basic, if not as spectacular. At issue is the difference between actualization as definition and actualization as determination. I find myself opting for determination, but only in ways chastened by Hartshorne's objections concerning the eternal objects and God. I seek a mode of determination utilizing temporal emergent forms of unity, which refers to God as an everlasting concrescence, yet providing a way in which this can interact with the world. Demonstrating this, however, is a task for another occasion.

LEWIS S. FORD

DEPARTMENT OF PHILOSOPHY
OLD DOMINION UNIVERSITY
JUNE 1985; REVISED JUNE 1988

*A NOTE ON REFERENCES

We shall be referring to these books by Alfred North Whitehead by the sigla:
AI   *The Aims of Education.* New York: Macmillan, 1929.
CN   *The Concept of Nature.* Cambridge: Cambridge University Press, 1920.
FR   *The Function of Reason.* Princeton: Princeton University Press, 1929.
PR   *Process and Reality.* Cited first according to the corrected edition of
              The Free Press, 1978, then by the original edition of Macmillan,
              1929.

RM   *Religion in the Making*. New York: Macmillan, 1926.
SMW   *Science and the Modern World*. New York: Macmillan, 1925. Cited ac-
            cording to the Free Press edition of 1967.

Books by Charles Hartshorne:
CSPM   *Creative Synthesis and Scientific Method*. London: SCM Press; La Salle,
            Ill.: Open Court, 1970.
DR   *The Divine Relativity: A Social Conception of God*. New Haven:
            Yale University Press, 1948.
MVG   *Man's Vision of God and the Logic of Theism*. Chicago: Willett,
            Clarke & Company, 1941. Hamden, Conn.: Archon, Books, 1964.
NTT   *A Natural Theology for Our Time*. La Salle, Ill.: Open Court, 1967.
PPS   *The Philosophy and Psychology of Sensation*. Chicago: University
            of Chicago Press, 1934.
WPE   *Whitehead's Philosophy: Selected Essays, 1935–1970*. Lincoln: Univer-
            sity of Nebraska Press, 1972.

Other books cited by sigla:
EWM   Lewis S. Ford, *The Emergence of Whitehead's Metaphysics, 1925–
            1929*. Albany: State University of New York Press, 1986.
EWP   Lewis S. Ford and George L. Kline, eds. *Explorations in Whitehead's
            Philosophy*. New York: Fordham University Press, 1963.
IWM   William A. Christian, *An Interpretation of Whitehead's Metaphysics*.
            New Haven: Yale University Press, 1959.
PS   *Process Studies*, for Charles Hartshorne, "Response to Neville's
            Creativity and God." PS 10/3–4 (Fall-Winter 1980), 93–97.
TPP   Lewis S. Ford, ed. *Two Process Philosophers: Hartshorne's Encounter
            with Whitehead*. American Academy of Religion: AAR Studies in Re-
            ligion, Number Five, 1973.
WP   Ivor Leclerc, *Whitehead's Philosophy: An Expository Introduction*. Lon-
            don: George Allen and Unwin, 1959. Washington: University Press
            of America, 1986.

NOTES

1. *Philosophical Review* 44/4 (July 1935), 323–44 (WP 21–40).

2. "Process and Nature of God," in *Traces of God in a Secular Culture*, ed. George F. McLean, O.M.I. (Staten Island: Alba House, 1973), pp. 131f.

3. These problems are examined in my survey, "God as a Temporally Ordered Society: Some Objections," forthcoming in the *Tulane Studies in Philosophy*.

4. I have proposed one, however, in "The Divine Activity of the Future," *Process Studies* 11/3 (Fall 1981), 169–79.

5. The last two paragraphs sketch some of the basic points of my essay on "The Non-Temporality of Whitehead's God," *International Philosophical Quarterly* 13/3 (September 1973), 347–76.

6. "My Enthusiastic but Partial Agreement with Whitehead," unpublished paper presented at the *XI. Congreso Interamericano de Filosofía*, Guadalajara, Mexico, 15 November 1985, MS. p. 7.

7. "Of What Use Are Whitehead's Eternal Objects?" pp. 102–16 in *Alfred North Whitehead: Essays on His Philosophy*, ed. George L. Kline (Englewood Cliffs, N.J.: Prentice-Hall, 1963).

8. This was my position in "The Non-Temporality of Whitehead's God" essay.

9. It is possible, however, to reconcile the claim that possibility and actuality cannot be formally distinguished with Hartshorne's demand that actualization should entail some qualitative enhancement. Let us suppose that possibilities consist solely of patterns, and are devoid of sensa. In that case sensa could be derived from past actualities, but they would need the specific patterns obtained by means of subjective aim to bring out any emergent qualities, hitherto inherent only undifferentiatedly in previous actuality. Then actual occasions would be capable of actualizing these newly differentiated sensa for God's and for our enjoyment. This would provide another reason why the world exists for God: apart from the world God would lack all enjoyment of qualities.

10. Personal communication to the author, December 1984.

11. "My Enthusiastic but Partial Agreement with Whitehead," pp. 7f.

12. Cf. CSPM, chapter 10, "The Prejudice in Favor of Symmetry."

13. This account of how Whitehead understands the atomicity of becoming is often overlooked because his final theory of concrescence is rarely in danger of being misunderstood as allowing for smaller acts of becoming. Yet his earlier theory, in which a physical occasion was superseded by a mental occasion (see the essay on "Time" of 1926: EWM 301–308) did just that (EWM 152–55). Furthermore, any attempt to combine his theory of transition in the Giffords draft, whereby the unified original datum of an occasion is constituted prior to its concrescence, with concrescence would constitute the sort of double unification within a single act of becoming excluded by this qualification (EWM 201).

14. Hartshorne recognizes that "the many become one and are increased by one" (PR 21/32) as Whitehead's novel insight (WPE 162), but does not take this process to be possibly gradual. Yet a great multiplicity might be first reduced to smaller and smaller multiplicities, before resulting in one final unity.

15. Early uses of 'perishing' and 'objective immortality' do not mention the 'perishing of *subjective* immediacy' (e.g. PR 60/94C, 81f/126C), while a later passage specifies that "actual entities 'perpetually perish' subjectively, but are immortal objectively. Actuality in perishing acquires objectivity, while it loses subjective immediacy" (PR 29/44). More precisely, but less pungently, the *subjectivity* (= becoming) of the actuality perishes in acquiring objectivity (= being).

16. Once the theory of consciousness is perfected by the introduction of intellectual feelings (in stage H), God as hitherto conceived as a concrescence of purely conceptual feeling could only be unconscious. To avoid this consequence, Whitehead experimented with the inclusion of divine physical feeling (stage I: see EWM 227–29).

17. 'Everlasting' is consistently presented in single quotation marks (PR 345–51/ 524–33).

18. *Review of Metaphysics* 5/4 (June 1953), 519.

19. In this sense, the medieval doctrine that evil is a privation of being finds an echo in this philosophy. For an analysis of the nature of evil and its overcoming in God, see my essay on "Divine Persuasion and the Triumph of Good," pp. 293–97, 299–304 in *Process Philosophy and Christian Thought*, ed. Delwin Brown, Ralph E. James, and Gene Reeves (Indianapolis: Bobbs-Merrill, 1971).

20. "Immortality of the Past," *Review of Metaphysics* 7 (1953–54) 108, citing AI 379.

21. Quoted by Hartshorne, ibid., p. 110.

22. Ibid., p. 105.

23. PR 220/336: "Its own process, which is its own internal existence, has evaporated, worn out and satisfied; but its effects are all to be described in terms of its 'satisfaction.'"
This is a change in the wider sense that there is a difference between successive states, if we take 'states' to mean both individual occasions and phases of concrescence. Yet since Whitehead has stipulated that 'change' applies only to the difference between successive occasions (PR 73/114, 79/123, 80/124), 'change' in his sense cannot apply here. We need a term for the wider sense. In one place Whitehead contrasts the macroscopic and microscopic senses of 'process' (PR 214/326f): in another place he terms it 'fluency' (PR 210/320). (Later on in the composition of *Process and Reality* macro- and microscopic are modified to macro- and microcosmic (PR 47f/75f, 215/327).) By this terminology, 'perishing' is an ontological transformation, which is an instance of microcosmic fluency.

24. See Jorge Luis Nobo, "Whitehead's Principle of Process," *Process Studies* 4/4 (Winter 1974), 275–84.

25. See my essay on "The Concept of 'Process': From 'Transition' to 'Concrescence'," pp. 73–101, in *Whitehead und der Prozessbegriff/Whitehead and The Idea of Process*, ed. Harold Holz and Ernest Wolf-Gazo (Freiburg: Verlag Karl Alber, 1984).

26. "The Immortality of the Past," p. 109.

27. Editors' notes to the corrected edition of *Process and Reality*, p. 396, ad 45.28.

28. Eugene H. Peters, *Hartshorne and Neoclassical Metaphysics* (Lincoln: University of Nebraska Press, 1970), p. 47, citing Hartshorne's *The Logic of Perfection* (La Salle, Ill.: Open Court, 1962), p. 165.

29. As a graduate student Hartshorne was convinced by William Ernest Hocking, one of his teachers, that "the future must be open, partly indeterminate, even for God" (TPP 7). But the means for developing this insight in terms of divine dipolarity and the asymmetrical nature of relations depended upon Whitehead's *Process and Reality* (cf. TPP 6–9).

30. As the third and final point of difference, Hartshorne writes: "I never cared for . . . his analysis of the becoming of an actual entity (a concrete unit-happening) into 'early' and 'late' phases" (WP 2).

31. See Frederic F. Fost, "Relativity Theory and Hartshorne's Dipolar Theism," TPP 89–99.

32. William A. Christian, *An Interpretation of Whitehead's Metaphysics* (New Haven: Yale University Press, 1959), 403–409.

33. See, e.g. Peters, *Hartshorne and Neoclassical Metaphysics*, Chap. 3.

17

Norman M. Martin

TAKING CREATIVITY SERIOUSLY: SOME OBSERVATIONS ON THE LOGICAL STRUCTURE OF HARTSHORNE'S PHILOSOPHY

1. A Reminiscence

B efore going into the main part of my discussion, I cannot resist the opportunity to express a personal appreciation of Charles Hartshorne.

My first contact with him was forty years ago as a graduate student in his seminar on Kant's *Critique of Pure Reason*. The course was admirably clear and thorough in its scholarly content. But perhaps of greater import was an exchange between him and me. In particular, he noted some logical problems in an argument in, if memory serves me, the Antinomies of Pure Reason. There was no question but that he was correct in his negative criticism. But then he proceeded to suggest, indeed it has always been a feature of Hartshorne that I admire that he typically will look for the positive content in others' thoughts, a revision of Kant's argument which Hartshorne said overcomes the difficulty he had discovered in Kant's original argument. Filled perhaps with the confidence imbued by a few courses with Carnap, I questioned whether Hartshorne had really succeeded in getting a logically correct argument for the point in question. Hartshorne took my objection as seriously as he would that of any colleague. Indeed after some discussion, he said he thought I was probably right and he would return to the question next time. The next session he started by thanking me, agreeing with my objection and presenting a revision, adding that he hoped he had it right this time. Unfortunately, he had overlooked yet another possibility which I then proceeded to point out. After a little discussion, he again thanked me, and the following time came back with an argument whose validity was indeed clear. The beauty of this exchange lay not only in his ability to take criticism from students, although I have known professors enough who could not, but that the whole exchange was carried out with total good humor and a total lack of defensiveness or hostility, certainly on his part and I hope also on mine. What was important to Hartshorne was the truth of the matter and it bothered him not at all that the criticism came from a baby-faced novice with more experience in directing artillery fire than arguing points on philosophy.

I finished the seminar and had yet another one (on metaphysics); then for a long time our paths diverged. When nearly twenty years later, I joined the faculty at the University of Texas, I again came in contact with him, this time as a colleague, I discovered that he not only remembered me, but that his memory of our exchange on Kant had been significant in convincing him to enthusiastically support my appointment. The last twenty years have taught me that this experience is in no way a "fluke"; Hartshorne is not only admirable in the creativeness of his thought, but also in the beauty of his soul.

2. Some Modal Logic

I now wish to turn to a review of some points on the semantics of modal logic. As will become clear, I have multiple reasons for doing so. I beg the indulgence of those of my readers who are already familiar with the subject.

One standard way of viewing the semantics of standard two-valued propositional logics is to consider it in terms of modal structures, sometimes called assignments, which are functions from the set of propositional variables to the set whose members are 0 and 1 (or alternatively, "true" and "false"). The values of complex sentences are of course determined from these "atomic" values by the usual truth table conditions. In the semantics of modal propositional logics, the modal structures are essentially the same as in standard logic except that we have in each case a set of assignments together with a relation (recently usually called "accessibility") defined on that set. The pair of a set of assignments and the accessibility relation goes under a variety of names—my own favorite is "modal assignment set". Modal operators are then specified using accessibility: for example, a sentence $\diamond S$—that is, "S is possible"—is true for an assignment A if and only if S is true in at least one assignment B which is accessible from A. Particular varieties of modal logic are specified by the restrictions on the accessibility relation (standard concepts remaining constant: e.g. a set of sentences is "contradictory" if it is satisfied by no assignment of any modal assignment set of the appropriate kind, a sentence is "entailed" by a set of sentences if every assignment of the appropriate kind that satisfies every member of the set also satisfies the sentence in question, and so on). In all of these, the assignments function rather like Leibnizian possible worlds and accessibility is from this point of view more or less relative possibility (i.e. A is accessible from B means, roughly, if B is the actual world, A is a possible world). In this way for instance, the system **K** is what is obtained by allowing all modal assignment sets, the system **D** those such that if for every A, there is a B such that B is accessible from A, the system **T** is what is obtained by requiring accessibility to be reflexive (i.e. A is always accessible from itself), **S4** with accessibility both reflexive and symmetric (A accessible from B implies B accessible from A) and **S5** with accessibility reflexive, symmetric, and transitive (A accessible from B with B from C implies A accessible from C).

When we turn to first order (or "predicate") logic, there are some special complications. As was the case in propositional logic, we would like the individual model structures to be like those of standard two-valued logic interrelated in the way model structures are related in propositional modal logic.

The standard model structure for first order logic consists of a non-empty set (ordinarily referred to as "the set of individuals", although there is no requirement or set of priorities that qualifies things as, or restricts things from being, individuals) together with a function which assigns an individual to every term and a set of n-tuples of terms to every n-place predicate; more clearly, if less accurately, it assigns a subset of the set of individuals to every predicate (less accurately, since this holds strictly only for one-place predicates). We are then able to define truth in a particular model structure as holding for an atomic sentence $Ft_1 \cdots t_n$ where F is an n-place predicate provided B is the set of n-tuples of individuals of A assigned by A to F, for each j, i_j is the individual of A which A assigns to t_j and the ordered n-tuple $<i_1, \cdots, i_n>$ is an element of B. As before connectives are treated by means of the truth-table definition and $\exists x B$ is true in a model-structure A if and only if B is true in a model structure which differs from A at most in the value assigned to B.

The above description spells out the structure of the semantics for first order modal logic, given as we have said that we want these semantics to be like that for modal propositional logic except for having first order, rather than propositional model structures as the elements of modal assignments sets related by accessibility. There is however one significant feature which our description has not clarified. If we take our current description literally, the set of individuals of each possible world is presumably chosen independently and it is unclear how individuals are to be associated from one "possible world" to another.

The simplest (and one of the most common historically) is to make the choice of set of individuals once and once only for each modal assignment set, thereby making the set of individuals the same for every "possible world". The disadvantage to this is that it excludes applications in which change involves change of individuals, such as ones in which the set of individuals is the (human) population of the earth and "possible worlds" are successive points in time. To see that this is not trivial, consider the so-called "Barcan formula":

$$\Diamond \, \exists x \, Fx \supset \exists x \, \Diamond \, Fx.$$

If $\Diamond$ indicates "true now or sometime in the future" and F will be true of my great-grandson, but of nobody else until he is born (and he will be, but is not yet), then there is a time in the future when $\exists x \, Fx$ is true but there is no present individual for which $\Diamond \, Fx$ is true. If however, the set of individuals remains constant and $\Diamond \, \exists x \, Fx$ is true in A, there is a "possible world" B accessible from A such that $\exists x \, Fx$ is true and hence an individual c in B such that Fc is true in B. But then if c is also an individual in A, there is an individual in A, namely c, for which $\Diamond \, Fx$ is true, i.e. $\Diamond$ Fc is true in A, and hence if the set of individuals is restricted in the indicated way, the Barcan formula is a logical truth. It is therefore clear that the interpretation above (about my great-grandson) cannot be represented if the set of individuals is restricted in the indicated way.

An alternative, in some sense, the opposite extreme, would be to make the status of being an individual belong critically to the particular "possible world" so that no individual is in two distinct "possible worlds" (at least in the same modal assignment set). One might term this alternative "the super-Hume-an model". In order to work modal semantics in this context, one must then introduce another relation defined on the union of the sets of individuals of the modal assignment set which we may term "representative of" and, for the present, represent with R. In the same rough intuitive sense for which accessibility can be said to be relative possibility, representativeness picks out that individual that for the purpose at hand (but not necessarily absolutely) can be regarded as being the same one in another "possible world". We can then adopt as interpretation of $\Diamond$D is true in A: There exists a model-structure B such that B is accessible from A and for every term in D, t_i, if a_i is the interpretation of t_i in A, there exists an individual b_i in B such that $Rb_i \, a_i$ (i.e. b_i represents a_i) and if B* differs from B (exactly) in that for every t_i in D, b_i is the interpretation of t_i in B* and D is true in B*. If it helps this can be expressed by saying that when D is reinterpreted such that whenever we referred to a_i in A, we now refer to b_i, D becomes true in B.

With this almost trivially modified interpretation of possibility we can adopt the same relativism with respect to representation as we did with regard to accessibility. There is at least one restriction on our relativism here: since we want it to be the case that if a "possible world" is accessible from itself, Fa $\supset \Diamond$ Fa should be true in that "possible world" with no further condition required. In order to guarantee this we must require the very plausible condition that R is reflexive—that is, that every individual represents itself (or, of course, herself or himself); this condition is especially trivial given that we are only talking about representing oneself in the same "possible world"; in this world at least, I must be me; I cannot help but be myself.

There are other conceivable restrictions which are plausible for many purposes, but not in my view as clearly neutral relative to all reasonable views of modal connection as to warrant "across-the-board" adoption. Two such (intimately related) are the principles that would require representation to be (relatively) one-many—i.e. [R(a,c) and R(b,c) and, a and b both in the same "possible world"] implies a and b are identical, or many-one—[R(c,a) and R(c,b) and, a and b both in the same "possible world"] implies a and b are identical. The principal reason for our hesitation is that it is not clear that we ought arbitrarily to exclude representation with division (as perhaps, in mytosis) or with merging.

For somewhat analogous reasons, it is not clear as to whether one should uniformly require R to be symmetric or transitive.

It might seem to many that we have overlooked the possibility of allowing but not requiring individuals to appear in more than one world. The reason why we do not is that if there is no other device—such as our relation R—to represent trans-"world" quasi-identity, we can capture the same effect by requiring R to be relatively one-one and an equivalence, while if there is such a device, the quasi-identity conditions are dispersed among two different devices, which seems to be at best an unnecessary multiplication of such devices.

Notice that the commonplace characterization of the structure of our semantics can be, to say the least, misleading. Our "super-Hume-an" semantic structure would seem to imply a metaphysical or epistemological view that individuals are ultimate particulars of such an extreme kind that it is impossible for any individual to exist in more than one possible world. Hence the issue between "super-Hume-an" semantics and semantics in which the set of individuals is constant (or for that matter, one in which individuals can occur in more than one, but not necessarily in all, "possible worlds") would appear to be a metaphysical question concerning whether the same individual (perhaps the same person) could—or indeed must—be in more than one world (note the similarity, for special cases perhaps even identity, to Heraclitus's question about whether someone can go twice into the river) or else perhaps the epistemological question as to whether it is possible to figure how to identify this when it occurs.

It is our contention that this simple identification of these technical choices with the metaphysical and epistemological questions they resemble is somewhat mistaken. In the first place we are no more required to interpret things in modal semantics than in two-valued semantics when there are significant linguistic or philosophical reasons against this. Neglect of this point has been the source of repeated mischief generated by assuming that some logical system is the only possible one and then attempting to derive important philosophical results from the special properties of a logical system (one might call this "the panlogical fallacy").

There is however a second objection, perhaps more important. Although in metaphysics and apparently also in epistemology, there is a real incompatability between the Heraclitean type of position correlated with "super-Hume-an" semantics and the alternatives we have mentioned, in semantics the relation is in fact simply that "super-Hume-an" semantics is more general.

To show that this is so, let us assume one believes in the kind of individuals that one has in the kind of semantics involved in the type of system in which the set of individuals is constant over all "possible worlds" (i.e. model structures) in a modal assignment set. Let us suppose that those individuals are i_j over an appropriate index set and the model structures are m_k over an index set. Then the ordered couples $<i_j, m_k>$ can be chosen to be the individuals of the correlated "super-Hume-an" semantics. Of course we then restrict R such that $R <i_j, m_k> <i_{j*}, m_{k*}>$ if and only if $i_j = i_{j*}$.

To express what is going on in somewhat less technical language, there is no necessary identification between a concept such as individual in a metaphysical sense (roughly, perhaps, things that are really and ultimately particular) or in an epistemological sense (perhaps, things whose concepts we are able to individuate) on one hand, and "individual" as it appears in semantics on the other. The latter is specified simply by being a member of a set which is otherwise quite arbitrary. In other words, a set of individuals in a semantic sense is not a set of things which have the properties of really being individuals, but is instead a set of things which will fill the semantic role of individual in the particular application. As a result, we are free to identify some notion of individual (perhaps metaphysical) instead with the cells of the partition generated by R when that is an equivalence relation, or indeed, yet other possibilities; we definitely do not need to identify metaphysical individuals with logical ones.

The point raised is of considerable generality. Just as "individuals" in semantics are not necessarily individuals (in some other sense), "possible worlds" are not necessarily possible worlds nor for that matter worlds at all, "accessible worlds" may not be accessible, while "possible worlds" may, for instance, be morally acceptable states of our world and so on.

The reason for this paradoxical condition is that the names used to refer to elements of a mathematical structure such as a semantical system have no fixed and necessary relation to the things normally referred to by those names; only the complex of relations specified is determined. To be sure there is usually *some* reason for the choice of names: sometimes that choice is actually the belief of the person who chose it that it really *is* exactly or something like the ordinary meaning of the term employed. But at times (as in our choice of "super-Hume-an"), it is an attempt to be amusing, or to be easier to remember, or to mark one of its standard applications—even if it is known that this is but one application among many. Thus, among algebraic structures, groups are not necessarily social, fields not necessarily rural, nor are spaces necessarily wide-open. Similarly, individuals may have a complex structure; they may be either concrete or abstract.

I grant that in other philsophical contexts this type of flexibility may be misleading or irresponsible and perhaps even impermissible.

In the same kind of way to assert that the semantics of a theory has a certain structure is not to claim any particular way by which that may be known. Again the names used for any particular structure in the semantics (say T) likewise normally makes no commitment as to who knows that this structure is the one that obtains or how this knowledge is acquired.

3. HARTSHORNE'S LOGIC

Let us now turn to Hartshorne's philosophy and more particularly to our views as to the logical structure it involves.

The first and most essential is that the basic structure is that of a modal semantics. More specifically, one in which possibility is associated with futurity. "Real possibility is real futurity,"[1] and he elsewhere clarifies that there cannot be eternal contingencies.[2]

In addition, Hartshorne makes clear that there are not alternative possible worlds, except in the sense of alternative "possible states of the actual world."[3]

The upshot of these specifications is that if we are to model this view of the world, we must have a modal assignment set whose members are possible states of the world. Viewing the situation from the present actuality, if something is now possible, this is because it is either now true or may become so in a state of the world which (if it actually occurs) will be a future to the present and that state is a possible future of the present state. This view of things allows us to specify that accessibility in a modal assignment set that models the world as Hartshorne sees it must be S4, i.e., accessibility must be reflexive and transitive. It is interesting and perhaps partially confirming that the varieties of modal logic which fit well with his discussions of the Ontological Argument appear always to be varieties of S4.

It is clear that the states of the world as so conceived are not intended to be restricted to some sort of snap-shot of the world but also to include assignments of truth values to sentences about the past and the future. There is however an important difference between the two. For a fixed present, there is one and only one past of that future. Relative to *our* knowledge, there may be indeed more than one conceivable past that may have led up to the present we actually have.

But only one of these is the actual past. At least one of the reasons for this is that the things now true were actualized at some time and so the set of present truths must include the statement of all those actualizations.

If you permit me a slight digression here, there is a structurally conceivable alternative that Hartshorne does not accept, although I am not absolutely sure why not. Suppose that at a certain possible state of the world A, there are two conditions X and Y which do not exclude each other and such that neither are true, but both possible, at A. Now imagine that someone makes a choice or performs an action that makes X become true and somewhat later, someone similarly makes Y become true. Now let us imagine that instead, starting from A, first Y is determined and then X. From many points of view, it would seem to be possible that the final set of determinations, viz. those all implied by A together with both X and Y, are the same and hence that the resulting state really has two possible pasts.

There are at least two ways of dealing with this, both of which are I think, generally in agreement with the views Hartshorne seems to want to insist on. The first one (which I think he would reject) would say that in principle this can and perhaps occasionally does occur, but of course in that situation we canot actually distinguish between the two pasts (since by assumption when both were true the world was determined in exactly the same way, *ex hypothesi*) and so the two are different only trivially. The second alternative is that for X and Y to be sufficiently specified, "X and then Y" is simply a different specification than "Y and then X" and hence we are left with only one past for each possible state of the world.

So we see that (either absolutely and in any event in all essentials), the state of the world includes the determinations that specify the past, since (at least in general) the present state differs from the past by having some things that were previously only possible, become actual, the state of the world acquires a sort of cumulative feature. Since Hartshorne holds that "the past is determinate, but the future is not"[4] and that "one-way dependence is the essence of time,"[5] we are not surprised to note that we have a structure similar to that of the semantics of intuitionistic logic.

This suggestion is further supported by Hartshorne's treatment of future propostions. Specifically the question involves the status of "X will do A" at the state of the world B, X doing A and X not doing A or both possible at B. Note in passing that his position is *not* dependent on the temporal indefiniteness of the example; all of the arguments involved apply *mutatis mutandis* to "X will do A at time t", where t is a future time. Hartshorne's position is that "X will do A" is true at state of the world B if what is already determined at B guarantees that every sufficiently long sequence of possible determinations includes one C such that "X did A" is true at C. In more colloquial terminology, if B is the state of the world, it is already (completely) causally determined that X will indeed do A. Similarly "X will not do A" is true at B if no sequence of the kind in question determines a state of the world in which X does A.

We have noted above the resemblance between what we have been developing and that of Kripke's version of semantics for intuitionistic logic. This resemblance is perhaps even more striking if we consider instead the interpretation of intuitionistic logic which originated with Brouwer and was repeatedly emphasized by Heyting: namely, the identification of "mathematically true" with the knowledge of an idealized mathematician who knew all constructions that have been made by any actual mathematician, together with their logical (or perhaps, computational) consequences. An alternative related account, which has been mentioned by Dummett and John Murphy, I am sure among others, identifies "true" with (likewise idealized but not necessarily mathematical) knowledge.

Like this view, as often formulated, sentences A and not-A are for Hartshorne, contraries rather than contradictories, although in general it remains correct to say that well-formed sentences are true or false.[6]

Some qualifications have to be made here: the first is that the model structures for Hartshorne, unlike in the Brouwerian or Brouwer-Dummett accounts, are *not* epistemic in any ordinary sense. If the model structures (as we have seen, these are states of the world) are to be considered as representing knowledge at all, that knowledge must surely be that of God, since it represents everything that is determinately true. (We will be returning to the question of God's knowledge presently). Any action, any decision, by anyone or anything, that makes a sentence determinately true which had been only probable, affects truth values assigned. The individuals which exist in particular states of the world do not necessarily, like mathematical objects in Brouwer's view, come into existence as the result of considered and conscious volition. Yet, it is part of Hartshorne's view that with the exception of new individuals whose existence is somehow predictable, no statements concerning such individuals are true.

A second, and somewhat more technical point, must be raised. In formally intuitionistic logics, such as that of Heyting, the set of well-formed formulae (sentences if you will) which are assigned the value "true" in A always includes that in B if A is accessible from B. While, as we have seen, there is a class of statements for which this is true for Hartshorne: presumably, this class includes all modal-free sentences. It is however clear that the situation is different for modal statements. It is indeed central to Hartshorne's view of the world that decisions and actions make some things which were possible, no longer so. Consequently, statements concerning possibility, impossibility, contingency and the like *can* be true in state of affairs A, but not in some state of affairs B accessible from A provided something has occurred which excludes that condition. E.g., at state of affairs A it may be true that X can have a child (is not sterile), but say as a result of an accident or operation at state of affairs B (some later time), X may become sterile. As Hartshorne expresses it, "The items are contingent in that the decisions are free. But the decisions once made, the possibility of making some alternative decision is gone forever. It remains true that there was such a possibility."[7] The upshot is that since presumably modal statements are among those that can be made and such statements *can* become false after being true, the logical structure of Hartshorne's philosophy, although closely related to that of intuitionism, is not identical to it.

It is incidentally worth mentioning, if only in passing, a terminological peculiarity of Hartshorne, which I do not believe has any important theoretical consequences, but could conceivably mislead some readers. The most standard terminology in modal logic has necessity (perhaps symbolized as $\Box$) and possibility (perhaps $\Diamond$) as dual concepts; in particular, such that $\Box A$ is logically equivalent to $\sim\Diamond\sim A$ and $\Diamond A$ is logically equivalent to $\sim\Box\sim A$. This tendency is typically maintained through the whole range of accessibility relations and indeed even for those formal modal logics (e.g. Lewis's S1) which are not readily interpreted in terms of Kripke-style semantics. Hartshorne has (at least) two related modal notions: on one hand he has the possibility related to the accessibility relation on the modal assignment set which represents the states of the world (possible or actual); on the other, the possibility relation associated with being a member of that modal assignment set at all (roughly, something is possible in this second sense if and only if it is or ever was possible in the first sense). Now Hartshorne most usually uses "possible" in the first sense, although occasionally (usually in metatheoretical connections), in the second sense. On the other hand, he virtually always uses "necessary" in the second sense, and virtually never in the first, preferring for that notion, locutions like "determinately true" to which (for non-modal statements in this case) it corresponds. It is, it should be noted, true that necessity in the second sense implies necessity in the first. Consequently true assertions of necessity in the second sense imply the truth of the corresponding assertion of necessity in the first sense (of course the converse holds for denials). It should be added that it is *not* claimed that any error in Hartshorne has its origin in this (as it appears to me) ambiguity.[8]

There is one additional restriction which Hartshorne perhaps makes which (if indeed true) takes him even further from the intuitionists. Eugene Peters claims, and Hartshorne does not challenge this in his comments on Peters's article, that "there can be no eternal contingencies."[9] This however raises the question whether it is possible for the modal assignment set that represents the actual world, including the entire history of how it may develop and how it could have developed (but didn't), to have as an element a model structure B such that for some (modal free) proposition A, A is not presently true (i.e. true in B), but there exist accessible states (from B) for which A is true and none for which not-A is determinately true, and that nonetheless, if C is a state of the world accessible from B and A is not true in C, A is possible in C and there exists a state D (not identical with C) which is accessible from C for which A is false. If the modal assignment set that "represents" the world could have this character it could be the case that it is impossible that A is impossible, but that nevertheless, it is not true that A will be the case (hence, intuitionistically, not-not-A is the case at B, but not only is A not the case, but it might never be the case).

To clarify consider two forms of religious Universalism: in both, if you are not (yet) saved, you will have a chance to be later. In the first, however, if you are stubborn enough, you may forever refuse to reform and be saved; in the second, even now we can assert, you *will* be saved, even though there is no way for you or perhaps even God to know when until you do actually reform. While I see no obvious belief central to Hartshorne's philosophy which seems to me to rule out as possibilities the kind of structure involved in the first kind of Universalism, I do not know any good reason for his insisting on it either. In this connection, we must make a few observations: propositions which could satisfy that kind of logical structure must have a certain type of indefiniteness. For example, the proposition that X will do A at time t (for, of course, particular X, A, and t), could not be an example, since the "impossibility" of the "impossibility" of A will at times starting with t exclude the possibility of it being false, while the fact that t is already past will exclude the possibility of it being false, but possible, leaving only the possibility of its determinate truth. For similar reasons, propositions like X will do A by 2000 A.D. must be excluded. In order to qualify a proposition must express a condition, like salvation for our Universalist, which could happen at *any* time in the future and Hartshorne at least sometimes appears to feel that this may not represent a real proposition.

In summary we can say the following concerning the apparent semantics underlying Hartshorne's philosophical views:

The world (in the broadest sense) can be represented by a modal assignment set with an accessibility relation of the S4 type. The individual model structures of this modal assignment set represent possible states of the world, possible not only in the sense used by formal logicians, but also in a somewhat causal sense. This might be expressed by saying each model structure represents a state of the world which is or was really possible. Propositions referring to events future to states of the world are only true if true in all states of the world accessible from the given one. In addition, this modal assignment set has the property that for every state of the world, there exist at least two states B and C, neither the same as A and such that there are propositions true in B, but not in C (and such that the two refer to the same time). To this characterization, there are two additional conditions concerning which we are uncertain, namely: 1. Can any state of the world have two different pasts? If not (and I think that Hartshorne's position on this will be negative) we can assert that (in graph theoretical terms) the modal assignment set is a non-trivial tree (and the tree whose root is the present state of the world is non-trivial for every state of the world). 2. Does the certainty of the possibility of A imply that every possible future include a state of the world for which A is true (as it does, as we have seen, only include states of the world for which A is possible). Notice that the non-triviality requirement excludes determinism, and hence guarantees that some things at least are determined "as we go along".

In connection with Hartshorne's theological interests, it may be of interest to speculate what concerning the structure we have been talking about God might be claimed to know (and which might be claimed to be known by non-divine beings).

The second of those questions is, I believe, the easiest: Since the model structures are intended to represent an entire state of the world, I presume even the best of us mortals know only a very small number of propositions. What knowledge we can ascribe to God is somewhat less clear. We can consider the following possibilities:

1. God knows everything true in the present state of the world. Since this includes modal statements and statements about the past, He also knows many things about the past and future.

2. God knows everything in the modal assignment set plus which state of the world is the actual one; that is, for every state of the world which is or ever was possible, God knows what would be true if that were the actual state of the world and furthermore knows which of these *is* the actual state of the world.[10]

Are these two characterizations of divine knowledge really different? The answer is not unambiguously provided by the characterization I have given so far. The reason is that we have not fully characterized either the mathematical structure of the modal assignment set or how complex propositions can be. If we assume the strongest reasonable assumptions concerning propositions and require all accessibility paths in the modal assignment set to be discrete, everything true in the modal assignment set might be representable by a possibly complex proposition true in the present state of the world. But I personally find the first of these assumptions a little arbitrary and the second an extremely dubious, perhaps even blasphemous attempt to make God limited in *exactly* the ways in which we are. As a consequence, I see little reason to accept that. (We shall see if Hartshorne has an opinion on this one.) If the two are different (as I suggest), there is I think little reason not to prefer the second view. (Among other things, it ascribes to God some kinds of infinite knowledge which we lack.) One thing that neither view claims is that God knows which real choices will be made, and so God, like us, gets to know things. (He, of course, gets to know many more things than we do.)

Before closing, I should like briefly to discuss the relevance of what I have been saying to an issue which has been raised repeatedly to and concerning Hartshorne's views on these issues, most notably by the late Richard M. Martin. According to the objecting view, propositions in their most "primitive" (in the logical sense) and specific form are timeless and their truth and falsity are likewise timeless. Those who hold this position of course do not generally intend thereby to deny that there are sentences like "it is raining in Austin" which are sometimes true and sometimes not. Leaving to the side the fine grain of the discussion not, in my opinion, relevant to the issue (e.g., Is the sentence in question a proposition?, Does it express the same proposition as "it is raining in Austin now"?, etc.), the serious issues involved, seem to come down to this:

Since in general, there are really multiple possible futures, a proposition like "My eldest great-grandson will be a famous mathematician in 2050" is not in general now determinate in its truth value (even if rather oddly amended by adding something like January 1, 2:30 P.M. E.S.T.). I am not hereby being pessimistic about my progeny. My oldest grandchild is now three. To express this more accurately in Hartshorne's terminology, it is now false, because its future status is indeterminate. To be sure if there were total causal determinism there would be only one possible future in Hartshorne's sense (sense one *supra*) and hence there would be only one possible state of affairs at 2:30 P.M. E.S.T. etc.; if that were the case, there would be only two possibilities. Either at that time, I have a great-grandson and he (or the oldest of them, if I have more than one) is indeed a famous mathematician and hence the proposition is true; or else either I have no great-grandsons then or I do, but the eldest one is not a famous mathematician and in this case the proposition is false. Now suppose for the sake of the argument, there were exactly two states of the world for January 1, 2050, etc. (Of course, the more expected situation is that there are many, probably infinitely many, such states.) Suppose further that in the first one, Norman Martin's eldest great-grandson is the Kurt Gödel of his period, while in the other, I have no great-grandchildren. Obviously we cannot with assurance now regard either the proposition or its negation as determinately true.

Now some of the complication of the situation is due to confusing two closely related situations. To explain, let me introduce a little additional terminology. Let us call a modal assignment set S of the kind we have been talking about **deterministic** if the accessibility relation is a simple ordering, i.e. if A and B both elements of S implies A accessible from B or B from A. (We have already guaranteed that A accessible from B and B from A guarantees A is B.) We will call a modal assignment set S* a **sub-modal assignment set** of S provided A an element of S* implies A an element of S and if A and B are elements of S*, A is accessible from B in S* if and only if A is accessible from B in S. Finally we will call a sub-modal assignment set of S, P, a **path** through S provided it is deterministic and provided if A and B are both in P and there is a C such that A is accessible from C in S and C is accessible from B in S, C is in P.

Now it is fairly clear that the set of paths through the modal assignment set which represents the possible states of the world are what is frequently called the set H of (complete) possible histories of the world (complete in the sense that they contain what would ordinarily be called the future). Now since H contains all possible complete histories of the world, it must perforce contain the actual complete history. Suppose P_0 were the actual history. By definition P_0 is a deterministic modal assignment (note that A being a model structure in P_0 will cause it to assign the same values to non-modal propositions in P_0 as it does in S (but not in general for modal propositions).

Now within P_0, statements about the future, if they are time-definite enough, have the timeless character that Hartshorne's critics like Richard Martin think they have in the actual world. One might, as John Calvin apparently did, believe that God really knows, not only that there exists a set H and all of the characteristics of its elements (God, at least in the second of our above Hartshornian alternatives, does indeed know all *that*) and which of them could not possibly be P_0 (God, on the same view, knows *that* as well), but also *which* element of H really is P_0. (On either Hartshornian view suggested, God would only know that if determinism were completely true.) If one believes *that*, one could express all of what we have said in completely timeless terms. But if one takes choice and determination seriously, those timeless statements which can be made are beyond knowledge, even divine knowledge; that is, in our technical terms, no one can ever know which member of H really is P_0. Notice that if someone did accept real possibility, but with some account which made the choice of P_0 possible, Hartshorne would (if he were convinced) have to modify his metaphysics and his theology, but as far as I can see, not his logic.

NORMAN M. MARTIN

DEPARTMENT OF PHILOSOPHY
UNIVERSITY OF TEXAS
JUNE 1986; REVISED MARCH 1987

NOTES

1. Charles Hartshorne, "Response to Smith" in John B. Cobb, Jr. and Franklin B. Gamewell, *Existence and Actuality: Conversations with Charles Hartshorne*, Chicago: University of Chicago Press, 1984, p. 110.

2. Charles Hartshorne, "Real Possibility", *Journal of Philosophy*, vol. 60 (October 1960), 602.

3. Hartshorne, "Response to Smith", op. cit.

4. Charles Hartshorne, *Creative Synthesis and Philosophical Method*, London: SCM Press Ltd., 1970, p. 222.

5. Ibid. A fairly thorough discussion of the cumulative nature of time that we are relying on here can be found in Hartshorne, "Creativity and the Deductive Logic of Causality", *Review of Metaphysics*, vol. 27 (September 1973), 62–64. See especially 68, "The past is found in the present, not vice versa; and only because the past is in the present is the future also, though only partially, in the present."

6. Charles Hartshorne, "The Meaning of 'Is Going to Be'", *MIND*, vol. 74, New series (January 1965), 48–49.

7. Charles Hartshorne, "Response to Alston", in Cobb and Gamewell, op. cit., p. 100.

8. It should be noted that unlike the first sense of possibility which is based on an accessibility relation of the S4 type, the second sense of possibility is based (if at all) on an S5 accessibility.

9. Eugene H. Peters, "Methodology in the Metaphysics of Charles Hartshorne", in Cobb and Gamewell, op. cit., p. 9.

10. For a discussion which seems to support position 2, see "Creativity and the Deductive Logic of Causality", 68f.

18

H. G. Hubbeling

HARTSHORNE AND THE ONTOLOGICAL ARGUMENT

In this article I want to discuss Hartshorne's important contribution to the revival of the modern interest in the proofs of God's existence and especially the ontological argument. I shall also give a short exposition of Hartshorne's philosophy as far as that is relevant to our understanding of the superiority of the neoclassical concept of God (in comparison with classical theories) in order to face critical questions as to the validity of the ontological argument. I shall try to show that Hartshorne's philosophy is able to refute the various objections.

As Hartshorne's ontological argument needs a supplementation by the cosmological argument I shall give a modal reconstruction of the cosmological argument of my own and I shall try to show that this establishes an argument for Hartshorne's concept of God too.

I shall also ask some critical questions. Hartshorne does not sufficiently acknowledge the fact that there is more than one logical system so that even in the most rational philosophies a choice must be made, which brings an 'existentialistic' moment into philosophy. Secondly I wonder as to whether Hartshorne's temporal interpretation of modalities is correct. I shall give the more technical logical details of the various proofs in an appendix so that the major parts of this article can be read without knowledge of symbolic logic.

There is an astonishing revival of interest in the proofs of God's existence. Hartshorne has contributed to this revival by his reconstruction of the ontological argument but even more by his showing that the neoclassical concept of God is able to face many critical questions. But it remains astonishing that in our time these arguments for God's existence have a kind of revival, for our time strongly emphasizes exactness and a scientific attitude! This revival can be traced back to the fact that Kant's refutations are considered dated now. Kant founded his refutations on his epistemology, which in turn was based on a Peano-like arithmetic, Euclidian geometry, Newtonian mechanics, and Aristotelian logic. As all these sciences are more or less dated now, Kant's epistemology has lost its sacrosanctity.

Even more important are the following considerations. In his epistemology even Kant presupposed that the logical relations are always valid and that they are not influenced by the forms of perception and the categories. In Kant's view these forms and categories are the constituents of human experience. With their help the human mind is able to bring an order into the multitude of chaotic sensations. Kant infers these categories from Aristotelian logic, which is therefore presupposed. In other words even for Kant the logical relations must be applied to the Thing as such (*das Ding an sich*). In this respect Kant agrees with Leibniz. Further, with the help of modern logic one can show that logical statements can be made about the Thing as such, hence about God's world. Logical relations are true in all possible worlds, hence also in God's world. And even if one applies the important rule *ex nihilo nihil fit* and interprets this rule timelessly, a Kantian epistemology cannot overthrow it!

One of the first scholars who called our attention to Anselm's ontological argument in a modern way, was Charles Hartshorne in an article in the *Philosophical Review* (May 1944, Nr. 3, pp. 225–245) with the title "The Formal Validity and Real Significance of the Ontological Argument". Also in a book, he has written together with W. L. Reese, *Philosophers Speak of God* (Chicago, 1953) Anselm's argument was considered in a new way. Hartshorne got support from an unexpected side, viz from the Wittgensteinian Norman Malcolm who wrote an article "Anselm's Ontological Arguments" (*Philosophical Review*, January 1960, Nr. 1). (The article is also included in the volume containing Malcolm's collected articles, *Knowledge and Certainty*, Englewood Cliffs, 1963, 2nd edition 1964). Like Hartshorne, Malcolm showed that Anselm's argument in *Proslogium* 2 is not valid, but that the argument in *Proslogium* 3 is indeed valid. In the history of the Anselmian argument all the attention has been focussed on the argument in the second chapter. The difference between the two arguments is that in chapter 3 no longer the mere existence is the focus of interest as in chapter 2, but God's *necessary* existence.

Then Hartshorne published his famous reconstruction of the Anselmian argument in his book *The Logic of Perfection* (La Salle, 1962), in which he uses modern modal logic. I shall discuss this argument later on in this article. The quintessence of the reconstruction consists in the fact that Hartshorne shows that for God, i.e. for a perfect being, the following theorem is valid: *Either he (it) exists necessarily or he (it) necessarily does not exist*. I shall call this theorem Hartshorne's central thesis or simply *central thesis*, abbreviated CT. This CT is very important, for if we could show that God's existence is at least possible, i.e., that it is not self-contradictory, or in other words that it is not true that it necessarily does not not exist, then we may prove his existence with the help of CT in the following way:

(1) CT: Either God exists necessarily or he necessarily does not exist.
(2) God's existence is possible (by hypothesis).
(3) It is not true that he necessarily does not exist (from 2).
(4) God exists necessarily (from (1) and (3) by *modus tollendo ponens*).

Now Hartshorne is of the opinion that from the cosmological argument it at least follows that God's existence is possible. But is this correct? Kant has tried to show that the cosmological argument presupposes the ontological argument; do we not get into a *circulus vitiosus* in this way? Hartshorne has solved this problem, by pointing out that Kant's analysis should have shown that what the other arguments for God's existence borrow from the ontological argument is not the steps towards the conclusion, i.c., the steps which follow the demonstration of CT in the argument (i.e., the steps 7, 8, and 9 in Hartshorne's reconstruction (*vide* Appendix, section 2). What is borrowed from the ontological argument is the exclusion of contingency from perfection, i.e. the proof of CT and this again is a logical transformation of Anselm's Principle, to which we come in a moment. According to Hartshorne in this way there is no *circulus vitiosus*, if we use both arguments together. They are both complex and where one is weak the other is strong, and vice versa, (cp. *The Logic of Perfection and Other Essays in Neoclassical Metaphysics*, La Salle, 1962 [abbr. LP], p. 52). In other words the ontological and the cosmological argument together form a cumulative argument. In the argumentation above premise 1 (= CT) is proved by the ontological argument independently of the cosmological argument. The latter argument proves premise (2), independently of the ontological argument. Put together they have as a result a valid argument for God's existence.

Before we face the various objections against the ontological argument, we will outline some main features of Hartshorne's neoclassical concept of God, because with the help of this concept the various problems with respect to the ontological argument can be solved. The details of Hartshorne's reconstruction will be dealt with in the appendix. In my view Hartshorne's proof of the CT is flawless. Hartshorne continues the thought of Whitehead and Peirce. He has also studied with Husserl and he knows continental philosophy excellently. In his discussions he considers also continental positions. Hartshorne is a metaphysician and he defends the possibility of metaphysics against various criticisms. Metaphysical statements express necessary truths which cannot be falsified by contingent experience. In logical positivism it is taught that for a statement to be meaningful it is necessary that it must be falsifiable, at least in principle. A meaningful statement denies another statement. But then this other statement must be a real possibility, at least in principle. Hartshorne accepts the thesis that a meaningful statement denies another statement. But this alternative ought not to be a real (logical) possibility. It might be a purely verbal possibility that is logically contradictory. Whiteheadian tradition goes back to Leibniz at this point, who defended a metaphysics of all possible worlds, a concept that we find also in the semantics of modern modal logic (among others in S. Kripke). Metaphysical statements have thus a referent. They refer to states of affairs in all possible worlds. On this basis Heinrich Scholz in Germany wrote his *Metaphysik als strenge Wissenschaft* (Metaphysics as a Strict Science) in 1941. An example of such a metaphysical truth is the statement: 'There is something'. Some central metaphysical doctrines in Hartshorne are the following: The final (or in another order: the first) metaphysical states of affairs are actual entities. As synonyms for actual entities are given: least unit of Process, unit-becoming, unit-happening, unit-event, and quantum-process (*vide* Hartshorne's *Whitehead's Philosophy* (Lincoln, 1972 (= WP), p. 119f). As it may be inferred from the given synonyms Hartshorne sees not things but events as the last realities. Here Hartshorne stands in a great modern philosophical tradition. Who does not remember the beginning of Wittgenstein's *Tractatus Logico-Philosophicus*: "Die Welt ist alles, was der Fall ist. Die Welt ist die Gesamtheit der Tatsachen, nicht der Dinge" (The world is everything that is the case. The world is the totality of facts, not of things, *Tractatus* 1 and 1.1)? Hartshorne defends a genetic or event theory of identity against a substantial theory of identity. I am the same in my identity, but different in my actual states of affairs. I am the same person as ten years ago, but I am also different: I have different ideas, another knowledge of the world, my relations to other persons and things are different, etc. When I nevertheless intuitively understand the identity of my 'ego' then this is based on the fact that I make an abstraction from the various states of affairs and thus reach a permanent ego: "Identity is a somewhat abstract view of personal history" (WP, 181). Experience is the foundation of our knowledge of the actual entities, the unit-events. Hartshorne characterizes these actual entities also as 'occasions of experience'. When Berkeley sees *being* as *being perceived* ('esse est percipi'), Hartshorne could say: 'esse est possibiliter percipi'. Hartshorne interprets human experience as a paradigm for general experience. What is experienced by a subject (the object) is in its turn subject for experience. Human experience is not the only form of experience: " 'Inherent in experience as such' means exactly what it says; 'inherent in *human* experience as such' would mean something else" (*Creative Synthesis and Philosophical Method*, La Salle, 1970 (= CS), p. 25). Hartshorne also teaches what is called in Husserl's phenomenology the *intentionality* of experience, i.e., 'experience' is always 'experience of'. Further: experience is self-reflexive. "Experience must have stimuli; there must be objects of experience, data which are already there, ready to be experienced. Yet in this philosophy there is nothing in the world but creative experience.

What, then, are the objects that are there to be experienced? Simply, previous cases of experience!'' (CS 7). Memory is the clearest example of an experience of an experience. This intentionality refers in two directions. In the first place it indicates that there is no experience possible without previous experiences. Whitehead calls this *prehension*. In the second place every experience is determined to be a *datum* for following experiences. Whitehead calls this *objective immortality*. Prehension is never fully determined by the previous experiences. The latter are necessary, but never sufficient conditions for prehension. There is always a *creative synthesis*. Besides the metaphysical truth that there is necessarily something that exists it must be stated that there is necessarily experience. Further Hartshorne states that metaphysical categories always appear in pairs of contrasts: 'being-becoming', 'necessary-contingent', 'unchangeable-changeable', 'cause-effect', 'eternity-time', 'absolute-relative', 'unity-variety', etc. In Goethe we find analogous polarities. One might expect that Hartshorne will introduce a kind of Goethean dialectics or, even worse, a kind of Hegelian dialectics. But this is not to be feared because for Hartshorne ''logic is the backbone of philosophy'' (CS xvii). He interprets these polarities, unlike Goethe, as asymmetrical relations, so that a kind of dialectics is not necessary. Hartshorne calls this the *law of inclusive contrast*. The relation between the two contrasts is not that of a conjunction, but that of an inclusion: not A *and* B, but A *in* B. Being is in becoming, the necessary in the contingent, the unchangeable in the changeable, the absolute in the relative, etc. An example: The statement: 'two dodos + two dodos = four dodos' contains a contingent constituent, viz the existence of dodos. Still it contains at the same time an absolute necessary truth, viz that '2 + 2 = 4'. We must acknowledge that of the polarities mentioned above there is always one abstract and one concrete. 'Being', 'necessary', 'unchangeable', 'eternity', etc. are abstract terms. Their opposites are concrete. The concrete terms are fundamental, the abstract ones are derived from them. The abstract is *in* the concrete. With respect to the doctrine of God this means that we have to distinguish two fundamental aspects in God: God's *primordial nature* (to use Whitehead's concepts) which is abstract, eternal, unchangeable, etc. and God's *consequent nature*, which is present in contingent states of affairs. The future is open also for God, because mankind is free and can take creative decisions. Therefore he can also take morally wrong decisions without God's being blamed for that. Therefore the future is not fully determined. God, however, knows all that is abstract as abstract; he knows completely what is determined; he knows all the possibilities as possible. Hartshorne does not deny that the future is in God's hand in the sense that his love will be victorious and defeat all our resistance at the end. But God is not a God in a world of puppets. Therefore mankind also determines the future, at least partly. God's relation to us is not simply an external relation. For the more the partners in a relation have

consciousness, the more this relation is internal. A stone which stands to the left
of another stone, stands in an external relation. When the relation changes and
the stone comes to the right of the other stone, the stones themselves do not
change. This is different when a person loves another person. When this love is
broken the people change. God as the person who is at most conscious will
change when his relation of love towards mankind will change. God who stands
in a relation to mankind that is disobedient is different from God who stands in
a relation towards mankind that is obedient. Here I want to indicate that
Hartshorne's interpretation is closer to the biblical view of God than classical
metaphysics. In Hartshorne's view the history of God and the chosen people of
Israel is not a pseudo-history, in which everything was predetermined. It is a
history of the covenant in which man receives new chances again and again. He
could have taken these chances. It was not absolutely necessary that Christ would
come. Hartshorne's philosophy delivers us from philosophical essentialism that
has crept into theology. Many theologians think that we must deliver ourselves
from this philosophical essentialism by opposing biblical thinking against
philosophy. Philosophy leads us nowhere; we should leave it and keep to what
is called purely biblical thought. But, of course, it is better to replace onesided
essentialist philosophical thought by a better philosophical system. No theology
can do without philosophical notions, concepts, ideas, etc.

Further it is important in Hartshorne's philosophy that he gives a temporal interpretation of the modalities. Time is an objective modality and we
may not interpret eternity in an a-temporal way. Hartshorne also sees the relation of future and past as a-symmetrical. The modality of the past is
actuality. It is fixed and cannot be changed. The future has the modality of
possibility and eternity has the modality of necessity. As is well-known there
are thinkers who state that this relation between future and past is symmetrical.
And here we can distinguish between two trends. Some state that as the past
is fixed the future is also determined (Spinoza, Hegel, and others). But others
say that as the future is open, so must be the past (e.g. Kierkegaard in his
masterly 'Mellemspil' in his book *Philosophiske Smuler*). A consequence of all
this is that Hartshorne weakens the distinction between logical and real
possibility (cp. his article "Necessity" in the *Review of Metaphysics*, Dec. 1967,
pp. 290–296 and his article "Real Possibility" in the *Journal of Philosophy*,
Oct. 1960, pp. 593–605). This distinction is a consequence of our incomplete
knowledge. For the rest Hartshorne keeps to the usual distinction: logically
possible is what has meaning and is not logically contradictory; really possible is
what is compatible with the actuality, the past of our world until this moment.
But according to Hartshorne logical possibilities must refer to something in order
to be meaningful and in the last analysis they have therefore to refer to real
possibilities.

But let us now return to Hartshorne's ontological argument. My exposition of Hartshorne's philosophy was restricted to our goal: a better understanding of Hartshorne's new defence of this argument. Hartshorne starts with the premise that is called by him: Anselm's Principle, viz that perfection (God) cannot exist contingently. From this he deduces CT. He gives his argument in a logically technical way that we will give in an appendix at the end of our article. In his article "Contemporary Metaphysics in the United States" (F. H. Donell, Jr., ed., *Aspects of Contemporary American Philosophy*, Würzburg/Vienna 1965, pp. 18–27) Gustafson gives a translation (p. 21) of Hartshorne's argument in ordinary language, which does not mean that it is easier to follow now! As the reader can see Hartshorne starts with Anselm's Principle (step 1) and from this he deduces correctly CT (step 6).

1. If God (or absolute perfection) exists, then His existence is necessary, not contingent,
2. It is axiomatic that either it is necessary that God exists, or it is not necessary that God exists.
3. It is a postulate of modal logic that a proposition with a modal status has this status necessarily. Thus if it is not necessary that a thing exists, it is necessary that it is not necessary that the thing exists.
4. From (2) and (3) it follows that either it is necessary that God exists or it is necessary that it is not necessary that God exists.
5. But if the latter clause is true, then it can be deduced from (1) that it is necessary that God does not exist.
6. So that from (4) and (5) it follows that it is necessary that God exists or it is necessary that God does not exist.
7. But it is surely true that God's existence is possible and hence that it is not true that it is necessary that God does not exist.
8. Thus, from (6) and (7) it follows that God's existence is necessary.
9. If this is so, then by a modal postulate God exists.
10. God exists.

Now we shall face the various objections against the ontological argument.

(i) The best known is that from Kant, viz that existence is not a predicate. Therefore one cannot say that God lacks perfection, if he does not exist. This objection, however, is only relevant for Anselm's *Proslogium* chapter 2. And even here arguments in defence are possible. Kant's argument runs as follows: Existence is not a real predicate. A hundred thalers which are thought of have exactly the same properties as a hundred real thalers. If I add existence to the hundred thalers in my mind I do not add a new property. I only state that the hundred thalers which exist until then in my mind only, now also exist in reality. But a counter-argument presents itself immediately: With the hundred real

thalers I can pay my bill, at least in the time of Kant. Kant made the mistake of considering the things in themselves and not taking their relation to other things into consideration. Thus a hundred real thalers have some properties in addition to the hundred in my mind, viz e.g. that they are a means of payment, etc. But again a counter-objection against the counter-argument is possible, viz that relations are not properties. And this is certainly true for external relations, but also for internal?

We can also approach this problem from another side, viz with the help of set theory. In set theory sets are constituted (i.e. defined) by means of an unambiguous criterion with the help of which one may decide whether a certain object belongs to a certain set or not. Whether or not the set is empty is a question which does not belong to the definition of the set. Insofar Kant is apparently right. But, there are also sets in which 'to exist' or 'to be present in reality' belongs to the definition. One might e.g. speak about the set of the now living Americans. There is nothing contradictory in such a definition. One can operate meaningfully with such a set. As the definitions of sets mark their properties, must we now say that existence is a property or not?

G. E. Moore gives a famous example in order to show that existence is not a property. Compare:

(i) Some tigers exist
(ii) Some tigers growl

Now it may be obvious that (i) is a senseless statement, whereas (ii) is meaningful. But this only shows that there are restrictions in the use of the word 'exist'; it does not show that '. . . exists' is not a predicate. (i) is only without meaning if we have beforehand restricted the use of the word tigers to in reality living tigers. If we include in the term tigers also toy-tigers, painted tigers, etc., statement (i) becomes meaningful!

But whatever that may be, Hartshorne defends that with respect to God we have to do with necessary existence and that is certainly a property! "That modality with respect to existence is a predicate is assumed by the critics of the Argument themselves. For they hold, in effect, that to every predicate there is attached the status of contingency, i.e., its existence and non-existence must alike be conceivable. Obviously, if 'contingent' is a predicate, so is 'non-contingent'; just as, if 'perfect' is a predicate, so is 'imperfect' "(LP 52).

(ii) Another very important objection is that the concept of a being 'greater than which nothing can be thought of' is not very well conceivable, because something like a greatest possible number is not conceivable either. Also Hartshorne's concept of a most perfect being seems to be self-contradictory. In his well-known work *The Nature of Necessity* (1974) Plantinga has tried to show that this concept is not self-contradictory. He reduces *perfection* to a function of

omniscience and he is of the opinion that this can represent a closed set in contradistinction to the set of natural numbers. But is this true? One could at least in my view defend the thesis that the number of possible states of affairs known to God is at least countably infinite, i.e., that they form a one-one correspondence to the series of natural numbers. And if the latter does not form a closed set, why should the first form a closed set? With Hartshorne's neoclassical concept of God the difficulties disappear. God is perfect in the sense that he cannot be surpassed by any other being outside himself. But he may surpass himself! A God, who at the end of time has a mankind before him that responds to his love in a loving way is more perfect than a God in which this is not the case. We have shown above that in Hartshorne's process philosophy God's relations to people belong to God's properties.

(iii) Another objection is that of logical type. A universal like 'perfection' cannot be instantiated in an actual individual. An individual cannot represent a universal. Humanity is not human and why should the universal 'perfection' be perfect? According to Hartshorne, however, we must distinguish between *existence* and *actuality*. God is indeed perfect, but strictly speaking only in his primordial nature, i.e., in his abstract, eternal unchangeable being. But the concrete divine states of affairs (with respect to God-now) *have* perfection. They include perfection, which may be abstracted from it. Now, what has perfection (the *de facto* state of affairs) is *per definitionem* perfect and cannot be surpassed by the state of affairs of another individual, but only by the future states of affairs of that same individual. God-now and God-tomorrow can only be the states of affairs of the same individual. "God is the one individual in respect to whom the line between property and instance falls only between individual and state, not also, as it usually does, between individual and some broader class property, such as humanity. Perfection is not a class of similar individuals, but only a class of similar and genetically related states of one individual" (LP 67). What the ontological argument proves is not the false conclusion that there is a necessary instantiation of perfection, but that the set of instantiations of perfection is not empty and that this set must necessarily belong to one individual.

(iv) Related to the preceding objection is that of the paradox of the abstractness of the necessary. Logical analysis is said to teach us that the meaning of necessary is what all possible contingent alternatives have in common. In this view God as an *ens necessarium* can only be interpreted as abstract, without concrete contents. But here too the neoclassical view can solve this problem by making a distinction between God's primordial and consequent nature. God's primordial nature is an *ens necessarium*, but this is never without concrete instantiations.

(v) One of the objections that has been raised against the ontological argument in its modal form was that in this way one has to accept an Aristotelian

essentialism. It is supposed that a certain individual may be the same in all possible worlds. And at first sight this essentialism leads to insurmountable difficulties. Suppose that Eisenhower had been born in the Middle Ages, how would he have acted? How could we have recognized this individual as Eisenhower? Such questions are not meaningful! And if they are not meaningful then this means that there is no individual with an identical essence that can be identified in all possible worlds. Hartshorne, however, can answer this question very well. With the help of the distinction between existence and actuality, mentioned above, it is certainly possible to speak of an existence that remains the same in all possible worlds and to speak of instantiations (actualities) which include this existence that is everywhere identical. This holds both for the course of this world and for the various possible worlds. For we have seen that Hartshorne gives a temporal interpretation to the modalities. The past is fixed. Therefore questions about Eisenhower in the Middle Ages cannot be asked meaningfully, for there is no continuous stream of experience which makes it possible to speak of a set of actualities which includes the existence of 'Eisenhower in the Middle Ages'. But this does not mean that there cannot be an existence which remains the same in all possible worlds, for such a continuous stream of actualities is indeed, in principle, possible. A condition for this is, however, that there is a connection with our actual world. Here, G. L. Goodwin is able to show, in his interesting work *The Ontological Argument of Charles Hartshorne* (American Academy of Religion, Scholars Press, Missoula Montana, 1978), that Hartshorne's philosophy of the temporal interpretation of the modalities can be supported by the well-known Kripke semantics, in which also our actual world has a special indexed place in the series of possible worlds. This includes, however, a difficulty to which we will come in a moment.

(vi) A usual distinction is that between logical (*de dicto*) and real (*de re*) modalities. Now a frequent objection against the ontological argument is that it has shown the *de dicto* necessity of God's existence and therefore only the logical existence of God, not his real existence. But we have seen that for Hartshorne this distinction vanishes. But even if one objects to this, the objection does not hold ground, for a *de dicto* necessity would include its *de re* necessity! This is not true the other way round: A *de dicto* possibility does not involve a *de re* possibility. A precondition for all this is, however, that we accept a 'platonic' view in the foundations of logic and mathematics and not a 'conventionalistic' view. And here we come to the real weak point in Hartshorne's argument (but also in mine!).

In modern logic one has to distinguish between stricter and less strict systems. In the stricter systems less theorems can be proved and thus less theorems are valid. In propositional logic the most important difference is that between intuitive (constructive) logic (and mathematics) on the one hand and classical logic (and mathematics) on the other. The set of theorems of intuitive logic are a subsystem of that of classical logic. What can be proved in intuitive logic is also a theorem in classical logic, but the reverse is not true. The principle of intuitive logic (and mathematics) is that one has to give a positive proof for a positive theorem. It is not allowed to start with a negative hypothesis, e.g. non-p and then with the help of a *reductio ad absurdum* to prove p. It is allowed to start with p and then to prove non-p with the help of a *reductio ad absurdum*. Thus in intuitive logic the law of excluded middle: either p or non-p is not valid. In mathematics the concept of actual infinity is rejected. In classical logic the method of *reductio ad absurdum* is allowed without restrictions and thus the law of excluded middle is valid and also the concept of actual infinity. Also a certain philosophy is connected with these systems. In classical logic the logical laws are valid independently of the human mind. In most cases classical logic is connected with a certain 'platonic view' in that a certain existence is granted to logical laws, irrational numbers, etc. Intuitive logic is usually connected with a conventionalistic view. Logical laws are an invention (construction) of man. They do not exist independently of man.

Now, also in modal logic there is a distinction that according to standard theory runs parallel to that of the distinction between intuitive and classical logic. The three main systems are T, S_4, S_5. The difference is that in S_4 the following axiom is valid:

$Lp \rightarrow LLp$, i.e., if p is necessary then it is necessary that p is necessary. This axiom is also valid in S_5, but not in T.

In S_5 the following axiom is valid too:

$Mp \rightarrow LMp$, i.e., if it is possible that p, then it is necessary that it is possible that p. This axiom is not valid in S_4 (or T).

Now, according to many scholars the distinction between S_4 and S_5 runs more or less parallel to the distinction between intuitive and classical logic. Also the semantics of S_5 and S_4 are different. In S_5 we have to do with a more or less free view on our possible worlds. That is, we may for example say that it is still possible that Napoleon did not die on St. Helena in 1821, i.e., there is a possible world in which this is not the case. There are, however, semantics, in which our actual world is especially indexed. That is the case with the famous Kripke semantics, which Hartshorne needed for his temporal interpretation of the modalities as we have seen. Now, in Kripke semantics certain theorems of S_5 cannot be proved, i.e., the Kripke semantics are stricter than S_5. And here my critical questions for Hartshorne come forward. In the first place, in my view Hartshorne should have pointed out more clearly with what logical system he works. Such a system is connected with a whole philosophy and with various philosophical presuppositions, as we have seen. That means that Hartshorne's proof is only valid within a certain system! I, myself, have no objection to accepting S_5 and the platonic world view connected with it, but I think it is fair to acknowledge that Hartshorne's (and my!) arguments for God's existence lose their validity in a stricter system.

In the second place, and this is even worse in my view, Hartshorne gives his proofs in the system S_5, whereas he needs a stricter system for his temporal interpretation of the modalities. In other words Hartshorne builds his system with presuppositions that make his ontological proof nonvalid. That Hartshorne needs system S_5 is clear in his step 3. Hartshorne formulates this as follows: "a modal status is always necessary". But this is only true in S_5 and step 3 is indeed only allowed in S_5 and not in S_4. Moreover step 2 is not allowed in intuitive logic. So Hartshorne needs S_5.

In the third place Hartshorne should have acknowledged that even in a rational philosophy like his choices must be made, as we have seen above. Thus he should acknowledge the moment of truth in existentialism, where much emphasis is laid on the necessity to make choices. My three 'objections' are closely connected, as the reader may see.

Therefore I myself reject the temporal interpretation of the modalities. One may assume (with Kierkegaard) the openness of future and past. Of course, what has happened has happened and nothing can change that. That Napoleon died on St. Helena in 1821 (in the course of our history) is unchangeable. But in that case we consider the past events isolated. The past events have, however, their relations with innumerable other events, and by means of these other events, which may lie far in the future, these past events may change in their objective and subjective meaning. That is, the *objective* meaning of an event in the past may change insofar as its consequences may be different, etc. But also its *subjective* meaning may change: we can experience an event in the past differently. In 1821 on St. Helena was it a criminal who died, a dictator, a victim of unjust vengeance, or a misunderstood genius? To use Kierkegaard's terminology, of the past events the 'that', not the 'how' is fixed. Moreover God has another time. He may call back the past and make it real again. This is the central theme in the Christian doctrine of redemption, for example. With all this not only philosophical objections have been eliminated, there are now greater possibilities for theology. However, it is fair to say that my non-temporal interpretations lead to difficulties that Hartshorne had so beautifully solved. Especially I have difficulties with objection (v) mentioned above. For in my system asking for 'Eisenhower in the Middle Ages' is indeed possible as our concept of logical possibilities is much greater. But I think that in my system the problem can be solved too. We may also make Hartshorne's distinction between existence (in the Hartshornian sense) and instantiations (actualities). But in our system reincarnations are, at least logically, not excluded and then it is possible to speak of an abstract existence, which remains the same in changing instantiations. Thus it is possible to think of a person Y in the Middle Ages, who is later reborn in the twentieth century as Eisenhower. Both this Mr. Y and Eisenhower may have an abstract personality in common. In passing: I do not want to defend the claim that there are reincarnations, but I do not want them to be excluded logically.

As we have seen above Hartshorne's ontological proof needs the support of a cosmological argument. In the following I shall give a new cosmological argument of my own. It can be given in a technical modal variant and this will be done in the appendix. Here I shall give a more informal version based on set and lattice theory. Further I shall show that this new version of the cosmological argument needs Hartshorne's concept of God in its interpretation.

One of the main counter-arguments against the cosmological argument is that it is never necessary to stop the chain of arguments at a first or last mover, a first or last cause, or a necessary being. I too take as a principle the axiom: '*ex nihilo nihil fit*' or formulated otherwise 'for every state of affairs there must necessarily be a ground'. The renewal consists in the fact that we will apply this principle not only within the various chains of grounds (causes), but also to the sets of these chains in their relations to each other. That means that we presuppose the multiple application of the principle '*ex nihilo nihil fit*'. We can seek the cause (ground) of existence of, for example, a human being. It is his parents. We can then seek the cause of existence of the parents. We must then again refer to a couple of parents, etc. In this way we remain in a linear line of causality. But we must also seek the cause of the fact that two parents produce a human being. In that case we seek a kind of *second order* cause, i.e., we seek the cause of a certain causation.

In this way we get the following argument: We presuppose that the set of states of affairs in this world together with the relation 'to find its ground in ' (and this is a translation of the principle '*ex nihilo nihil fit*') constitutes an ordered set. This ordered set is a directed set by which we mean the following: If there are two states of affairs within the set, say A and B, and A does not find its ground in B nor B in A, then there is a third state of affairs, say C, which is the ground of both A and B (there might, of course, be intermediate grounds between C and A/B). In passing: as we shall see, the directedness of ordering is not yet decisive here, but it is tempting to start with it immediately from the outset. Now this whole set of states of affairs, which is ordered by the relation 'to find its ground in', has an infinite number of subsets ordered by the same R relation. And each of these ordered subsets again has an infinite number of states of affairs as its elements, so that in spite of our assumption that the set is a directed set, we are far from arriving at a last element. And that is the reason why in this modern reconstruction the traditional Thomistic variant of the cosmological argument cannot be proved.

But now we make another assumption, viz that there are subsets of the same type. Such a subset is, for example, the subset characterized by the relation 'being generated': a child is generated by his parents, who are themselves generated by their parents, etc. We now presuppose that it is possible to recognize types of ordered subsets. All generations of children by their parents constitute one type of a subset. All kinds of things causing heat constitute another type, all kinds of magnetic attraction another, etc. In this way we can make a partition within the whole set of states of affairs ordered by the relation 'to find its ground in'. We thus get a number of subsets characterized by a certain type of ground-consequence relation. Now the fundamental idea of my reconstruction of the cosmological argument is that this number of subsets is not infinite, in other words, that there is only a limited number of types of grounds.

Once more we seek the ground of these subsets. By doing so we apply the principle 'ex nihilo nihil fit' in a multiple way. That is, we say that the relation 'to find its ground in' is not only applicable within the various subsets, but also to the subsets as a whole, as described above. We seek the cause of causation. So this set of subsets is again a directed ordered set and because this directed set has a limited number of elements (the elements are here the subsets, each of a different type) this set has a last element according to modern set and lattice theory (vide e.g. H. Gericke, *Theorie der Verbände*, Mannheim, 1967, p. 38). I may even weaken my original premise in that the requirement of being a directed set is only needed for the ordering of the subsets (each of a different type). This requirement is not needed for the ordering *within* the subsets themselves in order to get the cosmological argument valid. Thus we arrive at a last element and this element is a ground that we might interpret as God (last or fundamental ground of all being). In passing: one may speak of God as a first or last ground. That depends on the direction of the ordering. If we speak of the ordering relation 'to find its ground in', we have to do with God as a last ground. If we speak of the ordering relation 'is the ground of', we have to do with God as a first cause. This direction is, however, a matter of convention and not really important.

As one can see, we have made the following assumptions (premises) in the course of our argument:

(i) the principle 'ex nihilo nihil fit' is applied in a multiple way, i.e., it is applied also to the set of subsets, and it is also applied to the causal (grounding) relations themselves, not only to the causes (grounds);

(ii) the number of types of grounds is not infinite;

(iii) the relation 'to find its ground in' constitutes a directed set (as we have seen, this is only needed for the ordering of the set of subsets);

(iv) we can distinguish various types of grounds;
(v) as we presuppose actually infinite series of causes we have to do with classical set theory, not with intuitive set theory.

If one does not want to accept the cosmological argument, one must try to reject one of these premises. And, of course, this is always possible. One should, however, consider the price one has to pay for this rejection, because then one is not allowed to use one of these rejected premises oneself! In my opinion all the premises have a sufficient grade of plausibility. Premise (v) can of course be rejected and one can remain within the limits of intuitive mathematics and logic. But one should realise that the price is high. The empirical natural sciences, for example, use classical mathematics! Premise (iv) will hardly meet a definite objection. I do not pretend that we can always give a theoretically exact definition of each type of causation (grounding) but a workable definition can certainly be given here and is given in ordinary science, because we always work with types of causes. Presupposition (iii) in the weak form given here, is not likely to be objected to. Premise (ii) cannot be proved exactly, but it is at least plausible. The number of states of affairs might be infinite, the number of *types* of grounds should be taken to be finite. The various sciences also presuppose this premise. They order according to causal principles and in doing so they only presuppose a limited number of them. If they did not do this, if in other words the number of types of grounds is infinite, then one must introduce in his system a whole series of unknown grounds (causes) and this is implausible and unnecessary. Premise (i) might be labelled plausible too, but I think that this is the weakest point of the argument. For I am convinced that the following attitude is certainly rational: Good, we admit that if we continue looking for grounds (i.e., if we apply the rule '*ex nihilo nihil fit*' in a multiple way) we finally arrive at a last ground. But why continue seeking grounds? For the construction of a science this is certainly not needed. In science we have nothing to do with last grounds or last causes. Naturally we admit that there are boundaries in our science, but we will remain within these boundaries. Even stronger: it is wrong to transgress these boundaries. Science made its great progress in the seventeenth century, when thinkers like Galilei and Newton renounced seeking complete explanations including last grounds. Descartes still made the mistake of building his physics on metaphysics. He was of the opinion that one should first of all know the last metaphysical principles in order to construct a physical system. One should, for example, first know what gravitation essentially is, before one could go on to work with it. This proved to be a wrong point of view. One can very well work with gravitation and make calculations without exactly knowing what exactly caused gravitation and without going further to the last ground: God. Moreover, some states of affairs in physics do not seem to fall under the rule '*ex nihilo nihil fit*'. For in quantum mechanics some states of affairs escape our possibilities of a causal ordering.

I immediately admit all this. I do not claim that modern reconstructions of the argument for God's existence are relevant to science. But in my view (and Hartshorne's) the problem of God's existence and other metaphysical questions have their own rights independent of the question as to whether these problems are relevant to science or not. These are problems that man struggles with and we must try to solve them in the best possible way. And then we must say that presupposition (i) has enough plausibility to be applied. Besides we may even indicate that this principle is silently presupposed in science too. That this principle is used within science is no problem; asking for causes or grounds is normal procedure here. But in science we presuppose that grounds for explanation do not change. That finds its ground in the fact that we tacitly take it for granted that, if A is grounded in B, this will not change without ground. But if the principle '*ex nihilo nihil fit*' cannot be applied in a multiple way we are never sure of this! And as for the unexplained states of affairs in quantum mechanics, this does not refute our cosmological argument which has to do with second order causes.

But this gives us some difficulties in the interpretation of this concept of God. For it may be clear that the *ens necessarium* and the last cause that is proved with the help of this argument is not a directly acting being in the world thanks to presupposition (i). It does not stand in the same line with the other causes. Now one can interpret this in various ways. One can give a deistic interpretation of this concept of God. But also a Spinozistic interpretation is possible. He who reads the scholium to the twenty-eighth proposition of the first part of Spinoza's *Ethics* will see that in Spinoza's system God as a cause (ground) is evidently not a member of the series of causes, not the first or last member of such a series but like in our cosmological argument a second order cause. Now many objections can be raised against a deistic or Spinozistic concept of God. But here Hartshorne's concept of God can also give the solution. He offers an excellent alternative. In my view what has been proved in the cosmological argument is God's primordial nature, the necessary aspects of God's nature, not the whole essence of God. That the cosmological argument proves a God with less properties than the ontological argument is no wonder. The argument is stricter, the number of presuppositions is less, but one has to pay for this! The ontological argument proves a perfect being, the cosmological argument only a first or last cause (first or last ground). Now the primordial nature of God has evidently a second order character and thus this new cosmological argument is a clear support for Harthorne's view.

Thus, although I think that Hartshorne's philosophy can be improved in some points, it is in my view one of the best systems in philosophy of religion we have at this moment.

H. G. HUBBELING

PHILOSOPHICAL AND THEOLOGICAL INSTITUTES
UNIVERSITY OF GRONINGEN
SEPTEMBER 1986

APPENDIX

In this appendix I will give the more technical proofs, both of Hartshorne and myself. For the technical details I may refer to a standard work on modal symbolic logic, viz G. E. Hughes and M. J. Cresswell, *An Introduction to Modal Logic*, London, 1968.

1. *Hartshorne's reconstruction of the ontological argument* (LP 50f):
The logical structure of the Anselmian argument in its mature or 'Second' form, may be partially formalized as follows: 'q' for '(Ex)Px' there is a perfect being, or perfection exists:

1. $q \Rightarrow Lq$	'Anselm's Principle': Perfection could not exist contingently
2. $Lq \vee \neg Lq$	Excluded Middle (only valid in classical logic!)
3. $\neg Lq \Rightarrow L \neg Lq$	Form of Becker's Postulate: modal status is always necessary (This is Hartshorne's formulation. I would indicate that this step is only valid in S_5)
4. $Lq \vee L \neg Lq$	Inference from (2, 3)
5. $L \neg Lq \Rightarrow L \neg q$	Inference from (1): the necessary falsity of the consequent implies that of the antecedent (Modal form of *modus tollens*)
6. $Lq \vee L \neg q$	Inference from (4, 5). This is CT!
7. $\neg L \neg q$	Intuitive postulate or conclusion from other theistic arguments: perfection is not impossible
8. Lq	Inference from (6, 7)

9. $Lq \Rightarrow q$	Modal axiom
10. q	Inference from (8, 9)

(Here the sign '$\neg$' stands for negation and the sign '$\Rightarrow$' stands for strict implication. This is at least the custom among logicians. In mathematics one may find the latter sign for material implication!).

Given Anselm's Principle (step 1) the proof runs unobjectionably until step 6, if we may presuppose classical logic and the system S_5. This step 6 may be considered as the central thesis (CT) of Hartshorne's proof. It is a major achievement of Hartshorne to have proved this important thesis (proposition). Step 7 is the weakest step in the argument, also acknowledged as such by Hartshorne.

2. *Hartshorne's simplified version of the proof*

In a letter to me Hartshorne himself proposed the following simplified version of his proof. The explanations are mine:

1. $\neg L \neg q$	Assumption. God is possible
2. $L (\neg q \lor Lq)$	Transformation of Anselm's Principle
3. $L \neg q \lor LLq$	From 2 by Theorem T29 of Hughes and Cresswell, op. cit., p. 5 (only valid in S_5!)
4. $L \neg q \lor Lq$	From 3. In S_5 (and S_4) LLq is equivalent with Lq
5. Lq	By 1 and 4
6. q	From 5

Indeed Hartshorne once more showed his genius in constructing a simpler proof. Here one can see the two fundamental presuppositions immediately (steps 1 and 2).

3. *Modal reconstruction of the cosmological argument*

Various reconstructions of the cosmological argument with the help of modal logic are possible. We will discuss two kinds of them, viz that with the help of modal predicate logic in which a primitive concept 'active working ground' is introduced, referred to with the symbol G. 'Gx' means now 'x is an active working ground'. In the other kind of proofs modal propositional logic is used. Here we do not need this primitive concept, for now the relation ground-consequence is expressed by the implication or equivalence relations. Here we have to do with the concepts of sufficient and necessary conditions.

4. *Proofs with the help of modal predicate logic*

We may prove God's existence here in a system stricter than S_5 and, as we have seen, this is an advantage. The difference is, however, not so great, for we have to use the Barcan formula, which is provable in S_5, but not in S_4. But still we have thus proven God's existence in a system stricter than S_5, for we have now proved it in S_4 + the Barcan formula! But, unfortunately we have to 'pay' for this stricter system with a less plausible premise. If we introduce a second variant in which this premise is replaced by a more probable one, we are in S_5 again! Further we will consider some other translations of the relation 'being the ground of'. But we shall see that then the proofs go more easily.

For a technical exposition of the Barcan formula and for some other technical details of the argument I may refer to the work of Hughes and Cresswell mentioned above. The Barcan formula is treated on pages 142–145. It may be represented in the following way:

(i) $(x)\, Lfx \rightarrow L(x)fx$

As is well-known the reversal is without problems and is valid in all modal systems:

(ii) $L(x)fx \rightarrow (x)\, L\, fx$

The structure of the proof is the same as in set theory, i.e., here too we need to recur to a multiple application of the principle '*ex nihilo nihil fit*'.

VARIANT A

1. $(x)\, L\, (fx \leftrightarrow Gb)$ *Premise*: There are states of affairs which have necessarily a certain ground, i.e, that in all worlds in which fx occurs b, its ground, also occurs. For the proof it is irrelevant whether we take this ground as a necessarily necessary condition $L(\rightarrow)$ or as a necessarily sufficient and necessary condition $L(\leftrightarrow)$. Here b is a constant parameter and G a constant predicate-symbol 'ground'. The domain of interpretation of f is limited, i.e., the premise is not necessarily valid for each predicate. If it were this would be the better for the proof!

2. (Ey) L ((x) L(fx ↔ Gb)   *Premise*: There is a ground for premise 1
   ↔ Gy)   and as the state of affairs in 1 is necessary,
the functor that expresses this ground must
also be necessary L (↔), because something that is necessary cannot have a contingent ground. Here too it is irrelevant
whether we take this to be a necessarily
necessary ground or a necessarily sufficient
and necessary ground. This premise expresses the multiple application of '*ex nihilo nihil fit*'

3. L (x) fx ↔ Gb   From 1; application of the Barcan formula

4. L (Ey) ((x) L(fx ↔ Gb)   From 2; application of Thesis T4 in
   ↔ Gy)   Hughes and Cresswell, op. cit., p. 144

5. L (L (x) (fx ↔ Gb) → Gc)   From 4; Existential Instantiation and again
application of the Barcan formula

6. L (x) (fx ↔ Gb) → LGc   From 5; derivation of the strict implication
from the strict equivalence. Further appli-
cation of the distribution axiom (T6)
(Hughes and Cresswell, op. cit., p. 31)
and T19 (op. cit., p. 46)

7. LGc   From 3 and 6 (*modus ponendo ponens*)

8. (Ex) LGx From 7; Existential Generalisation.

We may interpret this conclusion (Ex) LGx as 'There is a necessary ground, i.e.,
a ground in all possible worlds, an *ens necessarium* and a *causa necessaria*'.

Perhaps not everybody will consider premise 1 given above plausible. We
may, however, weaken it by considering it only as a possibility and as this
premise is not logically contradictory, it is then very convincing. The proof now
runs as follows:

VARIANT B

1. M (x) L(fx ↔ Gb)   Premise

2. M L(x) (fx ↔ Gb)   From 1; Barcan formula

3. L (x) (fx ↔ Gb)   From 2; Hughes and Cresswell, op. cit., T25
(p. 25), which theorem is only valid in S_5.

and this is again step 3 of the proof in variant A. Together with premise 2 (step 2) the rest of the proof is the same as the proof above. But this second variant is, however, less strict, for we have to do here with system S_5, and no longer with the system S_4 to which the Barcan formula has been added.

VARIANT C

The translation of the rule '*ex nihilo nihil fit*' in step (premise) 2 of variant A is not necessary. It is also possible to translate it in a weaker way, i.e., in such a way that the premise says (presupposes) more. Step 2 in variant C now runs:

$$2.\ L((x)\ L\ (fx \leftrightarrow Gb) \leftrightarrow (Ey)\ Gy)$$

This translation says more than the translation in variant A, for now it is already presupposed that this active working ground is in all worlds the same. It is no wonder that now the proof runs a little bit more easily for we may make the same steps as in variant A, but step 4 can now be inferred without an appeal to theorem T4 of Hughes and Cresswell.

VARIANT D

Not only step 2 can be translated differently, but also step 1. In a personal communication G. I. Mavrodes and A. O'Hear required that the translation should be done in the language of the *Principia Mathematica*, i.e., so that all existential statements should be translated with the help of the existential quantifier $(\exists x)$. I do not think that this is necessary; what is more, I think that one should distinguish between the statements 'there is . . .' and 'some . . .'. That we may do so, has been demonstrated sufficiently by the Polish logician Leśnievski. But on the other hand I have no objection to using the language of the *Principia Mathematica*. In this way step 1 is translated $(\exists x)\ L\ (fx \leftrightarrow Gb)$ instead of $(x)\ L\ (fx \leftrightarrow Gb)$. This has even the advantage that now the proof can be given in S_4 even without using the Barcan formula. The proof now runs:

1. $(\exists x)\ L\ (fx \leftrightarrow Gb)$	1st premise in the new translation.
2. $L(\exists x)\ (fx \leftrightarrow Gb)$	From 1; Hughes and Cresswell, op. cit., p. 144 (T4), (valid in S_4).
3. $(\exists y)\ L(L(\exists x)\ (fx \leftrightarrow Gb) \leftrightarrow Gy)$	2nd premise. There is necessarily a ground for the state of affairs mentioned in step 2 (and 1).
4. $L(L\ (\exists x)\ (fx \leftrightarrow Gb) \leftrightarrow Gc)$	From 3; existential instantiation.

5. $L(\exists x)(fx \leftrightarrow Gb) \leftrightarrow LGc$ From 4; derivation of the implication from the equivalence. Further Hughes and Cresswell, p. 31 (A6) and p. 46 (T19). Both the axiom A6 and the theorem T19 are valid in S_4.

6. LGc 2, 5. *Modus ponendo ponens*

7. $(\exists x) LGx$ From 6; existential generalization.

The great difference with the proof in variant A is, that now the whole argument is valid in S_4, which is an advantage.

5. *Proofs with the help of modal propositional logic*

We can also give the proof by using modal propositional logic only. From the premises 'there is a (certain) state of affairs' and 'for the *possibility* of this state of affairs there is necessarily required a necessary (or a necessary and sufficient) ground' we may infer that there must be an *ens necessarium*. The multiple application of the principle '*ex nihilo nihil fit*' is introduced here when we formulate in our second premise 'for the possibility of this state of affairs' and not simply 'for this state of affairs'. Since we may represent beings as states of affairs (like Hartshorne, Scholz, Carnap, and others!), we can formulate an *ens necessarium* by Lq. So we have to prove the following thesis:

$$(p \& L(Mp \rightarrow q) \rightarrow Lq$$

We do this by using a system of natural deduction. For the technical details of this we must again refer to Hughes and Cresswell, op. cit., pp. 331ff.

1. $p \& L(Mp \rightarrow q)$ Premise

2. p From 1; elimination of the conjunction

3. $L(Mp \rightarrow q)$ From 1; elimination of the conjunction

4. Mp From 2; theorem T1 of Hughes and Cresswell, op. cit., p. 33

5. $\square$ | $Mp \rightarrow q$ From 3; strict reiteration

6. Mp From 4; strict reiteration (only allowed in S_5

7. q From 5 and 6; elimination of the implication (= *Modus ponendo ponens*)

8. Lq From 7, introduction of necessity.

By inferring Lq from the premises $p \& L(Mp \rightarrow q)$ we have proved our thesis.

19

Robert C. Neville

TIME, TEMPORALITY, AND ONTOLOGY

A lthough he has been the first to credit his intellectual antecedents, sometimes lifting them from historical obscurity, Charles Hartshorne is a focal thinker for our century on the topic of time. Modestly characterizing his view as a simplification and logical clarification of Peirce and Whitehead, Hartshorne has articulated what I take to be the essential twentieth-century contribution to a metaphysical theory of time, and he has done this again and again.[1] The process of time is incremental, he says, and therefore asymmetrical. The past consists of fixed facts, and the future of possibilities. Since the present is the occasion of change that reduces possible future options to an achieved definite singularity, change has the structure of freedom, and in human beings with a capacity to employ propositions to anticipate the future (and know other things), this freedom can be significant human freedom. These are the simplified essentials of a metaphysics of freedom with which I am in full agreement. The purpose of this essay is to extend Hartshorne's conception to the full range of temporality and to inquire into its ontological foundations.

I. Timeliness and Temporality

Present Timeliness. It can hardly be doubted, after Hartshorne's contribution to process philosophy, that the present is the temporal mode in which change takes place. The special timeliness of the present, then, is the decision-making action that renders given conditions into a new situation. Present-timeliness cannot be analyzed as earlier and later, since that would require two different actions (one which is finished earlier so the later can begin), hence two presents. Rather, present-timeliness can be analyzed in two aspects. Objectively, it consists in a series of stages before and after decisions are made to reduce the relative indefiniteness of the before-decision stage to the relative definiteness of the after-decision stage; the stage achieving complete definiteness or individuality is not before any other stage in that present. Subjectively, present-timeliness consists in the decidings; correlated with objective stages are many decisions, but none earlier than another; the immediate subjectivity of a present moment is simply the active intention to wreak this immediately given set of conditions into some this-determinate outcome.

Present Temporality. I've used the word "timeliness" to indicate the mode of time for the present, and will shortly characterize the timeliness of the past and future. "Temporality" by contrast I use to mean the way by which something relates to time as such, or is constituted by time. The temporality of the present thus includes an earlier past and a future which shall come after. This temporality is internally constitutive of the present as present. It includes causal conditions as past, with their own timely and temporal structures. Part of the temporality of the present is thus to have a history leading up to it, providing its situation and its multitude of contents to be resolved. Although the timeliness of the present as such is decisive action, the temporality of the present includes an inherited past with which to act.[2]

Whitehead's analysis of concrescence in Part Three of *Process and Reality*, beginning with initial data in subjective unity and ending with the satisfaction of subjective harmony, is an exclusively timely analysis. Although the initial data are themselves past entities, this is an external point to the analysis of concrescence, and is to be accounted for by means of transition, another kind of process in Whitehead's view. With respect to the *temporal* aspect of the present, the past is ingredient as genuinely past.

Past Timeliness. The timeliness of the past is objective everlastingness. Once having happened, a change is an addition to what had happened before, fitting in according to its character. To call the past "objective" is to indicate its fixed character that can be an objective condition for subsequent present moments of change. It has that character by virtue of being a finished change, not by actually being involved in a subsequent change (although it may in fact be so involved). The asymmetry of time, to which Hartshorne has so eloquently and often argued, demands that the past have whatever character it has irrespective of what comes after; and it has that character everlastingly: nothing can change it. That a past moment is objective does not entail that a subsequent moment in fact is able to accept it as a condition; its causal influence might in fact stop with itself, and still it would be objective; ready to condition anything that could accept (or as Whitehead and Hartshorne would say, prehend) it.

It might be argued, as Hartshorne has, that any completed, and therefore past, change must in principle exist in a subsequent event which it conditions. There are two main lines of argument for this thesis. The first is that the objectivity of the past simply requires an actual subject in which to inhere;

otherwise it passes away. This is to affirm what Heidegger and others deride as the "metaphysics of presence." Thus, some process theologians argue that since ordinary things might neglect something from the past, there must be a God who assumes all finished things as conditions, else they would have no being. This argument, however, assumes without warrant that only present existence is real. The past is real precisely as past, as finished fact, as Hartshorne would say, and it is this whether or not anything else comes along, and whether or not the past makes a difference to anything else. The past, in becoming itself makes a difference to itself, and that difference is everlasting even if uninfluential. To assume that only the present is real constitutes a special danger for process philosophy; for, if the present is becoming, not being, and other things are real only insofar as they register in the present, then the whole of things threatens to slip into Maya.

The second argument to the effect that a past thing must be ingredient in some present thing stems from an interpretation of creativity itself. Following Whitehead, Hartshorne and many others say that any given plurality, *any and all*, requires unification in a subsequent event. Hence, at least some (immediately) subsequent event by definition must include the whole past in some guise or another. Since finite events transmute and distort their conditions, there must be a divine event that is incapable of losing anything. There is a hidden supposition of totalization in this argument, however, of which Whitehead was aware.[3]

In the train of finite events, some elements of the past are obviously lost. There are two ways of accounting for this. One is that present events simply cannot find a place within themselves for some past thing and prehend it negatively. In this case, the internal constitution or subjective form achieved by the negatively prehending present reflects the absence of the past thing; in this diminished sense, the past is objectified as particularly missing in the subsequent event. The other account of loss is the limitation imposed by what Whitehead called subjective unity, the limited set of initial conditions given as an occasion's data. If two contemporary occasions had exactly the same initial data, and if they include nothing of one another's creative contributions because they are each, in the present, still becoming, then it would be conceivable that there be numerically distinct but fully identical things, or otherwise contradictory things in the same space and time. The differences between contemporaries therefore consist not only in their doing different things with many of the same data, but also in their having slightly different sets of data to begin with, different subjective unities. An accomplished past thing, therefore, might not occur among any subsequent thing's initial data.

To say that God in principle must include everything is simply to beg the point here. Is it not the case that creativity requires only that, given a plurality of things, something new must emerge from it, perhaps neglecting some of the plurality? There must be some diversity for the sake of the emerging present event, but not necessarily including the whole of the things that have been achieved. As a picture of the creative advance, therefore, we may entertain a rather loosely connected universe, with pockets of order constituted by lines of conditioning, separated by relative neglect and low levels of order. If a past thing is completely and totally ignored by subsequent events, of course we would not know of it, and would call it part of the universe only "on principle." But for itself, and as the inheritor of its own past, it is objectively and everlastingly real, ready to condition anything ready to be conditioned by it.

Past Temporality. In contrast to its timeliness, the temporality of the past is to exhibit matrices of cohabitation among its own elements and in relation to the present and future. These matrices are structures of togetherness, such as temporal relations of precedence and consequence, spatial relations, and all kinds of causal relations in terms of which one thing conditions another. All disciplines of inquiry contribute their own matrices which, to the extent they are truthful, pick out dimensions of coordinate structure; physics treats many more dimensions of space-time than the usual four of common sense. Since each past thing was once a present moment, each has a wholly determinate relation to what was in its own past. Apart from the fact that a past thing once was present, and determined its relations in its present timeliness, the borders of past things are trivial relative to the matrices constituting their togetherness. In reference to the past, therefore, it is unimportant which were the items or events that had individual present immediacy. What is important are the structures they variously constitute together. A present moment in its own temporality receives the past not as a set of individual past "presents" but as a structured environment, a complex group of lines of influence, a unified past set of growing identities.

With respect to the temporal past, it is important to modify process philosophy's characteristic use of the notion of "thing." It is pointless to speak of actual occasions in the temporal past. The point is to speak of the actual things constituted by the coordinating structures of space, time, and causal inheritance. The structured things may have been made by the actions of many actual entities in their present moments, but how many and which ones do not matter except for identifying continuing individuals with responsibility. What matters is the kind of structure actualized, how tight it is, how the structured group interacts with others, and so forth. Science, which models its notion of "thing" on the past (as process philosophers since Bergson have noted), deals with reality insofar as it can be identified and manipulated according to its coordinate structures. (So it is a total mistake to attempt to identify a Whiteheadian actual occasion as an atomic particle; atomic particles and processes are structures characteristic of the temporal past.)

Because the structured thingness of past temporality is what environs, calls up, and funds all present moments, present actions should be thought of as actions of temporally thick things; similarly, the temporal future is structured by the ongoing careers of temporally thick things, acting moment by moment. "Temporal thickness" is not the specious present (a characteristic of the timeliness of the present) but rather is the character of things whose identity includes some past, present, and future, temporally related and comprehensively including the diverse timeliness of past, present, and future.

This recommendation about the language of "things" qualifies the extension of the use of the term "actual occasion (or entity)" as characteristic of process philosophy without in the least diminishing its importance. The role of the process analysis of actual occasions is to explain existence and change, two absolutely central topics. The analysis of present moments in what I have called their timely aspect is a signal contribution of process philosophy, addressing a disastrous lacuna in both the classical and the modern notion of substance and change. By generalizing the account of concrescence in a present moment to the past as merely finished, however, and to the future as not yet concrescing, process philosophy has opened itself to attacks from thinkers such as Paul Weiss and David Weissman who fix upon the "equal" truth in the substance emphasis on temporally thick structured identities and interactions.[4] The dominating focus on the timely structure of the present, characteristic of much process philosophy, has also made it difficult to register the sense of past and future temporal horizons elaborated by Husserl and Heidegger, and the sense of contemporary bodily thickness discussed by Merleau-Ponty. That exaggerated focus has given rise to accusations of overweening atomism, despite the fact that Whitehead, Hartshorne, and others emphasize the immanence of the past in the present and the superjective character of the present toward the future. "Immanence" and "superjection" are simply not persuasive under the influence of an over-emphasis on the timeliness of the present, on concrescence. They require an acknowledgment and analysis of what I have called temporality. Whitehead felt this need, I believe, and responded with the passages cited so beautifully by Wallach in her defense of the thesis that actual occasions can be of any temporal and spatial size whatsoever, and can include other occasions wholly within them; she in fact was pointing to the temporality of present, past, and future, but analyzing it with process philosophy's limited thematic tool, the timely structure of the present, concrescence.[5]

The temporality of the past relative to the present is to be structured potentialities for change, maybe with important vagueness for present decision making; the temporality of the past for the future beyond the present is vaguer potentialities waiting upon the present.

Future Timeliness. The timeliness of the future is the subjunctive normativeness of good ways of harmonizing things. That is, the future's timeliness is the non-date-referred condition that pattern x harmonizes a, b, and c with m value, y harmonizes them with n value, z harmonizes b, c, and d with o value, and so forth. This is the realm of Platonic forms, wholly subjunctive and not very timely in any usual sense at all. Normative patterns are wholly indeterminate without a multiplicity to harmonize, and by itself the future's multiplicity is strictly hypothetical. In itself, the future is not in time except negatively, by being not yet.

Future Temporality. The temporality of the future, however, is to be those patterns that integrate the past as it is being changed in the present. Therefore the temporal structure of the future is to be a constantly shifting set of patterns of possibilities for which the past provides and the future exercises potentialities. More specifically, the far future consists of very vague patterns for achieving value. The immediately next future consists of patterns only so vague as can be resolved by the present decisions. In between are patterns of intermediate vagueness that shift as things become determinate. That a pattern is vague means that it can be actualized in more than one way (the morrow can see either a sea battle or no sea battle—Aristotle). The temporal structure of the future is thus extraordinarily dynamic; the future is always changing, depending on what is happening. This dynamic quality, providing present moments with possibilities, can be seen as an aspect of sheer creativity, and it has led Lewis Ford to call it God.[6]

The temporalities of present, past, and future are related. The temporality of the present is to inherit the structured past and to determine the vague normative future by its decisions. The temporality of the past is to be its fixed self, providing structured, achieved actuality for subsequent events and delimiting hypothetical normative possibilities into actual but not actualized potentialities. The temporality of the future is to provide ways by which dated decisions can combine the structured conditions of the past into new achievements of value; the shifting temporality of the future comes from the fact the different presents of decisions come each with its own date. The temporality of dating consists of the timeliness of the now, the timeliness of the past fixed timeline, and the timeliness of the logical relations of vagueness and specificity relative to harmonizing pluralities. The timeliness of each mode is special to itself. Temporality involves the unity of time in all its modes, from the standpoint of each one.

Hartshorne rightly has focused on the present as the arena of action. By complementing his account by reference to the temporality of the past and future we can see how a temporally thick enduring individual is possible. In any given present moment, a discursive individual is also its achieved past and is faced with a partially structured future which likely contains its own future states. (Hartshorne sees the importance of acting for the future in his doctrine of the superject; but, de-emphasizing Whitehead's eternal objects, he gives little acknowledgment to a reality for the future save as an anticipation in a present concrescence.) The togetherness of present, past, and future temporalities provides for a temporally changing structured actuality that embodies a definite value moment by moment and at every moment is normatively affected by commitments arising from its own achievements.

Perishing. Two senses of perishing are paramount for an understanding of time: the perishing of subjectivity and the perishing of achieved value.

Following Hartshorne and the process philosophers, it almost goes without saying that the subjective immediacy of the present moment perishes with the achievement of finished satisfaction. When a moment has finished becoming and is ready to condition subsequent moments of creativity, it has lost its subjective immediacy. That immediacy consists in the intentional dynamism of working the plurality of conditions into a definite harmony: it is the aim at the elimination of vagueness, and its activity is decision-making. In the case of the higher creatures, subjective immediacy can have the sense of an experiential orientation to the world in the diverse modes of temporality. Both past and future have their own essential features, and therefore are "subjects" of their own characters; but neither has the subjectivity of the act of existing characteristic of the present. The past is thus "dead" and the future "unborn."

From a theological motive, some philosophers have argued that the subjective immediacy of a present moment is itself ready to be prehended by subsequent divine (if not finite) moments. Hartshorne has written:

> I hold that the satisfaction contains its process of becoming ("the being cannot be abstracted from the becoming"), so that to prehend a past satisfaction is to prehend the becoming, the subjective immediacy itself, of the past actuality. The past presentness, the past becoming (which did not prehend itself, it simply was itself) is now prehended. And I see Neville's and others' arguments against this as verbal confusions. Nothing is lost, with the qualification that all non-divine prehending is more or less indistinct (Whitehead's "negative prehensions") so that, except for God, much of the past is dismissed as irrelevant and in this sense is indeed lost. But not for God, by whose adequate prehending actualities "live forevermore."[7]

John Cobb has continued the line of argument:

> For Whitehead, the way in which one moment of my experience flows into its successor is not denuded of immediacy by the fact that it has attained satisfaction. What is felt by the later occasion are the feelings of the earlier occasions. It is true that modifications are introduced into the later occasion and that in the temporal flow the immediacy of the earlier feelings fades. Whitehead's intuition is that in God this immediacy does not fade.[8]

Hartshorne and Cobb both admit that the only elements in the present available as subsequent conditions are those that are objectified in the finished satisfaction. This may well include the elements (propositions) which function at intermediate stages in concrescence, and hence are still partially indeterminate. It may also include whatever elements of subjective form accrue to the process of deciding out the indeterminacies—the "how" of a process is contained in the "what" that is produced. In this sense, the objective satisfaction of a moment might include whatever the concrescing moment thinks "about" its own process (if anything—Hartshorne doubts self-awareness within concrescence itself). But what is not objectified is the immediate process itself, including its own affect where the process is experiential. (Rather than construing natural process on the analogy of human experience, as process philosophers sometimes do, I would construe experience as a complicated natural process whose temporally present key elements come from the immediacy of the process of decision-making. Thus, rather than claiming, with Hartshorne, to be a pan-psychist for whom material nature is a special case, I would claim to be a pan-naturalist for whom cases run from mere matter with no psychic development to psychically subtle nature in which matter is no longer "mere." Models of nature from, say, physics, deal with the special cases for which they are designed.) What is lost for any moment, when it becomes past, is its own subjective immediacy of changing. This is the very heart of process philosophy's crucial distinction between the modes of time.

The second important sense of perishing is the loss of structure. As past achievements, of course, the valuable structures are everlastingly what they are. But the issue regarding this kind of perishing is whether they continue to be important conditions for the present and future. "The grass withers and the flower fades." Evil structures perish as well as good ones, and since evil so often consists in misplaced structures it might have even less adaptive advantage than the good. But all achieved value loses enduring effects, and change is not always for the better. Process theology mitigates this sense of loss by saying that all achieved structured value continues always to be enjoyed subjectively by God. If we accept that such a God is real, then the divine experience is cumulatively rich without end. But the loss of achieved value is felt by the finite world irrespective of the divine experience, and for the world the past involves perishing. From the worldly standpoint there is the constant problem to determine whether the loss is bad or good, and what to do about it. The perishing of achieved valuable structures raises practical questions about whether to recreate them, or to mourn or celebrate their loss. The poignancy of this comes in large measure for the contrast between the temporality of the present, impoverished by the perishing, and the temporality of the past in which the perished achievements have slipped to ineffectual fixities. To remark that "the word of the Lord remains forever'' need not mean that God learns and never forgets; it can mean that the creative word is what it is outside of time such that it relates the components which severally compose time.

II. Time's Ontology

What is the being of time? This is its ontological question. To set the context for its discussion certain metaphysical distinctions are useful.[9] In the most abstract sense of "thing," abstracting from time and temporality, a thing is a harmony of essential and conditional features. The essential features are those it has unique to itself; the conditional ones are those it has by virtue of which it is relative to or "conditioned" by other things. Since a thing's identity is always determinate with respect to something, it needs conditional features relating it to the something with respect to which it is determinate. Since a thing cannot merely sum up its relations but must be something which does the summing, it needs essential features. The features of a thing are themselves things in this abstract sense, and so have their own conditional and essential features. A thing is a harmony of essential and conditional features in the sense that they simply fit together; there is no "third term" required to relate them because that would be just another thing to be related to them (implying an infinite regress of relations).

With regard to time, the timeliness of the modes—present, past, and future—display the respective essential features. In a present moment, what is essential is the actual deciding that creates a new determinate state of affairs out of past potentials. Among the essential elements are the novelties of subjective form as they develop, and the creative energy, as it were, in the decision-making. Whereas the creative energy may have a field-character common to many present moments, it is essential to a given moment by virtue of being creative with its initial data, its decisions, and its individual outcome. With regard to the past, what is essential is its objective, everlasting fixity. It lacks the present's capacity to change and to participate actively in any existential field, although it exhibits the structured coordinations of its temporality. Among the essential elements in the past are its structures and the values achieved by having those structures. What is essential to the future is the normativeness of its logically possible ways of harmonizing hypothetical multiplicities. Without reference to the other modes of time this hardly has determinate status except as conventional articulations are imagined for it; hence the essential features of the future are often taken to be merely the realm of formal logic.

According to the distinction between essential and conditional features, the modes of time could not be what they are without the conditional features as well. So the essential decisive dynamism of the present could not be itself without the conditions of the past to give it specificity, to supply initial data, and without the normative structures of the future to provide potential outcomes to be decided upon. The essential features of past fixity could not be distinguished from mere arbitrarily identified logical possibility without the decisions of those moments when present, and could not even be logical possibilities without the future. The normativeness of the essence of the future would be wholly indeterminate without the fixed characters of the past to provide the multiplicity to be realized and the dynamism of the present to make the logical normativeness relevant to realization. So each mode of time contributes conditional features to the other modes, making them what we commonly know them to be in conjunction with their essential features.

Temporality is the harmony of the respective timely essential features and the conditional features the modes of time give one another. The temporality of each mode is precisely its own essential features as harmonized with the other modes, and temporality as such is the harmony of all the modes of temporality as characterized above. That is, the present inherits the past and acts decisively now further to determine the future; the past provides actual content as causal ground to the present, and structures the future with its multifariousness; the future provides the ideal, normative and logical structure exhibited in the past and luring the present decision-making.

Time is the sum of the temporalities of all things, in all their temporal modes. For each thing within time, there is a shifting locus of its temporal embodiment vis-à-vis past, present, and future depending on which moment is the relevant present now. Since Hartshorne and the other process philosophers are exactly right about the way by which the present ''now'' cuts between a determined past and partially indeterminate future, the shifting locus of the now shifts not only the date but the determinate reality of temporal beings. As Kant pointed out time is concrete and single (though perhaps not as consistently unified by coordinating structures or geometries as he thought). The question of the being of time therefore is how the temporalities of all things can be real as a sum. ''Sum'' is a cheat word in this context, and needs an analysis.

The temporality of each mode of time (past, present, future) provides one form of togetherness for the three kinds of temporality. The past unifies the temporalities according to the chronological time line (and perhaps other more sophisticated coordinates). This does justice to the essential fixity of the past, and to the conditional traits of the present as fixing thing, to be past and to the conditional traits of the future as providing possibilities for future extensions of the coordinates. But the past's temporality does not touch the essential inner decisive dynamism of the present nor the essential normativeness of future form itself. And therefore the temporality of the past cannot successfully provide the togetherness needed for the three temporalities, although it is easy to see how people enamored of coordinate temporality would try to make it do so. Existentialists and process philosophers rightly protest the deadness of the past relative to the present; ethicists and artists rightly protest its "mere factuality" when severed from the normativeness of the essential future which any past once included.

The temporality of the present unifies the three temporalities as inherited past and future potentials for present action. This does justice to the essential dynamism of the present, to the conditional readiness of the past to influence the present, and to the conditional structures supplied by the future for possible actions. But it neglects the essential objective, everlasting fixity of the past, and also the past's achieved values, because it treats both only as potentials for modification in the present's creative actions. And it neglects the essential intrinsic normativeness of the future by transforming it into what merely satisfies the need to achieve determinateness, relative to past conditions, in the present moment. From the standpoint of present temporality, past and future function as horizons for identity in the now. The past merits a respect, however, and the future a sense of obligatoriness that are not registered within the temporality of the present alone. Philosophies emphasizing present temporality tend to collapse the fixity of given fact and the normativeness of external obligations—science and ethics—into an aesthetics of the moment. By neglecting the essential features of past and future, the temporality of the present cannot fully or adequately unify the three temporalities.

The temporality of the future unifies the three temporalities as the lure for increasing ideal definiteness, the final cause. This does justice to the future's essential normativeness, to the conditioning of the future by the past as providing multiplicities, and to the conditioning of the future by the present as constantly shifting the relative determinateness and indeterminateness of possibilities. But it fails to recognize the essential objective fixity of the past's temporality insofar as it treats the past merely as potentials for limiting logical possibility. And it fails to recognize the essential dynamism of present temporality which it treats as the principle, not the action, of selection. From the standpoint of future temporality, past and present are merely specifications of ideal possibility.

That each of the three modes of temporality is insufficient to unify the three into one temporality (or, concretely, time) illustrates an important characteristic of the problem of the one and the many. Stated abstractly, if there are two things, each with essential and conditional features, each can include the other with itself by means of the other's conditional features; but by definition it cannot include the other's essential features, without making the other just a proper part of itself. Therefore, a solution to the problem of the one and the many cannot be reached from the standpoint of any one of the many alone. We have seen how any attempt to define time from the standpoint of the temporality of any mode of time, present, past, or future, leaves out exactly what is essential in the other modes of time.

Therefore, that time which is the unity of the three kinds of temporality is somehow simply a fitting together of those three, a harmony of them. But how can this be characterized? Not by appeal to any of the senses of temporality within the harmony, by virtue of the above arguments. Must we then adopt the classic position of defining temporality in terms of "eternity"?

I believe we must indeed appeal to eternity to understand time. For, there is a togetherness of the modes of time that is not a function of any of the kinds of temporality. Put most paradoxically, there is a togetherness of a thing's youth, when its maturity is still undetermined, with its age when nearly everything is fixed. Temporal sequence is not the whole of the togetherness because the thing's determinate character is different at different stages in the sequence. Being horizoned by past and future is not the whole, because the center constantly shifts and the horizons gain and lose. The process of determining vague possibilities is not the whole because it neglects achievement and the action of decision. Therefore there must be some kind of non-temporal or eternal togetherness, not abstract as Hartshorne would say, but more concretely inclusive than any being in a given temporal mode.

But what can eternity be? It cannot be the *totum simul* eternity opposite present temporality precisely because there is no "at once, no *simul*," that registers that a thing which is indeterminate at one date becomes determinate later; *totum simul* eternity presupposes complete determinism in the temporal process, and cannot account for the passage of time making any difference. This eliminates many theological answers to the question of time. Nor can eternity be the opposite of past temporality, the eternity for which time is its moving image; for by citing eternal coordinates, this answer separates eternity from the actual movement required, and cannot account, for movement; the eternity of coordinates is in fact as deterministic and static as that of the *totum simul*. Nor can the eternity be the Aristotelian completeness of the final cause which moves by attraction, not moving itself; for that eternity accounts neither for the existence of actual things to be moved nor for the moving, and hence is too vague to relate to time at all.

The eternity making sense of time, I suggest, is that of an ontological or divine creative act which creates things that are in time, with successive present dates, etc., but which is itself not in time and hence not temporal. Only the created things are in time. As such, temporal created things succeed one another in timely fashion. Each present thing, as present, has a fixed past and a perhaps partially open future. Each past thing, or part of a thing which is past, has a character achieved in itself and also available to enter into and condition subsequent entities, and to restrict future potentialities. Each future thing is a normative way of harmonizing increasingly determinate possibilities that are in the way of being actualized. As time passes, a self-identical thing shifts temporal modes from future to present to past, changing its nature as it does so. There is no ontological date at which a thing's participation in time is simply what it is; there is only the temporal date, when it is past, at which the thing no longer can participate in time in a changing way. Time simply does not exist wholly at a time.

Ontological divine creation is temporal only because temporal things are created. To ask, for instance, whether the future is divinely determined presupposes a present to which that future is relative; and from the standpoint of that present, of course the future is indeterminate in part. But that present does not register the whole of time. The act of creation is temporal only in its products, not in its actions.

The unity of the act of creation consists in whatever is involved in the diverse essential features of what is created. With regard to time, this means that the divine creative act provides a context of mutual relevance in which the essential features of the present (decision-making, etc.), those of the past (objective fixity, etc.) and those of the future (normativeness, etc.) are together. Because the essential features are together, it is possible for the three modes of temporality to condition one another and therefore have the conditional features required for each to be itself. Each mode of temporality is a harmony of its essential and conditional features. The conditional ways by which the modes are together constitute our three temporal ways of unifying time. But the very existence of the conditional ways presupposes a more basic togetherness in which the diverse essential features are unified. Without the togetherness of the essential features, there could be no togetherness of the conditional features. The ontological divine creative act is eternal in the sense that its function as a context of mutual relevance is a precondition for all temporal relations, as displayed above.

Apart from creating things, there is no character to the ontological ground or divinity, since all "character" requires essential and conditional features, all of which must be created. The identification of the ontological ground comes from noting that there are indeed finite, temporal things which must be grounded. I call that ground "divine" because creation makes the affinity of essential features for each other that have no worldly contact save through conditional features; this is profound love or compassion, deeper than the conditional connections of things which can be brutal beyond belief.

Time is simply the created togetherness of the modes of temporality. Things participate in time by having those modes, all three modes. But the modes are not determinately consistent within time. From any point within time, regardless of the mode, the essential features of the other modes are opaque. The modes are determinately consistent only within the eternity of the ontological, divine creative act by which the things are made to be together each with its own shifting dates. To say anything simpler than this is to render impossible the recognition of some essential part of temporality, which is to be strangely untimely.

Time is real enough. But it is not difficult to see why it appears unreal if one starts with a prejudice for some one mode of temporality over the others, or if one starts by taking definite reality to be the capacity to create ontologically. The creator is unreal except as actually creating, and the individual modes of temporality are partial embodiments of what we know of the fullness of time.

Ontological creation commonly is construed as bringing something into existence, and this is an adequate construction for those things which exist. In a present moment, for instance, the dynamic decision-making brings a new entity into existence out of the resources of the past things; what is new is spontaneously created. The past resources in turn were themselves once new, with their novelty being an existential spontaneity at the date of their emergence, combined with their own antecedents, and so on back. The creation of actual existence takes place in present dated moments through the spontaneous harmonization of previous entities, which themselves were once created. The future does not exist, and hence is not created as an existent. It is real, however, since it has identity, shifting identity even. The creation of the future therefore has to be appropriate to future reality, to normativity. The generic notion of creation required is that the ontological creative act makes a thing's essential features in harmony with its conditional features; since the latter entail other things to provide the conditioning, the same creative act must create those other things, with their essential and conditional features. This creation of all related, different things together, with their individual harmonies of essential and conditional features, is the ontological ground functioning as the context for mutual relevance. Only a theory which acknowledges the mutual relevance of diverse things with uncommunicating essential features can do justice to the metaphysical pluralism our world displays, especially with respect to time.

The remarks about existence and the future in the previous paragraph reflect a construction of creation from the standpoint of the temporality of the present alone. It is more or less consonant with process philosophy which emphasizes that standpoint. Hartshorne, following Whitehead, sharply distinguishes onto-logical creativity from God. But on his scheme they work together to create in much the way the text here depicts. That is, creativity always makes a spontaneous new one out of the previous many; God lures each spontaneous process of concrescence. Therefore God plus creativity account for everything new in any entity, and they also account for what is old in that entity by having cooperated to create it in its own dated present.[10] From the standpoint of the temporality of the past, creation means sustaining the objective fixed contingent actuality of things everlastingly; and it means connecting the coordinating structures of the past to future possibilities and present actions. This sense of creation has been associated in the West with the creative mind of God, from the speculations of Augustine through those of Newton. In the East it has been captured in large part by the idea of the Buddha-world. Deep as these metaphors for creativity in the temporality of the past might be, they display only part of ontological creativity.

Creation in the mode of future temporality has not received the attention it deserves because of the prejudice that believes only presently existing things are created. Plato was getting at it in the *Philebus*, however, when he talked about the cause of mixture which achieves value in combining the limited and the unlimited; he also knew to say, in the *Republic*, that the Form of the Good creates both the visible world and invisible world (the forms), as well as our capacities to know them. Creation of future temporality alone is just as limited a sense of ontological creativity as that of present and past temporality.

At the heart of the deep mystery of time is the fact that time's true and whole creation, the creation of all three modes of temporality mutually conditioning one another, can be apprehended only at the metaphysical level in which their essential and conditional features are acknowledged and distinguished. Time does not exist within time, nor is its creation temporal. Whether by metaphysical dialectic or mystic vision, one must attain to the juncture of eternity with time to appreciate time as such. It seems that every major civilization has done that.

III. NOTES ON THE TEMPORAL STRUCTURE OF HUMAN BEING

Twentieth-century accounts of human time have been decidedly anthropocentric. This may not seem surprising since the topic is *human* time. But it is one thing to say that the contours of human life are shaped within time and quite another to say that time is a construct of the ontological character of human life. Insofar as process philosophy emphasizes the temporality of the present and interprets present concrescence on the model of abstracted human experience, its time sense is decidedly human. Existential and phenomenological approaches to time agree with the process focus on present temporality by their attention to consciousness (consciousness is an exclusively present temporal phenomenon); an interpretation of time in terms of horizons for awareness repeats the anthropocentrism. Even linguistic philosophy, when it pays attention to time at all, does so in terms of its embodiment in human language.

The most striking feature of the account of time in three temporal modes is that it makes time the measure of human embodiment rather than the other way around. The temporality of the past presents a nature measuring human life, a nature to be respected for itself, irrespective of human interests except insofar as contained there. The temporality of the future presents a realm of norms obliging human life by their intrinsic worth, irrespective of human interests except as those interests lie among the future possibilities. The temporalities of past, present, and future together present an objective, dynamic, value-laden time in which human beings find roles appropriate to their personal and social natures. The eternity of the togetherness of the modes of time is the ultimate measure of human truthfulness about the topic.

An account of human time relative to past temporality must emphasize the obligation to truth, both to representing things truly and to being true. Truthfulness is not the temporal mode of relation only to the past, but also to present and future insofar as these exhibit the coordinate objectivity of the temporality of the past. We are to be true to present and future insofar as they have objective characters that will or may become achieved. Both in representation and in life, past temporality implies a kind of piety toward the objectively real, toward nature. Past temporality means that there are things to which we must conform if we are to realize human time. This stands in contrast to the diminished position which says that there are only things which we are to use, things whose reality is exhausted in their being conditions for our own present existence. Whether in past, present, or future, the temporality of the past gives things a dignity to which human time implies respect. How paradoxical it is that the cry, "to the things themselves!" was uttered by philosophers who limited things to their appearance within human experience. Because of the temporality of the past, human experience should be conformed to the things, and we are untimely until we do so, as if we seek to escape the full dimension of human time. The aesthetics of present temporality is insufficient for truthfulness.

The temporality of the future lays an objective normativeness on human experience. Both interpretations (that might be true or false) and the selective directions of human life are guided by interests. As the pragmatists pointed out, truth is always qualified by the limited respects in which that which claims to be true selectively represents its objects. As they also pointed out in their more careful statements, the basic issue about human interests and purposes is not how to fulfill them but whether they are the best ones. The normativeness in future temporality is not reducible to human purposes, but measures them. Human timeliness is thus in a double consideration of purpose: from present temporality comes the human constitution as being essentially interested or purposed, and in relation to future temporality these interests and purposes are normed as justified or not. Because the future exhibits structures crossing possibilities for everything, the norms for human purposes respect private human interests only incidentally. Human purposes are judged by norms for the good of all. No one has stressed this more than Hartshorne.

The temporalities of past, present, and future together constitute human timeliness as respectful of the values achieved in process and the obligations devolving upon the decisions of life. Process philosophers, particularly in the work of Hartshorne, and pragmatism have distinguished themselves in this age of scientific and phenomenological positivism by their stress on the value-laden quality of life. Even when their expressions have emphasized the contours of present temporality, they have understood that value is characteristic of nature, not just the human sphere. To recognize the three-fold character of temporalities, past, present, and future, is to be in a position to characterize the values of things as normative for human life.

Process philosophy, especially that of Hartshorne, has rightly seen that present temporality displays the only time in which people are free to do something about their circumstances. Without creative freedom, people would not be responsible: responsibility would be traced back to the indefinitely far past through the lines of coordinate connection. Without creative freedom, the norms of the future would never become anyone's personal responsibility. The temporality of the present is indeed the existential center of all human temporality.

Although the present moment of becoming might be isolated in its timeliness, its past and future constituents (the only objective constituents it has) are interrelated and social. The structuring of the past and interpretation of the future are both learned from socially developed structures. The time of human persons is thereby a social time, not of individuals alone but of individuals constituted in part by their interactions with social artifacts such as signs. As a consequence, the time-sense of human life is social, not individual per se.

If the account given above is on the right road, human being in time has not one temporality but three. As a result, being in time is not only temporal but an eternal togetherness of three temporalities. Neglecting the eternal dimension, one either falls into confusion about the temporal dimensions or acknowledges one to the exclusion or distortion of the others. The age of science emphasized the temporality of the past, and translated the other temporalities into past terms insofar as it recognized them (e.g. deterministic interpretations of choice). The jaded post scientific age of our own time emphasizes present temporality where the translation of truth and moral value into aesthetics seems proof against de-existentialized past temporality. Not since the Christian middle ages has a concern for the normative future dominated the sense for truth. A balanced view of human time requires all three modes of temporality. This is a complex way to live—balancing incommeasurables as it were. But the search for simplicity is merely an aspect of present aestheticism from which reverence for truth and commitment to real norms must rescue us.

ROBERT C. NEVILLE

DEPARTMENTS OF PHILOSOPHY AND RELIGION
THE SCHOOL OF THEOLOGY
BOSTON UNIVERSITY
JUNE 1986

NOTES

1. Among Hartshorne's many discussions of time are: *The Divine Relativity: A Social Conception of God* (New Haven: Yale University Press, 1948), passim; *The Logic of Perfection and Other Essays in Neoclassical Metaphysics* (La Salle, Ill.: Open Court Publishing Company, 1962), Chapter Ten, "Time, Death, and Everlasting Life"; *Creative Synthesis and Philosophic Method* (La Salle, Ill.: Open Court Publishing Company, 1970), passim; *Insights and Oversights of Great Thinkers* (Albany: State University of New York Press, 1983), especially Chapter Four, "Aristotle's Modal View of Time and Eternity"; *Omnipotence and Other Theological Mistakes* (Albany: State University of New York Press, 1984), passim; and *Creativity in American Philosophy* (Albany: State University of New York Press, 1984), especially Chapter Seven, "A Revision of Peirce's Categories."

2. George Allan has performed a remarkable service in calling attention to the role of the past for any processive view of nature and history in his excellent book, *The Importances of the Past: A Meditation on the Authority of Tradition* (Albany: State University of New York Press, 1986).

3. See my essay, "Hegel and Whitehead on Totality: The Failure of a Conception of System," in *Hegel and Whitehead: Contemporary Perspectives on Systematic Philosophy*, edited by George R. Lucas, Jr. (Albany: State University of New York Press, 1986).

4. See, for instance, Paul Weiss's *Reality* (Princeton: Princeton University Press, 1939), passim, or *First Considerations* (Carbondale, Ill.: Southern Illinois University Press, 1977), pp. 223–237. See Weissman's essay, "The Spiral of Reflection," in *New Essays in Metaphysics*, edited by Robert C. Neville (Albany: State University of New York Press, 1987).

5. See F. Bradford Wallack, *The Epochal Nature of Process in Whitehead's Metaphysics* (Albany: State University of New York Press, 1980).

6. See Ford's "Creativity in a Future Key" in *New Essays in Metaphysics*.

7. In "Three Responses, cited above, pp. 93–94.

8. Ibid., p. 100.

9. These distinctions can be defended on their own but they are part of a speculative metaphysical theory I have developed elsewhere. See *God the Creator* (Chicago: University of Chicago Press, 1968), Chapters Two and Three; *The Cosmology of Freedom* (New Haven: Yale University Press, 1974), Chapters Two through Six; *Reconstruction of Thinking* (Albany: State University of New York Press, 1981), Chapters Three and Four.

They are applied specifically to time in *Recovery of the Measure* (Albany: State University of New York Press, 1989), where Chapters Nine and Ten are developments of the present essay.

10. See for instance Hartshorne's *The Logic of Perfection* and my *Creativity and God* (New York: Seabury Press, 1980). For Hartshorne's presentation of his own specific position relative to my own criticism of it, see his contribution, with John B. Cobb, Jr. and Lewis S. Ford, to "Three Responses to Neville's *Creativity and God*," in *Process Studies* 10/3–4 (Fall-Winter, 1980), and my response, "Concerning *Creativity and God*: A Response," in the same journal, 11/1 (Spring, 1981). Because my criticisms of Hartshorne's theology have been expressed and discussed elsewhere, my emphasis here has been on conciliatory positive construction.

20

T. L. S. Sprigge

HARTSHORNE'S CONCEPTION
OF THE PAST

Hartshorne is very probably the most important living metaphysician. He has developed a metaphysical system in the great tradition of such thinkers as Spinoza and Leibniz, but which breaks fundamentally new ground. From his writings a new theology has been born. He has added to the great alternative systems of the universe. His metaphysics is closely related to that of Whitehead, but the argumentation in its support is much clearer, as is also the way in which it is situated in relation to other systems.

I accept substantial parts of Hartshorne's metaphysics, in particular his panpsychism or psychicalism. Although I arrived at my panpsychism independently of his advocacy (as he arrived at it independently of Whitehead's panpsychist position, if such an interpretation of Whitehead is correct) I might not have had the courage to advocate it on my own behalf without his powerful advocacy, while the particular form in which I hold it owes, I do not know how much, but certainly a good deal, to Hartshorne. His lucid insistence that the doctrine does not imply that there are no unconscious beings, since a collective of sentients need not be, and indeed in a sense cannot be, itself sentient has been particularly helpful. Moreover, in trying to understand how a universe of pulses of experience can have the structure of a physical world, I have gone above all to the work of Hartshorne, together with that of Whitehead. Very helpful also is Hartshorne's account of metaphysical methodology.

In the context of contemporary British philosophy in which my lot has been cast that might make me seem almost a follower of Hartshorne. I would be glad to bear that title. However, I have found myself unable to accept an aspect of Hartshorne's thought which he may well regard as one of his main contributions. This is his view of time and his closely related views about relations and the way in which the universe as a whole is in God. I see some of the emotional appeal of Hartshorne's view, and the panentheism as opposed to pantheism, which it makes possible. I also see how, if it could once be accepted, it solves certain recalcitrant problems in metaphysics. But, whichever is the most appealing, I find a more traditional pantheism of the sort found in Bradley and Royce more finally convincing. I shall indicate some of the reasons why, in the hope that Professor Hartshorne will confirm or deny that I have understood his position, and say something about my difficulties with it.

Philosophers have sometimes asked, concerning both past and future, whether they are 'real'. The question is not much asked about the present, for (except insofar as all temporal phenomena are condemned as unreal by some) it is assumed that that at least is real.

The question whether the past or future is real might quite promisingly be interpreted as querying whether there is a quite determinate truth about them. Perhaps we cannot quite identify the questions but they are certainly closely related, even if not equivalent, and the second may be the clearer. In asking whether the past or future is real I think I am asking whether they are included in the totality of being I find myself in the midst of. If they are, and only if they are, is it to be concluded that there is a quite determinate truth about them. Actually, I think there are certain difficulties in clarifying precisely what is meant by there being a determinate truth about something. The fact that there may be no real answer to certain questions about something does not necessarily imply that it is indeterminate in any proper sense, for it may supply no hold for these kinds of questions without failing to be a quite definite something in its own right. However, although it may be difficult to make what is in question absolutely precise, I think it clear enough in practice what is meant by saying that the past is an absolutely determinate reality with a quite definite character, even in all the details of which humans may have to remain for ever ignorant, and in asking whether the future is not similarly definite, in spite of the necessary limitations of advance knowledge of it.

Granted the reality of the present, there are four possible positions concerning the reality of the three different time modalities. (1) Both past and future are unreal, and only the present is real. This is the philosophy of the present as advocated by Mead. (I think that is his view, as Hartshorne does, though I found it very difficult to understand his *Philosophy of the Present*.) Oddly enough, since he puts it forward as the doctrine that time is unreal, Schopenhauer sometimes seems to be advocating this view. (2) Both past and future are real. This is the eternalistic view of time, according to which past and future are simply events which are earlier or later than the phase of consciousness which calls them so, while the presentness of that phase is basically the fact that it supplies the point of view from which other events are being conceived as past, present, or future. This is more or less vaguely implied by many metaphysical systems, and definitely stated in a few. Santayana seems to have been the clearest proponent of this view, though it is required for the metaphysics of Bradley and Royce, and it is also found in Russell, Quine, and Ayer (after his first book) and many others. It needs to be enriched, I believe, by a richer phenomenology of time than is implied in such common definitions of past and future as merely 'earlier or later than *this*,' one to which Santayana in particular pointed the way. (3) The future is real, but the past is not. It may seem that no one has held this strange view. However, something rather of this sort seems to be implied by pragmatic and verificationist views which equate facts about the past with that which would ordinarily be regarded as evidence for them obtainable or existing in the present or future. One finds such a view in C. I. Lewis, in the very early A. J. Ayer, and it is vaguely suggested in James and Peirce. It is also implied at times in the statements of 'anti-realists', in Michael Dummett's sense, about a range of ordinary facts. (There are hints that Dummett himself may hold a theistic view of the reality of the past, not so far from Hartshorne's.) Santayana's discussion of such views is particularly entertaining. (*Character and Opinion in the United States* [London, 1924], p. 160) Let us call it the pragmatist's view. (4) The past is real, but the future is not. This is the view of Hartshorne. I shall call it the philosophy of becoming, since Hartshorne's view of time is one version of it and he describes his philosophy as one of becoming rather than being. Also C. D. Broad's version of this view was called a theory of absolute becoming.

Let us see how these four views bear upon such a case as the following. There is a shipwreck and a lone survivor is left on a boat. Believing that he has no hope of rescue, he plunges to his death in the ocean leaving a note in the boat. But just before he plunges in, he recites to himself (whether merely in his head, or aloud but unheard by any finite being who will remember it, makes little difference) a certain favourite poem. Friends of his learn of the basic fact of how he died from his note. They discuss his death, and one of them says, "Knowing him I bet he recited a poem before he died, and I bet it was Tennyson's *Break, break, break*". Others say that they think it unlikely that he did this, and as tempers fly some say he did, some say he did not. Now is not one of them stating the actual truth of the matter, and is not the fact that there is an actual truth of the matter quite independent of there being any way in which any finite individual can definitely discover it? Indeed, even if no one ever thought about anything bearing on it at all, it would, surely, remain for ever true that he did make this recitation.

It is surely the common sense view that there are definite truths about past events such as this which no one will ever know. But that is what is denied by the philosophy of the present and the pragmatist's view of past, present, and future. Both of the other two philosophies support this common sense stance. For myself it seems about as basic a truth as any can be that if I once do something it remains for ever true that I did it, however little trace of it may be left as time unrolls.

If we are suspicious of the idea of unformulated truths, we may qualify the above to the extent of saying that it is the common sense view that when a properly formulated proposition is articulated about the past it will always have a definite truth value even where there is no way of discovering what that is. I said that there were some problems about the notion of determinateness, and one of them concerns quite what a properly formulated such proposition is. Suppose I shuffle a face down and jokerless pack of cards and two of us guess whether the one on top is red or black. Then I shuffle again without our looking. Is there a definite truth here? Most would think so, but this does not follow merely from the reality of the past. Some kind of realist view about the physical world is required too. A realist about the past may think that only mental events are quite real and, not holding a panpsychist view of the physical, may think there is no definite truth about the cards. He will, however, think there is a definite truth about the recitation, since this was—if it occurred—experienced. However, certain way out physicalists and behaviourists might look at it the other way round, and regard the private mental recitation as an indeterminate fact, counting only a physical recitation as the sort of reality concerning which there is a determinate truth.

However all this may be, so far as it is the status of the past as such that is in question, it seems clear that the common sense view is that the past is determinate in every way that the present is. There is a quite definite truth about it, whether anyone knows it or not. If down to earth people sometimes seem to deny this, I believe it is because they find it so hard to concentrate on the issue of what truth there is, as opposed to what is discoverable, although they do not really identify them.

That this is the common sense view does not establish that it is right. I am no great believer in common sense, considered as a body of claims rather than as a quality of mind. But it does put the *onus probandi* on the contrary views. Thus the *onus probandi* is on the philosophy of the present or the pragmatist view, and unless they are strikingly convincing it is the other two views which will hold the day. And indeed I think anyone with common sense, understood as a desirable mental quality, will dismiss these views. Can you really suffer some pain now, which you do not tell others of, and believe that one day it will not even be true that you had the pain? To me the idea is quite absurd. Therefore, I take it that the past is determinate and real, and that our choice must lie between the eternalistic view of time and the philosophy of becoming.

Of these two I believe the philosophy of becoming is the more common sense one. The idea that there is a definite truth about the past, that past events are somehow there to settle the truth value of claims about them as future ones are not, accords better with our ordinary way of looking at things than the eternalistic one. This becomes even clearer, if we set aside what in the end are somewhat irrelevant points about determinism. To the extent that some fairly non-metaphysical people may flirt with the idea that the future is fully determinate it is almost always an the grounds of inclination to believe in some sort of determinism. However, the basis for belief in the determinate nature of the past does not lie in any belief that it is lawfully related to the present in such a way that a state description of the present plus the laws of nature entails every truth about the past. No, however loose we believe the lawful connection to be between one moment of time and another, we remain quite sure that there is a definite truth about what happened. For we think of the past as an independent part of reality with its own character, just as we think of a far off country (the determinateness of what is going on in which has nothing to do with how closely knit it may be to what is going on here). The basic question whether there is a determinate truth about the future is similarly distinct from the issue of determinism. It concerns whether the future is a definite reality which we can now be determinately right or wrong about, in guesses if not in knowledge claims, not how far that future is causally determined by what has happened so far. The fact that the existence of a determinate truth about the future is so often taken as standing or falling with determinism only shows that our common sense unwillingness to think of it as a reality in its own right makes us think that it can only have a determinate character if that is somehow determined by what has happened up till now; it does not settle the metaphysical astuteness of that unwillingness. It is true some eminent modern logicians have confused the issue of the determinacy of the future with the issue of determinism, but it is still a confusion.

It is not surprising that we are reluctant to think of the future as determinate, for we can hardly help thinking of it as indeterminate while we are wondering how to act, and are in the process of settling what the future will be. (Nonetheless, determinacy of the future is not incompatible with that determinate character being something which springs in part from what we are now doing.) However, of the two components of the philosophy of becoming, namely the reality of the past and the unreality of the future, it would be harder for common sense, and more unacceptable to a person with a common sense quality of mind, to give up the first than the second. Therefore, if it appears that the past can only be given reality by giving reality to the future also I think it is more the path of common sense to move forward to the eternalistic view than move back, say, to the philosophy of the present. That this is the only condition under which the past can be given the required kind of reality is the claim of the eternalist. One way of looking at Hartshorne's theory of the past is as a denial of this. There is a lot going for such a denial, since it gives us more of the common sense conception than any other view. But I am not convinced that such a denial can be made out.

One more preliminary remark before coming to grips with this issue. I have suggested that the most common sense view is that past and present are real, as opposed to the future which is not. That seems beyond doubt if 'real' simply means quite determinate in character. (It is very difficult to get people of a not very metaphysical turn even to see what you are getting at when you ask whether once a thing has happened it will always remain true that it did. The fact seems so obvious that they think you are discussing a question of knowability.) Yet it also goes against the grain of common sense to say that the past is 'real' in quite the same way as is the present. People want to say that there is a definite truth as to what happened. But they do not quite like the idea that the past is part of reality in just the same way that the present is. They like to think that it has a more shadowy, even if just as determinate, a reality. Thus 'determinateness' and 'reality' seem to carry slightly different meanings.

That points to another way in which Hartshorne's view gives common sense what it wants. Both Hartshorne and the eternalist think that there is a determinate truth about the past, however remote from our knowledge it may be in many details, and both agree that there must be a reality, of which we, as we are now, are part, which contains that real past, in virtue of correctly or incorrectly characterising which, propositions formulated now are true or false. But for the eternalist that real past is *in its own being* present, and has not undergone some change to be as of now the past. For Hartshorne, in contrast, it has undergone a certain change of status, so that it exists only as 'contained' or 'retained' in wholes of experience other than itself. That might justify saying that it is not real in quite the same way as it was. This may be another way in which his view accords well with common sense, though, at the cost, so I shall argue, of great difficulties.

Those stronger on common sense than metaphysics may challenge the notion that there has in any sense to be a real past by corresponding to which propositions formulated about it now are true or false. They may say that a proposition can be true because it describes correctly what was, and that this does not mean that this which *was* in any sense *is*. The past is what did exist or occur, not what does exist or is occurring, and to say that there is a definite truth about it does not imply that there has to *be*, only that there *was*, something which gives that truth its truth.

But note that we say that there *is* a truth about the past. It will not do to say merely that there *was* one. But what is the force of this *is*? Is it the *is* of presentness, or is it some sort of timeless *is*? Not that even the meaning, let alone the answer to, this question is unproblematic, for people differ as to whether a timeless *is* is just a disjunction of *was*, (tensed) *is*, and *will be*, or something of a different order, or whether the tensed *is* is merely the timeless one supplemented by an indication of simultaneity with this instance of the word. But whatever the temporal status of the *is* in 'There is a definite truth about the past', surely the past must *be* in a sense with the same temporal status.

It is all too easy to blind oneself to what is at issue when one asks whether the past is real. If one claims that the past is real one is not claiming that it is now. Rather one is claiming that it is now true that in some important sense there is a total reality which includes past and present, what is now and what was then. The issue between the proponent of the philosophy of becoming and the eternalist is as to whether there is in the same sense a total reality which includes the future. Similarly, if one contends, as both philosophers do, against say the philosophy of the present, that the past cannot have simply become nothing, else there would be no truth about it, as there indubitably is, one is not considering whether it has become nothing in the sense in which the traditional believer in material substance thinks that a broken physical object cannot become nothing. That is, one is not concerned with the issue whether its matter has become something else. One is simply saying that if the past is simply nothing, then it is as true that one thing happened as that its contrary did, and therefore the past must in some sense be something, indeed be what it always was, except perhaps for the sheer loss of presentness.

The case for eternalism turns upon rejecting the coherence of any such idea as the loss of presentness. For eternalism the past must in some sense be. But the only way it can be is as something which is, from its own point of view, present, from which it follows that we now are the future of something which is in itself as present as we are now. So we are as genuinely future as anything can be, namely the future of something intrinsically present, from which it follows that our future is just as determinate as our present. For if our future were indeterminate there would be some present events (those previous to us) which have a determinate future, and others which have an indeterminate one. That would mean that something very peculiar happens to time at time T (whatever the time at which all this is being thought about): namely, that the relations between past, present, and future radically change then.

In the present context, of dialogue with Professor Hartshorne, and those familiar, and many of them endorsing, his work, I need not be too concerned to put things in a way satisfactory to those who believe in a physical world which is quite unconscious, much of it, through and through. However, the same essential points could be made even within the context of a more materialist view of things, for which, expressions like 'from its own point of view' would, for the most part, have only metaphorical application. That understood, I can say that, for the eternalist, every ultimate individual, that is, every pulse of experience, is eternally present from its own point of view. That is, it is of its essence to experience itself as something which is occurring here and now as the ephemeral point of transition between a past from which it has emerged and a future into which it is debouching and helping determine. It is an eternal truth that it is a part of the eternal system of things looking out at other things as past and future (or perhaps contemporary) and that it feels itself to be passing away. Thus the passage of time is a real felt quality of every finite individual, each of which has its eternal unchanging place and character in the total eternal scheme, that unchanging character including its own sense of passage and of being ephemeral. The main reason for maintaining this is that the fact that there is a definite truth about the past requires that it still be true that the past in some sense is. The sense of 'be' or 'is' must be a timeless sense, since certainly the past is not there at the time I 'now' call now. But what *is* in this eternal sense cannot be something other than the experiences which make it up and these experiences cannot be anything other than the fleeting transitory experiences they always were. Among things in the past are the excitement a child felt as the curtain went up yesterday at a Christmas show. This excitement would not be itself if it were anything other than the fleeting but present experience it felt itself to be. So the past must consist of experiences which eternally are fleetingly present in their own being, and, as said, that means that this experience now, as the future of what is present in itself, gives us a perfect example of what future events are, namely, experiences which are fleetingly present but quite determinate in their own being. (Eternalism, as I understand and advocate it does not hold that consciousness somehow shifts in its survey of a static universe of being, as Hartshorne half suggests at times. (See *The Logic of Perfection*, p. 249.) There is no shift from one moment of consciousness to another; each is eternally there feeling itself as the fleeting transition between other moments and, for the absolute idealist, experienced as such by the Absolute in union with all other such moments.)

This is the view I hold, but I grant that it conflicts with our ordinary conception of things, for which the past is real in a sense in which the future is not. Has Hartshorne given us a satisfactory alternative to it?

According to Hartshorne, the ultimate constituents of the world and true subjects of experience are momentary pulses of experience or sentience. Each of these experiences more or less fully other such pulses, experiencing them in its own particular way and making its own particular synthesis of the multiplicity of experiences it experiences. Having made its own synthesis of other experiences it becomes available as an experience to be experienced by other experiences.

The other experiences which an experience experiences cannot be later experiences. They must therefore either be earlier experiences or contemporary ones. Whitehead dismissed (at least some of the time) the latter and said that an experience cannot experience its contemporaries. Hartshorne hesitates over this.

(See *The Divine Relativity*, p. 98 et ff and p. 140.) However, I do not think we will go far wrong if we simplify a little and take it that the experiences which are object of a certain experience must be earlier than it. The qualifications required if an experience can experience its contemporaries would make it more cumbrous to formulate my argument without affecting its essential thrust.

For Hartshorne, if I follow him, when I now experience other realities this is not, at least in the metaphysically most significant cases, a matter of there being some kind of representation of them in me. The other realities I experience are past experiences which really enter into, even if only in a partially and mutilated way, my present experience and help make it up. (See, for example, 'The Immortality of the Past', *Review of Metaphysics* 7, 1, 1953 at page 103.) Thus past experiences do not become nothing. They can remain part of reality as objects incorporated in later experiences.

However, if there were only finite experiences, even high grade ones like ours, still more if there were only lower grade ones, much would be lost and there would not be a fully determinate truth about the world. That there is such a truth rests on the existence of an infinite mind, or—more precisely—series of all comprehensive experiences each containing the divine essence, and hence a phase in God's history. At every moment the total divine experience contains all past experiences within it as part of what makes it up and what it unites into a fresh synthesis. Within each total divine experience the whole of the past is thus contained, and not in a partial or mutilated form. The next divine experience will contain the previous one, as its incorporated object, including therefore all its incorporated objects, but it will also include all finite experiences which were contemporary with it (and which made their own more limited but freely chosen synthesis of their more limited incorporated data) and will make its own fresh synthesis of all this. Equally each finite experience, in a series of finite experiences, will have as well as its own unmediated incorporating experience of certain past experiences some very limited experience of the previous divine experience. (I think this is right, and that we are not supposed only to have access to the past via God.)

The crucial point is this. If it were not for God, the past would only be there and be determinate to the extent that it had been incorporated into subsequent finite experiences. Since, however, God exists it remains in its complete determinateness as something which is there whether known about by finite minds or not. I take it that for Hartshorne this is one way in which one can argue for the existence of God. (See, for example, loc. cit. at p. 103 again.) (1) The past is determinate, and (2) it could not be so if it were not experienced by an infinite mind (retained along a series of omniscient experiences incorporating the divine essence), therefore God exists. (See, for example, *The Logic of Perfection*, pp. 152–53 and Chapter Ten.) This is not, of course, Hartshorne's main argument for God's existence, but it is a perfectly respectable argument, logically compulsive for anyone who accepts its two premisses.

If we accept this line of thought we can hold the philosophy of becoming. We can think of the past as being real and determinate, and of the future as being indeterminate. Moreover, we can do justice to the common sense feeling that though the past is determinate, and somehow real, it is not real in quite the way the present is. For the past exists as incorporated object, not as subject as yet unincorporated into any other experience as its object.

Does the view give us any positive ground for thinking that the future is indeterminate or does it merely allow us to think this? If the past exists as remembered by God, may not the future exist as anticipated by God?

I believe that there are really two distinct views which Hartshorne wishes to exclude. (1) First, he wants to exclude the view that the future is incorporated in the being of God in the same sort of way as the past is. He wishes to deny that it could have status as something about which there is a determinate truth and falsehood in virtue of being literally present in God's perfect anticipation of it, as the past is literally present in God's perfect memory of it. (2) Secondly, he wishes to deny any view, such as determinism, which holds that the character of the future is somehow settled by what has happened already without actually somehow pertaining to reality. Such a view would allow God to foretell every detail of the future without actually presently experiencing it. (Of course, he would also reject the third eternalist view about the future according to which it is simply the same as the present in its own being, but once this view has been dismissed about the past it scarcely needs separate discussion as one about the future, and so can be left out of account for the moment.) Let us take these two points in turn.

(1) Hartshorne holds that proper scrutiny of our own experience shows that we are always in process of making something new out of the data constituted by the past experiences we experience. Thus our own direct experience of the nature of the passage of time rules out the idea that the future is a determinate reality incorporated in present experience, for to be thus incorporated in present reality as a datum for a fresh creative synthesis is just what it is to be past. If the past lives as a whole it must be in some more comprehensive present divine experience in a manner of which its partial living in our present experience gives us some inkling; to think of the future, in whole or in part, as thus living belies our whole sense of what distinguishes it from the past.

Thus attention to the nature of consciousness shows that 'it is inseparable from decision, and it must lapse the instant action becomes merely inevitable'. (*The Logic of Perfection*, p. 17) Decision would make no sense if the future were somehow incorporated in advance in present experience and a God acting now must therefore be external to the future which he is in process of creating along with his creatures.

A more formal defence of the point that the future cannot be incorporated in God's present consciousness, as is the past, would show how this view would destroy the very distinction between past and future, and make it impossible to give any adequate explanation of the direction of time. To understand Hartshorne's views on this one must take account of his insistence that relations, of the most basic sort, are internal at one end and external at the other. That is, they pertain to the inherent nature of one of their terms but not to the other. If they did not pertain to either, they would have no place in reality. (He is appealing to a principle like that of Whitehead that everything—other than actual entities— must have a home in some actual entity or entities. This also reflects the puzzlings of Leibniz and others on the problem as to 'where' relations are.) But that does mean that they have to make a real difference to both terms, and in the most basic cases they do not.

Grasp of this logical point prepares us to see how an earlier event is never internally related to a later one, as later events are internally related to many past ones. This was true of past events when they were present and continues to be true of them when they become past. George Washington neither was nor is coloured in his being by Reagan's later knowledge of him, but Reagan is coloured in his being by the knowledge he has of Washington. Thus the relation of knowing Washington is internal to Reagan, but that of being known by Reagan is not an internal relation of Washington, and in an important sense has nothing to do with him, does not really help to characterise him. Hartshorne believes that the clue to the whole nature of the past is that it is what is incorporated in some experience as its object. When some totality of individual experience was present it was not thus incorporated, that is precisely what its being present was; now that it is incorporated it is past, for that is what it is to be past. The past is determinate but has a status distinct from that of the present in that it is incorporated in another experience, and is not composed of experiences which are totalities in their own right as it was when present. If the future was thus incorporated its status would be indistinguishable from that of the past, while if it consisted of experiences which were totalities in their own right, it would be indistinguishable from the present. As it is, the future is really nothing more than the existence of certain constraints upon what present creativity can set out to make of itself.

A persuasive case can be made out along these lines, partly phenomenological, partly logical, for denying that the future can exist in the present in the same way as Hartshorne believes that the past does. But does that rule out every kind of determinism, or indeed some other view for which God perfectly foretells the future without actually now experiencing it as He does the past?

(2) The fact that the *later* is internally related to the *earlier*, while the converse does not hold, would rule out any determinism for which causal relations are genuinely necessary. But what of the more usual modern variety in which causal laws relate what is not otherwise intrinsically related? Might not a determinist of this sort contend, along lines I have already indicated, that determinism has been true so as far as time has unrolled to date, and that the betting is it will hold for ever into the future. I think Hartshorne would reply that belief in this kind of rigid causal linking of what is not internally related is incoherent. For him causation requires some intrinsic connectedness, but when we look into it we see that it is only the effect which is intrinsically connected to its cause, and that the cause can only imply generic features of its effect. Since each new pulse of experience is a unification of a plurality of previously unsynthesised data from the past, the precise task it has in unifying them is a quite new one, underivable from the past by abstract formulae. (*Creative Synthesis*, pp. 2–6 et ff) To investigate this further would take us beyond our main theme into Hartshorne's detailed views on causation. I agree with Hartshorne, however, that there is an oddity in the combination of the view that determinism holds rigidly with a belief that the laws of nature are merely contingent generalisations about what always happens to have been, and may be expected to go on being, the case.

One fundamental objection Hartshorne has to determinism is that it implies that God can foretell the exact nature of the future, which (he claims) is an incoherent supposition. This does not dent God's omniscience. Since the future is nothing, not knowing is not failure to know something.

Hartshorne's main argument here is that a God 'who eternally knew all the fulfillment of his purpose would bring could have no need of that fulfillment or of purpose.' (*The Logic of Perfection*, p. 205) In a somewhat similar vein he suggests that if the future were determinately known by God all time would dovetail into one and nothing would be really earlier or later than anything else. (*The Divine Relativity*, p. 110; see also *The Logic of Perfection*, p. 165) The idea is that perfect knowledge of the future would render pointless the actual coming into being of the future.

I find it hard to evaluate this argument. It depends on how far one thinks merely conceptual knowledge can grasp the whole detail of actual experience. To the extent that it can, prediction need not make fulfilment otiose.

It is worth noting that for an eternalist who believed in an absolute consciousness and believed in determinism the problem would not arise. The absolute consciousness's knowledge that what I now call the future is determined would be its direct experience of both now and then as present in their own being, and of the one as following with causal necessity from the other. Not that such an eternalist need espouse determinism; he could equally suppose that both times were present for the absolute consciousness but were experienced as having a certain looseness of relation one to another, and even an aspect of eternal spontaneous self creation. Another view, which I favour, that is open to the eternalist, is that determinism in accordance with abstractly formulable scientific laws is untrue, and essentially falsified by the existence of creativity, but that a deeper sort of unpredictable necessitation of an event by its predecessors, as their necessary, in a broad sense aesthetic, synthesis and fulfilment, may tie things together where 'scientific' laws leaves slack. (Compare and contrast *The Logic of Perfection*, p. 314.) After all, absolute idealists have especially proclaimed that necessity does not work according to abstractable rule.

At any rate, for Hartshorne indeterminism is a corollary of the view that the future is not real as the past is. If it were already settled what the future would be, there would be little significance in its becoming, and such merely senseless becoming can be ruled out by the theist. But I hope that Hartshorne agrees with me that one cannot equate the issue between eternalism and the philosophy of becoming with that between determinism and indeterminism. Combination of some version of the philosophy of becoming with the view that determinism is true of the past, and that the betting is it will hold throughout the future, is not an absurdity at first blush, but must be argued against as a distinct position from that of eternalism. Equally rejection of determinism cannot be made an immediate ground for rejection of eternalism, since one can be an eternalist who rejects any notion that there are laws in virtue of which the character of one moment of time could always be read off from that of an earlier.

In view of this let us set the issue of determinism largely aside, and concentrate on the key thesis of Hartshorne's theory of past and future, namely, that the former has determinate reality in virtue of being retained in every detail in God's present consciousness, while the latter only has being as a set of constraints which the present places upon the creativity of God and of his creatures.

There is much that is appealing in this doctrine. It probably does more for common sense than most other theories do, so far as the sort of reality ascribed to each of past, present, and future goes. It also has for Hartshorne and others great religious and moral appeal in that it both meets the dissatisfaction with an entirely Heraclitian view of the universe as in a flux where nothing is ever won for the universe for good, while avoiding that muffling of the call to action and creativity which Hartshorne, in common with William James, and other Americans he has hymned for their belief in the central place of creativity in the scheme of things, see as the consequence of acceptance of the 'block universe' of eternalism. Nonetheless for reasons which I shall now give I have found it impossible to accept this view.

Hartshorne, just like the eternalist, holds that past events must be a definite reality if statements about the past are all to have a determinate truth value. On his account, this definite reality is the past as remembered by God. Our statements about the past are true or false because they correspond or not with the past as it exists in God's memory of it. (See, for example, *The Logic of Perfection*, p. 252 et ff.)

My first objection is that if God's memory is to play this role it must be entirely full and correct. That it is so is, of course, asserted by Hartshorne, for whom God's memory is infallible. My difficulty here is not one as to the possibility of an infallible memory. I am inclined to agree with Hartshorne that to a limited extent we can find even ourselves possessing this. My point is rather that in calling God's memory infallible we are saying that God is necessarily right about what happened and to me this seems to imply that He is right about events as they existed in the past (in the state Whitehead called that of subjective immediacy) and not merely as to how they exist as internal objects of his memory. God's necessarily being right about the past cannot be merely his necessarily being right about what objects are now incorporated in his being. To be right he must be right in thinking these incorporated beings had the status earlier of subjectively immediate beings in their own right. That they had this status must lie in their relation to something other than themselves as they are now, and that implies that it is still true that the past in its original subjective immediacy pertains to reality. If not, there is nothing but the objects in their present incorporated state, which is as much as to say that there is no truth to the effect that these incorporated objects existed previously to their being incorporated.

Perhaps Hartshorne will object that I am treating the objects as known by God, as part of his present being, as something different from the original objects which occurred in the past and thereby making it seem that to know the past God must know of something besides what is immediately present to him. That makes it look as though his knowledge of the past were mediated by exact icons of it so that the knowledge is only genuine if there is something beyond the icons which they represent. In contrast to this view, so perhaps Hartshorne will say, his position is that the very past, the very experiences of Julius Caesar, say, are now elements in God's experience. It is the very past which God retains, accumulating all events to date in ever fresh presents in which subsequent events enter into relations with them originally undreamt of. (See *Creative Synthesis*, pp. 16 ff.)

I am not sure how far this objection expresses Hartshorne's view. Sometimes he talks as though the divine consciousness of every moment synthesises all the finite experiences previous to it, only in the sense that it synthesises elements reflecting them in their past actuality. (*The Logic of Perfection*, p. 200) In that case it is admitted that there is something other than the elements of God's consciousness which is reflected by it, namely the past as it was. If so, it follows immediately that the past has an ontological status not derivative from God's knowledge of it. However, at other times the claim seems to be that it is the very past experience itself, not anything which represents it or into which it has changed, which somehow becomes part of God's later experience. (See *Creative Synthesis*, p. 118.)*

I do not see how a reply along these latter lines can meet the point at issue. It is hard to see how Hartshorne can deny that, for him, in becoming past, events which were originally present have somehow changed. I will not insist that they change because they enter into relations with later events which did not belong to reality when they were present, for Hartshorne holds that it is only the later events which are really in relation to the past ones and that that does not imply that the past events are really in that relation to the present ones. The relation only genuinely pertains to the later term. But without insisting that as time goes on the past events which are present in God change simply in virtue of entering into fresh relations I still claim that, as Hartshorne depicts them, they suffered at least an initial change when they ceased to be present and became elements in God's consciousness (and perhaps up to a point in the consciousness of various finite beings). This is, surely, the change which Whitehead describes as passing from subjective immediacy to the status of object for later subjects.

True, Hartshorne rejects Whitehead's talk of the 'perishing' of actual occasions. Yet he sees them as passing from 'is', or the fresh front of reality, in its limited creaturely aspect, to the 'has been', or the embedded in God's consciousness. It can hardly be denied that that is some kind of change of status. That means that they either change or are replaced by something 'corresponding' to them, and Hartshorne rejects the second. (*Creative Sythesis*, p. 16) (Something of this sort is perhaps recognized at ibid, p. 13.) But if they change in this way why cannot one ask whether they have changed in any other way? We are assured that a past pain remains precisely the same specific pain (ibid, p. 16). It is somehow metaphysically impossible for any change to take place other than whatever is strictly involved in becoming past and becoming something having status only within God's consciousness (or conceivably other later moments of consciousness).

I am happy to grant this. My point was not seriously to suggest that as it becomes past, or gets more past, a pain might cease to be a pain and become a

---

*At *Creative Synthesis*, p. 88 Hartshorne talks of past events as being 'present to or in' memory. 'In' suggests that memory includes them as parts, and Hartshorne often speaks thus. 'To' does not so clearly suggest this, but suggests, what is just as difficult for the enterprise of grounding the being of the past in God's memory of it, that what is presented to memory, even God's, has its own separate reality, so that it is not essentially God's consciousness which grounds the determinacy of the past.

pleasure. But I do claim that however necessary it is, it is still a substantial truth (if it is a truth at all) that the past experiences of finite beings, when they come to have the status of objects within ensuing states of the divine consciousness, are exactly like what they were when they originally occurred as separate wholes (or elements in separate wholes) of limited finite experience.

To assert this truth, with whatever degree of insistence on its necessity you like, is to admit, after all, that in an important sense, there are these two different, however exactly alike, things there to be referred to. Thus there are, say, Julius Caesar's experiences as retained in moments of God's consciousness belonging to the twentieth century and Julius Caesar's experiences before they had any such status, in particular as they were when they were present. But it can only make sense to say that there are these two things, and that they correspond to each other, if it is still true that the experiences in their original state of being present, and while not included in subsequent experiences, are and pertain to reality in the largest sense. This, so the eternalist argues, they can only do if reality, in the largest sense, eternally includes all past events as events which in their own essential being are present. But then, as I have said, we must say the same of the future, for this pulsating present (me trying to articulate my thoughts about Hartshorne's philosophy) is a perfect example of what it is to be a future.

Hartshorne may charge me with still not realizing that there is no question of the past changing in any way whatever when it becomes past. (See "The Immortality of the Past" at p. 109.) Nothing happens to what has already become, it is merely that more is added.

> 'When the past event was present' means . . . when the event was a whole which nothing possessed as a part; that the event is 'no longer present but past' means that now a new and more inclusive whole possesses it as part. (*The Divine Relativity*, p. 68)

Thus nothing happens to an event when it becomes past; it simply becomes part of a larger whole, as it was originally not, but while it is a real part of the nature of the larger whole (the divine consciousness of a later time) that it contains that part, it is never part of the nature of the included that it is so. Being included is an external relation.

This is quite similar to the doctrine of absolute becoming espoused by C. D. Broad in his *Scientific Thought*. On that view, if time is to be thought of as a line, it must be as a growing line. The present is the endpoint of the line. Each other point on the line was present when it was the endpoint, but it did not change in any way when the line grew beyond it. Both Hartshorne and Broad are inclined to claim that an event's being present is a matter of there not being anything in a certain relation to it and that being past is a matter of there being something in that relation to it. For Hartshorne the relation is that of including it in a certain sort of larger whole of consciousness; for Broad it is that of there being something beyond it at the growing end of time.

One puzzle about these views is this. If it makes no difference to an experience that it is past, *how do I know that the pain I am experiencing now is not past?* For when it becomes past nothing happens to it, it is simply part of a larger whole. There is no "change from vital actuality to a corpse or skeleton, . . . merely the fact that the definite actual subject is now also object for further subjects. No longer is it the latest verge of actuality, since there is now a richer reality, including the once latest one." (*Creative Synthesis*, p. 118) This seems an odd question but it certainly arises if one insists that the past is just what it was when present, that there is no "inner shrinkage or impoverishment" (ibid).

If Whitehead's notion of subjective immediacy is endorsed, the question does not arise. But then when one brings in the notion of subjective immediacy one admits that something does happen to an event as it becomes past. It becomes object rather than subject. But then I insist again that what is objective can only be what makes statements about the past true or false, if it is like itself when it was subjectively immediate, and that this implies that reality includes it in its subjectively immediate state and not only in its objective state.

However, what I am considering now is the possibility of avoiding this problem by denying that there is any such change to the experience itself as it becomes past, since all that has happened is that more reality has been added alongside, or on Hartshorne's view, around it. And when that is done I think my curious question really does pose itself, as to how I know from within my own experience that it is not already past through being included in a larger experience. Personally, as an eternalist, I do hold that reality includes past events in their state of subjective immediacy, but I infer from this that every event is eternally subjectively immediate in its own being, but past or future from the perspective of other events.

The view that reality accumulates with the passage of time, that nothing is lost, but is simply wrapped in fresh layers of reality, or fresh surrounding envelopes, is put forward by many philosophers I find highly sympathetic. Hartshorne is one of these philosophers, Bergson another. Such language may well capture some truth, but I believe it must be one better expressed in a more eternalistic way. It is interesting that McTaggart held a kind of eternalistic view of this doctrine. For the C series which is the reality of the temporal series is supposed to be ordered by a kind of relation of inclusion, the apparently later events being those which include the apparently earlier ones. McTaggart's extravagant metaphysics has little hold over me and his account of the C series will hardly do. Yet it does suggest that the eternalist may make something of the notion of inclusion as illuminating time. For myself I would draw rather on Hartshorne's view that later events are internally related to earlier ones in a way that does not hold vice versa, although I would see this as a matter of degree, not a matter of the relations being sheerly external at the earlier end.

I do not see how Hartshorne's view of earlier experiences being included as literal parts of later experiences can explain time, and the contrast between present and future. As an attempt to analyse time it seems to beg the question. *First*, an experience occurs as part of no larger totality. *Then*, it becomes a part of a larger totality, and *then* of a still larger one as that one becomes part of a larger one in its turn. If we do not rely on the independent intelligibility of the 'first' and the 'then' we can make no sense of this. But perhaps we are not supposed to get our whole understanding of time from this notion of inclusion, only to recognize that this is what happens in time. But surely that shows that the concept of the past is not explicated by talking of it as what is included in God's memory. And in that case we must acknowledge that propositions about the past cannot be true in virtue of anything which belongs to any consciousness existing now. Once this is granted I am led again back to eternalism as alone making sense of there being a truth about the past. (In fact, even the denial by the philosophy of the present that there is any truth about the past, secretly implies that there once was a past, and that makes no sense as a statement if the previous to this now is not eternally a part of reality there to be spoken of.)

The whole question of the nature of time, of the status of past, present, and future, is one of the most difficult in metaphysics, one which philosophers hardly come in sight of who expect to deal with it at the level of the mere analysis of temporal language. There are all sorts of superficial linguistic objections which can be raised both to the kind of eternalism I favour and to the theory of becoming as advocated by Hartshorne. There must be some people who have thought about the matter hard and got it wrong, and I am not foolish enough to think myself less likely to be such a person than Charles Hartshorne. Besides, I recognize that, for those who believe in any kind of divine consciousness, a philosophy of becoming allows a satisfying solution to the problem of evil not available to the eternalist. All the same, this particular element of Hartshorne's metaphysics is one that I have found I cannot accept, for the reasons I have given.

T. L. S. SPRIGGE

DEPARTMENT OF PHILOSOPHY
UNIVERSITY OF EDINBURGH
APRIL 1986

21

Paul Grimley Kuntz

CHARLES HARTSHORNE'S THEORY OF ORDER AND DISORDER

F ew philosophers have written so broadly about order. Charles Hartshorne's philosophy is in a class with St. Augustine's *De Ordine* and the writings of Whitehead since both of them write of different kinds of order. But what is most distinctive is the Peircian emphasis upon law (or regularity) and chance (or indeterminism). Although he sometimes entitles a chapter "order," one pole of the contrast, the treatment makes both poles equally necessary. His title that expresses the dipolarity of the category most adequately is "Order and Chaos." "Chaos" is not sheer nothingness. "Disorder" is not the mere denial or negate of "order." In this emphasis the philosophy of Hartshorne is remarkable.[1]

As with other philosophers who use "order" as a category, when we read Hartshorne on order and disorder we are in what may be considered the areas of logic, and of epistemology, and philosophy of nature, and aesthetics, and theology. Two remarkable things about Hartshorne's writings on order-disorder occur in every chapter or essay. The first is that the philosopher relates order-disorder in at least two fields generally now kept separate by present academic boundaries. The second is that the fundamental treatment is metaphysical, in the sense of dealing with what Hartshorne called "cosmic variables," characteristics found throughout the universe. Of course the interdisciplinary or cross disciplinary character of the factual references follows from the transdisciplinary character of metaphysical inquiry. Since every cosmic variable is of infinite range, like being that refers to everything, we must study it in many local variables, which bear to one another likenesses and differences.[2]

The author thanks the Emory Research Committee and the American Philosophical Society of Philadelphia for continued support. This paper was prepared for a special session of the Society for Philosophy of Religion in honor of Charles Hartshorne, 1972, Savannah, Georgia.

The first essays in which Charles Hartshorne made explicit his theory of order-disorder are those remarkable general chapters on "Nature," part II of *Beyond Humanism*, published in 1937, and republished with a "Preface" that stresses the bipolarity of necessity and contingency in God and man as well as in nature.[3]

We cannot, of course, cover all the writings of Charles Hartshorne, a dozen books and two or three hundred articles, and we can be sure that every one of them deals in some way with order-disorder. Not to deal with an important cosmic variable would be not to treat anything at all. All we can attempt here is to suggest the inter-relations of the theme in selected essays. On the logic of relations, in which "order," or more precisely "serial order" is defined, we have "The Prejudice in Favor of Symmetry."[4] On philosophy of nature we have not only "The Cosmic Variables" but also "Order in a Creative Universe," which is followed by "Indeterminism in Psychology and Ethics."[5] On beauty as the balance between order and disorder securing maximal value we have "God and the Beautiful,"[6] and "The Aesthetic Matrix of Value."[7] On theology we have a new conception of the argument from the order of nature to an orderer in "The Theistic Proofs."[8] On metaphysics we have an interpretation of the dipolar concept of order and disorder as crucial to becoming, particularly the commentary on C. S. Peirce.[9] These are not exhaustive of the important chapters and essays, especially since the philosophy of Charles Hartshorne is a philosophy of harmony, balance, and hierarchy and he has with his unique interests in man's relations to nature, addressed himself as no other philosopher to the ecological crisis. In the final practical application, Hartshorne's philosophy of order-disorder issues in an appeal to man to respect and protect nature's balances; *The Logic of Perfection* ends with "The Unity of Man and the Unity of Nature."[10]

I cite my sources with no attention to the order in which the essays were written and published, because with regard to order-disorder, there have been no fundamental changes between 1937 and the 1970s.

It is highly significant, in spite of the fact often confessed in prefaces that our philosopher sought rigor through logic, that he does not begin any discussion of "order" with a definition from the logic of relations. The early Whitehead and the early Russell often begin essays by defining order as a relation that is asymmetrical, transitive, and connected. It is not that Hartshorne did not know the logic of relations or consider it important and still neglected by philosophers.[11] Far from it, for he writes in a way that presupposes that we know that x and y are well ordered if and only if $xRy \neq yRx$. "Symmetry," the case of $xRy = yRx$, "is in a sense a lack of order. The equality of x and y puts them in no definite order, relative to one another. But the superiority of one to the other orders them. To exalt symmetry is to depreciate order. Those who exalt symmetry are advocating chaos.''[12] We should add that rank ordering is only one kind of principle that establishes a sense of direction, and there are temporal, spatial, causal relations as well as relations among sensed qualities such as "higher than in pitch" (or its opposite) and relations of magnitude (or its opposite) that also ground the asymmetry.

Why did Hartshorne only in 1970 deal explicitly with "order" as a relation defined in the logic of relations? Let us consider the relevant passage from *Beyond Humanism*. In considering a cosmic variable, "absolutely infinite in range,"

> we must face the objection that such a range would imply emptiness of all definite meaning. Do we not define a thing by contrast with something else, and must not all-inclusive variables, since all contrast is within them, be absolutely neutral and colorless, equivalent to bare 'being'? If this be so, philosophy is indeed a waste of time, for concepts are philosophical only if they are universal, cosmic. But the truth is that *a variable is not a mere common element among all its values, to be conceived by abstracting from them.*[13]

The logic of relations uses the contrast of asymmetry to symmetry as above, and of transitivity to intransitivity. Transitivity is when the same relation holds between a and c because it holds between a and b and b and c: if a is ancestor of b, and b is ancestor of c, then a is ancestor of c, but this does not and cannot hold for the specific relation "father of" or "mother of." Perhaps Hartshorne preferred the more specific causal relations to more general classification. Perhaps also he didn't see connexity, the feature of an ordered series that gives a term one and only one place in the series. Perhaps that seemed deterministic, or at least the metaphysics implicit in "a place for everything and everything in its place." That principle is a prejudice of strict determinism and against alternatives between which agents may choose. Obviously the notion of a "causal chain" does not allow that the next link may be this or that link. There is one and only one next in a serial chain.

So, although Hartshorne's theory of order-disorder sometimes explicitly appeals to Whitehead, it never makes the use of the logic of relations that we find in Whitehead (and also in Russell) and very strongly in Josiah Royce, especially *Principles of Logic* and "Order." Royce even views the moral life as a chain of command on the military model.[14]

Hartshorne's indebtedness here is more to C. S. Peirce than to anyone else and this is worth documenting and commenting on.

Hartshorne and Peirce introduce order and chaos together, like the Bible: "in the beginning the earth was without form and void, and darkness was upon the face of the deep. God said, Let there be light and there was light."

Peirce speculates on the meaning of primeval chaos, and how chaos is ordered. Hartshorne quotes Peirce, but more significantly the philosophizing flows from Peirce to Hartshorne with only quotation marks to differentiate one from the other.

What this means is that the process "proceeds [as] from the question to the answer—from the vague to the definite. And so likewise all the evolution we know of proceeds from the vague to the definite. The indeterminate future becomes the irrevocable past. . . . The undifferentiated differentiates itself. The homogeneous puts on heterogeneity. . . . As a rule the continuum has been derived from a more general continuum, a continuum of higher generality." The process "extends from before time and from before logic, we cannot suppose that it began elsewhere than in the utter vagueness of completely undetermined and dimensionless potentiality." "The evolutionary process is, therefore, not a mere evolution of the *existing universe*, but rather a process by which the very Platonic forms themselves have become or are becoming developed."[15]

Let us now restate the vision of order emerging out of chaos. In the beginning the word was only a question. The question is vague and indeterminate and undifferentiated. By chaos is meant the homogeneous and dimensionless. The answer to the question follows: it is definite and determined and differentiated. By order is meant the heterogeneous and the dimensioned.

Hartshorne quotes this version of the creation myth with approval. It is a meditation upon the categories, relating them to "the idea of God." It would explain how knowledge is possible: there is "a similarity between the operation of the human mind," says Hartshorne, "and the processes of nature."

The order of the universe that we attempt to state in our categories is *a continuum*. Chaos may be translated "undifferentiated continuum." To be ordered is for the multitude of dimensions to become distinct, definite, contracted. This process is "the evolution of forms." Our universe is "a continuum of forms," either originally or in an early stage, says Peirce. Hartshorne, I believe, prefers the latter, for only the latter avoids identifying God with absolute order. Every order is limited, otherwise God would not be the supreme exemplar of the categories.

What is it for a continuum to be contracted, hence, less vague? Quality is vague. Potentially it is anything we can sense of anything. It does not tell us what we feel.

In the myth of order out of chaos we are presented with the plenitude of creatures which inhabit sea, land, and air.

Peirce renders the splendor of the new creation and in his philosophic myth includes the notion that what we now inhabit is fallen:

> We can hardly but suppose that those sense-qualities that we now experience, colors, odors, sounds, feelings of every description, loves, griefs, surprise, are but the relics of an ancient ruined continuum of qualities, like a few columns standing here and there in testimony that here some old-world forum with its basilia and temples had

once made a magnificent *ensemble*. And just as that forum, before it was actually built, had had a vague underexistence in the mind of him who planned its construction, so too the cosmos of sense-qualities, which I would have you to suppose in some early stage of being was as real as your personal life in this minute, had in an antecedent stage of development a vaguer being, before the relations of its dimensions became definite and contracted.[16]

Hartshorne's theory of the continuum is continuous with Peirce's theory of the continuum. Hartshorne develops the theme thus:

> What we should do is look for the continuity (which is not bare identity) among sensations by which we can pass insensibly from one to another, as from red to yellow through orange—in fact, from any color sensation to any other. It may appear that we could not in this way get from color sensations to those of taste or smell. But, as I have shown elsewhere, this is because there are gaps in our human sensory experience, not because there are gaps in the possibilities of sense experience as such. Again, to see how all memories are alike, we should not try to cease imagining particular memories; rather we should imagine how our human memories could continuously expand or contract in various directions, or could have been greater or less in various continuous respects. *'Being' is the total system of all cosmic dimensions of continuous variation*. It is not the abstraction from these dimensions, nor even in every sense from all particular values among them. To be aware of the dimension of brightness from black to white, we need some values, a fairly 'pure' black, a good white, a few grays, but it does not matter just *which* grays, and certainly, we cannot possibly have all the infinitude of possible grays before us as definite items. Thus to be aware of a variable involves neither complete omniscience of its concrete values nor absolute abstraction from the concrete. As for contrast, there can be plenty of it—contrast between the dimensions, between cosmic and local variables, between variables and sample values, between all these and 'being' as their mode of integration.[17]

The more evident continuum is that between sound and feeling as when the bass notes of an organ can be felt as well as heard.

The important Hartshornian shift is not, however, to restore the original lost continuity, but rather the reinterpretation of the subject matter of metaphysics. It amounts to "'Being' is the total system of all cosmic dimensions of continuous variation." What we can talk about is the orders we experience and contrast and we analyze how different orders together constitute a world.

Not only are different orders contrasted with each other, but there is a contrast between *ordering and the ordered*.

One metaphysical concept of chaos is that it is sheer absence of all order. "We can think of [chaos] only negatively, indirectly, as the opposite of all that characterizes God. . . . God and chaos constitute the world. . . . All unity and universality come from God, all manifoldness from chaos. Without chaos God would be just as incapable of producing a world, as chaos without God." This view Hartshorne quotes from Ehrenfels, and he finds it close to Peirce, for there are randomness and law, both real, and each relatively present in all cosmic process. But is Ehrenfels correct that we can think of chaos only negatively, and does all order come from a single principle, God?[18]

Hartshorne's Law of Polarity says something quite different. The conjunction of order and chaos is the conjunction of two positive principles, as opposed to determinism. To deny the meaning of chaos is also to deny the meaning of order. Determinism does not simply interfere with "some special value of freedom but . . . denies even the value of order, which is significant because there is something to be ordered, and this something is spontaneity, creation of novelty. Causality is the *imposing of due limits upon unpredictable-novelty, not the negation of such novelty.*"[19]

Neither order nor chaos is absolute. The theological consequence of making order absolute would be that

> the Cosmic Orderer is responsible for all evils. But suppose determinism to be false, in the radical sense that not only human beings but all individuals, nay more, all events, have some degree of self-determination not wholly controllable by any cosmic principle or power. Then the cosmic principle of order consists, not in a determination of all events just as they occur, but in the setting of limits to the self-determination inherent in each event. *Order is thus the limit imposed upon chaos. It is not the alternative to or the absence of chaos, but its qualification as limited or partial, rather than absolute or pure chaos.* That evils take place is then due to the chaotic element. And if it be asked, *"Why does God not eliminate the chaos entirely?"*, the reply is, *"Because this is meaningless." Order is just the limiting of chaos*, as a river is the channeling (not the absence) of water. God's power cannot be exercised upon nonentity or upon the powerless but only upon lesser powers.[20]

This is perhaps the most clarifying single passage. The category might better be called ordering-ordered rather than order and disorder or order and chaos, to stress that we are dealing with activities in a process. I believe now we can see why Hartshorne did not begin with a definition of order from the logic of relations. A logical definition considers an arrangement of terms in a timeless and abstract way. Formal logic, as Hegel taught us, ignores becoming.

The metaphysical development of the banks-and-the-water image is particularly apt because of the etymology of "chaos" from older terms meaning a yawning gap.[21] In this context we might well think of evil as the overflowing of the banks, the excess of energy, typified in the destructiveness of a flood. But is the sole excess the uncontrolled? Why not also the frustration of too much control? Too much order as well as too little is evil, and too many different kinds of control are also frustrating. Particularly if this relative chaos is spontaneity, it must be protected against being overwhelmed by order. So I think Hartshorne would want to change the sentence "That evils take place is then due to the chaotic element."

The logic of relations aids us in thinking that bad chaos is produced by too many orders at the same time. Hartshorne refers to "three people filing through a narrow doorway." They may proceed "in the order of their ages, or in the order of their heights, or the alphabetical order of the first letter of their last names," etc.[22] This paradigm is similar to that used by Whitehead to show the relativity of kinds of serial order. Suppose that Mr. A, Mr. B, and Mr. C are not oldest, older, and least old, tallest, tall, and least tall, as well as first letter, second letter, and third letter of the alphabet; but we want them to observe all three principles at once. We might think that if a little order is good, more order is better, and most order is best. If we attempted to produce this maximization of order, we should produce only confusion and frustration. No purpose could be served, and there would be aesthetic delight in the melee only if we wanted a Donnybrook.

Hartshorne often tells us that we have entered a new intellectual phase in our thinking about order and chaos. Certainly it is correct that tradition teaches us to identify order with a single principle, a unitary principle, the sole source of good, and to identify chaos with sheer multiplicity, the sole source of evil.

Why have we so far failed to do justice to chaos? One reason is that we often identify the orderly as alone intelligible. The search for knowledge is often thought of as the result of a faith in order. As Whitehead says most beautifully, "There can be no living science without a widespread instinctive conviction of an order of things, especially an order of nature."[23] Hartshorne says why this should be so. ". . . A 'chance order' of events, if that is all it is, gives no information as to the future."[24] If we know that persons file by in order of the alphabet, and there is one for each letter, then, Mr. Hartshorne is the eighth in the procession. But suppose any given number of persons filing through the door. Suppose that either they are Hartshornes or Weisses. If there were no ordering principle, say alternation between Hartshorne and Weiss, we couldn't tell whether the eighth would be Charles or Paul. Chaos seems to leave us ignorant and without the ability to predict. But there is another way of thinking of chaos, as randomness. Says Hartshorne: "We seem now to be entering upon an essentially new intellectual phase, in which terms like 'chance,' 'randomness,' 'probability,' 'possibility,' are no longer to be dismissed, without fear of reproof, as but 'words for our ignorance.'"[25] What we can know about a random ordering of Hartshornes and Weisses is that the more perfectly chaotic, the more orderly the proportion of one to the other in the long run. Somehow Hartshorne does not seem to have made the point that randomness is a kind of order.[26] It allows a kind of lawfulness which is most valuable to know. Says Hartshorne: "statistical predictions can be tested, and in the more complex sciences and the sciences of living things they are about all that are tested. One speaks of 'statistically insignificant' versus 'statistically significant' correlations. Statistical determinism suffices. And, theoretically, even the absolute predictions of astronomy are probably to be interpreted as statistical.''[27]

Not only does Hartshorne press the case for the presence of chance or randomness as a form of chaos present in all nature, thus knowable only by forms of thought appropriate for such happenings, but also he argues for a truer understanding of values and a truer understanding of God.

Each agent in the universe is a creator, some like the non-human animal "in its humble little way.''[28] It is not only man who chooses (pure anthropomorphism) or God who can choose (pure theologism).[29] The old mistake was that of opposing chance to purpose. *"In reality, neither causality nor purpose is intelligible without chance."*[30]

> If *all* creatures have their little purposes, then in this sense teleology is universal. But so, we have seen, is an element of chance and partial "chaos," for these are inherent in the notion of multiple purpose. That chaos has narrow limits set to it is what all science seems to exhibit; the statistical laws express these limits. But how are the limits maintained? Surely not by virtue merely of innumerable little purposes in nature. The only explanation has to be in terms of supreme purpose. This is the theistic account of order. But it destroys its own foundation if it ends by denying the reality of the little purposes it is to harmonize, or to whose discords it is to set limits. The old teleology, by implication, made the divine purpose the only efficacious one. This meant that the very idea of divine purpose had no human basis of meaning.[31]

To those who prefer determinism, Hartshorne says that it adds, as Darwin's preference, nothing to the theory, as Darwin admitted.[32] What if the scientist says that determinism is preferable "on aesthetic grounds?"

> My objection is that his aesthetics [is] unsound. Artists and enjoyers of art do not seek absolute order, order at all costs. Quite the contrary. . . . The open secret of art is in a judicious mingling of regularity and irregularity, of the forseeable and the unforseeable. It is second-rate musicians who play in the most nearly predictable fashion; superb musicians continually deviate from the expected. As the religion of absolute law is a false religion, so the aesthetics of absolute law is a false aesthetics. . . . Writers on aesthetics in the deterministic ages tended to overstate the aspect of regularity in art . . . . They have learned to be more balanced in this respect.[33]

What is possible is an infinite range between absolute order and absolute chaos. What is impossible is absolute order or absolute chaos. Hartshorne pointed out in *Beyond Humanism* exactly how he was departing from tradition, particularly insofar as God was once identified with absolute order or with absolute freedom, or both.

> One of the most difficult of the cosmic variables has been the idea of law or order. The question is whether this order is absolute, or whether it admits of a measure of disorder, of unpredictable novelty and irregularity. Descartes treated absolute order as a local variable applying to non-human nature and (partial) freedom from order he regarded as another local variable, applying to man. God he apparently thought of as

wholly free. This made it difficult if not impossible to find any cosmic variable applicable to the causal problem. Spinoza sought to solve this difficulty by denying freedom, except in the sense of internal necessity ("self-determination"), some degree of which he granted to all things, and a supreme degree to God.[34]

Hartshorne's solution is to grant everything, including God, some measure of both order and disorder, insisting on man as an "example of the coexistence of life and law in the same objects."[35] We never therefore have a dilemma with regard to man, is he (or his act) determined or voluntary? We must always say, to a degree spontaneous, and to a degree, within limits.

Hartshorne is willing to accept Spinoza's analogy of the world to a mathematical system.

> Modern mathematics has . . . shown that the choice of premises for a mathematical system falls outside of mathematical rationality, being a matter of 'taste' or 'convention' or 'elegance.' But it does not fall outside of the real world, since choices are real events. Mathematical rationality is accordingly only one aspect of things, and it is the business of philosophy to show how other aspects are also real. [There is volition in the universe, just as in mathematics there is] "Let there be non-Euclidean geometry," so in the theistic universe there is "Let there be light." Why? There is no complete why. *Preference is ultimate*. It is presupposed in the purest of rational sciences.[36]

Everything in the universe shares in both order and disorder. There is nothing then to be characterized as either absolute order or absolute chaos; and we need to speculate, as I believe Hartshorne has not, on whether there is not an identity between absolute order and absolute chaos. To be an absolute order is to be orderly in every possible way. One type of order would be serial, requiring asymmetry. Another type of order would be balance, requiring symmetry. For the relationship to be both asymmetrical and symmetrical in the same respect at the same time for the same observer is a contradiction. Q. E. D.

Hence Hartshorne must persuade his reader to abandon the link between perfect order, perfect beauty, and God. Hartshorne knows he is apparently opposing what Einstein called "cosmic religious experience," the "deep faith in the rationality of the structure of the world," which motivated Kepler and Newton and other founders of modern science. Einstein called it "the strongest and the noblest driving force behind scientific research."[37] "Einstein said, against indeterminism, that he could not believe 'in a dice-throwing God.' But to have free creatures is, in effect, to throw dice. So why not a dice-throwing God? I fear the great Albert—and he was indeed great—fell into the idolatry of identifying deity with absolute law or non-chance. We may be afraid of chance, but God need not be afraid even of that."[38]

If the tradition was to ascribe the origin of the world to absolute order and then to puzzle over disorder, is Hartshorne turning tradition on its head and ascribing the origin to absolute chance and then puzzling over order? Hartshorne faces this charge. "Chance is inescapable. The only question is, Where is it to be located? Shall we suppose that the world as a whole is one vast throw of the dice, and yet within this whole all is the purest order? Or shall we not rather say that the whole is irrational, lacking 'sufficient reason,' because each part of it is devoid of such reason and incapable of furnishing it to any other part?" Is Hartshorne's position either a Lucretian or a Sartrian absurdity? Hartshorne is true to his Law of Polarity. The same principle order-disorder applies to the part and the whole. "Should not properties of the whole be magnified versions or superstages of the properties of parts? If the All has, in colossal fashion, an aspect of chance, then has not Each, in a humble and even minute way, its own share of this aspect?"[39]

Order is not absolute in the sense that laws are eternal in nature. Hartshorne's argument here is that laws of nature are "only the habits of the species of which nature is composed." ". . . Habit is never . . . that of an absolutely inflexible rule." Hence we have "a more or less flexible and modifiable habit or custom or decree. . . ."[40] Everything in nature has a history and has developed the habits it now has. There is always an alternative law, and since "many laws are conceivable, . . . no one of them can have any reason to be eternal, and hence no one of them can be absolute. . . ."[41]

In *Beyond Humanism* Hartshorne spoke of the "aesthetic and ethical necessity of irregularity."[42] The idea is not really developed beyond the point that

> Life is a blend of order and caprice, of pattern and its creative transcendence. These are all relative concepts, limiting each other, and in this mutual limitation contributing essentially to each others' significance. Control, prediction, classification of individuals are not the whole end of life. Nor are machine-made rugs, by virtue of their greater regularity, more satisfying than handmade ones. Would it not be a humorless and ugly world if (*per impossible*) determinists were its creators?[43]

Absolute order isn't really admirable, and Hartshorne deliberately uses an *ad hominem* appeal. Each reader may consult his own experience. If the world were more orderly, this means things would be more alike, and thus there would be less difference between things. Although sometimes Hartshorne may be repelled by "almost chaotic variety" (e.g., of philosophic views), he has a way of regarding this as a glory (e.g., of the American philosophic scene).[44]

The two fullest expressions of Hartshorne's aesthetic principle that beauty is unity in variety are "God and the Beautiful"[45] and "The Aesthetic Matrix of Value."[46] Between these two chapters come most of Hartshorne's articles on birdsong, a considerable contribution to both aesthetics and ornithology, again a study of order in nature that unites fields commonly unrelated. "The more highly developed the song, i.e., the more extensive the repertoire, the less predictable will be the next item. Thus the evolution of singing is towards maximizing unexpectedness, though always within limits, since the repertoire is essentially fixed in maturity, and since there is a general similarity of style. 'Theme with variations' is a very natural phrase in describing many songs."[47]

When Hartshorne makes explicit his view that beauty is a balance between order and chaos, the meaning of the contrast shifts to unity and variety.

The core of the argument remains identical: aesthetic satisfaction lies between pure order and pure chaos. The excess of order produces boredom, for there is too much unification and too little variety and contrast. The excess of chaos produces confusion, for there is too little unification, and too much variety and contrast. Hence pure unity is valueless and pure variety is valueless, and in balance lies rich satisfaction. But the later essay considers the criticism that the formula is empty and to say "unity in variety" (or "variety in unity") is insufficient. There must be the harmonization of contrasts and intensity of difference, otherwise there is triviality rather than profundity. Whereas in the earlier version, we have a doctrine of beauty, in the later there are many aesthetic modes, such as the "neat" (close to the orderly extreme) and the "ugly" (close to the chaotic extreme), with the addition of another polarity, between the "Hopelessly Complex or Profound" and the "Hopelessly Simple or Superficial." There are the "Magnificent," the "Sublime," and the "Tragic" on the Profound side and the "Commonplace," the "Pretty," and the "Ridiculous" on the Superficial side.

Further Hartshorne deepens his theory that if one grasps aesthetic balance, then one has the principle of intellectual worth and moral value. This is necessary if the early program is to be fulfilled in terms of order and disorder, and we are to have a unified theory of value. Whether the theory succeeds or not is too complicated to unravel in this brief account. The basis of the theory is that "nature, including man, is a mixture of order and randomness."[48]

What can be done further with a theory of order and disorder is exciting. For example: the differences between the sexes are good, for sex "difference . . . tends more to unite than to divide, to harmonize more than to produce discord."[49] Hartshorne could develop arguments against unisex as monotonous, and condemn homosexuality, and condemn artificial egalitarian equality, such as demanded by women's liberation.[50] Another application of the evil of excess is to the excessive discord of a newly caged wild animal. The other extreme is the resignation or at least mild boredom of the old. "Young animals find plenty of diversity in life, for so much is new. Old animals tend to find too little diversity, so much is old. They look on mildly bored while the young eagerly play. This gives . . . the ultimate reason for death, and for me makes the idea that death is essentially or in principle an evil, a sheer mistake. Death at a certain time, or in a certain way, may be a great evil, but death as such is a good."[51]

Does order-disorder also apply to God? Hartshorne holds in both essays that order-disorder is a key, if not the key, to understanding God's motivation and experience of the world. "God is not the super-staleness of the new, the never young, the monomania-like poverty—vainly called superrichness—of the merely absolute (just as he is not the blind chaos of the merely relative). . . . Every child . . . brings a new note of freshness, every youth for whom the world looks young, contributes this freshness . . . to God, who is literally the youngest and the oldest of all beings. . . ." Hartshorne's argument that unlike the old animal, bored because he has experienced everything (as he thinks it), God's richest accumulated experience makes him the most capable to assimilate further variety.[52] The depth of Hartshorne's aesthetic theology can be seen in his metaphor: "God . . . is an artist fostering and loving the beauty of the creatures, the harmonies and intensities of their experiences, as data for his own."[53] God enjoys infinitely, and in this is God's righteousness.[54]

Hartshorne's God cannot be adequately characterized in the old terms of power to judge, to condemn, and to reward. The reason for this is the chaotic. If we underestimate "randomness in life," then we may search for a scapegoat to blame (and would it not be also true, saints to exalt?). "But no one intends events as they happen."[55] "All are caught in a web of mixed intentions, blind necessity, and chance."[56]

We need however to balance these statements of randomness against other statements of the ordering process. ". . . We . . . add to the definiteness of the world, . . . decide the previously undecided, . . . settle the unsettled, . . . close some previously quite open alternatives . . . ."[57] ". . .To do anything at all is to do something to God, to decide anything is to decide something of the content of the all-inclusive awareness. Our deeds are instantly written in strictly indelible ink."[58] So on aesthetic grounds, Hartshorne has rethought a kind of day-of-judgment responsibility for our acts.

God on this theory is "both relative and absolute, conditioned and unconditioned, mutable and immutable, contingent and necessary. He is individual, but *the individual with strictly universal functions*. . . ."[59] The relevance here is that God is not merely a principle of order (Hartshorne says "not a mere or universal form, pattern, system, matter, or force"). But characterizing this supreme or unsurpassable individual are both order and disorder. ". . . God alone is both contingent and necessary."[60] Traditional proofs argue from the contingent world to a non-contingent deity. This argument tries to show that "purely contingent existence is not self-sufficient or intelligible by itself, so that to deny God would be . . . to reject any and every form of existence. . . ." It is an absurdity to say that nothing exists. "Something exists" is an a priori truth.[61] Again, the traditional proof argued that the order of the world is so good and beautiful that only a divine orderer could have produced it.

But what of the flaws? This argument of Hartshorne is that there must be partial disorder. ". . . It is not God alone who acts in the world; every individual acts. There is no single producer of the actual series of events; one producer, to be sure, is uniquely individual, unsurpassably influential."[62]

Hartshorne's cosmological argument is best formulated:

> The order of the world requires a divine orderer, not because the order is perfect, or because there is nothing chaotic or unfortunate in the series of events, but because apart from God there is no way to understand how there could be any limits at all to the confusion and anarchy implied by the notion of a multiplicity of creative agents, none universally influential or wise. And that there are such limits to anarchy is no mere fact; for there would have to be limits in any genuinely conceivable state of reality. But to understand this necessity is to see it as one with the necessity of God as cosmic orderer.[63]

The traditional proof from order claimed that "God's ordering [was] in eternity, entirely uninfluenced by any creaturely decisions. Indeed, the creaturely decisions were themselves divinely chosen. But then the divine cause of all things was a sheer exception to the rule that concrete effects are also concrete causes, and vice versa, and also to the rule that the cause precedes, the effects follow."[64] Hartshorne's argument is that "localized interaction cannot of itself make intelligible the possibility of any order and that without some order the concept of interaction itself lacks definite meaning, so that the denial of a strictly universal yet individual form of interaction would be the denial of any interaction at all."[65] The question is, why is not reality a "shapeless chaos?" "Only universal interaction can secure universal order, or impose and maintain laws of nature cosmic in scope and relevant to the past history of the universe. . . . The alternative to God's existence is not an existing chaos, but rather, nothing conceivable. The very concept of reality (and any significant 'unreality' as well) implicitly involves order and an orderer. Apart from God not only would this world not be conceivable, but no world, and no state of reality, or even of unreality, could be understood.It is not any mere fact that must be rejected . . . but the basic concept by which alone we can conceive even possible facts. All the arguments are just as truly a priori as the ontological."[66]

Hartshorne's argument is, in essence, twofold. First, the order-disorder of the world is not mutual adjustment of agents to each other.[67] Second, the order-disorder of the world requires one among the agents to be unsurpassable, what he calls a "chairman." "Order is in principle 'the rule of one.'"[68] Hence, a "world not ordered by God" is a contradiction like an "unordered but ordered" system of things."[69]

The universe, as Hartshorne presents it, is not only a continuum with many dimensions, it is an hierarchical order and a serial order. In all these orders Hartshorne has stressed asymmetry. Whenever we have such a relation as "better than" or "later in time and more developed" we have an irreversible direction, a one way relation.[70] Hartshorne has also stressed harmony and balance in the universe.[71]

I wish at the end to say that no contemporary philosoplier has devoted himself as profoundly as has Hartshorne to the concepts involved in the ecological crisis. One kind of ordering is that of growth, and the unlimited growth of man's population and production has resulted in pollution that, if unchecked, will render life itself impossible. In this respect what is needed is a balance between population and resources. Therefore I believe there needs to be a companion essay from Hartshorne called "The Prejudice in Favor of Asymmetry."

The subject order-disorder in the philosophy of Charles Hartshorne is far too rich and complex a topic for one brief exploratory essay. Both because of its vision, its techniques, and its practical application, it deserves sustained examination and criticism.

PAUL GRIMLEY KUNTZ

DEPARTMENT OF PHILOSOPHY
EMORY UNIVERSITY
JUNE 1985

WORKS BY CHARLES HARTSHORNE FREQUENTLY CITED, WITH SHORT TITLES

BH　　　　*Beyond Humanism: Essays in the Philosophy of Nature*, Lincoln: University of Nebraska Press, 1968, referred to as BH '68; other than preface same pagination as original edition, Chicago: Willett, Clark and Co., 1937.

CSPM　　　*Creative Synthesis and Philosophic Method*, La Salle, Ill.: Open Court Publishing Co., 1970.

LP　　　　*The Logic of Perfection and Other Essays*, La Salle, Ill.: Open Court Publishing Co., 1962.

MVG　　　*Man's Vision of God and the Logic of Theism*, New York: Harper and Brothers, 1941.

NTT　　　*A Natural Theology for Our Time*, La Salle, Ill.: Open Court Publishing Co., 1967.

PSG　　　*Philosophers Speak of God*, Chicago: University of Chicago Press, 1953 (with William L. Reese).

RSP　　　*Reality as Social Process*, Glencoe, Ill.: Free Press, and Boston, Mass.: Beacon Press, 1953.

OC   "Order and Chaos," in Paul G. Kuntz, *The Concept of Order*, Seattle: University of Washington Press, 1968, pp. 253–267.

ERT   "The Environmental Results of Technology," *Philosophy and Environmental Crisis*, Feb. 18–20, 1971, Athens, Georgia: University of Georgia Press, 1976, pp. 69–78.

NOTES

1. Charles Hartshorne, "Order and Chaos," in Paul G. Kuntz, *The Concept of Order* (Seattle: University of Washington Press, 1968), pp. 253–367. Cf. Paul G. Kuntz, "Religion of Order or Religion of Chaos?" *Religion in Life*, Vol. XXV, No. 3, Summer 1966, pp. 433–449.
2. BH 112–114.
3. BH '68, vii–x, "I still view man, nature and God in much the same way and for much the same reasons, although I think that the argument can be strengthened in certain ways," pp. vii–viii.
4. CSPM, X, pp. 205–226.
5. BH, VIII, IX, X, pp. 111–164.
6. MVG, VI, pp. 212–229.
7. CSPM, XVI, pp. 303–321.
8. NTT, II, pp. 29–65.
9. PSG, pp. 436–437.
10. LP, XIII, pp. 298–323.
11. CSPM 205.
12. CSPM 221.
13. BH 114–115, emphases mine.
14. Josiah Royce, *Logical Essays*, ed. Daniel S. Robinson (Dubuque, Iowa: Wm. C. Brown,1951), pp. 223–224.
15. PSG 267.
16. Ibid.
17. BH 115, emphasis mine.
18. PSG 353–354, 352.
19. PSG 484, emphasis mine.
20. PSG 436, emphasis mine.
21. Chaos, χαος "any vast gulf or chasm, the nether abyss, empty space, the first state of the universe" from χα—to yawn, gape, *New English Dictionary*, Vol. II, Clarendon Press, Oxford, 1893, p. 273.
22. OC 254.
23. A. N. Whitehead, *Science and the Modern World* (New York: Macmillan, 1926), p. 6.
24. OC 254.
25. OC 258.
26. This is a familiar point in Peirce: The odds in perfectly random sequence are that it will be one of two kinds or 50–50.
27. OC 264.
28. Ibid.
29. OC 265.
30. OC 260.

31. OC 266.
32. OC 267, see LP 206–211.
33. OC 264.
34. BH 125.
35. BH 127.
36. BH 132.
37. BH 19–20.
38. NTT 92.
39. BH 133.
40. BH 139.
41. BH 141.
42. BH 142.
43. BH 158.
44. LP 10, The chaotic aspect of variety is the excess of kinds, irreducible to types, but the rich plenitude is the contrasting goodness of variety.
45. MVG VI, 212–229.
46. CSPM XVI, 303–321.
47. CSPM 307.
48. CSPM 318.
49. CSPM 314–315.
50. Ibid.
51. CSPM 309.
52. MVG 228.
53, CSPM 309.
54. CSPM 310.
55. CSPM 318.
56. CSPM 319.
57. LP 19.
58. NTT 113–114.
59. NTT 36.
60. NTT 50.
61. Ibid.
62. NTT 58.
63. NTT 59.
64. NTT 60.
65. NTT 49.
66. NTT 53.
67. LP 157.
68. NTT 61.
69. LP 156.
70. "The Prejudice in Favor of Symmetry" argues this in great detail, CSPM X.
71. "Harmony in Life and Nature," RSP II.

22

Sterling M. McMurrin

HARTSHORNE'S CRITIQUE OF CLASSICAL METAPHYSICS AND THEOLOGY

Perhaps no living philosopher has made a more serious or more successful effort to define, elucidate, and criticize his own position by contrast and comparison with others than has Professor Charles Hartshorne. His extensive explications of his own thought exhibit an impressive grasp of not only earlier treatments of the issues which concern him, but as well the major trends and variations that characterize recent developments in metaphysics and theology. For six decades metaphysics has been for Hartshorne nothing less than a solemn vocation—as a philosopher, the pursuit of the nature of reality, and as a theologian, the search for a rational foundation for religion. Hartshorne philosophizes with his fist on the table. His extensive and at times intricate logical analyses of the problems of metaphysics and their scientific, moral, and religious implications are not the intellectual exercise of the typical analytic philosopher. They are a deadly serious effort to achieve substantive knowledge and truth.

By his comparative method Hartshorne has both sharpened his own concepts and brought attention to often overlooked or neglected facets of major philosophies of the past and has thrown new and interesting light on the classical thinkers and their influence from Aristotle through Aquinas, Leibniz, Kant, and Hegel to the present. He never fails to acknowledge his indebtedness to others and to disclose the worth of their ideas, even when he is critical of them. Hartshorne's indebtedness is great, of course, to Peirce and Whitehead, whose recondite philosophies he has known at close, even intimate, range— philosophies which have been made more understandable, and in some ways more meaningful, by his writing. But he is at pains as well to recognize his obligation to G. T. Fechner, William James, and Henri Bergson, to mention only a sampling of those who are frequently referenced in his work.

I regard Hartshorne as pre-eminent among living philosophers of religion. That he is the foremost representative of the "process theology" that now promises to effect large reforms in religious thought is a commonplace, but I rather think that it is sometimes overlooked that his "neoclassical metaphysics," which exhibits his uncommon philosophical insight and logical skill, is logically basic to his theological and moral concepts. No philosopher since Whitehead has done more to produce the renascence of responsible speculative thought that has followed upon the recent era of neopositivism and linguistic analysis and is today still gaining strength in academic circles.

Throughout his published work Hartshorne has exhibited an acute sensitivity to the classical absolutistic metaphysics that has generally characterized occidental thought, a metaphysics rooted historically in both Platonism and Aristotelianism, and transmitted especially by Stoicism and Neoplatonism. It was this metaphysics that became the chief philosophical foundation of the early church, infecting the entire theological structure of Christianity and the dominant culture which nourished and perpetuated it, an absolutistic interpretation of ultimate reality that still controls the conservative cultural and religious tradition. The sources of the absolutism which so clearly defines the classical metaphysics upon which Hartshorne has so vigorously made war are somewhat more complex than his writings usually indicate, considering the nature of the polygenetic intellectual cultures out of which the Christian philosophy and theology issued. But certainly in fastening his criticism on the slavish adhesion to the Greek concept of static, immutable, timeless being, free of all contingency, that has dominated the mainstream of occidental thought, he has targeted the chief villain on the metaphysical and theological scene.

It is to the great credit of Professor Hartshorne that his criticism of classical absolutism, though stern and unrelenting and obviously fired by considerable passion, has throughout been grounded in a commitment to reason that at times seems almost to absorb him in meticulous logical distinction and argument. While I question some of his premises or presuppositions, I can only admire the rational criteria which guide his thought and the rigorous adherence to strict logical inference that controls his method. One may not agree with Hartshorne, but no one seriously interested in metaphysics or theology can afford to ignore him. His philosophy is a carefully crafted systematic argument that incorporates in an original form much of the best thought of the past hundred years. His neoclassical metaphysics and process theology are philosophy on a high level. Hartshorne insists, in agreement with Peirce, that real progress in philosophic thought, even in speculative metaphysics, is not only possible but is actually taking place. In my opinion, he is a factor in that progress.

I will hazard the opinion that Professor Hartshorne's concern for theology is in fact not subordinate to his metaphysical interests, and that his theology, despite the logical structuring of his philosophy, is not originally a deduction from his metaphysics. But rather that his instinct, good sense, intuition, or whatever one cares to call it, has over the years driven home to him on grounds other than strictly logical, but nonetheless rational, that there must be a God and that God must be both absolute and finite, absolute in his goodness and finite in his power. Professor Hartshorne is a humane and compassionate person, and it would be a grievous error to see him as a kind of logical machine whose opinions on the world and God are basically a product of his powers of logical analysis and deduction. I mention this because the extensive and at times involuted logical analyses supporting his primary theses and their implicates can almost suggest that his conception of God is simply the end product of a chain of reasoning. I rather think that not only his ideas on the nature of God but also his position on the existence of God, despite his attachment to the ontological argument, are grounded more in a basically religious faith than in logic. It would be interesting to have him address this question directly.

It is not likely that anyone has worked over the theological problem more thoroughly or with more commitment to logical accuracy and detail, and in this pursuit Hartshorne has surely not only gained logical support for his ideas, he has also honed his definitions and arguments to a fine point as well. More than that, his logic has, I am sure, turned up new ideas and arguments in quite unexpected places, for even the simplest syllogism may, on careful examination, disclose ideas that are entirely new and unforeseen. Yet it seems to me that Hartshorne's panentheistic theory, which is based on a Law of Polarity and describes God as both absolute and relative, is in principle widely held in the occident by countless religious believers who know little or nothing of logic and are not given to rigorous theological reasoning, but whose beliefs are tempered by good judgment and common sense. My point is that Hartshorne's brand of theism, at least in its basic character, has large acceptance among the rank and file of those who are thoughtful in such matters but have neither philosophical nor theological cultivation—at least those who are not victimized by the cerebrations of the theologians or by an abject bibliolatry and are committed to some degree of independence and reasonableness in their religious views. His kind of theology is not in any strict sense revolutionary, except as a sophisticated logical formulation and argument and as a clear statement of radical departure from the classic tradition. In much of its basic character it conforms to the liberal forms of Judeo-Christian theism that have been around for some time. But in Hartshorne's work, the theology of an absolutely good Creator, supreme but limited in power, has achieved both logical respectability and a meticulous delineation of meaning.

Hartshorne has classified not only the Judeo-Christian scriptures as quasi-panentheistic, but as well some ancient Hindu, Egyptian, and Chinese scriptures, and, of course, he has acknowledged his agreement with any number of recent philosophers and theologians, to say nothing of his great respect for the work of Socinus and his followers and for the non-substantive metaphysics of the earlier forms of Buddhism. In view of this, and considering his penchant for referencing the work of others, it would be interesting to learn from Hartshorne himself just where he regards his work as breaking entirely new ground, apart from his logical structuring of the problems and his providing a rational basis for ideas that in principle, at least, already have wide acceptance among those who are trying to make sense of their religion.

The basis of Hartshorne's argument, which brings logic into conjunction with intellectual history, is his persuasive case that the chief error of classical metaphysics and theology has been to treat contraries as if they were contradictories, to fail to recognize that the ultimate reality is both absolute and relative—absolute in some respects and relative in others—that God, who, contrary to the traditional theology, is essentially diverse rather than simple, is both absolute and relative or finite—absolute in some respects and finite in others. Hartshorne is entirely right in holding that the so-called monopolar logic dominated much of the history of metaphysics and theology from Aristotle on, and his identifying prime examples of this has been an important contribution to scholarship. He has recognized three types of theistic theology around which much of his discussion and argument is structured. They can be briefly stated: 1. "There is a being in *all* respects absolutely perfect or unsurpassable, in no way and in no respect surpassable or perfectible." 2. "There is no being in all respects absolutely perfect; but there is a being in *some* respect or respects thus perfect, and in some respect or respects not so. . . ." 3. "There is no being in *any* respect absolutely perfect . . . " (*Man's Vision of God*, 1941, p. 11f.).

I am sure that Professor Hartshorne would be the first to acknowledge that in this kind of logical structuring of opposite categories, in cataloging actual instances of theological and metaphysical theories which are often lacking in definiteness, distortions, especially because of the necessity of oversimplification, are inevitable. Philosophic thought cannot escape some degree of confusion in its efforts to structure its problems and arguments. But his setting the categories in this simple triadic fashion and following through over the years with extensive logical analyses and historical studies has done much to clarify an immensely complex problem.

The essential character of the neoclassical metaphysics is perhaps best seen in Hartshorne's panentheistic theology, the second of his three types, where his principle of dipolarity breaks away from the classical absolutism while still avoiding the more extreme nominalistic pluralism that has throughout this century been set against absolutism, as in the instance of the radical empiricism of William James. Hartshorne may be on sound ground in his criticism of both the philosophical and theological mainstream for failing to pursue this middle course rather than opposing one extreme with another when both extremes produce problems that defy resolution whenever a serious attempt is made to reconcile reason with experience. Here is an important strength of his position, for his pantheistic theory is an attempt to satisfy both the rationalistic demand for necessary being and the empirical insistence on contingency and becoming.

The implications of Hartshorne's absolute-relative theory for theology and religion are, of course, both fundamental and far-reaching. If his metaphysics is sound, he may have found a way out of the major theological pitfalls that have plagued religious thought and practice in the past, difficulties resulting from a concept that must disclaim any compassionate relationship of God to the world and individuals, that makes the human experience of moral endeavor ultimately meaningless, and that logically entails a denial of the reality of evil and human tragedy. It may be a way out of the clutches of classical absolutism without acceding to the thoroughgoing nominalism that, despite the empirical tempera-ment of our culture, fails to satisfy the demands of reason. Hartshorne's kind of theology, whatever its problems, is not only an antidote to the absolutism of the past, but is as well a reply to the nominalistic death-of-God craze that justifiably objected to an absolutism which denied God's relevance to human experience but overreacted in the opposite extreme.

Hartshorne's own list of what he has rightly called the "deficiencies of inherited religions" is well worth repeating here: Other-worldliness, Power Worship, Asceticism, Moralism ("the notion that serving God is almost entirely a matter of avoiding theft and adultery and the like, together with dispersing charity, leaving noble-hearted courageous creative action in art, science, and statesmanship as religiously neutral or secondary"), Optimism ("the denial that tragedy is fundamental in the nature of existence and God"), and Obscurantism ("the theory that we can best praise God by indulging in contradiction and semantical nonsense") (*The Divine Relativity*, New Haven and London: Yale University Press, 1948, p. 148f.). I fully agree with this catalogue of dire consequences of what Hartshorne calls the "neglect of divine relativity," which he has correctly identified as the chief deficiency of traditional occidental theology.

Hartshorne claims for his dipolar (absolute and relative) metaphysics that it overcomes the traditional antinomies of unity and plurality, being and becoming, the infinite and the finite, eternity and time, necessity and freedom. His attempt to justify this immodest claim by logical analysis is impressive. I find it rather surprising, however, considering his habit of frequently referring to the work of others, that in this and in other connections he appears to make no reference to the work of Borden Parker Bowne, whose personalistic world ground was intended to serve the same purpose—the resolution of the metaphysical antinomies. He refers on occasion to the work of Bowne's successor, Edgar S. Brightman, but usually in consideration of Brightman's somewhat unique finitistic theology. Of course, Hartshorne gives considerable attention to the concept of God as personal, and he might well be regarded as a personalist, though he doesn't fit the idealistic mode typical of American personalism. It would be interesting to have his comparative commentary on Bowne's personalistic idealism which, though in a manner different from the influence of James or Hartshorne, has had, through Brightman and Ralph Tyler Flewelling, a considerable impact on the philosophy of religion. I can see marked similarities as well as differences in comparing Hartshorne with Bowne.

A central theological implication of Hartshorne's dipolar metaphysics is his attack on the traditional idea of divine omnipotence. It has been this facet of absolutism more than anything else that has played havoc with the efforts of the theologians to defend free will, to face honestly the problems of theodicy, and in general to make sense of the meaning and worth of human existence and moral experience. In their pluralistic finitism, James and others—William Pepperell Montague, for example—have faced these matters squarely and have made a place for man and his freedom while still defending a radically different, and thoroughly refreshing, theism that breaks clear of the classical tradition. From the standpoint of religious belief and worship, however, neither that finitism nor the absolutism-finitism of Brightman's God with the irrational Given has had much appeal beyond limited academic circles. The typical religious believer wants to worship a bona fide Absolute who has the whole world in his hand. He doesn't like to take his problems to a finite God who has problems of his own. But Hartshorne's theology, it seems to me, retains that measure of absolutism which may inspire worship and provide the worshiper with a sense of cosmic security and at the same time, through its relativism, allow adequate space in the universe for the reality of evil, suffering, and human creativity. The James-Whitehead-Hartshorne theology may well provide the possibility for liberal religion to be not simply the route of an inevitable transition from orthodoxy to naturalistic humanism, but rather a religion of both faith in God and faith in man. This may be the case at least for those, always a bare minority, whose religion is thoughtful and for whom theology makes a practical difference.

The chief factor in Hartshorne's metaphysics and theology that gives them relevance to religion is his insistence that action and passion in God are contraries, not contradictories, and that while God is supremely active, his is not the only creative will, and while he is the supreme cause and influence, he is affected by the contingent world, a world which is external as well as internal to him. God is both cause and effect. God influences us eminently, but we also influence God, something that the devout worshipers have always believed, or at least hoped, but which their technical theologians, with their creeds that God is without passion, have usually denied. It is here that Hartshorne provides for the divine compassion and makes his God, to use Whitehead's famous words, "available for religious purposes." With Whitehead, Hartshorne is far removed from Aristotle with his unmoved mover. I will not say that they are poles apart. James was poles apart from the classical position, but Hartshorne is somewhere down the middle. He seeks the best of both worlds—the absolute and relative, infinite and finite.

"I hold that if we could not influence God," Hartshorne wrote in his critique of Gabriel Marcel, "our existence would be simply vain" (*The Philosophy of Gabriel Marcel*, 1984, p. 360). Taken by itself this is not a persuasive argument for the divine passion, but it is a challenging idea. We are in a dialogue with God, who is effect as well as cause. Otherwise, says Hartshorne, God would not be a "Thou." This dialogue is religion. God creates us as free creatures, but in our free creativity we add to the divine life. Our creativity is God's potentiality being actualized. In this way, though nothing surpasses God, he surpasses himself. This is an element in the divine process.

God conceived as process or becoming rather than static being, despite his necessary existence—for the classical tradition a most radical heresy—is a central element of Hartshorne's theology, and his persistent and persuasive arguments in providing logical support for it and in refining its meaning have placed him at the center of the process theology movement, a movement which has had a marked impact on Jewish and Catholic as well as Protestant thought. Hartshorne holds that God is unsurpassable, but he means by this that he cannot be surpassed by anything other than God. He is not immutable, because he can surpass himself. God is not, in the Aristotelian mode, pure act without potentiality; he possesses all actual value and as well all potential perfections. But he does not have absolute maximum value, because not all possible value is actual in God. He is perfect, but his perfection does not mean the actualization of all potential value. "But God, and only God, can actually enjoy all actual values and potentially enjoy all potential ones" (ibid., p. 364). The free creativity of God's creatures adds to his value because he is in a sense a social being and his relation to his creatures is integral to his being. This fact of interaction and dialogue with God is the basis of Hartshorne's ethical theory, which is grounded in the relationship of love. God is in process, a process that issues from his contingent nature and the contingent world, even though in his determinate, necessary being he is absolute.

I fully agree that a theology of this kind makes more sense than the traditional doctrine, and it gives meaning to religion and life. There remains, however, the fundamental and perpetually vexing question of how these ideas can be known to be true. Surely Hartshorne's logic cannot establish that God is a loving being even if it could establish his existence, which even he does not claim. And despite his logic which makes a place for interaction with God, on what ground, rational or experiential, does Hartshorne base his claim that there is in fact such a reciprocal interaction? There are almost countless unanswered questions of this kind, but, of course, I am not suggesting that any philosopher should be expected to provide an answer to every question which his theories generate. There is inevitably a speculative character to metaphysics that must be taken for granted unless we simply rule out the entire discipline on positivistic grounds.

Hartshorne's assault upon the classical absolutistic metaphysic of being is a many-sided systematic attack, but in addition to those I have mentioned, two other factors are of such importance and interest that they deserve attention: his commitment to temporalism and his insistence that creative freedom is genuinely real. Nothing is more indicative of the full character of a metaphysical or theological system than its resolution of the issues of time and eternity and freedom and determinism, for certainly these lie at the heart of the matter whether reality is defined as event or substance. And they are of major importance when the implication of a theory of reality for actual value is of primary concern.

Hartshorne's description of God and ultimate reality implies the strongest emphasis on temporality. Here certainly is a major strength of his metaphysics and theology, though I believe that he might make even more of his position on time than he has done. The traditional theory inevitably either denied or in various ways downplayed the reality of time. This was due, of course, largely to the domination of Platonic and Aristotelian metaphysics, mediated through Neoplatonism to Christianity, which denied the temporality of the ultimately real, a necessary correlate of the denial of process and becoming, and reduced the time dimension of the events of the natural world to cycles in imitation of the timelessness of the universal reality. Notwithstanding the temporal character of the Hebrew scriptures which provided the religious foundation of Christianity, this timelessness became the eternity of God in Christian theology—a hallmark of the classical theology supported by most major theologians, including Augustine, Aquinas, Luther, and Calvin. In the moment of incarnation, declared the theologians, there was an intersection of eternity with time, but for the eternal God there is no past and no future, just a timeless present that embraces the totality of temporal reality. In such a system it is difficult to invest human history with any kind of meaning, or to find real value in the life of the individual or society. Moreover, the very concept of personality or person, whether human or divine, requires temporality, as it requires both freedom and passivity. The classical idea that God is a timeless person is in effect a contradiction. It seems to me that Hartshorne might well make more of this point. He holds that there is a divine analogue for human temporality, and I am sure that by this he means that he considers God to be genuinely temporal, having a genuine past and a genuine future, at least in his contingent nature. His conception of the immortality of man, and presumably of all contingent beings, is that everything is in some way preserved in the divine knowledge, for despite his temporality God is omniscient in a rather unorthodox way. This conforms to the idea that there is an eternal-temporal character of the divine. At any rate, without time in some sense or another, there is no process, only immutability, and Hartshorne's war on immutable being necessarily entails a battle with non-temporality. The free creative will is a central factor of his metaphysics, theology, and ethics, and without temporality both freedom and creativity would be quite meaningless, the freedom and creativity that make a difference for the world, that make a difference in God.

Having said that "it is trifling with philosophical problems to accept as valid questions and answers that have no conceivable bearing on how we propose to live" (*Insights and Oversights of Great Thinkers*, p. 373), Hartshorne makes the rather strange comment that *"Determinism is useless because it becomes applicable too late"* (loc. cit.). I say strange because, with due respect for Hartshorne's pragmatic temperament, I fail to see that the truth or falsity or meaningfulness of a proposition is relevant to how we propose to live. Certainly determinism is useless in affecting human decisions, and I regard it as false if not actually meaningless, but I cannot agree that its truth value in any way depends on its use value. I am not sure what Hartshorne means here by "useless" or "applicable."

I certainly would offer no defense for classical determinism, though I believe its defenders are quite understandable, and I fully agree with Hartshorne when he insists on freedom of the will. I like his definition of classical determinism as having a tautological structure, where all relations are internal and all events are interdependent. But I have some difficulty in understanding his denying determinism while defending universal causation and at the same time arguing against what he has termed "compatibilism," the reconciliation of freedom and causation by distinguishing causation from coercion. I fail to see on what ground, while acknowledging what he is willing to call universal causation, he can reasonably in some way dissociate events from the causal chain where this seems necessary to make the case for free will.

There is a sense in which Hartshorne does not deny that all events are caused. He acknowledges universal causation, using that term, but with a meaning quite different from that usually found in discussions of determinism and indeterminism. In the context of his theology, he holds that God is the cosmic cause, or, as he sometimes prefers to say, "influence." Causality is the influence of the past on the present, or the present on the future, and is treated temporally. Causality is present in all events, says Hartshorne, but causality does not determine the precise event or occurrence. Rather it determines the "real" possibilities for what occurs, the kind of event that will occur. Actual particular past events are "definite," but possibility is "indefinite." Free creativity yields the definite actual occurrence, which becomes past. Freedom is "becoming," which is the creation of definiteness where causation has made alternatives possible to free decision or action. The future is open, indefinite, and indeterminate; the past is closed, definite, and, I presume, determined.

I find this both appealing and confusing. Appealing because I admire Hartshorne's ingenuity in developing a theory of freedom while at the same time acknowledging universal causation; confusing because I fail to understand the principle on which he grounds his argument. I recognize, of course, that his temporalistic and creative conception of freedom, which I regard as one of the strong points of his philosophy, is entirely consonant with his basic theory of reality and his conception of God and man. And I realize that this is central to his whole metaphysics of process with its emphasis on creativity and an open future. But it doesn't seem to me that he makes a clear case. Rather, the shift from cause to influence and the distinction between indefinite and definite tend to confuse the issue and lay him open to the possible charge that he is begging this all-important question.

Universal causation, whether it is God or nature, is one thing. We are accustomed to it. And we at least have some grasp of what is intended by these words. But the free decision that chooses among the alternatives—what is it? Is it an uncaused, free-wheeling cause in the libertarian sense? Surely it is not chance, or it would not be responsible freedom. It seems to me that Hartshorne has not adequately explained himself at this point.

In his concern for reconciling freedom with universal causation, Professor Hartshorne may have given too little attention to the opportunities provided by a consideration of the nature of mental activity in decision and the utter complexity of brain activity in interaction with the environment. I have in mind the crucial problem of what constitutes the self taken as the agent of free decision and action. Considering the constant barrage of causal factors converging at every moment, a recognition of which satisfies the principle of universal causation, the very meaning of selfhood, of personality and creativity, of the free agent, may be located in the decision and action that issue from this massive conjunction. Hartshorne may well argue that this is simply a way of disguising determinism, but I believe that within the framework of his metaphysics there is here a better possibility than in the course which he has followed of defending free will against the equation of universal causality with classical determinism. His conception of God as both absolute and relative, as both necessary and contingent, requires universal causation and free creative will, and it may well be that the reconciliation of the two can be found in the nature of personality, the self as the conjunction of the vast congeries of causal forces, forces which in this complex combination produce movements in new directions which could not have been foretold even by the divine mind. A theory of this kind seems to be consonant even with Hartshorne's conception of God's omniscience.

Hartshorne has made much of the denial of classical determinism by many twentieth-century physicists, but there is still some question whether indeterminism in the sense in which this term is commonly employed can be established by the physical sciences. Despite the verdict of many physicists and some philosophers, I have never been fully persuaded that the uncertainty principle in quantum mechanics justifies a metaphysical doctrine of indeterminism, and even if there is in fact an indeterminate factor in sub-atomic physics where events are uncaused, I fail to see that this can justifiably be used as an argument for free will in human beings. Of course, Hartshorne's panpsychism, which seems to me not to be justified by his arguments, apparently extends some kind of freedom throughout the totality of the real. In affirming panpsychism he has immeasurably complicated everything. I find it impossible to follow him in that direction.

Hartshorne has treated the matter of physics and indeterminism in some detail, but not, I think, persuasively. He says that although quantum mechanics is not the last word, it may have sounded the death knell of classical mechanics. Like many others he appears to enjoy the presumed support of quantum theory and finds genuine support for creativity in the biological sciences with their emphasis on temporality and evolution. But I believe that free will is not for him an issue to be decided on scientific grounds, but rather is a speculative matter that conforms to personal experience and is consonant with his logical premises as well as his basic theological concepts. Hartshorne holds that metaphysical truths cannot be established or disproved by empirical science, but that does not mean that metaphysics is or should be indifferent to empirical considerations. Perhaps he would not regard the fact of free will as a metaphysical truth, but I am sure that he would not base his case for it entirely on scientific evidence.

It seems to me that our best, and probably only, justifiable ground for believing in the freedom of the will is our experience of feeling free in our decisions, an experience of free choice even when we are under physical or other duress in making the choice. But, of course, this is not an experience of our decision being uncaused. On the contrary, it is not difficult, though the complications are countless, for us to identify some of the causes of our choices on at least a gross level. Our failure to give a complete account of the causes is not an argument against causation but is simply the consequence of the utter complexity of the mind in its processes and in its relation to the body and the countless forces that impinge upon it. The question of moral choice is often the arena in which the hassle over freedom and determinism takes place. The choices are free because the person makes them. They are creative because something new has been added. But if they were not caused, there would be anarchy rather than morality. This is an old argument, as old as Aristotle, and I believe that Hartshorne would agree with it, for he does not deny a causal factor in free decision. Nevertheless, I get lost in some confusion of meaning when he comes to the heart of his argument for free will because he has inadequately stated his case for the nature of the free creative self or person.

Perhaps I should conclude these comments on Professor Hartshorne's philosophy by an admission that in my early years I was slightly infected by the views of logical positivism, and the scars of that infection are still with me, at least to the extent of my being a quite confirmed empiricist. I have, therefore, a lingering suspicion of all speculative metaphysics. Yet I believe that a carefully controlled, contrite metaphysics is possible. And this is what I have found in Hartshorne: a mastery of logical principles and analysis far superior to that of most speculative philosophers and a kind of earthy common sense that is a major plus for any philosopher, or for anyone else for that matter. I have sometimes felt that he was too much committed to logical distinctions and analyses in his treatment of theology, but his methods are so commendable and refreshing in comparison with the work of most others in that arena that I can only admire what he has done.

However, considering the large element of logic and rationalism in Hartshorne's method, something that seems to leap from almost every page, I have been somewhat disappointed that he has not given more explicit attention to the empirical foundations of his speculations and, indeed, to the intuitive or mystical ground of some of his ideas. There are many questions, it seems to me, on how Hartshorne reaches some of his conclusions regarding such things as the nature of God where they do not depend logically on his premises. But then he does not pretend to be a thoroughgoing rationalist to the exclusion of other ways of knowing. He has made it clear that "The unconditionally necessary could not be known empirically, nor could the contingent be known a priori" (*Creativity in American Philosophy*, 1984, p. 283). Even God, says Hartshorne, is bound in his knowledge to this restriction. "God must directly perceive the contingent creatures by contingent acts of prehension" (loc. cit.). But Hartshorne seems to have much to say about contingent facets of God without giving us the empirical ground for his knowledge claim.

My primary concern here has not been to discuss Hartshorne's methodological principles, and I have avoided commenting on his defense of the ontological argument, certainly a matter central to his interests and basically important to his metaphysics and theology. I agree with Hartshorne that an empirical proof of God's existence is an impossibility if God is defined in any way that is acceptable to cultured religion. And he is perhaps warranted in holding that the traditional cosmological and teleological arguments are at base rational rather than empirical. But I fail to see that his own a priori treatment of the problem is successful. Even if his defense of Anselm's second argument is accepted and Kant's objection is set aside on the ground that "perfect existence" *can* be a predicate, it seems to me that at best there has only been a clearing of the way for the God of religion. I think Professor Hartshorne agrees with this judgment.

Much that Hartshorne has to say is related to the ontological argument and, in a sense, dependent on it; or perhaps it would be more accurate to say that his system depends primarily on the large ontological assumption that the world is what reason finds it to be. This, of course, may well be the case. Rationalism has for some time been out of style, but with some of our leading thinkers, such as Brand Blanshard and Hartshorne, it seems to be making a comeback. This is by no means a disaster as long as it is a penitent rationalism carefully blended with the virtues of empiricism. But there seems to be a kind of massive begging of the question in rationalism, as perhaps there is in empiricism, or in mysticism, that what is to be accepted or proved is in some way, however well hidden, built into the initial assumptions or method. I recall one of my early teachers saying that "in the last analysis all knowledge is circular; it is simply a question of who has the biggest circle." If this is true, I can only say that Hartshorne has drawn a very big circle. He has made impressive contributions to metaphysics and is our foremost living specimen of a philosopher of religion. And, not least, he has contributed greatly to philosophical scholarship and understanding.

STERLING M. MCMURRIN

E. E. ERICKSEN DISTINGUISHED PROFESSOR
UNIVERSITY OF UTAH
OCTOBER 1986

23

Reiner Wiehl

HARTSHORNE'S PANPSYCHISM

1. RATIONAL AND EMPIRICAL METAPHYSICS

Hartshorne has ordered his philosophical thinking into a system of ideas which he calls neoclassical metaphysics. This term neoclassical is in itself philosophically significant. It implies that metaphysics, contrary to the views of many influential thinkers, especially in Europe, is by no means antiquated and superseded. A neoclassical metaphysics is, according to its own characterization of itself, indebted to classical metaphysics. Its classical status is less its historical-epochal locus than its canonical-normative role. The reference to the classical in the neoclassical designation indicates that the mode of questioning and the problems of the former are still relevant: questions about the essence and existence of a highest being (God), about causality and freedom, time and matter, the place of the human species in the creation and its relation to the other creatures. The "neo" implies that these age-old questions still call forcefully for an answer, though they require new answers so far as the old answers have shown themselves insufficient. Thus the most important aspect of the idea of a neoclassical metaphysics is that metaphysics is regarded as capable of renewal and steady progress, whether this progress consists in the working out of a hitherto unthought of metaphysical alternative, or in a new synthesis of already available doctrines. If—precisely in old Europe—metaphysics is taken to be a more or less complete affair, with no room for further development, and if therefore deconstruction or dismemberment is the need of the hour, and metaphysics is evaluated as a sickness, to the cure of which philosophy itself is called, then the neoclassical metaphysics opens up a new prospect of experimentation or exploration far more ample than the hectic destructiveness of the spirit of the age would like us to believe.

Translated from the German by Charles Hartshorne.

Among the many significant thinkers to whom Hartshorne feels his neoclassical metaphysics is indebted, the speculative philosophy of Whitehead plays a prominent role. If one asks for the most important features of the new metaphysics, two such features can be specified: one more negative and the other more positive. The more negative is the critical revision of the concept of substance, according to which things are enduring, not to say timeless, bearers of properties; the more positive is the critical revision of the traditional idea of time, according to which time is one-dimensional, linear, and homogenously absolute. The neoclassical view is that the traditional substance concept is an abstraction which, in the final analysis, is not the reality the substance idea seeks to express. This consists rather in elementary processes that internally are non-spatial and non-temporal, but which produce space and time.

Although Hartshorne repeatedly emphasizes the importance of Whitehead for the neoclassical metaphysics, he also has given the Whiteheadian metaphysics a number of special accents, above all one of content and one of form. On the side of content, Hartshorne has, much more strongly than Whitehead, stressed that the key to the renewal of classical metaphysics is the renewal of the idea of God. This shift of emphasis is connected to a distinction between metaphysics and cosmology which, in this form, is not found in Whitehead. The metaphysics has the concept of the idea of God to deal with, the cosmology the scientific knowledge of the world from the metaphysical standpoint. Metaphysics and cosmology differ conceptually but belong together in metaphysical thought. If Hartshorne stresses the key role of the God idea more strongly than Whitehead the background for this emphasis is the peculiar tension between metaphysics and cosmology. To be sure Hartshorne has been able to accept the fundamental features of the Whiteheadian idea of God but he stresses the distinction just referred to. Here it is not Hartshorne's attempt to renew the ontological argument, employing modern modal logic, that I have chiefly in mind. Rather it is a basic assumption that is presupposed by the argument. Hartshorne distinguishes two natures of God, one is God as independent of the world, the other is God as related to the world and as sharing in its temporality. Thus we have the difference between a formal-conceptual and a material-actual side of God.

One may ask whether the assumption of a pure form or formal essence of God requires a special logic that admits an ontological difference between form and matter [*Stoff*]. In my opinion an everyday prescientific logic can suffice to give the distinction a sense. It is the formal side of God that makes the renewal of the ontological argument possible. Yet the two natures belong inseparably together. This inseparability illustrates a fundamental feature of the Hartshornian thinking, and it explains the special emphasis on the idea of God. Hartshorne himself, in connection with this feature, speaks of the principle of relativity. He here does not mean the relativity of God in relation to the world, not like Whitehead, a universal relativity principle of creatureliness according to which relations are grounded in original facts of connectedness. Rather he means by relativity a principle of metaphysical rationality, to which Whitehead gives the name of coherence in his metaphysical cosmology. According to this principle the great metaphysical opposites exhibit themselves as abstractions and as errors when they are taken as absolute and separated from each other. Onesidedness in metaphysics serves as an indication of failure to achieve coherence and of irrationality. Hartshorne pleads emphatically and convincingly for the ideal of rationality in metaphysics. What distinguishes neoclassical from classical metaphysics is not the giving up of this ideal but a greater agility and subtlety in the characterization of the ideal. Here belongs most immediately, and above all, the renewal and strict modal-logical revision of the old ontological proof as formulated by Anselm. Here belongs also the fact that the argument is given a much larger place than it is by other thinkers of the neoclassical metaphysics, for example James and Whitehead. The latter is less concerned to argue than to allow the coherence of the metaphysics to speak for itself. Even in cases in which the difference between proofs and arguments is perhaps not a definitive one, we still find Hartshorne explicitly distinguishing them. Arguments in metaphysics are instrumental to the achievement of relativity in the sense of coherence. They are arguments against onesidedness, or the absolutizing of one pole of a metaphysical opposition at the expense of the other and thereby arguments in favor of the enlargement of one of a pair of metaphysical opposites through the other, and in favor of their mutual limitation. What distinguishes argumentation in general and in metaphysics from ontological proofs is this, that elsewhere than in these proofs an entirely exclusive or irreducible opposition cannot be found. This is the strength and also the weakness of a good argument. A good argument makes the presuppositions of a contrary argument and also its own presuppositions manifest. What even the best argument cannot do is this: to prove the completeness of all contrary arguments and therewith the completeness of all excluding premises [literal translation].

Hartshorne's distinction between metaphysical proofs and metaphysical arguments renders the question of the metaphysical conditions of such a distinction inaccessible. These conditions are manifestly to be sought in a metaphysical difference between form and content and between necessity and contingency.

In addition to the metaphysical proofs and the metaphysical arguments one finds in Hartshorne a further procedure, intended to promote the achievement and preservation of rationality. One encounters this procedure not only explicitly but also implicitly. More precisely: that this procedure can be wholly successful is the presupposition of Hartshorne's speculative metaphysics. At first glance this third procedure seems similar to that which phenomenologists, with Husserl in mind, call eidetic variation. Also there is affinity with Whitehead's speculative method. In all these cases the object is to transcend a given knowledge in the direction of additional cognitive possibilities and thereby transcend limited knowledge in the direction of greater universality. Hartshorne's procedure differs from Husserl's phenomenological method and also from Whitehead's speculative method. In Husserl Hartshorne finds an overestimation of common sense and everyday experience which gives the category of *thing* an inappropriately great import at the expense of the scientific insight into the microstructure of what is; further he finds the phenomenological method inadequate in that it considers subjectivity primarily only as either human or else as transcendental ideal of validity. These two prejudices are overcome in Whitehead's cosmology. Nevertheless between the Husserlian method of eidetic variations and the Whiteheadian method of speculative leaps there is an affinity, despite the methodical and ontological differences. In both cases one never comes to a final grasping of an absolute and all-inclusive dimension of universality. Husserl's phenomenology claims to give a priori validity precisely with regard to the singular and special, and with regard to singular and special regions of possible objects. This philosophical knowledge does not need an original all-inclusive knowledge of all horizons that form the backgrounds for definite objects and regions. It is left somewhat open whether and how far there is an absolute all-inclusive horizon. Whitehead's metaphysical speculation in his cosmology seeks to achieve such an all-inclusive horizon of world knowledge. Herein his metaphysics distinguishes itself from phenomenology. However, precisely this ultimate all-inclusive horizon cannot be an adequately given object of human understanding. Limitations of language and limited insight into the ultimate generalities form unsurmountable barriers. Human knowledge remains dependent upon the conditions of its own cosmic epoch; it remains limited by the conditions of its own historicity.

Here, if anywhere, I see a difference in principle between Husserl and Whitehead and another such difference between Hartshorne and Whitehead. In contrast to Whitehead's cosmology, Hartshorne's neoclassical view insists upon a difference in principle between metaphysics and cosmology and a difference of both from the empirical sciences. The former difference is in the kind of knowledge and of validity. Metaphysical knowledge is purely a priori. This means it can in principle not be falsified through empirical experience and its truths are exemplified in some manner by every experience. Cosmological knowledge is interpretation of the most universal results of science through metaphysical principles, and so, one might say, it is an applied metaphysics. This distinction is not without qualification to be equated to that between analytic and synthetic knowledge. If there is, for Hartshorne, an index for human inadequacy in knowledge, it is with respect to the difference between purely a priori knowledge and a knowledge that is constituted by a mixture of the a priori and the empirical. However, despite occasional lapses from clarity as to the difference between these two forms of knowledge, Hartshorne insists on its necessity. Whereas, for Whitehead, the level of final universality behind which one could not go is a speculative extrapolation of the most general actualized cognitive possibilities and insofar a regulative principle of progress in the achieving of cognitive generalizations, Hartshorne starts from the outset on the level of universal and strictly a priori, purely metaphysical knowledge. From this universal metaphysical standpoint every datum of experience is nothing more than a particular instance of metaphysical knowledge. Now this difference between metaphysics and cosmology is for Hartshorne by no means only a difference in principle between different forms of knowledge and in their validity. Rather for him the cognitive-methodological difference between a priori and empirical presupposes and is based on an onto-theological difference. It is through this primacy of the onto-theology that Hartshorne's metaphysics is neoclassical. This is no transcendental philosophy with hidden metaphysical premises.

Certainly in this fundamental point there is no difference, at least no essential one, from the Whiteheadian metaphysics. In that too the cognitive difference between the knowledge of the given and knowledge of the not given goes hand in hand with an original onto-theological difference. So Hartshorne has taken over from Whitehead the doctrine of the double nature of God. God is, for one thing, the all-embracing possibility of definiteness in general, the content of all possibilities, which transcends every historical epochal actuality of the to us familiar cosmos. For another thing, God is the all-embracing and all-pervasive actuality, the actuality which corresponds to each concrete singular actuality in that it takes this actuality into itself, and retains it as datum and starting point for the production of new actualities. In this fashion are united in the double nature of God not only all-inclusive actuality and all-inclusive possibility, but also timeless being and perpetual further creation.

2. Is Panpsychism a Monism or a Dualism?

If there is a basic difference between the metaphysics of Whitehead and that of Hartshorne, it consists in the more precise definition of the onto-theological difference above referred to. At first glance this difference between the two great thinkers is as follows. Whitehead contents himself with asserting the two natures of God. In contrast Hartshorne takes it to be the main point of his neoclassical theism that it grasps the double divine nature in a single concept.

This unitary conception of God is that of an absolutely perfect being, whose perfection, in contrast to the traditional definition of an *ens perfectisimum*, by the necessity of its existing does not exclude contingency in its actuality [*aktualer Existenz*]. The basic difference between Whitehead's and Hartshorne's metaphysics can be derived from this construction of a unitary concept of God. If one wants a sharp formulation of this difference it is that between an empirical (Whitehead) and an a priori (Hartshorne) metaphysics. To avoid a false estimation of this difference, however, we must recall a basic similarity between the two systems. Hartshorne follows Whitehead in one, and perhaps the most important, metaphysical assumption; namely in the tenet that all concrete actuality has the character of experience. This doctrine, in contrast to the one-sided idealistic doctrine, holds not only that all experience is of reality and all reality is experienced reality, but in addition that all reality is experience, that is, experiencing reality. This doctrine, which overcomes the one-sidedness of idealism and is a realistic idealism or idealistic realism, is the basic theme of panpsychism. By this definition, Whitehead and Hartshorne are panpsychists.

And yet there is an important difference, which gives one pause, both with reference to metaphysics in general and to the problem of the psychophysical problem in particular. If one compares the above sketched features of the Hartshornian and the Whiteheadian metaphysics, one has the impression of an appearance of a contrast between the two like that between rationalism and irrationalism arising from this ideal-real experiential actuality. On one side, with Hartshorne, we find proofs and arguments, and an obligation in metaphysics to the ideal of clarity, definiteness, and intelligibility to all; on the other side, with Whitehead, we are confronted with an unintelligibility which is directly related to the basic role assigned to the concept of experience. At the same time, this impression of a difference between a rational metaphysics of Hartshorne and an irrational metaphysics of Whitehead is more than misleading. Whitehead himself has emphatically proclaimed the idea of a rational metaphysics and no less a person than Hartshorne has defended Whitehead against the frequently raised accusation of irrationality.

If we may consider a difference in style in the metaphysical writings of Whitehead and Hartshorne, this is not so much connected to a different ideal of metaphysical rationality as to a different evaluation of the various criteria which must in principle come together to give a metaphysics the character of rationality. It can be shown that Hartshorne tends to identify the criteria of consistency and coherence, while Whitehead distinguishes them in order to give coherence the primacy. This difference goes with that indicated in the idea of metaphysics. There is a further consequence. As said above, we find in Hartshorne a constantly renewed self-obligation to clarity, definiteness, and intelligibility, whereas Whitehead repeatedly, especially in late writings, stresses the unavoidability of dimness and indefiniteness. The unintelligibility of his writings is in his view scarcely avoidable. This emphasis is anything but the necessary expression of a thoughtless irrationalism. Rather there is here a conscious critical attitude, a methodical element of possible criticism arising from the criterion of coherence, a criticism of the unnoticed abstractions, "the fallacies of misplaced concreteness." According to Whitehead all reality is experiential. A concrete experience is always in a world specific to itself and to which it belongs. Each experience senses, however dimly and indistinctly, the entirety of the world to which it belongs. That this world whole can be sensed only dimly and indistinctly is the sign of the finitude of creaturely beings. If there are differences in the creatures' capacity to grasp the world, this does not mean that there is in any of them an experience which is able to grasp the entirety of its world with full distinctness and in all details. Capacity for clarity and definiteness in experience is reserved for the more highly evolved creatures, but in them it is never complete. Furthermore they pay a price for this capacity. This price is superficiality, in two senses. The clarity of experiencing reaches only the higher, obvious levels of experience, not the original, deep levels of the experienced world. Clarity and distinctness as specific ordering structures of experience, as is true of all ordering, is only relative, a matter of more or less in comparison to more or less of disorder. There are only specific degrees of order under definite conditions and at the cost of other ordering possibilities.

If Hartshorne stresses not only the requirement of clarity and definiteness in metaphysical knowledge, but also the validity of the metaphysical principle of relativity, it follows that the contrast between the clarity and definiteness he seeks in metaphysics and the dimness [*Dunkelheit*, darkness] and indistinctness regarded by Whitehead as unavoidable can be no absolute opposition, nor is it an opposition between rationalism and irrationalism. Rather, in the two systems various criteria of rationality receive different evaluations. But the contrast between clarity and definiteness on the one hand and dimness and indefiniteness on the other hand has another important aspect. There is also a contrast between rationalism and empiricism *in* metaphysics. This contrast has a close relation to the already mentioned difference between a purely rational or a priori and an empirical or a posteriori metaphysics, although it is by no means identical with this epistemological difference. Rather, the difference between rationalism and empiricism *in* metaphysics arises from the difference between rationalism and empiricism *of* metaphysics as applied to certain fundamental metaphysical theorems. One such fundamental theorem, which in spite of their differences is common to both Hartshorne and Whitehead, is panpsychism, according to which all concrete actuality is experiential and every concretely actual existence is a subject of experiencing. The rational-empirical distinction, in application to the theorem of panpsychism, produces in metaphysics a distinction between a non-empirical and an empirical concept of experience. And this distinction has consequences not only for the concept of experience as such that it employs but also for the meaning of the metaphysical import of the panpsychism, and in the end for the conceptual import of the difference between a non-empirical and an empirical metaphysics. The empirical concept of experience in its universality necessarily has a different import for a non-empirical than for an empirical metaphysics. To be sure there may be various metaphysical concepts which are not noticeably affected by the difference between the empirical and the non-empirical concept of experience, at least not in their content, their conceptual specifications. The distinction between a non-empirical and an empirical metaphysics is purely formal and methodological. And I do not say that to this formal and methodological difference under all circumstances a difference of content is coordinated. However, the just named difference with respect to the formal, methodological determination of metaphysical knowledge is in both kinds of metaphysics presupposed and the possibility of corresponding differences of content must be regarded as no less important than the metaphysical difference itself.

The difference between Hartshorne's non-empirical and Whitehead's empirical metaphysics does not exclude the possibility of more or less important differences in the conceptual determination of the theorem of panpsychism. The following considerations presuppose that the possibility for a fundamental difference in the two panpsychisms is partly obscured by the lack of clarity concerning the formal, methodological difference between the two metaphysical systems. However this fundamental difference to some extent reveals itself in the contrasting ways in which panpsychism is explicated (by the two authors). For Hartshorne panpsychism is essentially equivalent to the idea that every concrete, actual existent is living, has the character of a living being. This panpsychism is based on his neometaphysical theism. Not only is God living, his aliveness arises from living connection with the world and the living creatures in it. The living connectedness between God and his creatures requires the pervasive aliveness of the creatures of the world. Where there is no life but only dead matter, there is no possibility of the aliveness of God, which involves a living interaction between creator and creatures.

However it may be with the cogency of this argument for panpsychism, we are here concerned with something else which that argument presupposes, namely the original meaning of "panpsychism." Hartshorne bases his criticism of materialism and dualism, as metaphysical doctrines, on his neoclassical metaphysical theism. His panpsychism and his theism are very closely interconnected. Here there seems to be complete harmony with the corresponding criticism by Whitehead who had rejected materialism as an unusable and antiquated theory as shown by developments in physics, especially in the electromagnetic field theory, theory of relativity, and quantum theory. Hartshorne follows Whitehead in this rejection of materialism. His arguments are not, as one might expect, taken from biology. They have their source, like those of Whitehead, in the most recent conceptual developments in theoretical physics. Also in the criticism of metaphysical dualism Hartshorne has extensively followed Whitehead. This criticism directs itself first of all against the metaphysics of substance, according to which the final manner of existing is that of substance, that is, of a thing, which perpetually endures and the endurance of which is based on its essential and persisting properties, whereas its changing is as inessential as the specifications which alter with the changes. For Hartshorne as for Whitehead such substances are only abstract constructions. Their foundation is concrete actual entities, which have the pattern of processes with the capacity to form groups (nexus). Accordingly change must be conceived otherwise than in classical metaphysics. Change is not accidental exchanging of accidental properties, but entering or departing from a concrete group of actual entities.

The above sketched common factor between Hartshorne and Whitehead in rejecting materialism and substance dualism almost inevitably awakens an impression of a positive agreement concerning a certain metaphysical tradition, so-called panpsychism. This impression is strengthened through an argument, found in both authors, against every kind of metaphysical dualism, and therefore against psychophysical dualism. Like Whitehead, Hartshorne sees in every metaphysical dualism the violation of one of the most basic criteria of rationality, and insofar the impairment of the rationality of metaphysical theorizing. What is at stake here is the criterion of coherence, according to which abstract entities are no less devoid of meaning than abstract principles when they are regarded as independent of all other abstractions and detached from concrete actuality. Universal contraries must be interconnected to form definite unities if they are to achieve their meaning as metaphysical principles. This unification is required for the universal contrariety of physical and psychical actuality in the totality of metaphysical principles, a totality that can be said to constitute a meaningful metaphysical theory. Accordingly one may formulate a concept, universal and formal, of panpsychism: panpsychism is that totality of metaphysical principles within which the universal contrasts of physical and psychical actuality can form their unification in singular cases and hence be taken as metaphysically applicable. The fundamental criticism which Whitehead and Hartshorne have both given of metaphysical dualism necessarily gives rise to a question: is the criticism of dualism the basis for a metaphysical monism? Have both thinkers so viewed the matter? And is this monism, so far as it is not that of materialism, that of a spiritualism? Or instead, does the criticism of dualism lead to a position that may be described either as a relative and limited dualism or as a relative and limited monism? Is there not, for the overcoming of psychophysical dualism, a need for the founding of a relative dualism and monism, according to which a distinction between physical and psychical reality is required so that talk of possible psychophysical unities can make sense?

3. THE SEVERAL MEANINGS OF PANPSYCHISM

In their answers to the above question the two authors seem to agree. Both are moderate dualists in the indicated sense, according to which metaphysical contraries have their relative validity, and only in their interconnectedness possess metaphysical significance. This general principle, however, gives rise to a number of theoretical options. The introduction of a general principle of relativity in metaphysics does not guarantee that all contraries without exception will conform to the principle. We cannot be sure that in a metaphysical theory there will be no unnoticed contraries which, so treated, will render the system incoherent. Moreover, there are various possible ways of interrelating the contraries and thereby achieving unity so that not all may occur in every metaphysical theory. So we should not be surprised if a closer look at Whitehead's and Hartshorne's theories finds substantial differences in the import of the panpsychistic theorem. These differences are so substantial that they cause us to ask how far the agreement in criticizing materialism and dualism has concealed differences in the application of the principle of relativity. In considering this question one must reckon with the possibility that the metaphysical theories here compared are not sufficiently definite to furnish satisfactory solutions to the problems involved.

Undoubtedly the metaphysical theorem of panpsychism, even in the form of a moderate and relative dualism, can take on various meanings, according to how the interrelatedness between a physical and a psychical entity is viewed. It is precisely the relativizing of the contrast between the physical and the psychical that opens up possible and impossible unifications of the two modes of being in various single cases. There are above all two different ways of construing panpsychism that are relevant to the a priori, non-empirical metaphysics of Hartshorne and the speculative, empirical metaphysics of Whitehead. The first way proposes this theorem: the concrete, actual form of being is that of the living, and so every concrete and actually existing entity is a living being. On the contrary, according to the second way, the concrete, actual form of being is organic being, and all concrete and actually existing entities are organisms.

Such a difference in the meaning of the panpsychism theorem obviously presupposes a difference between living being and organism, whether the difference is in the concepts or in the actualities. Accordingly we may specify the difference between the two doctrines as follows. In one doctrine panpsychism means the equivalence of living being and organism. That is, living beings are organisms and organisms are living beings. In contrast, in the second version of panpsychism there is a definite difference between living beings and organisms. When Whitehead calls his metaphysics a philosophy of organism and not a philosophy of life, he is taking for granted that the concrete mode of being is the organic and that life can be understood only in terms of the givenness of organisms and the formation of concrete groupings of organisms. In making this distinction between the two panpsychisms we must not lose sight of a fundamental agreement between the two metaphysical theories, apart from which the distinction made would be unintelligible. On both sides a criticism of the classical substance concept is presupposed and with this criticism comes the introduction of a new, neoclassical concept which, on the two sides, takes contrasting forms, on one side that of a "cosmological ideal" and on the other of an ontological principle. On one side the objection to substance is its indefiniteness or ambiguity concerning the ontological status of substance, because of which metaphysics is unable to overcome the dilemma of an absolute monism and an absolute dualism. Above all, there is objection to the metaphysical assumption that the final primordial concrete reality has the form of an all-embracing and immutable being, a being that transcends all time and endures in time and in which timeless attributes and changing properties are to be distinguished, of which the former constitute the time transcendence and the latter the time-endurance.

The fundamental metaphysical difference between thing-in-itself and appearance is here given the form of that between eternity and temporality. Through Whitehead's "cosmological ideal" a distinctive type of metaphysics is established, which takes the form of a speculative cosmology. This cosmology is such that, in harmony with the natural sciences, it assumes as the elementary form of reality an infinite multiplicity of singular existing entities, and that these entities are best conceived as all of the same type. The cosmological ideal justifies us in classifying the corresponding cosmological metaphysics as a scientific realism. In Whitehead's metaphysics the ontological principle supplements the cosmological ideal by endowing it with a formal status. According to this principle, the elementary concrete entities do not have the character of immutable, surviving and enduring substances, but the form of singular elementary processes. These processes are not defined by endurance and change but by coming to be and perishing. They come to be through external conditions and they constitute a definite union of their coming to be and perishing by their internal self-determination.

Whitehead's and Hartshorne's common criticism of the classical substance idea allows endurance and change, in comparison with becoming and perishing of the elementary processes, to appear as secondary and derivative. Returning now to the above described difference of meaning (in the two ideas of panpsychism), taking into account the shared ontological foundation, it is natural to surmise that the difference must arise from some hidden difference of the seemingly common ontological foundation, and that the difference of meaning is somehow at work in the difference in the foundation. This would imply the following; in the universal characterizing of the elementary processes as living beings on one side and as organisms on the other side, either a difference in the formal concept of elementary process or a difference in the application of the concept or perhaps both are at work. As has been said, the most basic difference between the two systems is between the speculative-empirical and the non-empirical, a priori-valid theory of knowledge. But this metaphysical-epistemological difference is in neither the one nor the other theory definite enough to give us the basis for a more exact specification of the difference in the panpsychism theorem. Thus Hartshorne's a priori metaphysics does not exclude the possibility that the idea of living being as applied in the theorem of the universal aliveness of actuality is taken from experience and insofar is an empirical concept which through its metaphysical application acquires a priori validation. On the other side, Whitehead's panpsychistic theorem of the universal organicity of actuality is quite compatible with the presupposition that the here applied concept of organism is a formal, non-empirical one, a universal structural concept which by its metaphysical application acquires a function in empirical knowledge and an experiential content. What distinguishes metaphysical from mathematical knowledge is precisely this, that the former does not abstract from every experience, and accordingly cannot exclude experience as such from its purview. Insofar there is no strictly a priori metaphysics independent of all experience. Rather all metaphysical knowledge is related to a possible or actual experience. Metaphysical theories therefore may be distinguished according to the way they distribute the empirical and the non-empirical perspectives among the various components of the realities to which they have access. Particularly effective in this respect is the theoretical distinction introduced by Kant's critique of reason between empirical origin and a priori validity. However, this way of dividing the empirical and the non-empirical aspects of metaphysics is not the only possible way. Kant himself, in his metaphysical-scientific theory of motion, felt himself driven to such a differentiation to the extent that the necessity of connecting the empirical idea of motion with a priori validity made the introduction of special metaphysical requirements imperative. If then between the speculative-empirical metaphysics of Whitehead and the a priori metaphysics of Hartshorne an epistemological distinction is made, it must be presupposed that there is no such thing as a purely empirical or a purely a priori metaphysics. There is needed a more definite key to the distribution of a priori and empirical aspects among the theoretical components of a particular metaphysical theory. Only with such a key can one say to what extent one metaphysical theory is more empirical and another is more a priori. As in theories in general so in metaphysics, one makes a distinction between concepts and basic assumptions (theorems) and likewise between possible applications and conceptual and basic conditions of application. The distribution key for the difference between empirical and non-empirical is related to such and still other theoretical elements.

However it may be with the metaphysical theories of Whitehead and Hartshorne, such a distribution key seems not present in either one to explain the difference between the two panpsychisms. Not only can the shared panpsychistic concept, or the concept of an elementary subject of experience, be taken just as well as an empirically universal concept as it can be taken to be an a priori universal concept; similarly, it is on neither side clear whether the ontological idea of the goal-directed process, with its conceptual traits, is to be reckoned among the concepts to be applied, or under the conceptual conditions of possible application—in other words, among the conditions of various possible analyses and descriptions of given living or organismic experiences. And as for the key concepts of one panpsychism or the other, the concepts of living being and organism, the two metaphysical theories permit various possible functional specifications. One may take the concepts as concepts to be applied, or as concepts that define definite metaphysical realms. This openness of the metaphysical principles for various metaphysical functions corresponds to the openness of the metaphysical theories with respect to the epistemological difference of the empirical and non-empirical. This many-sided indefiniteness and openness suggests the question, whether it should be seen as a strength or a weakness of the two theories; whether for these theories greater definiteness is needed, or instead, whether the distinction between empirically universal and a priori universal has less importance for neoclassical metaphysics than traditional metaphysics led us to think it should have. Were this the case, the utterances of Whitehead and Hartshorne concerning this traditional distinction would have only subordinate importance.

4. The Philosophy of Organism as Alternative to a Metaphysical Panpsychism

Classical metaphysics was more than secondarily determined by its specific relations to the various sciences and their interrelationships and orderings. However these relationships were conceived, always there was an ordering in terms of values. One science was for metaphysics more scientific or more fundamental than another. It was not left to the sciences to order themselves, their ordering was also and primarily a topic for metaphysics. The idea was to interpret the obtaining order and to explain it. The emergence of a neoclassical metaphysics renders the question unavoidable, to what extent the revision of the metaphysical principles changes not only the principles of science but the relations between metaphysics and science. The extent of the agreement between the metaphysical theories of Whitehead and Hartshorne seems to involve also the relation of metaphysics to science. Both see a particular affinity, a theoretical correspondence, between traditional metaphysics and mathematical physics as the paradigmatic science. Both acknowledge the need to revise this metaphysics in view of the profound revision of basic concepts in recent and most recent scientific developments [some of which came after Whitehead's attention to physics had lapsed]. Both, finally, sought in the idea of a neoclassical metaphysics the overcoming of the scientifically antiquated materialism as well as the overcoming of the "bifurcation of nature," a dualism that does not do justice to the observed phenomena. At the same time, however, the above indicated diversity in the meaning given the panpsychistic theorem with respect to the various possible ways of relating metaphysics and science, a diversity hidden behind the semblance of conceptual agreement, makes itself apparent. If the neoclassical metaphysics renounces the phenomenological distinction of common sense between the unliving and the living and grants that all concrete and actually existing entities are living beings [*Lebewesen*], the conclusion is not far off that, contrary to the tradition, the paradigmatic science is not mathematical physics but biology. It is then the concern of neoclassical metaphysics to make this change of paradigm in science intelligible and to clarify its consequences in altering the priorities between physical and biological knowledge. If, however, the neoclassical metaphysics takes as the primordial form of actuality a basic organismic structure, and accepts as the concrete actual entities organisms, without identifying these directly with living beings, thus retaining the distinction between the living and the unliving, then the possibility is given to allow the traditional scientific paradigm of theoretical physics to retain its validity, and thus the change of paradigm is accepted only as an internal change within this fundamental science, long recognized as such. This paradigm change is then simplified as that from a mechanical to an organismic model.

Both Whitehead's and Hartshorne's philosophical theories give sufficient room for both the just specified modes of relationship between metaphysics and science. On the one hand, because of its recent and most recent advances theoretical physics appears to be the standard-giving basic science by which the principles of the neoclassical metaphysics, including the principle of panpsychism, must be justified. From this basic science important arguments for panpsychism are taken. On the other hand, such a neoclassical physicalism and materialism contrast sharply with the idea of overcoming the "bifurcation of nature." This idea seems rather to speak for a metaphysical biologism, or even for a metaphysical spiritualism. However, we have not exhausted the free play involved in the indefinite relationship of neoclassical metaphysics and science. In Whitehead's and Hartshorne's metaphysics we find traits that support the acceptance of a neoclassical basic science that includes both physics and biology, a scientific cosmology occupying a peculiar intermediate position between a rational metaphysics on the one side and the numerous sciences on the other.

Finally, however, still another relationship of neoclassical metaphysics to science is thinkable. According to this thought-possibility, there is no longer an absolute, universally valid and acknowledged standard of scientificality, and therefore a universally valid, basic science by the contents and methods of which the hierarchically ordered single sciences orient themselves. Instead of such an ideal-typical hierarchy based on a metaphysics, from now on there obtains a relative equality of all sciences in relation to metaphysics and one another. According to this possible way of thinking neoclassical metaphysics furnishes only an extremely general conceptual framework with various possible conditions of application, to which the various single sciences, in accordance with their specific contents and in their specific manners, do justice. Here there is no privileged science for which the pretension of a canonically valid paradigm could be made. Instead, every single science has the property of exemplifying the neoclassical metaphysics after its own manner. Of these thought possibilities for a relationship between metaphysics and science, Whitehead's metaphysics seems to be closer to the last mentioned and Hartshorne's to the next to last. In any case the relative indefiniteness of the two metaphysical theories raises anew the question about the relation of metaphysics to the sciences and also the question of the essence of metaphysics and the extent to which this essence is definable by the relation to the sciences.

If Whitehead's speculative metaphysics displays itself primarily as empirical and Hartshorne's primarily as rational, we must nevertheless bear in mind that the difference between empiricism and rationalism affects not only, or in general primarily, the theoretical status of the current metaphysical theory, but relates first of all to the objects of this theory, the concrete actual entities which, in the neoclassical metaphysics by its ontological principle are taken as elementary. Talk about a possible empiricism and rationalism in metaphysics refers to the original elements of experience. What is at stake is not only whether the origin of the concept of the elementary processes of experience is empirical or rational. Rather the empirical-rational difference relates to a definite analysis of these processes as well as to their definite components. In this fashion this distinction between empiricism and rationalism in metaphysics becomes relevant to the various meanings assigned to the panpsychist theorem. The most important function of panpsychism is the overcoming of the "bifurcation of nature" and the elimination of the antinomies which are unavoidably involved in such a doubling of nature.

If there are, in classical as well as in neoclassical metaphysics, various meanings for the theorem of panpsychism, this multiplicity of meanings arises by no means exclusively from the various formal-ontological possibilities of obtaining a unitary conceptual perspective by which an absolute opposition of metaphysical ideas can be relativized. The possible multiplicity of meanings for panpsychism presupposes a possible multiplicity of meanings for the "bifurcation of nature" which panpsychism criticizes and seeks to overcome. This presupposed multiplicity is primarily in the content, for the very idea of any such doubling of nature concerns some definite, absolute, and absolutely dominant metaphysical opposition, to which the various metaphysical categories are conformed. In the metaphysical and scientific actuality, however, various conceptions of a 'bifurcation' are possible, of which each has its most appropriate metaphysical opposition. Such possible metaphysical oppositions for various ideas of a 'bifurcation of nature' are the oppositions of physical and psychical, material and spiritual, extended and inextended. Yet the real ground of the multiple meanings [of panpsychism] and of its presupposed multiplicity [of bifurcations] lies still deeper. The current metaphysical and scientific reality of a definite 'bifurcation of nature' does not, by the dominance of a particular metaphysical opposition, exclude every other metaphysical opposition. Talk of the dominance of such a contrast tells us rather that other oppositions are present but given subordinate status and by the type of their presence the type of dominance is made specific. It may even be that several such oppositions dominate others, and that the bifurcation in question in general cannot be defined through any single opposition. This polyguity [translator's neologism: extension of 'ambiguity'] necessarily goes into the panpsychism that by its unitary perspective overcomes the doubling of nature.

In every thinkable panpsychism, one may distinguish formal and contentual grounds of a possible polyguity. In doing this one must take into account a possible reciprocal interdependence of these grounds. Whitehead's and Hartshorne's panpsychism is, as I have said, no absolute panpsychism. Their doctrine is rather relative to the multiplicity of grounds for various possible meanings relative to the specific grounds for each particular meaning. If various possible meanings of a neoclassical panpsychism are distinguished, this happens against the background of the difference of meaning between classical and neoclassical panpsychism. What distinguishes the two panpsychisms is not only this, that the old ontological principle of substance is replaced by the new principle of process. The difference is also not exhausted by this, that in place of an ever and perpetually enduring thing, which is altered only in its contingent properties, there is a creation that, in the course of its becoming, achieves its essential definiteness and with this achievement comes to its end, yet as datum in other similar creations continues to exist. Even this does not suffice to distinguish the new panpsychism from the old, for other metaphysical oppositions arise which produce quite other bifurcations and therewith demand solutions to quite other problems of overcoming bifurcation. Contrary to what we might have expected, we come at last to the conclusion that it is the same elementary metaphysical oppositions with which both the old and the new panpsychism struggles, such as those of actual and potential, material and spiritual, bodily and mental, extended and inextended, composite and single, universal and particular, etc. Above all, it is the old opposition living and nonliving, which, in both views, goes through the entirety of metaphysical oppositions and dominates it. In its way of overcoming this dominant opposition, the new shows its real essential difference from the old panpsychism. Here must be shown its superiority in solving the problems, compared to the old solutions. For traditional panpsychism the basic opposition (of living and nonliving) was in principle absolute. Because of this, its overcoming, and the solution of its antinomies, could be thought only by reducing one of the two sides, namely that of the unliving, to a mere appearance, a marginal case of the living. In contrast, for the new panpsychism this opposition is only relative. Accordingly, we do not need to suppose that obviously unliving things like mountains, stones, or artifacts are in fact living things, and only in deceptive appearances are unliving. Here it is a matter of "more and less of life rather than either or." In this manner and thanks to the principle of relativity the reality of the unliving can be acknowledged besides that of the living.

The reason for the validity of this principle of relativizing the idea of life is to be found in the application of the new ontological principle of "process" to all metaphysical oppositions. According to this neoclassical application, any actual entity unites in a process all of the elements required for the actualization of its essence. These elements are in themselves ordered in metaphysical oppositions which, in the given actual entity, are always bound together in a definite way and are relativized in a definite perspective. Thus an actually existing entity is as process the place of unification of all important opposites in its constitutive elements and the ground of their relativizing. Against the background of this peculiarity of neoclassical panpsychism the specific difference in meaning between the panpsychistic theories of Whitehead and Hartshorne can be seen. Both agree in the thesis that the apparently absolute opposition between the unliving and the living is entirely relative. However, this agreement is such that it might conceal the initially affirmed difference of meaning. Not only can the relativizing of the opposition take many forms, what is most important is whether or not the relativizing is bound up with the assumption that the difference between the living and the unliving is the most important and basic metaphysical distinction. One can think the relativizing of the opposition of the living and unliving only on condition that other metaphysical oppositions are more elementary and basic. And in fact for Whitehead the living-unliving opposition is no elementary opposition or difference. It certainly is less elementary than some other oppositions and differences. More elementary differences in his speculative metaphysics are: 1. between physically actual and conceptual; 2. extended and inextended; 3. external, causal, and internal, teleological; and 4. bodily and unbodily. None of these elementary differences can be reduced to one of the others. The peculiarity of Whitehead's conception of the overcoming of bifurcation consists above all in this, that it relates to all the just mentioned oppositions and differences and equally relativizes them all by binding them together. So far as I see, the essential difference between Whitehead's and Hartshorne's panpsychism consists in this, that for one of them but not for the other the distinction between the unliving and the living remains fundamental compared to those four other distinctions mentioned above, and particularly so with respect to the idea and actuality of God. If the idea of panpsychism is united with the acknowledging of the concept of life as the most elementary and fundamental concept, then Whitehead's alleged panpsychism is no panpsychism. And one of the basic differences between his metaphysics and Hartshorne's is that between an organic and a panpsychistic theory. Precisely this essential difference between Whitehead's and Hartshorne's neoclassical metaphysics leads in the end to the question: has Hartshorne succeeded in justifying panpsychism on the basis of a process ontology, without becoming involved in the antinomies which Whitehead through his philosophy of organism wanted to eliminate?

REINER WIEHL

DEPARTMENT OF PHILOSOPHY
UNIVERSITY OF HEIDELBERG
JULY 1987

D. HISTORICAL ANTECEDENTS

24

Daniel A. Dombrowski

HARTSHORNE AND PLATO

1. Introduction

B ecause of his famous remark that all of Western philosophy is a series of footnotes to Plato, and because of his equally famous defense of eternal objects, Whitehead is often thought of as a Platonist. Yet despite Hartshorne's use of Plato's thoughts on the World-Soul in the *Timaeus*, he is hardly ever compared to Plato because he is some sort of critic of eternal objects. My thesis in this article is that Hartshorne is every bit the Platonist as Whitehead. I am not alleging that Hartshorne is a centripetal thinker who moves away from his dearest concerns. Rather, I suggest that all one has to do to notice Hartshorne's Platonism is to read carefully Hartshorne's own explicit references to Plato, a type of careful reading which has not yet, to my knowledge, been attempted.

2. Asymmetricality in the Dialogues

The word "Platonist" is assuredly vague. Hartshorne himself is very much aware that the dialogue style suggests little intention of formal unity, and that implicit in the character of Socrates is a denial of rigid system. Although a completely satisfactory resolution to the problem of whether there really is one Platonic philosophy will continue to elude scholars, there is nonetheless sufficient unity of an informal type that one can talk of a philosopher as a Platonist. At least three different approaches to Plato can be imagined: (a) The dialogues can be considered stages in the intellectual development of Plato, whereby if one looks at Plato's later dialogues one finds the most significant account of his position.[1] (b) The dialogues can be viewed as complex aspects of a unified system, such that the content of all the dialogues must be unified in any systematic interpretation of Plato.[2] And (c), the dialogues may merely express a set of loosely related and perhaps conflicting themes such that no relational whole may be found.

Hartshorne favors the first of these three views. The principles in the early dialogues are retained in the later, but they are used within a more profound system of concepts, just as Plato's thoughts can be used by neoclassical metaphysicians like Hartshorne without Plato being affected by their speculation. (It should also be noted that Hartshorne's thoughts on the asymmetricality of Plato's dialogues—PS, 38–39—are perhaps the best clues we have as to how Hartshorne would have us regard his own philosophic career, particularly the flurry of works he has published after he turned seventy.) Hartshorne traces Plato's development through three periods: the early dialogues up to and including the *Republic*; the Eleatic dialogues, where the "system" of the *Republic* is criticized; and the later dialogues, particularly the *Timaeus* and *Laws*. The traditional objections to Plato's philosophy do not apply with the same force by the time we reach the late dialogues; and it is no accident for Hartshorne that it is in these dialogues that God becomes a central concern for Plato. Although it is too simplistic to say that there is an inverse relationship between the emphasis placed on the theory of forms and that placed on God, it does seem fair to say that there is a shift in meaning in Plato's thought when teleological explanation according to forms is modified by teleological explanation in terms of God.

Obviously Hartshorne is not the sort of historian of philosophy who offers detailed textual arguments in favor of his appropriation of an author. Rather, he seems to exemplify in a Nietzschean way the dictum that the purpose of doing history of philosophy is to serve present philosophizing and life, not the other way around. And his thoughts on Plato should be evaluated according to this standard. One fruitful result of Hartshorne's thesis regarding the asymmetricality of the dialogues is that it offers a mode of resolving the seemingly interminable debates regarding the question of system in Plato. The final dialogues retain in *some* fashion all of the categories of the earlier dialogues, such that with a bit of qualification the second view of Plato mentioned above can be seen as an adjunct or internal corrective agent to the first. So also, alternate principles of explanation lead to alternate conceptions of soul and God; hence conflicts appear, which easily lead many scholars to posit a particular dialogue as early or late. But these conflicts are often found in the final dialogues themselves, making it possible to claim that the third position mentioned above is virtually contained in the first. These tensions in Plato's thought should not cause astonishment (or deconstructionist anarchy), but rather should give us confidence in the philosophical adequacy of Plato's thought in that he elaborated all (or most of) the necessary themes to do philosophy well *now* (PS, 40).

3. Forms as Items in Psychical Process

What does it mean to explain the world? At the very least it means to elucidate the unitary principle behind the apparent duality of mind and matter. Plato wavers, for Hartshorne, between seeing this principle in the forms and seeing it in soul (*psyche*). Hartshorne emphasizes the difficulty in offering an explanation through a form which is not really an explanation through soul. The neoplatonists were justified in interpreting the forms as divine ideas, inseparable from intelligence (*nous*); and Plato gives some warrant for this interpretation when he makes the Demiurge ideally aware of the highest form, that of the good. That is, the forms are items internal to psychical process (IO, 23–24).

This view obviously conflicts with the standard account that for Plato the forms are "independent" even of God. Hartshorne thinks Plato was brighter than this, even if many passages from Plato can be cited which *seem* to support this account. If "*X* is independent of *Y*" has a sharp logical meaning it must be that *X* could exist even if *Y* did not, which implies that *Y* is contingent. If *X* stands for the forms and *Y* for God, then the nonexistence of God is being taken as possible. But this "possibility" conflicts not only with the treatments of God in the *Timaeus* and Book Ten of the *Laws*, but also with Plato's flirtation with the ontological argument, to be discussed later. If the Demiurge is not contingent, then not only are the forms envisaged by deity, they *could not* lack this status.

It is true for Hartshorne that things which are more abstract than events (or events collected together as an individual) may be primordial in a vicarious way if they are always found embodied in inherited events. But he only sees the *most* abstract universals—the metaphysical principles themselves—as "eternal" in this sense. "They precede *every* event, but not *all* events, because every event has predecessors and any event must instance the metaphysical universals." Further, this Hartshornian doctrine is a version of Plato's view that forms are known by reminiscence in that memory is an ingredient in thought as such. But it is an "unplatonic platonism" (CS, 121–122); unplatonic, at least, on most interpretations of Plato. Abstraction from the concrete proceeds backwards in time and depends on memory because one may abstract from each instance but not from all—another instance will always do, but none at all will not do (WP, 76). It is true that for Plato mathematical forms "are not literal descriptions of things, but unattainable limits, *ideals* to which things may approximate in varying degrees" (BH, 148; IO, 230). For example, the ideal of absolute equality discussed in the *Phaedo* (74) is so unattainable that any sufficiently accurate measurement will reveal some slight difference between two "equal" things; or at least no measurement is accurate enough to prove that there is not a difference. So also with the form of straightness, et al. Hartshorne's disagreements with Whitehead on eternal objects are largely due to Whitehead's "Platonic" fascination with this particular ("atypical") feature of mathematical universals, i.e., their extreme abstractness and generality. Hartshorne does not think that Whitehead's notion of God would be hurt if one eliminated the idea of eternal species, for example, while retaining that of eternal highest genera, including the genus of specificity as such (WP, 97). Even with regard to mathematical forms there is a sense in which these ideals are "literally actualized" (MV, 324). For example, if there are two horses and two cows in a field, then the number of horses is *exactly*, not approximately, equal to the number of cows. It is because concrete things can be equal to each other that the abstraction "equality" is made possible (DR, 120). And it is Plato, at least "as he is usually interpreted," who is responsible for the error that what one knows in mathematics is pure being above becoming, devoid of life and power (MV, 28). Hartshorne agrees with Körner that Plato not so much discovered ideas as ideals (IO, 38).[3]

As before, however, this theory of forms as items in psychical process gives us a different view of Plato, a view which depends on the necessary existence of deity. If one asks whether the forms have supremacy over God, Hartshorne's response would be that "the issue is secondary and largely verbal" (PS, 56–57). The good and God are both eternal, and "independence" has no clear meaning between eternal (or everlasting) things. Because God *always* contemplates the good, it is in that sense an idea (of an Idea or Form). What could be gained by asking if forms would exist if they were not divine ideas, except the (erroneous) conclusion that God is a mere fact that perhaps comes to be, perhaps not? But for Hartshorne (and Plato, he alleges) there is never an alternative to the contemplation of the good by the supreme being. Only the most extreme types of "Platonism," not necessarily held by Plato, would see abstract entities as real in themselves apart from *all* concrete embodiment, say in some concrete process of thinking. The basic reality is concrete even if the most fundamental abstraction is concreteness as such. Metaphysics itself is "the study of the abstraction 'concreteness'." Hartshorne is not so bold to claim that Plato *quite* saw that concrete actualities are the whole of what is, but he came close enough to seeing this in his thoughts on God in the later dialogues so as to confound traditional interpretations of Plato's forms as absolutely independent of concrete embodiment (CS, 22, 100).

How does Hartshorne's treatment of Plato's forms in his own philosophy (he refers to them as "ideas") differ from Whitehead's? Whitehead believes in many eternal realities, including the metaphysical categories, the primordial nature of God, and eternal objects.[4] For Hartshorne the metaphysical categories (and mathematical ideas) are eternal, but only in the ways elucidated above. He rejects, however, Whitehead's term "eternal objects" and usually returns to the traditional term "universals." Although the metaphysical categories are time independent, and hence eternal, the other universals are emergent and contingent, as in "different from Shakespeare," or as in the precise shade and hue of blue in a certain iris or in a certain experience of the flower. Hartshorne cannot call these universals "eternal," as would Whitehead in his "extreme form of Platonism." But in this rejection Hartshorne nonetheless thinks he has Plato on his side. Hartshorne is not convinced that all truths, even those concerning universals, are timeless for Plato (CS, 59, 64; CA, 276).

From Peirce Hartshorne has learned that the past is the sum of accomplished facts, but there are additions to the past which occur at every moment. These actualities (events, not things) become but they do not change, in that change refers to the succession of these events. Once an actuality comes to be, it remains forever an indestructible item in the past. Thus it is false to say that all actualities change—none of them do!—and false to say that the past never really is. Plato is correct, on Hartshorne's view, that what is worth knowing is permanent, for past events and "emerged" universals have a reality that is forever. "Change is addition to, not subtraction from, reality. . . . Plato's greatness is that, more than anyone else, he almost saw even the things that he failed to see." Over and over Plato insists that unless we know the past of something we do not understand it.[5] This is another way of saying that the past of something is included in deity, and only in a profoundly different way is the future so included. Much of what Whitehead wants from eternal objects can more reasonably be gained from the everlasting and the theory of emergent universals. Presumably Whitehead would say that God could not know which eternal object an occasion will select, but God could know all the possibilities. Hartshorne's point is that the occasion "does not merely 'select' from fully determinate potentialities, but that it renders the determinable determinate."[6]

Of course I have presumed too much in alleging what Whitehead's relationship with Plato is; indeed it is a complex relationship.[7] My point has been to claim that Hartshorne's theory of emergent universals and his theory of forms as items in psychical process do not necessarily make his debt to Plato less than Whitehead's. Hartshorne's distaste for eternal objects is meant as a criticism of a certain variety of "Platonism," which distorts what is central in Whitehead's philosophy: creative synthesis (WP, 153, 186–187). Hartshorne does believe that Whitehead follows the neoplatonists and Plato himself (and, indeed, Hartshorne himself) in holding that forms or eternal objects are divine ideas, "nothing simply by themselves" (WV, 9). And our physical or hybrid prehensions of God as having these ideas are our best clues as to how to acquire them for ourselves. The disagreement between Hartshorne and Whitehead has nothing to do with the latter relying on Plato and the former eschewing Platonic influence. Rather, the major point of difference seems to lie with the question as to which ideas are eternal in God and which are acquired (divinely or humanly) as the creative process goes on.

4. SOUL AS SELF-MOVED

Cosmological speculation must, for Hartshorne, be in terms of: (a) soul— including Platonic forms; (b) matter; or (c) both soul and matter. Did Plato make his way to the first, psychicalist option? (IO, 24). Not quite, although he came rather close on Hartshorne's view. That is, because the second option would have been anathema to Plato, he was left with a confused version of dualism. This is not surprising for dualism. (Consider the evidence of the *Epinomis* 983D, where there is no *tertium quid* common to both soul and body, *yet* soul is the universal cause of body.) Without modern science, however, the inability of Plato to overcome dualism is quite understandable.

The question is, how close did Plato come to psychicalism? His view seems to have been, at first glance at the *Phaedrus* (245E) and Laws (896A), that souls initiate change and transmit it to others; whereas bodies merely receive and transmit change. But what does it mean to be self-moved? If the theory of forms is stressed, it might mean that bodies can only be moved by other moved things, whereas soul can also be moved by the motionless forms. Yet if the forms are items in (divine) psychical process, then soul in some sense is fundamental for cosmological speculation, and hence Plato comes quite close to psychicalism. For cosmological purposes the word *psyche* is used by Plato to refer to experiencing, thinking, remembering, feeling, etc., and only for ethical or religious purposes does he use the term to refer to an entity behind these processes (IO, 364). The view that a so-called substance is a new concrete reality at each moment is not necessarily incompatible with Plato's philosophy. Plato is well aware of the fact that the transition from motion to rest occupies no stretch of time at all, but occurs in an instant (*exaiphnes—Parmenides* 156). Hence it is not illegitimate to "read into" Plato's philosophy certain Whiteheadian notions (WV, 4).[8] A defect in Plato's treatment of these psychical processes would occur if he assumed that they are only examples of self-motion and not also examples of being moved (AW, 29). Indeed in the *Sophist* (248–249) Plato indicates that he thinks of knowing in these terms, i.e., it is active whereas being known is passive. The problem here is that to think of soul as influencing others without being influenced is to reduce soul to an object. But surely Plato does not always exhibit this tendency. For example, in the *Republic* the degree of adequacy in the mind of the knower is due to the adequacy of influence it receives from the object known. In fact, Hartshorne admits that the soul's ability to receive influence is *the* most obvious of the psychical powers. "For what else is perception?" (IO, 25).

Plato's definition of being in the *Sophist* (247D–E), the most sophisticated definition he offers, is that being is power (*dynamis*)— which is not accidentally the root of our word "dynamic" — specifically the power to affect *or* be affected by others. I take it that this "or" (*eite*) does not refer to mutual exclusivity between influence and being influenced. Plato's dialogue style betrays this point. One does something with (not to) one's dialectical partner. This makes the dialogue style a good model for the general nature of reality. As opposed to authoritarian dictation, in dialectic it "will not do to reason as though to speak and be heard are noble, while to listen and hear are not." Plato makes this explicit in at least one dialogue, the *Gorgias* (508A). Further, to speak of the supreme soul as persuading other souls is to suggest that each lesser soul has the power to be moved (IO, 26–27).

Hartshorne thinks that Plato hints at the psychicalist position (in which only concrete singulars feel, and in which the abstract is real only in the concrete, thus soul is the inclusive form of reality) when Plato indicates that soul is coincident with every action and passion. But no Greek was in a position to fully understand the difference between singulars and aggregates in the smaller parts of nature. That is, there is a vast difference between soul as such or soul as a generic principle, on the one hand, and animal soul (including human soul), on the other. Hartshorne's "(revised) Platonism" holds that it is the lack of self-motion in macroscopic inanimate things that has caused materialistis or dualists to suppose that the microscopic parts of these things also lack self-motion.[9] It should be remembered that in Plato's dialogues we learn that soul is the universal cause (*aitias tou holou—Epinomis* 988D), that it is (metaphysically?) prior to body (*presbyteras e somatos—Laws* 892A), that bodies are derived from soul (*soma de deuteron te kai hysteron—Laws* 896C), that we receive our being from soul (*Laws* 959A), and that soul is the primary source of all things (*psychen genesin hapanton einai proten—Laws* 899C). So although Plato could not fully understand the cosmological significance of psychicalism, it would be a mistake to think that he was totally ignorant of such significance, either by returning to primitive animism or by defending dualism *simpliciter*.

The meaning usually assigned to Plato's theory of forms was really born in the first book of Aristotle's *Metaphysics*, according to Hartshorne, with McKeon on his side. Hence the greatest problem in Plato's cosmology (which is the greatest ancient metaphysical scheme, in Hartshorne's view), is not this theory of forms, but that of sufficiently grasping the functions of soul as both creative and receptive, and the related problems of understanding internal and external relations and how the soul interacts with body (IO, 27–28; CA, 208–209).

Plato's analysis of becoming remains incomplete (see the *Sophist* 248–249) because if knowing something is to change that something, as Plato sometimes indicates, then past events go on changing when we think about them. Plato probably flirted with this idea (that knowing something changes it) as a reaction against the opposite view that the past completely determines the present, in souls as in bodies. The self-motion of soul must mean that the soul originates change, which is at least compatible with the view that necessary, although not sufficient, causal conditions are inherited from the past. The soul does not merely transmit tendencies from the past, nor just receive them, as in bodies. Though with less than optimal clarity, Plato anticipated the process transcendental "creativity" (IO, 32–33).

It is an error to assume that Plato's alternative to being determined by the past is to be determined by an ideal, for no ideal can be applied without *creative* particularization (IO, 34). It is instructive that the five major forms of Plato's *Sophist* (248–264) do not offer a definitive model for the world, but rather offer abstract principles of relation among things, general principles of harmony and diversity which can be realized in widely divergent ways. These forms are: existence, motion, rest, sameness, otherness. There are ideals of harmony and intensity of experience, but there is no uniquely right way of realizing these ideals; yet despite the absence of the form of the good and that of beauty, these thoughts obviously have great consequences for ethical and aesthetic issues, as Hartshorne's own ethics and aesthetics exemplify. But Plato's approach in the later dialogues is so novel it is no wonder that it was largely left untouched for two thousand years, and that the academy in short order fell into the hands of the cautious empiricist Carneades.

Hartshorne's theory of creativity can readily be seen as "the Platonic one" when "create" is substituted for "move" in Plato's defense of souls having the ability to at least partially move themselves (CA, 150). An understanding of soul as self-creative sheds light on at least three additional areas: (a) Plato had at least an inkling of the truth that "the creative, temporal character of experiencing yields all the light upon modality as ontological that we are going to get" in that "particular and actual are essentially one, and so are universal and potential" (CS, 225). (b) The lack of complete order in the world is explained by there being many souls. These many self-active agents imply indefinitely great if not complete disorder unless there is a "supreme soul to 'persuade' the many lesser souls to conform to a cosmic plan. They cannot completely fit such a plan for then they would not be self-determined." That is, Hartshorne's theodicy is essentially Platonic because the divine plan cannot be completely definite and detailed (WV, 23). And (c) the meaning of "God has power over us" has a meaning only if we return to Plato's notion of a self-moved mover of others which is also partially moved by these other self-movers. God can "rule the world" by setting optimal limits for free action. The divine can control the changes in us by inspiring us with novel ideas; by molding *itself* God presents at each moment a partly new ideal (DR, 139, 142). *Omni*potent power would therefore be a monopoly of power over the powerless; but Hartshorne agrees with Plato's claim that being *is* power, hence "to be an individual is to decide" (IO, 367).

5. REALITY AS DYADIC

Like a child begging for both, Plato declares in the *Sophist* (249D) that reality (as dynamic power[10]) is both at once: the unchangeable and that which changes. In this dyadic reality can be distinguished a thing's abstract "essence" from its being-in-a-context-of-relations. Because our knowledge itself is relational, we can never *fully* know the essence of a thing, only an endless series of relations. This intimates how Plato still retains in the later dialogues the notion of separation (*chorismos*). This distinction between a thing's "in itself" and its "in relation" is expressed in the *Philebus* (23–25) as an indeterminate dyad. That is, in addition to the determination "given" to being by number, measure, and limit, there is also an unlimited factor of multiplicity. That the dyad is indeterminate perhaps indicates which side of the dyad (becoming) is more inclusive. The same point was hinted at—but confusedly so—as early as the *Republic* (501B), where the philosopher is supposed to keep one eye on the forms and the other on the images of these forms in "this" world.[11]

Hartshorne especially likes to use these Platonic insights to illustrate the aesthetic core of reality in that an individual is a functional unity-in-diversity, "so long as it endures at all." Plato's basic idea of beauty as integrated diversity and intensity of experience is truly metaphysical: "valid for any possible state of reality" (CS, 307–308). And as is perhaps the case in Plato's *indeterminate* dyad, although there can be no assurance here, one pole in the dyad is more inclusive than the other, although this does not necessarily mean that there is no sense to be made of the notion of polar equality in Harthshorne's dipolar theism.[12] It *is* clear to Hartshorne, however, that dipolarity can be traced back to Plato, and this dipolarity is manifest in all reality, supremely so in God (PS, 2, 5). Each category and its contrary—e.g., being and becoming, unity and diversity, etc.—admits of a supreme case or a supercase. This is true whether we speak univocally or analogically about God. Therefore we are left with either two supreme beings or one supreme being with two "really distinct aspects." Only a superficial interpretation of the *Timaeus* would allege that Plato took the first option. Relying on Cornford, Hartshorne holds that Plato took the second option, albeit vividly presented in myth as if the first option were chosen.[13] Such is

Plato's wisdom, never so bold as to give all the answers, and always a playful source for continued philosophic conversation.[14]

For the sake of argument, Hartshorne would drop his thesis regarding *phases* of Platonic development, but he refuses to give up the thesis that there are two *facets* in Plato's thought (PS, 39–40, 43). The first is a diaeresis of existence into the quantitative and the qualitative, the mutable and the immutable, or better, the material and the formal (or ideational). Both soul and God are put in the latter (immobile) pole of these pairs. However, in the second facet (or phase) of Plato's thought, motion is granted to both soul and God. The "real opposition" here is between dependent and independent mobility, i.e., between body (taken as an insentient aggregate of sentient constituents) and soul (including divine soul). *Within* the World-Soul there is a principle of immutability, a principle which characterizes soul per se in the first facet (or phase). This complex of opposed concepts cannot be simplified by reducing God to the idea of the good. Not even in the first facet (or phase) did Plato ever clearly make this equation.[15] Rather, the good, although it is not God, is nonetheless compatible with the rule of a supreme conscious being. In short, "the conflict of opposing categories must, then, be viewed as inherent in the Platonic framework." Reality, including divine reality, is one, but this unity can only be discursively or metaphysically revealed as two, like centripetal and centrifugal forces in equilibrium.

6. Dipolar Theism

Having explored Hartshorne's debt to Plato's notions of soul and dipolarity, we are now in a position to look profitably at Hartshorne's use of Plato's World-Soul. I would like to emphasize, however, that Hartshorne's debt to Plato is *thoroughgoing* and that he has not, as some Hartshorne interpreters might assume, arbitrarily plucked the World-Soul out of the *Timaeus* so as to read Plato only to confirm his own beliefs. Further, Hartshorne views Plato not only as a dipolar theist, but also as a panentheist, such that all is *in* God (PS, 17).

There are two principles upon which Plato's theology turns: the "pure being" of the forms and the "supreme mobility" of soul (PS, 54). The unchanging deity of the *Phaedo*, *Republic*, and *Parmenides* is the supreme instance of fixity; the self-moving deity of the *Phaedrus* and the *Laws* is the supreme instance of mobility. Alluding to the aforementioned passage in the *Sophist* (to the effect that Plato, like an entreating child, says "Give us both"), Hartshorne claims that the two poles of Plato's theism are brought together with almost equal weight in the *Timaeus*. But the word "together" is problematic in that Plato mythically fixes the correlative categories in different beings, the Demiurge and the World-Soul, with the latter seemingly providing an answer to the criticism of the *Parmenides* that an absolute God could not know or be related to the world. (Hartshorne is not alone in thinking that Plato's myths and images stand for his real interest: concepts. See PS, 357).

The path of much later philosophy was to seek "consistency" and sacrifice one of these poles, and this path was in some ways encouraged by Plato himself in that the two poles cannot be related if both are considered concrete divine natures. This is why Hartshorne sees the Demiurge, which mythically makes the World-Soul, as eternal and the World-Soul as everlasting (PS, 55–57). And this is what he thinks Plato could or should have done, for if Platonism means anything it is that there are distinct levels of ontological abstractness. Relying on Wolfson,[16] Hartshorne thinks of eternity as the absence of temporal relations, hence God's eternal aspect cannot be concrete; yet the World-Soul is obviously concrete.[17]

Hartshorne is confident that his treatment of the Demiurge and World-Soul follows from basic Platonic distinctions, and that it continues the direction of Plato's logic in the *Timaeus*, which attempts to render consistent the inconsistent positions on God of the *Phaedo* and *Republic*, on the one hand, and the *Phaedrus*, on the other. This is not to suggest that all of the threads in Plato's view of God have been picked up, even by Hartshorne. For example, Plato sometimes multiplies gods into a pantheon of astral spirits, but these are mythical expressions which have never detained philosophers. Also, in the *Laws* the relation of self-motion to fixity is confusedly expressed in the figure of circular motion, etc. But even a multiplication of astral spirits is not incompatible with a monotheistic intent, for to call these "deities" or "gods" in a loose way is a "passing concession to ordinary language where precision is not sought." Monotheism is close to the surface of Plato's approach in that God is not posited by Plato as a mere fact to explain some other observed facts; rather God must comprehend the *entire* realm of forms, for God is the very principle of order in the world, the means by which the totality of things is one cosmos, a *uni*verse. Our task now is to zero in on Plato's notion of perfection so as to understand why both the Demiurge and World-Soul are needed.

God's immutability is inferred from God's perfection in the *Republic*. This ascendency of the principle of fixity has been taken throughout most of the history of philosophy to be the Platonic view of God *simpliciter*. It is helpful to notice that the World-Soul is the supreme example of soul but it is not perfect *if* perfection entails immutability; or, mythically expressed, the World-Soul is merely the most perfect of created things. Absoluteness (or perfection, as traditionally conceived) only belongs to an abstract, eternal aspect of God., i.e., God's essence rather than God's concrete actuality. Hence, Hartshorne finds no fault with the view of perfection in the *Republic*, but he tries to place it within a more inclusive view of God (PS, 31, 56; AW, 4–5, 30). If Plato is to be faulted it is because his spokesman in the *Republic* misleadingly talks of a being— instead of a mere abstract aspect of a being—so "perfect" that it could not change for the better or worse. That Hartshorne is not imposing his dipolar view on Plato is supported by the following consideration. If God were an *ens realissimum*, a most real being that could not change, either by improvement or by influence from others, God would come dangerously close to violating the definition of real being as dynamic power in the *Sophist* (CS, 69, 229). "The absolutely insensitive is the absolutely dead, not the supremely alive. The Platonists (perhaps not Plato) are blind to this truth" (AD, 232).

The two "Gods" of the *Timaeus* (the creator God and the created God—the Demiurge and the World-Soul, respectively) are aspects of one and the same deity. The *uni*verse as an animate and rational effect is superior to all other effects "as the whole or inclusive effect is superior to parts or included effects" (DR, 79–80).[18] But as in the *Republic* (381B), God is in every way the best possible (*ta tou theou pantei arista echei*). It is for this reason that Plato does not think that certain things are shameful in God merely because they are shameful in human beings; rather, anything less than the best possible is shameful in God because it is incompatible with the divine nature itself. And "best possible" has implications not only for ethical issues, but also for God's knowledge of the forms. Mathematical forms are not, on Hartshorne's interpretation of Plato, *directly* pictorial or imaginable. Lines, for example, are only intuited as ideal limits such that "even omniscience would have them as data only in a very special way," which is still compatible with the view that God is the measure of perfection and imperfection in the world (BH, 27–28, 63, 276).

Hartshorne has spent a good deal of his career criticizing the neoplatonic and medieval worship of being as opposed to becoming—"a doctrine riddled with antinomies"—a worship largely due to the influence of Parmenides on Plato, and the assumption that such influence constitutes Plato's entire philosophy. Hartshorne criticizes most interpreters of Plato in assuming that Plato's last word on God was that in the *Republic* to the effect that God, being perfect, cannot change. To a lesser extent he also criticizes Plato for going so far down this road before realizing that "an absolute maximum of value *in every conceivable respect*, does not make sense or is contradictory" (WP, 167; OO , 2–3). Like the "greatest possible number" the words "absolute maximum value" can be uttered, but they do not say anything if finite beings contribute something to the greatness of God, as they do to the supreme memory of the World-Soul.

Process theology in general "can be regarded as a partial return to Plato" because of his World-Soul as the divine self-moved, but not unmoved, mover of all other self-movers, and as the soul aware of all things. To help explicate Hartshorne's views on Plato, three sorts of sentiency (S) can be distinguished, all three of which can be found in Plato and Hartshorne in various ways under different labels. S1 is sentiency at the microscopic level of cells, atomic particles, and the like, where contemporary physics has vindicated Plato's flirtation with psychicalism, treated above. The nightmare of determinism has faded as reality in its fundamental constituents itself seems to have at least a partially indeterminate character of self-motion. That is, the sum total of efficient causes from the past do not supply the sufficient cause to explain the behavior of the smallest units of becoming in the world. Plato was wiser than he knew; little did he know that in twentieth-century physics universal mechanism would give way to a cosmic dance. S2 is sentiency per se, sentiency in the sense of feeling of feeling, found in animals and human beings, whereby beings with central nervous systems feel as wholes just as their constituent parts show at least prefigurements of feeling on a local level. And feeling *is* localized. Think of a knife stuck in the gut of any vertebrate,[19] or of sexual pleasure. S2 consists in taking these local feelings and collecting them so that an individual as a whole can feel what happens to its parts, even if the individual partially transcends the parts.

In the *Republic* (462C–D) Plato makes it clear that if there is pain in one's finger (note, not the whole hand) the entire community (*pasa he koinonia*) of bodily connections is hurt; the organized unity of the individual is such that when one part is hurt there is a feeling of pain in the *man* as a whole (*hole*) who has the pain in his finger (MV, 153). S3 is divine sentiency. If I am not mistaken, Plato shares with Hartshorne the following four-term analogy: S1:S2::S2:S3. The universe is a society or an organism (a Platonic World-Soul) of which one member (God, or the Platonic Demiurge) is preeminent just as human beings or animals are societies of cells, of which the mental part is preeminent.

Because animal individuals must, to maintain their integrity, adapt to their environment, mortality is implied. But if we imagine the World-Soul we must not consider an environment external to deity, but an internal one: the world-body of the world-mind. This cosmic, divine animal has such an intimate relation to its body that it must also have ideal ways of perceiving and remembering its body such that it can identify the microindividuals (S2) it includes. We can only tell when cells in our toe have been burned by the fire; we cannot identify the microindividuals as such (IO, 30, 366). It is true that the Demiurge is hampered by necessity (*anangke*) in the effort to conform the world or the contents of the receptacle to the ideal. Yet the Demiurge is not impeded by an environment external to deity, but by a plurality of self-movers. The value of contrast and richness provided by "cosmic 'creativity'" also provides the "recalcitrance of the 'material'," just as there is the "familiar difficulty of eliciting harmony among a plurality of creatures each having its own freedom." Although the evidence from Plato is somewhat unclear as to how matter "could consist of multitudinous 'souls' of extremely subhuman kinds," and as to how the order of the universe could be a static good forever (which Hartshorne thinks is impossible), he had at least a glimmering "that it was the multiplicity of souls that made absolute order impossible" (CS, 116).

On Hartshorne's view philosophers have myopically focused on the Plato they could understand, and ignored the Plato who was too profound for them. This is most evident with respect to Plato's panentheistic conception of a divine soul for the world, which even contemporary scholars of Plato's cosmology find odd.[20] But Hartshorne has taken the World-Soul as a clue for present philosophizing. For example, each new divine state harmonizes itself both with its predecessor *and* with the previous state of the cosmos. This is analogous to a human being harmonizing itself with its previous experience and bodily state, but with a decisive difference. The human being must hope that its internal and the external environment will continue to make it possible for it to survive, whereas God has no such problem in that there is no external environment for God (AD, 293). But the differences between God and human beings (e.g., God knows the microindividuals included in the divine life and God has no external environment) should not cloud the important similarities (e.g., the facts that self-change is integral to soul at all levels and that the soul-body analogy used to understand God does not preclude the person-person analogy — which links the divine person with human beings). The most important similarity lies in the fact that one's bodily cells are associated, at a given moment, with one as a conscious, supercellular singular, just as all lesser beings are associated with the society of singulars called God (CA, 203, 251, 274). In a way, all talk about God short of univocity contains *some* negativity, in that God does not exist, know, love, etc., as we do. With regard to the divine body, however, almost all theists have allowed this negativity to run wild (MV, 180).

Plato offered a "striking anticipation" of the doctrine of the compound individual, even if he ultimately fell short of the principle that individuality as such must be the compounding of organisms into organisms; but this is not surprising because cells were not yet discovered (WP, 53–54). In the case of the divine individual, where all entities are fully enjoyed, there can be no envy of others or conflict with them in that they are integral to the divine goodness. Less completely are a human being's cells internal to the individual, e.g., bone cells in one's arm are less internal and less fully possessed by the individual than are the brain cells. These considerations regarding divine inclusiveness also explain why the cosmos could not be held together and ordered by a malevolent God or a plurality of gods, in that these deities are always partly divided within or among themselves, and are incapable of an objective grasp of the forms. The cosmos can be held together only by an all-sympathetic coordinator (RS, 138, 190). Plato also came closer than any other philosopher to Hartshorne's notion that God is *whole* in "every categorial sense, all actuality in one individual actuality, and all possibility in one individual potentiality,'' albeit tempered by Harts-horne's own understanding of the potentiality inherent in God, somewhat less extensive than that found in Whitehead's view. And because of this wholeness God is not an organism of a loose kind which must await the light years it takes for cosmic interactions to take place, in that these interactions are all internal to the divine ''ideal animal'' itself (NT, 21, 99).

One of the reasons Hartshorne thinks of Plato as among the ''wisest and best'' of theologians is that he thinks Plato may have realized that the Demiurge *is* the World-Soul in abstraction, i.e., is that part of the World-Soul considered as having an eternal ideal which it is forever engaged in realizing. This process of realization is what Plato meant in the *Timaeus* by the ''moving image of eternity.'' Hartshorne's tempting way to read Plato alleges that God, utilizing partly self-created creatures, ''creates its own forever unfinished actualization.'' Thus, God is aware of both us and other noncosmic animals and the lesser souls, on the one hand, and eternal ideals, on the other. Even though God is the ''individual integrity'' of the world, which is otherwise a concatenation of myriad parts, Hartshorne's view is easily made compatible with the claim that God does not survey all events in the future with strict omniscience (OO, 52–53, 59, 94).

7. THE DIVINE BEING AND NONEXISTENCE

Belief in a World-Soul is connected in the divine animal with a belief in a World-Body, which is superior to our bodies because there is nothing internal to it (e.g., cancer cells) which could threaten its continued existence, *even if* the divine body is spatially finite. Further, our bodies are fragmentary, as in a human infant's coming into the world as a secondary lifestyle expressing its feelings upon a system which already had a basic order in its cells; whereas the divine body does not begin to exist on a foundation otherwise established. When an animal dies, its individual lifestyle no longer controls its members, yet the result is not chaos, but ''simply a return to the more pervasive types of order expressive of the cosmic mind-body.'' The World-Soul is aware of the divine body, and can vicariously suffer with its suffering members, but it cannot suffer in the sense of ceasing to exist due to an alien force. ''An individual can influence it, none can threaten it.'' Not even brain death can threaten it because the soul-body analogy cannot be pushed to the point where a divine brain is posited. As before, the contrast between the brain and a less essential bodily part only makes sense because an animal has an external environment. Consider that the divine body does not need limbs to move about, for it is its own place: ''space being merely the order among its parts.'' It does not need a digestive system or lungs to take in food or air from without in that there is no "without." So it is with all organs outside the central nervous system, which, as we know but Plato did not, is the organ that adapts "internal activities to external stimuli," a function which is not needed in the inclusive organism. The only function of the divine body is to furnish the World-Soul with awareness of, and power over, its bodily members. So although there is no special part of the cosmos recognizable as a nervous system, every individual becomes, *as it were*, a brain cell directly communicating to the World-Soul, and likewise receiving influences from divine feeling or thought (OO, 133–135; IO, 348).

These thoughts on the divine body are not just consequences of Hartshorne's use of the soul-body analogy to understand God; they are also logically entailed by his metaphysics. Hartshorne has often claimed (contra Kant, et al.) that there are necessary truths concerning existence, e.g., "Something exists." The absurdity of claiming that "there might have been (absolutely) nothing" is derived from Plato himself (and Bergson), who, when he commits parricide on father Parmenides in the *Sophist* (241–242), only admits the existence of relative nonbeing or otherness, not the existence of absolutely nothing, which would be a logical contradiction in that *it* would then be something (IO, x–xi). Along with Plato and Spinoza, Hartshorne agrees that all determination is negation, but this inescapable element of negation is precisely Plato's form of otherness or relative nonbeing. The statement "Nothing exists" could not conceivably be verified, i.e., a completely restrictive or wholly negative statement is not a conceivable yet unrealized fact, but an impossibility (CS, 22, 159). Particular bodies can pass out of existence (or better, pass into an other sort of existence), but the divine body of the universe itself has no alternative but to exist.

8. Proofs for God's Existence

It is not surprising that Hartshorne treats two arguments which appear, or are alleged to appear, in Plato: the ontological argument and the argument from order. J. Prescott Johnson's excellent article on the ontological argument in Plato provides a focus: Johnson alleges that Plato's dialectic in the *Republic*, used as a means to know the good, amounts to an ontological argument for the necessary existence of the good.[21] That is, supreme reality is not a mere hypothesis; and knowledge of this reality "requires no assumptions" and "makes no use of images, relying on ideas only," thus distinguishing *noesis* from *dianoia*. No merely contingent existence could be known in this a priori manner, nor could any contingent existence be *hyperousia*, as Plato says of the good (509B). Only a necessary and underived thing could be to the whole of reality as the sun is to life on earth.

Hartshorne commends Johnson for defending Plato's procedure against the Kantian criticism that "the merely possible and the existent cannot differ qualitatively. In regard to the supreme conception, the *merely* possible is indistinguishable from the impossible." The merely possible is precisely what hypothetical knowledge (*dianoia*) deals with in contrast to the object of the highest knowledge (*noesis*). At least one feature is missing in Johnson's analysis, however: the relation of the good to God. If one identifies the good with God, then Plato in effect looks like a classical theist, with God as a necessary existent with pure absoluteness. But, as we have seen, this is a difficult view to defend on textual grounds (pace More, Eslick, etc.). If the good is a necessary feature or idea in God, then God for Plato may well be absoluteness necessarily existent somehow, but with the particular actuality of God contingent and relative. It is this latter interpretation which Hartshorne adopts in an attempt to reconcile Johnson's insights, the *Republic*, and the *Timaeus*. What in Plato himself was probably an unresolved ambiguity regarding the relation between the good and God—a wise restraint on Plato's part—tended in his followers to become a "premature and unwise" decision in favor of the first interpretation, hence the "fatal onesidedness" which has "exacted severe penalities" in the history of thought about God (AD, 139–141).

Hartshorne agrees with Esser[22] that there was no explicit statement of the ontological argument before Anselm, hence his great "discovery," yet the very notion of the Demiurge as a creator God presupposes modal concepts which at least make the argument implicit in Plato. If the Demiurge's reality actualized a potential that could have been unactualized, then the Demiurge is just as much in need of a creator as any other being. Thus the Platonic argument from order in Book Ten of the *Laws*, the oldest formal proof for God, to be treated in a moment, "breaks down if Anselm's discovery is a mere sophistry" (AD, 148–149, 307). Plato (or better, Platonism) misled Anselm at several points, e.g., in assuming that reality does not admit of increase in the way that we can always conceive of a greater for any conceivable number. It will not do to assume, as many followers of Plato have done, that deity's qualitative supremacy transcends magnitude altogether. Quantity may have a value which is not attainable without it, as in appreciating more moments of a creature's life rather than fewer. This defect is closely connected with the monopolar prejudice in favor of mere unity, as though absence of contrast could make sheer unity intelligible. A related Hartshornian criticism would apply to the Platonic vision of "absolute beauty," which is a contradiction if in fact beauty entails variety, for "all possible variety" is full of mutual incompatibilities (AD, 27–31).

Hartshorne explicitly asks, "Is the proof Platonic?" (AD, 55–57). All classical theists are Platonists, in a certain sense, in that they believe that "the universal principle of being can be a sort of superconcrete yet eternal reality," immune to becoming, but not an abstraction. They think that goodness itself is the most good thing, which exemplifies what Hartshorne calls the "homological fallacy": eternal principles (*logoi*) are in no way abstract or inferior to, but quite *like* concrete actualities. As should now be obvious, Hartshorne is not convinced that Plato committed this fallacy. Hartshorne only argues against the "Platonizing" procedure, not Plato, in the following way: contingency is in the step from universal to particular, a step from the more abstract to the more concrete. Hartshorne realizes that the view that forms are not ultimately separable from concrete instances is "often termed the Aristotelian view," but the belief that universals must have *some* embodiment—say in a mind thinking them—can be fairly termed, as Hartshorne puts it, a "moderate Platonism." The contrast between "predicates" and "exemplified predicates" is not the ground for contingency because of the priority which must be given to the latter: some predicates *must* be exemplified or there would be nothing to talk about. Rather, the ground of contingency is in the distinction between: (a) specific predicates, which always involve mutual exclusiveness, competitive ways of instancing more general notions, alternative "determinates" under higher "determinables," and (b) generic predicates, which are less determinate. But only an "ultra-Platonic negation" would view forms as not specialized or concretized at all. The contingency of each step toward particularity does not mean that no definite step might have been taken, but that "other *equally definite* steps" might have been taken. "Not even Plato" believed in the complete self-sufficiency of the abstract or universal; Plato was never "ultra-Platonic."

How do these considerations relate to the ontological argument? For Hartshorne the argument is valid only if the individuality of God is conceivable as a pure determinable which must be particularized and concretized somehow. God's bare *existence* is quite abstract, about as noncompetitive as "reality as such." It has an infinite range of variations and flexibility. But God is not characterless or "flabby" because of God's *actuality* in some embodied state. The definitive functions of deity are strictly universal and coextensive with modality as such: God is related actually to all actual things and potentially to all potential things. God is—à la the *Sophist*—influenced by and influences everything. Thus, modal coextensiveness is equivalent to the notion of the unsurpassable. The mistake of "Platonism" in the bad sense is the notion that all beautiful things must preexist in the Absolute Form of Beauty, an ultimate determinable which somehow issued in determinations. But this is to deny any intelligible creativity, divine or creaturely. "To be creative is to add positive determinations to reality, to enrich the totality of things by new values." Hence the ultimate determinable is the supreme creativity, abstractly conceived. In the neoclassical, "moderately Platonic" use of Plato, we can see that Plato avoids not only the homological fallacy, but also the formal fallacy whereby formal reality gives to concrete reality what formal reality itself lacks (AD, 57–59).

Hartshorne notes that there were atheists in Plato's day, and even before that (*Laws* 887C), so that Plato's argument from order—blended with the cosmological argument—starts the important tradition of knowing how rationally to answer nonbelievers (NT, 125; PS, 25). Plato's use of this argument in Book Ten of the *Laws* shows that he had "one of the most penetrating of all intelligences," a mind with "imaginative subtlety" which dwarfs his most famous followers. Further, the proof is intended as a series of hints, to be filled in by the reader's meditations, which Hartshorne is obviously willing to do. But even though the proof is really an outline, it furnishes the material for an argument stronger than any stated by Aristotle or Thomas Aquinas, and stronger than any criticized by Hume or Kant (IO, 35–36). The outline looks something like this: 1. Psychical process or soul is the only self-explanatory process, the only self-determining type of change. 2. Order among souls, and hence in reality generally, can be explained only through a supremely good soul, which persuades the others to conform to its decisions. 3. Disorder and evil are not due to the supreme soul's decisions, but to the conflicting decisions of other souls.

Although Plato came too close to identifying disorder and evil (for Hartshorne partial disorder is needed to balance order so as to produce beauty), his wisdom is seen when Hume and Kant suggest that the disorder in the world might be explained polytheistically. This is an extreme and inadequate way to put Plato's very point, if by "gods" is meant souls. And we have already seen why order cannot be explained by a divine committee. One further reason for this claim needs to be stated here: because the higher the consciousness the more "widely and abruptly" it can disagree with other consciousnesses which are its peers, a pantheon of gods would be even more in need of a single superior to understand the world as a cosmos than a plurality of earthly animals.

Hartshorne agrees with Burnet[23] that Plato's greatest discovery regarding God does not concern the forms but soul or psychical process. This discovery allows us: to understand the primordial and everlasting ideal for the cosmos—the good—in the supreme soul; to realize that "creativity" is the true transcendental, which applies to creator and creatures alike; to claim that cosmic order requires one soul to order the others, yet disorder does not require one soul (e.g., Satan), only a multiplicity of agents able to get in each other's way; to urge that the classical theistic "problem of evil" could not so much as arise in Plato's thought because God is not totally responsible for the world (IO, 36–38). (Although Plato does waver between attributing evil to "matter" and to the freedom of souls—OO, 53). Nor does Hartshorne think that it would be a good thing for God to be so responsible: beauty requires partial disorder and cosmic creativity per se is a good thing. This is no trivial attempt at theodicy on Hartshorne's part in that there are metaphysical reasons for these claims. From Plato Hartshorne has learned[24] that every negation (relative nonbeing or otherness) implies an affirmation, i.e., there are no merely negative truths. To say that "divinity does not exist" is to say something positive about the reality whose existence is incompatible with God. Usually it is the positive existence of evil in the world which is assumed to be incompatible with (an omnipotent) God, but if there is no such incompatibility, then Plato's argument from order stands, as does the tragic view of life because there are "pervasive elements of chance, partial disorder, and frustration in reality."[25]

9. Conclusion

Colin Gunton is typical of many scholars who have ignored the relationship between Plato and Hartshorne. Even when discussing the World-Soul, Gunton only notices the similarity between Spinoza and Hartshorne, despite Hartshorne's repeated citations of Plato as the source for his belief in the World-Soul. Gunton does notice that Hartshorne is like Plato in believing that the clue to the metaphysical understanding of reality is in the concepts of the mind,[26] but this, I hope I have shown, only scratches the surface of the relationship between these two thinkers. Once this surface is scratched, one finds that Hartshorne believes the theory of time as asymmetrical has profound consequences not only for how we interpret Plato's works (and, I would add, Hartshorne's own works), but also for how we interpret the history of philosophy in general. It is "only in the relative sense in which philosophical conceptions are likely to have novelty." Hartshorne is explicit that he means relative to Plato (RS, 169; DR, ix). From Hartshorne's early encounter with the Platonism of Emerson, to his doctoral dissertation in 1923 (where Plato is cited as "the great founder" of Hartshorne's own teleological monism and monistic principle[27]), to all of his books throughout his career, *especially* his works after CS in 1970, Hartshorne has been in the process of trying to understand and, where necessary, improve upon Plato.[28] Yet how odd it is that Hartshorne has to remind even a thinker as familiar with his work as John Cobb of the importance of Plato for his idea of God. I hope we are now in a position, however, to take Hartshorne seriously when he says in 1984 that : "I have always been something of a Platonist" (EA, 164–165).

DANIEL A. DOMBROWSKI

DEPARTMENT OF PHILOSOPHY
SEATTLE UNIVERSITY
JANUARY 1987

ABBREVIATIONS OF WORKS BY HARTSHORNE
IN CHRONOLOGICAL ORDER

BH = *Beyond Humanism* (Lincoln: University of Nebraska Press, 1968), originally published in 1937.

MV = *Man's Vision of God* (N.Y.: Harper & Brothers, 1941).

DR = *The Divine Relativity* (New Haven: Yale University Press, 1948).

PS = *Philosophers Speak of God* (Chicago: University of Chicago Press, 1953).

RS = *Reality as Social Process* (Boston: Beacon Press, 1953).

AD = *Anselm's Discovery* (La Salle, Ill.: Open Court, 1965).

NT = *A Natural Theology for Our Time* (La Salle, Ill.: Open Court, 1967).

CS = *Creative Synthesis and Philosophic Method* (La Salle, Ill.: Open Court, 1970).

WP = *Whitehead's Philosophy* (Lincoln: University of Nebraska Press, 1972).

AW = *Aquinas to Whitehead* (Milwaukee: Marquette University Publications, 1976).

WV = *Whitehead's View of Reality* (N.Y.: Pilgrim Press, 1981).

IO = *Insights and Oversights of Great Thinkers* (Albany: SUNY Press, 1983).

EA = *Existence and Actuality* (Chicago: University of Chicago Press, 1984).

CA = *Creativity in American Philosophy* (Albany: SUNY Press, 1984).

OO = *Omnipotence and Other Theological Mistakes* (Albany: SUNY Press, 1984).

NOTES

1. Hartshorne relies here on the work of Julius Stenzel, *Plato's Method of Dialectic*, trans. by D. J. Allen (Oxford: Clarendon Press, 1940).

2. Here Hartshorne cites Schleiermacher's view of Plato and the work of Raphael Demos, *The Philosophy of Plato* (N.Y.: Scribner's, 1939).

3. See Stephen Körner, *What is Philosophy?* (London: Penguin, 1969), p. 255.

4. See David Griffin, "Hartshorne's Differences from Whitehead," in *Two Process Philosophers*, ed. by Lewis Ford (Tallahassee, Fla.: American Academy of Religion, 1973), pp. 37–38.

5. See my *Plato's Philosophy of History* (Washington, D.C.: University Press of America, 1981). The above quote is from Hartshorne's review of this book in *Process Studies* 12 (1982), pp. 201–202.

6. Griffin, pp. 39–40.

7. See, e.g., Lewis Ford, "Whitehead's Differences from Hartshorne," in *Two Process Philosophers*, who argues that Hartshorne is not very much at odds with Whitehead regarding eternal possibilities. And Ivor Leclerc, "Whitehead and the Theory of Form," in *Process and Divinity: The Hartshorne Festschrift* (La Salle, Ill.: Open Court, 1964), notices that Whitehead is not necessarily committed to the notion that forms are *ousiai* or separate actualities, in that he is an Aristotelian to the extent that he insists that forms are forms of *ousiai*; nor does Whitehead believe—as does Plato, according to Leclerc—that forms are perfect archetypes or specific in number. Nonetheless, Leclerc admits not only that Whitehead, along with Plato, saw that to recognize an element of form exhibited by many actualities necessitates that we acknowledge form as a distinct metaphysical category. (Even Hartshorne could admit this much.) Whitehead also believes, according to Leclerc, that form, although not separate from actualization, *does*

have some "nature" transcending actuality. It is perhaps because of this "nature" that A. W. Levi calls Whitehead a "Platonic realist." See Levi's "Bergson or Whitehead?," in *Process and Divinity*.

8. No less a scholar than A. E. Taylor has tried to interpret Plato on such terms. See *Commentary on Plato's Timaeus* (Oxford: Clarendon Press, 1928), pp. 71–73, where it is claimed that change for Plato is the process through which reality (as dynamic power?) effects ingression into the world of becoming. Cornford rejects this view, but Hartshorne nonetheless notes certain concessions made by Cornford to the process interpretation of Plato, as we will see. See F. M. Cornford, *Plato's Cosmology* (London: Routledge and Kegan Paul, 1937), pp. xi–xii. Also see another favorite source for Hartshorne, R. B. Levinson, *In Defense of Plato* (Cambridge: Harvard University Press, 1953), p. 630.

9. Here Hartshorne argues against Thomas Gould, *Platonic Love* (London: Routledge and Kegan Paul, 1963), Ch. 9.

10. Hartshorne often refers to Plato's notion of being as dynamic power in his articles, which I have mostly left out of my treatment in that they reiterate or anticipate points made in his books. See, e.g., "God and the Meaning of Life," in *On Nature*, ed. by Leroy Rouner (Notre Dame, Ind.: University of Notre Dame Press, 1984), p. 158.

11. See Leonard Eslick, "The Dyadic Character of Being in Plato," *Modern Schoolman* 21 (1953), pp. 11–18. Also James Reagan, "Being and Nonbeing in Plato's *Sophist*," *Modern Schoolman* 42 (1965), pp. 305–314.

12. See my "Polar Equality in Dipolar Theism," *Modern Schoolman* 62 (1985), pp. 305–316. Cf. Eugene Peters, *Hartshorne and Neoclassical Metaphysics* (Lincoln: University of Nebraska Press, 1970), pp. 80–81.

13. See Cornford, p. 39, who claims that *in* the divine soul of the universe is a divine reason, the latter symbolized by the Demiurge. Also see AW, 4–5 and IO, 70–71.

14. See my "Rorty on Plato as an Edifier," in *Doing Philosophy Historically*, ed. by Peter Hare (Buffalo: Prometheus Books, 1988).

15. Hartshorne relies here on P. E. More, *The Religion of Plato* (Princeton: Princeton University Press, 1921), p. 120. Also see *Republic* (508–509), the probable source of this identification. A. Boyce Gibson, "The Two Strands in Natural Theology," in *Process and Divinity*, pp. 472, 475–476, notes that in the *Timaeus* Plato makes a statement of the conception of God as outgoing and an attempt to connect this conception with God as self-sufficient (*autarkeia*), and that Plato puts soul on the "same level of being" as forms; thus, Plato "was able to explain what in the earlier dialogues remained a mystery."

16. H. A. Wolfson, *The Philosophy of Spinoza* (Cambridge: Harvard University Press, 1934), I, p. 358–360.

17. The most recent work in this area is by Richard Mohr, *The Platonic Cosmology* (Leiden: Brill, 1985), who offers a different interpretation from Hartshorne's, but the two are compatible at several points. Mohr reminds us that the Demiurge appears, in a way, in the *Republic* VII, *Sophist*, *Statesman*, and *Philebus* as well as in the *Timaeus*, and that the Demiurge exists independently of soul and withdraws from the world. The World-Soul is found not only in the *Timaeus*, but also in the *Statesman* and *Philebus*. For Mohr the World-Soul is primarily the *maintainer* of order in the world; which entails that the World-Soul has a supreme memory; it does not really communicate motion *to* the body of the world, hence, one assumes, it receives or transmits it. To do this the World-Soul must be immanent in the corporeal, but not exactly as the actualization of body as in Aristotle. A few points remain unclear, however, in Mohr's otherwise fine work: He does not explicate the relationship between the Demiurge and the World-Soul, but states only that the division between the two is more than mythical. Are they two gods for Mohr? Or

if only one god, how are they related? Mohr is also unsure as to why the World-Soul must succumb to the bodily world. The dipolar logic of Hartshorne's theism (see the introduction to PS) is especially helpful here. And Mohr is at a loss to explain how we could possibly take the World-Soul seriously today because most of the world is "clearly inert." *Is* this clear?

18. Hartshorne relies here on Cornford and Demos. Also see MV, 52. From Demos, pp. 120–125, Hartshorne's view that God is not omnipotent, thus preserving divine goodness—see CA, 266—is reinforced in that Plato held the same view. Demos is clear that God is dipolar for Plato because reality is dipolar, and this without contradiction. Finally, Demos offers *some* support for Hartshorne's position on the relation between God and the forms: "But though irreducible each to the other, they may both be regarded as abstractions from one ultimate complex fact of patterned activity." This is not exactly Hartshorne's view in that Plato's "real God" is the World-Soul and it is from this that the Demiurge and the forms are abstracted. Levinson is closer to Hartshorne on the point than Demos. See OO, 53; IO, 37.

19. See my "Was Plato a Vegetarian?," *Aperion* XVIII (June, 1984), pp. 1–9; and *The Philosophy of Vegetarianism* (Amherst: University of Massachusetts Press, 1984). Also see *Hartshorne and the Metaphysics of Animal Rights* (Albany: SUNY Press, 1988).

20. Again, see Mohr. Also, in the discussion of the person-person analogy which follows, it should be noted that for Hartshorne the best example of a person-person analogy with respect to the God-creature relationship is a mother-fetus example (assuming, for the moment, that a fetus late in pregnancy is a person), *not* a father-child or king-subject example. Male bias in theology (largely absent in Plato) has prevented us from seeing this (OO, 60).

21. J. Prescott Johnson, "The Ontological Argument in Plato," *The Personalist* 44 (1963), pp. 24–34.

22. M. Esser, "Finden sich Spuren des ontologischen Gottesbeweises vor dem Heiligen Anselm?," *Jahrbucher fur Philosophie und spekulative Theologie* 29 (1910).

23. See John Burnet, *Platonism* (Berkeley: University of California Press, 1928), p. 119.

24. Hartshorne relies here on Lewis Campbell, "Plato," *Encyclopaedia Britannica*, eleventh edition.

25. Eugene Peters, pp. 34–35, connects Plato's and Hartshorne's concepts of negation with panpsychism. Just as uttering a falsehood (what is not) is to say something—contra the sophist—so also we cannot know what the *complete* absence of experience or life would be like.

26. See Colin Gunton, "Rejection, Influence, and Development: Hartshorne in the History of Philosophy," *Process Studies* 6 (Spring, 1976), pp. 33–42; and *Becoming and Being: The Doctrine of God in Charles Hartshorne and Karl Barth* (Oxford: Oxford University Press, 1978), pp. 85–88. I think it is misleading, however, for Gunton to suggest that Plato has a doctrine of innate ideas like Descartes.

27. See William Sessions, "Hartshorne's Early Philosophy," in *Two Process Philosophers*, pp. 10–34.

28. Space limitations have forced me to omit the relationship between Plato and Hartshorne in two important areas: (a) love and ethics; and (b) the history of philosophy, whose progress is judged by Hartshorne against the standard of "the genuinely Platonic program."

25

John E. Smith

NEOCLASSICAL METAPHYSICS AND THE HISTORY OF PHILOSOPHY

M y aim in this essay is to consider some of the judgments passed by Hartshorne in his book, *Insights and Oversights of Great Thinkers*, a book, which as the subtitle indicates, is also meant to be an appraisal of Western philosophy—with some references to Eastern thought as well. It is important to notice at the outset that, in addition to certain considerations about the history of philosophy, how it has been written and what uses it has, that are to serve as criteria of judgment, there is the underlying touchstone of Hartshorne's neoclassical metaphysics. The great thinkers, in short, will find themselves at the bar of this position and it is upon this basis that the reader will find the definite reasons why a given philosopher is credited with an insight or charged with an oversight. This is as it should be if we are to avoid what has been described in philosophical criticism—I believe by Michael Foster—as "shooting arrows from a concealed position," a practice much in evidence some decades ago by those who claimed merely to be "doing" philosophy while purporting to know nothing about "presuppositions." Curiously enough, however, Hartshorne does not articulate his position, except in a general and vague way, at the beginning of the discussion, although anyone familiar with his thought will detect its presence, but only in his final summary where we are told that the arguments advanced in connection with the rationality of the views he has considered have been "influenced by the work of a group of philosophers, sometimes called philosophers of Process" (p. 364) and that his own version of this position is called "neoclassical metaphysics" (Ibid.). Perhaps this postponement was meant to keep the discussion from becoming a didactic "application" of principles to the philosophical positions discussed and indeed it must be acknowledged that Hartshorne's metaphysics is rooted in his critique of past views and in his acceptance of those put forth by thinkers—Bergson, Peirce,

James, Whitehead—in the past century. Nevertheless, it needs to be kept in mind that the appraisals of philosophers in this book are made in terms of the central ideas of Hartshorne's metaphysics. And I believe that he would agree that in making judgments on this basis his own philosophical standpoint is also being brought before the bar of reason. Insight into the viability of any philosophy is provided by the critical judgments on other views dictated by that philosophy.

Since, as we all know, the history of Western philosophy is a long and intricate story, it would be folly to attempt to cover it all. Hence I have selected Hartshorne's treatment of three major philosophers—Aristotle, Kant, and Hegel—for special consideration. I choose Aristotle because there Hartshorne gives a first-rate account of what is living (or should be) in Aristotle's theory of modality, a doctrine that forms an important part of neoclassical metaphysics. I choose Kant because Hartshorne has some illuminating and novel things to say; not much Kant interpretation has been carried out from the perspective of process metaphysics. I choose Hegel, I hope not unfairly since I regard this chapter as quite inadequate for so monumental a thinker, because I believe it reveals some of Hartshorne's "oversights," especially his failure to appreciate fully the distinction between understanding and reason and its bearing on the transition from Kant to Hegel. This failure, moreover, casts some doubt on Hartshorne's sanguine belief in formal logic and what he considers to be argumentation in philosophy.

In order to put the discussion that follows in a proper perspective it is necessary to call attention to Hartshorne's views about the nature and uses of the history of philosophy and especially how he proposes to approach the subject. Hartshorne makes some most illuminating remarks about how the history of philosophy has been written in the past and, by implication, how it should be written in the future since these remarks cluster about a "three-fold complaint" concerning the way most previous historians have treated the subject. His first criticism has to do with the belief that the most attention has been focused on those philosophers (and their systems) who have exerted strong influence on both contemporaries and successors. While not denying that this influence is a reason for being interested in a philosopher, Hartshorne contends that it is not the only reason for such interest and that, in some cases, it may not be the best reason. Acknowledging that it is impossible for any single philosopher to encompass the long history of doctrinal possibilities in order to determine which views are to be regarded as most plausible and capable of surviving careful scrutiny, Hartshorne maintains that every philosopher will have to make his or her own decision on the matter. Such a decision, he believes, must and can be made by a proper *use* of past thought. What this means is made clear in the claim that "what we want from the history of philosophy is knowledge not merely of influential views and arguments but of possible ones" (p. 1f.). This claim, as we shall see, is central to Hartshorne's entire approach. The illustration offered in support of this contention seems to me essentially sound for making the basic point. According to Hartshorne, both Spinoza and Leibniz, under the long-standing conception of God as the Unmoved Mover, could not conceive of God as, for example, Socinus did, as gaining any new knowledge through the medium of the emergence of new facts and creative human decisions and actions. The result, says Hartshorne, was that Socinus and his views were ignored by historians who could not themselves envisage any possibilities other than the one represented by the classical view set forth by two most influential thinkers.

Hartshorne's second complaint is less clear. He tells us that the majority of those writing the history of philosophy have been insufficiently analytic by which he means that they have presented philosophies "en bloc"—Platonism, Aristotelianism, Hegelianism, etc.—as if they were organisms all of whose features are interdependent and equally important so that we have either to choose between these wholistic alternatives, or start over again, or perhaps try a piecemeal approach—all of which Hartshorne rejects. As far as I can tell, he regards a properly analytic approach to the subject as the giving of an account of historical answers to definite questions which means that what we need is the history of problems rather than of systems. That this approach has merit can be seen in the significant contributions made by the two historians he cites— Lovejoy and Wolfson—but it may lead us to suppose that there are previously packaged versions of historical problems which remain the same regardlesss of the historical periods in which they appear (G. E. Moore, for example, was most severe in his seminar on those who referred to the "problem of X" while supposing that everyone knew what that meant without further explanation). There are, to be sure, historical *continuities* in philosophical issues so that, for example, one might regard the question at the center of discussion among logicians some decades ago as to whether the counterfactual conditional can be expressed in an extensional language as an essentially nominalistic formulation of the Aristotelian problem of the nature of potentiality. But even in this instance the conditions of "the problem" were greatly altered; Aristotle was giving a metaphysical account of what is, while the logicians were mainly concerned to avoid "metaphysics" and to construe everything in terms of a present, actual fact. The point is that the approach through problems, while clearly contributing something of importance to the study of the history of philosophy, tends to become *ahistorical* to too great a degree.

To take another example, Kant could consider the question whether the world had a beginning in time (even if he was using it only in order to exhibit the "natural dialectic" of human reason), whereas that question could have had no meaning for Aristotle in the sense that he could not have envisioned time as having a "beginning." The reason, of course, is that Kant like many others had inherited the Judeo-Christian tradition and the problems it raised; no one prior to that tradition could possibly have thought in terms of its doctrines and philosophical problems. If philosophy, as Hegel showed, has a genuinely historical development, we must be wary about thinking of "timeless" philosophical problems that confront every thinker in the same way. A more circumspect approach would be to attempt to identify in any historical period *analogous* formulations of issues that have been raised in the past as in my example of the counterfactual. The modern issue was neither the same as the ancient one, nor was it entirely different, something that preserves the historical continuity.

There is, however, something more involved in Hartshorne's criticism, namely, that even the two historians commended for their approach through problems are said not to have paid sufficient attention to "conceptual possibilities" (p. 3). By a "possible" view Hartshorne means one that is "not too hopelessly absurd" as a minimal criterion, but also one determined by logical means. Thus we are told that in the case of the conception of God there are only three doctrinal possibilities—(1) No God; (2) A simply and wholly immutable God; (3) A God not wholly immutable. These alternatives, but especially (3), are understandable from *a present standpoint* informed by the developments of process thought and neoclassical metaphysics. However, is it legitimate to suppose, as Hartshorne apparently does, that these alternatives were present as actual possibilities for thought to past thinkers regardless of the "climate of opinion" marking the historical period in which they thought? It is clear from the record that, given the general shape assumed by Christian theology from, let us say, the Christian Platonists of Alexandria to Thomas Aquinas, the third possible conception of God cited would be bound to be regarded from that standpoint as virtually the same as the first—No God. The question is not whether they were correct in their view, but whether they could reasonably have been expected to envisage such a conception under the *historical* conditions. Hartshorne himself knows, because he took part in the discussion, that some three decades ago two eminent thinkers—Tillich and Maritain—expressed serious objections to his process conception of God claiming, to put it simply, that he was "changing" God. I am not joining this issue here; I wish merely to point out the ahistorical character of Hartshorne's approach. He seems to think that the possibilities for thought which he *presently* envisages were always "there" in some timeless sense and that all seriously concerned thinkers "could" (should?) have considered them as real possibilities for interpreting reality.

Hartshorne's third charge against many historians of philosophy is that they have given insufficient help in the difficult matter of deciding what positions should be taken seriously and which may be safely discarded. In making this criticism, however, Hartshorne notes quite fairly that if the historian goes too far in this critical direction he may fail in the primary historical task. In the end he looks for some compromise between extremes. I would suggest that, in agreement with Hartshorne, Passmore's work represents one extreme—he exhibits a remarkable capacity to express clearly and accurately the distinctive features of widely contrasting views and approaches, but with virtually no critical appraisal. While I am uncertain about whom to place at the other extreme, I am confident that Hegel, both in the *Lectures on the History of Philosophy* and other works, is a good candidate for the middle position. Contrary to the opinions of those who have not studied Hegel and simply assume that he wrapped his own "system" around the history of thought, the fact is that his treatment of the major thinkers is at once well informed and critical in the sense that he penetrates to the central principle of a position and seeks to show the extent of its consistency, comprehensiveness, and accord with experience. He leaves the reader in no doubt about what is living and what is dead in the philosophical tradition. In this regard, I see Hegel as having fulfilled in his own time Hartshorne's main demand when he says about a philosophical view, "what is important is *why* it was held, and whether the supposed reason stands up in the light of our knowledge today" (p. 5).

Since Hartshorne proposes to illustrate in the body of the book the main use of the history of philosophy, "a laboratory for testing truth," a brief comment on this principle is in order. On his view, we should ask of any philosopher, past or present, what questions has he put deliberately, including possible answers and arguments, and what questions has he either ignored or perhaps merely noticed and not dealt with carefully. This seems to me a sound approach and Hartshorne illustrates it nicely with examples from Leibniz and Hume. Leibniz, he points out, announced the Principle of Sufficient Reason and took it as an axiom without considering it as a response to the question of rational explanation, a question, admittedly, allowing of more than one answer. The same is said to be true of Hume's assumption of strict causal determinism with an absolute minimum of discussion of the principle itself, since his main concern was to find a justification for it in "experience."

Leibniz, as Hartshorne rightly points out, did consider with care the question, "How does matter differ from, or resemble, mind?" and gave an answer that was found to be significant by later thinkers such as Peirce and Whitehead. Hartshorne's point is that to ignore what all three thinkers had to say on the topic is to waste philosophical resources. Needless to say, I agree with him.

At this point I wish to pursue briefly the idea that Hartshorne's approach is ahistorical by means of a comparison with that of Hegel. Hegel saw the history of philosophy philosophically or as the cosmic and creative development of ideas in which successive systems do not simply cancel each other out—the skeptical view—but instead interact in bringing about newer and more adequate or concrete accounts of the nature of things. Hegel's method here was two-fold; on the one hand, he sought to detect, and ultimately to "cancel" limitations and errors in previous views, while preserving the element of truth they contain. His treatment of empiricism furnishes an excellent example. While recognizing its concreteness in contrast to what he called the previous metaphysics of the understanding, its demand that the individual be presented with what he or she is asked to believe, and its belief in the importance of analysis, Hegel nevertheless insisted that empiricism falls short in a number of particulars, including its inability to unite what analysis has dismembered and its failure to do justice to the "proper infinites" — self and God — because of its adherence to the domain of sense as the ultimate criterion of meaning and truth. The usual mistake here is to emphasize what Hegel negated over and above what he sought to preserve. On the other hand, he sought to test philosophical positions by asking not merely what success they enjoy in illuminating the features of reality they select, but in asking how they fare, how adequate and comprehensive they are, when they are forced to interpret reality as a whole. Nothing, incidentally, is changed in this process by insisting, as Hartshorne does, that the "whole" is not static and "all there" but a creative advance instead, since that simply means that there is more to interpret. Hegel's second demand is what he regarded as the self-criticism of the position, its criticism at the bar of reality. He held that philosophical positions are thus made to reveal their own inadequacy within an immanent, historical dialectic as distinct from being judged inadequate (if they are) by some external judge applying wholly antecedent criteria.

Hartshorne's treatment of the history of philosophy is not historical in Hegel's sense at all, since, once he has developed the basic ideas of neoclassical metaphysics — there are some twenty of them presented in his final chapter, even if only two of them are pivotal — he goes back with the wisdom (?) of hindsight (a "sight" overlooked!) to judge previous positions acknowledging their "insights," i.e., their accordances with, approximations to and anticipations of the truths of neoclassical metaphysics — and exposing their "oversights," i.e., their failures to see the truths of neoclassical metaphysics by persisting in adherence to other, less valid alternatives. I do not deny that there is much to learn from this procedure and I am much in sympathy with Hartshorne's avowed aim which is to discuss not what the great philosophers did for their ages, but what we can learn from them in solving our own philosophical problems. The inquiry is said, nevertheless, to focus on the way "some great philosophers furnish an illuminating background for a type of philosophy distinctive of this century" (p. ix), the most brilliant example of which is said to be the system of Whitehead. It would seem, then, that the history of Western philosophy, instead of being a series of footnotes to Plato, is rather a series of prophetic anticipations if not of Whitehead, then, of Hartshorne's neoclassical metaphysics.

The approach, however, is ahistorical, first, in that the appraisals of past philosophers are less rooted in the historical development or dialectic of ideas than in the criteria applied, as it were, *ab extra* from the standpoint of what Hartshorne regards as a superior process philosophy; what is valid in all thought, past or present, is what is in accord with, or does not preclude or contradict this position. There is a second sense in which the approach is ahistorical in that Hartshorne underestimates the actual force of historical conditions summed up in that happy phrase of his favorite philosopher, "the climate of opinion." He seems to think that every philosopher could have (should have) envisaged a far greater range of philosophical alternatives than he actually did—an important basis for many of Hartshorne's criticisms—and the question is whether this is reasonable to assume. Could Kant, for example, the philosopher of Newton, have *actually* (I mean "actually" and not in Hartshorne's hindsight), seriously entertained the indeterminate world of Bergson, Peirce, James, and Whitehead? Granted that he encountered insuperable problems with regard to freedom in not having done so and thus had to resort to the two story universe, the question remains, nevertheless, whether Hartshorne's method of supposing that at every juncture a philosopher's considering of a large range of philosophical possibilities (some of which may well have been "inconceivable" at the time) was itself a real possibility for each individual thinker. Hartshorne sees Hegel as imperious in his approach and grandiose in his vision, but there seems to be something of both in Hartshorne's ahistorical view of reason as largely that of formal logic, including, to be sure, modal logic and the logic of relatives, presenting to each thinker the theoretical possibilities that should have been envisaged.

Hartshorne's treatment of Aristotle forms one of the best chapters in the book, not least because of his appreciation for Aristotle's approximation to an important doctrine of neoclassical metaphysics, but also because of his modal view of time and eternity. As regards the doctrine, Hartshorne maintains that Aristotle did not know that both plants and animals are colonies of cells each of which is a living organism and not a mere organ. He was, moreover, unaware that plants, having no nerve cells, cannot, like animals possessing such cells, summon the entire colony to act as a single agent. Consequently, Hartshorne's claim, "the vegetative soul as a single entity is a myth" (p. 41). Aristotle did, however, according to Hartshorne, come close to the true insight when he claimed that a tree is "like a sleeping man who never wakes up" (Ibid.), because in deep and dreamless sleep the human body is like a multicellular plant, no more than a society of cells lacking a dominant monad—Leibniz—or a presiding route of occasions—Whitehead. Hartshorne rightly concludes that in such circumstances the conscious individual is in abeyance, a fact that should indicate the relativity of personal identity since the unity of the body exceeds that of the mind in any form of change. Or, as Hartshorne puts it, "Our (almost) vegetative individuality is never in abeyance'' (Ibid.), whereas our dominant monad is deposed from its king-like status many times during the year. This reasoning seems to me to exhibit the sort of synthesis of empirical knowledge and philosophical insight that we much need at present and do not often find.

As regards Aristotle's modal logic of becoming, Hartshorne stresses, above all, the emphasis he placed on the relation between modal and temporal distinctions, and especially his view, now mostly ignored, that modal concepts are about the structure of existence and not language. Hartshorne finds five ''Laws'' of objective modality in Aristotle, among which are the claim that an ''occurrence strictly presupposes its causal antecedents; but not vice versa, or given the present the past is wholly necessary but not the future'' (p. 44), and the claim that ''the future is a mixture of contingency and (conditional) necessity relative to the present'' (Ibid.). Since I cannot consider all five Laws here, and these two are most closely related to Hartshorne's concern to retain real possibility and creative becoming, I shall focus attention on one central point which has to do with Aristotle's seeming to suspend the law of excluded middle in expressing the indeterminacy of the future. Here, in my view, Hartshorne has succeeded both in preserving Aristotle's essential meaning and in showing why only two values are needed for propositional logic.

I shall set forth Hartshorne's main point by restating his argument. Aristotle begins by saying that either ''The fight will occur'' is true or ''The fight will not occur'' is true, but that which is true is indeterminate. Hartshorne finds this analysis ''unclear'' by which he means, I take it, that it erroneously places propositions about the future beyond the scope of excluded middle. Not wanting to allow that, Hartshorne proposes the ascription of a qualified ''indeterminacy'' to future reality, illustrated in the following way: If it is causally possible that at a time in the future I decide to do X, and also possible at that time that I decide to do something other than X, there arises the question of what the *truth* is about the future decision. Hartshorne's answer is that the truth is, I *may* or *may not* decide to do X— these being the range of present possibilities open. If, however, the assertion ''I *will* do X'' is made, that implies that non-X is already (eternally?) ruled out, and that conclusion is *false*, if the future is indeterminate in the relevant respect. So far, so good, Hartshorne, however, goes further (and this has got to be one of his best insights) in pointing out that the foregoing means *not* that a certain proposition is neither true nor false, but rather that one proposition ''I *may* or *may not* do X'' is true, while the two propositions ''I *will* do X'' and ''I *will* do either nothing or something instead of X'' are both false. This solution preserves both the logical principle and the conditional indeterminacy of the future. Aristotle's eternalistic bias led him, in the example of the sea fight, to ask which of the two propositions expressing the alternatives is true *now,* antecedent to tomorrow and indeed to all tomorrows, with the result that he lost sight of his own principle that the future is a mixture of contingency and conditional necessity.

Hartshorne's appraisal of Kant's thought has the great advantage that comes from confronting his doctrines directly and making reasoned judgments about their viability. He does not become mired in detail and, while his approach must omit a great deal—there is no mention of the transcendental deduction—it is in the end more fruitful than that of a Paton, helpful as his commentary is, who considers every detail in exposition without making definite assessments of the validity of Kant's claims. In this chapter, focusing on what Hartshorne calls Kant's "traditionalism," we can see Hartshorne's neoclassical metaphysics at work in forming the basis of his critical judgments. I cannot hope to deal with all of them; hence I shall select for comment the following topics: Kant and classical theism; Kant's phenomenalism; time and modality and substance and creativity or becoming.

Hartshorne is quite right in saying that Kant's conception of God as expressed in the Ideal of pure reason is essentially the same as that of classical theism (especially the formulation of Leibniz), except that he denied the possibility that belief in the reality of God could be justified on any grounds other than as a postulate of practical reason. In asserting human freedom, Kant, according to Hartshorne, saw it in exclusively noumenal terms and thus could not show its intelligibility in experiential terms. Hartshorne is also correct in regarding this view as traditional since, as he says, Augustine, Calvin, and Jonathan Edwards (I would not include Luther here as Hartshorne does), for example, were also hard put to find any place for phenomenal freedom or creative initiative in the face of the doctrine of predestination. Moreover, it cannot be denied that Kant was at something of a loss in explaining how noumenal freedom is related either to his phenomenal determinism or to the creative power of God.

As regards Hartshorne's account of Kant's phenomenalism or the, once again, traditional view that we cannot know the grounds of phenomena but only the relations between appearances, I believe that he is correct, but not entirely so. He says that Kant added another "traditional" element in the idea that what we experience is experience. "He had," Hartshorne writes, "the all too common conception of experience as not immediately and effectively aware of anything but itself and its own adjectives . . ." (p. 171). And he goes on to attribute this view to Descartes, whereas I would say that it is the underlying view of British empiricism, articulated in different ways by Locke, Berkeley, and Hume, and continued to the present. I entirely agree with Hartshorne that this conception of experience is, as he says, the "disease" of modern philosophy and I have argued in numerous writings that it is the same disease that the Pragmatists and others sought to stamp out. I am, however, reluctant to identify Kant wholly and unequivocally with that empiricism, and for at least two reasons. First, one cannot ignore the fact that for Kant, experience (*Erfahrung = empirische Erkenntnis*) is *not* the same as the immediate sense component alone, but is rather a synthesis of what he called the matter of intuition determined by the pure categories of the understanding. This point is expressed in Kant's claim that the minimum valid unity of experience is a *judgment* and not the atomic ideas of the classical view denoted by a *term*. The entire intent of Kant's deduction is to show that to think an *object* as an intersubjective reality and not merely as a set of subjective impressions, requires the universality and necessity bestowed by the categories; they are the necessary conditions both for something to *be* and to *be thought of* as an object. Therefore, in fairness to Kant it is essential to note that he has an ''objective'' phenomenalism and, while I agree with Hartshorne that Kant mistakenly thought the relation between the appearance and the in-itself to be a mystery, we should not overlook the unique sort of ''phenomenalism'' Kant espouses and place him in the same category with the empiricism he was criticizing, even if he accepted more of it than he realized.

My second reason for hesitation in accepting Hartshorne's interpretation of Kant as ''extreme'' phenomenalism is that, unlike Descartes and British empiricism from Hume to Russell and Ayer, Kant does not pursue the problem of how to reach the ''external world.'' For those thinkers for whom the object of knowledge is some immediate impression or idea on the ''inside,'' so to speak, there is the unavoidable problem of how to surmount that starting point and reach the external world. So stated, this problem can be seen to be insoluble in advance because the only sort of data one might cite in making the transition to an outer world would be more of the same, i.e., those same immediate impressions. Curiously enough Kant, though he did hanker after the in-itself—a mistake on my view—always regarded the phenomena as having intersubjective status through the force of the categories and, except in the problematic section on the refutation of idealism, he does not envisage reaching the external world as the sort of problem that it was for Russell. Kant's conception of the nature of knowledge and hence of experience may indeed pose its problems, especially since it depends entirely on identifying ''object'' with ''object of knowledge,'' but I do not believe that his *criticism* of classical empiricsm should be ignored.

In his pursuit of the appearance-reality relation in Kant, Hartshorne makes two points that I believe are correct and important. First, he is right in saying that, for Kant, it is our involvement in *passivity* that leads to our being able to know no more than appearance (whereas God alone knows reality), and that, by combining Aristotle's Unmoved Mover with the scholastic idea of divine knowledge, Kant ''discredit(ed) our human form of knowing'' (p. 172). Consequently, since he rightly proposes to give up the unmoved but omniscient deity, Hartshorne looks for a new way of understanding the limits of human knowing.

The second point has to do with perception and passivity. As against Kant, Hartshorne maintains that our limitation in experiencing is not our passivity but rather that we are not passive enough. Hartshorne's point is that we cannot submit sufficiently to delicate stimuli and thus that we fail to record the micro-constituents of nature so that ultimately "our responses are crude simplifications" (p. 174). This point has a measure of truth to the degree that we obviously omit much that comes within the actual purview of experience because it is not noticed. If, however, Hartshorne means something more than this, as he certainly appears to do when he says that in pain "it is not alone we that suffer," but "certain of our cells," then the question must arise as to whether we can be said to "experience" the suffering of the cells in the same sense as we experience the pain. Is it really illuminating to say, largely in order to avoid "idealism," that our pain appears in "blurred fashion" as the suffering of the cells? The same goes for colors and their correlative wave-lengths on the colorimeter. Is my experience of a red object the appearance to my visual apparatus in "blurred fashion" of light having a certain wave-length? I realize that this issue—the problem of pan-psychism, or whatever term one wants to use—is too extensive to be joined here, but it deserves to be mentioned at least in connection with Hartshorne's criticism of Kant's emphasis on passivity.

Since I want to consider Hartshorne's discussion of Kant on time and modality in more detail below, I shall pass on to the third topic of substance and creative becoming. Here I believe that Hartshorne is right in his criticism of Kant and that hence he must be credited with an important insight (hindsight?). Arguing for the asymmetry required for cumulative creativity with directionality, Hartshorne rightly points out that in Kant's arguments for causality aimed at distinguishing objective from subjective succession, he retained the classical view of causality that runs counter to his own argument since that view was aimed at reducing the relation to symmetry (p. 181). Kant's limitation here stems from the primacy he accorded mechanics and physics and, while he did introduce the biological dimension in *The Critique of Judgment*, the concepts of becoming and of process as we know them today, and indeed as they figured in Hegel's thought, did not play a prominent part in Kant's philosophy. In this regard, I can wholly agree with Hartshorne when he says of the age of Newton—and of Kant—"The concept of reason of the age was inadequate to this task [of understanding the soul's self-creation]. The ultimate function of reason is to guide the creation of additional definiteness and therefore new values, not to prescribe or compel the derivation of equivalences, of effects merely equal to their causes" (p. 184). Another way of saying this is that Kant, as Hegel saw, opted in the end for the primacy of the understanding as *the* criterion and, consequently, for the subordination of reason. One of the major problems of our time is that we have followed Kant's lead and there has been a widespread loss of faith in the reason that Hegel, Whitehead, and Hartshorne, each in their own way, hold to be essential.

Hartshorne commends Kant's treatment of the modal categories in terms of temporality—correlating possibility with *some time* or other; existence with a *determinate time*, and necessity with *all times*—which is in effect the determination of time through the three quantifiers of the Aristotelian logic, some, one, and all. I have no quarrel with this correlation and I am at one with Hartshorne in holding that, while there can be a formal treatment of modality (p. 43), modal concepts are not primarily about either formal logic or language, but about, in his phrase, the temporal-eternal structure of existence. This point is reenforced by his discussion of Aristotle's (p. 47) view that whether something is to be called contingent or necessary "is to be determined by inspection of its nature" — the doctrine of objective modality. Hartshorne goes on to say that this doctrine is the answer to Kant's claim that an ontological argument must start with the premise that existence is always a predicate. What Hartshorne does not notice, however, is that Kant's rejection of an ontological argument is bound up with his denial of the objective modality that Hartshorne, in company with Aristotle, maintains. In considering the modal categories, Kant held that they are different from those of quantity, quality, and relation in one crucial respect— "they do not in the least enlarge the concept to which they are attached as predicates. They only express the relation of the concept to the faculty of knowledge" (A 219–B 266). The consequence of this difference becomes evident in Kant's schematization of the modal categories where "existence" appears in all three. "The schema of possibility," he writes, "is the agreement of the synthesis of different representations with the conditions of time in general . . . The schema is therefore the determination of the representation of a thing at some time or other" (A 144–B 184). True, he does not here say "existence" at some time or other, but if we consider the characterization of possibility in the postulates of Empirical Thought, it is clear that it is existence that is involved. He writes: "That which agrees with the formal conditions of experience, that is, with the conditions of intuition and of concepts, is *possible*" (A 218–B 266). Since "experience" was understood by Kant as *empirische Erkenntnis* or knowledge of objects the material for which is given in intuition, possibility here can mean nothing other than "possibility for *existing* as an object at some time or other." Nothing, in short, can be "possible" but an object as defined by the conditions of possible experience.[1]

The recurrence of existence in the explication of the modal categories is more perspicuous in the schemas of existence and necessity. There we are told that "The schema of actuality is existence in some determinate time" and "The schema of necessity is existence of an object at all times" (A 145). Two further consequences follow; first, the separation of the modal categories from the content or nature of an object makes it impossible to determine whether something is contingent or necessary by an inspection of that nature, and, second, it is clear that Kant has only one "real" mode, namely, existence understood in the sense in which it is legitimately applied to spatio-temporal objects, the only things that, according to Kant, we can know. Thus there can be, on Kant's view, no distinction between the *natures* of things insofar as they fall under the modal categories since the only distinction involved is the temporal quantifier. Hence the idea of the necessarily existent as in the case of God whose *nature* determines the mode, could be understood by Kant in no sense other than that there is some object that "always" exists, except that this "existence" is not that of a necessary being, but only of an *object* that is at "all times." In the end, Kant's elaborate attack on the idea that existence is a real predicate in the refutation of the ontological argument is not as important as the fact that this conclusion is a direct consequence of his non-objective conception of modality and his restriction of "existence" to objects whose sensible material can be given only in intuition.[2]

Hartshorne hits upon this point himself in his discussion of what he calls Aristotle's "First Modal Law" — the equivalence of "necessary" and "eternal" — when he rightly points out that necessity is the criterion and is a matter of the examination of concepts, whereas eternity, if taken as an observable fact, can never be such a criterion. "We cannot," he writes, "watch something existing and go on watching it forever and thus eventually find out that it never fails to exist" (p. 48). But this is precisely what Kant would have to rely on for the support of his "at all times," and this is another way of saying that Kant's "necessity" has to be of some empirical sort since it is determined by a theory of knowledge within the bounds of sense.

There is a considerable danger that Hegel's thought will be misunderstood at the most basic level if one approaches him, as Hartshorne clearly does, with the idea that his philosophy deals primarily with "polarities" or "contrasts" and that it has the aim of providing a "synthesis" of the two elements. Apart from the fact, now well known, that the "thesis-antithesis-synthesis" rubric of the textbook histories of philosophy is virtually absent from Hegel's writings, there is the not less important consideration that he goes out of his way in many passages to distinguish the development that is truly dialectical in character from the sort of thing represented by the confrontation of polar opposites. Following is one such passage from *The Philosophy of Nature* in the *Encyclopedia*. Before quoting it, however, I must emphasize the fact that I am not concerned with his concept of necessity for present purposes, but only with what he says in criticism of polarity. Hegel writes:

> There has been a lot of talk in physics about polarity. This concept is a great advance in the metaphysics of the sciences; for the concept of polarity is simply nothing else

but the specific relation of necessity between two different terms, which are one, in that when one is given, the other is also given. *But this polarity is restricted to opposition*. However, through the opposition there is also given the return of the opposition into unity, and this is the *third term* which the necessity of the Concept (*Begriff*) has over and above polarity. . . . In Spirit (*Geist*), *the fundamental form of necessity is the triad.*'' (*Encycl.* 248, *Zusatz*; emphasis added).

If we add to this the numerous passages in which Hegel describes the Concept as a *development* through stages or ''moments,'' we can see both the difference between dialectic and polarity and the inadequacy of the latter as a key to Hegel's thought. To begin with, polarity as such is a dyad where the two members are *symmetrical*; if A is the polar opposite of B, B is the polar opposite of A and on this conception there can be oscillation, but no *advance*, whereas Hegel tells us repeatedly that the essence of dialectic is an advance to a definite result, something that *has become*. This can be understood only if there is an *asymmetrical* relation in the triadic form of dialectic wherein the first member is to become by incorporating the second into itself and returning to itself as the third member in the form of the concrete unity that is the result. The process has a unique direction and cannot be reversed. Thus, for example, if we were to conceive of abstract freedom and necessity as no more than a polar dyad, there could be no advance to what Hegel calls concrete freedom, or the unity of abstract freedom and necessity or determination, just because the dyad leaves us with nothing more than the opposition between the two and no basis for a passage to the future result.

An even clearer illustration of the point is to be found in Hegel's reconstruction of Kant's triad—unity, plurality, totality. First, there is the abstract unity of, say, Socrates (Socrates *is* Socrates), and then there is the advance to the abstract plurality resulting from analysis (Socrates is a philosopher, Athenian, gadfly, etc.) and finally to the concrete totality which is at the same time the concrete unity of Socrates the individual whose concrete unity as such is the togetherness of his abstract unity and just that plurality. Again, the development is asymmetrical in that we attain the totality only through the movement of mediation or analysis that issues in a higher unity embracing both the abstract unity and the abstract plurality. Without the asymmetrical process there can be no final result.

None of this can be understood either through polarity or the principle of contrast alone because both place the opposition in a symmetrical relation within a dyad where nothing is to be found but the opposition and hence there can be no linear movement beyond. Stated in the most general terms, the one principle at work throughout Hegel's philosophy is that there is always a something that is to become and then an other through which this something must pass as the medium for its development, but it is not the case that that other is to become in the same sense. It is for this reason that one has to speak of an *asymmetry* in the process; without that there is either no becoming with a definite outcome or mere becoming with no result.

Against this background, let us see how Hartshorne interprets Hegel. For a start, it is necessary to see what Hartshorne means by the principle of contrast since he credits Hegel (along with Whitehead) with grasping this principle while at the same time charging Hegel with applying it without proper restriction. As far as I can see, Hartshorne understands the principle of contrast as essentially a dyad. The occasions of its application bear this out. In his discussion of tbe Stoics (Ch. 5), but pointedly against Blanshard (this is a history of philosophy to conjure with!), Hartshorne maintains that necessity is a "special case" and makes sense only in contrast with there being many things not necessary. This would seem to be a "bare" contrast. In his consideration of the upshot of Medieval thought (p. 77), contrast is exhibited in the distinction between the essence of something and its accidents or contingent qualities. Once again, bare contrast. In the section on Hume (p. 141); it is said that *meaning* requires contrast such that if there were no independence, to say that "*X* depends on *Y*" would say "nothing distinctive" about *X* and *Y* since there would be only one organic whole in which nothing is independent of anything else. Again, the contrast appears as no more than a dyadic relation between dependence and independence. Incidentally, I am not objecting to the points Hartshorne is making in these particular applications; I am merely trying to understand what he means by the principle of contrast. In the discussion of Hume and Bradley (p. 260), the contrast is between the extremes (polarities?) involved in the pluralism and monism issue, and it appears that the contrast intended implies that there is nothing in between (dyad?). In the discussion of Spinoza (p. 369), Hartshorne claims that his denial of all contingency deprives the contrasting term or necessity of its meaning. Throughout all these instances, the principle of contrast is understood as dyadic and, while it serves to call attention to the existence of polar opposites, it will not suffice as it stands to point the way to the proper resolution of any of the problems posed by these opposites. The conclusion at this point is that something in addition to this principle will be required for understanding Hegel in view of what I have shown above about his criticism of polarity in favor of dialectic. The curious fact is that, while criticizing Hegel for an "unlimited use of contrast" (p. 205)—Hegel is said to have taken the "other" to mean "other than" *all* the others in a wholesale sense, whereas the proper contrast is with *some* others (see below), Hartshorne does see that, for Hegel, "in the opposition of subject-object, the subject overlaps" (p. 196). This, of course, is just what Hegel maintains throughout and points to precisely what I suggested previously in calling attention to the asymmetry involved in dialectic. Hence I find it difficult to understand how Hartshorne can say several pages later on that "where opposing predicates apply" we can always ask, "which predicate describes the togetherness of the two? . . . With ultimate contraries, one pole is the inclusive one" (p. 206). And Hartshorne goes on to say that, for Aristotle, the individual includes the universal, whereas Hegel is said to hold the opposite. But of course Hegel has indicated the inclusive category and that is precisely where the asymmetry comes in—freedom is the inclusive category in relation to the opposite, necessity, and the subject is the inclusive category with regard to the opposite, object. As regards the individual, for Hegel the full *triad* in question is *universal*, *particular*, and *individual* by which he understands the universal here to be the abstract individual—I = I—the particular to be the realization or self-specification of that universality, and the concrete individual the unity of the two. Hegel, therefore, has his own version of how the individual "includes the universal." Hartshorne, however, has only a dyadic model—universal and individual—and then asks which of the two is the inclusive one, whereas Hegel indicates quite clearly that the universal is the inclusive category, *although not in the abstract sense of a common feature*, and that the individual is the concrete result of the specified universal. One cannot fit Hegel's Concept into a dyadic schema (his *dyads* are developed in the section on "Essence" in the *Logic* where they are predominantly oppositions and hence fall short of the further mediation provided by the Concept for which the minimum unit of meaning is the *triad*), and therefore Hegel's asymmetries focus on the first that is to become, the second or other as the medium of realization, and the third as the return on a higher level to the first as the concrete unity of the two. Hartshorne misses this and says (p. 211, n.2) that Hegel did not distinguish between symmetrical and asymmetrical views of otherness. This is indeed odd when the entire dialectical movement depends on asymmetry and Hegel always indicates the inclusive term, for that is precisely what determines the actual development represented in the triad.

What Hartshorne fails to see in his treatment of Hegel is what may be called the kind or degree of otherness articulated in the particular phases or "moments" in the process of becoming. The point is that all of Hegel's categories develop in richness of content as they proceed from each other in the dialectical advance, and hence one cannot think of any category as simply recurrent with an abstract identity that expresses sameness without difference. This is true of otherness as well. At the lowest level (i.e., the most abstract) of articulation—the contrast of Being and Nothing —we come as close to "bare" otherness as it is possible to come; in the *Logic* the categories of Being are taken as monads and pass into each other with an absolute minimum of specification. When we come, however, to the categories of Essence all of which are manifested as dyads, it is possible to refer not merely to otherness as such, but to "its other" or a new degree of otherness, something that could not be articulated in the earlier phase of the processs. And, of course, as one moves from Logic on to Nature and Spirit, otherness becomes increasingly specified and internalized. Nature, as the assundered form of the Idea in space, is described by Hegel as the Idea in its "extreme" otherness, and yet Nature as such is also a manifestation of Spirit in the form of genera, species, and laws, so that in the end it is not *alien* to Spirit as in the Cartesian dualism where thought and extension are so "barely" other that they can be related only by the conjunction.

Spirit, morever, is said to be other than Nature with respect to Spirit's proper essence, but in the development in Nature from mechanism through chemism to what Hegel calls teleology, there appear the phenomena of life and the animal soul which are, for want of a better term, "closer" to (i.e., "less other than") Spirit than what we find in the inorganic world. The point is made in an even more forceful way in the triad of Spirit as such—subjective Mind—objective Mind—Absolute Mind—where Hegel says that in this sphere there is "no out and out (*durchaus*) other," because *all* Mind is self-determined, and yet subjective Mind is only potentially Mind because it lacks the degree of unity (i.e., degree of otherness incorporated) possessed by objective and Absolute Mind. Hence, although in the sphere of Mind as such there is no totally other, subjective Mind is still to a degree other than the succeeding two forms.

One must pay attention to these degrees of relevant otherness in Hegel and this I believe that Hartshorne does not do. The reason seems to be that he makes an all or nothing demand (curious for Hartshorne) on Hegel's system as a whole that there be a distinction between "all" and "some" (dyad?) with respect to otherness, as can be seen from the following passage:

> The Hegelian paradox that things imply their own others is derived from the argument: X cannot be other than Y unless there is Y for X to be other than: hence, Hegel concludes, *difference entails dependence* of each thing on every other. However, as we saw in chapters 13 and 14, although each thing must contrast with many other things to be what it is, it need not and cannot contrast with every other thing past, present, or future . . . (p. 205).

Here it seems that Hartshorne is concerned mainly to attack what he takes to be the main thesis of Hegel, namely, the totally internal relatedness of everything or the "block universe" that James objected to so strenuously in the form of Royce's Absolute. Whether Hegel's view is correctly represented by Hartshorne in the highly abstract and general formula of the dependence of every thing on every other is open to question and is too complex a matter to be settled here. But my contention is that in fastening on this point with his "all" or "some" alternative (Hegel's "either/or" of the understanding) addressed to the system as a whole, Hartshorne fails to see the subtlety of Hegel's treatment of otherness in the particular stages of the dialectical advance. For Hegel, otherness is never a wholesale affair.

There is much to be learned from Hartshorne's treatment of the history of philosophy, unconventional and uneven though it may be. He exhibits a seriousness and a candor that are sometimes lacking on the present philosophical scene where so many tend to mistake intellectual fireworks for philosophical illumination. I applaud him for these virtues. And yet I cannot avoid the sense that he betrays an excessive self-confidence in his logical argumentation, and a severity in exposing the oversights of others which at times borders on the sort of moralism we associate with Fichte for whom philosophical error was tantamount to moral deficiency. The self-confidence, as is evident throughout the book, stems from Hartshorne's firm belief that he is virtually alone among those who still pursue the metaphysical quest in exhibiting the logical rigor that, in conversation at any rate, he always associates with Carnap. I hope that the preceding discussion, especially in connection with Hegel, will raise some doubts about the viability of so formal a logic for dealing with metaphysical issues. As William Barrett has pointed out, it is curious indeed that philosophers with such diverse philosophical positions as Russell, Wittgenstein, and Whitehead should find themselves appealing to essentially the same formal logic. This suggests that the relation between such logic and philosophy can only be quite external.

As regards Hartshorne's firm judgments concerning the oversights of others, it is not without significance that those of us who have known him over the years have often wondered why he never seems to look puzzled or in doubt regardless of the objections raised against his views. Raphael Demos many years ago said, in a response from the audience to which Hartshorne had just given a paper, "Charles, you know too much about God!" It is noteworthy in this regard that, according to the Bible, God was sometimes said to be "torn within" in the face of a difficult judgment.

JOHN E. SMITH

DEPARTMENT OF PHILOSOPHY
YALE UNIVERSITY
FEBRUARY 1987

NOTES

1. It is worth noting here that in dealing with Kant it is necessary to distinguish "possibility" as a modal category from the "possibility" that figures in the transcendental enterprise of discovering the conditions for the "possibility" of experience as objective knowledge.

2. It will not do to call up, in Kant's defense, his own claim that the modal categories (A 220–B 267) are not to have a merely logical significance expressing the form of *thought*, but are to refer to the possibility, actuality, and necessity of *things*, since in order to have this reference the modal categories "must concern possible experience and its synthetic unity, in which alone objects of knowledge can be given." Once again we are confined to objects that may be, are, or must be, except that these determinations are *extrinsic* to the natures of whatever objects are in question.

26

George R. Lucas, Jr.

HARTSHORNE AND THE DEVELOPMENT OF PROCESS PHILOSOPHIES

T hroughout his long and distinguished career, Charles Hartshorne has made substantial constructive contributions to the tradition of process philosophy. He has also, on numerous occasions, made energetic and enthusiastic attempts to interpret the historical development of this tradition. Motivated by a sense of intellectual and historical justice, inspired by a passionate concern that achievements of genuine value should not be lost, he has called attention to creative and original thinkers whose contributions to philosophic insight are customarily overlooked, including Faustus Socinus, Ramanuja, the Buddhists, G. T. Fechner, and Friedrich von Schelling.[1] He has gone beyond the traditional mythical ascription of the origins of process philosophy to its patron saint, Heraclitus, and suggested instead that the history of this movement stretches back even further to Ikhnaton of Egypt (ca. 1350 B.C.E.).[2] Finally, Hartshorne has aroused genuine controversy by castigating many of the main figures in the history of philosophy for their intellectual weaknesses or failures of imagination and insight at strategic junctures in that history. Those unfortunate enough to receive a poor grade on one of Hartshorne's infamous historical "report cards" may find the origin of their failure not merely in what they *did* say—but in what they could have or should have been able to say, but *didn't*.[3]

My aims in this essay are modest by comparison. I will offer a brief outline of the historical development of process philosophy, and suggest the place of Professor Hartshorne's own contributions within that larger history. My approach to the history of process philosophies is more narrowly focused than Hartshorne's own. I locate the origins of modern process philosophies in a series of intellectual revolts, beginning in Enlightenment Europe midway through the eighteenth century, and extending throughout most of the nineteenth century in a variety of forms. While I cannot offer an extensively detailed treatment here,[4]

I will suggest that the tradition encompasses four distinct schools of thought, motivated by quite different philosophical agendas. While it has been customary to link Hartshorne with Whitehead in this tradition, my interpretation will lend support to those few dissenters, recently including Hartshorne himself, who have stressed his differences from Whitehead and his radical transformation of the scope and direction of contemporary process thought.[5]

With a more detailed historical schematic background in place, we will be able to view Hartshorne's own contribution as the vigorous defense of an historically distinct school of *idealistic* process metaphysics. While it once constituted a lively philosophical alternative early in this century in the works of W. E. Hocking, E. S. Brightman, A. S. Pringle-Pattison, Bernard Bosanquet, H. H. Joachim, W. P. Montague, R. G. Collingwood, and a host of other idealist defenders of personalism and pluralism,[6] this particular "process" strand of idealism has all but disappeared today.

I. FROM PRE-DARWINIAN EVOLUTIONISTS TO HEGEL

Process philosophy is customarily delineated through the specification of a series of descriptive categories, stressing in particular: the central metaphysical importance of time and change; the ontological primacy of events in place of an underlying and static substance; flux, becoming, novelty and finite freedom or partial self-creativity; internal relatedness, organicism and holism; a doctrine of critical realism which emphasizes the phenomenological interconnections of subject and object, knower and known; and finally a doctrine of "experience" understood as co-extensive throughout the whole of nature, rather than inexplicably limited to an arbitrarily narrow range of entities.

This list of descriptive categories and dogmatic perspectives is by now all too familiar to disciples and critics of the process tradition alike. What is less often appreciated, however, is that virtually all of these familiar categories arise in a wide range of polemical or rhetorical reactions against the prevailing mainstream philosophical and cultural worldviews of Enlightenment Europe. The consolidation of these different polemical movements into a recognizable "process tradition" occurs gradually, and is only recognizable as something of a unified tradition by the end of the nineteenth century. Prior to the twentieth-century revolutions in astronomy and physics which inspired the philosophy of Whitehead, this consolidation and unification were achieved primarily by devotees of the life sciences: vitalists, emergent evolutionists, and in general, those philosophers whom I have elsewhere termed "evolutionary cosmologists."[7]

Evolutionist doctrine of one sort or another constituted the chief rallying point of the earliest process revolutionaries. This fundamental point is often lost in the aftermath of Thomas Huxley's dramatic defense of Darwinian naturalism against its theological critics. The culturally visible but intellectually spurious opposition of Darwinism and Christian theology masks a covert and far more profound transformation of evolutionist theory effected by later neo-Darwinians, such as Weissman and Ernst Haeckel. That is, these later scientists developed a "defense" of evolution which achieved a rapprochement with precisely the sort of reductionism and mechanistic materialism that evolutionist theories originally intended to *supplant* as conceptually inadequate. The central issue here is thus *not* primarily theism versus atheism, for Diderot, Lamarck, de Maillet, and other early advocates of "evolutionary transformism" were every bit as hostile to Deism and Christian creationism as the most radical contemporary neo-Darwinian defender of biological evolution. At stake, rather, was what counts as acceptable scientific methodology, and what sort of larger cosmology underlies the investigative methods that are finally employed. These early "prophets of evolution" found reductionism and mechanism utterly deficient and unsuitable in every respect.

Against what they perceived as the intellectually stifling and politically enervating conception of a static, fixed, closed, deterministic universe assembled and relentlessly operated by Divine Providence, eighteenth-century French philosophes and encyclopedists marshalled philosophic argument and preliminary geological and paleontological evidence to suggest that the earth was vastly older, and infinitely more changeable and mysterious than this prevailing cosmology would suggest. Benoit de Maillet's *Telliamed* (1748) offered a fantastic, speculative, and highly imaginative account of the origins of species in vast primordial seas impregnated with the "seeds" ("semences") of all life forms, which have largely receded and left the earth covered with fossil remains. Maupertuis, in the *Venus physique* (1745) and more forcefully in *The System of Nature* (1751) offered a quite different and extraordinary account of genetic mutation and recombination in living species, mediated by "particles" with prehensive or low-grade sentient properties. And in *Thoughts on the Interpretation of Nature* (1751), Diderot brought to a focus these revolutionary intellectual currents in what one prominent intellectual historian has called "the most complete and brilliant speculative exposition of [evolutionism] in his time."[8]

Diderot's doctrine of "transformism" stressed the dynamic and self-generated properties of living organisms, and postulated the lengthy primordial history and gradual evolutionary development of each distinct species. Years later in the *Dream of d'Alembert* (1769), as well as in his *Elements of Physiology* (c. 1780), Diderot explored the wider cosmological implications of his evolutionary transformist approach. He postulated a radical reformulation of "materialism" emphasizing an organic conception of the universe—self-sufficient and perpetually organizing and re-organizing itself—a concept of "matter" as entailing either inert or "living" sensitivity, and an organizing principle inherent in all living bodies, "un principe vital," which pervades, animates, vivifies, and unifies the functioning of a living organic whole.

It is likewise this spirit of protest and revolution, more than the elegant and systematic details of his chemical, biological, and physiological theories, that animates Lamarck's evolutionary hypothesis. Biologists then and now concentrate on the details of Lamarck's functional theories about the decay of vestigial limbs and organs through disuse, and the inheritance of acquired traits. These particular details of "Lamarckism" follow, however, from Lamarck's broader metaphysical commitments to the continuity of nature as an active, self-organizing, organic whole, characterized by a dynamic reciprocity and interconnectedness among all the constituent parts.[9]

Johann Wolfgang von Goethe, pursuing studies of botany early in his career, offered a highly fanciful account—which many subsequent commentators interpret as proto-evolutionary—of the development of existing botanical species from primal botanical forms or *Urpflanze*.[10] In physics, Goethe's novel approach to optics in his celebrated *Zur Farbenlehre* (1810) suggested that the spectrum of colors was a manifestation of the subjective experience of light. His masterfully artistic portrayal in *Faust* (1831) of nature as a vast cosmic organism characterized by strife, suffering, and ceaseless metamorphosis and becoming, is metaphysically of a piece with Lamarck's concept of nature—so much so that an influential American geologist and naturalist later in the nineteenth century held that Lamarck and Goethe were scientific collaborators.[11]

The example of Goethe in particular suggests how the revolutionary themes (and the categories of process metaphysics) contained in proto-evolutionary accounts almost a century before Darwin were subsequently taken up as weapons in the hands of later Romantic philosophers, who were less interested in the radical re-interpretation than in the total undermining of scientific methodology. Those Romantics whose radical humanistic values had been forged in the aftermath of Rousseau and the French Revolution, rightly discerned allies among the proponents of these early speculative evolutionary cosmologies emerging from the life sciences. The latter movements seemed to expose, on experiential and empirical grounds, the moral and intellectual bankruptcy of the earlier dehumanizing synthesis of mathematical and physical analysis developed by Galileo, Newton, and Laplace.

Schelling, in his *System of Transcendental Idealism* (1800) brought to a focus his own earlier works (which had emphasized the role of "force" rather than "matter" as the unifying conception of the physical sciences) in order to elaborate and defend a mystical Romantic conception of Nature as the infinite and restless self-activity of a living, organic Whole.

Hegel, by contrast, sharply rejected the anti-intellectual and anti-rationalistic implications of Schelling's romanticist approach, even as he dismissed as fanciful the notion of actual biological evolution. But Hegel's *Encyclopedia* discussion (ca. 1817–1831) of the philosophy of nature is replete with appreciative references to Goethe's physical and biological theories, which partially explains why few commentators today are led to read and take this material seriously. While he decisively rejected the specifics of the Lamarckian-romantic theory of evolutionary transformation in nature (*Enc.* sec. 249, 252, 339), Hegel nonetheless adopted many of the same underlying metaphysical positions, both in criticizing the explanatory and conceptual shortcomings of materialism, mechanism, and reductionism in physics, chemistry, and especially in biology, as well as in developing an alternative methodological approach which he termed "Organische Physik" (cf. *Enc.* sec. 337–376).[12]

Hegel evidently eschewed the idea of a real, temporal process or flux of organic forms in nature. Nevertheless, he developed a kind of "organic teleology" or "organic mechanism" (to utilize Whitehead's later phrase) applicable throughout the natural realm, which he proposed as a conceptually more adequate model of explanation than that afforded by Galileo's and Newton's metaphysics of mechanism and causal determinism.[13] Hegel's elaborate theory of teleological explanation emphasized precisely the protest of early evolutionists and Romantic philosophers against inert matter, vacuous actuality, and their attendant conceptions, and proposed simultaneously an alternative account of real internal relations in organic unities which was in most essential respects hospitable to the evolutionist and Romantic conceptions of nature. Moreover, he adapted the idea of "evolutionary transformation" to firmer empirical ground as a mode of interpreting cultural and historical development, and thus offered one of the clearest and most influential models of "historical process." His family of concepts—negation, alienation, and dialectic—and his interpretation of history as the emergence, through dialectical struggle, of competing forms of cultural self consciousness, manifest a strong resemblance to the metaphysical tenets of struggle, strife, and evolutionary emergence in Romantic *Naturphilosophie* and Lamarckian evolutionist theory. I suggest that these concepts outline a dynamic and temporal "logic of process" over against the static subject-predicate Aristotelian deductive logic characteristic of the more prevalent and traditional methods of analysis, which Hegel had likewise dismissed as inadequate in his lengthy *Science of Logic* (1812–1816).

II. Post-Hegelian Idealism and Later Evolutionary Cosmology

Hegel's theories of organic purposive behavior in nature and history, and his sweeping conceptions of historical evolutionary development of nations and cultures exerted profound influence on subsequent idealists of both "left" and "right" persuasion. The theological and politically conservative reading of the Hegelian right wing retained principally the notions of organism, teleology, and interconnectedness, while extensively downplaying the more disturbing notions of finite freedom, novelty and creativity, contingency, temporal flux and becoming.[14] Especially in the hands of later English interpreters, such as McTaggart and Bradley, this was effected by virtually ignoring the *Jenaschriften* and the *Phenomenology* in favor of the *Encyclopedia*, and even there passing over the extensive discussions of *Naturphilosophie* which were technically difficult and obscure—and by the late nineteenth century, no longer very meaningful. It is, of course, primarily this reading of Hegel which is familiar to Anglo-American audiences, and which was rejected by early twentieth-century realists and empiricists, including Whitehead. What is important and rather ironic in historical perspective is that, in rejecting the dominant Anglicized interpretation of Hegel based on a selective reading of the *Encyclopedia,* many later realist critics and idealist revolutionaries inadvertently recovered the more salient features of this earlier metaphysical revolution originally effected by the younger Hegel and his Romantic and evolutionist predecessors, as I suggest below.

In the political and anti-metaphysical left-wing interpretation of Hegel, by contrast, emphasis was placed instead precisely on the notions of the emergence of finite freedom and liberation through historical struggle and transformation. But this emphasis (most notably by Arnold Ruge and the young Marx) on the importance of time, freedom, change, and history as novel teleological process tended to come at the expense of organic interrelatedness and holism—those essential but metaphysical properties of *Geist* in the *Phenomenology* and *Rechtsphilosophie* which these later critics dismissed as reactionary and oppressive. It was instead the retention of the notion of dialectical process and progress in history and culture that identifies Hegel and his left wing interpreters as contributors to the process tradition. In light of these historical developments, it is not surprising that contemporary process philosophers, including Hartshorne, have intuited some common metaphysical ground, even though they might not otherwise completely agree with this strand of Romantic-political idealism.

I have suggested that evolutionist theories initially were not so much a matter of scientific controversy as they were a rallying point for anti-scientific sentiment. Early evolutionists were attacking the inadequacy of prevailing assumptions about the nature of scientific method, and the concept of nature such methodological assumptions underwrote. As this reigning natural worldview was also strongly associated with the prevailing political and religious ethos to which these critics took strenuous objection, the evolutionists from Diderot to Lamarck intended nothing less than a wholesale overthrow of the established Enlightenment cultural order.

I have also suggested that this underlying agenda meshed well with the more explicitly revolutionary agenda of Romantic philosophers and litterateurs. Through the natural allegiance of these two cultural currents (aided by the fluctuation between both camps of influential figures like Goethe), the main insights of the early speculative evolutionists came to exert a powerful influence on the development of post-Kantian German idealism, even when, as in the case of Hegel himself, the central tenet—a temporal flux and gradual transformation of form in nature—is rejected. Hegelian idealism, with its focus on the rise and variation of forms of self consciousness in the historical process—indebted as this approach was to early evolutionists and Romantics—in turn exerted a powerful imaginative influence on later evolutionary cosmology.

In *The Origin of Species* (1859), Darwin finally managed to set the basic evolutionist hypothesis on firm empirical and scientific footing, and thereby apparently removed it once and for all from the sphere of Romantic or speculative cosmology. Afterwards, however, the central remaining scientific and speculative problems seemed constituted around the post-Hegelian issue of *how* to account for the emergence of *mind and consciousness* in the evolutionary flux. Darwin had accounted for a great deal of extant paleontological evidence on a purely naturalistic basis with his twin principles of random variation and natural selection. But lacking the subsequent studies on genetic inheritance of Father Gregor Mendel, Darwin's hypothesis seemed hopelessly improbable in accounting for the evolution of such complexity and diversity as was actually observed, particularly at the higher reaches of the "great chain of being" where mind and consciousness seemed to dominate. In fact, the whole evolutionist hypothesis seemed contradictory in light of the development of the theory of entropy in thermodynamics and statistical physics. Such problems drove both Darwin and Thomas Huxley further toward a Lamarckian formulation in later years.

These critical issues became the cornerstone of the later evolutionary cosmologists, the "vitalists" and "emergent evolutionists" of the turn of the century. They accepted the basic evolutionist approach, and by and large acknowledged their indebtedness to Darwin. However, as with him, they felt compelled in the light of these paradoxical results to "rescue" the theory by recourse to a variety of ad hoc hypotheses: élan vital (Bergson), evolutionary love (Peirce), emergents and resultants (C. Lloyd Morgan), the inexplicable but stubborn tendency toward the formation of wholes (Jan Smuts), "telefinalism" (Lecomte du Noüy), the "nisus" or creative urge of primordial space-time (Samuel Alexander), the non-material agency of "entelechy" particularized in individual organic forms as "psychoids" (Hans Driesch), or the hypothesis of "orthogenesis" with its attendant notion of a convergent theological "Omega-point" (Teilhard de Chardin).[15]

It is vital to appreciate the sharp differences and disagreements among these thinkers. While Bergson, Hans Driesch, and Teilhard are vitalists, others, including Morgan and Smuts, were sharply critical of ad hoc vitalist hypotheses. While the "orthogenesis" or "nisus" approaches are convergent and monistic, Peirce, Morgan, and Smuts were ontological pluralists. Morgan, Smuts, and Bergson were not especially motivated by (and in the case of Smuts, apparently quite hostile to) traditional theistic interpretations of evolution, while a kind of evolutionary natural theology is central to the otherwise distinctive theories of Alexander, Teilhard, and Driesch.

It is only really in the last few years, in the wake of Ilya Prigogine's Nobel prizewinning studies of nonlinear dissipative systems in biochemistry, that evolutionary theories have been demonstrated as compatible with, rather than radically opposed to, physical thermodynamics. Combined with our understanding of the "quantum" theory of genetics, from Mendel to Watson and Crick, we are only now beginning to forge a conceptually adequate synthetic theory of evolution sufficient to account for the novel emergence and transmission of complex physiological traits. Given the recent nature of these discoveries, we can account in historical retrospect for the legitimate variety of evolutionist hypotheses which focused on a more "Hegelian-Aristotelian" teleological approach to creativity and emergence, or which stressed the dialectical opposition of the material forces of brute nature and the "upward thrust" of some vital evolutionary principle.

While the issue may no longer be so sharply drawn, it is small wonder that the details of rival evolutionist hypotheses, with their vastly different metaphysical assumptions and implications for the significance of value, consciousness, and the dignity of life, sparked such heated controversy between radical mechanists and self-styled "social Darwinists" on the one hand, and their more humanistic opponents on the other. The noble example of Darwin's gracious competitor, Alfred R. Wallace, deserves special mention in this context.[16] To a large extent, this protest against radical mechanism and in behalf of the central importance of humanistic values in the life sciences continues as a major emphasis in the writings of more recent exponents of evolutionary cosmology, including such distinguished scientists as Theodosius Dobzhansky, W. H. Thorpe, C. H. Waddington, Julian Huxley, and Rene Dubos.

III. The Realist Revolt and the Reformulation of Idealism

The realist revolt against idealism at the beginning of the present century was forged in the crucible of the larger debate detailed in the preceding two sections. What was being rejected, however, was the *Anglicized* variety of the Hegelian right wing, of which F. H. Bradley was the principal champion. William James and Ralph Barton Perry, for example, repudiated the metaphysical views common to McTaggart, Bradley, and Josiah Royce, centered on a timeless and monistic doctrine of thoroughgoing internal relatedness. In place of this view, the realist revolutionaries stressed the independent ontological status of the external world, temporal passage, and the experience of pluralism and genuine difference. In particular, as Perry himself observed, realism tended toward "identifying reality with the elements, processes and systems of experience. But it maintains that these elements, processes and systems are independent of being experienced."[17]

The metaphysics of American realism, in contrast to the British counterpart represented by Moore, Russell,[18] and Broad, is distinctly post-Hegelian, even though it is by no means post-idealistic. Peirce, James, and Dewey all had read Hegel and been influenced by subsequent themes in the various strands of idealistic metaphysics, and all saw themselves as rejecting Hegelian absolutism and monism—at least in the form current under the aegis of Bradley and Royce. In contrast, they embraced pluralism, presupposed the notion of creative evolutionary advance, and saw themselves as radical empiricists. In the aftermath of the Hegelian developmental account of varieties of levels of conscious experience, as well as the impact of evolutionist debates about the emergence of experientially-oriented entities from seemingly inanimate matter, it was inconceivable for the American realists to recur (as their British counterparts did) to the naive and unsophisticated account of experience presupposed by Descartes and Locke. John E. Smith vigorously emphasizes that the unique innovation of American realists and pragmatists was their radical reconceptualization of the very notion of "experience" consistent with more recent advances in evolutionary biology, physiology, and experimental psychology.[19] In particular, the American realists collectively developed a radical critique of simplistic models of visual sense perception and notions of "calculative rationality" which had functioned as the foundations of epistemology in the modern era.

The characteristic emphasis of C. S. Peirce and William James on change and emergent novelty, together with the unique insistence that even change and emergent novelty are bounded by laws or principles which themselves evolve, suggest—again, in contrast to the British counterparts—that American realism and pragmatism are also distinctively "post-evolutionary." While many of the central features of the evolutionist approach are presupposed in the metaphysics of American realism, no single theory of evolution is emphasized, nor is "evolution" as such the central defining metaphysical category for any of the realists or pragmatists—with the notable exceptions of the refined evolutionary cosmology of the later Peirce, and the reinterpretations and popularizations of Herbert Spencer effected by John Fiske.[20] While John Dewey cites numerous examples of the impact of evolutionist doctrine on the development of pragmatism and his own instrumentalism,[21] it is likewise evident in the social philosophies of Dewey, Lewis, and G. H. Mead—stressing the evolution of values, social systems, and the changing nature of truth—how far these pragmatists had extended the implications of evolutionist doctrine on a tangent which led far from the original ideas of Darwin.

Perhaps the most striking historical revelation, however, is the remarkable correlation of positions representing later critical realism with the reformulated metaphysical views of post-Hegelian idealism. I have already intimated the manner in which Hegelian idealism, together with aspects of its left wing interpretation, and its influence on later evolutionary cosmology, already tended toward many of the themes which were subsequently taken up as central to this "realist revolt." Moreover, in seeking to recover the importance of time, the reality of finite personal experience, and also to account for the obvious features of historical flux and ontological pluralism, many idealist philosophers in Britain and America were "revolting" against the same implications of the Anglicized right-wing interpretation, and hence re-introducing into philosophical debate many of the same motifs, as were the realist revolutionaries. Chief among these personalistic and pluralistic idealists were Collingwood and Pringle-Pattison in Britain, and William Ernest Hocking and Edgar Sheffield Brightman in America.

On the other hand, it is ironic to note how, during the formative period from the early 1900s until about 1930, the ongoing revision of untenable positions in the realist movement itself gradually led to the qualified re-admission of many of the idealist doctrines that realists had intended initially to deny.[22]

Initially, the metaphysical foundations of the realist revolt comprised four essential claims: (1) a rejection of "mystical monism" in favor of ontological pluralism; (2) a rejection of internal relatedness in favor of the view that perceived objects are themselves undisturbed by their inclusion in a relation with a knower; (3) an avowal of epistemological monism (over against Kantian dualism) arguing that knower and known are part of a homogeneous environment; and (4) a final remarkable, and ultimately fatal tenet of neo-realism, a belief in a realm of universal Platonic forms.[23]

The first claim constitutes the "realist manifesto" against idealism. But it is essential to recognize that claim (3) regarding epistemological monism was *also* the cornerstone of *Hegel's* philosophy—the spearhead of his reaction against the epistemological dualism of Descartes and Kant. Ironically, the attack upon

Bradley and Berkeley embodied in the conjunction of (2) and (1) renders it impossible to defend either (3) or (4). The denial of internal relations re-introduces precisely the sort of epistemological dualism between knower and known, subject and object, which (3) denies. And, as Bertrand Russell later realized, it is impossible to explain the participation or "ingredience" of universals in particulars apart from *some* kind of doctrine of real *internal* relatedness. In addition, the failure to distinguish between epistemological and ontological monism led to a great deal of confused and largely pointless debate among realists themselves.[24]

These conflicts led to the dissolution of neo-realism and the rise of critical realism in both America and Great Britain. This movement retains a commitment to ontological pluralism and epistemological monism by postulating a logical entity—an intermediary "object"—between knower and known: an "essence" (Santayana) or sense-datum (Moore, Broad, and Russell). While it seemed to solve the problem of perceptual veridicality, this approach ended up replacing the question of the relations between objects and knowers with the problem of analyzing the relation between real objects and their logical "essences," in turn raising a further question about the ontological status of the latter. Apart from re-admitting a doctrine of internal relations, this dilemma could only be solved by postulating an ontological plethora of entities where relatively few had been needed before—in retrospect, initiating an amusing episode of conundrum, particularly in the British pursuit of sense-data theory early in the present century.

In America, the Cornell psychologist and philosopher, Charles A. Strong, offered a vigorous interpretation and defense of Santayana's views by explicit appeal to panpsychism.[25] As he was a prominent member of the new group of "critical realists" formed at the December, 1916 meeting of the American Philosophical Association (which also included such luminaries as Santayana, Drake, Perry, and Roy Wood Sellars), his advocacy of this approach appeared to re-introduce into later realism the criteria of universal sentience and internal relatedness which *earlier* realists had sought to refute.

In both countries the idealist leanings of critical realism came to be of sufficient embarrassment to force the abandonment of the theory by the early 1930s. Some American realists, such as Spaulding, Montague, Morgan, Strong, and Drake turned increasingly to emergent evolutionism to account simultaneously for epistemological monism (3) and ontological pluralism (1). Other developments included what A. E. Murphy described at the time as "objective relativism," of which Victor Harlow gave a revealing account in 1931:

> This is an attempt to turn the at present dominant physical theory of relativity into a philosophical system of relativity. It asserts the reality of a pluralistic world, yet asserts with it a relativity of characters which would make relations the essential

elements of that reality. It takes two forms. The first . . . is that presented by Alfred North Whitehead, which though pluralistic is essentially a philosophy of an organic world—and immediately suggests memories of Hegel—and which he admits to be very similar to the conclusions of Bradley. Murphy, who holds essentially the same position, includes Dewey among the "objective relativists." The other, which is presented by F. S. C. Northrop, a pupil of Whitehead, and supported by F. E. Hoskyn, presents a type of atomism or monadism that is strongly reminiscent of Leibniz. . . . Both . . . might be considered types of neo-realism in their assertion of epistemological monism, their [ontological] pluralism and their denial of traditional substance.[26]

In sum, what is, on the American scene at least, sometimes referred to as the "metaphysics of pragmatism" turns out to be a conglomeration of views drawn either from evolutionary cosmology or from the neo-realist resurgence against idealism. These metaphysical foundations do not include specific commitments to process and change, so much as to ontological pluralism, epistemological monism, some variant of Platonism regarding universals or what Whitehead termed "forms of definiteness" in experience, and a denial of internal relatedness. Finally, the historical development and demise of realism illustrates the conceptual incoherence of these views.

IV. WHITEHEAD AND HARTSHORNE

Whitehead's philosophy attempts to encompass all of these important realist commitments, save the antipathy toward internal relatedness. Indeed, his philosophical development can be portrayed in part as an attempt to restate the fundamental metaphysical commitments of realism on a more coherent basis. It is evident, moreover, that many leading realists of the time, most notably Ralph Barton Perry, regarded Whitehead's metaphysics as the logical culmination, and perhaps the last hope, of their philosophic revolution.

The continuity of Whitehead's position with the larger development of realism is almost as remarkable as are his unique and creative innovations. His recursion to "pre-Kantian" modes of thought intends (as the realists did as well) to re-conceptualize the foundations of experience in order to avoid the epistemological pitfalls into which subsequent modern philosophy had fallen. His Leibnizian quantization of experience—undertaken in part to avoid the otherwise paradoxical result that novelty cannot emerge out of undifferentiated continuity—ended up asserting the primacy of "unobservables" in order to account for actual experience. Whitehead's innovation here, in a sense, was to substitute a single species of "actual occasions" in place of the bewildering ontological plethora of entities characteristic of British sense-data theory. Finally, Whitehead's puzzling adherence to his strange doctrine of "eternal objects" can be viewed as of a piece with the larger realist presumption of the necessity of Platonism in some form to account for similarity and forms of definiteness in experience. John Dewey once remarked that superfluous philosophic positions are never actually refuted so much as simply abandoned. Had Whitehead's doctrine of eternal objects not been canonized and scholasticized out of historical context by subsequent Whiteheadian disciples, in all likelihood it would simply have "withered away," as did the unnecessary, untenable, and ultimately fantastic realist commitment to Platonism generally.[27]

The stubborn antipathy of realists toward internal relatedness had proven their downfall, and Whitehead did not emulate this. Instead, he re-introduced the doctrine, central both to idealism and evolutionary cosmology, of "organism" and fundamental experiential interconnectedness. However, he apparently recognized that the entire notion of internal relations would itself have to be radically recast, in order to account simultaneously for causality and freedom, actuality and potentiality, and particular discrete occasions or episodes of experience simultaneously exhibiting non-unique and non-discrete forms of definiteness. The result, as Hartshorne subsequently observed, was Whitehead's "revolutionary doctrine" of temporally asymmetric "prehensions," externally related to their (temporally prior) "objects," but internally related to their (temporally consequent) "subjects."[28]

As a result of Whitehead's historical and literary grounding, many of the essential "process" themes developed over a century earlier as protests against "scientific materialism" were re-discovered in his own independent assessment of the conceptual inadequacies of that worldview. Because he was in part sensitive to the earlier historical revolt against these views by Romantic and idealistic poets and litterateurs, Whitehead's own revised metaphysical perspective exhibits a number of Romantic and idealistic undercurrents, and explicitly compares with the move away from absolutism and monism proposed by later personal idealists. I have already specifically cited Andrew Seth Pringle-Pattison in Great Britain, and students of Hermann Lotze in America, including Borden Parker Bowne and Edgar Sheffield Brightman, and, after Josiah Royce, the major exponent of idealism at Harvard, William Ernest Hocking.

Hartshorne's influences, as William Ladd Sessions has demonstrated,[29] were drawn almost exclusively from these teachers and associates. Furthermore, he engaged in his formative studies and wrote his doctoral dissertation while steeped in the atmosphere of the intense debate between realism and idealism which I have portrayed as the most characteristic element of early twentieth-century Anglo-American philosophy. In light of the foregoing account, it is not surprising to discover, as Sessions does, that Hartshorne attacks the positions of Perry and James, and appears to draw inspiration from Hocking, Bradley, and other contemporary idealists.

Based on the preceding analysis, however, it is *also* not surprising that Hartshorne, without contradiction, subsequently gleaned the more congenial insights stemming from a fundamentally distinct, and in many respects even alien tradition through his later encounter with the thought of C. S. Peirce and Whitehead. Both of these had, in effect, helped to establish a kind of realist rapprochement with the most essential doctrines of later idealism and evolutionary cosmology, to which Hartshorne already had vigorously committed his own philosophical career. Finally, Hartshorne himself has often testified that his personal perspective was shaped quite independently from his boyhood study of the same basic literary and artistic sources which Whitehead had earlier come to appreciate, thus accounting for the remarkable similarity in aesthetic intuitions and commitments.[30]

Hartshorne is the chief heir of a process tradition which he received primarily from the later pluralistic and personalistic idealists. Together with his distinguished British colleague, Errol E. Harris, he is one of the few surviving representatives of what once was a flourishing school of systematic and speculative inquiry earlier in this century.

Whitehead, by contrast, founded a distinct and original school of process thought—albeit one which was likewise grounded in the attempt to develop a coherent synthesis of critical realism and idealism, incorporating many of the main insights of the original process school of evolutionary cosmology. His orientation in mathematics, logic, and the physical sciences, however, offered a perspective seldom achieved before or since by disciples of process thought, and marked a sharp departure from the more traditional descriptive and intuitive philosophic methods practiced by the evolutionary cosmologists. Like his colleagues in American realism, he did not make "evolution" itself the central category of his metaphysical system. Others who rank with Whitehead in this regard are Arthur Eddington, James Jeans, Werner Heisenberg, Louis de Broglie, Milič Čapek, Ilya Prigogine, and David Bohm.[31]

The longstanding customary, but decidedly inaccurate portrayal of Hartshorne as the heir and disciple of Whitehead and Peirce[32] has had an interesting effect upon the subsequent development of contemporary process philosophy. On the one hand, Whitehead's highly technical notions of epochalism, temporal asymmetry, and prehension provided Hartshorne with more precise conceptual and linguistic equipment with which to render intelligible his idealistic commitments to internal relatedness and theism, and suggested how he might simultaneously develop precise analytical concepts of finite freedom and individual creativity while adhering to the more traditional idealist notions of community, society, and God.[33]

Hartshorne's fundamental stress on panpsychism (or what he prefers to call psychicalism) and his vigorous extension and defense of an all-embracing conception of divinity are thoroughly consistent with the idealist background I have cited. But Hartshorne's single-minded advocacy of such views represents a radical departure from the more measured realist sensibilities of Whitehead and Peirce. This tension is very much alive today: the forceful impact of Hartshorne's own personality on the pursuit of philosophy in America, and the ongoing careers of his numerous students and disciples, have cumulatively transformed process philosophy from a speculative cosmology into a sophisticated philosophical theology.[34]

V. Conclusion

While Hartshorne has occasionally been attacked or dismissed as an "idealist," such classification has heretofore not been perceived as very meaningful. Even its sharpest critics usually take for granted that process philosophy is an heir of the early twentieth-century realist revolt against idealism, and recognize that, apart from F. H. Bradley, Whitehead was not particularly hospitable to, or conversant with, idealist philosophers such as Hegel. My historical analysis of the movement, however, delineates four distinct schools within the larger process tradition: evolutionary cosmology, idealism, realism, and Whitehead's novel synthesis of these consonant with recent developments in mathematical physics rather than with earlier developments in the life sciences. This analysis suggests in particular that post-Hegelian idealism represents a legitimate but quite distinct school of process philosophy, of which Hartshorne has emerged as one of a very few surviving contemporary representatives.[35] This in turn legitimates other analyses of his philosophy which have stressed his differences in method and agenda from both Whitehead and Peirce, and helps account for the subsequent radical transformation of emphasis in post-Whiteheadian process thought from cosmology to theology.

George R. Lucas, Jr.

Department of Philosophy
Clemson University
May 1986

NOTES

1. "Ideas and Theses of Process Philosophers" in Lewis S. Ford, ed., *Two Process Philosophers: Hartshorne's Encounter with Whitehead* (Tallahassee, FL: American

Academy of Religion, 1973), pp. 100–104; also *Philosophers Speak of God*, ed. Hartshorne and Reese (Chicago, IL: University of Chicago Press, 1953), passim.

2. See "The Development of Process Philosophy," in *Philosophers of Process*, ed. Douglas Browning (New York: Random House, 1965), pp. v–xxii.

3. To my knowledge, this aggressive and tendentious approach to the interpretation of the history of philosophy was first manifest in *Philosophers Speak of God*. More recently, see *Insights and Oversights of Great Thinkers: An Evaluation of Western Philosophy* (Albany, NY: State University of New York Press, 1983); *Creativity in American Philosophy* (SUNY Press, 1984); and *Omnipotence and Other Theological Mistakes* (SUNY Press, 1984).

4. I offer a more detailed outline, with annotated bibliographical sources, in my preliminary study: *The Genesis of Modern Process Thought: An Historical Outline with Bibliography* (London and Metuchen, NJ: Scarecrow Press, 1983), hereafter cited as GMPT. A full exposition of this history, however, remains to be carried out.

5. E.g., Lewis Ford, *Two Process Philosophers*, passim. Hartshorne himself has referred to his own view, in contrast to Whitehead's, as a "realistic idealism," although he has never offered a detailed analysis of this oxymoron. While his marked differences from Whitehead are pointed out on several occasions in his major systematic work, *Creative Synthesis and Philosophic Method* (London: SCM, Press, 1970), Hartshorne explicitly began to distance himself from Whitehead in a 1977 lecture at Leuven, Belgium: "Whitehead's Revolutionary Concept of Prehension," *International Philosophical Quarterly* 19, no. 3 (September 1979): 253–263. In his review of my GMPT, Hartshorne cited numerous other influences on his thought, and sharply objected to the customary conflation of his interests with those of Whitehead and Peirce: *Process Studies*, 13, no. 2 (Summer 1983), 176–179. In a less flattering mode, the late James K. Feibleman attacked the Hartshornian turn in contemporary process metaphysics as radically non-Whiteheadian: cf. "Why Whitehead is not a 'Process Philosopher'," *Tulane Studies in Philosophy* 23 (1970): 48–59.

6. Cf. the more extensive historical analysis of this tradition in GMPT, pp. 181–211.

7. See my "Evolutionist Theories and Whitehead's Philosophy," *Process Studies* 14, no. 4 (Winter 1985): 287–300.

8. Lester G. Crocker, "Diderot and Eighteenth Century French Transformism," in *Forerunners of Darwin: 1745–1859*, ed. Glass, Tempkin, and Straus (Baltimore, MD: Johns Hopkins University Press, 1959), p. 129.

9. Cf. the *Hydrologie* (1802) and *Philosophe zoologique* (1809) for Lamarck's views on non-reductionistic chemical analysis, the symbolic importance of fire as an example of "animate matter," and his synthesis of these perspectives on materialism into an evolutionary account opposed at once to dualism, mechanism, and vitalism.

10. Cf. *On the Metamorphosis of Plants* (1790).

11. Joseph LeConte, *Evolution: Its Nature, Its Evidences and its Relation to Religious Thought* (New York: Appleton, 1888). However, I have found no other evidence for this view. Rather, I suspect that, at minimum, the closeness of their respective evolutionary perspectives reflects the extent to which such speculative cosmologies were rooted in the prevailing intellectual climate of opinion by the early nineteenth century.

12. In addition, there are appreciative references to Lamarck in the lengthy *Zusatz* to *Enc.* sec. 370. See also Leo Rauch, "Hegel and the Emerging World: The Jena Lectures on *Naturphilosophie* (1805–06)," *Owl of Minerva* 16, no. 2 (Spring 1985): 175–181.

In the absence of this historical perspective, it is easy to misunderstand and dismiss Hegel's views on science and the philosophy of nature, as, most recently, Milič Čapek has done: "Hegel and the Organic View of Nature," *Hegel and the Sciences*, ed. R. S. Cohen and M. W. Wartofsky (Amsterdam: D. Reidel, 1984), pp. 109–121.

13. Cf. G. R. Lucas, Jr., "A Re-interpretation of Hegel's Philosophy of Nature," *Journal of the History of Philosophy* 22, no. 1 (1984): 103–113.

14. Dieter Henrich has called attention to the manner in which such notions associated with finitude and contingency are central to Hegel's own thought, and have been systematically overlooked by most interpreters. Cf. "Hegels Theorie über den Zufall," *Kant-Studien* 50 (1958–59): 131–148.

15. It may seem puzzling to mention Teilhard at this juncture, but despite the comparatively recent public fascination with his thought, his views on evolution were actually formulated much earlier in the century. Intellectually, he is in every respect a contemporary of the other evolutionary cosmologists cited above.

16. While Darwin wavered in his estimate of the popularized "social" or cultural extrapolation of his theory of natural selection, Wallace clearly saw the radical fallacy and dangerously ethnocentric and politically abusive implications of social Darwinism, and repudiated it out of hand. He linked this issue with the need to discern an adequate scientific account of the emergence of mind in evolution, which he was never able successfully to accomplish. As the human brain seemed vastly superior in capability to anything required for mere survival, towards the end of his life Wallace fell back on the postulate of a "divine influx" to account for the elevation of homo sapiens above the rest of nature. Cf. *Social Environment and Moral Progress* (New York: Funk and Wagnalls, 1913).

17. "A Realistic Theory of Independence," in Holt, Marvin, Montague, Perry, Pitkin, and Spaulding: *The New Realism* (New York: Macmillan, 1912), p. 103.

18. Russell in particular was very uneasy with the more explicitly metaphysical (and, from his standpoint, anti-epistemological) turn of American realism. In a letter to Ralph Barton Perry [from, Harvard University's Pusey Library collection, dated August 30, 1912] regarding the publication of *The New Realism* (from which the preceding quotation was excerpted), Russell discusses the American realists' combination of a style of logic "that I heartily agree with" with a metaphysic, derived from William James, denying the old mind-matter dualism. Russell comments on the latter even then: "So far I have not been able to agree with this metaphysic, but I am open to conviction; it is only on logic that I have really decided opinions."

19. "The Reconception of Experience in Peirce, James and Dewey," *Monist* 68, no. 4 (October 1985): 538–554.

20. Cf. Philip P. Wiener, *Evolution and the Founders of Pragmatism* (Cambridge, MA: Harvard University Press, 1949); also James Collins, "Darwin's Impact on Philosophy," *Thought* 34 (June 1959): 184–248.

21. E.g., his title essay in *The Influence of Darwin on Philosophy* (New York: Henry Holt, 1910). Also "The Evolutionary Method As Applied to Morality: Its Scientific Necessity," *Philosophical Review* 11, no. 2 (March 1902): 107ff.; and "The Philosophical Work of Spencer," *Philosophical Review* 13, no. 2 (March 1904): 159ff.

22. I give a more detailed analysis of the degeneration of realism in GMPT (pp. 136–149) from which the present account is distilled. A sense of the frustration with this state of affairs is evident in Ralph Barton Perry's requiem for realism in 1939: "American Philosophy in the First Decade of the Twentieth Century," *Revue internationale de philosophie* 3 (April 15,1939): 423–443.

23. Victor Harlow, *Bibliography and Genetic Study of American Realism* (Oklahoma City, 1931), pp. 54–56. See also John H. Muirhead's discussion of *The Platonic Tradition in Anglo-Saxon Philosophy* (London: George Allen & Unwin, 1931) for an account of this view common to virtually all realists through about 1925.

24. In response to John Dewey's initial claim to assert realism and pluralism, without recourse to monism or dualism (by which Dewey refers to his realist *ontology*), A. O. Lovejoy reponds that pluralism *is* a species of dualism, which realism is supposed to *deny*. But Lovejoy is clearly referring to the *epistemological* position, and not ontology, a confusion which Dewey likewise fails to appreciate. For a succinct record of the ensuing foolishness, see the following exchanges in *The Journal of Philosophy*: Dewey, "Realism without Monism or Dualism," 19, no. 12 (June 8, 1922): 309–317 and 19, no. 13 (June 22, 1922): 351–361; Lovejoy's rejoinders are published in 19, no. 19 (September 14, 1922): 505–515, and 19, no. 20 (September 28, 1922): 533–541. Dewey's surrejoinders appear in volume 21, no. 8 (April 10, 1924): 197–204; and 21, no. 22 (October 23, 1924): 601–611.

25. Cf. *The Origin of Consciousness: An Attempt to Conceive the Mind as a Product of Evolution* (New York: Macmillan, 1918).

26. Harlow, op. cit. 103ff. The term "objective relativism" is applied to both Whitehead and Dewey by A. E. Murphy, "Objective Relativism in Whitehead and Dewey," *Philosophical Review* 36 (1927): 121–144. John Dewey puts the matter somewhat differently in discussing the relative distinction between "subjects" and "objects": "The Objectivism-Subjectivism of Modern Philosophy," *Journal of Philosophy* 38, no. 20 (September 25, 1941): 533–542.

27. Hartshorne offers a cogent critique of the metaphysical incoherence of Whitehead's platonism, arguing in this case for the primacy of a more Peircean-nominalist view of forms of definiteness in experience. *Creative Synthesis and Philosophic Method* (London: SCM Press, 1970), ch. IV; see p. 59, also p. xv. He repeats this attack on eternal objects and his preference for Peirceanism a decade later in a critical rejoinder in *Process Studies* 10, no. 3–4 (Fall-Winter 1980): 95.

28. Again, see Hartshorne's "Whitehead's Revolutionary Concept of Prehension," loc. cit. In the case of prehensions of eternal objects, which are non-temporal, the prehensions are externally related to the eternal objects themselves, but internally related to the wholly temporalized relational essence of these forms and their temporalized "ingredience" in some particular episode of subjective experience.

29. "Hartshorne's Early Philosophy," *Two Process Philosopers*, ed. Lewis S. Ford, pp. 10–34. Cf. Sessions's discussion of Hartshorne's influences and contemporaries in his review of Bruce Kuklick, *The Rise of American Philosophy in Process Studies* 8, no. 1 (Spring 1978): 57f.

30. Hartshorne suggests these influences, especially on the development of his panpsychicalism, in his review of GMPT, loc. cit. Cf. also Eugene H. Peters's very personal account of these influences on Hartshorne in the opening chapter of *Hartshorne and Neoclassical Metaphysics* (Lincoln, NB: University of Nebraska Press, 1970).

31. I do not mean to imply that these are somehow Whitehead's disciples; rather, they are independent thinkers who have pursued cosmology from much the same background orientation and perspective as Whitehead. Eddington, Jeans, Prigogine, and Bohm were in fact influenced by Whitehead; Heisenberg acknowledged his philosophical debt primarily to Hegel; while de Broglie and Čapek are both distinctive interpreters of Henri Bergson.

32. Despite having edited the monograph which decisively demonstrated the inaccuracy of this constant conjunction, Lewis S. Ford later joins Hartshorne's principal student, John B. Cobb, Jr., in citing this customary background in their tribute to Hartshorne in the special *festschrift* issue of *Process Studies* 6, no. 1 (Spring 1976).

33. Theodore R. Vitali provides a careful analysis of these appropriations and refining influences on Hartshorne's philosophical views: "The Peirceian Influence on Hartshorne's Subjectivism," *Process Studies* 7, no. 4 (Winter 1977): 238–249.

34. Victor Lowe has called attention to this bias and principal preoccupation of contemporary process philosophers, and has suggested by way of contrast how measured and modest was Whitehead's own philosophical interest in theism: Cf. "A. N. W.: A Biographical Perspective," *Process Studies* 12, no. 3 (Fall 1982): 137–147; esp. 146. Cf. the gentle rebuke on this point in Lowe's *Understanding Whitehead* (Baltimore, MD: Johns Hopkins University Press, 1962).

35. Hartshorne's embarrassing lacuna and stubborn antipathy towards Hegel becomes all the more difficult to account for in this light. A perfectly plausible interpretation of the Hegelian stress upon *Geist* and self-conciousness is that what is fully actual is *not* inert, "immediate" matter at a simple location undergoing purely external relations, but rather only that which is *fully mediated*: i.e., that which affects, and is affected by, all other actualities. There are, in addition, relatively few significant differences discernible by any but the most devoted disciple of either between Hegel's Absolute (Spinoza's Substance become Subject, and given an historical, proto-evolutionary autobiography) and Hartshorne's dipolar theism, stressing God as Supreme and Absolute, yet indebted and internally related to every aspect of actuality. Cf. Hartshorne's *The Divine Relativity: A Social Conception of God* with the treatment of Whitehead and Hegel on theism which I outline in *Two Views of Freedom in Process Thought: A Study of Hegel and Whitehead* (Atlanta, GA: Scholars Press, 1979). Such comparisons are vindicated by several other commentators on this issue in *Hegel and Whitehead: Contemporary Perspectives on Systematic Philosophy*, ed. George R. Lucas, Jr. (Albany, NY: State University of New York Press, 1986).

27

Donald S. Lee

HARTSHORNE AND PRAGMATIC METAPHYSICS

1

There is a strong sense in which Charles Hartshorne is a distinctly American philosopher. He has shown how to preserve and enhance intellectually the central ideal with which the American experience began and still continues: the ideal of freedom. He has not written persuasive tracts on the political liberty and psychological freedom of choice worshipped by Americans. Rather, he has penetrated through the everyday experience of free choice and self determination to a ground of metaphysically real freedom. "Here is the ultimate meaning of creation — in the freedom or self-determination of any experience as a new 'one', arising out of a previous many, in terms of which it cannot, by any causal relationship, be fully described." [1]

Hartshorne is not the central figure in unfolding the idea of genuine freedom — Whitehead was. Whitehead constructed a philosophic system in which process supervenes over static substance, and freedom (creativity, novelty) is ultimate in moving from the present to the future. Unfortunately, Whitehead's obscure terminology placed the bulk of his writings beyond the grasp of almost the entire intellectual community. Fortunately, some interpreters of his work have brought its meaning within reach. Among the best of these is Hartshorne. He has developed several core ideas of Whitehead's system, particularly the notion of freedom, which he often called 'creativity'. He speaks of " . . . the doctrine of 'creative synthesis' or 'creativity' as the 'ultimate' abstract principle of existence." (CS&PM xv) By making creativity, freedom, intelligible he has rationally grounded the political, moral, and psychological freedom we Americans cherish but are hard put to defend rationally in an atmosphere of scientific determinism.

2

Hartshorne's full metaphysical meaning of freedom is often vague due to using "creativity", "self-determination", "spontaneity", "novelty", and even "chance" as synonyms. Moreover, he is not very precise in distinguishing when those terms refer to the phenomenal experiences to be explained by his metaphysical theory from when he is using them as part of his theory's explanatory apparatus. In either case, he tries to remain close to their intuitive meanings familiar to us.

Freedom experienced in our choices of everyday life vaguely stands over against our commonplace experience of being coerced. Experiencing freedom (or seeming to) is one thing, getting a conceptual grip on it is another. In our scientific era, rooted in the intellectual tradition of Galileo, Descartes, and Newton, we tend to believe that any event can be explained by deterministic laws. Since freedom as creativity falls outside such laws, any appeal to it flies in the face of scientific understanding.

The conflict between scientific understanding and freedom finds sharp expression in a dilemma of modern man: how can man be morally responsible? Determinism precludes genuine choice while, on the other hand, freedom from determination by the past precludes depending on previously established moral character. Hence determined or free, men seem cut off from moral responsibility. Deterministic philosophers contend that the freedom felt by men is illusory. Opposing them, non-deterministic philosophers say only selected aspects at most are determined. The upshot is that the intellectual understanding of freedom seems impossible, yet the recognition of our feeling of its operation poses no difficulty.

Hartshorne deals with freedom by following the Whiteheadian orientation: deny that the Newtonian model of scientific explanation is the model for metaphysical explanation. The scientific account of events should fall within the wider scope of a metaphysical account. Whitehead placed the idea of creativity (freedom) at the axiomatic level in his system as an ultimate category along with the idea of inheritance from the past. Hartshorne has taken the two ideas and developed their joint operation with a slant all his own. Events progress within broad patterns of inheritance from the past while their fine tuning is spontaneous, generating novelty. Hartshorne adopts Whitehead's program of placing creativity and inheritance at the axiomatic level of his system. That is, he does not try to explain how novelty can exist within a totally lawful course of events, he simply says there is no reason, apart from slavishness to the Newtonian world scheme, to believe the course of events is totally lawful. If one substitutes for the Newtonian axiom the process axiom of the joint operation of wide-pattern inheritance and fine tuning novelty, paradoxes such as the moral dilemma of modern man need not arise.

Once the axiom of joint inheritance and novelty replaces the axiom of strict causal determinism, the rest of the older metaphysics cannot be left intact. Such a mixed set of axiomatic ultimates would result in a scheme ill fitted for interpreting both ordinary and sophisticated experience. Virtually all the ultimate axioms need radical revision to yield a system providing a coherent yet very different interpretation of experience. The radical revisions Hartshorne adopts are Whiteheadian: replace the traditional idea of fixed substance by that of creative process and the traditional idea of the ultimacy of reason by that of the ultimacy of feeling. From this new perspective the world is not comprehended as separate substances with essential attributes, but as a *process* of distinct events, each connected to preceding and succeeding ones. Nor is experience guided at bottom by structures analogous to reasoning. Rather, present *feeling* appropriates the outlines of past events and, supplied with a dose of spontaneity (creativity), aims toward the future. In this metaphysical scheme both determinism (inheritance) and freedom (novelty, spontaneity, creativity) obtain consistently side by side.

3

In order to bring out Hartshorne's distinct American flavor I will stack him up against the school of thought in American philosophy which best captures its spirit, pragmatism. I have adopted this strategy because Hartshorne's philosophy is so highly systematic that without the pronounced interconnections among his metaphysical ideas, the philosophy would be sapped of its strength. To appreciate Hartshorne's niche in the American tradition, his philosophy requires comparison with a systematic school of American philosophic thought, and pragmatism fills that bill very well.

Hartshorne is no stranger to pragmatism. Working as co-editor of the first six volumes of the *Collected Papers of Charles Sanders Peirce* exposed him to the originator of pragmatism as methodologist and metaphysician. He often cites Peirce as his second place hero with only Whitehead ahead of him. Though this makes Hartshorne neither a Peircean nor a pragmatist it does mean that Peirce's thought influenced him greatly: "From Peirce and James I accept a basic pragmatism . . . ideas must be expressible in living and behavior or they are merely verbal." (CS&MP xvi) His adoption of this central theme of pragmatism leads us to expect that he agrees with pragmatism in many ways and will address the several ways he disagrees. Interestingly, he sees himself potentially coinciding with the instrumentalist and developmental brand of pragmatic philosophy if he were without his theism: "If we must settle for a non-theistic view, then I question if Dewey and Mead have been surpassed."[2] But, the theistic motivation drives

Hartshorne, so this invoking of Dewey and Mead is a hypothetical comment, to be entertained only. Yet, it is not merely a throw-away remark; it reveals his affinity to American strains of thought and to pragmatic themes in philosophy.

4

Pragmatic metaphysics is not the system of just one philosopher who elicited the underpinning of pragmatic methodology and epistemology. Rather, the general features of such a metaphysics can be abstracted from a consistent position encompassing most of the fundamental pragmatic ideas of the five "classical" pragmatists: Charles Peirce, William James, John Dewey, George Herbert Mead, and C. I. Lewis. I presume with Peirce but not James that pragmatism is systematic and not merely a patchwork of philosophic doctrines and themes.

Pragmatism stresses first and foremost that thinking is an organismic procedure for adjustment to environmental demands by beings who become human by virtue of that procedure. The key element in thinking is the concept, the meaning of a written or spoken term. Each concept has meaning dependent on some others in a network of concepts, and each by virtue of its position there has its own distinct meaning. Concepts function as pre-set criteria for attending to and focusing on whatever is presented. With them one selects from the abundance of stimulation surrounding him to anticipate what is coming so that behavior can be adjusted accordingly. Pragmatism maintains with Kant that mental activity structures experience, but breaks with him by maintaining that the structuring concepts arise from interaction with the environment rather than from inherently fixed reason. Accordingly, pragmatism is an empiricism: meanings and knowledge originate from sense experience and ultimately refer back to it for application and validation.

For pragmatism, the scientific method of validating general beliefs as knowledge is central to the entire enterprise of philosophy, either natively as reflective thinking (Dewey), or sophisticatedly as deliberate experimentation (Peirce). Scientific method yields conceptions on high levels of generality while keeping in touch with activity. These conceptions are tools for adjusting to the incessant changes in environmental conditions.

With its stress on thinking and knowing, pragmatism is primarily an epistemology emphasizing meaning and method with metaphysical themes low in the background.

5

The metaphysical framework underlying the epistemology of pragmatism consists of four different types of categories: global, descriptive, compositional, and ordering. The only global category is "being", the descriptive categories concern the general appearance of the system; the compositional categories spell out the ingredients of being; the ordering categories indicate very generally how the other categories are arranged.

5A. Global Category

Being. I shall call the totality of everything "being". *Being* is not a property to predicate of anything; rather, it indicates everything of which anything can be predicated. To avoid the nonsense of indicating that there is something over against the totality of everything, the term "non-being" will not be used. "Non-being" utilizes the concept of denial or negation, but for that concept to be meaningful some distinctions need to be made within being. Another term, "experience", is used globally by all pragmatists, but its universality lies in the epistemological realm not the metaphysical realm.

5B. Descriptive Categories

Naturalism. Pragmatism is decidedly naturalistic. *Naturalism* on a universal scale is the claim that the character of each aspect and portion of being is similar in some ultimate way to the character of all other aspects or portions. The similarity is usually a matter of regularity by constant laws or classification, or of connection by continuity, or of sameness by homogeneous physical composition, or even of systematic randomness.

That which is non-natural is what violates any of the similarities just noted, and it comes in several varieties; namely, the *unnatural*, the *artificial*, and the *supernatural*. "Unnatural" refers to whatever violates any kind of similarity to a distorted extent. Monstrosities, deviations from physical laws, and the sudden appearance of regularity where randomness once reigned, are unnatural. The non-naturalness of "artificial" things consists in their existing in nature only by virtue of man's purposive activities. Though thinking is a natural function of man, the products of his thought are considered to be artificial. Mathematics is artificial, so is a book, and a bridge. Another variety of non-naturalism is "supernaturalism", the belief that some power, agency, or entity beyond the natural world (ultimate similarity) is responsible partly or wholly for what exists and happens in the natural world.

Emergence. Pragmatism recognizes that properties and things form together in new ways, producing genuinely novel properties and things. When material becomes organized and so functions in specific complex ways, specific properties (wetness of water, for instance) are sometimes manifested which are never present in the components (hydrogen and oxygen) of the complex.

Mead in his genetic psychology of social behaviorism, in *Mind, Self, and Society*, constantly invokes emergence. Minds and selves along with significant symbols emerge from specific physical and biological conditions obtaining in social settings.

Pluralism. Pragmatism presumes that being is irreducibly *pluralistic* in that undissolvable differences lie within the totality of being. Among the classical pragmatists James was most insistent in championing pluralism over any philosophic theory promoting a monolithic 'block' universe. One important cue that a pragmatic metaphysics takes from James's pluralism, is his dismissal of plurality as atomistically separate entities, qualities, and functions, interconnected only by artificial 'unreal' devices.[3] Such an unconnected universe, though possible, is antithetical to pragmatism.

5C. Compositional Categories

Process. Pragmatism presumes all being to be process; process is a primary *MODE OF BEING*. Process stands in contrast to metaphysically independent substances. A substance does not really change with respect to what makes it the substance it is; rather, change is something non-essential to substance *qua* substance.

Process presents an uncompromisingly different picture. It is directional change in which earlier differentiations lead into later ones connected to them, gradually flowing into them. All development presumes that being is process. For instance, evolution is the process by which forms change quickly or slowly into other forms; in fact, forms (species) are relatively static stages in continuing development.

Event. The process of all being is differentiable into partial processes each of which is an *event*. "Differentiation" and "partialness" are not categories but are bound up in the category of event. The process as a whole is not metaphysically prior to the events composing it, nor they to it. Events differ but are not set off from one another by absolute boundaries; they gradually merge into one another. Smaller events may occur together as parts of larger events, and two events may overlap by having one or more of their smaller events in common. And, some events may be excluded from others.

Relation. For there to be events and their inclusions, overlappings, and exclusions there must be *relations* among events and between events and the process as a whole. There are also relations among relations and relations between a relation and an event.

A relation is *not* an event; it is *not* a process. Though the totality of being is process as a whole it is not exhaustively identified as that, for if it were, then a relation, in order to *be*, would have to be a process. It is not a process, yet it is being in *some* way. It is the second primary *MODE OF BEING*. Process and relation are co-ordinate ways of being—they are not opposite each other.

Two relations stand out: (i) *sameness/difference*, and (ii) *connective continuity*. (i) For events to be related, they must be the *same* in some respect and *different* in another. Sameness and difference are relations primordial to any other relation: all events are the same inasmuch as each is an event, and all are different inasmuch as each is not identical to any other. (ii) Any event as part of the process as a whole is directly *connected* to at least some other event(s) and indirectly connected to all events. The connectivity can be guaranteed only if the process as a whole is *continuous* and each event itself is internally continuous, i.e., without gaps or ultimate boundaries. Sameness/difference and connective continuity are primordial relations grounding other pervasive relations such as quality, regularity, structure, and function.

Act and feeling. I will assume that quality, regularity, structure, and function can be derived and elaborated to focus on the kind of event central to pragmatism; namely, an *act*. Acts are located in *organisms*, themselves emergent events exhibiting qualities, regularities, structures, and functions. Also located only within organisms are feelings. *Feeling* falls within the mode of process, but cannot be further explained in terms of already introduced categories and conceptions—it is metaphysically primitive, emerging in organisms. An organism registers feelings and directs its activities on cues from them, *interacting* with its *environment*. Interaction by organisms capable of thinking is *transaction*.

Mead divides an act into four continuously connected stages: (1) an *impulse* of the organism, (2) its *perception* of the environment, (3) its *manipulation* of the environment, and (4) its felt *consummation*.[4] An act, accordingly, is functionally demarcated by feeling an impulse at its start and then feeling a consummation at its end. A *significant symbol* emerges in a social act when one stimulates oneself the same as others so that a common response is established among all the participants, including the stimulator. With it, cognitive behavior becomes possible.

Potentiality. Among the modal concepts, potentiality, actuality, possibility, and necessity, only potentiality is a rock-bottom category. It is the third *MODE OF BEING* alongside process and relation. The other three modal concepts are derivative from it and other categories.

Within pragmatism, *potentiality* is the idea of different anticipated responses to a stimulus. In a *deliberative* act, an agent symbolizes several responses (called 'alternatives'), each of which he *feels* as a *tendency*, and none of which he carries out immediately. Potentiality is roughly synonymous with tendency and refers to the direction which one event has toward alternative later events.

Actuality refers to the process itself, the concrete ongoing flow of events. The present is actual; the future is not actual nor is it yet process. *Possibility* in the pure sense of logical possibility omits by abstraction the ideas of "feeling" and "directionality" from potentiality. Thus, logical possibilities do not concern plausibility nor reference to time. They are abstractions valuable for mathematics and logic, but it is a serious confusion to treat them on the same metaphysical level as conceptually formulated felt tendencies. Finally, necessity can be accounted for as the impossibility of non-actuality.

Negation and existence. Some historically familiar categories, negation and existence, have not been included as basic in the foregoing account. They can be sufficiently accounted for by categories already cited or implied.

Negation can be derived from the primordial relation of difference and aligned with other derivative features such as oppositeness and polarity. Negation is not global; it must always be qualified within being. *Existence* can be understood as that which is actual in space/time location.

5D. Ordering Categories

An adequate metaphysical account of the world should provide an explanatory conception of the *real*. To make sense of "real", two other conceptions are needed: *category* and *system*. These three conceptions are categories underlying order in being, making arrangement possible.

Only when categories interlock in a system is the meaning of "real" coherent—unless it has been stipulated as synonymous with "being", "actual", or "existent". Apart from such stipulation, the word "real" has meaning only relative to whatever category is applied in a given case. As C. I. Lewis says:

> The ascription of reality to the content of any particular experience is always elliptical: some qualification—material reality, psychic reality, mathematical reality—is always understood. And whatever is real in one such sense will be unreal in others . . . the problem of distinguishing real from unreal. . . is always a problem of . . . referring the given experience to its proper category.[5]

Generally, anything is real relative to its own category in a system of categories, and can be contrasted to what is not real there. Things in the world need not be dichotomized into the absolutely real and unreal. Accordingly, "reality" is a *metaphysical index* or ordering category; it indicates when a category is properly applied. For pragmatism, "reality" indicates which category sets the context of a particular situation.

6

Hartshorne can be compared to pragmatism by examining him on each of the pragmatic categories just presented. Those ideas of pragmatism to which he has a reasonably close fit will be examined first and those with which he has significant differences will be examined afterward.

6A. Global Category

Being. Hartshorne recognizes the word "being" as having two different meanings: being as reality or being in contrast to becoming. (CAP 249) Since process philosophy takes becoming as primary he assigns the latter non-becoming meaning of being as secondary[6] and suitable as a primary category. Insofar as he thinks of being as reality and reality as becoming he transforms the traditional intension of being to mean becoming.

It might seem that reality means for him what pragmatic metaphysics means by being, but that is not possible because it so often refers to concrete actuality while pragmatism's "being" refers to more than that. For the pragmatists abstractions have being but under Hartshorne's concrete actuality sense of "reality" abstractions are not real.

A term of Hartshorne's that approximates pragmatic metaphysics' "being" can be found in the statement "something exists". For him this is a necessary statement—its denial being impossible. (CS&PM 161ff) In it the term "something" means the bare idea of something; (CS&PM 246) it is "something or other". (CS&PM 14) This idea of "something" abstracted from "something exists" is global for Hartshorne's metaphysics; it indicates whatever there is.

6B. Descriptive Categories

Naturalism. Hartshorne's God-dominated metaphysics is not naturalistic so this topic will be discussed later.

Emergence. Hartshorne's metaphysics, based on Whitehead, takes creative synthesis to be the cornerstone of his philosophy. "To be is to create." (CS&PM 1) He sees "creative synthetic experiencing . . . as the most powerful metaphysical generalization ever accomplished." (CS&PM 107) Creativity occurs in every event ranging from very weak to very strong. It is freedom, chance, novelty, emergence. Hartshorne not only agrees with pragmatism on emergence, but carries it beyond the minimum set at a general level by pragmatism.

Pluralism. Hartshorne takes events as the basic elements comprising reality, what Whitehead called actual entities. There are innumerably many of these, not constituted by matter but by momentary feelings. Each one pulls aspects of its past events into itself by prehension but does not fully determine the next one to come along. Because the future is indefinite, events do not form a fixed process, a monolith of feeling. Thus, Hartshorne's philosophy is unquestionably pluralistic.

6C. Compositional Categories

Process. Hartshorne's Whiteheadian philosophy is a process metaphysics the details of which go far beyond the general designation of "process" called for by any pragmatic metaphysics. Process, for him, is indeed directional change; in fact, it always moves from one state into its successors with the introduction of novelty (creative synthesis) however mild. Underlying the gradual change on the surface of experience is a hidden structure of discrete events that do *not* merge but are connected in that each is internally related to its immediate antecedents, but externally related to its future successors.

Event. All of what is actual, was actual, or will be actual are "events" for Hartshorne. He agrees with pragmatic metaphysics that these events compose process. However, he disagrees with pragmatism in taking events to be ultimately discrete and thereby metaphysically more basic than the process as a whole. For the pragmatic metaphysician, the process as a whole is as ultimate as the divisibility of the process, while actually dividing it is relative to circumstances and thereby not as primordial as process or the potentiality for dividing it. This disagreement will be gone into later.

Insofar as events may compose societies or societies may overlap by having events in common or some events may exclude others, both Hartshorne and pragmatism agree.

Relation. For Hartshorne relation is a fundamental category, since he holds relations among events are not reducible to the events themselves. The two most important relations among actualities are successiveness of some events to others and contemporaneity among some events. There are also relations among relations (e.g., logical) and relations between concrete actualities and relations themselves (e.g., application).

As for the specific relation(s) of sameness/difference, Hartshorne can place it among the most important relation(s) in his logic of contrasts (CS&PM Chap. VI) where "difference" would be correlative with and dominant to "sameness". As for the specific relation of connective continuity fundamental to pragmatism, Hartshorne's position that events are ultimately discrete is diametrically opposed to pragmatism. This disagreement will be discussed later.

The relation of asymmetry is held by Hartshorne to be primordial among all relations. Pragmatic metaphysics has no trouble agreeing with him here. In fact, any process philosophy is committed to the primacy of asymmetry over symmetry because process is *uni-directional* (earlier going to later).

In sum, Hartshorne and pragmatic metaphysics fit each other well with respect to the category of relation except for the relation of continuity.

Act and feeling. For pragmatism the term "act" is limited to behavior by creatures capable of at least low level rational behavior. Hartshorne uses "act" much more widely, holding that every actuality acts by virtue of its freedom and feeling. Regardless of his use of the term, he places what the pragmatist calls an act at a categorial level in his philosophy. He says in agreement with pragmatism, "ideas must be expressible in living and behavior." (CS&PM xvi) The meaning of an idea is anchored in acts. For him, the acts that pragmatism talks about are special societies of events, societies demarcated within human activity by the special type of feeling which grounds cognition.

Hartshorne's theory of organisms and feeling extends far outside pragmatism. Pragmatic metaphysics limits "organism" to the ordinary idea confined to plants and animals, and limits "feeling" to animals. Organisms and feelings emerge from non-organismic conditions. In contrast, Hartshorne considers *every* event to be organismic and shot through with feeling. Pragmatism cannot agree that all process is feeling. This is a disagreement between them to be discussed later. In any case, because all reality is feeling for Hartshorne, the circumscribed ideas of organism and feeling embedded deeply in pragmatism are not deep in his metaphysics.

Potentiality. Concerning the modal concepts, potentiality, actuality, possibility, and necessity, Hartshorne and pragmatism agree on actuality and necessity. Actuality is the process itself, while necessity can be defined as the impossibility of non-actuality. Potentiality and possibility present difficulty.

For pragmatism, potentiality is a tendency in an event toward more than one alternative later event. Hartshorne would have no trouble with this inasmuch as for him any event has novelty in it and so is not forced into any definite later event. However, a close reading of Hartshorne shows that he rarely clearly distinguishes potentiality from possibility. (CAP 225; CS&PM 225, 282) He says there is no difference between possibility and reference to the future: "the possible is the future." (CS&PM 61, also 115, 133, 222) Furthermore, he says, "Those who insist on the difference between logical and real modalities . . . have usually been determinists." (*Monist* 334) Thus, there is no ultimate distinction between logical possibility and potentiality. Yet, it appears that he appreciates the distinction between the traditional meanings of potentiality and possibility by calling potentiality "real possibilities" (CAP 271) and by declaring "real potentialities" to be distinct from "logical possibilities in general".[7] These distinctions and denials of distinctions between possibility and potentiality are confusing. Hartshorne should tell us the difference between possibility, real possibility, existential possibility, logical possibility, open possibility, universal possibility, potentiality, pure potentiality, and real potentiality—all of which he mentions.

In any case, Hartshorne could probably be fitted, after considerable jimmying, within the pragmatic position on potentiality.

Negation and existence. The pragmatist does not take negation to be global. As discussed earlier, Hartshorne, too, rejects the concept of total nothingness. Moreover, he can derive the abstract idea of negation from difference, polarity, and opposition just as the pragmatists do.

Though he means something different by "existence" (*Monist* 331) than the pragmatist's "that which is actual in space/time location," he would be able to admit the great importance of the latter—especially with his emphasis on actuality being concrete. He says, "No actuality, nothing concrete, . . . is identifiable unless empirically." (*Monist* 332) And, "empirically" usually involves space/time location.

6D. Ordering Categories

Pragmatism holds that in a system of categories "real" is an index term indicating that a given category is properly applied. "Reality" has no fixed referent; there is no absolute reality over against an absolute unreality.

Hartshorne does not differ essentially from pragmatism on "category" and "system", but he uses "reality" equivocally. For instance, from "acts of fancying or mistakenly believing are real occurrences," he concludes, "that the unreal is also a form of reality." (CS&PM 99) The first use of "real" (and "unreal") is indexical while the last is absolute. Usually, his "reality" is equivalent to "actuality". On occasion, he uses "total reality" (CS&PM 14) to include not only actuality but also possibility. Clarification is needed here. Insofar as he promotes the absolute sense he falls outside the pragmatic framework.

Summary

Hartshorne agrees with many more points in pragmatic metaphysics than he disagrees with. His global category "something or other" matches closely with pragmatism's "being". Descriptively, his system is pluralistic and emergentist but his supernaturalism contrasts sharply with pragmatism's naturalism. Compositionally, his Whiteheadianism is one of process, event, relation, and potentiality; it counters pragmatism's continuum of actuality with discrete actual events. He also disagrees by taking feeling to be in all actuality, whereas pragmatism restricts feeling to animal life. As for ordering categories, he agrees with "category" and "system", though his equivocal use of "real" creates some problems.

7

Hartshorne disagrees strongly with pragmatism on three categorial issues: (A) supernaturalism versus naturalism, (B) total presence of feeling versus its partial presence, (C) discreteness versus continuity. Discussion of these issues shall be limited to how they distinguish Hartshorne from pragmatism.

(A) Hartshorne's metaphysics is a pronounced theism in which God transcends the natural world. If naturalism states that each part of being is similar in some ultimate way to all other parts, then his metaphysics is supernaturalistic for it asserts that some power, agency, or entity beyond the natural world (ultimate similarity) is responsible partly or wholly for what happens in the natural world. He states that there is an infinite gap between finite individuals and God and between divine cause-effect and ordinary cause-effect. (CS&PM 156–57) He also criticizes Dewey's naturalistic conception of God as metaphysically unsatisfactory. (CAP 95) A theism of an all-encompassing deity transcending human existence is needed to permanently preserve all the values ever achieved.[8]

Despite Hartshorne's assertions about the transcendence of God, one may nevertheless be hesitant to grant that his deity is infinitely beyond whatever ultimate similarity constitutes the natural world. His notion of God is so different from the Judaic-Christian God that the definition of supernatural only partly fits his deity.

What is it in human experience that indicates to someone that he is referring to God? Hartshorne appeals mainly and repeatedly to one phenomenon experienced by feeling, attitude, and behavior; namely, worship. God is worthy of worship due to being unexcelled relative to all else in human experience. In addition, he claims two other kinds of experience deliver a sense of deity: (a) felt regularities basing "the laws of nature as the chief indentifiable aspects of God's creative action" (CAP 224) and (b) felt participation in a reality wider than personal experience, "To be religious . . . is to find, or hope to find, a 'connaturality' of ourselves with the rest of reality." (CAP 260) In brief, different people know they are talking about the same thing, deity, when they refer to experiences of worship, nature's regularity, and participation.

The phenomenal experiences do not reveal attributes which uniquely characterize God. Such characterization requires defining God abstractly, yet this does not imply he is a "merely abstract entity." (CS&PM 246) In fact, Hartshorne proclaims God to be the totality of ultimate concreteness (his consequent nature). Since we can grasp God rationally only in terms of abstractions, our *knowledge* of God is theoretic rather than empirical. The theoretic grasp is a priori necessary relative to the terminology, semantics, and logical structure of process metaphysics. In short, God can be understood as the most concrete being grasped by abstractions interrelated by a priori necessity within process philosophy.

Hartshorne's God, conceived within the idea of reality as emergent process (not as fixed substance), turns out to be far removed from the garden variety Judaic-Christian God. To begin with, God cannot foresee the *actual* future inasmuch as part of what determines it is the novelty occurring in the present and future. Accordingly, God is not *omniscient* in the traditional sense. Nor is he *omnipotent* in the traditional sense because the genuine creativity in each event is independent of God's power. Nor is God a final perfection, even though he is the *most perfect* being at any given time he can be yet more perfect later.

Hartshorne infuses his reconstructed idea of deity into attributes normally predicated of God, thus revealing how non-traditional his God is. According to tradition, in addition to being omniscient, omnipotent, and perfect, God is, among other attributes, necessary, absolute, immutable, uncaused, existent, independent, and eminent. Hartshorne, reinterprets these as follows. The *necessity* of God lies in the class of his possible states not being empty even though any actual state is contingent. This necessity lying in God's primordial nature (as potentiality for qualities and relations and order among them) is abstract and so not real as his contingent concreteness. Regarding *absoluteness*, God in his consequent nature (as the totality of present actuality absorbing the past), is not absolute but relative to both his prior states and to the autonomous creativity within present events. God is *immutable* in the minimal sense that his primordial nature as the totality of potentiality has general characteristics that never change. On the other hand, God's consequent nature (the totality of present actuality) is definitely mutable as process goes on; the unified prehension of all events at one present passes into a changed later present.

The traditional idea of God as *uncaused* and hence eternal is an abstract definition which avoids his contingent and actual consequent nature. As contingent, God at each moment in his consequent nature is caused, and there never was a first cause—process goes back infinitely. God's *existence* is universal, not particular: his nature must be actualized somehow but the specific states he passes into are contingencies. God is *independent* of the world insofar as he contains the entire continuum of possibilities (his primordial nature) that the world might actualize into. On the other hand, God's consequent nature is dependent on the world because any state God is now in depends partly on earlier states and partly on the autonomous creativity in each event composing them. God's supreme *eminence* is his complete superiority in value to any event or society of them. Such eminence does not, however, place God's value incomparably beyond creaturely value, for his eminence derives partly from participation in him by the value experiences of creatures.

From the above it is obvious that Hartshorne's God is not nearly as transcendent as God traditionally understood. The line separating God as natural from him as supernatural is further blurred by Hartshorne's agreement with Whitehead that God is the supreme exemplification of Whitehead's categories rather than a transcendent exception to them. God is supreme in at least six ways: (1) as the ground of all possibility, (2) as an all-inclusive event (society for Hartshorne), (3) as the agency transforming possibility to actuality, (4) as total memory, (5) as perfect purpose and love, and (6) as the supreme orderer. (WP 79) These six supremacies fill out the metaphysical system of process philosophy by appealing to wholes and completions. So, they smack little of genuine transcendence while appealing to ultimates within immanence.

The limitations put by Hartshorne on the omnipotence and omniscience of God realign two famous paradoxes of traditional theology: the problem of evil and the problem of free will. Hartshorne has no problem with the existence of evil in a universe guided by a benevolent God—evil is due to the conflict between the creative results of partially autonomous events. Since God does not control the creativity in each event, he cannot guarantee total harmony. He optimizes it as best he can. Hartshorne has even less difficulty with the problem of free will because by making it axiomatic that freedom is in each event, he concludes that God can neither foresee a rational creature's decision nor determine what it must be.

Hartshorne's God is far enough removed from tradition to urge not calling him "God", a name packed heavily with nuances inappropriate for the deity Hartshorne believes encompasses the world. Everywhere the term "God" is used, and the pronoun "he" in referring to God, the terms "deity" and "it" should be substituted. Such wording would go a long way towards demythologizing and increasing the understanding of Hartshorne's deity. I believe this deity would be revealed as minimally transcendent: bordering closely to ultimates in most naturalistic aspects and transcendent in relatively few supernatural aspects. This blurring of the line between natural and supernatural puts Hartshorne closer to a pragmatic metaphysics than first suspected, though it must be admitted pragmatic metaphysics has no inner drive to speculate about completions and wholes to the point of constructing a naturalistic theology.

(B) A second conflict between Hartshorne and pragmatism concerns the status of feeling. Pragmatism in accord with common sense limits feeling to animal life, while Hartshorne, with Whitehead, says all individual actualities feel, extending the concept of organism to universal categorial scope.

Surely, the Hartshorne-Whitehead position is distant from common sense, so their radical stance needs a closer look. Hartshorne believes that every philosopher should have a stance on the mind-body problem; (CAP 5–6) he takes an idealistic position as opposed to a materialistic or dualistic one. By idealism he means that actuality can be explained at bottom only by psychicalistic terms with physical terms being derivable from them. He apparently accepts Descartes' dichotomy between mind and body regarding terminology, for he lumps feeling or sentience in with mind (CAP 96, 129, 147, 258–59; CS&PM 141, 145, 154), taking thought to be doing on a higher level what feeling does on a lower level. In any case, it is feeling, not thought which pervades all events including atoms or molecules. Hartshorne quotes Whitehead approvingly as saying reality is an "ocean of feelings". (WP 148)

The question is whether such a position is "idealism" inasmuch as "mind" for him does not explain all actuality—feeling, sentience, explains it. Apart from including feeling under the Cartesian rubric "mental", misunderstanding results from calling a sentience-based metaphysics idealism or psychicalism. Wouldn't Hartshorne be better off selecting a set of properties from both the Cartesian physical and mental domains and declaring them to characterize feeling or sentience. He could do this since he thinks that some mental attributes have extension (CS&PM 113–14) and some purely physical entities (atoms) have feeling. (CAP 258) The set of selected properties, incompatible for Descartes but compatible for Hartshorne, would characterize feeling and thereby generate a position called "sentientism", a name free of the mentalism and rationalism suggested by the term "idealism". Hartshorne and Whitehead are sentientists, not idealists.

Pragmatism has no Cartesian dualism, for it holds that mind emerges from complex conditions of feeling in organisms which have certain properties in specific circumstances. For the pragmatist, feelings emerged within organisms, the organisms emerged from matter, and matter emerged from energy of some sort. Thus, the process of actuality has energy (activity) at its base rather than feeling. Whether Hartshorne would attack energy as a basis of explaining the way he attacks matter (materialism) I do not know. Regardless, pragmatists' intuition at this level directly acquaints them with energy (activity) as much as Hartshorne's intuition directly acquaints him with feeling, so for them energy (activity) is more basic on an explanatory level than feeling.

The difference between pragmatism and Hartshorne concerning the pervasive 'substratum' of process is between activity (energy) and feeling (sentience). The gap can be narrowed somewhat because for Hartshorne each event contains an ingredient of creativity as well as feeling. Creativity shows up as activity as distinguished from sentience, so activity is in there on a primitive level. He tells us that all feeling expresses itself in action, (CAP 241) and that feeling as one and acting as one are two sides of the same thing, namely existing as one. (CS&PM 143; CAP 130) I leave it to him to decide how much the gap between himself and pragmatism on feeling and action can be closed.

(C) A third categorial topic differentiating Hartshorne greatly from pragmatism concerns the continuity of actuality. He follows Whitehead's doctrine of discrete actual entities in holding that the events comprising actuality are not connected in a continuum. Hartshorne proposes that actuality comes into discrete existence from the indeterminate continuity of potentiality (or possibility). (CAP 84; CS&PM 122–26) In contrast, Peirce held that not only is potentiality continuous but so is actuality. (CAP 82, *Monist* 330) Mead held that actuality is continuous (CAP 134, 138) and Dewey also. (CS&PM 122)

Hartshorne admits experience seems to be continuous but claims that is due to its vagueness. (CS&PM 194) Vague intuition comes close to apprehending units of ongoing experence but they remain indistinct. (CS&PM 195, *Monist* 321) With all this indistinctness, (CS&PM 194) he cannot appeal to directly intuited experience to settle the issue. Beyond appealing to intuited experience, he says the mathematically refined meaning of continuity cannot be deduced from the looser more intuitive meaning of it, nor can the reverse deduction hold. Yet, he argues that mathematics *favors* actual event pluralism. (CS&PM 192–93)

To examine this dispute the meanings of "continuous" and "discrete" must be pinpointed. For Hartshorne a continuum has no actual parts, just possible parts (CS&PM 122), and any cut in a continuum is arbitrary (CS&PM 235, SPCSPSS 468). A continuum does not consist of a collection of points; (*Monist* 329) and, it is simple in that it is a single idea. (CS&PM 126) It is a matrix from which parts are produced.[9] "Continuity" meaning "any kind of intrinsic connectedness" (CS&PM 192) is too loose to distinguish the continuous from the discrete. As for discreteness, he takes it to mean mutually external units. (CS&PM 192) These units cannot in actuality be sheer points, for points are abstract ideals or limiting concepts. (CS&PM 193) Discreteness as discontinuity is complex. (CS&PM 126) He speaks of two kinds of discreteness: 1) definitely undivided parts, and 2) self-sufficient, merely externally related parts. (SPCSPSS 468) He rejects discreteness as *merely* externally related parts, claiming they are internally related, too. (SPCSPSS 468)

Hartshorne believes it is fundamental that events are discrete. No event is divisible into discrete parts (no sub-events) (CS&PM 193)—he chides Whitehead for speaking of phases in an actual entity (WP 178)—yet it has finite temporal spread. (CS&PM 123) With temporal extension but no sub-events it can be concluded that each event is internally continuous, and so a matrix from which parts can be produced, but that such parts are not themselves event-like. If an event were not internally continuous but point-like, then experience would not appear vaguely continuous—which it does. His picture of actuality, then, is of each internally continuous event juxtaposed to other such events with no continuity between it and them; in his terminology, there is no matrix, simple in itself, from which those events are produced as parts.

A question arises: How is any event connected to another juxtaposed to it? It cannot be jammed next to it so that its internal boundary is an external boundary to that next event. For, if that were the case, then the boundary is a Dedekind cut in what originally is a continuum.[10] Since Hartshorne rules out original continuity, *each* of the events has a distinct internal boundary and these two boundaries are juxtaposed with nothing in between. (Anything in between would be an actuality that is not an event—an impossibility.) The boundaries just rub up against one another. So, the question of connection between events remains.

For Hartshorne events are intrinsically connected by prehension, where the later of two juxtaposed events grasps the earlier. I hold that connection by prehension is more consistent with actuality being continuous than with it being discrete. Inasmuch as events are feelings, prehension intrinsically connects (uni-directionally) a later feeling with an immediately earlier one. Yet, *prehension itself is an activity of feeling*, it is the feeling of other (previous) feelings. (WP 11, 159; CAP 81, 262) Thus, the general picture of the relation of prehension between actual events is that of two units of feeling connected by—what else?—feeling. Feeling as prehension penetrates the boundaries separating two feelings-as-events. Hartshorne has connected two units by something having exactly their same nature. The characterization of an extended process where connectors and connectees have the exact same nature is far more intelligible as a continuum being cut by a boundary rather than as units connected by a non-unit. Hartshorne appears to have anticipated this problem: "That an event in one place prehends, internally relates itself to, an event in another place does not, by any logic apparent to me, entail that there is a continuum of actual events intermediate between the two!" (SPCSPSS 468) But he has not brought in the idea that events and prehension are in essence the same—feeling. Just by *calling* the relation of feeling between two feelings by one name and the related feelings by another does not overcome the logic that *does* entail their continuity. Where reality is an "ocean of feeling", reality must be continuous and not an aggregate of drops.

This, however, is not the end of the story. For if feeling is continuous then what is the status of the boundaries that divide it into events? They cannot be feelings. Earlier we saw that every event has two irreducible features: feeling and creativity (spontaneity). Accordingly, I suggest that creativity cuts the continuum of feeling, breaking it into segments, distinct but not inherently discrete qua feeling. *Feeling* as continuous *is* a matrix from which events are produced as parts while *creativity* is not continuous but comes in discrete form partitioning the continuum of feeling into segments containing both feeling and itself (creativity).

With this realignment of Hartshorne's position, the 'arbitrariness' of a cut (an imposed boundary) in a continuum (SPCSPSS 469; CS&PM 123, 235) takes an altered meaning. Considering that arbitrary means not regular, or not controlled, not constrained by an internal or external factor, there is a sense in which a cutting boundary is arbitrary: *relative to feeling* it is arbitrary inasmuch as the boundary is the insertion of creativity. And, creativity is spontaneous and spontaneity is arbitrary—irregular, uncontrolled, and not constrained by an internal or external factor.

The realigned picture is this: feeling is a continuum of difference of feeling; creativity is discrete; creativity is spontaneous relative to the continuum of feeling; instances of creativity are boundaries dividing felt experience into discretely focused event-experiences; the creativity boundary beginning one event-experience is within it but is an external boundary to the preceding event-experience. An event is new and different by virtue of a boundary of creativity inside it starting it off, but ends with no final boundary inside it—the beginning of a new event ends the immediately preceding one. Prehension is the active (verb) aspect of feeling while events are the segmented (noun) aspect of feeling where each segment is taken as a unity.

Pragmatism can be criticized on the subject of continuity for not coming to terms with discreteness in any programmatic way. It is one thing for a pragmatist to say that emergence occurs within continuous development,[11] but it is another thing to make sense of combining them. If development moves along continuously, then how can a new property emerge without cutting in to get started? Pragmatism should not make continuity so categorially fundamental as to render derivative status to segmenting.

Hartshorne and pragmatism have something to offer each other here, for discreteness and continuity are equally elemental in the flow of process.

8

It has been said that any metaphysical position can be boiled down to its stand on the issue of "the one and the many", or, in its dynamic version, "permanence and change". In ancient times, the main thrust of philosophy emphasized permanence, characterizing it in terms of staticness and sometimes of repetition or homogeneity. Change was regarded negatively as difference occurring through time. With the advent of empirical science in the sixteenth and seventeenth centuries, permanence became *regularity* in change through time. Scientific laws, the new permanencies, depend on change, not on staticness or homogeneous uniformity. These laws resolved the ancient problem of permanence and change, reconciling them with each other.

If scientific laws were the new permanencies, what were the new changes? Not the lawfully changing observed phenomena, for these were absorbed under the new idea of permanence; viz., regularity. It was not till the nineteenth century that ideas got sorted out well enough to discover that the new idea of change was that of chance. Gibbs with statistical thermodynamics based on probabilities and Darwin with variation (its source unaccounted for by him) in biological reproduction both took chance or spontaneity as the new type of change standing in contrast to the permanence of regularity. A new problem of permanence and change cropped up: how can the universe escape being completely determined? Process philosophy, taking chance variation and so genuine novelty and emergence seriously, reconciles the new permanence and the new change by shifting from individual substances being basic to events being basic. Timelessness gets replaced by time passage (beforeness and afterness) as fundamental. And, most importantly to our point here, spontaneity (chance) as creativity becomes an ultimate category, unexplained by anything else while working with other ultimate categories to explain everything else.

In both Hartshorne's metaphysics and that of pragmatism, spontaneity has ultimate categorial status: as creativity in Hartshorne and as emergence in pragmatism. For Hartshorne, creativity is combined with feeling in discrete events connected by prehension. For pragmatism, emergence is combined with the continuum of activity dividing it into events. The relation between the new permanence, scientific laws, and the new change, spontaneity, has received extensive philosophic treatment from these distinct quarters which agree on a vast majority of topics while differing on enough points to make their contrast interesting and their suggestions to each other illuminating.

Donald S. Lee

Department of Philosophy
Tulane University
June 1986

NOTES

1. Charles Hartshorne, *Creative Synthesis and Philosophic Method* (La Salle, Ill., 1970), p. 3. Hereafter cited in text as "CS&PM" followed by the page number.
2. Charles Hartshorne, *Creativity in American Philosophy* (Albany, N.Y., 1984), p. 282. Hereafter cited in text as "CAP" followed by the page number.
3. Joseph Blau, *Men and Movements in American Philosophy* (New York, 1952), p. 261.
4. G. H. Mead, *The Philosophy of the Act* (Chicago, 1938), pp. 3–25.
5. C. I. Lewis, *Mind and the World Order* (Dover paperback, 1956), p. 11.

6. Charles Hartshorne, "Categories and Creative Experiencing," *The Monist*, vol. 66 (1983), p. 320. Hereafter cited in text as *Monist* followed by the page number.

7. Charles Hartshorne, "Charles Peirce's 'One Contribution to Philosophy' and His Most Serious Mistake," *Studies in the Philosophy of Charles Sanders Peirce, Second Series*, ed. E. C. Moore and R. S. Robin (Amherst, Mass., 1964), p. 466. Hereafter cited in text as "SPCSPSS" followed by the page number.

8. Charles Hartshorne, *Whitehead's Philosophy* (Lincoln, Neb., 1972) pp. 109–10. Hereafter cited in text as "WP" followed by the page number.

9. Charles Hartshorne, "Twelve Elements of My Philosophy," *The Southwestern Journal of Philosophy*, vol. V, no. 1 (1974), p. 13.

10. A Dedekind cut is a boundary dividing an extension so that the boundary itself falls inside one of the two segments while at the same time being a limit of and outside the other segment with no gap between itself and the other segment.

11. S. Morris Eames, *Pragmatic Naturalism* (Carbondale, Ill., 1977), p. 17.

28

Matao Noda

A HISTORIAN'S SKETCH OF HARTSHORNE'S METAPHYSICS

Preliminary Comment

When I try to think about his philosophy it is the image of Professor Hartshorne himself that at once comes up and enchants me, so as to make me little able to keep proper distance from his thinking. I feel I must, in order to restore a historian's perspective, first pay my respect to his charming traits.

It was in the summer of 1958 that Professor Hartshorne for the first time came to Kyoto to give us a course of lectures at the American Studies Seminar held under the auspices of both Dōshisha and Kyoto Universities. One day we had free hours for an outing, to visit places of interest around Lake Biwa. We went first to Ishiyama Temple. One of the features of the place was an old room open to the lake, where Lady Murasaki is said to have written part of *The Tale of Genji*.

We were about to go up to the temple buildings when at the gate Professor Hartshorne caught, high up on a big cedar, some chirping of the bird ōruri, one of the five finest singers in the world as he would often mention. He was overjoyed and would remain there listening to the song. He would give up the visit to the temple buildings whereas Mrs. Hartshorne, interested in literature, was glad to go up. Professor Hartshorne said to me, "I have little interest in old wood."

On one occasion members of the class were discussing methods of philosophy, language analysis, phenomenology, and so on. But at the last Professor Hartshorne bluntly said, "The method of philosophy is quite simple. It is to try always to think about the same thing."

I

Hartshorne shows himself to be a historian of philosophy in a unique way in his *Insights and Oversights of Great Thinkers* (1983). In his treatment of past philosophers Hartshorne never fails to speak out his own evaluation of relevant points of each system, true or false, or rather good or bad. In this trait his history of philosophy is only equaled by those of Hegel and of Bertrand Russell.

Therefore in trying to ponder rather freely on Hartshorne's metaphysics I may after all be only picking up some of his own remarks on other philosophers and consequently on himself. I can only hope that the order and disposition of things may be somewhat new.

What I would notice here is very roughly that Hartshorne adopts in his metaphysics the idea of atomism in the widest sense, to cover the common structure of being in general. First, in his natural philosophy Hartshorne, following Whitehead, accepts modern physical atomism at its face value and tries to offer its ontological interpretation. Secondly, Hartshorne takes our 'self' as a temporal series of innumerable actual selves, emphasizing the ethical consequences of this atomistic analysis of our self. Thirdly and lastly, according to Hartshorne God himself, though immortal and everlasting, develops his creative acts of love *in time*. I think I may say that Hartshorne conceives God as having a temporal atomistic constitution similar to that of our human self. — These three points I would like to consider in some detail.

Whitehead and Hartshorne explicitly accept the idea of atomism in their natural philosophy. This contrasts them with other contemporary realists. For example, Merleau-Ponty emphasizes in his theory of perception the importance of the human body (flesh),[1] but does not go so far as to consider the cell-structure of our body, to which Hartshorne refers in considering our feelings of pain. In feeling pain we feel, according to Hartshorne, the feelings of some of our bodily cells. Realist phenomenology in general takes our perceptual 'life world' as somehow privileged over against the world of cells, molecules, and atoms, while Whitehead and Hartshorne would acknowledge the latter world as a natural extension of the former. Hartshorne often reminds us that our natural perception is not quite adequate to physical reality, so that it may well be aided by microscopes, for example.

As a matter of fact the view of Whitehead and Hartshorne was the view generally held by seventeenth-century philosophers, notably by Boyle, Locke, and Newton. But the theory they inherited from the Greek atomists did not do justice to chemical and optical phenomena. Locke tried atomistic analysis of physical substance but, so to say, had to retreat to the phenomenal analysis of the perceptual view of it. Newton went back to a reexamination of recipes of the alchemists. Atomism had to make a fresh restart at the beginning of the nineteenth century in order to be useful in modern science. And between Dalton's chemical atomism and present day microphysics lies, I think, the epochmaking fact that atoms came to be endowed with electro-magnetic properties. These came to be numbered among the 'primary qualities' of physical substance.

By the aid of electro-magnetic theory the fine constituents of matter came to be conceived as self-moving and active, in contrast to the inert atoms conceived by the Greek atomists. In modern physics atoms became 'active singulars' in Hartshorne's happy wording.[2] And as he very often notices, while stones and rocks are inert, their constituent atoms are quite active. A similar contrast we find even between our watch we used just yesterday and our watch we use today. And thus taking the atomistic idea in the broad sense that we should come down to the imperceptibly small constituents of things in order to reach the truth of the world, we also remember that since the nineteenth century, biology got remarkably vivified by the discovery of the cell as the unit of life.

Hartshorne's characterization of atoms in modern physics as active singulars goes hand in hand with the introduction of the concept 'event' as showing the atomic element of temporary processes. Without going into Hartshorne's and Whitehead's theoretical technique of constituting time processes, I would only notice here that while classical atomism conceived the *atom* as a unit of *space*, modern atomism gave justice to *time* with the idea of the *event*.

As for the causal workings of the active singulars, Hartshorne comes to the general conclusion that causes are never the sufficient conditions of the becoming of effects; causes offer no more than the necessary conditions for effects. Hence nature shows no strict causal determinism but allows a certain degree of randomness and chance. This probabilistic view of causation apparently suggested by the fact of indeterminacy found by microphysics, converges in the philosophy of Hartshorne with other evidences taken from biology and psychology, to the conclusion of the general creativity of nature.

II

Returning now to the level of the human world, we find Hartshorne applying atomistic analysis to our human self. When I say "I just remember so and so", 'I' means the subject of the unitary activity of perceiving, remembering, and so on. But when I say "I was born in 1910" the 'I' here means not a spiritual substance with various mental faculties as it was conceived by Descartes, but rather a temporal series of innumerable activities, a series as yet open to the future. This atomistic insight into the structure of the human self Hartshorne attributes to Hume and the ancient Buddhists. And what Hume neglected and the Buddhists attended to was the ethical consequences of this insight. It tells us that selfishness is an effect of our illusion and that our self is in truth as sympathetic with the interests of others as with self-interest. My series of actual selves has had in the past innumerable contacts and sympathies with other actual selves. My self-interest now is concerned with my future self which will in truth be a convergence of sympathies among many selves including me. So the argument which, presupposing human nature to be primarily concerned with self-interest only, tries to derive from it something of altruism by a round-about way, must be said to be doubly vain. Hartshorne, I remember, tells us somewhere that he owes this insight, always cherished by him, to the experience he had as a volunteer attendant in a military hospital in Normandy during World War I.

We now come to the last point. Needless to say, natural theology has always been his main concern. It led him to a radical critique of the concept of God held by traditional Christian theology. He tried to renew the theological concept of God so as to do justice to the concept of God entertained by actual religious experience. And his way was, as in the case of natural things and human beings, to give up the classical idea of substance and to have recourse to the idea of atoms or active singulars in their modern conception. The concept of God as the most perfect, purely active, eternal, and immutable, infinite and omnipotent substance, first conceived by Philo, shared by Augustine and inherited by medieval theologians, receives from Hartshorne a sort of analysis similar to that applied to the human personal self. God as eternal substance is not the God of love we are face to face with in our religious experience. This is rather God as temporal actuality. The eternal substance conceived by theologians as God is in truth a society of divine actualities, itself developing in time but immortal and everlasting in contrast with mortal creatures.

This way to conceive God is indeed to relativize him. But Hartshorne maintains that absoluteness is nothing but abstractness; relativeness on the contrary, as being in many ways related to others, means concreteness. Also the reason why God has to be temporal is that there are incompossibilities even among positive values and the realization of values cannot be all at once. A painter cannot use all colors in one picture. There cannot be all perfections at once realized in one substance.

Divine love means that God can be passive and sympathetic towards the sufferings of creatures. Classical theology would say[3] that God's compassion is only what He seems to be to the creatures and that for God himself it is not passivity, but only justice. But if divine love means forgiveness of sins and divine justice means punishing them, Anselm's distinction, in spite of his argument, may imply contradiction. The contradiction or rather incompossibility can be solved only by temporal succession of divine actualities.

As for omnipotence, if it means the absolute dominion over the world up to the predestination of all things, this attribute of omnipotence simply cannot be divine. God's love allows full spontaneity and liberty to all creatures. God leads them not by coercion but by persuasion. In this respect Faustus Socinus, the heretic theologian of the sixteenth century, is quite right. Hartshorne many times tells us his agreement with the Socinians.

We now ask how Hartshorne proves the existence of the everlasting God. He gives up both of the empirical proofs, the cosmological and the teleological, because, I surmise, these proofs presuppose a concept of nature too narrowly determined and lacking creativity. He has recourse to the ontological argument of Anselm.

Hartshorne concentrates upon the modal argument which Anselm added to his main argument from divine essence to his existence. The modal argument distinguishes God as necessary being, that is, as something whose nonbeing cannot be conceived, from the creature as contingent being, that is, something whose nonbeing can be conceived. From the fact that God is a necessary being it follows that God truly exists. As for the distinction itself of necessity and contingency, Hartshorne appeals to his principle of contrast, which in this case means that conceiving contingency requires conceiving at the same time its contrary, that is, necessity.—I can not go into more detail on Hartshorne's ontological argument, but I would say that as a whole he was candid enough in giving up empirical proofs and adopting an a priori argument.

In this paper I distinguished tentatively three levels of things, physical nature, the human world, and divinity. I found Hartshorne applying to each level similar ways of thinking which I would like to call the way of modern atomism. By means of this way of thinking I think Hartshorne has caught an analogical unity of being. But of course he would go further to reach the view of ultimate unity. And as for the first two levels I imagine Hartshorne has had two possibilities before him. One is the way to panpsychism which so to say identifies physical atoms with living cells. The other way, which is not necessarily an alternative to the first, is, I think, to conceive along the axis of time a universal cosmic evolution. It may lead to the evolution of the species of matter as well as to that of the species of life. It seems to me that Hartshorne in recent years has been interested in this second way.

On the third level of being Hartshorne could conceive divine life as the ultimate concrete unity of all things. God receives all finite lives as so many contributions to divine life and gives them immortality in divine memory.

I would close this story of my understanding of Hartshorne's metaphysics with a comment on atomistic philosophy. It seems to me that atomistic philosophy since Epicurus and Lucretius has always been in bad fame in the West and has been taken as essentially connected with 'materialism' and 'atheism', of course contrary to the Christian tradition. Even in the seventeenth century Descartes was eager to distinguish his physics from atomism. Boyle would not admit that he read Lucretius, etc., etc. Now it seems to me to be quite remarkable that Hartshorne applied atomistic ways of thinking in metaphysics in general and even in theology in particular. Though Hartshorne himself may prefer to call this way, for example, 'event pluralism' rather than 'atomism', and in his theology he refers, for example, to the distinction in modern logic between existential and singular propositions in talking about divine existence and divine actuality, I think these are on the same line with the modern atomistic way, and I would emphasize this point in order to show that Hartshorne is remarkably free from the traditional prejudice in the West against atomism.

MATAO NODA

FACULTY OF LITERATURE
KYOTO UNIVERSITY
NOVEMBER 1986

NOTES

1. Hartshorne, *Insights and Oversights of Great Thinkers*, p. 344.
2. Op. cit., p. 21.
3. Anselm, *Proslogion*, Chaps. 8, 9, 10.

29

Keiji Matsunobu

CHARLES HARTSHORNE'S IMPRESSION ON THE KYOTO SCHOOL

The song of "A Coconut"[1] which is thrown up on the Japanese shore after having floated on the warm, black Japanese Current of the Pacific Ocean far from the southern islands is one of those romantic childhood memories possessed by many Japanese. The Japanese Islands as a whole are a typical example of a society which has been gradually opened. The tiny harbor Shimoda, at the southern end of Izu Peninsula by the foot of Mt. Fuji, is a historical point where the U.S. iron ships ("Kurobune" or "black ships" in Japanese) anchored more than one hundred thirty years ago to urge the Shōgun to open his country. On the Izu Peninsula here and there we find old Shinto shrines, "Kinomiya Jinjya" in Japanese. These enshrined those oldest objects of worship which had been floating again and again on the ocean waves in ancient times. On the southern Okinawa Islands there exists also a legend that richness comes from over the sea. Recently, for more than two hundred years, the Japanese Islands were closed[2] with the strict prohibition of Christianity under the Tokugawa-Shōgun Government and the Japanese mind and society were hampered, though there was a strong integrity through responsibility among people with some Confucian discipline. Primarily, Japan on these beautiful islands with a mild climate was already a society with considerably mixed races about two thousand years ago.

With the background of the Tokugawa period with the central government of the Shōgun in a fairly modern-style state which still included a feudal social status system and feudal lords, the Meiji Restoration opened a new empire which marched on successfully towards a westernized modern nation to become one of the world powers.

It seemed that Japan achieved her subjective aim, but through the tragedy of World War II, she was forced to make a great change. Her present situation, however, is globally common, similar to other advanced parts of the world.

Then, what is her mission today in this globally interrelated world from her East Asian perspective? Human beings may survive only through mutual communication. Philosophical communication, which alone can support deeper understanding, nevertheless, is one of the most difficult tasks even today! It is my conviction, however, that the Japanese philosophic mind, which has been represented by Nishida's philosophy of the Kyoto School, is now approaching the pass where it can be objectified at last for an exchange with Western philosophy. This means that the Western way of thinking is also being objectified for an exchange with the Eastern. It also means, as I shall try to make clear in what follows, that Hartshorne's impression on the Kyoto School is by no means one on a *tabula rasa*.

Once, able students of philosophy, Kiyoshi Miki and others of Tokyo University, shifted to Nishida's place of Kyoto. This well known event meant that Kyoto University was actually becoming the center of philosophy in the first twenty years of this century. The significance of this group of most distinguished academic philosophers in Kyoto, however, has been critically reflected since World War II, and new researches on Western philosophy, especially historical investigations have been emphasized. The wealth of research on Western classics which had been accumulated in the past among Kyoto University humanistic scholars including philosophers, was soon illuminated with a new light in understanding Whitehead's and Hartshorne's insights. In particular, among researchers on Plato, there was a fresh awakening to new perspectives which would overcome simply hermeneutic dimensions. For example, Professor Yoshio Fujisawa of Kyoto University, in his essay "Plato and Whitehead" in the most representative magazine *Shisō* (*Thought* in English, published by Iwanami, Tokyo), No. 7, 1983, repudiated the subject-predicate logic or substance-attribute metaphysics and showed new perspectives.

Not only literary hermeneutics, but also cosmological plenitude has been suggested. Charles Hartshorne's arrival in Kyoto in 1958 as guest professor was just in time. It should be noted, moreover, that Kitaro Nishida developed his unique standpoint in terms of his predicate-logic of the Japanese language, which usually has no subject, with his background of Mahayana Buddhism, whereas Western logic before A. N. Whitehead's metaphysics had been centered on the subject—the only substance as individual. Now, among Nishida's and Tanabe's disciples from Kyoto and also even from Tokyo and elsewhere, there seems to be an increasing interest in cosmological process philosophy.

Nearly one hundred years have passed since Raphael Koeber[3] began to teach philosophy students at Tokyo University. Koeber from Germany lectured mainly on Western classic Greek and Latin texts, and his lectures on Aesthetics attracted young Japanese minds. Among them there was a genius Hidenaka Tanaka whom Koeber personally gave the name *festina lente*. This *festina lente* and another

Koeber disciple, Seiichi Hatano, became professors of Kyoto University, where all philosophy students attended their lectures on Western classics and Christian thought. Their teaching has been bearing fruits all these years. Among those able researchers we should mention the following: Professor Emeritus Saburō Takada of Kyoto University (Aristotle and Thomas Aquinas), the late Professor Tateo Kanda of International Christian University in Tokyo (New Testament), the late Professor Nobutoshi Nagasawa of Kyushu University (Plato), the late Professor Michitarō Tanaka of Kyoto University (Plato), Professor Katsumi Matsumura of Kyoto and later of Kwansei Gakuin University (Augustine and Christian theology. He held the chair of Christianity, formally arranged for the first time at Kyoto University), the late Professor Eijiro Hattori of Kansai University (Augustine), the late Professor Tetsutaro Ariga of Dōshisha and later of Kyoto University (Origen), and the present most distinguished professor on Plato, Yoshio Fujisawa of Kyoto University (now the president of the Japanese Philosophical Association), Professor Yūji Matsunaga of Kyushu University (Plato), and so on.

Based strictly on original texts, the scholars mentioned above prepared the way towards scholarly works for understanding modern Western philosophy.

Nishida's successor Hajime Tanabe was also a wonderful educator in philosophy and arranged a Japanese series on Western philosophers ("Seitetsu-sōsho" in Japanese, published by Kyoto Kōbundō Book Company). These volumes were written by his disciples, professors at representative Japanese universities. The topics and authors are as follows: Socrates (by Takatsugu Goto), Plato (by Nobutoshi Nagasawa), Aristotle (Saburō Takada), Plotinus (Jisuke Kano), Augustine (Katsumi Matsumura), Descartes (Matao Noda), Spinoza (Minoru Takamura), Leibniz (Torataro Shimomura), Hume (Torakazu Doi), Maine de Biran (Hisayuki Omodaka), Johann Joachim Winckelmann (Tsutomu Izima), Kant (Masaaki Kōsaka), Karl Wilhelm von Humboldt (Hisanosuke Izui), Hegel (Iwao Kōyama), Schleiermacher (Taizō Watanabe), Husserl (Yukichi Shitahodo). Bergson, Thomas Aquinas, and others were not published, though writers had been assigned. (For those unpublished, quite a number of fine studies have been produced since Tanabe's series.) Besides their earnest research on Western philosophy, the Humanities Division of Kyoto University made many sharply penetrating studies on Oriental thought—Indian, Chinese, and Japanese history of thought as well as archaeology and others.

Therefore, what was introduced by Professor Fritz Buri of the University of Basel, Switzerland, through his book[4] about Kyoto Buddhist philosophers explains only one side of the Kyoto School religious philosophy. We should not forget other aspects which signify our strenuous efforts to understand Western tradition.

Nishida's philosophy is not simply Buddhistic nor as Buddha-Christus, it is a marvelous, cosmological synthesis of East and West in Western style, though in logic itself there is no East and West. This importance was clearly mentioned by Nishida's intimate disciple Toratarō Shimomura (a member of the Academy, chief editor for the complete works of both Nishida and Tanabe, Professor Emeritus of Education of Tokyo University, most significant philosopher of mathematics and history of sciences among direct disciples of Nishida and Tanabe today, and a brilliant scholar on Leibniz with his new arrangement of the complete works of Leibniz in Japanese. His work in his old age—he was born in 1902—on Leonardo da Vinci amazed Japanese intellectuals and was highly praised by his other teacher Hajime Tanabe, who was still alive then at North Karuizawa Village after his retirement from Kyoto).

Naturally, Shimomura has been the supreme advisor together with Hartshorne to our newly established Japanese Society for Whitehead Process Studies (with an official organ *Process Thought*), for which I have had the honor of being president these several years. Professor Charles Hartshorne, together with other guests from Europe and America, attended our sixth annual meeting in 1984 at Nagoya where we held the first International Symposium on Process and Reality at Nanzan University.

Matao Noda (born in 1910, he is now an advisor to our Japanese Process Society), who was well known as a Cartesian because of his first successful work on Descartes in the series of "Seitetsu-sōsho", was adventurous enough to accept Charles Hartshorne on his philosophy faculty at Kyoto while he was active there. Some results of his acquaintance with Hartshorne may be found in his English and Japanese essays published in 1910 by Hakusuisha, Tokyo. I am happy to recollect my days at the University of Chicago in 1950–1952 as associate professor from the newly established National University Saga, leaving a position at Kyushu University, when I had the honor as the first Japanese to introduce three important aspects of Kyoto School philosophy: the panentheistic idea of God in Nishida's metaphysics, Metanoetik as the recent standpoint of my teacher Tanabe as successor of Nishida, and the emphasis of mystic elements in Seiichi Hatano's philosophy of religion at the Kyoto School. On my return from Europe where I stayed several years introducing Japanese language and culture, Hartshorne was called to Kyoto by Professor Noda. His distinguished lectures on Leibniz and Whitehead and his arguments on Anselm and others, which I had listened to at Chicago, were presented to Kyoto University students. Hartshorne's visit at Kyoto was quite timely, as it was just before the period of students' riots on Japanese campuses, and this period was longest at Kyoto University. Once (in 1919) John Dewey lectured on "Reconstruction in Philosophy" at Tokyo University on his way to Peking, China. Hartshorne's coming to Kyoto this time symbolized the actual construction of East-West, as his wisdom indicated to us that Creativity in the meeting of East and West which was extended by A. N. Whitehead's cosmology and was eagerly sought for in the Kyoto School.

Now, more than twenty years have passed since then, and it is my pleasure to sketch some aspects of Hartshorne's impression on the Kyoto School, including other philosophic tendencies in recent Japan. Our Society for Whitehead Process Studies has able philosophers as committee members, and they are all awakened to the necessity of promoting process studies in Japan. As you may have heard, Kyoto School philosophy had been much absorbed in dialectic logic, though, through Buddhist metaphysics of Nothingness. This way of dialectic, however, seems to be not so fecund to us, and we are now eager to learn some other creative process-approach instead of dialectic.

The late Professor Masaaki Kōsaka of Kyoto, who was most distinguished in Kantian studies under Nishida, suggested some similarity of Nishida's metaphysics to Whitehead's in his later work. He pointed out the common monadological implications and aspects in Nishida and Whitehead. Later, younger Professor Seisaku Yamamoto, who was once a student under Hartshorne at Kyoto and Emory, published a book *Whitehead and Nishida's Philosophy,* and it is also a fruit of the East-West encounter at Kyoto, in Nishida's tradition. The birth of Nishida's metaphysics itself had been really a meeting of East and West, and its significance was clearly mentioned in Professor T. Shimomura's unique work *Nishida Kitaro—Person and Thought,* published by Tōkai University Press in 1977.

A Study of Good was the starting point of Nishida's philosophical career, and its English translation is available in a newly revised edition by Professor V. H. Viglielmo of the University of Hawaii. In this work Nishida tried to explain his intuition in terms of William James's "pure experience" in accordance with radical empiricism. We are deeply stimulated by the fact that the empirical insight of Jonathan Edwards's philosophy of eighteenth-century New England was the glorious starting of American philosophy on the New Continent. It was almost a century before the rise of German Idealism, which also influenced philosophic discussions in the New World. Later, St. Louis became the center for the first academic journal of philosophy in America before the creative speculation of Charles Sanders Peirce (whose *Collected Papers* were published for the first time by Charles Hartshorne and Paul Weiss) and the appearance of the Pragmatists and the opening of the Golden Age of philosophy at Harvard University. It was quite lucky that Nishida could respond to James's radical empiricism from his Zen experience and consequently created his own philosophy, which again gradually produced the Golden Age of the Kyoto School with so many brilliant figures.

The synthesizing spirit in Hegelian dialectic which was found in later Nishida was originally from his disciple Tanabe's influence. Tanabe, primarily a Kantian philosopher of mathematics and natural science, was soon seriously absorbed in Hegel and persuaded his teacher Nishida into the Dialectic, though both philosophers accepted the Buddhistic traditions of Nothingness. Soon Nishida found his standing place different from Tanabe's and stopped discussions with him. The last systematizing in Nishida's metaphysics was in terms of Leibniz's monadology, and it was brought about by the penetrating research on Leibniz by the genius Shimomura, his disciple. Shimomura is really the living representative philosopher of the Kyoto School, in the continued Golden Age of Kyoto at present.

After World War II, the importance of British empiricism was newly understood and younger generations of Japanese philosophers became aware of the creative interpretations of Locke and Hume. The Philosophy of Science Association was also started, and Professor Emeritus Nobushige Sawada (one of the founding committee for our Japanese Process Society) of Keiō University is now responsible for it as president. The possibility of a new metaphysics or cosmology mediated by present day sciences, however, seems to be very difficult. Inquiries into new ways towards Eco-Ethica,[5] metaphysics, or cosmology have been cultivated by Tomonobu Imamichi and Makoto Yamamoto with their successors and also by the young professor Yōichiro Murakami (in the field of the history of natural science) at Tokyo University, and all of them have been interested in more concrete approaches through Process Philosophy.

The French-Japanese Philosophy Association, of which Hisayuki Omodaka (professor emeritus of Osaka University), a member of the Academy, has been president, involves many brilliant figures who are also deeply interested in the process approach. Omodaka has been cultivating contemporary philosophy of medicine, including the Oriental, especially Chinese, element. He was with Nishida, Tanabe, and Kuki of Kyoto School as their faithful disciple and later together with Hartshorne at Kyoto. Omodaka combines the French philosophical tradition with that of East Asia and insists on both individuality and process.

Well, let me here introduce some aspects of younger philosophers representing current discussions[6] in Tokyo:

> Because of its inability to respond to actual tasks, Nishida's philosophy should be understood as what has been linked with the 'Centricism of the Imperial Household' or Japanese racialism. Nishida's metaphysics is a frank expression of that Japanese mentality which is common to almost all Japanese, in spite of its dressing of Mahayana Buddhism or of German Idealism. Mr. Yūjiro Nakamura's indication that Nishida's philosophy has something in common with post-modern philosophy, means, on the contrary, that post-modern thought greatly resembles Nishida's standpoint. The present role of philosophers is to make Westerners understand the scope of Japanese thought. To overcome modern philosophy, we have to generalize once more those universal principles which modern times have generalized, so that we can pass beyond the boundary of 'Modern' or 'West'. It is the task of philosophers.

With regard to the above criticism by philosopher Yoshirō Takeuchi, Professor Yūjirō Nakamura of Meiji University (now vice-president of the French-Japanese Philosophy Association) argues as follows:

> Only through recent Western self-criticism after 'Structurism', it has become possible to criticise Nishida's philosophy for the first time in Japan. Because such thought as found in Nishida's always emerges among Japanese thought in the same structure, Japanese thought will never be newly created without positive criticism of or confrontation with Nishida's philosophy. Thought is a grapple with what is already in oneself. To philosophize without learning Nishida would be nonsense! Concrete experience is not only such one simple layer as social reality. Experience involves the reality of the soul. There is the depth of unconsciousness, too. Experience is multi-layered. The multiplicity of layers and complexity of daily life can never be explained or expounded upon if we try to interpret only through political, social experience or institutionalized experience. . . . The great problem of philosophy in Japan is the 'Eclecticism' in Japanese thought. . . . Post-modern thought is a style of Eclecticism, so it is fitted to Japanese. 'The self-identity of absolute contradiction' in Nishida's philosophy is also a sort of Eclecticism. Therefore, post-modern thought is a matter of course to Japanese, while it is just self-realized by Westerners.

The discussions cited above are a representative evaluation of Nishida's metaphysics by philosophers in metropolitan Tokyo and reflect the critical attitude of younger generations towards the Kyoto School. It is our present task to find how Whitehead-Hartshorne's organic speculation, especially on compound individuals, could successfully influence those discussions. The task involves an epoch-making significance in Japan and East Asia, where the Christian heritage of 'persona' as the ground of human right never existed and discrimination of all kinds is still strong. That is the reason why we need Hartshorne's Theism, with its social conception.

It is well known that Tanabe once raised a hot discussion against his teacher Nishida. Tanabe emphasized the copula in sentences instead of the predicate, which was the standing point of Nishida, and later developed his 'logic of species' against Nishida's 'topos of Individuals'. Nishida's last metaphysics was 'counter-correspondence' and his very last work was 'My Logic', which was not completed. Whitehead-Hartshorne's speculation leads to that last standpoint of Nishida, in a sense of counter-correspondence of East and West.

Nishida's successor Tanabe raised again an argument against the wholistic standpoint of Satomi Takahashi of Tōhoku University at Sendai, North Japan. In this argument, too, Tanabe insisted on the truth of dialectic on his side. Today, how easily we could join Tanabe's side in the argument! Tanabe retired at the age of 60 from Kyoto University in January of 1945, just before the tragic end of the war. His last lecture at Kyoto was 'Metanoetik'. His followers, who have held chairs at Kyoto University for many years, have been adhering to Tanabe's logic of species as mediating process, with creative interpretations. There is some similarity between Hartshorne and Tanabe, as Hartshorne insisted on *Divine Relativity* after *Beyond Humanism*, and Tanabe's concern was exactly the same—Absolute-Relative relation in logic. To the discussions raised by Tanabe, Whitehead's grouping of occasions and Hartshorne's social conception of the universe would correspond to a more desirable integrity of synthesis, as Creativity was the last concern to Tanabe and also to all other metaphysicians of the Kyoto School. With the discussions mentioned above as our background, Hartshorne's arrival in Kyoto was only in time and creative arguments between East and West had just begun! The Japanese Society for Process Studies, with deep gratitude to Hartshorne, continues such discussions among younger generations in East Asia, with different perspectives from the Claremont Process Center[7] in the U.S.A. and the Leuven Center in Europe.

Traditions have been much emphasized above. Let me conclude with a quotation from Whitehead's chapter on Foresight in *Adventures of Ideas*:

> Mankind is now in one of its rare moods of shifting its outlook. The mere compulsion of traditions has lost its force. It is our business—philosophers, students, and practical men—to re-create and reënact a vision of the world, including those elements of reverence and order without which society lapses into riot, and penetrated through and through with unflinching rationality. Such a vision is the knowledge which Plato identified with virtue. Epochs for which, within the limits of their development, this vision has been widespread are the epochs unfading in the memory of mankind.

KEIJI MATSUNOBU

DEPARTMENT OF PHILOSOPHY
KYUSHU KYORITSU UNIVERSITY, JAPAN
OCTOBER 1987

NOTES

1. A romantic poem by Tōson Shimazaki, put beautifully to music by Toraji Ōnaka. Poet T. Shimazaki was also a famous writer, whose work "Before the Dawn" symbolizes the summit of modern Japanese literature, graduated from Meiji Gakuin mission school in 1891. That school in Tokyo is the place where Edwin O. Reischauer was born as a son of a Presbyterian missionary and also the college where the late Toyohiko Kagawa, the great evangelist, studied.

2. During the closed period, only a small group of Dutch merchants, who were not interested in the Christian mission, were permitted exceptionally to stay on the tiny island Dezima in the harbor of Nagasaki. Japanese people were absolutely prohibited from going

abroad. No large boats were allowed to be built. Before the closing, Francis Xavier (1506–1552) once engaged in missionary activity in Japan.

3. Raphael Koeber was born in 1848. His father was a German-Russian, his mother a Russian-Swedish-German. He learned music at Moscow, studied philosophy and other subjects at Jena and Heidelberg, where he took his Ph.D. under the direction of Professor Kuno Fischer. While staying at Munich, which had a Catholic atmosphere, he was called to Tokyo University. He came to Japan in 1893 and taught at Tokyo University for twenty-one years, and stayed until his death in 1923. He was really the founder of Western philosophy in Japan. His fine essays were *Kleine Schriften*, published in 1918 by the Iwanami Book Company in Japan.

4. Fritz Buri's distinguished book is *Der Buddha-Christus als der Herr des wahren Selbst—Die Religionsphilosophie der Kyoto-Schulen und das Christentum*, published by Haupt, Bern/Stuttgart, in 1982.

5. Tomonobu Imamichi's advocacy of "eco-ethica" is found in Japanese in the magazine *Thought* (*Shisō* in Japanese), 1983, No. 1. His English essay will be found partly in *Acta institutionis philosophiae et aesthetica*, vol. 3, "Axiological Reflection on 'Language and Act'—From eco-ethical point of view—" (*Revue internationale de Philosophie moderne*, published by the Centre international pour étude comparée de philosophie et d'esthétique, Tokyo, Japan, and edited by Tomonobu Imamichi).

6. There were discussions between Takeuchi and Nakamura. First, Takeuchi's essay in *Sekai-World*, November, 1986. Nakamura's counter-argument in *Shisō* in January, 1987. Takeuchi's refutation again in *Shisō* in March, 1987. The evening *Asahi* on 20 March 1987 reported some concluding words of the two philosophers after Takeo Nishijima met directly with both thinkers.

7. Professor John Cobb, Jr. is directing the Process Center at Claremont. He was born in Kobe, Japan in 1905, as a son of a Methodist missionary and was a student of Charles Hartshorne at the University of Chicago. He represents the frontier of process theology today. In 1987 he lectured at Harvard University. Professor Jan Van der Veken is the director of the Leuven Process Center, where the Husserl archives also exist on the same Catholic university campus. He is the president of the European Whitehead League which sponsored the first Whitehead Symposium in 1981 at Bonn University, West Germany. At this conference I made a short speech on present day Japanese philosophy.

As for our Society for Process Studies in Japan, the seventh annual meeting (after the sixth which was the first international symposium at Nagoya), was held at Kyoto University on *Adventures of Ideas*. The eighth was at Waseda University on Nature, Man, and Society. In May 1987 the second international assembly on Process, Peace, and Human Rights was held at Kyoto (Shūgakuin Seminar House) with the participation of twenty distinguished American and European theologians, and of twelve elected members of our Japanese Process Society.

Whitehead and the World Order was the theme of the annual conference of our society for the meeting on 5 December 1987 at Kyushu University. Science, Technology, and Ethics will be the topic for our 1988 meeting at Tokyo University, just after our Bali Conference (Indonesia) in June on the Emerging Pacific Era. For the year 1989 the subject of the annual meeting at Musahi University in Tokyo will be the importance of mathematics in the philosophical career of A. N. Whitehead.

PART THREE

THE PHILOSOPHER
REPLIES

Charles Hartshorne

A REPLY TO MY CRITICS

PRELIMINARIES AND PRINCIPLES: REPLY TO EVERYBODY

I group my responses into four major classes, labeled Empirical Studies, Philosophy of Religion, Logic, Phenomenology, and Metaphysics, and Historical Antecedents. I put them in this order in spite of the obvious objection that the history group belongs first rather than last. My reasoning is that to deal with the history of something one must know what the something is. One must really start with the present. This is most true in the history of highly intellectual matters. Common sense may have some notion of what war is but not of what metaphysics or physics are. Sixty (plus?) years ago I heard Heidegger give a history of philosophy, beginning with Husserl and going back and back until he reached the pre-Socratics. I saw some sense in this. My main trouble was that he started with his German intellectual present, and a very special brand even of that, not with my Haverford- and Harvard-taught present. Another reason I put the history last is that in my philosophical thinking I often have historical antecedents in mind. When those reading my replies to the four groups in the order in which they stand arrive at group D, it will have become fairly clear to them what it is that is to be given an historical setting, and what a number of elements of the setting are.

I put Empirical Studies first because my earliest ambitious attempts to think in a disciplined intellectual way were partly in a branch of biology and partly in a branch of psychology. In both I was seeking to find hitherto overlooked or insufficiently clarified empirical truths. Also, two of the contributions in this group were the first two that I received and the first to which I wrote my responses. There are other reasons, which I think some readers will be able to guess, that led me to prefer beginning with this group.

I put Philosophy of Religion second because that is the other early strand of my endeavors, having been brought up by pious parents, who, unlike some pious persons, made religion attractive, and by a pious founder and director of a boarding school of whom the same could be said. Like my parents he accepted science, including evolutionary theory.

The third group, Logic, Phenomenology, and Metaphysics, is the heart of the philosophy of religion, and even the ornithology was guided by an application of the metaphysics, without compromising the empirical character of the former or the non-empirical character of the latter. As Popper (also Einstein) says, to try to purify science of all metaphysics is to hamper or cripple it. Apart from some glimmerings of metaphysical principles, one does not know what to look for observationally and experimentally. For example, the strictly deterministic causality of early modern science was a metaphysical doctrine or dogma that for centuries proved scientifically helpful. It was a metaphysical error, some of us think, and has been shown dispensable in science. We now begin to see what qualified form of determinism or sufficient reason we should substitute for it. Similar statements may be made about materialism. In metaphysics both doctrines have always been harmful, in theology, ruinous. Some forms of idealism are no better. I include in the third section logic and metaphysics because I hold, as I recall the British philosopher R. M. Hare once saying, that metaphysics is best conceived as (the search for) the logic of extremely general concepts, called categories by Aristotle and Kant. These include but are more than the "logical constants," as these are now usually listed. The "more" is furnished by phenomenology, or theory of experience as such. Here Peirce, Bergson, Croce, Heidegger, Ortega y Gasset, have helped me to correct what seemed, when I listened to Husserl and read his *Ideen zu einer reinen Phaenomenologie*, a remarkably artificial, falsely intellectualistic account of direct experience or givenness. My reaction to Husserl, I learned, was somewhat similar to that of the last two mentioned writers.

My four groups are only relatively distinct. As I, with some great precedents, define the two terms, 'empirical metaphysics' is contradiction or nonsense. However, human weaknesses are such that metaphysicians cannot afford to refuse to learn from scientists, who exercise great care about their language, and some of the greatest of whom have also been philosophically gifted. (There are similar relations between philosophy and theology.) The best philosophers have contributed to science. Plato, Aristotle, Leibniz, Peirce, Whitehead are outstanding examples.

The wide differences in length of the replies is more or less accidental and should not be taken as invidious or strongly evaluative either way.

I wish to give here one example of a metaphysical truth. It is the answer to the supposedly genuine question, "Why is there something rather than nothing?" I know of no ancient Greek, Hindu, or Hebrew who thought the answer to this question was a contingent truth. My answer is, there is something rather than nothing because the 'being of total nonbeing' is contradiction or mere nonsense. 'Nothing' is an essentially relative term (Bergson) and absolutizing it destroys its legitimate meaning. *'Something exists' states a necessary truth*. Let us call this principle *P* Zero. The proper metaphysical question is, "What is implied by 'something' in this necessary yet existential assertion?" The full answer to *this* question is the whole of metaphysics. I believe it implies God's existence and essence as defined by "dual transcendence," but does not imply God's total reality, which I call the divine *actuality* and which is infinitely more than Whitehead's Primordial and Consequent divine natures since it includes an infinity of divine instances or *states* of the consequent nature. It is further defined or explicated by two analogies, one being the interpersonal analogy, the ideal form of love or concern by one individual for other individuals, as in Old and New Testaments (and many other religious writings), and the other being Plato's analogy of the "World Soul" and the Universe as the body of this Soul. Both analogies, the Biblical and the Platonic, should be clarified in the light of what we now in a reasonable sense know but no human being did know thousands of years ago about the cosmos, and its macroscopic, microscopic, and megaloscopic structures, including something like neo-Darwinian evolution and our best knowledge of psychophysiology. These are all fallible, but we do what we can with them or we cheat ourselves.

To take the Bible as literally the Word of God is Bibliolatry, not worship of God, and taking some ancient Greek, Medieval European, or Marx or Lenin, as infallible is also idolatrous. It is the duty of theologians and philosophers to try to save us from religious or antireligious fanaticism and the resulting religious wars and near wars. It is God, not any book or set of books, that loves us and all beings as we cannot love ourselves or any human or subhuman reality. It is only God we should love "with *all* our being." It cannot be done with our species as the beloved, for something in us will love the other non-human animals and much more besides. Mere humanism is a glaringly inadequate religion. Nothing that is less than cosmic in scope will do. If not God, then at least the universe (Strawson) is the nontheistic second best. The other inhabited planets that, according to present knowledge, seem probable, are the minimal additions to the life on this planet and in this solar system that we cannot, without stunting our human nature, refuse to love in principle. Even this is not really enough. Both the Bible and ancient thought around the world is, I hold, on the side of this contention.

The reader now knows in outline where I stand—for the old *and* the new, religion *and* secular science, at their best as we can now see them—but not for secular humanism. I am far too much a biologist as well as too much a metaphysician to take that seriously, except as a danger. And the same for so-called fundamentalism, in which also I see a serious danger for us all. Now that I have given some outlines of my position, the question naturally arises (it is forcibly put by one contributor, McMurrin), "How do you know, if you do, that the position is sound?" I reply, "I know at least this, that for seven decades I have tried my best, in circumstances not unfavorable for the inquiry, to make it sound." A one-time student of mine, Richard Rorty, once remarked that in metaphysics there are no recognized principles, criteria, or rules of procedure, "not one." Well, I have been proposing some principles that I recommend and try to follow consistently. Here is a brief sketch.

P1. *Truth by Coherence.* With statements of metaphysical generality, given coherent meaning, there cannot be mere falsity. The alternative to truth in metaphysics is failure to talk sense. (Wittgensteinians state a half-truth here, as though there were no uniquely coherent way to combine the most general ideas. *Metaphysical abstractions entail their own mutual relations*, including their relation to actuality, which is one of them. Among the reasons why I admire Karl Popper is that he, first of all, pointed the way to the most appropriate epistemological definition of metaphysics: the search for generalities that are significant and important yet are not by *conceivable observations falsifiable*. They are, if wrong, falsifiable, but only logically (in the broadest sense)—by finding that terms are used either contradictorily, or so vaguely, unpragmatically, or ambiguously that nothing is said and "language is idling."

Truth by coherence is not truth without correspondence, nor is truth by correspondence truth without coherence. But on the metaphysical level of generality, coherence guarantees correspondence, as it does not on more specific, less abstract levels. That abstractions intermediate between metaphysical categories and the concrete are only contingently instantiated is for the same reason that concrete or actual entities are contingent, that they are *competitive* for existence with other possibilities on the same level of abstractness. For example, every animal or species of animal, by existing imposes some limitations (in spite of the truth in symbiosis) upon what other animals or species can coexist with it. But the metaphysical truth 'there are particular things' imposes no limitations upon anything save the absurd negation, 'there are no particular things.' I take as axiomatic that there are particular things and *could not not* be some such. This truth is also statable as, "there are *no merely negative truths*." This truth is itself not merely negative; for it implies for its own coherence that there are some truths, *all* of which are at least partly positive. Metaphysical truths are *wholly* positive, excluding nothing th at makes good sense. They could not have been untrue if they are true at all, and if they are false they could not have been true.

P2. We should apply to metaphysical questions the *pragmatic principle* first enunciated by Peirce as a criterion of belief, hence of meaning. It seems that we can show the content of our metaphysical beliefs only by other than merely verbal actions. For example, I personally see no conceivable way to act that expresses the often proclaimed conviction that there is a timeless knowledge of the contents of all time. It seems simply irrelevant to our living. What is relevant is that we can, by our living, *give* something, and can try to optimize our gift, to a life that is *everlasting*—meaning not timeless but unborn and undying. In short, we can serve a primordial, deathless, and all-cherishing mode of awareness. Still more briefly, we can serve God. Other than this I find no rational aim for our lives that can stand full analysis. This for me is what Kant ought to have meant (but was unable to, within his tradition) by the *summum bonum*, the Purpose by which all lesser purposes are to be evaluated.

P3. *The Phenomenological Principle.* Peirce, Bergson, Husserl (perhaps slightly dependent on Bergson), Heidegger, Merleau-Ponty, and Whitehead (essentially independently, I think, of the others) came to a partly common insight here. I have been exposed more or less intensively to the thought of these six men (Peirce and Bergson only through their writings) and have been influenced by them—least so by Heidegger, though I heard him lecture many times. All phenomenologists, so far as I know them, reject both materialism and dualism in their extreme forms, and only Husserl comes close to the Berkeleyan extreme of idealism. None are extreme monists or absolute idealists of the Bradleyan stripe. Whitehead and Heidegger see experience as essentially aesthetic and religious and regard poets as important witnesses. In this regard I think Whitehead is the best phenomenologist of the six. That this is possible with a mathematical logician is remarkable, although Mr. Dodgson (Lewis Carroll) is something of a precedent.

Whitehead's phenomenological power is seen in his discovery of *prehension*, the clue in direct experience to the nature of causality. Whitehead's phenomenological breakthrough came about as follows. First, he focused on memory in the extremely short-run, say a tenth of a second. It alone is memory in its purity. Here the so-called mistakes of memory can scarcely occur. All else is memory of remembering of remembering, in a maze of details lost in the pervasive *indistinctness* as to the concrete that Leibniz, Peirce, and, long before them, Plato, and especially Epicurus, thought characterized human experience in general. The atoms (or Plato's triangles) are always there; but we cannot intuit them one by one. Similarly, we cannot in long-run remembering pick out much detail. "Mistakes of memory" are errors of judgment, not about what is directly remembered in the simplest cases, but about what has happened after much intervening experiencing has still further hidden details. Memory simply as such has not been shown to be other than genuine (though only partially distinct) *givenness* of realities independent of the experiences to which they are given.

(The "myth of the given" refers correctly not to mere memory or any form of direct givenness but to *judgments* in complex, obscure cases that often, as Whitehead rightly remarks, are mistakenly taken as standard.) The past, so far as simply remembered, is indeed given or felt as independent reality.

What is called introspection is not simultaneous experiencing of that very experience—which implies a vicious regress—but an experiencing of *just preceding* experiencing. It is memory. Hence the given can be causal condition. *Cause* is at least a necessary antecedent condition of an occurrence; in immediate memory we have an experience as given in the following experience. Of course the later experience requires its predecessor as its given object. Whitehead takes as the aspect of givenness the relation between what is prehended and the prehending. It is easiest to discern in short-run memory rather than in perception or long-run memory.

In perception, it is often thought, the given is simultaneous with the perceiving experience. Yet we know that a seen event, even though near, occurs *before* we see it and a heard event much longer before we hear it. Why assume that extra-bodily events are the typical cases of perceiving? What about inner bodily events, particularly those in the central nervous system? If they are simultaneous with the perceiving, then perception cannot illustrate causality (if causes are antecedent conditions). Whitehead makes the contrary assumption: that the perceived data are antecedent and, in the most direct cases inner-bodily, events. Here we have human experiences directly conditioned not by previous human experiences but by physiological happenings. That we are not aware of any time difference here between perceiving and perceived is similar to our not being aware of the time difference involved in "introspection," except that we know that previous experiences themselves remembered, whereas we do not know that previous physiological events remembered. The difference in nature between a human experience and the inner actuality of cellular processes is too great for it to be obvious that anything remotely like memory is a capacity of cells taken as units. Whitehead's "subjectivism" is here far from Husserl's Berkeleyan type; atoms or cells, he thinks, are no mere "ideas" in divine or human minds, they have their own, if not ideas, then at least, feelings. They do not, as we do, think; but they do feel their immediate past. This is a crude sketch of how Whitehead discovers direct causal conditioning in both memory and perception and does so without falling into an ultimate hard dualism, or an extreme unrealism or epistemological solipsism. *His* idealism is a definite realism with realities given to, but independent of, the experiences to and in which they are given.

Hume could give no explanation of the past conditioning the present. But, if the present-past relation is a subject-and-given-object relation, of course the subject, to be what it is, requires its object. In memory we find this relation, just where Hume did not look for it. By subject-object relation we here mean, not (as in Husserl) the relation of a subject's thought or *intention* to what is thought or intended, but only the relation of a concrete prehending or intuiting to its antecedent data in memory or perception. Conscious thought or reference, sign usage, is both more and less than prehending. Even in dreams, besides thoughts there are given actualities, both mnemonic and perceptual, as Bergson (better than anyone else) in his essay on dreams shows.

P4. Causes are to be defined as necessary but *not strictly sufficient*, conditions for what concretely occurs. Note that 'sufficient' here simply means necessity in the forward temporal direction. Combining the two forms of necessity, we have classical determinism. We then have only necessity in the succession of events but no possibility in the Aristotelian sense of possibly yes and possibly no. Yet necessity, as logicians are rediscovering (Kripke and others), is only what all of a set of possibilities have in common. It is abstract. Peirce saw this and regarded possibility, not necessity, as the basic modal idea. It is a fallacy of ultra-rationalism (from the Stoics to Kant, Fichte, and, I think, Hegel) to exalt necessity as the key to intelligibility. Initially given possibility as a positive idea, we can understand modality; initially given only necessity, there is no way to go to find the real world. Life is a dealing with the contingencies presented by the creative process which is the positive locus of possibility. You see it or you don't. Aristotle did, Peirce (anticipated by Epicurus) generalized the idea; independently, Whitehead (a third scientist and logician) arrived at a similar standpoint, helped by Bergson, James, and Dewey. Since these, Karl Popper, in his insightful and important essay *Of Clouds and Clocks*, reinforces the position.

Are there sufficient causal conditions? Sufficient to make happenings possible? Yes, for happenings occur. Events have *enabling* conditions. But whether or not their conditions make them happen just as they do is a distinct question. Perhaps in part they make themselves happen. Just this is the issue of determinism and *freedom*. Are there more than merely enabling conditions? In a sense, obviously yes. We do make successful predictions. But this fact leaves wide open a range of possibilities between strict and *qualified determinism*. No one in his or her senses sees it as a goal of life to acquire power to predict all happenings in detail. We know that the experience of unanticipated novelties is a good part of the charm of life, including the life of scientists who hope to make surprising discoveries. Only a very one-sided aesthetics or ethics can have made determinism-to-the-limit seem a genuine ideal. Even the physicists are coming to see this. But Epicurus, Peirce, and some others saw it well before the physics of this century. How far Whitehead needed that physics to see it is a nice question.

I *know* that, helped by Bergson and James, he arrived at it *before* Heisenberg's uncertainty article.

That present actualities are subjects experiencing previous subjects implies, I have argued (in the 1973 essay "Creativity and the Deductive Logic of Causality"), that the future cannot be wholly unpredictable, taking into account basic aesthetic principles motivating experiencing. Single actualities—and only they can literally prehend—must achieve some "satisfaction" in making the creative synthesis of data from the past that an experience is. Whitehead avoids the obvious errors here. He knows that beauty is not the same as sheer order but, as a musicologist has said, is "the vast realm between mechanism [mere order] and chaos." In addition, there is no conceivable way to formulate a precise quantitative law to render in principle predictable the precise creative process whereby "the many become one and are increased by one." The new unit is a creation. No psychologist has really dreamt of such a law. If a determinist, he drops experience and talks about behavior. But as absolutely ordered, that, too, is a dream and a bad one.

P5. *The Principle of Moderation.* Wilfrid Sellars has remarked that errors come in pairs of opposite extremes, the truth being somehow *between the extremes.* One way of supporting this assumption is as follows. Respect for those holding an extreme view, say Hume with his radical pluralism (followed by Russell and many other great thinkers) should lead us to reject the extreme opposite view, radical monism. Similarly, respect for radical monists, some also great minds with many disciples, leads us to reject radical pluralism. If we adopt either extreme, we imply that those holding the opposite must be hopelessly irrational. Instead, we should say, "These people (on either side) may have been a bit crazy or odd, but not *that* crazy or odd." In spite of this light-touch way of putting the matter, I am entirely serious about it. (My 1987 book, *Wisdom as Moderation,* is on this subject.) Unless we go at such issues in this way we seem to show insufficient trust in human rationality, thereby condemning ourselves along with the rest. The explanation, compatible with respect for both extreme parties, is that each sees how wrong the other is, but somehow fails to note that the dichotomy is an inexhaustive division of possibilities. Doctrinal contraries may both be wrong, but cannot both be right. This elementary logical truth is remarkably neglected in metaphysics, for example by F. H. Bradley and Bertrand Russell. There are extremes of materialism and of spiritualism; nor is dualism the mean, for it embodies some of the extremisms of both sides.

P6. *The Principle of Inclusive Polarity.* The contrasting concepts that generate extremes are related not by a mere symmetrical "and" embracing the poles but by one pole in a sense including the other and *not vice versa,* as the contingent includes the necessary or as a subject includes (Hegel: "overlaps") its object. The contrasting concepts become contraries in the sense of propositional logic (both cannot be true but both can be false) only when wrongly combined to characterize the same (or every) aspect of what is described. When one concept is applied only to extremely abstract aspects of things and the other only to concrete or intermediately abstract aspects, there is, by standard logical rules, no contradiction. No special logic, à la Hegel or Marx, need be invoked. Nor is there need to blur the distinction between conflicts among individuals and logical contradictions. To assert that two individuals' aims, when stated, are such that their joint realization would be contradictory does not violate the rule that contradictory statements are in all cases false. "I say P and you say not-P" is not contradictory and is often true. I am fond of the statement by a royal personage, "My brother Henry (perhaps it was another name) and I are of one mind; we both want Milan." He may not have been wise in this statement, but he was not talking nonsense and what he said was probably true. I completely accept the logical law concerning contradiction.

P7. *Simple but not too simple.* Another rule I rely on and that history shows the wisdom of, is Whitehead's maxim, "Seek simplicity— and distrust it." Why the seeking? Because if we do not try to simplify the welter of ideas under higher unities, we get no useful grip on reality. Both extremes in ultimate contrarieties are in a sense simpler than the moderate position they both overlook. Why the distrust? Because mere dichotomies are always crude. A trichotomy, as Peirce sagely held, is vastly closer at least to what is needed. For instance, "all, some, or none." Sometimes we need a more numerous, yet finite and manageable, set of options. For example, it can be shown that there are exactly sixteen ways of trying to describe God and what is not God, or the world, in terms of traditional contraries such as necessary or contingent, absolute or relative, infinite or finite, eternal or temporal, and still others. The true way is in a sense the most complex of the sixteen, and yet not unmanageably so. Most of the combinations have low plausibility and have scarcely been defended. But several have been powerfully espoused.

P8. *Doctrinal Matrices* It seems to me evident that from purely mathematical premises nothing extramathematical can be proved. But I hold also (with Peirce) that simply without mathematics virtually nothing can be reasonably argued for, I do not say proved, in metaphysics. Mathematical analysis is the only way to *exhaust logical possibilities*. Arguments about God, for example, do involve just sixteen combinatorial possibilities for employing conceptual contrasts, such as necessary-contingent, infinite-finite, traditionally used to define the word 'God', and we are not wholly rational if we fail to consider all of these combinations in distinguishing God from all else. In this analysis I seem to have no close historical antecedents.[1]

P9. Kant's principle that we can apply our categories only through the *temporal structure of experience* is relevant to metaphysical issues. Here I cite Aristotle for the, to me, intuitive truth that only in temporal terms can modal contrasts make existential sense. Accidents do not happen in pure eternity. They happen in temporal actuality, in becoming. To swallow time up in something eternal is either to deny contingency altogether or to try to tuck contingencies into the texture of the merely eternal. I cannot see much hope for metaphysics on either basis.

P10. Another intuitive clue is that *necessity*, since Leibniz, has been rightly analyzed as *what a set of positive possibilities have in common*; unconditional necessity is what the universal set of positive possibilities have in common. From this I deduce that the wholly necessary is extremely *abstract*. To make deity wholly necessary is to make it an empty abstraction. It follows that the inclusive or concrete reality must be contingent if anything is contingent. 'Two and three are five, and it is raining here-now' is contingent if that it is raining is so. "The Encompassing" must, as such, be contingent.

P11. On formal-logical grounds I argue that *symmetry is a derivative form of relatedness*, always explicable as a two-way functioning of what in general is a nonsymmetrical or asymmetrical relation. Thus equality of X and Y is that neither is greater than the other. In contrast, we cannot define greater or better than by merely denying equality of the things compared. Symmetry seems a positive word; but this is deceptive. It is really a negative idea: that there is *no direction* to the order of the terms. "A equal to B" is the same as "B equal to A," but "A greater than B" is very different from "B greater than A." In truth, symmetry is always an abstraction. As Plato said, no two things are absolutely equal in nature. (We may for some purposes so regard them, particularly in microphysics.) If A and B interact, this is not a single action going in two directions. If A and B know each other, this is two knowledges, not one. Directional, one-way order is the key to reality. Even in God there must be some analogy to the arrow of time.

---

[1]My best formulation of this doctrinal matrix is "Metaphysics and Dual Transcendence," *Tulane Studies in Philosophy*, 3, 1986. Or see Ch. 13 in *CS*. See also the article "Pantheism and Panentheism," in *The Encyclopedia of Religion*. Senior Editor, Mircea Eliade. (New York: Macmillan Publishing Co.; London: Collier Macmillan Publishers, 1987), vol. 11. In this article, seven of the sixteen possible combinations of the four concepts C, N, n, c are not considered. They are the three atheistic cases, omitting N, C, and NC; three acosmic cases omitting c, n, and cn; and the all-zero case, rejecting all four modal concepts—on the ground, presumably, that modality is merely syntactical or linguistic. This fashionable notion rules out rational discussion of theism and its denial a priori. It also cannot do justice to the pragmatic truth that life simply is a process of deciding between real possibilities for the future.

Given a symmetrical concept, we should look for its nonsymmetrical explicans. "Necessary and sufficient causal condition" is a symmetrical formula, implying necessity in both temporal directions. This is already suspicious. But there is more. Our natural intuitions of memory and expectation, of causes and possible effects of the present, also support a basic asymmetry. Since we exist our parents must have been; but our parents might never have had us as their children. Current science, with its concept of Mendelian inheritance and quantum theory, both involving discreteness and chance, supports this. No science and no human need requires absolute order. What they do require is causally significant freedom, without which life does not make sense.

P12. Since combinatory or systematic coherence is the meaning of metaphysical truth, answering objections in metaphysics has the difficulty that one cannot restate one's metaphysical system each time one is challenged. Gilbert Ryle once admitted that *philosophical problems are interconnected* so that *piecemeal disposal of issues one by one* is scarcely possible. He thereby shocked some of his fellow nonmetaphysicians. The English tradition, with its radically pluralistic trend, has always somewhat favored piecemeal strategies. The German tradition in Fichte and Hegel (influenced by Spinoza) went to the opposite extreme. As usual, wisdom is between the extremes (cf. P5). We do have some concrete phenomenological insights and some abstract formal insights. If we take both of these seriously and put a burden of proof on what violates them (as much of Hegel and, at the opposite extreme, of Hume, does), then we may have a chance to approach the truth. This, I hold, is also more likely if we use the history of philosophy as well as our own and our contemporaries' ingenuity, in searching for the coherence of our basic concepts. (See P19.)

P13. Another basic truth that helps in metaphysics is that concepts express distinctions, from which some critics of metaphysics derive *"the principle of contrast."* To say that "everything" is such and such—for example, is necessary, or is contingent; absolute, or relative; one, or many—is scarcely to say anything. Unity simply apart from plurality, or vice versa, is nothing coherently conceivable. Blanshard's "to understand is to see to be necessary" is a perfect example of a metaphysical error. ("Perfect" here is meant as a compliment. Clarity is a virtue. Only good writers can be so clearly wrong as he is on this issue.) To understand is to see some things or aspects of things as necessary and some as contingent; neither term would function existentially if the other did not.

The principle of contrast is a powerful metaphysical resource, not a weapon against all metaphysics. It, and not overgeneralized necessity, is the principle of reason. It corrects Hume *and* Spinoza, Leibniz (or Royce) *and* William James (or J. S. Mill). To say, "everything is necessary," or "everything is contingent" is to say something significant only if the connotation of 'everything' is somehow limited. Everything *concrete* may significantly, and I believe truly, be called contingent, and only the extremely abstract can be strictly necessary. To say, "God is exclusively necessary," or "exclusively contingent," is to destroy the religious meaning of 'God'. And what is not God is, in its most abstract sense of "some world or other," necessary; God must be *actually*, not merely potentially, creator (*pace* thousands of theologians).

P14. *Logical Strength implies Contingency.* No axiom is more clearly valid than this: *The logically weaker form of a statement can be deduced from the stronger form, but not vice versa.* Thus from 'this is a fox' one can deduce 'this is an animal', but the reverse deduction is a nonsequitur. It follows that *either* everything is necessary, violating the principle of contrast, itself a more evident axiom than some of the traditional ones, *or* only logically very weak statements can be unconditionally necessary. The contingent is richer than the necessary can possibly be. To suppose that the entire content of reality is necessary is by implication to reduce actuality to an empty abstraction. To say that God is wholly necessary is to do the same with God.

P15. Among the necessary truths this must be one: necessarily there are some positive contingent truths. The job of the metaphysician is to make as clear as possible, rather than to blur or deny, the distinction between the two sorts of truths. Hegelians have tended to deny, or at best to blur hopelessly, this distinction. *Metaphysical* truth is indeed "truth by coherence." "Rationalism is the search for the coherence of the [most general] presuppositions of civilized living." This is one definition of metaphysics, stressing the pragmatic criterion of meaning. As Peirce put it, the meaning of an idea is its contribution to the *summum bonum*. Peirce does not say, the *truth* of an idea is this contribution. However, in metaphysics meaning and truth are one, falsity here being incoherence or simply lack of meaning. When bad metaphysicians speak, they use words in ways that contradict or nullify their meanings. William James, by trying to treat all truth as contingent and empirically testable (Quine's holism, taken literally, comes to this also), got into what Montague called the "pragmire" of confusion that made some of James's writings on pragmatism largely a sad wasteland. Until we know that a contingent statement is true, we cannot know its full contribution to the good; but in metaphysics, given coherent meaning there cannot be falsity. The alternative to truth in that subject is failure to talk sense. Wittgensteinians seem to think that there are no coherent necessary ways to combine the most general ideas. They give a mischievously persuasive definition of metaphysics.

P16. The principle of sufficient reason in its strong Leibnizian form must be given up. It not only contradicts freedom or (if you prefer) hopelessly trivializes it, but also raises the question, does the sufficient reason itself have a sufficient reason? If there is an infinite regress of reasons, what is the reason for the entire series? True, any weaker version also raises such questions, for the real possibility of what happens here and now must have depended upon what went before. Causality means *at least enabling conditions*, without which the happening would have been impossible. But the weaker version has the advantage that it admits *freedom in the strong sense* of power to turn mere indefinite possibility of a certain abstractly characterized *kind* of happening into more specific abstractions or into fully particularized concrete happenings. This opens the door, otherwise closed, to conceiving an eminent, divine form of freedom able to decide such limitations upon mere logical possibility as make *cosmic* orderliness (probabilistic natural laws) effective from the beginning of a cosmic epoch, though not for infinite time. Talk about "eternal laws" of happenings is bad metaphysics.

P17. The weakened version of Leibniz's principle implies a weakened version of sufficient conditions justifying *partial* prediction of the future. Given a certain situation, a certain range of possible sorts of outcomes obtains, out of which some one sort must occur; in many cases the range may be so narrow that for certain purposes one may treat it as though it were the same as what actually happens. In an atomic explosion, or in the movements of heavenly bodies, we are not concerned about the behavior of this or that atom, molecule, or particle. There is no great mystery about the plausibility of strict determinism in such contexts. If this led to overgeneralization by many thinkers of an apparently absolute order, this seems entirely compatible with what we know about how human beings tend to use their intellects.

Already with Maxwell and Peirce the possible fallacy was pointed out, and it was Peirce who, with a few French writers (and some German and Italian writers whom he probably did not know), began the long slow process of rethinking the entire causal idea. The news that this has been happening seems scarcely to have reached the general educated public. Several recent books on causality leave open or assign to physics the determinism question. The current popularity of "compatibilism," that it does not really matter for freedom whether or not determinism is true, I regard as a typical rearguard action by nostalgic proponents of a lost cause. If the natures of causality and of freedom are not philosophically important, what is? Allowing for a reasonable indeterminacy, or qualification of "sufficient" causation, they must indeed be compatible.

P18. *Causal or Real Possibility (or Necessity) as more than Logical Possibility.* This distinction, commonly made, I have sometimes seemed to reject; and this has caused some confusion for which I partly blame myself. There is certainly a very real difference between the necessity of a conclusion (given the truth of the premises of a valid deductive argument) and the necessity of the required causal conditions of an event. The difference is in levels of abstractness or generality in contrast to the concrete or particular. What actually happens concretely transcends verbal description and must be intuited or prehended for its relations to be known. Only divine intuition is adequate to the richness of actuality. Of course, we cannot see by mere sight what is required to make possible what we see happen since we do not see a single one of the particles, atoms, molecules, or cells involved, much less a single one of the motivating animal or subanimal feelings or thoughts involved. Above all, we do not see the divine feeling and thought involved in maintaining the natural laws of our cosmic epoch. Finally, my attempt to generalize the causal notion of possibility so that it attains the generality of conceivability itself requires the idea of other cosmic epochs and laws. (I am here following Whitehead and a few other thinkers who have held that all definite quantitative laws are *finite* in their time scope.) Only in a highly complex and subtle manner am I claiming to transcend the usual distinction, and the reason I need to do this is to justify the metaphysical applicability of the most clearly valid axioms of modal logic; for instance, that the inclusive and concrete truth must be contingent and that the necessary must be exclusive and abstract.

The modal structure of causality, so far as now known to science, is that of quantum physics. It is closer to logical requirements than was Newtonian physics in that it no longer limits the modalities to two, necessary and impossible, but allows for open possibilities and probabilities. Further progress will not, I venture to say, be in the direction of a return to the modal paradox of positive and negative necessity with no place for possibility, the manifest key to all modalities. We have explored that necessitarian blind alley for twenty-five centuries. Plato, Aristotle, and Epicurus thought they knew better. We have their reasons and more.

I would like to suggest to anyone who finds my reply to a contributor unsatisfactory that he or she read, or reread, this general reply to see if it does not helpfully supplement my specific reply to that contributor.

Of the twenty-nine contributors my overall impression is one of pleasant surprise. They are more cordial toward my writing and thinking than I dared to hope; the misunderstandings are fewer and the criticisms mostly less harsh than I was inclined to fear. My earnest desire to communicate and to think and write with honesty and clarity has, it seems, achieved some success. More important, the view, as old as Greek skepticism and cleverly expounded by prominent colleagues today, of the vanity of the philosophical enterprise is, one may hope, slightly counterbalanced by the way in which a highly speculative and bold form of philosophizing can still meet with a good reception.

P19. *The history of ideas is a testing ground.* Consider, for example, the following. Greek materialism began as deterministic (Democritus) but ended in qualified determinism (Epicurus, Lucretius). Epicurus took chance to be an aspect of freedom, as much later did Peirce and James. Whitehead agrees with them, though he prefers 'disorder' to 'chance' or 'randomness'. That this does not contradict responsibility I try to show in reply to Kane. As Bishop Butler said, probability (not necessity of events) is the guide of life. Again, modern science began as strictly deterministic and modern theology as largely so. First the Socinian theologians, then Kierkegaard, then more and more theologians; first Maxwell and Peirce, then Heisenberg, then more and more scientists, broke with the tradition of unfreedom. Sheer determinism is not a survivor in the evolution of ideas. Whatever can be done with it has been tried and found wanting. One could say the same of certain forms of theism, and some forms of idealism and materialism.

For convenience I restate the principles.

PRINCIPLES IN METAPHYSICS

P0. Necessarily Something exists.
P1. Metaphysical Truth by Coherence of universal categories.
P2. Pragmatic Principle: metaphysical truths must be expressible in manner of living.
P3. Phenomenological Principle, Prehension or Feeling of Feeling.
P4. Causes as necessary but not strictly sufficient conditions; indeterminacy of the future in its concreteness.
P5. Principle of Moderation: truth and value as between extremes.
P6. Inclusive Polarity. (CS, pp. 99–100.)
P7. Simple, but not too simple.
P8. Doctrinal Matrices: exhaustive sets of theoretical options. (CS, pp. 266, 271.)
P9. Temporal structure of experience as clue to categorial contrasts.
P10. Necessity as common factor of possibilities.
P11. Symmetry as Derivative form of relatedness. (CS, Ch. X.)
P12. Interconnectedness of philosophical problems. (P1.)
P13. Principle of Contrast. (CS, 139f.)
P14. Logical Strength implies contingency: logical poverty of the necessary. (P10.)
P15. That there are some positive contingent truths is not contingent. (P0, P13.)
P16. Incompatibilism: freedom implies real chance. (P4, P9, P10, P11.)
P17. The Qualified Principle of Sufficient Reason.
P18. Causal or Real possibility as more than logical possibility.
P19. History of Ideas as testing ground.
P20. The foregoing nineteen principles must, if true, be mutually compatible; any one fully understood is, except in emphasis, equivalent to any other. They all define that abstract Something that could not fail to have instantiation or concrete realization.

ABBREVIATIONS FOR TITLES OF BOOKS CITED IN THE REPLIES

AD	*Anselm's Discovery*
W, AI	(A. N. Whitehead's) *Adventures of Ideas*
AW	*Aquinas to Whitehead*
BH	*Beyond Humanism*
BS	*Born to Sing: an Interpretation and World Survey of Bird Song*
CAP	*Creativity in American Philosophy*
CP, CSP	*Collected Papers of Charles Peirce* (ed. Hartshorne, Weiss, Burks)
DR	*The Divine Relativity*
IO	*Insights and Oversights of Great Thinkers*
LP	*The Logic of Perfection*
MN	*Mind in Nature: Essays on the Interface of Science and Philosophy*, ed. John Cobb and David Griffin (See Dorothy C. Hartshorne's Bibliographical Addenda, 1977)
W, MT	(A. N. Whitehead's) *Modes of Thought*
MVG	*Man's Vision of God*
NT	*A Natural Theology for our Time*
OMN	*Divine Omnipotence and Other Theological Mistakes*
PPS	*The Philosophy and Psychology of Sensation*
W, PR	(Whitehead's) *Process and Reality*
RSP	*Reality as Social Process*
WM	*Wisdom as Moderation*
WP	*Whitehead's Philosophy*

A. EMPIRICAL INQUIRIES

R1. Birch on Darwin, Chance, and Purpose

Although my first book (*PPS*) scored no great successes in this country or in England: it achieved one success in Australia that was fortunate for me. It appealed to the professor of biology at the University of Melbourne, W. E. Agar, who convinced his student L. Charles Birch that my book, as an application of Whitehead's philosophy, was significant for biological theory.[2] Readers of Birch's essay will not be surprised to learn that I am pleased with it. Birch is professor of biology in the University of Sydney. When I went to Australia as Fulbright lecturer in philosophy I was accepted personally ("that chap Hartshorne was certainly a nice chap," to quote one friendly philosopher at Melbourne) but, except for Alexander Boyce-Gibson who had invited me, and

---

[2]W. E. Agar, *A Contribution to the Theory of the Living Organism*. 2nd. ed. (Carlton, Victoria: Melbourne University Press, 1951). Unfortunately the remoteness of Australia, and perhaps even the extreme modesty of the title helped to prevent much attention from being given to this book. Ernest Nagel wrote a very negative review of it, which is no surprise to anyone who has read much of Nagel. As a friend of his who knows him well has said, he is a kind man who could write unkind and (I think) somewhat unfair reviews.

who was himself a voice in the wilderness in Australian philosophy, and except for Birch whom we came to know in Sydney, my kind of philosophy did not take hold. In addition to any limitations in my presentations, there were two main reasons: the influence of G. E. Moore in Brisbane and Sydney, and of Wittgenstein in Melbourne. There was also John Smart developing his materialism in Adelaide. In contrast, ornithologists in that far-off country gave me the best response I had had from specialists in that subject. And I recall a physicist there who said that he was glad to learn of "a philosopher who was interested in living things." Indeed, I respond warmly to both the title and the contents of E. O. Wilson's book *Biophilia*. His mistake is in supposing that there is any simply nonliving and insentient, yet concrete and singular reality.

Since I agree so thoroughly with Birch, I shall not take much space to go into details. I will say something about the fact that, as Birch makes clear, Charles Kingsley, contemporary of Darwin, not only accepted Darwinism, pious clergyman though he was, as God's way of creating, but did so in a way that partly anticipated the process doctrine of *universal* creativity. That nobody saw the significance of this until recently is an example of what I call the "cultural lag" characteristic of philosophy. Over and over, one finds that someone saw the point long before scholars generally caught on. Epicurus took chance seriously literally thousands of years before Peirce proposed his doctrine of tychism with forceful arguments on the level of (or above) the science of his time. And Epicurus and Lucretius related chance to freedom, just as James and Peirce later did. But our culture generally is still pre-Epicurean, also pre-Aristotelian (for the great philosopher-scientist partly saw what Epicurus saw), as well as pre-Peircean.

Of all Birch's formulations there is only one that I would even mildly criticize. Twice he says that creatures have freedom "to respond or not to respond" to the divine persuasion. This for me is too close to the traditional notion, obey or disobey God's command. Whitehead and Berdyaev have taught me that the divine imperative is to "be creative and foster creativity in others." An artist, scientist, or statesman, a husband, wife, or friend is not just obeying or disobeying someone or something. All are *creating experiences* in themselves and helping others to do the same. Even an atom of uranium is not just deciding whether or not at a given moment to change into an atom of lead. That is but a partial aspect of what is being decided. Whitehead soared above all previous thought when he said, "The many become one and are increased by one." The new unity is not a mere rearrangement of old units, it is a new single actuality. No unqualified determinism can construe this, and so the reduction by determinists (including Skinner) of feeling to mere behavior is not surprising. Even so they do not get rid of the indeterminacy of quantum physics and, as I believe, with Bergson and Whitehead, the greater indeterminacy of animal behavior. Feeling is no "idle wheel" in nature but the universal driving force. And it comes in finite unit-cases, not in infinitely divided portions. All concrete plurality is finite except that already actualized in the beginningless past. And even that is forever being increased. This topic will recur again in the replies.

R2. Skutch on Bird Song and Philosophy

Alexander Skutch is a name well known to students of the behavior of birds; he is also a distinguished botanist. Neotropical nature has been his specialty; he has lived with it during many decades. He is well read about bird behavior in various countries. To have him comment on my bird-song book is very good luck indeed. This is especially so because Skutch is a philosopher as well as a scientist, as one can see from several of his books.[3] He has, however, taken pains to discuss, in dealing with my ornithological writings, only those aspects of his philosophy that are closely relevant to *Born to Sing*. There are other aspects; but he has generously put them aside almost entirely in the present case. I shall not altogether imitate him in this.

I find no misinterpretation of my views about bird song in Skutch's account and feel, as he has often told me, that on this subject our views harmonize well. I am aware that by one measure of "short-term memory" we and birds are not far apart. To detect how many successive musical tones one has just been hearing, for instance, *without counting, using words or other symbols*, birds can get to five, and we do little better. However, we can memorize a very long pattern, musical or verbal, while parrots, for example, seem to stop at five seconds; thus, a short nursery rhyme spoken rapidly. Continued fear of a snake in the brush seems rather different. I do agree that for a bird more happens in a brief time than for us. Still birds have no symphonies or long reproducible musical compositions.

If E. A. Armstrong (whom I knew well) and Skutch have not been wholly convinced by my evidence that birds who sing well also sing more in a year, this has to be taken seriously. I think, however, that there is justification for my "elaborate formula" for measuring amount of singing—including length of song season (rather few species sing appreciably in every month), a fraction to discount long pauses not part of the musical pattern, and ways of allowing for species known to sing with some freedom in winter quarters or in migration. Having lived in quite a number of parts of this country and the world I have a more adequate base for statistical estimates than Armstrong, or even perhaps Skutch, has had, or more chances to make such comparisons as his, between the two thrushes near his house in Costa Rica (which I have visited). And I wonder

---

[3]See especially Alexander F. Skutch, *Life Ascending* (Austin: University of Texas Press, 1985).

if he has allowed adequately for the (if I recall rightly) shorter pauses of Clay-colored (Skutch's Garden) Thrush, implying more actual singing in a given "performance." Where I live now, Mockingbird, Cardinal, and Carolina Wren sing much of the year and with fairly high continuity. In central California, Mockingbird, Hermit Thrush, and Fox Sparrow have long seasons and high continuity (short pauses), all singing far better than merely mediocre singers. At least the case for my "correlation of quantity and quality" is still open.

Perhaps Skutch's tropical observation station may in this matter be less favorable than my predominantly nontropical one. The rigors of cold winters, or of migration to escape winter, are severe tests of the power of aesthetic sensitivity to overcome distracting forces and maintain singing zeal. Life is easier (as shown by fewer or smaller clutches of eggs) "where winter never comes"; hence the luxury of singing outside the breeding season is more affordable. The same difference is shown by the much greater amounts of that other luxury, female or dual singing, duetting, in the tropics. I owe this argument to the stimulus of Skutch's skepticism; it occurs to me now for the first time. Skutch's opinion of its validity would be of interest.

As to whether our "characters" must determine our choices, or we would make more mistakes than we do, this approaches one of our philosophical differences. Our characters and circumstances certainly have a lot to do with our choices, but how close this comes to strictly "determining" them is the question.

In the breadth of his interests Skutch reminds me of two other writers, E. O. Wilson, justly famous "sociobiologist," and Rudolf Jordan, South African grape grower and writer of philosophical books appealing to science rather than metaphysics to settle questions.[4] I mention Wilson here because he has given the best account I have read of what we can infer from neurophysiology and evolutionary theory about human freedom. It shows how wide open the issue, as an empirical scientific one, still is.[5] Jordan holds a view, congenial to me, that causal determinism is nowhere absolute.

Skutch would, I think, like (and I am still more strongly inclined) to attribute a psychical aspect to even the least of the truly integrated actualities (acting as one) in nature, taking particles, atoms, cells, and animals generally, as singular in this dynamic sense. As the reader perhaps knows, I treat causal freedom, creativity, in the same generalized way.

---

[4]Rudolf Jordan, *The New Perspective* (The University of Chicago Press, 1951). For his penetrating and informative discussion of individuality as a fifth dimension see pp. 36–38; of randomness or the accidental and freedom, pp. 76–91. Jordan's *Autobiography* (New York: Frederick Fell, 1981) is a truly wise man's reflections upon his career. See pp. 100, 153, 180, 198, 201. In the last page cited I think he somewhat overstates the "vagueness" of theism as defined by dual transcendence and the interpersonal and mind-body analogies.

[5]E. O. Wilson, *Biophilia* (Cambridge, Mass. and London, England: Harvard University Press, 1984). Also *On Human Nature* (same press, 1978).

Skutch and I could probably agree that biological generalizations are likely to have exceptions. That is one of the reasons why I tried to use statistical methods, sometimes requiring a computer to handle easily. There are many variables; one cannot expect the neatness of some truths of physics. My attempt to find correlations among quantified variables of singing behavior, drawing data from many regions and many writers, is the first of its kind and so far seems the only one. The ball is now in the court of those who wish to check my results. Concerning the Spot-breasted Oriole of tropical Middle America, it has a beautiful song but stereotyped, lacking in variety or complexity, and not high in continuity, hence rather low in quantity per minute of performance. This is true in general of the colorful orioles. Beauty is not the only variable I take into account in rating singing skill as a biological concept. This is relevant to the Tinamous example.

Thinking of Skutch, I recall the lines of William Cullen Bryant: "To him who in the love of nature holds/ communion with her visible [and audible] forms she speaks a various language." If anyone has loved nature in recent times it is Skutch—with the serious qualifications, however, that he thinks there should be no limit to the determination of events by the past, no possibility of destructive interindividual conflict, no multiple freedom or creative decision-making to cause disorder or conflict, and—here like Schweitzer—no predation. That I fall into conflict with him on these points is an example of what I am talking about. To make such disorder or conflict impossible would, on my view, be to make life itself, and any positively conceivable world, impossible also. My view furnishes a model of much that Skutch thinks to be erroneous and his view a model of much that I think erroneous. Yet we can coexist and to a considerable extent appreciate each other. And after all, between us we cover energetically both sides of three great controversies, those over theism and the goods and bads in nature, determinism and freedom, and mortality and immortality of individuals (and species—he seems to object to *their* mortality also).

A reader opposed to theism will find in Skutch's book *Life Ascending* the most vigorous account I have read of the atheistic argument from evil. One who favors theism should note how dependent the argument is upon the assumption (which Darwin could be comfortable neither with nor without) that divine power must be a monopoly of decision-making, leaving no genuine options open for creaturely freedom. Skutch seems innocent of Darwin's misgivings on this topic and quite fails to envisage what Birch and I see as the key to the evolutionary scheme—it might be called the Charles Kingsley principle—of creatures "making themselves," hence in some degree their descendants, their species. (Kingsley, a clergyman and literary genius, was not wholly clear in his view, but then who was, in those years?)

One who believes neither in God nor in human careers extending beyond death should note how Skutch's feeling that death should not terminate our careers is nourished by his disbelief in God and consequent inability to find in objective immortality of all experience in divine experience the remedy for temporal finitude. For God our earthly actuality will be everlastingly there, as Whitehead was first to say clearly and with adequate systematic context. Lacking this, what remedy is there but endless individual careers? I see in Skutch, as in the Jain religion that he knows and admires, an example of how belief in human survival, individual or specific, is a rival to theistic belief, not its supposed proper complement, as in conventional Islam and Christianity— also in Kant's second Critique! By ascribing immortality to oneself (or one's species) one challenges the distinctiveness of a divine attribute. I mention here Heidegger's recognition that deity is "infinite temporality," not sheer eternity. If we, too, have this infinity for the future, then in so far we are as God. I think a more humble role is the appropriate one. The Jains are candid about their contrary position: they hold that after death they may, forever, more and more fully divinize themselves. We do not need God, we shall become gods ourselves.

If I have been less generous to Skutch's philosophy than he to mine, I hope this is partly balanced by the fact that I have sought to introduce him as writer to philosophers, most of whom will probably not have heard of him. Reading his work, whatever one's beliefs, one will share in the spiritual adventures of one of the great field naturalists of all time.

R3. Chiaraviglio on Song, Evolution, and Theism

Although *Born to Sing* has been reviewed or discussed by many, no one, I think, has so accurately and succinctly summarized what is distinctive about it as Lucio Chiaraviglio does in the first two brief paragraphs, and almost in the first sentence, of his essay. He notes that the work embodies an *empirical* investigation by a *philosopher* of an aspect (the auditory "expressions") of the *behavior* of a group (a very large world-wide one) of animal species; that it seeks to *quantify* the variables of behavior studied and looks for *correlations* among these variables, and also between one of them and an aspect of the behavior of a species in a widely different group (the human species of the mammals), its *aesthetic* judgments as applied to bird song. Aristotle and a scholastic philosopher had done empirical work in ornithology; some ornithologists had given attention to a possible aesthetic sense in birds, but none of these writers attempted to quantify the behavior variables involved. The combination of the six factors I have italicized is indeed unique. In prefacing my book with Fermi's pronouncement, "To know is to measure," I meant to call attention to the centrality of quantification. Modern science is essentially a measuring of empirical facts as means to the discovery of otherwise hidden structures of reality.

What has all this to do with aesthetic ratings of bird song? I have heard Paul Dirac say to an audience of philosophers and scientists, "It is more important that Einstein's theory is beautiful than that it is true." Mathematicians, physicists, biologists, often speak of the beauties of their theories and discoveries. One definition of science might be: "The search for the hidden beauty of the world, so far as discoverable by close observation, open discussion, and the use of rigorous logic and mathematics."

As I have explained in the last chapter of my book *Creative Synthesis*, all value, including the value of truth, is, at least indirectly, aesthetic, the value of experiences as such, and I hold, with idealists or psychicalists generally, including Leibniz, Peirce, Whitehead, and Bergson, that simply apart from experience on some level, human, subhuman, or superhuman, apart from all experiences there is nothing. Experiences are intrinsically valuable so far as they are harmonious and intense. The most general principles of harmony and intensity are more ultimate than the laws of physics and are the reasons for there being natural laws. Chiaraviglio, basically knowledgeable in the exact sciences, especially logic and physics, information theory, and recent evolutionary theory, is philosphically sophisticated and aesthetically sensitive, especially to music. He is familiar with the metaphysics of Whitehead, some aspects of which he has formalized according to a logical scheme. Of all my former students he was probably the one whose technical competence most transcended that of his teacher. I am not surprised that it is he, not anyone else, who sees most exactly what I was trying to do in my ornithological work. Considering its brevity, I find no flaws in his account of that work. I have tried to find correlations (or their absence) among the following variables: degrees of song development or "singing skill," territorial individualism (or its opposite, gregariousness), inconspicuousness, and some other behavioral-ecological variables. The correlations mostly come out strongly positive, in some cases according to a computer as used by a trained operator (not by me).

One hypothesized correlation, for which I am chiefly known to ornithologists, that concerning monotony-avoidance in singing, turned out only weakly positive for one large group of singers, those not classified as true songbirds or oscines. These non-oscines (including the suboscines), some species of which do sing monotonously, lack highly-developed muscle systems for controlling utterances. I therefore revised my theory to run: the development of muscles for singing evolved together with the development of neurones for aesthetic discrimination and enjoyment. The crude and the subtle physical requisites evolved at much the same pace.[6]

After my book was published, some experiments by Fernando Nottebohm and others on bird brains showed that in the songbirds tested the number of neurones in the areas of the forebrain involved in singing varied seasonally by hundreds of thousands from the period of abundant singing to that of little or no singing. This explains a fact that had puzzled me, why species that sing and sing well part of the year may cease almost entirely for months. I wondered why (if, as I believe, they enjoy singing) they give up this enjoyment for protracted periods. If the brain cells concerned are lacking, perhaps the very "idea" of, or feeling for, the song pattern could not be had; the birds could not even *want* to sing. Actually, the best singers statistically sing much more of the year than poor singers. They also have life-strategies that make distinctive singing unusually needful. Above all, they are strongly territorial, rather than gregarious, and are inconspicuous in their natural habitats. (Modern lawns are somewhat unnatural.) If territorial possession must be advertised and cannot be made apparent visually, it must be proclaimed by sound. Thus our human judgment of singing goodness or skill is confirmed by behavioral and ecological correlations. The human judgments of "good" singing that yield such correlations cannot be as "subjective" as many suppose. Some ornithologists saw the point, especially those that have focused on song.

I am slightly (and perhaps wrongly) uneasy about Chiaraviglio's carefully guarded substitution of "intelligence" for my "mind," "psyche," "soul," or "experiencing." One is reminded of Descartes' "cogito" to cover also feeling, volition, desire. I see a point in Whitehead's (also Peirce's and Bradley's) preference for *feeling* as the universal aspect of the psychical. An infant surely feels; but how much does it think? True, there is learning at least down to the protozoan level, but 'intelligence' is perhaps a bit misleading for such adaptive capacity. Whitehead's "intellectual feelings" and "symbolic reference", or Peirce's theory of signs, seem to me to take care of the cognitive aspect, retaining feeling as including an at least slight aspect of memory (present feeling of past feelings) and a minimal sense (Whitehead's "mentality") of open

---

[6]My "Monotony-threshold in singing birds" (Auk, 83, 176–92) was published in 1956. Twenty-six years later, in a two-volumed work on *Acoustic Communication in Birds*, Ed. Kroodsma et al. (Academic Press), Vol. II, containing essays by nine authors on "Song and Its Consequences," about twenty references to my work on song, especially with reference to the avoidance of monotony, are scattered through the volume. Kroodsma defends my primary thesis that high continuity in singing (very brief pauses) correlates well with "immediate variety" (avoidance of excessive repetition except after sufficient time-lapse to escape monotony in the psychological sense). A biologist known for his work on song, in reviewing *BS*, wrote, "The author is a very capable ornithologist." Another wrote, "He has certainly read about these birds."

possibilities, and "decision" among them, for the primitive levels, as well as necessary aspects of all higher ones. Life is enjoying-suffering, with at least some slight sense of actual past and possible future events, whatever else it may also be. *Mere* thinking or knowing may be left to computers, which in the literal sense do not think at all but only enable us to do so faster and more powerfully. Here as at many points I am glad to agree with Karl Popper.

Apart from these semantic questions, I appreciate and find educative— though strenuous to grasp—Chiaraviglio's account of the evolution of intelligence. I have never consciously disbelieved in evolution and have, nearly as long as I can recall, felt myself to be a member of one—a curiously eccentric one—of the multitude of animal kinds, all of them products of evolution. I have also long believed in the evolutionary role of "culture," in the generalized sense of learning from one's elders and peers, or, on the human level, from ancestors. In this way some of the results formerly expected from genetic inheritance of acquired characters can indirectly be obtained. As new forms of adaptive behavior happen to emerge in individuals, and are imitated, or learned from, by others, any genes that favor such behavior also become adaptive. That culture in this general sense has "costs" and "may be a dead end" reminds me of something I once heard G. F. Moore, historian of religion, say: "It is civilization that destroys nations. What else could destroy them?" The extravagant resort to drugs today looks like an illusory flight from a scarcely bearable civilization. Chiaraviglio is troubled, as I am, by the thought that we may have fallen into dangerously unnatural ways of living.

In the section on feelings and algorithms, my commentator hints at some disagreement with my thought; but I find nothing to quarrel with him about in this section, nor in the next, on algorithms and adaptation, which closes with a careful summary of some investigations on the brains of certain songbirds. I am happy that Chiaraviglio finds the results of these inquiries supportive of my views about the relations between singing skill and facts of neural anatomy. I may be the first to use the expression "singing skill." Swallows fly more as well as better than most birds, some of which are flightless, or fly only slowly and under pressure. Swallows fly fast (and gracefully, to our perceptions), and we sense that their doing so is no hardship and probably at least mildly enjoyable. Singing skill, like any other, must have degrees, and for wide variations in the degrees there must be adaptive reasons.

In the latter part of the last section, on complexity, chaos, and order, my commentator indicates some misgivings, not about my ornithological ideas but about my theistic metaphysics—which was at most barely hinted at in the book on song, but of which Chiaraviglio, as my former student, and a reader of *The Logic of Perfection*, is well aware. As he knows, metaphysics in my view has important relations to logic (and mathematics), also to experience, but is not open to observational falsification. Chiaraviglio's introduction, late in the essay, of the name of Anselm is his way of recognizing my position on this topic. He knows my (partial) defense of Anselm. But, being less sympathetic to this side of my work than to my analysis of aesthetic ideas in their empirical applications, he may somewhat oversimplify the problem he finds in my application of these ideas to deity.

I agree, perhaps more than my critic realizes, with his point that aesthetic principles do not justify the idea of deity, *if* that is taken as simply identical with what Plato once called perfection, meaning a value so absolute that any addition or change would be irrelevant or worse. This simple identification I do not accept. On the contrary, I hold that there is no coherent way to conceive an absolute terminus to the series of more and more beautiful concrete actualities. I hold, rather, that deity is the kind of actuality whose beauty can be surpassed *only by itself*. The actual divine beauty includes (by prehending or intuiting them) all other actual beauties, hence no other actual beauty can rival it. However, as new actualities (new even for God) are created (partly by themselves as acting freely), the divine life is "enriched." In any actual state of reality God is the *de facto* terminus of "more beautiful than." An eternal, hence (Aristotle) strictly necessary, terminus to this series is a non-idea (contra Aristotle) and makes no consistent sense. Aesthetic value, in the primary concrete sense in which a total experience is good in itself, admits of no absolute maximum. Nor can any concrete experience, divine or otherwise, be necessarily existent. What can be necessary is that there be *some* concrete and intrinsically good experiences, some of them divine and some not divine. The divine experiences that there are could have been unactualized; but the class of divine experiences as well as the class of nondivine experiences could not have been empty. The nondivine experiences, however, do not, whereas the divine experiences do, form a single individual life, ideally self-identical, not in the strict logical or Leibnizian sense of there being no contingency of qualities but in the sense of an ideal and everlasting retention of all qualities once acquired.

My concept of divine transcendence is "dual," involving a uniquely excellent way of being complete and unsurpassable (even by itself) but also a uniquely excellent way of being forever further enhanced and in this sense self-surpassed. Classical theism was oversimple, one-sided in trying to define deity by putting God on one side only of the ultimate polar contrasts, in spite of the evidence that both poles are required to constitute a concrete meaning for the term God or any other name of an individual being. I am far from alone in this contention, although no one has generalized and clarified the principle, which I call "dual transcendence", as I have done. Socinus (sixteenth, seventeenth centuries), Berdyaev, E. S. Brightman, Bergson, Peirce, Whitehead, a number of others, some in India, also Japan, have in one way or another broken with the simple one-sided classical views. The old labels do not pick out the real issues. My view is as definitely different from classical pantheism as from classical theism, and also quite different from what was meant in other times by the idea of a simply "finite" God. Brightman had already written about his "finite-infinite" God. And Whitehead clearly affirmed or implied both finitude and infinity, necessity and contingency, independence and dependence, of God.

I believe Chiaraviglio will not disagree with me when I say that it is a logical truism that contrary properties may be consistently applied to a subject, provided they are attributed to the subject in diverse respects. The contingent, dependent aspect of God is concrete and all-inclusive of other dependent, concrete actualities; whereas the necessary, independent aspects are abstract. Thus my dual theory of transcendence is not a simple "coincidence" of opposites in God.

There are two kinds of beauty: beauty of abstract ideas, as in mathematical theories; and beauty of concrete experiences. God's purely necessary and therefore eternal 'essence', as I call it, is abstractly beautiful in an absolute sense; for it includes whatever else is strictly eternal, hence all extremely abstract beauty; it does not include the incomparably richer beauty of the actual developing cosmos and God's enjoyment of that cosmos, in which contingent harmonies are enjoyed as well as the necessary and eternal ones. What my friend Lucio Chiaraviglio mostly discusses in his essay is the contingent beauties, and I agree, so far as I understand it, with much that he says.

It is true that theism attributes some forms of excellence to deity that are terminal. These are abstract and negative aspects of value, such as the impossibility of divine error and ignorance. They are abstract for they tell us nothing about the concrete features of the world that is divinely known and upon which the concrete aesthetic value of the knowing partly depends. Similarly righteousness, or right-ness in responding to and influencing the world, is abstract. One can rightly respond to the suffering of others, but this will not make the suffering responded to other than suffering. Indeed I hold with Berdyaev and Whitehead (and some ancient heretics) that God sympathizes with and in that sense *shares* the suffering.

A similar distinction can be made between abstract and concrete aspects of aesthetic value. Not only can abstract objects be found beautiful but there is an abstractable aspect of enjoying even concrete beauties and this aspect can be maximal or nonmaximal. A bird cannot enjoy the beauty of a symphony, but only at most of simple, brief tunes or bits of rhythm; no human being can enjoy the concrete beauty of the cosmos in anything like its fullness; God can be distinguished from all else by the divine ability to *adequately* enjoy the cosmos in its *de facto* entirety. Each newly created creature will be an addition to the value thus divinely enjoyed; but the ability to respond ideally well to each new creature can at all times be unsurpassable absolutely.

What my critic writes about the components of nature needing no container, nothing to hold them together, I find brilliantly put, but less than conclusive. The components do prehend their predecessors and (after a time-lapse) their near contemporaries (as in their previous states); but the entire scheme of natural laws is taken for granted in the account. If the type of order (the system of laws) in our cosmic epoch is contingent, then it is as if a decision had been made. The creatures mutually adapt; but one cannot adapt to mere chaos. The critic says the distances between worlds (inhabitable planets?) saves diverse, mutually incompatible life-webs from disrupting each other. This is part of the basic order that theism attributes to a divine orderer. The spaciousness of the cosmos makes possible a vast variety of life-systems.

There is little in Chiaraviglio's essay about freedom. I find instances of this even in birds' or other animals' singing. In my Peirce-Whitehead view, reality is composed of at least slightly free actualities (free in the libertarian, creative, causal sense), the necessary but not strictly "sufficient" or precisely determining conditions of each act of freedom being set only by acts of freedom already performed, whether by the same individuals or by others. If this is the whole story, what explains the possibility of the basic laws that make mutual adaptation possible, including the isolation of planets from one another that limits the disturbance of one life-web by another? The theistic answer is that "others" in the previous sentence must include a divine or all-surpassing form of freedom able to inspire the rest to conform to the divinely decided natural laws of their cosmic epoch.

My trust in metaphysics and in theism is not simply in Anselm's type of argument. For me that is but one of half a dozen theistic arguments from conceptual requirements. Each argument is strong where the others are weak by themselves; together they form a cable, not a chain as weak as its weakest link. No one of these arguments would entirely convince me; but none is without force and they are logically interconnected in intelligible ways. (*CS*, ch. 15.)

I agree that processes relate themselves to other processes, but I think this presupposes something not itself a localized process of specific worldly types only contingently instantiated, surpassable by others, fallible in wisdom and power. There is need for a process of the cosmic or supercosmic kind, forming the individual surpassable only by itself, its individuality necessarily somehow instantiated and able to make ordering decisions setting the kind of mixture of Epicurean "chance and necessity" (or probability) that gives a cosmic epoch its character. One of the theistic arguments holds that truth (or reality, they are interdefinable) is intelligible only in terms of something analogous to knowing or awareness as in us yet infallible in that error and ignorance are excluded, though not new knowledge, so far as what is there to be known is itself new. In the sense in which we *fallibly* "know" or are intelligent, the infallible wisdom does not know—or solve problems.

My basic conclusion from "Anselm's principle" is not that we certainly know the divine existence but that we can know, with reasonable certainty, that the only intelligible alternative to the divine existence is the divine impossibility, the incoherence of the idea itself. It is not easy to conceive God coherently, and Chiaraviglio's misgivings imply this. But, since Anselm, it is obtuse to suppose (I do not mean that Chiaraviglio supposes this) that there are two questions, "Can we make sense out of the idea of God?" and "Can we know that such a being exists?" The question of meaning is the entire question. In other words, the idea of divine existence is irreducibly metaphysical, transempirical.

Another argument tries to show that without the idea of God we cannot formulate a rational aim for living. It cannot be one's own survival; for we and all nondivine individuals die. For similar reasons it cannot be species survival. If all worldly experiences contribute to a form of experience that ideally retains their aesthetic richness, then all self-regarding and all other-regarding concerns are summed up in the one inclusive concern of serving God, who is not mortal and does not forget. It begs the question to infer that such an ability to avoid forgetting and death is impossible for God because it is impossible for nondivine beings. God, on any high religious standpoint, has some unique properties.

That the move to theism is "poorly motivated" by considerations of ordinary processes I connect with my insistence that theism is transempirical, though remaining experiential. Without percepts there are no concepts, and no percept could compel most of us to believe in the existence of God. However, I hold that no one could conceivably observe something incompatible with the divine existence. For both classical and neoclassical theism any conceivable world would be a God-ordered world. Worlds cannot be divided into those with God and those without. If this world is without God, then any world would be so. The existential question is "Which makes sense, the theistic idea of a world or the nontheistic idea?" Atheism has nothing comparable to the mystic's claim to intuit God. Nontheism is always argumentative, never essentially intuitive. As criticism of absurd or idolatrous notions of God, implying mean or absurd conceptions of human nature, or of nature generally, it may very well have an intuitive basis.

Chiaraviglio is rightly suspicious of any view that does not harmonize with the revolutionary origins of our and every species. Some theistic views do not so harmonize. But they are views I reject. The theist Charles Kingsley found a key to this problem in the lifetime of Darwin. (So did my father not long after Darwin's death.) It is the view that the divine making "makes things [to some extent] make themselves." If individuals have some degree of freedom in the creative sense, then in the long run they also partly make their descendants and may make new species. Theism is illuminating in this context. All self-making in nature is subject to laws of nature, expressive of the (approximate or statistical) cosmic orderliness without which no coherent system of partly free beings can exist? A theism that takes God as supreme example of self-making is uniquely able to explain how there can be such cosmic orderliness. Nondivine, localized, fallible individuals cannot reasonably be supposed to decide which among conceivable laws shall obtain in our cosmic epoch. Only a supreme freedom, supremely universal and unfailing in its influence because of its supreme quality, can meet this requirement. And the requirement must be met, not simply if there is to be a world, but no matter what. For I regard the being of total nonbeing, as well as the being of God without any world, as nonsense or contradiction. Hence the divine power to provide the necessary limits to disorder among the always partly self-made creatures must be infallible.

In addition an evolutionary reason can be given for the fact that our species of animal in all its branches, so far as we know its habits, has had some form of religion. Bergson, in his *Two Sources of Religion and Ethics*, his greatest work in my opinion, gives, so far as I know, the best explanation of why a species that develops our human degree of symbolic power will need guidance and motivation beyond that furnished by instincts tested by natural selection, and he shows how such guidance and motivation is provided by the religions, especially the theistic ones. He also suggests some explanation of the excesses, absurdities, and dangers posed by the religious imagination *(le fonction fabulatrice),* along with the elements of truth.

I add Whitehead's great chapter on "Peace" in *AI,* summed up by the splendid phrase that we can conceive our individual adventures as "included in the adventure of the universe as one." In my view (even more explicitly than in Whitehead's), the universe as one is God, analogous to the way I (or you) is my (or your) body as one. The animal body as merely a vast society of cells is a collective and does not act as one in the full sense in which a human or other higher animal acts as one. The divine integrity of the cosmos must be in principle infinitely superior to that of any animal body. It must be immune to destruction, insanity, malevolence, folly, but not to sharing in the joys and sufferings of its bodily constituents or "cells". I take even Plato, also Berdyaev and Whitehead, to have had rather similar views on these points. But Aristotle, Plotinus, Augustine, and Aquinas mistook metaphysical or theological half-truths for the complete truth so far as humanly knowable.

I feel grateful to my long-time friend and one-time student for his incisive and insightful discussion of two contrasting aspects of my work. If his appreciation of one of these aspects does not persuade him to follow me in the other, he is like Skutch and, for all I know, at least a third of the contributors, who apparently do not accept any positive version of the central idea of the theistic religions. Agreement in the philosophy of religion is not in sight in our present-day world.

On one point I can agree with my critic, namely that to justify a declarative proposition one must "exhaust the possible alternatives." This I attempt to do in my sixteen ways of applying, positively or negatively, to God and what is not God, modal or other comparably abstract polar categories. We must also find analogies between the divine, which we do not obviously experience as such, and things that we do obviously so experience, for instance persons or other higher animals. Without these analogies the idea of God remains an utterly empty abstraction and its existence would lack religious or ethical import and mean no more than that we conceive it. Classical theism and pantheism ignored most of the sixteen categorial ways and they also ignored or implicitly negated the most helpful analogies, including the mind-body relation in ourselves and, by reasonable inference, in other higher animals.

I have already indicated that, among my former students, the one to whom I am here replying was the one whose intellectual power seemed most apparent. I close this reply by saying that (I hope with due respect for the others) among the twenty-nine contributors to the present volume, I again find myself almost overwhelmed by the same impression of power. His objections to theism seem to me much more to the point than the most usual traditional ones. Mere empiricism cannot rationally deal with the theistic issue. Deity cannot be coherently conceived by ordinary empirical means of extrapolation, and neither its existence nor its nonexistence can be shown in this way. However, according to a number of great scientists and philosophers of science, including Karl Popper, neither can science be given full explication, nor can it flourish, without some transempirical principles, including a realistic view of human knowledge. The essential religious problems seem to me to make similar requirements even more manifestly. However, to argue this matter adequately with this critic on his high level exceeds my abilities. Chiaraviglio's contribution is worth careful study by readers who cherish intellectual aspects of philosophical problems.

R4. Viney on the Psychology of Sensation

Professor Wayne Viney, in his careful, understanding, and informative essay, is not quite the first or only psychologist to say some kind things about my first book *(PPS)* of more than fifty years ago. Koffka said it was worth reading, and Carroll Pratt, specialist in the psychology of music, an important theme in my book, told me, perhaps twenty years ago, that it was ahead of its time. But on the whole this new long-delayed discussion is the most encouraging one there has been. In empirical science, to be relevant after a half century is enough to give an inquirer the feeling that his or her hard work and thinking—and no one can read that book and not realize how much hard work and thinking went into it—were not done in vain.

I find no misinterpretations in Viney's account. What he says I did in the book is what—so far as a complex argumentation can be summarized in the space allowed—I think I did. And his explanation of the little attention the book has received (although, as he points out, it was reprinted after thirty-four years) is compatible with and helpfully supplements the explanation I would give. I was fascinated, for instance, by his account of William James's absurd impatience with sensory psychology. This seems one more instance of the distortions produced by an over-moralistic, rather than aesthetic, approach to problems of value and motivation. James has also been accused of being little interested in children and in genetic psychology. This I connect with his being a male chauvinist. These are all examples of the gulf some biologists see between their subject and psychology as so far developed. A related fact is the neglect of comparative psychology, or its reduction to concern for human beings and laboratory animals. From this point of view I value E. O. Wilson, with his sociobiology, as a needed counterbalance to all merely "humanistic" approaches to the social sciences.

First books are likely to have faults somehow connected to the fact that they are, in each case, an author's first big attempt. My first book had such faults. Not all the argumentation is clearly better than special pleading. And there was some bad luck in that it has the most misleading typographical error of my publishing career. On an early page (27) occurs the word *millimeter* where *millimicron* is required. In fact *millimeter* was not in my manuscript or in my mind; its occurrence in the printed book arose from an odd combination of an insufficiently legible handwritten abbreviation of mine (in Greek letters) expanded (on the supposition that the letters were English *m*'s) into the supposed complete word *millimeter* by an editor of the press, corrected by me to *millimicron* in galley proof, but somehow persisting in the printed version. Knight Dunlap cited the error as evidence of my ignorance.

Viney's essay speaks for itself so well that I could almost content myself with what I have already said about its merits. However, I will mention a few things he omitted. I would like sometime to know what he thinks of the experiments by F. R. Bichowsky, G. B. Phelan, and R. B. Cattell to check on the often alleged separability of affect and sensation, experiments done on both sides of the Atlantic and causing the important British psychologist C. Spearman, like the others mentioned, to adopt a psychicalist ontology.

I also wonder what he thinks of my analysis of loudness as a somewhat ambiguous term blurring the distinction between strength of a sound arising from its intensity per unit of volume and strength arising from volume, where volume or bulk means spread of activity throughout a portion of nervous tissue, and unit of volume means something like a nerve cell, or group of cells interacting in a certain way. Intensity per unit of volume largely coincides, as experiments have shown, with pitch, while physiological volume is what appears introspectively as voluminousness of sounds. Low-pitched sounds are diffuse, spread out; high-pitched are concentrated and at the upper limit point-like. These distinctions are entirely relevant to the musical effects of sounds and, I have no doubt, are essential to understanding the power of music. Pratt explains musical effects by the various ways tones are combined; however, single tones are already in themselves differentially expressive, emotional. Ordinary association theories miss the real point. No animal needs to learn the basic emotive meaning of loud snarls, whines, groans, or thunderclaps. An infant will cry upon hearing thunder.

The psychology of music, and of poetry, is still undeveloped because of poor understanding of the emotional character of sensory qualities. When Beethoven said, the tones made by musical instruments are ''primordial feelings of nature'' (Urgefühle der Natur) he was a better psychologist than many professionals. Classical composers knew these things. See the book by Deryck Cooke.[7]

Before I knew that Viney was to contribute to this volume I was already indebted to him as the admirable father of an admirable son, Donald, who has written a fine book on my global argument (or system of arguments) for theism. It is my observation of life, and of biographies, that unusual merit in a person usually means unusual merit in at least one parent. How far this is a matter of genes and how far a matter of learning after birth we cannot know; but we do, I think, know that it is partly both. Charles Peirce is not thinkable without the intelligence of his father Benjamin, whose view of reality was not far from that of his son's, and I am not thinkable without both my father's and my mother's personalities. The causes of a personality are other personalites even more than inherited genes.

R5. Hospers on the Aesthetics of Sensation

As Wayne Viney encourages the psychological author of PPS, so John Hospers encourages its philosophical author. The two papers are the most adequate and penetrating discussions of my aesthetic theory of experience that I recall reading. Professor Hospers makes many points that I take to be sound. As he realizes, our language for feelings and emotions is not easily made precise—if indeed precision means much in this difficult matter. He realizes also that the way he inclines to think about the role of affection in experience has a good deal of

---

[7]The Language of Music (Oxford University Press, 1959). My dear lamented aesthetician friend Douglas Morgan did not accept my interpretation of this book, which he made fun of by calling it ''The Cook Book.''

overlap with my theorizing. Where we differ is in some cases, I think, more a matter of emphasis, or of verbal habits than a clear contradiction.

First I take up his correct point that to say "sensory qualities are qualities of feeling" would be pointless unless there were some sort of distinction between the two sets of qualities, or between sensation and feeling. The usual view is that some at least of these qualities are not qualities of feeling; this I reject, and say: They are all qualities of feeling. However, and this seems fairly obvious, not all feelings are qualities of sensation. Feeling is the more *general* term. A feeling of disappointment is no mere sensation, nor is a feeling of satisfaction in solving a problem, or a feeling of anger. Sensations are feelings especially closely dependent upon functionings of the sensory apparatus, optical with colors, auditory with sound qualities, etc. They are also more sharply localized in phenomenal space. Pains or physical pleasures are examples.

Another way to formulate the difference is by using Whitehead's terms "objective" and "subjective" forms of feeling. All feeling, as Whitehead has helped me to see, is feeling-of-feeling, or, as he also says, sympathy. Implicitly I had long believed this, but lacked the wit to put it so neatly. (One must allow for antipathy as a complicated special case of sympathy.) The first-mentioned feeling is the subjective; the second-mentioned, the objective form of the feeling. In disappointment the objective forms are not normally disappointments; but they include sensory elements. In sensation the objective forms are on the neuro-cellular level and in that sense subhuman. One's physical pains are, as objects and in certain cells, vastly more primitive forms of suffering. My "sense data" are physical realities, not (as they seem to be for Husserl) mere adjectives of our experiences. I call this a semi-identity theory of the mind-brain (or nervous system) duality.

Hospers gives some account of my use of continuity in relating sensory qualities to one another but does not perhaps quite see how this supports my argument against a sheer dualism between sensation and affection. Consider his point that, although green is midway in its half-circle of hues between yellow and blue, if we had not seen green we might be surprised by this fact. Now I say that careful attention to blue and yellow would tell us not only that there must be an intermediate quality but also something about its properties. Yellow in saturated form is the brightest color (closest to white, farthest from black); blue is the opposite, farthest from white, nearest to black. In other words, yellow has the highest punctiform intensity, and blue the lowest. In between are red and green, equally midway between the most and least intense.

If red and green are midway in terms of one Cartesian coordinate, they must be opposites in another. In what terms are we to understand this opposition? My answer is, red somehow suggests aggression, warmth, or excitement, and green the relative lack of such qualities. The terms are vague; but there is experimental evidence in the physiological response to the long visible wave lengths that such terms fit better than their opposites. Since yellow is more intense in the brightness sense than blue, there are limitations in the possibilities of blue to even seem to express hostility. Hospers, however, thinks a strong blue can seem to "come at one." In my book I cite some experimental studies by psychologists that bear on such questions. I find them to give some support to my affective theory (e.g., *PPS*, pp. 76, 119–24, 135–36).

If all possible qualities (sensory or affective) form a continuum of possibilities—and I don't know how one could prove the contrary!—then whether we call them all sensory or all affective is in part a verbal matter. But I think the latter is clearly the better choice.

Bergson opposes the idea that black is less intense than other colors with the question-begging remark, "black is just as real as the others." It is as truly real yes, but as intense, no. To have a faint feeling is to *really* have that feeling. The proper contrary of 'real' is 'merely imagined', not zero in intensity. True, the difference is smaller with low intensities. This is a subtle semantical problem. But I refute Bergson, I think definitively, by the following: a *very bright* light can be yellowish, orange, or yellow-greenish, but scarcely bluish, and certainly not blackish. Ordinary indoor colors with usual indoor lighting are very unintense compared to direct light from sun, or electricity. There are bluish flames, thermally very hot indeed, but not very bright visually. Bergson was wrong. Thunder seems more or less dark (and massive) but not lightning or an intense shriek or whistle.

In discussions of sensory qualities it is important to note the distinction between 'quality' in this sense and what is meant by the word in the classical doctrine of "primary qualities" as the ones crucial in physics or chemistry. These are really structures rather than qualities in the most significant sense. The word 'property' can be taken to cover both the "secondary" and the (scientifically) primary attributes of things. Structures, such as vibration rates, or wavelengths, had best be called just that, or else properties; they are not simple in the same sense as blue, sweet, or pain. The difference between structure and quality is in some strong sense a logical-type difference, not at all like that between red and green, red and sweet, or blue and unpleasant.

Whitehead speaks of "intellectual feelings," and though we certainly think about both structures and qualities, we also feel the beauty or ugliness of both. Language to deal with all this is difficult to work out. Spinoza wrote of intellectual love. Descartes on the other hand tried to embrace feeling under his *cogito*. Bradley, Whitehead, and Peirce avoid this usage, I think wisely. Theists who believe in a God of love should see that feeling has to be the inclusive term for the psychical. In addition, it seems more reasonable to speak of infants and lower animals as feeling than as thinking. Feeling motivates behavior directly;

mere thinking may inhibit almost all behavior. Yet Hegel seems to try to swallow up feeling under mere ideas of reason. On the other hand he also said somewhere, I recall, that reality is "the play of love with itself." In some ways Hume is better than the great rationalists of the past in recognizing the inclusiveness of feeling. Plato was better in this than Aristotle. But even he did not dare to speak of divine love but only of divine "freedom from jealousy," envy, or something of the kind.

The reader will perhaps see from the above that there is no very definite issue between me and the commentator with regard to the intellectual aspects of art, or the moral or religious aspects. The various contextual aspects he speaks of all contribute to an experience as well as any directly sensory aspects. After all, "interesting" is an aesthetic term, making an experience intrinsically good to a certain extent.

Concerning the idea that Eskimos may experience whiteness differently from others, ditto desert dwellers and green, I have several remarks. First these people, too, spend part of their lives amid vegetation. The inhabited northern regions are not all snow and ice all the year; deserts have oases in which people live when they can. But more important, since my view is that the direct feeling qualities of color, sound, smell, and the rest are built into the sensory apparatus, the basic possibilities may have been settled almost millions of years ago before there were people in the far North or in deserts. (After this sentence was written a letter from Hospers showed that this point had occurred to him after he wrote the draft of his essay to which my sentence referred.) My view is biological as well as psychological.

As an example, I emphasize the way taste and olfactory qualities give direct motivation, apart from learning, to eat or drink some substances and avoid others. We need not learn that eating bananas is good, our taste buds tell us that. (Sugar of lead is not found in natural situations in which sense organs developed.) Harsh sound qualities naturally express harsh attitudes and spell danger, as all higher animals know. They are born partly ready to act accordingly. Bird songs advertising territory sound much less repellent, although they are used in a considerable portion of cases to warn off intruders. But since they are also often used to attract mates or preserve pair bonds they cannot be essentially expressive of hostility. Moreover, if the hearer and potential intruder is at a suitable distance, there is no evidence it is felt as an actual intruder. The singer may well feel no hostility. "There that one is, minding his business as I mine here, nothing wrong with that!" Quite likely something mildly right about it. "Counter-singing" seems to be enjoyed.

"Black" is deceptive. In metallic objects especially, or in skins, there are usually shiny bits. Teeth and eyeballs are conspicuously not black. Black, as Pikler said, encourages sleep and is in a sense restful. It adds greatly to the contrasts in experience, and the most "intense" black is attainable, one is told, only through contrast with bright colors. Of course many "blacks" are light or dark brown. Afro-Americans, some of whom say, "Black is beautiful," have not been shown in controlled experiments to have a different inherent feeling in sensory blackness than "whites." Do they prefer deep blue (the hue nearest to black) or disfavor pink, orange, yellow more than do "whites"?

Hospers understands my distinction between feelings that *are* the sensations and feelings *about* the sensations, such as those expressing a preference for one compared to other sensations. Personally I do not quite see having a favorite color as reasonable. It depends upon what you want the color for and when and where. If one likes to feel excited, thrilled, one would not prefer green; if one likes to feel serene one might prefer sky blue or green; if simply merry, yellow. This brings us to the curious business of so many today liking yellow least. There is the connection with cowardice, and this is indeed an association in the standard sense, individually and culturally conditioned rather than built in by the more or less remote evolutionary past. It is not clearly adaptive, like the sweetness of fruits or the serenity of green and blue.

Apart from the cowardice question, there are other things about yellow that may influence preference. Yellow is merry, light-hearted, not serious (farthest of the saturated hues from black), and some people are very serious. The sole case I have known of a person who preferred yellow (as he said, from the age of four) was a man who recollected a happy very early childhood with a much loved young mother. At the age of five he saw a book with a partly yellow bird pictured on the cover and asked his mother to buy it for him, which she did. He became eventually a superb field naturalist and nature study became almost his life. At fifteen the tragic death of his mother deprived him of his favorite object of affection. He became a serious, though not humorless, and at times witty, young man. A stepmother was little help to him. After some years, the older sister of his mother took the place, almost, of his mother. After twenty years she, too, died. Moreover, he was aware that her life had had tragic aspects. In addition, the nature that he loved was being increasingly marred by technological procedures, population expansion, and the general craving for luxuries, uninhibited by an appreciation of nature comparable to his own. I think that for him yellow was a symbol of the way life had once been for him and ought to be, but increasingly was not. In this case, and probably in general, preferring something as simple as a single sensation quality is not itself simple at all and therefore cannot coincide with any single quality.

To me all the hues are beautiful compared to blank nothing, but so is all experience in some degree. I accept Whitehead's "satisfaction" as universally applicable to actual entities, experient occasions. Hitler's deeds were monstrous; but his experiences were not wholly without intrinsic values. What was monstrous was the gap between what life was like for millions because of his deeds and what it could have been if he had not acquired and used power as he did. (Many others were partly responsible, both in Germany and in other countries, including my own, for his malevolent and hideous career.)

An adequate aesthetics recognizes the beauty of holiness, righteousness, love, wisdom, generosity, courage, dignity, humor, and a soul-searching sense of tragedy, as well as sensory beauty. Some great artists express almost all of these values—Shakespeare, Mozart, Jane Austen, for example. In the only sentence of Hospers that I had in my memory before I read his contribution to this volume, he managed to put several aesthetic values into seven words that he spoke to me about my *PPS*. It was at once the most generous and the most imaginatively humorous comment that I had received about that book. I am not quite the one to say that it was wise. But it was unforgettably beautiful. It was either "I will defend it with my life," or "I will guard it with my body." He may not himself remember either one, but that would be because for him such a response was less surprising than it was for me. It told me that his further comments on the book would be worth having.

That I am not sure of two words out of the seven is a nice example of the mixture of distinctness and indistinctness that characterizes our long-term recollecting. Many times I have thought of the incident, and one's experiencing is always *somehow* creative, one of the "hows" being the way in which we make definite descriptions of memory data that are less definite. In reciting poetry from memory one can check on this. One may recall the sense better than the exact wording, or vice versa. What is important philosophically is that it is the real past that is given, although never with godlike distinctness and adequacy.

Hospers is partly right about my circular diagram of aesthetic values, but in a way that does not refute the diagram so much as it shows an inadequacy of the verbal descriptions outside the circle.[8] The pretty differs from the beautiful and still more from the sublime, not merely or perhaps primarily in being simpler but in being less intense or profound, in drawing less upon the entire resources of the individual. 'Superficial' may be the best single word here. The value of the diagram is that it says vastly more, almost at a glance, than even a large number of words alone can convey. That the ugly is not mere lack of unity is correct. I sometimes cite the festive artists' award for the "ugliest object" to a statue of Venus with a clock in her stomach! As mere or absolute lack of variety puts an

---

[8]Of the three versions of my circle of aesthetic values, one in each of three of my books (*BS*, *CS*, *WM*), the one in my book on bird song does not mention simplicity or complexity as poles of the horizontal dimension. It is important to realize that all the aesthetic values are akin to beauty, even including the ugly. Where there is no suggestion of harmony there is no significant discord either. Literally unbearable pain is also unborn.

experience outside the circle, so does mere lack of unity. There really are no such experiences.

Individuals will always differ more or less in the extent to which they yield to what Hospers calls the temptation to attempt definite generalizations (in subjects far from pure mathematics and physics). Such generalizations are among the things we can scarcely live with nor without. I find Hospers admirably balanced here, but tilted more toward distrust than trust—in comparison to some of us. I still regard my diagram as a discovery (by three people, I being the third) of an important two-dimensionality and quasi-geometry of a subject thousands of years old: the functions of such terms as beautiful, pretty, comic, sublime, neat, or tidy. That beauty is (in at least two ways) the central or middle value and the others are extremes seems to me to survive what criticisms I have encountered. Aristotle knew this about certain virtues, but where does he say it about beauty?

In sum, Hospers shows that my aesthetic view of experience is open to honest doubt; but so is any other view that approaches it in clarity and definiteness. As G. E. Moore used to say, "I am puzzled"; but I have more confidence than Hospers that we can glimpse some ultimate truths about reality. Moore said he "devoutly hoped" that "reality is spiritual," but found himself unable to find cogent reasons for thinking it is. In my reply to McMurrin, I argue that a metaphysically general view which, upon careful thought, appeals to us as something that ought to be true is thereby shown to be probably true. Life itself implicitly affirms (Schweitzer) an eternal rightness in reality.

As so often in this volume, I feel inclined to thank the commentator for his painstaking and skillful analysis of the problems my writing about certain matters presented to him.

R6. Kane on Freedom and Sufficient Reason

Whether or not Robert Kane is right in rating my contribution to the free will problem at the top of my generation, I trust I am right in putting his work, in this context, at the top of his. (In [almost] my generation I rate Popper highly on the same subject.)

Kane's generation has been characterized by the extent to which it has made a radical distrust of metaphysical arguments the dominant fashion. Kane has taken this fashion more seriously than I have. I rather admire him for this. But I remain a convinced metaphysician and am not persuaded by his objections, well-formulated and subtle as they are, against my view that determinism, quite apart from the question of human freedom and ethical responsibility, does not make coherent sense. Here I need to slightly correct Kane's account of my reason for rejecting a priori arguments *for* determinism. His discussion could be taken to imply that my reason is what modern physics has shown about causality.

Hardly! Long before modern physics, Epicurus, Plato, and Aristotle saw conceptual difficulties in a strict determinism. Among the ancients only Democritus and the Stoics were determinists. And the conceptual difficulties the others saw in determinism were not limited to considerations of human ethical responsibility. Peirce summed up the pre-quantum physics case as only a genius could have done, and Clerk Maxwell strongly hinted at it. True they did argue from the laws of gasses, but this was only a part of their reasoning, especially of Peirce's. Bergson almost predicted the kind of change that quantum physics has brought about in scientific views of causality. Peirce (and Bergson) should, I hold, have predicted something like even the quantum idea itself, but Peirce had a prejudice, inherited from his father, against admitting discreteness as the basic principle of actuality, just as continuity is the principle of possibility.

My appeal to current physics, which I poorly understand, is only to counteract the traditional view (found in Hume for example) that science has shown the truth of determinism. Science has shown a great deal, but nothing so absolutely *definite* as unqualified determinism, the sheer zero of creative, causally somewhat transcendent determination *of the present by the present.* Absolute zero is a "quantity" to be affirmed only with certain precautions. Determinists have not taken these precautions. Nor have those, even Peirce, who have affirmed the absolute continuity (zero of discreteness) of actual becoming.

A metaphysical case against an affirmation has to be that no coherent metaphysics can contain the affirmation. Is Spinoza coherent? I think not, and so have many philosophers who have studied him. Was Leibniz coherent in his unqualified affirmation of sufficient reason? Same answer. Was Marx, in his materialistic determinism, coherent? If these attempts, made with such genius, failed, it is reasonable to suspect that it can't be done. Nor is there any need for it.

I salute Dr. Kane on his brilliant treatment of sufficient reason. The principle, he thinks, is too strong, an overstatement. So is causality if taken as meaning that there are always both necessary *and* sufficient antecedent reasons for *exactly* what happens. Becoming is not the unwinding of necessities. How could it be? It is always at least slightly creative.[9]

Since human beings exist in a world that once was without them, their existence is not a metaphysical necessity. Human freedom is a special case, knowable only by observation, not by consulting purely general conceptions. Only something like Kant's idea of "rational being" (other than God) enters into a purely metaphysical context. Kane's book is largely devoted to the study of the

---

[9]See R. H. Kane, "Nature, Plenitude and Sufficient Reason," *American Philosophical Quarterly*, 13, 1 (Jan. 1976), 23–31.

special and empirical human case. I have no doubt that he has dealt more adequately with it in important respects than I have ever done.

There is indeed a problem of "supervenience," or action of our experiencing on the cells of the brain. Eccles, Popper, Sperry have struggled with it; Wigner holds there must be such a thing. Although I am too little mathematical to do much with such a task, I can explain metaphysically why there must be actions of individuals on other individuals; however, I do not include under individuals an animal or human body, for that is a collective not a dynamically singular entity. Cells seem to act as units, but brain action or bodily action is a resultant of invisibly, small and rapid actors, together (except in dreamless sleep) with the one unitary actor which is our experience of the moment, the human form of Whiteheadian actual entities. (Quanta in the concrete are psychological; only the Buddhists among great traditions anticipated physics in their psychology.) We virtually intuit a momentary experience in the immediate memory of the next such experience a fraction of a second (perhaps a twelfth) later. We intuit it only indistinctly, but the indistinctness of all our concrete intuitions is a doctrine common to Leibniz, Peirce, Whitehead, and others. It was clearly implied by Democritus and Epicurus. This limitation is the explanation of the failure of attempts to make introspection the primary method in a science of psychology, also of the at best rather limited success of recent forms of phenomenology.

According to Kane, a deterministic theology is not as plainly absurd as I say it is. I think the absurdity has been made plain enough in two thousand years of intellectual history. God, acting freely in the sense that the action could have been left undone, produced us, whose actions are wholly determined by God. Or does one say with Spinoza that even God acts in the only way God could act? Either way you are in trouble and not making sense. You are playing fast and loose with words and doing so more than you quite realize.

Kane (playing 'devil's advocate', as it seems to me) argues that even if we cannot use strict determinism as applied to our own decisions to help us decide, we can use the doctrine to predict the decisions of others. I find this far-fetched. If we do not know our own detailed future acts in advance, far less can we know those of others whose pasts we know so much less well than our own. We can indeed predict some aspects of our own future acts and of the acts of others, but they are more or less abstract aspects, never the concrete decisions one in effect makes many times a second.

Kane and I are in fair agreement on the proposition that there are indeed universal principles of causality. Causal explanation shows why what occurs was *possible when and where* it occurred and would not have been possible elsewhere or elsewhen. Thus I have tried to partially explain my own intellectual growth as a *possible* outcome of my early upbringing and environment. Not only is it beyond present human capabilities to explain the actuality of my growth as determined, necessitated by that early kind of upbringing and environment (and the gene mixture of my mother's first male fetus), but there is no good reason to think there could or need be such an explanation. Real local possibilities are what science enables us to know, not necessities. However, these real local possibilities may in some cases be so narrowly restricted that the gap between possibility and necessity may for most purposes be disregarded. If there must be a tremendous nuclear explosion, who cares about what various individual atoms or particles may do? The hope of predicting the behavior of particular atoms or particles in the exact way we predict the movements of planets is no longer alive in science. Maxwell and Peirce gave it up more than a hundred years ago.

The most plausible criticism Kane makes of my a priori defense of my (Whitehead's, Peirce's, Bergson's, W. P. Montague's) doctrine of becoming as creative is when he says that the transition from the indefiniteness of potentiality to the definiteness of actuality is not required for becoming. All that is required is that the descriptively definite future events with their precise place in the A series (McTaggart) of before and after are not *now*. What is added to make them now is no new specific predicate but only *nowness*. I admit that my talk about definiteness has been somewhat ambiguous. (I sometimes think the role of ambiguity in philosophy can scarcely be exaggerated, it is so pervasive.) Here is the place to distinguish two aspects of traditional "nominalism."

Nominalists tend to take similarity as ultimate concept, not to be explained by partial identity through the "ingredience" of "eternal objects" or timeless universals. This aspect of nominalism has a deep truth in it, according to my form of realism. Universals also have similarities and differences; these relations have a certain ultimacy. The error of nominalism is not in stressing similarity.

The error is rather in not seeing that to be future is to be further determinable, and that becoming determinate or fully particular is the same as coming to be present or actual (and then past). It follows that there are (as Whitehead in one passage implies) ever-new forms of similarity, new universals. Being like or different from my present experience, for example, is not reducible to having or lacking certain abstract properties that might have been mentioned yesterday. The final beauty of reality transcends abstractable predicates.

If all the definiteness there could ever be were laid up in eternal arrays of definite qualities, why would there be any point in actual instances? And why would Whitehead's God, eternally knowing all eternal objects, need or want an actual world? The concrete is in this sense ineffable. Absolutely definite and repeatable qualities laid up in advance do not belong in a philosophy of process. Here I agree with Peirce (against Whitehead) and with Bergson, Dewey, and some others, including the psychologist-philosopher Stout. Whitehead himself should not, by his own analysis of continuity, have written of "eternal objects" as a definite plurality of single items. His "blue is an eternal object" refers to just what portion of the continuum of color hues between green and red? In any portion, however small, there would be an infinity, or (Peirce) a multitude beyond all multitude, or (Bergson) no definite number, of possible hues. If space is not a sum of points, why should color be a sum of definite and repeatable items? There are no perfectly definite "forms of definitness." There are unique concrete instances, every one of which adds something qualitative and valuable to anything merely eternal.

Several points are often missed in discussing freedom. (1) One is the difference between conscious choices with explicit options definitely in mind and definite reasons or motives being weighed pro and con, and the many times a second (mostly unconsciously) resolved indeterminacies for the very next momentary experience. Peirce even put the time lapse required as "infinitesimal." Whitehead thinks it is finite and in the human case roughly measurable. There is empirical evidence for this. Somehow each little new present comes to be as just what it is, with a unitary quale (Peirce writes about the "emotion of the ensemble") that no amount of talk can ever exhaust or duplicate. Nor do things exist for us merely to be talked about. The "linguistic turn" is a half-truth at most.

(2) If many times a second something not absolutely predetermined occurs, then what in the long run occurs may be very significantly different from anything that laws of nature would have made predictable.

(3) Some choices that deserve to be called free may have been already determined seconds, hours, or days, and perhaps at least probable for years, beforehand, without having been determined when one was born. But such choices are between rather abstract options. I struggled for weeks to decide, Should I leave Chicago for Emory (or, later, Emory for Texas)? For all I know, my affirmative decisions in these cases were already settled well before I stopped arguing the matter with myself. But each moment more particular issues had to be decided. Just what reasons should I take into account, how should I state my decision, and so on. The "fallacy of misplaced concreteness" is pervasive: language makes this more or less inevitable. What we actually *do* is never simply one of the options consciously considered. Language is incapable of stating anything so particular as what actually happens. How could it predict the happening? It predicts something less concrete, less particular. Popper makes this point in arguing about determinism. I've been trying to make it during much of my career.

If, on the most concrete level, there is always some transcendence of causal determination and if over half a million "decisions" are made in a day or two (ten at least per second), most of them with no conscious weighing of options (as Maeterlinck said, "it is necessary to live naively," spontaneously, and by feeling or impulse), it does not follow that we are not responsible for the general trend of the results. For, since early childhood we have been deciding somewhat consciously in what direction we shall encourage ourselves to develop, what ideals to adopt, what friends to select, what books to read, in short what Skinnerian reënforcements to use upon ourselves. It is only infants or subhuman animals that are not rationally somewhat responsible for being as they are. Adult human beings are responsible.

Lincoln once said, "I don't like that man's face." "He can't help his face," someone objected. "If this were a very young man," (or did he say, a child?), replied Lincoln, "you might say that, but not with a person of his age." We partly make our very faces! The Platonist Edmund Spenser wrote,

> For the body from the soul its form doth take,
> For soul is form and doth the body make.

According to Plato, soul is self-moved, and all change is initiated by soul. He failed to add, soul on some level, which may be vastly different from, and less complex or intelligent than, the human form of the psychical. If Plato was a mind-matter dualist, it was clearly because he thought inorganic matter was totally inert, did not move itself. We know through science that there is no such matter as Plato thought there was. Plato should have been a psychical monist, and only a scientific mistake barred the way to his being this. Epicurus guessed that all matter is self-moved and partly free from strict causal order. He should have guessed that it also has some lowly form of sentience or feeling. Not sticks and stones are sentient and move themselves, but particles, atoms, bacteria are and do.

(4) Another point often overlooked is that human freedom can be looked upon in causal terms in three ways: (a) classical causality applies universally, even to human choices; (b) classical causality applies to much of nature, but not to human beings (or perhaps the animals, or all of life); (c) causality as necessary, but not strictly sufficient or absolutely determining condition, applies to all nature (but not with the same degree of indeterminacy on all levels of nature). Thus we have two forms of causal monism, one deterministic, the other probabilistic or statistical, and with varying degrees of the indeterminacy; and a dualism, with predetermining causality in some portions of nature and probabilistic causality in other portions. As with so many issues, there are at least three basic options not just two. We know that the reason for the Greeks' dualism was their ignorance of the microstructure of nature, in which (as only the atomists guessed and more than guessed) there is no merely inert stuff unable to move itself. It is time to take seriously the fact that dualism has classically been based on sheer ignorance of truths we now know. It is no longer shrewd to take literally the concept of the inorganic, of lifeless mere matter, devoid of initiative, that most philosophers for two thousand years thought they had to accept.

Popper makes a sort of last stand here by holding that with life there are problems to solve but not on the level of atoms and the like. If he generalizes the idea of problems enough to cover plants (or plant cells?) and one-celled creatures, how can he know that a still further generalization would not take atoms into account? In the sun various atoms disintegrate, cannot survive. Do atoms have problems of adjustment and survival? Can we justify an absolute zero here?

The current fashion of compatibilism is one aspect of a general tendency to *trivialize* philosophical issues. I could quote Wittgenstein on this point and have done so elsewhere. He thought it made for "boring" writing. If the question is, "Were determinism established, would it then be rational to conclude that we are not ethically responsible?" then I say, certainly it would not. To give up ethical responsibility, or what Kant meant by practical reason, is irrational no matter what! From this we should conclude: either determinism is irrational and could not be justified, or compatibilism is correct. Since I find the arguments for compatibilism weak and those against both compatibilism (James settled that issue for me long ago) and determinism strong (Peirce settled that issue for me), why should I bother much with compatibilism? I find Kane on the right side of both issues, but over-generous to the defenders of compatibilism—a fault in a good direction I suppose. I hope his work will receive the attention it deserves, now that his book has been published.

I agree with Kane that chance interactions of my brain cells would not be my freedom. But if it is really chance, it is (an aspect of) their freedom. Chance is a negative idea, the absence of fully determining antecedent conditions. Freedom, however, is partly positive, the act of *self-creation* or self-movement of present experience not fully determined by anything anterior to or other than itself.

I do not see that Kane has shown strict determinism to have any pragmatic value other than that arising from its ultra-simplicity. We have to live partly by fictions, models that *could not* correspond exactly to reality. But we should know what we are doing in this. Determinism is the simplest model of causality. Given laws of nature, what happens is thought of as entailed exactly both by what happened previously and by what happens subsequently. I deny, however, that this doctrine rationally implies any useful conclusions about our decision-making that would not follow from a sensibly qualified view of causality, such as Kane himself holds. By inconsistent, irrational reasoning some may deduce pessimism (Schopenhauer is an example), others (Leibniz for example, whose superdeterminism included a miracle here and there), deduce extreme optimism. Neither view, as James shows, is rationally useful, and neither one is genuinely entailed. In Islam many claim to deduce that they can leave all to God, who is bound to do whatever divine wisdom and goodness is bound to do. Or, is God genuinely free in acting, as we, it is said, are not? In any case, believers in Allah (Omar

Khayyam said the bottom line here) still must make decisions in the light of *probable* consequences of their actions as apparent to them. We live by probabilities and not by fully particularized necessities. Determinism is not a usable chart of reality. It is make-believe, not genuine belief, as Omar, the English satirical novelist Peacock, Peirce, J. S. Austin, and Isaiah Berlin imply.

The entailment of details of the past by the present we can and do use all the time, but not details of the future. We know and act upon letters that we have received from others, we do not normally know or act upon letters we "are going" to receive. Finding dinosaur bones, we know (allowing for some improbable mistakes) a good deal about what kind of animal did live ages ago and where; we do not know anything remotely like this about what and where animals "will" live, even in the present century, come wars or destruction of habitats by the population explosion. Technology decreases the predictability of the future, and does this even for God, in my view.

In Kane's discussion of motivation as determining or not determining decisions, actions, or experiences, does he do justice to the point that if a motive is linguistically expressible it cannot be as particular as what realizes it? Motives, purposes, plans, are outlines; they leave the full quality of what realizes them more or less indefinite. I see no good reason to suppose that even a divine purpose could realize itself in a reality whose quality merely duplicated that defined by the purpose plus some wholly transparent "actuality" or "nowness." Leibniz's eternally and divinely envisaged possible worlds are not worlds at all. They do not consist of individuals or even definite species. They are highly abstract *kinds* of world. Individuals, as Robert Hartman used to insist, "define themselves." They are self-moved, not entirely made, moved, or defined, by others. Before Hartman, Plato, Aristotle, Peirce, and Bergson came close to making the same point.

To discuss a primary problem with a philosopher as knowledgeable and careful as Kane is a privilege. He has, I think, enabled me to clarify somewhat the position I hold. For this I can only be grateful, as well as for his early presentation of his contribution.

B. Philosophy of Religion

R7. Engelhardt on Theism and Bioethics

Of the living philosophers I have known who could be called Hegelian or to an important extent disciples of Hegel, the two who make most sense to me are John Findlay and a pupil of his and of mine, Dr. Tristram Engelhardt, Junior. He has an advanced degree in medicine as well as in philosophy. So far as I am aware there is no one of higher authority on the subject of bioethics. I wonder if he has a serious rival in this subject.

Engelhardt has no significant quarrel, it seems, with my writings and I have none with his essay. It is the second time that he has shown how well he comprehends what I have tried to do in natural or philosophical theology. I have a few mildly critical comments.

As Engelhardt is aware, the statement in his introduction that God creates all that God knows is the classical but not exactly the neoclassical doctrine. God creates the possibility of what God knows, but actualities are self-creative. The creatures are also creators and the creator is also creature. Deity is the supreme form of causing and the supreme form of being caused, of activity and passivity, of giving and receiving. This is dual transcendence. Love receives as well as gives, and God is love. A knowledge that is in no way receptive is meaningless or contradictory.

As the reader perhaps knows, I would not deny that God is omniscient but only that God is "omniscient" — that is, as this word has often been construed in the past. However, as it was used by the Socinians centuries ago and by some writers more recently, I affirm it. Similarly I would not simply deny that God is "all-powerful." Although not all-determining, God has ideal power, as my Father used to say, "over all." Divine power is unsurpassable in scope (not, like our power, localized in some fragment of space or time, but ubiquitous), as well as unsurpassable (and unequalizable) by others in quality. All-determining power is, in a philosophy of universal creativity, a non-idea, not a maximal degree of anything positive but only an absurdity. It makes divine freedom a monopoly; yet freedom, like life, is social in principle. It cannot be monopolized.

In all essentials I agree with and admire this essay. What a joy to read writing so free from wordiness and fuzziness; so readable and comprehensively knowledgeable!

R8. Cobb on My Theology

There are two contrasting ways in which comment by one thinker on the work of another can attain distinction. A very popular way, in which (I believe) I, too, have indulged, is with force and clarity to attack weaknesses, flaws, in the other's thought. The contrasting way is to restate and defend the thought of the other in some respects more clearly and persuasively than the one commented upon has done. This is how I view John R. Cobb's contribution.

One of my memories of him is of his behavior at the oral examination of his work for a Master's degree in the University of Chicago Divinity School. Another former student of mine, Bernard Loomer, much beloved and now deceased, in theology Cobb's principal teacher, was sometimes wordy in his queries to students. In the examination, Cobb several times responded to Loomer with some such phrase as, "If I may restate your question . . ." whereupon he gave a lucid, concise formulation of the teacher's query and then replied to it as thus stated. As Cobb finally passed out of the room so that we could discuss his performance, Loomer smiled to the rest of us and said, "He's a smart cookie. No one's going to push him around." The beauty of it is that if Cobb is one not likely to be pushed around, neither does he push others. But he does get things done and is a very constructive individual. He was one of the students whose later success has been a pleasure, but no great surprise, to watch.

I offer three minor amplifications of his account of my work in the philosophy of nature and of God. The first is that I have come recently to prefer 'psychicalism' to panpsychism. For this there are two reasons. As parallel to 'physicalism' or 'materialism', it seems neater; the more substantive reason is that, as Cobb says, I do not in the same sense attribute mind or psychological qualities to everything; for instance to stones, or even to trees, but only to what I call the "dynamic singulars" of which stones and trees are groupings or collectives.

My second amplification is that I see some danger in using 'part' and 'whole' as Cobb does. God is not simply the world-whole of stars, planets, and smaller or larger groupings, but, as Cobb makes clear, a supreme and all-embracing *experiencing* of the whole. I sometimes use Jaspers's "the Encompassing." Plato says, and in this shows his greatness, that the divine Soul includes the divine body, not vice versa. He does not explain; but my reason is simple: subjects include their objects (as Bosanquet said). If this seems not so in the human case, it is partly because most of what we take as objects are not only outside our bodies, but outside that body within the body which is the central nervous system. A single human experience can (indistinctly) prehend millions of nerve cells, and do so much more adequately than single cells prehend one another.

My third amplification is that my half-dozen theistic arguments as stated in canonical form, so to speak, in *CS* are all frank appeals to individual judgment in selecting one out of an exhaustive set of theoretical possibilities. No claim is made to start from self-evident premises, except those that set up the *exhaustiveness* of the set. Views A, B, C, D (the number varies with the concepts used) cannot all be false and only one can be true: take your choice. There is no compulsion to accept the choice that I take. But you are shown the price you pay if you reject it, namely the trilemma offered by the remaining views. If you refuse to employ the concepts that establish the set, then this is one more choice, and it too has its price. I submit that this mode of argument is a golden mean between traditional extremes of denial and affirmation concerning the importance or relevance of theistic arguments. (I now repent having called them proofs.)

I see a certain generosity in Cobb's concentration on my thought rather than Whitehead's, since his own work on Whitehead exalted Whitehead's rather than my philosophy, though it accepted some of my interpretations of Whitehead. Schubert Ogden, with some qualification, shows the opposite preference. Both understand me well, as do Cobb's colleagues David Griffin and Lewis Ford in the work of the Center for Process Studies and its periodical.

R9. Reese on Panentheism and God's Goodness

Three philosophical publishing events in this century have been collaborations between two authors. The first and best known was by Whitehead and Russell in *Principia Mathematica*. Later these collaborators drifted rather far apart. The next such event, *The Collected Papers of Charles S. Peirce*, edited by Hartshorne and Paul Weiss, also became rather widely known. The collaborators drifted apart, but less radically so than our illustrious predecessors. I have nothing but gratitude and admiration for Weiss's part in our joint endeavor. The third case, William L. Reese's and my *Philosophers Speak of God*, I consider to have been also a successful collaboration. In this case the collaborators scarcely drifted apart. Reese has demonstrated abundantly that my confidence in his understanding of my ideas was well-placed. His attractively written *Ascent from Below*, an introduction to philosophy, and his *Dictionary of Philosophy and Theology*, a wonderfully useful reference work, show his flair for entering into and formulating a variety of philosophies sympathetically and accurately.

Reese has two main problems in this essay. One is also a problem, even *the* problem, for me: how God as prehending, caring for, sensitive to, the creatures is to be conceived, given the current non-Newtonian idea of physical relativity, according to which there is apparently no unique cosmic present or unambiguous simultaneity. I am not able to think well enough about this problem to judge how far Reese's discussion helps to solve it. However, I consider his essay a marvelous example of a sincerely religious person, with keen intellectual and also vivid ethico-religious scruples, wrestling with a difficult philosophical conundrum. I think it deserves careful reading. Concerning the Ozark farmer's trouble with being too completely included, swallowed up, by God, I will just mention, what Reese well knows, that it is precisely not a Whitehead-Hartshorne doctrine that prehension of a creaturely actuality determines the actuality, or that in a case of feeling of feeling, the first-mentioned feeling, the subjective form, in any way alters the second-mentioned or objective form, the datum prehended. And this applies to divine prehensions no less than to nondivine prehensions. Classical pantheism negated the self-creativity which, according to the category of the ultimate, is the form of forms, transcendentally universal to all actualities. The inclusiveness of the divine body and the Platonic inclusion of a body in its soul (not vice versa) is fully achieved in the uniquely adequate divine case.

Concerning the phrase "divine event," I take this as an echo of the use of this phrase by Henry Wieman, to whose presence in the University of Chicago Divinity School Reese had been exposed.

I find myself essentially agreeing with many of the points Reese makes, and in some of them he gives a better formulation than I have done, particularly in his discussion of ethical goodness in God and the problem of evil. My reply to Jacquelyn Kegley (R11) on this topic is quite inadequate by comparison. In dealing with religious topics, Reese has the tune as well as the words, to adapt a metaphor of Mark Twain's.

When Reese writes that a person's body is personally ordered, he seems to forget Whitehead's use of words, which at this point is mine. A human person's body is a corpuscular, not a personally ordered, society. What is personally, that is, linearly ordered is the person's sequence of experient occasions; the occasions making up one's body form a vastly complicated society of interacting societies. When Reese writes that in perception we do not intuit as obvious the awareness of other persons or that of the universe, and that "philosophers agree we lack direct awareness of other minds," I am a little troubled. Whitehead and I hold that in all experience there is "feeling of feeling," where the second token of the word refers to feelings whose feelers are other actual entities. And some of these other actual feelers are not members of the sequence of actual entities forming one's own stream of awareness. So there is direct awareness of other minds. One intuits, I hold, the pleasant and unpleasant feelings of one's own bodily cells. They in their vastly inferior fashion feel our feelings, and, analogously, we feel God's feelings; and God in vastly, indeed ideally, superior fashion feels ours.

In the main, however, I admire Reese's contribution, as I do all his work, and at some points where there is perhaps a difference between our opinions, I am not at all sure of my exact view. As with some other contributions to this volume, my sense is that to have had such pupils and readers is to have labored far from in vain.

R10. Van der Veken on God and the Ultimate

Professor Jan Van der Veken's paper is impressive in its knowledge of intellectual history. Hans Gadamer once said to me, "We Germans are drowned in history." He might have said this of continental Europeans instead of merely Germans. Historical perspectives are never wholly free from distortion. Indeed, the use of language distorts, as deconstructionists emphasize and overemphasize. But (as they grudgingly admit) they could not do this if language were completely helpless to counteract the danger. My commentator locates my work in his perspective, but with more attention to my early and middle periods than to the last two decades. He refers to CS but only to a chapter that seems to me, taken together with the final chapter, to answer some of his criticisms.

I wish to make four principal points. One is that although all-inclusiveness, necessary existence, and unsurpassability (by others) are, I hold, divine properties, my primary move is not from these properties to God. Rather, I move *to* all-inclusiveness, etc., *from* the idea of "loving God" (who "is love") with *"all"* one's heart, mind, soul, and strength. I usually *start* with the religious idea. In addition, "ultimate reality" is not a favorite phrase of mine. Similar remarks apply to "the philosophical absolute." I regard "absolute" as a viciously ambiguous term, unless it is carefully explained in more ordinary language words, such as 'independent of all'. I also insist that this is not identical with "all-inclusive"; rather it is the opposite pole in the same ultimate contrast. (I do use 'ultimate' in *this* application.) My doctrine of dual transcendence is that the supreme reality is both all-inclusive (and therefore dependent upon all) and all-exclusive, and therefore independent of all. It is a silly tautology that the all-inclusive cannot depend upon anything "outside itself." This does not make it independent of anything, but only of nothing, whatever kind of thing that is. Real independence is of something, not of nothing. The apparent contradiction is removed by distinguishing the abstract, necessarily existent essence of God (which is nontemporal) from the concrete actuality of God, which is in some uniquely excellent fashion temporal, dependent or relative, and contingent. By the Aristotelian principle, the concrete (and relative) can include what is abstract and (in the sense of independent) absolute. By explaining some of my ideas with verbal usages that are slightly foreign to me, my extraordinary friend has unintentionally distorted somewhat my philosophy.

My second main point is that I do not think that the mere logic of modality would directly give us the full connotation of 'deity', 'divine', or 'God'. However, not only the word 'God' but any word has to acquire meaning from experience. And to show what this involves, we must have a theory of experience as such. Idealists have always known this, but some materialists and dualists seem to forget it. My theory of experience, as Hospers and Chiaraviglio have recognized, is aesthetic. Here I agree not only with Whitehead, but also with Croce and various others. I agree with Plato that, apart from all considerations of "good," nothing can be adequately understood or explained. In addition I view experience as pervasively social, feeling of feeling, that is, sympathy. "To know is to sympathize" (Carlyle). (See last chapter of *CS*.)

Does philosophy put the question and religion give the answer (Tillich), or does religion give the question and philosophy the answer? I have said the latter. But I now say, both. Human fallibility implies that philosophers and theologians do better trying to learn from each other than trying to go it alone. We know that religion came before philosophy (unless in an extremely undeveloped form). (Bergson has explained why, better than anyone else.) On the other hand, without philosophy, religions tend to quarrel in dangerous, destructive fashion. Some trust the Bible (Old Testament? New? Both?); others, the Koran or the Baghavad Gita. To what can we turn in this confusion if not to philosophy? To science, yes, so far as religion involves nonmetaphysical aspects—as it always does, since the existence of human beings is a contingent truth.

My fourth point is that, although the logic of modality does not directly yield the idea of God, it does take us closer to that idea than Van der Veken thinks, and this in two ways. First, it is an elementary modal law that necessary truths are what a set of contingent truths have in common and that what the universal set of *all possible* truths have in common is *unconditionally* necessary. The total truth is a vastly complex contingent truth; for, by another modal law, no strictly necessary truth can include a contingent one. By analogy, no necessary being, so far as necessary, can include anything contingent. From this it follows that if God is aware of all truth then the divine knowledge must have contingent aspects. The only nearly plausible way to evade this requirement is to hold, as Spinoza did, that there are no contingent truths at all. This, however, is extremely paradoxical, if not simply absurd. An ultimate contrast like necessary-contingent loses its meaning if one pole is denied application. This "principle of contrast" (P12), which I learned from an Australian disciple of Wittgenstein, seems to me a valid axiom. For me it renders Spinoza's extreme modal view a dead issue. The theological conclusion is that God must be supposed just as truly contingent as necessary; and the apparent inconsistency disappears when one takes into account the distinction between the divine existence and the divine actuality. If I have explained anything clearly, it is this distinction, which so far as I know I am the first to make definitely and clearly. All theology, I hold, implies it.

The other way in which the logic of modality helps in conceiving deity is by taking the modal polarity and its laws as a model of the generalized principle of dual transcendence. Just as there must be a divine form of necessity and also, one of contingency, so there must be divine forms of absoluteness or independence and also of relativity or dependence; similarly with quite a number of other extremely general polarities, including simplicity and complexity, abstractness and concreteness, infinity (in some senses) and finitude, activity and passivity, timelessness and temporality, being and becoming. Plato and Whitehead, more than most theologians, came closest to a full statement of this duality in the idea of deity.

I take Van der Veken's searching critique, as I think it was intended to be taken, as complimentary, and trust that he will take my counter-criticisms in a similar way. He, like many scholars in the smaller countries, has a fine capacity to mediate between languages and national traditions.

R11. Kegley on Royce and Community

Royce is certainly an appropriate topic for this volume; he is well represented by
Dr. Jacquelyn Kegley. I think she is right in suggesting that Royce did more
justice to some aspects of community than I have been able to do. The sociology
of religion seems even more difficult to deal with than the strictly metaphysical
aspect. I see important light on both subjects in Bergson's theory of *The Two
Sources*. Agreeing with Royce that mere intuition is not sufficient, I hold that
Bergson at his best (in his mature writings more than in his early ones) makes
good use of interpretation. But I am more of a metaphysician than an empirical
inquirer into the concrete aspects of human religions. Like Royce, however, I
have thought much (since 1916, when I read Tolstoi) about the war problem.
Royce's attempt to use the institution of insurance in the cause of peace is not
mentioned by Dr. Kegley. We desperately need light on the subject of war. Kant,
to his lasting honor, did his best to deal with it. Hegel gave it up as hopeless, if
my memory is correct. Neither one fully realized, nor, I suppose, did Royce, that
until that problem is more nearly solved the possibility of a significant future for
our species is at best extremely problematic. The mathematician Martin Hellman
of Stanford comes close to proving this. Paul Weiss, in his impressive book
Toward the Perfected State, has a discussion that for practical purposes seems
pre-nuclear and to that extent disappointing.

Concerning Royce's use of Peirce's three categories and W. L. Sessions's
comments on my neglect of Thirdness, I differ somewhat from all three writers
about this. My proposal is to relate Thirdness and futurity in a way that seems in
some respects more Peircean than Peirce's own version, somewhat as he said that
Herbert Spencer was "only a semi-Spencerian."[10] In all prehension there is an
aspect of free decision, using materials from the past to create the future. This is
certainly not merely dyadic; and indeed the concrete prehension of the past is
polyadic, not simply triadic. Since God also has a future, the analysis applies to
divine prehensions. Of course, God surpasses all else quantitatively *and*
qualitatively. God (and only God) is aware of all, and aware of each in an
unsurpassable manner. I hold that there are three basic categories, but that the
number of relata of the dyadic, triadic, polyadic, relations is not the main point,
which is rather the way the three ideas, dependence, independence, and the
intermediate idea of probability, or mixture of chance and necessity, appear in
phenomena. This is indeed a basic *modal* clue in phenomenology. Being second
illustrates dependence, but so do being third and more polyadic relative
properties. Being first does not depend on there being an actual second (under the
same classification); and so firstness illustrates independence. However,

---

[10]See my "Revision of Peirce's Categories," in *Monist*, 63 (1980):277–89; also in *Creativity in
American Philosophy*, ch. 7.

although the present does not depend on the particulars of what happens later, yet without possibilities and probabilities of later events the present would be as nothing. Peirce was only partly right: numerical relations furnish some clues to the supremely important aspects of dependence and independence in reality; but in phenomenology it is the modal-temporal, not the numerical, relations that we are trying to understand. And the modes of dependence, independence, and futurity-as-probability are indeed three. Otherwise numerical relations should be left to arithmetic and number theory.

Concerning sin, guilt, and salvation, Kegley's comments are somewhat like my clergyman father's comment on my *Vision of God* book: He: "You don't discuss sin." I: "I have a paragraph on sin." Father: "A paragraph!" End of that discussion.

Eugene O'Neill's mother was haunted by a sense of guilt that did neither her nor her son much good but probably much harm. Guilt feelings are not necessarily good things. Penitence is good, not self-flagellation or fear of an angry deity. I definitely disbelieve in a punishing deity, an idea that drove O'Neill to Nietzsche and similarly influenced James Joyce. Punishing parents and schoolmasters have done much harm. Positive reinforcement is best, as Skinner says; God knows this as well as any psychologist. The man who shot more than twenty persons from the tower of the University of Texas had a father who boasted he had disciplined his children. He taught at least one of them to hate life and everybody. It is a sad story and not a brand-new one. If we are a violent population, as we seem to be, it is partly, I have no doubt, because many of us had parents who were violent as parents. (I did not.)

What is salvation? I think it is achieving on a humanly reflective level what the sub-ethical wild animals have on their unreflective or less reflective one, an habitual feeling of their place in the world and the values of that place. We are the animals that, in outlines, know large portions of the entire terrestrial animal-and-subanimal scheme. We can also use our reflective powers, as Kant said, to become incomparably worse than wild beasts. Reinhold Niebuhr speaks to my condition when he says that our capacity (such as it is) for conceiving God-like powers may tempt us to want to be more than we essentially are: creatures, on a humble level co-creating with God and for God. We need to learn to enjoy being contributors to what is radically more than ourselves. We need to learn to love others in principle in the same way as we love ourselves, rather than partly hating ourselves and still more hating others.

I have a this-worldly view of salvation. Read Trollope or Jane Austen; they were Christians, surely; but they discuss salvation and damnation not as affairs to occur after death, but here in life between birth and death. They show the many ways we can mistreat even those close to us, lord it over others, despise others, blind ourselves to their needs and sufferings. They show that the selfish are often unkind to themselves as well as to others. They show the differences between "rational happiness" and various forms of misery, some of them self-inflicted. In Trollope's *Marion Fay* the heroine, but not the hero, believes in posthumous life in heaven. The outcome in this life is tragic.

What Whitehead calls "Peace," in the noble chapter of that name *(AI)*, is his view of salvation, and is mine. Austen's Fanny and Edmund Bertram attained something like it, as did Emma and Mr. Knightley. So did Trollope's saintly Mr. Harding. The parables of Jesus may be interpreted largely in this way, so far as I know. But so may the words of some of the famous Rabbis of this and some other ages; also of some founders or practitioners of various other religions.

When Mark Twain's wife, in her efforts to cure him of his profanity, resorted to the tactic of imitation, he replied, "You have the words, my dear, but not the tune." Sometimes when philosophers restate views of other philosophers, a similar situation seems to obtain. When Dr. Kegley presents Royce's views I feel both words and tunes in her exposition, and I feel the same in most of her exposition of my views. But when it comes to the relations of the ethical and the aesthetic in my writing, the tune seems sometimes lacking. (And in value theory tune is close to the heart of the matter.) After all "love" is at least as central in my thinking as beauty. Blake's lines, "Oh, he gives to us his joy/ that our grief he may destroy/ Till our grief is fled and gone/ He doth sit by us and moan" were cited at the beginning of my most religious book *(MVG)*. Clearly God is for me not merely analogous to an artist or playwright. The words of this poem, the players in this play, are beloved by the poet or playwright, and beloved as makers of their own decisions and to that extent of themselves. The details of the play are left to the players.

Is God ethical? Or only aesthetic? In all transference of terms from their human instances to the divine application, there is a difference in principle. God's aesthetic contemplation is qualitatively ideal as well as universal in scope. But even we human beings, in attending to Shakespeare's *Othello*, attend to Iago as well as to Desdemona. This does not mean that we are "impartial as to good and bad." Not at all. Neither is God. There is ambiguity here, as well as a slight deficiency of tune.

I grant to Kegley and to John Moskop that I have not adequately dealt with the role of justice in human affairs. I certainly think that there is a divine fairness or righteousness; but it has little to do with rewarding in our legal sense and nothing to do with punishing. It is other creatures that in detail reward or in any sense punish us. God gives us the infinitely precious gift of divine love without which nothing makes sense; there is no long-run achievement, no rational aim of aims or purpose of all purposes. "A man's virtue is his monument" said an ancient Egyptian. The only everlasting fame is before God.

As I explain in *CS*, goodness comes into aesthetics in two ways. A truly good will (a) is beautiful to contemplate and, as Plato says, means harmony in one's inner nature. As Spinoza said, those who hate their fellows partly hate themselves in doing so. Also, (b) acting from good will probabilistically means doing aesthetic good to others and to those who may come after us. The virtuous who make everyone miserable are less virtuous than they think. To this extent we should all be utilitarians. But there is a valid case for rule utilitarianism, as Bishop Berkeley as well as Kant saw. I have not worked out a complete ethics, true enough.

If even in us good will is a central element in beauty of experience, there must of course be an eminent form of this in God. Perhaps the Jewish idea of a covenant between God and those who worship God makes sense. However, I have not tried to work this out. What is clear to me is that in God the uneasy tension between self-interest and interest in others is transcended.

If neoclassical metaphysics has not entirely eliminated the classical problem of evil, it has at least radically transformed it. Since concrete details in the world are results of causally free creaturely decisions, there is no need to justify them theologically. Alas, however, as used in classical theism this "free-will defense" was weak; it allotted freedom at most only to human creatures. Neoclassicism, with Epicurus and Peirce, allots a measure of it to atoms and to every cell and animal. Ah, it is said, but indirectly God is responsible for the natural laws that make the results of such freedom possible. *If* 'responsible' has an ethical meaning here, then it implies that another set of laws, another kind of cosmos, was possible entirely without freedom, or with freedom that involved *less risk of evil, yet with equal opportunity for good.* I have not encountered the philosopher who can explain to me how we know there could be such a system. The justly famous naturalist and ornithologist, Alexander Skutch, who is not a theist, in his *Life Ascending* holds that there ought to be no predators in nature. How such a nature would look, he makes ingenious but not in my view convincing efforts to tell us.

I have seen little evidence that the book of Job was in error when it questioned our human ability to construct worlds, even in our minds. To conceive a natural system that would really work and really be better than ours is more of a task than some appear to think. And those are changing the subject who take for granted the coherence of the idea of omnipotence that either unequivocally or ambiguously denies creaturely freedom. It has not been proven that strict determinism makes sense as a genuine possibility. Like "perfect lever" it is a limiting idea that could not be literally instantiated. And the closer one came to it, the closer one would come to no good as well as no evil—simply no life at all.

R12. King on Buddhism, Hierarchy, and Reason

Dr. Sallie King's precise comparisons of my thought and Buddhism seem to me examples of scholarship on a high level. Her essay does us both honor and earns my gratitude. I select two topics for my reply: the indeed central questions of rationalism versus religious intuitionism, and of hierarchical order versus a doctrine of equality between human and nonhuman forms of life. I have written a good deal in defense of my method of metaphysical analysis as closely related to formal logic; but I have not adequately defended my hierarchical conception of nature. I begin with the latter.

I well remember how, in Japan, where I had been asked to address a Japanese group on the ideals of our Declaration of Independence, when I had explained in what sense human beings are superior to the other animals but (with certain qualifications) equal to one another, two members of the not large group asked why I did not defend the equality of *all* animals. I replied that at least they could not all be enabled to vote or run for political office. I did not then and do not now regard this as a trivial or irrelevant reply. I shall return to the pragmatic aspect of the problem in due course.

For a general doctrine of higher and lower, or more and less, important levels of reality, I have at least three lines of defense. The first is a point of formal logic. Equality is a special case, not a general principle. We say that two propositions are equivalent if each entails the other; entailment in general, however, is one-way. The biconditional is a special case of conditioning, not vice versa. Again, that 2-plus-3 *equals* 5 means that neither is more than the other. More, greater, or better than is the principle, not equality. An idea which is the dual negative of another idea is not the principle but a derivative. (Cf. P10.)

My second line of defense is implied by Plato's remark that nothing in nature is strictly equal to anything else. More generally, mathematical ideas are ideals, not literal properties of actual things. Two, three, and five are numbers, not actualities. A man who has two hundred dollars and gains three hundred more has greater reason to exult than one who has three hundred and gains two hundred more. Then, too, there are dollars and dollars, depending upon inflation. Also comparisons of size, time-spans, and other values of variables are known through measurements; and there are no strictly exact means of measuring. Plato was profound in stressing the gap between mathematical precision and the way the world knowably is. Strict equality, like other symmetrical notions, is a limiting case and an unverifiable one. Inequalities are verifiably there, not equalities.

My third line of defense is a pragmatic principle: what we have to be guided by in our decision-making, we should not pretend to reject theoretically. We have to be guided by judgments of unequal value. If we do not eat animals, we still have to consume plant cells, each of which is a living organism and, I am convinced, a sentient creature. Moreover, each of us includes in his or her individual being billions of animal cells. What sense does it make to say that each of these is equal to ourselves in value? This way madness lies. Is an embryo equal to a four-months-old fetus, the fetus equal to an infant, the infant to a child learning to speak, the child equal to an adult? Then indeed abortion is simply murder and the fanatics who bomb abortion clinics have a case. I hold the extreme pro-life theorists partly responsible, whatever they say, for such violence. They are talking nonsense, and harmful nonsense. Dr. King applies the word "wild" to the Buddhist doctrine that a rabbit might exemplify Nirvana. I think there is danger in this wildness.

To go from the human being to the single cells, from them toward molecules, then atoms and particles, is to go toward nothing at all, and cannot be from equals to equals. The zero of value is one limit of thought; and some such idea as that of God is the opposite limit. Some ways of defining deity make it as empty of content as the zero; my form of theism (close to Whitehead's) avoids this by the principle of dual transcendence, according to which God, the *all-surpassing* individual, in a certain way is *self-surpassing*. This enables God to have an endlessly increasing, concrete, contingent content: the divine experiencing of the by-others-surpassable individuals. A great advantage of a *theistic* hierarchical order is that it can furnish a universal measure and permanent register of value without which all value-comparisons seem hopelessly ambiguous or wildly relative. Wittgenstein's utter perplexity in discussing values, as recorded by Norman Malcolm, gives a fine example.

I credit Dr. King with having given me the stimulation I needed to reach a higher level of clarity on this entire matter than I had attained before. She was well advised in making this topic the subject of her principal criticism of my version of Buddhism. At this point I do indeed depart from that tradition. And my defense of hierarchy shows also why I cannot accept the Buddhist rejection of reason and extreme toleration of paradox. The Buddhists sought "the middle way" of sense between unwise extremes, but never quite found the golden mean. I suspect their nontheism stood in the way. If the Chinese were hierarchicalists they were also, as Herrlee Creel says, theists in their Confucianism. This is even more apparent in Mo Tzu. "Heaven" meant deity.

Still another line of defense for the hierarchical principle is the axiom that if A has value V and B has value V' as well as V, then A's is the greater value. One has to assume that the combination of V and V' is reasonably self-consistent and harmonious. Now we, as the intellectual, thinking animals par excellence, do not have our intellectuality or rationality *instead of* other merits, such as courage, fidelity, kindness, love, industriousness, but in addition to them. If our intelligence has more scope, so does our love. To this extent we are the other animals *plus*. Because the mutual compatibility between a high level of thinking and a high level of emotional life can be questioned, this defense is less cogent, perhaps, than the others. But it has to be considered.

To the charge that treating nonhuman animals as subhuman is simply species-prejudice I have a double answer. First, I by no means assume or accept the synonymity of 'nonhuman' and 'subhuman' animality, and this for the clear and definite reason that I take seriously the proposition, in good standing in current science and in no way incompatible with my metaphysics of religion, that there are billions or superbillions of planets in the cosmos, probably a significant proportion of which are capable of supporting animal life, a still not insignificant proportion of these actually have such life, and of these a significant proportion have life on high levels. Nor does it seem to me in the least likely that none of these nonhuman animal forms are superior to us. I have little doubt that some are superior. So the embarrassment that such an idea, according to Anthony Flew, has for Christians is no embarrassment for my religion at all. A cosmos in which so vast and complex a spatial array contained only one planet with highly conscious, intelligent inhabitants seems a far from satisfying notion. My second answer to the charge of anthropomorphic bias is that I have great respect for the porpoises and whales and hesitate to call them subhuman. Also the Chimpanzees and Gorillas are like small human children in their level of behavior. If an infant is in value terms not radically subhuman, then much less so are the other primates as adults. Nonhuman animal is one idea, subhuman animal is quite another.

I agree that animal suffering is an evil. The author of *Alice in Wonderland* thought that physical pain in us is no greater evil than such pain in another kind of animal. It is arguable, however, that by distracting us from more important matters it is greater. I am not wholly clear on this point; it worried my teacher, C. I. Lewis.

Let us turn now to the question of reason versus intuition or direct experience. Whitehead, who called himself a rationalist (as I regarded myself before my Whiteheadian period began) said that "philosophy is mystical, not in its method but in its conclusions." Buddhism is somewhat ambiguous on this matter, as it is on so many issues. I have similar trouble with Bergson, also and even more, with Heidegger. Bergson says metaphysics does without concepts, but of course he uses concepts and sometimes uses them badly.

I find in Buddhism a kind of false rationalism in the doctrine of Karma. A well-known Japanese scholar of our time once said to me, "If you had been born blind would you not want to know some reason why this misfortune had happened to you?" I told him that I would not look to Karma for help in such a case, nor want to be told that I had earned this evil by "my" behavior in a previous incarnation. I might be interested in the kind of causal analysis that medical science might furnish, but not at all in an attempt to moralize my handicap in terms of my preconceptional behavior. I regard as superstition the attempt to find moral explanations for all evils. Primitive witchcraft is scarcely worse so far as I am concerned. With Epicurus, Aristotle, and Peirce (who got it partly from those others, plus late classical physics), I am wholly convinced that creativity, however slight in some cases, is universal in nature, and that chance and freedom are inseparable. That a free act took place, and not some other act also compatible with the already formed character and circumstances of the agent at the time, is not fully determined in advance. That another act by a contemporary individual also occurred is doubly undetermined in advance. From these truly chance *combinations* of free acts everything proceeds. Common sense with its ideas of good and bad "luck" is sounder than deterministic theories. Our weal and woe depend partly on what happens around us and partly on how we use our freedom in responding to what happens. Good and bad luck, good and bad management of our responses to the luck—these two aspects make life. With both luck and management good we do well, with both bad we do ill; with either one good and the other not too bad we "may get by." I once said all this to a large audience of handicapped people. They saw the point and responded cordially.

I hold that it tends to discourage sympathy to give moral justifications for what comes to us from without. To say, "he deserved to be born blind" does not promote sympathy, but rather a smug, "That's his Karma." On this issue I am indeed non-Buddhist but also sharply opposed to much that passes for Christian. If Buddhists had been really clear about universal freedom as implying chance they would have avoided this trouble, and so would those Christians who have not avoided it. When I read in Popper's volume in this series his statement that success is "mostly a matter of luck," I thought, "one more example of how much sense this man has." Think of the fantastic luck I had in my parents. They were not perfect parents, but they were far, far better than most. Shall I claim to have deserved them? I ask the reader to recall or reread the first two sentences of this reply.

R13. Arapura on My Response to Vedantism

In preparation for William L. Reese's and my book *(PSG)* of readings on ideas of God through the ages and in East and West, we read some translations of works by founders of Buddhism and Hinduism. Somewhat later I began to meet living representatives of these religions, in this country, Japan, and India. My youthful reading of Emerson's essays and poems (especially *Brahma*) may have given me some inkling of the Hindu attitude. Some years ago, as consultant (by correspondence) for an East Indian University, I read a doctoral dissertation defending Advaita Vedantism. I have talked repeatedly with two Brahmins proud of their caste. From all of these proponents I received similar impressions of the doctrine and its manner of defending itself against Buddhism, Hindu pluralism, and some Western doctrines. I feel that Professor Arapura is a good representative of his form of mystical monism or anti-pluralism.

Difficulties of intercultural dialogue are perhaps at their greatest with Arapura's set of topics. Arguments that seem (combined with meditative experiences) conclusive to orthodox or Advaita Vedantists have left Buddhists unconvinced for many centuries; and, for a shorter but still considerable lapse of time, the case for Advaita Vedantism has seemed weak to most Westerners. One way to look at this is to say that metaphysical issues are not resolvable by reason. In a way Vedantists and Buddhists both say this; but then they, not wholly consistently I think, continue to argue as though reason had application. My view is that in metaphysics it is more difficult to think rationally than in natural science, but not impossible, and that, concerning intercultural dialogue, it is pertinent to emphasize the fact that the differences between geographically or linguistically separated cultures are to a considerable extent duplicated within each such culture. Arapura does not mention the fact for instance, that there is one strand of Vedantism, the Bengali School founded by Sri Jiva Goswami, that I for one find more congenial than the classical theism of the European Middle Ages. It is a good deal closer to my perspective than even Ramanuja was. There is also a fairly close match for the classical Western doctrine in medieval Indian theism. From such facts, and they could be duplicated even for Japan to some extent, and for China, I conclude that the intercultural problem is, at worst, not hopeless—unless indeed metaphysics is simply a vain enterprise, as some think it is, and this, too, in various cultures.

I incline to the view that the West, through its greater attention to mathematics and to observational and experimental tests of ideas, arrived at a somewhat more effective criterion of good reasoning than the Orient did. We are more wary of arguments that appeal *neither* to careful sensory observation of nature (conducted cooperatively for centuries and with the use, wherever applicable, of mathematically exact divisions and organizations of possibilities), *nor* to a logic whose operations can themselves be mathematicized (up to a point).

Arapura says that in happenings something more than just happenings must be produced. Whitehead says that what is produced is an actual entity. This is not a changing substance but a concrete reality, richer than any mere abstraction, such as being or becoming, simply as such. It is, further, an example of experience or subjectivity in a generalized sense. Its coming into being is a creation. Change is successive instances of creation. Arapura says there must be continuity, or 'succession' has no meaning. I agree. 'Continuity', however, has a number of senses. Which of these senses applies here is one of the questions answering which divides philosophers. My Whiteheadian view construes the continuity in the successive states of a changing individual in part as the Buddhists do; but the concept of prehension, by which past states become intrinsic to their successors as objectified data, gives the continuity a stronger sense than in the Theravada, while avoiding the extreme monism of some forms of the Mahayana. Whitehead's carefully qualified concept of genetic identity, or continuity in succession, is superior to any conception of this that I have found in Buddhism.

Against Buddhism, Vedantism has a case. But neither side has the clarity, in my view, that process thought has achieved on this issue. Prehension is a discovery with no adequate anticipation in East or West. It analytically isolates what memory and perception have in common, which is that in both the past is intuited (see P3). Hence in every experience the past is *given* as influencing the present. The present is new as a whole; but this does not mean that it is nothing but new, has no old constituents. On the contrary, it is an *emergent* synthesis of old elements. And these elements, so far as concrete, are previous syntheses of their predecessors. So the creative process feeds on its own already achieved products and on nothing else.

In Tibetan Buddhism there is said to be a doctrine that perception is always of the past, not of the absolute present. If so, then some Buddhists were close to a theory of prehension. New actualities are neither simply identical nor simply not identical with anything previous. They are partly identical and partly not. Moreover, this lack of absoluteness holds both for the distinction between old and new members of a sequence constituting the career of individual X and also between individual X and individual Y. Your past influences my present by the same general principle (but in specifically different degrees and ways) as that according to which my past influences my present. Individuals, that is sequential societies, are either "personally ordered" (as in the sequence of your or my experiences) or "corpuscular," which means not in linear order. A society has its "defining characteristics." These are abstract in comparison with their successive instantiations. What "exists" in actualities is less rich, more abstract, than the actualities. I propose my distinction between existence and actuality as clearer even than Whitehead's use of these words.

Arapura speaks of the indefinite. Whitehead's "form of forms," his ultimate abstraction, "creativity," is his and my indefinite. It is *infinitely* indefinite, because it abstracts from every actuality. But the infinitely indefinite is not more or greater or more real than the definite, any more than potentiality is more real than actuality. Mere possibility is the possibility of everything but the actuality of nothing. If actuality is not more than possibility, then why actualize? In short, why live? Most Westerners cannot understand what it means to live, while talking about something absolutely superior to life. They are likely to prefer either a mere humanism, or a theism of the living God who loves all and cherishes all in an everlasting life that loses nothing once achieved. This cannot be a mere absolute, or anything arrived at by dismissing everything concrete and rich in beautiful contrasts and relations, hence diversity and multiplicity. The other view looks like a pragmatically absurd living act of negating life. And it did not convince Ramanuja, still less Sri Jiva Goswami. None of all this is discreditable to Arapura. Other orthodox Vedantists impress me the same way or less well. And, alas, my favorite Hindu sect, the Bengali School, is a small sect in India—perhaps one percent of the many millions of people.

Do Professor Arapura and I understand each other? We have each other's English words to a considerable extent; but, in Mark Twain's metaphor, to which I resorted in two previous replies, we do not quite catch each other's tunes. I apologize to my commentator, who has wrestled strenuously and fairly with a most difficult topic. We are all to some extent victims of a bewildering array of traditions among which we have to try to select aspects of truth. Broadly speaking, we are making the same quest, from contrasting starting points.

C. LOGIC, PHENOMENOLOGY, AND METAPHYSICS

R14. Devlin on Metaphysical Asymmetry

If I were asked what student of mine, while still a student, showed the firmest grasp of my mature metaphysical system, I should have no hesitation in answering: "James P. Devlin." His term paper in my last seminar before I became emeritus at the University of Texas was in this respect unprecedented. That essay was only a premonition of the one I am now to respond to. Dr. Devlin focuses on the real center of the system, my list of "ultimate contrasts," expounded only in one chapter of *CS*, but in fragments suggested in many other writings. These contrasts take the place, in my thought, of Hegel's *Gegensätse*, also of Paul Weiss's "finalities" or "ultimates." Devlin sees sharply not only the relations of these essential elements of the scheme to one another but also some of their relations to the history of thought, especially to Aristotle. Here he most helpfully amplifies my chapter on Aristotle in *IO*.[11] I now regret the inadequacy of my treatment in that chapter (*pace* Paul Weiss and Andrew Reck)

---

[11]Another scholar who supports the view that Aristotle anticipated the insight which I find in Peirce, Bergson, and Whitehead into the indeterminacy of the future is Dr. Sarah Waterlow Broadie. See her wonderfully penetrating article, "On What Would Have Happened Otherwise: a Problem for Determinists," *Review of Metaphysics*, 39, 3 (March 1986), 433–54.

of the rightly famous theory of substance. In broad terms, Aristotle was, in that theory, in the sensible middle between two contrary extremes, along with Whitehead and many others, including Weiss. Compared to Leibniz and Hume, Aristotle was right. One mistake he still made was, as Devlin says, to miss or deny the distinction between the (temporal) continuity (in the strictest sense) of the possible and the spatio-temporal discreteness of the actual. Another was his supposition that the basic predicates, such as warm or moist, are nonrelative instead of relative, such as aware of or influenced by. Peirce and Whitehead with a logic of relative predicates (partly their own creation) to guide them, avoided this mistake. Not so Russell—a psychological paradox. (See *IO*, Ch. 10.) Each new present is for him logically independent of its predecessors.

In much of Devlin's paper (reduced, he wrote me, from ninety pages to twenty-five) there is a remarkable economy of words with a high level of clarity and precision. In a few places, however, the brevity does lead to loss of clarity or precision. For instance, when it is said that I accuse Aristotle of "assuming there could be a contingent knowing of something eternal." A human knowing of anything whatever is contingent in that the human knower or knowers might not have existed. Contingent knowing can embrace necessary truths; what is impossible, as Devlin himself makes clear, is a necessary knowing of contingent truths. Aristotle thought that we could know something to be eternal merely by observing that it appears not to change. Devlin's next sentence makes this point.

There seems some difference between Devlin and me concerning the deficiencies of ancient Greek thought as a whole. I think that Plato, unlike Aristotle, *almost* saw that "eternity is in love with time." His Soul of the World knows and cares about the creatures and is not simply timeless but a moving image of eternity. I count Plato and Whitehead as nonclassical theists. True, Plato is somewhat ambiguous here, so that it is easy to see how Aristotle could derive his view from one aspect of Plato. Another defect of Greek thought was its idea of inert matter. Epicurus guessed otherwise; but only in recent times has the idea of mere stuff, mere being, been overcome by cogent arguments.

Devlin and I perhaps disagree slightly at a few other points. He says "simultaneity" where I would say "contemporaneity." And he does not mention my puzzle over Bell's Theorem in quantum theory or my admitted inability to relate what I call divine time to worldly time as known to us through physics and common sense. That spatial relations, in contrast to temporal, are symmetrical, does not of itself tell us whether they are mutual relations of dependence or mutual relations of independence. As Milič Čapek insists, the structure of the world is essentially temporal; space is a complication of time, not vice versa. Both concepts express the causal order of the world; and causality is inherently asymmetrical, as time is. Individual existents can interact, but not the quantum actualities making up their careers. Both concepts (and all concepts) require that of experience, which is even more obviously asymmetrical. This brings us back to the ultimate contrasts. The abstract-concrete contrast is another asymmetry, as Devlin sees clearly, and the concrete is the richer, inclusive aspect, while the abstract is the thinner, included aspect. The famous "absolute," or wholly independent, is the most abstract, the thinnest of all. The worship of the merely absolute has had its adequate try-out and should be put in its proper subordinate place.

Devlin rightly says that there are far fewer individuals in Aristotle's world than in mine; he knows, of course, that there are for me a still much vaster number of concrete singulars, since an individual is not the ultimate concrete actuality or definite particular but a sequential grouping of one-way-dependent-independent particulars. Aristotle partly missed both the spatial and the temporal atomicity of reality. In several dimensions he missed the extent of plurality in the world. (Epicurus missed it in the temporal dimension and had no idea of the many levels of spatial atomicity. Who before Leibniz did?)

Where Devlin says Aristotle should not have affirmed the eternity of anything save "the essential nature of God and the structure of the universe," I would, to avoid a possible ambiguity, say, the essential nature of God and structure of the universe so far as common to all possible cosmic epochs. But this is nit-picking. Devlin has understood me very well indeed.

I think I follow his imaginative description of my typological rather than developmental view of the history of philosophy. I'm not sure about the "wheat" and "chaff" metaphor. But yes, I see intellectual history as neither simply random nor wholly coherent (rational). Since freedom is pervasive, chance intersecting of free acts is also pervasive. As Aristotle hinted, order in the world is one of probability ("for the most part"), something that Kant, in his Newtonianism, could see no better than Leibniz.

The typology comes in as follows: The history of philosophy is the history of concept formation on the most general level. The most general concepts express ultimate contrasts: hence they come in pairs. Given such a pair, there are a limited finite number of ways in which the concepts can be combined. I have shown, for example, that there are sixteen ways in which the basic contrasts of necessity and contingency, or absoluteness and relativity, or abstractness and concreteness, can be applied to the ideas of God and what is not God (the world). Of these ways one is exactly the view of Spinoza, another, the view of Aristotle (illustrating what Devlin calls the consistency of Aristotle's theology). The medieval classical theistic view (say Aquinas's) is Aristotelian minus some of its consistency, but plus a concession to religious requirements.

If you say, "But there is the further option of rejecting the concepts as wholly irrelevant or inapplicable to the question raised," I reply, "This is exactly the sixteenth or zero possibility." With each option one looks for possible counter-intuitive implications since only one of the options could be true. Intuition gives the final verdict. But logic will have defined the question that intuition is to answer, or the problem it is to solve. Is there any other equally rational way to deal with metaphysical issues?

My idea of the use of the history of philosophy as resource for present philosophizing is that the great philosophers can help us to find exhaustive sets of mutually exclusive theoretical options, such as the sixteen mentioned above, and to find intuitively supported axioms that rule out all views but one. To show the *complete set* of possibilities for combining concepts historically used to deal with a problem, it is only pure (in this case very elementary) mathematics, sheer logic, that can do this part of the job.

Devlin is far from the only one with a Roman Catholic background (University of Notre Dame, I recall) who finds process thought enlightening. For some of the others see *The New Schoolman*, 62, 4 (May, 1983). After all, these are people trained, as I was, to think historically in philosophy and theology. And since the good Pope John suggested that it might be all right to take Thomas Aquinas with less than absolute seriousness, Catholics have been relatively free of their worst metaphysical hang-up. Paradoxically it is Protestants and atheists who have no one to tell them to relax from theirs!

As an Irishman, Devlin has his own version of the insight of Socrates and Plato, who knew that wisdom is allied with wit and humor. It is said of the Irish that they value conversation as a precious art; Devlin has given me my best direct experience of that.

The former would-be poet in me enjoys the alliteration of Devlin's brief closing sentence, and the delightful ambiguity of its metaphor. Is the "blade" that of a soldier, or rather of a surgeon, medical student, anatomist, or pathologist who seeks to improve the health of the living by discovering the partly hidden ailments of the deceased? I think it is the latter. I do not wish to kill or wound but to help the living (or those who may come after us) partly by disclosing sound and unsound factors in the thought of those of whom we have only their writings. In doing this I am of course hampered by any unsound factors in my own equipment.

Like Martin and Chiaraviglio, Devlin is an expert in computer science, as well as a knowledgeable student of intellectual history.

R15. Frankenberry on Method in Metaphysics

Dr. Nancy Frankenberry writes about my "patient and thorough theory of metaphysics." I deeply appreciate her patient and, in its spatial limitations, remarkably thorough and understanding discussion of the theory, with special attention to my stipulations about method. In a few places I think her formulations are in need of some slight qualification; but this is scarcely avoidable in the subject. Like the two other feminine contributors to this volume, this one, I believe, has never been my student. Yet I think their contributions compare favorably with any three of the nonfeminine contributors. With Ashley Montague I find the negative description of masculinity more appropriate than the negative one of femininity. In principle it is women who most completely sum up the species as self-perpetuating, and what is a species if not a self-perpetuating group of creatures?

Of course I enjoy the complimentary passages and general tone of the vividly written essay. I will, however, focus on the suggested criticisms or calls for further clarification. These are mostly in the final pages. Before taking these up it seems appropriate to point out that the other contributor whose topic comes closest to Frankenberry's is Devlin. Donald Lee and Reiner Wiehl should also be mentioned.

I am somewhat surprised by the remark that actual examples of the pragmatic aspect I claim for my metaphysics are as rare "as the Dodo" in my writings. This suggests two different views of the import of 'pragmatic'. One of my objections to the invidious interpretation of categorial contrasts (other than expressly value contrasts, such as good versus bad, or better versus worse) is, in my sense, pragmatic, and is that no one can express in manner of living the alleged conviction that, for example, it is, universally and unqualifiedly, better to be independent than dependent, absolute than relative, infinite than finite, simple than complex, active than passive or receptive, and so on with still other ultimate contrasts. We show in living that this is not what we believe. I find that Peirce and James support me in this. Another example is my argument that nothing eternal and strictly necessary can be bad, a defect, or something that ought not to be. Negative value terms imply something that ought to be, or to have been, *prevented*, or put an end to; and this is nonsense if the something is eternal or necessary. Again, my basic clue in all my thinking is love, not mere knowledge, and love as, at a minimum, feeling of feeling, that is, sympathy. This surely has behavioral implications. So I am not clear as to what the criticism amounts to. Donald Lee, a specialist on pragmatism, finds a good deal of it in my writings.

The remark that I seem to take concrete actualities as mere exemplifications of metaphysical, that is (in one sense) extremely abstract truths, parallels a similar one by Dr. Wiehl. Both writers realize that I also hold that the abstract is in the concrete and nowhere else and that the concrete is infinitely more than the merely abstract, where the *more* includes better, or is also a value term. So I incline to think that my defense can be simply, "When one is doing metaphysics, partly by giving illustrations from experience, that is what one is doing." Nothing is implied against the overwhelming value of the concrete for life and its purposes, of which doing metaphysics is a very special case, as is doing physics with its severe abstraction from mind—apart from the minds of physicists simply as such.

Another surprise, which, however, on reflection I found illuminating, was the statement that one of my maxims of method was to attend to technical philosophical language more than to ordinary language. I had thought that I said rather the opposite. But in fact I say or imply both. Ordinary language is for ordinary purposes; for extraordinary purposes we may have to stretch language. However, in doing this we must not lose contact with the ordinary meanings of words. Historically misused technical words, such as 'absolute' and 'relative' need to be used with care. 'Absolute' has sometimes been used to mean at once all-inclusive and yet wholly independent or nonrelative, in spite of the logical truism that if something includes everything it cannot be independent of anything or in a significant sense nonrelative, for it must be made what it is partly by its relations to what it includes. So I restrict my use of 'absolute' for that which is not dependent upon, and does not include, *at least some* other things. Above all, I distinguish between descriptive and evaluative technical words. 'Independent' is not a synonym for 'good' nor is 'dependent' a synonym for 'bad'. Some forms of dependency are not bad and some forms of independency are not good. Traditional metaphysics almost hopelessly confused matters by ignoring these distinctions. 'Infinite' is not a synonym for 'supremely good' nor is 'finite' one for 'bad' or even for 'not supremely good'. By themselves they are not definitely evaluative terms and there is only confusion in taking them to be so. As some of the Greeks knew, mere infinity is empty, formless, not beautiful. Nor could the merely infinite know finite things, any more than it could know contingent things.

A third surprising passage in Professor Frankenberry's essay shows, I think, a misunderstanding by its writer, or a failure to communicate by me. In her note 50 she takes my "or nothing" (instead of "or something else," as she thinks it should be) for a statement of my view, when it is rather my polemic against those who seem to think it makes sense to ask, "Why is there something rather than nothing?" or who think that contingency means, "this or nothing." Except for the above-mentioned mild surprises, what I chiefly find in the essay and am delighted by are numerous flashes of insight into what I, perhaps immodestly, think my work amounts to and the ways in which it is revolutionary. In her comparison with deconstructionism, the "shift of emphasis," and other historical remarks she repeatedly relates neoclassicism to the history of ideas in ways that I venture to think show a mind that has read both me and many other philosophers far from in vain.

My emphasis on logic and mathematics as essential not only in all exact sciences but also in metaphysics is supported in principle by Peirce, Whitehead, and (to some extent) Plato. I think I have somewhat clarified the point by generalizing Fermi's dictum "to know is to measure" so that it runs, "to know is to order," of which quantitative analysis is a special case. (Abstract ideas other than numbers are subject to mathematical precision.) It is high time that philosophers realized that, whereas in physics the important mathematical orderings (e.g., group theory and calculus) are more difficult to work out and understand than simple, finite arithmetic, in metaphysics some extremely elementary and easily acquired logico-mathematical truths are very important yet sadly neglected. Peirce's theory of categories helped me to see this, and, I believe, to improve even upon Peirce's theory just mentioned. But none of this entails the unimportance of concrete experience for philosophy, for life, and for the philosophy of life. Metaphysics, though central in philosophy as I see the latter, is not the whole of philosophy. The inclusive human wisdom is more than science and metaphysics and is to some extent irreducibly intuitive and personal. Complete agreement cannot be secured by arguments or observation. Politics, the art of generous, judicious compromise, is also required to make group survival and achievement possible. Democracy, clumsy as it is, is feasible, whereas Plato's scheme of philosopher kings is not.

Frankenberry is not mistaken in thinking that my writings as she knew them were not adequate to the phenomenological aspect of philosophy which in principle I acknowledge. It is perhaps of some significance, however, that the last two chapters of CS (those, besides the first chapter, most relevant in this connection) were not referred to in her footnotes. Nor was my first book, PPS, mentioned. It too is relevant. Two long essays on phenomenology, written in recent years, are planned for publication, one in a book of essays by a number of authors, and the other in what, if I manage to complete some details of preparing it for publication, will probably be my last philosophical book, though possibly not quite my last book.[12] A long book of recollections of philosophers and other interesting persons may well be that, unless it proves possible to do the final work on a manuscript of a book on birds less technical than my Born to Sing.

Finally I will deal with a question which comes also from Donald Lee as well as from H. N. Lee (and is supported by Bergson and many others). Am I justified in accepting Whitehead's, or the Buddhists', radical temporal pluralism of distinct unit-experiences instead of the apparently continuous flow of experiences in waking life (note, not including dreamless sleep, if that is admitted)? The

---

[12]For one of these essays see "An Anglo-American Phenomenology: Method and Some Results," in *Pragmatism Considers Phenomenology*. Ed. R. S. Corrington, Carl Hausman, and T. M. Seebohm (Washington: Center for Advanced Research in Phenomenology & University Press of America, 1987), 59–71.

question is legitimate, but I take my answer to be also legitimate, as well as, on the whole, cogent.

It seems that there must be limits to the power of phenomenological inquiry to settle on its own all the important metaphysical questions. Otherwise it is not to be understood how disagreements in philosophy have persisted and been so great as they have been. Merely consulting what is directly and distinctly given cannot in human beings be an infallible method in philosophy. Indeed, as I like to repeat, one of the better definitions of God attributes to the deity just such an ability for definitive intuiting of reality. Things just as they are must indeed be directly given clearly and distinctly to the all-knowing. We, however, are not divine.

Democritus and Epicurus in ancient Greece were convinced that the realities given in perception were given unclearly and indistinctly. How else could they be given if the realities are atoms of imperceptible smallness? It is a tautology, but still a truth, that perception cannot tell us directly what imperceptibly small realities there are, or are not. Leibniz, who was a spiritualistic rather than materialistic atomist, agreed with Epicurus as to the indistinctness (he also said, "confusedness") of our direct intuitions of nature. Psychologists, almost uniformly, I think, reject the claims of introspection to tell us directly or definitively just what our experiences, or our personal selves, may be, not to mention what is going on in the experiences of other persons and animals generally. Peirce and Whitehead, also Bergson (with some inconsistency I feel) are with Leibniz and the psychologists. Obviously if God knows atoms directly, then for God they are not imperceptibly small. Still they remain so for us, although with fantastically elaborate apparatus of magnification we can almost see them one by one.

I may be the first person to formulate the following principle: What is *positively and definitely given* in perception must be accepted as really there; but what is not so given may yet also be there. When, for example, we feel physical pains or pleasures, something corresponding to them is there in our bodies and not just in our experiences. I reject "sense data" categorically if they are defined as only in our experiences but not otherwise in our bodies. The motto for pains is, hurt my cells and you hurt me. Pain is something *bad* in our bodies, namely in our cells, as well as in our experiences. It is in our experiences only because it is also and first of all in certain cellular or subcellular bodily constituents. Moreover, something of the quality of the pain is in these minute entities. I reject the Kantian notion that it is possible to experience something not in the least given, in either its qualitative or its structural aspects.

The problem of temporal discreteness was, in the West, long overlooked, from a logical point of view quite arbitrarily and with no explicit reasons given. The Greek atomism was purely spatial. Temporally there was supposed to be sheer continuity; in addition, change was reduced to mere alteration of spatial location. Only in space was reality a great multiplicity of unit instances; in time it was the relocation of sheer identities. Leibniz kept this bizarre scheme, with the half-remedy that there was a continuous flow of qualitative change within each spatial atom. Leibniz failed to see that he was treating spatial multiplicity according to the principle: "If there is definite multiplicity there must be definite unit cases." But he treated time in violation of the principle. Yet we do distinguish John sick from John well and remove the contradiction *either* by saying that John in the two cases is logically two subjects rather than just one, *or* by saying that "sick now" is one predicate and "sick yesterday" is another predicate. The choice between the two ways of removing the contradiction was made without reasoning. The Buddhists made it with reasoning, as did Whitehead. Peirce was for once off guard here, and Bergson was extremely careless and really kept the contradiction by talking about "interpenetration" of mental states, excusing himself by saying that logic does not apply in this case. Experiences surely are successive, but what are the unit terms of these relations of succeeding?

Not only Whitehead but also the logician von Wright argue that the contradiction, subject S has contradictory predicates, such as sick and not sick, is not legitimately removed by trying to put temporal location into every predicate; rather, one must take the final unit-subject to be a single experience, or quantum of experiencing that is not a succession of temporally smaller experiences, but occurs as a single undivided experience, yet is not punctiform or instantaneous. For me this reasoning is stronger than any negative verdict from the absence of *clearly* intuited quantizations of experiencing. Moreover, direct intuition can reasonably be said to come close to revealing the order of magnitude of the quanta. The number of successive distinguishable musical tones per second that can be humanly detected is clearly far fewer than one hundred and more than five. In a high fever the number may be greater and in abnormally low temperatures smaller than in normal temperatures. An information theory expert has said that Whitehead's idea is given some indirect support by empirical facts. There is good reason to think that birds can make somewhat smaller temporal distinctions than we can. With molecules, atoms, or particles as the unit spatial cases, the unit temporal ones would be vastly shorter; with cold-blooded animals in cold environments longer.

On the whole, it is not the phenomenological argument against the Whiteheadian or Buddhist theory that bothers me, it is the difficulty of putting together the various time differences between different levels of life with one another and with the application or non-application of the principle of quanta of becoming to the divine life. (Like Whitehead I am committed to a temporal aspect of that life.) The best I can say about this difficulty, which is not phenomenological in any direct way, is that we should not expect to find understanding of the temporal structure of reality to be easy. The physicists have trouble with it; and there are excellent reasons for supposing that time is the ultimate key to space, so that if time were easy to grasp by human means, everything would be. The whole notion that it is eternity, the timeless, that is hard to understand is wrong. It is precisely with the extremely abstract that our intellects are most at home, as in arithmetic. What is less temporal than numbers?

Augustine argued for the divine existence by almost equating the truth about God with truth about numbers. As though the divine all-knowing could be less complex or concrete than the cosmos that God knows! True, the uniquely divine defining characteristic of all-knowing*ness*, simply as an idea, is itself extremely abstract; hence it makes sense to take the divine existence as no less necessary than that $2 + 2 = 4$. Nevertheless, to equate the bare existence of God simply as all-knowing with the concrete actuality of the divine life is to reduce God to the combination: necessary existence (an extremely abstract property), all-knowingness, all numbers and other mathematical entities, but without any specific qualities of feeling, any definite genera or species of animals, any actual knowing of any actual cosmos.

My ad hoc principle, as the critic calls it, of least paradox and the way my methodological principles for metaphysics are more or less inseparable from my metaphysical conclusions, are, I submit, about what one should expect from the extreme generality and mutual inseparability of metaphysical categories, together with the fact that we are not God and things are not given to our direct intuition with unsurpassable clarity and distinctness.

Aristotle saw that each discipline must have the method appropriate to its subject matter. Yet he tried to treat physics as though sheer inspection of nature through vision and touch should almost tell us just how to classify what we perceive. He unconsciously slurred over the difference between necessary or eternal and contingent or temporal truth, even though he made that distinction in some respects more clearly than anyone before him and also than many who came after him. And he failed to deal with the atomist's argument that we manifestly do not detect by mere sense perception the real dynamism of nature. The admission that the operative structures below the animal level are microstructures is the only reasonable way to explain how little we know from their apparent sensory qualities as to how seen things will change under various conditions, such as high or low temperatures, under great pressures, in a vacuum, and so on. The atomists were partly right, and for partly right reasons, as against Aristotle. Modern physics had to start with them, not Aristotle, or even Plato.

I rest my case. Posterity, if we have one, will judge. Anyhow, God knows.

R16. Ford on Whitehead's and My Philosophy

In my recollection of Lewis S. Ford from his year of study at Emory (before he went on to his doctoral degree at Yale), he stands out as the obviously capable student whose special interest then was in the abstruse metaphysics of Schelling, but who, when he took a course in symbolic logic in the mathematics department, was given an A in it. As my title implies, he is more generous in his discussion than his title suggests, dealing with me as more than (though in some ways perhaps also less than) an interpreter of Whitehead.

Professor Ford, well known as editor of *Process Studies* and a very thorough scholar in the development of Whitehead's thought, in the present volume applies his scholarship to my thought. Although I scarcely disagree with anything in the first few paragraphs of his essay, I would like to elaborate some points. What I learned from "prehension" was not the mere ideas of asymmetrical awareness or of the essential asymmetry of time; I think I already had these and also the notion of external and internal relations as involved together in single two-term relations. What was new was the idea that this structure is illustrated in the most direct perceptions as well as in memory. The memory side was already in Hocking and others and is the natural intuitive view. What I needed to learn from Whitehead was that, even in the most direct *perceptions,* the data are before, not strictly simultaneous with, the perceiving. This fitted the conviction I had acquired from a now almost forgotten teacher at Harvard (who later gave up philosophy and became a country gentleman) and from a book by Lossky: that an experience is the dependent factor and what is directly given, intuited, or experienced is the wholly independent factor in the relation of the two. This, according to the teacher, was what almost everyone, from Descartes to Kant and Husserl, had missed. I still agree with him. And how can one change or create past happenings? We conform to them, not they to us.

To Ford's list of influences—James, Royce, Hocking—I would like to add my Haverford teacher Rufus Jones, and still earlier, two mystical poets, Emerson and Wordsworth, the second of whom was also important for Whitehead. In addition I was influenced by many of the same philosophers as the great Anglo-American was, including Plato (on whom, with Spinoza, I specialized as Ph.D. candidate); also, Leibniz, Hume, Berkeley, Kant, Bergson, Bradley, Russell, and some of the classical theists.

As teacher my primary objective has been threefold: to make students aware of Peirce, and/or Whitehead, and/or some of my ideas. Success with a student in any one of these aims was for me satisfying enough. One difference between me and Whitehead is that, as he once put it, he was "a baby in [technical] psychology" (he was, however, in my view one of the best amateur armchair psychologists there have been); in contrast, I had considerable exposure to several capable psychologists at Harvard and passed a general examination in the subject. I also wrote a book *(PPS)* in part dealing intensively with some experimental work bearing on the nature of sensation. It supported, as he recognized in a letter to me, Whitehead's view of sensation as a species of feeling. Whitehead's knowledge of natural science was best in physics, of which I know very little; but I have some intensive knowledge of a branch of zoology and its literature. (I had two admirable courses in biology.) Here, too, our views scarcely conflicted. Again, at first by a lucky accident, I taught many classes in aesthetics; but I found that Whitehead's system was more relevant to that subject, as well as to ornithology, than was any other system, even Hegel's, Kant's, or Schopenhauer's.

Another difference is that the theology Whitehead was brought up to know about was, it seems probable, classical theism, whereas my father, Francis Cope Hartshorne, a clergyman of the American branch of the same church as Whitehead's father, had learned from a theological teacher (trained in England) to believe a theology that in principle, apart from questions about Jesus, was what I call neoclassical. It proclaimed a God of love who was not immutable or uninfluenced by the creatures, and whose all-powerfulness did not mean that our decisions are uniquely determined by divine creativity. They are made possible by it, but we make them actual. To that extent *we make* the world. Creativity was for Father not a divine monopoly. What Whitehead had to fight for, against tradition as he knew it, was to some extent my birthright.

I do not recall thinking about Father's form of theism while working out my own philosophy at Harvard; and only by reading recently a letter of his on the subject have I come to realize to what extent I must have been indirectly influenced by a late nineteenth-century turn, in a branch of British theology (perhaps influenced by Martineau), away from classical theism. My religious quarrels with Father concerned only his Christology, his beliefs in personal immortality (but I recall no definite discussion with him about that), and something miraculous (he avoided making it more definite) back of the Resurrection story to explain how the church could spring from the death of its founder on a cross. But with my parents' faith in a God of love I have had no serious, prolonged disagreement. Moreover, they both lived their faith and made it attractive as a form of life. Whitehead's father did that too. About his mother, however, the evidence seems unclear.

Among the eleven differences that Griffin and Ford together see between my system and Whitehead's, I find some that seem largely matters of language, or emphasis. For example, I think that my psychicalism and Whitehead's reformed subjectivism are essentially the same. We both agree that much of the subjectivity in nature is nonconscious and mean by this the same lack of judgmental complications of mere feeling. To feel is not necessarily to know that or how one feels. Knowing is more than mere feeling. What Whitehead calls "mentality" is, in minimal cases, only a feeling, however rudimentary and unconceptual, of futurity or real possibility. All subjects in some way and degree have a feeling of past and future. Adult human beings cannot reduce their experience to anything so limited as the most primitive forms of such feeling; but then we have great trouble imagining or definitely remembering infant feelings. For us, feeling is always somewhat conscious; does it follow that all feeling must be so? Our "intellectual feelings" are emergents, but not feeling as such.

I now take up the four topics, alphabetically ordered, discussed by Ford.

(a) God. Whitehead's essay (in *Adventures of Ideas*) on "The New Reformation," and his chapter on "Peace" in that book, as well as the final chapter of *PR*, seem to me to express with sublime eloquence a view similar to mine. The main difference is that I find the idea of God as a single actual entity too close for comfort to classical theism and doubtfully consistent with the rest of the system. A subject that never reaches completion but "is always moving on" as it actualizes novel prehensions of novel states of the world is not a single subject or single actuality as Whitehead conceives these. This, to be sure, concerns an irreducibly mysterious matter: how in God alone all de facto actualities can be unified into a single (or multiple) creative synthesis that fully possesses and transcends their values. And of course, God as personally ordered society of subjects is very far from being *closely* analogous to a human person's succession of experiences—broken as that is by dreamless sleep, dreams, delirium, multiple personality, aphasia, all the while prehending nothing with full vividness or adequacy. I also agree that relating the divine becoming to the problem of simultaneity in physics exceeds my capacity. Paul Fitzgerald has tried to exhaust the possible theories here.[13] I feel incapable of solving the problem, and it seems clear that Whitehead did not solve it.

That the idea of God is analogical is traditional and is common to neoclassical or process theologians generally. But Whitehead, like classical theism, has only one basic analogy and I, thanks to Plato, have two. The shared analogy is the interpersonal one, loving relations between persons. I add as extremely important the soul-body analogy of Plato, modernizing "soul" to mean personally ordered experiences, Whiteheadian subjects or actual entities, and "body" to mean certain other and subordinate subjects on a lower level of conscious or nonconscious feeling. Whitehead rejects this analogy (for weak reasons), instead of translating it into his own terms. I see great advantages in this translation. Cornford and others have shown how Plato's Demiurge or Creator can be conceived as an aspect of the World Soul as acting according to

---

[13]Paul Fitzgerald was one of several physicists who discussed the bearings of relativity physics on the idea of God in *The Journal of Philosophy* 46 (1969), no. 11, 307–55.

the idea of Good. Here also, Whitehead is too close to classical theism, which rejected the World Soul, but too far from Plato, who can be viewed as, in his form of theism, the nearest to Whitehead of any of the other great thinkers who preceded Whitehead. It was Aristotle who muddied the waters, or rather, radically oversimplified the theistic problem as Plato saw it. The muddying was done by the Stoics, Manichaeans, Gnostics, and, on a higher level, Plotinus. Mere eternal being, unmoved yet moving all, was not the God that Plato worshipped. The *Timaeus* (and tenth book of *The Laws*) and the last chapter of *PR* stand out above all that came between them. I owe this thought to a student who was too skeptical to believe either formulation, but who saw their power.

Plato, Whitehead, and by implication Socinus, W. E. Hocking, and my father, accepted a duality in deity. Plato speaks of two Gods, the one creating and the other created, "the eternal God and the God that was to be." Whitehead speaks of two natures of God, but does not quite tell us how they form but one being. True, all his actualities are dipolar, with both mental and physical prehensions. I have tried to generalize and systematize the double duality, that which uniquely applies to God and that which applies to the nondivine actualities. The duality God-world, which is essential to both poles, I also accept. I call the entire theory the doctrine of "dual transcendence and (dual) immanence."

One side of dual transcendence is fairly traditional: God is unique by being necessarily existent, independent or absolute, infinite, eternal, immutable; the nondivine individuals exist contingently, are dependent, relative, finite, temporal, and (as societies or enduring individuals) mutable (as single actualities, they become but do not change). The other side of divine transcendence is that God is also uniquely excellent (beyond possible rivalry by another) in manner of being contingent (in actuality not in existence, a distinction I read into Whitehead); God is also uniquely relative, finite, temporal, and mutable (though only by increase, addition). Dual immanence means that the nondivine beings are, in less excellent ways (surpassable by others) contingent in their very existence (as individuals or societies), fragmentary (mere parts of the finite), changeable as individuals by loss and destruction as well as by increase or growth, yet absolute or independent (of remote contemporaries and successors). Existence and actuality are distinct because it is individuals (societies) or species that exist, while single actualities occur or are self-actualized. Less concrete entities than actualities exist if their defining characteristics are instantiated by actualities. There is in God an independence of *all* others and a dependence upon *all* others; in the nondivine, both dependence and independence are of *some* only. God is the *all* being, the others are the *some* beings. This is traditional enough: God knows all things, we know some things. I add, God is prehended by all, we by some, actualities.

I read the distinction between existence and actuality into Whitehead because his actual entities are not, I think, said to exist, and he makes it clear that the existence of an individual (or society) means that its ''defining characteristics'' occur in at least some actualities. His treating God as a single actuality makes trouble here and this is one reason I reject it. The ontological argument is also relevant. (Whitehead's rejection of that argument does not apply to it as I use it; for I argue, not from a mere ''verbal definition'' but, as Leibniz said, from the assumption, made explicit, that the definition has coherent positive sense (as 'class of all classes' does not).

How do the two natures, primordial and consequent, in God form one being? Analogously, how do the identity of my gene structure and the non-identity of many of my cells now with my cells as a child form me now? Or how does the fact that some of my purposes and traits of character are virtually fixed for years cohere with the fact that I now have a new experience and respond with a suitable new purposive action? Since the divine necessity or independence (in existence) is with respect to all others, and the divine contingency or dependence (in actuality) is equally with respect to all others, the first must be uniquely abstract and the second uniquely concrete. Well does Whitehead term the primordial nature abstract. But how concrete is the consequent nature? I see here a real ambiguity. A nature, an essence, is an abstraction. Traditionally no real distinction between the divine essence and the full actuality of God was admitted. Yet the point of the word essence is its contrast with accidents. And surely, Whitehead does not regard the concrete consequent reality of deity (prehending all actualities) as noncontingent; for then nothing could be contingent. Besides the two natures, we need something more. I call this more the consequent *states* of God—the God prehending our world now, for instance.

Perhaps some readers know or have guessed what my key to this problem is: the Aristotelian or ontological principle of Whitehead, that the abstract is in the concrete, not vice versa. (Incidentally I could have learned this asymmetry from C. I. Lewis rather than from Whitehead. Lewis says it in nearly the same words as Whitehead.) The independent factor in deity is abstract, and so is the consequent nature as a mere nature. Russell says, somewhere, ''concrete*ness* is an abstraction;'' what is concrete are the instances of this abstraction. The consequent nature is the divine concreteness. So there must be instances of the consequent nature, and these members of a necessarily non-empty class form the divine actuality. They are many, not simply one; I call them states.

It does not follow that the primordial nature is a mere inert object. Recall that ''God is not before but with all worlds.'' Always God was consciously prehending a world. Primordially, God was already actualized as consequent. Moreover, not only *we* have the concept of the primordial nature; God primordially knows the contrast between the divine essence and the divine accidents, or between the incomparable way (unsurpassable by others) of prehending and the by-others-surpassable ways; or between the divine way of changing (by increase only) and the ordinary ways of possible loss or corruption. Divine thinking thinks divine thinking, as Aristotle said; but it also thinks nondivine thinkings (as data, objective forms of feeling in the divine prehensions).

My enthusiasm is especially for Whitehead's making it clear that God is not merely creator and the creatures merely created, not merely cause while the creatures are merely effects. No, in relation to the creatures, God is partly created by them (God as consequent), and they are to that extent creative of something in God. Lequier saw this long before Whitehead. But it goes too far to call God a "primordial accident." The divine existence is strictly uncaused by anything prior to it. This is true of no other being. "The world" that God *must* have is no definite world rather than any other. It is not *a* being, *an* actuality, or *a* society, it is merely the abstraction, some world or other. But God is not just some God or other. And God's existence as the one and only divine individual is beginningless and endless, or "unborn and undying," as Buddha said of something, who knows what?

(b) My rejection of *eternal objects* is only partial. For one thing, mathematical objects are eternal possibilities, for example, Planck's Constant as a possible feature of some cosmic epoch. What I take not to be eternal is, for example, blue as a single definite quality out of the irreducibly vague continuum of possible sensory qualities. Only quite abstract structures can be (in a sense) definite yet timeless. But this does not mean that there is no eternal abstract ideal or purpose (Plato's Form of Good), and no eternal continuum (as a Peircean "multitude beyond all multitude") of qualitative possibilities, out of which fully definite single qualities emerge, are created, in their appropriate cosmic epochs. Qualitative definiteness is the final product of creativity, not its timeless storehouse. I follow Peirce here more than Whitehead; but Whitehead's theory of extensive abstraction seems relevant.

Ford's argument that if God's ideas are all derived from past actualities then God could not give us new subjective aims is searching. However, mathematical ideas are not copies of past experiences but are inherent in thinking enough about thinking. As Leibniz said, they are in "the intellect itself." Also, although the eternal continuum of quality does not include definite qualities, it can guide the creation of definite quality. Finally, qualitative creativity is not a divine monopoly, for we accomplish it in our final aims or satisfactions.

The continuum of colors in three dimensions found in some psychology or art books suggests the possibility of feeling a red more saturated than we can experience, or a much more numerous array of noticeable differences than we can have; also qualities intermediate between visual and auditory qualities. I find this a very mysterious topic and am not certain of any exact solution to the problem. I congratulate Ford for having so well formulated it. It is perhaps worth mentioning that Berdyaev is on my side in this question. He says that creativity produces new ideas, "new images," and does not, as he thinks Platonists suppose, simply actualize eternal ideas.

Verbal formulations of what happens in high-grade actualities are bound to be oversimplifications. The brain-cells must do much to help an experience of the human type to achieve its synthesis of its past. The laws of nature must go far toward explaining cellular functioning, assuming that cells or their singular actualities are subjects, not mere bits of stuff or value-free process. God as orderer of the world, the type of order differing in diverse cosmic epochs, determines the laws which, however, are not classical deterministic laws but are statistical, or somehow allow for chance and probability. Half-life laws seem to allow particles a sort of freedom, but the result is a great deal of order.

In describing the laws of nature as "imposed" I mean only that divine decisions are involved, and that these decisions work by persuasion. As a physicist said to me in this context, "It is as if an electron knew the mathematics of its behavior." It does not know this, but it feels in a way that gets the statistical result; and this is because it feels God so far as there is in God what is relevant to it.

That the divine lure is "irresistible" only means that no creature can threaten the integrity of the world order so far as aesthetically necessary for there to be a world. Even God requires a world, some world or other. In my view there is no contingency in the fulfillment of this requirement. Even God could not experience or prehend unmitigated chaos; but the divine power to prevent its occurrence is absolute. However, the divine adaptability is also ideally great so that universal freedom is still possible. Low-grade actualities have extremely slight creativity and with many of a kind individual eccentricities cancel out statistically.

An analogy to suggest how God could inspire a statistical result is this. I once took part in a test of marksmanship. We all aimed at targets. The shots went more or less close to the "bull's-eye", and the holes were concentrated more and more near the eye. Suppose then that the target was not seen, but vaguely or indistinctly felt under divine inspiration. Because of the vagueness and the creativity, however slight of the creature, the center would seldom be precisely hit but still more often so than any other tiny spot, and the distribution would be statistically calculable.

Remember, too, that God prehends all the past qualities of every past epoch and hence has far more, indeed in a sense infinitely more, at command than we can have. If Whitehead could formulate an eternal divine ideal of harmony and intensity of feeling, there seems no reason to doubt that God could have this ideal, or something like but superior to it. As eternal, it is nothing resembling a single definite quality or multiplicity of qualities. If God has this ideal, God can apply it to our situations. And if we prehend divine prehensions of the world, this could influence our behavior. But we would still have to take into account our memories of past experiences and our feelings of the effects of our past behavior on the society of our bodily micro-constituents in their just previous states. As Spinoza said, a human mind is the "idea" (modernized, "*experience*") of a human body, which is the portion of nature containing the actualities that we most directly and constantly prehend and are prehended by.

(c) Prehension and Causality. I am still not convinced, by Ford (or Jorge Nobo) that there can be *mutual* prehensions among actual entities.[14] I regard the asymmetrical structure of prehension as the clue to the subject-object relation and the solution of Hume's problem of causality—one of the greatest of all discoveries. Countless idealists and materialists alike had missed it. But I fail to see that either contemporary or future actual entities or subjects are in any literal sense intuited, experienced, prehended. Future actual occasions cannot be prehended; for there are none. Whitehead says so. As for contemporaries, Whitehead celebrates their independence from one another as the basis of freedom.

Why then the many assertions of *mutual* or *universal* extensive connectedness that Whitehead makes? As he was a great geometrician I feel my relative ignorance in that subject in criticizing him at this point. But the following is what I must conclude. It is true that an actuality has relations to, and prehensions of, some factors that later actualities, when they come to be, must include as aspects or constituents of themselves. But what is to be included is something less concrete than the later actualities, and the abstract is in the concrete, not vice versa. The very general kind of extensive connection that applies to every cosmic epoch is less specific than our spatio-temporal structure in this cosmic epoch, and even the latter as conceptualizable is abstract. (In the concrete, structure is also qualitative and transmathematical, transmetaphysical.) Since (as Whitehead wrote, and C. I. Lewis and Carnap as well) the abstract-concrete relation is external for the abstract term, the internal relation of prehension that qualifies a present or past actuality relative to some geometrical factor in future (and as yet nonexistent) actualities does not carry through to constitute a present prehension of future actualities. If A prehended B's prehension of C, then A would indirectly prehend C. But this is not the situation we are discussing in relating present to future occasions.

---

[14]Jorge Nobo, *Whitehead's Metaphysics of Extension and Solidarity*. Albany: State University of New York Press, 1986.

With contemporary actualities as distinguished from enduring individuals, or societies of actualities, I see the same lack of mutuality. What is mutual in space (which is indeed the way there are mutual relations) is that each of two contemporary actualities prehends much but not all of the past that is prehended by the other. In this way individuals interact. But that actuality A (say my experience now) prehends actuality B (say your experience earlier) does not entail that B prehends A. The two are in the same universe because they have a partly common past (and a partly common potential future); but calling this an "indirect connection" blurs the ambiguity involved. The geometrical part is covered by what has been said about abstract and concrete. To disagree with Ford, Nobo, and Whitehead is not an ideal position to be in; but it seems to be where I am. I may have missed the point. I suspect, though, that this disagreement with Whitehead is one aspect and the disagreement about eternal objects another aspect of the same issue.

Whitehead is one of the few great philosophers to see clearly that a cause should not be *defined* as strictly determining, but only as influencing or making a difference to, what happens later, so that without it the happening, just as it is, could not have occurred. Does the past make a difference to, influence, the present? Hume could find no logical reason why it should. But if the present-past relation is of a momentary experience or subject to its given (not merely thought or intended) objects, then, of course, the subject is influenced by these objects and could not be what it is without them. It makes no sense to deny this. In memory we see this relation, just where Hume did not look for it. By subject-object relation we here mean, not the relation of a subject's thought or intention to what is thought or intended, but only the relation of prehending or intuiting to its data in memory or perception. Conscious thought or reference, sign usage, is both more or less than prehending. Even in dreams, besides thoughts there are prehensions both mnemonic and perceptual, as Bergson (better than anyone else in history) in his essay on dreams shows (apart from the word prehend).

I entirely agree with Whitehead's statement: "The order of the world is aesthetic and is grounded in God." Without God the explanation of cosmic order through the subject-object-aesthetic theory of becoming is circular or begs the question. For it to be possible to achieve satisfaction in prehending the past, there must already be order in that past—order, but not too tight or complete order. "Disorder is as real as order"—and as necessary aesthetically. Besides, since no order could dictate the creative act, cosmic order must in any case involve some allowance for freedom in the libertarian sense. How, without a supreme or divine form of creativity, could the countless many subjects, most of them little conscious and narrowly limited to a tiny part of nature, somehow adapt to one another their ever-changing and interacting societies so as to make experiencing possible at all? A world of free but nondivine beings seems a formula for chaos or nothing genuinely conceivable.

Whitehead takes for granted, as do I, that the natural laws cannot be the only possible ones. They will differ in remote stretches of cosmic development. It is, as Fred Hoyle, the astronomer, argues (in *The Black Cloud*) as if there had been a choice of the basic rules for our world. What if not a supremely influential agent could make this choice? And what would make it supremely influential? Here I use the Platonic analogy. Why is it that my cells to a certain extent respond to my wishes or decisions? I am like a little deity in the mind-body system. Each decision we make creates something new in our personalities and in our bodies. In this sense deity is the analogically ideal case of what we are as animals. Our conscious feeling or thought is superior to that of our cells; therefore they are somewhat obedient to our imperatives. We persuade them. In Whitehead's Platonic scheme this is what God does to all subjects. If you say that this degrades God you are either forgetting that this is an analogy (controlled by the principles of dual transcendence) or you are degrading the true notion of our mind-body reality.

The wonder is not that the body does not always work well but that it works at all. I agree with a remark of Hume's Cleanthes and with Merleau-Ponty that apart from something like the relation of mind to body, or to "flesh," we have no experiential basis for the concept of mind. Hence it is an illusion to suppose that we exalt God by positing a divine analogue to our consciousness and feeling (love) but deny any divine analogue to the relation of animal minds to animal bodies. Tertullian thought that God was or had a body. A few theologians since Plato, in Germany and this country (Pfleiderer, D. C. McIntosh) that I admire have accepted Plato's analogy.

The divine body (or, as Goethe calls it, the living garment of deity) is not simply better or greater than ordinary bodies, it is in a sense absolutely different; for it has *no* external environment. Plato's clarity here was exemplary. Modernized a little, Plato disposed in advance of the objection that there is no cosmic nervous system. For God, unlike us, interacts equally directly with *every* individual, whereas our experiences directly and effectively influence, it seems, only a few billion of the hundred billion bodily cells, and the rest through these. God needs no brain to mediate between influences coming from without (for there is no without) and those coming from within. Moreover, *this* soul is defined as excellent beyond possible rivalry, and its creative influence upon its body therefore must be ideally great. Equally beyond rivalry must be its sensitive response to the weal and woe of its bodily parts, its love for them. However, on Whiteheadian principles each of its members must have some freedom; therefore the divine influence cannot simply eliminate risk of disharmony among the parts, or sufferings therein, and in these the divine feelings vicariously participate. So

God is the "fellow sufferer who understands." 'Fellow' here does not connote equality, that is the point of 'understands' (as we do not). However, all prehension, for Whitehead (and me), involves some kind or degree of sympathy. Since the cosmic soul is unborn and undying, there can be no absolute beginning of the creative process in a Big Bang and no cessation in a mere black hole or cosmic heat death. These must both be toned down to transitions between cosmic epochs.

(d) Perishing and Concrescence. Whitehead and some of his interpreters may be right in positing successive phases in the self-creation of an actual entity. I only find it difficult to be sure that the distinctions which save, if they do, the theory from contradiction can be maintained. Whitehead says that in metaphysics language is stretched to its limits, and this is one of the issues that for me illustrates what he is talking about. That there seems to be no perfect, trouble-free way of expressing the most universal truths does not, for some of us, mean that all ways are equally good or equally bad. There is no perfect way in political thought or much else outside of pure mathematics, and by some criteria not even there perhaps. But there are better and worse ways, at least taking the special needs of different cultural stages into account. Perhaps the distinction between transition, the actual succession of actual entities, and the non-actual but in some sense real succession of phases in the becoming of an actual entity makes sense. I'm not quite sure that it does or doesn't.

On "perishing": I never seem to get the point. By the "being" of past becoming I mean that, unlike many imagined or possible cases of becoming it really did occur and must henceforth be taken into account. Whitehead's own definition of 'being' comes to this. Plato's "being is simply power" comes close. So I do not see what has ceased to be. Everlastingly, from now on, past becoming is a potential datum for future becoming to prehend. That this becoming is there to prehend *is* its being. The becoming does not go on happening, but its availability is its having happened. Past happening seems to me genuine happening, not mere being. And Whitehead says "its being cannot be abstracted from its becoming." So I'm not sure what the point is that I miss. I admit that past means object, but what is taken as object, prehended, is past subjects.

I would like to say something about one difference between my work and Whitehead's that some may think as important as any difference in our conclusions. This is that I have gradually worked out, beginning with my dissertation over six decades ago, a method of argument in dealing with philosophical issues. Whitehead does give arguments for his views, but he gives to some readers, including unfortunately, Karl Popper, the impression of scarcely arguing his case. Popper is reported to have said of me, "He is a theologian, but—he argues." I take this as complimentary. Like Whitehead but even more so, I argue partly historically. I think many issues have been reasonably settled, each by one or more great philosophers. For instance, I hold that James's "Dilemma of Determinism" is close to conclusive against compatibilism (the consistency of deterministic theories of freedom). Combined with Peirce's essay on the "Doctrine of Necessity" and some remarks of Whitehead, it removes compatibilism from the class of live issues. If more is needed, add Popper's superb booklet, *Of Clouds and Clocks*.[15]

I have arrived, however, at a systematic form of argument (sketched in R14) that uses deductive logic not directly to prove a positive conclusion but to make entirely clear what more than such logic is needed to reach a reasonable decision. It is the idea of elimination from an exhaustive finite set of mutually exclusive theoretical possibilities, given a pair, or small set, of concepts traditionally used to state an issue. Thus, given the two pairs of concepts, Necessity applied to God, Contingency applied to God; necessity applied to what is not divine, contingency in that application, and symbolizing these four concepts by N, C, n, c, then as the mathematically possible combinations, including the all-zero case of no application, we have sixteen possibilities, no more and no less. We then look for reasons, intuitively credible, against one or more of these sixteen. For me there are credible principles with intuitive appeal which, usually several of them for a combination, rule out all combinations but one, symbolized by NC.nc, that is complete application. This illustrates the double duality mentioned above.

Instead of necessary and contingent, we can use absolute and relative, and a number of other conceptual pairs—with similar results. If this is not a rational way of dealing with metaphysical issues don't ask me what would be. It is the only one I can see as fully rational. Since to adopt one of the sixteen mutually incompatible possibilities is by implication to reject the other fifteen, not to know what these others are is to rely too heavily on an initial positive decision. I strongly support Popper's emphasis on negative decisions. Positive intuition must also be appealed to in the end; but it needs to be shown what it is doing in rejecting other possibilities. This, indeed, is what mathematics contributes to philosophy. It tells us exactly what, in our metaphysical affirmations, we are denying. How else is one to know?

I will give one other example of the method. We all deal with the idea of changing, yet through change in some sense or degree the same, individuals or things. Call this the problem of gen-identity, German *Genidentität*. There are two extreme doctrines, neatly incarnate in Leibniz and Hume. For the first, despite change, there is complete literal identity. I have always been the

---

[15]Karl Popper, *Of Clouds and Clocks: An Approach to the Problem of Rationality and the Freedom of Man.* St. Louis, MO: Washington University Press, 1966. The (Second) Arthur Holly Compton Memorial Lecture, presented at Washington University, 1965.

individual who at a certain time began to exist and at a certain other time (known to God) ceases (in the ordinary sense at least) to exist. This is what I already was when yet an infant. The "law of succession" of states is what defines me as the individual that I am. The close relation of this to the timeless view of divine knowledge and hence of truth is obvious enough. The view is extremely paradoxical.

The strict oppo•ite of complete identity is no identity. What then is individuality? Mere (partial) similarity through change? So we have the extreme pluralism of Hume, Russell, and many others. This too is paradoxical. Between the two extremes is the view that there is partial or qualified identity. Aristotle first carefully formulated such a view; a host of persons since have agreed with him. Besides essence, or what makes the individual that individual, there are accidents. Thus, I could have been myself had I not just now noticed a bit of white stain from liquid paper on a finger of mine. Sensible people tend to admit this kind of contingency. It is the commonsense view, as C. I. Lewis admitted, though he was then a Leibnizian on this question.

We have so far three views formally distinct. I see two other possibilities. There is radical monism: plurality of individuals is an illusion; indeed all multiplicity, spatial or temporal, is, unreal. (Leibniz could be termed a monist with respect to temporal, but [apart from the fairy tale of preëstablished harmony] a radical pluralist with respect to spatial, multiplicity.)

Where in all this is Whitehead? He admits accidents of an individual, and a somewhat relative or conventional form of essence remains as "defining characteristics." So far he is close to Aristotle and common sense. But he raises an issue not noticed by most of the others, except perhaps Hume and certainly the Buddhists. Is the becoming of an individual's states or experiences continuous or discrete? Aristotle, Peirce, Bergson, any number of others, assume sheer continuity. Whitehead and G. H. von Wright give formal arguments, related to Zeno, to show that this is illogical. I agree with them. If we experience continuously, then how is there any definite succession, or how are there any definite terms for temporal relations? Peirce held that each present is infinitesimal; so that there are an infinity of experiences in any finite time, however short. He used this to show that we have no identifiable immediate intuitions. His fallibilism rests on this argument. But fallibilism can be based on another idea which is that direct intuition of the concrete does not entail wholly *distinct* and *clear* intuition. Indeed, intuition of the concrete both direct and clear is what some of us would call divine intuition. (Leibniz would support this, I think.)

In any case, counting monism, there are (at least) five theoretical possibilities. I see excellent reasons against all but the Buddhist-Whiteheadian view. It has the great advantage, seen clearly by Buddhists and Whitehead, that (presupposing prehensions of the past, in some Buddhists denatured by notions of somehow involving future occasions before they come to be), we can say that what is called self-interest is really a kind of narrowly limited altruism, the concern of the present unit of self for future units in the same individual sequence. Moreover, since past actualities are prehended and future ones (as not yet realized but further determinable possibilities) are anticipated—in principle, whether they are, or are not, members of our own personally ordered series—and since we care about persons who will live after our deaths, it is a mistake to regard as the only, or even the chief, basis or justification for concern for others that it helps us to take care of our own earthly futures. Combined with ideas of heaven and hell, this self-interest ethics can result in what Berdyaev called "the most disgusting morality ever conceived."

Whitehead and I might both be called neorationalists, having learned (I partly with his help) the falsity of several assumptions of classical rationalism; for instance, the assumption that the function of deduction in metaphysics is to draw conclusions from easily arrived at and self-evident axioms. History shows this procedure to be unsafe. The primary function of deduction, in metaphysical, as in empirical, usage, is to test supposed axioms by their entailed conclusions. In metaphysics, seeking only necessary truths, everything is self-evident *if* you have enough insight, but only God has unlimited insight on this or any level. Also the principle of sufficient reason, as Robert Kane brilliantly shows, must be qualified to be a valid axiom.

One of the reasons why I admire Karl Popper is that he, first of all, gave the right definition of metaphysics: the search for generalities that are significant and important yet *not observationally testable*, that is, conceivably empirically falsifiable. They are, if wrong, falsifiable, but only logically (in the broadest sense)—by finding that terms are used either contradictorily, or so vaguely, ambiguously, or empty of practical import that nothing is said.

An axiom that seems to be sound is that metaphysical coherence or truth, like Aristotelian virtue, is a mean between extremes. My recent book *WM* deals with this. There are extremes of materialism and extremes of spiritualism; nor is mere dualism the mean, for it embodies some of the extremisms of both sides. Atheism is an extreme, and some classical forms of theism are so also.

I see why David Griffin says I am more rationalistic than Whitehead and why Ford says this is no great difference. I think Whitehead is sometimes uncomfortably close to blurring the distinction between metaphysics and empirical cosmology. (The British tradition disfavors metaphysics more than the American does.) But Whitehead, on occasion, admits the distinction. Victor Lowe, who understands Whitehead, thinks Whitehead ought to have been more wholeheartedly empirical. Whitehead might well, like Peirce, have had a keener sense of the experimental side of science (and of the importance of behaviorism as a method); but Lowe is clear that the thoroughgoing empiricist he would like him to have been is not what Whitehead was. An insightful passage on the nature of metaphysics is Whitehead's declaration that we should try to generalize our very general ideas just as far as they can be generalized and *still make sense*, for only in this way will we find their metaphysical truth. If, for example, we cannot simply deny experience, then we must generalize it, to see if it will not do the job that "matter" is asked to do. I say the same about matter; the World Soul doctrine, with the cosmos as divine body, matter interpreted as mostly extremely low forms of (nonhuman) experience or mind, is one implication.

Anselm and his critics early made me vividly aware of the problem of ontological necessity and contingency. Peirce reaffirmed the lesson. He held that, since it is the concrete that is contingent, determinism deprives us of any naturalistic approach to the problem of relating the richness and variety of the world to what is necessary, driving the origin of all that richness back infinitely, or positing a beginning that was purely arbitrary, a blind accident or a supernatural act of freedom. Instead we should see in each instance of becoming a new act of freedom (self-determination), however slight its novelty. And Peirce did not simply reject the ontological argument (indeed he said some things in its favor), or any theistic argument. "They all prove something." Whitehead seems to pick and choose here somewhat arbitrarily. By luck, in a class taught by C. I. Lewis I was confronted with Anselm's argument; I contended against Lewis's view that it was wholly fallacious. He said, some "scholastics went at it" as I was doing. Teaching Kant for some years forced me to stick to the problem. Whitehead is basically on the right side in all this, but he does not quite focus on the modal problem.

Perhaps I am more rationalistic, but then I had Peirce and Whitehead to learn from at the age of twenty-eight; earlier, C. I. Lewis and H. M. Sheffer. The bridge between logic and metaphysics has to be the idea of modality above all. So, of course, Quine, who pooh-poohs modal logic, cannot cross that bridge. Carnap admitted modal logic, but so grudgingly as almost to nullify his admission. And it is the great discoveries by the original pragmatist and the Anglo-American metaphysician that I primarily defend. The other bridge to metaphysics, that between experience (in its concreteness) and metaphysics has also to be where Peirce and Whitehead found it, in the idea of creative love (or feeling of feeling) as human, subhuman, and superhuman.

In such ways I try to argue reasonably for, and in some respects clarify or deepen, Whitehead's precious insights into the creative-prehensive structure of reality. Ford is to be thanked by readers who find this reply worth reading, since his careful questions were what led me to think intensively about matters of concern to both of us.

Supplementary Comment on Ford's New Version**. Perhaps Ford is the most rationalistic of the three of us, for he keeps trying to get a completely definite and verbally consistent account, with no loose ends at all. With Whitehead I hold that this is an unattainable ideal. Only God has either the perfect metaphysical, or the perfect physical, truth, and it is not verbal. Deconstructionism is partly correct; language is an imperfect, not a perfect, means to intuit reality. However, we can gradually, for those trained and apt in the matter, overcome some of the cruder mistakes. I think we *know* that causal order cannot be the absolute order that classical physics and metaphysics thought they could affirm. I incline to think we can know that localized, noncosmic, nondivine agents cannot suffice to decide the contingent aspects of natural laws (and we can know that there must be such aspects). Thus the laws cannot be merely immanent, if that means wholly decided by nondivine creatures. They must, it seems, be divinely decided, and by persuasion made effective. Also the contingency of laws means that they are effective only during a cosmic epoch, not eternally, and I am with Whitehead on a succession of cosmic epochs each with its own laws.

One point relevant to the problem of contemporaries is that, taking reality to be in principle spatially finite (as I hold we should take it), there may be no need for strict contemporaneity. God may take the creaturely actual entities one by one. However, since the divine past of the creative process must be beginningless, hence numerically infinite (in contrast to the spatial elsewhere), each new actual entity must be given an infinity of relations to its predecessors. What this means for relativity and quantum theories is beyond me. It must in some sense be beyond physics also. As Whitehead said, we are doing well to know a huge finite past, say back to the Big Bang (though I am not wholly convinced, as Hoyle is not, as to that) without claiming to know either that there was nothing before the B.B. or what was before it.

I congratulate Ford for his speculative courage. But we fragments of finite actuality do not have unlimited ability to grasp either the finite or the infinite aspects of cosmic and divine reality. We can know what we need to know for playing our optimal roles in our cosmic epoch. They are humble roles. As a physicist said, when commenting on such phrases as "the conquest of space," "How conceited can we get?"

Plato's mind-body analogy is primary for me, but neglected by Whitehead and perhaps by Ford. My or your bodily behavior is not merely physico-chemical. Every "decision," in Whitehead's extremely general sense, that you or I make, several times per second when awake, or while dreaming, slightly alters things in a way that physics, as now constituted, says simply *nothing*

---

*Presumably on Ford's June 1988 revision. —LEH

about. As Wigner emphasizes, the presence of (animal) awareness *must* make a difference. On the other hand, the physico-chemical forces are always there, with my (or your) special gene structure, and it is, to a substantial extent, these factors that communicate to us indirectly the divine persuasion to conform to the order of this cosmic epoch. The molecules have little range of decision-making, of creativity. Collectively their limitations limit our ranges. Cells also come in as agents on their own. No simple scheme can entirely cover all this. How could it?

I admit *mathematical* entities as eternal.

My best contribution may be in my sixteen-fold analysis of divine dual transcendence in terms of the polar contraries—absolute-relative, necessary-contingent, infinite-finite, possible-actual, universal-particular, and still others, as applied to God and what is not God, or the Cosmos. I here use rigorous, that is, mathematically exact, logic to exhaust theoretical possibilities, and then look for reasonable rules to eliminate all but one of the sixteen possibilities. For this procedure I find no close precedent. (For the duality there are precedents, and in many traditions.) Unluckily, only in one of my books do I present this scheme, and even in it (*Creative Synthesis*) my exposition is clumsy and inelegant (op. cit., pp. 266, 471). Thanks to Joseph Pickle of Colorado College, I now know how to arrange a neat table of the 4^2 combinations of the two concepts in their double applications or inapplications (zero cases) so that the logical relationships can be surveyed almost at a glance. Peirce's idea of a logical diagram is here illustrated in a simple but, it seems to me, very powerful example. If I had died in my seventies or early eighties I would not have fully reached this achievement. Modern medicine and hygiene enlarge the possibilities even for philosophical discovery. Indeed, especially for that, since Plato was not mistaken in holding that maturity is required for philosophical wisdom.

R17. Martin on the Logic of My Metaphysics

Norman M. Martin is a logical technician besides being philosophically sophisticated and profound. Among my former students, he, like Chiaraviglio, has always been able to think easily about more complex logical or mathematical problems than I have learned to handle. I hope this volume will have many readers able to do more justice to his contribution than I can. I take seriously the Socratic point that part of true wisdom is knowing what one does not know. My way of mitigating the effects of my cognitive deficiencies is to expose myself to those who know what I do not. If I do not well understand physics, higher mathematics, or advanced forms of mathematical logic, and yet have opinions to which these are relevant, at least I pay attention to what experts in the subjects say when they write or talk in a less technical vein. The nature of philosophy seems to me to make this attitude particularly desirable. To cover the whole philosophically relevant knowledge of one's own time as well as Plato, Aristotle, or Leibniz did becomes less and less possible. In recent decades Peirce and Whitehead have come nearest to doing it. I have just named the five most competent of the highly creative, speculative Western philosophers whom I know about and have implied some of my reasons for so regarding them.

Professor Martin's pleasant memories of early impressions of me match mine of early impressions of him. We felt that we had common values but somewhat different abilities and centers of interest—different but complementary rather than competitive. He delighted me by the smile of good will with which he corrected some mistakes of mine. That he focused on formal logic and was perhaps more Carnap's student than mine was all right with me, as it was in the case of the somewhat similar Abraham Kaplan. I had more difficulty happily sharing students with the learned and powerful pedagogue Richard McKeon, some of whose disciples seemed to go out of their way to learn nothing of my ideas. Rather than attribute this lack of harmony simply to faults in either of us, I prefer to think of it as partly bad luck for both of us. Our personalities were not a good combination. Partly, the trouble arose from the fact that McKeon was the protégé of President Hutchins. This also, I suspect, was partly good and partly bad luck for both of us. (Hutchins, too, had some bad luck. He was a superior administrator.) I am not sure, but I incline to think that I learned more from McKeon than he did from me. He was a learned and ingenious interpreter of the history of ideas. His "This is a new age of Sophists" (in the Greek sense) haunts me. I wish it were less true!

Some formal logicians and some linguistic analysts seem to fall into the idea that formal logic can all by itself somehow determine what one does with metaphysical questions. Some students of Wittgenstein act as if only one linguistic "form of life" is a correct use of language. Martin is not one of these. (Bertrand Russell hesitated on this matter. At his best he thought logic was permissive rather than dictatorial.) I wanted Martin's help against the idea that either no metaphysics or only one metaphysics could appeal plausibly to logic. My own view is neither that all sorts of metaphysical systems can be perfectly logical, yet mutually incompatible, nor that logic suffices in choosing a metaphysics. The relation is more subtle and complex than these extremes imply. A good metaphysics is a logic of categories additional to, but including, the recognized logical constants. It requires insight into ideas that cannot, as well as those that (in small finite cases) can be *diagrammed* (in the generalized sense of Peirce, anticipated by Lange) and are the subject matter of mathematics.

It seems true that modal logic as I use it is at least close to C. I. Lewis's logic of strict implication S4. In some contexts S5 comes in. (Billy Joe Lucas, in a dissertation done at the University of Texas at Austin, has worked this out.[16] I have never been frightened by the alleged paradoxes of strict implication. That deduction from illogical premises yields only the illogical conclusion, P & $-P$ for all values of P, seems in order to me; and that deduction from any premise whatever can yield, among its less obvious conclusions, all necessary truths seems even more clearly in order. If anything is true, strictly necessary statements are. That is their necessity. Moreover, in neoclassical metaphysics the unconditionally necessary consists of intrinsic relationships connecting abstractions so general that any and every possible state of affairs will instantiate them. (That is the sense in which God is "being itself," the individual with functions so completely general as to be relevant everywhere.) It is important that Quine's "no bachelor is married" is not unconditionally necessary. In some conceivable states of affairs there could be no such proposition with the meaning we give it.

I agree with Martin that unqualified determinism is incompatible with the temporalistic view of contingent truths. But then, overtly or covertly, determinism has always been qualified. It was always an artificial view that confused mathematical abstractions with concrete facts. (Plato knew this, many others have not known it.) For one thing, sensory and emotional qualities were always left out of the picture. And determinism was never consistently applied in the act of deciding. It is a pragmatically empty doctrine, except as it is inconsistently or irrationally handled, played fast and loose with. (See R6.)

That we must have "access" to possibilities from some actuality and cannot simply make possibilities (other than mathematical) out of terms or concepts thrown together, I agree. I understand what Martin means by the extreme view that every change means a new individual. At the opposite extreme is the view that there are no new individuals, but only exactly the same individuals in new states. I also see why he associates the first extreme (change as ever-new individuals) with the name of Hume. I associate the other extreme with Leibniz. However, Leibniz is, in an odd way, both an extreme (spatial) pluralist and an extreme (temporal) monist. In one possible world, ours, which is also the sole actual world, change is only of states of forever strictly the same individuals; but God might, except for the "moral necessity" of choosing the best possible world, have made a world with some individuals the same as in ours and some very different. Hume, also, in another way, was both an extreme pluralist, each moment considered a simply new entity (however similar to its predecessors) and an extreme monist, since the new entity is precisely determined—*how* we cannot understand—by its predecessors. Between the extremes in both respects were Aristotle and many followers: individuals are *in essentials* the same through change, but more or less sharply different in inessentials, and their changes are

---

[16]Billy Joe Lucas, "The Logic of Omniscience" (Ph.D. diss., University of Texas at Austin, 1981).

partly matters of chance. My Buddhist-Whiteheadian view concerning the temporal structure of individuals is between Hume and Leibniz and with Aristotle, *except* that the dichotomy universal-individual is enlarged to a trichotomy, universal-individual-particular, and that the becoming of states (particulars) of an individual is not continuous but in *least quanta,* finite in number in a given time span on a given level of reality; for instance, the flow of experiences in a human being, or an ape, or a whale.

It seems that I must make a confession, not only for myself but for process philosophers generally: we have not worked out the relation between this revised Aristotelian view and the technical procedures of recent mathematical logic. Whitehead said it should be done, but left the task for others. I have not done it either. This is an aspect of the movement that remains a "promissory note," to use the expression of Wayne Viney in his consideration of my psychology of sensation. If I had not tried to become expert in metaphysics, in the behavior of singing birds, and in the empirical psychology of sensation, but had sharply focused instead on the interface between metaphysics and formal logic, as my lamented friend Richard Martin thought I should have done, the situation might by now have been different. One has to put some trust in one's spontaneous interests.

What Norman Martin calls "absolute particulars" is what Whitehead calls actual entities or actual occasions. Change is the successive creation of these particulars. The enduring, changing individuals of common sense are sequential groups, called societies, of particulars; some groups are "personally ordered" and some are "corpuscular," not personally ordered. Your, or some other animal's, experiences throughout life form a personally ordered society. Your body with its subhuman (cellular, etc.) experiences form a corpuscular society. A tree is a corpuscular society with (probably) no personal order above the cellular level. Only a nervous system (it is reasonable to suppose) enables a multicellular creature to have a supercellular dominant "entelechy" (Leibniz).

What is lacking in the process movement so far is a decision of how actual entities, in contrast to societies, are to be symbolized in logic. Richard Martin and Chiaraviglio have done some work on this, but only on the level of nonmodal logic and on the assumption that truth about what happens in a given stretch of time obtains timelessly. No such timeless truth about temporal realities is appropriate to Whitehead's, Peirce's, or my metaphysics, and obviously not to Bergson's or Berdyaev's. This is what Martin means by my "taking creativity seriously." The truth about actualities is not timeless, because the actualities have being only in and after their temporal loci. Time is the incremental creation of realities and hence of truth about these realities. To eternalize all truth is to eternalize everything. Truth about timeless metaphysical and mathematical principles is indeed timeless. I have taken this for granted, and I attribute the view to Aristotle.

Individuals are neither wholly actual and concrete nor merely potential and abstract, but both. Only actualities, particulars, are wholly concrete or definite. By the time they are known (distinctly, only by God), they are past. "There are no occasions [or actualities] in the future" (Whitehead). There are no predestined actualities, nor are there predestined yet wholly new individuals. My first great grandson is a class of possibilities for an individual, not a definite individual. Individual uniqueness escapes conceptualization in advance.

Nixon as not resigning but impeached is a once possible state or state series of Nixon; but Nixon before his conception (and even as an infant in what most matters) was an individual possibility only in the weak sense discussed above. 'Julius Caesar' names a past actual society whose entire history is wholly definite (for God); but no still living individual's history is wholly definite. Aristotle's essentials of individuals are Whitehead's "defining characteristics," like "first son" of two given parents. But this identifies no actuality in advance. My parents could have had a first son with quite a different gene mixture from mine, and even the genes did not wholly determine the first actual experience in that embryo, fetus, or infant that began my career. The fact of identical twins makes that very clear. I had such a pair as brothers. Their experiences were by no means duplicates of one another.

That "Possible worlds are alternative states of the actual world" is the simplest way to state my view, but perhaps it is too simple. I take seriously the "cosmic epoch" idea of Whitehead. Perhaps our epoch began with the Big Bang and its set of laws. However, this was not the absolute beginning of the creative process. The category of creativity, with its aspects of actual entity, prehension, emergent synthesis, and the like, implies an infinite set of already actualized instances furnishing initial data for their successors. And definite quantitative laws are contingent, having other possibilities that may have once obtained or may in the future obtain. Cosmic epochs seem to have their relations less in any time we can know than in what I incline to call divine time, constituting the divine history, not just the history of our world. If this idea were much more lucid than I am able to make it, perhaps it would by that very fact be suspicious. As animals adapting to an environment, we have capacities primarily shaped to deal with our epoch, not the totality of epochs. Whitehead's "unimaginable past and unimaginable future" doubly refers beyond our epoch. Our interest in this beyond is religious, rather than narrowly practical. Niebuhr's "The end of history is beyond history" can be interpreted in this sense.

Positive modal statements that become false after being true I regard as incompletely formulated statements. Statements about contingent things presuppose some "actual world" in Whitehead's sense as their referent. An actual world in this sense is the actual past of a given actuality. "Rain is possible tomorrow," true here on Monday, becomes false on Wednesday if the state of the weather on Wednesday excludes rain here in the next twenty-four hours. But the statement is still true of the actual world of Monday. Statements made at a date and true of the world at that date become later false only if the date of utterance is left out of account. There are new but everlasting positive truths, about both actualities and possibilities; but only essentially negative truths become later false. "No one has ever done such and such" becomes false when someone does the such and such, but "someone has done such and such," if true, can never later become false. There is a radical asymmetry between assertion and denial, as well as between past and future. It is wonderful how many puzzles begin to dissolve when one frees oneself from the prejudice that symmetry is the basic principle, and asymmetry or directional order is derivative or unreal.

I am not sure that I fully understand what is involved in Martin's discussion of two senses of possible and necessary and the definitions of the two concepts in terms of double negation: possible meaning, not necessarily false, and necessary meaning, not possibly false. I hold with Peirce that this symmetry is misleading. The positive idea is "possible"; "necessary" is derivative, meaning what is true no matter what, the common factor of a set of possibilities. Potentiality, futurity, is inherent in the "form of forms," creativity.

One must also distinguish eternal, pure unconditional modalities from temporal, real, or conditional modalities. Eternal modalities are doubly modal; they could not have been otherwise. The necessary existence of God is an unconditional necessity; but the divine actuality is contingent and conditional in its particular aspects. The necessity of the particular past, given the particular present, is conditional, and so is the possibility of its partly predictable future. There might have been a different possibility for that future.

Can all truths be divided, as Aristotle implies, into temporal-contingent (or only conditionally necessary) ones and nontemporal necessary ones? For instance, suppose something contingent and possible never happens—but hold, *never* is a word about all time, and how is this different from eternity? My reply is, "What could make it true that it never happens?" For an example, by each one of your or my past free acts we excluded other ways of acting that had previously been possible. Neither we nor anyone else will ever be in a position to act as we might have done on that occasion. So it will never be done. However, this truth that it will never be done only *became* truth at the time of the act; it is indeed a truth *about* all time but not a truth that has obtained *in* or *at* all time. Even divine decisions cannot be timeless. God (who is good at no matter what time) cannot decide whether or not to do or be good, only *how* to do or be good. Deity is not tempted. Deity and unsurpassable kindness are the same.

Since the eternity that excludes contingency means "not only true for all the future but equally for all the past," the Universalist's problem about salvation seems scarcely relevant. It also is not a problem for my metaphysics since I am not committed to any salvation beyond what is involved in the objective immortality of the past in the divine prehensions. I believe also that the doctrine of Hell and of everlasting punishment to which the Universalists were objecting is not even a genuinely conceivable, coherent doctrine. No eternally and necessarily existing being could be so incoherent in its motivations as to will, whether contingently or necessarily, to treat creatures in any such fashion, whether or not the required form of immortality is conceivable. The view that Dante's genius made appear thinkable is ultimately not thinkable. It suggests pictures that can be imagined but not thought through as more than pictures, as concepts.

I have trouble with the set H of possible world histories, "complete" for all time, past and future. My rejection of determinism is not on merely contingent factual grounds. I think no possible world could be deterministic. The very idea of modality depends upon freedom or creativity. Only mathematical possibilities are (in a sense) as definite as their actualizations. Possible color qualities are in principle indefinite. The number of just noticeable differences that we can distinguish between red and yellow through the oranges is perhaps a hundred. None of the hundred would be as definite as, and yet identical with, the hue I experience right now in my typewriter tape. Actuality is not reducible to a set of repeatable predicates, eternal objects, eternally envisaged by deity. I am, even more radically than Whitehead, a philosopher of becoming and, on this issue, side with Dewey, Bergson, and also Peirce.

I agree with Martin that divine knowledge must be conceived as superior in principle to ours; but I hold that this means primarily that divine intuition, unlike ours, is not indistinct or blurred in its feeling of others' feelings. Here "others" include even one's own past subjectivities, those in the same personally ordered series with one's present ones. That "all hearts are open to God" I take seriously. Concrete knowledge is social, and God is the "Socious" unsurpassable as such. God, I suppose, knows what "would be true" if this or that happened tomorrow, but this *would be* is no very definite history. Tomorrow will define itself, it cannot be defined in advance plus some universal trait of "actuality." It will have new predicates, not merely new applications of old predicates. The meaning of life is that each of us can enrich reality with new definiteness, hence new beauties—new even for God. I do identify truth with what God knows; but the content of this knowledge increases, not only in its *true* propositions but in its propositions. I perhaps failed to provide Martin with my essay on "new propositions," the only writing of mine, so far as I know, that was ever mentioned in the *Journal of Symbolic Logic*.

I agree with Martin that only God can distinctly know an infinite complexity. Indeed, we can distinctly intuit no more than a quite small finite complexity.

Irrefutably the Greek atomists by implication maintained that, as is tautologically evident, objects too minute for human intuitions to grasp one by one are not and could not be shown nonexistent by our inability to intuit or perceive them. The atomists have also not been and could not be shown mistaken in holding that only such minute objects can explain what we do perceive of nature. Bishop Berkeley did not refute this contention by holding that the order of our perceptions is explained by imputing to God capacity to control the order apparent in our intuitions and to have the intuitions (miscalled "ideas"), even when we do not. Aristotle's physics is the most determined attempt to explain physical reality on the supposition that human perceptual intuitions are adequate to directly exhibit the natures of things. The failure of his physics was definitive. On some issues Epicurus was simply right and Aristotle simply wrong. If Berkeley's God has our intuitions, what are they intuitions of? There is no proper theory of *givenness* in any of the three great British empiricists. Hume's impressions are either impressions of themselves or of nothing—either way, language is idling. (Here Thomas Reid was right.) Kant's theory was in some ways worse still. Whitehead's "prehending" is the chief breakthrough in history on this point.

There is some analogy between my views and those of L. E. J. Brower and Saul Kripke. Also, I do seem to imply what Martin calls a "non-trivial tree." The difficulty of the latter is partly to harmonize it with the interpretations of relativity and particle physics. Although physics is an empirical science and metaphysics is nonempirical, empirical and contingent truths cannot contradict necessary ones. Besides, there is a metaphysical element in empirical knowledge. Einstein's view differed from Newton's not solely on the basis of empirical results such as the Michelson-Morley experiment. Einstein argued partly from results of an intellectual experiment, and quite consciously so. He saw that absolute simultaneity implied absurd consequences.

Putting the matter in another way, since a metaphysical or necessary truth is one that no genuinely conceivable possibility would, if actualized, contradict, it follows that metaphysical truths must harmonize with any physics that even makes sense, whether or not it is empirically confirmed. If the idea of simultaneity as relative in the Einstein fashion makes sense in principle, that is, apart from special quantitative aspects, then a valid metaphysics cannot be incompatible with it. The same holds of the quantum idea, apart from the special constant involved in Planck's formulation. I strongly incline to the view that the major changes in empirical science are partly metaphysical. Thus, the basic idea of evolution would, I hold, be valid in no matter what genuinely conceivable cosmic epoch or world-kind. Aristotle was, as anti-evolutionist, a bad metaphysician. Only deity simply in its defining traits, and what is nondivine simply as such, can obtain eternally and without change.

Although I did not invent the notion of metaphysics as the search for necessary and immutable truths, it seems that scarcely anyone in all the centuries since Aristotle has quite focused upon what this, taken seriously, by modal laws must entail. For instance, it requires us to distinguish between two meanings of "empirical." There is the broad meaning, in some fashion derived from perception, or "from experience," and the narrower and for some purposes crucial meaning, "negatively testable by perception, observationally falsifiable." Popper was the first to focus sharply on this narrower meaning as demarcating metaphysics from empirical science. All knowledge involves perception, and no word has meaning apart from all perception. If God has knowledge, then God has perception. All knowledge is "experiential"; but not all knowledge is empirical in the Popperian sense. Since, however, the total truth, by modal law, must be contingent, any knowledge that understands itself and its functions will have both a contingent and a necessary aspect, and the latter will be an abstract element in the former. Both aspects will be real. Metaphysician and biologist both interpret the same total reality, and both at their best know this. The difference is one of emphasis. All must refer to concrete examples; but for metaphysics these are to illustrate what words of extremely general import are to mean, while for the biologist they are to show what the actual world happens in particular to be like.

In a conference of two about modality, neither Martin nor I found it easy to translate from my language into his, or vice versa, my difficulty arising partly from an inability to fully assimilate the use of "accessible" for modal statements, never, so far as I recall, having happened to read anyone employing this term, although I have read some work by Carnap, von Wright, Kripke, Rescher, Lucas, and Kneale on the subject, as well as C. I. Lewis. It also appeared, however, that our two sets of beliefs were to a considerable extent mutually compatible. Certainly we are closer than Carnap, Quine, Richard Martin, or David Lewis and I are on the modal problem.

The harmony in difference that Norman Martin and I experienced at the beginning of our acquaintanceship seems in fairly good shape now after almost five decades. The gap in proficiency in logic has widened; but we still make sense to each other, although I am somewhat bewildered or dazzled by the more intricate details of his contribution.

R18. Hubbeling on the Ontological Argument

Meeting H. G. Hubbeling (alas now deceased) a few years ago in Belgium (he was, however, a professor of philosophy and theology in the Netherlands) was encouraging. A logician with a knowledgeable interest in metaphysics and theology is not an everyday experience. His essay, like that of Norman Martin, puts a strain on my ability, or lack of it, to think with technical competence in exact logic. I wish however, to emphasize my conviction that my chief contentions about the ontological argument can be put, and to some extent evaluated, informally. For one thing, this argument is not by itself the chief, or even one of the chief, reasons for theistic belief. My two primary reasons for belief are the arguments: (1) without God we cannot understand how cosmic order as such is possible; and (2) without God as recipient and objective immortalizer of our achievements, "all experience is a passing whiff of insignificance," considering our mortality and other basic aspects of animal life. (Both of these arguments, I hold, would apply to any genuinely conceivable kind of world.) Otherwise put, the question is, "Accepting creativity as ultimate category, how is cosmic order possible without a supreme form of creativity, a divine form, to persuade the lesser forms to conform to the minimal requirements of a viable universe?" And how, in a Godless cosmos, assuming that this is a coherent idea (which I doubt), could there be for decision-making any rational aim or measure of value?

On the other hand, that the ontological argument (OA) could be the mere vicious circle or formal fallacy that Kant and Hume took it to be, I find also incredible. The idea of God itself must entail a logical-type difference between God and all else. God taken as just another, though greater, being among beings, all contingent in their very identity or existence, is, as Peirce said, a fetish, and worship of it could only be idolatry. This was Anselm's discovery, though it is easy to show that Aristotle had virtually said it, as had Philo. And it has been reasonably read into Plato as well.

Formally, the OA requires two extralogical premises. One is the Anselmian principle that the concept of God is contradictory if taken as describing a contingently existing (or contingently not existing) being. The divine existence is either a necessity or an impossibility. The other premise is that at least some definition of deity that entails the noncontingency just referred to is not absurd and is consistent. This premise is not obviously self-evident, and in my opinion knowledgeable atheists will reject it, as Carnap, for instance, did. John Findlay at one time offered an ontological disproof of it.

If the two extralogical premises are accepted, a very important consequence must also be accepted, which is that the central theistic question is non-empirical (in Popper's sense) and is essentially metaphysical. Empirical science cannot settle it, nor can ordinary common sense, reasoning from empirical observations. In a broad sense, the question is exclusively conceptual or one of informal logic. Does theism make sense? To suppose that the answer to *this* question leaves any further question of 'divine existence' still open is to fail to comprehend the meaning of *divine*. To compare a deity that does not but might exist with one that might not but does exist is to change the subject from the doctrine of theism to some fancy like those producing the Greek gods and goddesses. And even with them, the question of clear and coherent meaning is formidable.

What also follows from the foregoing is that the problem of evil, when it takes as premises, observations about the amounts and kinds of suffering and wickedness in the world, is a product of poor theologies. And what has been wrong with the theologies is no longer a secret. It is the idea that creaturely acts could be strictly determined by a divine "Let it be so." Let this murder be committed, and it will be committed, exactly and only as divinely decided. Even apart from evil, this is an incoherent idea. Individual decisions in their concreteness are made by individuals themselves, not by another, even a divine other.

Considering that he is in a geographically, nationally, and linguistically different tradition, Hubbeling's understanding of my thought is remarkable and gratifying. I note a few topics where there is perhaps a slight misunderstanding. I do not take myself to "teach what is called in Husserl's phenomenology the *intentionality* of experiencing, i.e., that experience is always experience of." Husserl blurs a distinction that I make sharply, as Whitehead also does, between experiencing a *datum* and *meaning or intending an object* that may or may not independently exist. Husserl's "hyletic data" are sense data in the sense I reject—dependent upon the experiencing for which they are data. Husserl's all too Berkeleyan idealism is the result. Experiencing an *independent* datum is what I, with Whitehead, call prehension, and *never* call intention. If the datum is also intended, that is an additional fact. One prehends much that one does not intend and intends much that one does not prehend. I am not sure whether or how much this difference in terminology influences Hubbeling in his partial differences of opinion with me as to the modal status of the future and the past.

Another apparent difference is that I do not believe that "the future is open also for God because *mankind* is free." Rather, my doctrine, as were the doctrines of Peirce and Whitehead (also Epicurus), is that all actors in reality, all dynamic singulars, are in some measure (greater than zero) free in the libertarian sense. In most cases the freedom is unconscious; but it is always causally significant and leaves the future open even for God.

I have trouble with talk of God's love being "victorious in the end." With Whitehead, I deny that there is an absolute end (or absolute beginning, either) to the creative process. There may be an end of our cosmic epoch; but how far it helps to call this end a victory is not clear. (Each moment, God forms an ideal reception of the worldly process in the divine life, the divine Consequent State.) I also would not talk about "stones" as ultimate terms of external relations. Stones are only for rough common sense single entities; talk about them is shorthand for talk about atoms or molecules. A stone is nonconscious rather than unconscious, as a crowd of sentient individuals is nonsentient rather than insentient. It is not in the ultimate sense *an* entity. I take molecular, atomic, even particle, along with cellular and animal, language seriously; but ordinary inanimate physical objects are human makeshifts. They are not the doers of what is done in reality.

The distinction between logical and real possibility I dealt with in my reply to Norman Martin (R17). The notion of cosmic epoch is relevant, as are the notions of divine time and the relativity of simultaneity. These are among the not wholly finished parts of my metaphysical project.

That the past acquires new meaning and therefore is changed I regard as a result of ambiguity, not as a valid argument. Whitehead *defines* being in terms of *possible* uses in future prehensions. Whatever values the present *could* ever have are (as possible but not as actual) already there and are the being of the present. Possibility and being are always abstractions, and so is the past. To think the past we must abstract from what is new in the present. What the past *could* do for the new present was already in the past, but as possibility, not as actuality. And only the present in question has *this* actuality. I take these considerations to apply to divine past and present. But I admit that I have not told a very clear story as to just how this all fits together. What is clear is that, for example, the values we have from knowing about Plato are in us, not in Plato. True, divine prehensions of the past actuality of Plato were always much clearer for God than they were for Plato or his contemporaries; but they were still abstract, outlines, not fully concrete duplicates, of our or God's present experiences of Plato. As for what Kierkegaard meant by God changing the past, I give up on that. He did deny predestination and did believe in genuine freedom for human beings. But his dichotomy of the temporal and eternal was, in my view, too close to classical theism—like so many dichotomies, it is in need of triadic mediation.

Where Hubbeling says that the cosmological argument does not prove the "whole essence of God," I would say two things: no argument proves the whole divine *actuality* (which is infinitely more than *any* essence); but the cosmological argument as I state it in *CS* proves the same essence as does the ontological. I treat the conclusion, "there is a supreme agent making a cosmos possible but lacking the essential attributes of deity, including ethical perfection," as only the next to final, not the final stage of the argument. I can do this because I generalize the principle of which Anselm's is a special case, so that the mere idea of "something" entails necessary existence. The "being of total nonbeing" is contradiction; or no one knows what it could mean.

I also argue that to make a world possible means to create a definite type of cosmic order, the definiteness of which must be contingent; the theory is that all contingency implies decision somewhere. There can and indeed must be undecided combinations of decisions; but that decisions occur is an eternal necessity. It is no accident that accidents happen. "Just what accidents" is what is accidental. But cosmic *orderliness* cannot happen by mere accident or merely local decisions. Further, I argue that to explain how the supreme agent can persuade the deciders making up reality to conform to the minimal order without which nothing coherently conceivable would be possible, we must suppose an *absolute power to influence all agents sufficiently to guarantee this minimum.* Still further, I argue that the power you and I have over our bodies derives from the truth that we care about the constituents of those bodies and through our sympathetic prehensions of their values we have value for them. To explain an absolute power to guarantee some world or other, there must be an absolute form of the superiority that explains influence in general. It is what can *give* value because it *has* value that influences. Mindless matter could have no actual value, hence it could not be known. In its negativity it is a figment of our imagination.

I also argue that the necessity and eternity of the divine existence are incompatible with the least imperfection in the defining characteristics of deity. The argument is that the function of negative valuation is to guide someone in avoiding, putting an end to, preventing, improving, what is bad or regrettable. With the eternal and necessary, this is ruled out in principle. I gave this argument long ago. For me it is conclusive. The strictly eternal principles of existence must be exactly and entirely good and right. They are not merely neutral between good and bad; for life is in principle enjoyment, not suffering, good, not evil. Life's necessary aspects have a goodness, or beauty, that can be enjoyed. Mathematical beauty is of this kind. Classical theists and Aristotelian theists realized and were fascinated by the absolute but abstract beauty of deity; they failed to realize that there must also be concrete divine beauty and (my reply to Chiaraviglio again) this is contingent in its particularized forms and has no absolute maximum. God is concrete beauty in the form that is surpassable only by itself.

Professor Hubbeling's discussion of the comparative merits and problems of Lewis's S4 and S5 is no doubt relevant but perhaps less decisive than he supposes. In *CS* I give a version of ontological argument that (except for the parenthesized and inessential part of A3) is in ordinary language terms. It illustrates my method of arguing in metaphysics from exhaustive options, assuming that certain concepts, such as consistency and existence are used by parties to a dispute. All my reasons for theistic belief are, in *CS*, Chapter 14, put in this fashion. It is not clear to me that anything so technical as formal systems of modal logic are necessarily involved. My view of theistic argumentation is that it is essentially an appeal to individual judgment, not to mechanical (computerizable) manipulation of symbols as in mathematical deduction. What is thus deduced is only the exhaustiveness of the options, on the assumptions specified. Which three of the four options for belief are to be rejected is finally a matter of intuitive judgment. As I take Gödel to have shown, there is no merely formal way of eluding such appeals to intuition, even in mathematics itself, much more in metaphysics.

Here is the nontechnical, exhaustive options form of the OA.

A1 Deity cannot be consistently conceived.
A2 Deity can be consistently conceived, equally whether as existent or as non-existent.
A3 Deity can be consistently conceived, but only as non-existent (as an unactualizable or regulative ideal or limiting concept).
T Deity can be consistently conceived, but only as existent, somehow actualized.

Since the final appeal is to intuition, I no longer speak of "theistic proofs," but only of theistic arguments. I believe they are rational, but not coercive, methods of influencing belief. No one can be coerced into trust in God. No trust is sincere if it is not trust also in one's own intuitions.

As with Norman Martin's discussion, I rejoice in the technicality of part of Hubbeling's, even though it sets for me a test in which I can receive no high grade. I hope others better equipped, and with enough time to go into them, will find the issues intriguing.

R19. Neville on Temporality and God

Professor Robert C. Neville is a challenging critic of my philosophy but is aware that his own has a good deal of common ground with it. We agree that worldly reality, nature, is essentially an affair of varying levels of freedom, each of which is influenced though not entirely determined by at least some (I say all) of its predecessors. We both reject the Hume-Russell pluralism of events mutually external and the opposite monism of events mutually internal to each other, in the latter case forming a single reality of which all else is at most mere adjective. We agree that the actual past is, in some sense and degree, internal to the present; but the future as a set of events is not internal to the present. But Neville thinks the togetherness of past, present, and future cannot be in the present, the past, or the future, but must be in, or by virtue of, something eternal. As he says, I regard the strictly eternal as an abstraction; he thinks otherwise, it seems. How far is this difference a substantial one, apart from the mere words used? In metaphysics there is always danger of ambiguity, hidden inconsistency, or vagueness so great that affirmation and denial are equally vain.

"Eternal" may mean merely "unborn and undying" (Buddha), that is, ungenerated and indestructible. It may also mean immutable, "not in time," without distinction between earlier and later. Only the second meaning is the eternal as the extremely abstract. The first meaning can be concrete. Both the abstract and timeless eternal and the concrete but not simply timeless eternal are required to explain the world. Both are aspects of God as necessarily existing and necessarily having *some* contingent world or other, but contingently having the actual world.

If two philosophers differ verbally, the question is always relevant, ''Is it a difference between two equally clear and definite but mutually incompatible statements, or is one statement less clear than the other?'' If the philosophers are contemporaries, each may find the other unclear. Outside of mathematics and the least problematic perceptual statements, what is clarity? I have something of this trouble with Neville. He may have it with me. That is always possible in metaphysics.

I admit that, were I not a theist, I do not know what I would take the structure of time to be. I might feel that G. H. Mead was right, and that the truth about the past is whatever evidence still discoverable by our type of intelligence implies that it is, so that with each new present some details of the past drop out not only of our knowledge but of reality. David Miller thinks (alas, thought) that there are no everlasting, simply fixed truths about the past. Apart from God, this seems arguable. But I cannot see that it makes sense. ''It did happen, but (at a later time) it is no longer true that it did'' — What does that mean? This is one of my reasons for believing in God as concrete yet neither timeless, nor capable of being generated out of a previous Godless reality or of ceasing to exist. Past events that have become ''ineffectual'' in the world are not so for God, whose cherishing of actualities is everlasting (not timeless) and complete. Appearance and reality coincide for the conscious divine prehensions. ''To be is to be perceived'' is false of human perceiving but not of divine perceiving. Neville, in contrast, speaks of a divine creative act which is not in time. The modes of time are somehow together in, or brought together by, this timeless act. This combination of words does not communicate to me.

Neville argues that the past must be real in and for itself, not just in the sense that it continues to be prehended by subsequent actualities. It might not be so prehended, but still it was real in itself. My counterargument is, for one thing, What would make it *now* true that it *was* real, if it is simply absent from all present reality? And why is it important that it was real if it is wholly ineffectual for present reality? I am puzzled by Neville's talking of ''love and compassion'' in God, unless it means what I would mean, that God is not merely active, creative, in relation to creatures, but is also passive, allowing the self-creativity of the creatures to make a difference to God. And then why is that not my view? I hold with Berdyaev and Karl Barth that there is, in Barth's words, a ''kind of holy change in God.'' God, as required to make worldly process possible, is not something simply other than process, but the (by others) unsurpassable or eminent process, with a super-temporality free from the defects that Berdyaev sees in worldly time, such as loss of the vividness of the past, inability to predict even the truly predictable aspects of the future, and anxiety about the future interfering with the satisfactions of the present. If Neville's divine creating does what is needed, then I wonder how much it differs other than verbally from what I want to say. I am afraid though, that it does not do what is needed and is one more version of theological determinism; God literally making evil as well as good. To this I am, of course, sharply opposed.

I agree with Neville that much recent thought is anthropocentric. Whitehead's and my metaphysics are as free from this as any, so far as I can see. Nature once managed without us, and will again be able to manage without us. There are the quintillions of planets we have reason to postulate, a certain percentage inhabitable, of these, many inhabited, and of the latter, many inhabited by higher forms of life. It is not the human mind that is the key, but mind as such. Yet we have to start with the samples of reality that we have, and of these we ourselves are the ones we know most fully. Analogical generalization is the basic procedure of our knowledge.

I am not impressed by Neville's willingness to postulate mere matter, as if we had any basis for the idea of *concreteness* apart from experiences as such. Spatio-temporally extended and concrete stuff or process is a blank check apart from sensory-affective qualities that for physicists are not in mere matter. I see no evidence that either physics or psychology has made any serious effort to distinguish between mere matter and minded matter, or to draw a lower boundary to comparative psychology. Some leading physicists and biologists are psychicalists. The support of Leibniz, Peirce, Whitehead, some recent scientists I know about, is enough in my view to counterbalance the supposed commonsense objections to psychicalism. Either matter is we know not what or it is mind in some form.

Verbally we can, as Neville suggests, postulate two things having the same past initial data and making the same creative synthesis of these data; but I doubt if we know what we are saying when we do this. Since the data do not fully determine the synthesis, there would be no reason for the same result. And I also do not know what it means for the two actual things to be two if their spatio-temporal, that is causal conditions and their prehensions were exactly the same. Arguments in metaphysics are tricky. I can ask questions of my view that I cannot answer to my own satisfaction. But I do not know how far this discredits my basic position and how far it just means that my capacity to think clearly on certain complex and subtle levels is limited.

Concerning "temporally thick things," why need they be more than Whiteheadian societies, particularly those with strands of personal order? There are (pace Paul Weiss and Peter Bertocci) changing individuals for Whitehead, but they are not singular in the strict sense in which a single actual entity is singular. Buddhism is much the same on this point.

My partial rejection of eternal objects does not mean that there are no eternal principles. Nor have I any quarrel with Neville's idea of obligations in the structure of the world to which we ought to make suitable responses. I do not simply disagree even with Neville's proposition that a plurality cannot be totalized, or as I like to put it, be enabled to add up to something, by one member of the totality. In my own way I may be saying this. It is a similar issue to the one I have with Tillich's saying that God is "not a being but being itself." I say that God is both an individual being and being itself. God is both unsurpassably individual and unsurpassably universal. To be is to be for God (and God is for God); thus God is being itself. God is not *a* being but *the* being, the only individual with universal functions. No other individual is relevant everywhere and always, causative of all, affected by all, loving all and (unconsciously or consciously) loved by all. There is a difference in principle between God and any other individual.

My concept of "contributionism" is a temporalistic idea and is one way of summarizing my view. The present contributes itself to the future of life. This is its "being." But the definitive recipient of the contribution is the divine recipient. My sharpest objection to classical theism is its making God the giver of everything and recipient of nothing. I feel a need for a divine recipient of our contributions as definitely as I feel a need for a divine contributor to or enabler of our existence. We need a God to serve, not just a God who serves us. But a timeless God does not fit these requirements. A "first" cause is not enough; materialism's matter might be such a cause (if 'matter' meant anything apart from mind). There is equal need for a last effect, or rather an everlasting effect, to complete the ungenerated cause. We need God in all the past and all the future. Only abstractions can be both and yet timeless. The relations of numbers are undated; but they are empty by themselves. Concreteness means contingency and temporality. Modal logic in one of its most self-evident axioms supports me here. Combining the necessary and the contingent in propositional logic gives us a contingent conjunctive proposition. $(Np \ \& \ -Nq) \rightarrow (-N \ (p \ \& \ q))$ Necessity is abstract, non-inclusive. And, as Aristotle saw, the purely eternal is necessary. He failed only to see that it must also be abstract, in-actual, empty. Only in recent times has this insight dawned clearly on philosophers.

Otherwise I leave the issues between me and this very capable critic to the judgment of others.

R20. *Sprigge on Past, Future, and Eternity*

It is an example of the role of chance, the philosophical importance of which I learned from James and Peirce, that Professor T. L. S. Sprigge would probably not have been a contributor to this volume had I not happened to attend a meeting in New York at which Sprigge gave a talk showing good understanding of a representative group of American philosophers. His essay for this volume confirms my impression of his competence to make the sort of judgment he now makes about me as a metaphysician. I am indeed complimented.

It is especially pleasing that he is a psychicalist. I already knew that about him, but took his title to indicate that he chose some other topic for his commentary because it would give him the opportunity to avoid merely agreeing with me. However, I did not anticipate the direction of his disagreement. I thought he would think I have made too much of the internal relation of later to earlier actualities. Instead, he thinks I make too little of the relation of earlier to later entities. He wants relations to be symmetrically internal and, like Bradley, posits a timeless spiritual Reality beyond all relations and of which all else is less real appearance. Any contribution our descendants may make to this Reality it has never lacked. The God (or "Absolute," to speak with Bradley) of Abraham was or is no less than our God; any "addition" we make to Reality is a timeless possession of it. Yet we have (or have we?) had freedom to make a different, perhaps better or worse, contribution.

This disagreement is one more example of how difficult, if not impossible, complete agreement is among metaphysicians. It is, I think, relevant to bear in mind that since by definition (Aristotle, Kant) metaphysics is the attempt to discover necessary, not contingent, yet existential, truths, and since we are talking about truths that can be rationally evaluated in discussion with others, it must be verbally or symbolically formulated truths that are in question. But, as much recent discussion has made clear, and as Plato knew, communication or expression through language is a human function, fallible like other such functions. There is always a possibility that disagreement (or agreement), with others or oneself, is less about things or concepts than about just what words are to be used for things or concepts. Deconstructionists would be nearly right about this if they stopped exaggerating the point so grossly and one-sidedly.

I like Sprigge's attempt to give an exhaustive classification of views about past, present, and future. This method I use systematically. But it has to be done mathematically, however elementary the mathematics, to be rigorous in its exhaustiveness. The word 'real' (or 'being') is too slippery for this. Must the future be either simply unreal or simply real? "Tomorrow's events" are not nothing—far from it. What they are also not, on my view, is an extensive class with definite particular members. The past is indeed such a class. The future is real, but only as an intensive class with potentially extensive members. These potentialities for particular members cannot remain wholly unactualized. The *how* of actualization is for tomorrow's actualities to determine; today (still more, timelessly) they are indeterminate. Peirce, beyond perhaps all others, was clear about the essential *generality* of the future. It consists of real but intrinsically vague *Thirds*, universals, in the form of tendencies, purposes, or, to use Popper's term, "propensities." These real Thirds, these "objectively vague" possibilities or probabilities that *will* be superseded by definite actualities, are the basis of natural laws, contrary to fact conditionals, and also what gives sense to decisions or choices.

I understand the question, "How do we know that our present is not already in the remote past?" I've wondered about that myself. It is a fine example of how ordinary language, not normally used for such very abstract purposes, tends to produce paradoxes unless we are very careful. I think the first step here is to take seriously the Whiteheadian doctrine (hinted at by Peirce and Gilbert Ryle) that introspection is really memory used in a certain way. The prehended or known actuality is past actuality. The present (even in perception) prehends its predecessors, not itself—which would generate a vicious regress of knowing, knowing its knowing, etc. It *is* itself, but prehends (and, if on a high level of experience, can be said to know) its past, not itself. That the near past is given as near, not far, can I think be explained. That it is past, not strictly present, in the temporal sense follows from the analysis of becoming. Until an actuality has become, it is not fully itself, not really there to be known.

My second and final answer to the query about the location of the present is Whitehead's doctrine of actual, that is past, worlds. Temporal relations are in actual worlds, of which a slightly new one is prehended with each new experience. In which actual world is the "already" in the above question supposed to obtain? I conclude that the question is ill-formed, has no definite meaning. We know about where we are temporally in any given experience—for instance, now in the nearly ended seventh year of Mr. Reagan's presidency. Every now, by prehending its near past, locates itself temporally. Reagan is still president. Also I know that for months I have been eighty-nine years old, and that my ninetieth birthday is ten days in the future.

I can understand to some extent how Sprigge might find Bradley and Royce convincing, and I agree with him that their positions are similar in that neither admits any strictly external relations or any irreducibly temporal truths. I also see how Santayana helps to push him in the same direction, since Santayana holds the timeless theory of all truths, a theory structurally equivalent to classical theism. Truth is taken as though it were content of timeless knowing—without the knowing.

In my *Mind* (1965) essay on "The Meaning of 'Is going to be'" I argued against the timeless view of historical truths and offered a refutation of the defense of that view that had been published in *Mind*. If anyone in Britain dealt with the challenge, I missed his or her discussion. I take seriously the fact that neither Bradley's, nor Royce's system—also not McTaggart's arguments against the temporal theory of truths about particular temporal things, to which Sprigge relevantly refers—have proved to any notable extent survivors in the competition of ideas in Britain or America. I incline to think this matter is *une chose jugée*, as the French say.

Sprigge refers to pragmatism; but I think he underestimates the role of an element of pragmatism in metaphysics. How does it rationally illuminate behavior, actual living, to declare that the entire content of our decisions is timelessly there for truth or for knowledge? And how does one deal with modalities if one renounces the Aristotelian proposition that contingency is the openness, partial indeterminacy, of the future, and that what is eternally definite is noncontingent? I have yet to see a convincing answer to Peirce's argument for this Aristotelian position. And what Sprigge says about determinism and indeterminism being alike compatible with eternalism is for me metaphysical in the bad sense. Truth in metaphysics does not admit of such neutrality between similarly universal or abstract concepts. This is precisely the meaning of "truth by coherence." Properly understood, "internal relations" are not merely compatible with "external relations"; the two require each other (Principle of Polarity).

The logic of ultimate contrasts is for me *the* logic of metaphysics. However, the truth that metaphysical concepts symmetrically require each other implies an asymmetrical consequence, which is that instantiations of only one of a polar pair include instantiations of the other. If there are both an abstract and a concrete entity, the former is real only in the latter, not vice versa. Numbers are real in numberable things or in numbering agents, the necessary is in the contingent, the simple in the complex, and so forth. Necessity is a property of free actualities—that they *must* take into account antecedent cases of freedom. And some free actualities there *must* be. Hegel's "freedom is the understanding of necessity" is viciously ambiguous or simply wrong. It changes the subject from that of modal structure (piecemeal contingency here and now, rather than either no contingency, or only a unitary cosmic contingency of the entire space-time whole) to a merely psychological distinction (valid in itself though it is) between unwilling, unwanted behavior and that which is voluntary, wish-embodying, for one who understands reality.

As J. L. Austin said to Isaiah Berlin, people do not believe in determinism as they believe they are going to die. The latter belief is taken definitely and rationally into account by many things we do, but there is no reasonable pragmatic consequence of the belief that whatever one decides is eternally (not simply thereafter everlastingly) determined. Shortly before a decision it may be largely determined, and it will be entirely so ever thereafter. According to these beliefs we can and do act. Statements that are not rationally related to conceivable and more than verbal behavior are mere verbiage, mere talk, they are not demonstrably believed (Alexander Bain, Peirce).

I am glad Sprigge brings common sense into the equation. Here I take Peirce as my master, and value his "critical common sensism." Valid common sense is essentially pragmatic. The reason psychicalism is not quite common sense is that, for most human purposes, in dealing with inorganic or vegetable entities we do not need to consider what feelings may be in the entites, and indeed without science we do not know what, apart from visible animals, the dynamic singulars, the genuinely active agents are. Nor can we pay much practical attention to the question of feelings in the lower animals. But nothing is gained for behavior by definitely *denying* feelings (of an individually trivial kind) on these or any levels of nature. It transcends common sense to assert such a zero of the psychical. But it is well within common sense to admit feelings in other people and other higher animals. In the religions—even Buddhism—we encounter the question of a radically superhuman kind of feeling, divine love, and this raises the question, does God have two relations to creatures, one in which the deity sympathizes with creaturely feelings, and the other in which there is in some creatures a zero of such feelings. What then takes their place as the concrete, qualitative, more than merely structural properties of things? Here I see no good answer in materialism or dualism. So there is a pragmatic reason for rejecting the idea of absolutely inorganic, lifeless, insentient yet singular creatures. This makes it possible to view God as indeed loving the creatures, all creatures. And the view of freedom or creativity as form of forms enables us to get rid of the monstrous question, why would a loving God torture (punish or discipline) us with the ills from which we suffer?

Whatever happens to us comes from freedom, but not even divine freedom is a monopoly—indeed, divine love is least of all a will to monopolize decision-making. Neither the analogy of divine parent nor the truly Platonic soul and body analogy implies such a thing. The eminent body is the body of the universal, unborn and undying, necessarily somehow existing, or incarnate Soul, enjoying relations of appreciative sympathy with the members of its body, ruling over them as self-deciding, free subjects, not as slaves or puppets.

In addition to my partial agreement with Sprigge about common sense, I also accept part of what he says about the necessity of the past for the present transcending causal laws and all mere abstractions. Even God knows this relation in particular instances by intuition or feeling, not by concepts, by thinking. The necessity is, as my English commentator says, aesthetic. In the divine case it is God's sympathetic feeling of creaturely feelings as creaturely, for God objective forms of feeling. But, alas, my aesthetics not only does not require, it forbids (here again one metaphysical principle is nonneutral with respect to another metaphysical principle) the notion that the future is equally necessary to the present. It was the Greeks, and the old form of aesthetics, that identified beauty with sheer order, the absolute opposite of chaos. I have learned from Whitehead, from several musicologists, a German aesthetician, an artistic lady student, and my own aesthetic experiences that beauty, like Aristotelian virtue, is between extremes, a mean, the aesthetic extremes being chaos and absolute order. Precisely for aesthetic reasons, beauty cannot be absolute order, which would be zero value aesthetically. Short of that zero, cases of this extreme may be called the neat or tidy. A golf course, compared to a forest or wild savannah, is an example.

In addition to the Peirce-James criterion of meaning—that a doctrine must be conceivably and rationally relevant to more than merely verbal behavior—I have a number of other guiding principles in looking for sense in metaphysically general statements. One is (P5) that errors come in pairs of opposite extremes, the truth being somehow between the extremes. One way of supporting this assumption is as follows. Respect for those holding an extreme view, say Hume with his radical pluralism, followed by Russell and many other great thinkers, should lead us to reject the extreme opposite view, radical monism. Similarly, respect for radical monists, some also great minds with many disciples, leads us to reject monism's opposite, radical pluralism. If we adopt either extreme, we imply that those holding the opposite must be hopelessly irrational. Instead we should say, "These people (on either side) may have been a bit crazy or odd, but not *that* crazy or odd." In spite of this light-touch way of putting the matter, I am entirely serious about it. (My 1987 book, *Wisdom as Moderation*, is on this subject.)

Unless we go at such issues in this way, we seem to show insufficient trust in human rationality, thereby condemning ourselves along with the rest. The view compatible with respect for both extreme opposites is that each sees how wrong the other is, but somehow fails to note that the dichotomy is an inexhaustive division of possibilities. Contraries are not contradictories, they may both be wrong but cannot both be right. This elementary logical truth is signally neglected when it comes to metaphysics.

Another clue I put trust in is that history shows the wisdom of Whitehead's maxim, "Seek simplicity—and distrust it." Both extremes in ultimate contrarieties are in a sense simpler than the moderate position they both overlook. Yet if we do not try to simplify the welter of ideas under higher unities, we get no manageable grip on reality. However, mere dichotomies are always crude; and there are formal logical evidences of this. A trichotomy, as Peirce very sagely held, is vastly closer at least to what we need.

Sprigge began his discussion with a fourfold division. Sometimes we need a more numerous, yet finite and manageable, set of options. If divine necessity is

N, divine contingency C, nondivine or worldly necessity n and contingency c, then of the sixteen possible combinations the one that symbolizes my view (and Whitehead's by implication) is NC.cn. It is in a way the most complex of the sixteen! In terms of eternity and temporality, my view is ET.te. (The reversal of order between the two modalities is not part of the mathematics which yields the number sixteen but only a reminder that God and what is not God cannot be necessary (and eternal; or contingent and temporal), in altogether the same sense.) It seems evident that nothing extramathematical can be proved from *mere* mathematics. But I hold also that simply without mathematics virtually nothing can be reasonably proved in metaphysics. It is the only way to exhaust logical possibilities.

I notice that the word contingent does not occur in Sprigge's essay. If all truths are timelessly known or prehended, does this mean they are all necessary truths? If not, then I cite Aristotle and countless others for the to me intuitive truth that only in temporal terms can modal contrasts make sense. Accidents do not happen in pure eternity. They happen in temporal actuality, in becoming. To swallow time up in something eternal is to try to tuck contingencies into the texture of the merely eternal. I cannot see much hope for metaphysics on that basis.

Another intuitive clue is that necessity, since Leibniz, has been rightly analyzed as what a set of possibilities have in common; unconditional necessity is what the universal set of possibilities have in common. From this I deduce that the wholly necessary is extremely abstract. To make deity wholly necessary is to make it an empty abstraction. The inclusive reality must be contingent if anything is contingent. 'Two and three are five and it is raining here-now' is contingent if the raining is so.

Another clue. Symmetry seems a positive word, but this is deceptive. It is really a negative idea, that there is *no direction* to the order of the terms. "A equal to B" is the same as "B equal to A," but "A greater than B" is very different from "B greater than A." In fact symmetry is always an abstraction. As Plato said, no two things are absolutely equal in nature. We may so regard them for limited purposes. "A and B know each other" does not mean that the knowledge A has of B is simply B's knowledge of A read backwards. Directional, not directionless, order is the key to reality. Even the divine life must have a form of the directionality of time.

One final clue is the Principle of Contrast with which many try to discredit metaphysics but which is really a basic metaphysical truth. To say, "everything is necessary," or "everything is contingent" is to say nothing significant about anything, unless the connotation of 'everything' is somehow limited. Everything *concrete* may significantly, and I believe truly, be called contingent; but this is because only the extremely abstract can be strictly necessary. To say, "God is exclusively necessary," or "exclusively contingent," is to nullify the religious meaning of 'God'.

I am unimpressed by talk about change of status entailing intrinsic change. My argument that it is we who enjoy or suffer our relation to Julius Caesar, not Caesar, seems to me cogent. Any other view I regard as superstition. If 'internal relations' says anything, 'external relations' also says something. Relations cannot, as Bradley cogently argues, fall simply between terms; but they can and indeed in a large class of cases must fall inside one term and outside the other. If B possesses relation to A, then B possesses A as its relatum. It does not follow that A possesses any relation to B. Mere similarity or difference relations, such as Caesar's difference from me obtain only now that we are both parts of the actual world; and they affect me while doing nothing to Caesar. Thus in temporal relations of earlier and later there may be only the two terms and the later term as relative to the earlier. This asymmetrical internal-external relatedness is never explicitly mentioned, so far as I know, by Bradley, much less analytically shown to be absurd or impossible. The same oversight occurred in China a dozen centuries or so earlier in some arguments about relations by the great Buddhist Fa Tsang, and in India earlier still in that other great Buddhist, Nagarjuna. Philosophers have been overfascinated by symmetry! In some of Sprigge's phrases about temporal structure, I suggest that "language is idling." It does not say anything to the point of any more than merely verbal purpose. (Wittgensteinian principles can be used against Wittgensteinian charges against "metaphysics.")

Sprigge is well aware that his ultimate divine unity idea is strongly against the main British tradition. But does he adequately see that he may be merely countering an exaggeration with the opposite one? Both extremes may be right and both wrong, each as against the other. In Germany the opposite bias, overstress on unity, has been frequently defended. Leibniz tried to combine both contraries, but in part by accepting what was worst in each. He has windowless monads, an *ultra-unity* view of genetic identity, or individual continuity through time, but also *ultra-disunity between* individuals, rescued from utter absurdity only by the artifice of pre-established harmony. Hegel tried to unite the contraries, but who has ever shown a lucid logic in *how* he united them?

Wittgenstein (influenced, one guesses, by Russell as well as Hume) began as an extreme pluralist, gave this up, but never really tells us or himself what view between the extremes he adopts. The penalty is not surprising: that he cannot make up his mind about any religious question. Indeed he cannot come to anything much about ethical or aesthetic values. O. K. Bouwsma's little book makes this clear enough. Bouwsma himself remained a Presbyterian, but without positive benefit from metaphysical analysis. I agree with him, however, on one thing, that the highest sound ideal is that we should love God with all our being and our neighbor as ourselves. Nothing like this seems to come to the surface in Wittgenstein. He fails to see clearly that there is a value-asymmetry as between love on the one hand and hatred or indifference on the other. Life is in principle affirmative, not negative. We live primarily by hope, joy, and love, not fear, pain, and hate. Watch animals (especially females) with their young.

One more point about the British tradition (Occam to Russell and Wittgenstein). Of all the traditions this one has been the most unresistant to the doctrine of causal determinism. Not even the Germans have been so given to the deadly doctrine of "compatibilism": that to be significantly free we do not need to decide anything not determined in advance by the world before we came to be. This is not radical pluralism, but nearly the opposite. It is akin to Leibniz's "principle of sufficient reason," which (I agree here with Russell) is really the denial of genuine contingency (and genuine freedom). The final imperative, as Berdyaev says, is *"be creative"* of *new definiteness* (my word but Berdyaev's meaning). Hume, radical pluralist, yet affirms strict determinism. This incoherent combination is almost unique to Britain. True, something like it can be found in Jonathan Edwards; but American thought soon reacted vigorously and, in Peirce, James, and Dewey, broke free from any such idea. Thanks to Descartes, French thought is like ours or better in this respect. Even in Germany, Crusius definitely rejected the principle of sufficient reason in its unqualified form—on the simple, and I think adequate, ground that it contradicts freedom in any significant sense. J. L. Austin and Isaiah Berlin are on the right side in this question, but how many others in Britain? Locke is unclear, and I have found no defense of causal freedom in Berkeley. Wittgenstein inclines toward sanity here, but makes no general use of the principle which, according to Epicurus, Bergson, Peirce, and Whitehead, is a metaphysically universal category applicable to all actualities.

To deal explicitly with all the interesting points Sprigge makes would require more than the available space. I cannot adequately thank him for the stimulation of his well-written essay. Hearing him in New York years ago was a lucky "break." It is good to have an English philosopher who in this era can see the merits of psychicalism and who takes seriously metaphysical issues. Also one who has time and makes the effort to study American work in this field. I appreciate his vigorously argued commentary.

R21. Kuntz on Order and Orderliness

Paul G. Kuntz is a learned scholar with remarkably comprehensive interests. He must, I think, be the only philosopher who could publish a book on Whitehead and then, two years later, a book on Bertrand Russell in which, as he explained to me, he tries "to portray Russell with the breadth and sympathy of

Whitehead.'' (Actually, Whitehead largely gave up discussing Russell after their collaboration in logic ended.) Kuntz is probably also the only contributor to this volume who tries to do full justice to a basic fact about my intellectual development: virtually *simultaneous* intensive exposure to Peirce's thought and Whitehead's. He is partly right in saying that I am in some respects closer to Peirce than to Whitehead. He is also justified in remarking that I do not have much to say about the technicalities of the logic of relations, considering how important I say that that logic is. I have been somewhat casual, lazy if you wish to be severe, about such technicalities. My lamented and dear friend Richard Martin used to scold me for this.

By ''partly right'' in the fourth preceding sentence I meant, among other things, the following. I do accept Peirce's notion of the evolution of definite qualities out of a primordial continuum of possible qualities in which there is nothing so *definite* as the qualities that emerge out of the continuum. This is my partial or qualified rejection of Whitehead's eternal objects.

My agreement with Peirce is also only partial. For one thing, my view of the evolution of causal order is essentially non-Peircean—in the following way. Peirce conceives causal order as starting from an absolute minimum, an almost or quite complete chaos, and becoming ever more nearly complete in the ''infinitely distant future'' in an absolute rigidity of total order excluding consciousness altogether. I reject this scheme and accept Whitehead's theory of cosmic epochs differing less in *degrees* of orderliness than in *kinds* of order, in the specific natural laws that characterize them. I find very convincing Whitehead's idea that natural or causal laws are contingent, although that there are some laws or other is a necessity and is guaranteed by the wisdom and power of God. If other laws are possible, this is not an utterly idle possibility—as it would be if the laws were, as Leibniz thought, the best possible, and therefore by ''moral necessity'' for God the only possible ones. The other possible laws are fruitful possibilities which in infinite time will be made use of. Various possible order patterns for cosmic epochs have each their own aesthetic values and should not be excluded for all eternity by divine choice. Peirce's asymmetry in the advance from zero order to maximal order is too extreme for me. I systematically reject extremes in ultimate conceptual issues.

It is indeed easy to argue, as Kuntz apparently does, that if, in all becoming, reality receives new definiteness and only the indefinite continuum is primordial, then the remote past must be more and more like sheer indefiniteness. However, the reasoning assumes a wholly finite past. We here confront Kant's antinomy (anticipated by Jonathan Edwards) of the past. An absolute beginning of becoming would be different in principle from all later phases. Did Adam have a navel? On the other hand, can we conceive an actual infinity? Peirce says the beginning is ''infinitely distant.'' One still confronts the paradox of absolute yet actual infinity. My view is that we must admit an actual infinity of (past) time, though not of space. The infinity of the future, as Kant says, is no problem; for it is only a potential infinity. (Why did Kant not see that this modal asymmetry is incompatible with his acceptance of classical determinism, a symmetrical doctrine of causal necessity?) I find in Whitehead no statement that becoming had a beginning, and his accounts of prehension and creativity seem to entail that there cannot have been one.

G. E. Moore wrote an essay in which he defended the idea that the only actual infinity we need to admit is that of the past. This seems the least forbidding of the paradoxes one confronts in this matter. (Edwards gave up the problem as showing our hopeless limitations as human beings.) There has always been an in-a-sense-infinite definiteness, but not an *in every sense infinite* definiteness, and each of us increases it. Russell told me that he found this not mathematically impossible. Granted an infinite number of past items, he said, if new items are really new they can aesthetically enrich the totality. Nothing has been lost, something added; in some sense there must be more.

Another way in which I side with Whitehead and against Peirce is related to the continuity idea. If Whitehead makes too little of the continuity of possible qualities and therefore too much of the definiteness of the least parts of this continuum (contrary to his treatment of point-instants in "extensive abstraction"), Peirce makes too much of the continuity of actualities and too little of their discreteness. I hold that the multitude of these is spatially finite. Whitehead says that actuality is "incurably discrete," but Peirce's Synechism prevents him from seeing this and is his worst mistake. Neither of these great geometrical thinkers got both sides of the continuity problem right. Continuity of the possible, yes; continuity (in the mathematical sense) of the actual, no. Whitehead's eternal objects (in the plural) are only ambiguously discrete, Peirce's synechistically described actual becoming (with an infinity of presents in a finite time) is scarcely discrete at all. Hence succession relations have no definite terms.

In general, somewhat unlike Kuntz and many others, I find that the great thinkers tend to be definitely right on some points and definitely wrong on some others. They want to be clear and definite and it is their merit not to try to avoid definite mistakes by not being definite at all. Whitehead and Peirce both tried to be clear and definite. They ran the risk inseparable from this. Leibniz is the supreme example here. He was lucidly and usefully wrong about a number of things and wonderfully lucid and right about some others.

I cannot comment, for reasons of space, on all the many points made by Kuntz. But I will say two things about connexity. One is that I should, as he suggests, have alluded to it. The other is the following. It is only by mistake that connexity is made to seem to entail determinism. The entailment runs only the other way. An indeterministic form of connexity is quite conceivable. If *b* implicates or has internal relationship to *a*, and *c* to *b* and so on, then every item has the only place it could have in the series. But still, granted *a*, there might have been no *b* at all, with or without relation to *a*. Granted *b* it has to follow *a*, but granted *a* it does not have to be followed by *b*. Being predecessor of *b* is not intrinsic to *a* even though being successor of *a* is intrinsic to *b*. There is no contradiction here. One can see in Schopenhauer's *On the Fourfold Root of the Principle of Sufficient Reason* the clear commission of this logical fallacy of inferring lack of connexity from indeterminism. If I am related to my ancestors, and my descendants will be related to me, there is no other order in which all three could have been. If I had not been at all, I would have had *no* place in the series not some other place. I would have been indistinguishable from nothing, and nothing is nowhere.

It is pleasant to be reminded of Ehrenfels (pupil of Brentano), whom I, and perhaps nearly everyone else, had forgotten about. He did, independently of Whitehead, make clear his conviction that disorder is real. The limitation that I long ago felt in him (which may be one reason he made so little impression on the world) is that he seemed not quite to see that neither order nor chaos is anything in complete abstraction from what Peirce called the spontaneity of feeling (and of thought and volition). What orders is also what disorders, psychical creativity, on many levels, human and nonhuman. Apart from more or less free experiencing, sympathetically prehending its own previous instances, there is nothing, bare nothing.

"Love makes the world go round," but love sometimes takes a twisted form called hate, and there are multitudes of lovers, human, nonhuman, subhuman, superhuman, none of whom can fully determine the decisions of another. Out of all this some order and some disorder arise. The by-another-unsurpassable or divine form of creativity excludes both absolute (lifeless and meaningless) order and absolute (equally lifeless and meaningless) disorder. It guarantees an ever-increasing treasure of past achievements of aesthetic value in the all-surpassing experience, but it does not guarantee the exact forms or the extent or rate of the increase from moment to moment. It does, I take it, guarantee that the process of achievement will never cease and that no *eternal* deficiency can be the reason for frustration or suffering. Whatever is unborn and undying is altogether good and lovable; only what comes to be and is perishable can deserve criticism or dislike. There is no sufficient reason for what concretely happens; but for this negative truth there is indeed a sufficient reason. Robert H. Kane is right about that.

Kuntz's special and knowledgeable concern with types of order makes his contribution highly distinctive. While thinking about this (and listening to the inspiring musicianship of Placido Domingo), it occurred to me that when the illustrious Fermi said, "To know is to measure," he should have said, "To know is to order," for while quantification is ordering, it is not the only kind of ordering, and topology, the nonquantitative geometry, is just as lucid a branch of mathematics as arithmetic. Kuntz certainly has a point.

R22. McMurrin on Neoclassical Metaphysics

It is an honor to be seriously discussed by a scholar and public figure of such distinction as Sterling M. McMurrin. So far as I know, he is the outstanding scholar on Mormon theology; but only a look at *Who's Who in America* can enable one to do justice to the reasons for the previous sentence. His *Religion, Reason, and Truth: Historical Essays in the Philosophy of Religion* seems to me an illuminating book. He is a cautious admirer of philosophical speculation. I am glad to learn that he agrees with me that strict determinism is false. However, like Robert Kane, he is not convinced by my argument for the metaphysically general and necessary Epicurean-Peircean generalization of libertarian freedom to cover all conceivable natures or cosmic epochs. He also thinks that my theism is not a deduction from my metaphysics but has prior sources. I do not disagree sharply with this. There is no simple one-way order in metaphysics. Whitehead puts it neatly: "Rationalism is the search for the coherence of the [most general] presuppositions of civilized living." Coherence is a circle, not a straight line. On the highest level of generality, nothing is essentially premise or essentially conclusion. The metaphysical ideas mutually illuminate one another. What in a sense does come first is civilized living.

I wonder if McMurrin has thought carefully enough about the duality "necessary" and "sufficient" causal conditions (n.c.c.'s), and about the further ambiguity of the (at least) two meanings of "sufficient." Nicolai Hartmann tried to prove determinism by identifying the totality of necessary conditions with the sufficient condition. I have always thought this procedure of his an elementary logical blunder, such as one will scarcely find in Peirce or Whitehead—or, I hope, even in me. 'Sufficient' has at least two meanings. It may mean, sufficient to make the event possible; but then it is just the totality of necessary conditions. The question still remains, "Will the event happen?" If there is freedom, the event *may* happen, but also it *may not*. In other words, causal conditions are *enabling*, not compelling. This is creativity: that to some extent events make themselves happen. An event's antecedents make the event possible but do not turn the possibility into the actuality that then becomes. The present is, to some slight degree at least, its own master.

A still further distinction is needful. What concretely happens is one thing, the *kind* of happening, as specified by certain more or less abstract, approximate, or statistical criteria, is something else. On low levels of freedom, causal conditions *almost* determine what happens, and for many usual purposes this is all we care about. The movements of planets are good examples of this. What each atom does in a planet is beside the point in astronomical mechanics. The plausibility of determinism for many centuries arose in part from this obvious fact. But in organisms the somewhat indeterministic microstructure is by no means beside the point.

Another consideration is this. Dichotomous thinking is easiest. There is order or there is disorder. It is more complicated to consider degrees of orderliness or disorderliness. Ricoeur in an early book declared dogmatically that either causal order is absolute or there is only causal chaos. By the same principle, if political order is imperfect at all, there is political chaos. The crudity of this mistake, obvious as it seems to some of us, has by clear implication been committed countless times by defenders of determinism, or (not very different really) of compatibilism. When I reminded Ricoeur of his remark in the book referred to, he said, "It's nonsense. That book is full of mistakes." A philosopher who makes and persists in many mistakes on that level I have trouble in seeing as a great philosopher. I qualify this by remarking that each age is likely to have some fairly elementary mistakes that nearly everyone makes because of a complex of pressures characterizing that age. In Kant's day only Crusius saw what many see now, that the principle of sufficient reason, unless carefully qualified, is too strong to make coherent sense. It oversimplifies. For example, it is false that to act rationally one must know the best possible action. On that principle one could never act at all. And there is no need to know it. What one should try to know is some mode of action *about as good* as any other one possible in the circumstances.

It is no objection to an act that one could have done something else equally good. What regret or blame can arise from this fact, if it is a fact? There is no reason to think that every practical problem has but one optimally good solution. Did Leibniz see this? (Who did at the time?) He pictures God making no world if no single kind of world were the best possible. But *any* world is better than simply no world. (To doubt this is, I think, to deny in principle that our world has *any* value.) So God would do the worst possible thing because there is no best possible thing! Nor have I exhausted the arbitrary assumptions of the best-possible-world doctrine. In our age the pressures are different and the danger Leibniz fell into is not our danger.

I consider that Peirce gave cogent arguments against a dualism of nature wholly unfree except in persons, just as I consider that James (followed by Dewey and Whitehead) gave cogent reasons against the idea that persons are unfree. Compatibilists generally ignore both James's "Dilemma of Determinism," and Peirce's "The Doctrine of Necessity Examined."

Indeterminism is naturalized, piecemeal contingency; granted all the previous n.c.c.'s, what happens next is not necessary but a new instance of contingency. Determinism pushes effective contingency back and back into the past long before we existed and deprives contingency of naturalistic instances. Then either there is no contingency at all or it is back of everything, supernatural in status. We are never shown *contingent becoming* in action. The cosmos as a whole, all the way back, is contingent—or else Spinoza was right, only one modal pole has any reality. All of this seems to me, as it did to Peirce, a blind alley. Why enter it?

I agree with McMurrin that mere logic cannot tell us that God is love. Logic is not what tells us that there is such a thing as love. Logic presupposes life. Logicality is not the aim of life, which is rather happiness in the sense of harmony and intensity of experience. Aesthetic principles furnish the framework in which logic has its place. If Hegel knew this, he took odd ways of saying it. In my version of theistic arguments in *CS* I do not claim that certain premises must be accepted as self-evident and that from these premises the theistic conclusion follows deductively. Instead, I argue that from certain concepts used to explicate the idea of God it does follow deductively that a rather small number of mutually exclusive theoretical options concerning the existence of God and the world exhaust the possibilities. Since the options are mutually exclusive, to believe the truth of any one of them, is, by implication, to believe the falsity of all the others; and since the set of options exhausts the possibilities, disbelief in all but one of them puts one in the position of either believing the remaining option or of failing to take a stand. There is the further question of whether one accepts what I call the interpersonal analogy by employing terms such as love or sympathy of God, supplementing them by use of the Platonic mind-body analogy, modernized through usage of the cell theory, one of the greatest achievements of science: or instead tries to avoid the danger of anthropomorphism by utterly vague, ambiguous, or vacuous efforts to give content to such abstractions as "infinite", "pure actuality", "absolute", and the like. To understand this array of options and make a definite choice, considering more than one side of all the issues, is what I regard as a rational way to answer the theistic question. This sense of "rational" does not seem to me a trivial one. It takes into account that we cannot know God as God knows God, although mathematicians can be said to know, virtually as God knows, that $2 + 3 = 5$. Ideas defining God in the religious sense cannot have for us this degree of clarity. The essential religious problem is the sense of the idea of God, not whether the idea has instantiation in reality. The logic of the idea forbids a contingent relation in this case of essence and existence. That much *is* clear about the idea. But no verbal definition of deity can guarantee that the idea is internally coherent, as "class of all classes" is not.

I am in agreement with positivism (Carnap, Comte also, I think) on the point that the meaning question in this instance precedes the existence question.

Worship of God is rational only if God-talk makes sense. Merely formal logic cannot know the answer here. Nor can empirical science merely as such. This includes psychiatry, Freud did not know the answer. He admitted that he got his atheism from philosophers (e.g., Schopenhauer).

On what grounds can one accept or reject the various options? One can, of course, have arguments for one's decision with each option. I give some arguments for mine. But one cannot have an infinity of arguments for premises of argument for premises of argument . . . Life is not long enough for even a very large finite number of such steps. So one must simply find oneself believing, or give up the problem and try to avoid believing or disbelieving. However, since to live as conscious on a human level means to have some idea of what one is trying to do, and since religious and irreligious ideas do have implications for how one lives, and to what end or ends, it seems unclear how mere agnosticism can be a viable answer.

McMurrin seems to me to underestimate the rationality of the pragmatic principle that a metaphysics must be livable, must have a reasonable relation to how one lives. One who says, "Life has no meaning, in the long run no value: the universe is essentially lifeless and indifferent to value," yet goes on living, can be challenged to prove that he means what he (or she) says. Bain's definition of belief, "That on which a person is prepared to act" (I agree here with Peirce), is relevant and searching. Does truth have any relation to value? Suppose you say it does not. Then you can be asked to show why you concern yourself with truth.

I suspect that McMurrin has overlooked here my distinction between contingent, empirical values or truths and metaphysical or necessary values or truths. One should not argue, as James sometimes seems almost to do, "This contingent existential proposition [James thought they were all contingent] is pleasing, encouraging, satisfying, hence it must be true." If the proposition is such that it could only be true contingently then, in believing it, we run the risk that, sooner or later its falsity will get us into trouble, and in any case we shall have trivialized the distinction between fact and fancy, slurred over the difference between serious, intellectually honest scientific or philosophical thinking and prescientific, prephilosophical, wishful or fanciful thinking, such as may have predominated among our prehistoric ancestors. But if the proposition is so abstract and general that its only possible truth is that it makes sense and its only possible falsity is that it does not make sense, then, I hold, the idea of wishful thinking has a quite different relevance. It is still true that we may be led by emotions to believe falsely. But this will mean believing somewhat incoherently, confusedly, or self-contradictorily. Our believing will not be single-minded and we will play fast and loose with the terms in which we express it. The same will be true in what we say about the values of the belief. They will not be what they are taken to be, will not be genuinely positive or genuinely negative values.

I hold that a necessary and eternal badness, and this is what a metaphysically universal badness would be, is an incoherent idea. By what pragmatic criterion could it be bad? For instance, it could not be something we should try, or someone should have tried, to prevent, for it is not preventable, or try to improve for it is unalterable and would obtain just as it is no matter what. A necessary good can, however, be satisfying to contemplate as the presupposition of all other good, whether eternal or temporal, as well as the measure and guarantee of preservation for all achieved temporal good.

Perhaps we should try our best to forget the eternal badness, or pretend that it does not obtain? At this point I go with Albert Schweitzer: the declaration of totally hopeless despair cannot express life and is an existential contradiction of thought with the thinker's very life. The essential truths must be essentially good, or there is no use pretending to talk sense about them. We cannot really mean what we say. Even suicide does not express mere negation. "The world would be better without me" does not imply that the world had better not be, it means almost the contrary. One's own death cannot do *oneself* any good; for the merely dead have neither good nor evil. They have nothing. And that means just not having. Why not talk sense by having some faith in life and the cosmos?

McMurrin says many good things in his essay. This is not the first time I have been indebted to him. He is a fellow citizen one can be proud of.

R23. Wiehl on Whitehead's and My Psychicalism

Dr. Reiner Wiehl is the only survivor that I happen to know about of the students I had in Germany, during some months in 1948–49 in which I lectured and taught, not in English, but in German. President Robert M. Hutchins arranged for a group of us on the faculty of the University of Chicago to go to Frankfurt to help the university there to recover from the losses caused by the war. Wiehl's topic, involving comparison of my philosophical scheme with Whitehead's, partly overlaps that of Lewis Ford. Both writers somewhat underestimate my debt to Peirce and a number of other writers and teachers. I can hardly blame them for this. My career, as student, writer, and teacher, has been a complicated one. This should be borne in mind by any reader of my response to Wiehl. If I see both my agreements and disagreements with Whitehead in some respects otherwise than my German commentator does, my saying so is not to be taken as a complaint, but merely as an attempt to set the record straight. Although not even I can know all that is in my publications during more than sixty years, yet

I may know the contents better than anyone whose primary language is not English.

Dr. Wiehl's essay, which I have, somewhat reluctantly, translated (because it seemed there would otherwise be a delay) from the German presents me with something like the problem I felt in replying to Arapura. The German tradition in metaphysics, like that of India, is an intensely distinctive one and is rather widely different from that of my country. There is a cultural contrast between them that may cause him, or me, to "miss the tune"—even though we both know the dictionary meanings of the words. I shall try to be fair to his complex comparisons of my views with those of Whitehead. Here his topic overlaps not only with that of Ford, but also with Devlin's and Frankenberry's. To some extent my differences from Wiehl may be anticipated from what I have said in response to those others as well as in the Preliminary Reply.

There is indeed some difference between my metaphysics and Whitehead's. According to Wiehl the difference is not in degree of rationality but in our theories of what rationality in speculative philosophy is. I see Whitehead as sometimes almost, but not quite, making my Popperian distinction between empirical cosmology and a priori metaphysics. The latter seeks necessary positive truths about existence; these, of course, are not *falsifiable* by any *conceivable observations*. This criterion of the demarcation of metaphysics from empirical knowledge seems not to have been definitely made before Karl Popper, although it was almost explicit in Peirce, whom Popper has called a great philosopher. All knowledge is *experiential* in the sense that mere "thinking," apart from some form of perception, is a mythical something that had best be left to computers. Kant's "from experience" is ambiguous. All meaning comes from some form of perception (including the "nonsensuous perception" that we call memory); and hence, so does all knowledge. Moreover, while no conceivable genuine observation (correctly reporting its prehension) could contradict a metaphysical truth, it can of course help us to see why the contradictory of a metaphysical truth fails to make sense. My, after all, traditional definition of metaphysics as "seeking universal and necessary (existential) truths" is sometimes implied by Whitehead, as when he says that even arithmetic might not be metaphysically valid since it might not usefully apply to some possible world or to some conceivable "cosmic epoch." However, this to me is leaning over backward since Whiteheadian actual entities are by definition genuine singulars and so in principle countable, at least by God as recognized by Whitehead. My view is that Whitehead's categories in *PR*, Chapter 2, are supposed to apply to all truly conceivable cosmic epochs and to be necessary. Human fallibility entails that the supposition could be false; but strict necessity is what Whitehead was aiming at in those categories.

It is important that while no conceivable observation, properly formulated, could, and this is a tautology, contradict a strictly necessary truth, any observation, *fully understood*, would more or less confirm (Popper "corroborate") such truth. And the meaning of the terms in which any truth whatever is expressed presupposes observation in some form. I miss in Wiehl some mention of cosmic epochs, differing in their laws of nature, and the idea of falsification by *conceivable* percepts or observations.

As to my greater stress on the place of God in metaphysics, this is, so far as I see, a somewhat indefinite matter of emphasis. Whitehead takes his idea of God to be the necessary ground (by the Primordial Nature) of all forms of definiteness or eternal objects, hence of all purely eternal possibilities, those relevant to every cosmic epoch. Also, God is for Whitehead the ground of orderliness in the world, as well as the only way that our passing moments of experiencing can escape utter insignificance in the long run. It is not obvious how my view makes God much more essential than all this.

It is true that I stress modal concepts much more than Whitehead, but Whitehead nowhere denies and in a few passages affirms, that reality has an "essence" that could not have been otherwise. Indeed, if God is the ground of possibility, the possibility of no God is the possibility of no possibility, that is, non-sense. Again the concept of coherence or mutual implicativeness of the categories, not merely their mutual compatibility, is strongly affirmed by Whitehead and by me.

I do emphasize inconsistency between metaphysically general statements as an important sign of metaphysical error; but I agree with Whitehead that creative experience, as emergent synthesis of previous experience, is the form of forms, wholly apart from which there is "nothing, bare nothing." Since the categories are but aspects of creativity they cannot be independent of one another. Consistent meaning on this level *is* coherence and is truth.

However, Wiehl's main topic is panpsychism. He is correct that this is not separable from certain subordinate issues, or ways of stating the "bifurcation of nature" that a psychical monism is trying to overcome without falling into a materialistic monism. Other dualities than mind and matter need to be considered, including subject-object, singular-composite, dynamic-inert. Wiehl takes as crucial for me the duality, substance versus processes (in groups). In fact, however, I was (in 1918) a committed psychicalist (a term I prefer to panpsychist) before I had clearly faced the substance question or knew Whitehead. I knew Emerson's literary version of Berkeleyan idealism, Royce's doctrine of community (or the overlapping of purposes and memories among human individuals), the phenomenological idealism of Wordsworth, and Emerson's Brahmanic monism. Of Whitehead's actual entities, however, I had scarcely the vaguest notion, nor had he yet published on them. What really convinced me was my own form of phenomenological testing of the idea of mere *unfeeling yet directly given* objects of perception. I thought I had found that there were none.

Later, of my Harvard teachers, W. E. Hocking was a Berkeleyan idealist, so far as I could see, with some interesting new twists. C. I. Lewis was a phenomenalist, precariously trying to combine a theory of sense data with a realistic view of nature, without falling into Berkeley's trap, while R. B. Perry was a sharp critic of idealism from the standpoint of an extreme, and to me absurd, radical pluralism. As a relative of mine said, Perry's criticisms of the forms of metaphysics of his time were like a man of weak digestion visiting many restaurants and complaining about the food! Only one Harvard teacher, L. T. Troland, was a psychicalist. On my oral examination, he expressed his agreement with the doctrine. So the first scientist, but far from the last who agreed with me on this point was a leading psychologist. Much later I came to know well two biologists of note who rejected dualism and materialism without being mere Berkeleyans, but taking a realistic view of nature.

Wiehl stresses my agreement with Whitehead on the relation of physics to psychicalism. I am glad he does so, because it helps me to make a point that I have barely hinted at in my previous writings. In answer to the question, "Why go to physics to refute materialism (and dualism)?" I offer the following considerations. Early human societies had no clear notion of mere dead, insentient matter. It required an incipient science of so-called inorganic nature to produce the concept. So one appropriate way to argue against it is with the help of physicists. Peirce was just as definitely a panpsychist as Whitehead, but he had no theory like Whitehead's of actual entities. He had, however, a phenomenology that saw no basic duality of "feeling" and mere sensation. Although Peirce hinted strongly that the idea of individual identity in traditional substance doctrines was a gross exaggeration, he had no definite notion of concrete temporal singulars yielding definite finite temporal pluralities. James was closer to this than he was. The Anglo-American idealists I read also lacked that idea completely.

Of the dualities connected with psychicalism, the key one for me is, *singular and composite*. Groups of sentient entities are not necessarily also sentient (fallacy of composition), nor are members of a group that as a whole does not feel necessarily insentient (fallacy of division). From whom did I first learn about this? It was not Whitehead but Leibniz, who saw it with the clarity of genius nearly three hundred years ago.

So far from basing my psychicalism primarily on physics, I think that phenomenological and psychological reflection, generalized down through zoology and botany, and finally still further to include something like physics, has been my procedure. Wiehl's hint that something like this should have been my procedure was more right than he knew.

There are some other points on which Wiehl is right, again perhaps more than he quite knows. I do argue for psychicalism from my theism and have from the beginning. For example in a 1912 poem:

There's a spirit in the mountains,
    In every living thing,
And it sparkles in the fountains
    That from the hillsides spring . . .
It's the spirit of God's love.

If there are literary sources for this, they are the Bible, Emerson, Wordsworth, and Shelley. In my poem, as a fifteen-year-old, I did not mean simply that nature is beautiful and useful to human beings. I was already focusing on bird song as a revelation of aesthetic feeling in animals far from the human kind.

I may reasonably be criticized for introducing such personal items, which are, it could be held, irrelevant to the philosophical problem. I venture to hold a somewhat different view of philosophical discussion. We know, after twenty-five centuries of this discussion, that philosophical beliefs are to some extent personally conditioned. If we are to understand each other, or ourselves (here I agree with William James), we need to know how the personal factors come into the equation. With a highly articulate, intellectually trained father, I was brought up to reason my beliefs. Over and over, when I have found an agreement with another philosopher, I have found that some, at least, of the reasons that brought this other philosopher to the same belief as I held were not very different from the reasons that had already brought me to the belief. This was true with Peirce and Whitehead, in my exposure to their philosophies in my late twenties.

Not only did I reason to psychicalism from my theism, but the converse reasoning also was important for me. If, without psychicalism, theism is incoherent, so, without theism, is psychicalism. How can many psyches, each of whom (Plato) is to some extent self-moved as well as moved by other self-movers, constitute an orderly cosmos? Here Leibniz was exactly not the right guide. His actual world was completely determined by God's selection of the best possible assemblage of monads, each of which is absolutely controlled by the law of succession of states that is inherent in its very identity as that individual. Leibniz's *Theodicy* makes entirely clear that, unlike Plato, the seventeenth-century thinker identified freedom with mere voluntariness, doing what one wants to do, this wanting being fully determined by its sufficient reason. I was once briefly a psychological determinist but have never expanded the belief into a metaphysical system. Spinozism for me has always been primarily a magnificent example of how not to do metaphysics. I studied the *Ethics* to see just where the great lens-maker went wrong and where, despite his necessitarianism, he was a wise and good soul.

Wiehl is right in distinguishing the duality, extended-inextended from that of sentient or psychical in contrast to material or physical. However, the "moderate dualism" Wiehl (verbally correctly) attributes to me, though other than the Cartesian one of thinking-but-inextended versus nonthinking-but-extended, is not, I think, quite as Wiehl describes it. For me all singular actualities are in some sense extended; they have spatial and not punctiform places, and temporal, not instantaneous, durations. It is, however, only *composites* of such singulars that are extended in the *obvious* manner in which visibly large physical entities are. Space as viewed by common sense contains no clearly singular, dynamic, self-moved, or individually sentient entities other than multicellular animals. I call this a "mitigated dualism." It explains the plausibility of technical dualism before the modern discovery of self-moving (and sentient) microscopic or submicroscopic constituents of visibly large bodies.

Here seems to be the place to consider Wiehl's surprising contrast between my preference for "living" and Whitehead's "organic" as the keys to our respective panpsychisms. In fact both Whitehead and I make similar use of both terms! My essays, "Organic and Inorganic Wholes" (1942) and "A World of Organisms" *(LP)*, perhaps unknown to Wiehl, try to show that the "metaphor" (as Whitehead once called one of his analogies) of "organisms" can be used to state my view as well as to state Whitehead's. And Whitehead uses "life" as key term in parts of his *Modes of Thought*. Whitehead says that his is a "cell theory" of reality, and I say that we are as cells in the divine cosmic organism. I also argue that even atoms and particles are organisms in a generalized sense.

A metaphor or analogy that I, but not Whitehead, employ, but which I read into Merleau-Ponty's use of "flesh," is the mind-body analogy. Here I think Whitehead, like Merleau-Ponty, failed to notice how his own theory of the mind-body relation in a vertebrate or human animal can be generalized to include even deity. Instead he gave a weak historical reason for dismissing Plato's World Soul suggestion.

Wiehl is right that materialism and dualism alike give a very abstract formulation of merely physical realities, omitting *qualities* in the pregnant sense in which "secondary" (or tertiary) properties are, and so-called "primary" properties are not, qualities but only structures, relational patterns (expressible purely mathematically). Whitehead stressed this point, but here he only confirmed and sharpened what I already believed, and many others had told me about, including Berkeley, Bradley, and Troland. It is also in Leibniz, who defined space as simply "coexistence" of his monads, in contrast to time, which is successive existence—implying an asymmetry (time's arrow) to which a determinist, including Leibniz, could not do justice, but a Bergsonian, Jamesian, or even a student of W. E. Hocking could.

Troland distinguished between "sciousness" and "*con*-sciousness"; the former applies to the brain cells, the latter is our experiencing as conditioned by the cellular processes. Both "sciousness" and consciousness are psychical, but the latter is of course on a much higher level. Whitehead adds three ideas: temporal quantization of the humanly psychical into unit-instances, with different time-lengths on the two levels; prehension as feeling of antecedent feeling, a common factor of memory and perception; and creativity, which I try to read into Plato (his "self-motion" of soul). Troland was a determinist; James made that view impossible for me. Peirce and Whitehead enabled me to generalize the Jamesian antecedent indeterminacy of human action into a universal category—or even a transcendental, applicable also to God.

My initial commitment to psychicalism was on the basis of the phenomeno-logical and psychological inseparability of sensory qualities from a subclass of feeling qualities. This was, Whitehead told me in so many words, also his reason for rejecting materialism (and dualism). Wiehl, however, derives the rejection from Whitehead's substitution of process for the traditional notion of substance. This certainly helped, but Whitehead's psychicalism has an even closer relation to his preoccupation with aesthetic categories, and is above all embodied in the formula, "feeling of feeling," as powerful as it is simple, for the basic relation of experiencing to what is experienced or strictly *given*. It also relates both Whitehead and me—independent, in this, of one another—to Bradley's *Appearance and Reality*, a book that did something, and in some respects much the same thing, to both of us.

Furthermore, one reason for psychicalism relates Whitehead and me in a similar way to Wordsworth. When that poet wrote of seeing "into the life of things," he was not talking specifically about organisms, or life merely as found in animals and plants, but rather about feelings like "pleasure," which he attributed to moving animals and growing plants, or "delight," which he attributed to light coming from the moon *as we experience it*, or to dancing daffodils. Whitehead did not borrow the word 'organism' from Wordsworth, but he certainly was influenced by Wordsworth's attribution of feeling to the active agents in nature. Whitehead and I also explain our vague normal (and some very intense special forms) of physical pleasure from our participation in the "bodily life," the cells, in which there are, we hold, feelings, presumably not conscious in the Whiteheadian sense in which we, and probably some other higher animals, are conscious. In spite of the obvious charge that Wordsworth committed the pathetic fallacy, we found in him a valid account of the emotive content of those sensations that are the only directly perceived qualities (in the more than merely structural sense) of physical reality.

Croce had a similar reason for rejecting dualism and materialism; but he avoided psychicalism by an agnosticism as to what form of nonhuman feeling or mind other than human is the objective reality disclosed in our perceptions. In short, Croce was a phenomenalistic, not a realistic, idealist. He lacked the belief that the bodily actualities, whose societies form the most directly given parts of nature as we experience it, are directly prehended, that is, their feelings are indistinctly felt, in our perceptions.

Since I am arguing with a German writer, perhaps it will help to name some German philosophers who seem to me to have come closest to neoclassical psychicalism.

Leibniz saw that the account of nature by physics is a mere abstract skeleton, devoid of qualities in the pregnant sense that escapes merely mathematical definition. Yet Leibniz was as far as possible from seeing what was most wrong with the concept of substance, which was that users of this concept tended to *absolutize* individual identity, and thus to negate freedom, and in addition to deny or greatly underemphasize interaction between individuals. Whitehead's societal groupings are relatively, not absolutely, identical through change. Apart from the temporal quantization, they are Aristotle's changing and only relatively identical individuals and they definitely interact.

Kant did see (footnote in his *Dreams of a Ghost-seer*) that we must *either* remain agnostic about what constitutes the physical things we experience as more than data in our experiences, *or* agree with Leibniz that they consist of psychical individuals of a nonhuman kind. But then, Kant maintained, we cannot understand how they can interact to form a cosmos. In other words, the preëstablished harmony will not do. I, and I think Whitehead, would agree with Kant as against Leibniz at this point. And Kant had clearly no use for either materialism or a hard dualism of mind and matter.

Hegel criticized Leibniz for his extreme pluralism of monads related to one another only by divine choice, as many clocks might by a clockmaker be made to keep time together. But he was, it seems, not interested in Leibniz's great discovery of the possibility of a psychicalism that does justice to the insight of the ancient atomists that the dynamic singulars in nature must, in the vast majority, be supposed imperceptibly minute, and that seemingly inert portions of nature are composites whose singular constituents are not inert and so, for all we could possibly know, are instances of the psychical in the Platonic sense (self-activated and at least sentient)—thus doing away with the need for a materialistic or dualistic theory. Instead of enriching our obviously inadequate direct perceptions of dynamic agents in nature by conceiving a host of additional dynamic singulars below the threshold of our sensory capacity to distinguish them, Hegel, so far as I see, merely multiplies and interrelates conceptual abstractions.

The reason this difference could be made to seem slight or almost nil is that, of course, the mere *idea* of dynamic singulars endowed with concrete forms and cases of feeling does not give us distinct intuitions of any of these cases in its concreteness. Only deity could have such intuitions. However, in several ways the idea of concrete actualities too numerous and minute in their spatial and temporal extensions for us to distinguish them intuitively does enrich our understanding. It enlarges the significance of the distinction between our and the divine way of experiencing reality, the former radically unable to measure nature's variety of kinds and individuals and hence to fully enjoy its beauty. Thus it confirms the importance of stretching our minds to assimilate the sublime concept of deity and shows how badly Hegel has failed to rise to the majesty of this concept, lowering it so that his "God" seems scarcely more than an idealization of the conceptual powers of our kind of animal.

Another advantage of neopsychicalism, to invent a word, is that, unlike Berkeleyan idealism, it can support science as not only enlarging our understanding of commonsense realities, such as terrestrial persons, animals, plants, mountains, rivers, planets, stars, sun, but also radically extending the system of terrestrial animals and plants to include those that are microscopically small. Furthermore, to this planetary system with its one web of high level sentient life we can now add a probably vast number of other systems with very likely at least thousands of planets inhabited by webs of life whose upper reaches in some cases may well include creatures spiritually superior to ourselves.

Schelling is closer than Hegel to neo-psychicalism. Closer still, in their ideas of God, are Fechner, the psychologist, especially in his great chapter in *Zendavesta* on God and the world, the theologian Pfleiderer, and the Munich cosmologist and philosopher of religion, Alois Wenzl, who had some knowledge of Whitehead's work and in whose presence I gave a lecture on Whitehead in 1948. (It was published in *Zeitschrift für Philosophische Forschung*, 3, 4 [1949].) In vague ways Goethe was a psychicalist; his sublime line about the cosmos as the "living garment of deity" and his saying that he could *feel* the reality of God are suggestive. But on the whole, Germany has lacked any equivalent of Wordsworth. Heidegger's Hölderlin may have something to offer.

Nietzsche was in some ways a process philosopher; but—and this is a tremendous but—he was a determinist, and his eternal recurrence turns into absurdity his defense of becoming as primary and being as a mere abstraction. His eternal circling of time recalls the ancients' circling of heavenly bodies and was his substitute for God as a refuge from the ultimate perishing of achieved values. If the idea of God is difficult to make coherent sense out of, Nietzsche's alternative is at least as difficult a conundrum. And how does it really help to illuminate life's problems?

I have long been inclined to take as one reason why a good many contemporaries have put aside Whitehead's system and/or mine is that the sources and reasons for these rather complex systems are not very simple, so that criticisms of them are also not easily researched and documented. My voluminous and widely scattered publications do not help in this respect. So I do not particularly fault Wiehl if he has oversimplified or exaggerated my differences from Whitehead, as well as the diversity of considerations supporting, for both of us, our points of agreement.

Peirce had a definite doctrine, with which I am in sympathy, that a philosophical conclusion should not rest upon a single line, but a variety of lines, of argument. I also recall here Peirce's other doctrine that extreme originality in philosophy is a sign of eccentricity rather than of penetration. Many truths have been said, and rather well said, by one or more philosophers long before they have been generally assimilated by anything like the whole body of writers or teachers. Even my contention that the history of philosophy should be investigated partly by means of a purely logical (that is, mathematical) process of exhausting theoretical options is not quite without precedent. Another American philosopher had some such idea and, when he became aware of my version of it, he asked someone, "Who is this fellow that has my idea of how to go at the history of philosophy?" I have forgotten his name (or was it not Churchman?), but I think he was at the University of Pennsylvania. Peirce's theory of categories was also a precedent. As I try to show, it was too arithmetical but not too mathematical, by Peirce's own definition of that subject.

If Wiehl has somewhat misunderstood me, it may be partly my fault; but whatever texts he has in mind (he gives no documentation) it is for me certain that what he calls my panpsychism, according to a definition that is not stated or intended in any writing of mine, and according to which Whitehead is indeed, as Wiehl says, no panpsychist, is not my or anyone's panpsychism. I know about it only from Wiehl. What is fundamental in my metaphysics is not life *instead of* organicity, but *feeling* (which every actual entity, for me as for Whitehead, has) instead of insentience, and *activity*, the dynamic, instead of the inert. Whitehead, too, rejects "dead matter" in just the sense I reject it, that is, inert stuff, or process, devoid of feeling and intrinsic value ("vacuous actuality"). I never say or imply that stones are "living beings," and the only sense in which I say that atoms or molecules are living (and I can show that Whitehead sometimes implies that they are) is the extremely generalized sense that does not imply reproductive capacity, DNA, and other characteristics that occur only in plants or animals. Both of us accept the common sense and biological concepts of life that distinguish the subject matters of botany and zoology from that of physics.

One of many signs that Wiehl, in spite of his heroic attempt to be fair and accurate, has not correctly characterized my differences from Whitehead is the way in which he fails to take into account the following facts. Although the word psychology does not appear in his essay, it does appear in the title of one of my books *(PPS)*. A society of which I have been president is The Southern Society of Philosophy and Psychology. Several of my essays are definitely about problems of psychology; for example an essay on the group mind. The only scientific society of which I am a member or ever have been is the American Ornithological Union, in which I was elected to the élite minority that has voting powers. In the sciences of life, in the narrow sense the word normally has and that neither I nor Whitehead have any quarrel with, I have some inside knowledge. Whitehead's analogical use of 'society' (a key term in *PR*) is not mentioned by Wiehl—although without the concept of "social order" and its resulting definitions of sequential groups or societies, some "personally ordered" and some "corpuscular," little sense can be made of Whitehead's "Philosophy of Organism."

Psychicalism does, as Wiehl suggests, mean a definite view about the order of the sciences: which is that the only possible complete empirical knowledge would be a comparative social psychology, of which physics would be the branch dealing with the most widely distributed dynamic singulars. These are also those on low levels of experiencing (individually mere "trivial puffs of existence," as Whitehead says), with feelings but not intellectual feelings, in the absence of which Whitehead does not apply the word "conscious." Because of these limitations physics would be the most severely behavioristic branch of psychology.

Wiehl seems not to use the terms prehension, or feeling of feeling. In German there may be difficulties, but without some synonyms for these English words it is not easy to express either my view or Whitehead's. "Organism" is scarcely a technical term, a category, in Whitehead, as actual entity, society, and prehension, are. Nor is it the category of the ultimate, as creativity is.

The unique role my psychicalism assigns to psychology is spelled out somewhat in "Psychology and the Unity of Knowledge." As for biology, it is the intermediate science bridging the gap between physics, including chemistry and astronomy, and the science of mind as such, or what Peirce called psychics. The one very long and close scientific friendship I have enjoyed has been with Sewall Wright, great geneticist, evolutionary theorist, and experimental student of animal behavior. He shares my psychicalism, though without its theistic aspect. (See his essay in *MN*.) This is one example of the many ways of arriving at the realization that the idea of matter has no positive content to distinguish it from the idea of mind, generalizing this idea to the uttermost. What led Plato long ago to accept the idea of insentient, inert matter, was the apparent givenness of such inert stuff to our perceptions, plus his insight into the positive trait of mind that it is self-moved, that is, self-creative. Democritus had shrewdly guessed that the single constituents of which visible bodies are composed are not inert or without self-movement; though he failed, it seems, to say, therefore, not without soul or mind.

Forget about life, forget about organism, Whitehead and I can still express the central insight that we share; creativity as category of the ultimate, or experiencing as "emergent synthesizing" of antecedent experiencing, each instance of which is a unitary complex of prehensions of previous instances, where prehension is feeling of feelings other than those referred to by the first of the two tokens of 'feeling.'

It is important to realize that the opposition mind-matter is *not* one of the primary oppositions in either Whitehead's view or mine! Subject-object is indeed a primary opposition; but the object, if single, concrete, and actual, is another antecedent subject or actual entity as prehensive or sentient. An object, in this metaphysical sense, is no special kind of thing, but a thing of whatever kind in a certain relation. As for living-nonliving, this is, in terms of the common or biological sense of the word 'life', a somewhat secondary opposition. Where have I said otherwise?

Perhaps Wiehl has not read the chapter on "ultimate contrasts" in *CS*. 'Matter' does not appear in it, nor does 'life'. The following terms do appear: concrete-abstract, subject-object (where the object is abstract only relative to the subject prehending it but may be an antecedent actual entity), complex-simple, relative-absolute, finite-infinite, actual-possible, discrete-continuous. Matter in the ordinary physical meaning differs from mind (in the general sense of at least sentient or affective experience) in two ways: it is *for our senses* inactive though we now know it is a composite of active singulars, and its feelings are not appreciably conscious or thoughtful. A visible portion of it is not as a whole creative or self-determinative, and its components are only minimally creative or self-determinative; hence classical deterministic causality may seem to apply to it for most purposes.

One difference between mind and matter is, as Wiehl suggests, relative as between more and less rather than absolute as between yes and no. However, equally essential is the difference between wholes that do and those that do not act as one. The latter, which I call dynamic singulars, we intuit directly in our own case except in dreamless sleep, and by easy analogy perceive in the other higher animals. The analogy applies to single-celled animals and plants and to animal and plant cells, but probably not to multicellular plants, and surely not to mountains. Psychicalism extends it below cells to molecules, atoms, and particles, but not to crystals. The latter are organized but as wholes inert, in a sense in which white blood cells, for example, are not inert but highly active.

(Red blood corpuscles are said to be dead cells, and so no longer active or sentient as wholes.)

I hope I have made it clear that the "non-empirical" character of metaphysics does not exclude perceptual support for a positive metaphysical proposition; it excludes only an observational *veto* of a positive metaphysical proposition by some conceivable experiences but support for the proposition by other conceivable experiences. A metaphysical mistake fits *no* genuinely conceivable experience, whereas a metaphysical discovery fits *any* genuinely conceivable experience, though one may or may not be able to see that or how it fits or fails to fit.

As Wiehl says, cosmology is not exclusively empirical but involves, in ideal and in fact, metaphysical aspects and can be viewed as a branch of applied metaphysics. But then, so is all empirical knowledge, and here, too, Whitehead and I (and Popper) agree more than disagree. Simply without metaphysical as well as empirical elements, science cannot be. And this is logical, because contingent truth is the inclusive form of truth. In principle, or apart from human limitations, science includes and is more than metaphysics.

Whitehead calls his doctrine a "cell theory of reality," but it is I, not he, who says that we are as cells in the divine cosmic organism, an analogy I first heard from a psychiatrist I had an interview with in Germany in 1924. He was a disciple of Freud. In my writings, but not in Whitehead's, God is said to have a body, the cosmos. And it is Whitehead who stresses the applicability of categories to God. So by that test I am more of an organicist than he is! I also definitely speak of God experiencing, as well as prehending or feeling.

My ultimate intuitive clue in philosophy is that "God is love" and that the idea of God is definable as that of the being worthy to be loved with all one's heart, mind, soul, and entire being. This definition I owe to Paul Tillich. I conclude that therefore love in its most generalized sense is the principle of principles. It is creativity, stressing one of its aspects. Whitehead says that "Love, imperfect in us is perfect in God." It is with his help that I have been able to generalize this to apply to nondivine actualities generally, Peirce hints strongly in the same direction and so does Bergson.

Two important differences between my psychicalism and Whitehead's are that I conceive God as analogous to a "personally ordered society" rather than to a single actuality, and distinguish between God's Consequent Nature (CN), capturable in a concept, and the contingent states or instantiations of that nature—states knowable only intuitively and (to put it mildly) knowable adequately only by God. The CN in itself is part of the formal not the material side, in Wiehl's language. It is not contingent.

Because Whitehead does not distinguish between consequent *nature* and consequent *states* of God, or between divine concrete*ness* and instances of this abstraction, he obscures the truth that he also tries to affirm, that God was never (for Whitehead or for me), in Wiehl's phrase, simply "independent of the world, " or simply "before the world." The divine existential independence is of our actual world, but not of there being some world or other. On the contrary, the relation of God to worldly existence as such is necessary ("beyond the accidents of God's will"); moreover, God is "not before but with" all creatures, or all worlds. Here again cosmic epochs must come in. God primordially and necessarily has a consequent nature and some consequent states or other, responding to some world or other. The creative process has had no beginning.

Whereas Wiehl sees my concept of God as more "unitary" than Whitehead's, I should think it is in a way less unitary; and so I think would Whitehead have thought. I have the problems of the not unqualified unity of a personally ordered society (or linear sequence) of divine actualities, the consequent states, as well as of the two natures. Nor do I claim to have full clarity as to how this complexity is to be unified. I also want to point out that many before Whitehead had definitely implied a duality in God between the defining or necessary characteristics of deity, the famous divine attributes, which make God in any case God, rather than one of the creatures, and whatever it is that gives God unsurpassably appropriate relations to each of the actual contingent creatures. The attribute of unsurpassable wisdom and goodness is God's, whatever creatures happen to be or do, but the ideally wise divine awareness of, and good responses to, you or me, who might not have existed or might have made other uses of our freedom, can be as it is only because we contingently are as we are and act as we act. Whitehead and most process thinkers admit that God cannot be coherently conceived without this duality of eternal-necessary *and* temporal-contingent. Socinus clearly affirmed both sides of the distinction.

Whitehead, by his concepts of creativity and prehension, was able to give dual transcendency a place in a great system. But in principle it has been there in a centuries old tradition (indeed it is easily read into the Bible for instance), and a dozen writers have with some clarity affirmed it. My own father rejected the purely non-dual, merely necessary, merely eternal, merely absolute notion of deity. I appreciate Wiehl's raising of this issue (of the divine unity), even though I conceive it otherwise than he does.

Whitehead says, as I do, that our understanding of nature must take both directions, that of explaining the higher by the lower and the lower by the higher. The lower levels are in the higher, as atoms are in our bodily cells and our cells, so far as felt or prehended, are in our experiences. On the other hand, since we cannot distinctly and directly feel how other animals feel, vastly less how an atom feels, or what it is like to be an atom, we are left with the mere abstract patterns (whether with substance ideas or with process ideas instead) that physics offers us in purely mathematical terms (so-called primary properties), unless we accept some distant analogy between what it is like to be ourselves and what it is like to be an atom. This analogy, says Whitehead somewhere, is "a metaphor mutely calling for a leap of the imagination." Either that leap, or a confession of blank ignorance. We "ape-like" creatures are not God. This negative truth is a powerful safeguard against the hubris that is a human temptation. As Whitehead has also said, "We are little men against a vast universe" (and stretch of cosmic epochs). Even trying to understand the Soviets strains our comprehension, as trying to understand us strains theirs. We do the best we can and must hope it will suffice.

Has Wiehl understood me, or I him? To some extent. We have done the best we can, under the circumstances. Philosophical communication is not the easiest kind. Linguistic and national cultural differences magnify difficulties that are there without them.

In one perspective I can see value in Whitehead's and Wiehl's emphasis on 'organism'. The phrase "inorganic nature" is sometimes used to point to the sub-animal and sub-vegetable portions of the cosmos, which indeed are incomparably the largest parts of it. And common sense tends to see in this fact support for a dualism of mind and mere matter, a dualism brought seemingly close by the fact that even plants are not easily thought as sentient. The chief reason, however, for both dividing lines, that between animals and plants, and that dividing both from the elements and mere gasses, liquids, and solids, is the same. In both cases the point is simply the logical truth that groups of *imperceptibly* minute active constituents will not be perceived as active or sentient, merely because the minute constituents are active. The fallacy of division, assigning the (apparent) inertia of a group to its members, is at work, and fools many scholars as well as many more simple-minded persons. Leibniz is there for the asking. He applied a lucid logic to the problem. Renouvier, Peirce, Whitehead, I, and many others learned the lesson from him. One waits for the rest to do so. It is activity and feeling, not life (or inertia and insentience, not deadness) that need stressing, along with the dependence of animal perceiving on the magnitude of the perceived.

If this reply seems unusually replete with criticisms, this need not be taken as a negative valuation of Wiehl's painstaking, searching essay. He has caused me to work hard to explain myself, and that is an example of what this series of volumes, the idea of which was a creation of Paul Arthur Schilpp, was intended to bring about. My critic has worked hard; so have I. Philosophy puts a strain on human nature. So do most worthwhile things, as Spinoza implies at the end of his *Ethics*.

D. Historical Antecedents

R24. *Dombrowski on My Platonism*

I first encountered the remarkable scholarship of Dr. Daniel Dombrowski when I read his book *Plato's Philosophy of History*, which I admired very much. It seemed to me a much needed corrective of certain views about Plato. Now he shows how much new light he can throw upon one aspect of the theme of this present volume. Even I am surprised to find how well my interpretation of Plato survives the scrutiny of one who certainly knows Plato's work better than I do. He also knows my work well.

Considering the difficulties of communication between philosophers, unusual circumstances were required to make the essay before us possible. Between Plato and Dombrowski, also between Dombrowski and me, came a learned scholar in the history of ideas who is also a fine teacher, Leonard J. Eslick. Professor Eslick was, long ago, my student for a year. He became later a close student of Bergson as well as an expert in Greek philosophy. He also followed my work closely. It is precisely Bergson who stresses what pseudo-platonism has tended to miss: becoming as the concrete or complete mode of reality, and the aspect of self-creativity that Lequier earlier and Whitehead later found in experiencing as such. Peirce also had this insight.

In partly explaining circumstantially Dombrowski's achievement, I am not belittling it. Pupils sometimes equal or surpass their teachers. But how high one can climb in these matters does depend partly upon the level of teaching from which one starts. This pupil had a high starting-point. (He had the historical scholar James Collins, I assume, as well as Eslick.) I am in danger of immodesty if I pay him all the compliments I incline to feel are deserved, since his account is so favorable to me. I will say only that I claim no more validity for my references to Plato than he grants to them. I have no vanity in this regard that he does not satisfy.

To respond adequately to a great philosopher of the far past, especially if one is trying to learn not simply from one but from many of the great philosophers, requires much time. As Plato held, philosophical profundity usually requires longevity. In some respects, it is only somewhat recently that I have begun to sense the full scope of greatness in Aristotle or Plato, or even in Epicurus. That Whitehead had a decade more of active adult living than Peirce was an immense advantage. In this regard I have a similar advantage compared to both of them. Longevity is partly luck, like many other good things, and partly good management. Whitehead, for example, did not smoke or otherwise abuse his health.

Both Whitehead and Peirce had an attitude toward the history of philosophy that seems a good one. Peirce put it well: he said he tried to see each system as its maker saw it. Many historians could say this with some justification. But there is a further distinction. Peirce and Whitehead were not merely students of philosophy; they were mathematicians, logicians, physicists; and Peirce was a widely experienced experimental scientist. When they took a philosophy seriously, they also took some rather different kinds of knowledge or opinion seriously and from the inside. In a much more limited way, I went to the history of ideas with a perspective arrived at partly from biology and psychology, partly from intensive exposure to liberal theology and religion. And any dogmatic slumber in religious belief I might have been in danger of had been broken by R. W. Emerson and Matthew Arnold. So some issues in the philosophy of religion and of biological nature were already apparent and vivid to me. Also, where my science was lacking, Peirce and Whitehead had a lot of what I lacked. To put it all together took many decades.

I want to signify a strong agreement with Dombrowski's reference to the "anarchy" with which deconstructionists threaten us. Of course, there is some truth in what they say; but it is so overstated and misapplied that it is already time to declare a halt. Someone has said that "a fashion is a disease cured only by another disease." In recent decades the French thinkers have been giving us several instances of this. Derrida and his admirers are perhaps the latest examples. But I do think their fashion is a disease, like all overdrawn skepticisms.

If this volume proves anything, it proves two things: a philosopher can be understood in favorable circumstances, but also, how easily he can be misunderstood! A mathematician or physicist can change his field with a short article. The dictum, "What I say three times is true", of Lewis Carroll, quoted by Whitehead, applies to philosophy. It is my excuse for writing so much.

R25. Smith on the History of Philosophy

I am glad that Professor John E. Smith has chosen two of the best chapters in *IO*, those on Aristotle and Kant, for comment. Nor can I object to his choosing the chapter on Hegel, surely not one of the best, as a third topic. His discussion of the Aristotle essay shows the understanding I have learned to expect from him. (It agrees well with Devlin's treatment of the same topic.) Smith's discussion of the Kant chapter is also, for the most part, fair enough. In it, however, the formidable topic of a-historicity raises its head. His charge here, and his use of the cliché "wisdom of hindsight," might be appropriate in criticizing some books. However, wisdom of hindsight is precisely what that book of mine is deliberately about. I was seeking to find out what truths *we* can learn by looking back temporally, not merely truths about the past, though that is part of it, but above all, what we can learn about the present and future, including help in the search for eternal and necessary truths of existence; that is, metaphysical truths. In the process we learn also some things that are not metaphysical, e.g., the limitations and fallibilities of our human form of rationality.

There is between me and Smith a strange partial failure of communication—which, as always, may be partly my fault. Smith misses, as if (to adapt G. K. Chesterton) "by magic," the fact that he is offering coals to Newcastle when he tells me that what I call logical possibilities for theory were not "actually," that is psychologically or sociologically, possible, but rather were excluded by the spirit of the time. Thus Kant could not conceive that God might not be in *all* respects unchanging and Aristotle could not conceive that our world might have had a beginning. One of my principal points is here offered to me as a criticism. With the wisdom of hindsight we can see how philosophers sometimes fail to obey logical rules that they all acknowledge as valid.

By logically or conceptually possible options for theory I do *not* mean sociologically, psychologically, or historically possible. That is quite another matter. However, the Socinians did, long before Kant and even before Leibniz, conceive God as not in all respects immutable. So the historical impossibility was not absolute. The Socinians made their move for what still looks like a right reason: the freedom of the creatures.

There is no logical rule against holding that a predicate may apply positively to a subject in one of its aspects and negatively in another aspect. If the predicate is 'changing' and the subject is an individual being, then it is not usual that it applies to a subject in *all* aspects, nor is it usual that it applies in *no* aspect. True, God is exceptional in principle; for God alone is worthy of worship. Some ways of changing are certainly defects that God must not be supposed to have but which creatures often do have. Decay, corruption, are of course excluded by the divine essence. So is the change from wicked to righteous or vice versa. But what about growth in aesthetic richness of content? Either the idea of a greatest possible richness of content is logically impossible (as greatest possible number is) or it is possible. Need the high religions assume this possibility? Can one quote Jesus, Jeremiah, or the Book of Job, to this effect? I cannot see that theologians had any right to take the position they took on this issue in the name of Christianity or of Judaism. And many biblical scholars agree with me in this.

In a certain rather literal sense the wisdom of hindsight is about all we have. We judge the future by our knowledge of the past. As Ortega y Gasset said, "We do not have a nature, we have a history." Even our genes are pieces of physiological history. We got them by partly chance combinations of creaturely decisions, their results saved from the opposite evils of deadly monotony and deadly chaos by divine decisions concerning our cosmic epoch's type of order. These decisions appear to us as the laws of nature, of which, as I recall from Matthew Arnold, an ancient tragedian (Sophocles) said, "The power of God is mighty in them and groweth not old,'' from which it need not follow that the laws can never change. Other laws may take their place. But they can suffice for us.

No great religion asks us to worship a verbal abstraction, such as *"in all respects* perfect, and therefore incapable of increase.'' Instead, the great religions, with the problematic exception of Buddhism, ask us to worship a being functioning toward us as the ideal cosmic parent, ruler, friend, leader. Plato, with his wonderful wisdom, asked us to conceive a cosmic Soul whose body is the cosmos. Our relation to God, for Plato, is like that of a cell in our bodies to us. We *care* about our cells, and Plato uses the word *sympathy* to express the unity of the body. Modern cell theory helps here, I submit, to make this more concrete. A psychiatrist, disciple of Freud, whom I once talked to in Germany told me that this was his religious belief. If this analogy is rejected, I ask on what ground, or by what criterion, that would not also rule out the other analogies mentioned? I am convinced there is no such ground. All analogies are only our human makeshifts for what in God would be direct intuition, sheer experience. God is the One to whom ''all hearts are open.'' It is not simply concepts that God knows in knowing us, with our feelings and thoughts. It is those feelings and thoughts themselves. There is divine experience of our experiences, divine prehension of our prehensions. Surely we prehend what goes on in some, at least, of the constituents of our bodies—though not distinctly, or as though we had divine intuitions.

To Smith's objection to my view that we feel the sufferings of certain cells in feeling pain I reply that I have yet to hear of another theory of sensation that makes as good sense as this one does. It is implied by Whitehead's view of the mind-body relation, so far as I understand that. In sensing colors, what we feel directly is not light rays, but qualities of feeling in cells of our optical systems.

In discussing the Hegel chapter Smith is taking me not at my best, for I am not firmly enough convinced that Hegel is worth careful study to make such a study. Royce did make one, and he came out, as so many Hegel students have, where I think Hegel came out, with a theory of universally internal relations— unless the truth is rather that Hegel is too ambiguous to be even definitely wrong. If I am not at my best in this chapter, neither is Smith in his discussion of it. It is a case of talking at cross purposes. For instance, I am as insistent upon going beyond dyads, dichotomies, as anyone. A Peircean is bound to do this. Universal-individual-particular: this is a model of the logic of ''ultimate contrasts,'' as in my chapter on that subject in *CS.* I regret not having, in the Hegel essay, referred to that chapter. It is the only place where I give my alternative to Hegel's dialectic. The three concepts in the triad have certain interrelationships, and there is a fourth term involved, the vast *group* of particular or fully concrete actualities which are instances of particularity.

The principle of contrast does have a dyadic point; talk of necessity can be clarified only by talking also of contingency, and vice versa; but the Aristotelian or ontological principle also holds: that mere universals or concepts have reality only in concrete particulars. Individuals, too, have reality only in such particulars. Individuals are partly abstract or universal; an individual has its unique essence. This, however, is in ordinary cases a partly conventional matter. Only God has a wholly definite though extremely abstract essence.

I acknowledge that I made a mistake to emphasize that Hegel thought each thing had to include its contrast with *all* others. Many Hegelians did take this position, including Royce, Green, Bosanquet, for three. And I note that Smith is not ready to show that Hegel did *not* take this position. The fact seems to be that on this elementary issue it is hard to find him committed pro or con. What I should have stressed, however, is that Hegel never says clearly that X may be similar to or other than Y and depend on this relation for its own being, although Y does not depend upon any relation to X. Thus I depend for my very existence as a certain individual upon ancestors who did not depend upon me and would have existed whether or not I later came to exist. Here, too, Smith does not tell us where Hegel stands.

Nothing that Smith says allays my suspicion that Hegel's dialectic is not a presently very useful contribution to metaphysics, or to the logic of universal categories. His dialectic seems not an affair of individuals and actualities but an affair of conceptual entities dancing a peculiar sort of dance. F. H. Bradley said something about Hegel's remoteness from the concrete. Bradley is at least clear enough to be significantly wrong; I have yet to see that Hegel is.

The distinction of Reason and Understanding I first met in Coleridge's *Aids to Reflection* when I was about nineteen years old. Before I take seriously the idea of a logic beyond ordinary exact logic, I want to know whether ordinary logic is being violated to make room for the extraordinary logic. If so, I must be excused from going further.

I do think metaphysics transcends ordinary logic, but not by violating it. Ideas like becoming or creativity cannot be made clear enough to give truths as undeniable as $2 + 3 = 5$. But one can make clear the logical possibilities for combining certain concepts *about* becoming. The two terms "necessary" and "sufficient" conditions of events in their predecessors may be used to define strict determinism; each term may be affirmed or denied in a definite finite number of ways. Terms like independent and dependent, and surpass or better than, may be used in characterizing what makes deity different in principle from all other beings. This yields precisely sixteen logically possible combinations. Selection of the one true theory cannot be done by ordinary logic. However, by means of two basic analogies required to give content to the idea of God one can find that some of the combinations either violate logical rules or render the analogies hopelessly ambiguous or meaningless. One can also show the price of any one selection in ruling out the fifteen others. In this way by a combination of impersonal logic and personal intuition one may arrive at a decision that is as rational as human powers permit. I have never intended to claim more than this. I cannot absolutely prove to all competent persons that my or any idea of God worth considering makes fully coherent sense. If no such idea does, then no such being exists. If, however, there is a coherent idea of divinity, then the being does exist, since noncontingency of existence is inherent in any idea justifying the attitude of worship.

As for my seeming to be too certain, or seeming to think it a duty that others think as I do, this suggests that I have been expressing myself poorly. I may be guilty on this score. But it is not my *doctrine* that forces me to present it thus badly. I claim no infallibility.

Basic triads in my metaphysical logic, besides *universal, individual, particular*, are *essence, existence, actuality*; also, *dependence* or *relativity, independence* or *absoluteness*, and *probability*. As David Tracy says, the distinction: existence, actuality, is my "breakthrough," without which the ontological argument is unintelligible. To exist is to be actualized or concretized *somehow*; actuality is the *how*, or *in what concrete particulars*, an essence, universal, or individual is actualized. In ordinary language terms I have thus clarified a topic explored for millennia without reaching clarity. I can read the distinction into Peirce and Whitehead; but they did not make it, although Whitehead was the one who gave the right term for concrete reality. It is his "actual" entities that are how or in what an essence is actualized or a concept is instantiated. So long as an individual exists, it is never fully actualized but still has potentialities for further actualization. As Weiss says, "To be is to be incomplete."

If Hegel has his *Begriff* to account for everything, I, with Whitehead and others, have the creative process of experiencing on many levels, the highest level being the dually-transcendent or divine form. All abstractions are from instances of the creative advance. Consider Hegel's unity, plurality, and totality, as applying to Socrates. The abstract plurality is Socrates as a philosopher, gadfly, etc., and the totality is the unity of Socrates. What constitutes this concrete unity? Hegel gives us the two words concrete and unity, but not what makes the unity irreducible to any togetherness of conceptual entities. The unity that is Socrates at a given moment is a felt grasping of past feelings, or experiencing of past experiencings, some of them past experiences of Socrates, others, past experiences of many other individuals. Actualities are not measured by mere thought; they must be intuited, enjoyed, suffered.

It is not true that my dyadic relation of categorially contrasting concepts is symmetrical. On the contrary, in cases of subject-object, subjects overlap objects; in cases of contingency-necessity, it is the contingent realities that are the inclusive entities. See pp. 99–130 of *IO*.

I once talked at length with two Canadian Hegelians, one the teacher of the other, and over and over I found them arguing from premises that seemed to me devoid of clear warrant, or clear anything. I have read many Hegelians and have found them systematically unclear. As to the book, *The Secret of Hegel*, my comment is a quotation, "He kept the secret." When I was in Germany in the twenties, there was a leading expositor of Hegel; I found him like the others referred to. True, the fault *could* be in me.

We human beings have such extremely limited direct intuitions of the concrete, intuitions limited in scope of effective definiteness (and, even concerning the spatio-temporally nearest actualities, lacking as to fine details or nuances) that we have to make do with concepts *about* the concrete and inferences from the bits of definiteness our perceptual or mnemonic intuitions provide. Hence we tend to think that the comprehensive truth is found in the abstract. "Intellectual intuition" in Kant's or the Scholastic sense, in which the subject simply creates its objects, is not the measure of reality. All-cherishing love is that measure. It does not simply create the concrete actualities that are its objects; for they are in part self-creative. Rather it creates and sustains their possibility. But they produce the definite actualizations of this possibility. Love as free cherishing of the freedom of others is what all thought that understands itself is about. I agree with C. I. Lewis that Hegel's "freedom" is not what anyone else (except the Stoics, including Spinoza) had meant and not a meaning useful in cosmology, metaphysics, physics, or biology. When I have asked interpreters of Hegel whether he had a clear doctrine of modalities, they never seem to have a definite answer. Do the Marxists have one?

In my disagreement with Smith about the present (or future) usefulness of Hegel in metaphysics or cosmology I am not belittling Smith. In his enthusiasm for Hegel he is in good company. By the criterion of influence, Hegel is undeniably one of the great. Moreover, perhaps no one in his time had a comparable awareness of cultural history in the West. (On Hindu philosophy he was badly misled by British sources. Building an empire is one undertaking; doing scholarly research on the people conquered is a different and somewhat incompatible one.) Hegel took the medieval mystics into account as well as the Scholastics, Spinoza as well as Christians and Greeks. He inspired Zeller, superb historian of Greek thought, and other useful German historians of philosophy. Without Hegel, there would be no Feuerbach or Marx; also no Anglo-American disciples of Hegel: Green, Bradley, Bosanquet, McTaggart, the Cairds, Royce. I read them all and got help from them in my groping for an escape from the sterile trilemma: dualism, materialism, and extreme subjective idealism, as in Berkeley. Do I know what my work would have amounted to without these influences? Surely not. As Whitehead said, "Philosophy never fully recovers from the shock of a great philosopher."

For better or for worse, I have elected to take most seriously those philosophers who show that they know from the inside, and contribute to, the logic of the understanding and its applications in mathematics, metaphysics, and natural science (as these existed in and before their time), but who also are vividly aware of religion and art. That is why I give Plato, Aristotle, Leibniz, Peirce, and Whitehead unique importance, and why Spinoza, Hegel, and even Kant do not quite measure up. Hume also does not; but his originality and forcefulness, also neatness and readability (rightly praised by Kant), in expounding the skeptical vein that is necessary to keep speculative metaphysicians from excessive confidence or power, give him a special place. Hegel writes with literary power but is no mathematician or (in the normal sense) logician or scientist; his power is not that of clarity, and in his haste to transcend understanding he fails to show that he grasps or can contribute to its enormous achievements and potentialities. He does state two great metaphysical truths, (1) the inclusiveness of subject over object, and in general of one side of the ultimate contrarieties over the other, and hence (2) that the truth is the unity of these contraries. What he fails to see clearly is the radical inadequacy of human experiencing to disclose or measure the fullness of actuality and the impossibility that the remedy for this can be thinking in the merely human fashion, which is our way of trying to make up for our indistinct direct intuitions by a complicated use and interweaving of concepts.[17]

The Scholastics were right: the divine knowing is intuitive, nondiscursive. Alas, their worship of immutability, their ontolatry, prevented them from seeing, what Hegel in his way did see, that becoming is *more* than mere being and that even deity must have ideas, thoughts, ideals, as well as intuitions of the concrete insofar as the future is irreducibly a matter of possibility and probability, not of

---

[17]Those who think better of Hegel than I do might enjoy the essays resulting from a conference organized by Neville and Quentin Lauer and edited by George Lucas. See *Hegel and Whitehead: Contemporary Perspectives on Systematic Philosophy* (Albany: State University of New York Press, 1986). A minor illness kept me from contributing to this conference. The participants, as I rather expected, managed quite well under this circumstance. Besides Lucas, they included Van der Veken, J. E. Smith, R. C. Neville, and fifteen others from various countries. Interest in Hegel is indeed alive and well. One of the essays (I shall not otherwise identify it) seems to me doubtfully fair to Hegel and definitely unfair to Whitehead. What Whitehead means by Objective Immortality and the inclusion of the little adventures of our careers in the "Adventure of the Universe as One" is interpreted as depriving our careers of their unique, individual preciousness. What is missing in this author's caricaturing account is that the value of our experiences for God is precisely their unique, individual beauty. What God enjoys, and the divine happiness is enriched by, is precisely our joys. As for our sorrows, "God is the Fellow Sufferer who understands." In my psychology, sufferers find some "satisfaction" (Whitehead's term for concrete actualization) in even their worst experiences. It is tautology that "unbearable suffering" is not borne. Life is in principle creation or addition, not destruction or subtraction, of value. Past actuality is indestructible.

determinate actuality; and that the "lure" of ideals is the force that motivates the transition from the less definite future to the definite past—which alone is fully actual and is forever being enriched by additional definiteness, new concrete particulars—new even for God.

I agree entirely with Smith's remark that Kant rejected the idea of ontological modality and therefore, of course, had to reject Anselm's argument. Dieter Henrich made that clear to me long ago in his book on the argument.

On the whole I think that Smith has treated me well. He has given me a fine opportunity to express my faith that, in spite of Kant's denial of this, echoed by Popper, there is progress in metaphysics. Consider: if I, or you, have known the writings of Plato as a student, and since then in a long life have known many illustrious interpreters and critics of Plato, starting with Aristotle, and if we have done something similar with Leibniz, Peirce, Whitehead, and others, and yet have derived no advantage over these men from all this, then we are not only less brilliant than these great thinkers, we are downright stupid.

According to Max Fisch, Peirce probably got his theory of tychism from Epicurus. In spite of Thomas Kuhn, I think we can identify intellectual problems as persistent through the ages more definitely than even Lovejoy or Wolfson did. If there are only a finite number of possibilities, using concepts nearly everyone has used, we can see what happens to these at the hands of various writers. The Stoics did over-universalize, and thus, by the principle of contrast, nullify the term necessary, as Epicurus, Lucretius, Plato, and Aristotle did not. Spinoza reverted to the Stoics. This was regression. Aristotle and Epicurus did have

---

I admit some ambiguity in Whitehead's exposition of "Transmutation" in God as consequent. I think the best interpretation is that God's prehensions, or feelings of others' feelings, are without "negative prehensions" or loss of adequacy to the given actualities. I cannot see that adding God to the cosmology takes away anything positive from the nontheistic picture. It gives permanence to otherwise transient values, mere "passing whiffs of insignificance." Indeed, even the truth about or reality of the past is most intelligible as its togetherness in the divine life, which intuits distinctly that which, when we look at the stars (or even remember our own such past experiences) we intuit indistinctly. Also, God as ground of order explains how the many free creatures can avoid hopeless confusion and constitute a viable ongoing cosmos. Atheism takes much from this account, but adds nothing that I can grasp. Long, long ago when I was at Harvard a graduate student said, after a nontheist had spoken about the values he treasured, what for me became a bottom line, "The love of God includes all that."

Neville's essay is better argued than the one discussed above. It seems, however, to take away the idea of the universe as one. There is, we are told, no total cosmos, only partial cosmic orders. This is a real issue. Physics and metaphysics will be dealing with it so long as we can easily foresee. Whitehead's or my case is real, but somewhat unfinished at this point. I do think it manifest that the universe as one in Whitehead's theism can only be a modernized version of Plato's world soul and the divine body as the cosmos of nondivine actualities. The modernization includes the metaphysical, scarcely scientific, idea of cosmic epochs, particularized by the Big Bang hypothesis. However, I share Fred Hoyle's unwillingness to completely exclude views more like the Steady State Hypothesis. See his book *The Intelligent Universe*. He argues for a theism remarkably like the neoclassical notion of dual transcendence.

ontological modality; Kant did not, he was in thought pre-Aristotelian. There is regression in metaphysics, but Kant was wiser in some of his doctrines, for instance in his saying that categories must be given a temporal meaning to have concrete application. But in metaphysics he was no Plato, no Aristotle, no Leibniz. In some ways he is now a museum piece. He was even strongly opposed to an evolutionary view of species. He had the wrong absolutistic view of substance and the self-identity of persons through change, and the wrong deterministic view of causality. The reign of such Newtonian doctrines was nearing its end. He would be left behind, without Leibniz's genius in mathematics and logic, and his vision of a spiritualistic non-dualism.

R26. Lucas on Sources of Process Philosophy

To go deeply into Dr. George Lucas's historical account (which is further elaborated in his *Genesis of Modern Process Thought*) is more than I can undertake here. I find his list of antecedents and influences helpful. I do not take umbrage at his characterization of my approach to intellectual history as "aggressive and tendentious" or even his reference to my "infamous 'report cards' on the failures of the great philosophers." I assume he would admit that probably all of us are somewhat tendentious in doing history—and perhaps that he himself is not always unaggressive, for instance in "unnecessary, untenable, and ultimately fantastic realist commitment to Platonism generally," or in (my) "embarrassing lacuna and stubborn antipathy toward Hegel."

More seriously, I feel a subtle but significant distortion in the suggestion that I find "the failures of philosophers not merely in what they *did* say but in what they could have or should have been able to say, but *didn't*." Almost the contrary, I try in some important cases to show why it was *not* possible for them, in their culture, to see some things that it is now very possible to see. I try, for example, to sort out the issues that the ancient Greek philosophers were in a position to understand and those toward which they were not in this position. Similarly, with Leibniz and Kant. My discussion is in a sense more historical than Lucas allows it to be. However, I was not primarily discussing failure or success of philosophers in and for their time, but (so to speak) their failure or success in helping us in our time. I assume that the great philosophers hoped to find truths that would survive criticism. I think they did find some—that was in part their greatness. Another part was the way in which, by brilliant clarity or vividness in advocating error, they stimulated reactions leading to the eventual discovery of views at least closer to the truth. Greek materialism and determinism, Spinoza's and Leibniz's extreme rationalisms, were among my examples. Hume's extreme pluralism was another.

I have a similarly unbitter quarrel with Lucas about his to me somewhat fantastic list of "process idealists": W. E. Hocking, E. S. Brightman, A. S.

Pringle-Pattison, *Bernard Bosanquet, H. H. Joachim,* W. P. Montague, R. G. Collingwood. The by me italicized names seem not, almost extremely not, process philosophers. The others, taking things very roughly and broadly, might be accepted, especially Brightman, Montague, and Collingwood. I have read all seven men, and heard five of them.

Concerning the influence of my Harvard teachers, they all taught me things (perhaps most of all the logicians Lewis and Sheffer); but so did Emerson's *Essays,* Royce's *Problem of Christianity* (read at Haverford College), and James's *Varieties of Religious Experience* (read in the army medical corps), the reading of Wordsworth's poetry (at boarding school), and the hearing (in childhood and early youth) of my father's sermons, which were expressive of a virtually neoclassical perspective on the nature of deity.

To describe Whitehead's quantization of experience as Leibnizian is not absolutely wrong, but is scarcely a half-truth. Leibnizian monads were quanta from a spatial, but not from a temporal, point of view. On the contrary, Leibniz in his theory of time, was (so far as I know) a Synechist, with (though long before) Peirce.

That Peirce was less insistent and more ambiguous about the status of deity than I have been, I grant. He did, however, say that the cosmos is a divine poem (as by implication did Whitehead) and did call himself an idealist and make feeling a universal category.

I see no great difference between me and Whitehead concerning the way all things are together in the consequent aspect of God: they are in God in the sense of being data of divine prehensions—exactly my view. I also take to heart the statement that the order of nature is basically aesthetic and is "grounded in God." Whitehead showed how seriously he took his theism when he said that, apart from the creatures' "objective immortality" in God, "all experience is a passing whiff of insignificance." Whitehead once said, in my hearing, that, "as physics is the rational interpretation of the data of sense perception, so metaphysics is the rational interpretation of the data of religious experience."

Concerning Hegel, I am less negative about him than was Peirce (who showed, I think, that he knew what he was talking about—Hegel's method of reasoning, his "logic"), or than my teacher on Post-Kantian Idealism, C. I. Lewis—"In method Hegel was a very poor philosopher." Like Hegel, however, I argue from the entire history of philosophy in both Orient and Occident; like him I look for the truth in a "synthesis" or "unity of contraries." But I allow the logic of understanding—or what most people and logicians mean by 'logic'—a more important role than he does in speculative philosophy, and I see some basic fallacies in his *Logik der Vernunft.* After all, I had, as Hegel had not, the logicians Peirce, Lewis, Sheffer, Whitehead, and Russell, also Carnap, H. Scholz, Meyerson (I recall a careful essay of his on Hegel's dialectic), Tarski,

R. M. Martin, and Popper to learn from. I did not learn enough from them, but more than Kant or Hegel ever knew, about what Peirce called "exact logic." Lucas does well to mention S. Alexander. Whitehead's remark about him, the only one I recall, was simply, "It is obvious that I have read Alexander." I, too, have read him.

Between us, I venture to think, Lucas and I have given my kind of philosophy a reasonable historical setting in modern philosophy.

R27. Donald Lee on My Pragmatism

To have pragmatism represented in this volume seems appropriate. In my case the pragmatic influence came most directly from James, Peirce, and C. I. Lewis. I knew Dewey and Mead somewhat well and knew even better many of those influenced by Dewey or Mead. Apart from Peirce and James, the pragmatic writing that I have found most congenial was Dewey's essay "Time and Individuality." I read his aesthetics with appreciation, as well as *Experience and Nature*, and *The Quest for Certainty*—indeed, most of his chief works.

Reading Lee's essay a second time gives me a pleasing impression of a mind valiantly striving, with considerable success, to be clear, fair, and honest in comparing two ways of philosophizing. One of these he calls pragmatism and regards (as do many others) as the most characteristically American way, and the one in which he feels most at home. In contrast to it is my neoclassical way which he regards as a version of Whiteheadianism—granting, however, that it is also substantially indebted to Peirce, the founder of pragmatism. So far, so good. Reading the essay also causes me to have, as I repeatedly do in writing these replies, the thought, "the deconstructionists are partly right in holding that we cannot discern a clear and genuine distinction (yet also a correlation) between language and what language is about: the world that we experience." Deconstructionists themselves admit that the language they use in talking about language must itself be deconstructed, or is itself open to the same caveat. Hence what they claim is not the whole truth, even about language.

Some of Lee's distinctions between my views and pragmatic ones strike me as close to mere verbalisms, or matters of emphasis. This does not mean that I dismiss all his criticisms. Some of them I find deserved. I am partly to blame for some misunderstandings of the sense in which (influenced by Boutroux, Peirce, and Whitehead) I stretch "real" or causal possibility so that in a sense it covers the whole of the logically possible. Clarity on this point requires taking into account the notion of actual and conceivable cosmic epochs, as well as the divine capacity to experience various kinds of worlds of creatures, provide some supercosmic necessary conditions for them, and envisage conceptually the forms these worlds might take. In our actual cosmic epoch the humanly conceivable, still more the divinely conceivable, far transcends what is really, causally possible *in that epoch*. Also real possibility presupposes definite actualities, initial conditions, and these are not knowable, even by God, merely conceptually. They must be intuited, felt, not merely thought.

The ways in which the past is necessary condition for the present *in particular concrete cases* cannot be found by consulting ideas. Actualities are not knowable merely conceptually, even by deity. My past is implicated in my present (and not vice versa), although I cannot consciously detect the details of the past by intuiting my present (really just previous) experience. Only God has this degree of consciousness, but even divine "intellect" is not the ultimate wisdom; divine love of actualities is.

I see the similarities and differences between my thought and American pragmatism in part as Lee does. I will, however, to save space, emphasize only some differences between his description of them and the one I would give. The word *reality* I use as Peirce and, I think, Whitehead did. That is now, and in some cases eternally, real which *will influence* future prehensions by actualities, including God as actual. "To be is to be a potential [datum of prehension] for every [future] becoming." This defines being in the sense in which being is not in contrast to becoming and coincides with reality. "That is real," said Peirce, "which is what it is whatever anyone thinks it is." I express this by: "Reality is whatever there is truth about; if you know what truth is, you know what reality is, and vice versa; but neither truth nor reality can be defined apart from the idea of knowledge" — or better, of love as feeling of feeling.

I have not intended to say that only actualities can be real. Not at all, but what is inactual could not be real in some mere realm of essence, with no help from actualities. Numbers are real if there are numberable things, and things capable of numbering, where 'things' entails some actualities. (Whatever else God is, he-she has all the value that is in the thinking of mathematicians.) So mathematical entities exist. But they are not actualities, only realities. I take C. I. Lewis's remarks about reality to be compatible with my view. Fancied events have the limited reality of being actually fancied and of referring to the world of our cosmic epoch for the meanings of the terms used to describe what is fancied. Real unit events are actualities; real ideas are instantiated or thought by actualities.

Partly, no doubt, because of limitations of space, Lee somewhat oversimplifies his "pragmatism." He regards me as not a pragmatist in three respects. One is my universalizing of "feeling." Peirce, however, did this in about the same sense as I (and Whitehead) have done it. I do not say that every entity is sentient. Crystals are not, trees are not, only their atoms, molecules, or cells are. Only these are dynamically singular. Peirce and Whitehead imply much, perhaps all, of this. In this way we come closer to common sense than Lee quite realizes.

A mitigated dualism remains, as well as a vast deal of emergence of new kinds of feelings, new even for God.

Another nonpragmatic tenet is the doctrine of temporally discrete actualities. Here indeed I am emphatically not a Peircean. However, James's notion of drops, unit instances, of experiencing encouraged Whitehead to develop his proposition that actuality is incurably discrete. And both James and Whitehead related the problem to Zeno's paradoxes.

A third element of my thought that is not included in Lee's pragmatism is belief in God. However, Peirce and James were in some sense theists, and Dewey wrote a book on his philosophy of religion in which he even used the word God as capable of a legitimate positive meaning. I have elsewhere argued that the theisms of Peirce and James, and Dewey's philosophy of religion, could all be made pragmatically more significant and coherent if altered in the direction of my metaphysics of dual transcendence. By renouncing the search for necessary, non-empirical, yet existential truths James and Dewey made themselves unconvincing in religion. Peirce was hampered in this subject by a remarkable, slightly naive respect for medieval theology—surprising in his case. He failed to distinguish clearly between "necessary being" as denoting a being necessary in its entire reality, rather than only in its bare existence as *somehow* actualized concretely, but contingent in the concrete *how* (or *in what concrete states*) the abstract essence of the being is actualized. Also, as Peirce admitted, in his early period he was hampered by a nominalistic tendency.

I believe that James and Peirce both would have recognized the relevance of Whitehead's metaphysics more than Dewey was able to do, and I have shown that James seriously misinterpreted Fechner's theism, which gave much more than he realized of the pragmatic value James was looking for. Fechner's idea of deity was dipolar in somewhat the sense of my dual transcendence.

Lee does not fully see how dual transcendence is also a theory of dual immanence and can admit a universal sameness of actualities, even including divine actuality. My distinction between categories and transcendentals covers this. The categories specify similarities of all nondivine actualities; the transcendentals give similarities of all actualities including God. As to the extreme diminution that Lee thinks transcendence receives in neoclassicism, the only formulations I reject in the classical doctrine of transcendence are those that I hold lack coherent meaning. Either they are internally contradictory, or they use terms whose standard meaning has been lost and no new consistent meanings are provided, or, so far as I can see, are conceivable.

About "supernaturalism," there is a vagueness in my doctrine in that I am unable to decide how far to exclude or admit the possibility of miracles. I think Hume was largely right that miraculous happenings, such as are reported not only in Judaism and Christianity but in Buddhism, Hinduism, and about all the living religions, cannot be known to have occurred as related. The only definite "acts of God" we can be sure of are the laws of our cosmic epoch. There is a general deduction from the definition of God that every actuality is divinely prehended in an unsurpassably loving way and thus made "objectively immortal"; also that the reality of natural laws means that each actuality is divinely inspired to take its place in the cosmic order, where taking its place does *not* mean acting with divine wisdom and as determined by divine power, so that whatever happens is the best thing that could happen. This would exclude creaturely freedom and hence creaturely actuality. But it does mean that the cosmos cannot degenerate into mere chaos, any more than it can degenerate into a hopeless tedium of monotonous regularity.

Lee mentions but does not elucidate my distinction between existence and actuality. What exists is always more or less abstract. I have in mind here the symbolism of formal logic. If for some actual x, $\emptyset x$, then $\emptyset$ exists. (I agree here with Gustav Bergmann.) *Humanity* exists if there are human individuals; these are not single actualities but actualities socially linked and forming a group enduring temporally. Individuals exist if there are actualities embodying their "defining characteristics." This is purely Whiteheadian. Tomorrow I will exist if tomorrow there are actualities additional to those of my career up to now embodying (among many others) the characters of being the first male offspring of the two individuals who were my parents. Actuality is *how*, or *in what*, something less concrete is actualized. Existence is merely being *somehow*, or *in something*, actualized, concretely instantiated. In my theism, God is necessarily existent; but this is the *very* abstract aspect of God that the defining characteristics of deity could not be simply unactualized, although in just what concrete form actualized is contingent. I take Peirce to have been close to this view. Divine actuality is God as concretized, not merely somehow, but definitely; for instance as knowing you and me, who might not have and once did not exist to be known. My defense of the ontological argument is nonsense apart from these distinctions.

Let us turn to relations. For me, as for Whitehead and, I think, Peirce, *relations* are not additional entities over and above related things, they *are* the things as, in Peirce's excellent term, relative (Second or Third) to certain other things. Relativity is the key to relations. The logic of relations is "the logic of relatives," relative terms. A simply absolute term would be a pure first. I think Peirce made a mistake here. As found in phenomena, firstness is primarily not absolute or unlimited, but qualified. Each experience is relative to its predecessors, but not relative to its successors.

To relate a term to its predecessors, nothing is needed but the prehensions which make up the term as an actuality. It is related just in being what it is; time and space are the ordering of prehensive actualities. This ordering is partly self-enacted, the activity which *is* actuality. But the possibility of aesthetic harmony, without a minimum of which no actualization of feeling can take place, I refer to the inspiration of deity, much as Whitehead does.

In what Lee says about boundaries and continuity as "connecting" actualities I feel he is trying to explain prehension by space-time; whereas I think, and take Peirce and (more clearly) Whitehead to have thought, it is the other way. Prehending is ultimate, inherent in the meaning of psychical terms: experiencing, perceiving, feeling, remembering.

Lee follows Peirce (and Harold N. Lee) in taking continuity as the order not only of possibilities but also of actualities. This, of course, is Peirce's synechism. I follow not only Whitehead but von Wright, another logician, in rejecting the second of these two assertions. I have examined Peirce's arguments for synechism and find a clear logical fallacy in the most definite of them, something rare in Peirce. He says we should assume continuity until or unless we find observational reason for some definite discontinuity; because otherwise we would be settling a priori what should be left open for observation to settle. The fallacy is this: To assume any particular discontinuity a priori would indeed be wrong; but to assume discontinuity merely as such leaves open an infinity of possible, mutually incompatible forms of discontinuity. On the other hand, to assume continuity is to exclude all of the infinity (or superinfinity?) of possible forms of discontinuity. So I think it is synechism that closes what should initially be left open.

Peirce excluded what quantum theory asserts, as one of the vast multitude of possible forms of discontinuity. Yet Peirce wanted to anticipate and guide the development of physics! Were he alive today, I think he would reconsider. And he once said that there may be a minimal unit of experiencing (as James held), but that we do not know such a thing.

Whitehead and von Wright have similar arguments for the discreteness of actuality. Von Wright: if in any time, however short, experience changes, then for any two successive portions of experiencing, however short, "*E* is *P*" and "*E* is not-*P*" will both be true for some value of *P*. Only in an absolute instant (and not then either) will there be any truth conforming to the law of noncontradiction. Whitehead's argument is closer to the old Zeno arguments, to which he refers. Peirce himself says, "Continuity is a multitude beyond all multitude." I apply this aspect of Peirce against Whitehead's talk of eternal objects—as though they were a multitude of definite items. But Whitehead is a quantum physicist, and his eternal objects can be toned down to fit Peirce's insights into the "evolution of the Platonic forms themselves."

The consequences that Peirce derived from synechism, his fallibilism, for instance, are derivable quite well from the combination of discreteness and continuity, actuality and possibility, that appears in quantum theory. As for tychism, the reality of chance, that, too, follows from the combination. As Peirce said, probability (theory of chances) is a continuous quantity.

Lee does not mention the fact that in my psychicalism, or rejection not only of pure materialism but also of an emergent dualism of mind arising from mere mindless, unfeeling matter, I have Peirce clearly on my side and James only ambiguously against me. Neither James nor Peirce, especially not Peirce, admits the concept of mere insentient, unthinking matter as a well-formed formula. Everywhere, according to Peirce, there is feeling, also reaction, and representation. Whitehead's prehension, applicable to all actuality, divine or not divine, includes an essential aspect of value ("satisfaction"). Sharply he rejects "vacuous actuality," devoid of feeling or value. I once wrote Dewey about his opposition to psychicalism. He replied; but I found his brief answer opaque. Nor do I find clarity on the topic anywhere in his writings.

Marcus Ford makes a case for the view that James was a panpsychist, and I partly agree—in this way: either James has no coherent ontology, or it is psychicalism. His essay on pure experience is a masterpiece of ambiguity, by my standards. From Leibniz to this day there have been outstanding psychicalists among scientists (physicists, biologists, psychologists) and philosophers who have rejected the idea of vacuous actuality. They are a minority, but an elite minority.

Sewall Wright, with remarkable knowledge of the whole of science, was a convinced psychicalist. There are many others. Leibniz has been effectively refuted on other issues, but on the point that mere matter is an empty negation, devoid of positive concrete content, he has not been seriously refuted. It is not on this point that such competent judges as Peirce or Whitehead criticize him. Most philosophers do not seriously try. They are still pre-Leibnizian. As for common sense, it is, as Peirce held in his critical common-sensism, a judge only in matters quite other than this one. Apart from science, what does anyone know of the microstructure of nature? Almost nobody is saying that sticks and stones or multicellular plants as wholes feel or enjoy, but some have said or are saying that atoms and cells do so. What does ordinary experience tell us about these? The ancient Greeks knew not these entities; common sense is still on the level of Aristotle on some issues. Nor is there ordinary practical necessity to know better. Scientists, pure and applied, are there if needed.

By 1714 Leibniz virtually had a cell theory. Knowing of microörganisms from van Leeuwenhoek, he shrewdly guessed that visibly large organisms were made up of invisibly small ones. What a genius could see then, one might hope most scientists and philosophers would see now, the intellectually attractive possibility of getting rid of an absolute dualism of organic and inorganic, or mind and mere matter. There is still room for an infinite amount of emergence in the kinds and levels of organicity and mentality.

I have trouble with Lee's use of 'activity' and 'energy' as names for the original or primitive form of physical reality. Apart from experience, 'energy' is a word begging a sense. Experience reveals activity as experiencing, moved by values. This is the given; the rest is construction. Plato anticipated Whitehead here, apart from the hindrances of scientific ignorance. "Soul," he said, is what is "self-moved." We now know that nothing is merely inert. Had Plato known that, would he not have been a psychicalist? Although actualities are discrete, conceivable or *possible kinds* of actuality are continuous, degrees and forms of the psychical.

To me it seems rather clear that the very idea of atoms or particles is an idea of spatial discontinuity. Half a small portion of a continuum is a smaller portion, but half an atom is not a smaller atom. The same with half a cell, or a vertebrate animal. Then there is the all or none of nerve impulse.

That the cosmic process as a whole "is not prior to the events composing it nor they to it" is for me ambiguous or wrong. That spatially separate individuals are *symmetrically* related, or not related, to each other is indeed correct; but, as Lee seems to agree, the temporal aspect involves asymmetrical dependence. Each event is a new whole presupposing its predecessors. A prehends B which prehended C and so on. The infinite regress is exclusively retrospective. This is the one actual infinity. In all other spatiotemporal respects actuality is finite, even in the divine case.

I agree with Lee that similarity-difference relations are not "connective" (Hegel and Bradley went astray on this); but I find an ambiguity in his "connective continuity." Prehension is the concrete form of connectedness, as Whitehead says, but it has nothing to do with the idea of a continuum of actualities, as, for instance, infinitely divisible. Half a portion of a continuum is a smaller continuum, half an actuality is not an actuality. A later actuality can contain an earlier one as its prehended datum; and this grounds causal influence and, together with God as cosmic persuader, accounts for the causal order of the world. The persuading involves both creaturely and divine prehensions.

I wonder if Lee means what Whitehead and I do by internal relations between actualities. Whitehead sometimes speaks of these as mutual or symmetrical. I never do, but in the retrospective direction they connect if anything does or could. Infinite divisibility or complete gradualness (which seems implied by Lee's "merging") does not help with that, so far as I can see. It means that we can never come even close to truly single actualities as term of relations of succession. There is good evidence that we have no more than at most about twenty successive experiences in a second. In an indistinct way we almost introspect them, as in rapidly successive musical notes.

I confess that in two respects my view is unfinished and beyond my power to clarify satisfactorily. One is that the number of successive experient occasions or actualities in a given time-span varies widely on different levels of reality. On the higher animal and human level it is a small number per second, on the micro-level vastly more rapid unless at extremely low temperatures; and how to interweave these all into a spatiotemporal ever-enlarging whole as new actualities are created (partly self-created), and in accordance with the theories of physics, still in some respects in dispute, I do not know and Whitehead seems not to tell us. The other difficulty is how to conceive the temporal aspect (Whitehead says, and Berdyaev implies, there is such an aspect) of the divine life in relation to the worldly temporal structure.

Concerning the use of the word God: Whitehead said he regretted using that word so much in *PR*, and in *AI* he scarcely did use it. I differ somewhat here. I see this matter, not in the light of intellectual history of some previous centuries, or even two previous millennia, but of three millennia, in the thought of Ikhnaton of Egypt, Confucius, Mo Tzu, Plato, Aristotle, down to Tillich, Berdyaev, and since these. In that long perspective, it is Medieval and Reformation classical theism that misused the religious word. It invited us to worship the absolute, devoid of any intrinsic relativity. I do not find this in Old or New Testament, nor in Plato, (read as I and some others read him). I do find it in Aristotle and Plotinus. So much the worse for them, so far as I am concerned. My God is Plato's World Soul, not his Demiurge, which is an abstraction from the supreme soul and is almost all one finds in classical theism. The latter is not in any form of Buddhism, and not in the branches of Hinduism that I find most convincing. I think my view of God is really a religious view, the idea of a God who loves all creatures and should be loved by them all.

I close by expressing appreciation of the generosity of the final passages of Lee's stimulating essay, indeed of his entire essay.

R28. Noda on My Atomism

Like science, philosophy tries to transcend national and cultural limitations. It is less successful in this than science; but the effort is not in vain. Of all the philosophers I know, Professor Matao Noda is the best single example of this. In a few pages he says a great deal that I take to be true of my way of thinking and shows wonderful sensitivity to the history of ideas.

Like my long-time friend (since 1958, and when, even before meeting him, I received his first letter about my coming to Kyoto), I begin my essay with some reminiscences. In that first brief letter he made it entirely clear that he really did favor my expected visit and why. After one of my lectures, he remarked, "Yes, you are a philosopher *in our sense*."

Two of his recollections, based on casual statements of mine, need a little context. The Japanese Blue Flycatcher, *Ōruri*, is, by my six criteria, one of the estimated best *five per cent* (about two hundred) of the nearly four thousand songbirds (technically oscines) in the world. I could not narrow this élite minority down to so small a number as five. That would be like trying, without scientific instruments, to ascertain the five tallest mountains in the world. Singing skill is not subject to such exact comparisons. But, as common sense knows when an elevation is high, extremely high, or low (a mere hill) so, with sufficiently wide experience, helped by tape recorders and the like, one may be able to form reasonable lists of birds with very high levels of singing ability, as well as those with mediocre, and those with very slight, abilities.

The phrase Noda quotes, "always thinking about the same thing," had, I believe, the following background. I had read that a mathematician, not primarily a philosopher (I think it was Poincaré), when asked how he made one of his best discoveries, had said, "By always thinking about the problem." I suspect that my echo of this occurred during a second visit to Japan (1966) when I was asked to give a "Summer Seminar," between academic semesters. The group met five times a week and took all morning each time, with a comfortable rest in the middle. When this plan was told to me in advance, I said to myself, "That is the way to concentrate on a topic and go deeply into it." Poincaré's remark was, I believe, in my mind. Early in the seminar, we came upon the ontological argument. I had never so intensely concentrated on just that subject before, and the result was a flood of ideas such as I have had only one other time. (This was when I wrote my dissertation at Harvard. For five weeks I did just that.)

As Noda is aware, "atomism" can mean various things. Until Leibniz, in the West, atomism was always materialistic. What Leibniz did was, with only vague modern and still vaguer ancient precedents, to create a definitely spiritual or psychical atomism. His artificial theory of monads, with their lack of "windows" (no internal relations toward one another) and their preëstablished harmony, was a bizarre affair. It combined some of the mistakes of the Newtonian period in both philosophy and science. But it did express some still relevant ideas. It combined the Platonic insight that mind is the self-moved (or intrinsically active) mode of reality with the insight of the Greek atomist Epicurus that no portion of nature is simply without self-motion. Leibniz saw that the pervasiveness of self-motion, taken platonically, implies the pervasiveness of mind or soul. As if by magic, Epicurus had *not* seen this. Epicurus did, however, see that self-motion is incompatible with an absolute causal order in motion; for such an order implies that no causal distinction could be made between the cosmic whole (or some super-cosmic power) as determining, for example, the movements of the group of atoms constituting his own awareness and individual will and that atomic group as determining, moving, itself (themselves?). He believed in individual freedom; hence he was unwilling to admit a single absolute world-order as all-determining. At this point Leibniz was, in my view, below the level of Epicurus. God's choice of the best possible world must, he thought, determine everything.

Leibniz did see that the duality of mind and mere matter was made platonically groundless in view of the evidence of modern science that the reasonably assumed dynamic singulars of inorganic nature are imperceptibly minute. He knew also about the discovery in Holland of imperceptibly minute yet living, animate organisms. And he knew that Plato and his pupil Aristotle both gave a central place to the fact that we human animals come closest to understanding nature by generalized analogy with ourselves as active. His conclusion was that human perceptions fail to disclose directly what nature is. They are "confused" or "indistinct." Knowing or guessing that macroscopic organisms consist of microörganisms, he had the gist of the cell theory of animate nature and a clue to the ultimate denial of any absolutely "inorganic" part of nature. He was close to, yet far from, Whitehead's more complete Platonism, the "philosophy of organism." As if by magic, he could not quite take this step, since the spell of classical physics, with its strict determinism and lack of individual dynamic freedom, was too strong. Also, he could not, because of the power of classical theism, following Aristotle and Philo (not Plato of the *Timaeus* and *Laws* X), appreciate Plato's doctrine of the World Soul, with the cosmos its body. Deity as the "Ideal Animal," was beyond his power to conceive. God had to be wholly absolute and independent, the absolutely perfect, wholly uncreated reality, producing the best possible created reality. Sinner and saint were alike necessary elements in exactly the most-nearly-perfect-possible yet created cosmos.

History shows the lure of false simplicities: there is extended but insentient matter, and inextended but sentient mind; there is God simply cause, in no relation effect, simply Creator, in no sense created; and nature created, in no sense creative. Again, in reproduction the male element gives the form, the female only the matter. We now know that some of the forms (the genes in the *mitochondria*) *never* come from the male, and that, in general, both sexes contribute form. The male failure to provide any appreciable part of the matter or any of the mitochondriac genes comes closest to the traditional view, but almost reverses the sexes! And even this is too simple; for the sex determination comes (in our species) through the male. My final view about simplicity is, "simple, but not too simple." Reality has some intelligible universal traits; but it is a human weakness to fall too much in love with the first, all too simple, way we hit upon of characterizing these.

Let us return to Leibniz's spiritual atomism. One still relevant aspect of it is the insight that the Cartesian or Spinozistic 'extension' is not on the same level of concreteness as 'mind'. Spatial characters are purely relational; structural, not qualitative. The question, "What is it that is extended?" is not answered by the word matter or the word the Greeks used, translated as 'being'. Another still relevant aspect is that perception tells us little directly about nature's dynamic agents, other than animals large enough to be perceived as such. If we want to know the agents or active singulars, even most of those in animals (what digests our food or beats our heart, for example) our only intrinsically intelligible experiential illustrations for the idea of agency are ourselves and fellow animals. As Whitehead says, our theory must be a "cell theory," generalized by analogy.

Whitehead failed, indeed refused, to apply this to the cosmos, refused to think of himself and bodily constituents as cells in the divine organism. Here he departed from Plato just where in my view Plato was millennia ahead of his time, and even of Whitehead. True, the analogy was only that, but so, according to Whitehead, was his own statement that God sympathizes with our feelings. Without analogy, there can be no theology and also, I think, no science. Peirce said it: we must think "zoömorphically."

Hume's suggestion that the world may be a great vegetable can, I hold, be refuted. The visually discernible vegetable is a society of cells and, so far as has been shown, may be only that. It is nerve cells that make an animal able to act as one. The cosmos is an integrated whole, not only more so than a tree, it is incomparably more so even than a vertebrate animal. The vegetable analogy is poor. I admit, however, that to relate these contentions properly to relativity and particle physics exceeds my competence. In any case neither cosmic soul nor cosmic body should be supposed wholly open to our easy comprehension.

Leibniz rejected both Descartes's two kinds of substance and Spinoza's two-aspect view of his one substance. He did so for some of the right reasons that later led Peirce, Bergson, and Whitehead to do the same. Only relation to *experience* as such can give the pervasive union of structure and quality that—and here Bertrand Russell as well as Roy Wood Sellars and Wilfrid Sellars agree—is required for concrete actuality, at least *so far as we can know this union*. As Peirce put it, "the Kingdom of Mind and the Kingdom of Matter are one kingdom"; however, Peirce also said, it is mind that alone is "self-intelligible"; it is mind that understands both itself and matter. It does the latter by enlarging its idea of itself to cover all the forms that matter takes. Materialism and dualism embody arbitrarily truncated views of mind. Mind, Peirce concludes, is the "fountain of existence." In my philosophy, as in Whitehead's, monads are not only, as Noda says, pluralized temporally; they are also assigned asymmetrical relations of prehension in sequential groups (societies) of momentary actualities.

I am slightly uneasy when Noda says that a self is as sympathetic with the interests of others as with its own interest. As he and I know, there are some very selfish people. The point, of course, is the relativity of such distinctions.

Absolute lack of self-interest and absolute lack of interest in the interests of others are subhuman, indeed mere negative limits of thought. The right balance between the two forms of interest is the problem that religions and philosophies have long tried to solve.

It is partly my fault that the notion has arisen that the ontological argument is for me *the* reason for accepting theism. As readers of this volume (or of *CS*) know, I have half a dozen reasons, of which the ontological is only one. Its special importance is that it disposes of the notion that *any* cogent argument in metaphysical questions, of which the theistic question is one, can be merely empirical. But what I have come to hold is that the other classical arguments; cosmological, design, epistemic, aesthetic, ethical, are all best reformulated as a priori, that is, from concepts so general that we cannot repudiate them and still think coherently. They must be instantiated somehow, in some actualities; but how or in what is only knowable empirically. This scheme is spelled out only in *CS*, not in any other of my books. I worked on it for twenty years (1950–1970) before being satisfied with my formulations.

Noda does not quite say so; but I think he knows that my atomism is quite different from the "logical atomism" of those who follow Hume in supposing that genuinely distinguishable entities must be *mutually* separable or logically independent of one another. On the contrary, although A is aware of B does not entail that B is aware of A, it does entail that A and B are neither simply identical nor *mutually* independent.

Of all the philosophers that I know, none has a more subtle and ever-ready vein of humor than Noda. In a conference it is entertaining to watch his face for the smiles that show he knows when a speaker is not quite making sense. Once in a meeting in Honolulu where we were comparing Whitehead and Buddhism, a well-known expositor of Japanese neo-Buddhism began one of his illustrations of the wisdom of that tradition by a sentence beginning, "When one is learning to swim. . . ." Noda interrupted him by saying approximately the following, "Learning to swim is not to the point. We don't need Buddhism for that." Then, turning to the rest of the group, he said, "We say that in Japanese, too."

Noda himself once read an excellent paper in my department here in Austin on Whitehead's Philosophy and Nishida's. Although the department had had for years a Buddhist and a Vedantist, both East Indians, it was not so intercultural as to fully appreciate Noda's penetration and scholarship. Perhaps it was somewhat misled by Noda's characteristically Buddhist (and genuine) modesty. He knows enough to realize how much more there is to know.

Professor Noda's speciality is seventeenth-century French philosophy. His religious background is Buddhist. Although he once told my wife that he never heard me talk without learning something, he also has indicated to me that he is not a theist. Just where he draws the line I find an intriguing question. The scholarly expositor of Japanese Buddhism to the West, Suzuki, once wrote that he was not sure that Zen is nontheistic. If he is not sure about this, how can I be sure?

Professor Noda's younger daughter spent two years in our house while attending the university here. She soon became a most helpful and ever-tactful member of the family and continues to call us Aunt and Uncle. My wife was the non-family spokesman at her wedding to a Japanese engineer. All this is one of many examples I could give of how irrelevant and stupid racism or cultural arrogance comes to seem if one has wide experience of various nations, with various traditions. Among the political figures with whom I have felt deeply congenial when I heard or talked to them I count a Socialist from India, also Nehru speaking in the University of Chicago Chapel, and Sarvepalli Radhakrishnan before he became President. (I thought then and think now, he was a greater statesman than philosopher.) Never have I met anyone who seemed to me more immediately and permanently likeable than J. L. Mehta of Banaras, scholarly specialist on Heidegger. I know an Iranian student in my university who similarly appeals to me. The moral I draw is: individual value differences are the great ones.

Since Professor Noda was under considerable personal and family health difficulties in preparing this essay, I am especially grateful that he wrote it. It is one more proof that philosophical communication across cultural boundaries is very well possible.

R29. *Matsunobu on Philosophy in the Kyoto School*

Like Editor Hahn, I am grateful to Profesor Keiji Matsunobu for giving us his historical sketch of some philosophical developments in his country. Because of linguistic difficulties, I had little information, while lecturing in Kyoto during my first visit (in 1958), about the effects on students of my talks. In the second visit, in 1966, I had the students in an intensive two (or was it three?) weeks' seminar, meeting five days each week, responding in English (or with translations) so that it was more like teaching at home (or in Germany, where I had the language, especially after the first few weeks). It seems, from Matsunobu's account, that I had some effect on the thinking in his country.

I recall that, besides studying in Chicago, my one-time student has also studied in Germany. He is well aware of Christian as well as Buddhist and Shinto influences on Japanese philosophy. His essay brings to nine the number of essays written by scholars from other lands in this volume and to eight those by former students of mine.

Matsunobu refers to the "Eclecticism" of Japanese philosophers. I have been more impressed by their fondness for specialization. Before my first arrival in Japan I had somehow acquired the conviction that I would find there experts on every subject in which I had an intellectual interest, including Leibniz and ornithology. This expectation was not disappointed. Now I am pleased to learn about Japanese specialists in Plato. As Dombrowski shows, I am more of a Platonist than I have sometimes been aware of and more than many of my commentators have been aware of. I had Paul Shorey as colleague at the University of Chicago, and before that one of my closest friends, Ronald Levinson, was a learned disciple of Shorey. The latter's book, *What Plato Said*, was one of my earliest preferred secondary philosophical sources. P. E. More followed later, also Burnet and Cornford. I think they served me well. I did more reading in (translated) Plato (I know only a few words of Greek) than perhaps in any philosopher before Kant. For me Plato was *the* metaphysician and philosophical theologian before Whitehead. Between the two I incline, as it seems do the Japanese, to take Leibniz as next in importance.

Matsunobu mentions my notions of divine relativity (and yet also divine absoluteness) and the social structure of reality as of possible use in Japanese philosophy. In my reply to Sallie King (R12) on Buddhism I stress the relevance of neoclassical theism as correcting the insufficient acknowledgement of hierarchy in Buddhist ontologies, and also as showing that rationality and formal logic have more positive roles to play in metaphysics than most Buddhists have allowed. In regard to the doctrine of nothingness (or emptiness), it may be that the Japanese tradition makes these terms important for present-day Japanese thought, but I venture to confess my belief that whatever can be said in these terms can be said as well or better in other terms. Simply in itself, and apart from all else, anything you please is indeed no better than nothing. But why not say *that* by saying that everything is together with much else and could not have been what it is without its required contextual others. As Ortega y Gasset put it, "I am myself *and* my circumstances." Or, as Heidegger put it, the basic given is our "being-in-the-world." I would add, and here both Heidegger and Buddhists might hesitate or demur, the final context is not world but God-world. Even God, however, simply apart from all else is no better than nothing—there can be no such God. No power could prevent God from having some world or worlds, and it insults rather than praises God to suppose a possibility of a divine choice to create nothing, to be only potentially creative. A (merely) absolute God and a (merely) relative God—these are both half truths that become monstrous errors if taken as simply true.

On the other hand, I find talk about "absolute contradiction" perverse, or at best only a provocative way of saying what can be said as well or better without seeming to defy an elementary, and in truth valid, logical law. This law does not say that the attribution of two contrasting predicates to the same subject is contradictory. They must be applied "in the same respect" to the subject—for instance at the same time, or in the same part or aspect of the subject, if they are to make a contradictory assertion. The doctrine of a finite-infinite or relative-absolute or contingent-necessary deity can very well distinguish between aspects of the All-surpassing that are and those that are not dependent upon relation to particular other realities, or between those that are and those that are not contingent or finite.

That it is very difficult to work out a scientific cosmology abreast of current science I entirely grant. This is a job we are not likely to see accomplished once and for all in the foreseeable future. This does not mean that we are making no progress toward a better grasp of truth. There is here as in so many matters a judicious mean between extreme optimism or speculative daring and extreme pessimism or scepticism. We are not God, but we may be the only species of animal on this planet that can do anything much like making this negative statement, and our descendants may understand its meaning better than we do.

Although I have read some of Nishida, Tanabe, and the other neo-Buddhist Japanese philosophers, I have failed to internalize and remember it at all well. I agree with Matsunobu that "constructionism" and ("deconstructionism") and related, characteristically challenging (and, I think, one-sided) French intellectual fashions, can help us to attain some objectivity about our philosophical convictions or ways of thinking. But such fashions are always followed by others. My motto here still is, "accentuate the positive," dare to search for a livable view of the meaning of life in its comprehensive context of space and time, taking into account the mortality of nondivine individuals and species.

My commentator's emphasis on the thought of his country leads me to mention some impressions of mine concerning differences and similarities between our two countries. One impression is that in both there are now a great number of religious sects, perhaps greater than in any third country. And, since the Occupation, there is in neither a uniquely official religion. Another similarity is that both countries, in early phases, were heavily dependent on cultural importations, we in our colonial phases from Europe, Japan for several centuries, beginning in the time of Shotoku-Taishi (sixth century) from China and Korea. Still another is that both countries have had a phase of successfully defended military isolation, then a phase of successful imperialist extension, and a phase of dismal military failure (we in Southeast Asia). I sometimes think that Japan and West Germany are the two countries in the world today that see most clearly the twentieth-century discovery of the truth that technology has finally turned war, that age-old cross of humanity, into one of the principal enemies of mankind itself. In addition, our Southern States have in a manner of speaking experienced dismal military failure twice over. Both countries have been (and in spite of some faltering on our part still are) world leaders in technology, Japan for its size phenomenally so, like ancient Greece and Rome, and nineteenth-century England and Germany. Finally, and most important, between them, both Shinto and Buddhism have enabled the Japanese to give in some respects more impressive exhibitions of the kind of behavior our own principal religious traditions have recommended than our Christianity has produced among us at the present time. The Japanese people are among the most honest, polite, energetic, and least criminal or cruel there are in the highly industrialized peoples of the world.

One striking dissimilarity between our countries can be interpreted in almost opposite ways. From the standpoint of our feminism (and I regard myself as a feminist), Japan is still a male chauvinist country. But, and this is a significant but, the version of male dominance found today in Japan compares ethically and rationally very favorably with the versions found in other industrialized countries. I am thinking, for instance, of the gross wife and child abuses we hear about as distressingly common in my country. In addition, there are a few facts in Japanese history that might prove helpful in the future. There was the admirable Japanese Empress of Shotoku-Taishi's time and there was the perhaps first great novelist in the world (almost a Jane Austen), the Lady Murasaki-Shikibu. With us a woman president or head of state is still barely thinkable, in spite of Indira Gandhi and Mrs. Thatcher!

Our two countries need not be too proud to learn from each other. The Japanese might teach us to learn how to make everyday relations of individuals (including labor-management relations) more beautiful, less crude and ugly, than they can all too easily become. The Japanese know, better than we do, that aesthetic principles are ultimate, as well as ethical ones. The art of arts is life itself.

In one way, Japan's problem of acute population pressure on available land resources is bound to become more and more our problem. Our open spaces, so far as we still have them, beckon not only to our present citizens but also to the oppressed or unfortunate in many countries, some of which refuse to legalize birth control. Pollution (from population increase and luxury demands) almost rivals war as human enemy. We need to think more than we yet do of the one ship earth.

I charge philosophers as a class with having through the centuries been largely blind to several metaphysical truths, the recognition of which long ago might have saved us from part of our present danger; philosophers did not really and unambiguously believe in freedom of individuals; and they failed to think out the consequences of admitting the negative aspects of chance and risk inherent in that freedom; nor did they, in this connection, take seriously into account the evident truth that science and technology magnify the scope and consequences of freedom, its dangers as well as its opportunities.

The nuclear dilemma was in this sense foreseeable and by an English novelist (Thomas Love Peacock) was foreseen about 80 years before it came upon us. Peacock saw military weapons becoming more and more destructive. He asked, "What is the limit? Is it a weapon so destructive that it could destroy humanity itself?" Well, we have it. This humorous and incorrigibly sane writer made wonderful fun of compatibilism, the deterministic theory of freedom. All he lacked was only the generalization, made at long last by Peirce, Bergson, Varisco, and Whitehead, among a few others, that individual transcendence of causal necessity is only in degree unique to the human species, and is in principle inherent in individuality as such. Epicurus hinted at this. But no Greek, and not Leibniz, Hume, or Kant, simply no one, until about 120 years ago, even began to think out the pragmatic and theological implications of the idea. Is it not time to focus on this neglected task?

Matsunobu's references to recent French philosophy, and also to his countryman Noda's scholarship in Descartes, remind me of how little there is in this volume about the important contributions by French philosophers to metaphysics. There was Anselm's most famous of all theistic arguments (and deservedly so), also his classical summary of Augustinian neo-Platonism, illustrating both its excessive rejection of anthropomorphism and its indulgence in dubious forms of anthropomorphism (in the incarnation and atonement doctrines). There was Descartes, the first philosophical theologian since Philo Judaeus, who to my satisfaction defended both human and divine freedom. Descartes also, inadvertently, gave valuable evidence *against* the notion attributed to him of matter as having positive aspects not explicable by even the most radically other-than-human forms of mind. After Descartes, nearly every notable French philosopher (indeed I do not know of an exception) rejected both secular and theistic determinisms. The French also, since Descartes, have shown little fondness for reductive materialism or a hard dualism.

Two scholarly studies of Whitehead have appeared in the French literature: Alix Parmentier's *La philosophie de Whitehead et le problème de Dieu* (Paris, 1968); and Jean-Marie Breuvart's *Les directives de la symbolisation et les modèles de référence dans la philosophie d'A. N. Whitehead* (Lille/Paris, 1976, 775 pp.). Neither of these writers finds Whitehead's system convincing as it stands, Parmentier because of a classical theistic pre-conviction, Breuvart for reasons I have not managed to understand. He does say that Hegel's ontology seems to him a better guide than Whitehead's system in the fundamental speculative questions. This leads me to make a final attempt to explicate my attitude toward Hegel.

I am in three senses an Hegelian (and so was Whitehead). I believe that becoming is *more* than mere being; that metaphysical truth is in the unity of ultimate contraries; and that subjectivity is the key to objectivity, or that "subject overlaps object.'' But I definitely generalize this one-way overlapping to cover many other contrarieties. For instance, contingency overlaps necessity. Formal logic supports this by showing that the conjunct of a contingent truth and a necessary one is itself contingent. Hegel's ''freedom is the understanding of necessity'' needs to be revised, or taken to mean that necessity is merely what thinkable acts of freedom have in common. As subjectivity explains objectivity, so does creative experience, via its prehensive structure, explain its own limitations or necessities. There could not conceivably be a sheer absence of freedom from any part of nature. Time is ''objective modality'' (Peirce); all logic requires modal distinctions between dependence and independence among propositions; these require ontological distinctions between dependence and independence among things that propositions are about; and finally, propositions require objects, explained by subjects, none of which can be wholly uncreative, or unprehensive, totally without feeling of others' feeling. Apart from causally creative experience and prehensive experience there can be nothing, bare nothing, to constitute truth or falsity, reality or unreality. A noted scientist, Sewall Wright, has said it, ''There is nothing but freedom.'' All thought is about freedom limited only by other freedom. Plato, Aristotle, Epicurus, taken together, give support to these insights, and in the last hundred years speculative philosophy has been returning to this perspective. The notion that modality is merely linguistic, or how we talk, seems to me, as it did to Peirce, close to sheer silliness. Whether this fox *can* or *cannot* in this chase catch that rabbit surely does not depend on how we talk about foxes or rabbits. Without objective possibility and probability, life is meaningless. Probability is the guide to life and to the understanding of life's environment. That, I hold, is the logico-metaphysical message of the twentieth century.

Does subjectivity explain objectivity? Yes; for in knowing that you are my object, I also know that I am or may be your object. Moreover, there are many of ''you'' compared to one of ''me''; still more, the variety that may come under ''you'' (if that only means, cases, kinds, or aspects of subjectivity other than mine) is as great as the variety of positively thinkable realities. Sheer other-than-mind is a meaningless or contradictory phrase. Are these statements dogmatic? Yes, I suppose so. Could I be wrong in them? Same answer. But many great minds would also have been wrong. We are all fallible (Plato, Peirce, Whitehead, Popper); however, by learning from predecessors and contemporaries we can perhaps mitigate the effects of this fallibility.

According to an American visitor, Heidegger's final message to the world was simply, gratitude. This is my final word to those scarcely countable others who made this volume possible, thereby not only greatly honoring but also immensely stimulating me and, I hope, potentially benefitting many others wishing to reflect on our human condition.

PART FOUR

BIBLIOGRAPHY OF THE WRITINGS OF CHARLES HARTSHORNE

CHARLES HARTSHORNE: PRIMARY BIBLIOGRAPHY

Compiled by Dorothy C. Hartshorne

PART I—PHILOSOPHY

Books

1. *The Philosophy and Psychology of Sensation.* Chicago: The University of Chicago Press, 1934. Pp. 288. Reissued in 1968 by Kennikat Press.

2. *Beyond Humanism: Essays in the New Philosophy of Nature.* Chicago: Willet, Clark & Company, 1937. Pp. 324 + xiv. Bison Book Edition, with new Preface. Lincoln: University of Nebraska Press, 1968.

3. *Man's Vision of God and the Logic of Theism.* Chicago: Willet, Clark & Company, 1941. Pp. 360. After 1948 published by Harper and Brothers Publishers, New York. Reprinted, 1964, by Archon Books, Hamden, Conn.

4. *The Divine Relativity: A Social Conception of God.* The Terry Lectures, 1947. New Haven: Yale University Press, 1948. Pp. 164.

5. *Whitehead and the Modern World: Science, Metaphysics, and Civilization, Three Essays on the Thought of Alfred North Whitehead.* By Victor Lowe, Charles Hartshorne, and A. H. Johnson. "Whitehead's Metaphysics" by Charles Hartshorne, 25–41. Boston: The Beacon Press, 1950. Reprinted by Books for Libraries Press, 1972.

6. *Reality as Social Process: Studies in Metaphysics and Religion.* Glencoe: The Free Press and Boston: The Beacon Press, 1953. Pp. 223. Reprinted by Hafner, 1971.

7. *Philosophers Speak of God.* (With William L. Reese) Chicago: The University of Chicago Press. 1953. Pp. 535. Reissued in 1976 in Midway Reprints.

8. *The Logic of Perfection and Other Essays in Neoclassical Metaphysics.* La Salle: Open Court, 1962. Pp. 335.

9. *Anselm's Discovery.* La Salle: Open Court, 1965. Pp. 333.

10. *The Social Conception of the Universe* [3 chapters from *Reality as Social Process*], edited by Keiji Matsunobu. Tokyo: Aoyama, and New York: Macmillan, 1967. Pp. 78.

11. *A Natural Theology for Our Time.* La Salle: Open Court, 1967. Pp. 145.

12. *Creative Synthesis and Philosophic Method.* London: SCM Press Ltd., 1970. Pp. 337. La Salle: Open Court, 1970.

13. *Whitehead's Philosophy: Selected Essays, 1935–1970.* Lincoln: University of Nebraska Press, 1972. Japanese translation by Keiji Matsunobu and Minoru Ōtsuka, Kyōto: Kōrosha, 1989.

14. *Aquinas to Whitehead: Seven Centuries of Metaphysics of Religion. The Aquinas Lecture, 1976.* Milwaukee: Marquette University Publications, 1976. Pp. 54 + iii.

15. *Insights and Oversights of Great Thinkers: an Evaluation of Western Philosophy.* Albany: State University of New York Press, 1983. Pp. 393.

16. *Omnipotence and Other Theological Mistakes.* Albany: State University of New York Press, 1984. Pp. 144. Japanese translation by Minoru Ōtsuka. Kyōto: Kōrosha, 1991.

17. *Creativity in American Philosophy.* Albany: State University of New York Press, 1984. Pp. 299.

18. *Wisdom as Moderation: a Philosophy of the Middle Way.* State University of New York Press, 1987. Pp. 157.

19. *Collected Papers of Charles Sanders Peirce.* Edited by Charles Hartshorne and Paul Weiss. Cambridge: Harvard University Press.
    Vol. 1, *Principles of Philosophy,* 1931. Pp. 393.
    Vol. 2, *Elements of Logic,* 1932. Pp. 535.
    Vol. 3, *Exact Logic,* 1933. Pp. 433.
    Vol. 4, *The Simplest Mathematics,* 1933. Pp. 601.
    Vol. 5, *Pragmatism and Pragmaticism,* 1934. Pp. 455.
    Vol. 6, *Scientific Metaphysics,* 1935. Pp. 462.

Articles and Reviews

1. "Memory, Youth, and Age," *The Haverfordian* 37, 8 (Jan., 1916), 323.

2. "Barriers to Progress: Or Some Superstitions of Modernism," *The Gad-Fly* [Student Liberal Club of Harvard University] (1923), 1–15.

3. Review of A. N. Whitehead, *Symbolism, Its Meaning and Effect, Hound and Horn* 1 (1927), 148–152.

4. Review of Martin Heidegger, *Sein und Zeit* and of Oskar Becker, *Mathematische Existenz* from *Jahrbuch für Philosophie und phänomenologische Forschung,* Achter Band. Halle: Max Niemeyer, 1927, *Philosophical Review* 38, 3 (May, 1929), 284–293.

5. "Continuity, the Form of Forms, in Charles Peirce," *Monist* 39, 4 (Oct., 1929), 521–534.

6. Review of Etienne Souriau, *L'Avenir de l'esthétique*. Paris: Félix Alcan, 1929, *International Journal of Ethics* 40, 1 (Oct., 1929), 132–133.

7. "Ethics and the Assumption of Purely Private Pleasures," *International Journal of Ethics* 40, 4 (July, 1930), 496–515.

8. "Sense Quality and Feeling Tone." *Proceedings of the Seventh International Congress of Philosophy*, ed. Gilbert Ryle. London: Oxford University Press, 1931, 168–172.

9. "Contingency and the New Era in Metaphysics, I," *Journal of Philosophy* 29, 16 (Aug. 4, 1932), 421–431; II, Ibid. 29, 17 (Aug. 18, 1932), 457–469.

10. Review of André Lalande, *Les Illusions évolutionnistes*. Paris: Félix Alcan, 1930, *International Journal of Ethics* 43, 1 (Oct., 1932), 94–97.

11. "Four Principles of Method—with Applications," *Monist* 43, 1 (Jan., 1933), 40–72.

12. Review of G. Watts Cunningham, *The Idealistic Argument in Recent British and American Philosophy*. New York: Century, 1933, *International Journal of Ethics* 43, 4 (July, 1933), 447–449.

13. Foreword to Eugene Freeman, *The Categories of Charles Peirce*. Chicago: Open Court, 1934.

14. Review of R. G. Collingwood, *An Essay on Philosophical Method*. Oxford: Clarendon, 1933, *International Journal of Ethics* 44, 3 (Apr., 1934), 357–358.

15. "The Intelligibility of Sensations," *Monist* 44, 2 (July, 1934), 161–185.

16. Review of Ernest W. Barnes, *Scientific Theory and Religion*. N.Y.: Macmillan, 1933; J. E. Turner, *Essentials in the Development of Religion*. N.Y.: Macmillan, 1934; T. V. Seshagiro Row, *New Light on Fundamental Problems*. Madras: University Press, 1932, *International Journal of Ethics* 44, 4 (July, 1934), 465–471.

17. Review of Gerhard Kraenzlin, *Max Schelers Phaenomenologische Systematik*. Leipzig: S. Hirzel, 1934; Adolph Sternberger, *Der verstandene Tod*. Leipzig: S. Hirzel, 1934, Ibid., 478–480.

18. "Redefining God," *New Humanist* 7, 4 (July–Aug., 1934), 8–15.

19. "The New Metaphysics and Current Problems, I," *New Frontier* 1, 1 (Sept., 1934), 24–31; II, Ibid. 1, 5 (Nov.–Dec., 1934), 8–14.

20. "Ethics and the New Theology," *International Journal of Ethics* 45, 1 (Oct., 1934), 90–101.

21. Review of Louis Vialle, *Le Désir du néant*. Paris: Félix Alcan, 1933, Ibid., 116–117.

22. Review of William Pepperell Montague, *The Chances of Surviving Death*. Cambridge: Harvard University Press, 1934, Ibid., 120–121.

23. Review of John Nibb, *Christianity and Internationalism*. London: Elliot Stock, 1934; Georges Lakhovsky, *Le Racisme et l'orchestre universelle*. Paris: Félix Alcan, 1934, Ibid., 121–122.

24. "The Parallel Development of Method in Physics and Psychology," *Philosophy of Science* 1, 4 (Oct., 1934), 446–459.

25. "Pattern and Movement in Art and Science," *Comment* (The University of Chicago) 3, 2 (Winter, 1935), 1–2, 11.

26. Discussion: "Flexibility of Scientific Truth," *Philosophy of Science* 2 (1935), 255–256.

27. Review of D. Draghicesco, *Vérité et révélation*, Vol. 1. Paris: Félix Alcan, 1934, *International Journal of Ethics* 45, 2 (Jan., 1935), 248–249.

28. Review of Adolphe Ferrière, *Der Primat des Geistes als Grundlage einer aufbauenden Erziehung* (tr. Emmi Hirschberg). Berlin: Julius Beltz, n.d., Ibid., 250.

29. Review of Henry C. Simons, *A Positive Program for Laissez Faire*. Chicago: University of Chicago Press, 1935, *Christian Century* 52, 23 (June 5, 1935), 761–762.

30. "Metaphysics for Positivists," *Philosophy of Science* 2, 3 (July, 1935), 287–303.

31. "On Some Criticisms of Whitehead's Philosophy," *Philosophical Review* 44, 4 (July, 1935), 323–344.

32. Review of John Wisdom, *Problems of Mind and Matter*. Cambridge: University Press, 1934; Thomas Whittaker, *Reason*. Cambridge: University Press, 1934; Julius W. Friend and James Feibleman, *Science and the Spirit of Man*. London: Allen and Unwin, 1933, *International Journal of Ethics* 45, 4 (July, 1935), 461–465.

33. Review of Gajanan Wasudeo Kaveeshwar, *The Metaphysics of Berkeley Critically Examined in the Light of Modern Philosophy*. Mandleshwar, India: A. Kaveeshwar, 1933, Ibid., 494.

34. "The Compound Individual." *Philosophical Essays for Alfred North Whitehead*, ed. Otis H. Lee. New York: Longmans Green, 1936, 193–220.

35. "The New Pantheism, I" *Christian Register* 115, 8 (Feb. 20, 1936), 119–120; II, Ibid. 115, 9 (Feb. 27, 1936), 141–143.

36. Review of D. Draghicesco, *Vérité et rélévation*, Vol. II, Paris: Félix Alcan, 1934, *International Journal of Ethics* 47, 1 (Oct., 1936), 133–135.

37. "The Philosophical Limitations of Humanism," *University Review* 3, 4 (Summer, 1937), 240–242.

38. Review of Andre Cresson, *La Representation*. Paris: Boivin, 1936, *Philosophical Review* 47, 1 (Jan., 1938), 90–91.

39. Review of G. P. Adams, W. R. Dennes, J. Loewenberg, D. S. Mackay, P. Marhenke, S. C. Pepper, E. W. Strong, *Knowledge and Society*. New York: Appleton-Century, 1938, *Christian Century* 55, 30 (July 27, 1938), 917.

40. Review of Jacques Maritain, *The Degrees of Knowledge*. N.Y.: Scribner's, 1938, *Christian Century* 55 (Oct. 5, 1938), 1195.

41. "The Reality of the Past, the Unreality of the Future," *Hibbert Journal* 37, 2 (Jan., 1939), 246–257.

42. Review of Wilhelm Keller, *Der Sinnbegriff als Kategorie der Geisteswissenschaften*. Munich: Ernst Reinhardt, 1937, *Philosophical Review* 48, 1 (Jan. 1939), 95.

43. Review of Rasvihari Das, *The Philosophy of Whitehead*. London: James Clarke, n.d., Ibid. 48, 2 (March, 1939), 230–231.

44. Notes: Letter (Reply to Roger Holmes), *Philosophical Review* 68, 2 (March, 1939), 243.

45. "The Method of Imaginative Variations" in "Notes Concerning Husserl," *Journal of Philosophy* 36, 9 (Apr. 27, 1939), 233–234.

46. "Are All Propositions about the Future either True or False?" Program of the American Philosophical Association: Western Division, Apr. 20–22, 1939, 26–32.

47. Review of Alfred North Whitehead, *Modes of Thought*. N.Y.: Macmillan, 1938, *Review of Religion* 3, 4 (May, 1939), 494–496.

48. Discussion: "The Interpretation of Whitehead (Reply to John W. Blyth)," *Philosophical Review* 48, 4 (July, 1939), 415–423.

49. Review of James Bissett Pratt, *Naturalism*. New Haven: Yale University Press, 1939, *Journal of Religion* 19, 3 (July, 1939), 234–235.

50. Review of Ralph Barton Perry, *In the Spirit of William James*. New Haven: Yale University Press, 1938, Ibid., 247–248.

51. Review of Jacques Maritain, *The Degrees of Knowledge*. N.Y.: Scribner's, 1938, Ibid., 267–269.

52. Review of A. Campbell Garnett, *Reality and Value*. New Haven: Yale University Press, 1937, *The Scroll* 37, 3 (Nov., 1939), 93–95.

53. "A Critique of Peirce's Idea of God" in "Abstracts of Papers to be Read at the Joint Meeting of the Eastern and Western Divisions of the American Philosophical Association, Columbia University, December, 1939," *Journal of Philosophy* 36, 25 (Dec. 7, 1939), 683–684.

54. "Husserl and the Social Structure of Immediacy." *Philosophical Essays in Memory of Edmund Husserl*, ed. Marvin Farber. Cambridge: Harvard University Press, 1940, 219–230.

55. "Santayana's Doctrine of Essence." *The Philosophy of George Santayana*, ed. Paul Arthur Schilpp. The Library of Living Philosophers, Vol. 2. Evanston and Chicago: Northwestern University, 1940, 135–182.

56. "The Three Ideas of God," *Journal of Liberal Religion* 1, 3 (Winter, 1940), 9–16.

57. Review of Justus Buchler, *Charles Peirce's Empiricism*. N.Y.: Harcourt, Brace, 1939, *Ethics* 50, 2 (Jan., 1940), 248.

58. Review of Josef Maier, *On Hegel's Critique of Kant*. N.Y.: Columbia University Press, 1939, *Journal of Religion* 20, 1 (Jan., 1940), 106.

59. Review of *The Philosophy of John Dewey*, ed. Paul Arthur Schilpp. Evanston: Northwestern University, 1939, *Christian Century* 42, 10 (March 6, 1940), 313–315.

60. Review of Irwin Edman, *Arts and the Man*. N.Y.: Norton, 1939, *Ethics* 50, 3 (Apr., 1940), 369–370.

61. Review of Arthur Hazard Dakin, *Man the Measure*. Princeton: Princeton University Press, 1939; Archibald Allan Bowman, *A Sacramental Universe*. Princeton: Princeton University Press, 1939, Ibid., 363–366.

62. Review of Milton Karl Munitz, *The Moral Philosophy of Santayana*. N.Y.: Columbia University Press, 1939, *Journal of Religion* 20, 2 (Apr., 1940), 196–198.

63. Review of Charles M. Perry, *Toward a Dimensional Realism*. Norman: University of Oklahoma Press, 1939, Ibid., 214.

64. Review of Theodore Meyer Greene, *The Arts and the Art of Criticism*. Princeton: Princeton University Press, 1940, *Ethics* 51, 1 (Oct., 1940), 116–117.

65. "Whitehead's Idea of God." *The Philosophy of Alfred North Whitehead*, ed. Paul Arthur Schilpp. The Library of Living Philosophers, Vol. 3. Evanston and Chicago: Northwestern University, 1941, 513–559.

66. "Charles Sanders Peirce's Metaphysics of Evolution," *New England Quarterly* 14, 1 (March, 1941), 49–63.

67. "Anthropomorphic Tendencies in Positivism," *Philosophy of Science* 8, 2 (April, 1941), 184–203.

68. Review of Frederick J. E. Woodbridge, *An Essay on Nature*. N.Y.: Columbia University Press, 1940, *Ethics* 51, 4 (July, 1941), 488–490.

69. Review of DeWitt H. Parker, *Experience and Substance*. Ann Arbor: University of Michigan Press, 1941, *Christian Century* 48, 27 (July 2, 1941), 864.

70. "A Critique of Peirce's Idea of God," *Philosophical Review* 50, 5 (Sept., 1941), 516–523.

71. Review of Ledger Wood, *The Analysis of Knowledge*. Princeton: Princeton University Press, 1941, *Philosophy and Phenomenological Research* 2, 1 (Sept., 1941), 104–108.

72. Review of Gustaf Strömberg, *The Soul of the Universe, Review of Religion* 5, 3 (1941), 357–360.

73. "Organic and Inorganic Wholes." Program of the Fiftieth Anniversary Symposia, The University of Chicago, 1941, 12.

74. "A Philosophy of Democratic Defense." *Science, Philosophy, and Religion: Second Symposium*. N.Y.: Conference on Science, Philosophy, and Religion in Their Relation to the Democratic Way of Life, Inc., 1942, 130–172.

75. Review of *The Philosophy of Peirce: Selected Writings*, ed. Justus Buchler. N.Y.: Harcourt Brace, 1940, *Philosophical Review* 51, 1 (Jan., 1942), 92.

76. Review of Etienne Gilson, *God and Philosophy*. New Haven: Yale University Press, 1941, *Journal of Religion* 22, 2 (Apr., 1942), 221–224.

77. "Elements of Truth in the Group-Mind Concept," *Social Research* 9, 2 (May, 1942), 248–265.

78. Review of *The Philosophy of Alfred North Whitehead*, ed. Paul Arthur Schilpp. Evanston: Northwestern University, 1941, *Religion in Life* 11, 3 (Summer, 1942), 469–470.

79. Review of *The Philosophy of Alfred North Whitehead*, ed. Paul Arthur Schilpp. Evanston: Northwestern University, 1941, *Thought* 17, 66 (Sept., 1942), 545–547.

80. Review of DeWitt H. Parker, *Experience and Substance*. Ann Arbor: University of Michigan Press, 1941. Philosophical Review 51, 5 (Sept., 1942), 523–526.

81. Review of Stephen C. Pepper, *World Hypotheses*. Berkeley: University of California Press, 1942, *Ethics* 53, 1 (Oct., 1942), 73–75.

82. "Organic and Inorganic Wholes," *Philosophy and Phenomenological Research* 3, 2 (Dec., 1942), 127–136.

83. Comment on "Democracy and the Rights of Man." *Science, Philosophy, and Religion: Second Symposium*. N.Y. Conference on Science, Philosophy, and Religion, Inc., 1942, 292.

84. Review of John Blyth, *Whitehead's Theory of Knowledge*. Providence: Brown University, 1941, *Philosophy and Phenomenological Research* 3, 3 (March, 1943), 372–375.

85. Discussion: "Is Whitehead's God the God of Religion?" [Suggested by Ely's book], *Ethics* 53, 3 (April, 1943), 219–227.

86. Review of Lewis Edwin Hahn, *A Contextualistic Theory of Perception*. Berkeley: University of California Press, 1942, Ibid., 233.

87. Review of A. Campbell Garnett, *A Realistic Philosophy of Religion*. Chicago: Willett Clark, 1942, *Journal of Religion* 23, 3 (July, 1943), 70–71.

88. Review of Stephen Lee Ely, *The Religious Availability of Whitehead's God*. Madison: University of Wisconsin Press, 1942, *Journal of Liberal Religion* 5, 1 (Summer, 1943), 55.

89. Communication. Rejoinder: "Ely on Whitehead," *Journal of Liberal Religion* 5, 2 (Sept., 1943), 97–100.

90. Discussion: "Reflections on the Strength and Weakness of Thomism," *Ethics* 54, 1 (Oct., 1943), 53–57.

91. Review of Jacques Maritain, *Saint Thomas and the Problem of Evil*. Milwaukee, Marquette University Press, 1942; *The Maritain Volume of 'The Thomist.'* N.Y.: Sheed and Ward, 1943, *Ethics* 54, 1 (Oct., 1943), 53–57.

92. Review of A. Campbell Garnett, *A Realistic Philosophy of Religion*. Chicago: Willett Clark, 1942, Ibid., 62–63.

93. "A Mathematical Analysis of Theism," *Review of Religion* 8, 1 (Nov., 1943), 20–38.

94. Radio Discussion: "How Christians Should Think about the Peace." By Edwin Aubrey, Charles Hartshorne, and Bernard Loomer. Pamphlet. Chicago: *The University of Chicago Round Table*, April 9, 1944. Pp. 20, passim.

95. Review of K. R. Sreenivasa Iyengar, *The Metaphysics of Value*, Vol. 1. Mysore: University of Mysore, 1942, *Ethics* 54, 3 (April, 1944), 230–231.

96. Review of John Elof Boodin, *Religion of Tomorrow*. N.Y.: Philosophical Library, 1943, Ibid., 233–234.

97. "The Formal Validity and Real Significance of the Ontological Argument," *Philosophical Review* 53, 3 (May, 1944), 225–245.

98. "Philosophy and Orthodoxy," *Ethics* 54, 4 (July, 1944), 295–298.

99. Review of Werner Jaeger, *Humanism and Theology*. Milwaukee: Marquette University Press, 1943, *Journal of Religion* 24, 3 (July, 1944), 230.

100. "God and Man not Rivals," *Journal of Liberal Religion* 6, 2 (Autumn, 1944), 9–13.

101. Abstract: "Beauty as Balance of Unity and Variety." *Proceedings*, First Annual Meeting, The American Society for Aesthetics, Cleveland, Ohio, Sept. 11–13, 1944, 29–30.

102. Comment on "Philosophical Ideas and Enduring Peace," 557; on "Philosophical Ideas and World Peace," 597; on "In Quest of Worldly Wisdom," 719–721. *Approaches to World Peace, Fourth Symposium*. Ed. Lyman Bryson, Louis Finkelstein, and Robert M. MacIver. N.Y.: Conference on Science, Philosophy, and Religion, 1944.

103. Review of Henry Alonzo Myers, *The Spinoza-Hegel Paradox*. Ithaca: Cornell University Press, 1944, *Ethics* 55, 1 (Oct., 1944), 71–72.

104. Review of Adhar Chandra Das, *Negative Fact, Negation, and Truth*. Calcutta: Calcutta University Press, 1942, Ibid., 77.

105. Discussion: "On Hartshorne's Formulation of the Ontological Argument: A Rejoinder" [to Elton], *Philosophical Review* 54, 1 (Jan., 1945), 63–65.

106. Entries, *An Encyclopedia of Religion*, ed. Vergilius Ferm. N.Y.: Philosophical Library, 1945, acosmism; analogy; anthropomorphism; anthropopathism; Aristotle and Aristotelianism; axiom; Berkeley, George; Carneades; cause; Copernican astronomy; eternal; eternity; ether; etiology, aetiology; foreknowledge, Divine; Gerson, Levi ben; God, as personal; Hume; infinite; Kant, Immanuel; omnipotence; omnipresence; omniscience; panentheism; panlogism; pantheism; Peirce,

Charles Sanders; perfect, perfection; Ptolemaic astronomy; Renouvier, Charles; Spencer, Herbert; Spinoza, Benedict; time; transcendence; Whitehead, Alfred North.

107. Review Article: "Efficient Causality in Aristotle and St. Thomas" [By Francis X. Meehan. Washington: Catholic University Press, 1940], *Journal of Religion* 25, 1 (Jan. 1945), 25–32.

108. Review of Rudolf Jordan, *Homo Sapiens Socialis*. South Africa: Central News Agency, 1944, *Ethics* 55, 4 (July, 1945), 312–313.

109. Review of Jacques Maritain, *The Dream of Descartes*. N.Y.: Philosophical Library, 1944, Ibid., 321.

110. Review of *Vladimir Soloviev's Lectures on Godmanhood*, Intro. by Peter Zouboff. N.Y.: International University Press, 1944, Ibid., 322.

111. Discussion: "Professor Hartshorne's Syllogism: Rejoinder" [to Elton], *Philosophical Review* 54, 5 (Sept., 1945), 506–508.

112. Review of K. F. Reinhardt, *A Realistic Philosophy*. Milwaukee: Bruce, 1944, Ibid., 521–522.

113. "A New Philosophic Conception of the Universe," *Hibbert Journal* 44, 1 (Oct., 1945), 14–21.

114. Review Article: *The Philosophy of Bertrand Russell*, ed. Paul Arthur Schilpp. Library of Living Philosophers, Vol. 5. Evanston: Northwestern University, 1944, *Journal of Religion* 25, 4 (Oct., 1945), 280–284.

115. Communication: "Reply to Father Meehan," *Journal of Religion* 26, 1 (Jan., 1946), 54–57.

116. Review of Erich Frank, *Philosophical Understanding and Religious Truth*. London: Oxford University Press, 1945, *Review of Religion* 10, 2 (Jan., 1946), 182–189.

117. Review of William Ernest Hocking, *Science and the Idea of God*. Chapel Hill: University of North Carolina Press, 1944, *Philosophy and Phenomenological Research* 6, 3 (March, 1946), 453–457.

118. "Relative, Absolute, and Superrelative: A Formal Analysis," *Philosophical Review* 55, 3 (May, 1946), 213–228.

119. "The Common Good and the Value Receptacle," Program of the American Philosophical Association, Western Division, May 9–11, 1946, 10–11.

120. "Tragic and Sublime Aspects of Christian Love," *Journal of Liberal Religion* 8, 1 (Summer, 1946), 36–44.

121. "Theological Values in Current Metaphysics," *Journal of Religion* 26, 3 (July, 1946), 157–167.

122. "Leibniz's Greatest Discovery," *Journal of the History of Ideas* 7, 4 (Oct., 1946), 411–421.

123. "Ideal Knowledge Defines Reality: What Was True in Idealism," *Journal of Philosophy* 43, 21 (Oct. 10, 1946), 573–582.

124. Correction of "Ideal Knowledge Defines Reality," *Journal of Philosophy* 43, 26 (Dec. 19, 1946), 724.

125. Review of Henri Bergson, *The Creative Mind*, tr. Mabelle L. Andison. N.Y.: Philosophical Library, 1946, *Journal of Religion* 27, 1 (Jan., 1947), 64–65.

126. "Two Levels of Faith and Reason," Program of Week of Work of the National Council on Religion in Higher Education, 1947, 16.

127. Review of José Ortega y Gasset, *Concord and Liberty*. N.Y.: Norton, 1946, *Christian Century* 64, 7 (Feb. 12, 1947), 207.

128. Review of Gustav Theodor Fechner, *Religion of a Scientist: Selections from Fechner*, ed. and tr. Walter Lowrie. N.Y.: Pantheon, 1946, *Journal of Religion* 27, 2 (Apr., 1947), 126–128.

129. Review of Nels F. S. Ferré, *Faith and Reason*, N.Y.: Harper, 1946, *Review of Religion* 11, 4 (May, 1947), 409–413.

130. Review of Martin Foss, *The Idea of Perfection in the Western World*. Princeton: Princeton University Press, 1946, *Journal of Modern History* 19, 2 (June, 1947), 15.

131. "God as Absolute, Yet Related to All," *Review of Metaphysics* 1, 1 (Sept., 1947), 24–51.

132. Review of Henry N. Wieman et al., *Religious Liberals Reply*. Boston: Beacon Press, 1947, *Christian Register* 126, 9 (Oct., 1947), 412–413.

133. Review of *The Wit and Wisdom of Whitehead*, compiled by A. H. Johnson. Boston: Beacon Press, 1947, Ibid., 126, 10 (Nov., 1947), 446.

134. "Two Levels of Faith and Reason," *Journal of Bible and Religion* 16, 1 (Jan., 1948), 30–38.

135. Review of Paul Weiss, *Nature and Man*. N.Y.: Henry Holt, 1947, *Ethics* 58, 2 (Jan., 1948), 143–144.

136. Review of A. Campbell Garnett, *God in Us*. Chicago: Willett Clark, 1945, Ibid., 151.

137. "The Rationalistic Criterion in Metaphysics," *Philosophy and Phenomenological Research* 8, 3 (March, 1948), 436–447.

138. "Existential Propositions and the Law of Categories." *Fascicule* 1, *Proceedings of the Tenth International Congress of Philosophy*, ed. E. W. Beth et al. Amsterdam: North-Holland Publishing Co., 1948, 342–344.

139. "Aesthetics of Color," Program: Research in Textiles, Clothing, and Related Art, March 19–20, 1948, 2.

140. "Whitehead's Metaphysics," Program of the American Philosophical Association, Western Division, May 6–8, 1948, 13–14.

141. Review of Jean Wahl, *The Philosopher's Way*. N.Y.: Oxford University Press, 1948, *Philosophical Review* 57, 5 (Sept., 1948), 509–511.

142. "Das metaphysische System Whiteheads," *Zeitschrift fur philosophische Forschung*, 3, 4 (1949), 566–575.

143. "Le Principe de relativité philosophique chez Whitehead:" Lecture delivered at the Sorbonne, Feb. 4, 1949, announced in Bulletin. EC 1959.

144. "Ein theologisches Paradoxon. I Die Wissensform des Paradoxons. II Die Willensform des Paradoxons," *Philosophisches Jahrbuch* 59, 2 (1949), 250–251.

145. "Noch einmal die Zufälligkeit der Welt und Notwendigkeit Gottes: Erwiderung an Dr. Ferdinand Bergenthal," Ibid., 355–356.

146. "Ob Göttliches Wissen um die weltliche Existenz notwendig sein kann: Eine Erwiderung," Ibid., 60, 4 (1950), 469–471.

147. "The Synthesis of Idealism and Realism," *Theoria* (Sweden), 15 (March 12, 1949), 90–107.

148. "Chance, Love, and Incompatibility": Presidential Address, Western Division of the American Philosophical Association meeting at Columbus, Ohio, April 29, 1949, *Philosophical Review* 58, 5 (Sept., 1949), 429–450.

149. Review of Otis Lee, *Existence and Inquiry*. Chicago: University of Chicago Press, 1949, *Review of Metaphysics* 3, 1 (Sept., 1949), 107–114.

150. "Panpsychism." *A History of Philosophical Systems*, ed. Vergilius Ferm. N.Y.: Philosophical Library, 1950, 442–453.

151. "Le Principe de relativité philosophique chez Whitehead," *Revue de Métaphysique et de Morale* 55, 1 (Jan.–March, 1950), 16–29.

152. "The Divine Relativity and Absoluteness: A Reply [to John Wild]," *Review of Metaphysics* 4, 1 (Sept., 1950), 31–60.

153. "God in General Philosophical Thought." *The Encyclopedia Hebraica*, 3, 1951 (Jewish Calendar 5711). Jerusalem: Encyclopedia Publishing Co., 1951, 467–478.

154. "Strict and Genetic Identity: An Illustration of the Relations of Logic to Metaphysics." *Structure, Method, and Meaning: Essays in Honor of Henry M. Sheffer*, ed. Horace M. Kallen et al. N.Y.: Liberal Arts Press, 1951, 242–254.

155. "Philosophy of Religion in the United States," *Philosophy and Phenomenological Research* 11, 3 (March, 1951), 406–410.

156. Discussion: "Arthur Berndtson on Mystical Experience," *Personalist* 32, 2 (Spring, 1951), 191–193.

157. Review of Kelvin Van Nuys, *Science and Cosmic Purpose*. N.Y.: Harper, 1949, *Review of Religion* 16, 1–2 (Nov., 1951), 79–84.

158. "The Relativity of Nonrelativity: Some Reflections on Firstness." *Studies in the Philosophy of Charles Sanders Peirce*, ed. Philip P. Wiener and Frederic H. Young. Cambridge: Harvard University Press, 1952, 215–224.

159. "Radhakrishnan on Mind, Matter, and God." *The Philosophy of Sarvepalli Radhakrishnan*, ed. Paul Arthur Schilpp. The Library of Living Philosophers, Vol. 8. N.Y.: Tudor, 1952, 313–322.

160. "Tillich's Doctrine of God." *The Theology of Paul Tillich*. The Library of Living Theology, Vol. 1, ed. Charles W. Kegley and Robert W. Bretall. N.Y.: Macmillan, 1952, 164–195.

161. "La Philosophie de la religion aux Etats-Unis," *Les Etudes Philosophiques* 7, 1–2 (Jan.-June, 1952), 50–56.

162. "Time, Death, and Eternal Life," *Journal of Religion* 32, 2 (Apr., 1952), 97–107.

163. Review of Georg Siegmund, *Naturordnung als Quelle der Gotteserkenntnis: Neubegründung des theologischen Gottesbeweises*. Freiburg: Herder, 1950, *Philosophy and Phenomenological Research* 12, 4 (June, 1952), 584–585.

164. "Politics and the Metaphysics of Freedom." *Enquête sur la liberté, Fédération internationale des sociétés de philosophie*. Publié avec le concours de l'u.n.e.s.c.o. Paris: Hermann, 1953, 79–85.

165. "Noch einmal, das Wissen Gottes," *Philosophisches Jahrbuch* 62, 2. Freiburg-München: Verlag Karl Alber, 1953, 409–411.

166. "Spirit as Life Freely Participating in Life," *Biosophical Review* 10, 2 (1953), 31–32.

167. "The Monistic Theory of Expression," *Journal of Philosophy* 50, 14 (July 2, 1953), 425–434.

168. Review of John Wisdom, *Philosophy and Psycho-Analysis*. N.Y.: Philosophical Library, 1953, *Ethics* 63, 4 (July, 1953), 317–318.

169. "The Immortality of the Past: Critique of a Prevalent Misinterpretation," *Review of Metaphysics* 7, 1 (Sept., 1953), 98–112.

170. Symposium: "Are Religious Dogmas Cognitive and Meaningful?" *Journal of Philosophy* 51, 5 (March 4, 1954), 148–150.

171. Review of Risieri Frondizi, *The Nature of the Self*. New Haven: Yale University Press, 1953, *Philosophy and Phenomenological Research* 14, 3 (March, 1954), 419–420.

172. "The Kinds of Theism: A Reply [to Taubes]," *Journal of Religion* 34, 2 (Apr., 1954), 127–131.

173. "Mind, Matter, and Freedom," *Scientific Monthly* 78, 5 (May, 1954), 314–320.

174. Review Article: "Whitehead's Philosophy of Reality as Socially-Structured Process" (apropos *Alfred North Whitehead: An Anthology*, selected by F. S. C. Northrop and Mason Gross), *Chicago Review* 8, 2 (Spring–Summer, 1954), 60–77.

175. Review of F. W. Eggleston, *Reflections of an Australian Liberal*. Melbourne: Cheshire, 1953, *Ethics* 64, 4 (July, 1954), 332.

176. "Biology and the Spiritual View of the World: A Comment on Dr. Birch's Paper," *Christian Scholar* 37, 3 (Sept., 1954), 408–409.

177. "Russian Metaphysics: Some Reactions to Zenkovsky's History," *Review of Metaphysics* 8, 1 (Sept., 1954), 61–78.

178. "Causal Necessities: An Alternative to Hume," *Philosophical Review* 43, 4 (Oct., 1954), 479–499.

179. Review of J. Defever, S. J., *La Preuve réelle de Dieu.* Paris: Desclée de Brouwer, 1953, *Philosophy and Phenomenological Research* 15, 2 (Dec., 1954), 285–286.

180. Review of Brand Blanshard, *The Nature of Thought.* London: Allen & Unwin, 1959, *Philosophische Rundschau* 3, 1–2 (1955), 119–120.

181. "Process as Inclusive Category: A Reply [to John E. Smith]," *Journal of Philosophy* 52, 4 (Feb. 17, 1955), 94–102.

182. Review of Eranos [various authors], *Spirit and Nature, Papers from the Eranos Yearbooks*, Vol. 1. N.Y.: Pantheon, 1954, *Journal of Religion* 35, 2 (Apr., 1955), 106–107.

183. Review of Wilmon Henry Sheldon, *God and Polarity.* New Haven: Yale University Press, 1954, *Philosophical Review* 64, 2 (Apr., 1955), 312–316.

184. Panel Discussion: 1955 Edward Gallahue Seminar in Religion and Psychology at the Menninger Foundation. *Passim.* [Mimeographed.]

185. "Some Empty though Important Truths," *Review of Metaphysics* 8, 4 (June, 1955), 553–568.

186. "The Unity of Man and the Unity of Nature," *Emory University Quarterly* 11, 3 (Oct., 1955), 129–141.

187. "Some Empty though Important Truths: A Preface to Metaphysics" [reprinted from 185 *supra*]. *American Philosophers at Work: The Philosophic Scene in the United States*, ed. Sidney Hook. N.Y.: Criterion Books, 1956, 225–235.

188. "Royce's Mistake—and Achievement," *Journal of Philosophy* 53, 3 (Feb. 2, 1956), 123–130.

189. Panel Discussion: 1956 Edward Gallahue Seminar in Religion and Psychology at the Menninger Foundation. *Passim.* [Mimeographed.]

190. Colloquium No. 8: "The Idea of Creation," *Review of Metaphysics* 9, 3 (March, 1956), 464–465.

191. Review of Robert Leet Patterson, *Irrationalism and Rationalism in Religion.* Durham: Duke University Press, 1954, *Review of Religion* 20, 3–4 (March, 1956), 211–213.

192. "The Idea of God—Literal or Analogical?" *Christian Scholar* 29, 2 (June, 1956), 131–136.

193. Discussion: "New Propositions and New Truths," *Review of Metaphysics* 9, 4 (June, 1956), 656–661.

194. "Two Strata of Meaning in Religious Discourse." Symposium on Philosophy of Religion, *Southern Philosopher* 5, 3 (Oct., 1956), 4–7.

195. "Some Reflections Suggested by H. Wolfson's *Philosophy of the Church Fathers, Vol I: Faith, Trinity, Incarnation.*" Cambridge: Harvard University Press, 1956. *Collection of Reviews*, Southern Society for Philosophy of Religion, J. R. Cresswell, Bibliographer. March 9, 1957, 1–10. [Mimeographed.]

196. "Whitehead and Berdyaev: Is There Tragedy in God?" *Journal of Religion* 37, 2 (Apr., 1957), 71–84.

197. Review of William Ernest Hocking, *The Coming World Civilization*. N.Y.: Harper, 1956, *Chicago Theological Seminary Register* 47, 5 (May, 1957), 21–22.

198. Review of William Ernest Hocking, *The Coming World Civilization*. N.Y.: Harper, 1956, *Philosophy and Phenomenological Research* 17, 4 (June, 1957), 562–563.

199. Review of Gerda Walter, *Phänomenologie der Mystik*. Olten und Freiburg im Breisgau: Walter-Verlag, 1955, Ibid., 18, 1 (Sept., 1957), 140–141.

200. "Charles Peirce, Philosopher-Scientist." "Charles Sanders Peirce—A Symposium," *Journal of Public Law* 7, 1 (Spring, 1958), 2–12.

201. Discussion: "Whitehead on Process: A Reply to Professor Eslick," *Philosophy and Phenomenological Research* 18, 4 (June, 1958), 514–520.

202. "Science, Insecurity, and the Abiding Treasure," *Journal of Religion* 38, 3 (July, 1958), 168–174.

203. "Outlines of a Philosophy of Nature, Part I," *Personalist* 39, 3 (Summer, July, 1958), 239–248. "Part II," Ibid. 39, 4 (Autumn, Oct., 1958), 380–391.

204. "Freedom Requires Indeterminism and Universal Causality," *Journal of Philosophy* 55, 19 (Sept. 11, 1958), 793–811.

205. "Metaphysical Statements as Nonrestrictive and Existential," *Review of Metaphysics* 12, 1 (Sept., 1958), 35–47.

206. "The Logical Structure of Givenness," *Philosophical Quarterly* [Scotland] 8, 33 (Oct., 1958), 307–316.

207. "The Philosophy of Creative Synthesis." Symposium: Creativity as a Philosophical Category, *Journal of Philosophy* 55, 22 (Oct. 23, 1958), 944–953.

208. Discussion: "The Structure of Metaphysics: A Criticism of Lazerowitz's Theory," *Philosophy and Phenomenological Research* 19, 2 (Dec., 1958), 226–240.

209. "Four Unrefuted Forms of the Ontological Argument," *Journal of Philosophical Studies* [Kyoto, Japan] 40, 1 (Jan., 1959), 1–15. In Japanese, with English Summary.

210. "A Philosopher's Assessment of Christianity." *Religion and Culture: Essays in Honor of Paul Tillich*, ed. Walter Leibrecht. N.Y.: Harper, 1959, 167–180.

211. "John Wisdom on 'Gods': Two Views of the Logic of Theism," *Downside Review* [Bath, England] Winter, 1958–59, 5–17.

212. "The Principle of Shared Creativity." *Unitarian Symposia No. 6, What Can Religion Offer Modern Man?* April, 1959, 1–8.

213. "The Philosophy of Creative Synthesis" [207 *supra, reprinted*], *Americana: A Monthly Journal of Humanities, Social Sciences, and Natural Sciences* [Tokyo] 5, 8 (Aug., 1959), 80–90. (In Japanese.)

214. "The Philosophy of Creative Synthesis," *Americana: A Monthly Journal of Humanities, Social Sciences, and Natural Sciences* 5, 8 (Aug., 1959), 80–90. Tokyo, U.S.I.S. In Japanese. EC 1968.

215. "Freedom, Individuality, and Beauty in Nature," *Snowy Egret* 24, 2 (Autumn, 1960), 5–14. [Mimeographed.]

216. "Equalitarianism and the Great Inequalities," *Emory Alumnus* 36, 7 (Nov., 1960), 24–25, 49.

217. "Jinsei no mokuteki" ("The Aim of Life"), tr. Toshio Mikoda, *Tetsugaku Kenkyu* [Journal of Philosophical Studies, Japan] 41, 2 (Nov., 1960), 1–13.

218. "The Buddhist-Whiteheadian View of the Self and the Religious Traditions." *Proceedings of the Ninth International Congress for the History of Religions.* Tokyo and Kyoto, 1958. Tokyo: Maruzen, 1960, 298–302.

219. "Whitehead and Contemporary Philosophy." *The Relevance of Whitehead: Philosophical Essays in Commemoration of the Centenary of the Birth of Alfred North Whitehead*, ed. Ivor Leclerc. London: Allen and Unwin, 1961, 21–43.

220. "Metaphysics and the Modality of Existential Judgments." Ibid., 107–121.

221. "Hume's Metaphysics and Its Present-Day Influence," *New Scholasticism* 35, 2 (Apr., 1961), 152–171.

222. "The Social Structure of Experience," *Philosophy* 36, 137 (Apr. and July, 1961), 97–111.

223. "The Structure of Givenness," *Philosophical Forum* 18 (1960–61), 22–39.

224. "God's Existence: A Conceptual Problem." *Religious Experience and Truth: A Symposium*, ed. Sidney Hook, N.Y.: N.Y. University Press, 1961, 211–219.

225. Discussion: "Professor Hall on Perception," *Philosophy and Phenomenological Research* 21, 4 (June, 1961), 563–571.

226. "Tillich and the Other Great Tradition," *Anglican Theological Review* 43, 3 (July, 1961), 245–259.

227. "The Logic of the Ontological Argument," *Journal of Philosophy* 58, 17 (Aug. 17, 1961), 471–473.

228. Discussion: "Absolute Objects and Relative Subjects: A Reply" [to F. H. Parker], *Review of Metaphysics* 15, 1 (Sept., 1961), 174–188.

229. "Man in Nature." *Experience, Existence, and the Good: Essays in Honor of Paul Weiss*, ed. Irwin C. Lieb. Carbondale: Southern Illinois University Press, 1961, 89–99.

230.   "Whitehead, the Anglo-American Philosopher-Scientist." *Proceedings of the American Catholic Philosophical Association.* Washington: Catholic University of America, 1961, 163–171.

231.   Introduction to Second Edition, *Saint Anselm, Basic Writings*, tr. S. N. Deane. La Salle: Open Court, 1962, 1–19.

232.   "The Modern World and a Modern View of God," *Crane Review* 4, 2 (Winter, 1962), 73–85.

233.   "Religion and Creative Experience," *Darshana, an International Quarterly of Philosophy, Psychology, Psychical Research, Religion, Mysticism and Sociology,* (India) 2, 1 (Jan., 1962), 47–52.

234.   "What Did Anselm Discover?" *Union Seminary Quarterly Review* 17, 3 (March, 1962), 213–222. See item 295, this bibliography.

235.   "La Creatividad Participada," tr. Sira Jaén, *Revista de Filosofía de la Universidad de Costa Rica* 3, 11 (Jan.–June, 1962), 237–244.

236.   "Religion and Creative Experience," *Unitarian Register and Universalist Leader* 141, 6 (June, 1962), 9–11.

237.   "Mind as Memory and Creative Love." *Theories of the Mind*, ed. Jordan M. Scher. N.Y.: The Free Press of Glencoe, 1962, 440–463.

238.   Discussion: "How Some Speak and Yet Do Not Speak of God," *Philosophy and Phenomenological Research* 23, 2 (Dec., 1962), 274–276.

239.   "Present Prospects for Metaphysics," *Monist* 47, 2 (Winter, 1963), 188–210.

240.   "Individual Differences and the Ideal of Equality," *New South* 18, 2 (Feb., 1963), 3–8.

241.   "Martin Bubers Metaphysik." *Martin Buber*, herausgegeben von Schilpp u. Friedman. Stuttgart: Kohlhammer Verlag, 1963, 42–61.

242.   "Alternative Conceptions of God" [from *Man's Vision of God*]. *Religious Belief and Philosophical Thought*, ed. William P. Alston. N.Y.: Harcourt, Brace & World, 1963, 320–337.

243.   "Further Fascination of the Ontological Argument: Replies to Richardson," *Union Seminary Quarterly Review* 18, 3, Part I (March, 1963), 244–245.

244.   "Whitehead's Novel Intuition." *Alfred North Whitehead: Essays on His Philosophy*, ed. George L. Kline. Englewood Cliffs, N.J.: Prentice-Hall, 1963, 18–26.

245.   "Sensation in Psychology and Philosophy," *Southern Journal of Philosophy* 1, 2 (Summer, 1963) 3–14.

246.   "Rationale of the Ontological Proof," *Theology Today* 20, 2 (July, 1963), 278–283.

247.   "Whitehead's Conception of God" and "Whitehead's Theory of Prehension." *Actas: Segundo Congreso Extraordinario Inter-americano de Filosofía, 22–26 Julio, 1961.* San José, Costa Rica: Imprenta Nacional, 1963 [misprinted 1962], 163–170.

248. Communication: "Finite or Finite-Infinite?" *Philosophy and Phenomenological Research* 24, 1 (Sept., 1963), 149.

249. "Real Possibility," *Journal of Philosophy* 60, 21 (Oct. 10, 1963), 593–605.

250. "Man's Fragmentariness," *Wesleyan Studies in Religion* 41, 6 (1963–64), 17–28.

251. "Abstract and Concrete in God: A Reply" [to Julian Hartt], *Review of Metaphysics* 17, 2 (Dec., 1963), 289–295.

252. "Santayana's Defiant Eclecticism," *Journal of Philosophy* 61, 1 (Jan. 2, 1964), 35–44.

253. Discussion: "What the Ontological Proof Does Not Do," *Review of Metaphysics* 17, 4 (June, 1964), 608–609.

254. "From Colonial Beginnings to Philosophical Greatness," *Monist* 48, 3 (July, 1964), 317–331.

255. Comments and Criticism: "Deliberation and Excluded Middle," *Journal of Philosophy* 61, 16 (Sept. 3, 1964), 476–477.

256. "Thinking about Thinking Machines," *Texas Quarterly* 7, 1 (Spring, 1964), 131–140.

257. Replies to "Interrogation of Charles Hartshorne, conducted by William Alston." *Philosophical Interrogations*, ed. Sydney and Beatrice Rome. N.Y.: Holt, Rinehart and Winston, 1964, 321–354. Questions to John Wild. Ibid., 158–160; Brand Blanshard. Ibid., 205; Paul Tillich, Ibid., 374–375.

258. "Is God's Existence a State of Affairs?" *Faith and the Philosophers*, ed. John Hick. N.Y.: St. Martin's Press, 1964, 6–33.

259. "El valor como disfrute del contraste y la teoría acumulativa del proceso," tr. J. L. González, *Dianoia, Anuario de Filosofía* 10 (1964), 182–194.

260. "Charles Peirce's 'One Contribution to Philosophy' and His Most Serious Mistake." *Studies in the Philosophy of Charles Sanders Peirce. Second Series*, ed. Edward G. Moore and Richard S. Robin. Amherst: University of Massachusetts Press, 1964, 455–474.

261. "Negative Facts and the Analogical Inference to 'Other Mind'." *Dr. S. Radhakrishan Souvenir Volume*, ed. Prof. J. P. Atreya et al. Moradabad [India]: Darshana International, 1964, 147–152.

262. "The Idea of a Worshipful Being," *Southern Journal of Philosophy* 2, 4 (Winter, 1964), 165–167.

263. "God as the Supreme Relativity," *Japanese Religions* 4, 1 (Dec., 1964), 30–33.

264. "The Necessarily Existent" [from *Man's Vision of God*]. *The Ontological Argument*, ed. Alvin Plantinga. N.Y.: Anchor Books, Doubleday, 1965, 123–135.

265. "The Meaning of 'Is Going to Be'," *Mind* 74, 293 (Jan., 1965) 46–58.

266. "The Theistic Proofs," *Union Seminary Quarterly Review* 20, 2 (Jan., 1965), 115–129.

267. "Abstract and Concrete Approaches to Deity," Ibid., 20, 3 (March, 1965), 265–270.

268. "A Metaphysics of Individualism." *Innocence and Power*, ed. Gordon Mills, Austin: University of Texas Press, 1965, 131–146.

269. "Determinism, Memory, and the Metaphysics of Becoming," *Pacific Philosophy Forum* 4, 4 (May, 1965), 81–85.

270. "The Social Theory of Feelings," *Southern Journal of Philosophy* 3, 2 (Summer, 1965), 87–93.

271. "The Development of Process Philosophy": Introduction to *Philosophers of Process*, ed. Douglas Browning. N.Y.: Random House, 1965, v–xii.

272. "Religious Aspects of Necessity and Contingency." *Great Issues Concerning Theism*, ed. Charles H. Monson, Jr. Salt Lake City: University of Utah Press, 1965, 147–164.

273. "Criteria for Ideas of God." *Insight and Vision: Essays in Philosophy in Honor of Radoslav Andrea Tsanoff*, ed. Konstantin Kolenda, *Rice University Studies*, 51, 4 (Fall, 1965), 85–95. Also in *Insight and Vision*, as above, published in San Antonio by Principia Press of Trinity University, 1966, 85–95.

274. Comment. Eugene H. Peters, *The Creative Advance*. St. Louis: Bethany Press, 1966, 133–143.

275. "The Two Possible Philosophical Definitions of God." *Actas: XIII Congreso Internacional de Filosofía*. Mexico City: Universidad Nacional Autonoma de Mexico, 1966, Volumen 9, 121.

276. "A New Look at the Problem of Evil." *Current Philosophical Issues: Essays in Honor of Curt John Ducasse*, comp. and ed. Frederick C. Dommeyer. Springfield, Ill.: Charles C. Thomas, 1966, 201–212.

277. "Idealism and Our Experience of Nature." *Philosophy, Religion, and the Coming World Civilization: Essays in Honor of William Ernest Hocking*, ed. Leroy S. Rouner. The Hague: Martinus Nijhoff, 1966, 70–80.

278. "Tillich and the Non-theological Meaning of Theological Terms," *Religion in Life* 35, 5 (Winter, 1966), 674–685. Reprinted in *Paul Tillich: Retrospect and Future* [pamphlet]. Nashville: Abingdon Press, 1966, 19–30.

279. "Some Reflections on Metaphysics and Language," *Foundations of Language: International Journal of Language and Philosophy* 2, 1 (Feb., 1966), 20–32.

280. "Is the Denial of Existence Ever Contradictory?" *Journal of Philosophy* 63, 4 (Feb. 17, 1966), 85–93.

281. "The Idea of Creativity in American Philosophy," *Journal of Kamatak University* [India]: *Social Sciences II*, 1966, 1–13.

282. Review of N. S. Srivastava, *Contemporary Indian Philosophy*. Delhi: M. R. M. Lal, 1965, *Research Journal of Philosophy*, Ranchi University [India] 1, 1 (Sept., 1966), 110–111.

283. "Religion in Process Philosophy." *Religion in Philosophical and Cultural Perspective*, ed. J. Clayton Feaver and William Horosz. Princeton: D. Van Nostrand, 1967, 246–268.

284. "Royce and the Collapse of Idealism." *Revue internationale de philosophie* 23, 79–80 (1967, Fasc. 1–2), 46–59.

285. 'Kagaku, Geijyutsu, Shukyo-Kofuku no Gensen to shite no' ("Science, Art, and Religion as Sources of Happiness"), tr. Matao Noda, *Japan-American Forum* 13, 3 (March, 1967), 47–66.

286. "God and the Social Structure of Reality," "The Significance of Man in the Life of God," and Answers to Questions. *Theology in Crisis: A Colloquium on 'The Credibility of God'*. New Concord, Ohio: Muskingum College, 1967, 19–32, 40–43, 44–50.

287. "Pantheism." *Encyclopedia Britannica* (1967, vol. 17), 233–234.

288. "Psychology and the Unity of Knowledge," *Southern Journal of Philosophy* 5, 2 (Summer, 1967), 81–90.

289. "The Dipolar Conception of Deity," *Review of Metaphysics* 21, 2 (Dec., 1967), 273–289.

290. "Necessity," Ibid., 290–296.

291. "Rejoinder to Purtill," Ibid., 308–309.

292. "Martin Buber's Metaphysics." *The Philosophy of Martin Buber*, ed. Paul Arthur Schilpp and Maurice Friedman. The Library of Living Philosophers, Vol. 12. La Salle: Open Court, 1967, 49–68.

293. "Santayana's Defiant Eclecticism" [from *Journal of Philosophy*: Item 252, this bibliography]. *Animal Faith and Spiritual Life*, ed. John Lachs. N.Y.: Appleton-Century-Crofts, 1967, 33–43.

294. "What Metaphysics Is," *Journal of Kamatak University: Social Sciences III*, 1967, 1–15.

295. "What Did Anselm Discover?" [expanded form of item 234, this bibliography]. *The Many-Faced Argument*, ed. John Hick and Arthur C. McGill. N.Y.: Macmillan, 1967, 321–333.

296. "The Irreducibly Modal Structure of the Argument" [from *The Logic of Perfection*]. Ibid., 334–340.

297. "Process Philosophy as a Resource for Christian Thought." *Philosophical Resources for Christian Thought*, ed. Perry LeFevre. Nashville: Abingdon, 1968, 44–66.

298. "The Necessarily Existent" [from *Man's Vision of God*]. *Philosophy of Religion*, ed. George L. Abernethy and Thomas A. Langford. 2nd ed. N.Y.: Macmillan, 1968, 238–247.

299. "The Divine Relativity" [from *The Divine Relativity*]. Ibid., 321–329.

300. "Order and Chaos." *The Concept of Order*, ed. Paul G. Kuntz. Seattle: University of Washington Press, 1968, 253–267.

301. "Three Strata of Meaning in Religious Discourse" [from *The Logic of Perfection*]. *Philosophy and Religion: Some Contemporary Perspectives*, ed. Jerry H. Gill. Minneapolis: Burgess, 1968, 173–182.

302. "The Aesthetics of Birdsong," *Journal of Aesthetics and Art Criticism* 26, 3 (Spring, 1968), 311–315.

303. "Kant's Refutation Still Not Convincing: A Reply" [to W. H. Baumer], *Monist* 52, 2 (Apr., 1968), 312–316.

304. "Lewis's Treatment of Memory." *The Philosophy of C. I. Lewis*, ed. Paul Arthur Schilpp. The Library of Living Philosophers, Vol. 13. La Salle: Open Court, 1968, 395–414.

305. "Armchair and Laboratory: A Philosopher Looks at Psychology." *Newsletter. Division 24 of the American Psychological Association* 2, 3 (1968), 1–4.

306. "Born Equal: The Importance and Limitations of an Ideal." *Parables and Problems*. Winona, Minn.: College of St. Teresa, 1968, 59–71. [Mimeographed.]

307. "The God of Religion and the God of Philosophy." Broadcast Monday, June 10, 1968, BBC London Third Programme, *The Listener*.

308. "The Case for Idealism," *Philosophical Forum* 1, 1 n.s. (Fall, 1968), 7–23.

309. "The God of Religion and the God of Philosophy." *Talk of God: Royal Institute of Philosophy Lectures, Vol. Two—1967–68*. London: Macmillan, 1969, 152–167.

310. "Duality versus Dualism and Monism," *Japanese Religions* 5, 1 (Apr., 1969), 51–63.

311. "Leibniz und das Geheimnis der Materie." *Studia Leibnitiana: Akten des Internationalen Leibniz-Kongresses, Hannover, 14–19 November, 1966, Band II: Mathematik-Naturwissenschaften*. Wiesbaden: Franz Steiner Verlag GMBH, 1969, 166–175.

312. "Religious Aspects of Necessity and Contingency" [from *Great Issues Concerning Theism*]. *And More About God*, ed. Lewis M. Rogers and Charles H. Monson, Jr. Salt Lake City: University of Utah Press, 1969, 145–161.

313. Review Article: "Whitehead in French Perspective," *Thomist* 33, 3 (July, 1969), 573–581.

314. Response. *Directives from Charles Hartshorne and Henry Nelson Wieman Critically Analyzed: Philosophy of Creativity Monograph Series*, Vol. 1, ed. William S. Minor. Carbondale: The Foundation for Creative Philosophy, Inc., 1969, 33–42.

315. "Divine Absoluteness and Divine Relativity." *Transcendence*, ed. Herbert W. Richardson and Donald R. Cutler. Boston: Beacon Press, 1969, 164–171.

316. "Metaphysics in North America." *Contemporary Philosophy: A Survey*, ed. Raymond Klibansky. Florence: La Nuova Italia Editrice, 1969, 36–49.

317. "Whitehead and Ordinary Language," *Southern Journal of Philosophy* 7, 4 (Winter, 1969–1970), 437–445.

318. "The Social Theory of Feelings." *Persons, Privacy, and Feeling: Essays in the Philosophy of Mind*, ed. Dwight Van de Vate, Jr. Memphis: Memphis State University Press, 1970, 39–51.

319. Preface to *Berdiaev's Philosophy of History* by David Bonner Richardson. The Hague: Martinus Nijhoff, 1970, ix–xiii.

320. "Why Study Birds?" *Virginia Quarterly Review* 46, 1 (Winter, 1970), 133–140.

321. "Recollections of Famous Philosophers and Other Important Persons," *Southern Journal of Philosophy* 8, 1 (Spring, 1970), 67–82.

322. "Two Forms of Idolatry," *International Journal for Philosophy of Religion*, 1, 1 (Spring, 1970), 3–15.

323. "Equality, Freedom, and the Insufficiency of Empiricism," *Southern Journal of Philosophy* 1, 3 (Fall, 1970), 20–27.

324. "Eternity," "Absolute," "God." *Prophetic Voices: Ideas and Words on Revolution*, ed. Ned O'Gorman. N.Y.: Random House, 1969; N.Y.: Vintage Books, 1970, 130–148.

325. "The Development of My Philosophy." *Contemporary American Philosophy: Second Series*, ed. John E. Smith. London: Allen & Unwin, 1970, 211–228.

326. "Ontological Primacy: A Reply to Buchler," *Journal of Philosophy* 67, 23 (Dec. 10, 1970), 979–986.

327. "Charles Hartshorne's Recollections of Editing the Peirce Papers," *Transactions of the Charles S. Peirce Society* 6, 3–4 (Summer–Fall, 1970), 149–159.

328. "Deity as the Inclusive Transcendence." *Evolution in Perspective: Commentaries in Honor of Pierre Lecomte du Noüy*, ed. George N. Shuster and Ralph E. Thorson. Notre Dame and London: University of Notre Dame Press, 1970, 155–160.

329. "The Formally Possible Doctrines of God" [from *Man's Vision of God*]. *Classical and Contemporary Readings in the Philosophy of Religion*, ed. John Hick. Second Edition. Englewood Cliffs: Prentice-Hall, 1970, 336–357.

330. "Time, Death, and Everlasting Life" [from *The Logic of Perfection*]. Ibid., 357–369.

331. "Science, Insecurity, and the Abiding Treasure" [abridged from *The Logic of Perfection*]. *The Spirit of American Philosophy: An Anthology*, selected, ed., and with Introductions by Gerald E. Myers. N.Y.: Capricorn Books, 1971, 327–332.

332. "Mind and Matter in Ryle, Ayer, and C. I. Lewis," *Idealistic Studies* 1, 1 (Jan., 1971), 13–32.

333. "Are There Absolutely Specific Universals?" *Journal of Philosophy* 68, 3 (Feb. 11, 1971), 76–78.

334. "Can Man Transcend His Animality?" *Monist* 55, 2 (April, 1971), 208–217.

335. "Selfishness in Man," *PHP* 1, 8 (May, 1971), 24–25.

336. "The Formally Possible Doctrines of God" [abridged from *Man's Vision of God*]. *Process Philosophy and Christian Thought*, ed. Delwin Brown, Ralph E. James, Jr., and Gene Reeves. Indianapolis: Bobbs-Merrill, 1971, 188–214. Also paperback.

337. "Could There Have Been Nothing? A Reply [to Craighead]," *Process Studies* 1, 1 (Spring, 1971), 25–28.

338. "Expression and Association" [from *The Philosophy and Psychology of Sensation*]. *Artistic Expression*, ed. John Hospers. N.Y.: Appleton-Century-Crofts, 1971, 204–217.

339. "Obligability and Determinism," *Journal of Social Philosophy* 2, 2 (Oct., 1971), 1–2.

340. "The Development of Process Philosophy" [from the introduction to *Philosophers of Process*, ed. Douglas Browning]. *Process Theology: Basic Writings*, ed. Ewert H. Cousins, N.Y.: Newman Press, 1971, 47–61.

341. "Philosophical and Religious Uses of God'" [from *A Natural Theology for Our Time*]. Ibid., 101–118.

342. "Can There Be Proofs for the Existence of God?" *Religious Language and Knowledge*, ed. Robert H. Ayers and William T. Blackstone. Athens: University of Georgia Press, 1972, 62–75.

343. "Mortimer Adler as Philosopher: A Criticism and Appreciation," *American Scholar* 41, 2 (Spring, 1972), 269–274.

344. "A Conversation with Charles Hartshorne at Hiram College," ed. Eugene Peters, *Eclectic: A Journal of Ideas* 1, 1 (Winter, 1972), 1–18.

345. Review of Paul Ramsey, *Fabricated Man*. New Haven: Yale University Press, 1970, *Philosophy Forum* 12, 1 & 2 (Sept., 1972), 149–152.

346. "Paul Weiss's *The God We Seek*," *Review of Metaphysics* 25, Supplement (June, 1972), 108–116.

347. "Personal Identity from A to Z," *Process Studies* 2, 3 (Fall, 1972), 209–215.

348. Author's Abstract: *Creative Synthesis and Philosophic Method*, *Monist* 56, 4 (Oct., 1972), 626–627.

349. Feature Book Review: "Some Thoughts Suggested by Lieb's *Four Faces of Man*," *International Philosophical Quarterly* 13, 1 (March, 1973), 131–134.

350. "Some Thoughts on 'Souls' and Neighborly Love," *Anglican Theological Review* 55, 2 (April, 1973), 144–147.

351. "Analysis and Cultural Lag in Philosophy," *Southern Journal of Philosophy* 11, 2–3 (Spring and Summer, 1973), 105–112.

352. "Being and Becoming: Review of Harold N. Lee, *Percepts, Concepts and Theoretic Knowledge*," *Review of Books and Religion* 2, 9 (Mid-June, 1973), 7.

353. "Process and the Nature of God." *Traces of God in a Secular Culture*, ed. George F. McLean, O.M.I. N.Y.: Alba House, 1973, 117–141.

354. "Creativity and the Deductive Logic of Causality," *Review of Metaphysics* 27, 1 (Sept., 1973), 62–74.

355. "Pensées sur ma vie," 26–32; "Thoughts on my Life," 60–66, *Bilingual Journal, Lecomte du Noüy Association* 5 (Fall, 1973).

356. "Charles Peirce and Quantum Mechanics," *Transactions of the Charles S. Peirce Society* 9, 4 (Fall, 1973), 191–201.

357. "Husserl and Whitehead on the Concrete." *Phenomenology: Continuation and Criticism: Essays in Memory of Dorion Cairns*, ed. F. Kersten and R. Zaner. The Hague: Martinus Nijhoff, 1973, 90–104.

358. "Charles Peirce and Quantum Mechanics." *Abstracts of Communications Sent to the XVth World Congress of Philosophy*. Varna, Sept. 17–22, 1973. Bulgarian Organizing Committee, International Fedcration of Philosophical Societies. See item 356.

359. "Ideas and Theses of Process Philosophers." *Two Process Philosophers: Hartshorne's Encounter with Whitehead*. AAR Studies in Religion Number Five. Tallahassee, Florida, American Academy of Religion, 1973, 100–103.

360. "Science and Quality," *Sound Seminars:* Tapes in Philosophy. N.Y.: McGraw-Hill, 1954, 1973.

361. "Contribuciones Permanentes de Spinoza" [Spanish translation of "Spinoza's Permanent Contributions"], *Folia humanistica; ciencias, artes, letras* 12 (Feb., 1974), 121–129.

362. "Twelve Elements of My Philosophy." *The Southwestern Journal of Philosophy* 5, 1 (Spring, 1974), 7–15.

363. Abstract: "Do Philosophers Know That They Have Bodies?" *Abstracts of Papers, 1974 Annual Conference, Australasian Association of Philosophy*. Canberra: Australian National University, 1974, 7–8.

364. "The Modern World and a Modern View of God," *Philosophy of Religion: Contemporary Perspectives*. Ed. Norbert O. Schedler. N.Y.: Macmillan, 1974, 469–479.

365. "Philosophy after Fifty Years." *Mid-Twentieth Century American Philosophy: Personal Statements*, ed. Peter A. Bertocci. N.Y.: Humanities Press, 1974, 140–154.

366. "The Environmental Results of Technology." *Philosophy and Environmental Crisis*, ed. William T. Blackstone. Athens: University of Georgia Press, 1974, 69–78.

367. "Beyond Enlightened Self-Interest: A Metaphysics of Ethics," *Ethics* 84, 3 (April, 1974), 201–216.

368. "Perception and the Concrete Abstractness of Science," *Philosophy and Phenomenological Research* 34, 4 (June, 1974), 465–476.

369. "The Nature of Philosophy." *Philosophy in Context: An Experiment in Teaching*, Vol. 4, ed. Leslie Armour. Cleveland: Cleveland State University, 1975, 7–16.

370. "Love and Dual Transcendence," *Union Seminary Quarterly Review* 30, 2–4 (Winter–Summer, 1975), 94–100.

371. "Whitehead's Differences from Buddhism," *Philosophy East and West* 25, 4 (Oct., 1975), 407–413.

372. "Whitehead and Leibniz: A Comparison." *Contemporary Studies in Philosophical Idealism*, ed. John Howie and Thomas O. Buford. Cape Cod, Mass.: Claude Stark and Company, 1975, 95–115.

373. "Do Birds Enjoy Singing? (An Ornitho-Philosophical Discourse)," *Bulletin of the Texas Ornithological Society* 8 (Dec., 1975), 2–5.

374. "The Centrality of Reason in Philosophy (Replies to Questions for Charles Hartshorne)." *Philosophy in Context*, Supplement to Volume 4 (1975), 5–11.

375. "Beyond Enlightened Self-Interest" [item 367 reprinted]. *Religious Experience and Process Theology*, ed. Harry James Cargas and Bernard Lee. N.Y.: Paulist Press, 1976, 301–322.

376. Author's Abstract: LP, *Monist* 59, 4 (Oct., 1976), 596.

377. Author's Abstract: NTOT, Ibid., 594.

378. Discussion: "Synthesis as Polyadic Inclusion: A Reply to Sessions," *Southern Journal of Philosophy* 14, 2 (Summer, 1976), 245–255.

379. "Mysticism and Rationalistic Metaphysics," *Monist* 59, 4 (Oct., 1976), 463–469.

380. "Psychicalism and the Leibnizian Principle," *Studia Leibnitiana* 8, 2 (1976), 154–159.

381. "Why Psychicalism? Comments on Keeling's and Shepherd's Criticisms," *Process Studies* 6, 1 (Spring, 1976), 67–72.

382. "Additional Reflections," *Process Studies* 7, 4 (Winter, 1977), 271–274.

383. "Bell's Theorem and Stapp's Revised View of Space-Time," *Process Studies* 7, 3 (Fall, 1977), 183–191.

384. "The Books That Shape Lives: Book Choices of Charles Hartshorne," *Christian Century* 44, 30 (Sept. 28, 1977), 860.

385. "Cobb's Theology of Ecology." *John Cobb's Theology in Process*, ed. David Ray Griffin and Thomas J. J. Altizer. Philadelphia: Westminster Press, 1977, 112–115.

386. "The Duty to Happiness," *Catalyst Tape Talk* 9, 5 (May,1977), 4.

387. John Hick on Logical and Ontological Necessity," *Religious Studies* 13, 2 (June, 1977), 155–165.

388. "The Neglect of Relative Predicates in Modern Philosophy," *American Philosophical Quarterly* 14, 4 (Oct., 1977), 309–318.

389. "Physics and Psychics: The Place of Mind in Nature." *Mind in Nature: Essays on the Interface of Science and Philosophy.* Washington, D.C.: University Press of America, 1977, 89–96.

390. "Response to Koestler's Paper." Ibid., 66.

391. "Response to Rensch's Paper." Ibid., 78.

392. "Whitehead's Metaphysical System", tr. Schubert M. Ogden, from "Das metaphysische System Whiteheads" by Charles Hartshorne. *A Rational Faith: Essays in Honor of Rabbi Levi A. Olan,* ed. Jack Bemporad. N.Y.: KTAV Publishing House, Inc., 1977, 107–123.

393. "The Acceptance of Death." *Philosophical Aspects of Thanatology,* Vol. 1, ed. Florence M. Hetzler and Austin H. Kutscher. N.Y.: MSS Information Corporation, 1978, 83–87.

394. "Can We Understand God?" *Louvain Studies* 7, 2 (Fall, 1978), 75–84.

395. Foreword. *The Ontological Argument of Charles Hartshorne* by George L. Goodwin. Missoula, Montana: Scholars Press, 1978, xi–xviii.

396. "Foundations for a Humane Ethics: What Human Beings Have in Common with Other Higher Animals." *On the Fifth Day. Animal Rights and Human Ethics,* ed. Richard Knowles Morris and Michael W. Fox. Washington, D.C.: Acropolis Books, Ltd., 1978, 154–172.

397. "The Individual Is a Society." *The Individual and Society: Essays Presented to David L. Miller on His Seventy-fifth Birthday,* ed. Michael P. Jones, Patricia O. F. Nobo, Jorge L. Nobo, Yen-ling Chang. Norman, Oklahoma: *Southwestern Journal of Philosophy,* 1978, 73–88.

398. "A New World and a New World View." *The Life of Choice,* ed. Clark Kucheman. Boston: Beacon Press, 1978, 82–92. (First given as a speech at U.T. graduation convocation, 1976.)

399. "The Organism According to Process Philosophy." *Organism, Medicine, and Metaphysics: Essays in Honor of Hans Jonas on His 75th Birthday,* May 10th, 1978, ed. Stuart F. Spicker. Dordrecht, Holland: D. Reidel, 1978, 137–154.

400. "Panpsychism: Mind as Sole Reality," *Ultimate Reality and Meaning* 1, 2 (1978), 115–129.

401. "A Philosophy of Death," *Philosophical Aspects of Thanatology,* Vol. 2, ed. Florence M. Hetzler and A. H. Kutscher. N.Y.: MSS Information Corporation, 1978, 81–89.

402. Preface, *Process Philosophy: Basic Writings,* ed. Jack R. Sibley and Pete A. Y. Gunter. Washington, D.C.: University Press of America, 1978, 1–7.

403. "Beyond Enlightened Self-Interest," Ibid., 395–416.

404. "Present Prospects for Metaphysics," Ibid., 199–212.

405. "A World of Organisms," Ibid., 275–296.

406. "Rechte—nicht nur für die Menschen" (tr. Dr. Ilse Tödt), *Zeitschrift für Evangelische Ethik* 22, 1 (Jan., 1978), 3–14.

407. Reply to Eugene H. Peters, *Ultimate Reality and Meaning* 1, 3 (1978), 233–234.

408. "Theism in Asian and Western Thought," *Philosophy East and West* 28, 4 (Oct., 1978), 401–411.

409. " 'Emptiness' and Fullness in Asiatic and Western Thought," *Journal of Chinese Philosophy* 6 (1979), 411–420.

410. "Charles Morris," *Semiotica* 28, 3–4 (1979), 193–194.

411. "God and Nature," *Anticipation* 25 (Jan., 1979), 58–64.

412. "The Rights of the Subhuman World," *Environmental Ethics: An Interdisciplinary Journal Dedicated to the Philosophical Aspects of Environmental Problems* 1, 1 (Spring, 1979), 49–60.

413. "Metaphysics Contributes to Ornithology," *Theoria to Theory* 13, 2 (1979), 127–140.

414. "Whitehead's Revolutionary Concept of Prehension," *International Philosophical Quarterly* 19, 3 (Sept., 1979), 253–263.

415. "Process Themes in Chinese Thought," *Journal of Chinese Philosophy* 6 (1979), 323–336.

416. "Philosophy and Religion," Program of the International Congress of Philosophy on "Contemporary Problems of Philosophy and Religion" at Fu Jen Catholic University, Taipei, Taiwan, Dec. 28, 1979–Jan. 4, 1980, 26.

417. "James's Empirical Pragmatism," *American Journal of Theology and Philosophy* 1, 1 (Jan., 1980), 14–20.

418. "My Neoclassical Metaphysics," *Tijdschrift voor Philosophie* 42, 1 (March, 1980), 3–10.

419. "In Defense of Wordsworth's View of Nature," *Philosophy & Literature* 4, 1 (Spring, 1980), 80–91.

420. Review of Karol Wojtyla, *The Acting Person*, *Philosophy and Phenomenological Research* 40, 3 (March, 1980), 443–444.

421. "Das metaphysische System Whiteheads," *Whitehead: Einführung in seine Kosmologie*. Beiträge von Gernot Böhme, Charles Hartshorne, u.s.w. Herausgegeben von Ernest Wolf-Gazo. Freiburg/München: Verlag Karl Albers, 1980, 28–44.

422. "Ethics and the Process of Living." *Man and His Conduct: Philosophical Essays in Honor of Risieri Frondizi*, ed. Jorge J. E. Gracia, Rio Piedras, Puerto Rico: Editorial Universitaria, 1980, 191–202.

423. "Pepper's Approach to Metaphysics," *Root Metaphor: The Live Thought of Stephen C. Pepper*. PAUNCH #53–54, (1980), 80–81.

424. "Understanding Freedom and Suffering," *Catalyst Tape Talk* 12, 9 (1980), 4–5 [cut and edited without consultation with author]. Also recorded tape available.

425. "A Revision of Peirce's Categories," *Monist*, 63, 3 (July, 1980), 277–289. Reprinted in *The Relevance of Charles Peirce,* ed. Eugene Freeman, Monist Library of Philosophy, 1983.

426. "Understanding as Seeing to Be Necessary," *The Philosophy of Brand Blanshard*, ed. Paul Arthur Schilpp. The Library of Living Philosophers, Vol. 15. La Salle: Open Court, 1980, 629–635.

427. "Response to Neville's *Creativity and God*," *Process Studies* 10, 3–4 (1980), 93–97.

428. "A Conversation between Charles Hartshorne and Jan Van der Veken," *Louvain Studies* VII, 2 (Fall, 1980), 129–142.

429. "Concerning Abortion: An Attempt at a Rational View," *The Christian Century* 98, 2 (Jan. 21, 1981), 42–45.

430. "The Ethics of Contributionism," *Responsibilities to Future Generations: Environmental Ethics*, ed. Ernest Partridge, Buffalo: Prometheus, 1981. 103–107.

431. "Critical Study: A Neglected Nonacademic Philosopher," *Process Studies* 11, 3 (1981), 213–215.

432. "Whitehead in Historical Context" in *Whitehead's View of Reality*, Hartshorne and Creighton Peden. New York: Pilgrim Press, 1981, 2–24.

433. "Neoclassical Metaphysics," *Philosophers on Their Own Work*, Vol. 8. Bern, Frankfurt a.M., Las Vegas: Peter Lang, 1981, 63–104. Includes a list of publications. In French and English.

434. "Science as the Search for the Hidden Beauty of the World," *The Aesthetic Dimension of Science*: 1980 Nobel Conference Number 16. Published 1982, 85–106; see also 107, 108, 117, 119–120, 123, 124– 5, 128–9, 130, 131, 137, 140, 143.

435. "Creative Interchange and Neoclassical Metaphysics," *Creative Interchange*, Boston University Studies in Philosophy and Religion; General Editor, Leroy S. Rouner, 1982, 107–121.

436. "Grounds for Believing in God's Existence," *Meaning, Truth, and God*, ed. Leroy S. Rouner. Notre Dame: University of Notre Dame Press, 1982, 17–33.

437. "Concerning Abortion: An Attempt at a Rational View," *Speak Out Against the New Right*, ed. Herbert F. Vetter, Boston: Beacon Press, 1982, 152–157. (From *The Christian Century*, 98, 2, 1981—item 429 of this bibliography.)

438. Review of Daniel A. Dombrowski, *Plato's Philosophy of History, Process Studies* 12, 3 (Fall, 1982), 201–202.

439. "Ontological Primacy: A Reply to Buchler." *Explorations in Whitehead's Philosophy*, ed. Lewis S. Ford and George L. Kline. New York: Fordham University Press, 1983, 295–303.

440. "Anselm and Aristotle's First Law of Modality," *Anselm Studies: An Occasional Journal* 1, 1983, 51–58.

441. "Categories, Transcendentals, and Creative Experiencing," *Monist* 66, 3 (July, 1983), 319–335.

442. "Peirce's Fresh Look at Philosophical Problems," *Krisis* 1, 1 (Summer, 1983), 1–5.

443. "Obligability and Determinism." *Philosophy for a Changing Society,* ed. Creighton Peden. Reynoldsburg, Ohio: Advocate Publishing Co., 95–96. (From *Journal of Social Philosophy*, 2, 2 (1971), item 339 in this bibliography.)

444. "God and the Meaning of Life." *On Nature*, ed. Leroy S. Rouner. Boston University Studies in Philosophy and Religion, Vol. 6. Notre Dame: University of Notre Dame Press, 1984, 154–168.

445. "Toward a Buddhisto-Christian Religion." *Buddhism and American Thinkers*, ed. Kenneth K. Inada and Nolan P. Jacobson. Albany: State University of New York Press, 1984, 1–13.

446. "Indeterministic Freedom as Universal Principle," *Journal of Social Philosophy* 15 (1984), 5–11.

447. "Marcel on God and Causality." *The Philosophy of Gabriel Marcel*, ed. Paul Arthur Schilpp and Lewis Edwin Hahn. The Library of Living Philosophers, Vol. 17. La Salle: Open Court, 1984, 353–366.

448. "How I got that way," *Existence and Actuality: Conversations with Charles Hartshorne*, ed. J. B. Cobb and F. I. Gamwell. Chicago: University of Chicago Press, 1984. Responses to: E. H. Peters, 12–15; S. M. Ogden, 37–42; R. M. Martin, 66–77; W. P. Alston, 98–102; J. E. Smith, 109–112; Paul Weiss, 121–129; Manley Thompson, 143–148; J. B. Cobb, Jr., 164–166; George Wolf, 184–188.

449. "Whitehead as Central but not Sole Philosopher of Process." In *Whitehead und der Prozessbegriff,* ed. Harold Holz and Ernest Wolf-Gazo. Freiburg, Munchen: Karl Alber, 1984.

450. "Theistic Proofs and Disproofs: The Findlay Paradox." *Studies in the Philosophy of J. N. Findlay*, ed. Robert S. Cohen, Richard M. Martin, Merold Westphal. Albany: State University of New York Press, 1985, 224–234.

451. "Creativity as a Value and Creativity as a Transcendental Category." *Creativity in Art, Religion, and Culture,* ed. M. H. Mitias. K & N, Amsterdam: Rodopi, (Elementa; 42) (1985), 3–11.

452. "A Philosophy of Shared Creative Experience." *American Philosophy: A Historical Anthology*, ed. with commentary, Barbara McKinnon. Albany: SUNY Press, 1985, 414–427.

453. "Process Theology in Historical and Systematic Contexts." *Modern Schoolman*, 62, 4 (1985), 221–231.

454. "Scientific and Religious Aspects of Bioethics." *Theology and Bioethics,* ed. E. E. Schelp. Dordrecht, Boston, Lancaster, Tokyo: D. Reidel Publishing Co., 1985, 27–44.

455. "Our Knowledge of God." *Knowing Religiously*, Boston University Studies in Philosophy and Religion. See #444, Vol. 7, (1985), 52–63.

456. "Reeves and Stearns on my Idealism," *American Journal of Theology and Philosophy* (1986), 45–50.

457. "Perspectives on Chinese Philosophy," *Journal of Chinese Philosophy* 13 (1986), 267–270.

458. "Metaphysics and the Dual Transcendence of God," *Tulane Studies in Philosophy*, 34 (1986). *Hartshorne's Neoclassical Theology*, ed. Forrest Wood, Jr. and Michael DeArmey, 65–72.

459. Review of Stephen Toulmin's *Return to Cosmology*, *Philosophy and Rhetoric*, 19, 4 (1986), 266–269.

460. "Some Theological Mistakes and Their Effects on Literature," *Journal of Speculative Philosophy*, New Series, Vol. 1, No. 1, (1987), 55–72.

461. "Argument in Metaphysics of Religion." *Process Thought and the Christian Doctrine of God, Spirit and Word*, a monastic review. Petersham, Mass.: St. Bedes, publishers, 1986.

462. "Pantheism and Panenthcism," *The Encyclopedia of Religion*, Senior Ed., Mircea Eliade. New York: Macmillan Publishing Co.; London: Collier Macmillan, Vol. 11, 1987.

463. "Transcendence and Immanence," Vol. 15 of the same.

464. "Bergson's Aesthetic Creationism," *Bergson & Modern Thought: Toward a Unified Science*, ed. A. C. Papanicolaou and Pete A. Gunter. New York: Harwood Academic, 1987.

465. "Weiss After Fifty Years." *Creativity and Common Sense: Essays in Honor of Paul Weiss*, ed. Thomas Krettek. Albany: State University of New York Press, (1987), 262–269.

466. "Mind and Body: A Special Case of Mind and Mind." *A Process Theory of Medicine: Interdisciplinary Essays*, ed. Marcus Ford. Lewiston, N.Y.: Edwin Mellen Press, 1987, 77–88.

467. "A Metaphysics of Universal Freedom." *Faith and Creativity. Essays in Honor of Eugene H. Peters*, ed. George Nordgulen and G. W. Shields. St. Louis, Mo.: CBP Press, 1987, 27–40.

468. "Some Principles of Procedure in Metaphysics." *The Nature of Metaphysical Knowledge*, ed. G. F. McLean and Hugo Meynell. Lanham, N.Y.; London: University Press of America, International Society for Metaphysics, 1988, 69–75.

469. "Sankara, Nagarjuna, and Fa Tsang, with some Western Analogues." *Interpreting across Boundaries: New Essays in Comparative Philosophy*, ed. G. J. Larson and Eliot Deutsch. Princeton University Press, 1988, 98–115.

470. "In Dispraise of Empiricism," *American Journal of Theology and Philosophy*, 10, 2 (May, 1989), 123–126.

471. "A Dual Theory of Theological Analogy." *American Journal of Theology and Philosophy* 10, 3 (Sept., 1989), 171–178.

472. "The Organism According to Process Philosophy." *Process in Context,* ed. Ernest Wolf-Gazo. New York: Peter Lang Publishing Inc.

473. "Metaphysical and Empirical Aspects of the Idea of God," *Witness and Existence: Essays in Honor of Schubert M. Ogden,* ed. P. E. Devenish and G. L. Goodwin, Chicago: University of Chicago Press, 1989, 177–189.

474. "General Remarks." *Hartshorne, Process Philosophy, and Theology,* ed. Robert Kane and Stephen H. Phillips. State University of New York Press, 1989, 181–197.

475. *Whitehead's Philosophy,* translated into Japanese by Minoru Otsuka, 1989.

476. "Von Wright and Hume's Axiom." *The Philosophy of Georg Henrik von Wright,* ed. Paul Arthur Schilpp and Lewis Edwin Hahn. The Library of Living Philosophers, Vol. 19. La Salle: Open Court, 1989, 59–76.

477. "Some Causes of My Intellectual Growth." (1990);

478. "Replies to My Critics." Both in *The Philosophy of Charles Hartshorne,* ed. Lewis Edwin Hahn. The Library of Living Philosophers, Vol. 20. La Salle: Open Court, 1991.

Forthcoming also:

479. "God, Necessary and Contingent; World, Contingent and Necessary, and the Fifteen Other Options in Thinking About God." *Festschrift for Ivor Leclerc,* ed. Paul Bogaard and Gordon Treasch.

480. "Buddhism and the Theistic Question." *Essays in Honor of Nolan P. Jacobson.*

481. "Kant's Categories and Whitehead's." Ed. Ernest Wolf-Gazo.

482. "Thinking About Thinking Machines." Revised and updated by Ryan. See item 256.

PART II—ORNITHOLOGY

Book

Born to Sing: An Interpretation and World Survey of Bird Song. Bloomington: Indiana University Press, 1973. Pp. 304.

Articles

1. "First Encounter with Hawaiian Songbirds," *Elepaio* [Hawaii] 12, 12 (June, 1952), 76–78.

2. "A Foreigner's Impression of the Lyrebird's Singing," *The Victorican Naturalist* [Australia] 49, 5 (Sept., 1952), 73–74.

3. "Musical Values in Australian Bird Songs," *The Emu* [Australia] 53, part 2 (June, 1953), 109–123.

4. "The Monotony Threshold in Singing Birds," *The Auk* [U.S.A.] 73 (April, 1956), 176–192.

5. "The Phenomenon of Bird Song," *The Emory University Quarterly* [U.S.A.] 12, 3 (Oct., 1956), 139–147.

6. "Some Biological Principles Applicable to Song-Behavior," *The Wilson Bulletin* [U.S.A.] 70, 1 (March, 1958), 41–56.

7. "The Relation of Bird Song to Music," *Ibis* [Great Britain] 100, 3 (1958), 421–445.

8. "Freedom, Individuality, and Beauty in Nature," *Snowy Egret* [Shorter Apts., Rome, Ga.] 24, 2 (Autumn, 1960). [See item 215, Part I, this bibliography.]

9. Review of *A Treasury of New Zealand Bird Song: An Album of Three Records*, The *Wilson Bulletin* 72, 4 (Dec. 14, 1960), 421–422.

10. "Sketch of a Theory of Imitative Singing," *The Oriole* 26, 2 (June, 1961), 23–27.

11. "Why Study Birds?" *The Virginia Quarterly Review* 46, 1 (Winter, 1970), 133–140. [See also item 320, Part I, this bibliography.]

12. "Birds and Man in Nature," Review of *The Life of Birds* by Jean Dorst, *The Virginia Quarterly Review* 51, 3 (Summer, 1975), 494–496.

13. "Do Birds Enjoy Singing? (An Ornitho-Philosophical Discourse)," *Bulletin of the Texas Ornithological Society* 8, (Dec., 1975), 2–5. [See item 373, Part I, this bibliography.]

14. Abstract of *Born to Sing, The Monist* 59, 2 (Apr. 1976), 299.

15. Review of *North American Bird Songs, A World of Music* by Paul Bondesen, *The Wilson Bulletin* 90, 1 (March 1978) 153–155.

16. "Metaphysics Contributes to Ornithology," *Theoria to Theory* 13 (1979), 127–140. [See item 413, Part I, this bibliography.]

NOTE

Because of illnesses, Dorothy Cooper Hartshorne's work on the foregoing bibliography largely ended in 1980. Later items were added by Charles Hartshorne, with some able help from supertypist Colleen Kieke. I would like to call attention to the fact that Dorothy's part of the work covered fifty-two years of my publishing career and that this is longer than most scholars' publishing careers. In addition, during all that time, she was the professionally trained editor of the writings she listed, and that by the time she could no longer do either activity I had learned through her much about how to do them for myself. Only a wild guess is possible as to how much of the quantity and quality of the writings would have been possible without her assistance. What is most improbable is that anyone else would have done nearly as much to help me or my readers.

For a secondary bibliography, also by Dorothy Cooper Hartshorne, see *Process Studies*, 3/3 (Fall, 1973) and 11/2. The years covered are 1929 to 1973. There is an alphabetical list of authors, something like 460, who have published discussions of parts or aspects of my work in philosophy or theology (not counting those on my ornithological writings). Some authors have done this many times, in two cases ten each.

See *Process Studies*, 3/4, 1973 for a list of dissertations (1944–1972) and other unpublished secondary material (compiled by D. R. Fowler).

The contribution (potential or actual) of women to culture has always been underestimated by men, and even by women. Only in this century has the extent of this error begun to dawn on us all.

INDEX

(by S. S. Rama Rao Pappu)

294, 356, 359, 397, 431, 491, 493, 495,
520, 559f, 562, 573, 578f, 581, 590, 607f,
612f, 631f, 637f, 640, 645, 651f, 657ff,
671, 679ff, 691ff, 702, 705, 710ff, 723,
727
Lenin, V. I., 571
Leonard, C. M., 90n
Le Roy, Edouard, 22
Leśnievski, S., 375
Levi, A. W., 486
Levinson, R. B., 486n, 727
Lévy-Bruhl, Lucien, 22
Lewis, C. I., 15, 20f, 26, 399, 532, 536, 548,
626, 644, 647, 652, 654, 657, 664, 691,
709, 713ff
Lewis, David, 664
Lewontin, Richard C., 58f, 63n
libertarianism, 137, 140
life, 243; affirmation of, 680; human, 164;
meaning of, 687; sacredness of, 162ff; unity
of, 60ff
Locke, John, 94ff, 326, 497, 517, 552, 562
logic, 24, 288, 685, 687; and metaphysics,
707f; Aristotelian, 356, 513; classical, 365;
first order, 341; intuitive, 347, 364ff;
modal, 204f, 207, 210, 275, 285, 340ff,
356, 358, 434, 446, 582, 672; predicate,
372f; propositional, 279, 340f, 364, 372,
376, 496, 577; tense, 285; Vedantic,
267f
Logos, 209
Loomer, Bernard, 34, 37, 614
Lotze, Hermann, 521
love, 59, 62, 210, 552, 554f, 622, 634, 700;
and world, 683; divine, 44, 614, 676;
human, 61f; self, 245
Lovejoy, A. O., 526n, 711
Lowe, Victor, 25, 314, 527n, 653f
loyalty, loyalty to, 229
Lucas, Billy Joe, 657, 658n
Lucas, George R., Jr., 394n, 525n, 527n,
664, 710n
Lucretius, 555f, 583, 585, 711
Luther, Martin, 327, 438

Mackie, J. L., 41
Macy, Joanne, 251n
Mahayana (Buddhism), 236, 238, 241ff
Mahowald, Mary Brody, 224f, 232n
Malcolm, Norman, 356, 625

Marcel, Gabriel, 437
Maritain, Jacques, 31, 492
Marti, Fritz, 34
Martin, Isolde G., 102, 111n
Martin, R. M., 351f, 714
Marx, Karl, 514, 571, 577, 607, 709
mathematics, 295, 311n, 369, 423, 628; and
pluralism, 545; as eternal, 656
materialism, 31, 615, 693ff; dialectical, 210
matrices, doctrinal, 577f
Matsumara, Katsumi, 559
Matsunaga, Yūji, 559
matter, 18, 284, 512, 724; and evil, 483; and
mind, 699; properties of, 58
Mavrodes, G. I., 375
Maxwell, G., 5
Maxwell, Clerk, 581, 607, 609
Maya, 258ff, 268, 379; as absolute indefinite,
259
Mayr, Ernst, 76n
McIntosh, D. C., 649
McKeon, Richard P., 30ff, 44f, 471, 657
McLean, George F., 335n
McManus, I. C., 101, 111n
McTaggart, J. M. E., 146, 413, 514, 517,
609, 675, 709
Mead, G. H., 27, 31, 398, 518, 531f, 534,
545, 548
Mead, Margaret, 28
meaning, and concept, 532; criterion of,
677
mechanics, quantum, 370, 441
mechanism, 179f; and physics, 173; as world
view, 171ff; consequences of, 172f
meditation, 238
Mehta, J. L., 42, 726
Meland, Bernard, 171
meliorism, 227
Meltzoff, Andrew N., 96, 110n
memory, 83, 89, 183, 243, 262, 573ff; and
experience, 359; and perception, 300; loss
of, 88; short term, 586
Mendes, Aristides de Sousa, 200
mentality, 333f
Merleau-Ponty, Maurice, 44, 288, 290n, 381,
552, 573, 649, 670, 693
metaphysics, 36, 135, 212, 250, 261, 275ff,
321, 325, 358, 433, 445ff, 468, 570ff, 579,
580f, 595, 634ff, 653f, 668f, 671, 675,
678f, 700, 713, 727; and abstraction, 294;